PRINCIPLES of MARKETING

FOURTH EDITION

Thomas C. KINNEAR

UNIVERSITY OF MICHIGAN

Kenneth L. BERNHARDT

GEORGIA STATE UNIVERSITY

Kathleen A. KRENTLER

SAN DIEGO STATE UNIVERSITY

HarperCollinsCollegePublishers

D0101571

Executive Editor: *Anne Elizabeth Smith*
Senior Developmental Editor: *Arlene Bessenoff*
Senior Marketing Manager: *Kate Steinbacher*
Supplements Editor: *Julie Zasloff*
Cover Photograph: *Clint Clemmens, Inc.*
Photo Research: *Diane Kraut*
Electronic Production Manager: *Eric Jorgensen*
Manufacuturing Manager: *Lisa Kinne*
Publishing Services: *Thompson Steele Production Services*
Electronic Page Makeup: *Thompson Steele Production Services*
Printer and Binder: *R. R. Donnelley*
Cover Printer: *Coral Graphic Services, Inc.*

Principles of Marketing, Fourth Edition

Library of Congress Cataloging-in-Publication Data

Kinnear, Thomas C., 1943–
    Principles of marketing / Thomas C. Kinnear, Kenneth L. Bernhardt,
Kathleen A. Krentler. -- 4th ed.
      p.   cm.
    ISBN 0-673-46555-1
      1. Marketing.   I. Bernhardt, Kenneth L., 1944–   . II. Krentler,
Kathleen A. III. Title
HF5415.K5227   1995
658.8--dc20   94-24391
                                                                        CIP

94 95 96 97 9 8 7 6 5 4 3 2 1

To Connie, Maggie, and Jamie

To Kathy and Karen

Love to Rick, Sarah, and Hannah

To Dana, our sun, mountain, and water

Brief Contents

ConTenTs

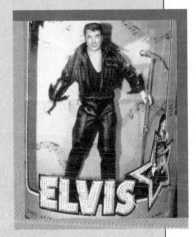

part II

The
Marketplace

 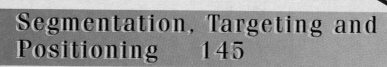

5

Segmentation, Targeting and Positioning   145

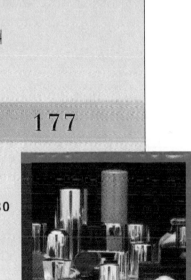

6   Consumer Buying Behavior   177

CHapTeR

CHAPTER 7

Business Markets and Organizational Buying Behavior   209

8 Information for Marketing Decision Making   239

CHapTeR

part III

Product

9   **Basic Product Concepts**   **277**

CHAPTER

10

Product Development and Management   309

part IV

Distribution

11   Channels of Distribution   351

CHAPTER

12 Wholesaling and Physical Distribution   391

CHApTeR

13 Retailing   429

CHAPTER

PART IV CASE
THE STORY OF HARLEY-DAVIDSON:
DISTRIBUTION
462

part V

Promotion

14   Communication Strategies   467

CHApTeR

15 Advertising, Sales Promotion, and Publicity   509

CHapTeR

16   Personal Selling   547

part VI

Pricing

17   Basic Pricing Concepts   587

CHApTeR

17 Fundamental Economic Analysis for Pricing Decisions   616

ApPendix

18 Pricing Procedures   633

CHapTeR

PART VI CASE
THE STORY OF HARLEY-DAVIDSON:
PRICING
664

part VII
**Marketing
Applications**

19   Marketing of Services   669

20 Marketing in the Social Sector   699

CHAPTER

Financial Concepts for Marketing Analysis   733

A
ApPendiX

B
ApPendix

Instructions for Using the Personal Computer Exercises Disk   747

Preface

In the five years since the third edition of *Principles of Marketing* was published, the world has undergone dramatic change. We live in a world without a defined set of borders, both politically and technologically, as the information highway stretches before us with untold possibilities. Recent changes have resulted in new and challenging developments in the field of marketing, which every student needs to learn and understand.

In response to these demands, we have created a book that is relevant and up-to-date. We've reorganized and expanded our coverage of global perspectives in the marketplace. We've included real issues that are important not only to you as professors, but also to your students—issues such as ethics, quality, customer satisfaction and value, careers, and the use of technology in marketing. And we've put together an outstanding ancillary package designed to extend the integration of theory and application that is a hallmark of our text.

WHAT'S NEW ABOUT *PRINCIPLES OF MARKETING, FOURTH EDITION?*

The fourth edition of *Principles of Marketing* represents a significant revision of the text. Here are a few of the major new features:

▪ New co-author, Kathy Krentler, brings a distinctive teaching orientation to the material. Kathy's experience in the classroom, her knowledge of students' needs and interests, and her joy in teaching the principles course combine with the traditional research base of the text to give this edition the best of both worlds: a strong theoretical foundation enhanced with compelling real-world applications and examples.

▪ An increasing focus on the globalization of marketing is reflected through the addition of international reviewers to our reviewer team, who contributed to the global marketing chapter (Chapter 4) and an array of in-text global examples.

▪ The strong integration of real-world examples and applications is reflected most dramatically in a new part-ending case, an overview of which is included on the front inside cover of the text. The compelling story of Harley-Davidson describes the superior marketing strategy that helped this exciting company not only increase its market share, but also surpass its earlier prominence. In addition, each text includes a survey that asks students to answer questions about Harley-Davidson. HarperCollins has arranged for Harley-Davidson to tabulate the national results of student surveys, which can then be used as an aid in demonstrating marketing research in action and in teaching Chapter 8, *Information for Marketing Decision Making*.

- New case applications at the end of each chapter enable students to apply the concepts covered in the chapter to actual situations faced by real companies.

- A new feature, Career Focus, appears at the end of each chapter. Written by Sue Cohn, Career Counselor, Stern School of Business, New York University, and Don Hudson, Career Counselor, School of Management, Yale University, the material demonstrates to students how they can apply the marketing concepts presented in the chapter in their own career search.

- The totally new ancillary package that accompanies the text extends the emphasis on the integration of theory with real-world applications and examples. Unique and all-new components include an international lecture series with eight lectures written by professors from different countries around the world; teaching notes for the Harley-Davidson case; sample articles from *American Demographics* magazine; and a laserdisc and video case study of the marketing plan for a full-length feature film, *The Last of the Mohicans*.

- A vibrant new design underscores the excitement of the marketing discipline and uses color to enhance the features of the text, while a new photo program illustrates the many timely marketing campaigns that are discussed. Tables and figures have been enhanced and rerendered to provide students with illustrative aids that facilitate learning.

HOW IS *PRINCIPLES OF MARKETING* ORGANIZED?

A number of organizational changes have been made to the text to help students understand the material in a logical sequence and to emphasize the critical topics in marketing as it is taught and practiced today.

- *Part One, Marketing and the Environment*, now includes four chapters. Global Marketing, previously Chapter 23, is now Chapter 4. The Marketing Environment, previously Chapter 3, is now Chapter 2, and we integrate topics from third edition Chapter 8—Public Policy, Regulation, and Ethical Marketing Practices—here. We devote an entire chapter to Marketing Planning (Chapter 3), which had been presented with marketing management in Chapter 2.

- *Part Two, The Marketplace*, previously five chapters, now includes four chapters. Third edition Chapter 8 is integrated into Chapter 2, The Marketing Environment. Ethics is also integrated throughout the text where appropriate.

- *Part Three, Product*, is similar to the third edition in structure.

- *Part Four, Distribution*, now includes three chapters. The third edition chapters on wholesaling and physical distribution are integrated into one chapter, Chapter 12.

- *Part Five, Promotion*, has a new chapter on communication strategies, which is Chapter 14. This replaces third edition Chapter 15, Promotion: Basic Concepts.

- *Part Six, Pricing*, now includes an Appendix to Chapter 17, which covers some of the more technical material on demand.

- *Part Seven, Specific Marketing Situations*, was reduced from four chapters to two, to cover marketing of services and marketing in the social sector.

- The careers material that appeared in Appendix A in the third edition is now integrated and appears as a Career Focus feature at the end of each chapter. This material is all new and now serves to reinforce marketing principles from each of the chapters. Appendix B of the third edition, Financial Concepts for Marketing Analysis, has been revised and is now Appendix A. A new appendix—Appendix B, Using the Personal Computer Exercises Disk—provides students with step-by-step instructions for using the software that is included with the text.

WHAT CONTENT CHANGES HAVE BEEN MADE WITHIN CHAPTERS?

▪ *Chapter 1, Introduction to Marketing*, provides students with an overview of the marketing discipline and current issues in the discipline. The chapter presents an expanded discussion of the production, marketing, and societal marketing concepts. The marketing mix (the four Ps) is now introduced in this chapter. New discussions reflect these concerns of marketers in the 1990s: the market-driven organization, relationship marketing, total quality management (TQM), green marketing, and global marketing.

▪ *Chapter 2, The Marketing Environment*, examines the key environmental forces that affect a firm. The chapter emphasizes relevant demographic factors such as the aging U.S. population, work force shifts, and the changing makeup of families. Current cultural factors, such as changing gender roles, cultural diversity, and changing values, are discussed. This chapter now treats issues such as consumerism, antitrust legislation, and ethics and social responsibility, the impact of the global economy on technological innovation, and ecoresponsibility and provides a global look at ecological factors. The material on environmental scanning, analysis, and diagnosis is treated in the context of putting together an environmental analysis.

▪ *Chapter 3, Marketing Planning*, examines the strategic marketing planning process as practiced by firms. The topics discussed provide a blueprint for the remainder of the book. The chapter uses examples from organizations that include Elvis Presley Enterprises, Philips International, the Disney Corporation, Gymboree, and American Express to explore the steps in the planning process.

▪ *Chapter 4, Global Marketing*, examines the framework within which global marketing occurs. This chapter looks at the implications of well-known global trade agreements such as the United States–Canada Free Trade Agreement and the North American Free Trade Agreement (NAFTA), the types of companies involved in global marketing, and methods of operation in the global arena.

▪ *Chapter 5, Segmentation, Targeting, and Positioning*, examines these three related processes. The chapter has been expanded to include material on geodemographic segmentation and criteria for selecting target markets. The authors discuss such targeting strategies as differentiated marketing, concentrated marketing, and disaggregation.

▪ *Chapter 6, Consumer Buying Behavior*, helps students understand the processes ultimate consumers go through in deciding to make a purchase. The chapter now includes a discussion of post-purchase dissonance as well as a description of the three types of reference groups: membership, aspiration, and disassociative. Situational factors are divided into five categories: physical surroundings, social surroundings, temporal perspective, task definition, and antecedent states.

▪ *Chapter 7, Business Markets and Organizational Buying Behavior*, focuses on those buying behaviors that are unique to businesses. The chapter has been reorganized and updated to include added coverage of relationship marketing and strategic alliances, a classification scheme for business market types, and business market segmentation. The section on the differences between business and consumer markets now includes in-depth discussions of demand, market size, and promotional techniques.

■ *Chapter 8, Information for Marketing Decision Making,* examines how marketers obtain the information they need to make decisions. The chapter opens with the impact of decision support systems and marketing information systems on marketing decision making. New topics focus on the relevance of personal contacts with other managers and personal experience, worldwide use of marketing research, using completed research, and the importance of qualitative and quantitative data. The discussion of forecasting methods has been updated to include a discussion of executive opinion and expert opinion surveys.

■ *Chapter 9, Basic Product Concepts,* takes a first look at the issues that are associated with marketing products. The chapter discusses the three-component definition of a product. Coverage of the classification of consumer goods and the product life cycle has been expanded. The chapter includes the latest research on the importance of brands and a section on new labeling requirements.

■ *Chapter 10, Product Development and Management,* discusses the process of developing new products and evaluating why products succeed or fail. The chapter now opens with a discussion of new product opportunities. We then address why new products succeed or fail and how to manage as well as modify existing products. The section on quality issues in product development and management has been rewritten to include current topics such as total quality management.

■ *Chapter 11, Channels of Distribution,* focuses on the issues that are critical in the channels of distribution. The chapter explores how goods and services move throughout the channels of distribution, how channels are organized, and what kinds of decisions are involved in managing channels of distribution. The chapter explores new systems of distribution and includes current information about electronic data interchange and strategic issues in market coverage.

■ *Chapter 12, Wholesaling and Physical Distribution,* combines the coverage of these two topics. The chapter explores how wholesaling works, as well as the objectives, management, organization, and operation of physical distribution systems. New discussions focus on retail-owned warehouses, distribution centers, independent wholesalers, channel integration, just-in-time distribution, and TQM as implemented in a market-driven physical distribution system.

■ *Chapter 13, Retailing,* focuses on this dynamic area of marketing. New topics in this chapter include global mail-order retailing and technological advancements as they relate to nonstore retailing such as teleshopping and retail management.

■ *Chapter 14, Communication Strategies,* introduces the concept of integrated marketing communications. The chapter includes an expanded examination of how the concept of response hierarchies helps marketers understand consumer responses to a particular marketing communication. Two new models are added to this discussion: the innovation adoption and the information-processing models. New topics under mix planning factors include the channel membership relationship and globalization.

■ *Chapter 15, Advertising, Sales Promotion, and Publicity,* focuses on those promotional tools. The chapter emphasizes the importance of integrating all promotional efforts into a single, integrated marketing communications plan. New discussions focus on ethical issues in advertising and how the monitoring of advertising ethics has become a global concern. New topics under sales promotion include contests and sweepstakes, bonus packs, price-offs, and event sponsorship.

- *Chapter 16, Personal Selling*, discusses the importance of personal selling to an organization, reviews the types of sales jobs, and examines the management of the sales force. The chapter has been updated to include the concept of team selling. We discuss ethical considerations in telemarketing and compare and contrast sales training in Japan with sales training in the United States and Canada. The chapter looks at the need for sales personnel to be trained to understand cross-cultural differences.

- *Chapter 17, Basic Pricing Concepts*, focuses on the basic concepts that underlie pricing decisions: pricing objectives, customer influences, cost considerations, product characteristics, competitive forces, and legal and regulatory constraints. The concepts of demand analysis, price elasticity, marginal analysis, cost analysis, and other economic principles are now covered in an appendix to this chapter. A Marketing in Action box on Wal-Mart's predatory pricing tactics highlights ethical pricing considerations.

- *Chapter 18, Pricing Procedures*, examines how costs represent a starting point for pricing strategy and then goes on to cover differential pricing, competitive pricing, product-line pricing, and miscellaneous pricing methods. New to this edition is a discussion of differential pricing for consumers such as second market discounting, periodic discounting, and random discounts. Other new topics include price signaling and the various product-line pricing methods, such as price bundling, premium pricing, image pricing, and complementary pricing.

- *Chapter 19, Marketing of Services*, examines the basic characteristics of services marketing. The chapter includes, as part of a broader discussion of the changing services environment, a discussion of Lovelock's six myths regarding the U.S. economy's service sector. Other topics new to this chapter include the growth of franchising, the expansion of leasing and rental businesses, and globalization.

- *Chapter 20, Marketing in the Social Sector*, examines the characteristics of social sector organizations and how marketing for those organizations differs from marketing in profit-making firms. The chapter has been updated to include a detailed discussion of the factors that have led to the rise in social sector marketing, and it includes material on strategic planning, consumer behavior, fund raising, and cause-related marketing.

HOW DOES THIS TEXT UNIQUELY AID STUDENTS IN MASTERING *PRINCIPLES OF MARKETING*?

Principles of Marketing, Fourth Edition, has been developed to assist students in mastering the concepts and topics that are presented in the text. These carefully constructed aids help to facilitate comprehension.

Learning Objectives. These objectives guide the student through the concepts presented in the chapter.

Marketing Profile. Each chapter opens with a Marketing Profile that previews the issues in the chapter. The profile presents a real situation in which marketing decisions were made. Examples include:

- an account of how the special distribution procedures implemented by Avon enable the company to gain market share in China (Chapter 4)

- an exploration of the factors considered in launching the Healthy Choice product line (Chapter 10)

- a discussion of how the Australian Tourist Commission uses an integrated marketing plan to streamline the tourism effort and to attract visitors "down under" (Chapter 14)

Marketing in Action. Each chapter contains at least two Marketing in Action boxes that provide concise illustrations of chapter concepts. Selected features, called "Spotlights," reflect coverage of special areas such as global marketing, societal marketing, ethics, green marketing, and technology. Examples include

- Are there Perfect Answers About Greenness? (Spotlight on Green Marketing, Chapter 2)

- Pepsico's Distribution Applications in Mexico (Spotlight on Global Marketing, Chapter 11)

- Electronic Retailing—Current Uses and Future Possibilities (Spotlight on Technology, Chapter 13)

- The Battle over Old Joe Camel (Spotlight on Ethics, Chapter 15)

Review Your Marketing Knowledge. These interim questions appear at least twice in each chapter. They are designed to challenge students to think about and review the material they have been reading.

Personal Computer Exercises. These exercises (one per chapter) allow students to explore issues presented in the chapter in more depth. The exercise is explained in the chapter and implemented on a self-contained computer disk (IBM version) that is included with the text. Examples include using actual demographic and sociocultural databases to analyze trends and an evaluation of alternative brands. These exercises are all new and provide a wonderful opportunity for students to apply the current technology to marketing principles. *The Macintosh version is available upon request from the publisher.*

End-of-Chapter Features. These features include the following:

- *Key Points.* These are presented at the end of each chapter to reinforce learning.

- *Key Terms.* A list of critical terms and concepts introduced in the chapter are provided, along with page references, and the terms are defined in the end-of-text glossary.

- *Issues for Discussion.* These questions help students think through the implications of the concepts introduced in the chapter.

- *Case Applications.* These cases (one per chapter) give students the opportunity to apply the concepts they have studied to real-world business situations. Examples include the environmental factors that affect marketing planning at Fisher-Price Toys (Chapter 3, Marketing Planning); the practices used by Illinois Bell to target the increasing number of telecommuters (Chapter 5, Segmentation, Targeting, and Positioning); the efforts of Barna Research Group, a firm that provides market research to churches and religious groups (Chapter 8, Information for Marketing Decision Making).

- *Career Focus.* These new end-of-chapter exercises reinforce the concepts presented in the chapter and enable students to develop marketing plans for themselves, as a career search aid. Selected chapters present information on related positions in marketing. Examples include applying the 4 Ps to one's own job search (Chapter 1, Introduction to Marketing); mastering the skills required in the global job market (Chapter 4, Global Marketing); and learning to research the hidden job market (Chapter 8, Information for Marketing Decision Making).

Harley-Davidson Case Study. This running case, found at the end of each part, highlights Harley-Davidson and helps demonstrate how marketing decisions led to the turnaround of this exciting company. Each installment of the case focuses on the elements of Harley-Davidson's story as it relates to the concepts presented in that part. After reviewing the installment, students answer questions that enable them to demonstrate mastery of the related marketing concepts.

End-of-text features. These features have been created to provide students with further support as they study *Principles of Marketing*.

- *Appendix A, Financial Concepts for Marketing Analysis*—This appendix introduces the student to the financial concepts necessary for an understanding of marketing.

- *Appendix B, Instructions for Using the Personal Computer Exercises Disk*— Appendix B provides instructions for running the PC Exercises.

- *Glossary*—An end-of-text glossary includes and defines all key terms that are boldfaced in the text.

- *Notes*—This section provides references for all items cited in the text.

- *Name/Subject* and *Company/Product/ Service Indexes*— Two indexes allow students access to specific companies and products and to subjects mentioned in the text.

HOW DOES THE *PRINCIPLES OF MARKETING* ANCILLARY PACKAGE UNIQUELY AID PROFESSORS IN THEIR TEACHING?

No marketing textbook would be complete without a comprehensive, up-to-the-minute ancillary package. Whereas an introductory marketing text should provide both the theory and the case examples which make major issues understandable and clear to the student, the ancillary package should show the real world of marketing in action through a wide range of media.

We are especially proud of the materials that accompany our fourth edition. We have placed a strong emphasis on integrating theory with real-world practice by including some of the most successful marketers in the business world today. By significantly expanding our package, we are able to offer a stimulating array of support materials which both instructors and students will find useful and exciting.

Printed Materials

Instructor's Manual (including Transparency Masters)

This manual was prepared by Catherine Glod of Mohawk Valley Community College. Its many features include:

- detailed chapter outlines

- hands-on assignments for each chapter

- a minimum of three original class exercises that stress cooperative learning, critical thinking, learning through writing, TQM, and classroom research. These exercises are specifically tied to concepts in the text and include complete answers.

- group-discussion exercises

- teaching hints and techniques

- answers to Review Your Marketing Knowledge questions

- guidelines for using the Career Focus sections in the main text

- experiential exercises

- small-business perspectives

- cultural and historical perspectives

- answers to the questions included in the part-ending Harley-Davidson case

The *Instructor's Manual* also includes many original transparency masters (see Transparencies and Acetates below).

Study Guide

Developed by Marjorie J. Cooper of Baylor University, the *Study Guide* features many valuable tools and exercises for the student. Sold as a separate saleable item, the *Guide* includes the following:

- fill-in chapter outlines and summaries designed to help students organize an overview of each chapter in their minds

- multiple-choice questions and true–false questions, including answers

- application scenarios in each chapter designed to help students apply concepts

- cases in each chapter that require in-depth understanding and application of marketing principles and concepts

- short-answer essay questions in cases, including suggested answers

Two Test Banks

Nearly 4,000 test questions are available in two separate test banks. *Test Bank 1* contains 2,000 all-new questions prepared by Steven A. Taylor of Illinois State University. *Test Bank 2* also contains 2,000 questions. Developed by André L. Honorée of Delgado Community College, *Test Bank 2* is based on the third edition's set of questions and is primarily intended for community college adopters.

Harley-Davidson Annual Report Teaching Notes

This guide, organized according to the seven parts of the main text, is offered to instructors as a complement to the running case on Harley-Davidson in the text. The *Teaching Notes*, prepared by Steven A. Taylor of Illinois State University, provide additional information about the company and helpful ideas for integrating material from the company's annual report in the classroom. Instructors can use excerpts from the report as handy teaching tools and as further sources of information for students. Transparency masters with additional Harley-Davidson material are also provided.

International Lecture Series

The purpose of the International Lecture Series is to enable instructors to provide students with a truly global perspective on marketing. Written by professors from around the globe, these lectures focus on marketing topics specific to the author's particular region and take roughly 20 to 40 minutes to deliver. Bibliographies are included in order to facilitate further research by professors and students. The series includes the following lectures:

- "Ecological Marketing: Euro-Marketing" by Manfred Kirchgeorg and Heribert Meffert, Universitat Munster, Germany

- "How *Newsweek* Was Successfully Launched in the Japanese News Magazine Market" by Ichiro Horide, Rcitaku University, Japan

- "The North American Free Trade Agreement" by Peggy Cunningham of Queen's University, Canada

- "Pricing in International Markets: A European Perspective" by John Fahy of Trinity College, Ireland

- "The Role and Nature of Brands" by Leslie de Chernatony of City University Business School, England

- "A Framework for Investigating the Option of Going Global" by Joel Saegert of University of Texas at San Antonio

- "How and Why to Develop a Company Image in Mexico (Using Sponsorships and Billboards)" by Arturo Z. Vásquez-Párraga at Florida International University

- "The Green Consumer in Europe" by Manfred Kirchgeorg and Heribert Meffert, Universitat Munster, Germany

American Demographics Sampler

Compiled by Paula Francese of the University of New Hampshire, this *Sampler* contains a variety of articles, tables, and graphs from recent issues of *American Demographics* magazine. These selections focus on trends in modern American society and relate not only to consumer behavior sections but to all parts of the text. Each article is, in essence, an extended example of a concept from the text. The *Sampler* also provides lecture notes and transparency masters which pertain to these excerpts and support the teaching of this material in the classroom. Each section includes at least three articles per topic, with supporting tables.

Software

TestMaster (IBM and Mac)

The HarperCollins TestMaster program is a computerized test generator that lets you construct tests by choosing questions from item banks that were prepared specifically for the textbook and course. The test construction process involves the use of a simple TestMaster Forum that is filled in on the computer screen, where test questions can be edited, saved, and printed. In addition, questions can be added to any test or item bank, or new item banks of test questions and graphics may be created.

Program Features. The TestMaster program offers the following features that are useful in test construction:

- Tests and item banks can include five types of questions: multiple-choice, true-false, matching, short-answer (any kind, including fill-in and completion), and essay.

- A supplementary page attached to each item bank question can contain its topic, objective, skill, difficulty, and other user-added information.

- Test questions can be chosen in a variety of ways including manual selection, random selection, choose while viewing, and choose by searching.

- Questions chosen for a test can be viewed and edited without affecting the original versions of the questions in the item bank.

- Test size is limited only by the memory capacity of the computer and the length of questions chosen.

- Test questions can be printed in the exact order specified or grouped and sorted automatically by the program.

- Test questions can be imported to or exported from the TestMaster program and the computer's own word-processing software.

- Printer files can be created or modified to take advantage of the capabilities of the printer.

Package Components. Each TestMaster package consists of

- the TestMaster program and the TestMaster utilities

- one or more TestMaster item bank disks

- a TestMaster user's guide

QuizMaster (IBM and Mac)

QuizMaster-TM is a program for IBM and Macintosh computers that coordinates with the TestMaster test-generator program. QuizMaster allows students to take a timed or untimed test created with TestMaster at the computer. Upon completing a test, a student can see his or her test score and view or print a diagnostic report that lists the topics or objectives that have been mastered or that need to be restudied. When QuizMaster is installed on a network, student scores are saved on disk, and instructors can use the QuizMaster utility program to view records and print reports for individual students, class sections, and entire courses.

MarketSim (IBM and Mac)

Developed by Stuart W. James and Michael Deighan of Interpretive Software, Inc., and Thomas C. Kinnear, co-author of the *Principles* text, this brand management computer simulation is based on the over-the-counter cold medicine industry. MarketSim can be used to accompany any principles of marketing text.

As members of a marketing management team, participants make decisions regarding product mix, pricing, distribution, advertising, and promotion. The simulation reveals how both the firm and its competitors perform over a ten-year period. Offered as a separate saleable item, the MarketSim package includes an in-depth *Student's Manual* and comes in three versions:

- Instructor's version, which includes both MS-DOS and Mac software, as well as an *Instructor's Manual* and transparency masters prepared by Ann Root, formerly of the University of Notre Dame

- MS-DOS student version, including student's manual

- Mac student version, including student's manual

A Windows version of the software is also available from Stuart W. James, Interpretive Software, 1932 Arlington Blvd., #107, Charlottesville, VA 22903.

Transparencies and Acetates

Four-Color Transparency Acetates

Figures, tables, and images from the text, including some original images, have been prepared as four-color acetate transparencies by Catherine Glod of Mohawk Valley Community College for overhead projection during classroom presentation of the materials.

Transparency Masters

Catherine Glod has also developed original transparency masters, which are included in the *Instructor's Manual* and can be photocopied onto transparency acetates.

Electronic Transparencies

Electronic transparency slides consisting of the transparency acetates and transparency masters are available upon request from the HarperCollins Software Services Group.

Laserdisc and Video

A *Teaching Guide* prepared by Catherine Glod of Mohawk Valley Community College and Gerard J. Tellis of the University of Southern California accompanies the following laserdisc and video materials.

Two-sided Laserdisc

- Side 1: A case study of the marketing of the film *The Last of the Mohicans* (Twentieth Century Fox)—This section, developed by Gerard J. Tellis of the University of Southern California, is a four-part case study of the marketing of a major motion picture, *The Last of the Mohicans*. The case allows students to solve real-life marketing problems according to concepts they have learned from the *Principles* text. Issues such as the timing of the release of the film, the film's positioning strategy, and the advertising and promotional campaign are discussed. Original film footage, behind the scenes footage, film and advertising stills, and interviews with Twentieth Century Fox executives are included. *The Last of the Mohicans* press kit and ads are included in the *Teaching Guide* to support the case in the classroom.

- Side 2: Lecture launchers, featuring Harley-Davidson—Side 2 of the laserdisc features video clips focusing on many companies, such as Harley-Davidson and the Girl Scouts of the U.S.A. The Harley-Davidson segment supports the running case in the book, while the other company clips, such as one about Loblaw's President's Choice brands, present assorted marketing issues which relate directly to the seven parts of the *Principles* text.

- Visual Stills—Both sides of the laserdisc also include visual stills taken from images (advertisements, graphs, charts, tables, etc.) in the *Principles* text and from the transparency acetates for classroom presentation and discussion. These stills include advertisements for Harley-Davidson motorcycles and promotional materials for *The Last of the Mohicans*.

Video Cases

Like the laserdisc, the video contains the motion picture case study and the company video clips, featuring Harley-Davidson.

HOW WAS *PRINCIPLES OF MARKETING, FOURTH EDITION,* DEVELOPED?

A critical part of the development of any text includes the contributions made by professors around the country and, in this case, around the world. The authors wish to acknowledge the contributions of Marjorie J. Cooper for her work on the product and pricing materials, of Sue Cohn and Don Hudson for the Career Focus, and of Stuart W. James for the preparation of the PC Exercises and MarketSim. The authors also acknowledge the contributions of those colleagues who reviewed earlier editions of the text.

C. L. Abercrombie
Memphis State University

Gerald S. Albaum
University of Oregon

Joe Cantrell
De Anza College

Wayne Chandler
Eastern Illinois University

Kent Claussen
Parkland College

William Curtis
University of Nebraska

Les R. Dlaby
Lake Forest College

Michael J. Etzell
University of Notre Dame

Cynthia Forbes
Golden Gate University

Peggy Gilbert
Southwest Missouri State University

Marlene Katz
Canada College

Stephen P. King
Keene State College

R. Eugene Klippel
Grand Valley State College

Duncan G. LaBay
University of Lowell

Ross Lanser
University of California Santa Cruz

Ford Laumer
Auburn University

Marilyn Liebrenz-Himes
George Washington University

Jill Long
Valparaiso University

Lynn J. Loudenback
New Mexico State University

Michael Mayo
Kent State University

Karen McDonnel Christensen
University of South Florida

Martin Meyers
University of Wisconsin–Stevens Point

Ronald Michaels
University of Kansas

Keith Murray
Northeastern University

Joseph Myslivec
Central Michigan University

Donald G. Norris
Miami University

Allan V. Palmer
University of North Carolina

Terry Paul
The Ohio State University

Judith Powell
University of Richmond

Robert Reuchert
University of Minnesota

Edward A. Riordan
Wayne State University

Bruce Seaton
Florida International University

Donald L. Shawver
University of Missouri, Columbia

Bill Tadlock
University of Arkansas–Little Rock

Burk C. Tower
University of Wisconsin–Oshkosh

Judy Wilkinson
University of Akron

We also acknowledge the comments and guidance of those of our colleagues on the reviewing panel for the fourth edition. These reviewers, located within the United States, provided invaluable support and advice.

April Atwood
University of Washington

Ronald Bauerly
Western Illinois University

Stephen Bell
New York University

Deirdre Bird
Northeastern University

Greg Black
Washington State University

Mary Jo Boehms
Jackson State Community College

Nicholas Brockunier
University of Maryland

Joseph D. Cangelosi, Jr.
University of Central Arkansas

William J. Carner
University of Texas, Autin

Richard P. Carr, Jr.
University of Arkansas at Little Rock

Kenny K. Chan
California State University, Chico

Paul Chao
University of Northern Iowa

Barbara Coe
University of North Texas

Catherine Cole
University of Iowa

Jane Cromartie
University of New Orleans

Douglas J. Dalrymple
Indiana University

William M. Diamond
SUNY-Albany

Dale F. Duhan
Texas Tech University

Basil Englis
Rutgers University

Leisa R. Flynn
Florida State University

Jeffrey P. Frank
St. Cloud State University

John F. Gaski
University of Notre Dame

Peggy S. Gilbert
Southwest Missouri State University

Marc Goldberg
Portland State University

David J. Good
Central Missouri State University

James S. Gould
Pace University–White Plains

Donald B. Guest
East Carolina University

Carolyn J. Hanka
Mankato State University

Nessim Hanna
Northern Illinois University

Susan E. Heckler
University of Arizona

Santord B. Helman
Middlesex County College

Paul Herbig
Jacksonville State University

Bernie Jaworski
University of Southern California

Jean Johnson
Washington State University

Marlene Kahla
Stephen F. Austin State University

Herbert Katzenstein
St. John's University

Tina Kiesler
Rutgers University

Irene Lang
California State University–Fullerton

Gary D. Law
Cuyahoga Community College–East

Richard C. Leventhal
Metropolitan State College

Bernard L. Martin
University of San Francisco

Melvin R. Mattson
Radford University

James McAlexander
Oregon State University

Ray McAlister
University of North Texas

Dennis R. McDermott
Virginia Commonwealth University

William C. Moser
Ball State University

Michael S. Noble
Sonoma State University

William Perttula
San Francisco State University

Lawrence Peterson
County College of Morris

Neal Proctor
Southwest Texas State University

Gary Reiman
City College of San Francisco

Robert G. Roe
University of Wyoming

John W. Schouten
University of Portland

Larry J. Seibert
Purdue University–North Central Campus

Chuck Slowe
University of South Dakota

Lois J. Smith
University of Wisconsin–Whitewater

Michael Solomon
Rutgers University

James V. Spiers
Arizona State University

Ronald W. Stampfl
San Diego State University

Philip J. Straub
Phillips Junior College

Harold Teer
James Madison University

Andrew J. Thacker
California State Polytechnic University

John Weiss
Colorado State University

Ron Weston
Contra Costa College

James H. Wilkins
University of Southwestern Louisiana

Jerry W. Wilson
Georgia Southern University

Timothy W. Wright
Lakeland Community College

We also solicited reviews and suggestions from professors at schools in various parts of the world. These reviewers were very thorough in their review of the manuscript and extremely forthcoming and generous in their suggestions for internationalizing the material. We owe a great debt to these colleagues at schools around the world.

Ida E. Berger
Queen's University, Kingston, Canada

Robert Carty
University of Greenwich

Peggy Cunningham
Queen's University, Kingston, Canada

Leslie de Chernatony
City University Business School, London

Nimr Eid
American University of Beirut

John Fahy
University of Dublin

J.D. Forbes
The University of British Columbia

John Hulland
University of Western Ontario

Neil C. Macpherson
Napier University

Paul Michell
Manchester Business School

Pete Naudé
Manchester Business School

Mike Shaw
Monash University

Ajay K. Sirisi
York University

Brock Smith
University of Victoria

Development and preparation of the text was truly an integrated team effort. We owe a great deal of appreciation to the staff at HarperCollins. We thank Anne Smith, our editor, for her creativity, determination, persistence, and courage for driving the book and associated aids to completion; Arlene Bessenoff for her outstanding insights and leadership as developmental editor; and Kate Steinbacher for her boundless energy in marketing the text. Jay O'Callaghan was an inspiration early on with this project, and Diana Acevedo provided marketing assistance. Nina Nowak, with her keen editorial eye and outstanding writing skills, was especially helpful with the Harley-Davidson case, the International Lecture Series, and related supporting teaching materials. We are grateful for the efforts of Eric Jorgensen in speeding the book through production. The advertising materials were enhanced by the efforts of Lisa Littman, Zina Scarpulla, Rob Westbrook, and Amy Spinthourakis. W. Jo Bakal-Schlomann put together a superb video and laserdisc package. We owe much to Susan Katz, Susan Driscoll, Mike Britton, and Bob Carlton for the support that they continue to give to this text.

Julie Zasloff masterfully organized each element of the supplements package within a tight schedule while working with a collage of authors and contributors: Marjorie J. Cooper, Paula Francese, Catherine Glod, André L. Honorée, and Steven A. Taylor. We'd also like to thank Peter Francese, founder and President of American Demographics, Inc., for his support and advice on including demographic and psychographic information throughout the text. The PC Exercises were designed and programmed by Michael Deighan, Mary Juraco, and Stuart W. James of Interpretive Software in Charlottesville, Virginia. Version 1.0 of the software was reviewed by Michael Mayo of Kent State University, David Stringer of DeAnza College, Ronald Michaels of Indiana University, Stephen Bell of New York University, and Richard Leventhal of Metropolitan State College.

At ICC, we acknowledge the efforts and talents of Sally Steele and Elinor Stapleton. Further, we know that the prose would not have read as well without the efforts of "supereditor" Steve Perine and without the talents of Becky Kohn, and the photo program would be sorely lacking without the vision of Diane Kraut. We thank Tim Becker for his efforts in researching many statistics and for his valuable contributions to the many up-to-date examples that are found throughout the book. These examples would lack richness and depth without Tim's input. We also thank Lee Young for checking the more technical figures.

We are indebted to Twentieth Century Fox for their help on *The Last of the Mohicans*. We thank the following individuals: Andrea Jaffe, President, Domestic Marketing; Tom Sherak, Senior Executive Vice President; Nancy Utley, Executive Vice President, Marketing, Media, and Research; Tony Sella, Senior Vice President, Marketing and Creative Advertising; and Bruce Pfander, Senior Vice President, FoxVideo Marketing. Most especially we appreciate Ira Rubenstein, Manager, Media Research, for his coordination of the video case.

Finally, and most especially, Harley-Davidson provided a tremendous amount of help and partnership, particularly the Brand Management Group. The company truly practices the best of marketing principles. Each person with whom we interacted was a pleasure. They are an extraordinarily professional group and just an especially nice bunch of people. For our wonderful relationship with Harley-Davidson, we are sincerely grateful.

We hope that each of you who uses this book learns from it and enjoys marketing as much as we have loved studying and living this discipline and, most especially, writing this text.

Thomas C. Kinnear
Kenneth L. Bernhardt
Kathleen A. Krentler
October 1994

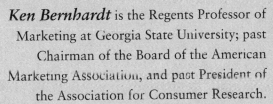

About The Authors

Tom Kinnear is Vice President for Development at the University of Michigan; D. Maynard Phelps Professor of Marketing; and former Editor of the *Journal of Marketing*.

Ken Bernhardt is the Regents Professor of Marketing at Georgia State University; past Chairman of the Board of the American Marketing Association, and past President of the Association for Consumer Research.

Kathy Krentler joins the fourth edition team by bringing invaluable insight as a teacher of the Principles of Marketing course at San Diego State University. She is a Professor of Marketing and also serves as Vice President for Programs of the Academy of Marketing Science. Kathy possesses an enthusiasm and commitment to the discipline that are evident throughout the text.

Discussing concepts and issues like relationship marketing, legal and ethical issues, green marketing, technology and total quality management, the fourth edition of *Principles of Marketing* represents a significant revision of this research-based text. Additionally, new co-author Kathleen Krentler brings a distinctive teaching orientation to the text. The fourth edition includes an increased focus on the globalization of marketing through an earlier placement of the global marketing chapter as well as an array of in-text global examples. The strong integration of real-world examples and applications is reflected most dramatically in the compelling story of Harley-Davidson. This running case details the superior marketing strategy that helped this company not only increase its market share, but also surpass its earlier prominence.

Principles of Marketing also provides students and professors with support through extensive learning aids like the "Marketing Profiles," "Marketing in Action" boxes, and "Career Focus" applications. The ancillary package that accompanies the text further extends the emphasis on integrating theory with real-world practice with an "International Lecture" series that includes lectures written by professors from around the world; teaching notes for the Harley-Davidson case; sample articles and information from *American Demographics* magazine; video laserdisc; and much more. Through each chapter and example, students learn how broadly marketing affects their everyday life. *Principles of Marketing*, 4e gives students an understanding of marketing in today's global economy as well as a glimpse of marketing in the 21st century.

HARLEY-DAVIDSON CASE STUDY

This running case, found at the end of each part, highlights Harley-Davidson and helps demonstrate how marketing decisions led to the turnaround of this exciting company. The Harley-Davidson story is further extended and integrated through the inclusion of a survey on students' perceptions of the firm, teaching tips in the Instructor's Manual, Teaching Notes for using the Harley-Davidson story, the Harley-Davidson annual report, and video footage of company events and advertising campaigns.

CHAPTER 3

Marketing Planning

LEARNING OBJECTIVES

Upon completing this chapter, you will be able to do the following:

■ **Describe** the steps involved in the strategic marketing planning process.

■ **Explain** the characteristics of a good business definition.

■ **Understand** the procedures involved in carrying out a situation analysis.

■ **Differentiate** between good and bad objectives.

■ **Discuss** the types of analyses available to aid marketing planners in formulating strategy.

■ **Identify** the differences between strategies and tactics.

■ **Understand** why control is so important to long-term success.

Marketing Profile

Keeping Elvis Alive Through Strategic Planning

Elvis Presley Enterprises (EPE) is far more than the purveyor of tacky mementos of the King of Rock & Roll. While it is true that EPE will gladly sell you a wide assortment of Elvis memorabilia including Elvis bracelets, scarves, and boxer shorts, it is equally true that EPE is a tightly run, aggressive, multimillion-dollar business that owes much of its success to careful planning.

The organization has been built around the image of Elvis Presley. The mission of EPE is to advance that image in a way that promotes the respectful and sincere persona that Elvis manifested throughout much of his career. The company has chosen this direction, the "high road" as CEO Jack Soden describes it, in recognition of the fact that Presley in the later years, before his death in 1977, portrayed an image inherently less marketable.

Elvis Presley Enterprises is organized around three divisions, each developed to advance Elvis's name and image in a different way. The three divisions are Graceland, Elvis's former home, now open for tours; licensing, the division that approves and allows the use of Elvis's name and image worldwide; and a music-publishing group. The music-publishing division works with RCA, which holds the rights to many of Elvis's songs, to oversee re-releases of the 750 songs Elvis recorded. The plans for each division are developed separately.

In the case of licensing, for example, there has been a move to increase the quality of merchandise bearing Elvis's name or picture. The organization is careful, however, to remember that products must be appropriate for the market. As one critic stated, "The challenge is making sure that [EPE] doesn't outclass its customers." Priscilla Presley, chair of EPE and Elvis's ex-wife, has said, "My staff tries to convince me . . . that the stuff is selling and we certainly don't want to put a stop to that."

The company engages in annual planning that includes decisions regarding which television shows, videos, and songs will be released in the upcoming year as well as where those releases will occur. People in upper management view this annual process as one of their most important jobs.

The payoff for this well-organized and aggressive firm has been significant profits. Although the firm divulges no financial data, estimates are that the Graceland complex (which includes not only Elvis's mansion but also an auto museum, an airplane museum, eight gift shops, the Heartbreak Hotel restaurant, Rockabilly's Diner, an ice cream parlor, post office, and movie theater) earns a minimum of $2.5 million annually. Furthermore, profits from Graceland and the licensing division are believed to pale in comparison to the earnings of the music-publishing division.

the past 20 years the television equipment market has almost gone completely to Japan. Only one U.S. company, Zenith, still makes television sets in the United States. However, with the introduction of HDTV, U.S. companies may get another chance to compete.

The process of technological innovation progresses from basic research to applied research to development and finally to production and marketing.[28] It takes time and money to carry out these four stages. Before biomedicine, energy, or any innovation reaches the marketing stage, years may have passed. For example, Xerography took about 18 years to move from the basic research stage to the development stage, and another 5 years to produce and market an office copier. In 1993, Polaroid introduced the Captiva, an instant camera with improved quality. The launch followed 3 years of development and an investment of more than $40 million.[29] Furthermore, other environmental forces such as the economy influence the innovation process. In an economic downturn, firms may invest less in research and development, opting instead to focus on proven products.

Marketing managers must be able to interpret technological changes and innovations in the environment. They must work closely with technological experts to translate knowledge and competence into marketable products and services. They must be aware of the interrelatedness of technological and other factors in the external environment. The potential problems of technological innovations like the commercial application of discoveries in HDTV need to be evaluated and understood.[30]

Global Technology

The advancement of technology is a global issue. The United States has been known as a world leader in the advancement of technology. To remain competitive, however, global research and development strategies must respond to changes in transportation, communication, information technology, and merged national markets. Intellectual capital is the critical resource in the global economy. The ability to generate, access, and rapidly use new knowledge and convert it (technology transfer) into marketable quality products and processes is the key to competitive advantage.[31]

Airbus Industrie is a cross-national European consortium that has developed and produced airplanes through support to its partner companies in the form of repayable loans.

SPOTLIGHT ON Societal Marketing

MARKETING IN ACTION

Marketing AIDS Prevention

Acquired immune deficiency syndrome, or AIDS, is a disease brought on by the human immuno-deficiency virus (HIV). The virus destroys the infected person's immune system, leaving the person susceptible to opportunistic infections, many of which can be fatal. There is no cure. The virus is most commonly spread through unpro-tected sexual activity or the sharing of needles. It is not spread by casual contact (e.g., kissing, hug-ging, holding hands).

The Department of Health and Human Services, the Public Health Service, and the Centers for Disease Control (CDC) along with public and private groups across the country are using mar-keting in an attempt to curb the spread of HIV. These groups are anx-ious to get out the mes-sage that each person in the country engaging in certain behaviors is at risk. However, everyone does not get the mes-sage in the same way. "Education efforts need to be community-spe-cific and sensitive to community standards and issues," states Tom Brandt, Associate Director of the National Commission on AIDS in Washington, DC.

Developing different messages for different groups allows hard-hitting communications to reach at-risk groups while minimizing the potential that they will reach others who might be offended. Intravenous drug users, for example, are the target of a pro-motional campaign spearheaded by "Bleachman," a Superman-like character with a bleach-bottle head who tells users to clean their needles before reusing or sharing them. Another at-risk segment of the population, homosexual men, is targeted with posters in gay bars and advertising in gay media. The group considered most at risk today,

adolescents ages 13–21, is targeted using HIV–AIDS awareness campaigns implemented in youth groups, boys' and girls' clubs, YMCAs, and other community-based organizations that meet the needs of teenagers.

The CDC does extensive market testing of the advertisements they produce before running them to determine their effectiveness and acceptability. They produced a TV spot that featured a young man infected with HIV holding a baby. The man tells the baby he'd like to be around to watch it grow up. While HIV-positive individuals found the ad effective, it bombed in test audiences repre-sentative of the general population. They ques-tioned how the man could have HIV or AIDS, while the baby did not. The CDC decided not to run the spot.

Other ads developed for general audiences have never run due to the difficulty of getting media to accept spots deemed controversial. This was the case with a poster developed by DDB-Needham, a large advertising agency, as part of an HIV–AIDS information campaign for the city of Chicago. The poster with the slogan Kissing Doesn't Kill depicted three cou-ples kissing: two men, two women, and a man and a woman.

The use of marketing to change behavior re-inforces the idea that the methods described in this book apply any time an exchange is occurring. Identifying a group of people and then developing a marketing effort directed at that group is a process that can be used whether your objective is profit, some other organizationally related measure, a decrease in consumption, or even a change in behavior.

"**W**hen I found out I had HIV at age 17, I learned that anyone can get it."

MARKETING TODAY AND TOMORROW

Marketing is a dynamic field. New ideas and philosophies regarding the best way to meet consumer wants and needs and provide customer satisfaction are constantly emerging. In this section we briefly introduce several issues that have emerged in the last few years. Each of these issues represents an idea or philosophy that will move marketing into the twenty-first century in a way that meets the evolving needs and concerns of consumers. Although the introductions in this section are brief, we will revisit each of these topics many times throughout the book.

The Market-Driven Organization

In the 1990s, organizations are increasingly attempting to implement the marketing concept by becoming market-driven or customer-driven. A **market-driven** organiza-tion is one in which all activities, by all functional parts of the organization, focus on the goal of customer satisfaction. Thus, research and development, finance, human resources, and production all view their mission as being to satisfy customers' cur-rent and potential needs. Marketing provides the key customer inputs and customer contact to guide this approach, typically through marketing research. Information obtained through research can be funneled to all parts of the organization, which

The Xerox Corporation is an example of a market-driven organization.

COMPLETE COVERAGE OF TECHNOLOGY

The text covers technology in marketing through the integration of in-text discussions (e.g., Chapter 2 discusses the implications of global technology) as well as through related "Marketing in Action" boxes. A related saleable supplement, *MarketSim,* based on the over-the-counter cold medicine industry, enables students to use technology to make decisions regarding product mix, pricing, distribution, advertising, and promotion.

MARKETING *IN ACTION*

SPOTLIGHT ON **Technology**

Advancing Technology Is Here: Are Consumers Ready?

More and more customers claim to want maturing technologies such as personal computers, networking, and electronic data interchange. The new into-the-future approach is, "Let the customer do it." Changing demographics such as declining numbers of adults and a low population growth rate combined with our increasing prominence as a service-oriented society means that fewer people are available to work as retail clerks and service attendants.

Businesses are implementing more self-service technologies for other reasons, which include cost leadership, product differentiation, bigger market share, and strategic advantage. Financial institutions originally intended that automatic teller machines (ATMs) would provide customers with convenient banking services at lower costs than tellers' salaries. Today about a half a trillion transactions are made by ATMs. Work is being done on voice recognition of ATM users. A chip in an ATM card will verify the voice of the cardholder. Withdrawals can then be made on "voice commands" without using the current keypad method. Now banks are attempting to join nationwide networks, such as Cirrus, that permit users to access cash outside of the bank's regional area. Another strategy is to increase the range of services and their attractiveness to ATM users and generate revenue from new fees.

Another new customer service technology is the Automated Checkout Machine (ACM) system offered by Checkrobot, Inc. ACM enables shoppers to check out their own merchandise before paying a centrally located cashier. The ACM System consists of automated checkout machine stations, a central computer linked to the stations, and a point-of-sale (POS) computer. It incorporates a security system to ensure that each item departing the store has been scanned and paid for. Checkrobot claims the ACM System offers the perception of improved customer service because the automated checkout machine is easy to use, decreases shopping time, and increases customers' control of their shopping forays.

Other self-service technologies include an automated scanning device that permits the exchange of money. For example, in a bank in Madrid, a customer can stack his U.S. dollars in a machine that returns pesetas and an itemized record of the transaction. The machine handles 16 currencies.

Marriott Hotels has automated guest check-in procedures to a point where average check-in time is one and one-half minutes. The hotel chain is developing a card that will enable guests to bypass check-in and go directly to a preassigned room. The card, similar to room key cards being used by many large hotels today, would contain all necessary information about the guest.

It is likely that new technologies that take into consideration demand, demographics, cost, competition, and other market information will appear every year. Marketers must be careful, however, to balance new technologies with consumer desires and their levels of comfort. As the global village becomes more of a reality, U.S. and foreign technologies should be incorporated to improve that customer service and comfort.

---

ages are legally required, Phillip Morris follows the rule to the letter. Many other countries, however, do not have such rules. In the African countries where Phillip Morris heavily promotes its cigarettes, the packs contain no health warnings.

Tenneco, Inc., matches contributions by employees to charities. The firm goes beyond what it feels is an obligation to support the United Way, Girl Scouts, and the Red Cross. However, the highest form of social responsibility is active contribution to society. An example of a social contribution is the Ronald McDonald House program. The McDonald's Corporation provides $25,000 seed money for each house. The rest of the funds are raised by a volunteer board, with significant contributions by owner/operators in each tri-state area. These facilities, located near medical centers, house families that have sick children in hospitals. This eases the family's burden while the children are receiving medical treatment.

Ethics and social responsibility are not only important for marketers to practice, monitor, and improve, but for all employees. The performance of a firm in terms of ethics and social responsibility influences employee behavior. Although there are arguments both for and against social responsibility and there is no one acceptable ethical behavior pattern, it makes sense to consider both areas very important. The society is demanding better performance from businesses and other institutions. It will either get better performance or the government will be asked to step in more aggressively.

PERSONAL COMPUTER EXERCISE

The use of demographic and social-cultural databases to analyze trends in the environment can be very useful to a marketing manager. This PC Exercise will help you evaluate the impact of current demographic trends on future consumer demand for various products and services.

KEY POINTS

- When a marketer is engaged in environmental scanning and analysis, he or she monitors, with whatever means available, the external environmental forces. The analysis involves finding threats and opportunities that the environment poses. The analysis also requires sifting through data, opinions, historical information, competitors' products and services, and anything available to help make a better decision.

- Changes in demographics and social values have an impact on how a market functions. These changes affect the products and services provided and the marketing tactics considered acceptable.

- There are four possible competitive situations: monopoly, oligopoly, monopolistic competition, and pure competition. The nature of competition a firm faces affects its marketing decisions.

- Buying power requires economic strength and the ability to make purchases. Economic strength is determined by a combination of factors such as income levels, inflation, productivity, and unemployment.

PERSONAL COMPUTER EXERCISES

PC Exercises provide students with the ability to manage information to make marketing decisions. These are found at the end of each chapter and are highlighted with an icon box.

INTEGRATION OF CURRENT RESEARCH DATA FROM *AMERICAN DEMOGRAPHICS*

The text integrates the latest data and research to support marketing topics and concepts to aid students in their research. The *American Demographics Sampler* supplement also focuses on trends in modern society relevant to these topics.

Demographic Factors

The study of people in the aggregate is called **demography.** A demographer is concerned about the size, birthrate, age, geographic migration patterns, and education levels of the population. Because the United States is undergoing a significant demographic transition in many areas, the analysis of demographic statistics can help marketing managers identify and understand market segments and plan strategies targeted to those segments.

In this section we briefly discuss some of the major trends in American demographics: changes in age, occupation, education, and family makeup. Recognizing these trends and looking at how marketers are responding should help marketers worldwide understand the importance of demographics.

Aging of the American population. The total population of the United States in the 1990s is increasing very slowly, at a rate of less than one percent per year. Population growth depends on the rate of births, deaths, and migration. Death rates are very predictable. Net migration to the United States has averaged about 500,000 persons per year.[6] Thus, the most important factor in predicting increases in population is the birthrate. Changes in the birthrate and the fertility rate—the number of children born to the average woman in her lifetime—have had a dramatic impact on the population during the past 25 years and will continue to have a major impact into the twenty-first century.

Increase in level of education. Demand for many products and services, such as books and magazines, travel, and entertainment, is influenced by the educational level of consumers. A person's level of education is closely related to his or her age—70 percent of those 65 years and older in 1993 did not finish high school, compared to less than 15 percent of those aged 25 to 44 years. In general, the U.S. population is more educated than ever before in its history. This trend toward increased education is expected to continue and, in fact, expand. Lifelong learning has become a necessity as improvements in technology and increased market globalization occur at increasingly rapid rates. No longer can employees graduate from high school or even college, get a job and stay there indefinitely without additional training. Figure 2-3 illustrates the increases in school enrollment predicted between 1991 and 2003. Although population is not anticipated to increase significantly, increases in school enrollment are evident in every age group and both genders.

For marketers, the trend toward increased education is important because higher levels of education produce consumers who are more sophisticated in evaluating product offerings, more receptive to new products, and more demanding of quality and performance. The Bureau of Labor Statistics reports that college-educated heads of households are more likely to buy services, spend more money

FIGURE 2.3
School Enrollment: 1991 and 2003

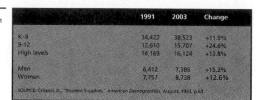

	1991	2003	Change
K–8	34,422	38,523	+11.9%
9–12	12,610	15,707	+24.6%
High levels	14,169	16,124	+13.8%
Men	6,412	7,386	+15.2%
Women	7,757	8,738	+12.6%

SOURCE: Crispell, D., "Student Supplies," *American Demographics,* August, 1993, p.63.

MARKETING ETHICS AND SOCIAL RESPONSIBILITY IN THE EXTERNAL ENVIRONMENT

Recognizing and acknowledging the importance of the external environment in making marketing decisions is not a one-way street. Not only must firms consider how the forces in the external environment affect their businesses, but they must also consider the impact of their decisions on the world around them. This consideration raises the issues of ethics and social responsibility. **Ethics** are a set of beliefs about what is right and wrong. They may be determined by a group or an individual. As introduced in Chapter 1, social responsibility is the obligation a business assumes to optimize the positive effects and minimize the negative effects of its actions on society. The marketing profession, like others, is concerned about ethics and social responsibility because of business issues, personal principles, and legal implications.

This definition of ethics has three implications. First, ethics may be individually defined rather than organizationally bound. Second, ethical behavior can vary from one person to another. Third, ethics are relative, not absolute. What a Japanese decision maker does to market sushi is probably different from what an Argentinean does to market beef. In Japan it is proper and almost expected to offer monetary incentives to suppliers to secure business. In the United States this action is not only seen as unethical but is generally viewed as anticompetitive and against the law. Ethical behavior is in the eye of the beholder, but it is usually behavior that meets generally accepted norms of a society. **Marketing ethics** is the application of ethical standards to all marketing activities and decisions.

Growing public attention to the ethics of business decisions and conduct has resulted in an increased interest among marketers in social responsibility, ethical ideology, and moral decision making. Boycotts, protests, personal and class action lawsuits, negative press, and falling profits have increased the awareness of managers about ethics and social responsibility.[10] The concepts of ethics and social responsibility are sometimes used interchangeably. As seen from their definitions, however, they each have a distinct meaning. Business ethics are individually based, while social responsibility concerns the decisions of the organization and their effects on society.

The idea of social responsibility became widely publicized during the 1960s as social values began to change. Today social responsibility is a consideration in decision making that organizations have generally accepted. The advertisement for Hoechst Celanese indicates that the firm takes its social responsibilities seriously.

An Ethical Framework

It is important to organize the concept of ethics as applied to marketing. Managers, students, and researchers could then consider the ethical implications of issues that face decision makers. Hunt and Vitell have provided a general theory of marketing ethics that is well organized, concise, and considers environmental forces.[11] Figure 2-5 presents this framework in which three major environments impact ethical decision making. The cultural environment (or cultural forces in the external environment), the industrial environment (the standards and nature of all competitors), and the organizational environment (characteristics and standards of the company itself) all shape perceptions of ethical judgments. The personal experiences of individual decision makers also affect perceptions and decision making.

The Hunt and Vitell framework introduces the notions of perceptions, norms, consequences, and decisions—all factors that affect ethical decision making.

ETHICAL BENCHMARK

Discussions are included throughout on the implications that ethics pose for marketing decision makers. An "Ethical Benchmark" (Chapter 2) provides a framework for marketing decisions, and "Geographic Segmentation Can Raise Ethical Issues" (Chapter 5) focuses on the ethical dimensions of the struggle to rebuild South Central Los Angeles.

F O Career U S

The Product Is You!

Welcome to the career *component* of this text. This special section provides you an opportunity to apply the principles of marketing to the activity that most of us spend the majority of our hours doing, namely WORK! At the end of each chapter we help you link the marketing concepts in that chapter to the *self-marketing* activities so critical to the career search process. Each "Career Focus" includes questions designed to give you the tools you will need to efficiently position yourself in a very competitive job market. For selected chapters, we present a brief overview of the specific positions in marketing that relate to the topics discussed in those chapters.

In a competitive job market, you need to "market" yourself. Review the definition of marketing. Career planning uses a similar process. Your job search will require that you understand how you can market yourself in a marketplace where there are many competing brands like yourself.

Chapter 1 describes one of the most talked-about principles of marketing, *the marketing mix*, comprised of the four Ps. We can apply these factors to the process of securing employment as follows:

- *Product.* Remember that the product in the job search is *you.* What characteristics would describe and define this product and its development? Which aspects would seem important to a potential buyer (employer)?

- *Place.* For your job search, place includes those channels through which you will promote yourself as a product. To paraphrase the text, place is the "set of individuals" who will connect you as the producer to employers as the users. Your network could include such contacts as placement offices, recent alumni, fellow students, executive recruiters, and human resource professionals.

- *Promotion.* This term refers to the methods you will use to get the word out about that "you" in the job market. Promotional tools include informational interviews, a professional résumé, and cover letters that highlight your constellation of skills and talents. All of these tools are advertisements that you as a product need to obtain job interviews. And finally, there is your direct promotion, your selling of yourself in the job interview.

- *Price.* This factor appears in negotiation of your salary, benefits, moving expenses, and other particulars of employment. To negotiate a fair price, you must understand the market range for you as a product, taking into consideration the value of your relevant education and experience.

Questions

Take a few moments to make a first pass at your job search as an application of the four Ps. For this purpose, just pick a dream job in terms of industry sector, professional function, and type of organization.

1. What are some target positions and who are some target employers that meet your dream job requirements?
2. Describe yourself as a *product* that could meet the needs of the employers you noted for the positions that you included. In writing your description, focus on your education, experience, and other relevant skills and attributes.
3. How would you define *place* for yourself? Be sure to consider the contacts that you would need to connect you to your prospective employers.
4. What would you feature in *promotion* of yourself to potential employers? Include the specifics you would highlight as your professional advertisement in cover letters and, eventually, in an interview.
5. What are the major factors that would determine *price* for yourself in your target job market?

Draft a summary of your answers to these questions and describe **your reactions** to this exercise. Include questions you have and any surprises that occurred during this process.

CASE APPLICATION

ILLINOIS BELL

TARGETING HOMEWORKERS

Illinois Bell, a division of Ameritech, has opened a Work-at-Home Planning Center in Chicago. The center is designed to assist consumers who work at home. Products such as telephones, fax machines, modems, and answering machines are targeted at three specific markets within this growing population:

- **full-time homeworker**—entrepreneurs who run their businesses out of their residences.
- **after-hours homeworker**—individuals who take work home with them
- **telecommuters**—workers who spend all or part of their work week working at home rather than at their employer's place of business

Approximately 35% of U.S. workers fell into one of these three categories sometime during 1992 according to LINK, a New York–based research firm commissioned by Illinois Bell to study the market. This represented an increase of 41% from 1990 and provided firms like Illinois Bell with an opportunity to respond to the growing trend. Laura Foote, marketing manager for Illinois Bell, predicts an 8% annual growth rate. Telecommuting, in particular, is expected to become a mainstream force in major corporations as we progress through the 1990s.

It is believed that growth of the "work-at-home" market results from the numerous benefits that working at home offers the employer, the employee, and society. Employers are better able to keep quality employees who are trying to balance their jobs with personal commitments like raising families or caring for elderly parents. Employees create more free and leisure time for themselves by avoiding long commutes. Society benefits environmentally in the form of fewer pollutants in the air and less gasoline used. Furthermore, the LINK study reported that the continued increase in working women and the growing desire of households to increase their income will also fuel the growth expected in the market.

Employers have also found that telecommuters can be more productive than other employees. The Los Angeles telecommunications department conducted a test of 500 city workers. The test found that telecommuting employees were 12.5 percent more productive than workers at central locations. Productivity was measured in terms of the number of reports the workers produced, the amount of material they reviewed, and the number of cases they closed.

Telecommuting received an unexpected promotional push when Los Angeles was shaken by a significant earthquake in January 1994. Closed freeways and impossibly long commutes were viewed by telecommuting advocates as opportunities to persuade Angelenos to try working at home. Pacific Bell responded to the opportunity by launching a radio and print ad campaign encouraging telecommuting. It even set up a special loan fund to outfit home offices.

Homeworkers have been aided by the growing market penetration of personal computers (PCs) which are found in the residences of 11.6 million home workers, according to the LINK study. The study also determined that this figure is growing rapidly. Such market penetration appears to provide opportunities to firms who target even the casual after-hours homeworker. According to Thomas Miller, director of the LINK study, "Two-thirds of all home computers and nearly three-fourths of all home fax machines are now owned by people bringing home work after hours. Also, casual after-hours homeworkers are involved in 85% of the job-related electronic data transfers now taking place from homes."

It would appear from the research that Illinois Bell could not go wrong in pursuing the homeworker market. Foote has acknowledged, however, that identifying the prospects in the target markets is difficult, making it extremely challenging to use such promotional techniques as direct mail. She believes that this difficulty is due to the fact that the market is still growing rapidly. According to Foote, as the growth continues, the market will identify itself, thus making marketing efforts simpler.

Questions

1. Is the purchase of equipment to set up a home office likely to represent extensive problem solving, limited problem solving, or routine response behavior? Explain.
2. Would your answer to Question 1 vary across the three target markets identified by Illinois Bell? How would this affect marketing strategy for the firm?
3. What consumer behavior concepts discussed in Chapter 6 are most relevant for Illinois Bell?
4. What additional information about buyer behavior would you want if you were in charge of marketing to the growing population of homeworkers?

part I
MARKETING AND THE ENVIRONMENT

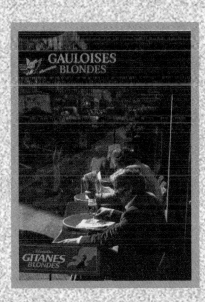

CHapTeR 1

Introduction to Marketing

LEARNING OBJECTIVES

Upon completing this chapter, you will be able to do the following:

■ **Define** marketing and the marketing concept.

■ **Explain** how marketing creates real utility or value for firms, consumers, and the economy.

■ **Compare** the production, sales, and marketing concepts of business operations.

■ **Discuss** the role of marketing in an organization and its relationship to other organizational functions.

■ **Describe** the prominent concerns and focuses of marketing practice in the 1990s.

■ **Understand** the importance of marketing to you, to the economy as a whole, and to business and not-for-profit organizations.

Marketing Profile

Carnival Cruise Line Uses Marketing to Sail to Success

At one time, thoughts of pleasure cruising conjured images of well-heeled, half-dead aristocrats sailing around the world in the lap of luxury aboard such great ships as the Queen Mary or the Queen Elizabeth II. Those days are gone forever. Nevertheless, the pleasure cruise business is thriving, to the tune of some $5 billion a year. It has found a new group of customers, the U.S. middle class. The number of middle-class Americans who board Love Boat-type cruise ships each year has increased by 600% since 1980. This is well above the growth rate for any other hospitality business. In 1992, 4.2 million Americans took pleasure cruises. Approximately 30% of today's passengers are between 25 and 39 years of age and 58% are under 60 years old. Their average household income is between $25,000 and $50,000 per year. Although only 5% of Americans have ever taken a cruise, 60% of U.S. adults report that they would like to take a cruise. Clearly, there is a huge untapped pool of potential customers.

Carnival Cruise Lines is directing its marketing efforts at these potential customers. Its approach is simple. First, it has ensured that it is offering a first-rate product. The line has made each of its ships a fun place to be. The ships offer casinos, movie theaters, discos, gyms with aerobic classes, and plenty of shopping. Entertainment is presented nightly, and food is served around the clock. Carnival maintains a guest-to-crew ratio of 2 to 1, so guests are swamped with service. The company also puts a great deal of emphasis on recruiting, motivating, and retaining an excellent crew. This emphasis on service allows Carnival to offer a unique experience with a minimum of hassle. Furthermore, cruises typically last three to seven days, making it possible for a younger customer to fit the cruise into his or her vacation time. Port visits occur almost daily, offering exciting sightseeing, water sports, and more shopping.

Second, Carnival has priced its cruises about 20% below those of its competitors, making them affordable to a wider range of middle-class customers. The typical seven-night cruise costs about $1000 per person, with airfare and unlimited food included.

Carnival has concentrated its cruises in the Caribbean and Mexico, which helps ensure pleasant sailing through calm seas and under sunny skies year-round.

To attract customers, Carnival advertises heavily, spending more than $15 million per year on television advertising and other promotional efforts. The typical television ad tries to create yearnings for glamour and excitement, as well as offer relaxation. Further, cash rewards are given to travel agents who book customers on a Carnival cruise.

As a result of Carnival's emphasis on product, service, price, place of distribution, and promotion, the firm's revenues have grown 30% annually since 1980. This rate is three times faster than the average for the cruise business as a whole. The firm's total revenue in 1992 was $1.47 billion. Carnival's eight ships carry more than one million passengers per year. The firm appears to have conquered the competitive seas of the pleasure cruise business. As the number one cruise line (in terms of total passengers carried), Carnival appears headed for even more lucrative seas. The industry predicts that by the year 2000, eight million North Americans will cruise annually.

The marketing profile you have just read describes the efforts of the Carnival Cruise Line to become competitive and to stay competitive through the use of *marketing*. This book introduces marketing to those who have not studied it before. As you read and learn from this book, you will discover that marketing is an important, dynamic, fascinating, and frequently frustrating subject:

- *Marketing is important.* It plays a major role in the success or failure of all organizations. It thereby affects not only the society in which we live but also our daily lives.

- *Marketing is dynamic.* It operates in the real world, which is constantly changing.

- *Marketing is fascinating.* Stories of marketing successes and marketing failures become part of business folklore all over the world.

- *Marketing is frequently frustrating.* It cannot be reduced to a set of equations that always yield right answers. Marketing is part science, but it is also part art.

The profile of Carnival Cruise Lines is but one of the hundreds of real-world marketing examples in this book. To appreciate fully not just the details of these actual examples but also their implications, try placing yourself in the situations described and think about what you would do. Picture yourself as part of the management team at Carnival, for example. Imagine that you are responsible for applying marketing principles to ensure that the company maintains or improves its position in the cruise line industry. This responsibility might be a bit scary, but it would also be exciting, wouldn't it? The small effort required to visualize yourself as a marketing manager will pay big dividends. When you have completed your study of this book, you will have a good basic understanding of the field of marketing. More important, you will also have developed a *feel* for marketing and be better prepared to make marketing decisions.

A note of caution: Many of the examples in the text are about organizations or products with which you are very familiar. Further, some of the concepts discussed may seem like little more than common sense. But beware. Don't fall into the trap of thinking that you already understand marketing and so underestimate the need to study and learn the material in this book. You will likely discover that your current ideas about marketing represent only the tip of the iceberg in this fascinating field.

DEFINING MARKETING

Long, long ago, our ancestors discovered that the specialization of labor was an efficient way to satisfy their needs for food, clothing, and shelter. If one person fished, another hunted, and a third farmed, all three would have more food than if each person performed all three tasks. As villages grew into towns and towns grew into cities, people set aside a central area—a *market*—where they could exchange the goods they produced for the goods they needed. Over the centuries the activities surrounding these exchanges developed into what we now call *marketing*.

There are many ways to define *marketing*. The first known reference to marketing dates from 1561, when it was defined simply as "the action of a market." According to the Institute of Marketing in England, "Marketing is the management function which organizes and directs all those business activities involved in assessing and converting customer purchasing power into effective demand for a specific product or service, and in moving the product or service to the final consumer or user so as to achieve the profit target or other objectives set by a company."[1] In this text, we use the much broader definition of *marketing* provided in 1985 by the American Marketing Association (AMA):

> **Marketing** is the process of planning and executing the conception, pricing, promotion, and distribution of ideas, goods and services to create exchanges that satisfy individual and organizational objectives.[2]

Notice that the AMA's definition does not limit marketing to businesses and so includes not-for-profit organizations as well as individuals. It recognizes that marketing is not limited to goods and services but can be applied also to ideas.

Regardless of how we define marketing, the common denominator of all marketing activity is exchange. **Exchange** refers to all activities associated with doing or receiving something of value from someone by giving or doing something in return. Figure 1.1 shows a few of the different types of things that can be exchanged. As you can see, what is received need not be a physical product or service and what is given in return need not be money. All that is necessary is that something of value be exchanged for something else of value.

For example, contributors of money to the World Famine Relief Fund (an organization that attempts to reduce world hunger) gain good feelings about themselves as caring human beings in return for their money. Similarly, a political candidate gains votes in exchange for promised action. For that matter, people looking for jobs or for spouses are also involved in marketing—the marketing of themselves.

Note that the intent of an exchange may not be increased consumption of a particular good or service. The directors of an antidrug campaign hope that a decrease in the use of drugs will be exchanged for information on drug abuse. When the objective of an exchange is to decrease consumption, it is commonly called **demarketing.** Of course demarketing one thing typically means marketing something else. In considering the "Spotlight on Societal Marketing: Marketing AIDS Prevention," you might ponder whether the objective is to demarket AIDS or market AIDS prevention.

At this point, it seems a good idea to point out that the term *market* has a somewhat special meaning when marketing is being discussed. In this text, **market** refers

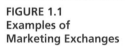

**FIGURE 1.1
Examples of
Marketing Exchanges**

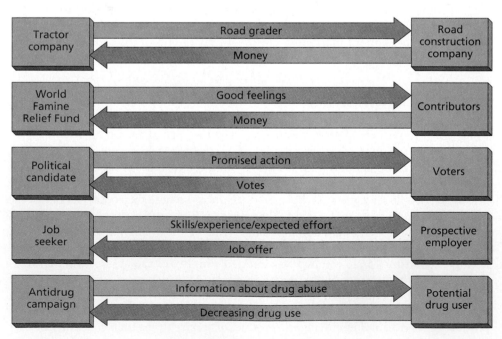

MARKETING *IN ACTION*

Marketing AIDS Prevention

Acquired immune deficiency syndrome, or AIDS, is a disease brought on by the human immuno-deficiency virus (HIV). The virus destroys the infected person's immune system, leaving the person susceptible to opportunistic infections, many of which can be fatal. There is no cure. The virus is most commonly spread through unprotected sexual activity or the sharing of needles. It is not spread by casual contact (e.g., kissing, hugging, holding hands).

The Department of Health and Human Services, the Public Health Service, and the Centers for Disease Control (CDC) along with public and private groups across the country are using marketing in an attempt to curb the spread of HIV. These groups are anxious to get out the message that each person in the country engaging in certain behaviors is at risk. However, everyone does not get the message in the same way. "Education efforts need to be community-specific and sensitive to community standards and issues," states Tom Brandt, Associate Director of the National Commission on AIDS in Washington, DC.

Developing different messages for different groups allows hard-hitting communications to reach at-risk groups while minimizing the potential that they will reach others who might be offended. Intravenous drug users, for example, are the target of a promotional campaign spearheaded by "Bleachman," a Superman-like character with a bleach-bottle head who tells users to clean their needles before reusing or sharing them. Another at-risk segment of the population, homosexual men, is targeted with posters in gay bars and advertising in gay media. The group considered most at risk today,

adolescents ages 13–21, is targeted using HIV–AIDS awareness campaigns implemented in youth groups, boys' and girls' clubs, YMCAs, and other community-based organizations that meet the needs of teenagers.

The CDC does extensive market testing of the advertisements they produce before running them to determine their effectiveness and acceptability. They produced a TV spot that featured a young man infected with HIV holding a baby. The man tells the baby he'd like to be around to watch it grow up. While HIV-positive individuals found the ad effective, it bombed in test audiences representative of the general population. They questioned how the man could have HIV or AIDS, while the baby did not. The CDC decided not to run the spot.

Other ads developed for general audiences have never run due to the difficulty of getting media to accept spots deemed controversial. This was the case with a poster developed by DDB-Needham, a large advertising agency, as part of an HIV–AIDS information campaign for the city of Chicago. The poster with the slogan Kissing Doesn't Kill depicted three couples kissing: two men, two women, and a man and a woman.

The use of marketing to change behavior reinforces the idea that the methods described in this book apply any time an exchange is occurring. Identifying a group of people and then developing a marketing effort directed at that group is a process that can be used whether your objective is profit, some other organizationally related measure, a decrease in consumption, or even a change in behavior.

"**W**hen I found out I had HIV at age 17, I learned that anyone can get it."

One in 250 Americans is infected with HIV.

"I'm 19 years old. And two years ago, I found out I had HIV, the virus that causes AIDS. Knowing that I could die has been scary. But what's even scarier is learning that my friends didn't learn a thing from all this. They're still doing what I did that got me infected."

"I think it's 'cause people my age think they're invincible. But I'm living proof that we're not."

To find out how you can prevent HIV, call the CDC National AIDS Hotline at 1-800-342-AIDS.

AMERICA
RESPONDS
TO AIDS

Peter Zamora, HIV Positive

U.S. DEPARTMENT OF HEALTH & HUMAN SERVICES   CDC
Public Health Service

The market for the Paris Metro (subway) consists of all those people who want or need to travel in Paris but who cannot afford or simply do not wish to use an alternative means of transportation.

to people or organizations who are ready, willing, and able to receive a product, service, or idea and to give something for it in return. For example, the market for the Paris Metro (subway) consists of all those people who want or need to travel in Paris but who cannot afford or simply do not wish to use an alternative means of transportation.

Exchange is, of course, not the only means by which individuals can satisfy their needs and wants. Self-production, theft, force, and beggary are other methods. In today's industrialized countries, however, self-production is rarely the most efficient means of meeting needs and wants. Further, theft and force are illegal and beggary is generally unacceptable. Hence, exchange is the primary means of satisfying wants and needs in the world today.

THE NEED FOR MARKETING

Whenever an individual or group of people has a good, service, or idea to distribute or disseminate and another individual or group would like to acquire that good, service, or idea, the necessary ingredients for a satisfactory exchange would seem to be in place. However, the exchange may not take place because of separations or gaps between the producers and consumers of goods, services, and ideas. There are five important types of separations:

1. *Spatial separation.* The parties to a potential exchange are usually separated geographically. Kellogg's produces Corn Flakes in Battle Creek, Michigan, but the cereal is consumed all over the country.

2. *Temporal separation.* The parties to a potential exchange usually cannot complete the exchange at the time the products are produced. The products must be moved from the location of the producer to the locations of the consumers, which takes time. Also, consumers want the products to be available when they need them. For example, most toy sales occur in November and December, but toy production occurs throughout the year.

3. *Perceptual separation.* Both producers and consumers may be unaware or uninterested in each others' offerings. There is thus a need for producers to obtain information about consumers and for consumers to know about product availability and price. Producers also need information about consumers to guide the production of goods, services, and ideas. Consumers find out about goods and services from a variety of sources including advertisements and independent media such as *Consumer Reports*. Producers, on the other hand, learn about consumers through marketing research and promotions. The airline industry's frequent flyer programs, for example, provide an excellent source of information about characteristics and travel habits of passengers.

4. *Separation in ownership.* There is an inherent separation of ownership between producers and consumers. Marketing systems facilitate the transfer of title for goods from producers to consumers. Campbell Soup Company, for example, produces soup. Ownership is transferred from Campbell to 7-Eleven stores (part of the marketing system) when 7-Eleven buys the soup. Ownership is transferred again when 7-Eleven sells the soup to a consumer who buys it for personal consumption.

5. *Separations in values.* Producers and consumers place different values on products. The producer looks at value in terms of production costs and competitive prices; the consumer values the product in terms of its usefulness and his or her ability to pay for it. For example, IBM placed high values on its PS/2 computers, based upon the cost of producing them and the activity of its competitors. Unfortunately for IBM, many American businesses placed much lower values on these machines, basing their judgments upon both their estimates of the increase in productivity the PS/2s would give them and their ability to pay.[3]

Marketing Bridges Exchange Gaps

By performing certain functions, marketing bridges the separations between producers and consumers. There are three basic types of **marketing functions**: transactional, logistical, and facilitating.

Transactional functions are the actual buying and selling of products. Selling involves the promotion of products through advertising, personal selling, publicity, and sales promotion. Buying involves seeking and evaluating alternative products. Selling helps to bridge perceptual, ownership, and values separations by making consumers aware of the existence and value of products and services. Buying aids in overcoming ownership and values separations by enabling consumers to understand the value of an item and ultimately possess it.

Logistical functions are the storage and transportation of products. These functions help overcome spatial and temporal separations by getting products to consumers at the places and times they desire them.

Facilitating functions include financing products, taking risks by holding ownership, providing market information, developing standards, and grading products against these standards. These functions are instrumental in overcoming temporal, perceptual, ownership, and values separations. A producer takes a risk when he or she decides to manufacture a product with the hope that the product will sell to consumers. Because the product may not sell, risk is incurred. When an industry or organization develops standards and then grades products against those standards, it is hoping to assure potential customers of the value of the goods.

Marketing Creates Utility

By bridging market separations, marketing creates **utility,** which is a measure of the extent to which a particular good, service, or idea satisfies the needs or wants of a particular individual or organization. Note that utility is a subjective evaluation. That is, a particular product may have different utilities for different individuals or even for the same individual at different times. For instance, a slice of cold pizza may have a high utility for someone who hasn't eaten all day, whereas its utility for a person who has just finished a big meal may be almost nil. Note also that, in creating utility, producers create real value. There are four basic kinds of utility: form, place, time, and possession.

Form utility is created by the production of the good, service, or idea itself. For example, a bushel of wheat has little utility for a hungry person. However, once the wheat has been processed into flour and then baked into bread, it has been transformed into something of substantial utility for a hungry person.

Place utility is created by making the product available *where* consumers need it. If you want to buy a car, for instance, you do not have to travel to Detroit, Michigan, to Kyushu, Japan, or to Stuttgart, Germany, to purchase it. Auto producers and dealers bring cars to convenient showrooms in cities and towns all across the world.

Time utility is created by making the product available *when* consumers need it. Thus, you can find a wider selection of swimsuits in Northern Hemisphere stores in May just prior to the summer season and overcoats in November even though the items may have been produced throughout the year. In the Southern Hemisphere, of course, the reverse is true.

Finally, **possession utility** is created by helping a consumer take title to a good. When a department store extends you credit so that you can own a couch even though you do not have the cash to pay for it, it is providing you possession utility.

Marketing alone creates place, time, and possession utility. Marketing can have a major impact on form utility as well. This happens when marketing input about the wants and needs of consumers affects the amount of or quality of production of a good, service, or idea. Figure 1.2 summarizes the relationships among the market separations, the functions performed by marketing to bridge these separations, and the utilities thereby created.

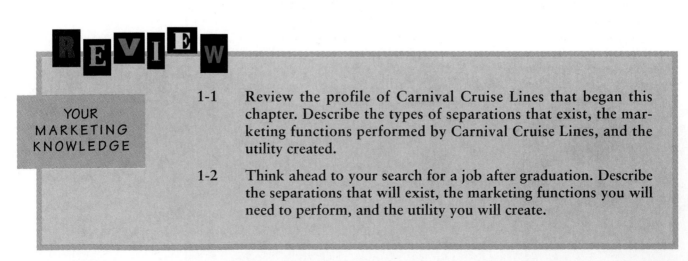

REVIEW

YOUR MARKETING KNOWLEDGE

1-1   Review the profile of Carnival Cruise Lines that began this chapter. Describe the types of separations that exist, the marketing functions performed by Carnival Cruise Lines, and the utility created.

1-2   Think ahead to your search for a job after graduation. Describe the separations that will exist, the marketing functions you will need to perform, and the utility you will create.

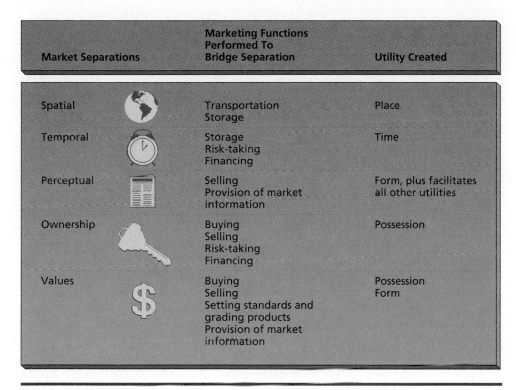

Market Separations		Marketing Functions Performed To Bridge Separation	Utility Created
Spatial		Transportation Storage	Place
Temporal		Storage Risk-taking Financing	Time
Perceptual		Selling Provision of market information	Form, plus facilitates all other utilities
Ownership		Buying Selling Risk-taking Financing	Possession
Values		Buying Selling Setting standards and grading products Provision of market information	Possession Form

FIGURE 1.2
Utilities Created by Marketing

MARKETING WITHIN THE ORGANIZATION

In one form or another, marketing has existed since our earliest ancestors first exchanged, say, saber-toothed tiger skins for woolly mammoth meat. However, the perception of marketing has changed dramatically over the years. A brief historical review of the way organizations have viewed marketing will help us to understand the current concepts of marketing.

The Production Concept

Up until about 1920, organizations in countries that had undergone the industrial revolution mostly had a production orientation. The **production concept** holds that a firm should produce and distribute those products it can produce most efficiently. Following the economic premise that supply creates its own demand, the firm simply assumes that there will be a market for its products. It has no need to be concerned about the preferences of potential consumers. Henry Ford was speaking from a production orientation when he said of his Model T automobile, "You can have any color you want as long as it's black." Demand for the Model T was so great that the fact that some customers might prefer a color other than black was not important to the success of the Ford Motor Company.

A production orientation works as long as a firm has a product that most consumers need, the demand for the product exceeds its supply, and there is little or no competition. For instance, if there is only one bakery in town, it will probably sell out of bread every day regardless of what kind of bread it bakes. Once a second bakery opens, however, if both bakeries wish to sell all the bread they bake, both will have to supply the kinds of bread customers want.

A production orientation is evident still among firms in some countries today. In Russia and other former Soviet Bloc countries, for example, basic staples such as meat and bread are in short supply. A butcher or baker in a small Russian town will have no trouble selling all of the meat or bread he or she can obtain or produce, regardless of the cut, type, or price.

The Sales Concept

By the 1920s, advances in manufacturing technology had given rise to widespread mass production in the industrialized countries of the world. Manufacturing firms could produce more than the markets would accept, so supply began to exceed demand. As a result, many businesses shifted from a production orientation to a sales orientation. The **sales concept** holds that just about anything can be sold to customers, whether they want it or not, if the sales approach is aggressive enough. During the time the sales orientation was in widespread use, the "hard sell" became almost synonymous with marketing. Unfortunately, many people continue to associate all marketing efforts with this approach. Indeed, it can be found still in many telephone solicitations and in the door-to-door selling of products. The objective of the sales concept viewpoint is to sell what is available, using all the advertising and personal selling skills one has, with little concern for the customer's postpurchase satisfaction.

With its very aggressive approach to selling, the sales orientation is the opposite of the production orientation, which has a very lackadaisical approach to selling. In one way, however, the two orientations are similar: Neither takes into account the wants and needs of consumers.

The Marketing Concept

In his book *The Wealth of Nations*, published in 1776, Adam Smith wrote:

> Consumption is the sole end and purpose of all production, and the interest of the producers ought to be attended to only so far as it may be necessary for promoting that of the consumer.[4]

Unfortunately, almost two centuries passed before a philosophy of doing business reflecting Smith's sage advice began to emerge in the early 1950s. This "new" philosophy is the marketing orientation. The **marketing concept** states that if all of an organization's activities, including production, are focused on consumer needs, long-run profits can be achieved by satisfying those needs. Organizations that have adopted the marketing concept are said to be marketing-oriented. One of the first corporations to adopt the marketing concept was General Electric. Its 1952 annual report stated:

> It [the marketing concept] introduces the marketing person at the beginning rather than at the end of the production cycle and integrates marketing into each phase of the business. Thus, marketing, through its studies and research, will establish for the engineer, the design and manufacturing person, what the customer wants in a given product, what price he or she is willing to pay, and where and when it will be wanted. Marketing will have authority in product planning, production scheduling, and inventory control, as well as sales, distribution, and servicing of the product.[5]

Many successful companies, among them Procter & Gamble and General Mills, have adopted the marketing concept. Procter & Gamble has always quickly responded to consumer wants and needs. It was the first firm, for example, to offer disposable diapers manufactured for the differing needs of boys and girls. General Mills and Kellogg's have responded to consumers' demand for healthier breakfast cereals by reducing the sugar and fat in many of their products.

Kellogg's has responded to consumers' demands for healthier breakfast cereals by reducing the sugar and fat in many of its products.

Marketing-oriented firms can demonstrate their commitment to meeting consumers' needs not only through the products they produce but also by adjusting prices to the purchase capabilities of consumers. Mercedes Benz, for example, introduced to the U.S. market its "C" Series, a line of cars is designed for the "first-time" luxury car buyer. The autos are priced just under $30,000 rather than about $45,000, a price common to many Mercedes (and other luxury) automobiles.

Customer service is another means of demonstrating adoption of the marketing concept. Companies whose personnel are easily accessible to their customers are generally thought to be marketing-oriented. Many firms that produce consumer products now offer an "800" number, which allows consumers to call the company toll-free with questions, ideas, and comments about the firm or its products. For example, Microsoft, a software producer, has an "800" number for consumers to call if they are having trouble with the firm's products. Technicians, sitting in front of computers, help the consumers.

The lack of success of other companies can be attributed, at least in part, to their failure to adopt a marketing orientation. Auto producers in the United States, for example, experienced serious declines in sales and profits during the 1970s because they failed to adapt as quickly as foreign manufacturers to consumers' demands for smaller, more fuel-efficient cars.

Harley-Davidson Motorcycles is a company that came close to failure due in large part to lack of a marketing orientation. The firm, established in 1903, had succeeded for many years, despite a production orientation, due to the demand for its products created by two world wars and lack of competition. In the 1950s and 1960s, however, U.S. consumers' perceptions of motorcycles became increasingly negative. Additionally, foreign manufacturers, especially Japanese, began introducing heavy competition into the U.S. market. Harley-Davidson failed to meet the needs and desires of the market. It did little to adapt its product, distribution, prices, or service to correspond to a changing market. The result was the near demise of the company. Only in more recent years has the firm adopted the marketing concept and met with renewed success.[6]

Marketing-oriented firms typically take a broader view of the business they are in than do production- or sales-oriented companies. This broader view allows them to adapt more quickly to changing consumer wants and needs because they are not locked in to seeing themselves as the producers of one specific product. Instead, a marketing-oriented firm sees itself as in the business of fulfilling consumers' wants and needs, whatever they may be. A music company, for example, that viewed itself narrowly as being in the business of producing records, would have travelled a difficult road when consumer preferences for recorded music changed from records to tapes and then to compact discs. A marketing-oriented company such as Paramount, however, views itself as being in the musical entertainment business. As consumers' demands for musical entertainment changed, Paramount's products also changed. Failure of an organization to take a broad view of its business is **marketing myopia.**[7]

The adoption of the marketing concept often results from increased competition in an industry. As a firm's competitors begin to focus their attention on customer satisfaction, the firm must do the same to compete effectively. Hence, an entire industry may adopt the marketing concept at roughly the same time. Banking is a service industry that has become marketing-oriented during the last 15 years. New products such as interest-bearing checking accounts and flexible certificates of deposit, extended banking hours, and 24-hour automatic teller machines are innovations designed to meet the changing needs of customers. Furthermore, several banks like Bank of America and Wells Fargo now enable depositors to check their balances and perform transactions over the telephone via computer.

Beginning in the 1970s and throughout the 1980s and 1990s, the marketing concept was increasingly adopted by not-for-profit organizations.[8] A **not-for-profit organization** is one whose objective is to attain some measure of success other than profits. A health-care clinic, for example, might measure success by the number of patients it serves. The slower acceptance of the marketing concept in this sector of the economy reflects the fact that competition was typically not intense, or was not recognized. Today, however, not-for-profit groups have come to realize that they do face competition. Consumers, for instance, have a variety of health-care options. With more knowledgeable consumers and the anticipated reforms in health care, the health-care providers who are not meeting the needs of consumers will have little business. Hence, the same focus on consumer needs found in most for-profit firms is shared by the majority of not-for-profit organizations today. Hospitals, churches, schools, and police departments have all benefited from the application of the marketing concept. Museums, once thought of by many as stuffy, boring places, have become increasingly responsive to consumer desires. The San Diego Aerospace Museum, for example, has installed many hands-on, interactive displays to entertain and encourage young visitors and to stimulate their interest in aviation. Likewise, the Aviation Museum in Noosa, Queensland, Australia, is popular worldwide, largely because it has developed displays to appeal to World War II survivors from all countries who served in Australia or fought alongside Australians throughout the Pacific theater.

The Societal Marketing Concept

While it is clearly important to respond to the wants and needs of consumers if an organization hopes to be successful, sometimes the wants and needs of specific groups conflict with the broader best interests of society. Consumers, for example, might desire the convenience of disposable bottles and cans for soda pop, yet improper disposal of those items produces an unsightly environment. Hence, in recent years the marketing concept has been expanded. Specifically, the **societal marketing concept** is an approach to decision making that integrates all activities of the organization to satisfy consumers' wants and needs in a way that is consistent with concern for broader societal consequences. This approach aims to achieve long-run objectives (profit or other) by satisfying consumers' wants and needs in balance with the needs of society as a whole.

The San Diego Aerospace Museum has installed many hands-on, interactive displays to entertain and encourage young visitors and to stimulate their interest in aviation.

This is a difficult standard to implement at times. The marketing decision maker may face consumer preferences that conflict directly with the broader interests of society. It is not always clear which should take precedence. Not all marketers even agree that implementation of this concept should be undertaken. The societal marketing concept implies that a firm might give up some sales or profits in order to meet the needs of society. As a company manager or owner, would you be willing to use only returnable bottles if it cost you some sales? Such decisions are difficult.

Governmental mandate might be viewed as taking the responsibility for such decisions from marketers. In New York, for example, although recycling is mandatory, marketing is still important to obtain compliance. New York City launched a marketing campaign to reach those citizens who might not be so environmentally conscious as others. Commercials were aired on local cable stations, ads were placed on the subway and on billboards, and the "recycling" truck showed up at most community fairs, festivals, and other activities to distribute information and stickers for trash cans.

Marketers should be expected to act in socially responsible ways. **Social responsibility** is the obligation a business assumes to optimize the positive effects and minimize the negative effects on society of its actions. The socially responsible choice is not always clear to decision makers. Social responsibility and the related issue of ethics are discussed in more detail in Chapter 2. Although this book focuses on the marketing concept, we do consider the broader societal consequences of the marketer's actions, as implied by the societal marketing concept, throughout the text.

MARKETING MANAGEMENT

An organization performs its marketing functions by determining the specific product that will be offered, how the product will be distributed, how the product will be promoted, and the price that will be charged. More formally:

> **Marketing management** is the planning, direction, and control of the entire marketing function, specifically the formulation and execution of marketing objectives, policies, programs, and strategy. Responsibilities include product development, organization, and staffing to carry out plans, supervision of marketing operations, and control of marketing performance.[9]

As you can see from this definition, a marketing manager (the person who manages the marketing efforts) is responsible not only for making decisions about what the organization will do (i.e., planning) in the areas of product offerings, distribution, promotion, and pricing, but also for overseeing the implementation and control of those plans.

Clearly, marketing management is a critical component of an organization's total management planning. It stands with functions such as production (manufacturing), finance, research and development, and human relations in the organization's management plan. The typical organizational chart in Figure 1.3 shows marketing as a prominent function. While it is true that marketing represents one of many functions, it is important to keep in mind that a marketing-oriented organization is one in which the basic tenet of customer satisfaction has permeated the entire organization. Such an organization sees marketing as the driving force behind the actions of all functions, not simply as a separate function whose role it is to sell products. Procter & Gamble, for example, focuses its entire organization on developing products to serve customers. Production, research, finance, and all other components of the firm are just as concerned with satisfying consumers as are marketing and sales.

It is not easy for a firm to maintain a company-wide commitment to customer satisfaction and the marketing concept. Departments other than marketing may

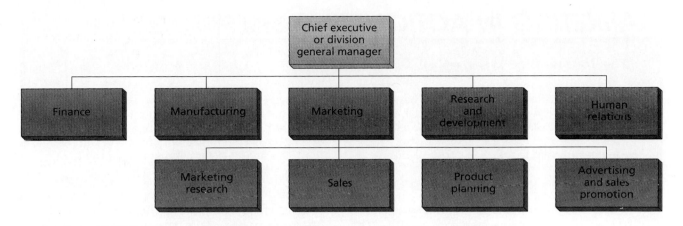

FIGURE 1.3
Functional Organizational Structure

initially find that such a commitment conflicts with their objectives. Production, for example, is interested in keeping costs low. One way this could be accomplished is through mass production of identical items. This approach, however, is likely to result in fewer styles, colors, and sizes for the consumer and is not a very marketing-oriented approach. Organizations can demonstrate their commitment to company-wide acceptance of the marketing concept by designating the top marketing officer in the firm as a vice president. By doing so, the firm acknowledges the importance of marketing to the overall success of the company. It does not, however, assure company-wide acceptance of the marketing concept.

The Marketing Mix

The activities about which the marketing manager must make decisions fall into four general categories: product, place (distribution), promotion, and price, often referred to as the **four Ps**.[10] These categories are **controllable variables** because they represent areas in which the marketing manager is in control of the decision. The activities encompassed in the four Ps are further referred to as the **marketing mix.**

Each of the four Ps represents a decision-making area that encompasses many related decisions. **Product,** for instance, includes such areas as new product research and development, product testing, development of service plans to accompany the product, and planning the management of a product over its lifetime. Packaging, branding, and warranty decisions are also often considered to be product issues. Since product actually refers to any part of what is being offered in exchange, product decisions entail issues that you may not think of as part of an organization's product. The "Spotlight on Global Marketing: The Toronto Blue Jays Baseball Team" illustrates this by showing that even with a losing team, other components of the product could be altered to attract fans.

Distribution, or place, addresses the where and when of product distribution. It is concerned with the selection, coordination, and evaluation of distribution channels. A **distribution channel** is the set of firms and individuals who participate in the flow of goods and services as they move from producer to user. For example, IBM produces computers that it distributes to CompUSA, a retailer, who in turn sells the computers to consumers. Distribution also encompasses decisions about transportation, warehousing, and inventory control.

MARKETING IN ACTION

The Toronto Blue Jays Baseball Team

The Toronto Blue Jays began playing baseball in April 1975. Despite early setbacks, which included a blizzard during the team's first home game and a less than stellar cast of everyday players, the Blue Jays were a box-office success story from the very start. Although never particularly good at attracting spectators when they played in other cities, the team's ticket sales at home have always been well above the league average.

In the early years, when the team's performance on the field was abysmal, the Blue Jays organization emphasized promotional give-aways (such as sun visors and plastic bats) and a family atmosphere. (Drinking beer was banned at Exhibition Stadium—the Blue Jays' original home—from the outset, and the stadium's small size promoted a feeling of intimacy.) Most spectators came to the stadium to have a good time with friends or family, and the Blue Jays' marketing plan in the early years catered to this need. As the first major league baseball team in English-speaking Canada, the Blue Jays also benefited from considerable media and spectator interest.

By the mid 1980s, the Jays had become a winning team. As the team's performance improved, more fans came to see the Blue Jays play, but by the late 1980s, the fans had become jaded. The team could perform well on the field during the regular season, but it had not been able to translate this into postseason success. Thus, the team's 1989 move to the Skydome was superbly timed. The Skydome stadium included a retractable roof, which could be opened during warm sunny days and closed during poor weather; an attractive and entertaining outfield video display board; and many other amenities common to modern stadiums.

Individuals who had had little interest in a Blue Jays game now had a reason to buy a ticket—to see the Skydome. This interest translated into a league record for home attendance in 1989, a feat that has been duplicated every year since the stadium's opening. During the 1990s, the Blue Jays also managed to exceed their best previous on-field performance, winning the World Series in 1992 and 1993.

As the 1994 season began, the Blue Jays franchise was one of the most valuable in major league sports. The organization's annual revenues (ranked as one of the top three in organized sports) come from many sources, including ticket sales, food concession sales inside the stadium, sale of broadcast rights to television and radio, and licensing fees. Licensing fees are payments made by manufacturers and retailers to the Blue Jays in exchange for the right to use the Blue Jays' name and logo. As the team's on-field performance has improved, licensing has become a particularly lucrative source of revenue for the organization.

A winning team is undoubtedly the best marketing tool for any baseball team. However, the Toronto Blue Jays have shown that, through the superior use of marketing, a baseball team can experience financial success despite a losing record. In fact, winning may be a bit of a curse. Although the Jays managed to repeat as World Series champions in 1993, their player payroll soared from $10.6 million in 1985 to almost $50 million in 1994. The task now facing the Jays is to continue to field a winning team without alienating fans through excessive price increases. This task is, of course, further complicated by the actions of players and owners that resulted in the cancellation of the 1994 season. Will the fans continue to support professional baseball in the future? Marketing may be a key to this question.

Promotion is the component of the marketing mix that communicates information to potential customers. Decisions regarding advertising, personal selling, publicity, public relations, and special promotional activities such as trade shows and product displays are part of this quarter of the marketing mix.

Price decisions involve price determination as well as setting price policies and developing specific pricing strategies, including choices about discounts. Some

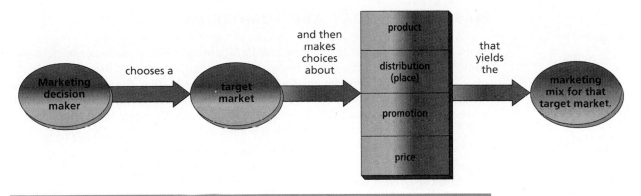

FIGURE 1.4
The Marketing Decision Maker and the Marketing Mix

companies, such as Sam's Warehouse, survive by maintaining everyday low prices. Other retail outlets, such as Broadway or Hudsons, may use a strategy of higher prices with occasional sales.

Decisions regarding the activities in the marketing mix must be made with a market in mind. A marketing manager will find it difficult, if not impossible, to make decisions regarding issues such as how best to advertise or what price to charge if he or she is not thinking of satisfying a certain group of potential customers. Hence, a marketing mix developed for a specific group of people is known as a **target market**. The marketing manager must identify a target market before making decisions in each of the controllable areas. Indeed, it is incorrect to think in terms of a marketing mix for a product or for an organization. The product is part of the marketing mix. An organization might have many marketing mixes depending on the number of target markers it is attempting to serve. Revlon Corporation, the cosmetics manufacturer, offers different lines of cosmetics targeted at different ethnic and racial groups. The firm has recently developed products specifically for African American and Hispanic consumers. Figure 1.4 illustrates the marketing decision maker's role in relation to a target market and the controllable variables

1-3   North American Honda has been extremely successful in the U.S. automobile market without the designation of someone as Vice President of Marketing. How is this possible?

1-4   Describe the marketing mix of the Toronto Blue Jays baseball team.

YOUR
MARKETING
KNOWLEDGE

MARKETING TODAY AND TOMORROW

Marketing is a dynamic field. New ideas and philosophies regarding the best way to meet consumer wants and needs and provide customer satisfaction are constantly emerging. In this section we briefly introduce several issues that have emerged in the last few years. Each of these issues represents an idea or philosophy that will move marketing into the twenty-first century in a way that meets the evolving needs and concerns of consumers. Although the introductions in this section are brief, we will revisit each of these topics many times throughout the book.

The Market-Driven Organization

In the 1990s, organizations are increasingly attempting to implement the marketing concept by becoming market-driven or customer-driven. A **market-driven** organization is one in which all activities, by all functional parts of the organization, focus on the goal of customer satisfaction. Thus, research and development, finance, human resources, and production all view their mission as being to satisfy customers' current and potential needs. Marketing provides the key customer inputs and customer contact to guide this approach, typically through marketing research. Information obtained through research can be funneled to all parts of the organization, which

The Xerox Corporation is an example of a market-driven organization.

can in turn use that information to carry out their tasks in response to consumer wants and needs. Marketing is also charged with delivering a program to the customer. The program, however, has been developed as a result of input from all the functional parts of the organization, not just from marketing. The Xerox Corporation is a market-driven organization, which conducts more than 40,000 surveys monthly in an effort to identify future and present needs and to ensure that existing customers are satisfied. The information is funneled to production, where it is used to make decisions about copier design and quality. Decisions about delivery, pricing, and sales effort are made only after thorough consideration of the customer. Furthermore, all employees are fully trained to serve consumers and build relationships with customers.

A market-driven organization may sound simply like an organization that has adopted the marketing concept. The two concepts are interrelated. A market-driven approach, however, goes beyond the mere notion of being marketing-oriented. The objective is to develop loyal customers and to develop relationships with customers that transcend a series of independent transactions based on exchanges. We proceed throughout this book on the assumption that being market-driven is a desirable goal for organizations.

Relationship Marketing

Market-driven organizations typically proceed by engaging in **relationship marketing,** in which marketing activity is seen as part of a pattern of interactions with the customer that form a continuing relationship.

These relationships with customers are intended to be so strong that customers and marketers will jointly solve problems. Marketers will anticipate customers' needs and set up mechanisms to make the relationship work easily and last a long time. For example, American Hospital Supply put its computer terminals in its customers' offices to allow the customer to check inventory status, verify prices, and place orders. Relationship marketing requires that all parts of the organization be coordinated to work with the customer, with marketing playing a key role.

Total Quality Management

Another means for implementing the marketing concept in an organization is acceptance of the management philosophy of **total quality management (TQM),** an operating philosophy that strives to imbue every aspect of organizational activity with quality. Acceptance of this philosophy by all departments in the organization generally produces an environment where all employees work together to create products and provide service that will please the customers. A university, for example, might institute a TQM program that would set goals within each department of the institution regarding how quickly students are seen, how rapidly inquiries are responded to, how few mistakes are made, and so forth. As each department strives to achieve its own quality goals, the institution as a whole provides better service and produces greater customer satisfaction.

Green Marketing

Green marketing refers to the carrying out of marketing activities with consideration for the environmental consequences. A laundry detergent manufacturer, for instance, is practicing green marketing when he or she produces phosphate-free, nonpolluting soap. Likewise, any firm that encourages recycling and makes it easy for the consumer to recycle its products could be viewed as a green marketer. Competitors in the photocopying industry, for example, have recently collaborated to develop an ink that can be washed off copies and reused up to ten times. Furthermore, soy-based ink, which is more easily biodegradable, is being used by the industry. The music industry has begun to change the packaging of compact discs, using less disposable paper and cardboard. The need to practice green marketing has become increasingly clear in the 1990s as the consequences of ignoring the environment have become frighteningly evident. Green marketing, however, is really just an ongoing development in the growth of socially responsible organizations. This book proceeds with the assumption that marketers, indeed everyone within organizations, have a basic responsibility to act in socially responsible ways.

Global Marketing

The need for marketers to think and plan in terms of a world market is increasingly apparent. **Global marketing** is the practice of marketing with a view to the entire world as a market. That does not mean that a marketer would choose to treat everyone in the world the same. It does mean, however, that marketers are commonly thinking about marketing activities and opportunities that transcend national borders. The opportunities inherent in global marketing have come about as the result of many factors, including improved worldwide communication and transportation and purposeful efforts such as the European Community and the North American Free Trade Agreement.

Marketers worldwide are taking advantage of marketing opportunities in all parts of the world. Firms such as Xerox, McDonald's, Radisson Hotels, and Procter & Gamble have operations in former Eastern and Soviet Bloc countries such as Poland and Russia. Likewise, many companies from Japan and other countries have followed the lead of successful giants such as Sony and Toyota in marketing their products in the United States.

Throughout this book we consider the world as a global market, using examples of companies from all over the world who are marketing to customers all over the world.

THE IMPORTANCE OF MARKETING

Perhaps when you began reading this book you asked, "Why should I study marketing?" Marketing is an important area for you to learn about for three basic reasons: (1) it is a major component of all economic activity; (2) it is critical to the success and failure of all organizations; and (3) it has a direct personal impact on you.

Importance to the Economy

Marketing is important to the economy as a whole. It helps support the high level of economic activity in most industrialized countries. Using the United States as an example, some additional facts will help point out marketing's importance to the economy:

- Approximately 25 to 35% of employed people in the United States are engaged in jobs that are directly or indirectly related to marketing.[11]

- On average, approximately 50% of every consumer dollar spent is related to marketing activity.[12] This value varies by product type. For example, in the marketing of cookies, marketing costs as a percentage of retail sales are broken down approximately as follows: advertising, 5%; shipping and distribution, 5%; packaging, 7%; manufacturer's sales force, 20%; and retail expenses and profit, 16%. This totals 53%.

▪ About 45% of family expenditures in the United States are for services such as transportation, health care, education, and recreation. With services, marketing's importance relative to other activities is apparent. Peter Drucker, a well-known author of books about general management, has said, "Any enterprise has two—and only two—basic functions: marketing and innovation."[13] This is especially true of service organizations, where "production" plays less of a role.

Importance to the Organization

The success or failure of specific products, or even of whole organizations, depends on many factors including management skills, production capabilities, financial resources and management, and marketing skills and programs. To say which is most important in a given situation is difficult. Clearly, however, meeting the wants and needs of customers, the basis of a marketing-oriented firm, is the action that keeps the entire organization moving along. Drucker said it well when he noted:

> Marketing is so basic that it cannot be considered a separate function. . . . It is the whole business seen from the point of view of its final results, that is, from the customer's point of view. Concern and responsibility for marketing must therefore permeate all areas of the enterprise.[14]

Accountants, managers, computer specialists, financial experts, and others in a firm will not have a job for long if the firm's marketing efforts prove ineffective.

Importance to You

In the past day or two, you may have listened to a radio ad, seen a television ad, or read a newspaper or magazine ad; stopped by some stores to buy food, books, or clothing; attempted to sell your old books or stereo system by placing a flyer on bulletin boards; or contributed blood at a Red Cross blood drive on campus. These are but a few of the direct ways marketing affects you on a daily basis. We all react to marketing activity (seeing ads, buying goods at a store, or giving blood), and we make use of it ourselves (selling books and stereo equipment). All of these activities encourage and facilitate exchange.

There are two other major dimensions of marketing that influence you directly: career possibilities in marketing, and your need to market yourself for the job you want. Career opportunities in marketing include retail merchandising and store management, brand management, buying advertising media or account management, marketing research, sales, public relations, and physical distribution management, among others. These careers need people with different interests and skills. A career in any aspect of marketing is dynamic and people oriented. Outgoing people are often attracted to marketing though, of course, the diversity of career opportunities in marketing means there is something for just about everyone. At the end of each chapter in this book, the "Career Focus" reinforces the concepts in the chapter and enables you to apply them to your job search.

THE STUDY OF MARKETING

Marketing is a relatively young discipline. It has been studied seriously in colleges and universities only for the past 100 years or so. Initially, marketing was a subspecialty in the field of economics. However, as economies became more complex, more questions about the dynamics involved in the exchange of goods, services, and ideas began to arise. Because these questions were not easily answered with the existing economic concepts and theories, marketing began to develop as a separate discipline. Today, there are at least five possible approaches to the study of marketing:

1. **Micromarketing** focuses on the way decisions are made about the marketing mix—product, distribution, promotion, and price. It is sometimes referred to as the **managerial approach.**

2. **Commodity marketing** concentrates on the functions performed in moving specific goods from producers to the ultimate consumers. This approach, for example, might study the roles of channel members in transporting products.

3. **Functional marketing** emphasizes the basic functions of marketing and how they are performed by various institutions. Information provision, for instance, might be analyzed in terms of all the different organizations that perform this task.

4. **Institutional marketing** concentrates on the organizations that perform various marketing functions. These include wholesalers and retailers, transportation companies, and warehouse systems. Here, study focuses on the organizations themselves rather than the tasks or functions they perform.

5. **Macromarketing** concerns the broader aspects of marketing and its effects on groups within society (such as children), on the economy, or on society as a whole. Macromarketing concentrates on legal and public policy issues, economic development, aggregate consumption patterns, and similar matters.

The views provided by these approaches are somewhat like those of five blindfolded people trying to describe an elephant on the basis of touch. Their descriptions will be very different, depending on whether the person is touching the trunk, tusks, ears, sides, or legs. So it is with the different approaches to marketing. Each gives a different perspective, and each has its merits.

OVERVIEW OF THE BOOK

This chapter has explained the basics of marketing: what it is and how it can benefit all types of organizations, society as a whole, and you as an individual. It has also introduced you to some issues at the forefront of marketing today that are predicted to move marketing into the twenty-first century. The rest of the book presents a more detailed look at the various aspects of marketing. The issues highlighted in this chapter in "Marketing Today and Tomorrow" are integrated throughout the book to emphasize their roles in the future of marketing.

Chapter 2 focuses on the marketing environment faced by a marketing decision maker. The trends affecting marketers worldwide as well as the issues of ethics and social responsibility are also considered in Chapter 2. Chapter 3 focuses on the managerial approach by looking at marketing management and presents a process for making ethical and socially responsible decisions. Chapter 4 is devoted to global marketing. The study of the consumer, the heart of marketing analysis, is discussed in Chapters 5, 6, and 7. Chapter 8 looks at marketing research as a means of obtaining the necessary information to allow better decision making.

Chapters 9 through 18 discuss specific marketing management decision areas. Chapters 9 and 10 focus on product aspects, and Chapters 11, 12, and 13 deal with distribution decisions. Chapter 11 presents a functional view of marketing channels and looks at physical distribution. Chapters 12 and 13 provide an institutional look at wholesalers and retailers, respectively. Chapter 14 examines promotional procedures in marketing, while Chapters 15 and 16 explore the individual elements of the promotional mix. Chapters 17 and 18 discuss pricing decisions.

The last part of the book discusses specific marketing situations, trends, and issues. Because we believe that marketing of services and not-for-profit organizations are all part of the mainstream of marketing, these topics are integrated throughout this book. But we also believe that these topics deserve special attention, so Chapters 19 and 20 explore marketing in services and not-for-profit organizations.

Each part of this text concludes with a segment of an ongoing case. The case focuses on the story of the Harley-Davidson organization. Each segment of the case asks you to apply the concepts presented to the issues that Harley-Davidson faced in its quest to gain market share and regain its early prominence.

The text presents relevant concepts along with real-world applications within each chapter through textual examples and the longer "Marketing in Action," and through one case at the end of the chapter. In addition, within each chapter you are given a chance to think about what you are learning in the "Review Your Marketing Knowledge" sections. The "Career Focus" exercise helps you to apply the topics of each chapter to your job search. One other feature designed to help you develop a deeper understanding of the material in the text is the "Personal Computer Exercise" at the end of most chapters. These exercises give you a chance to use marketing data to explore marketing concepts in depth. These exercises are included on the computer disk that comes with this text.

KEY POINTS

■ Exchange involves all the activities associated with receiving something from someone by giving something in return. This activity is an essential function of all aspects of our society.

■ Marketing includes all the activities designed to make exchange occur and work better. It thus affects each of us in our daily lives, the economy and society in which we live, and the success or failure of organizations.

■ Marketing is involved in the exchanges of physical goods, services, and ideas.

■ Marketing functions are designed to fill the gaps or separations that exist between producers of goods, services, and ideas and the consumers.

■ In performing these functions, marketing creates time, place, and possession utility, and to some degree, it contributes to form utility.

■ The application of the marketing concept is a key factor in the performance of organizations. This concept focuses on consumer needs and integrates all activities of the organization to satisfy these needs while achieving long-run profits or other objectives.

■ In applying the marketing concept, a manager needs to be concerned about the broader societal consequences of satisfying consumer needs.

■ Specific decisions related to the functions of marketing fall within the domain of marketing management. The marketing manager makes decisions about which consumers to target and what products, distribution, promotion, and price will appeal to that target market.

■ A key approach to the implementation of the marketing concept involves relationship marketing where organizations strive for such a strong link between the marketer and customer that purchases are seen as part of a continuing relationship and not a series of independent transactions.

■ A fundamental component of relationship marketing is a market-driven or customer-driven organization. In these organizations all activities are focused directly on satisfying and anticipating the needs and wants of customers.

■ Total quality management is a philosophy that can aid the implementation of the marketing concept.

■ Marketing in the 1990s and beyond must be attentive to the concerns expressed through the concepts of green marketing and global marketing.

KEY TERMS

marketing (6)
exchange (6)
demarketing (6)
market (6)
marketing functions (9)
transactional functions (9)
logistical functions (9)
facilitating functions (9)
utility (10)
form utility (10)
place utility (10)
time utility (10)
possession utility (10)
production concept (11)
sales concept (12)
marketing concept (12)
marketing myopia (14)
not-for-profit organization (14)
societal marketing concept (15)
social responsibility (16)
marketing management (16)
four Ps (17)
controllable variables (17)
marketing mix (17)
product (17)
distribution (17)
distribution channel (17)

promotion (18)
price decisions (18)
target market (19)
market-driven (20)
relationship marketing (21)
total quality management (TQM) (21)
green marketing (21)
global marketing (22)
micromarketing (24)
managerial approach (24)
commodity marketing (24)
functional marketing (24)
institutional marketing (24)
macromarketing (24)

ISSUES FOR DISCUSSION

1. For the "Marketing Profile," the "Spotlight on Societal Marketing," and the "Spotlight on Global Marketing" in this chapter, describe what is being exchanged.

2. For the "Marketing Profile," the "Spotlight on Societal Marketing," and the "Spotlight on Global Marketing" in this chapter, indicate what separations exist between producers and consumers, and indicate what utilities are created by marketing.

3. In your search for a job upon graduation, what market separations will exist? What marketing functions could bridge those separations?

4. A social critic commented: "Marketing . . . something like three-quarters to nine-tenths of it is idle waste." Discuss.

5. Ford Motor Company recently announced the intention to use only one supplier as its source for certain parts and supplies. What are the relationship marketing implications of this decision by Ford?

6. What is the difference between marketing and marketing management? How are the two related?

7. Using Figure 1.4, explain how accounting firms like Ernst & Young and Price Waterhouse practice marketing.

8. Give examples from your own experience of the marketing concept, the sales concept, and the production concept in action.

9. Could an organization be socially responsible without being marketing-oriented? Explain your answer.

10. Should marketing managers make judgments about the broader societal implications of their marketing decisions? Why or why not?

CASE APPLICATION

Los Angeles Rescue Mission: Helping the Needy

The Los Angeles Rescue Mission, a not-for-profit organization that provides food and shelter for the homeless, was in desperate need of marketing to help its fund-raising activities in 1989. New building codes required the mission to spend $500,000 in building improvements, an amount four times greater than the organization's annual income. Previous fund-raising activities consisted solely of sending an annual newsletter and request for support to a loyal but small group of individual and corporate donors.

To raise the necessary funds, the mission instituted a two-pronged marketing-based strategy: identify two target markets and then develop different marketing mixes for each.

The first target market the Rescue Mission focused on was existing donors. For this group, no services needed to be adjusted, only the timing and means of communicating the mission's needs. Appeals for donations were sent through the mail on a monthly basis. This action generated $85,000 immediately and showed that the tiny donor file was loyal.

The Rescue Mission also targeted people who had not donated previously, which required a different marketing approach. After deciding that a mailed appeal to this target market would be too costly given the results it could be expected to produce, the mission decided to undertake an advertising campaign in local newspapers. Newspaper advertising could reach potential donors for a much lower cost than could a direct mail approach. For example, instead of spending $15,000 to $20,000 to mail 50,000 requests for donations, the mission could run a small advertisement that cost about $100. The ad could be expected to reach approximately the same number of people as a direct mail piece. Because most people know what a rescue mission does, the advertisement did not need to include a lot of information. This strategy yielded 29,119 new donors and generated net income of $326,523.

Following its initial efforts with the two target markets, the Rescue Mission has instituted a regular monthly appeal and newsletter to all contributors. This effort has resulted in doubling the mission's monthly income.

With the money received, the mission has refurbished its old building and is in the middle of an $11 million campaign to generate funds for a new facility to house and serve 300 men, women, and children every night. With the help of the money raised thus far from this campaign and the increased donations produced by its marketing efforts, the annual budget is now more than $6 million, compared to $125,000 before the mission began its marketing efforts.

Questions

1. Describe the exchange process taking place between the Los Angeles Rescue Mission and a donor. What is the mission offering as a "product" to a potential donor? What "price" is that potential donor being asked to pay?
2. What types of utility have been created through the Los Angeles Rescue Mission's marketing efforts?
3. Does the mission appear to be a market-driven organization with respect to its fund-raising efforts? Explain.

The Product is You!

Welcome to the *career component* of this text. This special section provides you an opportunity to apply the principles of marketing to the activity that most of us spend the majority of our hours doing, namely WORK! At the end of each chapter we help you link the marketing concepts in that chapter to the *self-marketing* activities so critical to the career search process. Each "Career Focus" includes questions designed to give you the tools you will need to position yourself effectively in a very competitive job market. For selected chapters, we present a brief overview of the specific positions in marketing that relate to the topics discussed in those chapters.

In a competitive job market, you need to "market" yourself. Review the definition of *marketing*. Career planning uses a similar process. Your job search will require that you understand how you can market yourself in a marketplace where there are many competing brands like yourself.

Chapter 1 describes one of the most talked-about principles of marketing, *the marketing mix*, comprised of the four Ps. We can apply these factors to the process of securing employment as follows:

- *Product.* Remember that the product in the job search is *you*. What characteristics would describe and define this product and its development? Which aspects would seem important to a potential buyer (employer)?
- *Place.* For your job search, place includes those channels through which you will promote yourself as a product. To paraphrase the text, place is the "set of individuals" who will connect you as the producer to employers as the users. Your network could include such contacts as placement offices, recent alumni/alumnae, fellow students, executive recruiters, and human resource professionals.
- *Promotion.* This term refers to the methods you will use to get the word out that "you" are in the job market. Promotional tools include informational interviews, a professional résumé, and cover letters that highlight your constellation of skills and talents. All of these tools are advertisements that you as a product need to obtain job interviews. And finally, there is your direct promotion, your selling of yourself in the job interview.
- *Price.* This factor appears in negotiation of your salary, benefits, moving expenses, and other particulars of employment. To negotiate a fair price, you must understand the market range for you as a product, taking into consideration the value of your relevant education and experience.

Questions

Take a few moments to make a first pass at your job search as an application of the four Ps. For this purpose, just pick a dream job in terms of industry sector, professional function, and type of organization.

1. What are some target positions and who are some target employers that meet your dream job requirements?
2. Describe yourself as a *product* that could meet the needs of the employers you noted for the positions that you included. In writing your description, focus on your education, experience, and other relevant skills and attributes.
3. How would you define *place* for yourself? Be sure to consider the contacts that you would need to connect you to your prospective employers.
4. What would you feature in *promotion* of yourself to potential employers? Include the specifics you would highlight as your professional advertisement in cover letters and, eventually, in an interview.
5. What are the major factors that would determine *price* for yourself in your target job market?

Draft a summary of your answers to these questions and describe your reactions to this exercise. Include questions you have and any surprises that occurred during this process.

CHapTeR 2

The Marketing Environment

Upon completing this chapter, you will be able to do the following:

■ **Explain** the relationship between a firm and its external environment.

■ **Identify** the sources a marketing manager could turn to for environmental scanning.

■ **Discuss** some of the social-cultural factors that affect you as a consumer.

■ **Describe** how economic and competitive factors in the external environment affect marketing decisions.

■ **Comment** on the reasons for the rise of consumerism in the United States.

■ **Explain** the impact of the global economy on technological innovation.

■ **Understand** a firm's ecoresponsibility.

■ **Describe** briefly the ethical framework used to organize and evaluate individual behavior in the face of ethical dilemmas.

Marketing Profile

Who's Eating What, and Why in the United States and Europe?

Do European and U.S. consumers eat alike? Yes and no. People's eating habits are strongly influenced by a number of factors besides taste. Cultural values, demographic characteristics, personal finances, and concern about the environment all help determine what you eat. Furthermore, advances in technology, laws, and competition are factors in what foods are available to you. To the extent that U.S. and European consumers are influenced similarly by these factors, you would expect and, indeed, would find their eating habits to be remarkably similar. However, because the relative influence of many of these variables differs on the two sides of the Atlantic, U.S. diners and Europeans often find themselves eating different things.

Perhaps one of the most significant factors that appears to account for differences is the variation in social values. Consumers in the United States, for example, have been interested in the health and fitness aspects of their food for some time. This interest has resulted in a deluge of diet and other types of "lite" food on U.S. grocery shelves. European consumers, however, are just beginning to get interested in diet and "lite" foods. A recent study found both U.S. and European consumers primarily interested in the fat content of foods. After this commonality, however, the concerns of the two groups diverged. Europeans want (in descending order) freshness, vitamin and mineral content, and nutritional value while Americans look for foods low in salt, cholesterol, and sugar.

Ironically, as European interest in diet and "lite" goods is increasing, many U.S. consumers appear to be switching back to what has been called real food. Increasingly, healthy eating in the U.S. alternates with the consumption of heartier fare. Like other food producers, McDonald's appears to be responding to this move by downplaying its reduced-fat McLean Deluxe Burger (dubbed the McFlopper by some cynics) and introducing the Mega Mac, a half-pound hamburger patty.

Recent statistics reveal a demographic difference that may also account for variation in eating habits. A study found that 44 percent of Western European women reported being homemakers and only 33 percent said they worked outside the home. This is approximately the reverse of U.S. statistics on these same factors. Marketers realize that the presence of a full-time homemaker in a home is likely to account for different shopping, cooking, and eating habits for the entire family.

Economic and ecological factors can also help shape our eating habits. Consumers in the United States have traditionally been concerned with price. In the last few years, European consumers have become increasingly cost-conscious as well, due in large part to a recessionary economy throughout the early 1990s. Consumers with less money to spend and less optimism about the economy are likely to eat differently. Consumers on both sides of the Atlantic are also increasingly concerned about the environment. Marketers have found themselves having to respond to demands for reductions in excessive packaging, for example.

Advances in technology mean changes in what consumers eat. The introduction of the microwave oven, for example, has affected what's for dinner in U.S. households for the last twenty years. Microwavable food is a relatively new phenomenon in Europe, however.

Traditionally, European consumers have claimed that having a wide variety is much less important to them than it is to residents of the United States. However, increased competition from popular private-label products is pushing producers in industries like breakfast cereals to introduce more products into the European market. Time will tell whether European consumers will become more like U.S. consumers and respond to broader product offerings or whether they reject the strategy.

The changes in the European market brought on by economic, competitive, and social upheaval is providing opportunities for marketers who respond appropriately. Pepsico Corporation, for example, entered the Polish market in 1993 with "3-in-1" outlets combining Pizza Hut, Taco Bell, and KFC. The outlets have been very successful.

Smart marketers should be less concerned with whether U.S. and European consumers are alike and more concerned with monitoring the variety of factors that account for potential similarities and differences. Attention to the dynamic nature of those factors will produce opportunities for the alert marketer.

arketers must be aware of the key environmental forces that affect a firm. This chapter examines six of the most important external environmental forces that marketing managers face: social-cultural, economic, competitive, legal-political, technological, and ecological. Marketers must analyze and diagnose each of these forces to fully utilize data and information in a timely manner. Because environmental forces are external to the firm, they are not controllable by the firm. Indeed, environmental forces have been referred to as **uncontrollable variables.** Although basically uncontrollable, marketers cannot ignore these forces. The marketer's response to the impact of an environmental force will largely determine whether that force represents an opportunity or a threat to the firm. Although environmental forces are considered uncontrollable, firms sometimes try to influence these variables. A company, for example, might attempt to influence legal-political forces through lobbying efforts. Such influence, however, is typically long-term.

The record of business successes that has resulted entirely or partially from properly gathering and analyzing environmental information includes firms of all sizes. For example, through information gathering, United Airlines recognized that its customer base to certain destinations was changing. In response, the airline joined with McDonald's to offer an Inflight Happy Meals program on flights to Orlando, Florida, home of Disney World. DEVCOR, a small software development company, also achieved success by responding to changes in technological, competitive, and economic environmental factors. Analyzing and understanding these environments enabled DEVCOR to identify the need for compact disc-based maintenance manuals for automobiles and airplanes.

On the other hand, marketers who fail to properly gather and analyze environmental information often fail to find opportunities that translate into increased market share, customer satisfaction, and profit margin. The downturn experienced by the U.S. automobile industry during the 1970s and early 1980s resulted from the

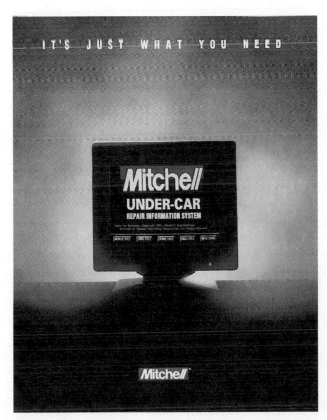

DEVCOR, a small software development company, achieved success by responding to changes in technological, competitive, and economic environmental factors. Analyzing and understanding these environments enabled DEVCOR to identify the need for compact disc-based maintenance manuals for automobiles and airplanes.

failure to respond to a changing environment. Oil prices were increasing worldwide and consumers were demanding smaller, more fuel-efficient automobiles. Problems for some parts of the industry have continued, again due to misreading environmental factors. In the early 1990s, for example, General Motors underestimated the public's interest in dual-side air bags. As a result, 44 percent of the firm's cars in 1992 offered only single-side air bags and more than 20 percent had no air bags at all. Competitors benefited from this error.

ENVIRONMENTAL CHANGE IS INEVITABLE

Change is perhaps the most powerful force of present-day life. The United States is now facing change in its economic stature, competitiveness, and productivity relative to other countries such as Germany, Japan, and Korea. These changes alter the level of confidence in U.S.-made products. Thus, quality has become an important issue that marketing managers are seriously evaluating. Regaining market share in the automobile industry, competing effectively with the Germans and Japanese in the high-technology industries, competing with European and Asian airlines for transatlantic traffic, and taking ethical and socially responsible acts are relatively new issues that marketing managers must now consider in a constantly changing world.

In the past, change often came at a much more leisurely pace; yet even then, the inability of individuals, cities, and nation-states to adapt to evolving trends resulted in a loss of power or even destruction. The Athenians did not understand why their city-state declined; the same was true of leaders in the crumbling Turkish empire many centuries later.

Like their historical predecessors, marketing managers do not have the luxury of ignoring or disregarding the forces of change. Managers must make decisions about product, promotion, place, and price in an environment engulfed by continual change, uncertainty, and varying degrees of turbulence. A recent example of a sudden change came with the Persian Gulf War in 1991. The cities of Carlsbad and Oceanside, California, are located very close to Camp Pendleton, a large Marine base. When thousands of troops were deployed to Saudi Arabia, the communities lost a substantial number of residents. Domino's Pizza nearly shut down operations in those cities due to the loss of soldiers who had been moonlighting as delivery men. Such shifts and events are not only uncontrollable but also beyond the marketing manager's ability to forecast precisely.

The external **marketing environment** of an organization includes all those factors that may affect the organization directly or indirectly in any perceptible way.[1] The environment can influence the factors that enter an organization. Such input includes people with values, needs, and goals; limited natural resources; and equipment and procedures.

The organization transforms the input to produce an output. The output (Macintosh personal computers, Kellogg's Low-fat Granola, a room at a Hilton hotel) goes back into the environment, again affecting the organization as the output is consumed, utilized, and evaluated. Thus, organizations and their environments are inseparable, each affecting the other. The difference between an organization's success and failure is often determined by the skill of its marketing managers in observing, analyzing, and forecasting the environment.

ANALYZING THE ENVIRONMENT

The process of analyzing the external environment begins with **environmental scanning,** the process of collecting information about the elements of a firm's environment. Once the information has been collected, an environmental analysis can take place. **Environmental analysis** is the monitoring and evaluation of external environmental forces. It is designed to determine the source of a firm's opportunities and threats. **Environmental diagnosis** is the process of making marketing decisions by assessing the significance of the data (opportunities and threats) in the environmental analysis.[2] The diagnosis is an opinion resulting from an evaluation of the available facts. The three components of analyzing the environment are closely related. The decision-making team responsible for analyzing the environment may include marketing experts, financial specialists, human resource managers, production planners, and research and development scientists. Each team member must weigh the facts, market conditions, the bargaining power of constituents, and alternatives available to consumers. Each individual must understand that market-driven forces will impact how successful the firm will be in the marketplace.

Figure 2.1 shows the relationship of an organization to the major forces of society, which are designated as the **external environment.** The importance of this

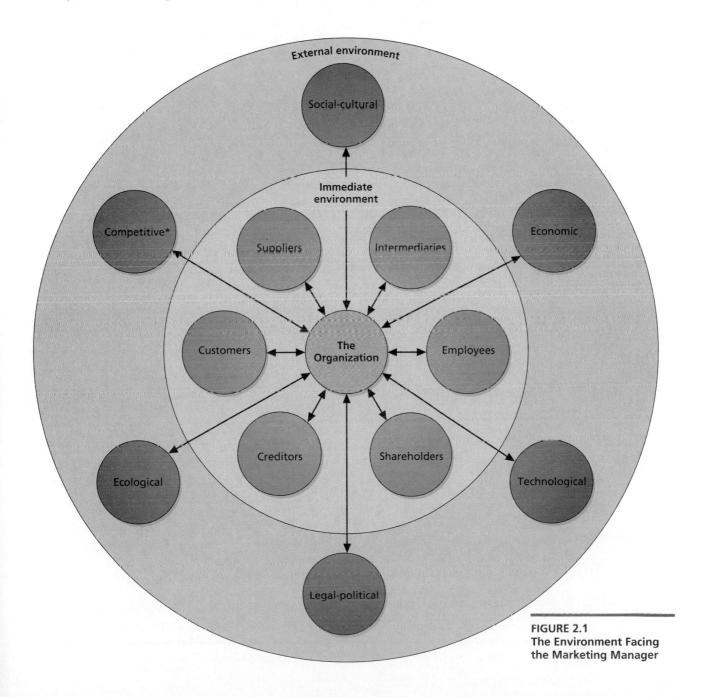

FIGURE 2.1
The Environment Facing the Marketing Manager

figure will become evident as each force is clarified in the chapter. For the time being, think of every marketing decision maker as being in the middle of the figure. Notice that Figure 2.1 includes an immediate environment with which the marketer and firm interacts: suppliers, customers, intermediaries, employees, creditors, and shareholders. The immediate environment is included in Figure 2.1 because the external environment affects the organization both directly and through the immediate environment. For example, changes in the social-cultural environment can affect the number of customers available for a product and the marketing manager's decisions about new product development or advertising expenditures.

An example of how changes in the external environment affect marketing decision makers will better illustrate the interrelatedness of the external environment and a firm such as Glaxo, a pharmaceutical manufacturer. In recent years, firms in the pharmaceutical industry have experienced changes in several external environmental forces. Critics of the industry have raised social and ethical issues. The industry has been attacked for conducting promotional drives disguised as education, for offering doctors hard cash rather than pens and notepads, and for distorting data to suit its promotional needs. Contentions that pharmaceutical companies have not always publicized the side effects of drugs has also caused legal-political forces to criticize the industry. As this environment has caused competition to become fiercer, some firms have been accused of bad-mouthing rival products.

In this environment, Glaxo's chief executive officer at the time, Ernest Mario, stated his belief that the laws of the marketplace required aggressive marketing tactics.[3] Mario decided that Glaxo must quickly establish its market share before competitors produced rival brands. Mario studied the competition, Glaxo's financial position, statistics concerning ulcers, patient complaints about the disabling effects of ulcers, and research and development reports about medications for ulcers.

As a result of the analysis, Glaxo moved quickly to establish itself as an industry leader in ulcer medication by promoting directly to consumers rather than through doctors. This approach not only provided a competitive edge but also avoided claims of unethical or illegal interaction with physicians. Glaxo was one of the first firms

Table 2.1
Important External
Environmental Factors

Social-Cultural	Economic	Competitive	Legal-Political	Technological	Ecological
Demographic • Aging of the population • Shifts in the work force • Increase in level of education • Changing makeup of families and households **Cultural** • Changing gender roles • Cultural diversity • Changing values	Income and the new economic realities Inflation Productivity Unemployment	Nature of competition Entry and exit of competing firms Major strategic changes by competitors	**Consumerism** • Marketers' responses to consumerism • Government's responses to consumerism **Legislation** • Antitrust legislation • Consumer protection legislation	The impact of technological innovation Global technology	Improving eco-responsibility Global look at ecological factors

to advertise on American television. According to Glaxo estimates, the commercials generated more than 500,000 visits to doctors. Today Glaxo's product, Zantac, is the world's top-selling brand of Ranitidine (an ulcer drug) with a 31.8 percent market share.[4] Zantac has been financially successful for Glaxo. In 1992 it had sales of $1.9 billion.[5]

This example illustrates a firm's response to environmental forces. Chief Executive Officer Mario believed his decisions represented decisive action in the face of a threatening external environment. The actions themselves, however, have raised questions regarding social and ethical issues. Is what Glaxo did with Zantac creating markets rather than responding to the needs of existing markets? Is the creation of markets in the pharmaceutical industry ethical behavior? This is a question that competitors and Glaxo management continue to face as they respond to the dynamic external environment in which they operate.

The six factors in the external environment that we consider in this chapter are each comprised of a number of issues. Table 2.1 identifies many of these issues for each of the six factors. A marketing manager's decisions should come only after carefully weighing and evaluating the factors and issues in Table 2.1.

SOCIAL-CULTURAL FACTORS

Social-cultural factors consist of institutions, people and their values, and the norms of behavior that are learned and shared. It is the people—who they are, where they are, how they live, what they think, and what values they hold—that make up the social-cultural fabric of society. The social component describes the characteristics of the society, its demographics. The cultural component deals with people's values and the behavioral norms. **Values** are defined as the likes, dislikes, beliefs, and prejudices that determine a person's view of the world.

Social-cultural factors affect marketing decisions across all four Ps because they establish limits regarding what a society finds acceptable and fair. For example, a highly affluent society is likely to accept more elaborate products than a less affluent society. An aging society may require distribution systems that make it more convenient for the members of that society to acquire goods and use services.

Demographic Factors

The study of people in the aggregate is **demography**. A demographer is concerned about the size, birthrate, age, geographic migration patterns, and education levels of the population. Because the United States is undergoing a significant demographic transition in many areas, the analysis of demographic statistics can help marketing managers identify and understand market segments and plan strategies targeted to those segments.

In this section we briefly discuss some of the major trends in American demographics: changes in age, occupation, education, and family makeup. Recognizing these trends and looking at how marketers are responding should help marketers worldwide understand the importance of demographics.

Aging of the American population.   The total population of the United States in the 1990s is increasing very slowly, at a rate of less than one percent per year. Population growth depends on the rate of births, deaths, and migration. Death rates are very predictable. Net migration to the United States has averaged about 500,000 persons per year.[6] Thus, the most important factor in predicting increases in population is the birthrate. Changes in the birthrate and the fertility rate—the number of children born to the average woman in her lifetime—have had a dramatic impact on the population during the past 25 years and will continue to have a major impact into the twenty-first century.

High fertility rates between 1947 and 1961 produced what is known as a "baby boom." The nearly 60 million Americans born during this period (age 34 to 48 years in 1995) account for about 40 percent of the U.S. adult population. Following the baby boom, fertility rates dropped in the 1970s, producing a "baby bust." In the 1980s and 1990s, a small increase in the fertility rate coupled with large numbers of women of childbearing age (those born during the 1947–1961 baby boom) has produced higher numbers of annual births.

The impact of these changes in fertility and birthrates is that growth in the population has not been and will not be comparable across all age groups. During the period 1987 to 1993, the largest percentage increases came in the group aged 35 to 54 years. The average age of the U.S. population was 28 in 1970, 30 in 1980, and 33 in 1990. The median age should reach 37 years by the year 2000. The number between the ages of 45 and 64 years will increase to 22 percent of the population by 2000 and to 26 percent of the population by 2010. Meanwhile, those between the ages of 25 and 34 years will drop by 4.9 million, to 38.2 million by 2000.[7] Figure 2.2 illustrates this maturing.

Many firms have already altered their marketing strategies to respond to the aging of the population. Levi's Dockers line, targeted at middle-aged consumers, has been very successful. Sharp Electronics recently introduced a VCR targeted at mature consumers that speaks the directions for ease of programming. Even advertising is changing. Reebok has used the tagline, "Not sensible. Just slightly rational," for its line of walking shoes in an attempt to appeal to baby boomers looking for comfortable walking shoes.[8]

Shifts in the work force. According to the U.S. Census Bureau, about one-third of today's work force are blue-collar workers, one-quarter are sales and clerical workers, one-quarter are managers or professionals, and the remainder are service workers or farmers. The blue-collar market is decreasing during the 1990s due in part to the shift away from manufacturing and to services, but will still make up one-quarter of the work force in the year 2000. This latter market—craftsmen, first-line supervisors, machine operators, and laborers—is important because of the large increases in blue-collar income in recent years. Furthermore, nontraditional blue-collar workers—those with technical and computer skills—will be in high demand in such growth industries as biotechnology, telecommunications, and computers.[9]

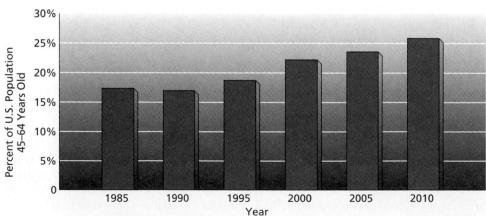

FIGURE 2.2
The Aging U.S. Population

Source: "Special Issue: The Tough New Consumer," *Fortune*, Autumn–Winter 1993, p. 87.

Increase in level of education. Demand for many products and services, such as books and magazines, travel, and entertainment, is influenced by the educational level of consumers. A person's level of education is closely related to his or her age—70 percent of those aged 65 years and older in 1993 did not finish high school, compared to less than 15 percent of those aged 25 to 44. In general, the U.S. population is more educated than ever before in its history. This trend toward increased education is expected to continue and, in fact, expand. Lifelong learning has become a necessity as improvements in technology and increased market globalization occur at increasingly rapid rates. No longer can employees graduate from high school or even college, get a job and stay there indefinitely without additional training. Figure 2.3 illustrates the increases in school enrollment predicted between 1991 and 2003. Although population is not anticipated to increase significantly, increases in school enrollment are evident in every age group and both genders.

For marketers, the trend toward increased education is important because higher levels of education produce consumers who are more sophisticated in evaluating product offerings, more receptive to new products, and more demanding of quality and performance. The Bureau of Labor Statistics reports that college-educated heads of household are more likely to buy services, spend more money on housing, spend two times as much on furniture and appliances, and two times as much on entertainment as do households headed by people who did not graduate from college. They also invest more in personal insurance and pensions. Households headed by those not graduated from college spend more on tobacco while households headed by college graduates spend more on alcohol.[10]

Changing makeup of families and households. The traditional definition of a typical U.S. household was one that contained a husband, a nonworking wife, and two or more children. That type of household accounts for only about nine percent of households today. In its place we see many single-parent households, households without children, households of one person, and other nontraditional households. The growth rate of households in general has far exceeded the growth of the population. For many companies, such as General Electric and AT&T, the number of separate households is a much better predictor of their sales than raw population totals. This is certainly true for companies in the housing and appliance industries. A household is likely to buy only one dwelling unit, washing machine, and dishwasher, no matter how many people live there.

A number of trends have combined to create these changes in families and households. Americans are staying single longer—more than one-half of the women and three-quarters of the men between 20 and 24 years old in the United States are still single. Divorce rates are at an all-time high. It is predicted that almost two-thirds of first marriages may end in divorce. There is a widening gap between the life expectancy of males and females. Currently average life expectancy in the United

	1991	2003	Change
K – 8	34,422	38,523	+11.9%
9 – 12	12,610	15,707	+24.6%
Higher Levels	14,169	16,124	+13.8%
Men	6,412	7,386	+15.2%
Women	7,757	8,738	+12.6%

Source: D. Crispell, "Student Supplies," *American Demographics*, August 1993, p. 63.

FIGURE 2.3
School Enrollment: 1991 and 2003

States is 74 years for men and 78 years for women. Widows now make up more than one-third of one-person households in the United States. These trends have produced a declining average size of household. It is interesting to note that despite this statistic, recent research shows many young and middle-aged adults and families moving back into their parents' households. Historically, this type of movement has been temporary. Cultural and ethnic differences also account for differences in this trend. Individuals of Hispanic and Asian background are often part of large, extended families.

The impact of all these changes is significant for marketers. Nontraditional households have different needs for goods and services than do traditional households. Smaller households often have more income per person than larger households, and require smaller houses, smaller cars, and smaller package sizes for food products. Households without children often spend more on personal entertainment and respond more to fads than do traditional households. More money may be spent on travel as well.

Cultural Factors

People's values and their behavioral norms comprise the cultural component of social-cultural factors from the external environment. In the following discussion we will consider three such factors that have influenced the U.S. population.

Changing gender roles.   Gender roles have made a significant and well-documented change over the last 30 years. As the traditional family has continued to decline, so have stereotypical views of men's and women's roles. Today more than one-half of the mothers (59 percent in 1992) of children under 5 years old are in the work force. Women are increasingly holding jobs that used to be held by men. Many men are taking a far more active role in parenting and housekeeping than their fathers did.

These changes may find some basis in changing economics. The household of today may require two incomes to manage higher living expenses. Many of the changes in gender roles, however, can be attributed to changes in the beliefs, prejudices, and values of the population regarding the proper roles of males and females in society. Marketers have found it necessary to respond to these changes in many ways. Products and services designed to provide convenience and efficiency of time have become virtual necessities in households where both husband and wife work. Personal shoppers are becoming increasingly popular because they assist consumers by doing the work of locating and comparing goods and services. They then contact the consumer who makes the final decision about whether to purchase.[11] Retail environments that make one-stop shopping possible also appeal to the working couple of the 1990s. Great success has been realized by warehouse clubs like Price/Costco, which offer customers food, clothing, electronics, and appliances as well as services such as pharmacies, eye care, travel, and auto repair. Promotion has also had to change. As the ads that follow show, women and men are depicted differently today in advertising than they were a generation ago.

Cultural diversity.   Although the population of the United States as a whole has been growing slowly, growth among minority groups has been much greater. While the growth rate for the white population between 1990 and 2000 is predicted to be only 4.4 percent, the African-American population is forecast to grow 20.7 percent, the Asian population 35 percent, and the Hispanic population 48 percent during that same period.[12] This trend is projected to continue into the next century.

African-Americans, Hispanics, and Asians are important for many consumer product categories. African-Americans, for example, represent a $280 billion market in the United States. They account for 34 percent of the hair care market and have

Just because it costs a bit more is not the reason your husband wants this cordless shaver for Christmas.

He's got reasons you've never even heard of:

Guess Where Rob And Kathy Will Be Enjoying Their Next Few Hundred Saturday Mornings.

Thomasville
Beautiful furniture, beautifully made.™

Next time insecurity creeps up on you,
STOMP

TODAY'S WOMAN

Nothing makes you feel better about yourself than being in charge and staying in shape. Weider makes it easier for you to take control with in-home equipment that's sturdy, dependable and affordable. The Club Stepper pictured here delivers the same aerobic benefits of machines costing far more, yet is remarkably priced at just $249.00 (plus shipping). It's all part of our commitment to value and quality. So call 1-800-220-WEIDER and get ready to do some stompin'!

weider.
The Total Fitness Company.™
In Canada: 2875 Bates Rd., Montreal P.Q. H3S1B7

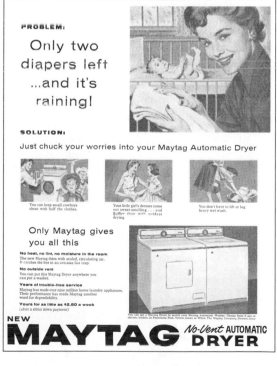

PROBLEM:

Only two diapers left ...and it's raining!

SOLUTION:

Just chuck your worries into your Maytag Automatic Dryer

You can keep small cowboys clean with half the clothes.

Your little girl's dresses come out sweet-smelling . . . and fluffier than with outdoor drying.

You don't have to lift or lug heavy wet wash.

Only Maytag gives you all this

No heat, no lint, no moisture in the room
The new Maytag dries with sealed, circulating air. It catches the lint in an oversize lint trap.

No outside vent
You can put this Maytag Dryer anywhere you can put a washer.

Years of trouble-free service
Maytag has made over nine million home laundry appliances. Their performance has made Maytag another word for dependability.

Yours for as little as $2.50 a week
(after a small down payment)

NEW
MAYTAG *No-Vent* AUTOMATIC DRYER

As these ads show, men and women are depicted differently today in advertising than they were a generation ago.

been found to be particularly strong consumers of candy bars, nondairy substitutes, corn, sausage, and freeze-dried coffee.[13] One reason the African-American, Hispanic, and Asian markets offer so much potential is that they are very accessible. The vast majority of these groups live in metropolitan areas.

Changing values.   Over time the values of a society can change dramatically. As demographics change, which they are doing around the world, the way consumers purchase products and services, think about products and services, and use products and services changes. Collecting information about changing values is difficult. It requires a concerted effort at surveying, observing, tracking trends, and using informed sources such as customer complaint lines.

Numerous changes in the way people live have forced marketers to adjust and try new approaches. These shifts in values were difficult to anticipate and not many firms were prepared for the changes. For example, increased education has resulted in new attitudes among employees about hours they wish to work, the quality of life they expect, and the kind of fringe benefits they desire. Leisure activities have been planned to attract people who take brief vacations. Three- to four-day vacations are more common than one- or two-week vacations.

Gatorade has countered competition from Coke and Pepsi in the sports drink market with increased advertising using sports celebrities such as former basketball star Michael Jordan.

One dramatic shift in values in the United States is in the area of fitness and health. Exercise, eating healthily, and preventive health care have become major concerns of a growing portion of the population. Coca-Cola and Pepsi want a bigger share of the growing sports drink market.[14] This market has been dominated by Gatorade, which is owned by Quaker Oats. Since Quaker acquired Gatorade in 1983, sales of sports drinks have soared from $85 million to more than $1 billion. More than 80 percent of this market is still in Quaker Oats' hands.

Coca-Cola has introduced Power Ade and Pepsico has launched All Sport, both believing that their vast distribution networks will take some of Gatorade's market. Gatorade has countered with increased advertising using sports celebrities such as former basketball star Michael Jordan and by introducing new flavors. The market is so large and is growing so fast that Quaker is pulling out all the stops. Developments in this market illustrate that marketers must monitor the changing values and tastes of consumers and take a proactive approach if they are to gain and keep market share. It is important for marketers to recognize that changes in values can come quickly or can be spread over long periods of time.

ECONOMIC FACTORS

Economic factors are an external force that consists of all variables that affect the buying patterns of consumers and the marketing plans of businesses. Economic factors include income, inflation, productivity, and unemployment. Generally a healthy economy is good for consumers and marketers alike. Consumers are able to buy more goods and services, so companies are able to make higher profits. Furthermore, consumer spending shifts away from an emphasis on the basic necessities of life—food, clothing, and shelter—to the purchase of such nonessentials as an additional television set or a vacation. Greater consumer demand also facilitates the establishment of new companies. During an economic downturn, such as the worldwide recession of the early 1990s, both consumers and businesses retrench. Consumers spend less and what they do spend, they spend on the basics. Businesses must adjust to the lower sales and profits that come with lower consumer demand. If the downturn lasts long enough, it can result in widespread business failures. Effective marketers try to anticipate changes in economic factors so that they can maximize the advantages offered by good times and minimize the damage caused by bad times.

REVIEW

YOUR MARKETING KNOWLEDGE

2-1   What social-cultural factors would be most important for a marketer of day care services to consider?

2-2   Would the impact of these important factors represent threats or opportunities to the day care provider? Explain.

Income and the New Economic Realities

Although consumer income is a demographic factor, it is so significantly influenced by the economy that we will consider it in this section. Despite the recession of the early 1990s, the U.S. population is gaining in affluence. By 2000 there will be more than 25 million households in the United States that earn more than $50,000 annually. That's almost a 100 percent increase from 1985 even after adjusting for inflation. The number of households earning $35,000 to $50,000 per year will also increase while those earning less than $15,000 and between $15,000 and $35,000 per year will decrease. Much of the gain in high-income households will be attributable to the aging of the population (older people typically hold higher paying jobs) and to the continued increase in the number of households with two incomes.

Marketing managers are most concerned with a consumer's disposable personal income (DPI). **Disposable personal income** is a consumer's total after-tax income to be used for spending and savings. This income, available to individuals and families, provides a marketing manager with information on the general health and potential of markets. Managers attempt to determine how income is divided among families. In 1990, disposable income per capita in the United States was $29,943.[15]

Marketers can prepare for increasing levels of affluence in many ways. Already we see improved customer service and a focus on higher quality and dependability in goods and services.[16] Home builders frequently use income figures to determine when, how many, and what types of homes to build. In the late 1980s as incomes rose substantially, home builders produced a ready supply of vacation homes. Unfortunately, as the U.S. economy fell into a recession in the early 1990s, many of these homes remained unsold.

Inflation

Inflation is a general rise in the prices that people must pay for goods and services. Inflation affects everyone. Since the Great Depression of the 1930s, average prices in the United States have moved steadily upward, almost never downward. The rate of inflation was relatively modest during the 1940s and 1950s but in the 1960s and 1970s prices increased at a faster rate. The cost of most goods and services today is about ten times higher than it was during the 1930s. Then a haircut, for example, cost about $.75, a meal in a comfortable restaurant cost $.50, and a pair of durable and stylish shoes cost about $4.95. Inflation in 1993 was below 4.0 percent, which is down significantly from the double-digit rate of 12 percent in 1981.[17] Even at the modest inflation rate of 3 percent, however, higher prices, represented in Figure 2.4, will become a reality by 1998.

Productivity

Most economists agree that inflation becomes worse with decreasing productivity. A sluggish, or flat, productivity rate can slow the growth of the entire economy. **Productivity** is an estimate of output per labor hour. Certainly it is a crude measure, subject to short-term error. However, over the long-term, productivity measures can clearly show trends. Productivity in the United States has gone through some ups and downs over the past 30 years. For years prior to 1970, the rate of productivity increased at an annual rate of approximately 2.5 percent. From 1970 to 1978 that growth rate slowed to around 2.0 percent. Productivity was virtually flat from 1978 to 1985. Since 1985 it has shown steady growth again. In 1993, U.S. manufacturing productivity grew by 4.2 percent, well above both Germany and Japan.[18]

Marketers must be concerned when productivity growth is sluggish or flat. When workers produce more, total output grows and employers can increase wages

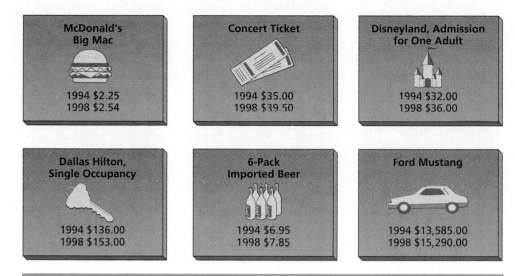

FIGURE 2.4
The Result of Modest (3%) Inflation Between 1994 and 1998

without raising prices. The rise in revenue from increased output will offset the higher wage costs. If productivity is flat, almost every dollar of wage gains is translated into price boosts. Goods and services that cost more will not be purchased because consumers do not have enough dollars to purchase them.

Unemployment

Shifting world population, rapid industrialization, and the diffusion of knowledge and technology around the world are creating a global work force. The distribution of global population is shifting toward the third world, which by the year 2020 will be home to five sixths of the world's people. Workers in these underdeveloped countries earn much lower wages than U.S., Canadian, German, and Japanese workers.

Automation, computerization, and robotization are spreading throughout the world. American business is applying new technology in an effort to cut costs and remain competitive. Corporate restructuring through mergers and acquisitions has shrunk employment by 2.8 million people in Fortune 500 firms since 1980.[19]

The new global arrangements, automation, computerization, robotization, and mergers and acquisitions have contributed to a reduction in the work force called *downsizing*. Not only have many blue-collar jobs been eliminated, but a growing number of managerial and professional jobs have been cut as well.

Downsizing, or the reduction of available jobs in Fortune 500 companies (larger firms), has resulted in unemployment. Marketing is affected because the buying power of unemployed individuals is significantly reduced. Even when workers become re-employed, their return to previous purchasing rates is often slow as they pay backed-up bills. Unemployment results in reduced buying power of employed individuals also. The employed individual is usually asked to pay higher taxes so the unemployed can receive welfare, compensation, and social services to meet the basic requirements of life.

Increasing opportunities with smaller firms and job creation in such firms will likely offset and exceed the unemployment occurring in larger firms. In the 1992 presidential campaign all three candidates emphasized the importance of job creation. Marketers must track both unemployment rates and job creation rates to determine the amount of consumer purchasing power.

COMPETITIVE FACTORS

Competition, domestic and international, is another important part of the external environment. Three competitive factors are the nature of competition, the entry and exit of competitors, and major changes of strategy by competitors.

The Nature of Competition

There are four widely described competitive environments: the **absolute monopoly, oligopoly, monopolistic competition,** and **pure competition.** Table 2.2 presents some of the main features of each of these environments. At one extreme is the absolute monopoly (public utilities, local telephone companies, and cable TV firms), with only one seller. In this market, there is little concern about promotion or price competition. Having control over a needed and unique product, these sellers can virtually dictate to others how their product or service is to be provided, priced, and promoted to consumers.

At the other extreme is the purely competitive environment. A large number of sellers are selling virtually identical products. Price competition is not possible because all sellers have the same product and must keep their prices at the level of the others. If one seller raised prices, buyers would purchase from another seller who had not. If this seller reduced prices below the level of competition, it would be swamped with orders that produced little or no profit. Farm commodities are a good example of products operating in this environment. The seller in the purely competitive environment is not able to influence others who help in getting the product to consumers because each seller sells only a small percentage of the total.

The two midrange environments, oligopoly and monopolistic competition, are the most common competitive situations in the United States. In the oligopolistic environment, a few large sellers account for a high percentage of the market. Promotion is a very important part of the marketing mix. Buyers typically view the products of oligopolists as having important differences. General Motors, Ford, and

Table 2.2
Possible Competitive Situations

	Absolute Monopoly	Oligopoly	Monopolistic Competition	Pure Competition
Number of sellers	One	Few	Many	A very large number
Concentration of total sales	100 percent of sales by one seller	High percentage by each seller	Small percentage by each seller	Very small percentage by each seller
Buyers' view of product differences	Unique product (no substitutes)	Highly differentiated	Few differences	No difference
Importance of Promotion	Low level of importance	Very important part of marketing mix	Less important	No importance
Importance of price competition	Not important	Avoid price competition	Very important	Unimportant
Relations with distribution channel	May be able to dictate terms	Considerable influence	Less influence	Very little influence

Source: Based on D. Robin, *Marketing* (Harper and Row, 1978), p. 137.

Chrysler are oligopolists. Their combined total of annual U.S. car sales is over 70 percent. Their products are perceived by consumers to have important differences. Ford's edge over General Motors in profits for 1993, for example, has been attributed to the fact that virtually all 1994 model Fords had at least one safety air bag while General Motors could make that claim for less than 60 percent of its products. In addition to the auto industry, the airline, oil, computer, and chemical processing industries are controlled largely by oligopolists.

In the monopolistically competitive environment, there are many sellers who each account for smaller percentages of total industry sales. The differences among competitors' products are not crucial to consumers. Shampoo is an example of a consumer product that faces this situation. The top ten brands of shampoo in the United States account for only 58 percent of market share. The leading shampoo, Procter & Gamble's Pert Plus, holds a 10.7 percent share of the market. Although many shampoos exist, they are all fairly similar in terms of what they contain and how they work. The monopolistically competitive firm often works to differentiate its product through promotion. Shampoo marketers promote features such as cleanness, shininess, squeakiness, and other factors that are difficult to differentiate. Price is an important consideration for many consumers.

Marketing managers must carefully examine the nature of domestic and foreign competition. Specifically, they need to determine what kind of market exists. For example, the domestic automotive industry must consider not only new competitors in the United States, but also foreign competitors (Toyota, Nissan, Honda) who are very active in the small car market.

Entry and Exit of Competing Firms

Of great concern to marketing managers is the changing nature of competition. That is, what new competitors are entering our business and which ones are leaving? If competitors leave, the probability of accomplishing corporate objectives related

Shampoo is an example of a monopolistically competitive industry. Shampoo marketers promote features such as cleanness, shininess, squeakiness, and other factors that are difficult to differentiate.

to market share and profitability increases.[20] When Pan American Airlines liquidated in 1992, the remaining U.S. airlines experienced an increase in passengers. A competitor's exit may concern a firm, however. Pan Am's departure left British Airways in a vulnerable position, inviting closer governmental scrutiny of charges of having a monopoly on Eastern European markets.

When new competitors enter, the opposite effect occurs. New competitors make it tougher to accomplish objectives. Companies like Bulova and Timex weren't pleased when Texas Instruments and Swatch entered their business of producing watches.

Whether a firm enters a market depends on the ease of entry. Firms are reluctant to enter a market if there is a scarcity of raw materials or if the structural barriers are high. Structural barriers are high when there is strong customer loyalty to existing brands, when large existing firms are enjoying significant economies of scale, and when existing firms are realizing cost advantages. Biotechnology is an example of an industry that is difficult to enter due to the necessity of large capital expenditures and the long-term nature of payback. Government inspection and monitoring adds greatly to the cost of entry. Within a biotechnology firm, four to six years of research often precede a sale. During this time there are no interim revenue infusions. These factors make entry into the industry risky and often questionable.

Major Strategic Changes by Competitors

Marketing managers want to know what major competitors are doing. Microsoft was very concerned when Apple introduced Macintosh with its simple, icon-based software. Apple's efforts resulted in lost market share for Microsoft until it developed the icon-based Windows program. Windows allowed Microsoft to recapture much of its market share. Today, firms and industries are concerned not only with competitiveness across companies but also with a nation's competitiveness, which is the extent the country's industries compete with those of other countries.

To be successful a company must pay attention to its competition and look for its mistakes, weaknesses, and problems. Then it must launch programs and make decisions that hit weak points such as flawed product design or overpriced products. In 1980 and 1981 Apple attacked the home computer field, a weak point in the IBM line. In 1990 Apple had more than $5.6 billion in sales. Steven Jobs, Apple's former chairman, saw and seized the opportunity to market a computer that could help people keep track of their personal finances in their homes.[21] Today Apple and IBM seem much closer than they were during the fiercely competitive environment of the 1980s. Both firms restructured in 1993 and 1994 to be more responsive to their customer bases, eliminate "dying" products, and deal with diminished customer loyalty. Furthermore, the two firms have forged an alliance to build common hardware and software.

Companies have always kept a close watch on what competitors were doing. Some of the main collectors of competitive information and intelligence are Ford Motor Company, Marriott Hotels, Rockwell International, Pepsico, Union Carbide, Revlon, and Gillette. These firms are known to have batteries of competitor analysts. How much of what these analysts learn is worth their salaries? When the information leads to the introduction of highly successful products, the answer would appear to be, all of it. Gillette, for example, expedited its introduction of the Sensor razor after learning that Schick, a major competitor, was also developing new products. The Sensor has been very successful for Gillette, which has gone on to develop a range of equally successful shaving and skin products to complement the razor.

Intelligence gathering has resulted in the theft of competitor's ideas and innovations. Montedison, Italy's largest chemical firm, was caught using unlicensed software, mostly Lotus 1-2-3. In 1986, the U.S. International Trade Commission estimated that American companies lost about $60 billion to foreign piracy each year.[22] The hardest hit are the most innovative, highly competitive firms in computer software and pharmaceuticals.

LEGAL-POLITICAL FACTORS

Legal-political factors consist of the government rules and regulations that apply to organizations. The very words *rules and regulations* often make marketing and other executives uneasy and resentful. No one likes being regulated. The American manager, for years, has been a staunch theoretical supporter of a hands-off government policy, that is, not interfering in any way with business activity. Yet most managers know that the business system cannot work without some government rules and regulations to organize and monitor the marketplace.

Governments have intervened in the marketplace principally in two modes: regulation of marketing conduct, and regulation of marketing institutions and industry structure. Some industries are now highly regulated by government policies. In late 1993 the over-the-counter vitamin industry became subject to federal regulations regarding the claims manufacturers could make about their products.

While marketers respond to increasing government involvement in marketing, they have to pay just as much attention to governmental developments in consumer purchasing behavior or competitive behavior. Marketing decision makers have been the objects of criticism from several societal groups, as well as from governments. Community members, in their roles as citizens rather than customers, have become upset about issues such as package pollution, advertising to children, and the quality of breakfast cereals. Paradoxically, while citizens often seek marketing practices consistent with public needs, as consumers with private wants, these same people act differently. For example, the controversy about soft-drink containers has clearly demonstrated that individuals say they want returnable bottles, but they buy nonreturnables.

Consumerism

Over the last 20 years, consumers have increasingly voiced their dissatisfactions with marketing practices and institutions. The overall term given to this customer reaction is **consumerism,** the movement to aid and protect consumers from business practices that infringe upon their rights.

A host of reasons have been cited for consumerism, but most boil down to the increasing complexity and impersonality of the marketplace. In short, consumers often find shopping such a complicated phenomenon that many feel they have "been had" through no fault of their own.

Marketers' responses to consumerism. Marketers have responded to consumerism in three basic ways: by regarding it as a threat to be opposed vigorously; by ignoring it, hoping it will disappear; and by regarding it as a signal that something can and ought to be done to improve the buyer-seller relationship. Those who have adopted the last stance and regard consumer dissatisfaction as a marketing opportunity have fared far better than those marketers who have responded negatively or not at all. In many instances, companies have found it difficult to respond alone to consumer problems and have gone to industry associations and other groups, urging industry-wide self-regulation. For example, the videogame industry is wrestling with the best way to handle consumer concern. Consumer complaints regarding the violence in

Over the last 20 years, customers have increasingly voiced their dissatisfactions with marketing practices and institutions. In this photo, consumers in Madison, Wisconsin, protest the addition of bovine growth hormone (BGH) to milk.

some videogames has caused some manufacturers and retailers to stop carrying particular games. Toys "Я" Us and F.A.O. Schwarz both removed Sega Genesis' Night Trap from their shelves during the Christmas 1993 selling season after considerable complaints. Sega has developed a rating system, much like the one used by the movie industry, for its games. Sega and Nintendo, another manufacturer, and large retailers like Toys "Я" Us, who carry the games have agreed to develop a voluntary labeling system.[23] The videogames industry as a whole began development of an industry-wide rating system in early 1994. Meanwhile a survey of 1000 adults in late 1993 indicated that 81.3 percent felt videogames should be rated.[24]

Self-regulation is often difficult. Consumers and politicians are skeptical of marketers' motives from the outset. Often there are no effective sanctions to impose on those who do not abide by the agreed-upon standards of conduct; and very often, it is virtually impossible to get agreement on a set of standards. In the survey cited above, only 18.1 percent of the respondents felt that makers of videogames should do the rating, 59.6 percent felt that rating should be done by an independent council, and 15.8 percent felt the government should do it.[25]

Government responses to consumerism.   The two most important government responses to consumerism are consumer protection and consumer education.

Consumer protection makes buying less risky and mistakes in buying less costly, usually through legal action. **Consumer education** refers to informing the buyer so he or she can buy wisely.

All levels of government have become involved in consumer protection, especially in assisting consumers with postpurchase problems. Additionally, the government has moved to protect consumers by acting against companies and industries that make promotional claims they cannot substantiate. The weight-loss industry, for example, has battled with the federal government about its promises and guarantees of successful weight reduction. Courts have generally settled problems by restricting any statements that are not substantiated.

Consumer education appears to be a potentially useful long-run response to consumer problems, but it involves several operational difficulties. Where do we begin? How should it be done? How do we know if it is being done correctly? Who pays for it? Many attempts have been made by governments and private concerns. Most of us have encountered labeling changes, product fact sheets, *Consumer Reports*, and the like. Additionally, some companies, such as J.C. Penney, have been very active in consumer education by publishing materials and running educational workshops. Added to all of these, the media perform their role by reporting allegations of marketing wrongdoing and highlighting needed or attempted reforms. This is their function in a free society, but it makes them part of the public arena of marketing.

Legislation

Marketers must operate within the constraints of laws and ethical behavior. To understand how the legal environment affects the way marketers compete, it is necessary to examine (1) relevant statutes, (2) their related interpretations by the courts, (3) the nature of enforcement by the Department of Justice and other agencies, and (4) the willingness of individual marketers to bring suit against one another.[26]

The statutes relevant to marketers can be categorized into two groups: laws affecting competition (antitrust legislation) and laws affecting consumers (consumer protection legislation). Table 2.3 summarizes the current major laws in both of these categories.

Antitrust legislation. Antitrust laws are designed to prevent or break up monopolies and deal with unfair methods of competition and deceptive practices. This category of legislation began with the Sherman Act (1890), which was a response to widespread monopolistic activity. Antitrust laws are still very important. The government-imposed breakup of AT&T and the consequent restructuring of the long-distance telephone industry is a modern example of antitrust laws at work.

The Congress of the United States has provided many exemptions to antitrust laws. Some of these exemptions relate to foreign trade, tariff policy to exclude foreign competition, and labor policy to protect workers.

The Antitrust Division of the Department of Justice has sole authority for enforcement of the Sherman Act and shares enforcement of other antitrust laws with the Federal Trade Commission. The Antitrust Division may bring criminal actions to punish violations or civil actions to restore competition and provide relief to those injured. In a criminal action, the case must be proven beyond "a reasonable doubt," whereas in a civil action, guilt must be established by "a preponderance of evidence."

Consumer protection legislation. Consumer protection legislation consists of laws passed to protect consumers against unfair and deceptive practices by firms. An important player in the enforcement of consumer protection legislation is the

Table 2.3
Major Antitrust and Consumer Protection Legislation

Area of Concern	Year	Act	Main Features
			Antitrust Laws
Restraint of trade and monopoly	1890	Sherman Act	Prohibits contracts, combinations, or conspiracies in restraint of trade (Section 1); monopolizing; attempting to monopolize, combinations or conspiracies to monopolize (Section 2)
Price discrimination	1914	Clayton Act	Prohibits price discrimination among purchasers that cannot be justified either by a difference in cost or as an attempt made, in good faith, to meet the price of a competitor (Section 2, as amended by Robinson-Patman Act of 1936, Section 2-a); payment of a broker's commission if an independent broker is not employed (Robinson-Patman, Section 2-c); providing supplementary services or allowances to a buyer unless such concessions are equally available to all buyers on a proportional basis (Robinson-Patman, Sections 2-d and 2-e); geographical price discrimination, except under conditions presented in the first clause (Robinson-Patman, Section 3); knowingly inducing or receiving an illegal discrimination in price (Robinson-Patman, Section 2-a); tying and exclusive dealing contracts (Section 3); mergers formed from acquisition of stocks or assets when the effect may be to lesson competition substantially, or to create a monopoly in any line of commerce in any section of the country (Section 7, as amended by Celler-Kefauver Act of 1950). Pre-notification of intent to merge is required under the Hart-Scott-Rodino Antitrust Improvement Act (1976).
Unfair methods of competition and unfair or deceptive practices in commerce	1914	Federal Trade Commission Act	Creates a commission whose orders are binding if not appealed to the courts by the defendant, and prohibits unfair methods of competition (Section 5); unfair or deceptive practices in commerce (Section 5, as amended by the Wheeler-Lea Act of 1938)
			Consumer Protection Legislation
Food, drugs, and cosmetics	1906	Food and Drug Act of 1906	Regulates interstate commerce in misbranded and adulterated foods, drinks, and drugs
	1906	Meat Inspection Act	Provides for sanitary and standardized meat products
	1938	Federal Food, Drug and Cosmetic Act of 1938	Strengthens the Food and Drug Act of 1906 by extending coverage to cosmetics; requires pre-distribution clearance of safety on new drugs; provides tolerance standards for unavoidable or required poisonous substances; and authorizes standards of identity, quality, and volume of container for foods
	1958	Food Additives Amendments	Amends the Food and Drug Act by prohibiting use of new food additives until the promoter establishes safety and the Food and Drug Administration (FDA) issues regulations specifying the conditions of use

Table 2.3
(Continued)

Area of Concern	Year	Act	Main Features
		Consumer Protection Legislation (Continued)	
	1960	Color Additives Amendment	Amends the Food and Drug Act, allowing the FDA to regulate the conditions of safe use for color additives in foods, drugs, and cosmetics
	1962	Kefauver-Harris Drug Amendments	Requires manufacturers to file all new drugs with the Food and Drug Administration; to label all drugs by generic name; and to pretest drugs for safety and efficacy
	1966	Drug Abuse Amendment	Sets up regulations for the sale of amphetamines and barbiturates
	1967	Wholesale Meat Act	Sets requirements making states' meat inspections meet federal standards, and orders unsanitary meat plants to be cleaned up
Fabric identification	1939	Wool Products Labeling Act	Provides for proper labeling of the kind and percentage of each type of wool
	1951	Fur Products Labeling Act	Provides that all furs show the true name of the animal from which they were produced
	1959	Textile Fiber Products Identification Act	Covers the labeling of most products not covered by the Wool or Fur Products Labeling Acts
Adequate and accurate consumer information	1914	Federal Trade Commission Act	Establishes the Federal Trade Commission (FTC) to control, among other responsibilities, "unfair methods of competition," such as deceptive advertising
	1958	Automobile Information Disclosure Act	Requires automobile manufacturers to post the suggested retail price on all new passenger vehicles
	1968	Consumer Credit Protection Act (Truth-in-Lending Act)	Requires full disclosure of annual interest rates and other finance charges on consumer loans and credit buying, including revolving charge accounts.
	1971	Fair Credit Reporting Act	Regulates the reporting and use of credit information
	1975	Magnuson-Moss Warranty/ FTC Improvement Act	Requires warranty terms to be in easy-to-understand language, limits the ability of companies to restrict their warranty liability, and sets strict guidelines for what is a "full" warranty
	1975	Fair Credit Billing Act	Sets up mechanisms for consumers to correct mistakes in their credit reports
	1976	Energy Policy and Conservation Act	Requires the FTC to set rules requiring disclosure of energy efficiency ratings for appliances
	1980	Fair Debt Collection Act	Makes it illegal to harass or abuse debtors; prohibits the use of falsehoods or other unfair methods to collect a debt

**Table 2.3
(Continued)**

Area of Concern	Year	Act	Main Features
Consumer Protection Legislation (Continued)			
Consumer Safety	1953	Flammable Fabrics Act	Prohibits shipment in interstate commerce of any clothing or material that could ignite easily
	1966	National Traffic and Motor Vehicle Safety Act	Authorizes the Department of Transportation to establish compulsory safety standards for new and used tires and automobiles
	1966	Child Safety Act	Strengthens the Federal Hazardous Substances Labeling Act of 1960 by preventing the marketing of potentially harmful products and permitting the Food and Drug Administration to remove inherently dangerous products from the market
	1969	Child Protection and Toy Safety Act	Amends the Federal Hazardous Substances Labeling Act to protect children from toys and other articles intended for them that have electrical, mechanical, thermal, or other hazards
	1970	Council on Environmental Quality Act	Authorizes the Secretary of the Interior to conduct investigations, surveys, and research relating to the nation's ecological systems, natural resources, and environmental quality and to establish a Council on Environmental Quality
	1972	Consumer Product Safety Commission Act	Creates a permanent Consumer Product Safety Commission, which identifies unsafe products and warns consumers of their hazards
	1976	Consumer Product Safety Commission Improvement Act	Expands the powers of the Commission and allows consumers to file suit against the Commission

Federal Trade Commission (FTC). The FTC is an independent administrative agency composed of five commissioners who are appointed by the President, with the advice and consent of the U.S. Senate, for terms of seven years. The President designates the chairperson. The FTC has a staff of about 800 people, consisting of lawyers, economists, and even some marketers.

The agency uses both voluntary and involuntary compliance methods for enforcement. Voluntary compliance methods include:

▪ *Conferences.* The agency conducts dialogues with affected businesspeople regarding the desirability of certain marketing practices.

▪ *Trade practice rules.* Since 1919 the agency has been publishing codes of suggested marketing practice, which were formulated in conjunction with businesspeople.

▪ *Guides.* Since 1958 the agency has been issuing administrative interpretations of its rulings prepared by the FTC.

▪ *Advisory opinions.* The agency issues statements, prepared by the staff for a long time and by the commissioners since 1961, about the legality of proposed business activities. These statements contain no assurance that the FTC will not take action.

Involuntary compliance methods include:

- *Preliminary injunctions.* The agency obtains temporary court orders requiring a firm to cease a marketing practice.

- *Cease and desist orders.* The agency obtains permanent injunctions against practices by firms subsequent to administrative hearings.

- *Consent orders.* The agency negotiates specific agreements to resolve a dispute without requiring admission of guilt.

- *Miscellaneous remedies.* The agency obtains corrective advertising or monetary refunds to consumers.

- *Trade regulation rules.* The agency issues statements prescribing a standard of conduct for a group of firms or an entire industry.

TECHNOLOGICAL FACTORS

Technology is a nation's accumulated competence to provide goods and services for people. When a better product or procedure is found, it is called **innovation.** **Technological innovation** includes all the activities involved in translating technical knowledge into a physical reality that can be used on a societal scale. Technology has touched almost every aspect of life in industrialized nations. In the process, it has made possible widespread affluence. The Brookings Institute estimated that nearly one-half of the increase in American national income between 1929 and 1969 came from advances in knowledge, or in other words, technology.

The importance of technological factors to marketers is captured in the classic comment, "Businesses that have been slow to react when major innovations have invaded their industry have often relinquished hard-won positions in a very few years, while companies that have successfully exploited the technological and business opportunities such innovations posed have rapidly become industry leaders."[20] A few technologies having the kind of success predicted by their originators are presented in the "Spotlight on Technology: Advancing Technology Is Here: Are Consumers Ready?" Trends and data suggest that a lot of customers want technologies that save them time and money.

The Impact of Technological Innovation

Technological innovations can have long-term effects on society and the purchasing patterns of consumers. Consider the impact of such innovations as the automobile, telephone, airplane, radio, television, computers, and various medical technologies.

Television is one example of a technological innovation that has continued to evolve. It is currently undergoing a technological breakthrough with high-definition television (HDTV) transmission. In 1994, a completely new way of broadcasting images began. The picture is much clearer and provides a more detailed wide-screen view. Like compact disc technology, HDTV is all digital. Instead of being transmitted like radio as continuously varying waves, pictures are transmitted as a pattern of numbers symbolizing the shade and color of each point on the screen. In essence, television sets are computers under this new technology. The shift to a digital system moves us toward the marriage of television and computer technologies.

The cost of an HDTV set can exceed $3000. What the consumer gets is a movielike format, CD-like sound, less flickering, and a perfectly clear picture. Over

MARKETING IN ACTION

Advancing Technology Is Here: Are Consumers Ready?

More and more customers claim to want maturing technologies such as personal computers, networking, and electronic data interchange. The new into-the-future approach is, "Let the customer do it." Changing demographics such as declining numbers of adults and a low population growth rate combined with our increasing prominence as a service-oriented society means that fewer people are available to work as retail clerks and service attendants.

Businesses are implementing more self-service technologies for other reasons, which include cost leadership, product differentiation, bigger market share, and strategic advantage. Financial institutions originally intended that automatic teller machines (ATMs) would provide customers with convenient banking services at lower costs than tellers' salaries. Today about a half a trillion transactions are made by ATMs. Work is being done on voice recognition of ATM users. A chip in an ATM card will verify the voice of the card-holder. Withdrawals can then be made on "voice commands" without using the current keypad method. Now banks are attempting to join nationwide networks, such as Cirrus, that permit users to access cash outside of the bank's regional area. Another strategy is to increase the range of services and their attractiveness to ATM users and generate revenue from new fees.

Another new customer service technology is the Automated Checkout Machine (ACM) system offered by Checkrobot, Inc. ACM enables shoppers to check out their own merchandise before paying a centrally located cashier. The ACM System consists of automated checkout machine stations, a

central computer linked to the stations, and a point-of-sale (POS) computer. It incorporates a security system to ensure that each item departing the store has been scanned and paid for. Checkrobot claims the ACM System offers the perception of improved customer service because the automated checkout machine is easy to use, decreases shopping time, and increases customers' control of their shopping forays.

Other self-service technologies include an automated scanning device that permits the exchange of money. For example, in a bank in Madrid, a customer can stack his U.S. dollars in a machine that returns pesetas and an itemized record of the transaction. The machine handles 16 currencies.

Marriott Hotels has automated guest check-in procedures to a point where average check-in time is one and one-half minutes. The hotel chain is developing a card that will enable guests to bypass check-in and go directly to a preassigned room. The card, similar to room key cards being used by many large hotels today, would contain all necessary information about the guest.

It is likely that new technologies that take into consideration demand, demographics, cost, competition, and other market information will appear every year. Marketers must be careful, however, to balance new technologies with consumer desires and their levels of comfort. As the global village becomes more of a reality, U.S. and foreign technologies should be incorporated to improve that customer service and comfort.

the past 20 years the television equipment market has almost gone completely to Japan. Only one U.S. company, Zenith, still makes television sets in the United States. However, with the introduction of HDTV, U.S. companies may get another chance to compete.

The process of technological innovation progresses from basic research to applied research to development and finally to production and marketing.[28] It takes time and money to carry out these four stages. Before biomedicine, energy, or any innovation reaches the marketing stage, years may have passed. For example, Xerography took about 18 years to move from the basic research stage to the development stage, and another 5 years to produce and market an office copier. In 1993, Polaroid introduced the Captiva, an instant camera with improved quality. The launch followed 3 years of development and an investment of more than $40 million.[29] Furthermore, other environmental forces such as the economy influence the innovation process. In an economic downturn, firms may invest less in research and development, opting instead to focus on proven products.

Marketing managers must be able to interpret technological changes and innovations in the environment. They must work closely with technological experts to translate knowledge and competence into marketable products and services. They must be aware of the interrelatedness of technological and other factors in the external environment. The potential problems of technological innovations like the commercial application of discoveries in HDTV need to be evaluated and understood.[30]

Global Technology

The advancement of technology is a global issue. The United States has been known as a world leader in the advancement of technology. To remain competitive, however, global research and development strategies must respond to changes in transportation, communication, information technology, and merged national markets. Intellectual capital is the critical resource in the global economy. The ability to generate, access, and rapidly use new knowledge and convert it (technology transfer) into marketable quality products and processes is the key to competitive advantage.[31]

Airbus Industrie is a cross-national European consortium that has developed and produced airplanes through support to its partner companies in the form of repayable loans.

The diffusion of technological capabilities and expansion of the technically trained work force worldwide have strengthened the competitive position of industrialized countries and enabled many more to enter the marketplace. As a result, dominance by the United States in nearly all high-tech markets is being challenged.

In many countries, government-sponsored programs have reduced the costs and risks associated with technological development by assuring long-term financial commitment. Airbus Industrie, for example, is a cross-national European consortium that has developed and produced airplanes through support to its partner companies in the form of repayable loans.

Technoglobalism refers to the internationalization of industrial activities due to technological needs.[32] It is the antithesis of **technonationalism,** which refers to efforts to maintain domestic technological competitiveness. Many corporations worldwide have employed global strategies such as trade, foreign investment, licensing, and joint ventures that have improved technological competitiveness. They have been able to accomplish this because of the increased returns to research and development costs and the sharing of costs in the spirit of technoglobalism.

Technologically, it is becoming inaccurate to speak of discoveries and breakthroughs by the United States relative to those of Japan, Germany, or any friendly nation. Technological development is becoming a technoglobal phenomenon involving a joint product of multinational institutions—universities, research laboratories, corporations, even defense programs—that link skilled people through computers, satellite communications, and jet airplanes.

Technological information is disseminated in blueprints, codes, and institutions that reach Tokyo or Berlin almost as soon as they reach Cleveland or Boston. Technonationalism is becoming less attractive and less tolerated in the interdependent world economy. Companies worldwide are beginning to realize this principle as they form more technology partnerships with multinational firms. For example, in the late 1980s, Mazda, a Japanese auto manufacturer, joined forces with Ford Motor Company to form Auto Alliance International Inc., an equal partnership. In 1989 Mazda, through Auto Alliance, began producing Ford Probes in Michigan. The American partner offered highly developed technical facilities while the Japanese partner offered production and sales expertise. The partnership has been so successful that Probes are now being exported to Japan and Europe.[33] Boeing Aircraft also partnered with a Japanese firm to co-produce the Boeing 777 aircraft. The partnership was good for Japan because it brought skill in commercial aircraft manufacturing and marketing to the country. Boeing benefited by having a home country advantage in terms of sales in Japan. Additionally, Japan provided a "jumping-off point" for Boeing to reach the huge Chinese aircraft market where today Boeing is a strong force.

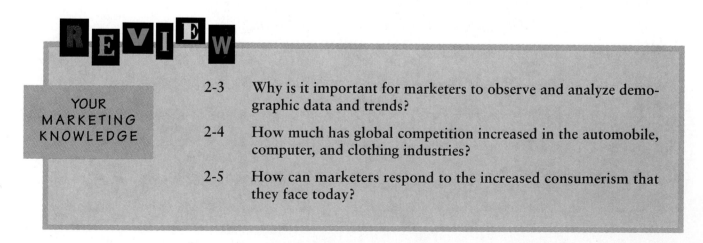

REVIEW

YOUR MARKETING KNOWLEDGE

2-3   Why is it important for marketers to observe and analyze demographic data and trends?

2-4   How much has global competition increased in the automobile, computer, and clothing industries?

2-5   How can marketers respond to the increased consumerism that they face today?

ECOLOGICAL FACTORS

Ecological factors consist of our natural surroundings. **Ecology** is the branch of natural science devoted to the study of the relationship between living things and their environment.[34] Today more and more marketers make decisions that incorporate ecological or environmental considerations. Due to public opinion, legal compliance, cost-effectiveness, competitive advantage, and responsible citizenship, marketers are paying more attention to the ecological factors. The ecology movement is worldwide, although some parts of the world are more progressive than others, and some firms are more progressive than others.

Four informal laws of ecology were suggested in 1971.[35] Their relevance for marketing managers is still significant.

1. Everything is connected to everything else.
2. Everything must go somewhere.
3. Nature knows best.
4. There is no such thing as a free lunch. Anything of importance has a cost.

These laws, when translated into marketing language, suggest that every company has pollution problems that must be assessed and controlled. The marketing managers and other executives must minimize the negative impact of business operations on the natural environment (water, air, plants, and wildlife) despite the fact that doing so will incur costs.

Improving Ecoresponsibility

Some forecasters and government officials believe that the 1990s will be known as the "earth decade" and that ecological environmentalism will be a major global force.[36] Many firms and organizations are working to make this prediction a reality by redefining the 3 Rs to stand for Reduce, Reuse, and Recycle.

- Egghead Discount Software operates a chain of 182 stores and a mail-order business. It used to generate a lot of packaging waste. Now it reuses packaging materials several times to reduce its waste. Its credo has become "Reuse It, Don't Lose It."[37]

- The 3M company is investing in pollution-control devices beyond what the law requires for its manufacturing facilities.

- In September 1990 the Air Resource Board in California imposed air quality standards that dramatically reduced auto emissions. In 1997, California will require that emissions of hydrocarbons and nitrogen oxides, the main components of ozone, be cut by 40 percent and 50 percent, respectively.[38]

- Wal-Mart asked its 7,000 suppliers to provide more recycled or recyclable products.

- The Body Shop, a manufacturer and worldwide retailer of skin and hair care products, places display literature on environmental and social issues alongside products in-store and fills its windows with information on issues such as rainforest destruction and ozone depletion. Every employee is assigned to spend half a day each month on environmental activism and other work in the community.

- General Motors, Ford, and Chrysler joined 14 oil companies to form the Auto/Oil Air Quality Improvement Research Program to search for new gasoline formulas. They hope to find a way to produce and process clean gasoline.[39]

Ecological environmentalism is likely to become a top priority for a number of reasons. First, concern for maintaining the ecological balance is widespread. Calls for

The Body Shop, a manufacturer and worldwide retailer of skin and hair care products, places display literature on environmental and social issues alongside products in-store and fills its windows with information on issues such as rainforest destruction and ozone depletion. Every employee is assigned to spend half a day each month on environmental activism and other work in the community.

organizations to be more ecologically and socially responsible are coming from a broad base of the population, not just from social activists and environmental groups like Greenpeace. Second, many environmentalists are attempting to work with business to solve the problems. Ecoresponsibility is being recognized as good business. Third, increasing government scrutiny and regulation is occurring only when necessary. Instead of immediately using laws, the government and some environmentalists have adopted the position that if a firm pollutes, it must pay a tax. If the firm doesn't want to pay, it solves its own pollution problem.[40] Fourth, leaders in businesses such as Apple Computer, Procter & Gamble, and Du Pont are emphasizing ecoresponsibility in their performance evaluations of managers. Although ecological decisions frequently involve a large gap between incurring the cost and reaping the benefits, decision makers seem more willing to say yes to increased expenses.[41]

There are no perfect answers to ecoresponsibility. The "Spotlight on Green Marketing: Are There Perfect Answers about Greenness?" raises some points that need to be considered when looking for solutions.

MARKETING *IN ACTION*

Are There Perfect Answers About Greenness?

A growing list of U.S. firms have decided—for public relations, staff morale, and other reasons—to be socially responsible about the environment. This is called going "green." For example, Lever Brothers, a manufacturer of household products, has led the pack in recycling plastic bottles. Du Pont has campaigned for chemical companies to take voluntary environmental initiatives. Monsanto, a chemical giant, took the lead in reducing air pollution long before passage of the Clean Air Act of 1990. Downy Fabric Softener can now be purchased in a "refill" pack.

Also, small firms in many businesses—bakers, painters, dry cleaners, and printing companies—have taken steps to comply with the law. Kinko's, a copying and business services firm, recycles paper and toner. Hannaford Brothers supermarkets, located in New England, offers shoppers canvas bags rather than plastic or paper bags. There is a lot of interest in and action toward being a responsible business and in achieving a "green," livable environment. However, there is also some debate about what is best.

In November 1990 McDonald's Corporation said it would phase out its use of polystyrene foam containers in favor of paper. McDonald's decision was based on evidence suggesting that the chemicals used in producing polystyrene were harmful to the environment. Now studies and researchers have suggested that the foam containers may be better for the environment than paper ones because the loss of trees used to produce paper is environmentally destructive. To settle similar debates, researchers have used a life-cycle analysis procedure to tote up every environmental risk associated with making, using, and disposing of products. In an unpub-

lished study it sponsored, McDonald's claims that paper has lower environmental costs in most, if not all, respects. Therefore McDonald's will stick with paper.

The environmentally correct decision regarding greenness is equally unclear in the diaper industry. In a study sponsored by Procter & Gamble, the manufacturer of Luvs and Pampers disposable diapers, it was found that cloth diapers consume more than three times as much energy, cradle to grave, as disposables do. But a study sponsored by the National Association of Diaper Services found the opposite.

The diaper duel illustrates the toughest issue in life-cycle analysis: how to compare different kinds of environmental harm. Cloth diapers use about 60 percent more water and create a greater volume of water pollution than disposables do. But disposables generate more than seven times as much trash, hence filling landfills, and they take more energy to produce. Biodegradable disposables, the hoped-for compromise, only biodegrade in the sunlight, not when buried in a landfill.

Can all products be separated into good and bad categories? The public would like simple answers: foam or paper? disposables or cloth? It doesn't appear, however, that life-cycle analysis or any present analytical methodology is going to provide simple answers. Costs, green benefits, research to support and oppose, common sense, and leadership are all factors that society, the government, and individuals will have to weigh in making decisions about ecological issues.

A Global Look at Ecological Factors

As formerly communist countries make the transition to free-market economies, they face serious environmental problems.[42] Some observers believe that if ecological problems are not addressed by Eastern Germany, Romania, Russia, and other republics in the former Soviet Union, there will be no need to worry about free markets. The former Soviet Union has been referred to as an environmental nightmare that threatens the world. In Russia, cars still use leaded gasoline, manufacturing industries use more than four times as much energy per unit of gross natural product as in the United States, and nuclear power plants are poorly maintained. The Chernobyl accident dumped an estimated 700,000 curries of radioactive dust on the continent. (The 1979 accident at Three Mile Island in the United States released less than 30 curries.)

The United States and other economic leaders in the international community must help solve the problems in Russia and other polluting nations. Cleaning up and stopping environmental abuse are concerns for everyone, not only marketing decision makers.

PUTTING TOGETHER THE ANALYSIS

Earlier in this chapter we introduced the concepts of environmental scanning, analysis, and diagnosis. Marketing decision makers must identify the critical environmental factors that affect the attractiveness of the firm.

Collecting the Information: Environmental Scanning

In environmental scanning the organization collects information on factors in the external environment that are relevant to that organization. Some companies use sophisticated forecasting and market research techniques to gather information about the external environment. Other firms do not have the resources or talent to employ sophisticated techniques. All organizations, however, use available verbal and written information to scan the environment. Sources of such information include radio and television, employees, customers, competitors, consultants, and government employees, newspapers, trade journals, and annual reports.

Levi Strauss is a firm that believes environmental scanning should be done domestically, internationally, and across industries. The firm regularly collects information on topics such as fashion trends across Europe, tax laws in foreign countries, rates of international monetary exchange, demographic statistics by country, and rates of inflation. Levi Strauss closely monitors the economic indicators in the U.S. economy. Decision makers attempt to find trends or signals that can be used to make design, distribution, pricing, promotion, and inventory selections.[43]

Identifying Opportunities and Threats: Environmental Analysis

Once it has gathered the relevant information about the external environment, the firm should evaluate each environmental force and identify (extract) specific opportunities and threats it implies for the firm.

Evaluating the attractiveness of each environmental force must take into consideration several aspects. For example, in evaluating competition and governmental forces, such factors as competitive numbers, barriers to entry and exit, availability of substitutes, government funding support, taxation, legislation, and regulation, must be considered.

Extracting from the evaluation opportunities and threats that face the firm can lead a company to a joint venture with a foreign partner.[44] For example, AT&T was anxious to enter the semiconductor business, but did not have a broad enough product line to be a major factor. The answer for AT&T was to form a partnership with Japan's NEC Corporation: AT&T traded some of its computer-aided design technology for some of NEC's advanced logic chips.

Failure to read, interpret, and act in a changing situation means that marketing opportunities will probably be missed. A **marketing opportunity** is "a challenge to specific marketing action that is characterized by a generally favorable set of environmental circumstances and an acceptable probability of success."[45]

There are no guarantees that marketers will do a good job of observing, analyzing, and forecasting environmental forces. However, it is necessary for firms to monitor environmental forces so they can seize the best marketing opportunities.[46] Without some form of environmental scanning program, the organization is not likely to adopt timely, efficient, and profitable marketing strategies. In fact, scanning the environment and collecting information on individuals has become a big business. It has also raised ethical issues regarding the invasion of privacy.

The process of analyzing the external environment and identifying opportunities and threats requires a realistic assessment of a firm's position. The following are some questions to help decision makers with this assessment.

1. What is the nature of the industry in which the organization is operating? Is there much innovation taking place? Is sophisticated technology employed? Is it subject to legal constraints? Is the industry marked by great diversity in the demands or needs of the customers?

2. What is our firm's bargaining power in the industry? Do we use our power efficiently? Does the organization have special advantages in the industry: managerial talent, location, experience with markets, reputation?

3. What is the mix of attributes of the environment? How much turbulence exists? Is it dynamic, unpredictable, expanding, fluctuating? How much hostility exists? What is the range of characteristics and needs of the markets? How much technical complexity exists? How sophisticated are the information, equipment, and processes needed to make and carry out strategic decisions? How much restriction exists? What are the legal and political constraints?

4. Given the environmental forces that affect the firm, what is the range of strategies available in the short- and long-run? Does the firm have distinctive competence that a well-designed and implemented strategy can enhance? Are there weaknesses that can be overcome by better quality and more timely environmental screening?

Decision makers must continually ask and answer those questions so they can observe, analyze, and forecast shifting environmental forces. Managers are not machines who automatically "check in" and respond. They perceive, feel, think, solve problems, as well as distort, misinterpret, become frustrated, and react emotionally. Any organization's environmental analysis is a reflection of its managers, time and resources, and techniques. In fact, the timeliness, thoroughness, and style of seizing marketing opportunities is largely dictated by top-level decision makers.

Making Marketing Decisions: Environmental Diagnosis

Ultimately, the organization must use the results of its environmental analyses to plan a response. Organizational styles of response come in many forms. At one pole (end point) is the reactive organization. This type of firm primarily reacts to innovations and is reluctant to try something new. The philosophy is that environmental forces are so uncontrollable that the organization has little effect on them. In the early 1970s, Ford, GM, Chrysler, and American Motors fit this description (reactive) in the downsized car market.

On the opposite end of the continuum are firms that are aggressive and forceful in pursuing their objectives. Toyota, Nissan, and Honda responded this way in the small-car market in the 1970s. These manufacturers of foreign cars believed they could influence environmental forces by making sound and timely decisions. This proactive style is used by organizations that take purposeful action to meet challenges or create marketing opportunities.

Saturn is pioneering improved market share by paying attention to relationships with dealers (Saturn calls them "retailers"), suppliers, and workers.

America's "Big Three" automakers—Ford, GM, and Chrysler—today are using a proactive style in the world car market.[47] They realize, in retrospect, that their biggest failure to adapt to the environment was their unwillingness to confront the threat of Japanese automakers. The Big Three are taking a more aggressive approach to pricing and design. They continue to monopolize sales of six-passenger cars and full-size pickup trucks. They also have a big lead in sport-utility vehicles and mini-vans. Ford has lifted its quality standards, Chrysler is now organized around information flows, and the Saturn Corporation (a wholly owned subsidiary of General Motors) is pioneering improved market share by paying attention to relationships with dealers (Saturn calls them "retailers"), suppliers, and workers. After 20 years of losing market share to foreign competitors, the Big Three are taking a proactive rather than a reactive approach.

Today a number of organizations would be classified by most observers as proactive. A sample of these firms includes Apple Computer, Intel, American Express, Reebok International, Super Valu Stores, McDonald's, General Electric, and 3M. These and other organizations on the proactive side of the continuum apply environmental scanning and analysis techniques and then make the necessary adaptations to the changes.

The continuum of proactive to reactive is used to illustrate the range of marketers' decision-making styles. Of course, most firms are not completely reactive or proactive. The response mode of most marketing managers lies somewhere between the two poles or changes from one style to another style. For example, Gillette seemed like a sleepy, nonaggressive company. Around the mid-1980s Gillette became aggressive and today is known as a major collector of competitor information. The success of the Sensor razor is an example of the result of this change in stance. Conceived in 1979 and developed in top secrecy at a cost of about $200 million, the Sensor razor was introduced in January 1990 in the United States, Japan, and Europe.[48] Instead of selling 18 million Sensor razors as the firm predicted in 1990, it produced and shipped more than 24 million. Schick, Gillette's competitor, has tried to imitate Sensor's success. It introduced the Tracer, which through 1992 had fallen flat, taking just 2 percent of the market. The Sensor was a technical success, but it was a market success because Gillette took a proactive approach, spent heavily on its brand name, and beat the competition in delivering a product that lived up to its advertising.[49]

Marketing decisions about price, place, product, and promotion take place in a continually changing environment. As you read this book, think about the powerful impact of environmental forces. Think also about the differences in reactive and proactive decision making. Each marketing decision is linked in some manner to the external environment, the forces in the market that drive decisions. To make successful decisions, marketers must invest time and effort to understand the environmental forces. Business successes such as the Japanese auto invasion of the American market, Quaker Oats' success with the sports drink Gatorade, and Levi Strauss's entry into markets around the world point out the importance of analyzing and gathering information about the environment.

MARKETING ETHICS AND SOCIAL RESPONSIBILITY IN THE EXTERNAL ENVIRONMENT

Recognizing and acknowledging the importance of the external environment in making marketing decisions is not a one-way street. Not only must firms consider how the forces in the external environment affect their businesses, but they must also consider the impact of their decisions on the world around them. This consideration raises the issues of ethics and social responsibility. **Ethics** are a set of beliefs about what is right and wrong. They may be determined by a group or an individual. As introduced in Chapter 1, social responsibility is the obligation a business assumes to optimize the positive effects and minimize the negative effects of its actions on society. The marketing profession, like others, is concerned about ethics and social responsibility because of business issues, personal principles, and legal implications.

This definition of ethics has three implications. First, ethics may be individually defined rather than organizationally bound. Second, ethical behavior can vary from one person to another. Third, ethics are relative, not absolute. What a Japanese decision maker does to market sushi is probably different from what an Argentinean does to market beef. In Japan it is proper and almost expected to offer monetary incentives to suppliers to secure business. In the United States this action is not only seen as unethical but is generally viewed as anticompetitive and against the law. Ethical behavior is in the eye of the beholder, but it is usually behavior that meets generally accepted norms of a society. **Marketing ethics** is the application of ethical standards to all marketing activities and decisions.

Growing public attention to the ethics of business decisions and conduct has resulted in an increased interest among marketers in social responsibility, ethical ideology, and moral decision making. Boycotts, protests, personal and class action lawsuits, negative press, and falling profits have increased the awareness of managers about ethics and social responsibility.[50] The concepts of ethics and social responsibility are sometimes used interchangeably. As seen from their definitions, however, they each have a distinct meaning. Business ethics are individually based, while social responsibility concerns the decisions of the organization and their effects on society.

The idea of social responsibility became widely publicized during the 1960s as social values began to change. Today social responsibility is a consideration in decision making that organizations have generally accepted. The advertisement for Hoechst Celanese indicates that the firm takes its social responsibilities seriously.

There Is More Than One Way To Climb The Corporate Ladder.

When Hoechst Celanese executives climbed these ladders armed with hammers and paint brushes, it was really no surprise. They had taken time off from a meeting to renovate the Nevins Center, a North Carolina facility for adults with special needs. This is just one of the many ways Hoechst Celanese men and women volunteer to improve the quality of life in the communities in which they live and work.

Whether they are educating schoolchildren on science or senior citizens on health care, our employees are dedicated to helping people and making a real difference. And that's really no surprise either. Because being a good corporate citizen is an important part of who we are at Hoechst Celanese.

Hoechst Celanese

Hoechst 🔁

The Name Behind The Names You Know

The Hoechst name and logo are registered trademarks of Hoechst AG

This advertisement for Hoechst Celanese indicates that the firm takes its social responsibilities seriously.

An Ethical Framework

It is important to organize the concept of ethics as applied to marketing. Managers, students, and researchers could then consider the ethical implications of issues that face decision makers. Hunt and Vitell have provided a general theory of marketing ethics that is well organized, concise, and considers environmental forces.[51] Figure 2.5 presents this framework in which three major environments impact ethical decision making. The cultural environment (or cultural forces in the external environment), the industrial environment (the standards and nature of all competitors), and the organizational environment (characteristics and standards of the company itself) all shape perceptions of ethical judgments. The personal experiences of individual decision makers also affect perceptions and decision making.

The Hunt and Vitell framework introduces the notions of perceptions, norms, consequences, and decisions—all factors that affect ethical decision making.

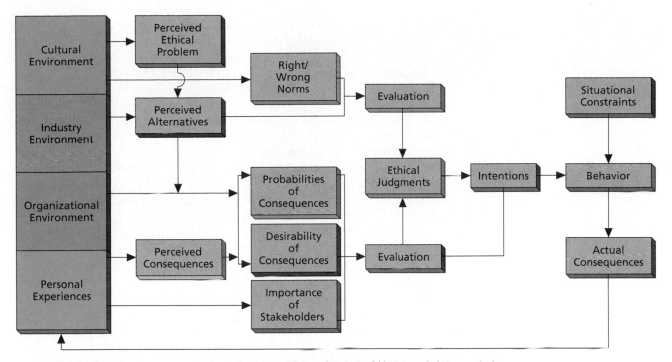

Source: Adapted by the authors from S. D. Hunt and S. Vitell, "A General Theory of Marketing Ethics," *Journal of Macromarketing*, Vol. 6, Spring 1986, p. 8. Reprinted by permission.

FIGURE 2.5
A General Theory of
Marketing Ethics

Ethical Dilemmas

Marketers constantly face ethical dilemmas. For example, should marketers advertise state lotteries, alcohol products, or cigarettes? Should marketers promote products (such as candy) to children that may have long-term health consequences? Should marketers pay large retailers a kickback to obtain shelf space? Ethical dilemmas mean that conflicting viewpoints on an issue exist.

The Hunt and Vitell framework can be applied to ethical dilemmas. For example, at the beginning of this chapter we discussed Glaxo's advertisements to patients and raised the issue that some believe the ads motivated more than 500,000 visits, many unnecessary, to doctors about ulcers. Did Glaxo's then president, Ernest Mario, think about the consequences of Glaxo's behavior? Of course we do not know whether he carefully weighed the consequences. Glaxo has been criticized for making the decision to advertise the ulcer medication and suggest that individuals visit their doctors. Since Mario was the chief executive officer, he is responsible for the decision. Glaxo's stockholders wanted a dividend and wanted the company to be successful; however, did they bargain for attention and criticism? The desired consequences and actual consequences at Glaxo can impact on how future dilemmas are resolved.

Determinants of Responses to Ethical Dilemmas

The standards and attitudes of the firm and the value systems of decision makers will largely determine how ethical dilemmas will be resolved. Several questions can guide behavior:

1. Does the decision violate someone's rights or the law?
2. Is everyone who is affected by the decision treated fairly?
3. Would you mind reading about the decision and its consequences in the newspaper?

When we apply these guidelines to Dow Corning's handling of silicone-gel breast implants, we see that the company failed. Dow was faced with a serious ethical dilemma when medical research began to indicate that the implants, which the firm manufactured, could leak after being placed in a woman's body. This leakage had major negative health consequences for the implant recipients. Because lawsuits are still being filed, it is not yet clear whether Dow violated the law. Dow Corning did mind when it read news accounts of its reaction to the product defect claims for the implants. Dow Corning didn't attempt to soothe some of the early complainants who felt disfigured or victimized by the product. It is obvious by the number of complaints and lawsuits that the decision to market the silicone-gel implants was one that victims claim treated them unfairly. Dow Corning is now dealing with being characterized as a careless and heartless company. Dow Corning's ethical reputation has been dramatically damaged and will be difficult to correct.

Public outcry regarding a firm's ethical decisions has resulted in more organizations adopting, publicizing, and refining an official code of ethics, which are written statements of the values and standards that guide the firm's actions. Table 2.4 presents the Code of Ethics of the American Marketing Association (AMA), members of which include businesspeople and academics who commit to statements in the code.

Despite the potential negative consequences of unethical and socially irresponsible behavior, there are still those who question whether it pays to be ethical and socially responsible. One way to consider this issue is in terms of the cost/benefit ratio of ethics and social responsibility. This approach has been used to consider the Exxon Valdez incident.[52] The supertanker Exxon Valdez spilled its load of crude oil into the waters off the Alaskan shoreline. Exxon had made an economic decision to reduce the crew size of its supertankers from 36 to 22 people. It also used single-hulled, not double-hulled, ships. It did not test its crew or officers for substance abuse. The tankers sailed late at night, when navigation is difficult. Exxon saved money, but the probability of an accident increased. Bottom-line profit, not the probability of an accident, was the main consideration in Exxon's decision. The result of this type of short-term thinking was disastrous for the natural environment.

Lyondell Petrochemical (LP) has taken a more long-term approach to social responsibility. The Atlantic Richfield Corporation created LP in 1985.[53] The company has worked on its technology to make its refinery the only one in the world that can process all types of crude oil. The firm has decided to be socially responsible and has figured out how to make isobutylene, a chemical used in the gasolines that were reformulated for the Clean Air Act of 1990. The company is recycling used lubricating oil into gasoline. It is also selling an environmentally benign lubricant to offshore rigs to help cut water pollution. Although LP has had problems in profitability, it has elected to take a long-term view of socially responsible citizenship.

The shrinkage of the world and the emphasis on globalization pose ethical dilemmas in terms of the Hunt and Vitell framework's perceptions, norms, and consequences. Should a U.S. firm use U.S. norms or Japanese norms when doing business in Japan? Should Union Carbide, an American firm, have used U.S. safety standards or Indian safety standards at its plant in Bhopal, India? Perhaps U.S. standards would have prevented the disaster that occurred when a chemical explosion killed many people. When operating in a global market, there is no single ethical standard.[54]

The United States, Mexico, and Canada have signed the North American Free Trade Agreement (NAFTA). Some people believe that if the Mexican economy improved, the United States would enjoy an expanding market for sophisticated products and services. However, critics of the agreement believe that Mexican

TABLE 2.4
America Marketing Association Code of Ethics

> **Members of the American Marketing Association (AMA) are committed to ethical professional conduct. They have joined together in subscribing to this Code of Ethics.**

Responsibilities of the Marketer

Marketers must accept responsibility for the consequence of their activities and make every effort to ensure that their decisions, recommendations, and actions function to identify, serve, and satisfy all relevant publics: customers, organizations and society.

Marketers' professional conduct must be guided by:

1. The basic rule of professional ethics: not knowingly to do harm;
2. The adherence to all applicable laws and regulations;
3. The accurate representation of their education, training and experience; and
4. The active support, practice and promotion of this Code of Ethics.

Honesty and Fairness

Marketers shall uphold and advance the integrity, honor, and dignity of the marketing profession by:

1. Being honest in serving consumers, clients, employees, suppliers, distributors and the public;
2. Not knowingly participating in conflict of interest without prior notice to all parties involved; and
3. Establishing equitable fee schedules including the payment or receipt of usual, customary and/or legal compensation for marketing exchanges.

Rights and Duties of parties in the Marketing Exchange Process

Participants in the marketing exchange process should be able to expect that:

1. Products and services offered are safe and fit for their intended uses;
2. Communications about offered products and services are not deceptive;
3. All parties intend to discharge their obligations, financial and otherwise, in good faith; and
4. Appropriate internal methods exist for equitable adjustment and/or redress of grievances concerning purchases.

It is understood that the above would include, *but is not limited to*, the following responsibilities of the marketer:

In the area of product development and management,

- disclosure of all substantial risks associated with product or service usage;
- identification of any product component substitution that might materially change the product or impact on the buyer's purchase decision;
- identification of extra-cost added features.

In the area of promotions,

- avoidance of false and misleading advertising;
- rejection of high pressure manipulations, or misleading sales tactics;
- avoidance of sales promotions that use deception or manipulation.

In the area of distribution,

- not manipulating the availability of a product for purpose of exploitation;
- not using coercion in the marketing channel;
- not exerting undue influence over the reseller's choice to handle a product.

In the area of pricing,

- not engaging in price fixing;
- not practicing predatory pricing;
- disclosing the full price associated with any purchase.

In the area of marketing research,

- prohibiting selling or fund raising under the guise of conducting research;
- maintaining research integrity by avoiding misrepresentation and omission of pertinent research data;
- treating outside clients and suppliers fairly.

Organizational Relationships

Marketers should be aware of how their behavior may influence or impact on the behavior of others in organizational relationships. They should not demand, encourage or apply coercion to obtain unethical behavior in their relationships with others, such as employees, suppliers or customers.

1. Apply confidentiality and anonymity in professional relationships with regard to privileged information;
2. Meet their obligations and responsibilities in contracts and mutual agreements in a timely manner;
3. Avoid taking the work of others, in whole, or in part, and represent this work as their own or directly benefit from it without compensation or consent of the originator or owner;
4. Avoid manipulation to take advantage of situations to maximize personal welfare in a way that unfairly deprives or damages the organization or others.

Any AMA members found to be in violation of any provision of this Code of Ethics may have his or her Association membership suspended or revoked.

The Ronald McDonald House program is an example of a social contribution. The McDonald's Corporation provides $25,000 seed money for each house, and the majority of funds are raised by a volunteer board, with significant contributions coming from owner/operators in each tri-state area.

environmental pollution will become worse, and that American businesses will flock to Mexico to take advantage of cheaper labor and lax pollution laws. Which code of ethics and sense of social responsibility should take precedent—Mexican or American? Marketing decision makers need to monitor their foreign operations, environments, and behavior so their performances in global markets is acceptable and responsible.

An Opposing View

There are arguments against organizations being immersed in socially responsible strategies, goals, and implementation. Nobel prize-winning economist Milton Friedman argues that business exists to earn profit. Thus, focusing on social responsibility detracts from the primary mission. Another argument is that business already is a powerful force in society. Promoting more business involvement in social programs, (e.g., feeding the homeless, K–12 education, child-care support programs) gives business even more power. Another argument against business involvement in social programs is that they do not have the expertise. What do companies know about charitable causes?

Some Concluding Thoughts

Although there are arguments on both sides, business plays a growing role in terms of social responsibility, ranging from accepting a social obligation to making a social contribution. For example, Phillip Morris conforms to obligation regarding its global marketing efforts. In the United States, where warnings to smokers on cigarette packages are legally required, Phillip Morris follows the rule to the letter. Many other countries, however, do not have such rules. In the African countries where Phillip Morris heavily promotes its cigarettes, the packs contain no health warnings.

Tenneco, Inc., matches contributions by employees to charities. The firm goes beyond what it feels is an obligation to support the United Way, Girl Scouts, and the Red Cross. However, the highest form of social responsibility is active contribution to society. An example of a social contribution is the Ronald McDonald House program. The McDonald's Corporation provides $25,000 seed money for each house. The rest of the funds are raised by a volunteer board, with significant contributions by owner/operators in each tri-state area. These facilities, located near medical centers, house families that have sick children in hospitals. This eases the family's burden while the children are receiving medical treatment.

Ethics and social responsibility are not only important for marketers to practice, monitor, and improve, but for all employees. The performance of a firm in terms of ethics and social responsibility influences employee behavior. Although there are arguments both for and against social responsibility and there is no one acceptable ethical behavior pattern, it makes sense to consider both areas very important. The society is demanding better performance from businesses and other institutions. It will either get better performance or the government will be asked to step in more aggressively.

PERSONAL COMPUTER EXERCISE

The use of demographic and social-cultural databases to analyze trends in the environment can be very useful to a marketing manager. This PC Exercise will help you evaluate the impact of current demographic trends on future consumer demand for various products and services.

KEY POINTS

- When a marketer is engaged in environmental scanning and analysis, he or she monitors, with whatever means available, the external environmental forces. The analysis involves finding threats and opportunities that the environment poses. The analysis also requires sifting through data, opinions, historical information, competitors' products and services, and anything available to help make a better decision.

- Changes in demographics and social values have an impact on how a market functions. These changes affect the products and services provided and the marketing tactics considered acceptable.

- There are four possible competitive situations: monopoly, oligopoly, monopolistic competition, and pure competition. The nature of competition a firm faces affects its marketing decisions.

- Buying power requires economic strength and the ability to make purchases. Economic strength is determined by a combination of factors such as income levels, inflation, productivity, and unemployment.

■ A list of legal-political factors that affect marketing decisions could fill a book. Notable factors include laws, regulations, tax requirements, and the status of relationships with other countries.

■ Technology is a nation's accumulated competence to provide goods and services for people. Marketers need to monitor and adapt to technological changes that they find through environmental scanning and analysis.

■ Concerns about the protection of the natural environment have swept across the world. It is likely that all marketing decisions will include concern about and specific attention to the natural environment.

■ Ethical dilemmas are faced by individuals and firms. The Hunt and Vitell framework and the three-question format present methods for thinking about marketing ethics. The framework highlights environmental forces, perceptions, norms, consequences, and decision making. When faced with an ethical dilemma, individuals must make ethical judgments or decisions. Marketing poses many ethical dilemmas about the product or service being marketed and the tactics or techniques used to market it.

KEY TERMS

uncontrollable variables (33)
marketing environment (34)
environmental scanning (34)
environmental analysis (34)
environmental diagnosis (35)
external environment (35)
values (37)
demography (37)
disposable personal income (DPI) (44)
inflation (44)
productivity (44)
absolute monopoly (46)
oligopoly (46)
monopolistic competition (46)
pure competition (46)
consumerism (49)
consumer protection (51)
consumer education (51)
technology (55)

innovation (55)
technological innovation (55)
technoglobalism (58)
technonationalism (58)
ecology (59)
marketing opportunity (62)
ethics (65)
marketing ethics (65)

ISSUES FOR DISCUSSION

1. What do you feel is missing in the Hunt and Vitell ethics framework? Does the framework cover all of the environmental forces that play a role?

2. What changes in social values have affected the purchase of: Hershey candy bars? FAX machines? golf clubs? Rolex watches? medical services?

3. Identify the factors that you believe have contributed to U.S. productivity outpacing that of Japan and Germany in the last few years.

4. Imagine that you are the marketer of a product that faces a pure competition situation. Would it be desirable to attempt to shift the market to monopolistic competition? How might you attempt to do so through marketing actions?

5. Sophisticated technological improvements will likely result in high-definition television sets. Why is disposable personal income (DPI) an important data point in predicting the success of HDTV in the marketplace?

6. As a soft drink manufacturer, how would you deal with the fact that consumers claim to want returnable bottles because they are good for the environment, while sales show that, given a choice, they continue to buy throwaways?

7. Some people believe that the U.S. government places U.S. pharmaceutical firms at a disadvantage in the marketplace. While drugs are being tested in the United States, foreign competitors are marketing them and gaining a foothold in the market. Should the U.S. government do something about this complaint? Why?

8. Assume that you are a marketing specialist at Compaq Computer, the number three personal computer manufacturer (after IBM and Apple). What type of information would you hope to collect during an environmental scan? How and where would you seek this information?

9. Should condom advertisements be shown to children ages 12–16? Does this situation create an ethical dilemma? Why or why not?

10. What demographic factors do you believe would be the most relevant to your decision making if you were marketing CD players? camping equipment? frozen dinners? lawn mowers? housecleaning services?

CASE APPLICATION

Disney: Growth or Problems?

Michael D. Eisner, Chief Executive Officer of the Walt Disney Company, wants the company to become the marketing wonder of the 1990s. He has a plan of proactive market-driven growth. Since Eisner took over the reins of Disney in 1984, revenues have sky-rocketed, the firm's stock has climbed over 700 percent, and people are talking about the Disney miracle.

The start of the Eisner-led campaign was the aggressive Disney move into the movie business. After years of simply rolling along, Walt Disney Company began producing top-grossing movies. In 1990 *Pretty Woman*, produced by Touchstone Films, Disney's adult label, grossed more than $126 million. The company has also had several animated hits in the 1990s, including *Beauty and the Beast* and *Aladdin*.

Another move by Disney's was the introduction of the Disney Television Channel. In the fall of 1985, Disney approached independent and affiliate television stations with Disney-Magic-1, a collection of 25 films, including *Dumbo*, *Splash*, and episodes from *The Wonderful World of Disney*, which ran on network television from 1954 to 1983.

Eisner believes that the Disney Channel both sells merchandise based on Disney characters and promotes Disneyland and Disney World. The theme parks stoke up enthusiasm for the movies and the inventiveness that goes into the movies can be diverted to keep the parks fresh. Most observers believe that Eisner has put some of founder Walt Disney's magic back into the company.

Despite the unprecedented growth in the Walt Disney Company, there are some critics and some potential for problems. By scanning environmental forces, one is left with the question of whether Eisner's growth strategy can be sustained.

Disney's purchase of Jim Henson Productions is leading some critics to question the company's goodwill. Disney bought the Henson film library, along with merchandising rights to such Henson characters as Kermit the Frog and Miss Piggy. When Jim Henson died in 1990, his family became embroiled in a dispute about the deal. Legal teams became involved in the Henson-family-versus-Disney fight about Jim Henson's characters, how they are used, and fees that will be paid. A settlement was reached, but only after some negative publicity tarnished the Disney image. In the past, Walt Disney Company didn't want to become involved in publicly debated and legal controversies.

The largest problem appears to involve Euro Disney. At a site 20 miles east of Paris, France, Euro Disney opened in 1991. Euro Disney is a $2.6 billion extravaganza and the first company-owned theme park outside the United States. Disney trained 12,000 Europeans to work in the theme park. Euro Disney has a golf course, a Davy Crockett campground, an ice skating rink, and six Disney-owned hotels with 5200 rooms.

Eisner would have liked Euro Disney to be as successful as Tokyo's Disneyland has been. Some 16 million visitors per year come to Tokyo's Disneyland. Mitsubishi Research Institute says Tokyo's Disneyland has a $6.3 billion impact on the Japanese economy.

Euro Disney, however, appears to be in deep trouble. The park lost $921 million in 1993, a staggering loss of $2.5 million per day! Eisner reaffirmed the company's commitment to keeping Euro Disney afloat "for a while." A shutdown of the park would clearly be an embarrassment for Disney.

Why hasn't Euro Disney been the draw that was predicted? Here are some points to consider:
1. The French take vacations en masse. In August, everything closes up.
2. French workers are not accustomed to abiding by strict work codes and regulations. Not smoking, not chewing gum, and not conversing with coworkers will strain morale. Unions are already angry that Disney is telling job candidates what they must look like.
3. There are arguments about French being the main language in the park. French critics believe that English names are used too frequently.
4. Although the Japanese like American culture, the French are not so impressed. Some, in fact, refer to Euro Disney as a "cultural Chernobyl."
5. Paris's weather conditions are not like Anaheim, Orlando, or Tokyo. Chill and rain will keep people away from the park.
6. Competition is on its way. MCA-Universal plans to open a studio and park close to Euro Disney.

Whether the problems can be solved remains to be seen. Disney claims to be moving ahead and working hard to succeed with Euro Disney. Despite what critics say about the pace at Walt Disney Company, the Eisner philosophy remains the same: "As long as you act as if you're coming from behind, you have a shot at staying ahead." He has taken a proactive approach in dealing with the external environment.

Questions

1. What environmental forces could indicate to Michael Eisner that Disney is growing too fast?
2. What mistakes appear to have been made in the environmental analysis that preceded the building of Euro Disney?
3. What cultural factors would a company like Disney need to consider if it were thinking about establishing a theme park in Mexico City?

Know Your Environment

Chapter 2 discusses the importance of knowing the environment in which your product competes. To be successful in your job search, you must pay attention to your competition. You need to define yourself in terms of your interests and capabilities, and identify opportunities that match your talents. Chapter 2 suggests that success or failure in business is determined by skills in observing, analyzing, and forecasting the environment. Environmental analysis also determines success in your career search.

Just like companies look for market opportunities, you must be aware of how you can capitalize on a career opportunity. To do so, you can use the environmental scanning approach to your career. When you think about employment, conduct a market scan of the industry you have chosen. The scan will prepare you to understand the market and how you can help to further a particular company's growth by knowing yourself and the company's competition.

In conducting a market scan and analysis of a target company you should consider these factors:

- *Social-Cultural.* Where might you find a comfortable functional/organizational culture? Factors to consider include formal versus informal structure, individual versus team emphasis, close versus limited control. Which organizations are likely to have values (likes, dislikes, beliefs, prejudices, etc.) that are acceptable to you?
- *Economic.* Which sectors/organizations have the underlying strengths to best support your career advancement? Factors to consider include domestic growth, global expansion, product edge, market position, social needs, regional trends. How is the company health: what are its projections for growth, what are the external factors that may affect it? Also, how does the company compensate its employees: is it competitive with others in the same industry?
- *Competitive.* How strong is the competition for entry-level positions (i.e., number of applicants versus number of openings)? What distinctive experiences and competencies can provide you a competitive edge (summer jobs, part-time work, dual degrees, extracurricular activities, leadership roles)?
- *Legal-political.* How might current and emerging federal, state, and local government rules and regulations affect your career opportunities? Factors to consider include industry controls, employment positions, environmental restraints, consumer protection, social settlements, tax requirements, trade agreements.
- *Technological.* Where can you find the emphasis on technology or innovation that you desire? Factors to consider include high-tech versus low-tech, service versus product, industrial versus consumer products, short versus long product life, high versus low reliance on new products.
- *Ecological.* Which of your sector/organization options offers a level of ecoresponsibility acceptable to you? Factors to consider include a sector leadership role, advanced operating practices that are pollution preventive, manufacturing that continually meets compliance regulations, minimal use of natural resources.

You need to consult many sources of information to conduct a thorough environmental scan of career opportunities. Some of the best sources include sector and organization surveys (obtainable in most libraries), literature searches (available through various computerized information services), and personal contacts with friends, acquaintances, and faculty who have knowledge of or direct experience in your fields of interest.

Questions

Make a trial run at a scan of external environmental factors that relate to career opportunities. For this exercise, use the dream job that you selected as part of the Career Focus in Chapter 1.

1. What sources of information will you use for your environmental scan (printed materials, information systems, and personal contacts)?
2. What are your *social-cultural* requirements and how does your target job rate against your needs?
3. Looking at the underlying *economic* strengths and weaknesses of your target organization, what are the major opportunities and threats for your career advancement?
4. What is the probable level of *competition* for your job and what are your best current or potential (i.e., could be developed before graduation) distinctive experiences and competencies?
5. How important are *legal-political*, *technological*, and *ecological* factors to your evaluation of your target job? How important is the emphasis on technology and innovation?
6. Based on this exercise, how would you weight the six external environmental factors in your career search?

CHapTeR 3

Marketing Planning

LEARNING OBJECTIVES

Upon completing this chapter, you will be able to do the following:

■ **Describe** the steps involved in the strategic marketing planning process.

■ **Explain** the characteristics of a good business definition.

■ **Understand** the procedures involved in carrying out a situation analysis.

■ **Differentiate** between good and bad objectives.

■ **Discuss** the types of analyses available to aid marketing planners in formulating strategy.

■ **Identify** the differences between strategies and tactics.

■ **Understand** why control is so important to long-term success.

Marketing Profile

Keeping Elvis Alive Through Strategic Planning

Elvis Presley Enterprises (EPE) is far more than the purveyor of tacky mementos of the King of Rock & Roll. While it is true that EPE will gladly sell you a wide assortment of Elvis memorabilia including Elvis bracelets, scarves, and boxer shorts, it is equally true that EPE is a tightly run, aggressive, multimillion-dollar business that owes much of its success to careful planning.

The organization has been built around the image of Elvis Presley. The mission of EPE is to advance that image in a way that promotes the respectful and sincere persona that Elvis manifested throughout much of his career. The company has chosen this direction, the "high road" as CEO Jack Soden describes it, in recognition of the fact that Presley in the later years, before his death in 1977, portrayed an image inherently less marketable.

Elvis Presley Enterprises is organized around three divisions, each developed to advance Elvis's name and image in a different way. The three divisions are Graceland, Elvis's former home, now open for tours; licensing, the division that approves and allows the use of Elvis's name and image worldwide; and a music-publishing group. The music-publishing division works with RCA, which holds the rights to many of Elvis's songs, to oversee re-releases of the 750 songs Elvis recorded. The plans for each division are developed separately.

In the case of licensing, for example, there has been a move to increase the quality of merchandise bearing Elvis's name or picture. The organization is careful, however, to remember that products must be appropriate for the market. As one critic stated, "The challenge is making sure that [EPE] doesn't outclass its customers." Priscilla Presley, chair of EPE and Elvis's ex-wife, has said, "My staff tries to convince me . . . that the stuff is selling and we certainly don't want to put a stop to that."

The company engages in annual planning that includes decisions regarding which television shows, videos, and songs will be released in the upcoming year as well as where those releases will occur. People in upper management view this annual process as one of their most important jobs.

The payoff for this well-organized and aggressive firm has been significant profits. Although the firm divulges no financial data, estimates are that the Graceland complex (which includes not only Elvis's mansion but also an auto museum, an airplane museum, eight gift shops, the Heartbreak Hotel restaurant, Rockabilly's Diner, an ice cream parlor, post office, and movie theater) earns a minimum of $2.5 million annually. Furthermore, profits from Graceland and the licensing division are believed to pale in comparison to the earnings of the music-publishing division.

arket-driven organizations rely on strategic marketing planning to formulate their plans and to make their marketing management decisions. The success of Elvis Presley Enterprises illustrates the benefit of strategic marketing planning. Organizations that plan carefully and thoughtfully possess a competitive edge over firms that do not. Figure 3.1 illustrates the steps in the strategic marketing planning process. In this chapter we examine both marketing strategy and marketing tactics. Marketing strategy is the long-term plan for developing a marketing mix that will achieve the organization's objectives. Marketing tactics include the short-term specific details of the plan. An early discussion of these issues will provide a foundation for the specific marketing mix elements covered in the remaining chapters of the text.

Our discussion begins with an examination of the development of a business definition. We then identify the components of a situation analysis and we consider the importance of establishing objectives. Next, we present several tools to aid marketers in formulating a marketing strategy. We also discuss how to create, implement, and control a marketing plan. This chapter concludes with an example of a strategic marketing plan for American Express.

FIGURE 3.1
The Strategic Marketing Planning Process

DEFINING THE BUSINESS

Every successful organization, whether for profit or not-for-profit, has a vision of what it is all about. The organization's **business definition** (sometimes called **mission statement**) answers the question, "What business are we in?" It provides thrust and direction to the organization, and is the cornerstone of its marketing strategy. Southwest Airlines defines its business as "the best alternative to car and bus travel." This definition provides direction for the firm's marketing activities.

A firm's business definition, of course, may change over time. Such changes are typically reflected in changes in marketing strategy as well. The Xerox Corporation, for example, has redefined itself from "a copier manufacturer" to a "supplier of automated office systems" and most recently to "the document company." Such changes in its business definition are reflected in the changing products and services the firm markets. A company whose business definition positions it as a document company would be expected to have a far greater range of products and services than a firm whose business definition focuses on the manufacture of copy machines.

Table 3.1 provides a detailed example of how a business definition directs marketing strategy. For Owens-Corning, the strategy developed to market fiberglass could have varied significantly depending on how it defined its business. Robert Davis states:

> Had the company taken the position that it was in the business of supplying a raw material to processors, its strategy would have differed enormously from the actual strategy based on the concept of "bringing better end products to the ultimate user." Because Owens-Corning put the ultimate user first, it manufactured the first Fiberglas fishing rods and luggage when the traditional manufacturers delayed adopting the new material. It launched consumer marketing programs to establish the new applications and then "gave" the business back to the normal suppliers.[1]

Components of a Good Business Definition

A good business definition should be:

- specific enough to impact the behavior of the organization
- focused more upon the satisfaction of customers' needs than the characteristics of the company's product
- able to reflect the essential skills of the organization
- attainable
- flexible.[2]

Let's look at each component of a good business definition.

Be specific enough to impact the behavior of the organization.   If an organization's business definition is too broad, it will fail to give adequate direction for strategy planning. Consider the experience of the Gillette Corporation. The firm expanded its business definition in the 1970s by defining itself as a producer of small consumer products. This expanded definition did not preclude Gillette from continuing to produce the men's and women's grooming and cosmetic products it was famous for. The definition was, however, sufficiently broad and ambiguous to allow the firm to venture into such product areas as digital watches, calculators, and smoke alarms. This was not successful for Gillette—the firm did not have experience with the markets for such products, nor in their production. In the late 1980s Gillette decided to return to its original business definition as a producer of men's and women's grooming and cosmetic items, and to the development and marketing of products for the markets it knew best. The firm's highly successful Sensor razor came from this retrenchment.

Basis of Possible Definition	Strategic Implications
Supplier of a raw material	Concentration on production, contract selling, long-term contracts
Bringing greater efficiency and profits to the manufacturers who elect to adopt Fiberglas in their finished products	Interfacing of seller's technical expert with customer's technical expert; trial installations, processing research
Better end products for consumer	Consumer marketing programs, joint ventures, manufacturing of final products

Source: Adapted from R. T. Davis, *Marketing Strategy (A): A Note* (Graduate School of Business, Stanford University, 1975), p. 3.

Table 3.1
Fiberglass: Alternative Business Definitions

United Airlines is another firm that ran into problems when it defined its business too broadly. In the mid-eighties the company redefined itself as a "full service connection for travelers." This definition resulted in the company's attempts to serve customers by doing everything—providing air transportation, lodging, and car rental services. United Airlines bought Hertz Rent A Car and Westin Hotels and changed its corporate name to Allegis. The change was not successful. The diversity of businesses incorporated under the broader business definition did not produce an integration of skills or a competitive advantage. Hertz and Westin were sold, the Allegis name was dropped, and the CEO behind the change was forced to resign.

Focus more on the satisfaction of customers' needs than the characteristics of the company's product. A business definition should focus on needs that the organization satisfies rather than describe a particular product, process, or set of procedures. This characteristic echoes the observation in Chapter 1 that marketing-oriented organizations are more likely to have broad definitions of their businesses. A business definition that is too narrow can produce the type of problems encountered by the railroad industry. As Theodore Levitt points out in his classic article, "Marketing Myopia," "they let others take customers away from them because they assumed themselves to be in the railway business rather than in the transportation business."[3] Levitt's remark points to the fact that the railroad industry continued to define itself in terms of trains when consumer needs were turning to fast, efficient transportation, something the airline industry was able to provide in a superior way.

Reflect the essential skills of the organization. A good business definition focuses on meeting consumers' needs within the skill levels and competitive advantage of the organization. Consider the experience of Quaker Oats. In the 1970s the firm attempted to recast itself from a marketer of such staple foods as oatmeal, pancake mix, and dry cereals into a marketer of toys (Fisher-Price) and theme restaurants (Magic Pan). Both ventures were failures. Much of the problem can be attributed to the fact that Quaker Oats had no expertise in either of the two industries it attempted to enter. The late 1980s saw the firm retreating to its core business of staple foods, and enjoying renewed success. The firm sold Fisher-Price to the Mattel Corporation. Fisher Price is featured in the Case Application at the end of this chapter.

The parent company of American Airlines, AMR Corporation, has been highly successful by branching into businesses that have enabled it to reflect its essential skills. The core strength of AMR is its skills with automation and service. In 1992 the firm owned 16 subsidiaries, which provided these skills to a variety of organizations in the travel industry. These subsidiaries include public warehousing and distribution services, training and consulting services, data processing facilities, telecommunications, and investment services. The subsidiaries, while comprising only 7 percent of AMR's revenue, accounted for 100 percent of its profits in 1992.

Be attainable.   While it is commendable for organizations to be ambitious, it makes little sense for them to define their business in terms that are not attainable. A business definition should be realistic. A small pharmaceutical company specializing in the manufacture of drugs targeted for people with asthma is not likely to meet with success by defining itself as a producer of prescription and over-the-counter medications to meet the needs of the general public.

United Parcel Service (UPS) is a firm that has defined its business in an ambitious yet attainable way. The organization defines itself as working to be the

United Parcel Service (UPS) defines itself as working to be the Number 1 choice of consumers and businesses when it comes to package delivery.

©1993 United Parcel Service of America, Inc.

Both circle the earth. Ours just happens to do it daily.

With all deference to the people at NASA, there's a big difference between shuttling astronauts and shuttling important international business packages.

To begin with, astronauts don't have to clear customs. Packages do. That's why UPS has developed the most comprehensive worldwide customs clearance network.

Our ground support is also unrivaled. With our familiar brown vehicles in the U.S., tuk-tuks in Bangkok, even gondolas in Venice, nobody is more reliable. In fact, UPS has over 270,000 employees serving more than 185 countries and territories. So it's no small wonder we make more on-time deliveries worldwide than anyone else.

Whatever corner of the earth you're shipping to, Singapore, São Paulo or Stockholm, send it UPS. Unlike NASA, we have a mission that's down to earth: to serve you better around the world. **The package delivery company more companies count on.**

Number 1 choice of consumers and businesses when it comes to package delivery. The firm supports this effort by allocating the funds and personnel necessary to make it happen.

Be flexible. A good definition defines the organization's business in a manner that allows change. Too rigid a definition can thwart a company. In the example of the Xerox Corporation, the firm's business definition has become increasingly flexible over the years. To be in the document business provides the firm with far greater latitude than does a business definition as a producer of copiers.

Strategic Business Units

Many companies are diversified into a number of different businesses and still more have a number of different products. All of the various businesses or products should, of course, be consistent with the organization's business definition. To facilitate strategic marketing planning, however, such companies often view themselves as comprised of separate strategic business units. A **strategic business unit** (SBU) is a self-contained part of a larger organization. Each SBU has its own set of customers and competitors, separate costs, and a distinct marketing strategy. It may be a company division, a product line within a division, or even a single product. Disney is an example of a company that has a number of SBUs, each representing a distinct business, though all fall under a general business definition of quality entertainment for the entire family.[4] Disney owns, among other things, theme parks, movie studios, a cable television channel, retail stores, and a record company. Johnson & Johnson is another company with many strategic business units. The company has more than 180 SBUs that produce and distribute products worldwide. Their products include such items as shampoos and baby-care goods but also range to nonprescription drugs, orthopedic equipment, and a variety of business-to-business products.

In essence, each SBU should be viewed as a completely separate business. Therefore, each SBU should have its own business definition within the context of the business definition of the parent company. The business definition for Touchstone Pictures (one of Disney's strategic business units), for example, is to provide entertainment for adult tastes while remaining consistent with the overall Disney focus on wholesome family entertainment.

The "Spotlight on Global Marketing: Tightening up What Business It's in Works for Philips," illustrates the value of a clearly defined mission statement and strategic business units that flow naturally from that statement.

3-1 What is the business definition of Elvis Presley Enterprises? How is that business definition used to guide the company? Describe an Elvis product that would be inconsistent with the organization's business definition.

3-2 Is EPE organized around the concept of strategic business units? If so, what are the organization's SBUs?

YOUR
MARKETING
KNOWLEDGE

MARKETING IN ACTION

Tightening up What Business It's in Works for Philips

At one time Philips, the Dutch electronics giant, made everything from saxophones to televisions. This conglomeration of unrelated product lines evolved because the firm had a very loosely defined mission and paid too little attention to its competitive strengths. This uncontrolled growth resulted in meager profits and low return on investment for the firm.

When increased competition (especially from Japan) began to threaten the consumer electronics division that had been Philips's strength, the firm decided it was spread too thin. The firm reworked its corporate mission to emphasize consumers' needs in the electronics field. The new mission statement also stressed a commitment to continuous innovation.

As a result of the new mission statement, Philips decided to sell unrelated SBUs that were diverting its attention from the product lines that represented the firm's core competencies. The company sold its record/CD recording label and several defense-related businesses. It chose to concentrate on five SBUs, all in the electronics field. The SBUs were televisions, compact disc (CD) players, semiconductors, computers, and commercial and residential lighting (light bulbs, etc.). The similarities among these five SBUs enhanced the possibility for synergy in manufacturing, distribution, research, and marketing.

The reworked mission statement provided the guidance Philips needed to pioneer the videocassette recorder and invent the compact disc player. The firm has also worked to improve its marketing research techniques so that it can better understand consumers' needs. Based on consumer input, the firm has developed a tiny CD player and a miniature color television.

The results of all this change have been phenomenal. Philips is currently the global leader in televisions with a 10 percent market share. The firm is part of a trio of consortia that are competing to develop a digital HDTV transmission standard for the United States. Philips light bulbs are number one in the world, although they lag behind General Electric in the U.S. market. Philips has recently released a line of "smart" light bulbs that have built-in computer chips. The line includes the Auto-Off bulb, which turns itself off after 30 minutes and the Dimmer, which drops from 100 watts to 70, 40, or 20 watts. The company is also moving forward on a joint venture with Osram, a German firm, to produce leadglass tubing that will be used in incandescent, fluoresent, and other lamps. Magnavox, Philips's brand of CD player, is gaining ground in the United States from Sony and Matsushita, formidable competitors. Philips's new digital compact cassette is competing head-on with Sony's mini-compact disc.

Semiconductors and computers have not fared so well. Philips's semiconductors are number ten in market share worldwide. This SBU has been losing money while locked in a heavy battle with Japanese competitors. Computers, also, are losing money. They are ranked 12th in market share in the world behind such major players as IBM and DEC. However, the company remains committed to these SBUs. It is currently concentrating dollars for research and development in both businesses. Philips's chairman believes that Philips can become the market leader in all five interrelated SBUs in the future.

PERFORMING A SITUATION ANALYSIS

Consider the following quote from the 1992 annual report of Apple Computers, Inc.:

> The Company's future operating results may be affected by a number of factors, including uncertainties relative to global economic conditions; industry factors; the availability and cost of components; the Company's ability to develop, manufacture, and sell its products profitably; the Company's ability to successfully increase market share in its core business while expanding its product base into other markets; the strength of its distribution channels; and the Company's ability to effectively manage expense growth relative to revenue growth in anticipation of continued pressure on gross margins as a percentage of net sales.[5]

Before an organization can begin to plan its strategy, indeed before it can even state, realistically, what it hopes to achieve, it must analyze the environment in which it is operating. This is called a **situation analysis.** The quote from Apple's annual report indicates that the firm has given careful consideration to the environment that will affect its future results. Factors operating within the firm (internal factors) and factors operating outside the firm (external factors) must be considered if the firm is to perform a complete assessment of the environment it faces.

Internal Factors

A number of internal factors affect marketing plans. Business definition, financial resources, cost structure, and competitive advantage are some of the internal factors. A marketing manager must make decisions consistent with these existing variables.

The firm's business definition, as discussed previously, provides guidance for and imposes limitations on marketing plans. Decisions regarding what products and services to develop should be made in light of whether the products or services being considered are consistent with the organization's business definition. Marketing planning cannot and should not proceed without due consideration of the firm's business definition.

Financial resources also affect marketing mix decisions. The organization may not have the funds to support its own sales force or a large advertising program. Consequently, the marketing manager may be limited in the types of promotion he or she can implement. In some instances, an organization might have considerable financial resources but top management may choose to allocate funds to different groups or products based on the desire to push a particular item. In this situation one marketer may have the money to aggressively market his or her product, while another manager in the same organization may have such limited funds that only a small marketing program is possible. Procter & Gamble is a large firm with considerable financial resources. Still, when making strategic decisions, it considers carefully the limitations implied by potential financial constraints. The firm, for example, will not enter the market with a new or extended product unless it can afford to appropriately promote that product for at least one year. If the resources are not readily available to saturate the market with promotion, Procter & Gamble postpones the market entry.[6]

Lack of resources can drive strategic decisions of an organization. For example, Aer Lingus, the national airline of Ireland, found itself in trouble when its core business, passenger transport, continued to sustain losses. As a result, the firm was forced to sell a profitable division, its hotel chain, to maintain its core business.

The cost structure involved in producing a product also influences marketing. **Cost structure** refers to the balance between fixed costs (costs that do not change in the short run regardless of output level) and variable costs (costs that vary directly with output level). When a product's fixed costs are high relative to its variable costs, the firm can handle additional customers at almost no additional costs. The airline industry is an example of this situation. The additional cost of one more passenger flying on a plane that is not full is negligible. For many firms, funds not needed to cover additional variable costs are available for marketing. Alternatively, when variable costs are high the firm may feel it can devote less money to marketing.

Competitive advantage refers to an organization's ability to operate in a way that makes it superior to its competition in the eyes of consumers. According to Michael Porter, a firm can achieve competitive advantage by offering consumers benefits equivalent to those offered by its competitors but for a lower price or by offering benefits distinct enough to offset a higher price.[7] Long distance competitors MCI and Sprint, for example, have competed effectively against AT&T by offering similar services at a lower price. Federal Express, on the other hand, provides benefits sufficiently superior to the U.S. Postal Service in the minds of enough consumers to allow FedEx to charge a rate 50 times higher than the post office.

Competitive advantage can also come from other components of the marketing mix. Coca-Cola and Kraft Foods, for example, maintain competitive advantages over other firms due to the strong relationships they have with several supermarket chains. This relationship results in Coke and Kraft being able to command prime display space in these supermarkets.

External Factors

External factors are variables that operate in the external environment, outside the firm. Typically the firm has no control over these factors. Social-cultural factors, economic factors, competitive factors, legal-political factors, technological factors, and ecological factors comprise this environment. (See Chapter 2 for a discussion of each factor.)

SWOT Analysis

As the marketing manager proceeds to analyze and evaluate the various internal and external factors that affect marketing planning, he or she begins to draw conclusions regarding the extent to which each factor's effect is positive or negative. A useful way to organize such conclusions is through a **SWOT analysis.** SWOT is an acronym for strengths, weaknesses, opportunities, and threats.

Internal factors that are positive represent strengths for a firm. A strong business definition that provides direction for product planning, for example, represents a strength. An organization like Southwest Airlines, with a decidedly competitive edge due to its ability to undercut the prices of competitors, would count competitive advantage as an organizational strength.

Negative internal factors are weaknesses for the organization. A cost structure with heavy emphasis on variable costs or a weak financial picture represent weaknesses that a marketing manager will have to work to overcome in marketing planning. In 1993 IBM faced both of these situations and has had to work aggressively to overcome these weaknesses.[8]

Opportunities and threats are typically found in the external environment. Opportunities form the basis of future success for an organization. An upswing in the economy, for example, could provide opportunity to a marketer of luxury goods such as fur coats. Consumers are more likely to indulge in luxuries in prosperous economic times. Opportunities, however, are most often realized only if the marketer takes advantage of them. A consumer may be more inclined to buy a mink coat when the economy is up, but he or she may actually buy it only if an enterprising marketer reminds the consumer (through promotion) that times are good and indulgence is okay.

Kentucky Fried Chicken has responded to the trend toward healthier eating by changing its name to KFC and introducing new products such as skinless chicken and rotisserie-cooked chicken.

Threats are problems that must be dealt with if the organization is to improve its performance. A social trend that discourages the wearing of fur coats because some consumers associate it with cruelty to animals represents a threat to the marketers of mink coats. In this instance, the marketer has many choices regarding how to respond to the threat. One alternative would be to attempt to convince consumers that wearing mink is acceptable. Another alternative would be to focus on consumer groups that do not follow the social trend against the product. The manager could even decide to introduce new, fake fur products. Similarly, medical reports indicating health concerns about caffeine represent a threat to coffee growers. The growers might decide to ignore the reports, hoping consumers will discount them, or they might decide to respond through product changes (decaffeinated coffee), promotional efforts ("Occasional indulgence is okay"), or other marketing approaches.

Many times, the impact of an external factor could be characterized as either an opportunity or a threat depending on how the marketer responds to it. A national trend toward healthier eating, for example, could easily be perceived as a threat to a firm such as Kentucky Fried Chicken. The firm has responded, however, by changing its name to KFC and introducing new products such as skinless chicken and rotisserie-cooked chicken. The firm's response to the trend has turned a threat into an opportunity to introduce new products. Pen manufacturers like Parker and Pilot have found opportunities to reposition their products in what at first appeared to be a threat to the industry. As consumers turn more and more to the use of computers, the writing instrument industry has been concerned that demand for pens will plummet. Several producers have responded to this threat with attempts to reposition pens as fashion accessories. This approach has allowed Parker to successfully market upscale pens that sell in the $250–$1000 range.[9]

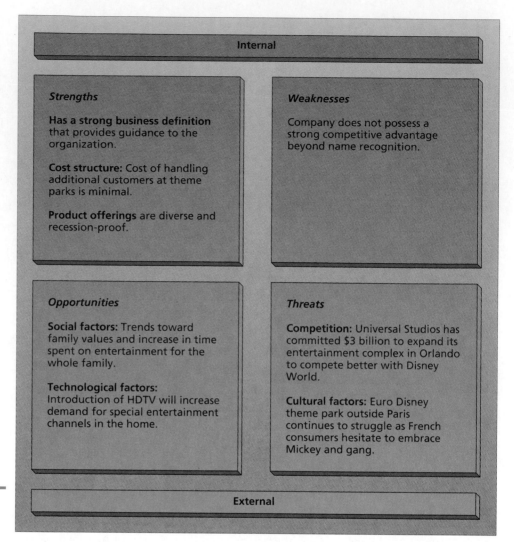

Internal

Strengths

Has a strong business definition that provides guidance to the organization.

Cost structure: Cost of handling additional customers at theme parks is minimal.

Product offerings are diverse and recession-proof.

Weaknesses

Company does not possess a strong competitive advantage beyond name recognition.

Opportunities

Social factors: Trends toward family values and increase in time spent on entertainment for the whole family.

Technological factors: Introduction of HDTV will increase demand for special entertainment channels in the home.

Threats

Competition: Universal Studios has committed $3 billion to expand its entertainment complex in Orlando to compete better with Disney World.

Cultural factors: Euro Disney theme park outside Paris continues to struggle as French consumers hesitate to embrace Mickey and gang.

External

FIGURE 3.2
Possible SWOT Analysis for Disney

Figure 3.2 illustrates the outcome of a possible SWOT analysis for the Disney Corporation. The situation analysis, of which SWOT is a part, is critical to an organization's ability to proceed with conscientious marketing planning.

ESTABLISHING OBJECTIVES

Once the situation analysis has been performed, the organization can decide what it hopes to achieve with its marketing efforts. Thus, the next step in the marketing planning process is to establish objectives. Objectives translate the business definition of the company into specific goals. This is done in light of the information uncovered by the situation analysis.

Good objectives must (1) specify exactly what is to be accomplished, (2) designate a quantitative level to be attained, and (3) specify a time frame for meeting the objective. For example, the statement "to increase return on investment" does not meet the last two criteria of level and time. But the statement "to increase Cheerios' market share of the ready-to-eat cereal market to 7 percent in the next year" does meet all three criteria. Apple Computer, Inc., established the following objective for

1993: to introduce as many personal computing products in fiscal 1993 as [the company] introduced in fiscal 1991 and 1992 combined.[10] This meets the three criteria for a good objective. It specifies what the firm will accomplish, it designates a quantitative level to be attained, and it specifies a time frame.

Objectives provide the baseline against which actual performance is measured, and as such, they are necessary to control the business. Therefore, it is important that objectives be attainable. The "Marketing in Action: Bic Corporation Sets Objectives" illustrates the Bic Corporation's position on the importance of establishing objectives.

Most organizations have multiple objectives. When this is the case, it is necessary for the objectives to be consistent with each other. A firm might, for example, state positive cash flow and increased market share as objectives. These goals are typically inconsistent with each other. Because it generally takes considerable funds to increase market share, it is unlikely that a positive cash flow would be produced if market share is increased. One way a firm could deal with this would be to order the objectives in terms of importance or time. Thus the firm might designate increased market share as the most important, or the short-term, objective while designating positive cash flow as a longer-term objective.

Objectives are established at various levels within an organization. Top management is most likely the source of overall business objectives, which must be filtered down into objectives for the various functional areas within the organization. A marketing manager might be responsible for establishing marketing objectives that derive from and are consistent with the overall business objectives. Hence, a company objective to increase market share might spawn marketing objectives within each component of the marketing mix, such as a sales objective to open 20 percent more accounts, an advertising objective to increase consumers' awareness by 40 percent, and a distribution objective to increase retail outlets that carry the product by 25 percent.

MARKETING IN ACTION

Bic Corporation Sets Objectives

"Without a clear, concise statement of objectives, there can be no viable strategy," states Donald M. Wilchek, a marketing manager at the Bic Corporation. "At Bic, specific objectives are set before a project is undertaken." This is just as true for small projects such as the development of a selling sheet as it is for the major launch of a new product. The corporate philosophy is that if money is spent, the firm must know what it hopes to achieve by the expenditure. This has been true at Bic since the company first began with the introduction of simple stick pens.

The disposable "crystal" stick pen, still Bic's largest seller, was regionally launched in 1959 and nationally launched with a retail price of $.19 in 1964. The company's objective was clear and concise—dominate the ballpoint pen market. Utilizing a straightforward strategy of producing a product that draws a line as well or better than anything on the market, pricing it significantly lower than the competition, making it almost universally available, and letting consumers know about it, Bic has clearly succeeded in achieving its objective. Today, Bic accounts for about two of every three ballpoint pens sold at retail.

FORMING A MARKETING STRATEGY

After establishing objectives, the marketing manager is ready to plan a strategy to accomplish those objectives. **Marketing strategy** is the long-term plan for developing a marketing mix that will achieve the organization's objectives by meeting the target market's needs. Marketing strategy, hence, must begin with the identification of the target market. Answers to the questions, "Who is the intended audience of the marketing mix?" and "What are its basic requirements?" must be addressed.

Once the target market has been defined, the marketing manager plans the marketing mix. Recall that a marketing mix is comprised of decisions in each of four areas: product, distribution, promotion, and price. Marketing strategy should define the product and its characteristics (product decisions), it should explain how the product will be brought to the user (distribution decisions), it should describe how the target market will be made aware of the product and persuaded to buy it (promotion decisions), and finally, it should specify the relative value of the offer vis-à-vis alternatives (price decisions).

An example of marketing strategy may help to clarify the concept and its components. The Lexus automobile was successful in achieving Toyota's objective of gaining the biggest share of the import luxury car market in the United States less than five years after its introduction. This objective was achieved through a wise, integrated marketing strategy:

- *Target market identification.* Toyota identified luxury car buyers as a target market and then conducted the most extensive market research ever undertaken for a car. Toyota gained a thorough understanding of the needs of the luxury car buyer.

- *Product decisions.* Toyota developed the Lexus LS400 (full-size sedan) to meet virtually all needs of the targeted consumers. The location of the instruments, the quiet ride of the car, and the capacity of the seats to adjust were designed in response to consumers' preferences indicated by the marketing research.

- *Distribution decisions.* Toyota created a dealership network especially for the Lexus. Lexus dealers were encouraged to provide a level of service and customer attention that are typically unheard of in car dealerships.

- *Promotion decisions.* Lexus advertised heavily with an emphasis on the quality, luxury, and driveability of the car.

- *Price decisions.* Lexus was initially priced more than $20,000 less than German-made competitors (particularly Mercedes) that featured similar performance characteristics.

The Lexus example illustrates that all the components of the marketing mix must be integrated to serve the needs of the target market and the company.

Organizations without a well thought-out, integrated marketing strategy can easily flip-flop in their marketing actions, causing confusion for potential consumers. In the early 1990s, for example, McDonald's introduced McDonald's Express outlets that featured a limited menu and drive-through service exclusively. At the same time the company was experimenting with expanded menus and table service at some restaurants. The question became, for many consumers, "What is McDonald's?" This does not mean that an organization's marketing strategy should be set in stone for all time. Indeed, as the internal and external factors change, so too must strategy. For example, Lipton (owned by the Pepsi Corporation) sold iced tea and iced tea mix for many years with only moderate advertising in a market where its only significant competition came from Nestlé (owned by the Coca-Cola Corporation). In the late 1980s the Snapple Beverage Corporation introduced Snapple Iced Tea with heavy advertising and positioning as an all-natural beverage. By 1993, Snapple had

The Lexus automobile was successful in achieving Toyota's objective of gaining the biggest share of the import luxury car market in the United States less than five years after its introduction.

soared to the top industry market share (36.2 percent compared to Lipton's 23.5 percent and Nestlé's 20 percent). Lipton fought back in 1994 with $30 million of advertising aimed at questioning Snapple's brewing process and its claims of all-natural beverages.[11] The result of all this activity appears to have benefited the entire industry, which represented $1.3 billion in sales in 1993.[12]

Sometimes changes in the internal or external environmental factors (or both) can occur very quickly. Thus, an organization should have a contingency plan that will help it to adapt. With contingency planning, changes in strategy are developed before environmental and internal factors change. If these changes do occur, the new strategy is implemented. Asian and African coffee producers found it necessary to implement such a contingency plan in 1993. Greater competition, depressed economic conditions in many parts of the world, and changing demographics accounted for declining consumer demand, and resulted in downward pressure on world prices of coffee. This situation caused the Association of Coffee Producing Countries to institute what it referred to as a "retention scheme." The scheme or strategy, which the Association had held in abeyance as long as world prices were acceptable to member countries and companies, called for coffee-producing countries to hold back as much as 20 percent of their coffee exports in an effort to push up the price worldwide.[13]

Strategic Marketing Tools

You may wonder how a marketing manager identifies the correct strategy to accomplish the firm's objectives. There is, of course, no textbook answer. Knowledge, experience, and mistakes all contribute to effective strategy planning, but nothing can guarantee success.

Several approaches have been developed to help in the area of strategic planning. Although these approaches do not guarantee success, they do serve as tools that aid planners in decision making. The tools that we consider here are all forms of portfolio analysis. **Portfolio analysis** is a method of assessing a firm's strategic business units and then using that assessment to guide overall strategy planning. Overall SBU strategy planning such as a decision to build, hold, or reduce market share, will have a major impact on that SBU's marketing strategy and plan. Share gains are typically obtained by increases in marketing activity and vice versa.

The Boston Consulting Group growth–share analysis.   Growth–share analysis was developed by the Boston Consulting Group (BCG) in the 1960s.[14] It is used to evaluate strategic business units (SBUs) in terms of either their ability to supply cash to the parent organization or their need to receive cash from the organization. Each SBU is positioned on a matrix like the one in Figure 3.3. Because the matrix is a prominent component of the analysis, this tool has come to be known as the **BCG matrix.** The size of the circle representing the SBU indicates its level of sales. The horizontal axis shows the market share of each SBU relative to the industry's largest competitor. The vertical axis shows the growth rate of the market in which each SBU competes. In general, the higher the market growth rate, the greater the investment required in plants, equipment, and working capital must be. As you can see, the matrix is divided into four quadrants.

Those SBUs with a big share of a low-growth market fall in the lower-left quadrant of the matrix. They are called **cash cows** because they generate more cash than they need to operate. This cash can be used by the parent organization to support SBUs that need cash infusions. Pepsico's Doritos snack chips are an example of a cash cow.[15]

FIGURE 3.3
Market Growth–Market Share Analysis: The BCG Matrix

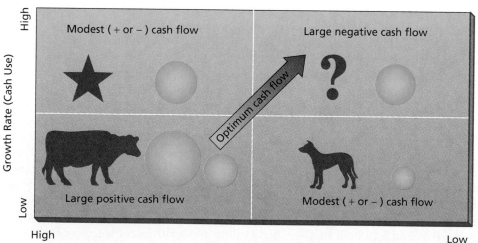

Source: Boston Consulting Group, 1970.

SBUs that fall in the lower-right quadrant are **dogs.** They have a small share of a low-growth market. Although they usually neither generate nor require large amounts of cash, they often have poor profitability. Lever's Pepsodent toothpaste is an example of a brand the firm has chosen to discount heavily due to its position in this category.[16]

Question marks in the upper-right quadrant are SBUs with a small share of a high-growth market. They typically require large amounts of cash, much more than they can generate, just to hold their market share because they have to grow with the market to do so. Increasing market share requires even more cash support. These SBUs present a dilemma to the parent organization. How much cash should be invested in the hope that those units will generate excess cash in the future? For this reason, these SBUs are referred to as **problem children.** St. Joseph's aspirin for children and Aqua Velva are such SBUs. In both cases their parent companies have decided to recommit resources in the hopes that the SBUs will gain market share.[17]

With a large market share of a high-growth market, the SBUs in the upper-left quadrant are **stars.** They tend to produce a lot of cash, but they also need a lot of cash to hold their own in a fast growing market. Generally, the amount of cash they generate and the amount of cash they require are more or less in balance. TravelPro's "Roll-Aboard" suitcase, a suitcase designed to roll down the narrow aisles of airplanes and fit under airplane seats, is a product that has proved to be a star.[18]

Typically, an SBU begins its existence as a question mark or a dog, requiring large infusions of cash from the parent company. If it successfully increases its share of the market, the SBU will become a star. As the growth of the market slows, the star of today may become the cash cow of tomorrow and generate large amounts of excess cash for the parent company. Eventually the cash cow may dry up and become a dog.

An organization can use the BCG matrix to plan its strategy at the corporate level. Because the organization's goal should be a balanced portfolio, there must be enough cash cows to support the question marks the firm is maintaining. Stars, which bring attention to the firm and may become cash cows, are also desirable. An obvious strategy regarding dogs is to get rid of them. Of course, it's not always easy to find a buyer! An organization with more cash cows than it needs to maintain its question marks may divest itself of some cash cows, because other firms are likely to find such SBUs highly desirable and the seller could get a good price for them. Procter & Gamble, the giant consumer goods producer, recently reevaluated many of its SBUs. The result was identification of some products to drop, some to "give more time to," and others to emphasize and heavily support. The firm sold Lilt (Home Permanent, a hair care product), killed White Cloud bathroom tissue, and merged Puritan cooking oil into its Crisco line.[19]

The BCG matrix was instrumental in establishing the concept of portfolio analysis as an aid to strategic planning.[20] In recent years, however, it has been criticized as too limited because it focuses on only two dimensions. Looking only at market share and growth rate, many argue, ignores other important strategic factors.

Market attractiveness–business strengths analysis.   The General Electric Company and the consulting firm of McKinsey & Company developed a strategic planning tool that relies on a larger number of factors than the BCG matrix.[21] As illustrated in Figure 3.4, the **GE Screening Grid** places an organization's SBUs on a grid comprised of two dimensions: company strengths and industry attractiveness. Each of these dimensions is an index that summarizes the combined impact of a number of factors.

The company strengths index is determined on the basis of an assessment of internal factors. The marketing manager would consider those factors we discussed

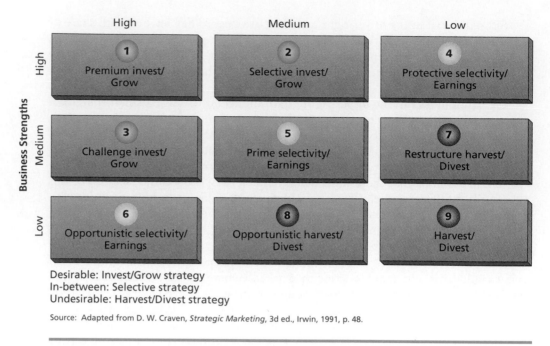

Desirable: Invest/Grow strategy
In-between: Selective strategy
Undesirable: Harvest/Divest strategy

Source: Adapted from D. W. Craven, *Strategic Marketing*, 3d ed., Irwin, 1991, p. 48.

FIGURE 3.4
Market Attractiveness–Business Strengths Analysis: The GE Screening Grid

earlier: business definition, financial resources, cost structure, and competitive advantage. Additional internal factors such as company market share, sales growth rate, customer loyalty, marketing skills relevant to the business, fit with distribution structure, and technological capabilities might also be considered. To form the index, the marketing manager must select the relevant factors, rate his or her organization on the factors, weight each factor in terms of importance, and then combine the weights and ratings. This combining procedure can be a simple weighted average or some more complex operation, depending on the manager's judgment.

The industry attractiveness index is a similarly combined summary of such external factors. The number and nature of competitors, technological developments, government regulations, economic fluctuations, and any other external variables deemed relevant by the marketing manager would be included in the index.

The two axes are combined to form the nine-block matrix shown in Figure 3.4. Each SBU is placed on the grid, in one of the nine blocks, based on the way that SBU is assessed according to the two summary dimensions. Placement in cells 1, 2, and 3 define the SBUs that will receive the resources to grow, the so-called "green light" SBUs. The market is high or medium in attractiveness and the organization has high enough skills and resources to take advantage of the market. Procter & Gamble is currently exploring environmentally safe disposable diapers. This product is a green light for the firm. SBUs placed on the diagonal (cells 4, 5, and 6) should receive selective investment. Caution (the yellow light) is the operating style. Laundry detergents such as Tide fall into this area for Procter & Gamble since the highly competitive market suggests only moderate industry attractiveness. Finally, placement in cells 7, 8, or 9 indicates that the SBU lacks opportunity in terms of either market capabilities, industry capabilities, or both. These "red light" businesses are managed to harvest their resources or are just divested. As the market has moved to liquid handsoaps, bar soaps such as Camay have moved into this category for Procter & Gamble.

Product–market opportunity analysis.   When an organization's stated objectives are related to growth, product-market opportunity analysis can be useful in plotting the appropriate strategy. This analysis is performed through the use of a classification scheme that represents alternative growth strategies a firm might implement. The scheme, presented in the form of a two-dimensional matrix, is illustrated in Figure 3.5. The dimensions in the matrix are markets and products. An organization can choose to grow by building a relationship with existing or new groups in either category.

The strategy implied when the decision is to focus growth efforts on existing markets and existing products is **market penetration.** With this strategy, the organization increases sales by getting greater market share with present products in current markets. For example, Crest toothpaste might attempt to increase its market share through more effective advertising. Furthermore, Crest might encourage consumers to brush more often, potentially increasing sales. Hershey temporarily increased the size of its chocolate bar while holding price steady. The "extra candy" was promoted as free in an attempt to lure candy bar purchasers to Hershey. Market penetration represents a relatively low-risk strategy for a firm. The organization is not breaking new ground in terms of people or products. While the low risk aspect of market penetration may be appealing to an organization, it is also true that the opportunity for significant growth may not be great with this strategy.

In the lower-left quadrant of Figure 3.5, the strategy is market development. **Market development** increases sales by taking present products to new markets. New markets may be found in many places like other segments of the population or through global expansion. Apple Computer announced plans in September 1993 to expand into China. Many computer companies are seeking market share in China. Similarly, Coca-Cola is entering the market in India, a move expected to greatly increase the firm's international market share; and Ben & Jerry's ice cream is attempting to build markets in Europe and Asia.[23] Firms sometimes find that market development can be accomplished expediently by working with another company that is familiar with the new market. Pier 1 Imports, for example, announced plans in late 1993 to expand into México, a previously untapped market for them. The expansion will be accomplished through an agreement between Pier 1 and *Sears de México*. Sears will carry Pier 1 goods in its Mexican stores.

Not all market development is accomplished through international expansion. In some cases a firm may identify new markets within existing geographical boundaries. The University of Phoenix, a private college, has expanded its market share by targeting adults who work full time and have inflexible schedules. The school offers weekend and other flexibly scheduled module courses. Many companies are targeting children, who offer the double benefit of money to spend now and the hope of becoming future loyal customers. Hyatt Hotels has used this strategy with its Camp Hyatt package that provides special services to children who are guests of the hotel.[24]

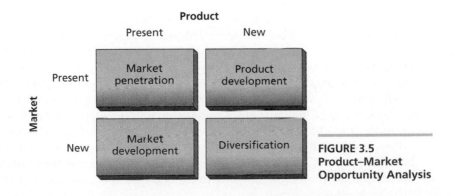

FIGURE 3.5
Product–Market
Opportunity Analysis

"You either get people with a MBA or an Engineering degree. But in real life, technology and marketing are integrated. The University of Phoenix came up with an excellent solution."

Ray Powers - US West Communications

Customized
Corporate
Education
Programs

University of Phoenix

Your Company's Corporate Classroom

The University of Phoenix has expanded its market share by targeting adults who work full time and have inflexible schedules.

The opposite of market development is **product development.** With this strategy sales are increased by introducing new products into present markets. Mrs. Field's cookies is committed to a strategy of product development. In the last several years the company has developed products such as muffins, biscuits, and specialty coffees. These products have been introduced into existing Mrs. Field's locations with the intent of increasing overall revenues per store.[25]

Both market development and product development are higher risk growth strategies than market penetration. In both cases the organization is exploring new ground. Its venture, however, is undertaken with the security of either a familiar market or a familiar product in tow. The two strategies could be characterized as medium-risk strategies.

The final growth strategy that a firm might consider is **diversification.** With this strategy, sales are increased by introducing new products into new markets. Diversification clearly carries the highest risk of the four alternative growth strategies considered. The organization is breaking new ground on two fronts, products and markets. The organization may choose to manage and minimize the risk by diversification through acquisition. In this situation a company grows by buying an SBU from an existing firm. Seagram's acquisition of Taylor wines from Coca-Cola is an example. It is also helpful if the firm's diversification involves products whose technology is related to technology currently used by the organization, or if the markets being entered are similar to the firm's existing markets. In this type of situation, diversification allows the company to expand into new products and markets while building on the strengths and skills of the organization. Maytag's acquisition of Hoover Vacuums, for example, allowed the firm to diversify while taking advantage of its strengths in production skills.[26] Toshiba, the Japanese electronics giant, is marketing an ashtray with a built-in fan that sucks up cigarette smoke.[27] While this represents a departure from the firm in terms of both product and consumer, Toshiba's production expertise allows easy manufacturing. Furthermore, the product may appeal to many consumers who have purchased Toshiba electronic equipment.

Sometimes even with these factors in the firm's favor, diversification proves too great a challenge. Coca-Cola's failure with Taylor wines has been attributed to the fact that wine production and marketing were too different from soda pop production and marketing for Coke to be able to make it a success. Diversification, on the other hand, does provide the opportunity to spread out a company's risk related to external factors and an industry's ill health by not keeping all its eggs in one basket. Anheuser-Busch, maker of Budweiser beer, found success diversifying with the acquisition of SeaWorld Parks around the United States.

Diversification can result in significant changes in an organization. General Cinema Corporation, a movie theater business, began diversifying in the late 1980s into insurance and retail businesses. In 1991 it acquired Harcourt Brace Jovanovich, Inc., a book publisher. Having moved far afield from its original business definition, the firm changed its name in 1991 from General Cinema to Harcourt General, Inc. The company's transformation was complete in late 1993 when it sold its General Cinema division.

A marketing manager who uses product–market opportunity analysis in planning a growth strategy must consider the resources of the firm, the potential for growth vis-à vis the firm's objectives (for example, market penetration may not offer sufficient growth potential to a firm with lofty objectives), and the amount of risk the organization is willing to incur. An organization may, of course, choose to attempt growth by implementing more than one strategy at the same time. The "Marketing in Action: On the Fast Track at Gymboree" describes the use of three growth strategies by an up-and-coming marketer of children's goods and services.

Profit impact of market strategies. The final marketing strategy tool that we will consider is **Profit Impact of Market Strategies (PIMS)**. PIMS is a computerized data bank of strategic information that is collected and analyzed by the Strategic Planning Institute. The institute gathers information, via questionnaire, from companies whose combined businesses represent more than 2500 SBUs. Information is gathered on a variety of factors including the amount of investment the firm has in a given SBU, the quality of the product or service that the SBU represents, the amount of growth in the market being targeted, and the amount of current strategic effort being exerted. The institute also gathers information on measures of financial performance (for example, return on investment and net cash flow). The data is analyzed for relationships among the various potential predictors of profitability and the financial performance of the participating organizations. The Strategic Planning Institute has been able to account for as much as 80 percent of the variation in profitability among the SBUs they've analyzed by looking at nine strategic influences.

Member firms are provided a wide range of information based on the output and analysis of the PIMS data. They are told what normal return on investment should be for a business of their size and type. Furthermore, strategies to improve financial performance are suggested. PIMS gives its members information about companies and SBUs that are strategically similar to them, reporting on strategic and operating characteristics that have helped the "look alikes" to achieve success.

Using PIMS data, a public accounting firm in Canada determined that the company's performance depended on service and the quality of products. It was further determined that a direct relationship existed between customer service and profit.

MARKETING IN ACTION ▬▬▬▬▬▬

On the Fast Track at Gymboree

Children are proving to be big business for Gymboree. Since its founding in 1976, the company has grown by leaps and bounds. Net income for the fiscal year ending in January 1995 is predicted to be $17.7 million, a 29 percent increase from the previous year. At the same time revenues are expected to surge 35 percent to $173 million.

What has fueled such success? No single thing, but rather a combination of growth strategies accounts for the health of Gymboree. The firm, begun in northern California, started by offering play and exercise classes to preschool aged children and their parents. The concept was successful for Gymboree, who went on to further penetrate the market for preschool play by opening play centers. Today there are 370 Gymboree play centers scattered across the United States and seven other countries. The centers serve 100,000 children annually. Only six of the centers are company-owned. Franchising has allowed Gymboree to further penetrate its original market.

In 1986 Gymboree decided to attempt additional growth through a product development strategy. Secure in the belief that it understood the preschool market, the firm expanded into clothing for children younger than 6 years old. The company markets its clothing in its own stores, located primarily in shopping malls. Gymboree's clothing stores have been an enormous success for the company, accounting for most of the firm's growth since their opening. In 1992 the company had 112 stores and by the end of 1993 it had expanded to 152 and planned to add 40 to 50 stores during 1994. The company designs the clothes at its headquarters in California and then contracts the manufacturing to Asian firms. The firm is considering further product development by testing shoe sales in some of its stores.

While product development has proved very successful for Gymboree, the firm is not satisfied to stop there. Market development is also being considered. On this front the company is planning to move beyond the preschool set and target older children, up to age 7. Additionally Gymboree is exploring the possibility of selling its products on cable television, thus allowing the company to reach a different group of parents.

IMPLEMENTING MARKETING TACTICS

Having a marketing strategy does not guarantee success. The strategy itself may be ill conceived, and there are many possible ways to implement it. While strategy provides guidance regarding how to accomplish objectives, the firm must make specific decisions about each element of the marketing mix before implementation. These pre-implementation specifics are called **marketing tactics.** Marketing tactics bring an organization's marketing strategy to life. As one marketing scholar stated,

> If a given strategy doesn't contribute to tactical results, then the given strategy is faulty, no matter how brilliantly conceived or eloquently presented. . . . The objective of a strategy is to make the operation work on a tactical level.[29]

Tactics form the heart of the organization's short-term marketing plan. This plan takes the long-term marketing strategy, the strategic marketing plan, as a given and develops detailed executions on each marketing mix element. These executions become a blueprint for implementation.

Tactical decisions in the area of product would include specifications regarding the number of different product items the firm will carry, the styling, and the functional features of each item. In the case of the Lexus, described earlier, while strategy involved designing features that targeted consumers wanted, tactics involved such decisions as the type of material to use for the seats. Honda's decision to increase the color selections for the Prelude from the limited choice of three it had initially offered is another tactical decision.

Distribution tactics revolve around issues such as the choice of which specific wholesalers and retailers to use and the types of programs that will be necessary to motivate those intermediaries. In the case of the Lexus, at the tactical level, Toyota had to determine how to interest potential dealers, how many dealerships were desirable, and how it could entice dealers to provide extremely high levels of service. Specific site location decisions would be an example of a tactical distribution decision for a service provider. Blockbuster Video, for example, specifically chooses to locate its stores near banks, pizza shops, and other highly frequented retail outlets.

Promotional strategy specifies the types of promotion to use. Toyota decided on significant advertising as well as personal selling for the Lexus. Strategy further specified that Lexus advertising would emphasize quality, luxury, and driveability. It was left to promotion tactics, however, to specify which creative presentation to use in the ads, in other words, exactly what would be said to consumers to emphasize these three features. Other promotion tactics would include choice of media (television? magazines? both?) and timing of the ads. The nature of sales promotions is also an example of a tactical decision. Kodak, for example, made a tactical decision when it decided to emblazon more than 5,000,000 raw eggs with the Kodak logo for a local promotion.

Tactics in the area of price specify the exact retail price for an item as well as whether special discounts, sales, introductory offers, and such will be offered. While Toyota's price strategy for the Lexus focused on significantly undercutting German competition, the decision to charge a sticker price of $33,500 was tactical.

Note that the tactical decisions described deal with the details and short-run aspects of a marketing program. An advertising program can be changed in the short run, as can the price or color of a product. These types of tactical changes can take place within a given marketing strategy.

The importance of effective marketing tactics should not be underestimated. A carefully thought-out marketing strategy that does not translate to equally well thought-out tactics has little chance for success.

3-3 Use product–market opportunity analysis to describe the various growth strategies the post office could use.

3-4 Describe the overall strategy and tactics used by the American Red Cross or your local blood bank to attract blood donors.

YOUR
MARKETING
KNOWLEDGE

MARKETING CONTROL

The marketing manager must control marketing plans once they've been implemented.[30] The function of **marketing control** is to give the manager feedback on how the plans are progressing. The purpose of marketing control is to maximize the probability that the organization will achieve its short-run and long-run objectives in the marketplace.[31] With the feedback that marketing control provides, the manager is in a position to know whether adjustments are needed.

Figure 3.6 illustrates the control process. The objectives established earlier in the strategic planning process answer the question, "What do we want to achieve?" Hence an organization's objectives set the standards against which performance will be evaluated. To maintain control, systems must be established to measure organizational performance. The issue of concern at this point in the control process is, "What is happening?" The next part of the control process involves a diagnosis of performance. Here the question being addressed is, "Why is it happening?" Finally, in the last component of the control process, appropriate corrective action is suggested as the planners consider the question, "What should we do about it?"

The organization should undertake two types of control: tactical (short-run) control and strategic (long-run) control. **Tactical control** is concerned with the short-term marketing plan of the organization. It assesses the effectiveness of the tactics developed to carry out strategy. **Strategic control** assesses the effectiveness of the organization's long-term marketing strategy. A good way to distinguish the two types of control is to consider which question the control is addressing:

- Are we doing the right things? (Strategic control)
- Are we doing things right? (Tactical control)

Tactical Control

At the tactical level, control most often is accomplished through the use of various sales and profitability measures. Such measures include revenue analysis, market share analysis, and marketing expense-to-sales analysis.

Revenue analysis is the measurement and evaluation of actual revenue in relation to the revenue objectives. **Market share analysis** is consideration of how the firm is doing compared to the competition. Is it gaining or losing ground? **Marketing expense-to-sales analysis** compares the ratio of various marketing expenses (such as advertising, marketing research) to the sales being generated.

The comparisons in tactical control analyses should be made not only on a company-wide level, but also at the geographic level (states, cities, sales territories),

---

FIGURE 3.6
The Control Process

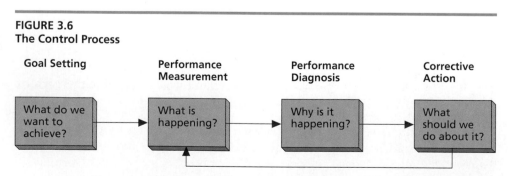

Source: P. Kotler and A. Andreasen, *Strategic Marketing for Nonprofit Organizations*, 4th ed., Prentice Hall, 1991, p. 617.

by product line or item, by customer type (steel industry, automobile industry), level of trade (retail versus wholesale), order size, and financial arrangement of sale (cash versus charge, and commission rate). The results of all these analyses should be available on a monthly, or at least quarterly, basis to marketing managers.

As an example of tactical control, a marketing manager for Apple Computers may receive a report that compares the sales and profit objectives for PowerBooks set in the Denver territory to actual sales and profits in that region. If sales or profits are either lower or higher than expected, the manager can investigate the causes. The manager may determine that sales are low because of poor account coverage, and can then rearrange sales territories to improve account coverage.

Strategic Control

A firm must periodically appraise the effectiveness of its long-term marketing strategy. The fundamental tool for doing this is the marketing audit. A **marketing audit** is an overall assessment of the organization's marketing environment, organizational capabilities, objectives, and strategy. It measures whether the firm is on track and if not, where it should focus attention. Philip Morris undertakes regular marketing audits. The organization believes that regular assessment by both internal and external sources is critical to keeping the company on target.

A marketing audit should possess four key characteristics:

1. The audit should be *comprehensive*. A marketing audit should assess all aspects of the organization's marketing efforts rather than look just at trouble spots.

2. The audit should be *systematic*. A marketing audit should proceed through a series of planned steps, in an orderly fashion.

3. The audit should be performed by an *independent* agency. To ensure objectivity, a marketing audit is best performed by personnel other than those currently responsible for marketing strategy. Outside consultants are often used.

4. The audit should be performed *periodically*. A marketing audit should be performed on a regular basis (for example, annually or biannually). This schedule should be maintained even when things seem fine.[32]

A STRATEGIC MARKETING PLAN FOR AMERICAN EXPRESS

As a conclusion to this chapter, let's consider the strategic marketing plan developed for 1992 by the American Express Company. American Express is a worldwide corporation that realized revenues of almost $27 million in 1992.[33] The company views itself as the global leader in the financial services industry. The various businesses that comprise American Express are all positioned to contribute to the advancement of this corporate business definition.

In 1992, the company was made up of five distinct and separate businesses. Each business possessed its own vision, objectives, and strategies and each was separately accountable for revenues or losses. According to the firm's 1992 annual report, "Each American Express business unit is responsible for developing and putting in place strategies to strengthen its franchise."[34]

The five businesses (or SBUs) that comprised American Express in 1992 were (1) Travel Related Services (TRS); (2) IDS Financial Services; (3) American Express Bank; (4) Shearson Lehman Brothers; and (5) First Data Corporation. At the strategic level, President and Chief Executive Officer Harvey Golub explained his responsibility as being "to ensure that the business unit and corporate strategies are executed with the appropriate degree of rigor, discipline, and urgency."[35] Furthermore, in Golub's view, strategies developed at the corporate level help direct the amount of attention each strategic business unit gets. For 1992, American Express adopted three strategic business priorities: (1) build the American Express brand franchise; (2) move Shearson Lehman Brothers farther along the road to sustained profitability; and (3) strengthen overall capital structure.

Objectives and strategies were also established for each strategic business unit. To illustrate how this was carried out at American Express we will consider one SBU, Travel Related Services (TRS). American Express's Travel Related Services is, according to CEO Golub, the business that symbolizes the company. TRS is the division of American Express that issues credit cards, identifies and contracts with service establishments (SEs) to accept those credit cards, and offers traveler's checks. The TRS division experienced problems in the late 1980s and early 1990s. A number of service establishments stopped accepting the American Express® card, resulting in a decrease in the number of places "cardmembers" could use their American Express credit cards. A situation analysis showed that these problems primarily resulted from intensified competition from Visa, MasterCard, and the Discover Card.

Travel Related Services identified five objectives for 1992:

1. Strengthen relationships with service establishments that accept the Card.
2. Reengineer business processes to improve customer service, reduce cycle time, and lower costs by $1 billion by 1994.
3. Increase Cardmember loyalty.
4. Reposition consumer lending products to increase profitability.
5. Build leadership positions in Travel, Travelers Cheques, and Corporate Card.

American Express proceeded to develop strategies and tactics to accomplish these objectives in 1992. To strengthen relationships with service establishments, the firm reorganized its SE marketing and sales organization. It implemented creative approaches such as specialists trained to serve specific industries and reduced discount rates for SEs that electronically submitted card charges.

To improve customer service and build cardmember loyalty, the business redesigned its revolving credit card, the Optima Card. It instituted tiered pricing based on tenure, spending, and past performance. Cardmembers who had held their

The introduction of American Express® Travelers Cheques *for Two* was designed to move American Express to a clear leadership position in the traveler's check business.

cards longer, who charged more, or who had a history of paying on time were charged less than others who did not meet these criteria. Cardmember loyalty was promoted by designating U.S. clients with high volume and long tenure as Members of Distinction, the distinction affording special personalized customer service.

The organization introduced American Express® Travelers Cheques *for Two*, a new product that allows two traveling companions to sign and use the same set of their traveler's checks. This new product was designed to move American Express to a clear leadership position in the traveler's check business.

TRS sought to establish a leadership position in the industry through promotion as well as changes and introductions of products and services. The company launched a U.S. advertising campaign designed to reinforce the value of the American Express Card to both members and merchants. This strategy was carried out through television commercials and printed advertisements.

The result of all these strategic efforts is documented by the progress TRS made toward achievement of its objectives for 1992. The organization reported strengthened SE relationships. Major new SEs were added (Kmart, the German rail system, and major oil companies) and the firm reenlisted some high-visibility SEs who had left. Reengineering efforts reduced costs for the firm by well over $1 billion in 1992. Furthermore, cardmember loyalty, as measured by average spending, was up at the end of 1992. The firm realized an 11.5 percent increase in spending per U.S. cardmember.

The results of TRS's strategic efforts in 1992 provided feedback that helped American Express to plan for the future. Based on the progress toward objectives in 1992, the firm created a vision to develop a set of products and services that will allow TRS to capture all of the credit card spending that its cardmembers engage in. Furthermore, specific financial objectives of 15 percent per year earnings growth and a return on equity of 18–20 percent have been established for the next several years.

To further illustrate the dynamic nature of strategic planning, let's consider the changes that have occurred at American Express since 1992. At the corporate level, the company has altered its SBU mix by divesting itself of Shearson Lehman Brothers (SLB). In 1993 American Express sold its Shearson retail brokerage to Primerica Corporation. In mid-1994 the Lehman Brothers investment firm was spun off from American Express to its shareholders and became an independent company.[36] Tactically, within the Travel Related Services Division, American Express introduced "The Plan" in 1993. "The Plan" is a series of service packages offered to American Express cardmembers designed to help the firm compete more effectively in the face of stiff competition from new bankcards.[37]

PERSONAL COMPUTER EXERCISE

Developing a comprehensive marketing strategy often involves the use of portfolio analysis. This PC Exercise allows you to analyze a company's strategic business units (SBUs) using a BCG growth–share matrix and a market attractiveness–business strengths matrix. After completing this exercise, you will understand better how portfolio analysis provides important insights into marketing strategy.

KEY POINTS

■ Strategic marketing planning involves a series of steps: determining a business definition, performing a situation analysis, establishing objectives, formulating strategy and tactics, implementing the strategy and tactics, and finally, assessing performance through a control system.

■ Business definition identifies the customer needs that an organization satisfies, while keeping those needs consistent with the organization's skills. The definition provides direction for the firm in formulating strategy.

■ Firms involved in multiple businesses often view each business separately, as strategic business units (SBUs). The firm must plan separately for each SBU but must also determine how the individual SBUs relate to each other.

■ Before formulating strategy, the organization must analyze factors that affect its decisions. Internal factors include business definition, financial resources, the cost structure of the firm, and whether the firm possesses a competitive advantage. External factors are uncontrollable factors from the outside environment.

■ A SWOT analysis can be used to characterize internal and external factors as either positive or negative.

■ Objectives set the standard against which an implemented strategy will be judged.

■ Marketing strategy establishes the basic logic, but not the specific details, of how the organization intends to compete. It identifies the target market and presents an overview of each element of the marketing mix.

■ Portfolio analysis provides a way for planners to evaluate and plan strategy for the organization's SBUs. Specific types of portfolio analysis include the BCG matrix, the GE grid, product–market opportunity analysis, and PIMS.

■ Marketing tactics set down the specific details of each element of the marketing mix, taking the marketing strategy as a given. These form the heart of the organization's one-year marketing plan.

■ Marketing control provides the feedback that allows an organization to assess whether its efforts have been successful. It provides direction for what needs to be changed. Without a control system, an organization's planning efforts can never benefit from experience.

KEY TERMS

business definition (80)
mission statement (80)
strategic business units (SBUs) (83)
situation analysis (85)
cost structure (85)
competitive advantage 86)
SWOT analysis (86)
marketing strategy (90)
portfolio analysis (92)

BCG matrix (92)
cash cows (92)
dogs (93)
question marks (93)
problem children (93)
stars (93)
GE Screening Grid (93)
market penetration (95)
market development (95)

ISSUES FOR DISCUSSION

1. As baby boomers have matured into middle age, Levi Strauss has found itself with falling sales in its mainstay product, jeans. What alternative opportunities for growth could Levi's pursue? Cite a specific example of each and speculate about the outcomes.

2. What internal factors would be important to consider as part of a situation analysis if you were planning to market yourself to law schools after obtaining your degree? Characterize each factor as a strength or weakness.

3. What external factors would affect your hopes of being accepted into law school? Does each represent a threat or an opportunity?

4. General Mills was a conglomerate composed of many divisions, including cereals, toys, clothes, wallpaper, and other food products. General Mills sold all but its food businesses. Why might it do this?

5. Pick one factor from the marketing environment that might affect the Hertz Rent A Car Company. Note how this factor might change and how Hertz's strategy might be affected.

6. What might the business definition of the United Way be? How could the United Way use this business definition to guide its strategic decisions?

7. Give an example of a strategy and a tactic that each of the following organizations might adopt:
   (a) Bank of America
   (b) San Diego Zoo
   (c) Reebok footwear
   (d) Caterpillar Tractors

8. Describe the control system that a library might institute. Be sure to include elements of both strategic and tactical control.

9. Some firms with very small market shares earn high returns on investment (ROI). This conflicts with the PIMS results that suggest that market share and ROI are positively related. What are the implications of this for the summary results from PIMS?

10. A common strategy for SBUs identified as dogs in the BCG matrix is harvesting (selling off). However, this is not always the case. Why might a firm choose to keep an SBU that was a dog?

CASE APPLICATION

Fisher-Price Toys:
Turmoil in Toyland

During the 1980s, while other toy manufacturers saw decreases in profit margins, sales growth, and market shares, Fisher-Price, the premiere global marketer of infant and preschool toys for more than 60 years, enjoyed outstanding financial results. Acquired in 1969 by the Quaker Oats Food Company, Fisher-Price provided significant profits to Quaker for many years. Ultimately, however, Quaker found Fisher-Price to be inconsistent with its business definition and lacking sufficient profitability for the firm. Quaker sold Fisher-Price to Mattel Corporation in 1992.

Early Business Definition

Fisher-Price, as an SBU of Quaker, established its own business definition, "to make long-lasting, high-quality, affordable and simple toys." The company focused on toys with intrinsic play value, ingenuity, and strong construction. The organization maintained the quality and reputation of its traditional products and consistently introduced innovative products for the infant and preschool aged groups. Fisher-Price emphasized expansion through extensive marketing research. This strategy allowed Fisher-Price to flourish during the early 1980s. In 1987 the firm had captured 64 percent of the preschool toy market.

As a result of the sales and profit potential in the preschool market, Fisher-Price found itself challenged in the late 1980s by a host of strong, well-established toy manufacturers. Playskool introduced an array of lower-priced products and Mattel obtained the licensing rights to include Disney characters in its product lines. This competion eroded Fisher-Price's market share (to 44 percent in 1990) and profits, and forced the company to post operating losses for all four quarters of 1990.

New Business Definition

Competition was not the only source of Fisher-Price's eroding situation. In the late 1980s, Fisher-Price strayed from its core product lines by introducing faddish toys for older children. Each year the company introduced an average of 60 new products that deviated significantly from its traditional, simple toys. The most visible failure was the electric sports car and child's camcorder. Neither product was consistent with the Fisher-Price strategy, nor did they capitalize on the significant brand equity of the Fisher-Price name. The sports car was expensive, of average quality, and aimed at older children who did not identify with the Fisher-Price name.

In attempting to market toys to a more mature audience (7-year-olds instead of 3-year-olds), the company ran into an image problem. "Fisher-Price is the preeminent preschool and infant brand. What it is not is a brand for older children. Kids have less preference for or even awareness of the Fisher-Price name than parents do, and for some kids, the name is too closely associated with babies," says Sean McGowan, a toy analyst at Gerard Klauer Mattison & Co.

Future Growth Opportunities

With its acquisition by Mattel, Fisher-Price is strategically placed to take advantage of significant growth opportunities. The company remains the worldwide leader in the preschool and infant market segments, manufacturing and distributing toys in the United Kingdom, Belgium, Canada, Germany, France, Italy, and Spain. The growth potential in these markets is outstanding given the open trade made possible by the European Community 1992 unification. Moreover, the recent opening of markets in Eastern Europe has provided an entirely new market with very low saturation levels and a propensity to buy anything American. Furthermore, Mattel's extensive global distribution system will enable Fisher-Price sales to further increase worldwide.

Clearly Fisher-Price's competitive advantage lies in the brand equity established with the infants and preschoolers of the first baby boom (1945–1964) generation. Parents have shown brand loyalty to toys popular during their childhoods. With the strength of Mattel supporting it, Fisher-Price is in an even stronger position to combat competition. Since acquiring Fisher-Price, Mattel has hired an expert toymaker from New Zealand to aid the company's return to its original goal of making simple, high-quality, affordable toys. With this support, Fisher-Price appears to have the potential to recapture market share and remain the leader in preschool and infant toy segments in the increasingly global marketplace.

Questions

1. How has the business definition changed at Fisher-Price? What have been the effects of these changes? Why?
2. How did internal and external factors affect the development of Fisher-Price's marketing strategy?
3. Looking at the BCG matrix, indicate which Quaker Oats quadrant Fisher-Price fit into. What does this placement suggest strategically for Fisher-Price?

Developing a Strategic Plan

Chapter 3 discusses the process that marketers engage in to accomplish strategic marketing planning. Every successful organization has a vision and definition that answers the question, "What business are we in?" Just like a business vision provides an organization with its thrust and direction, you, as a jobseeker, need to define who you are and what your career vision is.

The Career Focus in Chapter 2 helped you define yourself and examine the external factors in your target market. Next, you need to complete a *situation analysis* by looking at:

- *Internal factors*. These include your distinguishing experiences and competencies, as they would be valued in the marketplace for employment.
- *External factors*. These consist of your network of contacts in this marketplace. They can include resources provided by your school through on-campus recruiting, job posting, and alumni programs. Your own special array of friends, employers, classmates, and family are also considered external factors.
- *SWOT*. This analysis helps you evaluate the strengths, weaknesses, opportunities, and threats posed by the external and internal factors. In those areas where you identify internal negatives, you should seek ways to upgrade your skills and abilities and expand your networks. Strategies for upgrading could include obtaining additional work experience, selecting courses that will assist you, participating in school-sponsored programs, and pursuing additional career-directed contacts. It is important that you also recognize the limits of your schedule and arrange time to balance your career search with your schoolwork.

It is crucial that as you begin your career search, you develop a strategic marketing plan. If you do not take the time to do this, you will not be in a position to navigate your way through the rough seas of finding employment. Chapter 3 discusses steps that can be applied to your career search:

- *Establish objectives*. Define career objectives and set priorities that range from your ideal career to one that would be acceptable.
- *Form a marketing strategy*. Research your target markets and develop a list of target organizations that meet your objectives. Remember the four Ps as presented in Chapter 1. They will help you structure your job search.
- *Implement marketing tactics*. Establish detailed plans for developing the network you will need to reach the best possible contacts at your target companies. You should include a schedule of contacts, letters, telephone calls, and follow-up letters and calls. You also need to develop an advertising campaign for yourself that answers the question, "Why hire me?" Your campaign should focus on the entry-level needs at your target companies.
- *Marketing control* addresses both strategy (are we doing the right things?) and tactics (are we doing things right?). Because you and the marketplace are subject to change, you need to remember to periodically reassess your objectives, check your activities against your time frame for a summer job or employment, and adjust your plans accordingly.

Questions

1. What do you consider your internal strengths and weaknesses in obtaining your dream job? What can you do to enhance the positives and upgrade the negatives?
2. What are some acceptable alternatives to your dream job and the entry-level needs of the organizations you have targeted?
3. What strategy might you develop as an overall approach to these target companies? Use the four Ps as a frame of reference.
4. What steps would you take to build networks to employment contacts at your target organizations? Whom would you contact, what would you say, and when would you take each step?
5. Identify your strategic and tactical controls for this portion of your career search.

优 惠 广 场
9.5-9 折

Baby Gentle 寶柔系列

1 洗髮香波 原價：22元 優惠價：19.8元

2 浴露 原價：20元 優惠價：18元

3 潤膚露 原價：20元 優惠價：18元

4 爽身粉 原價：15元 優惠價：13.5元

CHapTeR 4

Global Marketing

Global
Marketing

Upon completing this chapter, you will be able to do the following:

■ **Discuss** factors that have contributed to the explosion of global business that has taken place since World War II.

■ **Explain** the significance for marketers of the major trade agreements that have occurred worldwide including GATT, the EC, and NAFTA.

■ **Identify** the types of companies involved in global marketing and explain how they differ.

■ **Describe** the ways in which three major external environments—cultural, legal/political, and economic—affect global marketers.

■ **Compare and contrast** four methods of operation in the global arena on the factors of control, risk, and commitment.

■ **Illustrate** standardized, localized, and combined approaches to global marketing across the four Ps.

*M*arketing *P*rofile

U.S. Companies Go Calling in China

Although in the United States Avon's direct sales method is somewhat out of date, it is now a revolutionary innovation in China. In late 1990, in the city of Guangzhou (Canton), capital of Guangdong Province in the People's Republic of China, Avon introduced the first direct selling operation in Chinese history. The company met its six-month sales projections in its first two months, and first-year sales were $4 million. In the next five years, Avon believes sales could reach $50 to $60 million. By that time Avon will have expanded into more cities and provinces.

Recruitment, increasingly tough in the United States, is a breeze in China. Avon's entrepreneurial, incentive-based selling system has helped attract an elite group of dealers that includes physicians, engineers, teachers, and computer scientists. One representative who makes about $120 a month as a pediatrician, earns ten times her salary as a part-time Avon representative. The lure of this kind of marketing and profit is taking China by storm.

One factor that has contributed to Avon's success in China is that Chinese women are anxious for a bit of glamour. After spending 40 years dressed in drab, unisex Mao suits with no make-up and uniform haircuts, the women of Guangdong provide a sure market for Avon's beauty products. Still, this was not an easy market for Avon to crack. In the mid-1980s, Avon spent five years negotiating with government authorities in Beijing for a venture in northern China. "We didn't get anywhere," says John Novosad, Hong Kong-based vice president in charge of Avon's Pacific operations. "They didn't understand the concept of direct selling and didn't know how to deal with it." Only after much frustration and considerable long discussions did Avon finally manage, in 1989, to hammer out an agreement for a joint venture (a partnership) with Avon holding 60 percent and Guangzhou's Cosmetics Factory the rest. A full line of Avon cosmetics is bottled and packaged in the Chinese factory.

There are some differences between the U.S. and Chinese operations. In the United States, Avon delivers merchandise directly to its representatives. In China, however, Avon has them pick up merchandise at branch depots, thus avoiding communication and transportation problems. Additionally, in China Avon employs salaried sales managers who recruit, train, and manage "franchise dealers." The franchise dealers cultivate clients and earn commissions of up to 30 percent of their sales, but they can also appoint additional sales representatives as a means of supplementing their commissions. A franchise dealer earns one-third of the 30 percent commission earned by his or her reps. On average, each franchise dealer appoints four representatives, giving Avon a sales force of more than 25,000 people in China.

Because door-to-door cold-calling arouses suspicion in China, Avon representatives do not ring doorbells. Instead, some sales are made to friends, relatives, and neighbors. The biggest volume of sales, however, comes from offices, factories, and schools. Franchise dealers are invited in by "danwei" (a term for work units) to give informal seminars on skin care, make-up, and grooming skills. Although there are some cultural differences, when it comes to selling hard, China's Avon reps can be as tough as any American Avon veteran. With an average per-capita income of only $350 to $400 a year for Chinese women, $2400 to $3000 in monthly commissions is a nice incentive in any language.

To many foreign companies, China is still the mysterious, inscrutable place it has been perceived to be for centuries. But for firms like Avon who are willing to commit the time and resources to understand China and the needs of its consumers, the country represents an opportunity of almost unimaginable proportion.

n the last 50 years since the end of World War II, a world marketplace has become reality. Organizations today face competition from around the world. *Competitiveness*, in fact, has been defined as the degree to which a nation, under free and fair market conditions, produces goods and services that meet the test of international markets while simultaneously maintaining and expanding the real incomes of its citizens.[1] Given the realities of global competitiveness and a world marketplace, marketers and consumers alike have come to accept the importance of global marketing. Large numbers of corporations and small businesses have moved across geographical boundaries and distributed their products to all parts of the world. American-made products can be found on every continent. Similarly, products produced in other countries are easily available in the United States.

Global marketing is the process of marketing outside national borders. The term is often used interchangeably with **international marketing.** Either term is correct when referring to marketing that takes place beyond the boundaries of an organization's home country. We will use the term *global marketing* because it emphasizes worldwide opportunities for a firm.

Many companies have found that global markets offer far greater potential than their domestic markets, especially for a product that has saturated that domestic market. Donald Keough, Coca-Cola's president commented, "When I think of Indonesia, a country on the equator with 180 million people, a medium age of 18, and a Moslem ban on alcohol, I feel I know what heaven looks like."[2] Figure 4.1 illustrates the differences in per-capita Coca-Cola consumption around the world. Clearly the potential for growth varies significantly across the globe.

Interest in global marketing has increased because trade among nations has exploded since the late 1950s. Nations have, of course, been trading for centuries. Improvements in communication and transportation since the 1940s and 1950s, however, have allowed consumers worldwide to learn about goods and services available beyond their national borders. Consumers have begun to demand these goods and services, thus creating the opportunities that have spurred growth.

In this chapter we examine the framework within which global marketing occurs. We begin with a look at trade among nations and the worldwide agreements that have enhanced it. We also discuss the types of companies involved in global

FIGURE 4.1
1992 Worldwide Per-Capita Consumption of Coca-Cola (8-oz. servings)

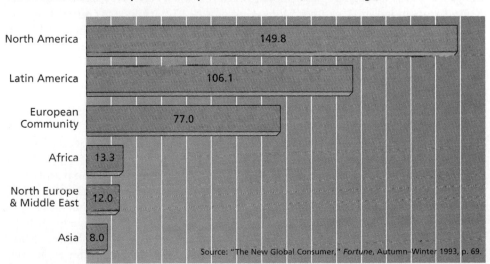

Source: "The New Global Consumer," *Fortune*, Autumn–Winter 1993, p. 69.

trade and marketing. The chapter then looks at the considerations involved in global marketing, starting with an examination of the external environment. Issues regarding the decision to enter an international market and methods of operating in the world market are discussed. Finally, we consider the development of marketing mixes for world markets. Global marketing is involved and complex and it is impossible to cover all of its intricacies in a single chapter. We hope, however, that the chapter will whet your interest enough so that you wish to learn more about global marketing, perhaps by taking a course dedicated to the topic.

GLOBAL TRADE AGREEMENTS

Trade among nations is the impetus behind global marketing. As trade among nations has increased over the last 50 years, global marketing has grown. It has been pointed out that improvements in communication and transportation have been largely responsible for this growth. Purposeful agreements between nations designed to enhance and improve trade have also contributed significantly to the growth of international trade and global marketing.

Since the end of World War II many countries have entered trade agreements to make international trading easier and more attractive. In many instances these agreements form trading blocs. A **trading bloc** is a group of countries, banded together, who trade as a single unit with other countries. The size of the trading bloc gives it economic clout in negotiating trades that a single country would not have. Similarly, nations sometimes form economic communities. An **economic community** is a group of countries that agree to operate as a single entity for economic purposes. Typically the economic community would agree to such things as no tariffs or trade restrictions among member countries.

General Agreements on Tariffs and Trade (GATT)

In 1948 23 nations signed the **General Agreements on Tariffs and Trade (GATT).** The purpose of GATT is to encourage unrestricted multilateral trade by binding participating nations to negotiating trade rules and by mandating penalties for any deviation. GATT established the **most-favored nation principle,** which ensures that all member nations receive the most favorable terms received by any nation from a GATT member. GATT members meet every two years to review existing agreements and negotiate new ones. Since its inception the GATT agreements have helped to liberalize world trade. The most recent round of talks, referred to as the *Uruguay Round*, concluded in December 1993. Currently 117 nations are contracting parties to GATT.[3] GATT, administered from Geneva, Switzerland, has been and continues to be a milestone in encouraging nations to conduct global business.

European Economic Community (EC)

In 1958 another important international agreement led to the creation of the **European Economic Community (EC),** also known as the **Common Market.** This agreement by Belgium, Denmark, France, Germany, Great Britain, Greece, Ireland, Italy, Luxembourg, the Netherlands, Portugal, and Spain, laid out a plan for a common antitrust law, removal of restrictions on the movement of capital and labor, and the imposition of uniform tariffs on imports from nonmember nations. At the beginning of 1993 virtually all remaining obstacles to free movement of people, goods and services, and capital within the twelve countries of the EC were removed. The EC forms a single market that is almost as large as the United States. Many Europeans anticipate that eventually Switzerland, Austria, and the remaining

Scandinavian countries will join the EC, which would make it the largest trading bloc in the world with 40 percent of the world's gross domestic product (GDP).[4]

Europeans generally like the idea of keeping pace in economic growth and technological innovation with the United States and Japan and feel that the EC is the key. A television commercial sponsored by the French government and intended to generate support for the EC opens with a skinny French boxer squaring off against a giant American football player and a huge Japanese Sumo wrestler. The boxer's future seems dim until his 11 EC partners arrive to help him. Faced with these 12 opponents, the football player and the Sumo wrestler turn tail and quickly leave the ring.

Because of its size, a strong EC will contribute to a healthy world economic system. The United States, in particular, stands to gain from a robust EC because of close U.S.–EC political, historic, and economic ties. In 1992, U.S.–EC trade amounted to $1,494 billion.[5] Many U.S. companies, including Lever Brothers, Procter & Gamble, and Quaker Oats, are working hard to increase their presence in Europe. Such firms often find that despite the EC agreement, Europeans see themselves as German, Greek, Spanish, and so forth, rather than as Europeans. Hence standardization of products, packages, and advertising across the EC must be undertaken cautiously.[6]

United States–Canada Free Trade Agreement

In January 1989 the United States and Canada reached a free trade agreement to remove barriers against trade and investment in the industrial, agricultural, and service sectors of their economies.[7] The agreement was intended, among other things, to increase business for Canadian firms and lower prices on both sides of the border.

Because the pact between the United States and Canada will not be fully effective until 1998, it is too early to say exactly how the two countries will benefit. Even before the agreement, about 75 percent of trade between Canada and the United States was free of duties. In the year following the agreement, Canadian reaction was less than enthusiastic. Although some companies gained business, others lost it. Furthermore, free trade did not immediately pay off in lower priced goods for Canadians.[8] Despite early skepticism, however, trade between the United States and Canada has increased from $153 billion in 1988 to $189 billion in 1992.[9]

North American Free Trade Agreement (NAFTA)

In February 1991 leaders of the United States, Canada, and Mexico announced they would negotiate a **North American Free Trade Agreement (NAFTA).** In October 1992 the agreement was signed by the three countries and in October 1993 the U.S. Congress approved it.

NAFTA is the product of long-standing trade trends in Mexico and Canada. Both countries historically have conducted more than 70 percent of their trade with the United States. Furthermore, Mexico and Canada have been heavily involved in production-sharing with U.S. companies for a long time. Production-sharing shifts labor-intensive production to less developed countries.

The move toward free trade in North America began in the 1980s. Mexico found itself in the midst of significant economic reform. Oil and commercial loans, the two products that had sustained Mexico's economy, were no longer sufficient to maintain its future economic growth. Foreign investment had become essential to the success of Mexico's economic reform. Hence the country began leaning toward free trade as a means of attracting foreign investment. Free trade with the United States would provide assured access to U.S. consumers, an enticement sufficient to encourage investors from outside Mexico.

The United States was also attracted to the idea of free trade with Mexico. In purely economic terms, the United States profits from Mexico's prosperity. Exports from the United States to Mexico increased from $12.4 billion in 1986 to $41 billion in 1992 as the Mexican economy improved.[10] This generated hundreds of thousands of jobs in the United States because about 70 percent of Mexico's imports come from the United States. Under NAFTA, Mexican tariffs on American-made products, which averaged 250 percent higher than U.S. tariffs on Mexican goods prior to the agreement, will be phased out over a 15-year period.

Proponents of NAFTA argue that the agreement will not only aid Mexico's growth but that it will also enhance the position of the United States in competitive world markets. Increased production-sharing between the United States and Mexico will allow the United States to lower prices for its goods on the world market. This type of arrangement has allowed countries in Europe and on the Pacific Rim to penetrate the U.S. market. Japan, for example, has deliberately shifted labor-intensive production to less developed neighbors in Asia.

NAFTA opponents argue that the agreement will take jobs away from U.S. workers. The U.S. labor force, it is argued, stands to lose from production-sharing between the United States and Mexico. Environmentalists have argued that NAFTA will lead American firms to relocate to Mexico in search of lower pollution-control costs, contributing to greater pollution of the North American continent.

The formation of a three-nation North American trading bloc creates a $7 trillion annual marketplace with about 380 million people. This is the largest economic community in the world. Opportunities exist not only for foreign-based marketers anxious to target all of North America, but also for Canadian, U.S., and Mexican marketers who are now more likely to market to their neighbors. Figure 4.2 illustrates differences in the spending patterns of U.S. and Mexican consumers. These differences, coupled with the lack of trade restrictions that NAFTA brought, should make marketers in some product categories anxious to target markets across the border. For example, as the figure indicates, Mexican consumers spend a larger per-

FIGURE 4.2
How People Spend in the U.S. and Mexico

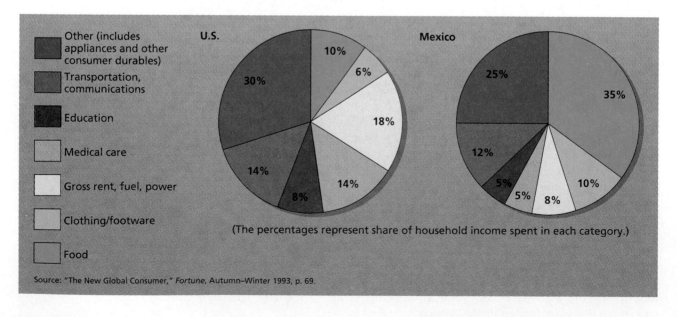

(The percentages represent share of household income spent in each category.)

Source: "The New Global Consumer," *Fortune*, Autumn–Winter 1993, p. 69.

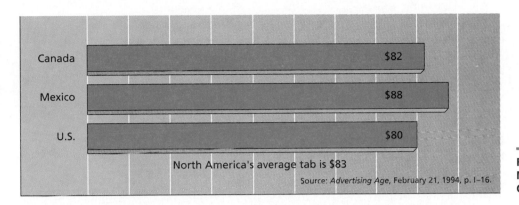

North America's average tab is $83

Source: *Advertising Age*, February 21, 1994, p. I–16.

FIGURE 4.3
North America's Weekly Grocery Spending

centage of their income on food. Figure 4.3 shows that this is not due solely to the fact that Mexican incomes are lower than those in the United States. In fact, Mexicans spend a greater number of dollars on groceries per week than do U.S. or Canadian consumers. Early marketing responses to this opportunity include the approach taken by Campbell's Soup. Anxious to expand its efforts in Mexico, the company created a North American division and a North American Marketing Council. The council focuses on all three countries in North America, exchanging brand data, product ideas, market research, and promotion concepts across borders.[11]

Other Trade Agreements

The Japanese are not sitting idly by while the Europeans, Mexicans, Canadians, and Americans form trading blocs and economic communities. Japan's approach is to integrate the Asian economies into a single economic unit. Led by Japan, and including Hong Kong, Singapore, South Korea, Taiwan (these four nations are known as the "Four Dragons"), Indonesia, Malaysia, the Philippines, and Thailand, the bloc will work to produce the highest value-added products in the world.[12]

With NAFTA, the formation of a three-nation North American trading bloc creates the largest economic community in the world.

Other nations of the world have also aligned to form trading blocs and economic communities. These include Mercosur (the four South American countries of Argentina, Brazil, Paraguay, and Uruguay). Furthermore, common markets exist among Caribbean countries, countries in Southeast Asia, and countries in West Africa.

COMPANIES INVOLVED IN GLOBAL TRADE AND MARKETING

Companies of all sizes and shapes are involved in global trade and marketing. Opportunities exist for large corporations as well as small businesses. Firms with significant experience in worldwide business as well as firms with little, if any, such experience engage in global marketing.

The nature of an organization's involvement and commitment in global trade and marketing defines the type of company it is. **Domestic firms** restrict their efforts to within the borders of the country in which they are based. **International firms** engage in trade and marketing outside the borders of their home countries. Generally these activities involve the selling of goods and services to markets in other countries. **Multinational corporations** engage in a variety of business activities outside the borders of their home countries. Multinationals not only sell in foreign markets but may also produce goods, conduct research, employ local work forces, and develop new products in a number of countries worldwide.

These three types of organizations represent a progression in terms of global commitment by a firm. Hence, an international company is a domestic company that operates in foreign markets. Its commitment to global business is limited. A multinational firm, on the other hand, has demonstrated a much larger commitment to global business by expanding operations beyond national borders.

It has been suggested that multinational corporations do not represent the ultimate commitment to global business.[13] A **world corporation** is a firm that has so fully

As globalization increases, companies find that as they pursue "foreign" markets, "foreign" companies pursue their home markets. Such a rivalry exists between Goodyear and Michelin.

integrated its operations into markets worldwide that its "home country" is of little consequence. World companies are integrated so well into worldwide markets that they appear localized even while operating on a global scale. One example of such a corporation is Unilever. The company is ostensibly based in Great Britain and the Netherlands. *Business Week*, however, estimates that 75 percent of its sales occur and 70 percent of its assets are held outside those two countries. Furthermore, five nationalities are represented on its executive board.[14] The country advertised in 32 countries in 1992.[15]

The transition from a multinational corporation to a world corporation may be a subtle one. It is still more common to hear the term *multinational*. Clearly, however, companies worldwide appear to be moving in the direction of greater and greater commitment to global business. In 1991, sales in foreign markets by U.S. multinationals represented 29 percent of sales by U.S. industries.[16] Table 4.1 lists the ten largest U.S.-based multinational firms.

Many of the world's largest corporations are not American. Nestle's, for example, a well-known name in the United States, is a Swiss firm. With only 2 percent of its sales occurring in Switzerland, however, Nestle's might certainly be considered a world corporation. While the United States tops the list of countries with the most companies among the 500 largest multinationals (with 161), Japan is not far behind with 128. Furthermore just three countries in the EC (Great Britain, Germany, and France) contribute another 102 multinationals to the top 500.[17]

Small Businesses and the Global Marketplace

Not all companies involved in global marketing are huge multinational corporations. As indicated at the beginning of this section, small businesses as well as large ones have found opportunities in the world market. Cohen's Fashion Optical, a midsize regional optical retail chain based in Long Island, New York, recently opened a store in Tashkent, Uzbekistan (a central Asian country that was formerly part of the

TABLE 4.1
The Ten Largest U.S.-Based Multinationals (1992)

Rank	Company	Revenue			Net Profit [1]			Assets		
		foreign ($mil)	total ($mil)	foreign as % of total	foreign ($mil)	total ($mil)	foreign as % of total	foreign ($mil)	total ($mil)	foreign as % of total
1	Exxon	79,227	103,160	76.8	4,207[2]	5,399[2]	77.9	48,205	85,030	56.7
2	General Motors	42,344	132,429	32.0	2,185	−2,621	P–D	44,472	190,908	23.3
3	IBM	39,890	64,523	61.8	−1,445	−6,865	D–D	46,597	86,705	53.7
4	Mobil	39,055[3]	57,389[3]	68.1	1,482[2]	1,710[2]	86.7	22,594	40,561	55.7
5	Ford Motor	35,700	100,132	35.7	−1,016	−502	D–D	49,414	180,545	27.4
6	Texaco[4]	26,311	50,041	52.6	712[2]	1,486[2]	47.9	11,155	29,813	37.4
7	Chevron[4]	20,573	46,612	44.1	872	2,210	39.5	12,311	36,423	33.8
8	Citicorp	19,249	31,948	60.3	1,266	722	175.3	105,564[5]	225,801[5]	46.8
9	E. I. du Pont de Nemours	17,468	37,208	46.9	685	975	70.3	16,011	38,870	41.2
10	Proctor & Gamble	14,582	29,362	49.7	428	1,872	22.9	10,389	24,025	43.2

[1]From continuing operations. [2]Net income before corporate expense. [3]Includes other income. [4]Includes proportionate interest in unconsolidated subsidiaries or affiliates. [5]Average assets. [6]Net income before minority interest. [7]Excludes Canadian operations. D–D: Deficit to deficit. D–P: Deficit to profit. P–D: Profit to deficit. NA: Not available.

Source: E. S. Hardy and S. Kichen, "The Forbes Foreign Rankings," *Forbes*, July 19, 1993, p. 182.

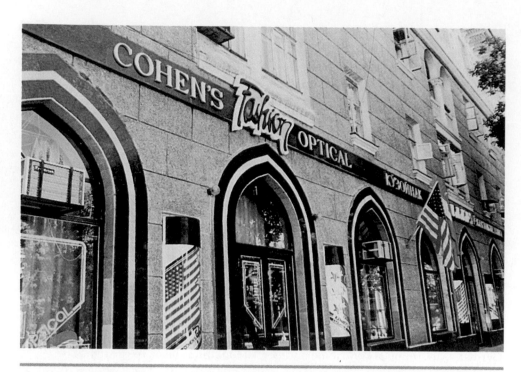

The Cohen's Fashion Optical store in Tashkent, Uzbekistan, sells an average of 250 to 300 pairs of glasses a day.

Soviet Republic). It was Cohen's first venture outside of the United States. The company found the Uzbek government a willing partner in opening the store, which sells an average of 250 to 300 pairs of glasses a day (compared to an average of 50 per day at its U.S. outlets).[18]

More and more countries in the world are aligning with each other to promote worldwide trade. More and more companies are developing operations that transcend national borders. These trends indicate that marketers must think globally when developing strategic marketing plans. A situation analysis must consider environmental factors on a worldwide basis. Market identification and evaluation must take on a global rather than national scope. Organizations must deliberate regarding the best methods of global operation. Marketing mixes must be planned with due consideration to world markets. This sequence of decision-making steps for global marketing is illustrated in Figure 4.4.

FIGURE 4.4
Steps in Global Marketing

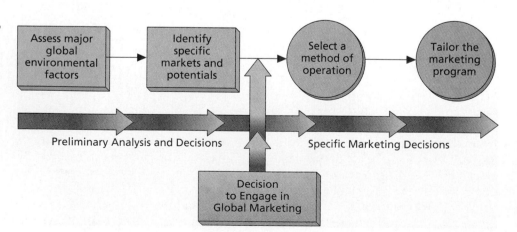

4-1   What factors have led to the controversies surrounding NAFTA?

4-2   Would you consider Avon (described in the "Marketing Profile" at the beginning of this chapter) an international, multinational, or world corporations?

YOUR MARKETING KNOWLEDGE

ASSESSING ENVIRONMENTAL CONDITIONS

The first step in developing a global marketing plan is to evaluate the environmental factors that may affect the plan. (Environmental forces were discussed at length in Chapter 2.) Three major environmental forces—economic, cultural, and political/legal—play crucial roles in global marketing. Changes in these three areas have been significant over the past four decades. Two recent changes are

- Asian countries such as Korea, Taiwan, Indonesia, Malaysia, and Singapore have experienced significant increases in their purchasing power. This increase makes those countries much more attractive as exporting targets.

- The overthrow of the Communist regime in the former U.S.S.R. has resulted in a struggle to establish free enterprise systems in the countries that comprise Eastern Europe and the Commonwealth of Independent States. This development has created both opportunities and headaches for many firms seeking to operate in this part of the world.

Economic Factors

Today there are more than 5.4 billion people in the world. Approximately 250 million, or only about 5 percent of them, live in the United States. Furthermore, population growth around the world far exceeds population growth in the United States. The worldwide rate of growth between 1980 and 1991 was 21 percent, while the growth rate in the United States during that same period was only about 10 percent.[19] Size and growth rate alone, of course, cannot account for marketing opportunity. The stage of a country's economic development helps determine the extent to which it represents a marketing opportunity.

Stage of Economic Development.   Several methods have been used to group the more than two hundred sovereign nations of the world according to economic development. According to one method, **developed nations** (sometimes called **industrialized nations**) include most of Western Europe, the United States, Canada, and Japan.[20] These nations are dominated by private enterprise and typically have a distinct consumer orientation. Their public sectors are also large and growing. Developed nations represent promising markets and investment opportunities.

The **developing nations** are moving from economies based on agriculture or the production of raw materials to economies based on industry. There are two groups of developing nations. In the first group are nations such as Australia, New Zealand, South Africa, Israel, Argentina, and Venezuela that enjoy a fairly high standard of living and are likely candidates for increased economic growth. The second group is still in the first phase of industrial development. Close to one-third of the world's population lives in such countries, which tend to have a low standard of living and little purchasing power. Countries in this second group desperately need the products and services of industrial nations, but have difficulty paying for them. Global marketing has not been an important consideration in such countries as India, Pakistan, Chad, Peru, Columbia, Sri Lanka, Tanzania, and Senegal. Even these countries, however, are beginning to join the global economy. For example, India with over 870 million people, includes the world's largest middle class, about 300 million strong. This largely untapped market is beginning to purchase more consumer goods.[21] Giants such as Coca-Cola and McDonald's are moving aggressively into India.

Also included in this second group of developing nations are many Eastern Bloc countries. As these countries have reformed from command economies to free enterprise economies, their struggles have been significant. Countries in Eastern Europe and the Commonwealth of Independent States are vast markets that have barely begun to be tapped. Consumers in these nations desire goods and services but typically do not have the money to pay for them. Additional difficulties are associated with doing business in these nations. For example, distribution systems are poor or do not exist and political and legal red tape can be daunting. Despite these problems,

Countries in Eastern Europe are vast markets that have barely begun to be tapped. Here, an ad for Kellogg's Corn Flakes, in Riga, Latvia.

many firms have worked to establish a presence in this part of the world. The United States Commerce Department reports that the value of American goods flowing into Russia totaled $3.625 billion in 1992 and $7.8 billion in U.S. goods flowed into Eastern Europe in 1993.[22]

A third stage of economic development is represented by the **less-developed nations.** Countries in this category contain populations with with very low literacy rates, limited technology, and low per-capita GDP. Many nations in Africa and Asia fit this description. In fact, more than one-half of the world's population live in less-developed nations. This large number of people, however, represents only about 15 percent of the world's income, hence their purchasing power is very small.

Not all marketers, however, see less-developed nations as poor marketing opportunities. Vodacom, the British cellular phone giant, is targeting rural communities in South Africa that currently have no telephones of any kind. The company is suggesting that such communities make communal purchases. Vodacom's objective for South Africa is to provide phone coverage to 70 percent of the population within five years. Currently 40 percent of South Africa's population has no phone service.[23]

Distinguishing among nations on the basis of stage of economic development is helpful to marketers. Such distinctions aid in assessing both the short-term and long-term opportunities that a nation represents. Developed nations represent the best short-term marketing opportunities due to the high standard of living and significant purchasing power enjoyed by the citizens. Developing nations, however, may represent the best long-term opportunities because they typically represent less saturated markets. As the standard of living and purchasing power of the developing nations increase, consumers will demand goods and services in large quantities.

Financial Aspects. Global marketers are also affected by the stability of the currencies in countries around the world and the exchange rates among countries. **Exchange rate** refers to the value of a country's currency relative to other currencies in the world. If the value of a country's currency fluctuates widely relative to the value of currencies in other countries, it will affect that country's sales and profit potential as a market. For example, in 1993 the value of the Uzbek ruble declined dramatically relative to just about every foreign currency. It took more rubles to purchase goods and services, especially from foreign countries. When this happened, Uzbekistan became a less desirable foreign market for global marketers. Currencies in developing and less-developed economies typically are less stable than those in industrialized nations. In recent years, however, even currencies such as the U.S. dollar, the British pound, and the Japanese yen have fluctuated rather widely. For example, in 1980 one U.S. dollar was the equivalent of 226.63 Japanese yen. In 1994, however, one U.S. dollar bought only 104.05 Japanese yen. Likewise, a British pound was the equivalent of U.S. $2.14 in 1980, but in 1994 a British pound could be bought with only U.S. $1.33.

All consumers are affected by varying exchange rates. As the value of a country's currency declines, imported goods become more expensive. Furthermore, global marketers may stop selling products in the market, since the higher prices result in decreased demand. Hence, consumers have fewer goods available and the ones that are available are expensive.

Many countries across the world have experienced recessionary economies during the early 1990s. A recession typically means decreased spending for consumers. It also affects the marketer's spending. Japan, for example, experienced a recession in the early 1990s which significantly affected marketers' advertising spending. In the 1980s, when things were booming in Japan, advertising rose by as much as 17 percent annually. That growth slowed in the early 1990s, however. In 1992, advertising dollars fell by 4 1/2 percent (to $33 billion), the first actual decline since 1965.[24]

Cultural Factors

Peoples' needs and wants and the way they satisfy those needs and wants—that is, the manner in which they consume—are in large part determined by culture. **Culture** is the sum total of a society's beliefs, morals, laws, customs, language, and art forms. It molds the way the people in a society behave, their standards for success and achievement, and even their view of what is good and ethical. Because every country has its own distinct culture and subcultures, the individuals in different countries often respond differently to particular marketing efforts. Thus, marketers must make sure that they understand a country's culture before planning and implementing a marketing program in that country. The failure to take cultural differences into account can lead to marketing problems and even marketing failure.

Cultural diversity can also create ethical dilemmas for global marketers. The "Spotlight on Ethics: Global Business Must Mind Its Morals" discusses the ethical issues faced by global businesspeople.

Language. The importance of language differences among countries should not be underestimated by marketers. The correct interpretation of words and phrases is crucial if promotional efforts are to be effective. Consider the way the literal translation of some American advertising messages, brand names, or terms might result in ridicule or even the rejection of products.

- When Coca-Cola first entered China, the company provided shopkeepers with signs printed in English. The Chinese added their own calligraphy, pronounced "ke kou ke la," which translated as "bite the wax tadpole."

- Herculon, a fiber used in carpets, and often referred to in describing carpeting, becomes "carpeting with the big derrière" when translated literally into Spanish.

- In Japanese, General Motor's slogan "Body by Fisher" translates as "Corpse by Fisher," and 3M's slogan that its Scotch tape "Sticks like crazy" comes out "Sticks foolishly."

In some instances, it may not be the literal translation, but rather the connotation of a phrase that is problematic. When Kmart entered Eastern Europe in 1992, it wanted sales clerks to wear name badges with the slogan, "I'm here for you." The slogan, used in the United States, is meant to connote friendliness and a consumer orientation. Female clerks in Czechoslovakia, however, were reluctant to wear the badges, fearing the slogan suggested an invitation to sexual harassment.[25]

Language can be particularly problematic when marketers are trying to sell products in multilingual countries. For example, all labels on goods sold in Quebec, Canada, must be in English and French. This problem is multiplied a hundredfold when products are marketed in India, where 203 dialects are spoken.[26]

Even a common language does not guarantee that a word or advertising message will be interpreted similarly in different countries. In England, for example, housekeepers hope that a furniture wax will not "tread off" rather than "wear off," and shoppers purchase a "tin" rather than a "can" of a grocery product.[27]

Color. Colors have different meanings in different cultures. Blue, which is considered a warm color in Holland, is seen as cold in Sweden. White is the color of death and mourning in China and Korea, and purple is an unacceptable color in many Spanish-speaking countries because of its association with death. In the United States yellow implies cowardice, while in India it carries religious and mystical overtones. In Malaysia green is associated with disease. Red is a popular color in China, but it is not well received in Africa.[28]

MARKETING *IN ACTION*

Global Business Must Mind Its Morals

As business goes global in the post–cold war world, executives could not be busier. They and their staffs are boning up on foreign languages, cementing local alliances, studying nations' licensing laws, assessing emerging markets and traveling to countries—Kazakhstan, Turkmenia—that didn't even exist a few years ago.

Tough stuff. But often neglected amid this busyness is another important and difficult task in global business: Developing moral standards.

Consider, for example, the basic question of which moral rules to follow. Our moral intuitions frequently blur when we cross national boundaries and our moral standards collide with those of other nations.

In Saudi Arabia, for instance, it is illegal to hire female managers for most jobs. But for an American company with operations there, is it immoral not to do so? Or: Is it immoral to avoid restrictive environmental laws at home by shifting facilities to developing nations? For answers to such questions, we cannot rely on national norms. We need principles that transcend boundaries.

But what are these principles?

Some executives might invoke cultural relativism, which holds that no culture's ethics are better than any other's. Under this standard, there are no international rights and wrongs. If Thailand tolerates the bribery of public officials, then Thai tolerance is no worse than Japanese or German intolerance. If Switzerland fails to find insider trading morally repugnant, then Swiss liberality is no worse than American restrictiveness. The concept of cultural relativism is simple and, unfortunately, fairly tempting when business is at stake.

For that reason, I and others reject cultural relativism. Its problem is that not all cultural differences lie at the fairly inconsequential level of bribery or insider trading. Cultural relativists must be prepared to tolerate all cultural differences. If one state endorses piracy—as some in history have—then one must grant piracy the same moral status as anti-piracy. Or look at crime prevention in ancient Rome. If a master was murdered, all the household's slaves were lined up and executed, without evidence or trial.

Moral absolutism has failings, of course. To measure all moral issues against a rigid, universal yardstick will disrespect valid cultural differences. For example, every nation wants to reduce pollu-

tion and to develop its economy. But different trade-offs of those goals may rationally be made by a third world country and by a developed one. The struggling nation, where people are starving, may tolerate more health-damaging smog in order to speed development.

So what is the answer? Clearly, to steer a middle course between moral relativism and moral absolutism. But where? Which moral values transcend national boundaries? We need rules that allow us to say to Union Carbide, "You committed a tragic mistake in letting safeguards lapse in Bhopal," while also respecting India's culture.

Many would say the transcendent values are those which are fundamental to the human condition—freedom, safety, dignity. Hard thinking is still needed to apply such a standard.

For instance, such fundamental principles probably require a company to help all customers injured by its own products, even accidentally. However, the help morally required can vary from culture to culture. A Japanese airline executive is expected to visit and make amends to the victims of an airplane crash, for example, but this is not so in the United States. The reason: America has a much more elaborate legal system for compensating victims than does Japan. Thus, the greater moral burden on the Japanese executives.

After a company establishes broad moral guidelines, it still must discover the best tools for making moral choices case by case.

One such tool is codes of ethics, such as the Sullivan Principles for the conduct of ethical business in apartheid South Africa, or the codes of individual companies, such as AT&T.

But ethical codes are inexact instruments. For example, IBM's renowned Business Conduct Guidelines are necessarily general. Also, codes usually speak in "thou shalt nots." Knowledge of the "no's" alone is often of little value in answering particular moral questions.

Guidelines that speak of rights can help fill the gaps in codes. For example, the average Central American begins work at age 11. If a company believes in the right to an education, then hiring children for full-time labor would violate this right, though hiring part-time might not.

In sum, ethical issues in international commerce go on and on. Thus, the best advice for executives, as they go about their busy global business, is to make time to study them.

Marketers must plan their products carefully, with full knowledge of the cultural implications of color. A product or even a package color that sends a negative message in a particular culture could spell failure.

Customs.   The customs of a society can and should influence marketing programs. The French, for example, are very interested and concerned about skin and body care. Both men and women tend to be heavy users of skin care products such as moisturizers. Cosmetics and toiletries targeted to the French market, consequently, are often positioned as aids to skin care. Promotionally, companies tend to move away from gimmicks and novelties. Scientific, almost paramedical approaches that emphasize products' features that enhance skin care tend to be most effective.[29]

Local customs regarding a single type of activity may vary significantly across the globe. Bribery is an example. **Bribery** is the act of giving, offering, or taking rewards for the performance of an activity that is known to be illegal or unjust. The practice of bribery in business activities dates back to ancient Egypt and Israel. Its acceptability varies significantly around the world. In 1977, the U.S. government enacted the Foreign Corrupt Practices Act, which made it illegal for U.S. firms to offer bribes to foreign government officials, regardless of local custom.

Values.   A person's values reflect his or her moral or religious beliefs and are learned through experiences within a culture. These values affect an individual's decisions to purchase certain products. They may also affect the type of promotions likely to appeal to the individual. For example, people in the United Kingdom tend to place a very low value on what they perceive to be vanity or superficial self-improvement. Hence, they prefer cosmetics and toiletries that are not perceived to be self-indulgent.[30] Calgon Bath's appeal to "get away from it all" in a bubble bath would not be likely to succeed in the United Kingdom.

Occasionally a company will challenge a cultural value in an attempt to be distinctive. Such was the case when Pepsico developed an advertisement for the Japanese market featuring rap singer, M. C. Hammer, who is shown singing an energetic rap song after drinking Pepsi. He then takes a few sips of Coca-Cola and immediately starts singing a slow ballad. After sipping more Pepsi, he regains his high-energy rap rhythm. The Japanese typically prefer ads that point out product benefits without criticizing competitors and this advertisement challenged those cultural values. In this particular case, however, Pepsi was ultimately successful in challenging the cultural norm. When Coca-Cola protested, Pepsi pulled the ads from the Japanese media. Later when Pepsi tried to buy media time to run the ads again, the Japanese media would not accept them. Pepsi returned to the airways, however, with a series of ads suggesting that Coke was fearful of the Pepsi ads, hence Japanese consumers would not be seeing them. When Pepsi offered a video of the ads that the media would not accept, more than 100,000 Japanese consumers responded. Pepsi sales in Japan increased 50 percent over the ensuing six months.[31]

Political-Legal Conditions

The political and legal environments faced by global marketers can present enormous challenges. Understanding and planning appropriate responses to the political-legal conditions within a single country is difficult in itself, hence dealing with these environments on a global basis creates a level of complexity that challenges even the most ambitious global marketer.

Political Stability.   The governments of countries around the world vary in terms of political stability. **Political stability** is the extent to which a country's government can be expected to remain strong and unchallenged. Instability is not limited to small, less-developed nations. Clearly the events that resulted in the breakup of the former U.S.S.R. illustrate the extent to which large, reasonably strong, and well-developed countries are vulnerable to political instability.

There can be no assurances that any particular country is immune from political instability. No doubt foreign companies that operated in such countries as Iran and South Africa felt they were doing so in reasonably stable environments. Political events in these nations over the past 15 years, however, have resulted in losses of money, equipment, and goodwill.

Although companies cannot guarantee that any foreign market will continue to be politically stable, efforts should be made to continuously assess the stability of any current or potential market. In recent years, many global marketers have hired staffs to monitor political conditions worldwide so as to better forecast the risks.[32]

Legal Considerations.   Global marketers must know how marketing is affected by domestic and international laws worldwide. Despite the rise in world trade and the agreements forged to encourage trade among nations, many countries, including the United States, have laws and regulations aimed at boosting firms at home. Such laws generally act to prohibit, or at least limit, foreign firms from doing business in home countries.

This move toward nationalism can take many forms. A country might, for example, institute requirements for minimum local ownership of companies, local product assembly, or local manufacture. Preference may be given to domestic suppliers for government contracts. Laws may place limitations on the number of foreign employees a firm can have. In Vietnam, a country just opening its doors to foreign investment, foreigners cannot own land. Business must be done through a Vietnam-based management company or in partnership with a local Vietnamese firm.

A country may also pass laws designed to be consistent with its political relationships (or absence of) with foreign countries. Hence, an American firm such as Caterpillar Tractor, is forbidden by U.S. law from selling its products to North Korea or Libya, because the United States does not maintain formal diplomatic relationships with these countries.[33] Likewise, for 19 years, since the height of the Vietnam war, U.S. companies were restricted by an American trade embargo from doing business in Vietnam. When President Clinton lifted the embargo at noon on February 4, 1994, Pepsico was ready. Just seven hours after the announcement that it was legal to operate in the country, bottles of Pepsi began rolling off an assembly line in Ho Chi Minh City. By the following evening, the company was running a television spot featuring Miss Vietnam.[34]

Political and legal maneuvers designed to shield a home country's businesses from foreign competition are referred to as **protectionism.** Protectionism is typically accomplished through the imposition of tariffs and quotas. A **tariff** is a tax imposed on products entering a country. The tariff is designed to result in higher prices for foreign products than for domestic products, thus encouraging consumers to "buy domestic." Trade agreements among countries typically reduce tariffs. The latest round of GATT talks resulted in an agreement by the EC, New Zealand, Japan, Canada, Australia, South Korea, Hong Kong, and Singapore to eliminate tariffs on products including pharmaceuticals, paper, and toys by 1999.[35]

A **quota** limits the amount of a product that can be brought into or sent out of a country. An import quota (a restriction on the amount brought into a country) aims to assure that domestic companies receive a certain portion of market share. Japan has for many years maintained strict import quotas on rice. Less than 1 percent of the rice consumed in Japan could come from sources outside the country. In late 1993 Japan relaxed its import quota on rice because heavy rains had wiped out more than 50 percent of the domestic rice crop.

ENTERING AND OPERATING IN THE WORLD ARENA

A company's decision to become involved in global marketing occurs in one of two ways. Either someone asks the firm to enter a foreign market or the firm decides for itself that the opportunities in global markets appear worth pursuing.[36] In the former case, the firm might be approached by an exporter of goods from its own country, an importer of goods from a foreign market, or even by a foreign government. A group of governments from countries in the Caribbean, for example, instituted the Caribbean Basin Initiative (CBI) in 1983. The CBI was designed to attract manufacturing companies from around the world to the Caribbean. By promoting the benefits of opening manufacturing facilities in Caribbean countries, the CBI managed to attract more than $2.2 billion in investment and provide almost 150,000 jobs by 1993.[37]

To assess the degree of opportunity in a foreign market, the firm needs to estimate the sales potential of that market. Forecasts and estimates are always subject to error, but they must be made to provide some picture of the opportunity a foreign market offers.[38] (Chapter 8 discusses the process of developing forecasts to estimate market and sales potential.)

Armed with forecasts of the market opportunity, a firm can decide whether to enter a given foreign market. If the decision is made to enter, the company must establish objectives and perform a situation analysis just as it would for any strategic planning effort.

Also critical for the company, once it has decided to go global, is the decision on the means it will use to enter foreign markets. There are four major alternatives: exporting, licensing, joint ventures, and direct ownership.[39] Which alternative a company chooses usually depends on three factors: the amount of control it wishes to maintain over its international marketing activities, the degree of commitment it wishes to make to international marketing, and the amount of risk it is willing to incur. Table 4.2 compares each of the four operating methods on these three factors.

Exporting

Exporting is sending products that have been produced in one country to a different country and selling them there. Exporting can be accomplished either directly or through intermediaries. In the latter case, the producing company sells the product to an intermediary such as an import-export agent (a specialist in the marketing of foreign-made goods in other countries). The intermediary thus assumes the responsibility for identifying target markets and for all other marketing activities required in the foreign market. If exporting is accomplished directly, the producing company retains responsibility for selling the product in the foreign market. This might be accomplished by establishing a sales branch in the foreign market or simply by

**TABLE 4.2
Comparison of Global
Methods of Operation**

Method of Operation	Control	Commitment	Risk
Exporting	Low	Low	Low
Licensing	Low to moderate	Low to moderate	Low
Joint venture	Moderate to high	Moderate to high	Moderate
Direct Ownership	High	High	High

Company	Export Sales $ Billions	Exports as % of sales
1. Boeing	17.49	57.5
2. General Motors	14.10	10.6
3. General Electric	8.20	13.2
4. International Business Machines	7.50	11.6
5. Ford	7.20	7.2
6. Chrysler	7.10	19.1
7. McDonnell Douglas	5.00	28.5
8. Philip Morris	3.80	7.6
9. Hewlett-Packard	3.70	22.6
10. E. I. du Pont de Nemours	3.50	9.4

Source: R. Farnighetti, ed., *Almanac 1994*, Funk & Wagnalls, New Jersey.

TABLE 4.3
America's 10 Biggest Exporters (1992)

sending salespeople into the foreign market on a regular basis. Table 4.3 provides information on the ten largest exporters in the United States.

With exporting, the actual presence of the producing company in the foreign market is minimal, hence the firm has limited control over international marketing activities. The way a product is promoted, distributed, and even priced in the foreign market is not controlled by the producer. In the case of exporting through intermediaries, the company has virtually no control over marketing once the product is sold to the intermediary. The presence of a sales force, as with direct exporting, results in slightly more control but it is still quite limited. Because the exported product is produced in the home country, however, control over production is great.

Exporting represents a limited commitment to global marketing. With this method of operation, it is fairly easy to exit a foreign market if sales or profits do not meet objectives. Because it represents only a small commitment, exporting is frequently the preferred method of operation for a company just beginning to explore opportunities in global business. This is especially true because limited risk goes along with limited commitment. With no investment in plant or equipment, the company risks little should the foray into the foreign market prove unsuccessful.

Many companies find exporting extremely profitable. Because this method of operation represents little commitment and risk for the firm, however, the profits realized through exporting are not likely to be so great as if the firm were willing to incur higher levels of commitment and risk. Hence, if a firm is successful with exporting, it may consider a method of operation that represents greater risk, a higher level of commitment to global business, and potential for even greater profitability.

In 1992 American companies exported goods worth approximately $448 billion, the European Economic Community nations exported goods worth $731 billion (including trade among EC members), and Japan exported about $340 billion in goods.[40] By comparison, the United States imported $533 billion worth of goods, the EC imported $764 billion worth of goods, and Japan imported $233 billion worth in 1992.[41] The difference between the values of a country's exports and imports is called its **balance of trade**. If exports exceed imports, there is a **trade surplus;** if imports exceed exports, there is a **trade deficit.** Figure 4.5 illustrates the balance of trade that existed among the United States, Japan, and the EC in 1992.

The United States has incurred a trade deficit since the early 1970s. This deficit had narrowed from a high of $170 billion in 1987 to approximately $85 billion in 1992. In 1993 the deficit increased to approximately $109 billion. Increased knowledge and increased interest by Americans in marketing products in the global marketplace has contributed to the trade deficit being smaller than it was in the late 1980s.

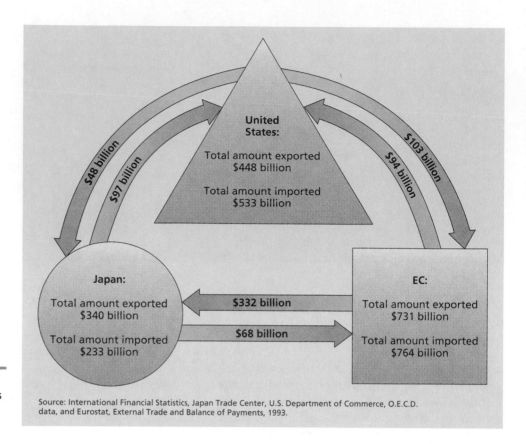

FIGURE 4.5
1993 Exports and Imports of Three Leading World Traders

The growth in U.S. exports has not occurred uniformly across all parts of the world. American exporters have taken advantage of growth opportunities in emerging global markets. Figure 4.6 compares various global markets in terms of share of U.S. export growth in 1992.

Licensing

Licensing is a practice whereby a company authorizes a foreign firm or individual to produce its product locally. The foreign licensee receives the right to produce the product as well as specifications for producing it. The licenser receives a fee or a royalty on products sold. A *licensing arrangement* may offer a foreign firm access to brands, trademarks, trade secrets, or patents. For example, Coca-Cola licenses firms around the world to produce Coke. The licensees not only receive the right to produce and market the product under the Coca-Cola trademark, but they also receive the secret formula for producing the drink. General Tire has licensed some foreign firms to use its tire technology and others to use its know-how to produce plastic film.[42]

   Licensing is attractive because it provides a means for companies to gain entry to foreign markets with little investment. The licensee bears the responsibility for supplying the capital to produce and market the product. Hence licensing can be an excellent method for a firm to expand rapidly with a minimum amount of money. To be successful, of course, the licenser must offer a product that interests consumers and licensees. To ensure this, a licenser might work to stimulate demand for the product in the foreign market. When the Berlin Wall fell, signaling the beginning of the end of communist rule in Eastern Europe and the former Soviet Union, Coca-Cola representatives were there passing out free six-packs.[43] Likewise, Coke has signed to sponsor the 1996 World's Fair to be held in Budapest, Hungary, where per-capita consumption of the soft drink in 1992 registered the third biggest jump in sales experienced in the company's 107-year history.

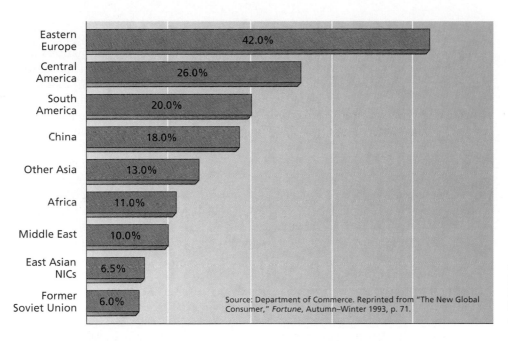

Source: Department of Commerce. Reprinted from "The New Global Consumer," *Fortune*, Autumn–Winter 1993, p. 71.

FIGURE 4.6
Emerging Markets for U.S. Exporters (share of U.S. export growth, 1992)

Licensing affords a company slightly more control over marketing activities in foreign markets than exists with exporting. This is because there is a formal contract between the licenser and the licensee. As part of the agreement, the licenser may choose to specify details of marketing activities that must be undertaken by the licensee. Coca-Cola might, for example, require a certain percentage of a licensee's sales be spent on promotion. If the agreement is not kept, the license could be revoked. Because licensees are operating in foreign markets without the continuous presence of the licenser, however, licensing cannot be characterized as a highly controlled method of operation.

An organization's commitment to global business is greater with licensing than with exporting. The firm's product(s) is now being produced in more than one country around the world. Some aspects of risk are also greater with licensing than with exporting. While it is true that a firm risks no capital in granting a license, there is risk to the company's image and goodwill should the actions of a licensee tarnish the reputation of the licenser. Many firms find licensing to be a very profitable method of global operation. Because it requires no investment by the licenser but allows international operations and sales, the profit potential, for a successful product, is significant.

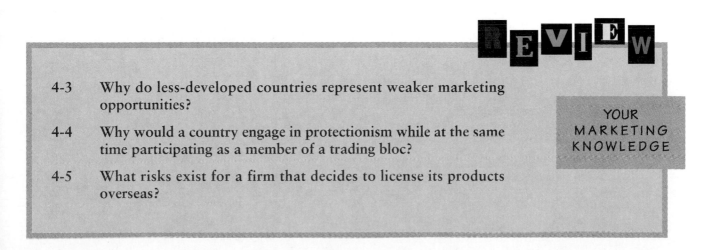

REVIEW

4-3   Why do less-developed countries represent weaker marketing opportunities?

4-4   Why would a country engage in protectionism while at the same time participating as a member of a trading bloc?

4-5   What risks exist for a firm that decides to license its products overseas?

YOUR MARKETING KNOWLEDGE

Joint Ventures

A **joint venture** is a company owned by two or more firms of different nationalities. It can be formed by one firm buying an interest in another or by two or more firms providing the resources to create a new and separate firm. When Toys "Я" Us entered the Japanese market by acquiring a Japanese partner, it used the first of these approaches. The second approach was used when Rockwell International, an American firm, coupled with Sumitomo, a Japanese firm. They formed a new venture to produce subway cars.[44]

Joint ventures can be formed to take a firm's existing products into a new market or to diversify into a new business. Kentucky Fried Chicken, a U.S. firm, achieved the first of these goals and the Mitsubishi Corporation of Japan achieved the second when the two firms joined forces to sell KFC chicken in Japan.[45] Each firm put up 50 percent of the capital to start the venture. In addition, KFC supplied the necessary marketing expertise and Mitsubishi provided the chicken, cooking equipment, and real estate for the store sites.

Joint ventures can also be formed to strengthen a firm's existing business or to obtain new products that can be sold in the firm's existing markets. Mexican-based Pacific Star de Occidente, a distributor of frozen and refrigerated products, entered a joint venture with U.S.-based Pillsbury in 1993. The partnership strengthened Pacific Star's business as distribution of Pillsbury products in Mexico doubled in the first year of the joint venture. Furthermore, Pacific Star was provided access to many Pillsbury products that were in demand by its consumers but previously unavailable in Mexico.[46]

For joint ventures to be successful, the two parties involved must maintain effective communication. Furthermore, agreement with respect to objectives, product specification, and marketing programs is important. Although it can be difficult to achieve all this between partners from different cultures, many successful joint ventures between seemingly diverse parties have been carried out. Coca-Cola, for example, has formed a joint venture with the city of Moscow, Russia. The partners formed a company that produces syrup and sells Coca-Cola from kiosks throughout the city.[47] The arrangement has allowed Coca-Cola to successfully enter a new market while providing employment (as well as Coca-Cola) to the citizens of Moscow.

Joint ventures provide a firm with a moderately high degree of control over international marketing activities. A firm that enters into a joint venture maintains a direct presence in the foreign market, along with its partner. Hence the firm shares direct control over marketing mix planning. This higher level of control (as compared to that enjoyed with exporting or licensing) allows the firm to ensure that desired standards for marketing activities are being met.

A joint venture represents the highest level of commitment to global marketing of the operational methods considered thus far. The two firms engaged in a joint venture have both made capital investments to cover plant and equipment. This higher level of commitment means that a joint venture carries with it higher risk than exporting or licensing. Should the economy crash, the political environment become unstable, or any other negative event occur, the partners to the joint venture must both bear the consequences. Of course, with the willingness to accept higher risk, comes the potential for greater profitability. A successful joint venture is likely to be more profitable for a firm than exporting or licensing in that same market would be.

Direct Ownership

Direct ownership occurs when a company owns and operates a facility in a foreign country with no local partner involved. The firm produces and markets products in the foreign country typically through a wholly owned subsidiary. Honda, the Japanese car manufacturer, produces automobiles in the United States. Its Tennessee-based operation has been so successful for the firm that some U.S.-produced Hondas are now exported to Japan.

Direct ownership provides the most control possible over the production, sale, and marketing of goods in a foreign country. Because the firm with direct ownership is solely responsible for planning marketing efforts, maximum control over such issues as price, promotion, and distribution method is possible. It is generally considered attractive to have such a high level of control because it allows the company to be absolutely sure that its plans are carried out. To be successful, however, the company engaged in direct ownership must work to make sure that its marketing ideas and plans are appropriate for the foreign market in which it is operating. Since there is no local partner to help the firm understand and adapt to the cultural, legal, and economic environments in the country, it is often a good idea to employ a work force that includes foreign nationals.

Commitment to a global marketplace is at its maximum with direct ownership. Firms engaged in direct ownership would typically be categorized as multinational corporations. Because of the high level of commitment that direct ownership represents, few companies would choose this method of operation for their first experience in global marketing. More likely, direct ownership would be the result of a progression of increasingly greater commitments to marketing in the world arena. A firm might, for example, begin its exploration of global marketing with exporting and then if that proves successful, increase its commitment through licensing or a joint venture, and ultimately go to direct ownership. Xerox Corporation operated in this manner when establishing itself in China. In 1987 the firm entered China strictly as a sales organization, exporting U.S.-made copiers to the country. After meeting with success and realizing the large market potential in China, Xerox established a joint venture with a Chinese company and began manufacturing copiers in China. In 1992 Xerox left its Chinese joint venture and established its own dealer network without a local partner.[48]

The main disadvantage of direct ownership comes from the risk that it involves. With this method of operation there is no one to share the burden of potential currency devaluation, declining markets, or government takeovers. For this reason it is important for a company contemplating direct ownership to carefully investigate the political and economic stability of the countries it is considering operating in. Of course, the increased willingness to take on risk that direct ownership represents is accompanied by an increased potential for profitability. While it is true that no one exists, under this method, to share the burden of risk, it is also true that no one exists with whom profits have to be shared.

Most countries have policies on the amount and types of direct ownership by foreigners. In Mexico, for example, The Law to Promote Mexican Investment and Regulate Foreign Investment formerly restricted foreign ownership to 49 percent of a business operating in Mexico. This law, in effect, meant that only joint ventures, not direct ownerships, were allowable in Mexico. President Salinas, however, enacted major revisions of the country's foreign investment regulations. Foreign ownership limits have been increased from 49 percent to 100 percent for businesses comprising about two-thirds of the Mexican economy. There are still some conditions foreign investors must meet. For instance, they must comply with environmental regulations, and their investments may not exceed $100 million. However, the fact that non-Mexicans can now own businesses outright, coupled with the easy trading policies that NAFTA has ensured, should make investment in Mexico and its future more attractive.

The United States is very open to direct ownership by companies and individuals from outside its borders. Restrictions on foreign investment do exist, however, in cases where the investor is from certain countries (Cambodia, Cuba, Libya, Nicaragua, and North Korea). Additionally, foreign investors cannot own more than 25 percent of a freshwater or coastal shipping enterprise, airline, or broadcast station. The government also closely monitors investment by foreigners in any company that affects national security. The relatively open policy maintained by the United States with respect to foreign investment and direct ownership has resulted in significant amounts of foreign-owned companies and property in this country. Cumulative investments by foreign-owned companies in the United States exceed $2 trillion. In 1992 alone, investment in the United States by foreign-owned companies exceeded $419 billion. While in the past direct ownership appeared to be a more popular method of operation for firms in other countries choosing to invest in the United States rather than vice versa, this balance appears to be changing as U.S. firms increase their level of commitment to global business. American direct foreign investments in 1992 totaled approximately $489 billion.[49]

TAILORING THE MARKETING MIX FOR GLOBAL MARKETS

Once the decision is made to enter an international market, the marketer must consider the components of the marketing mix. Marketing mix planning is important regardless of which method of operation is chosen for entering foreign markets. Research and discussion of global marketing has resulted in two opposing viewpoints of marketing planning for global markets. The first views marketing as a local issue, emphasizing differences among countries in customers, distribution systems, and marketing techniques, and advocates tailoring a marketing program for each country.[50] This is the **localized approach.** The opposing view considers marketing as know-how that can be transferred across borders. This view proposes that benefits accrue from using a **standardized approach** to global marketing.

The either-or debate between localized and standardized approaches to global marketing suggests too simplistic a view of this issue. A totally localized approach yields no competitive advantage in economies of scale, brand recognition, or market growth to a multinational firm. On the other hand, a standardized approach is not practical because of the differences in behaviors, customers, needs, marketing systems, and laws across the globe. Choosing between localized and standardized marketing will not help marketers develop a competitive strategy. Consideration of local issues and needs and using standardization to the degree possible must occur simultaneously.

Toyota is a company that has successfully combined localized and standardized approaches in global marketing. The Japanese auto manufacturer has used standardized channels of distribution and advertising approaches, but through research in local markets it has adapted its product to meet the needs of different consumers. In Canada, for example, Toyota tailors its cars to withstand severe weather conditions.[51] Usually tailoring a product for individual markets through product modification increases market share. Such adaptation, however, means additional costs. A company must determine whether the cost of a localized approach will be outweighed by the profits generated from increased market share.

Product

Marketers have several options as to the products they present in the global arena. They can sell the same product abroad that they sell at home, they can modify the product for foreign markets, or they can develop an entirely new product for foreign markets.

The simplest strategy is **product extension,** which involves offering the same product in all markets, domestic and foreign. This approach has worked successfully for companies including Pepsico, Coca-Cola, Kentucky Fried Chicken, and Levi's. Pepsi and Coke are currently battling for market share in both Russia and Vietnam, countries with small but growing soft-drink markets. Both firms are producing and selling the same cola to the Russian and Vietnamese markets that they sell to other markets around the world.[52] Not all companies that have attempted it, however, have found success with product extension. When Duncan Hines introduced its rich, moist American cakes to England, the British found them too messy to hold while sipping tea. Japanese consumers disliked the coleslaw produced by Kentucky Fried Chicken; it was too sweet for their tastes. KFC responded by cutting the sugar in half.

The strategy of modifying a product to meet local preferences or conditions is **product adaptation.** Cosmetics companies produce different colors to meet the differing preferences of European consumers. French women like bold reds while British and German women prefer pearly pink shades of lipstick and nail color.[53] Nestle's sells varieties of coffee to suit local tastes worldwide. Unilever produces frozen versions of local delicacies such as Bami Goreng and Madras Curry for markets in Indonesia and India.[54]

Product invention consists of developing a new product to meet a market's needs and preferences. The opportunities that exist with this strategy are great since many unmet needs exist worldwide, particularly in developing and less-developed economies. Marketers have not been quick, however, to attempt product invention. For example, despite the fact that an estimated 600 million people worldwide still scrub clothes by hand, it was the early 1980s before a company (Colgate-Palmolive) developed an inexpensive, all-plastic, manual washing machine with the tumbling action of an automatic washer for use in homes without electricity.[55]

Place

To succeed in a foreign market, a firm must have a good distribution system. The availability and quality of distribution channels, however, varies tremendously worldwide. Effective place planning in world markets usually presents a major challenge to global marketers. Three types of intermediaries are used most often by global marketers when penetrating international markets:

1. resident buyers within the international markets who work for foreign companies
2. international representatives of foreign firms
3. independent intermediaries who either purchase goods and sell them in international markets or arrange to bring buyers and sellers of goods together.

These intermediaries often sell products to wholesalers in the international market who, in turn, sell to retailers. Thus, a channel of distribution can be very long.

Allegiance to traditional methods of distribution in foreign markets can make global distribution planning a significant challenge. Some firms have been successful, however, in establishing distribution systems in international markets that differ from the established systems in that market. The "Spotlight on Global Marketing: Breaking with Tradition in Japan" discusses this challenge of distribution.

In general, the effectiveness of the distribution in a country depends on its level of economic development. Less-developed nations have less adequate distribution channels. In the Philippines, for example, Procter & Gamble sells soap products door-to-door, due to the country's poorly developed distribution system.

Promotion

Global marketers have long struggled with the issue of standardized versus localized approaches in promotion. Standardized promotion is not only less costly but also builds brand awareness and image worldwide. Unfortunately, the effectiveness of standardized promotional approaches is often limited due to the variety of cultural

MARKETING *IN ACTION*

Breaking with Tradition in Japan

Japan is a country known for its traditional ways. When it comes to distribution systems, however, tradition has meant inefficiency and high prices. All that may be changing.

Historically, Japanese distribution channels have been very long. By the time a consumer purchased a product, its title probably had passed through a minimum of six intermediaries. Some of these intermediaries may not have even had possession of the product. Each, however, added its markup to the item, resulting in not only a slow distribution process but also very costly goods for Japanese consumers.

The reasons for this cumbersome system are primarily political and social. Japanese economic policy since World War II has made nurturing an extensive array of small, neighborhood retailers a top priority. In order to serve the vast number of small businesses, sometimes on a daily basis, secondary and tertiary wholesalers have evolved. These wholesalers obtain goods from large wholesaling or trading companies and then distribute them to the hundreds of thousands of small shop owners throughout Japan. Socially, the traditional system nurtures business relationships, which are very important in Japanese culture. Many such relationships are based on long-standing personal friendships.

As the traditional system evolved, self-preservation became another factor in its continuance. With 20 percent of the Japanese work force employed in distribution, significant changes would mean the loss of many jobs. Japanese consumers, tired of paying high prices, are making demands that appear to be bringing about changes in the traditional system. A recent Gallup poll found that price, rather than quality, is the determining factor in purchases for a majority of Japanese consumers.

In response to their consumers' cries for lower prices, a growing number of retailers appear willing to buck the existing system. Discount retailers are springing up throughout Japan. Daiei Inc., for example, has opened Kou's, a wholesale membership club (similar to Sam's Club or Price Club in the United States),

in the Japanese port city of Kobe. Merchandise sold at Kou's is typically purchased directly from manufacturers in Japan or abroad (including the United States). Daiei's bypass of traditional distribution routes has resulted in prices to consumers that represent discounts of up to 80 percent over traditional retailers. In the first year of operation, 146,000 people became members of Daiei's club.

Such willingness of Japanese retailers to forge new alliances outside the traditional distribution systems has created considerable opportunities for foreign-based manufacturers interested in exporting to Japan. A dozen U.S.-made Spalding golf balls sell at Kou's membership club for the equivalent of U.S. $26.80. Elsewhere in Japan, where the balls have come through the traditional distribution system, their price is $72 per dozen. Not too surprisingly, the lower prices translate into higher demand for the imported products.

Some foreign companies have been able to establish their own distribution networks in Japan. One such company is U.S.-based Amway Corporation. Amway, a producer of cleaning products and other consumer goods, has been extremely successful in Japan using a distribution system that consists of local distributors who recruit additional local distributors. This system, sometimes referred to as **multilevel marketing,** has worked effectively for many products in the United States. The concept, however, was new to Japan when Amway introduced it. Amway uses no Japanese intermediaries and products are sent directly from the factory where they are produced in Michigan to Amway distribution centers in Japan. Salespeople obtain the goods from the distribution centers. Amway currently employs a sales force of 800,000 in Japan and has yearly sales of U.S. $1.25 billion. These figures make Amway the second biggest U.S. company in Japan (the biggest is Coca-Cola).

The changes occurring in the Japanese distribution system would seem to suggest that marketers committed to a market-driven focus will triumph, even if it means breaking with tradition in a country known for its traditional ways.

characteristics. Hence creativity and versatility are essential to developing effective international promotional campaigns. A 1988 study found that only 9 percent of U.S. multinationals claimed to use standardized approaches, 37 percent claimed to use localized advertising, and the remaining 54 percent used a combination strategy.[56] In 1992, it was found that a majority of U.S. manufacturers of consumer durables used localized approaches to advertising in global markets.[57]

Examples highlight the various approaches to promotion in global markets:

- Sciko used a standardized approach to sell its watches by launching an advertising campaign tied to the 1992 Summer Olympics. The slogan "The Measure of Greatness" was featured in centrally created ads that were shown worldwide.[58]

- Rimmel Cosmetics, marketers of Cutex brand, use a localized approach to advertising. In the United States, print ads feature glamorous, "perfect-looking" models, while in Europe ads feature models with more achievable, less perfect looks. The difference reflects the fact that European consumers tend to be more skeptical and more modest than American consumers.[59]

- Colgate-Palmolive combines standardized visual images with localized messages for many of its products. Colgate toothpaste, for example, uses a picture of a smiling globe in advertisements in almost every country where the product is marketed. The message that accompanies the picture, however, is localized to each market.[60]

Price

Prices in international markets are frequently determined by a cost-plus approach. This means that the price for the product is set by adding some level of profit to the cost of producing and marketing the good. Because market costs such as tariffs and shipping can be high for products sent into foreign markets, this approach can result in prices higher than those charged by local competitors. If consumers are willing to pay higher prices for imported goods, this may not be a problem. Often this is the case in industrialized nations. If, however, the foreign market is a developing or less-developed economy, global marketers must be particularly cognizant of the local market's ability to pay. Often firms will look for ways to cut costs, perhaps through simplified products or the use of local labor, in order to offer competitive prices. General Motors, for example, produces its S-10 truck for the Chinese market using local Chinese labor. This allows the firm to price the product competitively.[61]

The practice of selling products in foreign markets at prices well below that charged in a firm's domestic market is called **dumping**. Japanese firms have often been accused of dumping products such as VCRs and computer chips. Fuji, a Japanese firm, has been criticized for dumping fax paper in the U.S. market.[62] A firm might engage in dumping in order to build market share in the foreign market by offering a competitive price. Alternatively, dumping may occur because domestic demand has declined and the firm can no longer sell its inventory of the product.

PERSONAL COMPUTER EXERCISE

Globalization of marketing and manufacturing functions has increased dramatically in recent years. In this PC Exercise, you will be able to evaluate several international business opportunities. What sources of competitive advantage can globalization of a business create?

KEY POINTS

■ Trade agreements among nations worldwide as well as technological advances in transportation and communication have led to tremendous growth in global business since the end of World War II.

■ Trade blocs and economic communities are formed by groups of countries that band together to enhance trade among nations. The EC, comprised of twelve European nations, is probably the most prominent of these groups.

■ Major trade agreements include General Agreement on Tariffs & Trade (GATT), U.S.–Canada Free Trade Agreement, and North American Free Trade Agreement (NAFTA).

■ Companies of all sizes, worldwide, appear to be moving in the direction of greater commitment to global business.

■ The stage of economic development in a nation affects the extent to which it represents an opportunity for global marketers. Developed nations represent the most promising markets and investment opportunities. Less-developed nations do not offer very good opportunities.

■ Cultural factors including language, the meaning of various colors, and customs vary worldwide. It is critical for a global marketer to understand the cultural aspects of a market he or she is considering.

■ Cultural diversity makes decisions about ethical behavior more challenging to a global marketer than to a domestic marketer.

■ A country's degree of political stability as well as the laws and statutes it enforces affect its desirability as a global marketing target.

■ Exporting is a method of entering an international market that represents only a small risk. The exporter, however, has little control over marketing activities. Exporting represents a fairly small commitment to global marketing.

■ Licensing is a way of expanding rapidly in the world market with little capital investment. The risks are greater than with exporting (but still small). By licensing the marketer maintains some control of marketing activities. Licensing represents a slightly greater commitment to global marketing than exporting does.

■ A joint venture allows a marketer to exert a fairly large amount of control over marketing activities in a foreign market. It represents a significant commitment to global marketing. The risks inherent in operating in a foreign market are greater with a joint venture than they are with exporting or licensing.

■ Direct ownership represents the ultimate in control and commitment to global marketing. Because of the risk in this method of global operation, companies rarely engage in direct ownership as their first means of doing global business.

■ A standardized approach to global marketing requires a marketer to ignore the inherent differences among world markets when planning marketing mixes.

■ A localized approach to global marketing involves the assumption that there are few or no commonalities across markets worldwide. Hence this approach requires developing unique marketing mixes for each market.

KEY TERMS

global marketing (111)
international marketing (111)
trading bloc (112)
economic community (112)
General Agreements on Tariffs
    and Trade (GATT) (112)
most-favored nation principle (112)
European Economic Community (EC) (112)
Common Market (112)
North American Free Trade Agreement
    (NAFTA) (113)
domestic firms (116)
international firms (116)
multinational corporations (116)
world corporation (116)
developed nations (119)
industrialized nations (119)
developing nations (119)
less-developed nations (121)
exchange rate (121)

culture (122)
bribery (124)
political stability (124)
protectionism (125)
tariff (125)
quota (125)
exporting (126)
balance of trade (127)
trade surplus (127)
trade deficit (127)
licensing (128)
joint venture (130)
direct ownership (130)
localized approach (132)
standardized approach (132)
product extension (132)
product adaptation (133)
product invention (133)
multilevel marketing (134)
dumping (135)

ISSUES FOR DISCUSSION

1. What are some of the potential negative factors associated with the creation of blocs of free trade nations?

2. Describe the differences between an international firm, a multinational corporation, and a world corporation.

3. Multinational corporations have been accused by critics of earning high profits by utilizing inexpensive labor in less-developed countries so as to avoid high labor costs elsewhere. Supporters argue that multinationals are helping such less-developed nations by providing jobs. Which view do you support?

4. How should a global marketer go about evaluating the potential for microwave ovens in developing nations?

5. Global marketers have sometimes been criticized for introducing "non-necessity" products in less-developed nations. Does, for example, a less-developed nation need Coca-Cola? Comment.

6. What cultural factors should a U.S. producer of snack foods investigate before planning a marketing strategy for Russia?

7. Describe how a joint venture works. Is there a need for legal expertise to put one together?

8. Why might a marketer choose to license his or her product rather than export it to foreign markets?

9. Which of the three product strategies—extension, adaptation, or invention—would an exporter be most likely to engage in? Explain.

10. Is dumping an ethical practice? Why or why not?

CASE APPLICATION

Tobacco and Global Markets:
An Ethical Issue?

Are the ethics of U.S.-based tobacco companies, as well as the ethics of the U.S. government when it comes to the tobacco industry, going up in smoke? Consider the facts.

Tobacco companies in the United States have significantly increased their marketing efforts in global markets. These efforts appear to be in response to marketing research indicating that the cigarette business in the United States is getting weaker each year. Markets in Latin America, Europe, Africa, and Asia have been targeted. The Asian market, for example, where $90 billion worth of cigarettes are sold each year, has received considerable attention from U.S. producers Philip Morris and R. J. Reynolds. The companies have received support in their efforts from the U.S. government, which has pressured South Korea, Japan, and Taiwan to open their markets to the U.S. companies. The result of all these efforts? Smoking-related deaths have overtaken communicable diseases as Asia's top killer.

Another global market that tobacco firms have targeted for growth is Eastern Europe and the former Soviet Bloc. Seven hundred billion cigarettes are sold annually in this market, making it 40 percent larger than the U.S. market. Philip Morris and R. J. Reynolds, along with B.A.T. Industries of Britain and Reemstma of Germany, have entered this part of the world with a variety of operational methods. Philip Morris (PM), for example, invested $200 million in 1993 to acquire direct ownership of the Kazakhstan government-owned cigarette factory. The world's largest tobacco company, PM has also acquired factories in Russia, Krasnodar, Lithuania, Hungary, and the Czech Republic. Competitor R.J. Reynolds has acquired direct ownership in Russia, Poland, and Hungary, and set up two joint ventures in the Ukraine.

Promotion in these countries typically emphasizes the allure of western culture. For example, L & M cigarettes are touted as The Way America Tastes. Despite the efforts of world health organizations to stop them, tobacco companies continue to advertise on television in such countries as the Czech Republic and Hungary.

Tobacco companies, of course, are looking to make a profit. Thus, market development in global markets is an understandable, if easily criticized, strategy as western markets look less and less attractive. The actions of the U.S. government regarding this controversial industry may be more difficult to understand. Its signals appear mixed at best.

On one hand, the United States federal government, as well as state governments and local municipalities, have passed a myriad of legislation aimed at supporting the message Americans have received for years, namely: Smoking is hazardous to health. Smoking is now banned in most workplaces and in most public buildings in the country. It is also banned on all domestic airline flights with durations of fewer than six hours, which is enough time to get from coast to coast. In most states, cigarettes cannot legally be sold to individuals under 18 years of age, and by law every pack of cigarettes sold has to carry a warning from the U.S. Surgeon General. Furthermore, tobacco companies cannot advertise on television. However, while the government states that it supports anti-smoking campaigns, it provides millions of dollars in subsidies to U.S. tobacco growers and pressures foreign countries to open their markets to U.S. tobacco companies.

Questions

1. What might be the influence of economic factors on the acceptance of foreign-based tobacco companies in developing nations such as South Korea or Poland?
2. Why would Philip Morris and R. J. Reynolds use such a large variety of operational methods in marketing to countries of Eastern Europe and the former Soviet Bloc?
3. Present at least two arguments to advance each side of a debate regarding whether foreign-based tobacco companies' efforts in global markets are ethical.
4. For many people, the U. S. government's support of the tobacco industry both at home and abroad is ethically questionable. What do you think?

A World of Opportunity

As corporations face competition from around the world, they look to expand market opportunities and niches. Opportunities to position products in developing and less-developed nations will be the trend of the future. How do you harness this information and apply it to your career search? What career opportunities are presented by the globalization of marketing? The chapter discusses the importance of understanding cultural factors such as language, color, and customs to know the market that you will enter.

As industry becomes more global, there are increased opportunities for you to forge a career with an international focus. American products can be found everywhere. International experience can give you a competitive advantage in your job search, regardless of the area in which you plan to specialize.

- You can begin to pursue your interest in the international marketplace as an undergraduate. You might consider studying abroad for a semester or a year. Most colleges have an international office where you can speak with counselors about the educational and work-study programs available.
- On graduation, you might choose to travel extensively in a part of the world that interests you. You could gain international experience, learn or brush up on a foreign language, and develop sensitivity to a culture different from your own.
- One way to embark on an international career is to join a company that requires its employees to do some work abroad. Other ways include seeking positions in international nonprofit organizations, looking for foreign service opportunities, and considering the Peace Corps.

You can find information on job opportunities and career seminars with an international focus in your local bookstore, career office, and through continuing education programs.

Questions

1. Pick a country or area of the world that interests you and explore the programs that are available either through a semester abroad or through opportunities upon graduation.
2. Identify the materials that you used to get information about the opportunities suggested above.

Part One

The Story of Harley-Davidson Motorcycles

Overview

Harley-Davidson, Incorporated, the only remaining major American manufacturer of motorcycles, is riding the crest of success as measured by consumer demand, revenue, and profits. The company produces motorcycles and related products that espouse a unique attitude and inspire power, excitement, and individuality both in Harley-Davidson riders and in much of the nonriding public.

As a company, Harley-Davidson has evolved through stages of development that have affected business throughout the past century. When Harley first began to produce motorcycles in 1903, it entered the *production concept* stage, during which a company presumes that supply will create its own demand for a product. During this stage, there was no conscious effort to increase mass market sales; Harley-Davidson's primary goal was simply to develop a technically superior motorcycle. However, as the firm's success became more evident, it moved into the *sales concept* stage, during which improved manufacturing processes allowed supply to outpace demand. The natural response was to increase sales efforts, and at this time Harley-Davidson developed its worldwide dealership network.

Over the last two decades, Harley-Davidson has entered into the *marketing concept* stage, which involves a strong focus on consumer needs and has included developing the Harley Owners Group (H.O.G.), the world's largest organization of motorcycle enthusiasts. The company has also led a Continuous Improvement campaign for motorcycle quality and incorporates consumers' input into the design of its products. Currently Harley-Davidson is establishing itself as a relational marketer by nurturing customers' needs in motorcycling, parts, accessories, apparel, and club membership. The result of this relational focus is that Harley-Davidson has a loyal repeat-buyer group, with more than 90% of owners saying they intend to purchase another Harley-Davidson motorcycle.

How Did It Happen?

Harley-Davidson's success did not come overnight nor has it been sustained continuously. In the early 1900s, Harley-Davidson was one of more than 100 U.S. motorcycle manufacturers on the scene. However, when Ford Motor Company first introduced its Model T car, the motorcycle market was devastated, and most of the companies folded by 1920. Harley-Davidson did well in the 1960s and early 1970s in selling to an often misunderstood market. However, the company went from claiming 100% of the U.S. heavyweight motorcycle market to less than 25% in the early 1980s, when higher-quality and lower-priced Japanese offerings dominated.[1]

At the time, Harley-Davidson maintained that Japanese manufacturers were producing motorcycles at record rates and flooding the U.S. market, despite the fact that a sharp decline in new motorcycle purchases had been occurring. As a result, dealers of imported motorcycles resorted to intense price discounting to relieve their inventories, which created an unfair selling environment for Harley-Davidson. In late 1982, Harley-Davidson appealed to the International Trade Commission (I.T.C.) to increase tariffs on imported heavyweight motorcycles to help support the company against Japanese competition. Based on the I.T.C.'s recommendations, in 1983 the U.S. imposed additional tariffs, effective for five years. Buoyed by the tariffs, Harley-Davidson had regained the top position in the U.S. heavyweight market by the end of 1986. On firm financial footing, Harley-Davidson felt confident enough to petition the I.T.C. for early termination of the tariffs in 1987.

Over the years, Harley-Davidson's heavyweight motorcycle market share plunged from 75% in 1973 to 23% in 1983.[2] However, in 1994, Harley-Davidson held more than 60% of the heavyweight market in the United States[3] and claimed more than 50% of that market in Canada and Australia.[4] In addition, Harley-Davidson competes very effectively in Japan where its market share is more than 15%. In 1993 Harley-Davidson sold more than 3,500 cycles in Japan, a 17% increase over 1992.[5]

The Harley-Davidson Family

The first Harley-Davidson motorcycle was built in 1903 in Milwaukee, Wisconsin. There

William Harley and the Davidson brothers (Walter, Arthur, and William) designed and built high-quality motorcycles from scratch. The reputation of the bikes spread, and throughout the 1920s and 1930s police departments, postal workers, and even the U.S. military began to use the motorcycles. In WWII, all of Harley-Davidson's production (more than 90,000 units) was sold to the U. S. government for military use.

Postwar success brought about increased interest in product diversification. Harley-Davidson began an overseas expansion in 1960. The company bought half of the Italian cycle company Aeronautica Macchi S.p.A. in Verese, Italy, and created Harley Davidson International, based in Switzerland, to oversee operations. The new Acromacchi Harley-Davidson plant built smaller bikes for both European and domestic markets. During the early 1960s, Harley-Davidson also diversified stateside. Although the company's effort to produce snowmobiles ultimately failed, by 1976 they became the number one producer of gas and electric golf carts. In 1986, Harley-Davidson bought Holiday Rambler Corporation, a leading manufacturer of premium-quality motorhomes, trailers, and commercial vehicles. In 1994, this division represented more than 20% of Harley-Davidson's sales.

Harley-Davidson went public in 1965 and was bought by a diversified corporation, American Machine and Foundry Company (AMF), in 1969. Harley-Davidson then became one of the 70 subsidiaries of AMF that fought for funds, supports, and resources. In 1981, in a steeply declining market, a group of 13 Harley-Davidson executives bought the company back from AMF. The buy-back was a bold move that eventually paid off, and the Harley executives took the company public again in 1986. Harley-Davidson was listed on the American Stock Exchange in 1986 and moved to the New York Stock Exchange in 1987. In 1968, total sales exceeded $42 million; in 1993, they exceeded $1.2 billion.[6] In addition, a massive expansion to bring annual volume to 100,000 units is projected for completion in 1996[7], up from 37,000 units in 1986. These figures clearly reflect the dramatic changes made since the mid 1980s.

The Quality Approach Applied

In the 1950s Harley-Davidson built its motorcycles with "state-of-the-art" management and marketing practices. However, production and quality faltered briefly in the late 1970s and early 1980s due to a push for quantity that overshadowed quality. In response, the company embarked on a revitalization program with excellent results. Harley-Davidson followed the example of Japanese manufacturers and implemented the Materials-As-Needed (M.A.N.) system of assembly, a version of "just-in-time" inventory management. The company also instituted an Employee Involvement process, which encourages workers to take responsibility for continuously improving quality. All manufacturing employees were trained in Statistical Operator Control (S.O.C.), enabling them to identify potentially bad motorcycle parts.

According to Richard F. Teerlink, President and CEO of Harley-Davidson, the company has recognized the fact that "solutions lie in knowing the business, knowing customers, and paying attention to detail."[8] Teerlink is emphatic in his assertion that Harley-Davidson is "not just selling a motorcycle; rather, we're selling excitement, a life-style, a way for people to transform themselves." Through its motorcycles and related products, Harley-Davidson makes this excitement possible for an impressive legion of loyal customers.

Questions

1. What environmental changes in the United States might affect Harley-Davidson's growth in the next five years?
2. What consumer needs would you recommend Harley-Davidson address in order to increase sales to first-time riders?
3. In considering the firm's early international growth (it sold bikes in 67 countries by 1935), was Harley-Davidson ahead of the marketplace? Defend your answer.
4. What do you think is the ideal marketing mix for Harley-Davidson in the 1990s?
5. What recommendations would you make to Harley-Davidson for changing or maintaining its position?

part II

The MARKeTPLace

CHapTeR 5

Segmentation, Targeting, and Positioning

Upon completing this chapter, you will be able to do the following:

■ **Describe** the process used to identify a market.

■ **Explain** the concept of market segmentation and its value to a marketing-oriented firm.

■ **Discuss** how geographic, demographic, psychographic, and behavioral variables can be used to segment markets.

■ **Identify** the criteria that should be considered in selecting a target market.

■ **Define** the differences among the five targeting strategies.

■ **Understand** the role of positioning in developing marketing strategy.

Marketing Profile

Black & Decker Covers the Market, Segment by Segment

Are you a DIYer? A Do-It-Yourselfer? Do-It-Yourselfers are people who enjoy taking on home improvement projects themselves. If you fit the bill, you're not alone. In 1992 U.S. sales of home-improvement products totaled $73 billion. The Home Improvement Research Institute has predicted that such sales will grow at a rate of 6.3 percent annually through 1997.

Many companies are anxious to serve this growing market. Retailers like Home Depot and Sears, as well as Japanese manufacturers such as Makita, are working hard to meet the needs of Do-It-Yourselfers. One U.S. producer committed to satisfying the market is Black & Decker. Black & Decker, headquartered in Towson, Maryland, is well known for its variety of small electrical appliances for home use. It also has a well-known reputation as a producer of power tools and other products used to build and repair.

An analysis of the power tool market in the 1990s would suggest three major segments: the casual do-it-yourselfer, the serious do-it-yourselfer, and the professional craftsman/contractor. In mid-1991 the U.S. market was led by two major competitors: Makita and Sears's Craftsman line. Both competitors were producing mid-priced power tools aimed at serious DIYers. This segment wants a "better" quality product than the more casual enthusiast. Black & Decker, on the other hand, did not have a product positioned to meet the needs of this segment of the market. The firm produced modestly priced tools for the casual DIYer and was getting ready to launch a new product line, DeWalt, targeted at the professional craftsman/contractor segment.

Marketing research told Black & Decker that the serious DIYer segment was not likely to buy DeWalt tools, leaving this group to the competition. Retailers confirmed that the manufacturer was losing business by not offering products positioned to meet the desires of the serious DIYer. Black & Decker went to work. It began with extensive research, and a commitment to understanding the wants and needs of this market segment. It investigated everything from consumers' feelings about the first home project they'd ever done, to the colors and names they liked. The result was Quantum, a line of mid-priced power tools designed specifically to meet the needs of the serious DIYer. The line was positioned as a "step-up" from Black & Decker's existing line of power tools.

With the introduction of Quantum, just in time for the 1993 Christmas season, Black & Decker had the power tool market covered. The firm offers three lines of products, each positioned to meet the unique needs of a market segment to which it is targeted.

The Marketing Profile you just read used the term *market* in two different ways. First, it described people with a penchant for home improvement: Do-It-Yourselfers were referred to as a growing market. Second, it was used to describe people as a group with a demand for a certain product, the power tool market. Indeed, markets can be described in many ways. One way is size: the worldwide market for gasoline-powered automobiles exceeds 400 million autos. Every year in the United States, 7 percent of households purchase a new car or truck.[1] Another way a market can be described is by the characteristics of the buyers: "Married couples with at least one child at home buy 43 percent of the new vehicles sold in a year despite accounting for only 29 percent of the U.S. households."[2] Differences in consumer behavior—how frequently a buyer purchases gasoline, for example—is a third way by which a market can be described. We can understand markets by looking at the characteristics desired by consumers ("We have the premium market and they have most of the price-conscious market"). Finally, a market might be described by combining several factors across the categories.

Not all people in a market are the same, of course. The worldwide market for gasoline-powered automobiles is comprised of people with different ethnic backgrounds, different life-styles, and different likes and dislikes (just a few of the ways people in that market could differ).

To be able to serve a market, it is important for a marketer to describe the market accurately. It is also important for the marketer to understand the diversity in the market. Marketers today seem convinced that greater success comes with breaking up a large market into segments. This approach is called segmentation. More formally, **market segmentation** is the process of dividing large, heterogeneous markets into smaller subsets of people or businesses with similar needs and responsiveness to marketing mix offerings. Black & Decker used market segmentation when it identified three groups of consumers, each needing different power tools. While such an approach is undeniably more expensive than treating everyone the same, it is also true that this approach generally meets consumers' desires more successfully. Segmentation allows marketers to develop products that are uniquely positioned to meet the needs of a particular segment.

A marketer begins by segmenting a market. Once the market is segmented, the marketer must decide which strategic approach will best serve the market. Choosing the approach involves deciding which segments to target. Once target segments have been selected, the marketer must then decide how he or she wishes that target market to perceive the product. This involves positioning the product. The processes of segmentation, targeting, and positioning are three very important concepts to a consumer-oriented marketer.

WHAT IS A MARKET?

When marketers set out to sell a product or service, one of the most important things they must do is identify their market by determining who their potential customers are. To qualify as potential customers, persons or businesses must meet each of the following four criteria:

1. They must want or need the product or service.

2. They must be interested or potentially interested in buying the product or service.

3. They must have enough money or credit to buy the product or service.

4. They must be willing to buy the product or service.

For our purposes, then, a **market** consists of people or businesses with the interest or potential interest, the purchasing power, and the willingness to buy a product or service that satisfies a need or desire. Figure 5.1 illustrates the steps in defining a market.

Consider, for example, the market for motorcycle helmets. To be part of this market, a person would have to need or desire a helmet for his or her own use or for a gift and be interested or potentially interested in buying one. These criteria eliminate anyone who does not currently own a motorcycle or is not considering buying a motorcycle or who would not consider giving a helmet as a gift. It also eliminates people who have motorcycles, live in states without helmet laws, and do not like wearing a helmet while riding. Anyone who does not have the money or is not willing to spend the money to purchase a helmet is also eliminated from the potential market.

In this book we deal with both consumer markets and business markets. A **consumer market** consists of buyers who intend to use or benefit from the product or service themselves. Such consumers are often referred to as **ultimate consumers**. A **business market** consists of individuals or organizations that purchase products or services for use in the production of other products or services, for use in their day-to-day operations, or for resale. These consumers are referred to as **business-to-business** or **organizational consumers**.

Frequently, the same product is sold to both consumer and business markets. The wants and needs of the two types of markets are usually very different, however. The markets for fax machines are a good example. Consumer markets typically want low price, compactness, and ease of use. Business markets, on the other hand, are primarily interested in low cost per transmission and the quality of the transmission. Both markets want reliability.

Marketers use different strategies to reach consumer and business markets and to meet the needs of each market. The amount of personal selling required, the media used for promotional efforts, the packaging, the way prices are determined, the speed of delivery, and the credit terms available differ greatly between business markets and consumer markets. Because each type of market and indeed each market must be analyzed separately, market segmentation is important for both business and consumer markets. (This chapter focuses mainly on consumer markets. We will further explore consumer markets in Chapter 6. Then in Chapter 7 we will look closely at business markets.)

FIGURE 5.1
Steps in Defining a Market

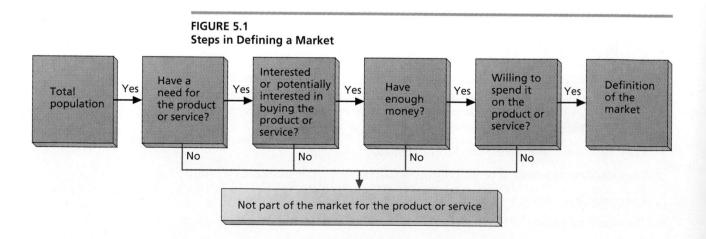

Camp Hyatt®

WHO'D HAVE THOUGHT WE'D TAKE CARE OF ALL YOUR LITTLE WORRIES?

At Hyatt, we know you want to spend your family vacation together. But sometimes, not too together. That's why we've created special programs like Camp Hyatt.® Where Hyatt Counselors will help your kids do everything from building sandcastles to building friendships. It's a blast for kids. And a break for you. To learn more about Camp Hyatt® and our other family programs, call your travel planner or Hyatt at 1-800-233-1234.

WE'VE THOUGHT OF EVERYTHING℠

HYATT
HOTELS & RESORTS ®

Frequently, the same product is sold to both consumer and business markets. The ad on the left stresses that Hyatt has programs and facilities that appeal to families with children, while the ad on the right emphasizes particular services and facilities that are attractive to business travelers.

BASES OF SEGMENTATION

Markets vary in the extent of their homogeneity. Some are comprised of people or businesses who have very similar needs, preferences, and desires. These homogeneous markets are fairly easy for marketers to please. A single marketing mix can be developed to satisfy everyone in the market. Most markets, however, are heterogeneous. The consumers in those markets differ from one another in buying characteristics, preferences, and the ways they respond to any given marketing mix. Meeting the needs of heterogeneous markets is a considerable challenge to marketers. One common way this challenge is met is through market segmentation. The goal of market segmentation is to identify market segments comprised of people or businesses with similar characteristics and therefore similar needs. Just about any identifiable human characteristic can be used as a variable to subdivide a large potential market into homogeneous market segments that differ from one another in terms of that characteristic. However, not all identifiable characteristics make good segmentation variables. Suppose you are given the assignment of creating consumer segments within your marketing class. How would you proceed? Perhaps you would divide the class into two segments on the basis of gender, putting men in one group and women in the other. This could be a good choice. In many product categories men and women have different needs and preferences. You might, on the other hand, choose to segment the class on the basis of an obvious external characteristic like hair color, putting blondes in one group, brunettes in another, and so forth. This would probably not be a good choice. Differences in hair color would seem to account for very few, if any, differences in consumer needs and preferences.

When deciding which variables to use to segment markets, the marketing manager's goal should be to identify market segments that differ from one another in the ways they respond to a particular marketing mix. If a variable cannot be expected to identify market segments that exhibit differences in their buying behavior toward a good or service, it is not a good choice as a segmentation variable in that particular case. Gender is often, but not always, an appropriate segmentation variable. The market for personal computers, for example, is not segmented on the basis of gender because differences in needs, preferences, and marketing responsiveness in this market do not differ by gender.

A number of characteristics are used as segmentation variables for both consumer and business markets.

Geographic Segmentation

When marketing managers divide the total market into segments on the basis of location, they are using **geographic segmentation.** Many types of locations can be used—regions, countries, states, counties, cities or towns, and even neighborhoods—depending on the goods or services being marketed. For example, a snowmobile manufacturer will likely concentrate on consumers living in the Snow Belt, but a water-ski manufacturer will probably concentrate on consumers living in the Sun Belt. Campbell's Soup uses regional segmentation to determine its marketing mixes. For instance, the Nacho Cheese soup it markets in the Southwest United States contains more jalapeño peppers than that marketed in other regions of the United States because people living in the Southwest tend to like spicier foods.

Other examples of geographic segmentation include:

▪ KIWI International Air Lines obtained mailing lists from various New Jersey country clubs to accomplish its mailing announcing flights into West Palm Beach, Florida, on October 31, 1993.[3]

▪ At its locations in predominantly black neighborhoods of Los Angeles, Denny's Restaurants offers a menu designed to appeal to African Americans.[4]

▪ The *Wall Street Journal* publishes 17 editions to accommodate the needs of readers in different geographical areas.[5]

▪ A leading public utility compares energy usage by geographic area to chart energy conservation campaigns and forecast energy needs.[6]

As the concept of global markets has grown, new opportunities to employ geographic segmentation have been created. Many marketers who had previously concentrated in their own country have found that market segments defined by world location have provided tremendous opportunities for products that may already have reached or surpassed their peak demand "at home." Manufacturers of such products as televisions, stereos, and radios, for example, have expanded to global markets.

Although KIWI International Air Lines is less than two years old, most KIWI pilots, mechanics and flight attendants — our 800 employee/owners — have been flying proudly for more than twenty years.

Except back then, we wore uniforms emblazoned with other airline emblems.

Today, most of those airlines are no longer around, and we've learned that there is a *better* way to run an airline. That's why we created KIWI.

We added legroom between the seats, replaced that old airline food with delicious healthy cuisine that you have to taste to believe, and threw in a big helping of friendly service.

Finally, we put the fair back into fares with enticing low pricing.

So fly with us... You can't beat the experience.

For reservations, call your travel agent or
1-800-JET-KIWI
1-800-538-5494

KIWI
INTERNATIONAL AIR LINES...
ATLANTA • CHICAGO • NEWARK • ORLANDO
SAN JUAN • TAMPA • WEST PALM BEACH

Kiwi International Air Lines obtained mailing lists from various New Jersey country clubs to accomplish its mailing announcing flights into West Palm Beach, Florida, on October 31, 1993.

The Australian producers of XXXX Beer decided to explore global markets after experiencing stagnant sales at home. In 1993 the company entered the U.S. market. It targeted cities on the West Coast, where a significant percentage of people have traveled to Australia and may have tasted the beer there. Early reports indicate that the product is selling well in the United States.[7]

Sometimes the decision to segment the market geographically raises ethical questions. The "Spotlight on Ethics: Geographic Segmentation Can Raise Ethical Issues," illustrates how this might be the case.

Demographic Segmentation

Dividing the total market into segments on the basis of such demographic variables as age, gender, income, occupation, education, race, nationality, and social class is called **demographic segmentation**. This is the most popular method by which marketers identify market segments. Demographic segmentation is widely used for two reasons. First, consumers' wants and needs are often closely associated with their demographic characteristics. For example, gender is an important segmentation variable for cosmetics, as is age for "heavy metal" music and income for luxury automobiles. Second, demographic variables are relatively easy to measure and are readily available to marketers. Sources such as U.S. Census data, Simmons Market Research, and Donnelley Demographics provide demographic information.

The following are examples of companies that have used demographics:

- The Ford Motor Company redesigned the Mustang in 1994 to appeal more to women, who represent a $65 billion annual market.[8] Design changes included switches with a softer feel (easier to use with longer fingernails) and more leg room (helpful for a driver wearing a skirt).[9] Using gender as a segmentation variable, Ford was better able to meet the needs of all drivers.

- Cane & Able, a firm that sells gadgets to make life easier (like jar openers) is targeting senior citizens by offering gadgets designed to ease the everyday problems associated with aging. The company is distributing items previously available only through medical supply houses (bathtub safety rails, for example) through outlets such as Wal-Mart and Kmart. Using age as a segmentation variable, the firm is addressing the shift to a growing senior population.[10]

- Cycle Dog Food offers four versions of its product, targeted to owners of puppies, young adult dogs, mature dogs, and overweight dogs. Using both age and physical size of pets as segmentation variables, the firm increased its penetration of the dog food market.

- Major cosmetic companies such as Revlon, Maybelline, and Procter & Gamble's Cover Girl line are beginning to formulate products for the needs of women from ethnic minorities. Cosmetics for Asian, Hispanic, and African American women can now be found in more retail outlets.[11]

Additional examples of demographic segmentation by ethnicity can be found in the "Marketing in Action: Opportunities Abound in Ethnic Markets." The Hispanic and African American markets have grown extremely fast in recent years. This growth has proved attractive for many marketers.

Geodemographic Segmentation

Geodemographic segmentation is based on the premise that people with similar economic and cultural backgrounds and perspectives tend to cluster together. It combines geographic and demographic information. A number of marketing research firms are now providing this sort of information. Two examples of geodemographic segmentation are Claritas' Prizm model and ACORN.

The Prizm model combines U.S. Census data and geographic information to identify 40 geodemographic categories in the United States. According to the Prizm model, for example, Chappaqua, New York, and Winnetka, Illinois, are classified as *Blueblood Estates*. This category includes "America's wealthiest socioeconomic neighborhoods, populated by super-upper established managers, professionals, and heirs to old money, accustomed to privilege." Weatherford, Texas, and Waverly, Ohio, are classified as *Shotguns and Pickups*. This category includes the "hundreds of small, outlying townships and crossroads villages that serve the nation's breadbasket and other rural areas." Residents in the Shotguns and Pickups category have lower middle incomes, are blue-collar craftspeople and service workers with household heads 35–54 years old.[12] Retailers and marketers of many consumer products and services use Prizm to define the characteristics of their customers.[13] The Arts and Entertainment Network credits an increase of 27,500 subscribers to use of the Prizm model.[14]

A Classification of Residential Neighborhoods (ACORN) is a European data base that also provides information that can be used to accomplish geodemographic

MARKETING IN ACTION

Geographic Segmentation Can Raise Ethical Issues

The riots that devastated Los Angeles in May of 1992 could have even more far-reaching business and economic effects than first imagined. Violence broke out following the acquittal of two police officers who had been charged with beating motorist Rodney King. In the time since the riots, the city has struggled to rebuild its South Central area, the section hit hardest by the destruction. The biggest struggle of all, however, continues to be convincing businesses to reinvest in the area. Geographical location is a common segmentation variable and one that has produced considerable success for many marketers.

The dilemma faced by marketers in evaluating certain areas of the Los Angeles market as a target for investment is, Where does good business judgment end and racism begin? Is it unethical for a company to choose not to reinvest in the predominantly low-income, high-crime areas that were hardest hit by the riots? Does the fact that many residents of these neighborhoods are African American or Hispanic make the decision a racial issue? Immediately following the riots several well-known African American entertainers, sports celebrities, and other notables were quick to announce that they would be investing in the riot-torn area. The retailers who provide the goods and services needed by consumers who live in these areas have not been so quick to follow suit.

Whether to do business in high-crime areas has raised ethical questions for many years. Consumer groups have long accused grocery retailers, especially small, independent proprietors, of taking advantage of consumers in high-crime areas by charging higher prices to those consumers least able to travel outside their immediate neighborhoods. The retailers often counter by pointing out the higher costs of doing business in such neighborhoods. The retailers maintain that greater shoplifting losses, higher insurance rates, and the need for more security all contribute to justify higher prices.

Is it unethical to vary pricing by segment when using geographics as a segmentation variable? Would it be more or less ethical for a retailer to choose not to serve some geographic segments at all? The decision by large grocery-store chains not to operate in high-crime areas is often cited as a factor in the high prices typically found in ghettos. The lack of competition allows existing retailers to charge higher prices. As you can see, the issue of whether to do business in a high-crime area is more complex than it may first appear to be.

---

segmentation. ACORN is country specific and, like Prizm, can be used to define the characteristics and locations of an organization's customers. ACORN uses 61 life-style characteristics to classify 226,000 neighborhoods into 40 segments. The characteristics include demographic factors such as income, age, education, value of home, and type of household. ACORN calculates Purchase Potential Indexes (PPI's) for various products, services, and activities in each of the segments. The model, for example, would allow a marketer to predict the purchase potential for appliances, cameras, or civic activities within a given segment. ACORN has been used to make site location decisions, to plan sales efforts, and to evaluate the potential of new products.[15]

Psychographic Segmentation

Another way markets are segmented is through the use of **psychographics,** segmentation variables based on consumers' personality characteristics and life-styles. **Lifestyle** refers to a set of values or tastes exhibited by a group of consumers, especially as they are reflected in consumption patterns.[16] A good way to understand the conceptual difference between the bases of segmentation we have already discussed and psychographics is to think of the former as states of being and the latter as states of mind.

MARKETING *IN ACTION*

Opportunities Abound in Ethnic Markets

Marketers today recognize the value of race and ethnicity as segmentation variables. Not only are certain population segments such as Hispanics and African Americans growing rapidly, but research indicates that the consumer characteristics of these segments are unique.

Hispanics represent the fastest growing ethnic segment of the U.S. population. By the year 2000 it is expected that Hispanics will comprise 9.4 percent of the population and by 2080, will grow to 20.4 percent. This growth is fueled by both immigration and an annual birthrate that far exceeds that of the non-Hispanic population. While the average number of persons in all U.S. households in 1992 was 3.17, in households headed by Hispanics the figure was 3.83.

Consumer research into the Hispanic market has increased in recent years. This research has discovered the following Hispanic preferences in advertising:

- Hispanic consumers desire detailed product information in advertisements directed to them. Comparative ads are well received by the Hispanic market.
- Hispanic consumers like testimonials that are generally perceived as honest and portraying real life. "Slice-of-life" testimonials by actual consumers appeal more to the market than ads that feature celebrities.
- Advertisements that relate a product or service to upbeat, happy people are well received by Hispanics. Because the consumers typically see themselves in these terms, they relate well to products associated with that view.
- The value of family is very important to Hispanic consumers. Advertisements that show products or services that provide the best (of anything) for a family are generally successful.
- Hispanic consumers are less likely than non-Hispanic consumers to identify with materialistic displays of success. Consequently, ads portraying affluent life-styles may not be well received.

- Use of informal, spoken Spanish rather than formal Spanish is generally better accepted. Hispanic consumers relate better to people in advertisements who speak as they do.

One of the earliest retailers to target marketing programs specifically toward Hispanics was the JCPenney Company. In 1978, JCPenney's catalog division produced a booklet in Spanish explaining how to shop with a JCPenney catalog in English. JCPenney was amazed at the overwhelming response. Although the booklet had been targeted to selected market areas, mainly in Florida, California, and Texas, requests for the booklet poured in from areas few people had considered important as Hispanic markets. Patricia V. Asip, the Argentinean manager of corporate Hispanic marketing for the company, noted, "This helped sensitize the company to the widespread existence of a customer out there who required a different kind of communication." Today JCPenney targets a diverse Hispanic market that includes different social classes, as well as the subpopulations of Mexicans, Puerto Ricans, Cubans, and other Latin Americans.

African Americans are also a fast growing minority segment in the United States. Furthermore, middle- and upper-income segments have grown significantly in the last ten years. Additionally, the percentage of African American families who earn $50,000 or more per year has grown faster than the percentage of white families earning that amount.

Studies suggest that black and white consumers cannot always be reached with the same advertising messages. African American consumers respond more positively than whites to ads emphasizing culture- and value-based messages.

African American consumers are good markets for services such as travel, health care, and financial planning. Research has shown that specific packaged goods such as candy bars, freeze-dried coffee, and canned meat appeal highly to African Americans.

5-1 Despite the opportunities cited in the "Marketing in Action: Opportunities Abound in Ethnic Markets," large numbers of companies have not rushed to embrace minority markets. List some reasons that companies might not target minority consumers.

5-2 Is it unethical or good business judgment for a retailer or other firm to avoid particular geographical locations that have high crime rates?

YOUR MARKETING KNOWLEDGE

Because psychographic variables are states of mind, gathering information about them can be a challenge for marketers. One of the most common ways of identifying psychographic variables is the **AIO** (activities, interests, and opinions) **inventory.** Such inventories are typically survey forms where researchers ask consumers to respond to questions that provide insight into the consumers' interests and opinions and the types of activities they like to engage in.

Table 5.1 provides an example of the types of questions that might be included on a typical AIO inventory. Respondents are asked to agree or disagree with each statement. By administering the inventory to a particular group of consumers, researchers could develop a *psychographic profile* of that group. If, for example, a group of "heavy renters" of movie videos (defined as renting more than ten videos per month) responded to the AIO inventory, a researcher could develop a profile of that category of consumers based on their levels of agreement or disagreement with the statements. Furthermore, two different groups, perhaps "occasional renters" as well as "heavy renters" could be asked to respond to the AIO statements. If the responses of the two groups differed significantly, their differing psychographic profiles could provide the basis for a segmentation strategy. Perhaps occasional renters are outgoing people who enjoy loud parties and think of themselves as

**TABLE 5.1
Typical AIO Inventory
Statements**

Statements
My greatest achievements are still ahead of me.
Five years from now, my income will probably be a lot higher than it is now.
I'd like to spend a year in Japan.
I like to be considered a leader.
I don't like to take chances.
I like parties where there is lots of music and talk.
I always have the car radio on when I drive.
Cosmopolitan is one of my favorite magazines.
I think I'm a bit of a swinger.
I like driving fast.
Liquor is a curse on American life.
People should not be banned from smoking in public.
If Americans were more religious, this would be a better country.

AGREE OR DISAGREE?

swingers while heavy renters are introverts who enjoy staying at home. Video rental companies might promote to the former group by suggesting they throw a "Night at the Movies" party while they promote the quiet appeal of "Just You and the Celluloid" to the latter group.

One of the most prominent and enduring uses of psychographic analysis (or *life-style analysis*, as it is sometimes called) has been by SRI International, a research firm.[17] In 1978 SRI developed a program called VALS (Values And Lifestyles). The program classified the American population into nine segments based on diversity in values and life-styles. In 1989 SRI introduced VALS 2, an updated version of VALS.[18] VALS 2 breaks the U.S. population into eight psychographic segments: the fullfilleds, the believers, the actualizers, the achievers, the strivers, the strugglers, the experiencers, and the makers. The eight segments are grouped into three categories based on primary orientation, which can be to principles, status, or action. Fullfilleds and believers make up the principle-oriented category. Actualizers, achievers, strivers, and strugglers belong to the status-oriented category. Experiencers and makers comprise the action-oriented category. Differences among segments within a category are based on variation in resources. Figure 5.2 describes some of the life-style characteristics of the eight segments.

American Airlines has used VALS to identify its frequent-flyer customer group, the business traveler, as "achievers."[19] Other marketers, particularly in the food industry, have indicated that segmentation using VALS does not work for products where consumers have little or no emotional involvement in the buying process.[20] Hence, staple products such as milk or bread are less likely to be sold successfully by targeting as a VALS segment. The lack of emotional involvement most consumers exhibit in deciding to purchase such products would make it difficult for a marketer to design separate, effective appeals for strivers, achievers, or any of the other segments.

This latter conclusion, in the food industry, illustrates the importance of selecting a segmentation variable, or set of variables, that is appropriate for the product or service under consideration. As we noted earlier, a variable that does not produce groups with diversity in marketing mix responsiveness for a given product or service is not a suitable segmentation factor in that instance.

Behavioral Segmentation

Behavioral segmentation is the last type of segmentation we will discuss. In behavioral segmentation, market segments are identified according to the actual behavior of consumers in the marketplace. Included in this category are usage rate, brand loyalty, readiness stage, and benefits sought.

Usage rate.   The frequency with which consumers buy or use a product or service is its **usage rate**. In many cases, 20 percent of the users account for close to 80 percent of the sales. In fact, this occurs so often that it is commonly referred to as the **80/20 rule.** When marketers choose usage rate as a segmentation variable, they first divide the market into three categories—heavy users, frequently called the *heavy half*; light users, frequently called the *light half*; and nonusers. Table 5.2 shows some product categories divided into these three segments.

To more easily identify the three segments, a marketer may attempt to find demographic characteristics that correlate with usage rate. A "heavy user" of cake mix, for example, is likely to be female, to be over 40 years old, and to be a full-time homemaker.

Different marketing mix strategies are directed toward each segment. Beer producers might use price promotions to attract the heavy-user segment (likely to be

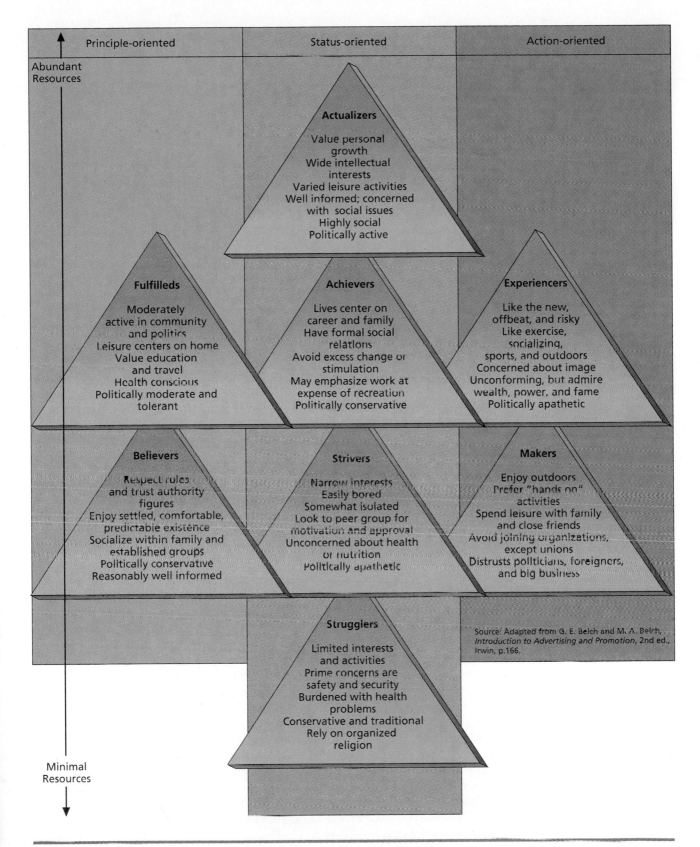

FIGURE 5.2
Life-style Characteristics of the VALS 2 Segments

	Nonusers	Users	
		Light Half	**Heavy Half**
Colas	H = 22%	H = 39%	H = 39%
	U = 0%	U = 10%	U = 90%
Bourbon	H = 59%	H = 20%	H = 21%
	U = 0%	U = 11%	U = 89%
Beer	H = 67%	H = 16%	H = 17%
	U = 0%	U = 12%	U = 88%
Cake Mixes	H = 27%	H = 36%	H = 37%
	U = 0%	U = 15%	U = 85%
Paper Towels	H = 34%	H = 33%	H = 33%
	U = 0%	U = 17%	U = 83%
Toilet Paper	H = 2%	H = 49%	H = 49%
	U = 0%	U = 26%	U = 74%

Note: H = Households
      U = Usage

**TABLE 5.2
Usage Rate
Segmentation for
Some Selected
Products**

particularly sensitive to price) while they target light consumers through ads that emphasize the taste of a new higher-priced product. Light users might also be a good market for smaller units: six- or eight-ounce bottles or cans. Nonusers might be attracted by the introduction of a nonalcoholic brew or a "beer that doesn't taste like beer." A marketer might, of course, decide to concentrate on just the heavy-user segment and ignore the other two segments.

Brand loyalty.   Consumers show different degrees of **brand loyalty,** which is a consumer's consistent purchase of a product or service that he or she prefers. For instance, some travelers will always stay at Holiday Inn if possible, some will stay at Holiday Inn if it is convenient, some will switch hotels for the sake of variety, and some will try to avoid Holiday Inn. Brand-loyal consumers are a valuable commodity to an organization. In addition to requiring less promotion, sales transactions with brand-loyal customers take less time and generally result in larger purchases.[21] Hence, it is important for marketers to identify consumers who are most loyal to their brand and to design marketing strategies to keep this group happy. ARYA cleaners in San Diego offers its regular customers a 10 percent discount. La Salsa, a fast growing Mexican food franchise in California, offers free tee-shirts to customers who have achieved a certain level of food purchases over time.

Marketers are also interested in encouraging consumers who are prone to switch brands to become loyal to one brand. Most airlines, for example, have initiated frequent-flyer programs designed to encourage flying only, or mostly, on that airline's flights. A customer who has accumulated 20,000 miles on American Airlines is entitled to a free flight. Additionally American and several other airlines offer discounted or free merchandise in exchange for accumulated miles.

Promotional messages directed to consumers who are brand loyal are likely to vary from those directed to others. A brand-loyal consumer should be reminded that she has made a good choice. A retailer like Sears, for example, might identify loyal shoppers by examining credit card usage and then send a direct mail advertisement to the loyal shoppers, thanking them for their patronage and congratulating them on a wise choice of stores. Consumers who switch brands frequently, on the other hand, might be targeted with advertising that shows the company's products in a positive light. Comparative ad campaigns such as those frequently used by Burger King, can be particularly effective in attracting frequent brand-switchers. This group would also be a good target for sales promotions like coupons. (The concept of brand loyalty is discussed again in Chapter 6.)

Readiness stage. For any good or service, different consumers will be in different stages of readiness to buy. Some consumers may be totally unaware of the product, others may be aware of it but not very knowledgeable about it, others may be knowledgeable but may have never tried it, some will intend to buy it, others will have actually bought it, and still others will be loyal users.

Different strategies are required for each of these segments. Heavy advertising might be required to reach the unaware and unknowledgeable segments. A firm might use radio advertising with frequent repetition, for example, to build awareness. Ads describing the product and its uses could help build knowledge. Sampling would be effective in reaching the knowledgeable nonuser of the product. Kellogg's mailed one-ounce sample sizes of its Low-Fat Granola to households across the United States as a way to get consumers to try the product. Personal selling might be required to convert people intending to buy into actual buyers. A consumer considering the purchase of a new automobile, for example, may become aware, knowledgeable, and even desirous of the product through advertising, but he is unlikely to purchase without the aid of some personal selling. Advertising different from that used to create awareness could prove effective in converting current buyers into loyal users.

Such advertising may use a more direct medium (for example, direct mail rather than radio) and emphasize the benefits of regular product usage.

Benefits sought. **Benefit segmentation** subdivides a market according to differences in the benefits that consumers are seeking when they buy a good or service. Because it uses causal rather than descriptive factors to segment markets, this approach to market segmentation is somewhat more sophisticated than the other approaches we have discussed. Proponents of benefit segmentation argue that the benefits sought by consumers actually determine their behavior, whereas demographic characteristics and other segmentation variables only serve as representatives that correlate with a type of behavior.

As with psychographic factors, it is not easy to observe the benefits that consumers seek. Identifying those benefits is a challenge to marketers who wish to use this approach to segmentation. Marketers typically employ marketing research to help them identify the benefits their target markets seek from products. One such technique is **laddering.** Laddering attempts to identify benefits sought by beginning with specific product attributes and then encouraging consumers to "climb the ladder" between these attributes and benefits or desired end states.[22] A consumer might, for example, begin the laddering process by indicating a preference for Oreo cookies over Hydrox cookies. Probing the consumer, the market researcher may determine that this preference is based on the fact that Oreos were his father's favorite cookie. When his mother bought Oreos his father was happy. When his father was happy, the family was in harmony. Hence, family acceptance and pleasure are the primary benefit the consumer seeks when selecting a brand of cookies to purchase. Figure 5.3 provides an illustration of laddering.

In the pioneering study that introduced the concept of benefit segmentation, Russell Haley identified four segments of the toothpaste market based on differences in the primary benefit consumers sought when buying toothpaste.[23] The four

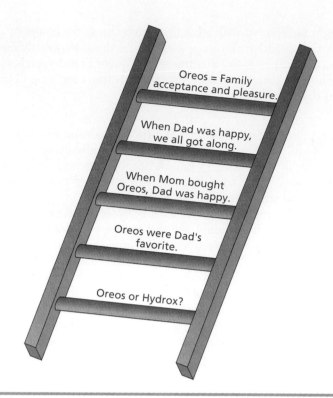

FIGURE 5.3
Laddering to Identify the Benefits Sought by Consumers

segments are given in Table 5.3. The table also breaks down each segment into demographic, psychographic, and other behavioral characteristics. The Worriers, for example, are typically members of large families. They are conservative, often hypochondriacs, and heavy users of toothpaste. However, the key factor that places them in the Worrier segment is that decay prevention is the principal benefit they seek from toothpaste. Note that benefit segmentation uses the *primary* benefit sought

TABLE 5.3
Benefit Segmentation of the Toothpaste Market

Segment Name	Principal Benefit Sought	Demographic Strengths	Special Behavioral Characteristics	Personality Characteristics	Life-style Characteristics
The Sensory Segment	Flavor, product appearance	Children	Users of spearmint flavored toothpaste	High self-involvement	Hedonistic
The Sociables	Brightness of teeth	Teens, young people	Smokers	High sociability	Active
The Worriers	Decay prevention	Large families	Heavy users	High hypochondriasis	Conservative
The Independent Segment	Price	Men	Heavy users	High autonomy	Value-oriented

Source: R. Haley, "Benefit Segmentation: A Decision-Oriented Tool," *Journal of Marketing* (July 1968), pp. 30–35.

to identify market segments. All consumers of toothpaste likely desire flavor, brightness of teeth, decay prevention, and low price. Only the benefit given top priority by an individual, however, determines the segment in which he or she is placed.

Segments identified by benefits sought should be targeted with marketing mixes that are appropriate for them. In the toothpaste market Crest would appear to be targeting the Worriers with its Tartar Control Formula, while Mentadent with peroxide for whitening teeth would seem focused at the Sociables.

Benefit segmentation has been used by the health industry to target segments of consumers for fitness centers.[24] "Dieters" are consumers most concerned with weight control and physical appearance. They use exercise to obtain those benefits. "Self-improvers" are concerned primarily with exercise as a way to feel better. "Winners" exercise to stay physically fit, a factor that they believe helps them get ahead in life.

Is There a "Right" Basis for Segmentation?

We've considered many variables that can be used to segment markets. The specific situation helps determine which of these variables the marketing decision maker should use in any given market. While geographics or demographics offer descriptive variables that are not in themselves the causes of behavior, they are often very reliable segmentation variables. While psychographic or behavioral factors, like benefits sought, represent variables more internal to the consumer and, perhaps, more related to actual purchase reasons, it is difficult to measure and collect data on such factors.

In the end, of course, the marketer should use the variable that will produce the best result—groupings of individuals who will respond similarly to marketing efforts. Most target markets are identified by using a combination of the various segmentation variables that we have discussed. The market for luxury cars for example, might be segmented by the behavioral factor, benefits sought (status, comfort, power, etc.), but marketers are also likely to use demographic and psychographic variables to describe the segments. The choice of a segmentation variable is not an "either-or" decision. The marketing decision maker should use the combination of factors that will produce segments for which marketing mixes can be successfully developed.

CRITERIA FOR SELECTING TARGET MARKETS

The fact that a market segment exists does not necessarily mean that a marketer should identify it as a target market. Each potential target market should be evaluated using at least three criteria—size, reachability, and responsiveness to marketing.

Size

For a market segment to be a good target market, the segment must be large enough to be potentially profitable and thereby justify the expenditure of marketing dollars. Consider, for example, two potential segments of the automobile market, very tall people and very short people. Each of these groups would be likely to desire an automobile designed specifically for its needs. Unfortunately, each comprises such a small segment of the total market that projected sales revenues would probably not justify the expenditures that would be necessary to produce and market automobiles just for that segment.

Size can be a tricky issue, however, so marketers should not evaluate potential target markets on the basis of size alone. The **majority fallacy** holds that it is a mistake to assume that the bigger a market is, the more potential it offers. A market segment may have many people in it, but those people may have low incomes or other characteristics that limit their buying potential. Furthermore, large market segments are likely to attract the attention of competitors. As a result, there may be more competition in larger segments than there is in smaller segments. Marketers of many products, for example, have targeted the baby-boom generation (consumers born between 1946 and 1963) because of the large size of the market. Competition in this market is typically very heavy, making success for any one company more of a challenge. Many hard liquor producers turned to baby boomers in the 1980s and early 1990s as their traditional, older market declined. Because so many producers were targeting the younger market, however, successful selling to baby boomers has been just as hard to come by.[25]

In recent years, many marketers have found it increasingly attractive to target smaller and smaller markets. As the U.S. market has become increasingly fragmented and global, marketers have often found it necessary to focus on very small segments in order to compete. Identifying a very small segment as a target market is termed **microniche marketing.** In the beer industry, for example, a number of microbreweries produce very small quantities of beer in comparison to the major breweries. These companies had great success during the 1980s and early 1990s with the strategy of targeting a small market. Despite the target market's small size, it was particularly desirable due to demographic characteristics such as high disposable income. Brooklyn Lager Beer, brewed in Brooklyn, New York, is an example of such a product. Microniche marketing is also practiced by First Cabin Travel of La Jolla, California. First Cabin arranges international travel tours for groups of

Brooklyn Lager Beer is an example of a product that has had great success by targeting a small market.

affluent tourists. The average price for a one-week trip arranged by First Cabin exceeds $5,000. The travel agency estimates the size of its target market at 1,000 to 1,500 people.[26]

Reachability

For a market segment to be viewed as a target market, the marketer must be able to reach it. Often, marketers identify segments that are large enough to be potentially profitable, but they cannot feasibly reach those segments through the available promotional efforts or channels of distribution. Several years ago, for example, a local chapter of Planned Parenthood wanted to provide birth control information to girls between the ages of 10 and 12 years. The organization found that schools were reluctant to allow it to distribute the information because it would likely upset some parents. Direct mail was also ruled out. Assuming that the organization could obtain a good mailing list, which would probably have been difficult, some parents were again likely to be upset if their daughters received the information through the mail. After evaluating all its options, the organization decided that the segment was not a good target market due to its inaccessibility.

Responsiveness to Marketing

Market segments make good target markets when the individuals in the segment are responsive to marketing efforts. A segment that derives all its product information through word-of-mouth communication, for example, might not prove to be a viable target market for a firm. The organization would find the segment unresponsive to any type of promotional effort.

To determine whether a segment will be responsive to an organization's marketing efforts, marketing research may be required. The company might investigate the segment's potential responsiveness through surveys or even through test marketing. (These and other research techniques are discussed in more detail in Chapter 8.)

TARGETING STRATEGIES

Once a market has been segmented, a marketer has several strategic options in selecting target markets. Figure 5.4 shows five targeting strategies.

Undifferentiated Marketing

Marketers who use **undifferentiated marketing**, also called **mass marketing**, offer consumers a single product or product line using a single marketing mix. This is a logical approach for markets that are generally homogeneous. It is not, however, a very marketing-oriented approach to a heterogeneous market. In effect, it responds to the market by ignoring its heterogeneity. Marketers who use undifferentiated marketing are not practicing market segmentation. The approach assumes that all consumers are sufficiently similar so that they will respond similarly to a single marketing mix. When competition is minimal or nonexistent, undifferentiated marketing can be a successful strategy even though the wants and desires of many consumers are being met only superficially. Henry Ford's statement about the Model T, "You can have any color you want as long as it's black," is a classic example of a mass marketing strategy. Mass marketing today is rare. A fast food restaurant such

A

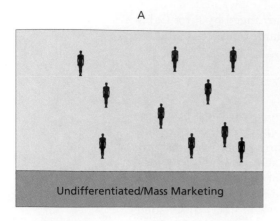

Undifferentiated/Mass Marketing

B

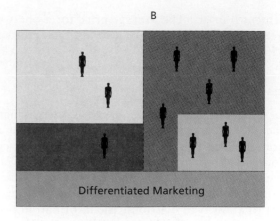

Differentiated Marketing

C

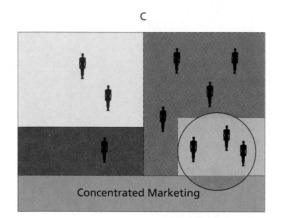

Concentrated Marketing

D

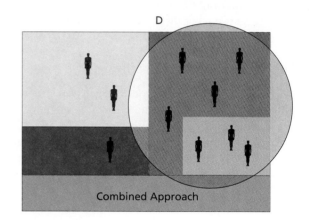

Combined Approach

E

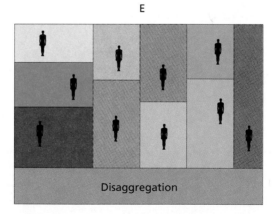

Disaggregation

FIGURE 5.4
Approaches to a
Heterogeneous Market

as In-N-Out Burger (in Southern California) that attempts to please the entire market with very limited menu offerings is practicing mass marketing. On the positive side, this strategy can save an organization the cost of marketing research and the administrative difficulties of segmenting a market. In addition, it can facilitate long runs in the production of manufactured goods and thus provide economies of scale. Undifferentiated marketing is illustrated schematically in Panel A of Figure 5.4.

Differentiated Marketing

A marketer may attempt to reach the entire market for a good or service by developing a unique marketing mix for each segment of the larger population. This approach is known as **differentiated marketing.** In this strategy, each segment becomes a target market for the firm. The strategy is illustrated in Panel B of Figure 5.4. Today, U.S. automobile producers such as General Motors and Ford use this strategy. For example, Ford Motor Company produces a variety of makes and models to meet the needs and preferences of consumers who vary with respect to many factors such as age, income, gender, and family status. The firm's Festiva, a subcompact, is targeted at younger, lower-income consumers without families. The Explorer, a sports utility vehicle and the WindStar minivan, on the other hand, are designed to meet the needs of families. Buyers are typically older and have higher incomes than the buyers of the Festiva. The Lincoln Towncar, a luxury car produced by Ford, appeals to older males with high incomes. Of the marketing mix variables, only the distribution strategy is the same for the different cars (all of Ford's offerings can be found at a Ford showroom); otherwise, the products, prices, and promotion strategies are different for each target market.

Although differentiated marketing generally does an excellent job of satisfying consumer needs, it can be a strain on a firm's resources. Planning and implementing multiple marketing mixes simultaneously may result in an organization's spreading itself too thin. Additionally, if the firm is unable to distinguish its target markets from each other, differential pricing or promotion strategies may cause discontent among consumers. For example, a firm that offers a discount for first-time buyers runs the risk of alienating its existing customers should those customers become aware of the promotion.

Concentrated Marketing

Marketers who have decided to use a segmentation approach, but who lack the resources or inclination to pursue a differentiated approach, may opt for **concentrated marketing.** Using this strategy, which is illustrated in Panel C of Figure 5.4, the marketer targets a single market segment from among the segments that have been identified. Concentrated marketing offers a compromise between undifferentiated marketing and differentiated marketing. It allows for the benefits of differentiated marketing in that it recognizes and addresses the heterogeneity of the larger market. At the same time, concentrated marketing allows marketers to focus on developing a single marketing mix for a single target market. This strategy may allow some economies of scale with fewer different production runs as well as a concentration of dollars on fewer promotion and distribution strategies. Automobile manufacturers such as Ferrari or Rolls Royce that focus on satisfying a single target market of affluent sports car or luxury car lovers are pursuing a concentrated marketing strategy. AIG Life Insurance Company targets women. It has developed products and promotional appeals emphasizing the target market's unique financial needs.[27]

The Combined Approach

Another compromise targeting strategy is the **combined approach.** With this strategy marketers determine whether they can combine identified segments into larger segments that will elicit a single consumer response despite some degree of heterogeneity. This strategy is illustrated in Panel D of Figure 5.4. The combined approach allows marketers to cover more of the total market with a single marketing mix than does concentrated marketing. The marketer using a combined approach might

Life's Changed.

The AIG Life Companies. What Makes Us Different Makes Us Better.

AIG World leaders in insurance and financial services

AIG Life Insurance practices concentrated marketing. The firm has developed products and promotional appeals that emphasize the unique financial needs of women.

choose to target a portion of the total market through combining (as in Panel D of Figure 5.4) or the marketer might choose to cover the entire larger market by creating as many combined segments as required to provide complete market coverage. Mercedes-Benz would be using this approach if the company targeted its 450 SL to both the luxury segment and sports car segment. These two market segments are often targeted separately, but they may be combined successfully to form a luxury sports car segment.

Disaggregation

The most extreme approach to targeting markets is **disaggregation.** The marketer using this strategy views each consumer or business in the total market as a separate market segment and develops a unique marketing mix for each one. This strategy is illustrated in Panel E of Figure 5.4. Clearly, disaggregation is the ultimate in customer-driven marketing. However, the cost and commitment of resources necessary to implement this strategy are so great that few manufacturers of consumer goods can afford to pursue it. We might argue, though, that manufacturers who allow consumers to alter goods to their own specifications are producing customized products and so are following a disaggregation strategy. Most automobile manufacturers, for instance, allow consumers to order cars with the exact set of options they desire. Similarly, the marketers of personal computer systems usually allow customers to select the exact configuration of memory, hardware, and software they want. Disaggregation also characterizes the marketing efforts of providers of specialized services, such as lawyers or tax consultants. Lastly, vendors selling to organizational consumers can use this approach successfully because their markets are frequently smaller and more concentrated than consumer markets. Boeing Aircraft views each major airline as a distinct target to be reached with an individual promotion, pricing, and distribution strategy as well as a customized product.

Choice of Approach

The marketing decision maker must consider many issues in deciding which targeting strategy is best. These issues include factors both internal and external to the company.

Internally, the firm must consider its goals and objectives as well as its resources. The organization's goals and objectives should influence its choice of a targeting strategy. A not-for-profit health clinic, for example, whose goal is to provide preventive health services to the entire community, might choose a differentiated strategy despite the fact that some segments of the market are expensive to serve or difficult to reach. A for-profit hospital, on the other hand, might choose a concentrated strategy, targeting its services to a small but affluent segment that offers significant potential for profitability. The availability of resources is also an internal factor that affects the choice of a targeting strategy. While the not-for-profit health clinic just described may wish to use a differentiated strategy to better meet the needs of the entire community, it may ultimately choose an undifferentiated strategy or a concentrated strategy. Either of these two strategies might prove less expensive or less labor intensive to implement.

Externally, the organization needs to consider the competition and the degree of heterogeneity exhibited by the market before deciding on a targeting strategy. The greater the competition in a market, the less likely a broad strategy like undifferentiated marketing will work. Similarly, combining could prove problematic in a market where competitors are focusing efforts on smaller, more precise target markets. The greater the degree of heterogeneity in a market, the more likely that a differentiated, concentrated, or disaggregated strategy would prove most effective.

Having considered all relevant internal and external issues, the fundamental basis on which a marketer should select a targeting strategy is cost–benefit analysis.[28] For each target market the marketer is considering, the costs of planning and implementing a marketing mix for the segment should be weighed against the revenues that segment will likely produce. To project the revenues a segment can be expected to produce, the firm should engage in forecasting. (Chapter 8 offers a thorough discussion of forecasting.)

5-3 Assume that you work for a company that makes kitchen knives. Your boss asks you to evaluate whether the company should target left-handed consumers. Ten percent of Americans, 24 million people, are left-handed. How would you go about determining if this segment of the population should be a target market for the company?

5-4 Would marital status be a better way to segment and target the market for kitchen knives? Why? What about targeting working women?

YOUR
MARKETING
KNOWLEDGE

POSITIONING

After choosing a targeting strategy and identifying target markets, a marketer needs to position his or her product in the minds of consumers. **Positioning** is the perception targeted consumers have of a firm's offering relative to that of competitors.[29] United Airlines, for example, positions itself as "the airline that's uniting the world." This positioning statement emphasizes United's commitment to a world market and seeks to differentiate the airline from competitors who have a less global focus. Organizations can use other factors besides product attributes and competition to position their products.[30] A company might, for example, position its brand as "the low price leader." Procter & Gamble has positioned its product, Nyquil, as "the nighttime cold remedy," hence positioning by time of use.

Perceptual Mapping

Since positioning is based on consumer perceptions, a useful way for marketers to choose a positioning strategy is through the use of a perceptual map. A **perceptual map** is a graph of consumers' perceptions of product attributes across two or more dimensions.[31] Perceptual maps can also be used to analyze the current position of a company's offerings relative to the competition and consumer demand. Figure 5.5 illustrates a perceptual map of department stores based on a study conducted by BBDO, an advertising agency.[32]

To construct a perceptual map, a marketer uses marketing research to gather three types of information from a target market. First, the marketer must identify product attributes that are important to the consumers. The perceptual map for

FIGURE 5.5
Mapping a Store's Personality

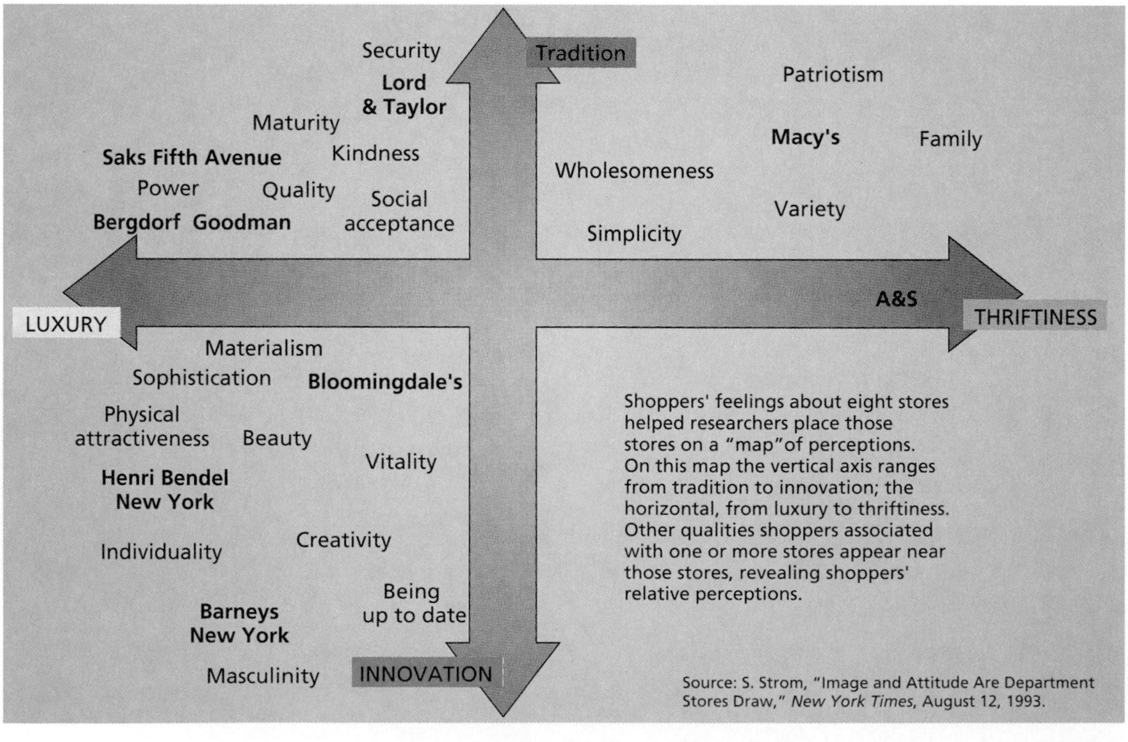

Shoppers' feelings about eight stores helped researchers place those stores on a "map" of perceptions. On this map the vertical axis ranges from tradition to innovation; the horizontal, from luxury to thriftiness. Other qualities shoppers associated with one or more stores appear near those stores, revealing shoppers' relative perceptions.

Source: S. Strom, "Image and Attitude Are Department Stores Draw," *New York Times*, August 12, 1993.

department stores in Figure 5.6 is based on two attributes: degree of innovation and degree of luxury. The second type of information required is consumer perceptions of various stores' brands relative to these two attributes. Henri Bendel, for example, is perceived to be a fairly innovative and very luxurious store. Macy's is perceived to be a traditional and thrifty store. The final type of information required to complete a perceptual map is the ideal point of the target market. An **ideal point** is the place on the perceptual map that represents the combination of attributes most desired by the consumer. This point describes the product the consumer would prefer over all others, even if such a product does not currently exist.[33] Figure 5.6 illustrates clusters of ideal points that might exist for department stores. Each cluster of ideal points is indicated by a numbered circle. The larger the circle, the greater the number of consumers in the market who find that combination of attributes ideal. By transposing Figure 5.6 onto Figure 5.5, a marketer could assess the market of existing department stores relative to consumers' preferences regarding what they perceive to be ideal department stores.

For existing products, a marketer can use a perceptual map that includes ideal point clusters to determine whether to consider repositioning a product. For example, Saks Fifth Avenue is perceived to be luxurious but not very innovative. Saks might consider attempting to reposition itself by introducing innovative services or by advertising that the store is indeed more innovative than shoppers think, especially if ideal point clusters indicate that consumers desire a department store with those features. A perceptual map can also be used to identify opportunities for new products. Cluster 2 desires a store that is thrifty and innovative. No current department stores are perceived to offer this combination of attributes. With this information, a marketer might choose to open a new store positioned specifically to

FIGURE 5.6
Ideal Point Cluster

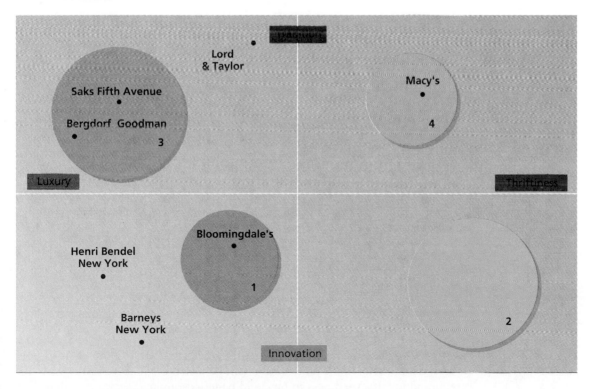

meet the needs of this cluster or to reposition an existing brand to focus better on this cluster.

This chapter has described segmentation, targeting, and positioning—three separate but interrelated processes. Identifying target markets is the cornerstone upon which marketing mix strategy is built. This identification, of course, cannot occur until the larger market has been segmented. Finally, a well thought-out positioning strategy provides the basis to develop a marketing mix once a target market has been identified. Although an organization will probably have some idea of what product it plans to market before it actually identifies target markets, the organization must remember that product strategy is a component of the marketing mix. Because a marketing mix is developed *for* a target market, target market identification should precede specific product planning. A clear understanding of the target market or markets makes development of the marketing mix(es) a much more straightforward task for the marketer.

PERSONAL COMPUTER EXERCISE

Forecasting market potential often involves the analysis of alternative market segments. Demographic data is frequently used to help determine the size of these segments, as this PC Exercise demonstrates.

KEY POINTS

- A market consists of people or businesses with the potential interest, purchasing power, and willingness to spend the money to buy a product or service to satisfy a need.

- Marketers typically divide markets into submarkets or segments, a process called market segmentation. Market segmentation allows a more efficient allocation of marketing resources, enables the marketer to understand better the needs of consumers in the market, and improves the organization's ability to satisfy the needs and wants of customers and potential customers.

- The major bases for segmentation are geographic, demographic, psychographic, and behavioral.

- Geographic and demographic segmentation variables are descriptive characteristics about people's states of being.

- Psychographic segmentation—using consumers' activities, interests, and opinions—enriches the description of market segments beyond simple demographics. It is useful to think of psychographics as states of mind.

- Behavioral variables enable managers to segment markets on the basis of consumers' actual behavior. Segmentation can be based on such variables as usage rate, brand loyalty, readiness to buy, and benefits sought.

■ For market segments to be useful, they must be of sufficient size and potential, they must be reachable, and they should show clear variation in responsiveness to marketing programs in comparison with other segments.

■ Once segments have been identified, a marketer has five targeting strategies to consider: undifferentiated, differentiated, concentrated, combined, and disaggregated.

■ Undifferentiated marketing is an approach to a market that assumes all consumers can be reached with a single marketing mix.

■ Differentiated marketing involves developing unique marketing mixes for each identified segment of the market.

■ Concentrated marketing occurs when the marketer selects one segment as a target market and develops a marketing mix for that segment alone.

■ The combined approach to marketing involves consolidating two or more segments with some similar characteristics into a larger segment that can be reached with a single marketing effort.

■ Disaggregation is a segmentation approach that views each individual in the population as a unique segment that requires its own marketing mix.

■ Positioning helps to clarify a product relative to its competition in the minds of the target market.

■ A perceptual map can be used to identify new opportunities for marketers or to determine if repositioning of existing products should be undertaken.

KEY TERMS

market segmentation (147)
market (148)
consumer market (148)
ultimate consumers (148)
business market (148)
business-to-business or organizational
    consumers (148)
geographic segmentation (150)
demographic segmentation (151)
geodemographic segmentation (152)
psychographics (153)
life-style (153)
AIO inventory (155)
behavioral segmentation (156)
usage rate (156)
80/20 rule (156)
brand loyalty(158)
benefit segmentation (159)
laddering (159)
majority fallacy (161)
microniche marketing (162)
undifferentiated marketing (163)

mass marketing (163)
differentiated marketing (165)
concentrated marketing (165)
combined approach (165)
disaggregation (166)
positioning (168)
perceptual map (168)
ideal point (169)

1. The advertising manager for a major consumer electronics company was recently quoted as follows: "I'd say that psychographics are a crock . . . With compact discs, we know we are going for the eighteen-to-twenty-four-year-olds; with TV and video-cassette equipment, it's older and more income—$25,000-plus and ages twenty-five to fifty. We've found a definite correlation between income and education levels and the market for our product." Do you agree with the advertising manager's views about demographic versus psychographic segmentation? Why or why not?

2. The director of marketing for Six Flags, a chain of theme parks, is intrigued by the projected increase in the percentage of senior citizens in the marketplace over the next decade. How might the company respond to this demographic information?

3. The O.M. Scott Company, a large marketer of grass seed, is concerned about the best way to segment its market. Through research the company has learned that the people spending the most on lawn care products care more about their lawns than the average homeowner, live in nicer neighborhoods, and earn above-average incomes. Should Scott segment the market using geographic, demographic, or psychographic segmentation? How should Scott define its target market?

4. In the past, hotel marketers (like Holiday Inn) used an undifferentiated strategy to market their services. Now many hotel companies have several types of hotels, each targeted at a different segment. For example, Holiday Inn markets the following products:

- Holiday Inn: "the world's leader in full-service, value-priced hotels"
- Embassy Suites: the leader in the all-suite hotel segment
- The Residence Inn: accommodations with a residential flavor
- Holiday Inn Crowne Plaza: "top-of-the-line hotels for the discriminating traveler"
- Hampton Inn: affordably priced hotels

What advantages does Holiday Inn gain by offering so many different types of hotels? What are the disadvantages? On what basis is Holiday Inn segmenting the market? Does this seem like a wise strategy?

5. A major insurance company is considering targeting the segment of the market that owns Chevrolets and lower-priced cars. It would only go after this end of the market, refusing to insure Porsches, Mercedes, and other high-priced cars. What questions should the insurance company ask before it implements this strategy?

6. Most of the airlines have frequent-flyer programs designed to appeal to heavy users of air travel and to generate increased brand loyalty. The rental car companies have begun to implement similar programs. Should retailers of men's and women's apparel undertake similar frequent-buyer programs, or are there other bases for segmenting and targeting that make more sense for the apparel marketers?

7. Use the concept of market segmentation to explain why Coca-Cola sells so many different drink products, including the soft drinks Coke II, Classic Coke, Diet Coke, Sprite, Fresca, Fanta in various versions, with and without caffeine, as well as Fruitopia, a noncarbonated drink containing 25 percent fruit juice.

8. Can all markets be segmented? Give an example of a product or service for which undifferentiated marketing might be an appropriate strategy.

9. A sporting goods retailer has decided to open a new store that will sell athletic shoes exclusively. She is evaluating the targeting strategies she might adopt. Consider the strategies available to her and make a recommendation.

10. Should the majority fallacy be a concern for a major auto manufacturer such as General Motors or Ford? How about for auto makers with a smaller, more specialized market, such as Porsche or Rolls Royce?

CASE APPLICATION

Taking Aim at Health-Conscious Consumers

In January, 1992, Tyson Foods, the number one chicken processor in the United States, was set to launch its chicken fajita and chicken stir-fry frozen dinners. The company had several options in selecting target markets for the new product. For instance, it could have targeted single people, working women, or college students, and positioned the two new products as easy-to-prepare and convenient alternatives to fast food. Instead, Tyson targeted "health-conscious" consumers and positioned the products as "low in fat" by emphasizing the calorie content on the packages and in its promotional efforts.

The firm was so confident that it introduced its new dinners without test marketing. Test marketing involves introducing a new product to limited markets to determine its likelihood for success before committing to full-scale introduction. Charles Grace, Tyson's product manager for frozen retail foods, explained that the firm decided to forgo test marketing because it did not want to slow down introduction of the products, given the growing popularity and consumer demand for healthier foods. Between 1989 and 1993 chicken consumption in the United States increased by 6 percent. This growth rate is expected to continue through the remainder of the 1990s.

Tyson has joined a growing number of firms who are producing food in a large variety of categories to target health-conscious consumers. Several firms, for example, have jumped into the fast growing "healthy soup" market. Campbell's Healthy Request and ConAgra's Healthy Choice accounted for 16.6 percent of the ready-to-serve soup category in the first two months of 1992. This is a 13.6 percent increase for the product category over 1991 according to Nielsen reports. ConAgra, again using the Healthy Choice brand, has also introduced an extra-lean ground beef containing oat gum as a fat substitute.

Fast food restaurants, long purveyors of high-fat, high-cholesterol, and high-calorie foods, may also be rethinking their targeting strategies. Traditionally, these companies have used demographics, mainly age, to define their markets. They have had good reason for doing so. A study commissioned by MTV, for example, found that 94 percent of teenagers in the United States had purchased fast food in the preceding three months. However, new product offerings such as salad bars and grilled chicken sandwiches suggest that the likes of McDonald's, Burger King, and Wendy's have also joined the march toward the health-conscious consumer.

The manufacturers and retailers who target health-conscious consumers are using both psychographic (life-style) and behavioral variables to segment their markets. The use of these variables appears to have brought much success.

Questions

1. Do health-conscious consumers meet the criteria for effective segmentation discussed in this chapter?
2. How might you identify a health-conscious consumer?
3. Which demographic variables do you think would be most useful for Tyson, if it chose to segment the market by demographics?
4. Which of the five targeting strategies presented in this chapter does Tyson appear to be using?

Know Your Markets

Chapter 5 discusses segmentation, targeting, and positioning as ways to fine-tune the approach to a product or service. Just as the marketer uses these processes, you, as a jobseeker, can use them to aid your search for employment.

Segmentation allows you to uniquely position yourself to meet the needs of a particular employer market. Bases for segmentation might include specific industries, organization size, the current success of the company, location of work, and company culture. The key is to identify segments that will influence how you approach your target markets.

In *selecting target markets*, you have a number of options: undifferentiated or mass marketing, concentrated marketing, or a combined approach.

- To use an *undifferentiated* or *mass marketing* strategy, you would advertise your product (yourself) through cover letters and résumés to companies and listings that you identify in books, directories, newspapers, and career offices. A small percentage of people find employment through this approach.
- The *concentrated marketing approach* is often used in conjunction with the undifferentiated approach. A concentrated marketing approach requires that you target a single industry and build a base of contacts. Usually, jobseekers find more success with this approach.
- For your job search, it is best to use a *combined approach*.

Positioning is a critical part of the job search. One way to get information on how you can best position yourself is to talk with an organization's representatives about how they would see you in relation to their newly hired employees. You would also need to learn what distinguished the entry-level persons hired from those not hired. You could review employment brochures to see what qualifications are highlighted for new hires and consult your college placement professionals about their evaluation of your qualifications in relation to the qualifications of the typical candidate. By obtaining this information, you will be prepared to anticipate what companies are looking for in new employees.

In your job search, remember to focus on attributes and skills that differentiate you from your competitors. One way to assess your attributes is through an *AIO inventory* (available in your college placement office). Your activities, interests, and opinions provide a clue to your values and skills, and to who you are. This provides an internal evaluation that is needed to know the product you want to sell. You also need to know the externals or the marketplace. You should assess a company's culture, business strategy, and competitors to understand better its needs, strengths, and weaknesses, and to create a broad strategy to promote your "product" (yourself) to your target markets.

CHapTeR 6

Consumer Buying Behavior

Upon completing this chapter, you will be able to do the following:

■ **Explain** why understanding consumer behavior is so important, yet such a challenge to marketers.

■ **Outline** the steps in the purchase decision process.

■ **Understand** the consumer information-seeking process, including internal search and external search.

■ **Identify** the types of problem-solving behavior used by consumers.

■ **Describe** the major influences on consumer behavior, including internal/psychological, external/social, and situational factors.

■ **Explain** the relationships among major categories of factors that influence consumer behavior.

■ **Describe** your own decision-making process, including the major factors influencing a recent purchase.

Marketing Profile

Can a Plastic Swan Make Scents?

Consumer decisions about what products to purchase are almost always influenced by the price of the product. That influence may not be what you would normally expect, however. A bargain price is usually very desirable, but not always. Some consumers feel a high price is desirable for specific products, because it connotes superior quality, status, and prestige.

Perfume has typically been associated with high prices, glitzy advertising campaigns, and expensive packaging. Hence when Lander Company of Englewood, New Jersey, introduced Swan Lake Perfume in 1992, it was forging a strategy different from that used by the rest of the perfume industry. Swan Lake was introduced with no advertising, no box, a simple bottle topped with a plastic swan, and a $5.95-per-ounce price tag. The perfume was intended as a stocking stuffer for Christmas 1992, but the company hoped it would be successful enough to survive past the holiday season.

Norman Auslander, the company's chairman, admitted that some buyers are attracted by the fancy packaging and the high prices of most perfumes. These buyers, the chairman believed, comprised "only about 10 percent of the market." Auslander, at the time of Swan Lake's introduction, described the perfume's marketing strategy as "staying within a price point that will attract the consumer segment." Product development decisions contributed to this strategy. While the raw ingredients of most perfumes may cost about the same, elaborate packaging and expensive bottles can account for much of the higher prices charged by many perfume makers. Lander's ability to charge a lower price could be explained by the simple, standard design of the product.

A break with the traditional marketing techniques that supposedly reflect consumer preferences and expectations made retailers nervous. Lander found retailers hesitant to stock Swan Lake because the company did not promise a multimillion dollar advertising campaign to support the perfume's introduction.

In contrast to Lander's low-keyed approach, Estée Lauder launched its newest perfume, Spellbound, with an extravagant media campaign. The most notable feature of the launch was a package that consisted of a two-minute video attached to a copy of the upscale fashion magazine *Elle*. The package was sent to 14,000 of Estée Lauder's select customers. Lauder also used plenty of print and television ads to promote the new fragrance, priced at $200 an ounce. Even firms who price their perfumes moderately still spend big when it comes to promotion. Revlon's Downtown Girl was introduced with a $3 million ad blitz.

According to Lander Company, consumers loved Swan Lake. The company contends that Auslander was correct in believing that most consumers would respond favorably to a bargain-priced perfume that lacked fancy packaging and a big promotional buildup. Unfortunately for Lander, the perfume did not survive past the 1992 holiday selling season. The company attributes its demise not to the consumer behavior of the targeted markets but to the intermediaries who would not carry the product. Ultimately Swan Lake was not able to achieve broad enough distribution to meet Lander's sales objectives. Did Lander accurately read consumer behavior or did the nervous retailers better understand how consumers would react?

Successful strategies in all aspects of the marketing mix—product, price, promotion, and distribution—depend on a thorough understanding of consumer behavior. **Consumer behavior** can be defined as the processes involved when individuals or groups select, purchase, use, or dispose of products, services, ideas, or experiences to satisfy needs and desires.[1] The "Marketing Profile" about Swan Lake Perfume shows the importance of understanding consumer behavior. For the perfume to be successful, Lander Company had to be correct in its estimation of consumers and what they wanted. Lander also had to convince retailers that its assessment of consumer behavior was correct. Retailers' beliefs that they understood better the behavior of consumers ultimately led to the product's demise.

The study of consumer behavior is really just the study of human behavior in the marketplace. In this chapter, we discuss many principles of behavior dealt with in psychology and sociology. Trying to understand these principles is a challenging endeavor. We can see what people do, but we cannot see the mental processes that underlie their actions. Often the best we can do is to infer the reasons for individuals' behavior from actions we observe.

Because we cannot directly observe what lies behind consumer behavior, the term **Black Box Model** refers to the process an individual goes through when making a decision.[2] A black box indicates that something is occurring that cannot be observed. Figure 6.1 could be described as a model of consumer behavior, though not a very enlightening one. The input is comprised of various types of information the decision maker will use. Input might include advertisements, presentations by salespersons, opinions of friends and family, and articles from *Consumer Reports*. As we discuss the principles and factors covered in this chapter, we will attempt to shed light on the inner workings of the black box.

To appreciate the challenges of trying to understand consumer behavior, let's look at a specific transaction:

> Late for class, Sarah Brown quickly stops at a vending machine. Pulling change from her backpack, she purchases two candy bars. She places one in her backpack and eats the second as she hurries off to class.

We clearly observe one component of Sarah's consumer behavior: She purchased two candy bars. Most aspects of her consumer behavior are not observable, however. We don't know whether Sarah intends to eat the second candy bar later or if she purchased it for someone else. We also know nothing about the "why" behind her decision to purchase the candy. Was she hungry? Does she particularly like candy bars? Did she buy them because the vending machine was on her way to class? How important was price in the decision? Did Sarah simply hope to put off class another few seconds by stopping? These are some of the many kinds of questions addressed by the study of consumer behavior.

This chapter will help you understand the processes ultimate consumers go through in deciding to make a purchase. **Ultimate consumers** are final users of goods

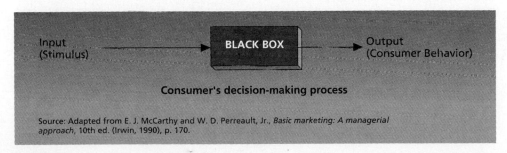

FIGURE 6.1
The Black Box Model of Consumer Decision Making

Source: Adapted from E. J. McCarthy and W. D. Perreault, Jr., *Basic marketing: A managerial approach*, 10th ed. (Irwin, 1990), p. 170.

and services. The chapter also explores many of the psychological, social, and situational factors that influence a consumer's behavior. Understanding the behavior of business consumers is also important for a complete picture of buyer behavior. Business consumers, as defined in Chapter 5, are individuals who use goods and services in the process of providing for the needs of ultimate consumers. (Because business-to-business buying behavior differs somewhat from that of ultimate consumers, we discuss it separately in Chapter 7.)

THE CONSUMER PURCHASE DECISION PROCESS

The definition of consumer behavior presented earlier stated that consumer behavior is a process rather than a discrete act. In fact, consumer behavior is a series of acts. Consumer behavior can be analyzed in terms of the **purchase decision process,** the series of stages (or acts) a consumer goes through in deciding to buy a product or service. As Figure 6.2 shows, the process consists of five stages: problem recognition, information seeking, evaluation of alternatives, purchase decision, and postpurchase evaluation.

FIGURE 6.2
The Consumer Purchase Decision Process

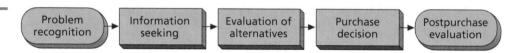

Notice that the purchase decision process begins long before the decision is made and continues after it. A marketer concerned with meeting the needs and desires of consumers should pay attention to all five stages of the purchase decision process. The market-driven concept, the idea that all activities of an organization should be focused directly on satisfying and anticipating the needs and wants of customers, is particularly relevant here. Not only does a firm need to take its customers into account at the various stages of marketing planning but, to be thorough, the organization must consider the various stages of the consumer's purchase decision process.

Recognizing a Problem

The first stage of the purchase decision process is problem recognition. It occurs when a person perceives a difference between some ideal state and his or her actual state at a given moment.[3] Consider, for example, a student who is in the market to rent an apartment. For her, the problem-recognition stage may have started when she decided that her dorm was too noisy or perhaps after an argument with her roommate. For a product like shampoo, problem recognition may occur when a consumer sees his favorite brand on sale, or it may be triggered when he notices that the bottle in his shower is almost empty.

Problem recognition may occur gradually. Several weeks may have passed before our student realized how much the noise in the dorm was bothering her. Sometimes, it occurs very quickly. When standing in the check-out line at the grocery store you see your favorite movie star on the cover of *People* and impulsively buy the magazine, you have experienced nearly instantaneous problem recognition. In fact, you have gone through virtually the entire purchase decision process in a matter of moments.

Marketing efforts can trigger problem recognition. Many buying decisions occur after consumers see an advertisement for a product or notice that an item is on sale.

Effective packaging can attract attention to a product. Personal selling can convince potential buyers that they have an unfulfilled need or want.

Seeking Information

After a consumer recognizes a problem, the next step in the purchase decision process is seeking information. Often, the consumer does not even know what alternatives are available. In such cases, much of the information search is concentrated on identifying products or services that will satisfy his or her needs. For example, a young couple expecting their first child might begin to resolve their diapering dilemma by reviewing the options they have observed other parents using. Perhaps they have friends who have diapered babies in disposables. As the couple begins to read parenting magazines and talk to parents of babies, they learn about other alternatives such as diaper services.

The amount and type of information gathered varies, depending on the product and the consumer. Some expectant parents might view the type of diaper to be used as an important decision with both economic and environmental implications, while other parents-to-be may see the decision as less important. For major purchases like stereo systems and automobiles, a great deal of information will be gathered from many different sources. A decision regarding a new car, for example, might cause a person to talk to friends and acquaintances, carefully read advertisements, visit showrooms to speak to salespersons, and seek information from publications such as *Car and Driver* and *Consumer Reports*.

For frequently purchased, low-priced products like shampoo and candy bars, only a minimal amount of information is typically gathered. When purchasing shampoo, for example, most consumers only seek information about the price and size (number of ounces) of one or two brands. Most often they obtain this information at the point of purchase.

After a consumer recognizes a problem, the next step in the purchase decision process is seeking information. The student who is searching for an apartment might consult local newspapers about available opportunities.

The information-seeking stage begins with a cognitive internal search. This is simply the process of searching the memory to see what one already knows about a product or service. Often, the consumer is not even aware of going through the process, particularly if the product or service is one that is consistently consumed. How much time do you usually spend searching your memory when you notice you are out of soap or toilet tissue? After the internal search, the consumer may have all the information that she needs. She can then proceed through the remaining stages of the purchase decision process.

If the consumer needs more information, he may undertake an external search for it.[4] There are four major sources of external information:

- *Personal sources.* Friends, relatives, and acquaintances often provide much information to the consumer. Personal sources are important because the consumer trusts them, even though the information is not always accurate.

- *Marketer-dominated sources.* These sources include advertising, salespersons, packaging, displays, channels of distribution, and pricing. Marketers try to make these sources as readily available as possible.

- *Public sources.* These sources include magazine and newspaper articles, product rating organizations such as *Consumer Reports*, and government agencies. Information from public sources is often important to consumers because it is usually factual and unbiased.

- *Personal interaction.* For a number of products, the most important information comes from the consumer's own interaction with the item (not including experience stored in the consumer's memory). Included in this category are handling the product, carefully examining its features, and actually using the product, as in taking an automobile for a test drive.

Table 6.1 presents the results of a study of appliance buyers, documenting the types of information used by the buyers and identifying the information sources that buyers found most helpful. (The sources of information available to organizations as buyers of products are somewhat different from the sources used by consumers. These are discussed in Chapter 7.)

TABLE 6.1
Information Sources Used in the Purchase of Appliances

Information Source	Buyers Who Consulted	Buyers Who Found Source Useful	Buyers' "Most Useful" Source
1. Appliance salesperson	59%*	49%	41%
2. Newspaper ad	39	28	13
3. Friend or relative	38	31	13
4. Catalog	35	28	9
5. Brochures/labels	28	25	9
6. Consumer reports	20	18	9
7. Appliance repairperson	14	10	5
8. Magazine ad	12	7	1
9. TV ad	10	5	1

* To be read: "59% of the buyers reported having consulted a salesperson as an information source. Almost all of these people (49% of the total sample) reported finding the salesperson to be a 'useful' source of information. When asked which source had been the 'most useful,' 41% of consumers reported that the salesperson had been."

Source: W. L. Wilkie and P. R. Dickson, "Shopping for appliances: Consumers' strategies and patterns of information search." *Marketing Science Institute Report,* No. 85–108, November 1985, p. 13.

Evaluating Alternatives

Once the consumer has gathered the information he or she deems necessary to make a decision, the evaluation of alternatives begins. The first part of this stage involves the identification of an evoked set. An **evoked set** is the group of brands the consumer will actually consider when making a purchase decision. Even when a large number of brands is available in a product category, consumers usually limit their evoked set to a relatively small number of brands.[5] Although there are literally hundreds of brands of cookies on the market, for example, you probably make a choice of which to buy from a set of six or seven brands.

Once the evoked set has been identified, the second step in the evaluation-of-alternatives stage begins. This step involves ranking the evoked set. To rank the alternatives in the evoked set, the consumer must identify the criteria to be used. For example, the student seeking to rent an apartment might use some combination of the following criteria:

- Price
- Location
- Size
- Amenities
- Demographics of others in building or complex
- Length of lease required
- Age of building
- Rules and regulations of complex

After identifying the criteria, the consumer determines the importance of each criterion. Although price is a criterion used by virtually all consumers, some people weight it heavily and others consider it a minor factor. Price is usually a minor factor if it is low relative to the buyer's income, or if the price differences among the alternatives in the evoked set are not significant.

For many consumer decisions, identifying criteria and determining their importance are done in an informal, almost subconscious manner. Consumers are unlikely to develop a formal list of criteria, ranked in order of importance, before purchasing a routine item that they have bought hundreds of times. In making the decision, however, the consumer is still guided by a set of criteria, no matter how informally the ranking of those criteria occurs.

Consumer perceptions and values influence the evaluation of alternatives. Two consumers may use the same criterion and give it the same weight but may view it differently. For example, two students may determine that demographics are very important when evaluating apartments. One student might assign a high rating to apartment complexes with lots of other students, while another student may feel that a complex with very few students is more desirable.

Advertising can seek to influence the criteria used to evaluate alternatives. Note how the brochure shown to the right informs consumers about the merits of Motorola Cordless Phones and stresses the importance of privacy when using a cordless phone.

Deciding to Purchase

By applying weights to the identified criteria, a consumer produces a rank order of items in his evoked set. At this point the consumer may arrive at a tentative decision to buy the top-ranked alternative. The final decision may vary from the intended one, however. If the preferred choice is not available, the consumer might purchase the second-ranked alternative instead of waiting for the top-ranked choice. The actual purchase might also be delayed until the consumer has selected a retail outlet and completed price negotiations.

Advertising can seek to influence the criteria used to evaluate alternatives. This brochure stresses the importance of privacy when using a cordless phone.

Postpurchase Evaluating

After completing the purchase, the consumer moves to the final stage of the purchase decision process, postpurchase evaluation. This process results in the consumer's satisfaction or dissatisfaction with the product or service. Satisfaction will occur if performance meets the consumer's expectations. If this is not the case, the consumer will be dissatisfied. Either way, information about the product will be stored in memory to be used the next time the consumer enters the problem-recognition stage of the purchase decision process. If, for example, a consumer purchased a Nissan automobile and was very satisfied with it, he might find out only about the new models of Nissans the next time he is in the market for a car. The evoked set in that future purchase decision process might include only Nissan products. If the consumer had been unhappy with the Nissan, he probably would consider many more alternatives and would undoubtedly seek more information when he's ready to purchase a new car.

Information that consumers store as a result of postpurchase evaluation can shorten their decision-making process in the future. Mentally, consumers may recognize a similar problem and then proceed directly to either the evaluative stage (if loyalty or satisfaction was not originally established) or to the decision stage (if no additional evaluation is necessary and satisfaction was achieved).

Consumers sometimes feel **postpurchase dissonance,** which is doubt or anxiety experienced after making a difficult, relatively permanent decision.[6] For example, after she signed the lease, the student who was searching for an apartment might agonize over whether she made the right decision. Will she be able to pay the rent every month? Will she be lonely living by herself? Marketers can aid consumers experiencing postpurchase dissonance by reassuring them that they made the correct decision. The leasing agent, for example, might assure the student that living alone provides more quiet time to study while informing her of the many social activities at the apartment complex.

Careful attention to the postpurchase evaluation, particularly to the alleviation of postpurchase dissonance, is an important part of the concept of being market-driven. Many firms today provide liberal warranties, return policies, and after-sale service to demonstrate their commitment to customers throughout the entire purchase decision process.

Types of Decision-Making Processes

Consumers respond differently to different types of buying situations. We have seen, for instance, that a consumer's behavior when leasing an apartment will be very different from her behavior when purchasing a candy bar or a bottle of shampoo. Most buying situations fall into one of three categories distinguished by the type of problem solving involved. They are extensive problem solving, limited problem solving, and routine response behavior.[7]

Extensive problem solving. For products like automobiles and housing, consumers spend a great deal of time and effort at each stage of the purchase decision process. Because consumers usually haven't bought these products in a long time, if ever, they tend to seek a lot of information, identify a relatively large evoked set, use many criteria to evaluate alternatives, and proceed cautiously in making their decisions. Purchases made in this way are sometimes called **high-involvement purchases.** High-involvement purchases are important to the consumer and are often closely tied to consumers' egos and self-images. A stereo system is a high-involvement product that is likely to involve extensive problem solving.[8]

Marketers of products and services that involve extensive problem solving must provide their target markets the information needed to make decisions. A stereo

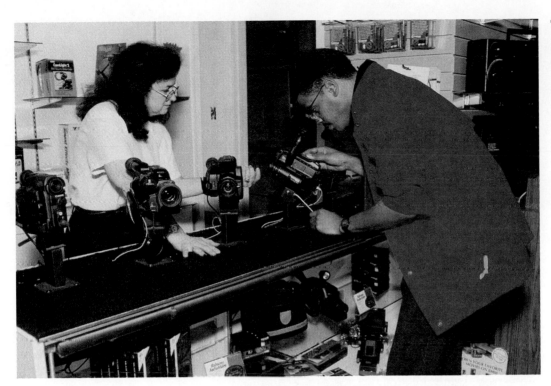

Electronics equipment is an example of a high-involvement product that is likely to involve extensive problem solving.

manufacturer, for example, might produce a print ad that compares its products and the products of competitors on a feature-by-feature basis.

Limited problem solving In situations requiring limited problem solving, like the purchase of small appliances or clothing, consumers are typically familiar with the product class, but they may not be familiar with all the alternatives. As a result, much less information seeking takes place, and much of it occurs at the point of purchase.

Take shoes as an example. Several alternatives are likely to be in the evoked set. Several criteria, such as style, color, price, and brand name, are used to choose from among the alternatives. Some effort is put into the evaluation of alternatives, although less than that typically exerted in the case of extensive problem solving. The purchase decision process is likely to take a moderately long period for limited problem solving. The shoe buyer, for example, may take a day or two to think about the alternatives before making a final purchase decision.

Routine response behavior. The purchase decision process for frequently purchased, low-priced products like toothpaste or shampoo is an example of routine response behavior, the least complex type of problem solving. For products in this category, consumers seek virtually no information and do not formally evaluate alternatives. Instead, their decisions are automatic. For example, a consumer glances at her gasoline gauge and notices it's on empty (problem recognition). She pulls into the first service station she sees and fills her car's gas tank. Almost no conscious thought is involved in the process.

Purchases by routine response are sometimes called **low-involvement purchases,** indicating the product is not very important to the consumer, the alternatives are perceived as similar, or the item is purchased frequently and does not require the consumer to go through the process each time. Examples include facial tissues, paper clips, and canned fruit.[9]

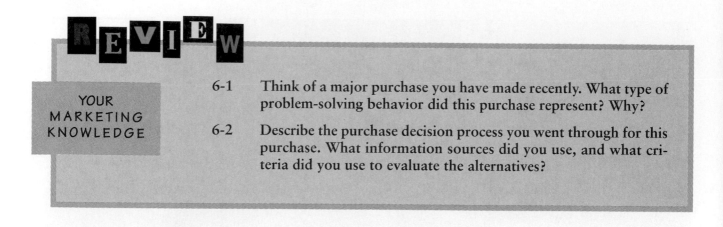

YOUR MARKETING KNOWLEDGE

6-1   Think of a major purchase you have made recently. What type of problem-solving behavior did this purchase represent? Why?

6-2   Describe the purchase decision process you went through for this purchase. What information sources did you use, and what criteria did you use to evaluate the alternatives?

INFLUENCES ON CONSUMER BEHAVIOR

So far in this chapter we have been discussing the stages of the purchase decision process. We now turn our attention to some of the many factors that influence that process. Figure 6.3 presents an expanded model of consumer behavior that includes the purchase decision process together with the many influences on it. These influences fit into five categories: demographics, marketing mix variables, psychological, social, and situational factors.

Demographic Factors

Demographic factors play an important role in the consumer purchase process. Income, age, occupation, and a myriad of other demographics can influence decision making at every step in the process. A very wealthy, retired consumer, for example, might engage in limited problem solving when deciding where to vacation this year. Due to unlimited funds and unlimited time, the consumer might seek only a small number of alternatives, like deciding between a luxury cruise around the world or an extended stay at a five-star resort. A less wealthy consumer with only two weeks of vacation for the year might view the decision as one that requires extensive problem solving. He may spend several months gathering information from a variety of sources and then spend weeks evaluating that information before making a decision. The "Marketing in Action: Winning, Losing, and Identifying the Players in the Senior Market" illustrates how marketers are targeting mature consumers by developing products and promotions designed to appeal to the buying process of older consumers. (To review the discussion of demographics see Chapter 2.)

Marketing Mix Factors

Another set of factors that marketers certainly hope will influence consumer behavior is the marketing mix itself. All four components of the marketing mix are planned to promote positive action. For example, companies may try to spur problem recognition by running a sale or offering a low, introductory price. The information in an advertisement can affect the information-seeking stage of a consumer's purchase decision process. Convenient home delivery may influence a consumer to rate a particular pizzeria high among the evoked set of restaurants he is considering. An extended warranty may serve to alleviate postpurchase dissonance. (As we discuss the various components of the marketing mix in Chapters 9 through 18, it will become clear to you how each part of the marketing mix affects the consumer decision process.)

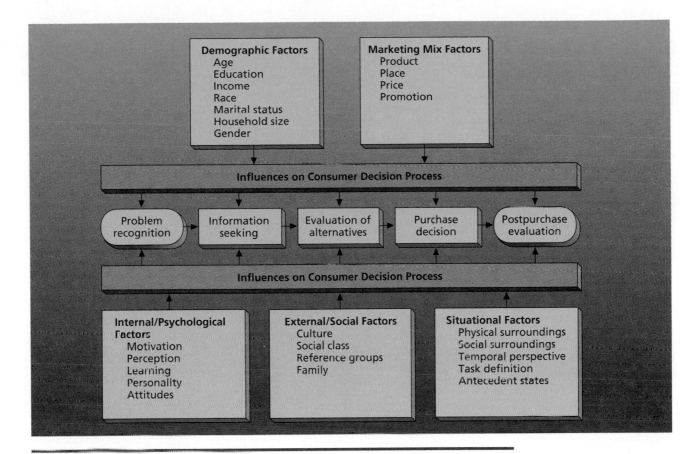

Demographic Factors
Age
Education
Income
Race
Marital status
Household size
Gender

Marketing Mix Factors
Product
Place
Price
Promotion

Influences on Consumer Decision Process

Problem recognition → Information seeking → Evaluation of alternatives → Purchase decision → Postpurchase evaluation

Influences on Consumer Decision Process

Internal/Psychological Factors
Motivation
Perception
Learning
Personality
Attitudes

External/Social Factors
Culture
Social class
Reference groups
Family

Situational Factors
Physical surroundings
Social surroundings
Temporal perspective
Task definition
Antecedent states

FIGURE 6.3
Expanded Model of Consumer Behavior

Psychological Factors

Much of what we know about how consumers behave is based on theories and research from the field of psychology, the study of individual behavior. When analyzing the process by which consumers make purchase decisions, marketers should understand such psychological factors as motivation, perception, learning, personality, and attitudes because they help explain the *why* of consumer behavior.

Psychological factors are sometimes called internal factors, that is, their influence occurs within the individual. Because their influence is internal it cannot be observed, but must be inferred from what people say or do. Often consumers themselves, however, do not know why they behave as they do. Other times they do know, but may not be willing to tell a researcher the true reasons for their behavior. Under these circumstances, you can imagine the challenge that marketers face when they attempt to understand the influences of psychological factors.

Motivation. **Motivation** is defined as activity toward a goal. It is the basis of all consumer behavior. A basic question marketers must answer is, "What will motivate people to buy my product or service?" When a consumer is motivated, he exists in a state called **drive**. Drive is generated by tension, which is caused by an unfulfilled need. Consumers strive to reduce the tension by satisfying the need. The need is thus a critical component in the motivation process. When a need is aroused, it becomes a motive or drive stimulating behavior. For example, hunger is a basic need that, when aroused, becomes a motive for satisfying the need, perhaps by stopping at

MARKETING IN ACTION

Winning, Losing, and Identifying the Players in the Senior Market

Thrifty Car Rental introduced its "Give a Friend a Lift" program in the late 1980s, around the same time that Southwestern Bell was touting the entrance into the marketplace of its *Silver Pages*. Both were targeted at mature consumers (i.e., over 50 years old). Thrifty has met with considerable success while Southwestern Bell has since dropped its product. "Give a Friend a Lift" is a promotional program designed to get older consumers to rent more cars from Thrifty. For every 25,000 cars rented by members of the American Association of Retired Persons (AARP), Thrifty donates a new Chrysler minivan to one of the Nation's 670 area agencies on aging. A recent study by Thrifty reported that 40% of consumers in the market would be more motivated to rent a car as a result of this program than if discounts were offered. The Southwestern Bell *Silver Pages* was a directory of retailers and the discounts it offered to older consumers. The directory folded in 1989, following undistinguished results. Such results contradicted the research undertaken prior to the introduction of the *Silver Pages*, which indicated that seniors as well as the advertising community were anxious for such a product.

In recent years, many companies have begun a hot pursuit of the so-called senior market. According to the 1990 U.S. Census figures, 64 million Americans are 50 years old or older. Although this represents only 25% of the population, the group has 75% of the nation's financial assets and about 50% of its discretionary income. Such figures may excite marketers. However, George Moschis, director of the Center for Mature Consumer Studies at Georgia State University, believes that the figures can be misleading. According to Professor Moschis, "The assumption now is that all older people are rich." Unfortunately, that is not the case. There exists, claims Moschis, "a great deal of variance of wealth among members of the mature market." Despite this fact, marketers are increasingly interested in targeting the segment.

Many firms besides Thrifty Car Rental have had success with the senior market. Nestle Foods' Tasters Choice coffee claims a market comprised of 50% over-fifty consumers. Its advertising, targeted at older consumers, was in response to research showing that seniors preferred subtle, understated ads that "tug at the heartstrings." Other firms who have had success in the mature market appear to be following the guidelines of David B. Wolfe who bases his contentions on the work of Abraham Maslow. Wolfe claims that older consumers have reached a point in their lives where "being" experiences rather than "acquiring" or "having-it-all" experiences are of primary importance. Products and services appealing to older adults' values (e.g., altruism or cooperation) provide opportunities for these types of "being" experiences.

With such knowledge available, what went wrong in the case of the *Silver Pages*? The problem, according to R.M. Jennings, president of AD/VENT, the unit of Southwestern Bell that published the directory, was that as the older population attracts more marketing attention, the discount promotions that were the directory's chief draw were undercut by the growing availability of such offers. In other words, Jennings states, "[An older person] can get a discount merely by looking like a senior and asking for it."

George Moschis might disagree. He warns against senior discounts and advertising in periodicals specifically targeting older consumers. "People in the mature market think of themselves as being 15 years younger than they actually are and may not care for being singled out on the basis of age." Southwestern Bell has not given up on the senior market. "We've got to go back to the drawing board and reformulate what we do," states Jennings. Acknowledging that the market is difficult and diverse, Mr. Jennings concludes, "We may never find what is the right product."

Recently, the Strategic Directions Group completed a study of seniors that yielded information to suggest that Southwestern Bell should stop trying to identify *the* product that will be right for all seniors. The study supports for Moschis's claim that much diversity exists within the market. Three thousand people over 50 years old were studied. The research found that people in the over-50 population cannot be viewed as a single group. Based on variations in the attitudes, lifestyles, and purchasing behaviors of the older consumers studied, the Strategic Directions Group has identified three general categories of consumers. Labeled *food*, *health*, and *self*, the groups reflected significant differences in consumer behavior across the population of seniors in the study. "Upbeat Enjoyers," a subsegment of the *self* category, for example, see themselves as growing more attractive with age and are more likely to buy "fun" products like imported automobiles. "Financial Positives," another subsegment of the *self* category, on the other hand, worry about aging and are more likely to consider plastic surgery.

a McDonald's restaurant. Of course, the consumer could satisfy hunger in many other ways. The specific decision to stop at McDonald's is influenced, in turn, by many additional factors.

Marketers attempt to stimulate drives and needs through advertising and selling. These activities can bring the consumer to a point where he or she recognizes the need as a drive and has the desire to satisfy it. As these drives increase to a point of being a problem, marketers provide the products and services to satisfy them.

There is no agreement among psychologists or consumer behavior scholars on the best way to classify consumer needs. Physiological needs are biologically determined and include the need for food, clothing, and shelter. Psychological needs are generated by one's social environment; among these are the need for affiliation, belonging, distinctiveness, individualism, personal fulfillment, and status. Abraham Maslow classified human needs into a hierarchy of five categories:

- *Physiological needs*: hunger, thirst, and shelter
- *Safety needs*: security, protection, order, and stability
- *Love needs*: affection, belonging, and friendship
- *Esteem needs*: self-respect, prestige, success, and achievement
- *Self-actualization needs*: desire for self-fulfillment[10]

According to Maslow, the lower order needs, such as physiological and safety needs, must be satisfied before higher-order needs can emerge. In industrialized nations such as the United States, Japan, and England, the majority of consumers have satisfied these physiological needs, and thus, the higher-order needs have become the driving force behind much consumer behavior. This is not necessarily the case in less-developed countries. Many third-world nations are still striving to satisfy the basic physiological needs of their citizens. Even countries such as Russia, Romania, Poland, and other former Eastern Bloc nations are primarily focused on lower-order needs. Table 6.2 presents three basic needs and a sample of promotional appeals directed at arousing these needs in certain product categories.

It is possible for a consumer to be at more than one level on Maslow's hierarchy of needs at the same time. This can occur because people operate in more

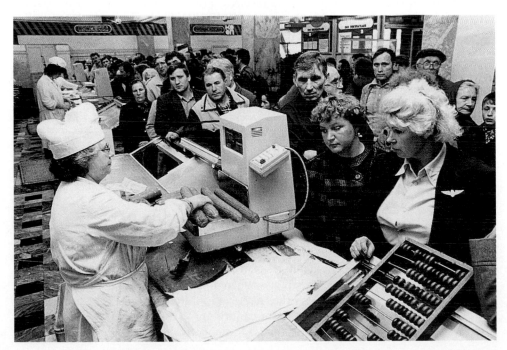

Many former Eastern Bloc nations are primarily focused on satisfying lower-order needs. Here people line up to buy sausages in Moscow.

Motive	Areas of Use	Illustrative Appeals
Affection	Telephones, liquor, greeting cards, automobiles, airlines, insurance, writing instruments, charitable organizations, and vacation resorts	Toyota: *"I love what you do for me."* United Airlines: *"Fly the friendly skies."* Hallmark Cards: *"When you care enough to send the very best."*
Safety	Appliances, toys, air travel, batteries, hotels, toothpaste, burglar and fire alarms, and traveler's checks	Children's Tylenol Tablets: *"The one most pediatricians give their own children."* Holiday Inn: *"Stay with someone you know."* Allstate Insurance: *"You're in good hands with Allstate."*
Achievement	Books, sporting equipment, lawn care products, computers, automobiles, colleges, liquor, and magazines	BMW: *"The ultimate driving machine."* Apple Computers: *"The power to be your best."* Wharton Executive Education: *"The learning experience of a lifetime."*

Source: Adapted from D. Loudon and A. Della Bitta, *Consumer Behavior: Concepts and Applications* (McGraw-Hill, 1979), p. 306.

Table 6.2
Examples of Motives and Promotional Appeals to Arouse Them

than one environment. For example, at work a new employee may be trying to satisfy social needs, with friends the same person may be seeking esteem, and personally she may be fully satisfied.

It is also possible for a consumer to move downward on the hierarchy, seeking to satisfy lower-order needs that were previously satisfied. This may occur as the result of events in the person's life such as divorce, marriage, loss of employment, a new job, the purchase of a new home, or a move to a strange city.

After needs have been aroused, they can be classified as *primary buying motives* or *selective buying motives*. Primary buying motives are associated with strong reasons to buy categories of products or services. For example, a desire for warmth and beauty in one's home might be a primary motive in the decision to purchase carpeting instead of other floor coverings. Selective buying motives refer to reasons for selection of particular brands within the product categories. Color, type of fiber, and price might be selective motives that determine the specific brand of carpeting purchased.

Another way to classify motives is to differentiate between *product motives* and *patronage motives*. Product motives are associated with the particular product or service being purchased. Ease of opening a package might be a product motive. Patronage motives are associated with the place the product or service will be purchased. Examples of patronage motives include the convenience of a store's location, friendly sales personnel, and the availability of a wide assortment of products and services.

Perception.   **Perception** is the process through which incoming stimuli, such as sights, sounds, tastes, or smells, are organized, interpreted, and given meaning.[11] In other words, it's the way people make sense of the stimuli they receive. An individual's behavior as a consumer is strongly affected by perceptions. If two consumers perceive a product, its price, or its other features in different ways, they are likely to behave toward it in different ways. Thus, marketers are generally very concerned about how people perceive their products. If one consumer, for example, perceives childproof caps on aspirin to be a safe way of protecting children, and a second consumer perceives the caps to be inconvenient and difficult to remove, the two individuals are not likely to act the same way when it comes to purchasing aspirin.

One important reality with which marketers must contend is that people have **selective perception.** That is, we actually perceive only a very small proportion of all the stimuli with which we are constantly bombarded. For example, most consumers are exposed to countless advertisements every day on billboards, in magazines and newspapers, and on television or the radio, but they actually are conscious of very few of them. Thus, an important goal for marketers is to make sure that the advertisements for their products are perceived by their target markets.

The nature of the stimulus itself and personal factors related to the target market are important in determining whether or not the stimulus is perceived.[12] Larger advertisements are more likely to be noticed than smaller ones. Color ads in magazines or newspapers are more likely to be noticed than black-and-white versions of the same ad. The frequency with which an ad is repeated can also be important in getting one's message perceived by consumers. Now you know why you sometimes see the same ad repeated over and over again during the commercial breaks for a single television program.

Personal factors strongly affect consumer perceptions. A person's needs, values, attitudes, experiences, and present situation affect whether he or she perceives various marketing stimuli. For example, a person who thinks of himself as being "with it" is more likely to perceive and pay attention to an ad for a sports car than to one for a station wagon. Similarly, a person is more likely to notice an ad on TV for a soft drink at 7 P.M. while cooling down after several sets of tennis than she would notice an ad on the radio for the same soft drink at 7 A.M. while she is getting ready to go to work. Past experiences also affect perceptions. People are more likely to perceive ads for products they have used and come to prefer.

Consumers respond to a product in terms of its **brand image,** the consumer's subjective evaluation of the brand based on the perceived benefits it provides. In marketing, a product's brand image is often much more important than its attributes. For example, Brand X of film might be comparable in quality to Kodak film but sell at a much lower price. However, if the consumer perceives that Kodak film is of much higher quality, the fact that Brand X is really the better value will be largely irrelevant. Brand image and consumer's self-concept sometimes work together in the consumer's purchase decision process. A classic study by Grubb and Hupp found that buyers of Volkswagens and Pontiac GTOs had different self-concepts and, therefore, had different perceptions of the owners of each model car.[13] The buyers of Volkswagens, for example, thought they had similar self-concepts to other Volkswagen owners, and they thought of themselves as different from owners of competing brands.

In another experiment on the impact of perception on buying behavior, Rolls Royce Motor Company ran an ad in *Architectural Digest* that let readers scratch a spot on the ad and smell the leathery Rolls interiors. Presumably the reader's perceptions of the car's luxury were enhanced. Calls to the company increased fourfold the month after the ad appeared.[14]

Consumers often perceive a positive relationship between a product's price and its quality, especially when limited information is available to them.[15] That is, in the absence of other evidence, consumers tend to assume that a higher price means higher quality. This perception is very important in product categories like diamond jewelry, where image and prestige are key factors.

Perception is also important in evaluating the risk associated with a purchase. **Perceived risk** occurs because consumers cannot anticipate with certainty the outcomes of their decisions. Furthermore, it is likely that some outcomes will be negative. There are several types of perceived risk. *Financial perceived risk* is associated with the cost of the product relative to the consumer's income—the higher the cost, the greater the perceived risk. *Functional perceived risk* is concerned with product performance—Will the product work the way it is supposed to? *Psychosocial perceived risk* is concerned with whether the product will enhance one's sense of self-concept or well-being—What will my friends think of me if I purchase this product?

Consumers generally strive to reduce risk in the purchase decision process by reducing either the negative consequences or the probability of the negative consequences. A marketer can aid consumers in their attempts to reduce perceived risk in a number of ways. To help reduce financial risk, for example, a firm might offer a money-back guarantee. Offering a free trial so that the consumer can see how the product performs might help reduce functional risk. An advertisement that assures a consumer that she will be the envy of her friends when using a particular product is aimed at reducing psychosocial risk.

Learning.   Consumers' perceptions of products and services and their motivations to buy or not buy them are primarily functions of learning. **Learning** refers to the changes that occur in an individual's behavior as the result of experiences. It affects values, attitudes, personalities, tastes, and almost every other aspect of behavior. Let's take another look at the purchase decision process. Consumers buying tennis balls for the first time will often do a considerable amount of information seeking. They also may have difficulty determining how to choose among alternatives. After they have purchased and used various brands of tennis balls a few times, however, they will have learned about the product category and the different brands. This learning will enable them to conduct the information search by examining their memories rather than by externally evaluating alternatives. Indeed, after many purchases, buying tennis balls may become a routine response behavior.

The stimulus–response model is one important way psychologists believe learning takes place.[16] The major components of the stimulus–response model are drive, cue, response, and reinforcement. We have already seen that a drive is a state of tension caused by an unfulfilled need. The drive will stimulate action to reduce the tension. Hunger, fear, and the desire for prestige are examples of drives. A **cue** is a stimulus in the environment that determines the nature of the response to a drive. Examples of cues include an advertisement for a fast-food restaurant, a coupon for $.50 off one's next purchase, or an in-store display. A **response** is an individual's reaction to a drive. A person who is hungry, for example, may purchase a Whopper at Burger King. When a direct relationship exists between a stimulus and a response to it, learning has begun to take place. **Reinforcement** is the reduction in a drive that results from a satisfying response. When reinforcement occurs, the probability that the same response will be repeated is increased. In other words, learning has taken place. Thus, if the Whopper is satisfying, the individual may buy at Burger King again when he or she becomes hungry. If the response if not reinforced over time, extinction occurs, and the learned habit ceases.

Consumers buy many products due to habitual responses resulting from previous satisfaction. The consumer demonstrates the close link between learning, habit, and brand loyalty. With continual reinforcement, learned behavior becomes habit. Habit can then lead to brand loyalty. **Brand loyalty** exists when consumers have a favorable attitude toward a single brand and purchase it consistently.

The Coca-Cola Company found out the magnitude of consumers' brand loyalty to Coke when it changed the formula for the product in 1985. Millions of consumers protested the change by refusing to buy the new product, even though blind taste tests had shown that the new Coke was generally preferred to the old Coke. The company was forced to reintroduce the old product, now renamed Coca-Cola Classic. In 1990 the company again began testing the reformulated product, dubbed Coke II, in Spokane, Washington.[17] Favorable reaction to the sweeter-than-Pepsi

The Coca-Cola Company found out the magnitude of consumers' brand loyalty to Coke when it changed the formula for the product.

formula led the company to expand distribution of the "new" product. By mid-1993 Coke II had been introduced nationwide and marketshare was increasing. This time around, however, it's unlikely that Coca-Cola will remove the revered Coca-Cola Classic.

REVIEW

YOUR
MARKETING
KNOWLEDGE

6-3   You are the head of marketing for a firm that produces ski equipment. How important do you think the concept of brand image is to your product and the product class as a whole?

6-4   How important is the perception of price to quality for your product? Would you market your ski equipment as a low-priced bargain or as an expensive prestige item?

Personality.   Unfortunately, psychologists have not been able to agree on any definition of the term *personality*. **Personality** reflects consistent and enduring behavioral responses to the stimuli an individual encounters. People tend to be consistently aggressive or submissive, extroverted or introverted, impulsive or orderly, or dominant or compliant. Marketers have long assumed that personality should be related to consumer behavior, even though there are very few examples from the research literature to support this conclusion.

Some two hundred studies have been reported in the marketing literature relating personality to such marketing concerns as consumer purchasing behavior, media choice, segmentation, and product choice. A review of these studies characterizes their cumulative findings as equivocal.[18] Another review article concludes, "A few studies indicate a strong relationship between personality and aspects of consumer behavior, a few indicate no relationship, and a great majority indicate that if correlations do exist they are so weak as to be questionable or perhaps meaningless."[19]

Attitudes.   Consumer **attitudes** are learned tendencies to perceive and act in a consistent way toward a given person, object, or idea, such as a product, service, brand, company, store, or spokesperson.[20] Attitudes are considered by many marketers to be accurate predictors of consumer behavior. This makes the study of how attitudes are formed and how they are changed important topics in marketing research.

According to traditional models, attitudes have three elements—a cognitive component (perceptions and beliefs), an affective component (evaluation, positive and negative feelings), and a behavioral component (intentions, preferences, or actions such as purchase).[21] The three components of attitudes are normally congruent, that is, the three components reinforce each other. People's perceptions of the world influence their evaluations, which, in turn, affect their behavior. For example, if consumers perceive that a product has the attributes they want, they are likely to have favorable feelings toward it and be inclined to buy it.

Attitudes are only tendencies to perceive and act in a given way. The actual behavior of consumers may be influenced more by a particular situation than by attitudes. For example, a consumer may believe that Sony makes a high-quality television at a reasonable price and may intend to buy one some day. However, whether or not she actually buys a Sony television will probably be determined by her financial circumstances and the condition of her present television. Thus, in any marketing study of attitudes, researchers must make sure they are measuring the appropriate attitude. Here, they should measure the consumer's attitude toward purchasing the Sony (which could be negative) rather than her attitude toward the Sony television itself (which may be positive). The fact that buying intentions and purchase behavior do not always follow consistently can be seen in a study of automobile purchasing. In the study, 63 percent of those who planned to buy a new car within the next year actually did while 37 percent did not. Additionally, 29 percent of those who did not intend to also purchased one.[22]

Once attitudes have been formed, they are not easy to change. One way to try to change attitude is to change one of the three components that make up an individual's attitude. The individual may then change her attitude in order to reestablish congruence among the components. For example, providing information that changes a person's perceptions or beliefs will alter the cognitive component and may result in a change in attitude. In "Marketing in Action: Relaunching P.F. Flyers," the company is attempting to change baby boomers' attitudes about its athletic shoes, which are currently viewed as old-fashioned, by focusing on the affective component of the attitude.

Social Factors

The psychological factors we have just discussed are internal factors, emanating from within the individual. This means that their effects are unique for each individual. Next, we will consider how social factors affect consumer behavior. The four primary social factors are culture, social class, reference groups, and family. These influences are external, emanating from outside the individual. This means that a number of different people may be subject to the same social influences. For example, almost everyone in a society is subject to many of the same cultural influences. On the other hand, as few as two or three people may be influenced by a particular family. Figure 6.4 illustrates how the four primary social factors relate to the individual and to each other.

MARKETING IN ACTION

Relaunching P.F. Flyers

Can fond memories from childhood and youth spark the revival of a product? P.F. Flyers is betting on it. In the 1950s and 1960s, P.F. Flyers were *the* athletic shoe to be seen in. Children and teenagers proudly sported the classic canvas shoes much the way young people today show off their Reebok Pumps and Nikes. P.F. Flyers' star began to fade, however. While its major competitors, like Converse, successfully adapted to consumers' changing wants and needs, P.F. Flyers lost more and more ground.

The baby boomers who grew up with P.F. Flyers, now ranging in age from 27 to 47 years, perceive the shoe to be old-fashioned. How can that perception be changed so that they, and eventually the next generation, will once again proudly wear the P.F. Flyer name across their heels? The company feels it can be done by evoking positive memories of their youth.

To help plan its promotional strategy, the firm undertook the P.F. Flyers National Nostalgia Report. The company queried baby boomers about things that most reminded them of their youth. The subjects were divided into two groups: younger boomers (27–35 years old) and older boomers (36–47 years old).

In both groups Coca-Cola ranked first among foods or beverages. The two groups differed,

however, on the number two ranking. The older boomers favored hamburgers; the younger set waxed nostalgic about pizza. When it came to advertising slogans, M & M's "Melts in your mouth, not in your hands," and "Oh I wish I were an Oscar Mayer wiener" ranked first and second. Boomers also had fond memories of Barbie dolls, bell-bottom pants, mini-skirts, and the Beatles. Of a more intimate nature, Led Zeppelin's "Stairway to Heaven" and Chicago's "Color My World" were remembered as the songs most boomers had enjoyed "making out to."

P.F. Flyers intends to use the findings of the nostalgia report to "tap into those things and have a much stronger way to reach them [boomers]," according to company spokeswoman Stacey Bender. The firm will initially target the boomer market because they remember P.F. Flyers. Once the shoes are reestablished in the marketplace, the firm plans to target younger markets as well.

In the meantime, the company is spending $2.5 million on a print campaign featuring ads it describes as "nostalgic in appearance, 50s and 60s oriented." The ads will run in magazines such as *People*, *Ladies Home Journal*, and *Parenting*.

Culture. **Culture** is the set of values, attitudes, and ways of doing things that are transmitted from generation to generation within a given society. It is learned behavior that includes the customs, morals, and habits of the individuals in the society. What we eat is an example of how culture affects our lives. Most Americans find the idea of eating horse meat repellent; however, many French Canadians consider horse meat a delicacy.

It is important for marketers to understand the culture of markets they plan to enter. This understanding must be translated into a marketing mix appropriate for the new culture. Wrigley Company, for example, has found Asia to be a hot market for its chewing gum. Part of the company's success may be attributed to the fact that it has been careful to adapt its advertising to suit the sensibilities of the market. A Chinese television commercial depicts a man eating smelly bean curd and then chewing gum. This action merits him a chaste kiss on the cheek from the woman in the advertisement.[23]

Not all companies have been as successful as Wrigley in making the adaptations necessary for success in different cultures. Consider the following blunders.[24, 25]

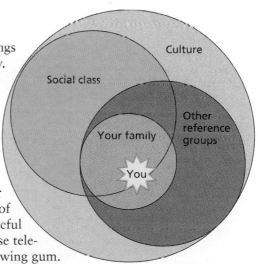

FIGURE 6.4
External/Social Influences and the Individual

- A firm trying to sell refrigerators in the Islamic Middle East promoted its product with ads showing the appliance full of food, including a giant ham. Muslims are forbidden by their religion to eat pork.

- A U.S. designer introduced a new perfume in Latin America with ads emphasizing its fresh scent of camellias. In this market, camellias are funeral flowers. Understandably, sales were slow.

- A baby food company whose label shows a cuddly infant encountered problems marketing its product in an African nation with a high illiteracy rate. Consumers assumed that this product was like other products they were accustomed to, with the label showing what was actually inside.

Although cultural values are relatively permanent, they do change as societies change. Marketers must understand cultural changes, and even anticipate them if possible, because such changes can have major effects on marketing strategies. A major cultural change in the United States in recent years involves women's roles in society. The accelerating movement of women into the workforce in the United States has resulted in significant differences in the structure of decision making in the family. Traditionally, for example, the man of the household was largely responsible for making decisions for the family regarding automobiles. Today, more than 45 percent of cars bought in the United States are purchased by women. Auto manufacturers have adapted cars to women by changing such things as the size and location of seats, mirrors, and radios. Car companies and dealers also target advertising toward women. Women were the primary target market of the redesigned Ford Mustang, introduced in 1994. The primary target market of the highly successful Mazda Miata was also women. The increasing influence of western values on culture in such countries as Russia and Japan may explain why firms like McDonald's and Levi Strauss have been so successful in these parts of the world.

Within any culture, there are **subcultures,** which are categories of people who share a sense of identity distinguishable from the that of the overall culture.[26] In the past 15 years marketers have become much more attuned to the importance of meeting the special needs of different subcultures. The most significant subcultures from a marketing perspective are those based on race, national origin, language, religion, and geographic location. In the United States, for example, the Hispanic sub-

Cultural values change as societies change. As more women purchase cars, car companies and dealers have adapted features for and targeted advertising toward women.

culture is becoming particularly prominent. (In Chapter 5 we discussed the growth of the Hispanic market and how market segmentation strategies might meet the needs of this subculture.) In general, subculture is an important consideration in the marketing of food products, clothing, furniture, and other items for the home. As subcultures become increasingly important to marketers through the 1990s and into the next century, more and more companies can be expected to design products, distribution channels, and promotion strategies to meet their special needs.

Social class.   Consider two households: Each earns $45,000 per year. Each consists of a husband and wife in their mid-30s and one child. Each lives in a suburb of a major metropolitan area. You might think that these households, on the basis of their demographic profiles, would have similar attitudes, values, and consumer behaviors. If another piece of information is added, however, your view might change. The first household consists of an assembly-line supervisor at the Ford plant and his wife, who works part-time as a waitress. The second consists of an attorney working in the legal department at Ford and her husband, a full-time homemaker. With this information, you might decide that the two households likely differ in attitudes, values, and consumer behaviors.

The reason for the differences in consumer behavior of the two households actually goes far beyond the occupational differences. It has to do with differences in the social class of each household. **Social classes** are relatively permanent and homogeneous divisions in a society into which individuals or families sharing similar values, life-styles, interests, and behavior can be categorized.[27] Although countries like the United States tend to view themselves as offering equal opportunity, numerous studies have shown that different social classes do exist and do influence consumer behavior.

The population of the United States has often been categorized into six social classes: upper-upper, lower-upper, upper-middle, lower-middle, upper-lower, and lower-lower. The population is not equally dispersed across these six classes. Typically, the upper classes account for a small portion of the population, while the bulk of the population resides in either the lower-middle class or the upper-lower class.

Social class can often be associated with a specific value system (for example, placing a high value on education), which leads to a specific life-style pattern (attending college), which leads to specific consumption patterns (buying textbooks). For this reason, social class is useful as a segmentation variable for some types of products.[28] For example, manufacturers of china, silver, ski equipment, and golf equipment tend to define their markets as upscale, meaning they consist of people in the higher social classes. The markets for air travel, real estate, and financial investments are also typically upscale. Products and services such as bowling, bus travel, and plastic dinnerware usually appeal to lower-class markets. The largest market for beer is the upper-lower class, and imported wines sell best to the upper-middle class. Social class also influences preferred types of media. The *New Yorker* and *Harper's* are read primarily by upper-class consumers. Thus, companies can reach a specific social-class target market by making the appropriate media choice. When Procter & Gamble, for example, decided to directly target lower social-class consumers, the company began advertising in the *National Enquirer*.[29]

Product acceptance often begins in higher social classes and then passes down to lower classes. For example, gourmet coffees such as cappuccino, espresso, and café au lait used to be consumed primarily by upper and some upper-middle class consumers. In recent years, however, gourmet coffee sales have risen meteorically as consumers in the middle classes have adopted them. Today, drinks such as cappuccino are increasingly available at reasonable prices in shopping malls, grocery stores, and food carts on heavily traveled roads and walkways.

Different advertising media often appeal to different social-class levels.[30] Thus, marketers can often reach a targeted social class by selecting the appropriate media.

Print media, especially magazines, tend to have somewhat higher social-class profiles than do radio and television, although this generalization must be qualified by the content of programming and the time of day. Talk shows such as those hosted by Oprah Winfrey and Geraldo Rivera attract primarily viewers in lower social classes while news show such as *60 Minutes* and the *McNeill/Lehrer Report* are typically watched by those in the upper social classes. Early evening television audiences tend to be heavily lower class, whereas late evening audiences tend to be middle class. Fashion, travel, and literary magazines are more often found in middle-class homes, while sports, outdoor, and romance magazines are more often found in lower-class homes.

Reference groups.   Have you ever wondered why so many fraternity and sorority members seem to dress alike and drive similar cars? These behaviors are indications of the impact of reference group influence. A **reference group** is a group that the individual uses as a reference point in the formation of his or her beliefs, attitudes, values, or behavior.

We can identify three types of reference groups, each of which exerts a different kind of influence:

- **Membership groups** are groups to which an individual currently belongs. A college student might belong to a fraternity or sorority that serves as a membership group for him or her. The student is then likely to choose clothing and a car similar to those chosen by other group members. A marketing major might join the student chapter of the American Marketing Association, making it a membership group.

- **Aspiration groups** are groups to which an individual aspires to belong. A medical school student might aspire to membership in the American Medical Association. Product endorsements by AMA members are likely to influence the student. American Express, which offers three levels of credit cards (green, gold, and platinum), advertises that "Membership has its privileges" and offers different services to the holders of the different cards. As a result, gold cardmembers may represent an aspiration group for green cardmembers. Likewise, platinum cardholders may represent an aspiration group for gold cardmembers.

A sorority is an example of a membership group. Such groups influence the beliefs, attitudes, values, or behavior of individuals.

- **Disassociative groups** are groups with which individuals wish to avoid identification. They may therefore behave in ways intended to establish distance between those groups and themselves. Some college students might view fraternities or sororities as disassociative groups. They may therefore dress and act in ways distinctly different from fraternity or sorority members.

The importance of reference groups in consumer behavior depends on the product category. In general, the more conspicuous a product is, the more important group influence will be. Reference group influence is probably limited in your decision regarding which brand of facial tissue to purchase. The make and model of the car you drive, however, is probably significantly influenced by your reference groups. Marketers may attempt to use the influence of reference groups in selling their products. A manufacturer of athletic shoes, for example, might advertise that its shoe is the one "all the kids at school" will be wearing.

Opinion leaders.   **Opinion leaders** are group members who are able to exert personal influence on the purchase decisions of other consumers because of their knowledge or expertise in certain product or service categories. For instance, an opinion leader who is an expert on computers will probably be consulted by people who know him before they buy new hardware or software. Normally, opinion leaders have rather narrow areas of interest. That is, the computer expert may know next to nothing about cars or clothes.

Opinion leaders are important to marketers because they are likely to be the first consumers to purchase new products, and they are likely to discuss these products with other potential consumers. Marketers will try to reach opinion leaders through the mass media, or personally, in the hope that the opinion leaders will pass on the information they have learned to other consumers. This process is referred to as the **two-step flow of communication.**[32] For instance, the Dunlop Corporation spent considerable resources trying to convince golf professionals that its new golf ball, the Maxfli DDH, was far superior to other golf balls on the market. Dunlop was successful convincing many golf pros, who then encouraged other consumers to purchase the new golf ball.

As you might expect, opinion leaders display certain product-related characteristics that set them apart from followers. These include more knowledge about the product category, greater interest in the product, more active information seeking about the product from personal sources, and greater likelihood to read magazines and other print media related to the product category.[33]

Family.   A person's family is a type of reference group. Like other reference groups, the family acts as a point of reference in the formation of an individual's beliefs, attitudes, values, and behavior. The influence of the family is so important that it merits separate treatment.

One important role the family plays is in the area of consumer socialization. **Consumer socialization** is the process by which young people acquire skills, knowledge, and attitudes that help them function as consumers. A study by Moschis and Moore of adolescents' purchasing behavior demonstrated the importance of parents in the consumer socialization process.[34] They found that parents were preferred almost twice as often as friends as a source of information. For products where price, social acceptance, and performance is of great concern (such as watches, dress shoes, pocket calculators, and hair dryers), preference for parental advice was substantial. Peers as a source of information were important in buying decisions for items where peer acceptance was important, such as sunglasses and wallets.

Not only do parents play an important role in influencing their children's consumer behavior, but children have been found to play an influential role in the

Children play an influential role in the purchasing behavior for a number of products consumed by the family, including snacks, candy, soft drinks, games and toys, toothpaste, and clothing.

purchasing behavior for a number of products consumed by the family. The extent of children's influence, however, varies dramatically by product category. One study found that 87 percent of mothers yielded to children's requests for specific breakfast cereals.[35] Children also had considerable influence on the purchase of products they consume, such as snacks, candy, soft drinks, games and toys, toothpaste, and clothing. However, children had virtually no influence on the purchase of such products as gasoline, laundry soap, automobiles, and cameras.

The family continues to influence an individual's consumer choices long after he or she has "left the nest." If you live in a house or apartment, separate from your parents, check the products and brand names in your kitchen cabinets. How many of them are the same as those you grew up with?

Situational Factors

The final category of factors influencing consumer behavior that we discuss in this chapter is the situational.[36] **Situational factors** are all those factors particular to a time and place of observation that do not follow from a knowledge of personal (individual) and stimulus (choice alternative) attributes and that have a demonstrable and systematic effect on current behavior.[37] In other words, these factors are influences on consumer behavior that aren't related to the individual buyer or the alternatives being considered. Such factors may affect the communications situation, purchase situation, or usage situation.[38] Situational variables have been described as falling into five classes: physical surroundings, social surroundings, temporal perspective, task definition, and antecedent states.[39]

Physical surroundings.   These include geographical and institutional location, decor, sounds, aromas, lighting, weather, and visible configurations of merchandise or other material surrounding the stimulus. The physical environment of a retail establishment, such as the lighting, the color of the walls, and the sounds, can affect the amount of time consumers spend in the establishment as well as the quantity of goods and services they buy. One study of the effects of physical surroundings found that restaurants that play slow background music had higher gross margins than those that play fast music. The slow music apparently relaxed the customers, so they spent more time in the restaurant and bought more drinks from the bar. Thus, restaurant managers who hope their patrons will linger over drinks would be well advised to play slow background music. Conversely, the managers of restaurants without bars might want to play fast music to turn over their tables as quickly as possible.[40]

Social surroundings.   These give depth to a situation. Examples are other persons present, their characteristics, their apparent roles, and the interpersonal interactions. When consumers hear or read an advertisement, shop, or consume a product or service alone, they are likely to behave much differently than they would if they engaged in these activities with others. Research has found that consumers look for different things in a dessert that will be eaten with guests than one they will eat alone or with family.[41] A "company" dessert, for example, should look pretty and appear to have required some effort to prepare. Consumer perception of television shows has been found to vary depending on whether the program was viewed alone or with another person.[42] Shopping behavior for products such as meat and cereal has been shown to be influenced by the presence of others.[43] Knowing the social surroundings in which their product will be consumed can help marketers plan appropriate product features.

Temporal perspective.   Temporal perspective may be specified in units ranging from time of day to seasons of the year. Time may also be measured relative to some past or future event for the situational participant. This allows for conceptions such as time constraints imposed by prior commitments. Have you ever found yourself grocery shopping when you were extremely hungry? Everything in the store looked good and you probably bought more products on impulse and spent more money than you would have had you shopped right after a big meal. Research has shown that, for most people, food shopping is affected by the time between shopping and eating.[44] Time of day can also affect consumer behavior. You may be more likely to linger over a leisurely restaurant meal late in the day than over one consumed earlier. Additionally, the season of the year, the amount of time you have to make a decision, and other aspects of time can affect the purchase decision process. For example, reducing the amount of time an individual has to shop can result in a less extensive information search.[45] The ad for Hunt's Ready Tomato Sauce shows an appeal directed at the person who has little time to shop and plan dinner.

Task definition.   Task definition includes an intent or requirement to select, shop for, or obtain information about a general or specific purchase. In addition, task may reflect different buyer and user roles anticipated by the individual. The reason for a purchase influences the purchase decision process. For example, selecting a product to be given as a gift is a quite different experience from selecting something for personal use. The features are likely to be more or less important in the two situations. If you're shopping for a sweater for yourself, price and durability may be the most important factors in your evaluation of the alternatives. For a gift, however, you may consider brand name and style of a sweater more important.

DINNER'S READY.

Really Ready Chili
Brown 1/2 lb. ground
beef; drain. Stir in Hunt's
Chunky Chili Ready Sauce
and 1 (15.5-oz.) can drained
Hunt's Chili or Kidney
Beans. Simmer, uncovered,
10 minutes and serve.

Minutes in the making, a pot of home-made chili simmers away on the stove. New Hunt's® Chunky Chili Ready Sauce is complete with chunks of vine-ripened tomatoes, onions and bell peppers, in a thick, well-seasoned sauce. All you add is your own ground beef and beans. Look for Italian, Mexican, and other Ready Sauce varieties in the tomato sauce section, next to other great sauces from Hunt's.

NEW HUNT'S READY TOMATO SAUCES

Temporal perspective is one situational factor that influences consumer behavior. This ad appeals to the person who has little time to shop and plan dinner.

Marketers may emphasize brand name over durability during the Christmas season when they know that many purchases will be given as gifts.

Several studies have found that not only whether the purchase was to be a gift but the occasion for gift-giving was important in product selection.[46] Respondents in one study felt birthday gifts should be "fun" and wedding gifts should be "utilitarian."

Antecedent states.   Antecedent states include momentary moods (such as anxiety, pleasantness, hostility, and excitement) or momentary conditions (such as cash on hand, fatigue, and illness), rather than chronic individual traits. Antecedent states are temporary conditions that can affect the purchase decision process. An individual's mood is an example. A person who feels lonely might go shopping in search of social contact. Retailers, hence, might emphasize that a trip to the mall can be a way to meet new people. A depressed person may hope to kick the mood by buying himself something. One researcher[47] pointed out that, in such cases, "the shopping trip is motivated not by the expected utility of consuming, but by the utility of the buying process itself."

In this chapter we have examined the purchase decision process and various factors that influence that process. Clearly, consumer behaviorists today understand far more about how consumers make decisions than was indicated by the Black Box

Model introduced at the beginning of the chapter. No one has yet provided the definitive answer to why and how consumers behave as they do in the marketplace. The study of consumer behavior is dynamic, with new research taking place continuously. Although marketers have progressed beyond the simple Black Box Model, a full understanding of consumer behavior is likely to be an eternal quest.

PERSONAL COMPUTER EXERCISE

The evaluation of alternative brands involves both subjective and objective factors. This PC Exercise enables you to see how subjective perceptions can be used together with objective measures of product attributes to evaluate alternative product offerings.

KEY POINTS

- The study of consumer behavior includes the actions consumers take in buying and using products, and the factors involved in the decision-making process leading to these actions.

- The purchase decision process is the series of stages consumers go through in deciding which products to buy. The five stages are problem recognition, information seeking, evaluation of alternatives, purchase decision, and postpurchase evaluation.

- Problem recognition occurs when there is a discrepancy between a consumer's actual and ideal states.

- The amount and type of information gathered and used by the consumer varies according to the type of product and the characteristics of the consumer. The information-seeking process begins with an internal search, supplemented by an external search of personal, marketer-dominated, public, and experienced sources.

- Evaluation of alternatives occurs after the consumer identifies an evoked set of possibilities.

- Three types of problem-solving behavior are extensive problem solving, limited problem solving, and routine response behavior.

- Influences on consumer behavior can be categorized into five groups: demographics, marketing mix variables, psychological factors, social factors, and situational factors.

- The psychological factors of motivation, perception, learning, personality, and attitude play an important role in determining consumer behavior. Because these factors are not directly observable, their influence must be inferred.

- Motivation is activity toward a goal designed to satisfy an unfulfilled need.

- Abraham Maslow classified needs into five hierarchical categories: physiological, safety, love, esteem, and self-actualization.

■ Consumers respond to product offerings in terms of brand images. The way consumers perceive the benefits of a product is much more important than the actual attributes of the product.

■ Consumers perceive risk to be associated with purchase decisions and act in ways to reduce the risk.

■ Brand loyalty exists when consumers have a favorable attitude toward a single brand, which they purchase consistently over time.

■ Consumer behavior is influenced by such social factors as culture, social class, reference groups, and family.

■ Subcultures have become increasingly important to marketers as they attempt to understand the impact of culture on consumer behavior.

■ The two-step flow of communication utilizes opinion leaders to reach the masses.

■ Situational factors such as physical surroundings, social surroundings, time, task, and antecedent states have strong impacts on consumer behavior.

KEY TERMS

consumer behavior (179)
Black Box Model (179)
ultimate consumers (179)
purchase decision process (180)
evoked set (183)
postpurchase dissonance (184)
high-involvement purchases (184)
low-involvement purchases (185)
motivation (187)
drive (187)
perception (190)
selective perception (191)
brand image (191)
perceived risk (191)
learning (192)
cue (192)

response (192)
reinforcement (192)
brand loyalty (192)
personality (193)
attitudes (194)
culture (195)
subcultures (196)
social class (197)
reference group (198)
membership groups (198)
aspiration groups (198)
disassociative groups (199)
opinion leaders (199)
two-step flow of communication (199)
consumer socialization (199)
situational factors (200)

ISSUES FOR DISCUSSION

1. Think back to your decision about which college to attend and describe what took place at each stage of the (purchase) decision process.

2. Consider your most recent clothing purchase. How was your purchase influenced by your (a) perceptions, (b) motives, (c) attitudes, (d) learning, and (e) personality? What roles were played by your family, reference groups, and opinion leaders?

3. Classify the purchase process for each of the following products as generally requiring extensive problem solving, limited problem solving, or routine response behavior for most consumers: (a) automobile tires, (b) fast food, (c) swimsuits, (d) compact disc player, (e) soft drinks, (f) life insurance.

4. The people who buy central air conditioners are high-income consumers who spend a considerable amount of time and effort determining which unit to buy. Buyers of room air conditioners, on the other hand, often buy on impulse during a heat wave. How does this difference affect the marketing strategies for a company like Fedders, which markets both products?

5. Give two examples of products that satisfy the needs at each stage of Maslow's hierarchy of needs.

6. Discuss the importance of social class and reference groups in the marketing of home computers.

7. Imagine that you are a retailer who sells fairly expensive athletic shoes produced by a variety of manufacturers. You have noticed that many of your customers seem somewhat anxious about whether they have made the right choice after purchasing a pair of shoes. Apparently many customers conclude that they made a poor choice, since returns at your store are quite high. What strategies might reduce the post-purchase dissonance of your customers, and the number of returns?

8. What problems, if any, would a bank have in trying to use the two-step flow of communication to market checking accounts to students by enlisting the help of campus opinion leaders?

9. Compare and contrast the importance of the various categories of influences on consumer behavior during the information-seeking stage for the purchase of a weekend vacation. Imagine that you are taking the vacation under each of the various circumstances:
   (a) You are going alone versus going with a friend.
   (b) You have recently inherited an unexpected $10,000.
   (c) You haven't inherited money.
   (d) You are planning the trip just after you received all A's for the term.
   (e) You are planning it after you failed an important exam.

10. Describe the differences between shopping for a shirt for your dad for Father's Day and shopping for a shirt for yourself to wear to school.

CASE APPLICATION
Targeting Homeworkers

Illinois Bell, a division of Ameritech, has opened a Work-at-Home Planning Center in Chicago. The center is designed to assist consumers who work at home. Products such as telephones, fax machines, modems, and answering machines are targeted at three specific markets within this growing population:

- *full-time homeworkers*: entrepreneurs who run their businesses out of their residences
- *after-hours homeworkers*: individuals who take work home with them
- *telecommuters*: workers who spend all or part of their work week working at home rather than at their employer's place of business

Approximately 35% of U.S. workers fell into one of these three categories sometime during 1992 according to LINK, a New York-based research firm commissioned by Illinois Bell to study the market. This represented an increase of 4.1% from 1990 and provided firms like Illinois Bell with an opportunity to respond to the growing trend. Laura Foote, marketing manager for Illinois Bell, predicts an annual growth rate of 8%. Telecommuting, in particular, is expected to become a mainstream force in major corporations as we progress through the 1990s.

It is believed that growth of the "work-at-home" market results from numerous benefits that working at home offers the employer, the employee, and society. Employers are better able to keep quality employees who are trying to balance their jobs with personal commitments like raising families or caring for elderly parents. Employees create more free and leisure time for themselves by avoiding long commutes. Society benefits environmentally in the form of fewer pollutants in the air and less gasoline used. Furthermore, the LINK study reported that the continued increases in working women and the desire of households to increase their income will also fuel the growth expected in the market.

Employers have also found that telecommuters can be more productive than other employees. The Los Angeles telecommunications department conducted a test of 500 city workers. The test found that telecommuting employees were 12.5% more productive than workers at central locations. Productivity was measured in terms of the number of reports the workers produced, the amount of material they reviewed, and the number of cases they closed.

Telecommuting received an unexpected promotional push when Los Angeles was shaken by a significant earthquake in January 1994. Closed freeways and impossibly long commutes were viewed by telecommuting advocates as opportunities to persuade Angelenos to try working at home. Pacific Bell responded to the opportunity by launching a radio and print ad campaign encouraging telecommuting. It even set up a special loan fund to outfit home offices.

Homeworkers have been aided by the growing market penetration of personal computers (PCs), which are found in the residences of 11.6 million homeworkers, according to the LINK study. The study also determined that this figure is growing rapidly. Such market penetration appears to provide opportunities to firms who target even the casual after-hours homeworker. According to Thomas Miller, director of the LINK study, "Two-thirds of all home computers and nearly three-fourths of all home fax machines are now owned by people bringing home work after hours. Also, casual after-hours homeworkers are involved in 85% of the job-related electronic data transfers now taking place from homes."

It would appear from the research that Illinois Bell could not go wrong in pursuing the homeworker market. Foote has acknowledged, however, that identifying the prospects in the target markets is difficult, making it extremely challenging to use such promotional techniques as direct mail. She believes that this difficulty is due to the fact that the market is still growing rapidly. According to Foote, as the growth continues, the market will identify itself, thus making marketing efforts simpler.

Questions

1. Is the purchase of equipment to set up a home-office likely to represent extensive problem solving, limited problem solving, or routine response behavior? Explain.
2. Would your answer to question 1 vary across the three target markets identified by Illinois Bell? How would this affect marketing strategy for the firm?
3. What consumer behavior concepts discussed in Chapter 6 are most relevant for Illinois Bell?
4. What additional information about buyer behavior would you want if you were in charge of marketing to the growing population of homeworkers?

Understanding Employer Behavior

Chapter 6 describes the stages of the purchase decision process. This process gives you an idea of what the customer, in this case the employer, wants and is looking for in a job candidate. If you use the Black Box Model approach to observe the behavior of your potential employer, you will understand that the employer is looking at your presentation, considering the opinion of others (his or her colleagues), and evaluating how you will fit into the organization's culture.

Ultimate consumers are the final users of goods and services. In your career search, companies are the ultimate consumers of your talents and skills. An employer goes through a *purchase decision process*, or a series of steps, in deciding to purchase your services. Here are the steps that companies may follow in making hiring decisions.

1. *Problem recognition.* Companies need workers. Their need for additional employees can occur gradually or rapidly, depending on industry need. That is why it is important that you network, to maximize your chance of "being in the right place at the right time."
2. *Information seeking.* Companies go "on campus," use head hunters, advertise, rely on word of mouth, and network internally to recruit new employees.
3. *Evaluation of alternatives.* A number of individuals are involved in evaluating alternatives, including:
   • the person who reviews résumés determines which applicants look "good" on paper and chooses the most qualified from the stack of résumés.
   • the person who conducts the screening interviews usually schedules 30-minute appointments to identify the "stars" who will be invited back for second interviews.
   • the person who makes the decision to hire is usually the last person to interview the final candidate. Reports from others involved in the interviewing process can help make the newly hired employee a success.
4. *Purchase decisions.* This process occurs when the company decides among alternatives and offers a position to candidates who have been rank ordered. A hiring (purchase) may be delayed until there is a final negotiation of salary (price) and benefits.
5. *Postpurchase evaluation.* This is the process where the consumer evaluates whether he is satisfied. Many companies evaluate performance by regular progress reports to monitor their ongoing commitment to purchase your services (i.e., keep you employed!).

Hiring people for jobs is a market-driven action. The organization is focused on satisfying and anticipating its needs and wants. As you market yourself, remember to think of how the consumer is making her decisions. Other factors that both you and the consumer need to consider are:
   • *Demographic*: age, background, social class
   • *Psychological*: motivation, perception, learning, personality, and attributes
   • *Motivational*: desire and ability to meet goals
   • *Social*: culture, family, how you fit into the culture of the organization

The study of consumer behavior has not yet provided definitive answers to why and how consumers behave as they do in the marketplace. Such a *je-ne-sais-quoi* element is also present in the process of securing employment, which involves some degree of chance and luck.

Question

Think back to your decision to choose the college you are attending. Describe what took place from the application process, to visiting the campus, to how you ultimately made your decision. This process of applying to a college and getting accepted or rejected is similar to the employment process.

CHapTeR 7

Business Markets and Organizational Buying Behavior

LEARNING OBJECTIVES

Upon completing this chapter, you will be able to do the following:

■ **Describe** the various types of business products and services.

■ **Differentiate** five types of business markets.

■ **Discuss** the differences among business and consumer markets.

■ **Explain** demand and comment on why it is important to business marketers.

■ **Define** the buying center concept and identify the various roles in the buying center.

■ **Understand** the ways business markets can be segmented including SIC codes.

■ **Compare** the buying behaviors of business markets and consumer markets.

■ **Understand** how strategic alliances between business marketers and their customers help firms become customer driven.

*M*arketing *P*rofile

Strategic Success at Duskes

For years following the death of its founder in 1983, Duskes, Incorporated, a Quebec-based distributor of industrial supplies, struggled to remain competitive. The struggle is over. In 1989 the firm was acquired by Ken Shulman and Steve Kornai, two savvy business marketers who increased sales by nearly 70 percent between 1989 and 1994. Duskes sells everything from hand and power tools to maintenance products and abrasives for cleaning large machinery. Also, fasteners and related items used in the manufacture of various products make up 40 percent of the company's inventory. Duskes will gladly sell a power drill or other tool to the ultimate consumer who wanders into the 3,000-square-foot showroom, but the focus of its efforts is large business accounts. Its clients include Molson-O'Keefe Brewery and Canadian Pacific Rail.

The dramatic turnaround in Duskes's fortunes is the result of several actions. All, however, are related to the firm's strong commitment to building partnerships (*strategic alliances*) with both the vendors from whom it acquires its products and with its customers. Duskes builds strategic alliances with clients by acting as their representative to manufacturers. Duskes's size and reputation enable the firm to negotiate better deals with manufacturers than either clients or smaller distributors could. In exchange for negotiating the best possible deal, Duskes asks clients to buy exclusively from them. Duskes works to build strong relationships between clients and the producers that supply those clients by including manufacturers' sales representatives in frequent visits to customers. All

three work to design strategies aimed at helping the client run his or her business more efficiently.

A commitment to technological improvements has also helped Duskes build strong strategic alliances. Prior to 1989, the firm had no computer system. The 40,000-piece inventory was managed by hand and frequent out-of-stocks left Duskes's clients unhappy and suppliers scrambling to fill emergency orders. The current state-of-the-art system eliminates these problems and allows Duskes to move ahead in such areas as electronic data interchange and inventory monitoring at customers' warehouses.

The high level of service by Duskes helps to solidify strong relationships between the company and its customers. Canadian Pacific Rail Manager of Materials, Wayne Hynes, states, "Any time we have a problem, they respond right away." The railroad, which maintains a mere three-day window for parts deliveries, claims Duskes is on time or early with 90 percent of the deliveries. "That's a real good service level compared to other companies," says Hynes.

Duskes's success has allowed the firm not only to increase sales but also to grow through acquisition. In late 1993 the firm bought Drummond Sullivan Company, another Quebec-based industrial supply house. Drummond Sullivan expanded the client base for Duskes since it sold to industries in which Duskes had not been heavily involved. Institutions such as hospitals were strong customers for Drummond Sullivan. Between the acquisition and the success experienced by aggressively building strategic alliances, Duskes expects its sales to increase another 25 percent in 1994.

Duskes's primary customers are other businesses rather than end users. In this chapter we look at business markets and the buying behavior of consumers in those markets. Some aspects of business markets and their buying behavior are very similar to that of their counterparts in consumer markets, but a number are substantially different.

The starting point in understanding how to market a business product is the same as for marketing a consumer product—segmenting the market and then defining a target market. For a business product, however, the process is often more difficult. For example, Duskes's marketers must first choose appropriate segmenting variables and identify businesses that are likely prospects for industrial supplies, and then identify the individuals in those businesses that should be targeted.

Marketing a business product, like the marketing of consumer products, requires understanding the decision-making process of buyers and the factors that influence that process. The nature and length of the decision-making process and the influential variables, however, are different for business products. As we saw in the Marketing Profile, building a strong relationship with a customer is often critical to the success of the business marketer. Furthermore, in contrast to the decision-making process of a consumer, decision making in a business is likely to require that specifications be spelled out and alternative suppliers be identified. The business may mandate a set of buying procedures, including requests for proposals, bids, and purchase orders, that have to be completed before the product is approved for purchase. Other individuals, including plant engineers, production workers, and purchasing agents, may be involved in the decision.

We begin this chapter by discussing the importance of building partnerships between business marketers and their customers. We then consider ways to classify business products and types of business markets. We then identify characteristics that distinguish business marketing from consumer marketing. We will then discuss marketplace issues as they relate to business marketing. We will revisit the two marketplace issues discussed in Chapters 5 and 6, segmentation and buyer behavior, with a focus on business marketing and the application of these issues to business marketers. While the process of market segmentation and the understanding of buyer behavior are equally important in consumer and business marketing, the application of these issues to business marketing produces some unique considerations.

BUSINESS MARKETS

Business markets consist of businesses, individuals, or organizations that purchase products or services for use in the production of other products or services, for use in their day-to-day operations, or for resale. Contractors who buy sheetrock for constructing walls in new houses, companies who buy personal computers for employees to use, and boutique owners who buy dried flower arrangements to sell in their stores all qualify as business markets.

One way to differentiate between business markets and consumer markets is to consider consumer markets as consisting of customers who buy goods and services to meet their personal wants and needs. As you recall, marketers refer to such customers as ultimate consumers. Business markets, on the other hand, consist of customers who buy goods and services that will allow them to produce or provide the goods and services that ultimate consumers purchase. Manufacturers, wholesalers, and retailers are types of business markets. In effect, we can consider **business marketing** to be marketing efforts aimed at any consuming group other than ultimate consumers.

Defined this way, it is important to recognize that business-to-business marketing includes efforts aimed at two substantial markets that may not be thought of as businesses in the traditional (motivated by profit) sense. These two markets are the institutional market and the government market. The institutional market consists of organizations such as educational institutions, hospitals, prisons, and not-for-profit organizations including museums, foundations, and libraries. The government market consists of the U.S. federal government, state governments, the thousands of county and local governments throughout the United States, and the governments of countries worldwide.

In the past, nonconsumer markets were commonly referred to as *organizational markets* and marketing directed at them was called *industrial marketing*. You are likely to encounter these terms in other books and articles about marketing. Today, the terms *business markets* and *business-to-business* (or simply *business*) *marketing* seem more appropriate and are rapidly becoming the accepted terminology for nonconsumer markets. As one marketer explains, "industrial marketing suggests marketing only to rust-belt heavy-manufacturing type industries and thus seems antiquated."[1]

RELATIONSHIP MARKETING IN BUSINESS MARKETS

Relationship marketing is developing a relationship between a marketer and his or her customers so that marketing activity becomes part of a continuing interaction. This form of marketing represents the ultimate for a market-driven organization because it makes the customer a full partner with the vendor in working to meet that customer's needs. Such an approach is critical in business marketing. Because the relationship between the business marketer and his or her customers is complex and because the business market is likely to be limited in size (making it difficult to just go out and find a new customer), the marketer must work to build strong and enduring relationships with customers. The importance of such relationship building is clear for Duskes's. Duskes's efforts at building strong relationships with its clients seems to account for the firm's success. The "Spotlight on Technology: Symbol Technologies Decodes Its Customers' Needs" also illustrates the benefit to a business marketer of building strong relationships.

An enduring relationship between a business marketer and a customer that represents a planned, mutual effort to solve problems and meet the customer's needs is a **strategic alliance**. Strategic alliances between business marketers and their customers can develop into true partnerships as the result of various types of supplier/customer interactions.[2] A business marketer might create ties with customers through advisory councils (as in the case of Symbol Technologies), joint promotions or development projects, or cooperative research and development efforts. Loctite Corporation, a producer of maintenance and repair items used by business customers, receives advice on product development and promotion from an advisory council of distributors. Because the distributors interact directly with the users of Loctite's products, they often have insights that the manufacturer does not. Using input from the advisory council, Loctite implemented a promotional campaign that featured six company products, bundled together, and billed as a Survival Kit. The promotion was highly successful for both Loctite and its distributors. Over the first four months, distributors earned more through the Survival Kit promotion than they had from any previous Loctite promotion.[3] Another successful strategic alliance was the relationship McKesson, a major distributor of drugs and health-care items, forged with its customers. The firm provided pharmacies with hand-held terminals that were linked to McKesson's computer.[4] Instead of waiting for McKesson's salespeople to call on them, the pharmacists could order by keying the items they wanted to buy into the terminals. This led to more productive salespeople, since they could

MARKETING IN ACTION

Symbol Technologies Decodes Its Customers' Needs

Symbol Technologies is the world's leading manufacturer of bar-code scanning equipment. Its U.S. sales have increased from $23 million in 1986 to $88 million in 1993. Worldwide sales are predicted to increase 5 percent annually through the 1990s.

Bar-code scanning equipment is used heavily at checkout counters in such retail operations as supermarkets and discount stores, as well as having many other applications. United Parcel Service uses bar-code scanners to track packages, Northwest Airlines uses them to route baggage and freight, and the Los Angeles County Court uses them keep tabs on trial evidence. Wholesalers use scanning equipment in warehouses to maintain inventory control. Hence the market for such equipment includes a wide range of business users from wholesalers and retailers to governments.

Symbol Technologies has had considerable success with just about every item in its product line. The company controls some 40 percent of the market for all types of scanning equipment, from the scanners themselves to the data terminals used to compute the information the scanners read. The firm's greatest success, however, has been its hand-held laser scanner, which maintains an 80 to 85 percent market share. The hand-held scanner resembles a gun and reads the Universal Price Codes (UPCs) on items. Another product enjoying significant success is Symbol Technologies's portable, wireless checkout scanner. The scanner is the size of a thick telephone book and can be used by roving sales clerks to ring up purchases for customers. Dayton-Hudson has made a commitment to purchase and use the scanners in its Mervyn's retail stores.

According to Stan Jaworski, the Senior Director of Marketing Communications for Symbol Technologies, the firm's achievements can be attributed largely to the way the company views its customers. "Basically, Symbol is a customer-driven company," states Jaworski. "The technological requirements of our scanners are strongly influenced by the demands and input of our customers." Symbol also recognizes that the demands of its customers are driven by the needs of the ultimate consumers those customers serve. Northwest Airline's use of bar-code scanning equipment helps ensure that its passengers' bags get to the right place. Symbol listens carefully to the needs of final consumers and then proposes ways that its business customers can meet those needs with Symbol's products.

The company believes that by forging a strategic alliance with its customer base, it can keep abreast of changes in the industry. To this end, the company maintains an advisory board comprised of 12 to 15 of its most important customers. The board meets at least twice a year to discuss trends in the marketplace and ideas for new products.

The information provided by the advisory board is disseminated to the appropriate divisions of the company. One of its most important destinations is the firm's research and development arm, where information from the advisory board is considered along with input from sales representatives in planning new products. One of the most promising of Symbol's new products is the Gladiator, a state-of-the-art scanner that uses a radio transmitter to pass scanned data directly to a computer. The Gladiator is worn on the head, allowing users to scan items without using their hands. This makes it particularly attractive to warehouse markets where the user needs both hands to move items while scanning.

Symbol Technologies's accomplishments have earned the company a Marketing Achievement Award from *Sales & Marketing* magazine.

spend more time selling new products and building personal relationships with new and existing accounts, instead of having to write up routine orders. The customers received faster service, when they wanted it, instead of having to wait for a salesperson to call. The computer also could be used to fill out insurance claims forms, saving the pharmacist time and speeding the reimbursements from insurance companies. Pharmacists soon found it very easy to order from McKesson, effectively shutting out other suppliers.

Another way to build a strong partnership is by sharing information. When a business marketer shares marketing and sales information with his or her suppliers and customers, a strong sense of cooperation and trust is established. Since many business marketers realize the benefit of such action, it is predicted that sharing information with channel partners will become the primary source of marketing and sales information in the future.[5] Figure 7.1 illustrates the results of a study regarding information sharing between business marketers, their suppliers, and their customers.

Because it is virtually impossible for a supplier to be the best on every dimension for every transaction, always offering the highest quality product with the most superior service at the lowest price, building strategic alliances is extremely critical. A business customer has to be convinced, through relationship marketing, that a given supplier will work to understand the customer's business and use that knowledge to meet the long-term needs of that customer better than an alternative supplier could. If a strong relationship is built, the benefits to both parties are significant. The key to being market/customer driven in this instance is that the transaction is not ended with the purchase order or sale—the relationship is ongoing, and what happens after the sale is as important as what happened before or during the sale. Theodore Levitt of the Harvard Business School has stated, "A company's most precious asset is its relationship with its customers."[6] Like all assets, of course, this relationship can appreciate or depreciate depending on the marketer's actions.

FIGURE 7.1
Information Sharing Between Partners

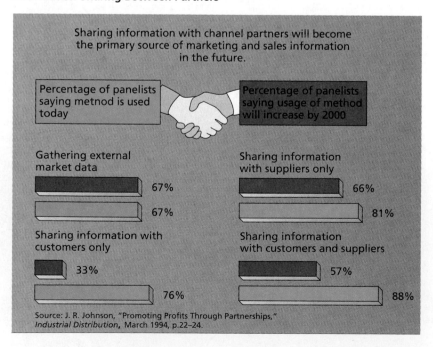

Sharing information with channel partners will become the primary source of marketing and sales information in the future.

Percentage of panelists saying method is used today

Percentage of panelists saying usage of method will increase by 2000

Gathering external market data
67%
67%

Sharing information with suppliers only
66%
81%

Sharing information with customers only
33%
76%

Sharing information with customers and suppliers
57%
88%

Source: J. R. Johnson, "Promoting Profits Through Partnerships," *Industrial Distribution*, March 1994, p.22–24.

CLASSIFICATION OF BUSINESS-TO-BUSINESS PRODUCTS AND SERVICES

The many kinds of products and services sold to business markets can be classified into seven general categories: business services, heavy equipment, light or accessory equipment, supplies, component parts, raw materials, and processed materials.[7]

Business Services

All the services purchased by businesses fall into the category **business services.** It can include legal and accounting services, maintenance and janitorial services, and advertising and public relations services. The Marriott hotel chain, for instance, relies on the Young and Rubicam agency for its advertising. Large firms often hire people to perform the services they require in-house. The communications and entertainment giant Time-Warner, for example, has entire departments to meet its legal and accounting needs. Smaller businesses, however, usually find it simpler and less costly to purchase the services they need from outside suppliers.

Heavy Equipment

Heavy equipment includes products used directly in the production of other goods, which are often attached to the physical plant of the businesses using them. This category is typically comprised of large capital goods, such as bottling equipment, printing presses, or blast furnaces. Heavy equipment can be purchased outright, but it is sometimes leased. A newspaper publishing company might, for example, lease the printing presses on which it prints its paper. Leasing can be more cost effective than purchasing heavy equipment, which typically involves large outlays of capital.

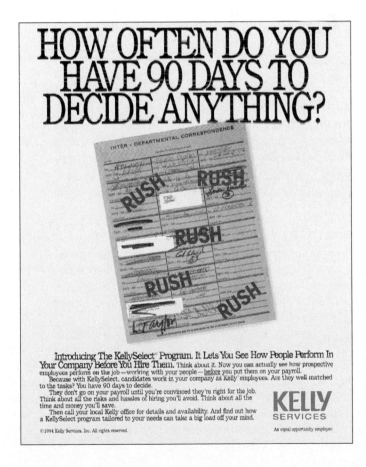

This ad for temporary employees shows one of the many services that businesses purchase.

Light or Accessory Equipment

Light or accessory equipment includes goods required for individuals in the firm to "get the job done" but which are not permanently affixed to the physical plant. Examples include power tools, copying machines, personal computers, fax machines, and automobiles. Light equipment can be purchased outright or leased, and is considerably less expensive than heavy equipment. A pharmaceutical company might lease a fleet of vans for its sales force. The regular users of items are often involved in selecting what to buy.

Supplies

Supplies are goods that are consumed by a business in its day-to-day operations. They include such products as cleaning compounds, drill bits, pens and pencils, business stationery, forms, and computer disks. Supplies are sometimes referred to as *maintenance, repair, and operating products*, which is usually shortened to **MRO products**. There are many firms whose entire business consists of providing supplies to other businesses. Office Depot, for example, is a major provider of office supplies to businesses throughout the United States.

Component Parts

Typically, **component parts** are goods marketed to **original equipment manufacturers (OEMs)**, who then incorporate them with little or no change into other goods. Examples include transistors, small electric motors, switches, and computer modems. Component parts are frequently sold to repair facilities, in which case they could be viewed as supplies. General Motors, for example, may purchase electrical systems or glass from suppliers and use them in the production of automobiles. The same suppliers may sell such component parts to auto repair shops.

Raw Materials

Raw materials are products mined or produced by extractive industries for use, with little or no alteration, in the production of other goods. Coal, crude oil, copper, lumber, and food crops are examples. These products are typically purchased by OEMs and other manufacturers. A steel producer might, for example, purchase coal to be burned for heating a blast furnace and a bread company might purchase wheat to use in baking bread.

Processed Materials

Processed materials are manufactured products used in the production of goods by OEMs and other manufacturers. They are usually produced to the specifications of a customer. Examples include chemicals, sheet metal, plastics, and specialty steel. A manufacturer of industrial cleaning components, for example, might purchase a specific formulation of chemicals to use in producing its cleansers.

Goods for Resale

In addition to the categories of business-to-business products listed so far, many business-to-business products are **goods for resale**. These are products purchased by wholesalers and retailers who will resell the items to other wholesalers, retailers, and ultimate consumers with no alteration to the product. The Broadway, a department store, purchases clothing manufactured by many companies and resells the clothing to ultimate consumers.

TYPES OF BUSINESS MARKETS

A marketer who sells to a business customer is called a **vendor.** Vendors sell to customers in several types of markets.

Manufacturers

Manufacturers make products that are sold to wholesalers, retailers, governments, institutions, and to ultimate consumers. They are a business market because they typically require goods and services in order to manufacture products. Hence, OEMs purchase component parts that are used in the manufacture of their products. Manufacturers represent a market for every type of business-to-business product except goods for resale. To give you an idea of the size of this market, in 1990, the most recent year for which statistics are available, 18,840,300 people were employed in manufacturing in the United States.[8]

Wholesalers

Wholesalers are intermediaries in a distribution system. These business consumers buy goods and services from manufacturers and from other wholesalers. Their functions in a distribution system include transportation and storage of goods for resale. Wholesalers purchase many categories of business-to-business goods and services. Chapter 12 provides an in-depth discussion of wholesalers.

Retailers

Retailers are intermediaries who sell goods and services to ultimate consumers. Hence, they purchase goods for resale from manufacturers and wholesalers. Retailers also purchase other types of business-to-business products such as light equipment, operating supplies, and business services, to facilitate their sales of goods to ultimate consumers. Chapter 13 provides an in-depth discussion of retailers.

Government Markets

Government buyers range from tiny towns to large cities, states, provinces, and of course, the federal governments of countries. Government markets can offer significant opportunities to marketers. For example, in 1993 the combined buying units of the U.S. federal government purchased $1.157 trillion in goods and services. That is more goods and services than any other single entity (government, business, industry, or organization) in the world.[9]

The buying process used by governmental units is typically more formalized than that used by most businesses. In the U.S. federal government, purchase decisions are based on an evaluation of bids submitted by sellers (or vendors). Vendors become aware of available government contracts, on which they can bid, in one of three ways. First, the vendor may become aware through the *Commerce Business Daily*, a publication that lists specifications and invites proposals from potential suppliers for all federal purchases of $5000 or more. Second, the potential supplier might request to be placed on a bidders' mailing list. Such mailing lists identify vendors interested in submitting bids on available government contracts for various types of goods and services. Finally, the federal government might send a potential supplier an invitation to bid after reading about that supplier in a directory or magazine, or after seeing an ad by the supplier. Interested vendors submit bids to the federal government based on precise specifications. Competing bids are evaluated and a purchase order or contract is awarded by the government. The contract typically goes to the bidder with the lowest price.

Government markets are very attractive to some business marketers because the information needed to sell to them is easily obtainable and their needs are usually consistent from year to year.[10] On the other hand, targeting government markets often means facing complex rules and regulations, typically demands that the seller bear all risk of such things as cost increases, and always involves mountains of paperwork. Although some companies have established their entire business around serving the government (General Dynamics, for example, which serves the defense industry), many other companies who sell to government markets are careful to avoid overreliance on such markets.

Institutional Markets

Institutional markets include all types of customers who serve the needs of large groups of people in institutional settings, such as schools, hospitals, and prisons. Such markets do not fall neatly into either the commercial or governmental sectors. Some institutional markets, such as public school systems, are viewed as part of the local government market. Other institutions, a private, not-for-profit hospital, for example, would be considered a noncommercial business customer. These discrepancies in classification make it difficult to estimate the total size of the institutional market. Its size has been stated to be as large as $1.2 trillion.[11]

Selling to the institutional market varies in complexity depending on the method of purchasing the institution uses and the means by which it serves people.[12] A university with multiple campuses, for example, might use centralized buying procedures, or it might allow autonomous purchasing decisions to be made at each campus. A public school system might cook meals in a centralized kitchen and then distribute the food to schools within the system, or individual schools might do their own buying and cooking. These decisions make an enormous difference in how a business marketer approaches the systems. In the case of centralized buying, a business marketer may be able to approach a single buying committee, submitting a bid similar to the method described for government markets. If purchase decisions are made autonomously by various units of the institution, the business marketer will need to determine whether a single set of buying criteria governs purchase decisions or whether each unit must be researched and approached separately. In targeting the institutional market, business marketers must gather information about the nature of purchasing and decision making before proceeding.

Small Businesses

Theoretically, any of the types of business markets discussed thus far could be **small businesses.** Whether a manufacturer, wholesaler, retailer, government, or institution, however, the fact that a business is small in size presents unique challenges to the marketer interested in selling to it. Practically, the largest number of small businesses are likely to be retailers. Small businesses have experienced significant growth in recent years even while larger firms have declined. Between 1987 and 1992, for example, firms of fewer than 100 employees on the average created jobs while larger firms lost jobs. Many small companies are as involved as their larger counterparts in global business. In 1993, small businesses in the United States shipped more than $110 billion in exports throughout the world.[13]

Small businesses are likely to have less formal purchasing processes. A small retail grocer might, for example, purchase a computer system after visiting a few suppliers to compare prices and features, while a large grocery chain might collect bids from a specified number of vendors and then evaluate those bids on pre-established criteria. Usually, fewer individuals are involved in the decision-making process for a small business. The owner of the small business, for example, may make all decisions, and a larger business may operate with a buying committee of several people.

These characteristics may make it easier for a vendor to deal with a small business customer. Submitting formalized bids or making sales presentations to a number of decision makers may not be necessary. On the other hand, the small business customer is likely to represent a smaller sale, which may be less attractive to the vendor.

DIFFERENCES BETWEEN BUSINESS AND CONSUMER MARKETS

In this section, we examine the major differences between business and consumer markets. They include variation in demand, market size, promotional techniques, the number of individuals involved in the buying process, and the amount of buyer expertise and rationality exhibited. Marketers must be aware of the differences if they are to understand both types of markets and plan effective marketing strategies.

Demand

Businesses do not purchase goods and services to meet their own wants and needs, but rather to produce or distribute goods and services to meet the wants and needs of ultimate consumers. Thus, we describe businesses' demand for goods and services as **derived demand** to indicate that it is determined not by the businesses themselves but by their customers. Business-to-business marketers must realize the success of a particular marketing effort may not depend solely on their efforts to meet the needs of their business customers, but can also be influenced by the customers of their business customers. Thus, if a marketer determines that consumer demand for the product of a particular business is off, he or she may want to target a different business.

Derived demand operates at several levels simultaneously. For example, the demand for ginned cotton is determined by the textile industry's need for cotton to make cloth. The demand for cloth in turn depends on the needs of the garment-making industry, which depends on the needs of clothing retailers, which ultimately depend on consumer's demand for cotton clothing.[14] These levels of derived demand are illustrated in Figure 7.2.

Derived demand is volatile. This means that a small change in consumer demand for a business's product can have a large impact on that business's demand for the goods and services it needs to make its product. For example, if consumers cut back slightly on their purchases of tires, tire retailers and wholesalers may find themselves with excess inventory. As a result, they may suspend their purchases from tire manufacturers until their inventories have been reduced. This could have a large impact on the number of tires produced by tire factories and an even larger impact on the factories' demand for raw materials.

An extreme example of the volatility of derived demand occurred during the Great Depression (1929–1933). The demand for consumer goods in the United States decreased by approximately 20 percent. The overall damage became much greater when the drop in consumer demand led to a 65 percent decrease in the demand for capital equipment to produce consumer goods.[15] More recently, General Dynamics, a major defense contractor to the U.S. government, laid off more than 6,000 employees in San Diego due to downsizing of the defense industry. The layoffs severely hurt the local economy. Not only did unemployed workers have less to spend, but suppliers who provided goods and services to General Dynamics suffered significantly.

Another important characteristic of the demand for business products is its inelastic nature. An increase or decrease in the price of an item will not have much

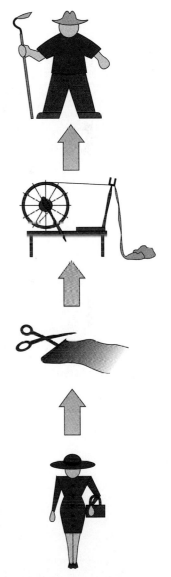

FIGURE 7.2
Levels of Derived Demand for Clothing

impact on businesses' demand for the item. For example, a large increase in the price of zippers would not change the number of zippers purchased by an apparel manufacturer. Demand is particularly likely to be inelastic when the item accounts for only a small portion of the total cost of the end product, as is the case with zippers. You should note, though, that such inelastic demand usually occurs at the industry-wide level, not at the level of the individual firm. Hence, even though apparel manufacturers will continue to buy the same number of zippers if prices go up, they will also begin searching for a cheaper supplier. Thus, the inelastic nature of the demand for business products does not give a firm carte blanche to increase prices and expect demand not to decline.

Market Size

Consumer products and services are often purchased by millions of people. In contrast, the base for business products and services is often very narrow. Boeing Aircraft, for example, sells its commercial aircraft to a total market of 200 airlines worldwide. Those 200 airlines, by comparison, sell tickets to more than 125 million people annually.[16] An active base of 4000 to 5000 customers is very large for some business products. It is not unusual for 100 to 250 customers to account for a substantial portion of a business marketer's sales volume.[17] In some cases a handful of buyers comprise the entire market. Jet engine manufacturers, for example, sell to a market composed of Boeing, McDonnell Douglas, Airbus, and a handful of other jet aircraft producers. This situation is rarely found in the consumer market. In these cases, each individual buyer is critical, thus he or she exerts a great deal of influence over the marketers. Boeing, for example, is no doubt able to specify product customization requirements, delivery schedules, and financing terms when buying jet engines.

Promotional Techniques

Because business markets are much smaller than consumer markets, there is more face-to-face contact between buyers and producers of business products. Most marketers of consumer products use advertising and sales promotion as the major means of communication with potential customers; most business marketers use personal selling as the predominant form of marketing communication, which makes many aspects of the selling and buying negotiable. Business marketers do use advertising when it is appropriate to reach their target markets as illustrated by the "Marketing in Action: Ryder Keeps on Truckin'." When business marketers advertise, they usually turn to magazines and trade journals as media vehicles. Table 7.1 lists the top five publications used by business advertisers in order of the value of advertising space purchased.

Publication	Value of Advertising Space Purchased by Business Marketers
Business Week	$79.91 million
Fortune	43.71 million
Forbes	37.26 million
PC Magazine	33.41 million
PC Week	14.55 million

Source: J. Jaben, "Marketing's New Fast Lane Emerges," *Business Marketing*, October 1993, pp. 20–25.

TABLE 7.1
Top 5 Publications for Business-to-Business Advertisements

MARKETING IN ACTION

Ryder Keeps On Truckin'

The Commercial Services Division of Ryder Truck Rental, Incorporated, leases trucks, one at a time or by the fleet, to business customers across the United States. In fact, full-service commercial leasing is a bigger part of Ryder's business than are the familiar yellow trucks leased by ultimate consumers. The segment accounted for about $600 million of the firm's revenue in 1993.

Ryder's success in the commercial market results from its use of such traditional business marketing techniques as personal selling plus some techniques not yet common in business marketing, especially market segmentation. Ryder uses company size as a main segmentation base because it indicates who in the company should be targeted for sales efforts. In midsized firms, for example, the Chief Executive Officer (CEO) or the Chief Financial Officer (CFO) typically makes the decisions about how the firm will meet its trucking needs. In large firms, these decisions are likely to be made by the Director of Transportation.

Ryder also segments by industry potential based on input from its sales force and marketing research department. The company targets high-growth industries and avoids low-growth or financially troubled industries. Bottlers of beer, soft drinks, and designer water have been a major target over the past few years. Truck leases by the bottling industry grew from 1000 to 8000 during a recent five-year period.

Geographic location is also a segmentation variable used by Ryder. The firm has recently targeted Great Britain, Germany, and Mexico for leasing operations. The firm believes international growth is vital to continued success.

Ryder's Commercial Services Division uses a considerable amount of advertising, even though its annual advertising budget is a modest $10 million. According to Bob Horton, Group Director of Marketing for Commercial Services at Ryder, advertising makes sense because much of the firm's strength comes from signing up small companies and helping them grow. Because it would be difficult to identify all the small companies that might be potential customers, Ryder finds that those companies are best reached through advertising, at least initially. Ryder advertises in newspapers, in the Yellow Pages, via direct mail, and on television. One animated commercial, created by the ad agency of Ogilvy & Mather and broadcast on network television, had a message that was short and to the point: "If the time you're spending managing your transportation needs could be better spent managing your business, talk to Ryder." The purpose of the ad was to increase potential customers' awareness of Ryder and get them to contact Ryder's sales force.

Number of Individuals Involved

Perhaps the most fundamental practical difference between consumer marketing and business marketing is the number of people involved in the purchase decision. In consumer markets, individuals or families make most buying decisions. In business markets, many individuals are involved. These people perform a number of distinctive roles in the purchase decision process that comprise the **buying center.** The roles in the buying center are users, influencers, buyers, deciders, and gatekeepers.[18] Several individuals may play the same role in any given purchasing situation. There is often, for example, more than one user of the good or service being purchased. Furthermore, you will see that a single individual may play more than one role. For instance, one person may act as both an influencer and a gatekeeper.

Users.   **Users** are individuals in the organization that actually use the product or service being purchased. In many cases, the users initiate the buying process or develop the specifications for the purchase. Users may also be important in evaluating the goods or services after the purchase. A sales rep who drives a company car is an example of a user.

Influencers.   **Influencers** are members of the firm that directly or indirectly affect the purchase decision process. They may develop criteria or may provide information to evaluate the alternatives under consideration. In manufacturing operations, for example, technical personnel such as engineers and operations managers influence many buying decisions.

Buyers.   **Buyers** are members of the organization that have formal authority for selecting the supplier and arranging the terms of the purchase. They typically have titles such as purchasing manager, purchasing agent, or buyer. The buyer's most important tasks are determining the set of possible suppliers and selecting the supplier to be used. Although the buyers are usually responsible for negotiating with suppliers, they are often constrained by the influence of others. For example, technical personnel may have established the specifications in such a way that the buyer is forced to deal with a particular supplier. As we will show later, the buyer's importance may be greater for the purchase of routine types of goods and services than it is for highly technical items being purchased for the first time by the organization.

Deciders.   **Deciders** are people who actually determine the final selection of products, services, and suppliers. The buyer may be the same individual as the decider, but often these two roles are played by different people, with the decider making the buying decision and the buyer making the actual purchase. Purchasing agents, for example, often have an upper limit to the dollar value for their authority to make purchase decisions. Decisions for purchases above this limit must be made by others in the organization, such as a vice president, president, or even the board of directors.

Gatekeepers.   **Gatekeepers** control the flow of information into the buying center. A gatekeeper is any individual within the organization who is in a position to have such control. Usually gatekeepers are purchasing agents or buyers who deal directly with vendors and potential vendors. A secretary, administrative assistant, or receptionist who screens calls for a user or influencer, however, is also a gatekeeper. Because the flow of information from salespersons to users and influencers is often controlled by the purchasing department, the purchasing agent's influence is strongest at the stage when buying alternatives are being identified.

Buyer Expertise and Rationality

Business buyers are professional buyers; buying is what they do for a living. Thus, they are typically far more knowledgeable than ultimate consumers about the goods and services they purchase. In addition, they have usually established (or had established for them) detailed specifications that suppliers of goods and services must meet. Therefore, their buying decisions are usually far more rational and less emotional than those of ultimate consumers. Impulse buying, which is common in consumer markets, is very unusual in business markets. Product quality, which is

This ad is typical of the rational appeal commonly used in business markets.

important to all consumers, is likely to be an even greater issue for business buyers because their jobs depend on their making good purchasing decisions.

The greater rationality of the business buyer is reflected in the types of promotion that marketers direct to business markets, where personal selling is far more common than mass media promotion. This is due not only to the differences in market size, as pointed out earlier, but also to the fact that mass media promotion often relies more on emotional appeals while personal selling provides an opportunity for more rational appeals. A sales representative for a pharmaceutical company, for example, can explain to a physician the merits of that company's products, counter concerns about side effects of medications, and describe the research and testing that occurred prior to commercialization. It would be difficult, if not impossible, to convey this same detailed information to the physician through an advertisement.

The advertising that is done tends to focus on product specifications and comparisons of technical characteristics among competing products. Emotional appeals, common in consumer advertising, are rare in business-to-business advertising. The advertisement for the Toshiba Satellite 486 is the kind of rational appeal commonly used in business markets.

Table 7.2 summarizes the differences between business and consumer markets discussed in this section.

	Business Market	Consumer Market
Members of the market	Manufacturers Wholesalers Retailers Governments Institutions	Individuals Households
Nature of demand	Derived	Direct
Reason for purchase	Production of other products Use in day-to-day operations Resale	Personal consumption
Market size	Typically small	Typically large
Promotional techniques used by producers to reach	Primarily personal selling	Primarily advertising
Number of individuals involved in buying process	Usually one or two	Usually several
Buyer's expertise	Generally significant	Generally limited
Type of appeal market responds to	More rational appeal	More emotional appeal

TABLE 7.2
Differences between Business and Consumer Marketing

SEGMENTATION IN BUSINESS MARKETS

Market segmentation (the dividing of large markets into smaller markets that are homogeneous in terms of the wants and needs of the customers) is just as important in business marketing as it is in consumer marketing. The process of segmentation in business markets, however, is often more complex.[19] This may be due to the fact that "[business] markets are highly heterogeneous, complex, and often hard to reach because of the multitude of products and uses as well as a great diversity among customers."[20]

Furthermore, even after segmentation is accomplished in theory, its implementation is frequently challenged by the fact that a business marketer's company structure, distribution system, and sales force may be geared to meet operational considerations rather than meet marketing considerations.[21] In a study of the market for construction equipment in Europe, researchers found companies resisted a market segmentation approach. The resistance existed in spite of the fact that the current approach to market division, by product type, sometimes resulted in a single customer being called on by several sales representatives from the same company.[22] Companies expressed concern about the disruption to the sales force and dealer network that would be caused by a reorganization based on differences in customer needs.

Nevertheless, segmentation is important to the success of a market-driven organization because it is more effective than mass marketing for meeting the customers' needs. The complexity of planning and implementing segmentation in business markets, along with few practical examples of segmentation, have led business marketers to be slow in developing strong segmentation approaches to their markets.[23] Concern has been expressed about how little effort many business marketers put into identifying segments within their broader market.[24] While broad-based approaches to market division are relatively common, segmentation using more narrowly defined variables to produce clearly defined segments is relatively uncommon. Business marketers must strive to understand the value and methodology of segmentation.

Bases in Segmentation of Business Markets

Business markets can be segmented using almost any of the bases of segmentation described for segmenting consumer markets. As Chapter 5 noted, these include geographics, demographics, and behavioral factors. Psychographics, described as consumer states of mind, and including personality and life-style characteristics, generally do not apply to segmenting business markets. On the other hand, buying process characteristics represent a segmentation base that is applicable to business markets but not consumer markets. As with segmentation in consumer markets, while just about any variable can be used to subdivide a market, effective segmentation occurs only when factors relevant to the similar needs, wants, and buying influences of segments are used.

Geographic segmentation.   Geographic factors can be extremely useful in segmenting business markets. Many industries are concentrated in certain geographical regions. For example, many apparel manufacturers are located in the southeastern United States, computer chip producers are commonly found in Asian countries, and the Bordeaux region of France is famous for its concentration of vintners. When a group of business customers with similar needs is located in a concentrated area, business marketers find it easier to develop focused promotion and streamlined distribution strategies.

Demographic segmentation.   Demographic segmentation is also a useful and common base of business market segmentation. Demographics such as company size (as illustrated in the "Marketing in Action" about Ryder), how long the business has been in existence, number of competitors, proximity to competitors, and other organizational characteristics can prove valuable in setting and implementing strategy and often to segment business markets.[25] A business marketer might, for example, use different selling techniques for the company's large accounts and small accounts. Large accounts may get personal sales calls on a monthly basis while smaller accounts receive only a monthly telephone call. The most prominent demographic factor used to segment business markets is the Standard Industrial Classification code. In fact, this system is so common and such an important part of business markets that it is discussed in detail in the next section of this chapter.

Behavioral segmentation.   Most of the behavioral factors appropriate for the consumer sector are also useful in the business market sector. Segmentation by volume of usage (usage rate), benefits sought, degree of brand loyalty, or buying readiness can work effectively for business markets. For example, usage rate segmentation can be used by a business marketer to differentiate heavy users, light users, and nonusers. Most major oil companies concentrate on the heavy-user market offering

Demographics such as company size are often used to segment business markets.

price discounts for greater volume of use. A smaller competitor like Superior Oil might find it profitable to concentrate on the light-user segment of the market. This could be done by providing frequent delivery regardless of volume purchased.

Segmentation by benefits sought can also be useful in the business market. Benefit segmentation often provides important information that is not obtained through segmentation methods such as demographic segmentation.[26] For example, some buyers of chemicals are interested in the finest quality available, often developing specifications with extremely narrow tolerances. Others, perhaps because of a lack of space for inventory or less working capital, are attracted by frequent, reliable deliveries of chemicals. Segmenting by these differences in benefits sought provides a clear distinction in the types of strategies that should be developed for the various segments.

Depending on the market, segmentation by brand loyalty or by stage of readiness might be important. For example, IBM has been particularly effective in developing and nurturing brand-loyal customers, trading them up to the faster, more expensive machines as their needs grow. IBM has also been successful in marketing to firms at various readiness stages through advertising, product demonstrations, strong personal selling, and user training.

Segmentation by buying process characteristics. Business marketers also segment by buying process characteristics.[27] This approach identifies a segment consisting of organizations with similar buying processes. Companies that rely heavily on gatekeepers to control information flow might, for example, be grouped into one segment. The marketing strategy for this segment would focus on heavy doses of personal selling directed specifically at the gatekeepers. Choffray and Lilien[28] performed a study that segmented the industrial cooling industry by differences and similarities in buying influences and buying processes. It found this approach produced segment distinctions closely related to differences in buyer behavior. Thus the method proved very useful as a segmentation base.

STANDARD INDUSTRIAL CLASSIFICATION SYSTEM

The **Standard Industrial Classification code (SIC)** is a detailed numbering system for classifying American establishments according to type of economic activity.[29] The SIC system is compiled by the United States Office of Management and Budget and divides the economy into 11 divisions. The divisions are agriculture, forestry, and fishing; mining; construction; manufacturing; transportation, communication, electric, gas, and sanitary services; wholesale trade; retail trade; finance, insurance, and real estate; services; public administration; and nonclassifiable establishments. A two-digit number is assigned to major industry groups within each division. Table 7.3 lists the division and lists the two-digit codes within each division. For example, Manufacturing, Division D, includes food manufacturers (SIC code 20); apparel manufacturers (SIC code 23); and fabricated metal products manufacturers (SIC code 34).

For each major industry group, total industry sales and employment are published. This information is compiled by SIC code for each county in the United States and is available by various geographical breakdowns. Revisions to the SIC manual, which lists the economic activity of businesses, institutions, and government agencies by SIC classification, are undertaken periodically.

TABLE 7.3
The Standard Industrial Classification System

Division	Industries Classified	First Two-digit SIC Numbers Involved
A	Agriculture, Forestry, and Fishing	01, 02, 07, 08, 09
B	Mining	10–14
C	Construction	15–17
D	Manufacturing	20–39
E	Transportation, Communications, Electric, Gas, and Sanitary Services	40–49
F	Wholesale Trade	50–51
G	Retail Trade	52–59
H	Finance, Insurance, and Real Estate	60–67
I	Services	70, 72–73, 75–76, 78–86, 88–89
J	Public Administration	91–97
K	Nonclassifiable Establishments	99

Classification	SIC Number	Description
Division	D	Manufacturing
Major group	34	Manufacturers of fabricated metal products
Industry subgroup	344	Manufacturers of fabricated structural metal products
Detailed industry	3441	Manufacturers of fabricated structural metal
Manufactured products	34411	Manufacturers of fabricated structural metal for buildings
Manufactured products	3441121	Manufacturers of fabricated structural metal for buildings—iron and steel (for sale to other companies): industrial

Source: R. W. Haas, *Business Marketing Management*, 5th ed., Boston: PWS-Kent, 1992, p. 247

TABLE 7.4
Samples of SIC Subgroup

After the initial major industry breakdown, the industry groups are divided into subgroups, which are given more specific numbers. Table 7.4 illustrates that the SIC system's level of specificity increases as the number of digits in the code increases.

The value of the SIC system in marketing segmentation is that companies in virtually every American industry have already been classified. Once a marketing manager identifies the SIC categories of interest, it is not difficult to combine SIC data with input/output analysis to develop market segments. **Input/output analysis** is based on the concept that the output (sales) from one industry is the input (purchases) of other industries. The Dallas/Fort Worth International Airport used input/output data regarding the increase in air travel to determine needs for expansion of jobs and buildings.[30] The U.S. Department of Commerce publishes national input/output models covering 83 primary industries.

While the SIC system remains a prominent system for understanding and accessing business markets, it is not without its critics. Marketers have argued that revisions to the system are not frequent enough. The most recent revision occurred in 1988. That revision was the first that had occurred in ten years. Furthermore, only one SIC code is assigned for the principal product per establishment, so if two or more products are produced at one location, the data for the secondary products are not captured by the SIC system. This can create underestimates for some industry categories. In spite of these criticisms, the SIC system remains an important source of information about business markets.

THE BUYING BEHAVIOR OF BUSINESSES

Understanding buyer behavior is just as important for business marketers as it is for consumer marketers. In many ways the buying behavior of businesses parallels the buying behavior of ultimate consumers. The types of buying decisions that businesses face vary based on the amount of experience they have with a decision and the amount of risk the decision is perceived to represent. Furthermore, the purchase decision process involves a series of steps including problem recognition, information gathering, evaluation of alternatives, decision, and postpurchase evaluation.

7-1 You have just been appointed director of marketing for a large corporate law firm. How might market segmentation help you develop a marketing strategy?

7-2 In your position as director of marketing, in what ways might the SIC system be helpful to you?

YOUR MARKETING KNOWLEDGE

Types of Buying Decisions

All the goods and services purchased by businesses fall into one of three buyclasses— new task buys, modified rebuys, and straight rebuys.[31] A **buyclass** is a type of buying decision based on the newness of the problem to the organization, the amount of information required, and the consideration of new alternatives. Some of the distinguishing characteristics of the three buy classes are shown in Table 7.5.

New task buys.   With **new task buys,** the members of the buying center face a requirement or problem that has not arisen before. They have little or no relevant buying experience, so a great deal of information is needed, and alternative suppliers are carefully considered. Many manufacturing firms are investing in complex computer systems that integrate all the automated processes within a factory into a single system referred to as computer integrated manufacturing (CIM). The purchase of a CIM system is a complex decision for a company. New task buys occur infrequently, but they are very important to marketers because they set the pattern for the more routine purchases that follow. New task buys in business marketing parallel extensive problem-solving behavior in consumer marketing. It has been suggested that efforts to build a strong strategic alliance are most important for business marketers when a new task buy such as a CIM is involved.[32]

**TABLE 7.5
Distinguishing Characteristics of Buying Situations**

Buying Situation (Buyclass)	Newness of the Problem	Information Requirements	New Alternatives
New task buy	High	Maximum	Important
Modified rebuy	Medium	Moderate	Limited
Straight rebuy	Low	Minimal	None

Source: P. Robinson, C. Faris, and Y. Wind, *Industrial Buying and Creative Marketing* (Allyn & Bacon, 1967), p. 28.

Modified rebuys.   **Modified rebuys** arise with continuing or recurring requirements where the buying alternatives are known but changed. A new evaluation of supplier offerings is done—prompted by the conviction that it is worthwhile to seek additional information and alternatives before a decision is made. Modified rebuys may arise internally because of new buying influences, potential cost reductions, quality improvements, or service benefits. They may arise because of external events such as an emergency or by the actions of a supplier. Growing concern by consumers, for example, about the environmental damage resulting from packaging might cause a business buyer to reevaluate suppliers with an eye to the supplier's level of environmental concern. Modified rebuys parallel limited problem solving for consumer markets.

Straight rebuys.   **Straight rebuys** are purchases that involve continuing or recurring requirements and are handled on a routine basis. They are the most common type of purchase by businesses and parallel routine response behavior in consumer buying. The company has a list, formally or informally, of acceptable suppliers and no new suppliers are considered. Buyers, often in the purchasing department, have a great deal of relevant buying experience, and little, if any, new information is needed. The item purchased, the price, or delivery time may change somewhat from purchase to purchase, as long as these variations do not cause a new source of supply to be considered. Apple Computers, for example, might have a list of several approved suppliers of computer chips. Orders may be given to all suppliers or the company may rotate orders among the approved suppliers, but never place an order with a supplier not on the list.

THE PURCHASE DECISION PROCESS IN BUSINESSES

The process by which companies purchase goods and services begins with someone in the organization anticipating a problem that can be solved through a purchase. Recognition of the problem may come from anyone in the organization: a user, an influencer, or even an individual not otherwise involved in the purchase decision process. For example, the president of the company might tell the vice president of operations that the cost of raw materials should be lower. The process is illustrated in Figure 7.3.

The second step is the development of specifications for products or services to solve the problem. At this stage, influencers such as technical and engineering

FIGURE 7.3
Organizational Purchase Decision Process

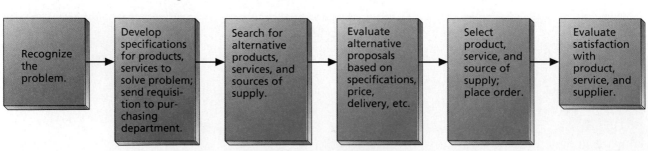

Source: Adapted from R. Haas, *Business Marketing Management*, 5th ed., Boston: PWS-Kent, 1992, pp. 273–176.

personnel may act as advisers. After the specifications are agreed upon, a requisition is sent to the purchasing department, and the search for alternative products, services, and sources begins. Gatekeepers are particularly important at this stage of the process, because they control the flow of information to the influencers, deciders, and others involved in the purchase decision.

The third step in the process is to evaluate the alternative proposals from the various sources of supply. The alternatives are evaluated in terms of how well they meet specifications, particularly with respect to performance. Other typical factors include price, delivery, seller reputation, and services provided. The actual price paid for a product may not be as important as the results of a value analysis of the product. A value analysis is a measure of all the costs involved in buying and using a particular item. These include the basic price of the item, any installation costs, any anticipated servicing costs, and replacement costs. The reliability of the item is also considered. As a result of a value analysis, a business may discover that a mechanical part that costs five times as much as an alternative may have a much greater value than the cheaper part if it results in substantially less downtime for the piece of equipment in which it is used.

After the alternatives have been evaluated, the decision is made and an order is placed. After the product or service has been received, it is evaluated, as is the supplier. This information will be compiled and used when this product or service is again needed.

Familiarity with the business purchase decision process and knowing how it works in a particular firm can be very useful to a business marketer in planning strategy. For example, at the second step of the process, influencers may wish to learn more about various product applications before developing specifications. If a vendor knows this, he or she may sponsor educational seminars to help the influencers learn about the latest product applications. A vendor who knows that his or her customers rely heavily on value analysis in evaluating alternatives at the third step of the process, might train sales representatives to acknowledge prices higher than the competition's and then emphasize the value of the company's products.

Just as with the consumer purchase process, a number of factors influence the business purchase decision process. In fact, there are usually more buying influences involved in business buying behavior, leading to substantial complexity from the seller's viewpoint. The "Marketing in Action: Know Thy Customers" discusses how to obtain information about the behavior of business buyers.

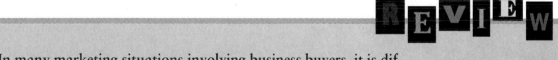

7-3 In many marketing situations involving business buyers, it is difficult to recognize the decision makers, gatekeepers, and key influencers. Why is it so hard to identify the various players in the buying center and their roles?

7-4 Is it easier to identify the members of the buying center and their roles for straight rebuys or for new task buys? Why?

YOUR MARKETING KNOWLEDGE

MARKETING IN ACTION

Know Thy Customers

The better business marketers understand the needs of their customers, the higher the level of customer satisfaction they can provide. Therefore, marketers are encouraged to read research studies that can help them learn more about their customers. One such study, titled "Know the Buyer Better," was conducted by the Penton Publishing Company. The researchers interviewed 104 members of buying centers representing ten industries. Among the findings reported were the following:

- Buyers look to sellers to aid them in areas where their time and expertise are limited. This situation is increasingly common as corporate downsizing spreads.

- Organizational buying is increasingly being handled by younger individuals at lower levels in the company. This provides opportunities for vendors because the "new" buyer is generally more open to new ideas and products.

- Buyers prefer viewing themselves as take-charge entrepreneurs rather than technicians, but at the same time they fear expanding beyond the safe and familiar. Hence suppliers who can operate in a buyer's "comfort zone" are most likely to get and keep the customer.

- Many buyers fear escalating technological complexity and thus shift their focus to "people issues" rather than "product issues." To be successful, suppliers must realize that customers buy relationships, not just products.

Understanding customers comes not only from wide-ranging cross-industry studies such as the Penton report, but also from a company surveying its own customers on an ongoing basis. DuPont Electronics, for example, conducts an annual customer satisfaction monitoring program. The program represents much more than just asking customers if they're satisfied. It carefully pushes to understand buyer behavior and reaction by inquiring about company performance versus expectations and asking questions customized to individual customers.

Other companies committed to understanding and hence satisfying their customers include the Industrial Services Division of Canada's Honeywell Limited. The firm, which has conducted customer satisfaction surveys annually since 1989, feels it is on its way to market-driven status.

Organizations should recognize that understanding the consumer behavior of their business customers does not imply an ability to change or adapt that behavior. After all, according to George U. Isaacs of Chicago Consulting, " . . . what might seem irrational from the supplier's perspective is rational behavior to the customer."

 PERSONAL COMPUTER EXERCISE

SIC Codes are important in determining the size of business markets. This PC Exercise allows you to use SIC data to examine the potential for each of several business markets. You will also learn how one can estimate a firm's market share using readily available SIC information.

KEY POINTS

- *Business marketing* and *business markets* are the names that have replaced the terms *industrial marketing* and *industrial markets*. The term *business* more accurately covers the breadth of marketing situations applicable in this case.

- Business products can be classified into seven categories: business services, heavy equipment, light or accessory equipment, supplies, component parts, raw materials, and processed materials.

- There are five types of business markets. They are manufacturers, wholesalers, retailers, government markets, and institutional markets.

- Government markets come in all sizes. The U.S. federal market is huge, and, therefore, attractive to many marketers. Many different products are bought, and much information about its buying process is available. The process is complex, however, and is different from typical commercial buying, often resulting in considerable risk.

- There are many differences between consumer and business markets and marketing. These include demand, market size, promotional techniques, number of individuals involved, and the degree of buyer expertise and rationality.

- An important difference between consumer and business markets is derived demand. With business markets, the demand for a product arises from the demand for another product.

- The demand for business products fluctuates, caused by the derived demand for those products. A small change in consumer demand can have a major change in the demand for business products.

- The demand for many business products is inelastic in nature, with price not having much impact on the level of primary demand (demand for the product category).

- The number of potential buyers is often small in business markets.

- A number of individuals are involved in most purchases made by business consumers. Those involved comprise the buying center. The roles in the buying center include users, influencers, buyers, deciders, and gatekeepers.

- Business buyers are usually more technically qualified than buyers in consumer markets, and buying motives are usually less emotional.

- Market segmentation is as important in business markets as it is in consumer markets. Bases for business market segmentation include geographic segmentation, demographic segmentation, buying process characteristics, and behavioristic segmentation (including benefit segmentation, brand loyalty, and readiness states). Demographic segmentation makes heavy use of the Standard Industrial Classification system (SIC).

- The steps in the decision process for business buyers are problem recognition; development of specifications; search for alternative products and sources of supply; evaluation of alternatives based on specifications, price, and delivery; selection of product/service, source of supply, and placing of the order; and the evaluation of the product and supplier.

■ There are three types of buying decisions, called buyclasses, made by business markets: new task buys, modified rebuys, and straight rebuys.

■ Strategic alliances between business marketers and their customers are important to the success of a customer-driven organization.

KEY TERMS

business markets (211)
business marketing (211)
strategic alliance (212)
business services (215)
heavy equipment (215)
light or accessory equipment (216)
supplies (216)
MRO products (216)
component parts (216)
original equipment manufacturers (OEMs) (216)
raw materials (216)
processed materials (216)
goods for resale (216)
vendor (217)
manufacturers (217)
wholesalers (217)
retailers (217)
institutional markets (218)
small businesses (218)
derived demand (219)
buying center (221)
users (222)
influencers (222)
buyers (222)

deciders (222)
gatekeepers (222)
Standard Industrial Classification Code (SIC) (227)
input/output analysis (228)
buyclass (229)
new task buys (229)
modified rebuys (230)
straight rebuys (230)

ISSUES FOR DISCUSSION

1. Give three examples of derived demand. How does derived demand affect the marketing strategies of these three products?

2. What types of actions might an accounting firm take to build strategic alliances with the small businesses that are its clients?

3. How might a marketer of facsimile machines like Xerox or Sharp segment the market?

4. How might the SIC system be helpful to a manufacturer of personal computers?

5. Describe similarities and differences between consumer and organizational buying behavior. Discuss how the purchase of automobiles might be different for the two markets, using the college student market and the rental car company market as examples.

6. Describe the likely members of the buying center for each of the following products and services:

   (a) Overnight mail

   (b) Annual contract with a major trucking firm

   (c) New personal computer for the marketing research department

   (d) New "super computer" system for the research and development laboratories of a major corporation

   (e) Legal pads and paper clips

7. Describe the buying process for the purchase of a $100,000 piece of medical equipment by a hospital. What information would be needed, and what criteria would be used to make the purchase decision?

8. What type of buying situation (new task, modified rebuy, or straight rebuy) would be represented by each of the purchases in question 6?

9. What is the impact of multiple buying roles on the marketing strategy of a postage machine manufacturer, a minicomputer marketer, and an office supplies distributor?

10. What considerations might a middle-sized manufacturer of office supplies have in deciding whether to attempt to sell to the federal government?

CASE APPLICATION

Hitting the Jackpot with a Customer-Driven Approach

When Tom Carns decided to open a quick-printing business in Las Vegas, his first move was to survey all the competition in town. He personally visited each of the 70 businesses offering quick-printing services and carefully evaluated their strengths and weaknesses. He soon realized that the way to make a difference was to set up an operation that was truly customer driven.

When Carns opened PDQ Printing the shop was fully stocked, well organized, and offered a full range of quick-printing services. The shop's staff was thoroughly trained and courteous. Most important, high-quality customer service was set as the number one priority from the day PDQ's doors first opened.

The success of PDQ Printing has been phenomenal. In 1991, sales rose by 19 percent over its 1990 level. In 1992, the company grossed $5 million, about 19 times the industry average. Even more impressive, PDQ's net profit margin is close to 20 percent, which is some 2.5 times better than the industry average.

The key to Carns's success may be his view of the product he provides. To him, a quick-printing service is more than a business that merely provides a commodity. Rather, he sees it as a "custom manufacturing business" with customers whose needs vary widely. Being customer driven means discovering those needs, working diligently to understand them, and then meeting them.

For Carns, an integral part of being customer driven has been the implementation of a carefully orchestrated segmentation plan. First, he defined his target market as businesses that provide professional services, such as medical facilities, legal and accounting firms, brokerages, and the like. Next, he identified specific market segments that promised to be profitable. Last, he developed procedures for discovering and meeting the needs of the targeted market segments. For example, he established a legal services division, which surveyed legal firms and then focused on producing the types of forms needed by attorneys.

No doubt Carns's wide-ranging promotional efforts have also played a role in his firm's success. Unlike most quick-printing services, PDQ advertises extensively through print and broadcast media and via direct mail. The advertisements stress product quality and image over price. This approach gives PDQ the latitude to charge somewhat higher prices than the competition.

Another of Carns's promotional innovations is the use of personal selling, which is very unusual in the quick-printing business. PDQ has seven sales-people, overseen by a sales manager, who call on customers and potential customers in the target markets identified by Carns. Carns believes that at least six or eight sales calls are required to land an account, so his sales force is trained to "keep calling" on prospects again and again.

The PDQ sales force is savvy about the buying center concept. PDQ salespersons realize that they must first get past the receptionist, who typically acts as gatekeeper. Therefore, on a first call the salespeople merely introduce themselves to the receptionist and ask for the name of the decider in the firm. The salesperson then has two sets of personalized notepads printed up overnight, one for the decider and one for the receptionist. When the salesperson returns the next day, only rarely does he or she have a problem getting past the receptionist.

PDQ is also on the lookout for unusual promotional efforts that might help land an account. When Carns targeted the ten largest litigation firms in Las Vegas through his legal services division, he had boxes of doughnuts delivered to each firm every morning for a month, compliments of PDQ. By the end of the month, PDQ had landed all ten accounts, which combined handled nearly 80 percent of the litigation work done in the city.

Carns is constantly looking for and implementing new ways to meet customer needs and thereby differentiate PDQ from its competition. The firm keeps binders of every form it has ever printed for its commercial clients so that reorders can be processed quickly. PDQ also proofreads its customers' jobs for them, an innovative service in an industry where the competition typically places the responsibility for proofreading on the customers. PDQ also routinely conducts extensive surveys of customer satisfaction.

Questions

1. Describe the steps in the organizational purchase decision process for a medical office buying printing services. What does PDQ do to influence each step of this process?
2. On what bases has PDQ segmented the market? What approach to segmentation is it using?
3. Explain the concept of derived demand as it would apply to PDQ. What might the firm be able to do to influence its demand levels?
4. How would an organizational purchaser of printing services differ from a college student using the services of a quick-print shop?

Career

UNDERSTANDING
THE BUSINESS

Chapter 7 presents characteristics of the business market, the arena in which you will market yourself to meet your career objectives. If you understand the properties of this market, you can be very competitive in your job search.

The better that marketers of business-to-business products and services understand the needs of their customers, the higher the level of customer satisfaction they can ensure. In your self-marketing activities, study your target organizations and conduct a true derived-demand analysis. The better you understand the opportunities and challenges of your target organizations, the better you will understand the opportunities and challenges that are available to you. One way to better understand your target organizations is to identify the organizations' specifications for hiring new personnel in your functional area.

Segmentation might not seem important in your job search, but in these highly competitive times, you need to investigate a wide market for yourself. Concentrate on your high-priority job targets, but also investigate some alternatives that "stretch" you a bit. For example, if you target large corporations because of their training programs, you might also consider smaller corporations because they could give you greater responsibilities.

The buying concept center also applies to your job search. You need to know who plays the role in the hiring process for your target organization. Larger organizations might use "gatekeepers." These human resource professionals conduct first-level screening interviews. You see these gatekeepers before you meet the employees who actually do the hiring. In smaller companies, one person might be in charge of screening applicants.

How can you use your knowledge of business-to-business marketing to gain the understanding of target organizations that you need to meet your career objectives? Gathering information on companies is one critical step. You can obtain company information from career resource libraries and annual reports as well as from other students, recent alumni, career counselors, and faculty and professional associations.

Questions

1. Which business markets interest you most? Which would be of least interest? Provide reasons for your preferences.
2. For one of your top-priority target organizations, describe the business situation and the specifications for new hires in your functional area. How do the two factors relate?
3. Describe the hiring process in one of your large target organizations. Identify each individual who plays a role in the process and tell which of the firm's needs and which of your qualifications that person would be likely to consider during the interview.

CHapTeR 8

Information for Marketing Decision Making

Upon completing this chapter, you will be able to do the following:

■ **Describe** the sources of information a marketing manager can use to make decisions.

■ **Explain** how a marketer uses a decision support system and a marketing information system.

■ **Understand** how a marketer would decide whether to do marketing research.

■ **Compare** the three categories of marketing research.

■ **Discuss** the steps in the marketing research process.

■ **Identify** the methods used to forecast market potential, sales potential, and sales level.

*M*arketing *P*rofile

Finding Out What Consumers Want

A Texas-based financial services company, USAA, does it by mailing out a half million surveys every year. Honda does it, in part, by videotaping consumers as they test drive new cars. Spiegel did it by analyzing the sales records of customers who ordered from its catalogue. Whether a company's style is asking people, observing people, analyzing what people have done or any of a host of other methods, the market-driven firm of the 1990s recognizes the importance of gathering information on what consumers want before making marketing decisions.

USAA is committed to listening to its customers. The company, which markets insurance, banking services, and mutual funds, mails 500,000 questionnaires annually to a sample of its 2.5 million customers. The surveys ask about customer satisfaction, future needs, and ideas for new products. The firm typically nets a 60 percent response rate (20 percent is considered good for mail surveys). USAA attributes the high response to the fact that the firm follows up on the information the surveys provide. Requests for more and different types of mutual funds, for example, resulted in a new product that was an immediate success for the company.

Honda uses a host of methods for gaining information on what consumers want. Customer surveys, focus groups (small groups of consumers invited to chat informally about products), and observation of drivers are all employed by the firm. In 1992 and 1993 the company sponsored a program it called the "E.T. Phone Home Project." During a three-month period, factory workers who produce Honda Accords put down their wrenches and picked up telephones instead. They called 47,000 recent Accord buyers (half of all the new Accords registered with the company during spring of 1992). The workers asked customers what they liked and didn't like about their new cars. The information gathered went to designers and will be reflected in changes on 1995 and 1996 model Accords.

Spiegel, the Chicago-based catalogue retailer, found that its company records contained a wealth of information that provided insight into consumers and ideas for new products. The firm, for example, was interested in targeting African American women. A data base was created by advertising the Spiegel catalogue in black-oriented publications such as *Ebony* and *Essence*. The firm then tracked the sales data on these clients and created a new product, E Style, a catalogue specifically targeted to African American women. Its pages are packed with offerings based on what sales data revealed black women desire. The catalogue has been an enormous success for Spiegel, outselling original forecasts by 50 percent.

The quality of marketing managers' decisions depends on properly obtaining and using information, which can be obtained in a variety of ways. Spiegel was able to introduce a successful new product based on information it had stored in its computer. Honda and USAA surveyed consumers to gather information that aided their decision making. An organization is not market-driven if it does not obtain and use information from and about the market to plan marketing strategy. Hence, information is desirable at every step throughout the strategic planning process.

In this chapter we examine how marketers obtain the information they need to make decisions, the sources managers use to get that information, marketing research (its role in aiding the decision maker), the marketing research process, and demand forecasting.

SOURCES OF INFORMATION FOR MARKETING DECISION MAKING

Marketers utilize three sources of information to aid their decision making. They are information systems (decision support systems and marketing information systems), contacts with other managers, and personal experience. These three sources are illustrated in Figure 8.1.

Decision Support Systems and Marketing Information Systems

Modern-day marketing decision makers are aided by the use of a decision support system.[1] A **decision support system (DSS)** is a system that collects and interprets information for decision making. It enables decision makers to interact directly with data bases and analysis models. The important components of a DSS include hardware, a communication network, a data base, a model base, a software base, and the DSS user (decision maker).[2] **Hardware** and a **communication network** refer to a computer that is connected to a larger system so it can receive and send information. A **data base** is the storage depot for the information flowing into the system.

FIGURE 8.1
Sources of Information Available to a Marketing Decision Maker

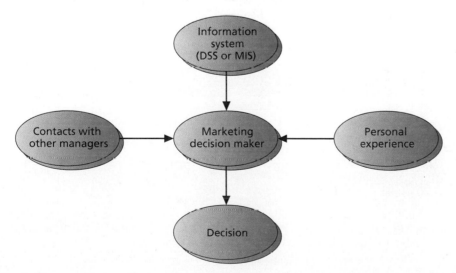

A **model base** contains operations research models that represent the real marketing world. For example, a marketer may have a model of his or her market in the bank. The model represents how consumers behave in the marketplace. A **software base** stores the programs needed to act on the data. It would contain programs to do statistical analysis as well as a spreadsheet program, a word processing program, and a presentation display package.

In essence, a DSS brings information from a wide variety of sources to a decision maker's fingertips through the use of computers. Decision support systems have evolved from another type of information system that aids marketing decision makers, a marketing information system. A **marketing information system (MIS)** is "a formalized set of procedures for generating, analyzing, storing, and distributing information to marketing decision makers on an ongoing basis."[3]

Both decision support systems and marketing information systems provide the information a marketing manager needs to make decisions in his or her area of responsibility. A sales manager, for example, might need sales information by product and by territory in order to assign quotas to the sales force. A DSS or an MIS could provide this information. The difference between a DSS and an MIS is that a DSS allows the decision maker to personalize the output by determining precisely what information he or she needs and then requesting only that information in the form that will be most helpful for decision making. Thus, a DSS is an interactive system. Using a DSS, the sales manager could look at the sales records for a specific territory and then request that they be broken down by quarter for each of the top five accounts. This information would be available instantaneously, on the computer screen. An MIS, on the other hand, provides information in a more structured manner, in a format predetermined to be useful. Table 8.1 details how the two systems differ.

Decision support systems are really just more sophisticated marketing information systems. The increase in sophistication has been largely due to technological achievements in the computer industry. It has been noted that thousands of smaller businesses today have information systems far more advanced than those that even the largest companies had ten years ago.[4] The use of CD-ROM has allowed storage of extremely large data bases right on a marketing manager's desk, as part of his or her PC.

The information that comprises an organization's MIS or DSS comes from many sources. These sources include accounting and sales reports generated within the company, published data about the industry (things such as market shares), competitor information (which might come from annual reports), government statistics, and marketing research findings. Figure 8.2 illustrates how these sources feed into the information system used by the decision maker.

TABLE 8.1
Management Information Systems versus Decision Support Systems

MIS	DSS
— Structured problems	— Unstructured problems
— Use of reports	— Use of models
— Rigid structure	— User-friendly interaction
— Information displaying restricted	— Adaptability
— Can improve decision making by clarifying raw data	— Can improve decision making by using "what if" analysis

Source: N. K. Malhotra, *Marketing Research: An Applied Orientation* (Prentice Hall, 1993), Figure 1.3, p. 14.

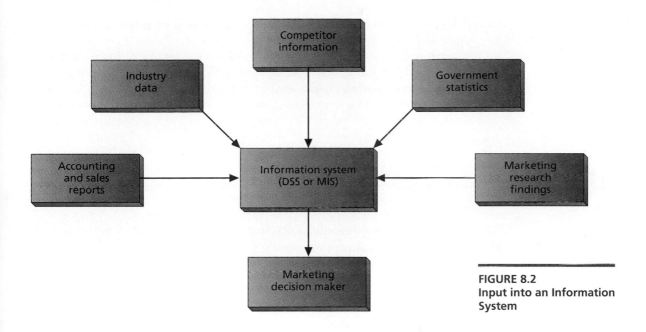

FIGURE 8.2
Input into an Information System

Personal Contacts with Other Managers

A second source of information is the decision maker's personal contacts with other managers within the company and within the industry. Many times the decision maker is faced with an issue that has been faced by other managers at other times. Thus, other managers may provide the information or at least suggest directions in which the marketing manager might look. Marketing managers are therefore well advised to cultivate personal contacts in their own and other firms. Of course, the manager must be cautious when discussing sensitive matters outside the firm so as not to give away company secrets.

Personal Experience

The final source of information the manager can call on to aid decision making is his or her own experience. Indeed, this may be the most important source of all. Personal experience is a very valuable source of information as evidenced by the high salaries that some organizations pay their experienced managers. Even when large amounts of information have been obtained from other sources, the marketing manager must rely on his or her experience to decide how much weight to assign that information and how to use it.

Sometimes marketing decision makers are so sure of their own judgment, based on experience, that they ignore other sources of information. The Edsel is a classic example where decision makers ignored other information and relied only on their own judgment and failure resulted. The Edsel was an automobile introduced by Ford Motor Company in 1957. The firm expected to sell 200,000 cars in the first year; instead it ceased production in 1959 after selling only 109,466 in three years. The name Edsel has become almost synonymous with failure. Part of the blame for the fiasco has been attributed to the fact that company executives ignored marketing research that told them the name Edsel would have a negative impact on consumers. The Ford executives were so sure they were right and their marketing research was wrong that they went ahead with the name Edsel anyway.[5]

Of course, decisions based solely on personal experience and judgment don't always turn out so badly. Later in this chapter we discuss cases where marketing research was ignored, sometimes with disastrous results, sometimes with good results. Most managers find that making decisions based on information from a combination of sources produces the best results.

Our focus in most of the remainder of this chapter is on marketing research. It is important to keep in mind, however, that marketing research is only one source of input into the information system used by marketing decision makers. Furthermore, the manager's information system is only one source of information that can be called on in decision making.

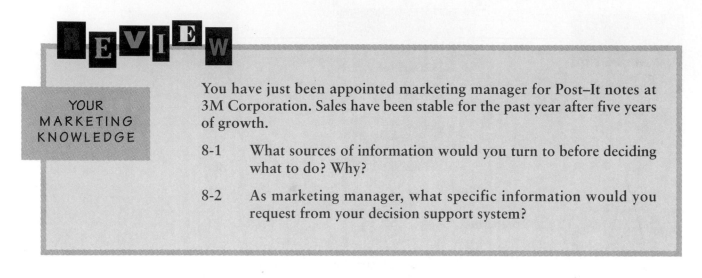

YOUR MARKETING KNOWLEDGE

You have just been appointed marketing manager for Post–It notes at 3M Corporation. Sales have been stable for the past year after five years of growth.

8-1   What sources of information would you turn to before deciding what to do? Why?

8-2   As marketing manager, what specific information would you request from your decision support system?

MARKETING RESEARCH AND DECISION MAKING

In 1987, the American Marketing Association adopted the following definition of marketing research:

> Marketing research is the function which links the consumer, customer, and public to the marketer through information—information used to identify and define marketing opportunities and problems; generate, refine, and evaluate marketing actions; monitor marketing performance; and improve understanding of marketing as a process.

> Marketing research specifies the information required to address these issues; designs the method for collecting information; manages and implements the data collection process; analyzes the results; and communicates the findings and their implications.[6]

For our purposes we will consider **marketing research** to be the systematic and objective development and provision of information to be used in the marketing management decision-making process. This may sound similar to the role of a marketing information system or a decision support system as described earlier. As pointed out, marketing research is a component of an organization's MIS or DSS. The firm's information system, however, provides continuous information whereas marketing research is undertaken periodically to provide information on a specific problem.

The requirement that marketing research be *systematic* means that it should be planned well in advance. The research design should be developed in detail, well before the research is actually begun. The requirement that marketing research be *objective* means that it should be conducted in an unbiased and unemotional manner. In other words, both the researchers and the marketing decision makers who order the research should ensure that their personal preferences do not inappropriately affect the results of the study. Finally, marketing research should be tied directly to a particular marketing problem. Research studies done without a marketing problem in mind are little more than exercises in data collection.

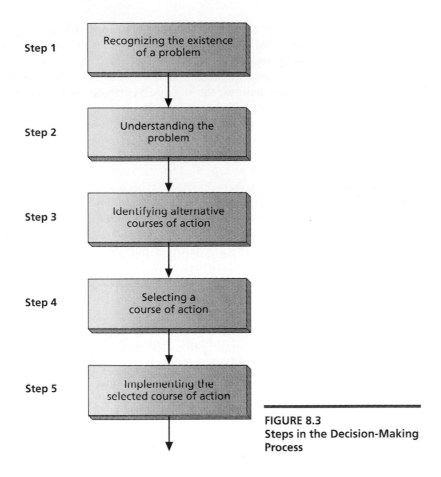

Step 1 — Recognizing the existence of a problem

Step 2 — Understanding the problem

Step 3 — Identifying alternative courses of action

Step 4 — Selecting a course of action

Step 5 — Implementing the selected course of action

FIGURE 8.3
Steps in the Decision-Making Process

When a marketing problem exists, there are typically five steps in the decision-making process used by marketing managers to deal with the problem. These five steps are summarized in Figure 8.3.

1. *Recognizing the existence of the problem.* The marketing problem-solving process begins when the marketing manager becomes aware that a problem exists. This may occur, for example, when the marketing manager is directed to develop a new marketing strategy or receives sales reports from the field indicating that a marketing strategy already in place is not working well. Imagine, for example, that the marketing manager of the Old Globe, a theater in San Diego, learned through an analysis of sales records at the close of the 1994 season that subscriptions were down 22 percent from 1993.

2. *Understanding the problem.* The manager must develop an understanding of the problem by, for instance, obtaining information though marketing research or by applying his or her own marketing expertise. The first step the Old Globe manager might take in attempting to understand why subscription sales are down is to consider what he knows about the organization's marketing efforts in 1994 and what he knows about the external environment. Advertising and telemarketing were cut back in 1994 and he suspects that may have contributed to the current sales problem. Furthermore, the economy in San Diego has been in a slump during the past two years. This personal consideration might be supplemented with some informal research aimed at better understanding the problem. The manager decides to call several former subscription holders and ask them why they didn't renew in 1994. He also decides to hold some informal discussions (focus groups) with current and former subscribers.

3. *Identifying alternative courses of action.* The marketing manager explicitly identifies actions that might be taken to adjust one or more of the four components of the marketing mix—product, price, place, or promotion. Research may play a role in these determinations. Based on the information obtained from the focus groups and discussions, the Old Globe manager designs a survey. He is interested in gathering people's perceptions of current Old Globe promotion and prices. From the survey results the manager formulates three strategies to reverse the declining sales: increase advertising, increase telemarketing, and reduce ticket prices.

4. *Selecting a course of action.* The marketing manager evaluates each of the possible actions and selects the one that seems best to solve the problem. Marketing research may again play a role. At this point the manager has decided to lower price. But how much? He undertakes an experiment whereby half of the 1994 subscription holders are offered an opportunity to renew for 1995 at 10 percent below 1994 rates. The other half are offered 20 percent off 1994 rates. The results of the experiment provide information on whether the lowest price being considered (20 percent off) produces enough additional subscriptions to make it worthwhile.

5. *Implementing the selected course of action.* The marketing manager takes steps to carry out the selected course of action. Based on the results of the experiment, the manager implements a 20 percent price decrease on Old Globe season subscriptions for 1995.

The Use of Marketing Research

The practice of marketing research is growing. The 50 largest U.S.-based marketing research firms increased revenues 3.5 percent in 1993 from 1992. The 1992 revenues, in themselves, represented an 11.1 percent increase from 1991.[7] The growth is occurring not only in the United States but worldwide. Of the $3.7 billion in revenues these top 50 firms had in 1993, 35 percent of it came from outside the United States. Despite this growth, many consumers are still skeptical of marketing research. The "Marketing in Action: Legitimizing Marketing Research—CMOR Fights the Good Fight" illustrates what the marketing research industry is doing to combat this skepticism.

Worldwide use of marketing research. Marketing research is a valuable input to marketing management decision making worldwide. Figure 8.4 illustrates the breakdown of marketing research expenditures on a global basis. As we can see, while the United States accounts for a major part of the marketing research in the world, it is far from the only place where marketing managers use research as an aid in decision making. The countries that account for most of the 40 percent of worldwide expenditures in Europe are Germany, the United Kingdom, France, Italy, and Spain.[8]

In sophisticated companies worldwide, the active integration of marketing research into decision making is a fact of organizational life. Consider the following examples of how marketing research has been used:

- Blue Diamond Almonds conducted marketing research in Russia before entering the market. The research determined that, in this market, it would be more effective to sell almonds based on their nutritive qualities than to position the product as a snack food (as Blue Diamond had done in the United States). Using this approach, Russia, in 1992, became Blue Diamond's third-largest overseas customer.[9]

- The Best Western Hotel chain conducted research worldwide on the composition of hotel business. The chain found that in North America 85 percent of its business was from domestic travelers. In the Far East, Australia, Africa, and the Middle East,

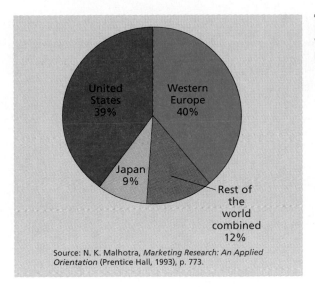

FIGURE 8.4
Worldwide Marketing Research Expenditures

United States 39%

Western Europe 40%

Japan 9%

Rest of the world combined 12%

Source: N. K. Malhotra, *Marketing Research: An Applied Orientation* (Prentice Hall, 1993), p. 773.

however, foreign travelers represented the majority of the chain's business. Based on these findings, Best Western targets domestic business in North America but targets foreign business elsewhere.[10]

- Volkswagen is conducting marketing research to determine the reaction of consumers in the United States to a new car, dubbed Concept 1. Concept 1 is reminiscent of the Volkswagen Beetle that was extremely successful in the U.S. market in the 1960s and 1970s. The research will help Volkswagen decide whether to produce the car.[11]

Despite the growing global prominence of marketing research, there are still many countries and many parts of the world where its use is not common, especially among small and medium-sized organizations. A study of 200 businesses with fewer than 200 employees in Ireland found that one-fifth of the businesses did not collect any market information. Among those that reported doing research, infor-

Volkswagen is conducting marketing research to determine the reaction of U.S. consumers to a new car, Concept 1. The research will help Volkswagen decide whether to produce the car.

© 1993 Rodney Rascona

Volkswagen Concept 1

MARKETING *IN ACTION* ■■■

Legitimizing Marketing Research—CMOR Fights the Good Fight

Despite the role marketing research can play in helping marketers to respond to the wants and needs of consumers, many people remain skeptical of the legitimacy of the marketing research industry. The Council for Marketing and Opinion Research (CMOR) is out to change all that. Founded in 1992, CMOR is a not-for-profit organization whose mission it is to promote awareness for and value of marketing research; enhance the marketing research experience; and establish a single unified industry voice on restrictive legislation and eroding respondent cooperation rates. The organization grew from a program initiated by the Marketing Research Association (an industry trade association) in the early 1980s called "Your Opinion Counts." The program sponsored advertising throughout the 1980s and early 1990s urging consumers to cooperate when asked for their opinions by a marketing research professional. Concern regarding the hesitancy of respondents to cooperate was industrywide at the time and remains a concern today.

CMOR hopes to increase respondent cooperation and decrease the likelihood of industrywide legislative regulation through lobbying, self-regulation, and consumer education. Legislation aimed at restricting the actions of marketing researchers is already in place in many states with more predicted at the local, state, and federal levels throughout the 1990s.

mation collection mechanisms tended to be informal rather than formal.[12] In less developed parts of the world, marketing research may not be undertaken because of the difficulties associated with carrying it out. In Pakistan, for example, it has been reported that researchers have a difficult time obtaining information from survey respondents for a number of reasons. These reasons include the low literacy level of the population and fear of giving information to strangers due to the unstable political environment in the country.[13]

The use of completed research. Carrying out marketing research, of course, doesn't always mean that it will be used in decision making. As pointed out in our discussion of personal experience, sometimes decision makers ignore the results of marketing research if they do not agree with the findings. Consider the following examples:

- When the electric refrigerator was invented, General Electric (GE) conducted marketing research on consumer response to the appliance. The results were overwhelmingly negative. Consumers did not want this noisy, expensive, and possibly dangerous appliance in their kitchens. The management at GE decided that the research results did not accurately reflect the way consumers would actually respond to the new product. The company introduced the refrigerator with great success and by so doing improved the quality of life of millions of consumers.

- Marketing research conducted prior to the introduction of MTV was not encouraging. Most consumers indicated that they would not sit and "watch" a song even if it were accompanied by a video. Research conclusions questioned whether the new concept would generate enough of a market to be economically viable. MTV was, of course, introduced despite the research findings. It has been enormously successful and is largely responsible for giving birth to the whole concept of music videos.

Of course, there are many examples of decision makers having ignored the findings of marketing research, and failure has resulted. The Edsel is one example. A second classic example is the introduction, in 1979, of the Susan B. Anthony dollar by the U. S. Bureau of the Mint. All the marketing research conducted by the Mint showed that the public would not be receptive to the new coin. Consumers disliked the size of the coin, thinking it would be easily confused with a quarter. Furthermore, consumers indicated that they felt dollar coins implied a weakening of the value of a dollar and reinforced the notion that little can be bought with a dollar anymore. The Mint went ahead and released the coin anyway. The dollar coin was a flop for the Mint. Of the 856 million Susan B. Anthony dollar coins that were minted, 757 million, almost 90 percent, were produced in 1979. Only 99 million more were minted before production ceased in 1981.

Unfortunately, deciding to go with the findings of marketing research is no guarantee of success. Coca-Cola introduced New Coke in 1985 only after extensive research that included thousands of blind taste tests. Two years and $4 million had gone into the marketing research effort. The research unequivocally indicated that consumers preferred the taste of New Coke over that of traditional Coke. New Coke was a major flop for Coca-Cola. In less than three months the company reversed itself and reintroduced its original formula under the name Coca-Cola Classic.[14]

Deciding to Do Marketing Research

Not every problem justifies carrying out a marketing research study. Before undertaking any kind of marketing research, the decision maker and the researcher must evaluate the problem carefully and determine the role marketing research will play in finding the solution to the problem. To make sure this is done, many organizations require the marketing manager to submit a formal marketing research request to upper management. These requests typically include as much of the following information as possible:

- a statement of the problem
- an explanation of the factors underlying the problem
- a list of alternative courses of action being considered
- a description of specific information that will be collected
- a statement of how the research findings will likely be used to solve the problem
- estimates of the costs and the value of the research

Assuming that the proposed research study is viewed as sound by upper management, the decision of whether to authorize the study rests on the money involved. If the estimated value or benefit of the research exceeds the estimated costs of conducting the study, the research request will likely be approved.

The costs of the research study can be assessed fairly easily. They include the expense of conducting the study, the loss of profits that might occur due to the delay in dealing with the problem, and the cost to the firm of the competitor's actions. In this last case, some types of research are undertaken in a public setting, thus alerting competitors to a firm's possible actions. A company might, for example, be conducting research to determine customer reaction to a new snack food. Competitors who become aware of the product may decide to use the idea and get the snack food to market first. The original company risks losing the profits that go to the first entrant in the market.

The value or benefit of marketing research is much more difficult to assess. Conceptually, research should increase the probability of selecting the best alternative or at least avoiding major mistakes. The difficulty arises because assessing the value of the increased likelihood of making a better marketing decision is a subjective evaluation. If marketing managers are confident that they can solve the problem using their own experience or with the help of other managers, then the findings of a research study would have little or no value and the study should not be undertaken. On the other hand, if managers are not sure they can solve the problem effectively, then a research study would be valuable. Indeed, as a manager's uncertainty increases, so does the value of the research and so does the desirability of conducting the study.

Market Size	Small Profit Margin	Large Profit Margin
Small	Cost likely to be greater than benefit; e.g., eyeglasses replacement screw	Possible benefits greater than cost; e.g., ultraexpensive sportswear
Large	Benefits likely to be greater than costs; e.g., Stouffer's frozen entrees	Benefits most likely to be greater than costs; e.g., medical equipment like C.A.T. scanner

Source: Adapted from C. McDaniel, Jr., and R. Gates, *Contemporary Marketing Research*, 2d ed. (West, 1993), Table 1.2, p. 17.

TABLE 8.2
The Decision to Conduct Marketing Research

Two determinants of the potential benefit of conducting marketing research regarding new product opportunities are the size of the market to be targeted and the size of the profit margin that can be expected.[15] Generally, the value of marketing research will be greater in cases involving larger markets and greater expected profit margins. Table 8.2 illustrates how these two factors can aid a marketing decision-maker in evaluating whether or not to conduct research.

Categories of Marketing Research

There are three general categories of marketing research—performance-monitoring research, exploratory research, and conclusive research. As shown in Figure 8.5, different categories of research are effective for different steps in the decision-making process.

Performance-monitoring research.   **Performance-monitoring research** provides feedback on an implemented marketing program. It answers the question: How well is the marketing program working? An organization might decide, for example, to study the effectiveness of its distribution strategy by doing research that compares sales under the current strategy to sales under strategies used in the past. Furthermore, it may survey customers to gain insight into their reactions to the current strategy. **Customer satisfaction measurement (CSM)** is an example of performance-monitoring research. The use of CSM, which provides an ongoing assessment of how satisfied customers are, increased by 28 percent between 1991 and 1992.[16] Frequently, some type of performance-monitoring research first alerts the marketing manager to the existence of a problem. In the example of the Old Globe theater, the ongoing analysis that informed the marketing manager that subscription sales were down 22 percent is an example of performance-monitoring research.

Exploratory research.   **Exploratory research** is research whose primary objective is to provide insights into the problem.[17] It is typically used in steps 2 and 3 of the decision-making process. In step 2, it is used to clarify the problem and to isolate the factors underlying the problem. The Old Globe marketing manager's use of focus groups and telephone discussions with former subscription holders are examples of exploratory research being used at step 2. In step 3, exploratory research is used to identify possible courses of action. When the manager did the survey to gain insight and help him plan possible alternatives, he was again using exploratory research. In either step, exploratory research can reveal new opportunities.

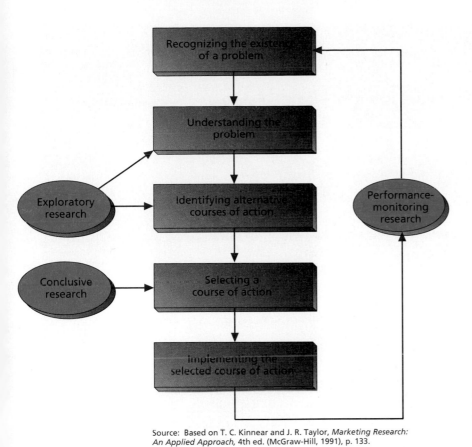

Source: Based on T. C. Kinnear and J. R. Taylor, *Marketing Research: An Applied Approach,* 4th ed. (McGraw-Hill, 1991), p. 133.

FIGURE 8.5
Types of Research in the Decision-Making Process

Conclusive research.   Conclusive research provides information to help the marketing manager evaluate the various alternatives identified in step 3 and select the practical alternative that promises to be the most effective. The experiment with the two different price reductions carried out by the Old Globe manager is an example of conclusive research.

THE MARKETING RESEARCH PROCESS

The process by which marketing research should be performed can be broken down into a series of stages as shown in Figure 8.6. Both the marketing manager and the marketing researcher are involved in the process, although the extent of their involvement varies with the stage. The marketing manager's level of participation is high during stages 1 and 2 because the basic direction the research will take is determined in these stages. The manager's level of participation is again high in the final stage, which is where he or she must interpret how the research findings can be applied to the problem at hand. The researcher's level of participation is high in stages 3 through 8, which involve the technical aspects of marketing research.

Stage One: Establish the Need for Information

Establishing the need for the information that marketing research can provide is a crucial stage in the marketing research process. The most important task at this stage is to correctly and clearly identify the problem. If possible, the factors underlying the problem and alternative courses of action to solve the problem should also be

FIGURE 8.6
Stages in the Marketing Research Process

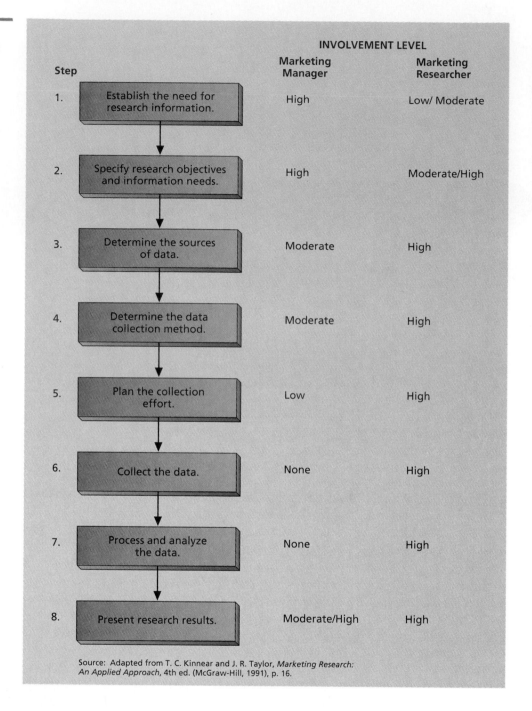

Step		INVOLVEMENT LEVEL	
		Marketing Manager	Marketing Researcher
1.	Establish the need for research information.	High	Low/ Moderate
2.	Specify research objectives and information needs.	High	Moderate/High
3.	Determine the sources of data.	Moderate	High
4.	Determine the data collection method.	Moderate	High
5.	Plan the collection effort.	Low	High
6.	Collect the data.	None	High
7.	Process and analyze the data.	None	High
8.	Present research results.	Moderate/High	High

Source: Adapted from T. C. Kinnear and J. R. Taylor, *Marketing Research: An Applied Approach*, 4th ed. (McGraw-Hill, 1991), p. 16.

identified. In many cases, however, exploratory research is needed to find this information. As we saw in the previous section, the need for research information must often be established before upper management will authorize the research study.

The failure to identify the problem correctly is one of the main reasons for unsuccessful marketing research studies. For example, when an ice cream manufacturer's market share began to decline, the marketing manager decided the problem was ineffective advertising. She convinced upper management to authorize a study of the company's mix of radio, television, and print media to determine how the company might more effectively spend its advertising dollars. The study was well executed, but it was essentially useless. The real problem turned out to be a shift in consumer tastes to low-fat and nonfat ice creams and frozen yogurts. More thorough investigation at the beginning would have identified the actual problem, which probably would have led to a useful research study.

Stage Two: Specify Research Objectives and Information Needs

The research objectives describe the purpose of a research study and give direction to a researcher regarding what needs to be accomplished. Consider the following objectives for three studies:

- Measure the market potential for solar energy equipment in the state of Maine.
- Determine which of three magazine advertisements generates the highest consumer recall.
- Measure consumers' preferences for alternative formulations of a new soft drink.

The information needs is a list of the specific information that must be found to meet the research objectives. For instance, the information needs for a study of the market potential for solar energy equipment in Maine might include the following:

- The percentage of Maine residents now using oil, gas, and coal
- The current market penetration of solar energy equipment
- The cost of solar energy systems currently available in Maine
- The identifying characteristics of the different segments of the total energy market in Maine
- The likely size of the market for solar energy equipment in 1995, 2000, and 2005

Stage Three: Determine the Sources of Data

The marketing researcher can obtain data from a variety of sources. Here we will discuss some of the more commonly used sources.

Secondary data. There are two basic types of marketing data—primary and secondary. **Primary data** are information newly collected for the problem at hand. **Secondary data** are information that was collected for another purpose. Secondary data can be collected more quickly than primary data and is also less expensive for the researcher to obtain. These two factors are powerful advantages of secondary data. Consequently, secondary data sources should always be searched thoroughly before the decision is made to gather primary data.

However, because secondary data were collected for purposes other than the problem at hand, they may not provide all of the information the marketing manager needs to solve the current problem. Furthermore, the data might be outdated or reported in a form that is not useful to the manager. For these reasons, secondary data sources are most commonly used for exploratory research. The major sources of secondary data are internal records, syndicated data, government data, and private data.[18]

Internal records. The company itself often has available very useful data such as sales and cost information organized by territory, customer, and product. This type of data can help identify areas of strength and weakness in the marketing program, and major trends in these areas. Internal records often play an important role in performance-monitoring research. Data indicating that sales are declining, for example, would alert the firm that a problem exists.

Syndicated data. A number of private organizations, such as A.C. Nielsen and Predicast, collect and sell standardized data designed to serve the needs of a number of organizations. This information is called syndicated data. A.C. Nielsen's Retail Index, for example, provides market share data on more than 2,000 product classes.

The data are collected in 25 countries worldwide.[19] A common method of collecting syndicated data today is through the use of a scanner, a device that reads UPC (Universal Product Codes) symbols on packages. Although this data have typically been collected in retail stores, SAMI/Burke, a market research firm, provides scanner wands to consumers for use in their homes.

Government data. All levels of the U.S. government—federal, state, and local—collect and make available many kinds of data relevant to marketing. The following sets of data are but a small part of the information available from the federal government:

- *Census of Housing* contains data on types of structures, year built, occupancy, appliances, value, rent, and ethnic category of occupant.
- *Census of Population* includes information on age, gender, race, national origin, employment, income, and family composition.
- *Census of Manufacturers* contains data on number, size, capital expenditures, output, inventories, and employment.
- *Census of Retail Trade* provides information on number, size, sales level, merchandise, and employment for retail stores.
- *Census of Wholesale Trade* provides information on number, size, sales levels, merchandise, and employment for wholesale operations.

At the federal level, The U.S. Department of Commerce is the clearinghouse for data from all censuses as well as data from other federal agencies and departments. Customer service representatives at the Department of Commerce gladly help marketers find the information they need.

Internationally, many governments have secondary information available. In the United Kingdom, for example, the Central Statistics Office is a government department responsible for collecting statistical data on the population. The level of data collected by governments and the frequency of its collection is extremely variable throughout the world. For example, the United States conducts a population census every ten years; the Republic of China last conducted one in 1982, 29 years since the previous Chinese census in 1953.[20]

Private data. Data are also published or made available for retrieval by many private organizations like magazine publishers, trade associations, advertising agencies, and research firms. In a single category such as magazines, marketers can find useful data in *Advertising Age, Forbes, Fortune, Business Week*, and *Sales & Marketing Management*, to name only a few of the many sources. A thorough search of secondary data requires access to an up-to-date and complete library of private data.

Primary data.   Primary data collection should be undertaken only after a thorough search of secondary data sources. It may turn out that the collection of primary data is unnecessary if the researcher finds all the data he or she needs from the secondary sources. If the researcher determines that primary data are necessary, there are two types to be considered, qualitative and quantitative.

Qualitative data. **Qualitative data** are not subject to quantification or quantitative analysis.[21] Research that involves qualitative data are called qualitative research. Such research typically involves input from small numbers of people in an unstructured format. It is designed to provide insight and understanding of the problem setting, hence it is commonly used for exploratory research.[22] Qualitative data are not appropriate for conclusive research because the number of respondents involved is so small.

A common vehicle for the collection of qualitative data is the focus group. A **focus group** is a group of eight to twelve participants who are led by a moderator in an in-depth discussion on one particular topic or concept.[23] The group is taped (either

Focus groups can be valuable for the collection of qualitative data. In this group, children taste test items for a hotel's children's menu.

audio or video) so the researcher can later analyze the discussion, looking for common themes. Focus groups can be valuable in uncovering ideas or thoughts that had not occurred to the researcher or decision maker. A paper products company recently nixed a toilet tissue commercial it had planned when focus groups perceived an unintentional sexual innuendo in the ad.[24] Costs for a typical focus group can run as high as $4,000, which has caused some research firms to experiment with electronic focus groups. These sessions involve participants speaking to each other via a networked computer system. Although this setup may reduce the group interaction that is an advantage of traditional focus groups, the cost is considerably less, approximately $1,500 per session.[25]

In-depth interviews are another common method of obtaining qualitative data. The interviews are lengthy, free-wheeling discussions between a researcher and an individual. A recent study found that such interviews produce as much information as focus groups despite the fact that only one subject is involved.[26]

Quantitative data. In contrast to qualitative data, **quantitative data** involve numbers. Quantitative research, which involves the use of quantitative data, seeks to measure the data and, typically, apply some form of statistical analysis.[27] Conclusive research and performance-monitoring research typically involve the use of quantitative research. Frequently researchers use qualitative data for exploratory research and follow it up with conclusive research that uses quantitative data.

The "Spotlight on Technology: Data Sources Today and Tomorrow" illustrates both qualitative and quantitative sources of data that are on the cutting edge of marketing research.

Stage Four: Determine the Data Collection Method

Quantitative data can be collected through observation, through experimentation, and through survey.

Observation. **Observation** is the collection of data with no communication between the respondent and the recorder of the behavior. Both humans and mechanical devices can be used to record the relevant activities. For example, a human recorder may note the number of brands tested and the amount of time spent at a cosmetics counter by customers. Mechanical devices can record the channel a television is tuned to. Observation provides an opportunity to collect data about behavior as it actually occurs. Thus it may provide more accurate data than would

MARKETING IN ACTION

Data Sources Today and Tomorrow

Marketing researchers are always looking for new sources of data to help them better understand consumers. While traditional sources such as focus groups and surveys to collect quantitative data are unlikely to become obsolete any time soon, new methods, both high- and low-tech, are in place today and will no doubt continue to grow in the future.

One relatively low-tech means of data collection is being practiced outside Chicago by marketing researchers at Foote, Cone & Belding, an advertising agency. The researchers have targeted a small Illinois town as a place to gather information on what drives small-town America. The town, dubbed Laskerville by the researchers (after Albert Lasker, the ad agency's founder), is unaware of its role as the object of intense observation. Researchers regularly visit the town, going to bars, car dealers, shops, and even funerals. The idea is that researchers will obtain insights into small-town life by anonymously observing it in action.

On the high-tech end of new approaches is SellCheck. SellCheck is a watch that does a lot more than tell time. Patented by Lee Weinblatt, the owner of PreTesting, a marketing research

firm in Tenafly, New Jersey, SellCheck is designed to record information on its wearer's media habits. The watch can record data on what television shows its wearer is watching and what radio stations he or she is listening to. It even has the capability to gather information on what magazines a subject reads.

All this is accomplished by having the gadget pick up nearly inaudible pulses that are emitted at regular intervals by televisions and radios. SellCheck would read the pulses much like UPC codes are read off packaged goods. SellCheck has the capability to distinguish between television commercials that its wearer actually watched and those that were "zapped." SellCheck could monitor magazine reading by placing tiny transmitters in the magazines' bindings. Marian Confer, Vice President of Research for the Magazine Publishers of America, states, "It, or something like it, will happen in the next five years."

For SellCheck to work, advertisers, media producers, and magazine publishers would all have to agree on a common set of signals and then agree to use those signals. So far that hasn't happened but it seems only a matter of time . . . .

---

be the case if respondents were asked to recall their behavior. On the other hand, if the observation is open, consumers may react differently than they usually would. Furthermore, data collection through observation can be a lengthy process. Perhaps most important, observation does not collect data regarding thoughts, opinions, and motivations.

Experimentation. An **experiment** is a means of data collection in which the researcher manipulates one or more independent variables and measures their effects on one or more dependent variables, while controlling for the effect of extraneous variables.[28] The objective of experimentation is to determine cause-and-effect relationships. For example, if we increase advertising expenditures by 10 percent, how will that affect profitability? The cause (a 10 percent increase in advertising expenditures) is the **independent variable**. The affected variable (profitability) is the **dependent variable**. In experimentation the researcher attempts to control all aspects of the situation so that he or she can be clear that the effect on the dependent variable is the result of the action taken on the independent variable. Procter & Gamble might, for example, test a new advertising theme for Pringles Potato Chips by choosing two similar cities and using the same marketing mix in each with the exception of advertising theme (the independent variable). The company would then monitor sales (the dependent variable) in the two cities to see how they were affected by the difference in advertising. Experimentation is appropriate for conclusive research because it directly tests cause and effect. It is the only type of research that does this. It is difficult, however, to be certain that all factors have been controlled. In the case of P & G's Pringles experiment, economic conditions and the actions of competitors cannot be controlled and might vary between the two cities.

Survey.   A **survey** is a structured questionnaire given to a group of people and designed to elicit specific information from them.[29] Unlike observation or experimentation, it involves asking people questions. Survey research is the most common method of collecting quantitative data, which is relatively easy to collect and lends itself easily to statistical analysis. Three modes of carrying out survey research are through the mail, over the telephone, and in personal interviews. These three modes are compared in Table 8.3.

Mail surveys provide no direct contact between the researcher and the respondent. This often results in a lack of motivation to respond. Average response rates for mail surveys are 10 to 20 percent.[30] Additionally, researchers have little control of a mail survey. They do not know who responded, the order the questions were answered in, or whether the respondent misunderstood some questions. Data collection through the mail also tends to be a lengthy process, often involving weeks or even months. Despite these problems, there are times when a mail survey is appropriate. Because respondents choose when they will sit down to answer a mail survey, they will usually be willing to answer a greater number of questions. Hence researchers can collect large amounts of data through the mail. Additionally, mail allows the collection of sensitive information that respondents may be reluctant to provide over the telephone or in person. A researcher interested in a person's expe-

TABLE 8.3
Three Modes of Data Collection

Criteria	In Person	By Telephone	By Mail
Cost	High	Moderately low	Low
Time	Moderately fast	Very fast	Slow
Control	High	Moderate	Low
Quantity of data that can be collected	Fairly large amount	Moderate amount	Large amount
Versatility to adapt to special needs of respondent	High (due to face-to-face contact)	Moderate	None
Effect on questions	Most biased for sensitive questions; confusing questions can be clarified	Moderately effective on sensitive questions; clarification possible	Best on sensitive questions; clarification not possible

rience as a shoplifter, for example, would probably use a mail survey. Respondents perceive greater anonymity when responding through the mail and may be more likely to give honest responses. Furthermore, data collection through the mail is generally less expensive than collecting data over the telephone or in person.

Telephone surveys are a fast and relatively inexpensive means of collecting data. The respondent is questioned and his or her responses are recorded on a paper questionnaire, or more likely today, on a computer screen. The use of computer-assisted telephone interviewing (CATI), which involves a data collector reading questions off a computer screen and typing in the respondent's answers, has grown tremendously in recent years and is now more popular than the traditional paper-and-pencil approach.[31] Many researchers, in fact, have moved beyond CATI to completely automated telephone surveys (CATS). CATS is an interactive technology that allows surveys to be conducted by a computer itself. A recorded voice asks the questions and respondents answer by pushing buttons on their telephones. Answers requiring more than the push of a button are recorded on tape.[32]

Telephone research is limited in the amount of data that can be collected and the degree of control the interviewer can exert. While telephone surveys remain a very popular method of data collection, researchers are increasingly faced with criticisms of this method. Consumers have complained that telephone interviewing is intrusive. Often the complainants do not distinguish between telephone research and telemarketing (the use of the telephone to sell goods and services). Many states have introduced legislation to restrict telephone surveying.[33] It has been suggested that by the year 2003, researchers using the telephone could be restricted in the following ways:[34]

- No calls between 5:00 and 7:00 P.M. or after 8:00 P.M.
- No calls on Sundays.
- No calls except to listed numbers. (Random digit dialing now allows researchers to reach unlisted numbers.)
- No calls to listed numbers if the person has indicated a wish not to receive such calls (by having an asterisk placed before his or her name) in the telephone book.

Personal interviewing provides the opportunity for the data collector to interact with the respondent face-to-face. Researchers have more control over the interview in such a situation. Personal interviews may take place in peoples' homes or elsewhere. Frequently mall-intercepts are used. In this situation a person is approached at a shopping mall. The interview may take place on the spot or the individual may be taken to a nearby test facility. Although personal interviews are traditionally conducted with a pencil and paper, computer-assisted personal interviewing (CAPI) is now common. With CAPI the respondent sits at a computer and responds to questions on the screen. A study comparing CAPI to traditional pencil-and-paper personal interviews, conducted by the First National Bank of Chicago, reported that consumers found CAPI more interesting and that they felt less inhibited than with the traditional approach.[35] CAPI was also found to save money when compared to the pencil-and-paper approach to personal interviewing, which is costly. Research using personal interviews can be completed relatively quickly, depending on the number of people to be interviewed. Furthermore, researchers can collect quite a large amount of data through personal interviews.

Deciding on the method of data collection that is right for the research being planned is not easy. The researcher must take into consideration the objectives of the research, any existing constraints (for example, time or budget), and the characteristics of the subject population. The "Marketing in Action: Collecting Data on Generation X Can Be a Real Challenge" illustrates how the subject population can affect the choice of data collection method(s).

MARKETING IN ACTION

Collecting Data on Generation X Can Be a Real Challenge

Marketers are interested in Generation X. Also known as baby busters, this is the population group following the well-documented baby-boom generation. There are 47 million people, aged 18 to 30 years, in Generation X. They represent an estimated $125 billion in spending power in the United States. Many companies, including Converse, Mazda, and Coca-Cola, are targeting Generation X. To increase the chances of success, marketing decision makers have turned to marketing research in an effort to understand this group. Researching the Generation X market, however, has proved to be a major challenge.

Traditional marketing research techniques, both qualitative and quantitative, have generally failed when researchers have attempted to use them on Generation Xers. Focus groups conducted at research facilities with clients behind two-way mirrors have not worked. According to Mitchell Fox, publisher of *Details*, a magazine targeted at Generation X, "We tried focus groups in a traditional conference room setting and it failed miserably. They understood we were there for something. It was like 'Big Brother.'" Telephone surveys, a common method of data collection, have also flopped with Generation X. David Morrison, President of Collegiate Marketing Company, states, "There's so much telemarketing that they [Generation X] are generally suspicious of anyone calling and addressing them as Mr. So-and-So." Nielsen Household Services (NHS), part of the A.C. Nielsen Company, recruits and maintains household panels (banks of consumers willing to respond to mail surveys). Here again, this traditional marketing research technique is not working with Generation X. Meredith Spector, Director of Data Services at NHS, admits that

Tracy in NYC. She said if she spits her gum out from up here and it hit someone below, the force would totally split them in half.

18- to 25-year-olds are not well-represented on the firm's panels. She attributes this to the fact that Generation Xers have been shown to live in their parents' homes longer than previous generations. Since NHS recruits heads of households for its panels, the technique misses a lot of Generation Xers.

These problems have not caused marketing researchers to give up on gathering information from Generation X. It has, however, caused them to be more creative in planning data collection. Focus groups are conducted among Generation Xers, but researchers often carry them out in nontraditional settings such as restaurants or private homes. One research company invites subjects to what they term, "really groovy slumber parties." Telephone surveys frequently give way to personal interviews. The personal interviews themselves often resemble friendly conversations and frequently occur in such nontraditional settings as bars, bathrooms, and lines of people waiting for concert tickets.

Researcher Irma Zandl, president of the New York-based research firm, The Zandl Group, cautions that unorthodox research methods should always be accompanied by solid (that is, more traditional) research. The use of such methods, however, does underscore the need to be creative and sensitive to the nuances of the market when planning marketing research.

Stage Five: Plan the Collection Effort

Once the data collection method has been determined, the researcher is faced with planning the specifics of the collection. Two basic tasks must be completed at this stage: data collection forms must be developed and a sample must be designed.

Develop data collection forms.   If a researcher is using the observation method, forms must be developed to record the observations of behaviors. The experimentation method will require forms to record the results of the experiments. The biggest challenge, however, is faced by the researcher using the survey method.

There are many issues in survey questionnaire design. They include how to word a question, how much information a question should attempt to obtain, whether a question should be closed-ended (check the appropriate box) or open-ended (what do you think?), and how the questions should be ordered. Some key issues to keep in mind are:

- Avoid leading questions. ("Doesn't this product work better than that one?")

- Avoid biasing questions. ("Do you agree with the American Medical Association that this drug is best?")

- Avoid double-barreled questions. ("What do you think of this product's taste and texture?")

- Use simple words that the respondent will understand. (The U.S. Census Bureau now uses "white" instead of "Caucasian.")

Design the sample.   The researcher must decide who should provide the data that will be collected. The researcher begins with a population, which is the entire group of elements, such as consumers, that the marketing manager wants to learn about. The researcher could take a census, in which case he or she would gather information from everyone in the population. Almost always, taking a census is impractical because of the time and expense involved. Therefore, the researcher usually selects a sample, which is a smaller group that is representative of the population. There are two basic types of samples, probability samples and nonprobability samples.

To obtain a probability sample, the researcher selects elements of the population according to explicit rules to guarantee that each element of the population will have the same known chance of being selected. For instance, a probability sample of 10 could be selected from a class of 100 students by putting each student's name on a slip of paper in a bowl and then drawing 10 slips at random. Each student would have a 1 in 10 chance of being selected for the sample. The main advantage of probability samples is that the information obtained from them can be analyzed statistically and the results can be generalized to the entire population. Thus, they are most often used in conclusive research studies. The main disadvantages to using a probability sample in a study are the time and expense involved.

A nonprobability sample is selected using any criteria the researcher wishes to use. For this reason, these samples are sometimes referred to as convenience samples or judgment samples. Selecting people who volunteer to fill out a questionnaire, or the first people to come by a table set up by a researcher in a suburban mall, would yield nonprobability samples. Studies that use nonprobability samples are far less expensive and far easier to conduct than are studies using probability samples. The trade-off is that the information gained cannot be generalized to a larger population. In other words, all the researcher discovers is information about the specific people selected for the sample. For this reason, nonprobability samples are most appropriate for exploratory research.

Stage Six: Collect the Data

Once all the plans have been made, it is time to actually collect the data. Data collection involves field work, contact with respondents. Because one researcher cannot possibly expect to contact each respondent, field work requires help. It has been suggested that, "the key to field work is investing in the selection, training, supervision, and evaluation of field workers."[36] A complete discussion of the processes of selection, training, supervision, and evaluation is not possible here. It is important, however, to note that if attention is not paid to ensuring that field work is carried out carefully, the planning that went into the marketing research process to this point has been wasted. Furthermore, if conclusions are drawn based on data that is not reliable due to poor field work, the marketing decision maker may be in a worse position than if no research had been done at all.

Nonresponse error is one type of error that can occur during data collection that is a potential source of bias. **Nonresponse error** is a systematic difference between those who do and do not respond to a survey.[37] Studies indicate that people with more education, higher-level occupations, women, and students are less likely to respond to surveys.[38] Researchers and field workers must guard against nonresponse error during data collection by attempting to interest all appropriate respondents in taking part.

A second source of potential bias during data collection is interviewing error. **Interviewing error** is error that results from conscious or unconscious bias in the interviewer's interaction with the respondent.[39] Interview error may be as innocent as the expression on the interviewer's face when asking a question or as serious as falsifying a response. In any case, careful selection and training of field workers can help overcome this potential source of bias.

Stage Seven: Process and Analyze the Data

Once the data is collected in the field, it must be prepared for presentation to marketing management. This involves two tasks: processing the data and analyzing the data.

Processing the data.   Data is often collected and put into a computer at the same time. When computer-assisted telephone interviewing (CATI), completely automated telephone surveys (CATS), and computer-assisted personal interviewing (CAPI) are used, no additional processing need take place before data analysis. If data was collected using paper questionnaires, it must be processed before it can be analyzed. Processing involves editing, coding, and data entry.

Editing is the process of checking for interviewer mistakes. Questionnaires should be reviewed to be sure that responses to closed-ended questions have been recorded correctly and that open-ended questions have legible and understandable responses. This process ensures completeness, accuracy, and clarity. Once edited, questionnaires are ready to be coded. **Coding** is the process of grouping and assigning numeric codes to the various responses to a particular question.[40] For example, for the variable gender, females might be given the number 1 and males, 2. The codes are the actual numbers that will be placed in the computer to represent responses. Figure 8.7 illustrates a portion of a coded questionnaire. **Data entry** is the process of converting information from a form that cannot be read by a computer to a form than can be read by a computer.[41] Data entry is accomplished by typing coded responses into a computer file. The file stores the data until the researcher is ready to analyze it.

FIGURE 8.7
Portion of a Coded Questionnaire

Please answer the following questions about yourself:

Circle one: Male   Code: 1 = Male
                  (Female)   2 = Female

Circle the highest level of education you have completed.

                          Code:
Graduate degree   **1**   Some college   **4**
Some graduate work   **2**   High school diploma   **5**
(Bachelor's degree)   **3**   Some high school   **6**

**Indicate the number of miles you drive one way from
where you live to your place of employment.**

                          Code:
Less than 1   **1**   (6 – 10)   **4**
1 – 3   **2**   More than 10   **5**
4 – 5   **3**

Fill in your age: 33 years   **Code:**
                                                **enter exact
                                                figure.**

Analyzing the data.   Data analysis involves applying statistical techniques to summarize the collected data. Its purpose is to transform the data into meaningful information that will help the marketing manager solve the problem defined at the beginning of the marketing research process. Some of the statistical techniques used to analyze data are relatively easy to apply. One-way tabulations or frequencies, for instance, answer questions such as the following:

- How many women were in the sample?
- What brand of toothpaste sold the most?
- How many respondents preferred Pepsi over Coke?

Two-way tabulations (cross-tabs) answer questions about relationships between two variables:

- What is the association between gender and brand choice? ("Do more men or more women prefer Pepsi over Coke?")
- Is higher income associated with greater use of credit cards?

More advanced statistical techniques may also be used with the data. These techniques are beyond the scope of this text.

Stage Eight: Present the Results

When the marketing researcher has completed the data analysis, he or she must prepare a report for the marketing manager. A two- or three-page summary that gives the most important findings of the research and their implications is usually all the marketing manager needs. The objective is to be as clear as possible. The technical details should be left to the appendices of the report.

The Marketing Research Process in Practice

In practice, the marketing research process may be repeated several times in finding the solution to a single marketing problem. For instance, a problem may be brought to the marketing manager's attention through performance-monitoring research. The problem may then be more clearly defined and alternatives may be discovered through exploratory research. The alternatives may then be evaluated through conclusive research. In each case, the entire marketing research process will be used.

American Airlines is an example of an organization that actively engages in all three types of marketing research. The airline regularly conducts customer satisfaction measurement, a type of performance-monitoring research, by having passengers fill out in-flight surveys. Additionally, the company conducts telephone surveys with specific groups of customers such as members of its frequent flyer program, in order to monitor customer satisfaction. Based on the feedback obtained through its performance-monitoring research, American carries out exploratory research to learn more about the concerns of passengers and non-passengers and to generate ideas for improving service. Exploratory research is conducted using focus groups and in-depth interviews. Finally, conclusive research is used to test ideas for new products and services.

8-3 Much marketing research that is technically well done fails to have a significant impact on the marketing decision being made. Why might this happen? How might this be prevented?

8-4 One of your friends has decided to run for president of the student government at your school. Design a marketing research study that will help define the main issues on students' minds and that will predict the outcome of the election.

YOUR
MARKETING
KNOWLEDGE

FORECASTING DEMAND

One of the key areas in organizations in which marketing information is needed is forecasting demand. Demand forecasting is critical to an understanding of the marketplace. A manager cannot hope to accurately evaluate marketing opportunities without a forecast of the potential that each opportunity affords. Forecasting can be a very complex topic because sophisticated statistical methods are normally used to develop forecasts. Here we take a general overview of forecasting and leave discussion of the technical complexities to courses in marketing research or statistical analysis.

Types of Forecasts

Three forecasts that are commonly developed are forecasts of market potential, sales potential, and sales levels.

Market potential. The **market potential** forecast for a product is an estimate of the maximum total sales possible for all sellers of the product to an identified customer group within a specified time frame. It may be given in terms of number of units, expressed as a dollar figure, or described in terms of number of users. For example, the 1995 market potential for cellular phones in the United States is estimated to be $21.5 billion. By 2000 the market potential is forecast to be $25 billion or more than 40 million subscribers.[42] A market potential forecast assumes a given marketing environment and a given level of marketing effort from all sellers.

Thus when the environment or the marketing efforts of competitors change, the market potential will also change. If U.S. West Cellular increases its advertising efforts, the market potential for the entire industry will change.

Sales potential. The **sales potential** forecast for a product is an estimate of the maximum sales to an identified customer group for one company during a set time period given a specified environment. If U.S. West possesses a 15 percent market share in the cellular phone industry, its sales potential in 1995 could be expected to be $3.23 billion (15 percent of $21.5 billion). Like market potential forecasts, sales potential forecasts change when the marketing environment changes. If government regulations make it more expensive to operate a cellular phone, not only is the industry market potential likely to decrease, but U.S. West's sales potential will also probably decrease.

Sales level. The **sales level** forecast is an estimate of the total expected sales of a company's product to an identified market in a particular time frame given an assumed marketing environment and a given level of company marketing effort. Although a sales level forecast assumes a given marketing effort, such forecasts can be used in marketing planning. Hence U.S. West might have three sales level forecasts for 1995, each based on a different level of advertising expenditure. The firm would then decide which level of advertising to do based on a comparison of these forecasts.

Approaches to Forecasting

Two general approaches may be used in developing forecasts of sales levels: the top-down forecasting method and the buildup forecasting method.

In **top-down forecasting,** an aggregate measure of expected sales is broken down to give the sales level forecast. For this reason, it is sometimes called breakdown forecasting. The forecaster begins by developing an aggregate measure, such as the market potential for a product. Usually, this measure is based on an empirically derived relationship between the product and some other measure. For example, the market potential for automobiles in the United States is closely related to the level and growth rate of the gross domestic product (GDP). Thus the forecaster would begin by estimating the level and growth rate of GDP for, say, the coming year. The forecaster would then use these estimates to estimate the total sales of automobiles in the United States. Next, the forecaster would break down the total sales into categories of interest to the company. These categories may be product lines or customer groups or geographic areas. The breakdown of the aggregate estimate of demand is usually based on some index that measures potential sales in the categories relative to each other. For example, an estimate of the total market potential for automobiles might be broken down into sales by geographic areas based on the size of the population within each geographic area. Once the market potential has been broken down by category, the company's market share of each category can be estimated and the sales forecast can be developed.

Buildup forecasting starts with estimates of sales at the lowest level of the categories the company has identified. Again, these categories can be product lines, customer groups, or geographic areas. These estimates are then added up to obtain the company's sales forecast. IBM might, for example, ask each of its sales representatives worldwide to estimate their sales for 1996. The sales reps could be expected to do this on the basis of their past experiences, their knowledge of their market and customers, and their plans for the year. The estimates of all the sales reps would be combined to form a forecast for the entire company. Buildup forecasting is frequently a corporate morale booster because it involves employees at all levels of the organization in the forecasting process.

Forecasting Methods

The forecasting of market potential, sales potential, and sales level that can be accomplished by looking at what has happened in the past and assuming something similar will happen in the future, by asking people what they think will happen in the future, or by testing to see what people do in a certain situation that might occur in the future.

Forecasting methods that focus on looking at what has happened in the past and assuming something similar will happen in the future range from very simple to fairly complex. Included in this category are trend analysis, general buying power indexes, and custom-made indexes.

Trend analysis. One of the simplest and least expensive forecasting techniques is **trend analysis.** This technique is based on the assumption that whatever unspecified factors caused sales in the past will continue to affect sales in the same way in the future. Hence, if sales increased 5 percent annually for each of the last three years, the forecast is that sales will increase 5 percent in the coming year. Trend analysis is also used by organizations to forecast things in addition to sales. Many companies, for example, use trend analysis to forecast workplace injuries. The frequency and severity rates of injuries in the past are used to predict future rates.[43] Trend analysis is unreliable except in very stable markets where environmental change is rare.

General buying power indexes. **General buying power indexes** attempt to identify factors that have affected past sales and use those factors to predict future sales. Such an index may use only one factor (a single-factor index) or it may use a combination of factors (a multifactor index). For example, a single-factor index might use income data to determine the market potential for a product in a state. Let us assume that the market potential for satellite dishes, among U.S. consumers with annual incomes over $50,000, is $100 million. We further assume that 20 percent of U.S. consumers with incomes over $50,000 live in California. Using 0.2 as our index, we can estimate the market potential for the product in California to be $20 million ($100 million times 0.2).

A source of data frequently used to construct buying power indexes is the "Survey of Buying Power," published annually by *Sales & Marketing Management*, a widely circulated trade journal. The Survey of Buying Power presents data on population, income, and retail sales broken down geographically by state, county, and city. These three pieces of data are used to construct a multifactor index called the *Buying Power Index (BPI)*.[44] The Buying Power Index is constructed by weighting population 0.2, effective buying income 0.5, and total retail sales 0.3. Using the BPI, the market potential for satellite dishes among consumers in California with annual incomes over $50,000, would be constructed as follows:

$$\text{BPI} = (0.2 \times \text{percent of population in category})$$
$$+ (0.5 \times \text{percent of effective buying income in category})$$
$$+ (0.3 \times \text{percent of retail sales in category}).$$

Forecasters can also construct their own multifactor index using buying power data by altering the weights of the factors to better reflect conditions in their industry. Multifactor indexes typically provide more accurate forecasts than single-factor indexes because they rely on a wider range of factors.

Custom-made indexes. The general buying power indexes may not provide accurate measures of the market potential for a particular product. In this circumstance, a marketer may want to construct a **custom-made index** unique to his or her product.

A **corollary product index** uses the known sales for one product to forecast the sales potential of another product. The two products must, of course, be related.

For example, the number of residential building permits issued in a given area is a good indicator of the potential market for electrical fixtures in that area. The exact relationship between the two products expressed as an index can be derived empirically from past data.

Custom multiple-factor indexes can also be developed. The researcher begins by identifying the most important factors that affect demand for the product and obtaining accurate data on these factors. The index is then derived by assigning each factor a weight that reflects its relative importance in determining demand and then combining the results. The validity of the index as a predictor of market potential must then be tested. Once validated, the index can be applied in the same fashion as any other index. A daycare provider, for example, might do research and then construct an index that weighted number of births 0.3, number of dual-income families in the area 0.4, and family income 0.3.

In order to use what people say as a basis of forecasting, a decision must be made about whom to ask. Methods that focus on asking people what they think will happen in the future include surveys of buyers' intentions, sales-force composites, surveys of executive opinion, and surveys of expert opinion.

Surveys of buyers' intentions.   Both market potential and sales levels can be forecast by **surveys of buyers' intentions** that survey prospective buyers about their purchasing intentions. They might, for instance, be asked to rate on a scale of 1 to 10 the likelihood of their buying a particular product or category of product in the next week or month or year. The results usually overstate actual purchases. However, if the researchers compare buying intentions to actual sales over time, they can derive a discount factor that can be applied to intended purchases to yield good forecasts. This buildup method works best for large durable products for which there are relatively few buyers.

Sales-force composites.   One buildup method of forecasting both sales levels and market potential is to obtain from all sales representatives **sales-force composites,** an estimate of sales in their territories for a specified future period. There may be a tendency for these estimates to overstate or understate actual sales. This can be corrected by applying an empirically derived adjustment factor to the total estimate. If the sales force is competent and if it is rewarded for making accurate estimates, then the sales-force composite can provide useful forecasts. The method is most effective when a company has a small number of large customers.

Surveys of executive opinion.   **Surveys of executive opinion** involve asking executives within the organization to predict sales in the coming period. Usually a number of executives representing a variety of functional areas such as marketing, production, and finance would be included. The quality of this method depends on the experience and expertise of the executives asked.

Surveys of expert opinion.   In **surveys of expert opinion,** independent experts are asked to predict. A common version of the method is the **Delphi Technique.** With the Delphi Technique, a group of experts are each asked their opinions separately. The anonymous opinions are then circulated to the group. Each expert is allowed to change his or her opinion after viewing the opinions of others. The technique continues until all experts have had an opportunity to see and respond to the opinions of each other. This method can be very effective.

Test markets.   **Test marketing** involves actually marketing a product in a few select cities and then using the sales levels in these cities to predict national sales. Hence this forecasting method is the only one we discuss that bases the forecast on current behavior rather than past or predicted behavior. This buildup forecasting method is most frequently used when a company is introducing a new product. KFC (Kentucky Fried Chicken) test marketed its Rotisserie Chicken in several cities, including Las Vegas, before introducing it nationally in 1993.[45] Pepsi tested a drink called Pepsi Max in the United Kingdom in 1992. It ultimately decided not to introduce the product.[46]

The main advantage of test markets is that they measure the actual purchasing behavior of consumers in the marketplace. The main disadvantages are time and expense. A test market may take a year or more to complete and may cost more than $1 million. Furthermore, test markets can be easily monitored by competitors, thus providing information about new products and giving the competitor a chance to reduce its competitive response time or even to beat the company to market with a similar item. Monitoring a competitor's test market recently allowed a cookie producer to reduce its response time to the competitor's new product from eight months to three months.[47] Sometimes, competitors may undertake unusual pricing or promotional activities in test-market cities, which can make the results of the test market unreliable. If, for example, Colgate-Palmolive became aware that a new flavor of Crest was being test marketed by Procter & Gamble, it might run a special sale, increase advertising, or offer coupons for Colgate in the test market city.

Test markets may be used to evaluate marketing strategies. A company, for example, might set up test markets in two similar cities. In the first city the test market might introduce a product at $2.99. In the second city, the same product might be introduced at $1.99. The results of the test markets could help the firm decide what price to charge for the product when it is introduced to the larger market.

Because of the disadvantages of test markets, many marketers now use simulated test markets. These are controlled laboratory experiments in which test consumers shop in a simulated store. The data from the experiments are used to forecast sales in the real market. Additional discussion of test markets can be found in Chapter 10.

PERSONAL COMPUTER EXERCISE

The use of marketing survey data can help determine the relative position that competing products hold in the minds of consumers. The PC Exercise gives you the opportunity to analyze some data from a consumers' survey of product perceptions of competing brands. Your analysis of this data should identify the perception problems and opportunities facing each brand.

KEY POINTS

■ Marketing managers draw information to use in decision making from multiple sources. These sources include information systems, contacts with other managers, and personal experience.

■ Decision Support Systems (DSS) and Marketing Information Systems (MIS) are two types of information systems that provide continuous information from many sources. A DSS is really just a more sophisticated MIS that allows the user to interact directly with the system.

■ Marketing research is one source of input to an information system. It is designed to provide information regarding a specific problem.

■ Because of its importance in the quality of management decisions, marketing research is widely used in organizations throughout the world.

■ Before requesting that marketing research be undertaken, a manager should always evaluate whether the expected benefits of the research outweigh its expected costs.

■ Marketing research can provide performance-monitoring information, produce insights by exploring new areas or ideas, and provide conclusive answers to well-defined alternative solutions.

■ Marketing research should follow the marketing research process. The stages in the marketing research process are: (1) establish the need for research information, (2) specify research objectives and information needs, (3) determine the sources of data, (4) determine the data collection method, (5) plan the collection effort, (6) collect the data, (7) process and analyze the data, and (8) present the research results.

■ Researchers should always search for and consider all possible sources of secondary data before deciding to gather primary data.

■ Observation, experimentation, and survey are the three means by which primary data can be collected.

■ One key managerial responsibility that requires research is forecasting demand. Top-down and buildup are the two general approaches to forecast market potential, sales potential, and sales level.

■ Forecasting techniques are based on what people have done in the past or what people predict will happen in the future.

■ Major forecasting techniques include trend analysis, general and custom-made indexes, surveys of buyers' intentions, executive opinions or expert opinions, sales-force composites, and test marketing.

KEY TERMS

decision support system (DSS) (241)
hardware (241)
communication network (241)
data base (241)
model base (242)
software base (242)
marketing information system (MIS) (242)
marketing research (244)
performance-monitoring research (250)
customer satisfaction measurement (CSM) (250)
exploratory research (250)
conclusive research (251)
primary data (253)

secondary data (253)
qualitative data (254)
focus group (254)
quantitative data (255)
observation (255)
experiment (256)
independent variable (256)
dependent variable (256)
survey (257)
nonresponse error (261)
interviewing error (261)
editing (261)
coding (261)
data entry (261)
market potential (263)

ISSUES FOR DISCUSSION

1. The level of technology that a well-developed DSS offers, in many cases, exceeds the management's capability to use the system. How would you see that such a system was effectively implemented in a business that you managed?

2. "A well-designed MIS or DSS requires an excellent marketing research department to work well. One should build the latter before undertaking the former." Evaluate this statement.

3. Only 9 percent of marketing research expenditures worldwide are made in Japan; the figure for the United States is 39 percent. Despite this difference, Japan has been enormously successful, far outselling U.S. competitors in many industries. How could this be explained?

4. Some managers use the results from focus groups to select among alternative courses of action. Why is this risky? Why would they do this?

5. Your instructor is interested in knowing how many students will take a senior-level course in marketing. What sources of data might be used to answer this question?

6. A clothing retailer is interested in whether the amount of time consumers spend in fitting rooms is related to the dollar amount they purchase. Which data collection method would be appropriate? Why?

7. A U.S. manufacturer of washing machines wonders if there is sufficient market potential in Eastern Europe to consider exporting. It has been decided to investigate this question through a survey. Which means (mail, telephone, or personal interview) of survey data collection would you recommend? Why?

8. You have been asked to design a study on student perceptions of the student lounge at your school. Outline all the dimensions of a study design. How would you ensure that the study would be used effectively by the managers of the lounge?

9. Forecasting has been described as "trying to drive a car by looking out the back window." Comment.

10. The Department of Motor Vehicles in your state is interested in developing a custom-made index to forecast annual demand for license plates. How should it proceed?

CASE APPLICATION

Researching Ways to Save Souls

George Barna's services are in hot demand these days. Mr. Barna is president of the Barna Research Group, a marketing research firm that provides services to churches and religious groups. The Hayward, California, firm conducts market studies to help churches understand their current members, attract new members, and evaluate existing and potential promotional vehicles.

Many traditionalists oppose the use of marketing techniques, including research, in churches. Parish consultant Lyle E. Schaller estimates that the majority of churches do not use marketing techniques and would rather see their congregations shrink rather than market themselves. As churches find marketing research and other marketing tools to be successful, however, the number of those opposed is likely to shrink.

Mecklenburg Community Church (MCC) in Charlotte, North Carolina, has been described as "the church that marketing research built." Before it ever opened for "business," the church hired a market research firm to find out what customers want. The newly founded church decided to target the "unchurched," those community members who had no current connection to a religious institution. The research firm hired by MCC used focus groups and personal interviews to learn what it would take to bring the unchurched into a church. Research results indicated that church was perceived as boring and that services were not relevant to people's everyday lives. It also revealed that the unchurched felt churches were always asking for money. MCC used the results of the research to design services and programs that appealed to the unchurched. After only 16 months of operation, Mecklenberg has 400 members. Eighty percent of the 400 come from the unchurched category.

The Willow Creek Community Church, located in suburban Chicago, is another tribute to marketing research. The church was founded in 1975. Before the church opened, researchers conducted door-to-door interviews to determine what people didn't like about traditional churches. Respondents told the interviewers that churches asked for money too frequently, that the music was dull, that services and sermons were boring, and that pastors made attendees feel guilty and ignorant. Willow Creek planned services that include dance, videos, soft rock music, and dramatic skits. While critics have dubbed services at Willow Creek "Church Lite" and "McChurch," attendance at weekly Sunday services averages 15,000.

Many, but not all, of the research techniques employed by churches are relatively unsophisticated by today's standards. The Mennonite Church, which has a separate marketing arm called Mennonite Media Ministries, researches advertising effectiveness by testing proposed broadcast and print ads before groups of targeted consumers. Its research is not infallible. Research suggested that an ad the church produced to emphasize its commitment to social services would be very successful. The advertisement carried a headline that read "Muscular Christianity" and featured a shirtless, muscular young man sawing a 2-by-4-inch board. The ad emphasized that church members often get their workouts helping others rather in gyms. Many church members disliked the ad, feeling that it used sex to sell their religious beliefs.

The use of marketing research by churches is likely to continue to grow in terms of both frequency and sophistication. If a church defines part of its mission as meeting the needs of its members, it stands to reason that marketing research can play a valuable role.

Questions

1. Some experts argue that churches can never be market driven because they are based on non-negotiable tenets. What role can marketing research play in such an environment?
2. Could a church benefit from a decision support system? What would such a system look like for a church? What components would it have?
3. Would there be anything wrong with a church conducting marketing research by surveying its members? Why?
4. Suggest a marketing research plan for a church to increase its penetration of the unchurched in the local community.

Researching the Hidden Market

Marketing research is as crucial to your career search as it is to consumer marketing. The first two steps in the decision-making process are recognizing the existence of the problem and understanding the problem. In examining these steps as they apply to your search for a position, you would probably conclude that today's job market is tight and highly competitive. Effective research can help you identify the best job opportunities and provide an edge over the competition. Three major sources of employment opportunities are on-campus recruiting, job postings (both on campus and in advertisements), and the "hidden market." Extensive market research will be required to tap into the hidden market so you can identify organizations where opportunities exist, even though they are not advertised.

The marketing research process of your job search will require you to review published information, contact individuals who can provide assistance, and rely on your personal experience. This chapter stresses the need for a well-defined plan for information collection. One way to begin is to speak with others who have recently gone through the career search process and to counselors who can assist you along the way. The product of your research should be a list of target organizations most likely to meet your career objectives and information on ways to gain access to those firms. You need to move beyond a simple list of organizations and obtain the following information:

1. *Product*: What skills are your targets seeking?
2. *Price*: What are the likely compensation packages?
3. *Place*: What are the optimal locations?
4. *Promotion*: What are the best ways to contact your targets?

The information you obtain becomes your foundation for selecting and implementing a course of action for your career and job search.

Questions

1. What conclusions can you draw about the competitive environment of your target job market (or markets)? What is your evidence for such conclusions?
2. What published information will you use for market research? Why have you selected these sources?
3. How will you use personal contacts in conducting market research? Why have you chosen these individuals?

Jobs in Marketing Research

Marketing researchers provide a great deal of the information that businesses need to make sound decisions about marketing their products. This involves analyzing data on products and sales, making surveys, constructing interviews, preparing forecasts, and making recommendations on product design, advertising, pricing, and distribution.

Skill requirements.   What do you need to undertake a career in marketing research? Skills in quantitative and behavioral sciences are important. You must be comfortable with numbers, and you must have an understanding of people's attitudes, tastes, and behaviors. Good communication skills are essential in gathering information and in presenting recommendations to management. Good interpersonal skills are also important, because the analyst often deals with managers in the firm and with outside research specialists.

Entering the field.   Entry-level opportunities in marketing research are fewer than in most other marketing areas. As the demand for new products and services grows, however, the need for information and identification of potential buyers increases.

Types of positions.   Most marketing research positions are available with "in-house" research staffs of manufacturing and marketing firms, marketing research consulting firms, or advertising agencies. Government agencies and university research centers are two other possible employers.

You are more likely to be involved with the actual mechanics of research if you join a research consulting firm, but no matter whom you work for, marketing research involves problem solving. Trainees generally start as research assistants or junior analysts. At first, this may involve performing clerical tasks such as copying data from published sources, editing and coding questionnaires, and tabulating survey returns. Trainees may learn to conduct interviews and write reports on survey findings. With experience, they may assume responsibility for specific marketing research projects or advance to managerial positions. A capable person may become marketing research director.

The Story of Harley-Davidson: The Marketplace

Historical Perspective

Harley-Davidson marketers repeatedly have to decide who they want to buy its products. This decision, for any company, is a formidable task. Throughout its history, Harley-Davidson has done a superior job of segmenting and targeting customers. In the early days, however, little sophisticated customer or market research (as we know it today) was conducted.

In the early 1900s, the motorcycle was essentially a bicycle with a weak internal combustion engine strapped onto it; a belt powered the rear wheel. Most of the 4,000 cycles registered in the United States in 1900 were used for transportation, rather than recreation.[1] Harley-Davidson knew how important durability was to motorcyclists. Riders relied heavily on a bike's ability to withstand the poor roads and paths of the day. Harley-Davidson enhanced the structure and safety of the bikes and then mass-produced them. It anticipated customers' needs and then developed durability to such a degree that the first bikes it produced were able to cover more than 100,000 miles.

The marketplace in the early days saw the United States evolving quickly following the Industrial Revolution. For its part, Harley-Davidson was busy responding to World War I with specially made motorcycles and surviving the Depression (mostly by establishing contracts with police departments and supporting the U.S. response to World War II). Meanwhile, other factors helped to heighten the motorcycle's popularity. Existing roads across the United States were being improved and new ones were being built. In addition, the U.S. population began to possess discretionary income. Because purchasing an automobile was beyond most peoples' means, many bought a motorcycle instead.

Primary Segments and Targets

Segmenting the market and targeting customers more effectively became critical to Harley-Davidson, especially after its 1981 buyout from American Machine and Foundry Company (AMF). Rather than promote its motorcycles to a huge and less responsive mass market, Harley-Davidson decided to build on past successes and sell to more people with similar characteristics. It chose not to seek sales aggressively from women, older people (over 55 years), or young (under 25 years) first-time riders. Instead, it opted to enhance the mystique of the traditional rider, the motorcycle, and all the trappings (camaraderie, adventure, and spirit) of the Harley-Davidson experience.

In 1981, the heavyweight motorcycle market was Harley-Davidson's target. The company identified the following "mininiches":
- customized bikes with specially designed accessories, bold paint schemes, and so on
- touring bikes for long-distance rides, with amenities such as stereo and saddlebags
- sport/touring bikes with many features of touring bikes but lighter and more agile
- sport/street bikes made for local cruising, with an emphasis on style and comfort.

As a result of good market analysis and customer research, Harley-Davidson was able to design and sell the right product to the right group. From 1983 to 1992 it increased its share in the heavyweight market from less than 15 percent to more than 60 percent.[2]

The average Harley-Davidson buyer is male, 41.6 years old, and shares an average household income of about $45,000 per year. Aging baby boomers are the heavyweight motorcycle's future lifeblood. Sales figures show this group increasing at least until the year 2000. Interestingly, Harley-Davidson does not target women differently than it does men. Rather, it finds that rider characteristics are not gender-specific, and that women ride their motorcycles for basically the same reasons that men do. However, the company provides an extension line of women's apparel and also sponsors the Ladies of Harley organization of motorcycle enthusiasts.

You will see Harley-Davidson bikes in municipalities and the military for police work, training, and other transportation needs. Although competition for such clients has been tough, many customers who switched away for price considerations return at the next "buy" for reliability, durability, response, quality, and value. Thousands of Harley-Davidson motorcycles are also sold annually to farmers, doctors, stockbrokers, teachers, retailers, secretaries, computer jocks, and almost every other occupational group. In addition, many well-known entertainers own Harley-Davidson bikes, including:

Muhammad Ali	Wynonna Judd
Ann-Margaret	Jay Leno
Dan Aykroyd	Tom Petty
Cher	Arnold Schwarzenegger
Billy Ray Cyrus	Bruce Springsteen
The Doobie Brothers	Sylvester Stallone
Goldie Hawn	Travis Tritt
Billy Joel	

Harley-Davidson sells about 70 percent of its bikes in the United States and roughly 30 percent abroad. The company has a strong international reputation. Riders abroad are usually professionals who can afford to pay up to $25,000 for a motorcycle and who thrill to the classic American image. In fact, export sales in 1993 equaled $283 million (24 percent of sales, up from 14 percent in 1989).

Harley-Davidson's marketers focus not only on demographics, but also on the psychographics of riders. The Harley-Davidson motorcycling life-style is reflected by those who have an "attitude" that stresses freedom, individualism, and a carefree approach to living. However, Harley-Davidson bikes are not intended for the reckless. Such riders are not part of the target audience, and Harley-Davidson consciously promotes safe riding. High safety standards typify owners of Harley-Davidsons and their performance on the bikes. One might say that Harley-Davidson wants its customers for life—a long one!

Secondary Segments and Targets

Besides Harley-Davidson owners, several other groups participate in the cachet of Harley-Davidson. These groups include relatives and friends of owners, or those who just go along to catch the spirit at numerous motorcycle events around the world. There are those who will never buy a Harley-Davidson, but wish they could. Instead, they will buy T-shirts, belts, vests, and jackets emblazoned with Harley-Davidson insignia and graphics portraying the spirit and camaraderie of the Harley-Davidson family. Many of these secondary enthusiasts will eventually buy a bike.

Marketing Research

Formal research conducted by Harley-Davidson consists of many ongoing focus groups and surveys of customer satisfaction. At Harley-Davidson, the key to any response to research and thousands of letters, surveys, and focus groups is that any change must help to get, serve, and keep customers. If recommended changes point to new product features that are not absolutely essential, Harley-Davidson probably will not make the change on all the bikes. Instead, the company might offer the change as a customer add-on through its profitable Parts and Accessories division. Thus, Harley-Davidson encourages riders to personalize their bikes and riding experiences.

Informal research, though highly structured, is gathered at Harley-Davidson events and Harley Owners Group (H.O.G.) gatherings. From April through October of each year, most of Harley-Davidson's management fan out across the country to participate in rallies, rides, parades, festivals, and "Town Hall Meetings." Here they offer demonstration rides and talk with customers to find out what they like and don't like, and what should be changed and how. The company listens very carefully to customers' comments. Likewise, owners take their relationship with the company seriously and provide valuable input. Other companies, including Ford Motor Company, seek to emulate this special customer-to-company relationship.

Questions

1. What role has market analysis played in Harley-Davidson's success?
2. If you had been the competition, what would you have done to minimize Harley-Davidson's success and maximize your own?
3. What other market segments might Harley-Davidson have approached in the past?
4. List and compare the segment characteristics of Harley-Davidson's customers and those of competitors' customers.
5. Based upon what you know so far about Harley-Davidson, what marketing recommendations would you make to ensure it succeeds in the future?

part III

PRODUCT

CHapTeR 9

Basic Product Concepts

LEARNING OBJECTIVES

Upon completing this chapter, you will be able to do the following:

■ **Understand** the definition of a product.

■ **Identify** how to classify products.

■ **Describe** the stages of the product life cycle.

■ **Recognize** the concepts of product line and product mix.

■ **Discuss** the alternative types of branding strategies.

■ **Define** the functions of packaging.

Marketing Profile

Skating to Success

In-line skates appear to have left traditional roller skates in the dust. Introduced in 1980 by Rollerblade, Incorporated, in-line skates sport wheels lined up in a row rather than two in front and two in back. The product class represents the fastest growing segment of the sporting goods industry according to American Sports Data, Incorporated. In 1992, 9.4 million skaters participated in the sport—a 51 percent increase over 1991.

Sales of in-line skates are almost as impressive as the number of participants who enjoy the sport. In the 12 months ending in September 1992, it is estimated that total industry sales amounted to $319 million—that's about 3.7 million pairs of skates. Rollerblade controls approximately 50 percent of this large and growing market. Competition, however, is significant. At last count there were 33 direct competitors, in addition to Rollerblade, also producing in-line skates.

Rollerblade faced a far different competitive situation when it introduced the first in-line skates in 1980. In effect, there was no direct competition. In the early 1980s, sales for Rollerblade grew very slowly and were made primarily to ice hockey players and skiers who used the skates for training. In 1986 Rollerblade decided it needed to raise general consumer awareness and build primary demand if sales were to take off. Mary Horwath, the firm's former Director of Promotion, describes the strategies that were implemented to grab attention and create a sport around the skate. The goal, as Horwath describes it, was to get the skate noticed.

To accomplish the goal, Rollerblade began by plotting ways to get people talking about in-line skates. Skates were given away to anyone deemed high-profile and consistent with the product's desired image of youthful sportiness. Cyclists, skiers, football players, and even pizza-delivery services fit the bill. Rollerblade also gave skates to rental shops located along trendy Venice Beach in California. Horwath estimates that the resulting publicity was worth the equivalent of $250,000 in advertising.

The firm also worked to establish promotional tie-ins with other companies whose target markets were consistent with Rollerblade's desired customers. Deals were cut with the likes of General Mills (for Golden Grahams cereal), Swatch watches, and Pepsi.

The company went on to demonstrate the product any place it felt the target market might congregate. The firm created Team Rollerblade, a group of the world's best professional in-line skate athletes. The team puts on demonstrations around the world. Specially equipped vans also took to the streets offering "free trials"—a welcome feature when consumers are being asked to part with as much as $300 for a product they understood little about.

The results of Rollerblade's efforts were astounding. From 1987 to 1991 the firm experienced a compounded annual growth rate of 135 percent. From an annual sales level of $3 million in 1987 the firm's sales had grown to more than $100 million by 1990 and more than $150 million by 1993. Not surprisingly, Rollerblade had trouble keeping up with demand through these years of growth. This opened the door for the competition. Despite the influx into the market, Rollerblade continues to prosper. Industry sales are growing at a rate that seems to accommodate all comers.

John Hetterick, President and CEO of Rollerblade, believes that the market is far from saturated. A recent study of U.S. households found that only 7 percent participated in the sport of in-line skating (versus 48 percent for bicycling). Hetterick, however, recognizes that "the business will not support 33 competitors in the long run." In fact, Hetterick was hired by Rollerblade in 1992 to lead the company through what he refers to as the "maturation process" of the industry.

Rollerblade has started to plan for the inevitable slowing of industry growth by targeting markets that the company has not previously focused on: in-line hockey players, children, and the international arena. The first two markets are being targeted through product development and promotion. The Powerblade Skate has been designed to meet the specific needs of hockey players while the Microblade Skate targets children 4 to 10 years old with an Extended Fit System™ that allows the skate to grow with the children's feet. Internationally, the firm is targeting Europe and Japan. In 1991 Nordica, the Italian ski boot manufacturer, bought a 50 percent interest in Rollerblade. This investment has enabled Rollerblade to tap into Nordica's extensive worldwide distribution network as well as its research and development capabilities. Things may slow down for this industry, but Rollerblade appears in-line for continued success.

Richard Teerlink, President and CEO of Harley-Davidson Motorcycles, has stated, "The first requirement of effective marketing is a solid product."[1] Teerlink believes that even if the rest of a firm's marketing efforts are world class, a company will die if product quality is poor. He should know; it almost happened to Harley-Davidson in the late 1970s. Your part-ending case talks about Harley-Davidson in detail, including its incredible comeback story. Today being market-driven at Harley means understanding what customers want and putting people first, starting with a quality product.

Marketers face a variety of challenges in the area of product decision making. Identifying products that meet the needs and wants of a target market and then managing those products appropriately in the face of competition are two of the biggest challenges a marketer encounters. As we saw in the Marketing Profile, developing and offering a product that catches the fancy of consumers can mean big business for a company. It also, inevitably, means big competition.

In this chapter we begin to look at the issues associated with marketing products. Specifically, we examine what is meant by the term *product* and consider how to classify consumer products. We consider a variety of ways to conceptualize products. This consideration includes the introduction of the product life cycle as well as the concepts of the product line and product mix. We conclude with a look at branding and packaging. Chapter 10 will complete our discussion of products with a look at product development and management.

WHAT IS A PRODUCT?

Jane buys a quart of Dreyer's Cookies 'N Cream ice cream at a 7-Eleven convenience store, paying $2.79. John buys a quart of Dreyer's Cookies 'N Cream ice cream at a Safeway supermarket, paying $2.49. Have these two consumers purchased the same product? The answer to this question depends on your definition of product. The narrowest definition would consider only the physical attributes of the purchase. On that dimension, both Jane and John have purchased the same product. But this narrow view does not take into account the concept of exchange, which is the essence of marketing.

In the transaction described here, each of the two consumers has exchanged money for a product. John paid thirty cents less than Jane but he also received less in return. Although both consumers received the same physical product, Jane received a number of other benefits. These include being able to park at the front door, avoiding a long wait, and being able to make the purchase late at night and very close to her home. Clearly these two consumers did not purchase the same package of benefits, and, thus, we say that they did not purchase the same product.

In this text we define **product** as every want-satisfying attribute a consumer receives in making an exchange, including psychological as well as physical benefits. This definition looks at products from the point of view of the consumer and includes much more than physical or tangible attributes.

Consider another example, the purchase of a videocassette recorder. When you buy a VCR you are receiving a metal box with electronic components in it (physical attributes). But this is not how you think of your purchase: you are buying a means of entertainment. Thinking of the VCR as an enhancement to your entertainment experience is an example of a want-satisfying attribute. Other want-satisfying attributes that a consumer of a VCR might seek include:

- special features, such as the ability to program 14 days in advance, stop action, and achieve special effects
- brand name of manufacturer and of retail outlet
- low price

- guarantee and/or warranty
- services, such as help in making decisions concerning which model to buy, installation instructions, and credit
- availability of service after the sale

Depending on the importance individual consumers place on each of these aspects, they will perceive the alternatives in the marketplace differently. For example, you may value a lower price and go to a discount store. You will perceive an RCA Model VR601HF videocassette recorder sold by a discount store as different from the same RCA Model VR601HF sold by a prestigious "full service" electronics retailer with highly knowledgeable sales and service personnel. The two retailers are selling different products even though the physical attributes of the two products are the same.

Philip Kotler, a leading scholar in marketing, has suggested that we should view the total product by thinking of each product as being composed of three components: the core product, the tangible product, and the augmented product.[2] The **core product** is comprised of the underlying benefits that a consumer is seeking in an exchange. In the case of the VCR, the core product would be the entertainment and satisfaction the buyer receives from the VCR. The **tangible product** is comprised of the actual features that facilitate the exchange of the core product. The VCR's electronic components, its program capabilities, and its simulated wood-grain finish are all parts of the tangible product. A product's color might also be viewed as a part of the tangible product although as the "Marketing in Action: Coloring Your Image" illustrates, a product's color may also connote its image. Image is an important feature that falls into the third component of product, the augmented product. The **augmented product** includes service-based and psychological features that enhance the complete product package from the customer's viewpoint. The brand name, the warranty, and the friendly, helpful service of the sales staff at the electronics store where the VCR was purchased are examples of augmented product. Figure 9.1 shows the three components that together define a total product and the various parts of each.

**FIGURE 9.1
Components of a
Product**

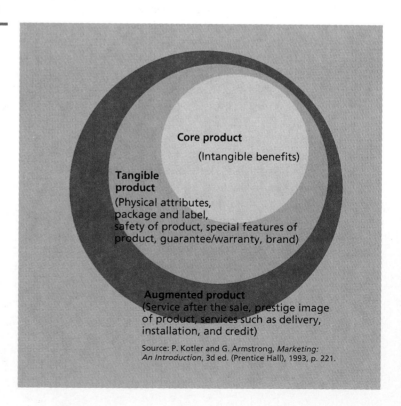

Core product
(Intangible benefits)

Tangible
product
(Physical attributes,
package and label,
safety of product, special features of
product, guarantee/warranty, brand)

Augmented product
(Service after the sale, prestige image
of product, services such as delivery,
installation, and credit)

Source: P. Kotler and G. Armstrong, *Marketing:
An Introduction*, 3d ed. (Prentice Hall), 1993, p. 221.

MARKETING *IN ACTION* ▰▰▰

Coloring Your Image

Does changing a product's color change the product itself? The answer is resoundingly *yes* if you consider the power of color to communicate image, an important part of the total product concept.

Firms as diverse as Reebok International, Best Western International, and Ford Motor Company agree that a product's color is a critical factor in its success. These firms are among a growing number of companies that have either hired an outside consultant or put someone on staff specifically to advise them on the colors their products should be. Pamela Boucher, a trend and color forecaster at Reebok International, recommended that the company phase out the bright reds, oranges, and yellows used in the 1980s in favor of back-to-nature colors. "Blackened green" is one of colors in the athletic shoe company's new offerings. A two-year research study at Best Western concluded that the bright yellow and black used in the Best Western emblem conveyed a low-quality image. The firm's updated logo features gold letters against a deep blue background.

In the case of the Ford Mustang, the firm consulted Carlton Wagner, a psychologist who bases his product color advice on the theory that certain colors and shades stimulate glandular action that in turn sends chemical signals to the brain. Wagner's ideas are considered questionable by many in the scientific community and by more traditional color consultants who rely on classic market research methods. His clients, however, have found his results convincing. According to Wagner, men prefer hotter shades and women prefer cooler shades. So he advised Ford to use a hot, yellow-based red for the Ford Mustang GT, a car targeted at men, and a cool red for the Probe, which is targeted at women.

Wagner has also been credited with a 5 percent increase in sales at Wienerschnitzel, the fast-food hot dog outlet. He advised the firm to add orange to the color scheme of its stores to build a stronger image as a purveyor of inexpensive hot dogs. Orange, it seems, means cheap. Color consultant Leatrice Eiseman, who also bases her work on the psychology of color, claims that orange and chartreuse are two of the colors most disliked by people. She attributes the dislike to the fact that the colors are commonly associated with bodily functions.

Many of the decisions regarding what colors will dominate the scene in products from clothing to automobiles to food are based on input from the Color Marketing Group. The Color Marketing Group is a trade association whose 1400 members include color marketers employed by many of the Fortune 500 companies as well as independent color consultants. The Group meets annually to predict which colors will be big sellers in the coming year. They forecast that earth tones will continue to flourish throughout the mid-1990s. Among the 15 colors identified at the 1994 meeting: 3 shades of gray, plantain (similar to an unripe banana), and winter moss (evergreen with a yellow tinge).

Color consultants offer the following general guidelines to marketers hoping to establish images and enhance their products through color:

- *rose putty*—a highly complex color popular with highly complex people
- *strong orange*—great around inexpensive products
- *prestige blue green*—a classy color, the highest indicator of financial success
- *pastel yellow*—a real attention getter, but it also induces stress
- *midrange blue*—an apple pie and mom color, America's favorite shade
- *dark blue*—conveys respect and responsibility, a good color for lawyers
- *bronze*—gets a negative response, useful when rejection is wanted
- *red violet*—a good fashion color for women, but men aren't wild about it
- *orchid*—an unpopular color that induces sensations of nausea

Our definition of product emphasizes the importance of concentrating on what consumers wish to buy rather than on what marketers think they are selling. The two are not always the same. Marketers sometimes overemphasize the technical aspects of their goods or services and underestimate the importance of the intangible benefits consumers are seeking. The intangible benefits may be far more important to the customer than the tangible aspects. For example, a consumer who purchases a microwave oven may not care about the delayed timer, the total wattage, and the cubic centimeters. The customer is seeking a convenient way to prepare a meal after a long day at work. A successful marketing campaign might then focus on the convenience of the microwave and leave the technical specifications for the fine print. Another important aspect of our definition of product is that it does not differentiate between goods and services. A product can be a good, a service, or a combination of the two. In fact, when you consider the three-component product definition, almost all products can be seen on a continuum from pure good to pure service.[3] Products we typically view as services, such as legal assistance, medical care, hair styling, and auto repair, fall closer to the service end of the continuum. This chapter will focus primarily on goods, while Chapter 19 highlights services. As we consider the basic product concepts, however, it is important to bear in mind that many of these concepts also apply to services.

CLASSIFICATION OF PRODUCTS

Classifying products helps us understand product decision making and plan strategies across all components of the marketing mix. Consumer attitudes and buying behavior form the bases for the various classification schemes marketers use. To classify products, we must use the same criteria that we use to classify markets. Products within a classification should be homogeneous, and the classification should be meaningful for product marketing.

To classify products, we first fit them into a user category. **Consumer products** are products purchased for use by ultimate consumers. **Business products** are products purchased by business consumers to be used in producing other goods or in rendering services.[4] This distinction can never be apparent from simply looking at a product; we must know something about who will be using the product, and how they will be using it. For example, when Heinz Ketchup is purchased by restaurants, it is classified differently from Heinz Ketchup purchased by ultimate consumers. In both cases the physical product is the same but the two are satisfying different needs. Restaurant owners purchase catsup to meet the desires of their customers and to offer a complete dining experience. Ultimate consumers purchase catsup to enhance the flavor of foods they eat. Given the differences in what the buyers are purchasing, different marketing programs must be developed. Business consumers may be more concerned about price and delivery options while ultimate consumers may be more affected by advertising and eye-catching packaging.

In some instances, of course, it may seem apparent from the product itself that the item is either a consumer product or a business product. Few ultimate consumers purchase Boeing 757 jets for their personal use. Be careful about assuming anything about a product without first investigating who will be using it, however. There are a few billionaires out there flying around in their own personal jumbo jets!

Classifying products as consumer products or business products is valuable, but the range of products within each of these categories is still very broad. Therefore, within each of these two broad categories, products can be classified further. The classification of business products was discussed in Chapter 7.

CLASSIFICATION OF CONSUMER PRODUCTS

Traditionally, marketers have classified consumer goods according to the way people shop for them. Three major categories are convenience goods, shopping goods, and specialty goods.[5] The amount of time and effort the consumer is willing to exert in obtaining the item determines which of the three categories the product falls into.

Convenience Goods

Convenience goods are products bought with a minimum of time and effort. Little forethought or planning occurs prior to the purchase of a convenience good. Convenience goods can be further categorized into three subtypes: staples, emergency goods, and impulse goods.

Staples.   **Staples** are convenience goods that consumers use on a regular and ongoing basis. They are typically goods that consumers have purchased many times before. This means the consumer already has a high level of knowledge about the product and does not need to do a great deal of shopping. Although staples are often heavily advertised, consumers tend not to have strong loyalty to any single brand and are relatively indifferent to which one of several major brands they buy. Staples are typically low-priced goods, a fact that also causes the consumer to feel that extensive shopping is not justified. Bear in mind, however, that it is the lack of effort on the part of the consumer, not the low price, that makes the item a staple. Examples of staples include milk and food products, newspapers, soft drinks, candy, and shampoo.

Emergency goods.   **Emergency goods** are convenience goods that consumers purchase with little forethought, planning, or effort because a situation arises that requires immediate possession of the item. If you are caught in a rainstorm while out of town you might purchase an umbrella even if you have one at home. In this case the umbrella is an emergency good. The consumer who purchases an auto battery from the closest service station after finding the battery in his or her car dead is

Newspapers are classified as staples, convenience goods used on a regular and ongoing basis.

also purchasing an emergency good. As you can see, emergency goods differ somewhat from staples. Because consumer demand for emergency goods is likely to be inelastic, consumers may be willing to pay a higher price for those goods. In many respects, however, the two types of goods are similar. In both subcategories of convenience goods, consumers do not exert effort in planning or shopping for the items.

Impulse goods.   **Impulse goods** are convenience goods that consumers purchase with no preplanning or thought. Seeing the item offered for sale is the stimulus that motivates the purchase. For example, have you ever stood in line at the checkout in a grocery store and added a candy bar, some gum, a magazine, or some batteries to your purchases? If so, you have bought impulse goods. Impulse goods are often small purchases that do not involve large amounts of money. However, this is not always the case. A consumer might, for example, purchase a fairly expensive piece of clothing after seeing it displayed in a department store window even though he or she was not shopping for clothes that day. Like the other two subcategories of convenience goods, the purchase of impulse goods involves little effort, planning, or forethought.

The key to marketing a convenience good is to have it readily available to the consumer. The product must be accessible in a convenient location when the consumer wants it or the sale will be lost. This requires intensive distribution. A convenience good like Coca-Cola, for example, is available in supermarkets, convenience stores, restaurants, service stations, stadiums, and in vending machines everywhere. The manufacturers of Coke know that while some consumers may prefer Coke to Pepsi, they are unlikely to go searching for it if a Pepsi machine is more convenient. The burden of the promotion for a convenience product is on the manufacturer. The retailer typically carries several brands and is indifferent to which one the consumer buys.

Shopping Goods

Shopping goods are products usually purchased only after the consumer has compared the price, quality, and style of a number of alternatives, often visiting several stores before making a purchase decision. Extensive information-seeking is necessary because the consumer has incomplete knowledge at the early stages of the purchase decision process. Thus, the decision process follows the limited or extensive problem-solving behavior described in Chapter 6. Shopping goods are less frequently purchased and are generally priced higher than convenience goods. Brand loyalty is minimal, and the goods are often products that others will see the consumer using. With shopping goods, consumers not only find it necessary to shop to increase product knowledge but want to "shop around" to feel they have made the best decision possible. Shopping goods can be subcategorized into two groups: homogeneous shopping goods and heterogeneous shopping goods.

Homogeneous shopping goods.   **Homogeneous shopping goods** are products that require considerable effort in the decision-making part of the purchase but present few choices in attributes. Consequently, the key factor in a consumer's decision in this category is usually price. Appliances such as washers and dryers are an example of homogeneous shopping goods. Since most manufacturers offer a range of models with similar features and colors, the average consumer in the market for a washer and dryer will base a decision on differences in price. The effort in shopping for this product will be focused on finding the best price.

Heterogeneous shopping goods.   **Heterogeneous shopping goods** are items purchased only after considerable effort is exerted and comparisons made of a number of product attributes which the consumer perceives to vary significantly among offerings. Clothing is an example of a heterogeneous shopping good. Most consumers are willing to exert some effort in shopping for clothes. While price is an important consideration in the decision-making process, other attributes such as fit, style, and color are also significant. A consumer may be willing to pay a higher price for an item because of the variation among these attributes.

The marketing strategy most appropriate for shopping goods is different from that used for convenience goods. Distribution does not have to be as intensive, because consumers will visit a number of retail outlets before making a decision. Thus, the goods only need to be in enough outlets so the consumer will encounter the product in at least one of the several stores visited. Promotion is often an important part of the marketing mix for shopping goods because of the need to inform consumers of the product and its price, but the retailer often plays the major role in this promotion. Price is also an important marketing mix component, especially for homogeneous shopping goods, for which it may be the sole determinant.

Specialty Goods

Specialty goods are products for which no reasonable substitutes exist, in the perception of the consumer, because of the unique characteristics or brand identification of the product. Consumers are thus willing to expend considerable effort to obtain these goods. A consumer who insists on a DieHard brand of car battery will accept no other, and is willing to search for the preferred brand has made the battery a specialty good. Other examples of products that are specialty goods for many people are expensive stereo and photographic equipment, designer clothing, specific restaurants, and certain brands of automobiles. In buying specialty goods, consumers are extremely brand-loyal. Because demand is virtually inelastic for this type of good, consumers are willing to pay premium prices.

Because consumers insist upon buying a particular brand, they will seek out the product from the retailer. Distribution is thus less important than it is for convenience and shopping goods, and relatively few outlets are needed. Advertising is used to let the consumer know where the product is, and the cost of this promotion is often shared by the retailer and the manufacturer.

A refrigerator is a homogeneous shopping good. The appliance is usually purchased after the consumer has compared alternatives and makes a decision, usually based on price.

Certain brands of automobiles, like this Porsche, are considered specialty goods by many.

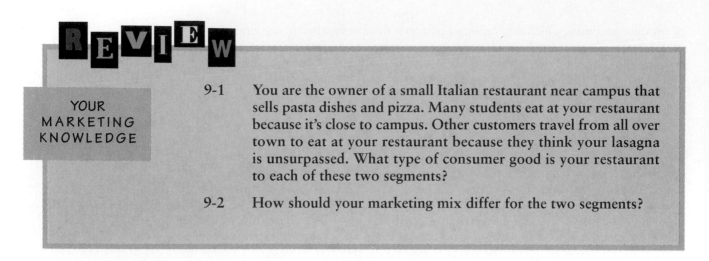

YOUR MARKETING KNOWLEDGE

9-1   You are the owner of a small Italian restaurant near campus that sells pasta dishes and pizza. Many students eat at your restaurant because it's close to campus. Other customers travel from all over town to eat at your restaurant because they think your lasagna is unsurpassed. What type of consumer good is your restaurant to each of these two segments?

9-2   How should your marketing mix differ for the two segments?

USING THE CLASSIFICATION SCHEME

The classification scheme for consumer goods is useful in planning marketing strategy and is the traditional way of categorizing such products. But the scheme has a number of problems. While it seems logical to base a classification system on consumer attitudes and buying behavior, we saw in Chapter 6 that not all consumers think and act alike. For example, for the consumer who would purchase only a DieHard auto battery, the product was a specialty good. Another consumer, however, knowing that he or she will soon need another auto battery, will visit a number of stores and ultimately buy the one that seems to offer the best value. In this case, the battery is a shopping good. Finally, the consumer who waits until his or her auto battery is dead and then replaces it with whatever the nearest service station sells is purchasing a convenience good. Thus, all products cannot be classified the same way for all consumers. This explains why different products are marketed with different marketing programs to reach different segments of the market.

Many consumer goods can be generalized to the shopping habits of most people. This helps make the traditional classification scheme more useful. The majority of consumers, for example, perceive milk to be a convenience good, a television to be a shopping good, and a Ferrari automobile to be a specialty good.

THE PRODUCT LIFE CYCLE

There are many ways to conceptualize a product that will help in marketing planning. The classification of goods scheme offers one approach. Another approach is the product life cycle. The **product life cycle (PLC)** is based on the premise that products change over the period of time they are in the marketplace. The product life cycle is the series of stages that a product class goes through from its introduction until it is taken off the market. It is usually divided into four stages: introduction, growth, maturity, and decline.

Movement through the stages of the product life cycle is unidirectional. It is also fairly predictable in the sense that a product class will progress from one stage to the next. For example, in 1982, retail dollar sales of waterbeds in the United States totaled $1,125 million; the market grew to $2,060 million in sales by 1985. The rapid growth attracted many competitors who flooded the market. The average price of waterbeds dropped during the 1980s as competition grew increasingly intense. In the peak year of 1988, the industry consisted of 326 manufacturers who combined to realize retail dollar sales of $2,200 million. The market then started to decline and level off. The industry had only $1,625 million in retail sales in 1990. By 1992 there were only 158 manufacturers and annual retail sales for the year were $1,450 million.[6] The waterbed market has moved through the product life cycle. Figure 9.2 illustrates a typical product life cycle.

While it is true that all product classes will move through the four stages, the PLC does not predict how long a product class will stay in any given stage. If a product class moved very rapidly through the stages, as in the case of a fad item, the shape of the PLC would be quite different from that illustrated in Figure 9.2. It might look more like Figure 9.3. When Essential Personal Items (EPI) introduced Epilady in 1987, an electric device that removed unwanted body hair, sales took off rapidly. By 1990 company sales exceeded $300 million. After being on the market for only five years, however, the product was removed in 1992 following a decline in sales that was almost as rapid as its ascent.

Conversely, a product class that started slowly, taking a long time to establish significant levels of demand, but which maintained steady demand over a long period

FIGURE 9.2
The Product Life Cycle

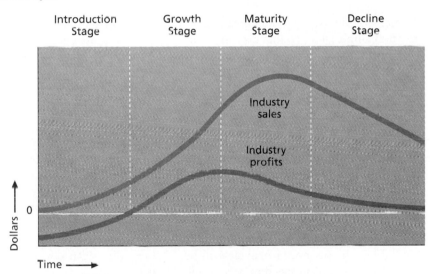

FIGURE 9.3
The Product Life Cycle of a Fad

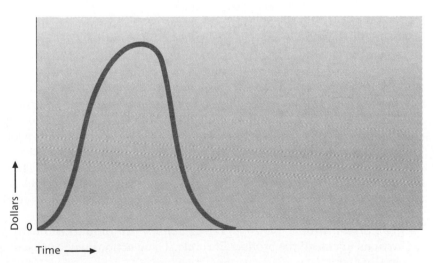

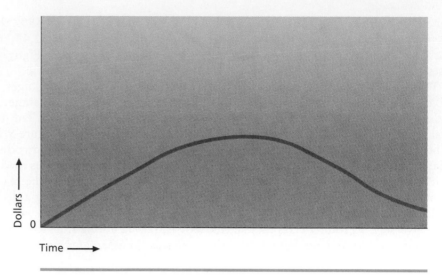

FIGURE 9.4
A Long Product Life Cycle

of time, would have a product life cycle that looked more like Figure 9.4. Typewriters are an example of a product class that enjoyed a lengthy life cycle. Their reign came to an end only when better alternatives (word processors and personal computers) were introduced and gained popularity.

Four important factors help determine the length and shape of the life cycle for a product class:

1. *Consumer needs, wants, attitudes, and behavior.* How quickly will a new product or a modified product be accepted by consumers? For example, consumers apparently want to be able to make and receive calls from their automobiles. So, sales of cellular telephones took off fairly rapidly and the product class moved quickly into the growth stage of the product life cycle. Demand for compact disc players, on the other hand, was initially slow. It took several years before the product class moved from introduction to growth.

2. *Rate of technological change.* The faster the rate of technological change, the shorter the product life cycle will be. The rapidity with which technological break-throughs in speed of processing and memory capacity have occurred in the personal computer market, for example, has resulted in a very short product life cycle for most forms of the product.

3. *Competitive activity.* If patents, tariffs, or access to raw material slow down the introduction of competitive products, the product life cycle will be much longer than it would be if there were ease of entry. The NutraSweet Company, for example, has enjoyed a patent on aspartame, the artificial sweetener. This patent has prevented competitors from introducing aspartame or products containing it. With the impending end of patent protection, NutraSweet is dropping prices in an attempt to discourage competition. The more vigorous the activity by competitors, the shorter the product life cycle will probably be, at least for individual forms of the product. The early 1990s saw a rush of competitive activity in the gourmet coffee and coffeehouse market. The enormity of the competition, however, appears to have rushed the coffeehouse concept through the product life cycle with some indication that sales are already flattening.

4. *The organization's own marketing action.* An organization can take many actions to extend the product life cycle. These actions will be described in detail in Chapter 10.

It is important for marketers to understand the different stages of the product life cycle because different marketing strategies are required for products at different stages. As we discuss the various stages of the product life cycle and their characteristics, remember that the life cycle refers to an entire product class, not the offerings of a single competitor. Thus, it is possible for a firm to find that the sales and profits of its product differ from the sales and profit levels being experienced by the product class as a whole at any point during the life cycle. For example, while sales may be low and profits nonexistent for typewriters in general, an individual producer might continue to market typewriters successfully. This could be the case because the producer faces little competition and is working hard to meet the needs of a small but loyal segment.

Introduction Stage

Introduction could be described as the pioneering stage of the product life cycle. At this stage the product is launched into the marketplace, often after a long period of development. As Figure 9.2 shows, sales are zero at first and are still low even at the end of introduction. Consumers are not aware of the product, its benefits, or potential uses. Thus, there should be an investment in advertising and promotion designed to educate potential customers and persuade innovators to try the new product. Promotion should seek to build primary demand for the product category. Since there are typically no important competitors, promotion to establish brand preference is relatively unimportant. As illustrated by the Marketing Profile, this is the stage that Rollerblade found itself in when it first introduced in-line skates. By giving skates away to high-profile people and rental shops, Rollerblade was able to establish in-line skates as a product class and build interest in them. The high promotion costs typical in introduction and the cost of establishing initial distribution for the product usually mean that profits will be negative during this stage.

Growth Stage

The growth stage can be thought of as the golden period of the product life cycle. More and more consumers are learning about and adopting the new product, hence sales volume increases rapidly. Profits are also increasing rapidly, particularly in the early part of growth. This rapid increase in sales and profits causes an influx of competition. As competitors enter the marketplace, a leveling of profits will occur. This happens because the increased competition puts downward pressure on prices and creates the need to spend additional promotional dollars to tell consumers why the firm's product is better than the competition's. Today Rollerblade faces challenges from 33 competitors. Almost all of the competitors offer in-line skates that sell for less than $100. This has forced Rollerblade to introduce Bladerunner, a new low-end product that is priced to match the competition.[7] Automatic bread machines are another example of a product class in the growth stage of the product life cycle. The machines were introduced to the U.S. market in 1988 by Welbilt, a New Jersey–based home appliance company. Sales began to take off and by 1993 Welbilt had 15 competitors. Industry sales of 2 million machines in 1993 exceeded the forecast of 1.75 million.[8]

Maturity Stage

In the early part of the maturity stage, sales continue to increase, but at a decreasing rate. By the end of the stage, sales have begun to decline. Profits of both retailers and manufacturers are declining in the maturity stage, and some manufacturers cease their marketing efforts. Because any company sales gains during the maturity stage typically come at the expense of a competitor, market share battles are common. Competition is very tough during maturity, and some competitors cut prices to attract or hold on to business. At this stage, brands have quite similar physical attributes, and it is difficult for marketers to differentiate their products. Sales promotions of all types are used to encourage brand-switching by consumers and to encourage retailers to promote and give shelf space to the company's brands. The soft drink industry is an example of a product class in maturity. Soft drink consumption, as a whole, has remained fairly stable for many years. *Beverage Digest* reports that bottle and can sales of soft drinks are growing at only 1.5 percent a year or less.[9] Hence Coca-Cola and Pepsi battle bitterly over existing cola drinkers. Coca-Cola, for example, spent $350 million during the summer of 1994 to sponsor a promotion that involved prizes such as Ford Mustangs and Kawasaki Jet Skis for consumers who found selected numbers on Coke products.[10]

Decline Stage

Eventually, product class sales begin to decline, sometimes even rapidly. The causes of the decline may be market saturation, new technology, or changes in social values. Since most homes have smoke detectors, sales in that product class have slowed considerably. Compact disc players have significantly slowed sales of cassette tape players. Health conscious consumers have caused a significant decrease in beef consumption in the United States. The decline in volume often results in higher costs. At this stage marketers must eliminate products that are no longer profitable or find ways of cutting operational and marketing costs. Some of these include eliminating marginal dealers and distributors, cutting advertising and sales promotion, and minimizing production costs. These cuts could result in renewed profitability. In effect, the product is "milked"; that is, it is allowed to coast with decreased marketing support as long as it remains profitable.

Of course it is possible that reducing marketing support will hasten the product's demise, and thus decline has been viewed as a self-fulfilling prophecy. Brands that have developed strong consumer loyalty decline slower than products that have not been differentiated from their competitors. It is even possible for individual competitors to do well for quite some time while the product class is in decline. They may be able to garner a larger market share, albeit of a smaller market, as other competitors drop out. Technics and Pioneer continue to produce stereo turntables although distribution is limited.

PRODUCT MIX

It is unusual today for a medium- or large-sized company to market only a single product. In looking at the multiple product offerings of an organization, we use the terms *product line* and *product mix*. A **product line** is a group of closely related products offered by an organization. A firm like Procter & Gamble has many different product lines that include laundry detergents, shampoos, and coffees. An organization's **product mix** consists of all the individual products available from the organization. In Procter & Gamble's case, there are many different products in its mix, counting all the different types of detergents, shampoos, coffees and other items it sells, as well as all the variety of package sizes.

A firm's **breadth of product mix** is determined by the number of product lines it markets. Firms such as Apple Computers or Kellogg's have a very narrow product mix, offering a limited number of product lines. Other companies, such as General Electric, have a very broad product mix. General Electric sells light bulbs, major appliances, heavy equipment such as power plant generators, small electrical motors, medical equipment, aircraft engines, repair services, and electrical parts. An organization's **depth of product mix** is determined by the number of individual product items, sizes, models, and colors available within each of its product lines. Thus, Kellogg's product mix is deep, because it markets several brands of cereal, each in packages of several sizes. Coors Beer has both a very narrow and a very shallow product mix, with a limited number of lines, and relatively few individual brands, sizes, and package types available for sale in each of its lines. Because depth refers to the number of products within a given product line, it is possible for a firm to have a product mix that contains some deep lines and some shallow lines. It would be difficult to generalize about the depth of such a firm's product mix.

A third characteristic that can be used to describe a firm's product mix is consistency. **Consistency of product mix** is determined by the degree to which the various products in the firm's product mix are related to each other in terms of use, distribution, target market, or some other means. For example, although General Electric has a very large product mix that is both broad and deep, almost everything that the firm produces has something to do with electricity. The firm's product mix can therefore be described as highly consistent. On the other hand, a company that is highly diversified, producing and marketing a vast range of products targeted at diverse markets, designed for diverse purposes, and distributed through diverse channels, would be described as having an inconsistent product mix. R. J. Reynolds manufactures many types of cigarette and tobacco products but its Nabisco Division also produces a wide variety of snacks, cookies, and other food items.

Decisions about the Product Mix

Decisions about a firm's product mix, its breadth, depth, and consistency are determined by the overall strategic plan and objectives of the organization, including the segment and needs of the target market(s) that the organization is trying to satisfy. A company might, for example, decide to add a new product line to its product mix in order to reach a newly chosen target market. When Sony decided to target young children, the company added a whole new line of products called "My First Sony." New product lines can be developed internally or they can be acquired. The same two options are available for expanding an organization's product offerings within each product line. Procter & Gamble, with an existing line of laundry detergents, might develop a new detergent to meet the needs of a newly defined target market. Conversely, they might acquire an existing laundry detergent from another company.

The firm's overall objectives should also guide its decisions regarding the consistency of the product mix. A highly consistent product mix may make it easier to introduce new items. Consumers in such a case may be more likely to perceive that the firm could do a good job of producing a new product that is consistent with products in the company's existing mix. When Cover Girl, for example, introduced a line of cosmetic brushes, the products were easily accepted by consumers who identify the company with cosmetic needs. Inconsistent product mixes, on the other hand, allow a firm to spread the risks of operation across a variety of industries and target markets. By diversifying into non-tobacco-related products, R. J. Reynolds Nabisco has been able to continue to prosper despite the declining tobacco market.

BRANDING

What products have you purchased recently? In answering this question, you undoubtedly remembered a number of brands. A **brand** is a name, term, symbol, design, or combination of these that identifies the seller's goods and services and

The logo for Coca-Cola Classic is an example of a brand mark.

distinguishes them from competitors' products.[11] A **brand name** is that part of a brand that can be vocalized, including letters, words, and numbers. A **brand mark** is a symbol, design, or a group of distinctive letters—the part of the brand that is seen but not spoken. Coke and Mercedes are both brand names. The distinctive lettering in Coca-Cola and the Mercedes symbol are brand marks. Services, as well as tangible goods, can be branded. MCI, for example, offers services with brand names such as Friends & Family and 1-800-COLLECT.[12] A **service mark,** similar to a brand mark, is a symbol, design, or a group of distinctive letters that designate a service rather than a tangible good. Hence while McDonald's is a brand name, the golden arches is the McDonald's service mark.

Consumers' perceptions of brand names can and do change over time. Table 9.1 lists the five strongest brand names in the United States in 1988, the five most powerful brand names in the United States in 1991, and the five brand names associated with highest quality in 1994. Note that while the 1994 and 1991 lists have four brands in common, none of the brand names on either of these lists is on the 1988 list.

If a brand or part of a brand is registered with the U.S. Patent and Trademark Office, it has legal protection for the exclusive use of a seller and becomes a **trademark.** There are currently about 1.65 million trademarks registered at the U.S. Patent Office. In 1993, 56,750 new trademarks were registered.[13] Trademarks are registered for twenty years and can be renewed for twenty years at a time if they have not been abandoned or surrendered through lack of use by the seller. A trademark may

TABLE 9.1
Best Known Brands in the U.S.

5 "Most Powerful" Brands in 1988	5 "Strongest" Brands in 1991	5 "Highest Quality" Brands in 1994
Coca-Cola	Disney World	Disney World
Campbell's	Kodak	Disneyland
Pepsi-Cola	Mercedes Benz	Kodak
AT&T	CNN	Hallmark
McDonald's	Hallmark	Mercedes Benz

Source: E. C. Baig, "Name That Brand," *Fortune,* July 4, 1988, pp. 10–12; *Marketing News,* September 16, 1992, p. 1; C. Miller, "Upscale Brands Regaining Popularity, *Marketing News,* May 23, 1994, p. 3.

be a brand name or a brand mark or both. Additionally, in recent years the trend has been toward allowing companies to trademark other aspects of their products. For example, Moen, Incorporated, a well-known producer of plumbing products, has a registered trademark that protects the distinctive shape of its Legend kitchen faucet and faucet handles. Similarly, Owens-Corning Fiberglas Corporation applied for and received a trademark for the particular shade of pink that distinguishes its insulation material from that of competitors.[14]

When a company obtains legal protection for a brand by registering it as a trademark, the company that has registered it may sue another firm for trademark infringement if the name or mark is used by the second firm. McDonald's Corporation is currently embroiled in a trademark infringement suit. The fast-food giant aired television commercials in 1993 featuring former basketball star Michael Jordan using the expression, "nothing but net." A 9-year-old New York girl, however, had received trademark approval for the expression in November 1992. McDonald's contends that the girl is too young to keep the trademark on the phrase because she can't use it in the ordinary course of trade.[15] The terms *brand* and *trademark* are comparable—brand is the commonly used term, and trademark is a legal term meaning those brands have been legally registered. Hence, all trademarks are brands but all brands are not necessarily trademarks.

The Importance of Branding

Brands are everywhere! It is estimated that the average American is exposed to 2100–2400 different brands every day.[16] Why is branding so prevalent? With increased technological capabilities enabling competitors to market extremely similar goods and services, a brand is often a product's most important distinguishing characteristic and may be the only part of the product a competitor cannot copy. Without the ability to use brand names, many organizations could not practice modern marketing.[17]

Branding has many advantages for marketers. Retailers, wholesalers, manufacturers, and other marketers can develop loyal customers who identify what to buy through branding. Advertising a brand encourages consumers to buy and continue buying products. Branding allows marketers to introduce new products more efficiently. For example, in 1993 when Skippy introduced peanut butter cookies, the product required less advertising and achieved faster consumer acceptance than it would have if it had not used Skippy's name. BankAmericard changed its brand name to VISA so it would be more effective in marketing the credit card throughout the world. Nissan introduced the brand name Datsun in the United States because it felt it would be more acceptable to American buyers, but eventually changed back to Nissan to establish a single brand name worldwide.

A hot trend recently has been co-branding between two well-known manufacturers. **Co-branding** is the pairing of two brand names of two producers on a single product. Pillsbury and Nabisco, for example, have partnered to produce Pillsbury Oreo Bars baking mix and frosting. Similarly, General Mills and Hershey Foods are now offering a co-branded breakfast cereal called Reese's Peanut Butter Puffs. Co-branding benefits manufacturers by extending brand awareness and allowing firms to enter new product categories with the help of a brand name already established in that category.[18]

Branding is also important for retailers. Consumers often select a store on the basis of the brands it offers. Thus, consumers who desire Craftsman tools or Kenmore appliances must shop at Sears because these brands are not available through any other retailer. The brands that a store stocks are an important part of its image for consumers. If retailers have exclusive rights to highly desired brands, they are less vulnerable to competition.

This co-branded breakfast cereal is offered by General Mills and Hershey Foods. Co-branding extends brand awareness and enables firms to enter new product categories with the help of a brand name that is already established in that category.

Branding also offers important advantages to consumers. A consumer is able to distinguish similar goods and services supplied by different producers because of branding. Consumers use brands to identify products they wish to purchase repeatedly, as well as those they wish to avoid. Brands simplify shopping, making the process much more efficient. Branding usually implies consistent quality, typically serving as a better indicator of quality than the price of a product. It also enables consumers to reduce the perceived risk in the purchase decision process.

Despite the advantages that branding appears to offer to all members of the distribution channel, there is disagreement among marketers regarding whether branding is a valuable process both today and into the future. According to recent studies, marketers feel today's consumers place less importance on brand names. In one study, national brand managers for consumer product companies reported that there seems to be a long-term trend for consumers to switch away from brand-named products to store-named products and generic offerings. Eighty percent of the brand managers surveyed attributed this trend to economic uncertainty and tighter family budgets.[19] In a second study, whose results are illustrated in Figure 9.5, both men's and women's level of agreement with the statement, "I try to stick to well-known brand names," dropped significantly between 1975 and 1993.[20]

FIGURE 9.5
Is the importance of brands declining?

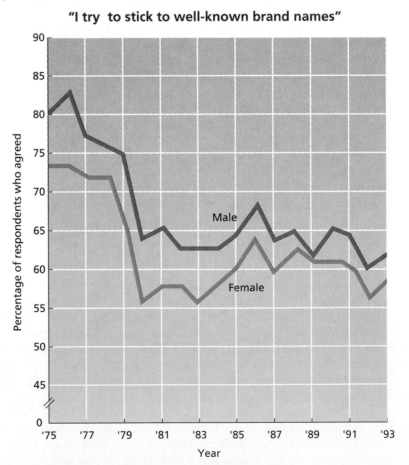

"I try to stick to well-known brand names"

Source: A. W. Fawcett, "Lifestyle Study: The Latest Results of DDB Needham's 18-Year Survey," *Advertising Age*, April 18, 1994, pp.12–13.

A third study, however, reported that the chief executive officers of 1,003 U.S.-based companies disagreed with the statement, "brand loyalty is dead." Their disagreement was supported in the research by findings that 70 percent of U.S. consumers agree with the statement, "I buy the same brand over and over again without really thinking about it." Furthermore, the research indicated that almost 75 percent of U.S. consumers agree that, "Once I find a brand I like, it is very difficult to get me to change brands."[21]

Branding Strategy Decisions

Marketers face a number of strategic decisions when it comes to branding. These include whether to use a manufacturer or a distributor brand, whether to use a family branding strategy or an individual branding strategy, and what name to use for their brand.

Manufacturer versus distributor brand.   One of the first issues a manufacturer must determine is whether to sell its products using a manufacturer's brand or a distributor's brand. A **manufacturer's brand** is owned by the manufacturer. These brands are sometimes called **national brands,** but in fact they may be distributed on a regional or national basis. Examples of manufacturer's brands include Cheerios, Tide, Sony, and Gillette. A **distributor's brand** is owned and controlled by a retailer, wholesaler, or other type of reseller. These brands are often called **private labels** or **store brands.** Examples of distributor's brands include Kenmore and Craftsman (Sears's brands), Radio Shack, and Kmart. Additionally, most grocery retailers carry one or more lines of private-label products. The Great Atlantic & Pacific Tea Co. (A & P), for example, offers three lines of private-label goods, Master Choice (premium), America's Choice (mid-priced), and Savings Plus (economy-priced).[22] Some distributor's brands are heavily advertised so that they resemble manufacturers' brands in the eyes of consumers. Two examples are Sears's DieHard battery and Radio Shack's Tandy personal computers. On the other hand, many distributors limit

Tandy personal computers are an example of a distributor's brand that is so heavily advertised that it resembles a manufacturer's brand in the eyes of consumers.

the amount of advertising they do, so they can keep prices lower than the national brands. This is often the case with grocery items.

Private-label brands are growing in popularity. In 1993 they enjoyed a market share of 19.7 percent of supermarket unit sales. That represented an increase from 19.4 percent in 1992 and only 16.4 percent in 1989.[23] Predictions regarding growth of private labels by the year 2000 range from a low of 23 percent to a high of 40 percent.[24] The increase has been attributed to many factors including increased economic concerns, improvements in product quality, and a decrease in network television usage by marketers of manufacturer's brands.[25]

The conditions that lead manufacturers to market products without using their own brands or adding to their brands are the same ones that result in retailers and wholesalers seeking products to market under their own brands. These conditions include:

1. The product class is past the midpoint in the growth stage of the life cycle; some market segments may be saturated.
2. Consumers are beginning to consider alternative offerings within the product class as undifferentiated substitutes for one another; that is, the product is approaching "commodity" status.
3. The reseller becomes more important than the manufacturer as a source of assurance of quality, style, or both to the customer and has greater economic power than the manufacturer.
4. Changes in the competitive environment stimulate manufacturers to provide distributors' brands, lest they lose distribution to competing manufacturers who will do so.
5. Economic slowdowns cause consumers to seek lower-priced products.
6. The distributors' volume becomes adequate to permit production of a custom product by the manufacturer and stocking and promotion by the distributor.[26]

With distributors' brands, more of the marketing is shifted from the manufacturer to the distributor. Small manufacturers in particular may find this desirable, especially if their marketing resources are limited. Manufacturers with excess capacity may also find that additional business from selling distributors' brands can improve profitability if additional sales can be made at a price above marginal cost of production. Distributors' brands offer the retailer and wholesaler a means of tying their consumers directly to them; if they are satisfied, consumers will return to them to buy the product in the future. Also, distributors' brands often enable retailers to earn greater profits while selling the product to consumers at a lower price than comparable alternatives.

Marketers of manufacturers' brands have been forced to respond to the growth of private-label brands. Those that perceive private labels as a threat are likely to increase the amount of advertising and sales promotions, such as coupons, that they engage in. Other manufacturers have increased their involvement in the production of private-label brands. This move may give a manufacturer leverage with retailers for shelf space as well as increasing overall sales revenue.[27] In 1993 Pillsbury Company decided to expand the number of products it produces under private labels. The company made the move for two reasons, to make money and to build partnerships with retailers.[28]

Consumers in North America sometimes perceive distributors' brands to be lower in quality than competitive manufacturers' brands. The opposite is the case in Europe. In many European countries, distributors' brands are perceived to be higher in quality than national brands. The American perception of inferior quality, however, may be changing as more retailers move to carry premium private-label lines. The "Spotlight on Global Marketing: Fit for a President" discusses the success that a Canadian retailer has had distributing premium private-label products.

Family brands versus individual brands. Marketers must also determine whether to sell products using individual brands or family brands. Companies having an individual branding policy use different brand names for each of their products. Thus, Procter & Gamble markets Pampers disposable diapers, Prell shampoo, and Pringles potato chips. With **family brands** a brand is applied to a line of products. General Electric, Scott Paper, Campbell's, Black & Decker, Xerox, IBM, Del Monte, and Kellogg's all use family brands. Some firms use a combination of individual and

MARKETING *IN ACTION*

SPOTLIGHT
ON
Global
Marketing

Fit for a President

President's Choice Decadent chocolate chip cookies are made with 100 percent pure butter and 40 percent chocolate chips. Nabisco's leading brand, Chips Ahoy, is made with vegetable oil and contains only 25 percent chocolate chips. Which would you choose? Oh by the way, President's Choice cookies are less expensive than Chips Ahoy. Are you still thinking?

Consumers in the United States typically have viewed private-label brands as economically priced alternatives to higher quality, nationally advertised, manufacturers' brands, President's Choice may change that. The premium private label is infiltrating grocery stores across North America. Prices are below those of manufacturers' brands and you won't see any national advertising. The quality of President's Choice products, however, is designed to be equal to or better than the manufacturers' brands with which they compete. The idea seems to be catching on. The line's U.S. sales volume rose 127 percent in 1993.

President's Choice, created in 1984, is the brainchild of the Loblaw Companies, Canada's biggest supermarket chain. The company was able to generate a large number of products in a relatively short time by raising the quality of existing store brands. Commenting on the success of President's Choice in the United States, Canadian food consultant John Winter stated, "There are not many Canadian ideas that you can export, but [this] is definitely one with some legs."

Retailers in 34 states have adopted President's Choice as their own. Converts include Lucky stores

on the west coast, Jewel stores in the Chicago area, Tom Thumb in Dallas, and D'Agostino in New York. Some of the retailers continue to sell other lines of private-label brands. Lucky stores, for example, feature Lady Lee products. President's Choice, however, is designed to offer an upscale alternative to traditional store brands and is not viewed as competing directly with a retailer's other private labels.

The success of President's Choice has, of course, spawned imitators. A & P stores offer Master Choice while Safeway stores feature Safeway Select. Wholesalers are also showing interest. Fleming Companies, a giant food wholesaler, introduced its line of premium private-label products in 1994. Under the brand name Marquee Premium, the line initially included 70 product items positioned to compete with manufacturers' brands. Like President's Choice, the imitators offer premium quality at prices below those charged for manufacturers' brands. This is possible primarily because of the absence of promotion and advertising budgets, which can run into the tens of millions of dollars for manufacturers' brands.

Despite the success being enjoyed by all of the premium quality private labels, President's Choice is clearly out in front. Brian Sharoff, president of the 1700-member New York–based Private Label Manufacturers Association, predicts that "it will probably take a long time for [the competitors] to catch up."

family brands. For example, automobile companies use names like Ford Taurus and Honda Prelude. General Electric uses the G.E. family name on one line of appliances and uses a separate name, Hotpoint, on a different line of appliances.

Individual brands are most appropriate when the products are not similar in quality or price. The use of individual brands minimizes confusion with other products of the company. Firms can appeal to different segments of the market with different strategies. This explains why Procter & Gamble uses individual brand names like Tide, Bold, Cheer, and Oxydol for its line of detergents. Each of these brands stands on its own and has its own image targeted toward its own segment of the market. An individual branding policy requires greater resources, however, because each brand must have its own promotional budget.

The use of family brands is most appropriate when the individual products are similar in quality and the firm's product mix is consistent. The family brand may offer greater economies in advertising and promotion as well as potentially higher impact. When the family brand is established, it is easier to obtain distribution, trial, and awareness of other new products that may be introduced with the brand. However, family brands also have potential disadvantages. If a new product introduced under a family brand fails, it may impact the perception of the rest of the product line. A watch company like Rolex, for example, should be very careful about introducing a new low-priced watch under the Rolex brand. If consumers perceive the new product as a cheap watch, it could ruin Rolex's reputation for fine watches. Family brands work best when the quality, target market, channels, product classification, and usage are all very similar, as with G.E. refrigerators, G.E. ovens, and G.E. washers and dryers. Honda, on the other hand, used a different brand name and set up a completely different dealer structure when it introduced its higher-priced Acura line of cars.

Brand name selection.   Think of the brand names SnackWell, Beautyrest, and Lean Cuisine. What comes to mind? Probably you thought of cookies and crackers, mattresses, and low-calorie frozen meals. This demonstrates the value of a good brand name. These three brand names are descriptive of the product benefits, are memorable, and fit the images the companies are trying to project. These three criteria were the most frequently mentioned in a study regarding brand name selection.[29]

There are four characteristics of a good brand name:

1. It should identify the product and set it apart from the competition.
2. It should describe the product or the function it performs.
3. It should communicate an important inherent quality of the product.
4. It should be memorable and easy to pronounce.[30]

Brand names with these characteristics seem to be more successful. There are many brands that have violated these rules and were less successful than their competitors. Consider for example, Colgate 100, Good News, or Mennen E. Do they describe the product? Does Max Factor describe product benefits as clearly as Cover Girl does?

There are, of course, many products that have violated the rules and still are very successful. For example, Häagen-Dazs, Riunite, Michelob, and Orville Redenbacher are neither short nor easy to pronounce. Thus, the criteria here should be considered guidelines, not hard-and-fast rules.

Generic Brands

Before leaving our discussion of branding, let's briefly consider generic brands. A **generic brand** or "no brand" is a type of brand used for products sold with no identification other than the contents. The products are labeled with names like Beer,

Generic brand products are sold with no identification other than the contents of the product. Recent studies indicate that market shares for generic products are dropping.

Corn Flakes, or Laundry Detergent. Generic brands originated in 1976 in France.[31] The products were an immediate success, accounting for an average 40 percent of sales in those categories where they competed with branded products.

The first generic brands appeared in the United States in 1977. The idea spread rapidly and within a few years generic brands became available in more than 320 product categories and in over 75 percent of the supermarkets in the United States.[32] On the average, generics cost about 40 percent less than nationally advertised brands, and 10 to 15 percent less than distributor private-label brands. Generic brands are generally of lower quality than manufacturers' and distributors' brands. Their level of quality may also be very inconsistent.

Studies conducted by Selling Areas-Marketing Incorporated, a marketing research company, have found that market shares for generic products have been dropping over the last 15 years.[33] They peaked in 1982 with $2.8 billion in sales and a 2.4 percent share of supermarket sales. By 1987, sales had slipped to $1.5 billion or about 1.2 percent of supermarket sales. Today, generic products are still found in a high percentage of supermarkets but represent less than 1.0 percent of supermarket sales. Sales have continued to be strongest in nonfood items such as paper bags, trash bags, coffee filters, and disposable diapers.[34] In some product categories, however, generics continue to thrive. Generic drugs, widely understood to be the equivalent of competitors' branded drugs, represent a growing market share in the pharmaceutical industry. Merck, a major pharmaceutical producer, recently decided to market both branded and generic versions of many of the drugs it manufactures in order to respond to this growing part of the market.[35]

REVIEW

9-3   What benefits do brand names and brand marks offer to companies? To retailers? To consumers?

9-4   Suppose you opened a retail store specializing in discount compact discs. How would you go about choosing a name for your store?

YOUR
MARKETING
KNOWLEDGE

PACKAGING

Marketers have increasingly recognized the importance of packaging. Traditionally, a package was perceived as a container, and the emphasis was on the ability of the package to protect the product. Today most marketers recognize that a package is also a presentation and welcome to customers. The promotional aspects of packaging are important because packages can contribute to substantially increased sales.[36]

A package has two important functions. First, it must have utility for the consumer and for the intermediaries in the channels of distribution. The package should protect the product, prevent breakage or spoilage, and extend the product's life. It should be convenient for the consumer to use and convenient for intermediaries to ship, store, and stack on a shelf. Resellers prefer packages that help cut shipping costs and reduce shoplifting. The package should also be easily disposable but not contribute to excessive waste.

Second, the package should facilitate promotional communication by allowing clear brand identification and promoting the product's features. A good label on the package, together with proper instructions on a product's use, for example, can reduce the amount of personal selling needed to convince the consumer to buy the product. Packaging such as an attractive Christmas box or a distinctive shape can lead to a substantial increase in a product's sales. These features, of course, must be weighed against the negative impact that charges of improper packaging can carry. L'Eggs pantyhose, for example, was successful for years with a distinctive, egg-shaped package. In 1991, however, the firm announced that the plastic L'Eggs egg would be scrapped in favor of a more environmentally friendly cardboard package.[37] A properly designed package can communicate the quality of a product, such as a slip-on box for a high-quality book. Also, there is no question that attractive, innovative packaging can help a marketer obtain additional shelf space for the company's products.

Some examples of successful packaging include:

▪ Vitel Mineral Water has distinguished itself from the competition by using a square plastic bottle rather than a round bottle. The company promotes, as a competitive advantage, the fact that its bottle will not roll when laid on its side.

▪ The success of Procter & Gamble's Pringles Potato Chips is largely attributable to packaging. The round can used for Pringles protects the chips better than traditional potato chip bags and takes less space on retailers' shelves and in home pantries.

▪ Numerous producers of motor oil targeted at the do-it-yourself oil changer have switched to packages with convenient built-in spouts for pouring. The spouts make it easier to use the product and have helped increase the number of consumers who change their own oil.

▪ Many frozen dinner manufacturers have replaced traditional aluminum trays with plastic so the consumer can pop the product, package and all, into the microwave.[38]

The "Marketing in Action: Dressing Up the Basics in Idaho" provides additional examples of how creative packaging has helped marketers increase their success.

Factors in Package Design

Several factors must be considered in designing and developing a package. These include environmental and resource considerations, financial and cost factors, governmental regulations, and consumer behavior.

MARKETING *IN ACTION*

Dressing Up the Basics in Idaho

In almost any grocery store across the United States, consumers can purchase ten pounds of Idaho-grown potatoes for less than $2.00. Despite this fact, Rolland Jones Potatoes, Incorporated, has been extremely successful selling a "baker's dozen" of Idaho potatoes for $18.95. The potatoes are wrapped in a decorative box that uses Easter grass.

The Baker's Dozen of Idaho potatoes is only one example of a growing phenomenon. Laura Hobbs, marketing specialist for the Idaho Department of Agriculture, reports that more than 200 Idaho farms produce specialty or value-added products. These goods typically consist of basic farm commodities that have been "dressed-up" with packaging. Consumers can choose from these products: microwave popcorn that comes on the cob and pops right off the cob, a bag of complete chili ingredients that makers claim won't cause embarrassing side-effects, and chocolate-covered "Couch Potato Chips."

Idaho farmers are supported by two groups, the Idaho Specialty Foods Association and Buy Idaho, whose goals are to help producers market and promote unique items. With the help of the groups, Idaho farmers are getting quite savvy. The marketers have discovered, for example, that packaging certain items together can increase their attractiveness. Hagerman's Rose Creek Winery found that sales of its wines soared when they were packaged in gift baskets with jars of Sun Valley brand mustard.

According to Hobbs, consumers attracted to the unique packaging provide a market for an endless variety of products, all of which are standard commodities transformed into new products through packaging. The value added through the unique packaging also provides opportunities to charge prices in ranges far above the prices of the standard products—like $18.95 for 12 potatoes!

Environmental and resource considerations. Marketers are under pressure to pay attention to the environmental impact of their packaging. Litter is always an important problem, and there is a growing concern about space for landfills. It has been estimated that packaging materials currently occupy one-third of all landfill space. Environmental and resource considerations have increased the use of recycled paper and recycled beverage containers. Patagonia, Incorporated, has begun producing jackets that contain polyester fiber spun from recycled plastic bottles.[39]

Financial and cost factors. Out of each dollar a consumer spends, approximately $.10 goes for packaging. In some product categories the figure is much higher. Packaging in the cosmetics industry, for example, accounts for almost 40 percent of the product's cost. A major change in packaging often requires new molds, dyes, and handling equipment, and thus can be very costly. For example, the cylindrical cardboard package used for Pringles potato chips costs almost twice as much as the traditional potato chip package. A marketer must be confident that a more expensive package will increase sales enough to justify the additional cost.

Government regulations. The U.S. government has been very active in regulating what marketers can and cannot say on packages. As of May 8, 1994, most food packages sold in the United States must carry a nutritional information label developed by the Food and Drug Administration.[40] Figure 9.6 illustrates the label and the information it provides. While these new requirements offer a major advancement in information for consumers, in fact the federal government has been regulating packaging for many years. The Federal Fair Packaging and Labeling Act of 1966 contained regulations about information that must be on packages. The Federal Hazardous Substances Act forbids the use of certain types of containers for

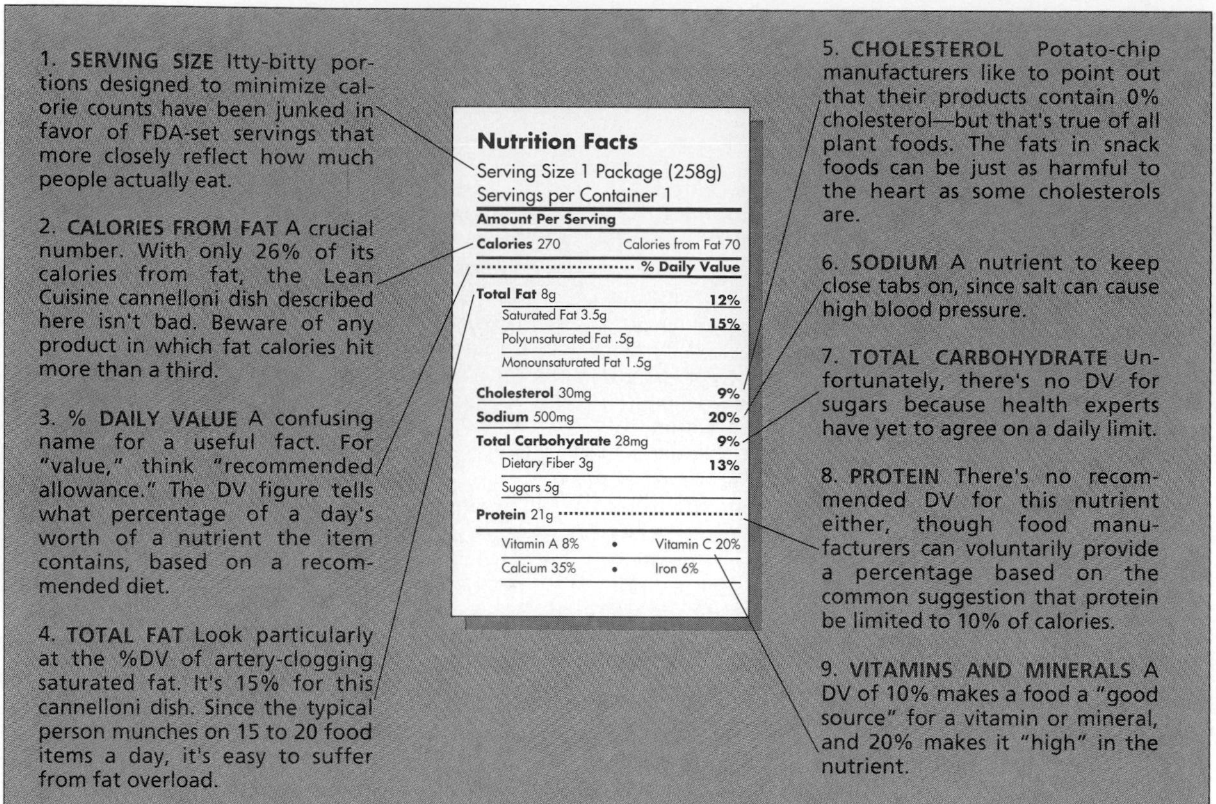

1. **SERVING SIZE** Itty-bitty portions designed to minimize calorie counts have been junked in favor of FDA-set servings that more closely reflect how much people actually eat.

2. **CALORIES FROM FAT** A crucial number. With only 26% of its calories from fat, the Lean Cuisine cannelloni dish described here isn't bad. Beware of any product in which fat calories hit more than a third.

3. **% DAILY VALUE** A confusing name for a useful fact. For "value," think "recommended allowance." The DV figure tells what percentage of a day's worth of a nutrient the item contains, based on a recommended diet.

4. **TOTAL FAT** Look particularly at the %DV of artery-clogging saturated fat. It's 15% for this cannelloni dish. Since the typical person munches on 15 to 20 food items a day, it's easy to suffer from fat overload.

5. **CHOLESTEROL** Potato-chip manufacturers like to point out that their products contain 0% cholesterol—but that's true of all plant foods. The fats in snack foods can be just as harmful to the heart as some cholesterols are.

6. **SODIUM** A nutrient to keep close tabs on, since salt can cause high blood pressure.

7. **TOTAL CARBOHYDRATE** Unfortunately, there's no DV for sugars because health experts have yet to agree on a daily limit.

8. **PROTEIN** There's no recommended DV for this nutrient either, though food manufacturers can voluntarily provide a percentage based on the common suggestion that protein be limited to 10% of calories.

9. **VITAMINS AND MINERALS** A DV of 10% makes a food a "good source" for a vitamin or mineral, and 20% makes it "high" in the nutrient.

Nutrition Facts

Serving Size 1 Package (258g)
Servings per Container 1

Amount Per Serving

Calories 270 — Calories from Fat 70

% Daily Value

Total Fat 8g	12%
Saturated Fat 3.5g	15%
Polyunsaturated Fat .5g	
Monounsaturated Fat 1.5g	
Cholesterol 30mg	9%
Sodium 500mg	20%
Total Carbohydrate 28mg	9%
Dietary Fiber 3g	13%
Sugars 5g	
Protein 21g	

Vitamin A 8%	•	Vitamin C 20%
Calcium 35%	•	Iron 6%

Source: A. Toufexis, "Know What You Eat," *Time*, May 9, 1994, p. 68.

FIGURE 9.6
New U.S. Labeling Requirements

products dangerous to ingest. The Consumer Products Safety Commission has requirements for packages, the most famous of which is the childproof aspirin bottle. Additionally, in the wake of the incident in the 1980s when Tylenol packages were tampered with, causing consumer deaths, many states have passed tamper-proof requirements for packaging. States have also outlawed certain types of packages such as nonbiodegradable packages and no-deposit, no-return beverage containers.

Consumer behavior and marketing strategy factors. A marketer is always interested in knowing how much a package will help sell the product. This, of course, depends upon consumer behavior. For example, several producers of laundry detergent have introduced highly concentrated products that can be sold in smaller packages. The smaller packages can reduce landfill space occupied by packaging as well as take less space on retailers' shelves and be lighter to carry and easier to use. It remains to be seen, however, how consumers will accept the new, smaller packages. Consumers accustomed to having a certain size package and using a certain amount of detergent per load of laundry may find it difficult to adjust their behavior to the new packaging.

Milk producers have encountered difficulties in gaining consumer acceptance of milk packaged in plastic pouches instead of plastic jugs or paper cartons. The pouches are better for the environment, more durable, space-saving, and tamper-evident. Milk in pouches stays fresh longer because of reduced potential for contamination. Despite these advantages, consumers have been slow to accept this new packaging.[41]

Consumer response to packaging can differ by country, making it important for global marketers to investigate variations in the markets they serve around the world. For example, more than 90 percent of the tennis balls sold in the United States come three to a can. Japanese consumers, however, prefer a two-pack and Europeans a four-pack.

PERSONAL COMPUTER EXERCISE

The stage of product life cycle in an industry is an important concept in determining marketing strategy for a product or brand. This PC Exercise will help you evaluate product life cycles by examining the industry characteristics of different products.

KEY POINTS

■ A product is the combination of want-satisfying attributes a consumer receives in making an exchange, including psychological as well as physical benefits.

■ Products can be described as possessing three components: the core product, the tangible product, and the augmented product.

■ Consumer goods are products purchased for use by households or ultimate consumers.

■ Consumer goods can be classified further as convenience, shopping, or specialty goods. Convenience goods can be subclassified as staples, emergency, or impulse goods. Shopping goods can be subclassified as homogeneous or heterogeneous. Different marketing strategies are required for each type of product.

■ The product life cycle consists of four stages from a product's introduction until it is taken off the market. The four stages are introduction, growth, maturity, and decline.

■ The length and shape of the product life cycle are determined by consumer needs, wants, attitudes, and behavior; the rate of technological change; competitive activity; and the organization's marketing actions.

■ A product line is a group of closely related products offered by an organization. A product mix consists of all the individual products available from one organization. Breadth of product mix is determined by the number of product lines marketed by the organization. Depth of product mix is determined by the number of sizes, models, and colors within each product line. Consistency of product mix is determined by the similarities in terms of use, distribution, and target market of the items in the product mix.

■ A brand is a name, term, symbol, design, or combination of these that identifies goods and services and distinguishes them from competitors' products. Branding has many advantages for marketers, resellers, and consumers.

■ A good brand name should identify the product and set it apart from the competition, describe the product or the function it performs, communicate the product's benefits, and be memorable and easy to pronounce.

■ Manufacturers may market their products under their own brands, or they may choose to use distributors' brands or generic brands. The organization may use individual brand names or it may apply a family brand to a line of products.

■ Packages have a functional role and a promotional role. Environmental and resource factors, financial considerations, governmental regulations, consumer behavior, and marketing strategy all influence package design.

KEY TERMS

product (279)
core product (280)
tangible product (280)
augmented product (280)
consumer product (282)
business product (282)
convenience goods (283)
staples (283)
emergency goods (283)
impulse goods (284)
shopping goods (284)
homogeneous shopping goods (284)
heterogeneous shopping goods (284)
specialty goods (285)
product life cycle (286)
product line(290)
product mix (290)
breadth of product mix (290)

depth of product mix (291)
consistency of product mix (291)
brand (291)
brand name (292)
brand mark (292)
service mark (292)
trademark (292)
co-branding (293)
manufacturer's brand (295)
national brand (295)
distributor's brand (295)
private label (295)
store brand (295)
family brand (297)
generic brand (298)
packaging (300)

ISSUES FOR DISCUSSION

1. General Electric announced it has developed a new type of lightbulb that will last five times longer than ordinary bulbs and will use only one-third the amount of electricity while generating the same amount of light. The bulb will cost $10 but will save $20 over its life in lower electric bills. Is this new lightbulb the same product as the company's traditional bulb? Describe the new bulb using the three components of product.

2. Using the classification of consumer goods, how would you classify each of the following products:
   (a) Vacation package to Hawaii
   (b) Paint for exterior of house
   (c) Leather wallet
   (d) Reebok shoes
   (e) Pepsi-Cola

3. How might your marketing mix differ if you were marketing business suits to three target markets: one that perceived the suits to be a convenience good? one that perceived them to be a shopping good? and one that perceived them to be a specialty good?

4. Where would you place cassette tape players in the product life cycle? What characteristics of that stage seem to support your view?

5. How valuable would advertising that compares your brand and a competitive brand be for a product class facing a "fad-shaped" product life cycle? Why?

6. Until recently, Kraft, Incorporated, marketed a number of food and dairy products such as Philadelphia Cream Cheese, Velveeta and other cheese products, Miracle Whip, Breyers Ice Cream, and Kraft Macaroni and Cheese. In addition, Kraft sold Tupperware products, West Bend appliances, and Duracell batteries. Recently, Kraft sold all of its nonfood product lines. Why might a company like Kraft choose to narrow its product mix? Is breadth of product mix or width of product mix more important for a company like Kraft?

7. What advantages might a company like Scott Paper see in selling distributors' brands? What are some disadvantages?

8. Coca-Cola recently introduced a fruit juice-based drink called Fruitopia. Why would the firm choose to use an individual branding strategy for the drink? What would be the advantages and disadvantages of individual and family branding in this case?

9. At the height of their popularity, research showed that there was often an inverse relationship between demand for generic products and a consumer's income. What might explain this?

10. Considering the functions of a good package, how would you rate the packages for the following products?
   (a) Pampers diapers
   (b) Coca-Cola
   (c) Yoplait yogurt
   (d) Kleenex facial tissues

CASE APPLICATION

A Growing Phenomenon—Bigger Is Beautiful

Women who wear larger than a standard misses size 12 constitute more than 30 percent of U.S. females. In the over-forty age group that figure increases to 40 percent. As a group, however, they account for only 15 percent of apparel purchases nationwide. For years, clothing manufacturers attributed this inequity to the fact that larger women were not interested in clothes. In the last five years, however, the simple truth has become increasingly apparent. Large women didn't buy much clothing because there wasn't much clothing for them to buy. Aside from Lane Bryant, the specialty retailer, for years larger women were relegated to choosing between elastic-waisted polyester pants and the inevitable muu-muu.

No more. Large-sized fashions are the hottest thing to come along in years. The trend traces its beginnings to designer Liz Claiborne. In 1989 the well-known designer introduced a line of clothing she named Elisabeth, specifically designed for and targeted to large women. Although the women to whom the clothes were targeted were not used to having such options, the line was a success almost from the beginning. By 1991, just two years after the line's introduction, sales had topped $100 million and represented 6 percent of Claiborne's volume.

Such phenomenal success, of course, has drawn the attention of other designers and competition for large-sized dollars is now fast and furious. Upscale designers such as Gianni Versace, Marina Rinaldi, and Givenchy have all begun to produce clothing for the larger woman. Industry sales grew to more than $10 billion in 1992 from a mere $2 billion ten years before. This growth, in 1990, represented a 25 percent increase in sales. During the same period sales of misses' and children's clothing increased only 7 percent.

Retailers have also responded to the phenomenon. Specialty retailers such as August Max Woman have joined Lane Bryant. The latter was purchased by The Limited in 1982 and has upgraded its merchandise to reflect the newly awakened demand sweeping the industry. Department stores have also responded by sig-

nificantly increasing the amount of floor space devoted to large-sized women's fashions. Bloomingdale's, the trendy Manhattan emporium, has expanded its Shop for Women from 8,100 to 13,500 square feet. Upscale retailer Saks Fifth Avenue, in 1992, opened an in-store boutique, devoted to large sizes, called Salon Z in many of its stores.

The target market for all these efforts at both the manufacturers' and retailers' level is clearly not only large but also affluent. The influx of competition has not, as yet, contributed to significant downward pressure on prices. August Max Woman's average-priced dress sells for $110, an average suit, $200. The Givenchy designer line, "Givenchy En Plus," ranges from $250 for a blouse to $600 for a dress. Despite these high prices, sales continue to soar.

The industry does appear to have one problem—deciding on the appropriate name for its large-sized clothes. Ever discreet, even in the face of evidence that big women are coming out of the closet, manufacturers and retailers have rarely used direct terms to describe their larger sized clothes. In addition to the aforementioned Salon Z and Elisabeth, Gianni Versace calls its line "Versatile" while Harvé Bénard has settled on "Pour la Femme." The slightly more direct "Plus Sizes" is in itself, of course, a euphemism for the large sizes. Target consumers are also "treated" to advertising that typically features models who wear size 10 or 12.

Questions

1. Describe the large-sized product lines offered by designers such as Liz Claiborne or Givenchy in terms of the total product concept defined in this chapter.
2. Using the classification of consumer goods, what type of good do you think the target market would perceive the large-sized apparel of Liz Claiborne or Givenchy to be? Why?
3. Evaluate the brand names for the clothing lines based on the criteria for a good brand name discussed in this chapter.

Moving Beyond the Core Product

This chapter has presented concepts basic to product decision making. These ideas can also be applied to you as a "product" in your career search.

The primary variables that define you as a product are your education, experience, and personal attributes. First, there is the breadth and depth of your education. What in your education demonstrates the range and focus relevant to your career objectives? Next, there is the length and level of your experience. What have you done that demonstrates your aptitude, or what you know you can do well? And finally, there are your personal attributes, with emphasis on communication and interpersonal skills. Where and how have you shown the capability to work with and through others?

The concept of the "augmented product" applies to your career search. You must distinguish yourself from others who have capabilities similar to yours, to move beyond the "core product." For example, your experience as a teaching assistant in college can add something extra to your academic record. This role indicates a special mastery of one of your key courses of study. Also, a series of internships that are tightly tied to your career objectives will distinguish you from others. Activities such as founding a professional organization or serving as a class officer can also set you apart.

The concept of "product life cycle" might seem to have little application to your career search. However, you need to have a long-range perspective of yourself as a product. Sometimes one's education can run the danger of obsolescence or one can miss opportunities to take courses that will be useful at a later stage in a career. In summary, you need to visualize yourself as a "product," from the viewpoint of your target employers. This understanding of self forms the foundation to effectively develop and manage yourself as a product, as covered in the next chapter.

Questions

1. Think of two or three of your target organizations that are significantly different. How would you describe yourself as a "product" (i.e., education, experience, and personal attributes) according to the needs of each organization?
2. As you consider your education, experience, and personal profile, what features might fall into the concept of "product augmentation" (that is, what are your significant extras)?
3. What examples can you cite where you have shaped your education or experience to meet longer range career needs or to expose yourself to a futuristic perspective?

CHapTeR 10

Product Development and Management

LEARNING OBJECTIVES

Upon completing this chapter, you will be able to do the following:

■ **Understand** the importance of product innovation.

■ **Identify** the types of new-product opportunities that exist for a firm.

■ **Describe** the development process for new products.

■ **Explain** why many new products fail.

■ **Identify** factors that contribute to successful new products.

■ **Understand** how the product life cycle concept can be used to plan strategy.

■ **Discuss** the process of modifying existing product lines.

■ **Describe** the importance of quality and marketing's role in delivering it.

Marketing Profile

Making a Healthy Choice When It Comes to New Products

According to Charles M. Harper, chairman of ConAgra, Incorporated, the Healthy Choice line of frozen dinners began with his own heart attack, which had been brought on by years of "eating anything I could get my hands on." As he lay in the hospital recuperating, Harper imagined a line of healthy frozen foods that tasted good. By 1991 the line, introduced in 1988, held a 40 percent market share with annual sales above $350 million. By 1993, Healthy Choice entrees represented annual retail sales that exceeded $400 million and a 12.8 percent share of the frozen dinner and entree market.

The Healthy Choice product line was carefully tested with consumers before being introduced to the general population. ConAgra's research and development staff spent a year working under the directive, "whatever the cost, don't sacrifice taste." The first test market results surprised even the ConAgra team. The low-sodium, low-fat, low-cholesterol frozen entrees sold much better than expected. According to the firm's vice president of marketing and sales, "We benefited from low expectations, [the products] were much better than people thought [they] would be." This finding supported ConAgra's decision to position the product against other high-quality frozen dinners rather than as a diet or health food.

The new product's brand name and packaging were an important part of the development process. The name *Healthy Choice* was chosen for the positive connotation it held for consumers. Because ConAgra felt the product would be an impulse purchase, it was important to make the items stand out in the freezer case. This was accomplished through the dark green packaging that not only differed from the competition but also suggested freshness and nutritive value.

In 1991 the firm expanded Healthy Choice to include soups, spaghetti sauce, seafood, and desserts. By 1992 Healthy Choice extra-lean ground beef, cold cuts, and hot dogs could also be found in your local supermarket. In 1993 the firm partnered with Kellogg's to introduce Healthy Choice breakfast cereal. The company plans to continue its expansion. States Stephen Hughes, the vice president of marketing and sales, "We're always looking for new opportunities; we feel there's still a lot of potential." New products all carry the Healthy Choice brand name, utilize the distinctive Healthy Choice packaging, and are targeted to the same health-conscious upscale consumer.

Despite the success that ConAgra has enjoyed with Healthy Choice, the company remains conscious of the high risk associated with introducing new products. Hughes recognizes that "The price of failure is very high, heads definitely roll [when a product fails]." Though it appears ConAgra left little to chance with Healthy Choice, the company still credits much of its success to good timing. "It was the right product at the right time," says Hughes.

he Marketing Profile on ConAgra's Healthy Choice shows that new products can rejuvenate humdrum sales and prove extremely valuable to an organization. However, successful new products do not just happen by chance. A great deal of research as well as careful design and planning—and perhaps a little luck—are necessary for a company to find the success that ConAgra has achieved with Healthy Choice.

Chapter 9 introduced the basic concepts of product, including branding and packaging issues. It also described the ways to classify and conceptualize products. In this chapter we discuss the process of developing new product and evaluate why products fail or succeed. We conclude with an overview of product management and a topic of growing importance—quality issues in marketing.

OPPORTUNITIES FOR NEW PRODUCTS

Rubbermaid, selected by *Fortune Magazine* as "America's Most Admired Company" for 1993, is an example of a company committed to new-product development. In 1993, the housewares division of the Ohio-based maker of rubber and plastic products averaged a new (not just improved) product for every day of the year. This would not be a particularly impressive feat if the products bombed, as so many products do in today's marketplace. But few Rubbermaid products are bombs; nine out of ten hit their commercial targets. As one of Rubbermaid's competitors puts it, "They're [i.e., Rubbermaid] in a class by themselves." The firm attributes its success ($1.8 billion in sales in 1993) to its dedication to new-product development and its commitment to habitually pumping 14 percent of profits into research and development (R&D).[1]

New Products Classified by Degree of Change

A new product may be classified as an innovation, a modification, or a "me-too." **Innovations** are products that provide new and different means of satisfying wants and needs. An innovation represents a completely new product category, one that is just beginning its product life cycle. Development of an innovation means high risk and demands a considerable investment of time, money, and other company resources. On the other hand, the introduction of a truly new product category usually means huge payoffs for the innovator. When they were first developed and introduced, televisions, birth control pills, microwave ovens, and fax machines were innovations. Now, changes in these products are modifications.

Modifications occur when an existing product is changed in some significant way. Modifications can be immensely profitable, if successful, and usually do not risk major losses of finances or other resources associated with innovation. The Healthy Choice line discussed in the Marketing Profile is a modification of existing products. Palmolive Ultra, a recently introduced, boasts a new enzyme technology to remove dried-on food and tough stains from dishes. Sterling Health introduced another modification, Bayer Select, a new line of cold and flu products developed to target specific symptoms.

Me-toos are products that are new to a firm but not new to the marketplace. Companies create "me-toos" because they believe there is room in the market for another competitor, and the projected returns outweigh the risks. For example, when McDonald's decided to enter the fast-food breakfast business, its product was new to the company even though a fast-food breakfast was not new to the market. Procter & Gamble has entered the "me-too" game with both disposable training pants and ultra-thin diapers—two offerings that enable the firm to play catch-up with diaper developments by Kimberly-Clark.[2]

New Products Classified by Role in the Product–Market Strategy

When a firm introduces a product that has a new brand name and is in a product category new to the organization, it is classified as a **new product**. Maxwell House's Cappio, a presweetened, ready-to-drink coffee product designed to be drunk cold, is an example of a new product of this type. If the product that is developed uses a new brand name, but is introduced into a category where the organization already has products, the new item is called a **flanker brand**. Hershey Foods' Hugs candy is a flanker to its Kisses and other candies.

If a firm produces new flavors, sizes, or models using an existing brand name in an existing category, they are called **line extensions**. Ben & Jerry's Chocolate Chip Cookie Dough ice cream, Kellogg's Rice Krispies Treats cereal, and Cool Mint Listerine are examples of line extensions. The strategy of continually expanding the line by adding new models has enabled companies like Seiko (watches), Casio (calculators), and Campbell's (soup) to tie up a substantial amount of shelf space and consumer attention in a product category.

A **technological extension** is use of an existing product in a new category, which then stimulates primary demand. Computer technology, through the development of word processing software, was applied to writing letters, memos, articles, books, reports, and other manuscripts. Thus demand grew for hardware and software systems that would take the place of typewriters. Table 10.1 gives examples of technical extensions in broadcast technology that should soon be evident in the marketplace.

The fifth classification is **franchise extension**. A firm introduces a product into a new category, using an existing brand name. Examples of franchise extensions

The introduction of new flavors using an existing brand name in an existing category is considered a line extension.

Technology	Status	Forecast
VCRs with commercial zapping ability	Introduced in Japan in 1990; currently not adaptable to U.S. TVs.	Most Americans, especially educated and upper-income people, would be likely to make this purchase. But ethical and legal questions may arise, and countertechnology may be developed.
"Intelligent" remote-control wands that can be programmed to operate a number of devices	Available since the mid-1980s. The Memorex CP8 can control television, VCR, satellite systems, cable television, CD, audio receiver, and two auxiliary inputs.	A large majority of young adults would like to purchase such a system, but acceptance declines with age. Blacks, Hispanics, and households with children are likely target markets. A prototype from Frox Inc. can read TV listings, select and record programs, and delete commercials.
Compact Disc Interactive (CD-I), a multimedia home entertainment/educational system	The Phillips CD1910, selling for about $1,000, is the only unit currently available to consumers. Software discs sell from $19.95 to $59.95.	When the price falls below $500, more will buy this new technology. The best customers are aged 18 to 44.
Flat Panel Television, thin enough to be mounted on the wall	Sharp and Matsushita have unveiled versions of this product in Japan, selling for about $4,000.	Available by the turn of the century. Acceptance will have an upscale skew, but will reach most Americans.
Cable radio for static-free listening	A handful of companies are currently transmitting, primarily in major metropolitan areas. More are on the way.	By 2001, a small number of cable radio companies will dominate the market in larger metropolitan areas. The prime users will be men aged 18 to 44.
High Definition Television (HDTV) with the clarity of film	The technology exists, and the FCC has ordered a 15-year transition period for the U.S. Japan has been broadcasting HDTV since 1990, but a typical set costs $35,000.	HDTVs will be operating in homes across the U.S. by the turn of the century. The cost of the technology will be a major factor influencing widespread acceptance, but 58 percent of Americans are potential buyers.

include the GM (General Motors) [credit] Card and Reese's Peanut Butter. Franchise extensions allow the organization to build on consumer awareness, goodwill, and image of its established brand name. Extensions also reduce the amount of money the firm needs to invest in the new product. A franchise extension quickly conveys to the consumer many of the attributes of the old product, allowing the organization to enter the new category from a position of strength. However, consumer perception of the new item must be consistent with perception of the brand name. Thus, Reese's Peanut Butter is a logical extension of the Reese's franchise, but Reese's ketchup would not be.

TABLE 10.1
What's Next and When: Here's the Forecast for Broadcast Technology in the 1990s

There is some risk in franchise extension—the potential of diluting the brand franchise in the long run. For years Coca-Cola has had a policy of limiting the use of its brand name to its flagship brand; after much debate, Coca-Cola executives decided to extend the brand name to Diet Coke.

Many companies work on a portfolio of new products so that at any one time they have a full pipeline of different types of new products in various stages of development. At 3M, for example, 10 to 15 percent of the budget for new-product development is spent on improving products in the company's existing product lines. Another 10 to 15 percent is spent on joint projects with manufacturing, pursuing ways to make 3M's products cheaper or better. Slightly more than 50 percent of the budget is aimed at finding completely new products both related and unrelated to the company's current lines of business. The remaining 15 percent is for longer term projects on the technological edge.[3] In contrast, some firms concentrate their new-product efforts on just one particular type of new product if they feel that strategy can best take advantage of company strengths. For example, a firm strong in the area of research and development may wish to focus its efforts on the introduction of innovative products. A second firm, weaker in technological research and development skills but strong in manufacturing skills that produce economies and lower prices, may decide to concentrate on the introduction of me-too products.

An example of the former situation is Glaxo, Britain's most valuable company and the world's second largest maker of prescription drugs. Glaxo marshalls its resources behind a few probable winners. And many industry observers believe Glaxo has the most promising pipeline of new products in the business. Three new drugs—Zofran, which is used in postchemotherapy recovery; Serevent, the long-lasting asthma treatment; and Imigran, an anti-migraine drug—are promising products that could each eventually reach annual sales of $1 billion. But Glaxo confines its research to a narrow range of about eight therapeutic categories: antiulcerants, respiratory drugs, and migraine treatment are examples.[4]

As discussed in Chapter 3, the product–market opportunity matrix, determined at the corporate level, is useful for many companies in planning strategy. The product–market strategy is associated with four approaches to managing products and markets: diversification, market development, product development, and market penetration. As Table 10.2 shows, different types of new products are most likely to be linked with specific approaches. For example, if a firm's objective is diversification, its strategy should be to develop a completely new product or a franchise extension. Consequently, this classification of new products helps marketers identify opportunities across a spectrum of strategic options.

TABLE 10.2
Types of Newness to the Firm

Corporate Strategy	New Product	Typical Extent of Newness
Diversification	• Completely new • Brand franchise extension	• New market • New technology probable
Market development	• Technical extension • Change in form	• New use • User-related technology
Product development	• Line extension • Flanker	• New segment • New technology possible
Market penetration	• Product modification (to meet or beat competition)	• No change in market • Small change in technology

Source: J. P. Guiltinan and G. W. Paul, *Marketing Management: Strategies and Programs,* 5th ed. (New York: McGraw-Hill, 1994), p. 198.

DEVELOPMENT OF NEW PRODUCTS

How do companies develop new products? The consulting firm of Booz, Allen & Hamilton has studied the product development process for more than 30 years, conducting numerous studies of the steps companies take to develop new products. The most successful developers of new products, the research has found, first clearly define the company's mission, objectives, and overall corporate strategy. They also define the company's commitment to new products and determine the current situation by analyzing the external environment and assessing the company's internal strengths and weaknesses with respect to new-product development. Once all this analysis is done, the most common process in product development consists of seven stages: new product strategy development, idea generation, screening and evaluation, business analysis, development, testing, and commercialization.[5] These stages are shown Figure 10.1.

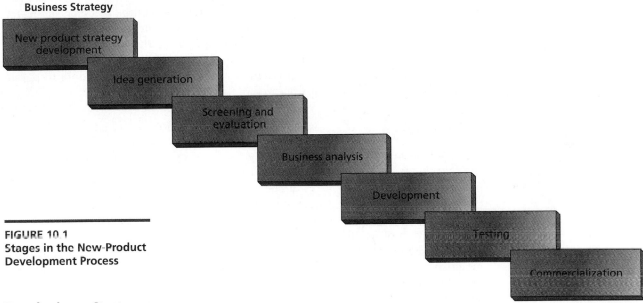

Business Strategy

New product strategy development

Idea generation

Screening and evaluation

Business analysis

Development

Testing

Commercialization

Commercialized Products

Source: Booz, Allen & Hamilton, Inc.

**FIGURE 10.1
Stages in the New-Product Development Process**

Developing a Strategy

A firm's new-product strategy is developed after having completed a situation analysis. The major parts of the strategy include defining parameters for the new products, the overall goals for the new-product activity, and the programs to achieve the goals. The strategy statement containing these parameters, goals, and programs is called the **product innovation charter (PIC)**.[6]

The parameters part of the PIC includes a definition of the product category or categories for the new products the company wants to develop and a definition of the customers for the new products. The product category may be defined by product type or class or by end-use application. For example, when Kellogg's announced it would concentrate its new-product efforts on developing new cereals, it was using a category defined by type or class. It was not interested in fast-food chains, toys, or other categories. Note that it did not refer to "breakfast meals" or to "products sold by supermarkets." Hence the development of Rice Krispies Treats cereal, which can be enjoyed for snacking, is consistent with this PIC. A cereal developed specifically for institutional uses would also be consistent with this PIC.

The PIC may also specify the technology that the firm will use to develop the new products. The definition of customers would include a statement outlining whether the company was seeking more business from current users or from new users. It might define the target customers in terms of demographics, psychographics, or other dimensions.

The goals of the new-product activity would be stated in terms of growth (rapid versus controlled), market share, (aggressively seeking an increase versus protecting current share), and sales and profit targets. Other goals might be to diversify, to add to current product lines, or to achieve a certain return on investment.

The last part of the PIC states specific programs to achieve the goals. This might include a statement of whether the new-product activity is to be primarily market-driven (guided by customers or competitors) or technology-driven (guided by the firm's technical capabilities). It might state the degree of innovation to be used, pioneering versus imitative, for example. A pioneering strategy usually has a higher payoff, but it is also much riskier than a strategy of imitating competitors. Many firms thus prefer to let their competitors innovate and then try quickly to copy and improve the innovation, thus producing a me-too product.

It is true that each company must develop a PIC that is compatible with that company's specific situation. However, many experts believe that U.S. managers avoid genuine innovation in favor of me-toos and line extensions, which are safe variations of existing products. For example, Japanese companies receive 44 percent of revenues from innovative products, while U.S. companies receive 28 percent of revenues from such ventures. Innovation experts say that the United States has brilliant scientists and engineers but few managers who know how to drive the creative process. Additionally, few companies allow executives the freedom to pursue a risky idea without penalty for failure.[7]

Idea Generation

Idea generation is the brainstorming stage of the product development process. It is the search for ideas for new products that are consistent with an organization's objectives. Because many ideas are needed, a firm cannot afford to rely only on its research and development people to produce an adequate number. Hence, many firms receive new-product ideas from a variety of sources. These include competitors, outside inventors, customers, intermediaries, and others.

Toro, a maker of mowers and other lawn equipment, keeps an independent inventor on retainer. Bob Comer, who has worked under contract for 23 years, invented an aerator for golf greens that did not tear up the green's surface. When launched, Toro's HydroJect outsold the competition two to one.[8]

Some firms even reward employees who come up with ideas for new products. Bell Atlantic uses a Champion program. Any employee who has a promising idea can leave his or her job for a specified time to receive training in writing a business plan and organizing a development schedule. The employee receives full pay and benefits during training. The champion can invest 10 percent of salary in the project, give up the bonus, and reap a 5 percent return on revenues (subject to restrictions) if the product gets to market. In its first two years, the program generated two patents and 11 more pending.[9]

Rubbermaid encourages its employees to look at what the company already does well. Bud Hellman, who used to run a Rubbermaid subsidiary, was touring one of the company's picnic-cooler plants when he had a great idea. Why not use the plastic blow-molding techniques to make a durable, lightweight, and inexpensive line of office furniture? The result: the Work Manager System, which now accounts for 60 percent of sales in Rubbermaid's furniture division.[10]

Ideas can also be the unexpected result of R&D efforts. In the case of 3M's Post-It Notes, for example, R&D personnel were attempting to produce a new super adhesive but kept turning up with one that would adhere easily, and detach just as easily. Only after shelving the product for a year did it occur to someone that while they had not produced what they had originally intended, there could be value in what *was* produced.[11] Figure 10.2 shows sources of new product ideas.

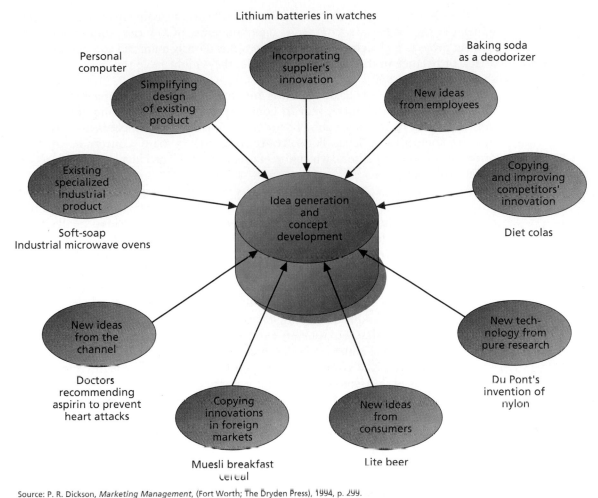

Source: P. R. Dickson, *Marketing Management*, (Fort Worth; The Dryden Press), 1994, p. 299.

FIGURE 10.2
Sources of Ideas for New Products

Screening and Evaluation

Screening and evaluation involve analyzing the ideas developed during the idea generation stage to determine which merit detailed study. Because the later steps in the process of product development—from business analysis through testing—can be very expensive, preliminary screening is essential to identify the better ideas from among the many possibilities. During the screening stage, an organization attempts to avoid two types of errors—a "go error," which occurs when the firm continues to evaluate an idea that will not be successful, and a "no-go error," which occurs when the firm discards an idea that might lead to a successful new product. It is important, therefore, that the criteria for the screening be neither too rigid nor too loose.

Early evaluation is designed to assess whether a true opportunity exists in the market. The firm's own technological resources will be considered as well as the competitive situation. Companies should also ask themselves whether the new idea fits into the company's PIC. The purpose of the evaluation step is to keep companies out of markets where they stand little chance of winning against competitors.

The new idea should be evaluated in the context of the company's product development portfolio. Healthy companies maintain a mix of low-risk, short-term development projects and high-risk, long-term projects. Poorly managed companies reflect a lack of balance in this area—for example, they might have too many high-risk, short-term projects.

One critical activity at this point is anticipation by project managers of major difficulties. These, of course, vary by company. For some food manufacturers, the difficulties may be creating a good flavor or keeping the cost of ingredients within the limits of competitive pricing. For software companies, a major concern has become price-cutting by competitors, which forces everyone in the product category to accept lower profit margins.

As you can see, companies should use a variety of evaluation procedures at this point in the development process. New-product ideas are often filtered through several successive evaluative tests before they are turned over for business analysis and then for development.

It is also important for an organization to identify the criteria to evaluate new ideas. One of the major approaches is to develop checklists to judge specific new-product ideas. A checklist used in the very early stage of the screening process would compare each idea with the objectives set for new products. For example, does the idea fit the type of products the company wants to introduce? Is the required production process one that the company can perform? Can the item be handled by the existing distribution channels and sales force? Is the potential market for the product large enough, and is the growth rate acceptable? The more thoroughly the organization has defined the criteria, the easier it is to screen out unacceptable ideas. Some organizations have separated the screening into two categories—criteria that must be met, and criteria that are desirable but not absolutely required. Table 10.3 presents screening criteria used by Johnson Wax Company.

TABLE 10.3
Screening Criteria Used by Johnson Wax

Product Criteria	Marketing Criteria	Financial Criteria
▪ Is it safe? ▪ How will it affect environment? ▪ Does it fit with existing technology, facilities, and skills? ▪ Is it high value added (vs. a commodity)? ▪ Is it a significant improvement for consumers? ▪ Is it compatible with packaging capabilities? ▪ Do we have a proprietary position? ▪ Is there opportunity for logical extensions? ▪ Is labor content average or below? ▪ What is the extended product life cycle (years vs. months)?	▪ Does it use marketing capabilities? ▪ Does it use existing sales force? ▪ Does it have high advertising/promotion content? ▪ Is there opportunity to expand overseas? ▪ Does it use existing distribution channels? ▪ Can we establish a leadership role in the market? ▪ Is it a major investment for consumers? ▪ Is there market growth potential?	▪ What is the potential for profit? ▪ What is the profit/risk ratio? ▪ How much working capital is required? ▪ Are capital requirements average or below? ▪ How much time to achieve positive cash flow?

Source: R. L. DeRose, "New Products—Sifting Through the Haystack," *The Journal of Consumer Marketing,* Summer 1986, pp. 81–84.

The other major part of the screening process is the use of **concept tests.** These consist of reactions from individual consumers or small groups of consumers to new-product ideas and concepts. A firm may use a focus group, as described in Chapter 8, personal interviews, or consumer panels to gather these reactions. Concept testing is especially relevant for new products that will require a change in consumer purchasing behavior. The success of Bayer Select, for example, depends on consumers adjusting to the purchase of several different Bayer products, keyed to different cold and flu symptoms. Concept testing would provide insight into consumers' reactions to this required change in purchasing behavior. Concept testing may not be applicable, however, to true innovations—products totally new to the marketplace—because consumers may have difficulty forming or even understanding the new concepts. For example, a concept test for facsimile transmission when the technology was being developed might have been of little value.

Concept tests are helpful in determining the relevant market for a concept, identifying product attributes or benefits that are likely determinants of brand choice, defining how the concept is perceived relative to existing alternatives, describing consumers' behavior with respect to the new concept, and predicting consumers' preferences.[12]

Business Analysis

At the **business analysis** stage, the surviving ideas are evaluated according to the organization's requirements for initial estimates of sales, market share, profit, or return on investment. This analysis often requires detailed studies of markets and competition as well as of costs and technical inputs. The purpose of this stage is to obtain a concrete business recommendation about the potential profitability of implementing the idea. The company must estimate sales, costs, and profitability before the product moves to the development stage. If the product clearly will not be able to meet the organization's objectives on these measures, then the investment in development can be shifted to products that are more likely to meet stated objectives. The key variables to determine are demand (sales), production and financial requirements, and compatibility with organizational objectives and policies.

Demand.   The key to determining demand is the estimation of market potential for the product and estimation of the company's anticipated market share. In the case of new products designed for markets with which the company is already familiar, it may be relatively easy to estimate market potential. But estimates for products in new markets, such as the first home computer, trash compactor, or a new chemical process, may be extremely difficult. The manager must not only estimate the sales of the new product, but also must evaluate its probable impact on the organization's other products. In particular, it is important to avoid the cannibalization of the company's other products. **Cannibalization** occurs when sales of a new product come at the expense of sales of other products in the product line. Thus, if Coca-Cola were to introduce a new root beer, it would want to make sure that the bulk of sales did not come at the expense of the company's Coca-Cola sales.

To estimate sales it is important to analyze four major elements: trial, first repeat, adoption, and frequency of purchase.[13] Early sales are primarily a function of the rate at which consumers try a new product and purchase it again. Over time, sales levels are determined by the proportion of consumers who adopt the product and the frequency with which they purchase it. In order to predict these sales, additional research may be necessary to determine consumers' behavior. This analysis is often easier for business products than for consumer products because information from a small number of potential customers may be all that is needed to make these predictions.

Production and financial requirements.   In addition to sales estimates, it is important to have a good estimate of costs to determine the likely profitability of a new product. The more similar the new product is to existing products, the easier it will be to estimate costs. Along with production costs, it is necessary to estimate capital and marketing costs. If new equipment or production facilities are required, and if substantial marketing costs, such as the establishment of new channels of distribution or extensive promotion, will be incurred, accurate estimates of the required capital must be determined. Marketing managers need to understand the financial investment required before approving or initiating substantial development expenses. If the company is unlikely to invest the required amount of money, the new product should not be developed.

Organizational objectives and policies.   Estimates of sales, costs, and investment must be examined in light of the organization's objectives and policies. For example, some companies have a policy that all new products can lose money for the first two years, but must break even by the end of the third year and must recoup losses from the first two years by the end of the fifth year. Other organizations have objectives that require a new product to have a given sales potential (for example, $1 million). Still other firms have a policy that allows development only of products likely to have a return on investment greater than 20 percent (or some other target number). Some organizations only look at profitability, others use return on investment, and still others discount cash flows to determine the present value of alternative new-product opportunities.

Development

After a product has made it through the business analysis stage, it then enters the development stage. Here the research and development (R&D) personnel, often with the help of engineers, will construct the actual product, transforming it from merely an idea or concept into a prototype model. At the same time, a tentative marketing mix is developed, including the package and label, brand name, advertising message, and distribution strategy. A firm that begins with product development, before passing through the stages already discussed, is operating with a production orientation.

At the development stage, the product's technical feasibility is determined. The company should be able to produce the good at a cost that will enable it to be marketed at an acceptable price to the consumer. The development stage often requires a large investment. It is not unusual to spend millions of dollars developing a new product, and many products take years to develop. One reason the process takes so long is that the firm must first build a prototype and test it with consumers, then it might develop a revised version which will be tested again with consumers. This process may occur a number of times, until the firm develops a product that meets consumers' needs, or until the project is abandoned. If the product requires approval from the government due to uncertainties regarding its safety in use, that approval can also slow the development process. The "Marketing in Action: Does Fake Fat Have a Future?" illustrates how lengthy the process of obtaining government approval can be.

The development process works best when the members of the research and development group are guided by marketing and financial considerations. They should be provided a detailed description of the product concept and the customer so they have some idea of the target market. The team should receive a clear statement of the benefits desired by the consumers and the relative importance of each benefit. They also need to be given targets for pricing and costs and variations in style, size, or flavor. Finally, they should know the probable channels of distribution and

MARKETING IN ACTION

Does Fake Fat Have a Future?

Just think of it . . . French fries, chocolate chip cookies, creamy salad dressings . . . all guilt-free because of olestra. Olestra is a fat substitute that exhibits fatlike properties (smells, cooks, and tastes like the real stuff) but passes through the body without being absorbed. The result: no-fat goodies that look and taste the same as their high-fat counterparts.

Sound too good to be true? That remains to be seen. Discovered in 1968 by two scientists employed, at the time, by Procter & Gamble, 26 years later the product still has not received approval from the Food and Drug Administration (FDA) of the U.S. government.

The history of Procter & Gamble's fight to win approval from the FDA to market olestra is rocky. The company started the process in 1975 by filing an application that defined olestra as a drug rather than a food. Actually, it preferred that olestra be accepted as a food, but the route to approval for a new drug seemed more direct. Because some studies had shown that olestra reduced cholesterol, the company felt a drug application was the best path to quick approval. This approach had to be abandoned in 1985 when additional tests could not support the claims for reducing cholesterol. In 1987 the company filed an application for olestra as a food additive. Confident that approval would be forthcoming, Procter & Gamble announced its new product to the world on May 7, 1987. Its stock jumped 10 percent in two days.

Believing that approval would come in 18 to 24 months, Procter & Gamble quickly assembled an 80-person team to begin marketing plans for the product. Brand names, positioning strategy (as a "food brand" or as an ingredient?), and promotion were debated. An advertising agency was retained. Meanwhile the firm pressed hard on the public relations and publicity fronts. The company was anxious to keep olestra on the public's mind.

Unfortunately the optimism was premature. In 1988 and 1989 it was announced that research studies performed on rats suggested that olestra was related to health risks including leukemia, premature death, and deformed offspring.

Consumer activists and Unilever, a Proctor & Gamble competitor that is also developing a fat substitute, called for more testing. The FDA agreed and in 1989 a new three-year study of effects in rats was mandated. In 1990 a three-year study on pigs was called for. A Procter & Gamble attorney, Peter Hutt, predicted in 1994 that approval could still be two years away.

As the drama to win FDA approval lengthened, the company's enthusiasm for committing resources to the development of a marketing plan waned. In 1989 the company eliminated the "stand-alone" division that had been created in 1987 for olestra. Olestra marketing responsibilities were taken on by its Edible Oils Division. Feeling that FDA approval was a long way off, in 1990 the company dismissed the advertising agency it had retained.

Procter & Gamble remains committed to its "new" product. To date the firm has spent almost $300 million on olestra. Marketing plans are moving much slower than they were in the late 1980s. However, despite talk that olestra, when and if it is approved, will first be introduced in Pringles potato chips, Pringles' ad agency claims it is not working on a campaign. Proctor & Gamble will not even begin to build a manufacturing plant—a process likely to take at least 18 months—until after FDA approval occurs.

All the excitement may be somewhat anticlimactic for Procter & Gamble. The company's series of patents on the olestra molecule were set to expire in 1994. It requested a special ten-year extension (to start when FDA approval occurs) citing delays in the review process that were beyond the company's control. Competitor Unilever protested the request, claiming the delays were the result of poor marketing decisions and lack of diligence on Proctor & Gamble's part. In December 1993, President Clinton agreed to two one-year extensions. If the FDA approves olestra by 1996, Proctor & Gamble can request another two-year extension. It seems clear that if olestra is approved, Proctor & Gamble will face competition before the year 2000.

how the product will be shipped. The more information that marketing provides, the more likely it is that the new product will meet the needs of the target consumers at an acceptable price.

An increasingly important aspect of development is product safety. The Consumer Product Safety Act of 1972 created the Consumer Product Safety Commission and gave it broad powers to mandate safety standards for virtually all consumer products. Manufacturers are required to conduct a "reasonable testing program" to ensure that their products conform to established safety standards. In addition, the law of product liability has been changing. The old rules held manufacturers and sellers liable only when they were negligent, or unreasonably careless, in what they made or how they made it. Today the courts are using a much tougher standard, **strict liability.** Under this concept, if a defect in a product is legally established, the manufacturer is liable, regardless of the precautions taken.[14]

Recently, a huge legal settlement was announced in the breast implant suit. The settlement is worth more than $4.3 billion. Under terms of the agreement, women who received silicone breast implants during the past 30 years will receive payments from $200,000 to $2 million for diagnosis, treatment, and removal of leaking silicone breast implants. Companies who will be contributing to the settlement fund include 3M, Dow Corning, Bristol-Myers Squibb, and Baxter International.[15]

Testing

After the product and marketing programs have been developed, they may be subjected to testing in the marketplace. A **test market** is the introduction of a product and marketing program to actual customers, under controlled conditions and in limited geographical areas, to determine its probable sales and profits. The test market is the firm's first chance to see how the product will perform in the actual marketplace before it commits to a national roll out. A test market reduces the probability of bringing out a new product that will eventually fail under normal marketing conditions.

Another benefit of test marketing is that the company can learn how to market the new product most effectively. For example, Vaseline Intensive Care Lotion was tested in three markets. In two of the markets advertising was used, and in the third market, a combination of advertising and sampling was tried. The greater success in the third market led the company to introduce the product nationally using a combination of sampling and advertising.[16] Lever left its Lever 2000, a combination deodorant and moisturizer soap, in the Atlanta test market for two years before its national introduction. Lever 2000 went on to become one of the biggest new-product successes in recent decades.[17] Similarly, Maxwell House's Cappio spent three years in the test market before being introduced nationally.[18]

At this stage of the new-product development process, the organization can test variations in the product or in the marketing mix, including alternative names, prices, and advertising budgets or messages. Depending on the results of the test market, the product can be introduced nationally, withdrawn, or sent back to the product development stage for modifications in the product or marketing program.

Despite the value of the information provided by a test market, this strategy is becoming increasingly uncommon.[19] Test marketing is very expensive and time consuming. A test market also provides the competition an opportunity to learn about the new product. A single test market typically costs more than $1 million and it is not at all unusual for the market testing of a given product to cost well over $2 million. The length of time required slows market introduction, and the visibility creates a risk that the competition will study the product, imitate it quickly, and enter the national market before the lengthy test market has even been completed. Furthermore, a competitor could invalidate a test market through various actions. A competitor, for example, could run extensive promotions, including coupons and mass media advertising, thus making it difficult for Maxwell House to determine the real sales of Cappio under normal market conditions.

Firms that decide to skip test marketing may decide to substitute an alternative means of testing. Alternatives to traditional twelve- to eighteen-month test markets include:

Before its national introduction, Lever 2000 was in the Atlanta test market for two years. The product subsequently became one of the biggest new-product successes in recent years.

- *Pretesting.* A few consumers are shown samples of new products along with ads for those products, to gauge probable response.
- *Computer modeling.* The firm uses historical data on similar products to compute small samples of data into sales projections.
- *Rolling the dice.* The company introduces a new product region by region, fixing ads and promotions along the way to a national launch.
- *Foreign fling.* The firm introduces the new product in one overseas market and then rolls it out globally if it meets expectations.[20]

Additional alternatives, including a simulated test market conducted in a store-like laboratory, may be used instead of a full test market.

In choosing where to test a new product, it is important to select "typical" markets. This means that the population in the cities selected should be representative of the national market—with respect to the product category—for such demographic characteristics as age, income, occupation, and buying habits. The competing products should be as similar as possible to those in the national marketplace, and the media available should also be representative. It is helpful if the test market city is relatively isolated, giving the firm better control of the distribution and media exposure, as well as making it more difficult for competitors to disrupt the test. In addition, the market must have retailers who will cooperate. Finally, the market should have research services that can collect the necessary information to evaluate the success of the new product on such measures as new-product awareness, trial, repeat buying, attractiveness to different market segments, and whether new-product sales are cutting into those of the company's other products or into those of the competition. Cities used recently for test markets include New Orleans, Louisiana; Denver, Colorado; Norfolk, Virginia; Rochester and Buffalo, New York.[21] Figure 10.3 shows

FIGURE 10.3
The Most Popular U.S. Test Markets

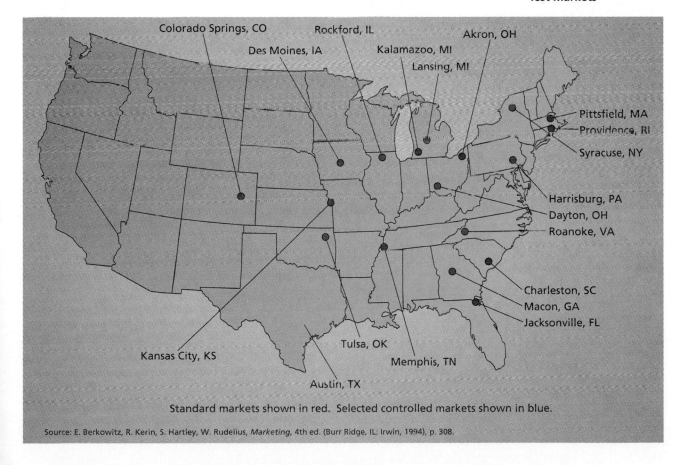

Standard markets shown in red. Selected controlled markets shown in blue.

Source: E. Berkowitz, R. Kerin, S. Hartley, W. Rudelius, *Marketing*, 4th ed. (Burr Ridge, IL: Irwin, 1994), p. 308.

Rank*	Place	1990 Population	Cumulative Index	Housing Value Index	Age Index	Race Index
1	Tulsa, OK	367,000	26.1	18.9	1.8	5.4
2	Charleston, WV	57,000	28.4	14.2	8.2	6.0
3	Midland, TX	89,000	31.4	18.2	7.4	5.8
4	Springfield, IL	105,000	32.4	22.8	3.4	6.3
5	Lexington-Fayette, KY	225,000	33.5	21.0	6.9	5.5
6	Wichita, KS	304,000	33.8	27.5	3.9	2.4
7	Bloomington, IL	52,000	34.0	17.3	6.1	10.6
8	Oklahoma City, OK	445,000	34.6	25.0	2.2	7.4
9	Indianapolis, IN	731,000	35.0	20.8	3.7	10.6
10	Rockford, IL	139,000	35.8	28.7	3.3	3.8
11	Longview, TX	70,000	36.0	25.9	2.3	7.8
12	Lafayette, LA	94,000	36.2	16.4	4.7	15.1
13	Omaha, NE	336,000	36.8	29.8	2.4	4.6
14	Phoenix, AZ	983,000	37.3	24.7	4.4	8.1
15	Gastonia, NC	55,000	37.4	21.4	3.2	12.8
16	Dallas, TX	1,007,000	37.8	4.5	7.3	26.0
17	Jacksonville, FL	635,000	38.4	21.2	4.0	13.2
18	Edmond, OK	52,000	38.8	17.7	7.9	13.2
19	High Point, NC	69,000	38.8	18.5	2.2	18.1
20	Salt Lake City, UT	160,000	39.1	21.5	7.3	10.3

* Top 20 places of 50,000 or more residents, ranked by cumulative index of dissimilarity, with population, cumulative index, housing value index, age distribution index, and race distribution index

Note: An index of zero indicates that the area's demographics match the U.S. perfectly

Source: J. Waldrop, "All-American Markets," *American Demographics*, January 1992, p. 26.

TABLE 10.4
Perfectly Ordinary Places: The Most Typical American Places Are Clustered in the South and the Midwest.

the most popular test markets in the United States, and Table 10.4 lists the most ordinary places in the United States, that is, the "most American" cities.

Commercialization

Only about one-half of the new products entering a test market show results justifying full **commercialization**—the introduction of the product into the marketplace. According to a study by Booz, Allen & Hamilton, it took 58 ideas to yield one successful new product.[22] Ideas for new products can be rejected at any stage of the product development process, although more are rejected at the early stages.

In 1981, the company updated the study by contacting 700 companies and found that an average of only seven ideas were required for every successful new product.[23] Booz, Allen & Hamilton attributed this dramatic improvement to the increasingly sophisticated way that companies develop new products, doing a better job at the very early stages of identifying areas for new-product development.

However, the latest research shows that these conclusions were premature and overly optimistic. Group EFO Ltd., a Connecticut-based consulting firm, has announced a major research study conducted with 166 managers of new products for some of the top manufacturers of packaged goods. This study found that only 8 percent of new product projects initiated at the major companies survived to reach the market. Once in the marketplace, only 17 percent of the new products met the major business objective that they were designed for. These figures translate into a failure rate of 83 percent. The cumulative result is that less than 1 percent of new projects initiated succeeded in the marketplace.[24]

Better concept and product testing and evaluation at the earlier stages may be needed for greater success at the commercialization stage, which can be extremely expensive. For example, a study in the grocery industry found that manufacturers paid an average of $5.1 million to get a new product on store shelves. When Bayer Select entered the national U.S. market, competing against aspirin-free Tylenol and Advil, its budget came to more than $116 million.[25]

Often firms must open new manufacturing facilities and produce large amounts of inventory to supply the channels of distribution. Costs for introductory advertising and sales promotion frequently exceed $10 million during the first year. In addition, it may be necessary to develop service facilities, produce spare parts, and conduct expensive sales training before the new product can be introduced. The firm must develop a thorough plan that indicates who will do what, when, where, and how.

Because of the great expense, a new product will often be introduced using a *regional rollout* strategy. A rollout is the introduction of the new product into the marketplace. Thus, it might take perhaps two years before the product is available nationally, as in the case of Lever 2000. A regional rollout reduces a company's risks and capital requirements. Cash generated from sales in one region can help finance introduction of the product into other regions.

After the introduction has taken place, the results must be carefully monitored. Consumer research may identify improvements that should be made in the product. Also, opportunities may exist for the introduction of new sizes, flavors, or styles. It may be profitable to direct the product or a revised version of it to new market segments, perhaps with a different marketing program.

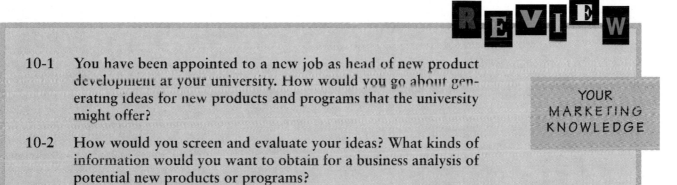

10-1   You have been appointed to a new job as head of new product development at your university. How would you go about generating ideas for new products and programs that the university might offer?

10-2   How would you screen and evaluate your ideas? What kinds of information would you want to obtain for a business analysis of potential new products or programs?

YOUR
MARKETING
KNOWLEDGE

WHY NEW PRODUCTS FAIL OR SUCCEED

There is no standard definition for the success or failure of a new product, but the product can be called successful if it meets management's original expectations in all important respects. If it does not meet management's original expectations, it can be defined as a failure.[26] A study by Chicago consultancy Kuczmarski & Associates supports the Group EFO's bleak findings on product performance. Kuczmarski studied success rates for 11,000 new products launched by 77 manufacturing, service, and consumer-products companies. The findings showed that only a little more than half, 56 percent, of products that actually get launched are still on the market five years later. Other studies peg the long-term success rate around 65 percent, but everyone agrees that something is not working right.[27]

Virtually no company expects a 100 percent success rate for new products. In the words of the marketing vice president for an office supplies manufacturer, "To target a new-product development program to expect a 100 percent success rate would be counterproductive—extreme conservatism would rule with very few, if any, projects reaching fruition."[28] Firms may have to accept a certain percentage of failed new products as the cost of increasing the probability of successfully introducing innovative new products into the marketplace. Nevertheless, most experts believe that efficiency needs to improve to reduce wasted resources in the new-product development process.

Executives at Hewlett-Packard's Medical Products Group studied 10 of their new-product failures along with 10 of their successes. They identified 14 tasks that were essential for success. These included identifying which projects play to a company's core strengths, accurately assessing how to sell the product, and determining early in the process what realistic costs would be. "We found if you missed on just 2 of the 14 factors, you failed with your product," says Mark Halloran, chief of research and development.[29]

It is also clear that companies should strive to minimize the cost of their failures and to maximize the amount they learn from these failures. Companies can also learn from the failures of others. Figure 10.4 lists some of the all-time great product flops.

Failure Factors

Nine factors are most often mentioned as the major causes contributing to the failure of new products.[30] They are lack of product uniqueness or superiority, poor planning, improper timing, technical problems, loss of objectivity, unexpected high product costs and prices, competition, company politics, and the need for government action.

Lack of product uniqueness or superiority.   Virtually every study of new-product failures identifies the lack of meaningful product uniqueness as the major cause of failure. Figure 10.5 shows the results of research conducted by Robert G. Cooper of McMaster University, Hamilton, Ontario, a recognized expert in new product marketing. Cooper has studied more than 1,000 business products in North America and Europe. He discovered that products not so new to the market—but that a company nonetheless thinks are innovative—have the poorest record of performance. In fact, they perform worse, on average, than simple, close-to-home line extensions.[31]

A frequent reason for the introduction of products that are not unique or superior is insufficient or faulty marketing research. After a product has failed to meet its expectations, marketers often confess to "a serious misreading" of consumers' needs, "too little field testing," or "overly optimistic forecasts of market need and acceptance."[32] Marketers and engineers, on occasion, simply decide what the marketplace wants without asking potential customers about their needs. This obviously can lead to disaster. For example, in the late 1980s, Frito-Lay introduced a collection of products that lacked unique or superior consumer benefits. Among these were cheese-topped crackers, cheese-filled snacks, and granola nuggets. When sales failed to materialize, these products were quickly dropped. Other notable flops include Toyota's T100 pickup truck; Coca-Cola's tiny soda fountain designed for office use; Rheingold's Gablinger, the first "diet beer"; and Simple Pleasure, NutraSweet's ice cream made with the Simplesse fat substitute.

Edsel and Friends: Ten World-Class Flops

FORD'S EDSEL	It had innovations galore—and quality problems from stuck hoods to defective power steering. Estimated loss per car—almost $1,117, or $250 million.
DU PONT'S CORFAM	A synthetic leather supposed to do for shoes what nylon did for stockings. Leather was just better. Cost: $80 million–$100 million.
POLAROID'S POLAVISION	Edwin Land used Polaroid's wet chemistry technology to develop an instant movie camera. But videotape technology was far better.
UNITED ARTISTS' *HEAVEN'S GATE*	Almost $30 million over budget, this western movie bombed so badly it almost destroyed UA.
RCA'S VIDEODISC	Supposed to capture the video recorder market. A tiny problem: It couldn't tape television shows. Loss: $500 million.
TIME'S *TV-CABLE WEEK*	A bid to outflank *TV Guide*. Cause of death: Ballooning costs to customize editions for each cable system. Loss: $47 million.
IBM'S PCjr	The awkward Chiclet keyboard. The slow microprocessor. The unattractive price. The late launch. IBM at its worst. Marketing cost: $40 million.
NEW COKE	Coca-Cola's answer to Pepsi's sweeter formula. Provoked a national uproar from old-formula loyalists. Watch for new formulation, Coke II.
R.J. REYNOLDS' PREMIER	This "cigarette" didn't burn. It didn't even emit smoke. It didn't taste good. Its failure persuaded CEO Ross Johnson to launch his equally disastrous buyout attempt.
NUTRASWEET'S SIMPLESSE	The fat substitute that would change the way we eat. But the market is swamped with substitutes, and many consumers like fat.

Source: C. Power, "Flops," *Business Week*, August 16, 1993, pp. 76–82.

FIGURE 10.4
Ten World-Class Flops

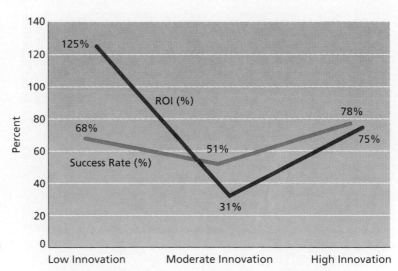

FIGURE 10.5
Impact of Innovativeness on Profitability

Source: B. Donath, "The Customer as Consultant," *Sales & Marketing Management*, September 1992, pp. 84–90.

Poor planning.   The second most frequently mentioned reason for new product failure is poor planning.[33] Included here is poor positioning and segmentation, under-budgeting, poor overall themes, overpricing, and inadequate handling of all other facets of a plan. The lack of adequate marketing research is often the reason why prices are set higher than consumers will pay and promotion or distribution efforts are inadequate or misdirected. Huffy Corporation did careful research before it launched the Cross Sport, a combination of the sturdy mountain bike popular with teenagers and the more sophisticated, thin-framed racing bike. Customers liked the bike, but Huffy made a gigantic mistake by placing it in mass retail outlets, such as Kmart and Toys "Я" Us. The hybrid bikes were aimed at adults and were priced 15 percent higher than other Huffy bikes. Customers needed individual sales attention that could be provided by the sort of knowledgeable salespeople who work in bike specialty shops. The result: a $5 million mistake. A study by Cooper of McMaster University shows that new-product managers double their chances of success when they match a new product with the right sales force and distribution system.[34]

Improper timing.   In many cases of failure, companies have been too slow or too fast to develop the new product, resulting in a poorly timed introduction. An example is the $25,000 DeLorean sports car that was introduced at the exact time that the economy was entering a downturn. Sales were so bad that the company was quickly put out of business.

Often, a new product will be hustled to the marketplace to meet or beat a competitive product. Sometimes the new product is not ready for introduction, because some of the important steps of the development process were skipped. Sometimes a product's time never comes. Remember the hypermarket, which was supposed to put the supermarket, drugstore, florist, bakery, and other specialty shops all out of business? It didn't. Products that have failed, along with some winners, are featured in the "Marketing in Action: Winning and Losing in the New Product Game."

Technical problems.   Sometimes design problems, technical difficulties, or manufacturing deficiencies contribute to the failure of a new product. Numerous products have had to be recalled from the marketplace because of unforeseen technical problems. Also, problems at a new production facility can doom a new product to failure. Sometimes it is just impossible to produce the product in the quantities necessary to serve a large marketplace, and the quality produced is not the same as it was during the test market. When Cadillac launched its Allante, the $50,000+ sports car that was supposed to rival BMW and Mercedes Benz, the car was underpowered, the roof leaked, and squeaks and wind noise marred the quiet that is expected of a luxury car.

Loss of objectivity.   Often the people involved in the new-product development process lose their objectivity. This can have several negative consequences. The firm may not do adequate marketing research on the size of the product's total market or managers may overestimate the product's benefits to consumers. Having invested so much time and effort in creating a new product, it is often difficult for the creators to see flaws. For example, marketers at RCA failed to recognize that consumers wouldn't value the higher quality picture of the videodisc player as much as the ability of a videocassette player to record TV programs as well as play prerecorded movies. RCA lost $500 million on the videodisc player.

Unexpected high product costs and prices.   Sometimes production costs are greatly underestimated, making it impossible for the new product to generate a profit at the originally intended price. One alternative is to raise the price, but this may yield a market price above what customers are willing to pay. Consider what happened to a large machinery producer:

> The problem developed while our new product was on exhibit. Many people liked what they saw—with the qualifications that just a few more functional capabilities would enhance its salability. Unfortunately, we listened to too many suggestions and proceeded to adapt additional features to the product. Its original $55,000 selling price became $80,000 as a result of these added features. We found the $80,000 product put us in a more unfavorable competitive position than if we had left it in its $55,000 configuration. The lesson learned was not to over engineer a product once it is developed for a specific market need.[35]

Competition.   Underestimating the effect of competitive actions can also contribute to failure of new products. Competitors may lower their prices, increase their promotional efforts, or take other defensive actions that may inhibit sales of the new product. For example, when Datril was introduced at less than half Tylenol's price, Tylenol lowered its price. But because Datril failed to anticipate Tylenol's price reduction, Tylenol, by combining its widespread brand recognition with a new, competitive price, was able to eliminate Datril's main advantage.

Company politics.   On occasion, the politics within an organization may require it to introduce a new product—to meet the company's objectives for introducing new products, for example. According to the Group EFO study, products are often rushed to market because management wants to fit the product into an agenda being driven by the budget.[36] In other cases, a new product may fail because no one in the organization had enough interest in the new product or enough clout to harness the resources necessary for a successful introduction. Group EFO found that few CEOs have had direct, hands-on new-product experience. Thus they do not know the terms or the concepts of new-product development. Additionally, the study found that at most companies, the best talent is put on established brands, and few who are assigned to new products see their work as a great career path.[37] All in all, the environment in many organizations is not conducive to effective management of new products.

MARKETING IN ACTION

Winning and Losing in the New Product Game

Every year, Food Marketing International (FMI) hosts a show to introduce wholesalers, retailers, and other interested parties to what's new in food products for the year. One of the hot new items in 1992 was alcohol-flavored lollipops. Margarita flavor appeared to be leading the pack in popularity though mescal-flavored pops, complete with a little worm embedded in the sucker, were also drawing a lot of attention.

While a variety of brand-new food items were getting their first exposure at the FMI show, many other new products were hitting the market in hopes of the success that company dreams are made of. Crystal Pepsi was fast out of the starting gate, having captured a 2.4 percent national share of supermarket soft-drink sales three months after its national rollout. But storm clouds quickly began to gather on the horizon. One year after Crystal's debut in its original test markets, its share was below 2 percent in those test markets. In Denver, considered a strong market for Pepsi, the combined share for Crystal and Diet Pepsi was only 1.5 percent. Marketers are predicting that clear beverages, briefly hot, will quickly fade from fashion.

Not all new products are found on grocery store shelves. Mattel Toys introduced Shani and friends in late 1991. Shani is a black fashion doll similar to Barbie. She and her friends, however, are designed, according to a company spokesperson, to "reflect the natural beauty of the African American woman." The line features dolls with different skin tones, hair styles, and facial features intended to represent the ethnic diversity of black women. Ethnic prints and influences are also prominent in the dolls' wardrobes.

Shani represents a departure for Mattel even though she is not the first African American fashion doll produced by the company. As early as 1968, Barbie's black friend, Christie, was introduced. Black and Hispanic versions of Barbie have also been available for many years. Concept testing for Shani, however, told Mattel that its earlier attempts had not captured any true ethnicity.

Christie was merely a white doll tinted dark.

Will liquor-flavored lollipops, Crystal Pepsi, and Shani succeed? If not, they may end up in the Museum of New Products. The Museum is the property of Marketing Intelligence Service, a company that monitors products in test markets for some of the nation's leading manufacturers of packaged goods. Five thousand products are on display at any given time but upwards of 75,000 items line the museum's storeroom shelves. The items displayed in the Museum of New Products represent primarily new product failures, though occasionally a success is also displayed.

Among the prominent failures of the past that have received the attention of museum goers is Singles, Gerber Products' food-in-a-jar that failed because consumers apparently associated it with baby food. According to a Gerber spokesperson, "As I understand it, it was very tasty, but it was a marketing and packaging problem." Heublein is on display with a product called Wine and Dine. It was a packaged dinner that included a bottle of cooking wine, Chianti or Burgundy for beef, Chablis for chicken. "A lot of people thought it was for drinking," states Richard Lawrence, Marketing Intelligence's president. "It wasn't clear until they read the fine print." Wine and Dine never got out of test market.

Some of the items that the museum has displayed in the past support the notion that product success or failure may have a lot to do with both timing and differences in product benefits. In the early 1980s, when Scott Paper introduced Raggedy Ann and Raggedy Andy disposable diapers, color-coded for each sex, they were a flop. The failure was attributed to retailers' refusal to double the shelf space available to the company and to the diapers' lack of a plastic backing, which required parents to use rubber pants over them. By 1989, however, when Procter & Gamble and Kimberly-Clark introduced male and female versions of Pampers, Luvs, and Huggies, respectively, the new products were hits.

Need for government action.   On occasion, government action may inhibit the sale of a new product, causing it to fail. Summit Technology, based in Waltham, Massachusetts, developed a laser technique for the removal of corneal scars. The laser procedure could substitute for risky corneal transplant surgery for as many as 20,000 U.S. patients per year. Summit has been trying for a year to win FDA approval for the procedure. But the FDA's ophthalmology panel, which usually meets at least four times a year, met only once in 1993 and did not even consider Summit's clinical results supporting its request for approval. Fortunately, Summit's laser device is used in 35 countries for refractive surgery to improve vision by changing the shape of the cornea. That foreign business accounted for virtually all of Summit's $30 million in sales in 1992. Were it not for the overseas business, Summit would be out of business.[38]

Success Factors

An investigation into the factors that separate successful and unsuccessful products tested a number of variables proposed by leading experts.[39] The research, based on more than 200 new products, identified eight factors that lead to success. Three factors most strongly related to success are:

1. *Product advantage.* The product offered unique features for the customer, was of higher quality, reduced customers' costs, was innovative, was superior to competing products in the eyes of the customer, and solved a problem faced by the customer.
2. *Proficiency of predevelopment activities.* For the most successful products, the firm proficiently conducted a set of upfront activities: initial screening, preliminary market assessment, preliminary technical assessment, detailed market study or marketing research, and business/financial analysis.
3. *Protocol.* Prior to the product development stage, there was a clear definition of the target market: customers' needs, wants, and preferences; the product concept; and product specifications and requirements.

Five other important success factors were having technical and production skills; incorporating proficient market-related activities, including marketing research and marketing communications skills; having a good fit between the project and the company's resources and R&D skills; being in a large, high-need, growth market; and having a good fit with respect to marketing resources and skills, including distribution and sales force. The support of top management was also studied and found to be important, but did not differentiate successes and failures.

Product superiority, in terms of unique benefits for consumers, innovativeness, quality, and superiority in the eyes of customers, was found to be the number one factor in new-product success. The proper management of the product development process, especially the early stages, was also vital to developing successful new products. These variables are within the control of marketing managers, and thus the success or failure of new products can be influenced by following the procedures.

MANAGING EXISTING PRODUCTS

Developing and introducing new products is challenging and critical to the long-term success of any organization. Equally challenging, and just as critical, is skillful management of the organization's existing products. Making correct decisions regarding the management of the firm's existing product mix is not an easy task. Chapter 9 presented a number of ways that a marketer can conceptualize products as an aid in identifying the appropriate strategies to use. By identifying which class a product falls into in the classification of goods, for example, a marketer gains some insight regarding appropriate strategies. A convenience good requires different distribution and pricing strategies than does a specialty good and so on. Furthermore, the product life cycle offers considerable aid as a tool in product management. Finally, analyzing a firm's product mix with respect to depth, breadth, and consistency of product lines can also help the marketing manager to plan appropriate strategies to meet his or her objectives.

Most marketers agree that it is possible to exert some control over sales of a brand as the product category progresses through the stages of the product life cycle. Each stage requires a different strategy. Table 10.5 shows the strategic implications of the various product life-cycle stages.

Here are examples of successful management of products through their PLCs:

▪ Tide detergent was introduced more than 45 years ago, and sales continue to increase year after year. The product has been improved some 55 times since its introduction, enabling the brand to forestall any decline in its market position. Figure 10.6 shows that Tide continues today as the number one brand in its category.

▪ Alpo canned dog food has been the market leader for many years. In spite of an explosion of competitors and sales in the dry segment of the dog food market, Alpo has maintained its volume through effective advertising that emphasizes the important dog food benefits of meat, protein, and quality. The brand's marketing program has resulted in significant brand loyalty, which has preserved Alpo's volume and position.[40]

▪ Research showed that 39 percent of Americans already use vinegar as a cleanser, so Heinz moved to cash in. Heinz Extra-Strength Cleaning Vinegar recently made its appearance in the cleaning products aisle as a floor-, window-, and carpet-cleaning agent. This is a good example of restoring luster to a stagnant product category.[41]

**FIGURE 10.6
Going with the
Tide**

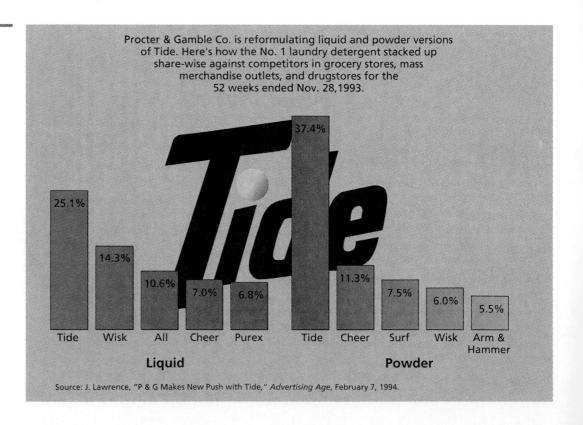

Procter & Gamble Co. is reformulating liquid and powder versions of Tide. Here's how the No. 1 laundry detergent stacked up share-wise against competitors in grocery stores, mass merchandise outlets, and drugstores for the 52 weeks ended Nov. 28, 1993.

Source: J. Lawrence, "P & G Makes New Push with Tide," *Advertising Age*, February 7, 1994.

TABLE 10.5
Implications of the Product Life Cycle (PLC) for Marketing Action

Effects and Responses	Stages of the PLC			
	Introduction	**Growth**	**Maturity**	**Decline**
Competition	None of importance	Some emulators	Many rivals competing for a small piece of the pie	Few in number with a rapid shakeout of weak members
Overall strategy	Market establishment—persuade early adopters to try the product	Market penetration—persuade mass market to prefer the brand	Defense of brand position—check the inroads of competition	Preparations for removal—milk the brand dry of all possible benefits
Profits	Negligible because of high production and marketing costs	Peak levels as a result of high prices and growing demand	Increasing competition cuts into profit margins and ultimately into total profits	Declining volume pushes costs up to levels that eliminate profits entirely
Retail prices	High, to recover some of the excessive costs of launching	High, to take advantage of heavy consumer demand	What the traffic will bear; need to avoid price wars	Low enough to permit quick liquidation of inventory
Distribution	Selective, as distribution is slowly built up	Intensive; employ small trade discounts since dealers are eager to store	Intensive; heavy trade allowances to retain shelf space	Selective; unprofitable outlets slowly phased out
Advertising strategy	Aim at the needs of early adopters	Make the mass market aware of brand benefits	Use advertising as a vehicle for differentiation among otherwise similar brands	Emphasize low price to reduce stock
Advertising emphasis	High, to generate awareness and interest among early adopters and persuade dealers to stock	Moderate, to let sales rise on the sheer momentum of word-of-mouth recommendations	Moderate, since most buyers are aware of brand characteristics	Minimum expenditures required to phase out the product
Consumer sales and promotion expenditures	Heavy, to entice target groups with samples, coupons, and other inducements	Moderate, to create brand preference (advertising is better suited to do this job)	Heavy, to encourage brand switching, hoping to convert some buyers into loyal users	Minimal, to let the brand coast by itself

Source: N. Dhalla and S. Yuspeh "Forget the Product Life Cycle Concept," *Harvard Business Review*, January–February, 1976, p. 104.

- Procter & Gamble repackaged diapers, marketing them to incontinent adults and calling the brand Attends. And Mars now sells M & Ms in the supermarket as a baking ingredient, with recipes on the back of the package.[42]

Extending the Product Life Cycle

As a product class moves through the maturity stage of the product life cycle, the future spells decline. But as the previous examples illustrate, marketers can intervene to slow movement into decline and thus maintain high sales and acceptable profits, at least for some period of time. In fact, many marketers, who anticipate movement of the product class, may begin to set extension strategies into place even during the growth stage of the life cycle. A firm can use a number of strategies to extend the length of time a product class remains in maturity. These include increasing usage by current users, finding new users, and finding new uses.

Increasing usage by current users.   One means of maintaining sales volume in a mature market is by attempting to increase penetration of existing target markets. By encouraging current users to use more of the product, a firm might even be able to raise sales. This could be accomplished through promotion by suggesting new use situations. For example, several years ago citrus growers began encouraging consumers to think of orange juice as more than a breakfast drink. By repositioning the juice as a good beverage to drink any time, current drinkers were encouraged to increase their consumption beyond breakfast.

A firm may also implement this strategy through such innovations as a change in package. For example, by packaging wine in single-serving cans, a producer makes it easier for consumers to take the product along on picnics or to places where a larger bottle may be inconvenient.

By attempting to increase usage by current users, the company is targeting a market with which it is familiar and has had some success. The product is one the firm knows and presumably produces well. This can be an attractive strategy for a marketer to employ since it is fairly low risk.

Finding new users.   This is the strategy Procter & Gamble employed for its baby diapers. By targeting a new market, the firm was able to counteract the effects of a declining birth rate. Several years ago, Yamaha attempted to tap homemakers, a user group not traditionally viewed as a market for motorcycles. Many firms in recent years have looked to global expansion for their products. This strategy, too, may represent an attempt to find new users for a firm's products when the company realizes that its domestic market has become saturated.

Finding new uses.   Finding new uses for an existing product can also help a company maintain sales volume in the face of a mature market. Dannon has begun pushing its yogurt as a substitute for high-fat eggs and oil in muffins and dips. It recently teamed with Duncan Hines to suggest using yogurt instead of eggs in a brownie mix.

These strategies represent creative approaches to the realities of a mature market, brought on by changing environmental situations. Heinz and its vinegar, cited earlier, is also an example of a company finding new uses for its product. By using a new-product approach to promoting the vinegar and by suggesting different ways to use the product, the firm successfully combated the likely decline of the product.

Some marketers have argued that since the product life-cycle concept should only be applied to product classes (for example, tires) or product form (radial tires, bias belted tires), the concept is not useful for a marketer in planning strategy for an individual brand.[43] However, brands that are market leaders may enjoy profits throughout every stage of the product life cycle, while weaker brands may never earn a profit. Sales of some brands continually increase even when the total market begins to decline. Opponents of the product life cycle marketing strategy argue that because of these exceptions, a marketer of an individual brand should not rely on product class generalizations to determine his or her product's strategy. While these arguments have some merit, it is generally agreed that the product life cycle concept can be of use to marketers of individual brands. If marketers remember that the product life cycle is only one tool in decision making and that it cannot dictate a particular strategy at any given point in time, they should find the PLC a useful aid to product management planning.

Modifying Existing Product Lines

There are a number of reasons for modifying an individual product or a product line. The firm may wish to increase sales, profits, or market share. It may need to support an overall marketing strategy. Or, the firm may make a change as part of reaching its objectives for its entire portfolio of products.[44] Clorox has always sold bleach as a laundry additive. But recognizing that many consumers use it to shine floors and windows, the company expanded the Clorox line by introducing the bleach-based liquid cleanser, Clorox Clean-Up. Because Clorox Clean-Up is a logical extension of the Clorox concept as a cleaning agent, the new product is selling briskly.[45]

Thus it should be noted that marketing managers can modify an existing product line by changing any one, or a combination, of the following attributes of a product line: positioning, physical characteristics, package, brand, amount and nature of value added, expansion or reduction of the product line, or composition of the product line.[46] The first five of these attributes apply to individual products and/or product lines; the last two apply only to the set of products within a product line.

Positioning. One way to modify an existing product line is to change the positioning of one or more products within the line. Mars repositioned its M & Ms as a baking product as well as a candy. Dannon is having similar success with its yogurt. The Las Vegas Convention & Visitors Bureau is working to reposition the city as a family vacation destination. Repositioning will require product changes. Las Vegas, for example, has had to develop family attractions, such as a water park and amusement rides. Often, a product can be repositioned by changing only the promotional strategy and/or distribution strategy. M & Ms and Dannon yogurt were not altered, only the advertising was changed.

Physical characteristics. Marketers may change the physical characteristics of a product, by altering quality, performance, and appearance. For example, Sunkist removed the caffeine from its orange soda, some cookie companies have removed tropical oils from their cookies, and Florsheim shoes introduces new styles each spring. A restaurant might improve the quality of its food, the attentiveness of its waiters and waitresses, or the ambiance of its interior. Each represents a change in a physical characteristic.

Alterations may be done to update the look of a product or to make it more attractive and appealing. Coke recently introduced bottles in the shape the firm had used previously, playing on customers' nostalgia.

Packages may be changed by altering attributes related to the function of the package or by altering attributes related to the use of the package as a communication vehicle. For example, Taylor California Cellars Wine changed a functional attribute of wine packaging when it introduced the product in aluminum cans for use by airline companies. Because this packaging was easy for flight attendants to store and dispense, the product became more attractive to airlines. Campbell's Soup increased sales of several of its products by stamping "The Lite Ones" on the packages of individual soups that were already low in calories. This was a change in a communications attribute.

Brand.   Many marketers who sell their own brand names have increased sales by marketing the same or similar products using private brands or distributor brands, and vice versa. The Whirlpool Corporation, for example, markets its products under its own brand name and under the Sears Kenmore brand. Pillsbury recently decided to add a private brand to its portfolio.

In Europe, a surge in private brands is taking a lot of credit for muscling major brands off the shelves. In the past five years, private brand market share has nearly doubled in the major European markets. [47]

Amount and nature of value added.   *Value added* refers to the change in the product characteristics from the time the ingredients enter the organization to the time the product is sold by the organization.[48] For example, Pillsbury changed its product line by altering the value added when it began marketing cake mixes in addition to flour. Sold as a cake mix, the flour (together with other ingredients) had much more value to the consumer. Many companies have made their products more convenient to use, thus adding value for the consumer. Hewlett-Packard's 2.9-pound OmniBook PC is really portable. Four AA batteries yield ten hours of work. Black & Decker's PowerShot heavy-duty stapler is redesigned for easy use; a side-window shows the staples.[49]

Expansion or reduction of the product line.   In many product categories, consumers have a strong desire for variety, and to satisfy them, marketers frequently add new styles, models, or flavors. For example, Kellogg's frequently adds new cereals to its product line, McDonald's introduces new items on its menu, and Ann Taylor adds new styles to her line of clothing. In the case of technical products, like computer hardware and software, one market segment will sometimes have more sophisticated requirements than other segments. Marketers in these industries will often expand the product line to include new products with the latest technical specifications while maintaining the old products in the line to satisfy the needs of the less sophisticated users.

Another way of expanding a product line is to include **complementary products.** Demand for these products is related to other products in the line. For example, the demand for brushes and clean-up supplies is complementary to the demand for paint, and a paint manufacturer may decide to satisfy the demand by introducing these complementary products. Complementary products do not compete with each other.

Marketers also reduce the product line on occasion by eliminating products.[50] Usually, companies only consider abandoning a product or product line after sales or profits have declined substantially. Managers often argue that they need a complete product line and that if they were to eliminate products in the line, customer ill will might develop. When GTE implemented its Installed Base Plan to upgrade business users' communications networks, the company was careful to give plenty of warning to customers. GTE wanted those users who would no longer be able to get parts and service for old systems to have advance warning, so they could plan for the changes.

Composition of the product line.   The composition of the product line may be changed by altering the individual products in the line. This can be accomplished by changing the product's style and characteristics, the options and accessories, or the pricing of the line. For example, a furniture manufacturer can change the composition of its product line by switching the emphasis from French provincial furniture to contemporary furniture. An appliance marketer can make certain features and accessories optional instead of standard, or vice versa. A producer of men's pants might alter the composition of its product line by emphasizing the $49.95 and $59.95 pants, instead of the $29.95 and $39.95 pants.

10-3 Suppose you are the new marketing manager for a company's line of fax machines. What stage of the product life cycle does the product line appear to be in and what promotional strategies would be appropriate for the line?

10-4 How can you use the concept of the product life cycle to help you determine your marketing strategy to increase sales of fax machines to the home (nonbusiness) market?

YOUR MARKETING KNOWLEDGE

QUALITY ISSUES IN PRODUCT DEVELOPMENT AND MANAGEMENT

In recent years the issue of quality has received a great deal of attention in companies. Quality is an important consideration for marketing managers in planning product strategy. When we speak of **quality,** we mean the collection of features and characteristics of a product or service that affect its ability to satisfy stated or implied needs.[51] In his book, *Quality Is Free*, Phil Crosby states that building quality into a product does not cost the company more because of the savings in rework, scrap, and servicing the product after the sale, as well as the benefits of customer satisfaction and repeat sales. Crosby goes on to state that if features are added to improve the product's fitness for use, fewer repairs are necessary and hence the customer is pleased. Even though adding a feature may require a manufacturer to charge a premium price, the product cost over its lifetime may really be lowered.[52]

Consumers' needs vary by target market. But even where low price is an important objective, consumers desire the best value for their money. Many consumers may be willing to compromise on durability in exchange for a lower price, for example. In such cases, the market-driven firm must determine the price level its customers find acceptable and then work to provide the highest level of quality possible at that price while still allowing the company to meet its profitability objectives.

Concern for quality is not restricted to product decisions, nor is it the sole concern of the marketing department. A market-driven firm strives for total quality management to permeate all parts of the company. **Total Quality Management (TQM)** refers to this philosophy. Under total quality management, everyone in the company must be committed to quality in every activity, from producing the product, to providing customer service, to sweeping the floors.

The responsibility for quality should permeate a market-driven organization. All functions and all individuals within the organization need to understand their roles in providing quality. It is true, however, that the marketing function in the organization bears responsibility for some specific aspects of quality, and for marketers this responsibility centers around marketing's role in product management.

Product Design

Both business consumers and ultimate consumers choose products based on their own subjective perceptions of desirable benefits, characteristics, features, and specifications. Companies that most nearly meet these expectations will be rewarded by selling their products; those who ignore these expectations do so at their peril.

This means that the first and most important step in designing a new product is to find out what customers want. But customers may not always know what they want; that is, they may not be able even to imagine product solutions to problems that they have accepted as inevitable. Yet, many current products represent advances that were not even imagined ten years ago. Examples include massive parallel processing computers, sophisticated database software, color-coded Legos, and the upcoming Simon wireless fax machine.

Engineering and Output

To be successful, a new product needs all the help it can get: superior design, superior materials, superior assembly, and superior quality control. If any element is weak, the overall quality is diminished. And today's marketplace can be very unforgiving when it comes to lesser-quality products.

Consequently, quality production demands a lot of cooperation and coordination throughout the development process and beyond. New product groups should include designers, engineers, production specialists, and marketers as well as a group manager who keeps everyone organized and moving forward on schedule.

Product groups must determine what cues customers use to judge quality. For many years, Chrysler was recognized as having the finest engineering among technical specialists, but customers did not see it that way. Not having a real first-hand understanding or appreciation of engineering, customers relied on simpler, more obvious product attributes, such as styling and appearance. The situation began to change when Lee Iacocca, committed to customer satisfaction, took over the company. The "Marketing in Action: Chrysler Minivan: A Quality Evaluation" shows how Chrysler's emphasis on quality led to success.

A product will develop a quality image if it excels on the attributes that customers use to judge quality. If it does not exhibit these attributes, all the selling in the world cannot save it. It is the responsibility of market research to provide this information to designers and engineers, so that these important characteristics can be engineered into the product. Yet, there are many ways of defining quality. Table 10.6 lists eight dimensions of quality, several of which may overlap in practice.

Service Quality

Services, whether products themselves or merely attributes connected to a tangible product, also vary in quality of dependability, speed, competence, courtesy, completeness, customization, and consistency. Services are obviously more difficult than goods to control, because services are provided by people. Researchers have identified five gaps between service provision and consumers' expectations that contribute to poor service quality in the minds of consumers.[53]

- GAP 1: *Consumers' expectation—management's perceptions.* Service providers do not always understand what features of the service connote high quality to consumers.

TABLE 10.6
Eight Critical Dimensions of Quality

Dimension	Definition
Performance	Refers to a product's primary operating characteristics. This dimension involves measurable attributes by which brands can be ranked.
Features	The features include the "bells and whistles" of products and services, those characteristics that supplement their basic functioning.
Reliability	This dimension reflects the probability of a product's malfunctioning or failing within a specified time period.
Conformance	The degree to which a product's design and operating characteristics meet established standards.
Durability	A measure of product life, durability encompasses both economic and technical dimensions. Technically, durability is the amount of use one gets from a product before it deteriorates. Economically, durability refers to the amount of use one gets from a product before it breaks down and replacement is preferable to continued repair.
Serviceability	This is the speed, courtesy, competence, and ease of repair.
Aesthetics	A matter of personal judgment, aesthetics refers to how a product looks, feels, sounds, tastes, or smells.
Perceived quality	Since consumers often do not have complete information about a product's or service's attributes, they use indirect measures for comparing brands. Perceived quality is inferred, rather than observed, from images, advertising, brand names, and reputation.

Source: D. A. Garvin, "Competing on the Eight Dimensions of Quality," *Harvard Business Review*, November–December, 1987, pp. 101–109.

- GAP 2: *Management's perceptions—service quality specifications.* Even when service providers understand what consumers expect, there are factors that may cause them not to establish service specifications to meet those expectations.

- GAP 3: *Service quality specifications—service delivery.* Standards for service quality are not always met by the actual service providers.

- GAP 4: *Service delivery—external communications.* Actual service performance does not always meet the standard suggested to consumers in promotion or, in other words, performance often doesn't match promises.

- GAP 5: *Expected service—perceived service.* Consumers evaluate service quality based on whether it met or exceeded the level they expected.

In order to provide quality, market-driven service providers must strive to close these gaps.

The discussion of product concepts and planning in this chapter and Chapter 9 pave the way for discussing the rest of the marketing mix. With a thoughtful product plan, the market-driven marketer is ready to begin planning his or her distribution, promotion, and pricing strategies.

MARKETING *IN ACTION*

Chrysler Minivan: A Quality Evaluation

Because quality is "in the eye of the beholder," it behooves us to examine quality issues in the light of one of the most profitable consumer products ever built—the Chrysler Minivan. Referred to by Chrysler executives as one of its "crown jewels," the minivan accounts for more than a quarter of the company's car and truck sales and perhaps as much as two-thirds of its profits.

The minivan's appeal is distinct from other automotive success stories, because its appeal is based almost entirely on utility rather than style or marketing. Based on extensive market research, the mini-van signifies a real breakthrough in efficiency due to its shape, function, and mechanical layout. Its high roof makes it easy to enter, and its combination of trucklike seating with carlike handling makes it easy to maneuver. Mainly used to haul passengers, the minivan is also roomy enough when the rear seats are removed to accommodate 4-by-8-foot sheets of plywood lying flat, an advantageous attribute that no station wagon and few small pickups can match.

The minivan is the most profitable line in Detroit. It sells in huge quantities, has changed little since its introduction, carries premium prices, and rarely requires rebates or other price-cutting incentives.

The minivan clearly illustrates design and engineering wedded to customers' needs and preferences. The roof is low enough to fit in residential garages, the hood is visible from the front seat, and the engine is positioned in front of the driver for protection in the event of a front-end collision. Buyers recognize the van as a passenger vehicle because designers added such cues as whitewall tires, wire wheel covers, and ersatz wood side trim. The single sliding door on the side saved weight and expense and added a measure of safety because it forced passengers to exit away from traffic on the sidewalk side of the vehicle.

By listening to customers, Chrysler was also able to avoid two crucial design errors that later befell its competitors. The silhouette with a long, wedge-shaped nose was rejected because drivers, especially short ones, couldn't see the end of the hood. GM made this mistake and its trio of long-snouted minivans were soundly rejected in the marketplace. Chrysler also scratched a design that placed the engine under a hump in the floor because it blocked passage from the front seats to the rear. Toyota originally tried that layout in its Previa, but the next version will use conventional front-wheel drive.

WE JUST MADE 2,400 CHANGES *in the* WORLD'S BEST-SELLING MINIVANS.

The new 1994 Plymouth Voyager

The new 1994 Dodge Caravan

THE FIRST MINIVANS *to* MEET 1998 CAR SAFETY STANDARDS RIGHT NOW.

Since inventing the first minivan back in 1984, we've sold over four million of them. And we've been relentless about improving our invention. We were the first with a minivan air bag. The first with driver and front passenger air bags. The first with integrated child safety seats. And now, for 1994, we've added dynamic side-impact protection—making ours the only minivans in the world to meet all 1998 car safety standards. And that's only the beginning. Other improvements include

a new 3.8-liter V-6 engine, a redesigned instrument panel and a new remote keyless entry system. And on top of that come thousands of other changes and refinements that demonstrate we're committed to continuous improvement. That's why our minivans remain the world best-sellers. For more information, call 1-800-876-MINIVAN.

THE MINIVAN COMPANY™

But Chrysler has found that it still needs to do some quality improvements. Although *Consumer Reports* gave the minivans one of its "recommended" ratings, the report still grades them below average in reliability, meaning they are more prone to breakdown than the typical new car. Also, the National Highway Traffic Safety Administration is studying whether the rear hatchback latches are prone to pop open and whether the antilock brakes are of acceptable quality. Finally, failures of a new electronic transmission in the 1989, 1990, and 1991 models undermined customer loyalty and nearly killed new sales. Chrysler launched a massive effort to placate owners by replacing the faulty units and providing free roadside assistance, but former CEO Lee Iacocca said the measures cost hundreds of millions of dollars—"more than Ford spent on the Edsel."

This example illustrates how design, engineering, production, and marketing worked together to create a successful new product for Chrysler. At the same time, the illustration shows that improved quality must be ongoing. Companies that will be most successful in the coming years will be those companies that listen to customers, design and engineer quality products, offer quality service, and constantly seek to improve what they have already produced.

PERSONAL COMPUTER EXERCISE

Screening and evaluating ideas for new products are important parts of the new-product development process. This PC Exercise allows you to rate a new product idea using the eight success factors cited in this chapter.

KEY POINTS

■ New products are essential for organizations that want to grow. The rate of new product introductions has been increasing.

■ The new-product development process consists of seven stages: new product strategy development, idea generation, screening and evaluation, business analysis, development, testing, and commercialization.

■ The Product Innovation Charter (PIC), defining the goals, product categories, and customers sought by the firm, is a key part of the new-product strategy development stage of the process.

■ New-product ideas are generated from research and development personnel, other company employees, customers, suppliers, consultants, distributors, and retailers. A formal process for generating new-product ideas is critical for new product success.

■ Ideas are screened to determine if they fit the type of products the organization wants to introduce. Other screening criteria include market size and growth, technical feasibility, fit with existing facilities and skills, and projected return on investment. Consumer concept tests are often used to help answer some of these questions.

■ At the business analysis stage, trial, repeat purchase, adoption, and frequency of purchase are estimated to determine probable demand. The product's anticipated production and financial requirements and its compatibility with the firm's objectives and policies are evaluated.

■ At the development stage, the product is transformed from merely an idea or concept into a prototype model. At the same time, a tentative marketing program is developed. The development stage often requires a large investment and may take a number of years to complete. An increasingly important aspect of product development is product safety and corporate liability.

■ Test markets help reduce the probability of introducing products that fail. They are also used to learn how to market new products most effectively. But companies sometimes decide not to use them, particularly if there is a risk that competing firms will find out about the new product and imitate it quickly. Controlled test markets and simulated test markets are used when the risk is lower. They are quicker and less expensive than traditional test marketing.

■ New products can be defined as successful if they meet management's objectives. Using this definition, about two thirds of new products are successful.

■ New products tend to fail if they are not unique or superior to competing products. Other factors contributing to new-product failure are poor planning, improper timing, technical problems, lack of objectivity, high costs, competition, company politics, and government actions.

■ Product advantage, proficiency of predevelopment activities, and a protocol describing the target market and product specifications are key factors leading to success of new products.

■ The length and shape of the product life cycle are determined by consumers' needs, wants, attitudes, and behavior; the rate of technological change; competitive activity; and the organization's own marketing actions.

■ The product life cycle can aid marketers in determining what marketing mix strategies are appropriate. Different strategies are called for at different stages in the product life cycle.

■ Product life cycles can sometimes be extended by employing the strategies of increasing usage by current users, finding new users, and finding new uses for the product.

■ Individual products can be modified by changing their position, physical characteristics, package, brand, or the amount and nature of value added. In addition, the set of products within a product line can be altered by expanding or reducing the product line or by changing its composition.

■ The quality of a product's development and management is a major factor in that product's success or failure. Quality reflects the product's ability to satisfy customer needs. Marketing personnel can play a key role in achieving product and service quality.

■ Total quality management represents a dedication on the part of the organization to focusing all efforts on providing quality products and services to consumers.

KEY TERMS

innovations (311)
modifications (311)
me-toos (311)
new product (312)
flanker brand (312)
line extension (312)
technological extension (312)
franchise extension (312)
product innovation charter
  (PIC) (315)
idea generation (316)

concept tests (319)
business analysis (319)
cannibalization (319)
strict liability (322)
test market (322)
commercialization (324)
complementary products (336)
quality (337)
Total Quality Management
  (TQM) (337)

ISSUES FOR DISCUSSION

1. Identify the following products as flanker brands, line extensions, franchise extensions, or new products:
   (a) McDonald's ham and cheese sandwich
   (b) Sears rental car service
   (c) Seiko computers
   (d) Trix yogurt

2. Oranamics, Incorporated, has the U.S. rights to distribute a new two-headed, Y-shaped, oversized toothbrush that cleans both sides of the teeth at the same time. What steps would you recommend before introducing the product?

3. How might a company like Xerox get ideas for new products? What techniques might it use to screen and evaluate the new ideas generated? What might be some of the more important screening criteria?

4. Sentinel Technologies has developed floppy disks for personal computers that are available in a variety of bright colors. How important is it for the company to test market the new product? What could Sentinel learn from a market test of the colored floppy disk?

5. Why is it important to develop the marketing program at the same time as the product?

6. Companies do a much better job of new-product strategy development and "front-end" thinking today, with the result that it takes only 7 ideas to generate one successful new product versus 58 ideas previously. The research techniques available have been improved substantially during this time period. Yet the success rate for new products has not improved over the years. Explain how this can be.

7. Holiday Inn markets hotel rooms under three strategies. Hampton Inns are budget motels, Embassy Suites offer a suite for the price of a quality hotel room, and Residence Inn is an apartment-like room for longer stays. The budget motel segment of the market has reached the maturity stage of the product life cycle, while the suite segment appears to be in the growth stage. The apartment-type motel is just being introduced into the hotel market. How might these three products (Hampton Inns, Embassy Suites, and Residence Inns) be marketed differently by Holiday Inn in the coming year?

8. What strategies for extending the product life cycle would you suggest to a manufacturer of personal computers?

9. Suggest some ways that the following products might be modified in order to increase sales:
   (a) Kraft Macaroni and Cheese dinners
   (b) Kenmore washers and dryers
   (c) Apple laptop computers
   (d) Honda Civic automobiles
   (e) Guess jeans

10. Why do you think the concept of total quality management has gotten so much attention in recent years? Do consumers care more about quality today than they did in the past?

11. Identify ways in which marketing personnel could improve customers' perceptions of quality for a dry cleaner.

CASE APPLICATION

Campbell's on the Move

To many, Campbell's will always be the soup in the familiar red and white can. Campbell's Soup Company certainly wants consumers to think of them when they see the familiar label—but for more than just soup. The firm has mounted an ambitious expansion of its pantry- and freezer-food lines, added new brands, updated its traditional labels, and increased promotional spending 5 percent and 8 percent respectively in the last two years.

Campbell's traditional red and white cans of condensed soup have been updated both inside and out. New flavors such as Broccoli Cheese have been added and labels have been dressed up by including photographs of the ingredients. The firm is marketing new lines of lower-fat, lower-calorie foods under the names Campbell's Healthy Request and Mrs. Paul's Healthy Treasures. The former features soup items but also such additions to the product mix as spaghetti sauce. Healthy Treasures add to the firm's existing line of Mrs. Paul's seafood products.

The company has decided to limit its product expansions to dry groceries and frozen foods, "[items] we know we're good at and can make lots of money at," according to Herbert M. Baum, president of the Campbell's North and South America division. Earlier attempts to expand beyond these core businesses, specifically a line of refrigerated salads called Fresh Chef, were unsuccessful and have been discontinued.

Campbell's has also found that economic conditions can affect the success of both new and existing products. The depressed economy faced by the United States in the early 1990s boded well for products such as condensed soup. Campbell's viewed this situation as an opportunity and began advertising a line of "family-sized" 26-ounce cans. According to Baum, "when you reconstitute two of those [26-ounce cans], they will fill your bathtub." Apparently this strategy is paying off—sales of the larger cans increased 64 percent between 1991 and 1992.

These actions by Campbell's appear to be in line with a recent survey performed by Group EFO Ltd., a marketing consulting company based in Weston, Connecticut. The survey found that for a majority of firms, 30 percent or more of their sales over the next five years must come from new products. Packaged goods analysts suggest that such goals, as well as the increased optimism that is represented by bigger promotional budgets for such firms as Campbell's and Procter & Gamble, may represent a rebirth of manufacturers' brands, which have suffered at the hands of dealer brands and generics over the last decade.

Questions

1. Classify the products introduced by Campbell's. Which are flanker brands, franchise extensions, line extensions, new products?
2. Why do you think Campbell's Fresh Chef line failed?
3. Campbell's original soups seem to be in the maturity stage of the product life cycle. What strategies, other than those listed in the case, might Campbell's consider to extend this stage for the soups?
4. How could repositioning help Campbell's?

Managing Your Product

The most successful companies adapt products to respond to market demands. With regard to your job search, you need to position yourself as an increasingly attractive package for a dynamic market.

In addition, you need to create a product advantage for yourself with your target organizations. This objective means going beyond the "must meet" criteria to the "desirable" criteria. To maximize your success in a job search requires that you create a continuing "product advantage" by modifying yourself to meet the needs of the employer.

How do you create a continuing market edge for yourself? As with business marketing, good market research and concept testing are critical factors in your career search. Contacting and listening to senior executives in your fields of interests can help you find out what they see as the management challenges ten years out. Then, you can try to fit these observations into your ongoing career preparations. You need to ask yourself how and where you can address these future management demands in your education, experience, and personal development. For example, in some fields, emerging international and environmental issues are likely to require a better understanding of cultural differences and resource limitations. You also need to maintain regular contact with other management people and recruiters to stay current on the needs for new hires. You should seek experience in your target field so that you will have a desirable edge and be able to exceed the needs of employers.

This chapter also highlights the importance of total quality. You might wonder what that theme has to do with your career search. Quality comes through the evidence or proof of knowledge and skills that you present in your cover letters, résumés, and interviews. The interviews assess your communication and interpersonal skills.

So far, the tie-in of career search to product management and development has emphasized content. Your packaging of your knowledge and skills is critical to success, especially if you are pursuing a career in some aspect of marketing. You need to be innovative in presenting yourself and in asking how you can be creative and stand out from others. One way to excel is to write cover letters that are reader centered: they state clearly how you meet the readers' key needs and wants. Another way is to include samples of your work, when appropriate. The idea is to package yourself in a way that is an attention-getting but honest representation of your skills and abilities.

You can maximize your career search success if you give continued attention to the development and communication of a product edge for yourself in your fields of interest.

Questions

1. What are the longer term trends in your fields of interest? How can you address these trends in your education, experience, and personal development?
2. What are your current and projected knowledge and skill edges in your career search?
3. Identify the proofs of your knowledge and skills. How do you know that this evidence will be acceptable to your prospective employers?

Jobs in Brand or Product Management

Brand managers, or, as they are sometimes called, product managers, are responsible for planning and directing the entire marketing program for a given product or group of products. In a way, working in brand management is like running your own business. A brand manager is involved in new-product ideas and research, advertising, sales promotion, packaging, pricing, inventory, sales, and the legal aspects of marketing a product. Companies such as Procter & Gamble, General Mills, and Du Pont use product managers.

Skills needed. An MBA is often a desirable credential for a brand manager, but some firms do hire marketers with bachelor's degrees. Other personal characteristics are of greater importance. One is the ability to identify and develop creativity—if not in yourself, then in those around you. An inquisitive personality, the ability to think like a consumer, political savvy, and passion for your work are qualities that will help you become a successful brand manager.

Entering the field. The entry-level position is generally as a brand assistant. You will be given both individual and team projects that pertain to all marketing decisions regarding your particular brand. If you perform well in this capacity, after about a year, you will be promoted to assistant brand manager, often for a different brand group. Your responsibilities will increase, and you will help train the brand assistants. After several years of highly rated performance as an assistant brand manager, you may be promoted to brand manager. You would then have total responsibility for the marketing effort and performance of your product. From brand manager, a logical progression might be to group brand manager, in charge of several brand groups, and then to general manager or vice president of marketing.

Atmosphere. In all of these positions, the hours can be long and the work can be frustrating. While you have responsibility for a product's performance, you do not have commensurate authority to see that your directives and plans are put into effect. Your work must be accomplished by dealing with other departments such as sales, marketing research, and production. Sometimes this can evolve into a political and competitive activity.

Part Three

The Story of Harley-Davidson: The Product

HARLEY-DAVIDSON®

Product Considerations

The core strength of Harley-Davidson is its excellent product—one that many thousands of people want to buy, and others who can't buy, still want. When purchasing a Harley-Davidson, you are not just buying a motorcycle, but also the heritage, image, service, and attitude that come with it. In order to stress their commitment to service, employees and dealers strive to build long-term relationships with customers. Management makes it a policy to attend Harley-Davidson's frequent "Town Hall Meetings," where Harley Owners Groups (H.O.G.) meet and share Harley stories and ideas for improvements in products and services.

The benefits of owning a Harley-Davidson include what the company believes is a unique combination of features: power, quality, reliability, size, consistency, and styling. In addition, other associated benefits of ownership attract consumers: more satisfaction and enjoyment than with other bikes; greater peace of mind due to quality and reliability; and a positive boost to one's status and individuality. Interestingly, Harley-Davidson has proprietary statistics showing that many non–Harley-Davidson owners switch to the brand soon after they get hooked on the motorcycling life-style. These newcomers quickly learn that Harley-Davidson has come to represent the height of the motorcycling experience—whether it be for quality and design, or image and attitude. Clearly Harley-Davidson has designed and delivered a product actively sought by customers—an enviable goal for a company to achieve.

Production Process

Today, demand for Harley-Davidson motorcycles exceeds the company's supply of bikes. This fact reflects well on the product, but puts pressure on production to make more bikes more quickly. Under such circumstances, a keen eye must be kept on maintaining the high quality of the bikes. Harley-Davidson continues to invest millions of dollars in production to ensure quality and consistency in the end product.

Between 1989 and 1993, more than $150 million was spent on capital improvements, including a new engine line that stops at planned computerized intervals, a new paint center in York, Pennsylvania, and robots that transfer heavy castings through the entire machining process. Further, Harley-Davidson has continued to implement formal programs such as Employee Involvement, Materials As Needed (a name for "just-in-time" inventory management), and Statistical Operator Control.[1]

Product Life Cycle and Line Expansion

The evolution of the Harley-Davidson motorcycle closely reflects the traditional product life cycle. The timeline for Harley-Davidson's product has lasted over 90 years, with peak sales and profits in the last six years. For more than 70 years, the heavyweight class of motorcycles has been in the mature stage of the product life cycle—when sales increase at a slower rate and profits begin to decrease.

With success often comes the desire to expand. Harley-Davidson has resisted this temptation and has been reluctant to stray beyond its traditional product line and expand into the lightweight motorcycle classes. The company feared expanding dramatically; it wanted to avoid entering a saturated market and diluting its core strength of traditional motorcycles. The resulting distraction (and loss in market share and revenues) could prove fatal if the core business were neglected. However, Harley-Davidson did expand sharply during the AMF years (1969–1981), when the company increased production capacity from 14,000 units per year in 1969 to 50,000 in the late 1970s.[2] The result was a decrease in quality for the sake of quantity.

Despite hundreds of riders' recommendations to expand into new products and markets, Harley-Davidson made it the company's mission to serve existing clientele, keep them loyal, get them to upgrade, and get new customers from traditional Harley-Davidson buyer groups. However, the company recently decided to stray from its usual path to meet the needs of people who have sought a sleek, performance-oriented product from Harley-Davidson. To that end, the company has acquired a 49 percent interest in Buell Motorcycle Company, a highly respected, American-based motorcycle manufacturer. This business move will extend Harley-Davidson's product life cycle.[5]

When Harley-Davidson looks at existing products and evaluates possible new ones, it looks not only at the physical feasibility of manufacturing the product, but also at who the customer will be. At least 1.5 years elapses between the time a new idea is introduced and when the item is produced. This time period takes into consideration the research, evaluation, testing, and production stages. Throughout the process, employees and customers are involved in development.

An example of bad timing for expansion was the introduction of the Cafe Racer, a high-performance motorcycle. It featured a Sportster engine, but the rest of the all-black bike resembled a racing motorcycle in shape and in style. Although the Cafe Racer became a cult classic, the bike was such a radical change from Harley-Davidson's traditional motorcycles that it was ignored by most customers and could not generate enough sales to survive as a new product. Essentially, the Cafe Racer arrived on the market at the wrong time and, therefore, was discontinued.

The Cafe Racer's troubles reflected the problems at Harley-Davidson of poor product management and poor quality during the late 1970s and early 1980s. The company was fortunate that, despite these difficulties, customer loyalty was high and the riders tolerant.

Harley-Davidson turned around the problems of the 1970s and early 1980s and eventually marketed its products more effectively. The result was a dramatically increased market share and record profits. The bottom line made it quite clear that marketing is almost useless with a badly timed product, whereas the right product matched with effective marketing nets success.

Product Changes

Major product changes are rarely made. Incremental technical and cosmetic adjustments are more frequent and have included new colors, different amounts and locations of chrome, and positioning and shape of handlebars and seats. The following is a list of enhancements, many suggested by Harley-Davidson owners, that have extended the life of the motorcycles for generations of riders:

- "V-Twin" cylinders in 1909
- saddle bags
- two-level seat for comfort and stability
- custom paint
- side cars
- balloon tires
- standardized parts
- streamlined gas tanks
- nonleak oil systems
- true wire-wheels
- electric start in 1965
- "anti-dive" air-assisted suspension system in 1983
- the first computer-controlled ignition system in 1983

Ancillary and Licensed Products

Licensing the trademark emblem and logos creates and increases an awareness of the brand among the riding and nonriding public and reinforces the company's image with customers. Harley-Davidson motorcycles are complemented in the secondary market with licensing arrangements to create such products and services as T-shirts and other apparel, collectibles, restaurants, and children's toys. These are target specific; not all consumers respond to each of these items.

The Brand

Harley-Davidson's brand is world famous and covers the company's motorcycles, Genuine accessories, MotorClothes, events, and even the motorcycling life-style itself. The company's management team takes this so seriously that it has created a department to monitor and control all brand-related issues. Worth billions and closely protected, the brand focuses on the image, consistency, quality, and presentation of all the company's products and services, as well as on the perceptions of customers and the general public. The importance of the brand proves that a quality product doesn't just happen. It is created, and it represents a response to the marketplace, the customers, and the environment.

Questions

1. List 25 features of Harley-Davidson's products and their associated benefits.
2. What additional products do you think would be beneficial to introduce in the next five to seven years? Why?
3. If you were the competition, what do you see as Harley-Davidson's weaknesses or as opportunities to increase your sales and profits?
4. What changes to both the Harley-Davidson company and its motorcycles would you recommend or anticipate in the next five years? Explain your answer.

part IV

DISTRIBUTION

CHapTeR 11

Channels of Distribution

Upon completing this chapter, you will be able to do the following:

■ **Identify** the distribution channel alternatives a marketing manager faces.

■ **Discuss** the factors that influence a marketer's choice of distribution channel.

■ **Compare** and contrast intensive, selective, and exclusive distribution intensities.

■ **Explain** why conflict is common in distribution channels.

■ **Understand** how a vertical marketing system can reduce conflict in a distribution channel.

■ **Describe** the common types of vertical marketing systems.

*M*arketing *P*rofile

Market-Driven Distribution Decisions: Thanks to Electronic Data Interchange

Have you ever wondered how some clothing stores seem to have such a good supply of the inventory consumers want while others run continuous clearance sales to get rid of the items that didn't sell last season? One reason is Electronic Data Interchange (EDI), one of the most popular communications concepts today.

EDI is the interchange of information from one company's computer to another's. EDI is not the same as electronic mail (e-mail). When using e-mail, one person enters information into a system so that another person can read it elsewhere. EDI involves a computer entering information into a system that will be read by another computer. Hence, EDI transmissions need not be in a language that people can understand; rather, the transmissions are done in standard computer formats. An example of EDI would be two computers communicating about a purchase order. When inventory in a store runs low, the retailer's computer might transmit a purchase order to the wholesaler's computer.

EDI links the members of a distribution system in one of two ways. Several members may exchange data directly or multiple companies may exchange information through a central clearinghouse. The following illustration shows these two approaches.

When using an EDI, a manufacturer enters its stock orders in a computer file, which is then forwarded to a supplier's computer. If the EDI system uses a central clearinghouse, the transactions are funneled through the third party's computer system, which then routes them to the appropriate supplier's computer. An EDI allows a manufacturer to communicate with an unlimited number of suppliers.

EDI is used at Benetton, the clothing manufacturer and retailer, to determine produc-

tion runs and to designate the optimum channels of distribution for routing finished goods. At each Benetton retail store, the point-of-sale cash registers maintain a running inventory of items, which they transmit via EDI to computers in branch offices. The branch offices, in turn, transmit the data to the central office computer. For example, if blue sweaters are selling fast, the computer tells the manufacturing system to produce more blue sweaters. The system determines the number of additional blue sweaters each individual store needs, and the best way to send the sweaters to the stores.

Ocean Spray, the producer of cranberry juice and other fruit products, also uses EDI for inventory planning. Retail grocers are able to manage their own inventories through computers at checkout counters and provide on-line shipping notices directly to Ocean Spray. Ocean Spray has found that having vendors provide this information through EDI enables the company to spend more time merchandising and marketing.

Selecting a distribution system is a difficult decision that managers must make continually. Computer-to-computer interchange makes the distribution task less complex, more accurate, and faster. It also provides an up-to-date picture of costs, routes, and efficiency. By linking the members of the distribution system via EDI, the system is better able to serve customers. It is no surprise, then, that market-driven organizations such as Benetton and Ocean Spray are heavily committed to the use of EDI. Manufacturers of consumer and business-to-business goods as well as those responsible for services such as banking and transportation will find EDI playing a large role over the next few years.

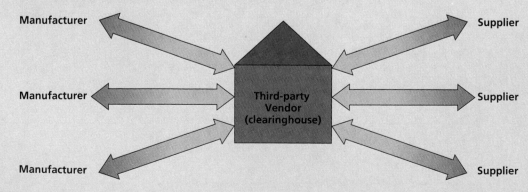

ow do goods and services move through channels of distribution? How are marketing channels of distribution organized? What decisions are involved in managing a channel of distribution? What new systems are replacing conventional channels of distribution? These are some of the critical questions about distribution that this chapter addresses. We will see that the functions performed by intermediaries, although costly, are necessary for the convenience they provide consumers and business-to-business users. Intermediaries are like highways—they are expensive, but without them we could not easily move things from place to place. The introduction of technology such as Electronic Data Interchange (EDI) is designed to make the job of intermediaries more efficient, less costly, and more customer-oriented. Intermediaries in the channels of distribution are crucial to improving customer satisfaction. In this chapter we consider some of the combinations of intermediaries that can form a distribution channel. (In Chapters 12 and 13 we will discuss major channel intermediaries, wholesalers, and retailers in detail.)

WHAT ARE CHANNELS OF DISTRIBUTION?

In any visit to a supermarket, department store, or hardware store, you may examine only some of the hundreds or thousands of items available. Most of these products have been transported from distant locations. The Sony television set on display in the department store in Fort Wayne, Indiana, may have come from a plant in Tokyo, Japan. The workbench in a hardware store in Brussels, Belgium, may have been shipped from a Black & Decker plant in Baltimore, Maryland. In each case marketing managers have determined the best method and route to bring products to us.

The delivery of goods and services, including automobiles, furniture, mass transportation, police protection, airline tickets, legal advice, and health care, is often delayed. Delays result in lost sales and disgruntled consumers. Through effective channels of distribution, some inefficiencies associated with moving goods and services from producer to ultimate or business-to-business consumer can be eliminated, and some delays can be significantly reduced.

Distribution involves getting products and services to people. A **marketing channel of distribution** (or just **channel of distribution**) is formally defined as the organizations or individuals who participate in the flow and transfer of title of goods and services as they move from a producer to an ultimate consumer or a business-to-business user.[1]

A marketing channel can be compared to a pipeline through which oil or gas flows. In a general sense, marketing channels of distribution make possible the flow of a product or service to a consumer. For example, Benetton uses electronic data interchange in order to have sweaters in stores when customers want to make purchases. This channel of distribution ensures a smooth and timely flow of products and services for customers.

Producers, intermediaries (also called middlemen or resellers), and buyers are channel members. **Intermediaries** are organizations or individuals that operate between the producer and consumer in a distribution channel. For example, a compact disc player may move from a plant (producer) in Taiwan, to a wholesaler (intermediary) in Hong Kong, a retailer (intermediary) in Los Angeles, and finally a consumer (buyer) in suburban Van Nuys, California.

The main concern in managing marketing channels is making an offering available for consumption.[2] Specifically, managing channels of distribution involves coordinating and directing the performance of all channel members so that the consumer receives the good or service in a reasonable amount of time.[3]

A marketing channel includes the producer and the ultimate user, as well as any intermediaries. Intermediaries can be wholesalers or retailers. **Wholesalers** are

The distribution of coffee can be used to illustrate the difference between merchants and agents. The coffee grower is a producer, the broker is an agent, and Starbucks is a merchant and retailer selling the gourmet coffee to consumers through company-owned stores.

intermediaries who do not sell to ultimate consumers. Instead, they sell to other intermediaries such as retailers and other wholesalers or to business-to-business consumers. **Retailers** are intermediaries who sell primarily to ultimate consumers (end users). Wholesalers can be **merchants**, people who take title and market (resell) on their own, or **agents**, people who do not take title but who facilitate the flow from producer to user. In the example of the compact disc player, the wholesaler was a merchant. An import-export business in Los Angeles that finds retail outlets in the United States to buy and carry goods produced by Asian manufacturers, however, would be an agent wholesaler rather than a merchant.

The difference between merchants and agents is further illustrated by following the distribution of coffee. Suppose a coffee grower in Guatemala sells coffee to Seattle-based Starbucks Coffee Company, which in turn provides it to its retail stores where ultimate consumers buy it. The sales transaction between the grower and Starbucks may be arranged by a broker, who may never take title to the coffee beans, but simply facilitates the transaction. The coffee grower is a producer, the broker is an agent, and Starbucks is a merchant and retailer selling the gourmet coffee to consumers through company-owned stores. The broker is like a real estate agent who brings coffee growers and coffee lovers together.[4]

The flow of some products involves numerous marketing intermediaries, many of whom are specialized by market, project, region, and even industry. In business markets (formerly called industrial markets), a distributor is an intermediary who often performs various activities in the marketing channel. Electrical device distributors, for example, sell products, maintain inventories, and extend credit to manufacturers who wish to buy electrical supplies.

WHY DO WE NEED INTERMEDIARIES?

Occasionally you hear the cry, "Get rid of the intermediaries; all they do is raise the price." However, the importance of channel intermediaries is clear from the coffee bean example. Growers cannot deal directly with ultimate consumers. They do not have the time or expertise to produce, package, shelve, and sell coffee to shoppers in stores. The costs of the intermediaries can seem high, but without intermediaries, the costs of bringing buyers and sellers together would be even higher.

Table 11.1 shows a breakdown of the costs involved in producing and marketing a compact disc. About 39 percent of the price paid by the consumer ($5.34) goes directly to intermediaries. Producers of compact discs could sell directly to consumers, but this would involve a number of inconveniences. Consumers would have to travel to warehouses or stores run by each manufacturer. Manufacturers would have to hire additional staff to deal with customers. Manufacturers would also need to spend more time and energy marketing their products, leaving fewer resources to improve the manufacturing process. In short, intermediaries make the manufacture and purchase of CDs more efficient for everyone.

As one researcher has stated, "The goal of marketing is the matching of segments of supply and demand."[5] Figure 11.1 shows how intermediaries simplify this matching process. Without an intermediary, each producer of discs would have to market directly to each consumer. In the figure, this would mean 12 transactions or contacts. However, with a single intermediary who, in turn, contacts each customer, there would be only 7 transactions. Paperwork, inconvenience, time, and travel expenses are significantly cut by intermediaries.

In recent years, some industries have started to eliminate intermediaries as a way to cut costs. One example is the life insurance industry. Veritas of Houston, Texas, and USAA of San Antonio, Texas, are now selling life insurance policies directly to the customer. After deciding that the costs of insurance agents were too high, and that direct selling would be effective, the independent insurance agent (intermediary) has been cut out of the process.[6]

TABLE 11.1
Intermediary Costs for a Compact Disc

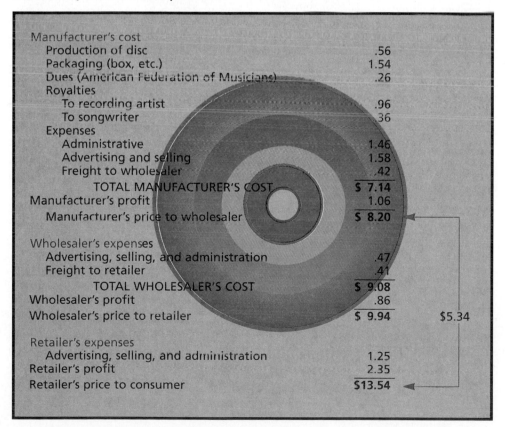

Manufacturer's cost	
Production of disc	.56
Packaging (box, etc.)	1.54
Dues (American Federation of Musicians)	.26
Royalties	
To recording artist	.96
To songwriter	.36
Expenses	
Administrative	1.46
Advertising and selling	1.58
Freight to wholesaler	.42
TOTAL MANUFACTURER'S COST	$ 7.14
Manufacturer's profit	1.06
Manufacturer's price to wholesaler	$ 8.20
Wholesaler's expenses	
Advertising, selling, and administration	.47
Freight to retailer	.41
TOTAL WHOLESALER'S COST	$ 9.08
Wholesaler's profit	.86
Wholesaler's price to retailer	$ 9.94
Retailer's expenses	
Advertising, selling, and administration	1.25
Retailer's profit	2.35
Retailer's price to consumer	$13.54

$5.34

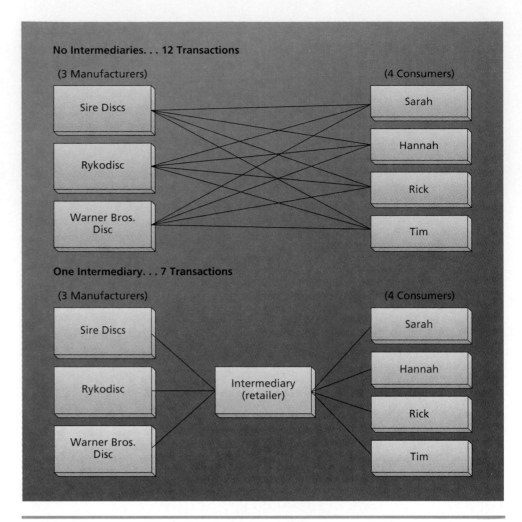

FIGURE 11.1
How Intermediaries Simplify Matching Supply to Demand

Personal computer marketers, facing stiff price competition, are also using fewer intermediaries. Many now use direct mail services instead of relying solely on retail sales and dealers. Apple distributes a catalogue to previous customers, potential new customers, and business customers. The catalogue features hardware and software products. By using primarily direct mail selling, Dell Computer Corporation of Austin, Texas, has built a business of approximately $2 billion annually in fewer than eight years.[7] This elimination of intermediaries can work effectively in some instances, but often producers find that operating without the aid of intermediaries is less convenient and more costly. This is due to the utility created by intermediaries. Despite its success with direct mail selling, many feel Dell must move on to additional distribution channels if it hopes for continued success.[8]

THE UTILITIES CREATED BY INTERMEDIARIES

The costs that intermediaries add are usually offset by the utilities they create. Intermediaries create form, time, place, and possession utilities for end users. These utilities are created through the transactional, logistical, and facilitative functions performed by marketers. You may wish to review Figure 1.2 (Utilities Created by Marketing) about the specific tasks associated with each of these functions.

The three functions (transactional, logistical, and facilitative) have three things in common: each uses up scarce resources, each can best be performed by specialists, and each is shiftable.[9] As it turns out, many of the tasks are most efficiently performed by intermediaries. If producers perform them, both costs and prices increase. When consumers are asked to perform some or all of the tasks, the result is often fewer sales. For example, most consumers do not like to travel long distances to get what they want, and they do not like to spend a lot of time shopping. One study, in fact, found that 65 percent of U.S. consumers find clothes shopping frustrating, and more than 47 percent dislike going to supermarkets to shop.[10] When intermediaries (the specialists) perform the tasks, the producer's costs and prices are lower and the consumers are happier. Of course, the intermediaries must receive some compensation for their work.

YOUR MARKETING KNOWLEDGE

11-1 Describe the channel of distribution that would most likely be used to bring a bicycle to a college student. A tube of toothpaste? An automobile?

11-2 What types of utility are created by retailers?

11-3 Give an example of a purchase by an ultimate consumer that probably involved an agent wholesaler in the distribution channel.

THE ORGANIZATION OF MARKETING CHANNELS

Channels of distribution vary according to the needs of a market and its consumers.[11] In this section we consider different ways marketing channels can be organized. A channel could involve a variety of intermediaries, or no intermediaries at all. An organization could use a single marketing channel or a number of different channels. Generally, manufacturers want to control the distribution channels in which they are involved because their distribution system represents an important part of their marketing strategy.[12] Hence, the manufacturer often tries to organize channels to ensure control.

Consumer Products: Marketing Channels

Figure 11.2 presents five patterns of distribution channels for consumer products. Channel I (the red arrow) is a **direct channel** from the producer to the consumer. Fuller Brush salespeople sell directly to the consumer, as do Mary Kay beauty consultants. **Indirect channels,** where intermediaries operate between producer and consumer, are illustrated in Channels II–V (the gray arrows). For example, Ocean Spray sells juices through brokers who sell to retail stores. This would fall under Channel III because there are two intermediaries: a broker and a retailer. Channel V is the longest channel of distribution; it includes two wholesalers (an agent and a merchant) as well as a retailer.

Although there are many ways that consumer goods pass through each channel, some patterns are more common than others. For example, fresh fruits and vegetables often flow directly from the manufacturer to the consumer. The longer the

In a direct channel, the product moves directly from the producer to the consumer. For example, Mary Kay beauty consultants sell directly to consumers.

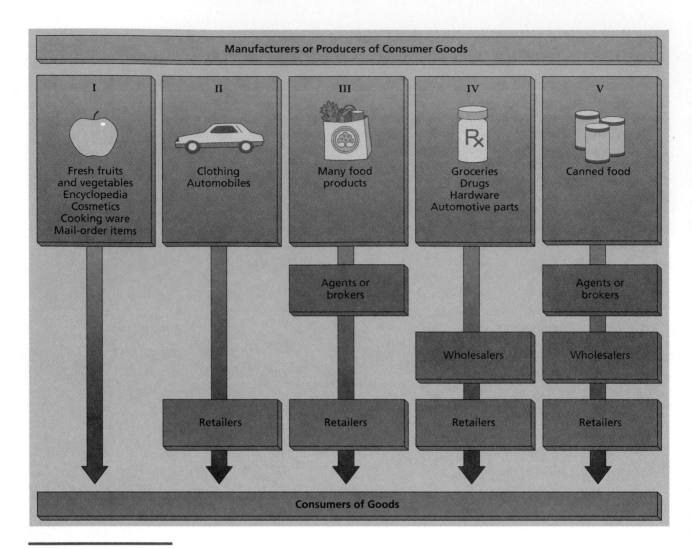

Manufacturers or Producers of Consumer Goods

I	II	III	IV	V
Fresh fruits and vegetables Encyclopedia Cosmetics Cooking ware Mail-order items	Clothing Automobiles	Many food products	Groceries Drugs Hardware Automotive parts	Canned food

Agents or brokers

Agents or brokers

Wholesalers

Wholesalers

Retailers

Retailers

Retailers

Retailers

Consumers of Goods

FIGURE 11.2
Marketing Channels of Distribution for Consumer Goods

channel, the more specialized are the functions performed by intermediaries. In most cases increased specialization means lower costs; each intermediary performs important functions in which he or she has become expert, and this efficiency results in prices relatively lower than if one person were performing all the functions.

Business-to-Business Products: Marketing Channels

In contrast to consumer goods, business-to-business goods most often use a direct channel of distribution. The manufacturer sells directly to the organizational user through a sales force or other direct marketing technique (for example, mail-order catalogues). In comparison to the consumer market, the business-to-business market is made up of a smaller number of relatively large buyers.[13] In addition, buyers often are concentrated geographically. Thus, the advantages of using intermediaries for manufacturers of business-to-business goods are not so clear as the advantages for manufacturers of consumer goods. Another reason for shorter channels for business-to-business goods is the complexity of many products, which require specialized knowledge or postsale service. Figure 11.3 presents three common channels of distribution for business products.

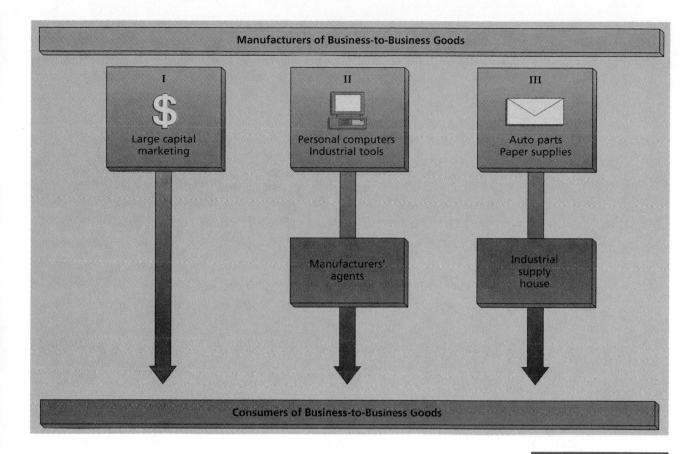

Manufacturers of Business-to-Business Goods

I
$
Large capital marketing

II
Personal computers Industrial tools

III
Auto parts Paper supplies

Manufacturers' agents

Industrial supply house

Consumers of Business-to-Business Goods

FIGURE 11.3
Marketing Channels of Distribution for Business-to-Business Goods

Specialized wholesalers such as manufacturers' agents will be defined and discussed further in Chapter 12. They are used to market some business products (Channel II in Figure 11.3) for the same reasons that agent wholesalers are used in consumer goods markets: the manufacturer is small, has a narrow product line, and sells in geographically dispersed markets. The industrial supply house in Channel III is a wholesaler. It is used primarily for supply and maintenance items and for low-cost, fairly standardized business equipment like lathe machines, shaft seals, electrical supplies, and grinding machines. Graybar Electric, for example, is a supply source for electric supplies. It advertises itself as a well-stocked, single source of electric supplies.

MULTIPLE CHANNELS

Some organizations use more than one marketing channel for similar products. For example, multiple channels are used when the same product is marketed to ultimate consumers and business consumers. STP Corporation sells oil and gasoline additives to service stations and supermarkets. The STP products reach consumers who may have different purchasing patterns. Some people do not buy STP-type products in supermarkets. However, there are some consumers who purchase what they need in any type of store because of the convenience.

In some situations the same product is marketed through a variety of retail outlets. Soft drinks, for example, are sold in almost all grocery stores, but they are also sold in drugstores, lounges, and vending machines. Additionally, restaurants sell soft drinks. In fact, 33 percent of soft drink sales come from fast-food restaurants alone.[14] Goodyear automobile tires are marketed through Goodyear-owned retail stores, tire wholesalers (who sell them to service stations), and franchised Goodyear stores.

The number of different channels used by an organization really depends on the number of different markets the organization is targeting. Each target market may require a unique distribution channel to meet its unique wants and needs. Hence, an organization that employs a differentiated segmentation strategy may use a number of different channels of distribution. Variation in choice of intermediary may also be accompanied by the use of different brand names to further distinguish target markets. The Hallmark Corporation, for example, markets its Hallmark cards in department stores and card shops while marketing its Ambassador brand cards in discount stores.[15]

REVERSE CHANNELS

Marketing channels are traditionally thought to make possible the forward movement of products or services from producer to consumers. However, there is increasing interest in **reverse channels,** in which goods flow back from consumers to producers or other marketing intermediaries. The recycling process is a good example of a reverse channel. The flow of materials, in this case, solid waste, must be reversed through a "backward channel." To do this effectively, however, the consumer must be motivated to become a producer who reverses this distribution process.[16]

Recently the marketing of trash (bottles, cans, and cartons) has become a focus of many consumers' and producers' efforts. Reverse channels have been given more attention as a result. For example, reverse vending machines placed next to machines selling soda pop encourage consumers to recycle their used cans. If an empty can is placed in the machine and a crank is turned, the recycler receives some change.[17]

The recycling process is an example of a reverse channel. This center in Omak, Washington, recycles old and crashed airplanes.

The intermediaries in reverse channels are unique. They receive products from the consumer and dispose of them or return them to the manufacturer. Some intermediaries who will play major roles as reverse channels increase in importance are trash-collection specialists, manufacturers' redemption centers, and trash-recycling brokers.

11-4   Describe a reverse channel of distribution that you have used.

11-5   Why are packaged food products typically sold through an indirect channel of distribution?

YOUR
MARKETING
KNOWLEDGE

MAKING DECISIONS ABOUT MARKETING CHANNELS: THE KEY FACTORS

Why is Tupperware sold directly to consumers at in-home demonstration "parties"? Why can one find Saint Laurent fashions in only a few stores in large cities? Why does Goodyear use multiple marketing channels to sell automobile tires? These questions can be answered if we understand how a marketing manager chooses a channel arrangement.

Marketing managers must consider a number of crucial issues if they are to avoid selecting inappropriate or inefficient marketing channels. Managers should examine past successes and failures. These prior events can reveal the factors that must be weighed in selecting appropriate channels.

Strategic Thinking

In a common scenario, a manufacturer uses incentives and other short-term solutions to improve its channel's performance. This is not always the best scenario, however. For example, in Japan, distribution is a crucial and difficult challenge for foreigners. Any attempt to unravel the Japanese distribution networks without a long-term strategy is doomed to failure. Samsung, a South Korean consumer electronics firm, worked out a strategic distribution plan by entering into long-term agreements with large department store chains instead of wading through layers of Japanese wholesalers.[18] Cannondale Corporation, an American producer of high-performance mountain bikes, established strong relationships with Japanese distributors by hiring Japanese professional bicyclists to enter races riding Cannondale bikes. As final consumers became aware of the company, the firm found it relatively easy to establish a distribution network in Japan.[19] In both of these cases, applying strategic thinking in planning distribution resulted in effective solutions for the firms.

In order to develop a strategic perspective it is necessary to consider any distributor as a partner.[20] Producers must first market to distributors by convincing distributors that it is important to be partners. Samsung was able to establish this type of relationship with the large department store chains in Japan. Next, the manufacturer must join distributors to market the product or service. Partnership, long-term thinking, and avoiding short-term incentives are ingredients of a strategic approach to distribution. If foreign firms are going to fare well in international markets, this strategic approach to distribution will have to be included in their decisions about marketing channels. American firms, in particular, generally benefit from adjusting their independent thinking when entering markets in other parts of the world.

Goals and Objectives

Every organization has goals and objectives. In selecting distribution channels, organizations must consider both general goals (such as earning a satisfactory profit, being socially responsive, minimizing complaints, and satisfying consumer needs and wants) and specific objectives (such as "increasing market share by 2 percent by the end of the current year"). The distribution strategy of the firm should be designed to contribute to the organization's attainment of its goals and objectives. To do so, channels must use available resources (human, technical, financial) and take account of constraints (legal, competitive, technological).

Company Characteristics

It is important to understand the characteristics of a company in selecting appropriate channels of distribution. A strong financial position and a strong marketing work force allow an organization to engage in costly, but profitable, direct marketing. For example, when Apple Computers decided to offer its computers directly to ultimate consumers through mail order (in addition to using independent retailers as it had done in the past), it meant more work for the company. Apple was required to deal directly with the users of its computers, working to convince them to buy an Apple computer. The firm's strong financial position allowed it to undertake this direct channel. With this strategy, Apple does not have to share profits with intermediaries.

Conversely, a company with weak resources may be forced to use powerful intermediaries, even when it requires giving up some power. A small, production-oriented firm with little marketing expertise may rely on a wholesaler to plan and carry out its entire marketing strategy. While this approach relieves the producer of concerns about marketing planning, it also removes much of the control the manufacturer might have over how and to whom its product is marketed. The greater a firm's financial resources, the more control it exercises over its channels of distribution.

Customer Characteristics

The ultimate users and buyers must be considered in making choices about channels. The identity of ultimate users must be precise and up-to-date. Who are they? Where do they live? What are their needs and wants? What appeals to them?

The buying specifications of customers must be studied in detail. Typical buying specifications for milk might be that it is purchased:

1. more than once a week
2. usually on Friday or Saturday, plus early in the week
3. in a supermarket along with other staples
4. as needed to replenish supply
5. according to an established brand preference, but brand preference may change if relative prices change

In contrast, the typical buying specifications for a high-quality personal computer system might be that it is purchased:

1. only from a well-established, reputable local dealer
2. only after considerable comparison shopping
3. after extended, thorough review and consideration
4. only from a dealer equipped to render prompt and reasonable product service

If the manufacturer knows something about users' buying specifications, it can decide on the type of intermediaries to use. By analyzing these specifications, many organizations have been able to develop very creative approaches to distribution channels that serve the needs and wants of their customers.

▪ Arby's, Taco Bell, and Pizza Hut have created their own double drive-through franchise stores. These limited-menu stores are built for a car to drive through the building and offer only drive-through service. Customers pick up their food and take it somewhere else to eat.[21]

▪ Glide dental floss, produced by W. L. Gore & Associates, was initially sold through dentists' offices. This strategy helped the small firm avoid competition from giants such as Johnson & Johnson and Gillette as well as develop an image of superior quality.[22]

▪ Girl Scouts offers scouting activities in classes during regular school hours. These projects have been developed to extend Girl Scouting to communities that are currently underserved.

These examples illustrate that target markets can be aggressively addressed by creatively establishing new channels of distribution. Differences in the needs and wants of customers require diverse channels of distribution.

Product Characteristics

The characteristics of a product play a role in the selection of appropriate channels of distribution. As discussed in Chapter 9, consumer goods fit into three categories: convenience, shopping, and specialty. These product categories can be combined with definitions of stores based on patronage motives.[23] Hence, retail stores can also be classified as convenience, shopping, and specialty stores. A 7-Eleven Store is a convenience store, while the local deli is a specialty store. Marshall Field's, Macy's, Sears, and Hudson's are shopping stores. Porsche dealerships and La-Z-Boy furniture stores are specialty establishments.

This classification scheme can be useful in choosing an appropriate channel. Convenience goods are best distributed through convenience stores, shopping goods through shopping stores, and specialty goods through specialty stores. Once a marketer has determined the type of good its product represents, he or she will know what type of store would be most appropriate for its distribution.

In addition to identifying the product's position in the goods classification scheme, the marketer's consideration of other product characteristics can also aid in the selection of distribution channels. Perishability, complexity, and replacement rate are all important product characteristics.

The more perishable a product is, the shorter the distribution channel it must use to reach final consumers. Marketers of products such as fresh seafood and cut flowers cannot send their products through a distribution channel consisting of multiple layers of intermediaries. Getting the product to the final consumer quickly is of utmost importance.

A product's complexity also affects the choice of channel. Generally, the more complex a product is, the fewer intermediaries will be in the distribution channel. Highly complex products such as mainframe computers or other technologically sophisticated equipment are likely to reach consumers through direct channels of distribution. Because extremely complex products are most often sold to business consumers, business-to-business consumers are more likely than ultimate consumers to be involved in direct channels of distribution.

Some experts believe the key determining characteristic of a good's or service's distribution channel is its **replacement rate,** the rate at which it is purchased and consumed.[24] Milk has a high replacement rate, a set of china has a low replacement rate, and a shirt has a medium replacement rate.

A good with a high replacement rate usually has four characteristics: low unit gross margin, low adjustment factor (amount of change required to meet customers' needs), short consumption period (a chocolate cake, for example, has a relatively short consumption period), and short search time (shopping time required to secure the good).[25]

A good with a high replacement rate requires more indirect routes of distribution. The reverse is true for goods with low replacement rates like china or automobiles. An evaluation of the replacement rate can guide decisions about distribution channels.

Market Characteristics

Knowledge of the characteristics of the market can help manufacturers make decisions about channels. Manufacturers should examine these characteristics:

- **market size,** both current and potential in units and dollars
- **market structure,** by geography, by account size
- **market share,** including direct and indirect competition
- **market stability,** the volatility of users' needs
- **market growth,** in units and dollars

Generally, the larger a market is (in terms of units, number of consumers, size of market share, etc.) the longer the distribution channel required to meet its needs. A very large market, with millions of customers, will probably use a distribution channel with several levels of intermediaries including a variety of wholesalers, each performing specialized functions, and an army of retailers. This complex channel will be required to reach such a large market. Kellogg's Corn Flakes, for example, may move from its producer in Battle Creek, Michigan, to wholesalers who provide warehousing facilities. A second, separate, wholesaler may provide transportation to get the cereal to markets nationwide. Once in a local market, the corn flakes may be moved by yet another wholesaler to the distribution centers of retail grocers. The retailers would then distribute the cereal to store shelves.

Likewise, a market that is widely dispersed geographically requires a distribution channel with more intermediaries. In marketing its vast line of consumer goods worldwide, Procter & Gamble relies on many intermediaries, using a long channel of distribution to reach its many customers.

Environmental Characteristics

In Chapter 2 we saw that environmental forces influence every part of the marketing function. Economic conditions and legal, political, technological, social-cultural, ecological, and competitive environmental forces affect the structure and efficiency of channels of distribution.

Channel competition can take four forms:

1. Competition among channel members at the same level. Retailers compete with other retailers, wholesalers with other wholesalers. One Walgreen's Drug Store may compete with another two miles away.

2. Competition among channel members at different levels. Manufacturers and retailers compete with wholesalers and with each other.
3. Competition among channels. The manufacturer-retailer channel competes with the manufacturer-wholesaler-retailer channel.
4. Competition among channel members for the use of other channel members. Manufacturers compete with other manufacturers for the use of a particular wholesaler or retailer, or wholesalers compete with other wholesalers for the use of a specific retailer.[26]

The competitive environment can result in decisions to change the pattern of distribution or the number of intermediaries. It can also result in conflict, which we will discuss later. Competition for the use of channel members can be as intense as price competition. In the supermarket field, for example, more and more retailers like Kroger (a national chain) and Dominick's (a Chicago-area supermarket chain) are reluctant to increase the number of brand items they carry because shelf space is limited. Thus, some brands will not make it to their shelves.

In a study of the supplier-retailer level of distribution, researchers examined the environmental factors that affect decision-making uncertainty in this channel relationship.[27] Four dimensions—diversity among consumers, dynamism, concentration, and capacity—are crucial to understanding decision-making uncertainty:

- *Diversity* is the degree of similarity-dissimilarity of such factors as needs, preference, and background of the customer.
- *Dynamism* is the frequency of change in competitive strategies and customer preferences.
- *Concentration* is the economic power of competitors.
- *Capacity* is the number of opportunities and resources in the environment.

These four environmental dimensions directly influence the degree of decision-making uncertainty expressed by channel members. Hence, the more diverse the customer base, the greater and more powerful the competition, and the more opportunities and resources (all environmental factors), the more difficult it is to plan a distribution channel.

The legal system that governs channels of distribution has evolved to encourage full interchannel and intrachannel competition. The deregulation of some industries has created an array of channels for a variety of goods and services. Federal, state, and local laws generally attempt to prohibit use of power that destroys competition in channels, and to prevent use of practices and enticements that actually or potentially injure competition in the marketplace. In the beer industry, for example, the U.S. Congress (in 1933) established a mandated distribution network that included independent distributors. This mandate, which is still in effect, was issued to encourage competition by keeping breweries from gaining direct control over the sale of beer to the final consumer.[28]

While governments are typically active in restricting many actions that would appear to reduce competition, some critics claim that through its inactivity with regard to mergers and acquisitions, the U.S. government has encouraged less competition. For example, Whirlpool Corporation acquired Kitchenaid Incorporated, another appliance maker, and within five months dismissed all of Kitchenaid's former distributors. Pepsico, which already owned the Taco Bell and Pizza Hut restaurant chains, acquired KFC (Kentucky Fried Chicken). Wendy's, a competitor of KFC, viewed this acquisition as a threat and banished Pepsico products and substituted Coca-Cola in its hamburger outlets.[29]

There are many other ways that environmental forces affect decision making regarding channels of distribution. In developing design and strategy, a marketing manager must carefully weigh environmental forces against each of the characteristics we have considered. The task of weighing each characteristic may seem impossible, or extremely complex, but failure to do so can result in the selection of improper, inefficient, or excessively costly channels of distribution. There is no one best channel of distribution, but some channels are better than others to meet an organization's general goals and objectives, as well as its marketing targets.

MARKET COVERAGE: HOW MANY CHANNEL OUTLETS?

Another important marketing channel decision is choosing the number of channel outlets or intermediaries needed for the desired degree of market exposure, the number of resellers to include in the channel.[30] This decision requires that the marketer determine the intensity of distribution to be used. How many retailers, wholesalers, and agents in a market should be included in the channel distribution network? There is no simple answer to this important question. The possibilities are limitless, ranging from distribution through numerous outlets to having only one outlet in a market area.

Intensive Distribution

The maximum market coverage occurs through **intensive distribution,** in which the manufacturer attempts to persuade as many retailers as possible in an area to carry the product. The advantages of intensive distribution are increased impulse purchasing, wider consumer recognition of the product, and greater consumer convenience. The disadvantages include lower margins, smaller orders, more problems with inventory control and reorders, and less overall control.

Some items that are intensively distributed are Coca-Cola, Pepsi Cola, Hershey's candy, Frito-Lay chips, Kodak film, Campbell's soups, General Mills Cheerios, and Juicy Fruit gum. Notice that all of these items would be categorized as consumer convenience goods. Convenience goods, you will recall, are products that consumers are willing to exert little, if any, effort to obtain. In the consumer market, almost all brand-name convenience items require intensive distribution because consumers will usually switch brands rather than exert energy searching for a specific offering. For example, most consumers will switch breakfast cereals rather than travel to another store to purchase a favorite. In the business-to-business market, office supplies, small tools, and standard-size fittings and seals are intensively distributed for similar reasons. The "Spotlight on Global Marketing: Pepsico's Distribution Applications in Mexico" illustrates how Pepsico has found success in Mexico by using the strategy of intensive distribution for its snack foods that the firm had refined in the United States.

Intensive distribution can result in large sales volume. However, it is expensive to advertise and maintain a large sales force. There is also the problem of motivating an intermediary to sell one's product more enthusiastically than another's. Gillette, Schick, and Wilkinson all want that extra push from intermediaries. The intermediaries for these intensively distributed products, on the other hand, may be indifferent with respect to which of these products their customers buy.

Exclusive Distribution

The use of a single or very small number of retailers or wholesalers in a particular geographical area is referred to as **exclusive distribution.** For example, New York City, with a population of about 7.5 million, has only one Beltrami fashion store and only a few Rolls Royce dealerships. If you would like to purchase Calèche Perfume by Hermès, you must visit the exclusive Hermès store on East 57th Street.

Exclusive distribution allows producers to choose the intermediaries whose images are most consistent with the image of their products. For example, Champ's Products markets its ice cream bars only at Chicago's Wrigley Field and Lincoln Park Zoo.

Exclusivity can provide significant marketing advantages for the manufacturer and intermediaries. Strong dealer loyalty and active sales support usually accompany exclusive distributorships. Exclusive intermediaries are motivated because they alone profit from their hard work and sales. Better forecasting and more efficient inventory control and retail control systems are possible when there is only one outlet. Exclusive distributors generally receive higher markups than other distributors. (The markup is the amount added to cost to cover expenses and allow a reasonable profit. See Chapter 18.) There is more consultation between producer and intermediary on decisions involving price, advertising, and inventory.

Exclusive distribution allows producers to choose the intermediaries whose images are most consistent with the image of their products. Champ's Products, for example, markets its premium ice cream bars only at Wrigley Field and the Lincoln Park Zoo in Chicago. The Chicago Cubs and the animals in the zoo are the association that Champ's wants for its ice cream bars.[31]

One disadvantage for a manufacturer in an exclusive distribution network is that sales can be lost because of the limited distribution. Thus, before deciding on exclusive distribution, producers must be sure that consumers are willing to take the time and effort to seek out their products. The need for a consumer to search out and travel to the location where a product is available suggests that exclusive distribution is most appropriate for specialty goods.

Exclusive distribution can help create an aura of specialness for a product. Exclusivity itself would appear to suggest that there is something about the product that is worth searching for. Marketers must be careful, however, not to attempt exclusive distribution with a product that consumers clearly do not see as special. When applied to a convenience product like a common snack food or shampoo, such an arrangement will probably result in lost sales rather than the creation of a specialty good.

Selective Distribution

Between the two extremes of exclusive and intensive distribution is **selective distribution.** This type of market coverage is used for products purchased by consumers who want to identify choices and make comparisons before purchasing. Consumer shopping goods and business-to-business accessory equipment typically are distributed selectively. Such products are often more expensive and are likely to be around longer than convenience goods or operating supplies. For example, durable goods

MARKETING IN ACTION

SPOTLIGHT
ON
**Global
Marketing**

Pepsico's Distribution Applications in Mexico

Pepsico sales in Mexico in 1991 were about $1.2 billion and are expected to grow to $2.0 billion by 1995. This growth reflects a trend for the company, which saw international sales and profits increase by 22 percent in 1992. The firm experienced double-digit growth in Mexico throughout the early 1990s. Mexico, with 84 million people, is expected to be one of the world's boom economies, and thus a significant opportunity for Pepsico throughout the 1990s. Pepsico is now Mexico's largest consumer products company, in part because of its excellent distribution system.

As the Mexican middle-class keeps growing, the demand for items such as chips and other snack food has also increased. The distribution channels have had to grow to keep up the supply. Pepsico acquired Sabritas, its Mexico City–based unit, through a joint venture in 1967. Then known as Productos Selectos, Sabritas had sales of less than $1 million, due in part to its outmoded distribution system. The firm regularly used bicyclists to deliver bags of potato chips to corner stores (*tiendas*).

Corner stores and mom-and-pop operations are a more common place to shop for groceries in

Mexico than in the United States. Pepsico faced the challenge of implementing an intensive distribution system that could guarantee efficient delivery to many small stores. Clearly, delivery by bicycle was not the method that would allow sales to grow. Today Sabritas has a sophisticated distribution network that carries its snack line by van from one of its four manufacturing plants in Mexico directly to supermarkets, as well as to 400,000 mom-and-pop shops around the country. Sabritas now has more than 70 percent of Mexico's salty snack market.

The improvement in Sabritas's distribution system has permitted it to do extensive distribution throughout Mexico. Now Pepsico is planning to distribute Sabritas to countries in South America. Based on its success in Mexico, Pepsico has entered into joint ventures in other countries. One such partnership is with Elena Chips in Brazil. From a distribution system that began with bicycles and progressed to trucks, airplanes, and ships, Sabritas can now be distributed efficiently and freshly to all the places where the vast Mexican market shops.

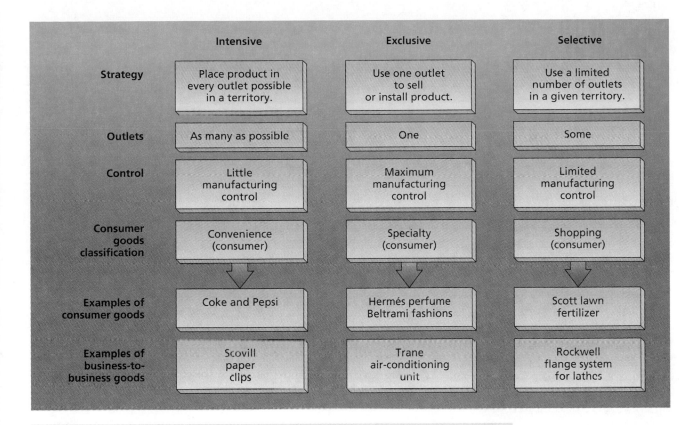

	Intensive	Exclusive	Selective
Strategy	Place product in every outlet possible in a territory.	Use one outlet to sell or install product.	Use a limited number of outlets in a given territory.
Outlets	As many as possible	One	Some
Control	Little manufacturing control	Maximum manufacturing control	Limited manufacturing control
Consumer goods classification	Convenience (consumer)	Specialty (consumer)	Shopping (consumer)
Examples of consumer goods	Coke and Pepsi	Hermés perfume Beltrami fashions	Scott lawn fertilizer
Examples of business-to-business goods	Scovill paper clips	Trane air-conditioning unit	Rockwell flange system for lathes

FIGURE 11.4
Intensive, Exclusive, and Selective Distribution

like personal computers, ceiling fans, stereos, and home appliances are distributed selectively.

With selective distribution, a manufacturer attempts to distribute only through outlets where sales volume, rate of inventory turnover, and order size result in a satisfactory profit. A selective distribution system is often profitable for manufacturers because it costs less than intensive distribution, there are fewer intermediaries to call on, and there is less intense competition and more cooperation among intermediaries.

Like exclusive distribution, selective distribution can connote an aura of exclusivity about a product. Perhaps you've seen or heard an advertisement for a product that is "available in better stores." The manufacturer in such a case not only benefits from the cost savings of less widespread distribution, but it also benefits from the connotation that its product is special because of its limited availability. Figure 11.4 summarizes the three market coverage choices that marketing managers face.

Strategic Issues in Market Coverage

Choosing the correct intensity of coverage for a product or service is not easy. Sometimes the intensity that initially appears best is not the correct choice. Honda, for example, considered a number of designs for the dealer network to sell Acura. It decided to use 270 dealers who pledged themselves to the exclusive sales of the Acura Legend and the Integra. Unfortunately, this strategy was not fully successful. By only selling a single car model, many dealers have not been able to generate enough revenue from service or used car sales to make a profit.

There is no formula to answer the question of what the best choice of market coverage is for a product or service. It has been suggested, however, that the following factors be considered.[32]

1. *The total market demand and growth rate.* The Saturn Corporation (a wholly owned subsidiary of General Motors) has estimated how rapidly demand will develop over time. From this estimate, it has identified key cities in which it requires dealers. At the end of 1993 there were 274 dealerships in the United States.

2. *How customers select dealers or outlets.* The rule of thumb is to ensure market coverage for products by customer segment. When Tandy decided to begin selling its computers at Wal-Mart, it saw this channel serving a different market segment from the one that is served by Radio Shack (hobbyists).

3. *The mix of dealers or retailers.* Relying too much on full-line or specialist dealers often results in missed market coverage. Full-line dealers often offer the manufacturer sales growth because they bundle products together. Specialists offer value-added expertise. By including both in a network, there is more coverage of the market.

4. *The capacity of each dealer or retailer.* Compaq Computer and Cooper Tire are renowned for their creative dealer support. Before adding new dealers, these two firms determine how they can boost dealer productivity.

CONTROL PROCEDURES AND LEGAL ISSUES

Manufacturers often use control procedures to influence the distribution of their product as it moves through the marketing channel. This section focuses on three ways they attempt to do this and the legal implications of each method.

Exclusive Dealing Contracts

With an **exclusive dealing contract,** the manufacturer prohibits an intermediary from carrying competing products. This type of contract is illegal in two situations. The first situation occurs when the manufacturer's sales volume is so substantial a part of the total volume in a market that competitors would be closed out of the market. Maybelline backed off from attempting to pressure retailers into carrying only a minimum number of competing cosmetic lines due to the questionable legalities. The second situation in which an exclusive dealing contract is illegal occurs when the contract between a large manufacturer and a much smaller intermediary causes the power imbalance to be a coercive threat and, possibly, a restraint of trade. This situation would be faced if a large manufacturer of athletic shoes such as Nike or Reebok pressured a small chain of shoe stores to carry only its brand of athletic footwear. The chain might feel it could not resist Nike's pressure and still survive.

Exclusive dealing is not always illegal. If equivalent products are available to consumers, or if the manufacturer's competitors have access to equivalent intermediaries, an exclusive dealing contract may be legal. Such a contract is also acceptable when a manufacturer is just getting started in a market or when a manufacturer's share of the market is negligible. Hence, the Old Snowmass Food Company of Aspen, Colorado, produces Crooked Spoke Barbeque Sauce and distributes it to the mountain states through an exclusive dealing contract with intermediaries in those states.[33]

Exclusive Sales Territory

When a manufacturer restricts the geographic territory of its intermediaries, it creates **exclusive sales territories.** The legal issue is whether restriction decreases competition and violates parts of the Sherman, Clayton, and Federal Trade Commission Acts. (These acts were discussed in Chapter 2.) The courts seek to encourage competition among intermediaries that handle the same brand, but exceptions are permitted when a manufacturer is new or its market share is negligible.

There are two types of sales territory restrictions: vertical and horizontal. With a *vertical restriction*, a manufacturer permits only one authorized intermediary. Many small manufacturers, for example, distribute their products exclusively through Wal-Mart. Wal-Mart encourages this type of distribution and is, in fact, anxious to deal directly with manufacturers rather than with a series of independent wholesalers who would be working to distribute the products to many retailers. Vertical restriction has usually been accepted by the courts because it promotes competing brands. A *horizontal restriction*, often judged unlawful by the courts, is an agreement among intermediaries (retailers and wholesalers) about who will market a manufacturer's products. In a case involving Schwinn Bicycle Company, the U.S. Supreme Court ruled against territorial restrictions imposed by Schwinn on intermediaries.[34] On the other hand, the court ruled that Sylvania could prevent expansion by one of its dealers into the territory of another. The court has stated that the rule of reason must be used to decide if exclusivity harms competition.[35] Thus, granting exclusive territories depends on whether a firm can legally justify its actions to the courts.

Tying Contracts

A **tying contract** is one in which a manufacturer or franchisor sells a product to an intermediary only if the intermediary also buys other (possibly unwanted) products from the manufacturer or franchisor or from another specified manufacturer. For example, Chicken Delight, a fast-food franchisor, obliged its outlets to purchase Chicken Delight's cooking and frying equipment, dips, and spices. The Supreme Court declared this tying contract system illegal and awarded the franchisees triple damages.

Tying contracts are often used when there are shortages of a desired product, and the manufacturer wants to push a less popular product. In franchise arrangements, franchisors often want each franchisee to purchase from them everything needed to run the business. In general, tying contracts of this type are illegal. On the other hand, tying contracts are often acceptable when a new firm is entering the market, the manufacturer (or franchisor) wants to maintain a quality product or service, or the exclusive intermediary is required to carry the manufacturer's full line of products but is not prohibited from carrying competing products. Magnavox might, for example, grant a retailer the exclusive right in a given geographical area to carry Magnavox televisions only if the retailer agrees to carry other products produced by Magnavox as well. Magnavox cannot, however, stop the retailer from carrying televisions produced by Sony and other competitors.

Retailers such as franchisees may actually benefit from tying contracts in that the franchisor can buy in larger quantities, thus realizing economies. Hotel management companies, for example, often require their properties to buy supplies through the corporate office. The net result may be that the corporate office makes a small percentage on the purchases but that the properties benefit from the lower bulk purchase prices negotiated by the corporate purchasing units. In addition to cost savings, the retailer saves the time and effort associated with doing its own purchasing.

MARKETING CHANNELS: CONFLICT AND COOPERATION

The need to manage channels of distribution is sometimes overshadowed by discussions of which pattern or how many intermediaries to use for optimal market coverage. Equally important to these strategic issues, however, is a strategy for managing the channel in such a way as to ensure cooperation rather than conflict among channel members. Conflict can arise because intermediaries, like manufacturers, are in business to accomplish goals and objectives. Unfortunately, the goals and objectives of intermediaries are not always the same as the goals and objectives of the manufacturer, thus the potential for conflict. Primary responsibilities of the key member (manufacturer, wholesaler, or retailer) in the channel are to plan, organize, control, and lead the channel so as to maximize cooperation and minimize conflict. The proper management of channels to ensure cooperation is essential if marketing mix objectives across all four Ps are to be achieved.[36]

Types of Conflict

In our earlier discussion of environmental characteristics, we saw a number of sources of interaction and conflict. The existence of competition suggests that a channel is more than a structure or set of interdependent parts. It can also involve horizontal or vertical conflict.[37]

Horizontal conflict.   **Horizontal conflict** occurs between or among intermediaries at the same level—two or more retailers (for example, Kroger and Winn-Dixie) or two or more wholesalers. This type of conflict also can be found between or among different types of retailers who handle similar products. Retail druggists (Eckerd's) compete with discount houses (Sav-On), department stores (JCPenney), quick-stop or convenience grocery stores (7-Eleven), and mail-order houses, all of which carry some of the same brands of products.

Vertical conflict.   **Vertical conflict** occurs between or among channel members at different levels—manufacturer with wholesalers, wholesalers with retailers, and so forth. It arises from differences in goals and objectives, misunderstandings, and poor communication. Because manufacturers often want to distance themselves from customers, manufacturers can have conflicts with dealers (retailers). However, in the current era of customer satisfaction and market-driven competition, the manufacturer is not generally able to pass the buck to intermediaries.[38] Consider, for example, a customer who purchased an American-made automobile. From the beginning, the remote entry system didn't work. The door locks would open and close at will while the car was moving. The dealer serviced the car again and again, but couldn't solve the problem. The customer called the factory only to be told that the firm did not deal with customers directly. The manufacturer would not talk with the customer. Is this the kind of image, reputation, and record that a manufacturer can afford in competitive markets? The "Marketing in Action: Tennis Racquets, Bicycles, and Channel Conflict" illustrates both horizontal and vertical conflict.

Since marketing channels consist of individual organizations, there is always the possibility of horizontal or vertical conflict among channel members. *Role theory* explains why the potential for channel conflict exists. In role theory terms, each member in the channel is expected by other members to perform certain roles or functions. However, members' role expectations are not always in agreement. When a member acts in an unexpected or abnormal way, dissatisfaction, frustration, and inefficiency emerge.

When channel members belong to different organizations, each may have its own view of how best to conduct business and what its role should be. For example,

MARKETING *IN ACTION*

Tennis Racquets, Bicycles, and Channel Conflict

Randy is the owner of the Racket Doctor Tennis Shop in Los Angeles. Randy devised a strategy to beat the competition by charging a few dollars less than the price being charged by all other retailers for prestigious Prince tennis racquets. In doing so, however, Randy became susceptible to problems. Prince (a unit of Italy's Edizione Holding Company) has a policy that states:

> Prince will not supply racquets to accounts which we believe will sell them at a price below the Suggested Range of Retail Pricing [established by Prince]. In the event Prince becomes aware of a dealer pricing a racquet below these guidelines, it will, following receipt of verification acceptable to Prince, suspend shipment to that account of that racquet and, in its sole discretion, any or all other racquets on this pricing policy.

Other retailers in competition with Randy began complaining to Prince when they became aware of Randy's pricing strategy. Thus, Randy's action caused horizontal conflict among the retailers in the Los Angeles area. Prince began investigating Randy's pricing and determined that he was not in accordance with its policy regarding the sale of Prince racquets. Thus, vertical conflict between the manufacturer (Prince) and a retailer (Randy) was also created.

The conflicts were resolved when a sales representative for Prince informed Randy that because of his price discount he would receive no more Prince racquets. Within a few weeks the Racket Doctor's supply of Prince racquets was depleted and Randy received no more Prince racquets to sell.

Gorilla Bicycle Company, a Salt Lake City retailer, faced a dilemma similar to that of the Racket Doctor. Gorilla was selling a popular brand of mountain bike, Specialized Mountain Bikes, at discount prices. Specialized, however, suggested the prices that retailers should charge for its product and preferred to do business only with retailers who followed those suggestions. Most retailers of mountain bikes, it seems, liked the Specialized policy of establishing prices and encouraging retailers to maintain them. When other retailers of mountain bikes complained about Gorilla's discounting of Specialized bikes (horizontal conflict), Specialized refused to supply bikes to Gorilla, and withheld tires and other accessories.

Gorilla agreed to sell at the manufacturer's agreed price if allowed to show customers that Specialized had ordered the price that must be charged and refused to allow the retailer to lower the price. Specialized would not agree to this and the vertical conflict between manufacturer and retailer caused an end to the relationship.

Mandatory pricing by manufacturers has prompted investigations by the Federal Trade Commission (FTC) in both the tennis racquet and bicycle industries. Currently no charges have been filed. The horizontal conflict between and among retailers caused by the pricing policies of manufacturers, however, has created disharmony in the industry. Additionally, the vertical conflict between manufacturers and retailers that has prompted some manufacturers to prohibit certain retailers from carrying their products has reduced the options for consumers in the market for either of these two products.

suppose a food producer like General Mills wanted intermediaries to promote Nature Valley granola bars in a particular manner. If a 7-Eleven store had a totally different picture of the best way to promote the product, a channel member role conflict would exist.

Resolving Conflict

When continual breakdowns in communication, agreements, and trust occur, conflict makes the situation dysfunctional. Reprisals, sabotage, anger, and frustration among manufacturers and intermediaries are not conducive to efficient marketing activities.

Wal-Mart is a powerful retail channel captain. All members of the channel are likely to cooperate with Wal-Mart's policies and strategies because they wish to continue doing business with Wal-Mart.

One way to resolve conflict is to follow the lead of a channel captain. A **channel captain** is often the member with the most power and authority, who directs, leads, and supports other channel members. IBM is a manufacturing channel leader, McKesson-Robbins is a dry wholesaler channel captain, and Wal-Mart is a powerful retail channel captain. For example, because Wal-Mart is a large and popular retailer that manufacturers and wholesalers wish to do business with, the discount retailer can set delivery dates, establish order policies, and plan promotion strategies for the whole distribution channel. All members of the channel are likely to cooperate because they respect Wal-Mart's ability to carry out these activities and, of course, because they wish to continue doing business with Wal-Mart.

A number of feasible strategies for conflict resolution exist for the variety of conflicts that might be encountered in a distribution channel. Two researchers have suggested that the different types of conflict can be categorized into "conflict zones."[39] Figure 11.5 summarizes the five conflict zones. The following examples describe some potential zones of conflict.

1. *Manufacturers bypass intermediaries and sell directly to users.* A manufacturer sometimes chooses to sell to intermediaries while at the same time competing with them and selling directly to consumers. This is referred to as **dual distribution.** For example, we noted earlier that several manufacturers of personal computers (including Apple) sell directly to consumers through catalogues; at the same time they distribute their products through intermediaries.

   Conflict often arises in this situation because intermediaries feel they are competing, at the retail level, with their own suppliers. One way to resolve the problem is for the manufacturer to sell only to intermediaries. In more than 65 years of business, SteelCase (an office-furniture manufacturer with $1 billion in sales), has never sold directly to users.[40] It has maintained that dual distribution activities are not good for business.

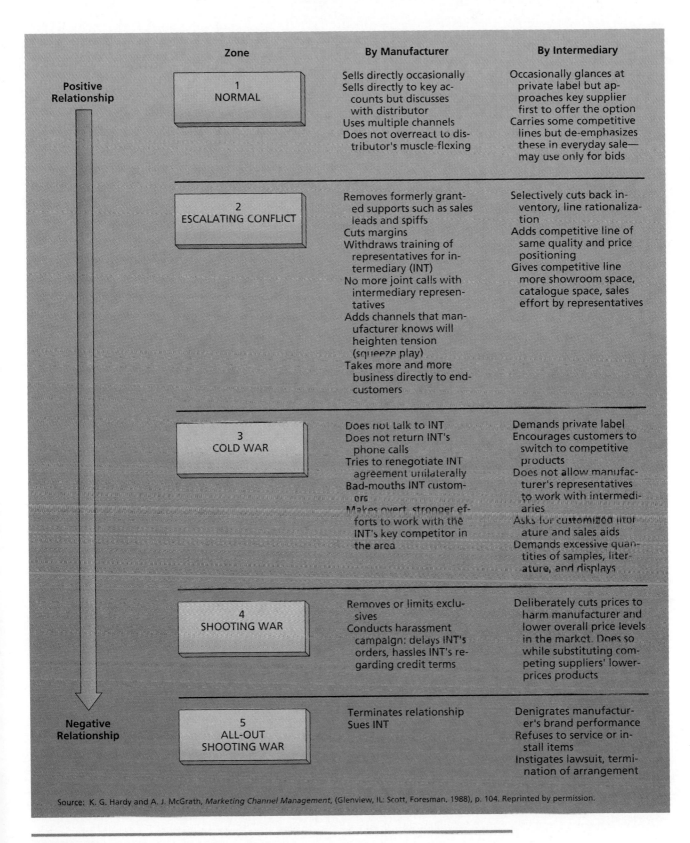

Zone	By Manufacturer	By Intermediary
1 **NORMAL**	Sells directly occasionally Sells directly to key accounts but discusses with distributor Uses multiple channels Does not overreact to distributor's muscle-flexing	Occasionally glances at private label but approaches key supplier first to offer the option Carries some competitive lines but de-emphasizes these in everyday sale—may use only for bids
2 **ESCALATING CONFLICT**	Removes formerly granted supports such as sales leads and spiffs Cuts margins Withdraws training of representatives for intermediary (INT) No more joint calls with intermediary representatives Adds channels that manufacturer knows will heighten tension (squeeze play) Takes more and more business directly to end-customers	Selectively cuts back inventory, line rationalization Adds competitive line of same quality and price positioning Gives competitive line more showroom space, catalogue space, sales effort by representatives
3 **COLD WAR**	Does not talk to INT Does not return INT's phone calls Tries to renegotiate INT agreement unilaterally Bad-mouths INT customers Makes overt, stronger efforts to work with the INT's key competitor in the area	Demands private label Encourages customers to switch to competitive products Does not allow manufacturer's representatives to work with intermediaries Asks for customized literature and sales aids Demands excessive quantities of samples, literature, and displays
4 **SHOOTING WAR**	Removes or limits exclusives Conducts harassment campaign: delays INT's orders, hassles INT's regarding credit terms	Deliberately cuts prices to harm manufacturer and lower overall price levels in the market. Does so while substituting competing suppliers' lower-prices products
5 **ALL-OUT SHOOTING WAR**	Terminates relationship Sues INT	Denigrates manufacturer's brand performance Refuses to service or install items Instigates lawsuit, termination of arrangement

Positive Relationship ↓ **Negative Relationship**

Source: K. G. Hardy and A. J. McGrath, *Marketing Channel Management*, (Glenview, IL: Scott, Foresman, 1988), p. 104. Reprinted by permission.

FIGURE 11.5
Manufacturer/Intermediary (INT) Behavior in Five Zones of Conflict

Another strategy to resolve or prevent this conflict is to adopt and use a policy of making direct sales only to a specific type or size of customer. A third strategy is to compensate intermediaries for all manufacturer-to-user direct sales, in which intermediaries are compensated at a lower rate than if they were in the channel.

2. *The manufacturer is perceived to have permitted too many intermediaries in a geographic area.* A major retailer such as Wal-Mart, for example, might object if its suppliers allowed a large number of other retailers in the same city or town to also carry items being carried by Wal-Mart. One method used to solve this problem is the establishment of "master dealers." These dealers are given commissions on the sales of other intermediaries in the area. Hence, Wal-Mart might receive a small commission on sales made by other retailers in the area. Another strategy is for the supplier to assess the area carefully to decide on the appropriate number of intermediaries.

3. *The margins that members in the channel receive differ.* In this case conflict arises because intermediaries compare their margins with those of other channel members. They may find that their margin is less than that of others in the channel. The key to resolving this form of conflict is to establish margins on the basis of effort expended and work performed. The manufacturer pays for work that is performed. If an intermediary doesn't stock an inventory, for example, it would not collect a portion of the margins for stocking.

4. *Sharing information on users' identities is in dispute.* Intermediaries are sometimes reluctant to share information that will identify their customers (users) to manufacturers. They may be concerned that the manufacturer would attempt to sell directly to the customer, bypassing the intermediary, if it possessed this information. Is user identity proprietary information?[41] When intermediaries and manufacturers have different views on this issue, conflicts can ensue. Strategies for resolving such conflicts include establishing trust with the intermediaries, increasing coupon redemption promotions, and jointly sponsoring intermediary–manufacturer marketing research.

Conflict will not spontaneously turn into neutral feelings or cooperation among channel members. Each channel member must work hard to create an efficient and cooperative channel of distribution. Each channel member views the conflict, the relationship, and the tensions differently. However accurate each perception may be, it represents reality to that channel member.

YOUR MARKETING KNOWLEDGE

11-6   Why would a marketing manager decide to intensively distribute a product? Give examples of products that are intensively distributed.

11-7   Describe factors that could contribute to vertical conflict in a marketing channel. Are these the same factors that are likely to cause horizontal conflict?

THE VERTICALLY INTEGRATED MARKET SYSTEM

After our discussion of conflict you may have the feeling that there is a prevalence of power struggles, disorganization, individualism at the expense of team play, and occasional chaos in marketing channels. The traditional view of marketing channels is that they are a loose confederation of independent operators (manufacturers, wholesalers, and retailers) who maneuver for position and bargain for a bigger margin. A more progressive approach to the design and strategy of marketing channels of distribution is found in vertically integrated marketing systems. According to this view, **vertical marketing systems** are "professionally managed and centrally programmed networks, pre-engineered to achieve operating economies and maximum market impact."[42] Compare this view of a distribution channel to one in which the manufacturer and any intermediaries just happen to come together with no plans for an ongoing relationship. Vertical marketing systems (VMS) offer an established and ongoing relationship among manufacturers and intermediaries that serves to reduce conflict and foster cooperation. All levels in the channel are working toward a single goal and one set of objectives. Three types of vertical marketing systems are the *corporate*, *contractual*, and *administered*.

Corporate Vertical Marketing Systems

A **corporate vertical marketing system** (or corporate system) achieves its operating efficiencies through single ownership of channel components. Typically the channel starts with independent levels but achieves corporate system status through integration. **Forward integration** occurs when a manufacturer operates its own distribution centers and/or retail stores. General Electric; Hart, Schaffner & Marx; and Walgreen's are manufacturers with corporate systems achieved through forward integration. They own most of their channel components, excluding retail outlets. Sherwin Williams Paint is a manufacturer with a corporate system that also owns its retail outlets.

A corporate system is formed through **backward integration** when a wholesaler or retailer owns a component upstream in the channel. JCPenney and Montgomery Ward own substantial interests in a number of their suppliers. Sears has gained significant control of its distribution system, from the production of goods to the sale to users, by owning wholesaling and manufacturing companies. Many of Sears's products are derived from firms in which Sears owns a part of the business.[43]

Administered Vertical Marketing Systems

With an **administered vertical marketing system** (or administered system), coordination is not achieved by ownership, as in the case of the corporate system, but through the size and power of the channel leader(s). Hence an administered system is similar in concept to an independent channel with a strong channel captain. Distribution functions are coordinated and controlled by the channel leader in order to develop a united team effort in the face of channel components with potentially disparate goals. Campbell's, Gillette, and Kraft are channel leaders that influence the policies of channel members, thus creating administered systems.

Kraft says its marketing goal is "to participate in all meals, whenever consumed." Sales in 1993 were more than $14 billion.[44] The company can command unusual cooperation from resellers in terms of shelf space, price policies, and promotional campaigns because its products account for more than 60 percent of dairy-case volume, excluding milk, eggs, and butter. The success of Kraft's administered system depends on the popularity of its brands, which include Velveeta (processed cheese), Parkay (margarine), Miracle Whip (salad dressing), Cracker Barrel (cheese), and Sealtest (ice cream).

Contractual Vertical Marketing Systems

In a **contractual vertical marketing system** (or contractual system), coordination of the channel is the result of a contract among channel members. The organizations at the different levels in the channel draw up a contract to perform certain marketing functions. This type of vertical marketing system has proved quite effective and influential. More than 40 percent of retail sales are accounted for by some type of contractual system. The three principal forms of contractual arrangement are wholesaler-sponsored voluntary groups, retailer-sponsored cooperative groups, and franchise systems.

Wholesaler-sponsored voluntary groups.   By organizing a number of independently owned retailers into a wholesaler-sponsored voluntary group, a wholesaler can provide goods and services far more economically than if it dealt with each retailer separately. Some better-known wholesaler-sponsored groups are Sentry Hardware, Western Auto, and Ben Franklin Stores. Sentry has more than 4,000 affiliated stores under contractual arrangement. It can exercise buying economies for products that will allow those stores to compete with large and powerful chains.

Retailer-sponsored cooperatives.   In a retailer-sponsored cooperative, retailers organize and operate their own wholesale companies, which then perform services for the member retailers. Each retailer is expected to purchase a minimum percentage of merchandise from the wholesaler. This type of contractual system came into existence because groups of retailers wanted to defend themselves against corporate chains. Retailer-sponsored cooperatives are most commonly found in the food industry. Two of the largest cooperatives are Associated Grocers and Certified Grocers, both of which serve several thousand retail outlets.

Franchising.   Franchising is a form of contractual system in which a parent company grants an individual (franchisee) or small company the right to do business in exchange for fees or royalties from revenues. The franchisee is given the right to use a seller's products, symbols, merchandise, and overall expertise in a defined territory. Furthermore, franchisors often offer management guidance and training. They (the franchisors) typically set standards and implement control systems to maintain a sought-after level of quality and consistency. If performance levels are not met, franchisees can be placed on probation. If deficiencies are not rectified, the franchisee may lose the franchise. Franchising offers the manufacturer (franchisor) opportunities to obtain some control over the distribution outlets without owning them.

Franchising has grown to be so successful that it is often viewed as a form of marketing rather than just as a type of contractual vertical marketing system. In 1992 franchising accounted for approximately 35 percent of retail sales. The International Franchise Association forecasts that by the year 2000, this figure will rise to 50 percent. There are more than 3,000 franchisors and approximately 480,000 franchised businesses currently in the United States. Additionally, more than 450 U.S.-based franchisors have worldwide operations.[45] Franchised business sales in 1992 were over $813 billion. They are predicted to reach $1 trillion by the year 2000. Services are the fastest growing franchise operations in the 1990s. For example, home health care franchises in the United States had sales of $10.3 billion in 1992, a 21.5 percent increase from 1991. Average growth in the industry throughout the remainder of the 1990s is predicted to be 16 percent annually.[46]

Franchisor	Number of Outlets Worldwide
McDonald's	13,000
7–Eleven	12,841
H & R Block	9,511
KFC	8,729
Subway	7,900
Pizza Hut	7,200
Burger King	6,600
Radio Shack	6,599
Century 21	6,041
International Dairy Queen	5,412

Source: Interview with Mr. A. Trincia, Director of Public Affairs, International Franchising Association, Washington, D.C. Interviewed by: T. A. Becker, spring 1994.

FIGURE 11.6
Top Ten Franchisors Worldwide in 1993

Figure 11.6 lists the ten largest franchisors, worldwide, and the number of outlets each had in 1993.

In most franchising arrangements the franchisor offers initial and continuing services based upon performance. These services are paid for (by the franchisee) initially with the start-up fee and then typically with the royalty based on sales or profits. Average start-up cost for a McDonald's franchise is $610,000. Average annual sales per store is $1.6 million in the United States.[47]

There is a growing interest among foreign countries in U.S.–franchised businesses. Increased levels of disposable income, a growing demand for consumer goods and services, expanding urbanization, and higher consumer mobility are reasons behind the global attractiveness of franchising. Like the economy, franchising is global. Entrepreneurs, consumers, and societies the world over are its beneficiaries. It has become not only a part of Europe, Japan, and Canada but also of Asia, South America, and Africa.

McDonald's opened its first "Golden Arch" in Russia in 1990 and has found the operation to be enormously successful.[10] This opening and the resulting success were possible only after McDonald's was able to finalize an agreement that there would be a reliable distribution system in Russia to secure the raw materials for processing meat patties, producing french fries, and receiving fresh dairy products and good apple pies. The assurance of quality products, on time, was vital for the success of McDonald's in Pushkin Square in Moscow.

South Korea has proved to be another country where fast-food franchises have met with success. The Korean fast-food market is small but booming as fast-food restaurants in the country have become popular places to spend time. Revenues in 1990 were about $615 million and are expected to grow by about 100 percent annually for the next few years.[49] McDonald's has pinpointed the Philippines, along with South Africa and the Baltics as major targets for expansion in the 1990s.[50]

As with any business, there are risks and pitfalls in franchising. Not every franchise is as well managed as McDonald's. Pizza Time Theater, Minnie Pearl Chicken, and Wild Bill's Family Restaurants were franchises that went bankrupt. Problems arise with contract interpretations. Franchisees may want to sell products other than those specified, or they may wish to buy nonfranchisor-supplied materials, items, or ingredients. Colonel Sanders of Kentucky Fried Chicken (now known as KFC) was known for checking on whether his "herbs and spices" recipe for chicken was being used properly. When it was not, the franchisee would hear about it immediately. In some cases franchisors do not deliver on promises concerning advertising,

There is growing interest among foreign countries in U.S.-franchised businesses. Shown here is the opening of the first McDonald's in China, on October 8, 1990, in Shenzhen.

training, and pricing. Disputes and conflict result in noncooperative behavior and, in some cases, legal actions.

The franchisor can occupy any position in the marketing channel. However, four types of franchise systems are especially popular:

1. *The manufacturer-retailer franchise*, as in automobile dealerships (Ford, General Motors, Nissan, Volkswagen) and service stations (Exxon, Shell).
2. *The manufacturer-wholesaler franchise*, especially common in the soft drink area. Coca-Cola, Pepsi-Cola, and Seven-Up sell syrups to franchised wholesalers who, in turn, bottle and distribute soft drinks to retailers.
3. *The wholesaler-retailer franchise*, as in Eckerd drug stores.
4. *The service-sponsored franchise*, such as Avis; Molly Maid; Jiffy Lube; Midas Mufflers; Holiday Camps, U.S.A.; and H & R Block Company.

Another form of franchising that has grown in significance in the United States and Canada is **standchising**.[51] The standchise is a modified, smaller retail outlet or kiosk, positioned in high-traffic areas in malls. Retailers have been known to sell everything from sweaters and jewelry to fresh fruit or cappuccino at the kiosks or carts. Given the increasing demand for retail space in prime malls, there has been a move to accommodate this type of retailing.

The standchising approach allows a small firm to set up a business without large outlays of capital. The kiosk can help reduce the costs of distribution and offer lower marketing costs than are possible with chain stores. Average costs per square foot are close to twice the mall average, but revenue per square foot may be three or four times greater than the norm. Lease costs and inventory costs are significantly less than for a full-scale retail outlet.

Kiosks located in malls are examples of standchises. The standchise approach allows a small firm to set up a business without large outlays of capital.

Vertical marketing systems represent attempts to improve the effectiveness of marketing channels of distribution. They have been created in response to changes in market conditions, environmental forces, and the desire to survive and grow. They are also responses to the need to make conventional distribution channels more dependent on team efforts. These two major forms of distribution are compared in Figure 11.7. Any benefits that accrue to members in marketing channels of distribution, conventional or vertically integrated, result from the quality of decision making. Decisions of such importance require information about the performance of channel members.

EVALUATING THE PERFORMANCE OF CHANNEL MEMBERS

The issues, problems, changes, and continual decision making that marketing channel managers face all emphasize the importance of performance evaluation. Changes in buying habits, laws, personnel, technology, competition, and other relevant factors necessitate constant monitoring of the marketing channel's design, effectiveness, and ability to adapt. Since channel members are involved in physical possession, promotion, financing, ordering, and payment functions, these areas can be monitored and described as marketing flows. It is difficult to obtain exact measurement of each of these areas because no quantitative measures yield perfectly reliable and valid data on the efficiency of marketing flows. Thus, managers of marketing channels must develop their own performance-evaluation programs.

It is extremely important for marketing managers who are supplying goods or services to intermediaries to be able to evaluate the performance of those intermediaries. Amount of sales is one indicator of the performance of marketing channel intermediaries. The manufacturer (or whoever is doing the evaluating) may decide to examine sales by an intermediary or sales of an intermediary to its customers.

The supplier can examine sales trends by comparing sales for a current period with sales for a comparable prior period, such as this summer versus last, one Labor

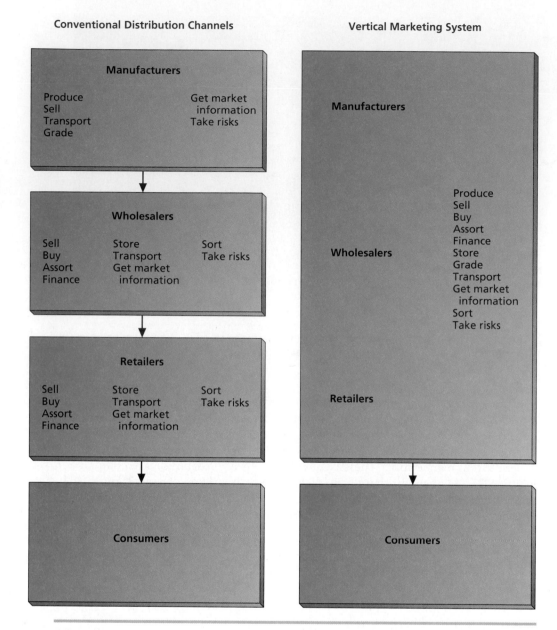

FIGURE 11.7
Comparison of Conventional Distribution Channels and Vertical Marketing Systems

Day versus another, or this year versus last year. Daily, weekly, monthly, or annual comparisons permit the supplier to examine trends.

Another method of evaluating marketing channel performance is to compare the sales performance of each member in the channel with that of all members. The manager can calculate the average sales for all members and then compare each member's performance to the average. This analysis can be used to examine total sales, sales by product or region, and sales growth or decline. A second approach to comparisons of channel members is to calculate the average sales performance of the best-selling members. This aggregate average serves as a standard to which the sales performance of other members can be compared.

Sales performance can also be evaluated on the basis of objectives achieved. Suppliers can set sales objectives alone or in consultation with channel members. Objectives can include the number of units sold in a period, total sales revenues, market shares, or ratios of total sales revenue to total sales cost. Actual achievements of each channel member can then be compared by looking at the percentages of objectives accomplished.

PERSONAL COMPUTER EXERCISE

The costs and benefits of using intermediaries vary with intensive, selective, and exclusive distribution. In this PC Exercise, you must analyze the importance of customers' needs and the company's distribution goals to arrive at the best distribution approach for a business.

KEY POINTS

- Marketing channels of distribution are pipelines through which goods and services flow from manufacturers to ultimate consumers and to business-to-business users.

- The use of intermediaries increases the cost of goods, but the increase is less than for other methods of distribution. Intermediaries also perform transactional, facilitative, and logistical functions in closing the gap between manufacturer and user. By performing these functions, intermediaries create time, place, and possession utilities.

- A direct channel is one that finds a manufacturer selling directly to a consumer. This type of channel is rare for consumer goods. An indirect channel has a number of intermediaries.

- Marketing managers, in deciding what channel is best at a particular time, consider such factors as goals and objectives, company strengths and weaknesses, customer characteristics, product characteristics, market mix characteristics, and environmental factors.

- The decision of market intensity involves determining how many channel outlets to use. Intensive distribution uses as many outlets as possible. Exclusive distribution uses a single outlet in a geographic area. Selective distribution involves a limited number of outlets.

- The decision regarding the appropriate intensity can be facilitated by considering the type of good being marketed, especially for consumer goods. If the product is a convenience item, intensive distribution should probably be used. Selective distribution is appropriate when marketing a shopping good. Specialty goods generally use exclusive distribution.

- Manufacturers often attempt to influence intermediaries by exclusive dealing contracts, exclusive sales territories, and tying contracts. The legality of these contracts must be checked carefully before contracts are negotiated, signed, and implemented.

■ Conflicts in marketing channels are inevitable but can be contained. Understanding vertical and horizontal conflict can help minimize conflict and improve cooperation.

■ Channel captains can also improve cooperation. Channel captains emerge because of their expertise or power, by virtue of which they can influence others in the channel. A channel captain can be a manufacturer, a wholesaler, or a retailer.

■ Vertical marketing systems are a formal means of encouraging cooperation and coordination among channel members. This can be accomplished through single ownership, through a contract, or through the influence of a powerful channel member.

■ Franchising is a popular form of vertical marketing system that has experienced significant growth worldwide.

■ No matter what type of channel is used, manufacturers need to evaluate the performance of members. Evaluation permits the manufacturer to make necessary changes or prevent unnecessary errors and losses.

KEY TERMS

(marketing) channel of
  distribution (353)
intermediaries (353)
wholesalers (353)
retailers (354)
merchants (354)
agents (354)
direct channel (357)
indirect channel (357)
reverse channel (360)
replacement rate (364)
market size (364)
market structure (364)
market share (364)
market stability (364)
market growth (364)
intensive distribution (366)
exclusive distribution (366)
selective distribution (368)
exclusive dealing contract (370)
exclusive sales territories (371)

tying contract (371)
horizontal conflict (372)
vertical conflict (372)
channel captain (374)
dual distribution (374)
vertical marketing systems (377)
corporate vertical marketing
  system (377)
forward integration (377)
backward integration (377)
administered vertical marketing
  system (377)
contractual vertical marketing
  system (378)
wholesaler-sponsored voluntary
  group (378)
retailer-sponsored cooperative (378)
franchising (378)
standchising (380)

ISSUES FOR DISCUSSION

1. At a family dinner recently, your Uncle Joe commented, "If we could just get rid of the middlemen (intermediaries), everything we buy would be a lot cheaper!" Comment.

2. What role might a retailer play in implementing a successful reverse channel for soda pop and beer cans?

3. What channel of distribution would you recommend for:
   (a) cellular telephones
   (b) Maine lobsters
   (c) dental services

   Explain your recommendations.

4. What distribution intensity is being used in the videocassette rental business? Do you agree with this strategy? Why or why not?

5. Give an example of a product or service that is exclusively distributed in your city or town. Why would you decide to purchase such a product when obtaining it requires extra effort?

6. Can the decision to use exclusive distribution create a specialty good? Discuss.

7. How can a manufacturer minimize horizontal conflict among wholesalers in a channel?

8. What type of vertical conflict is likely to emerge between a franchisor and a franchisee?

9. Which of the three types of vertical marketing systems is likely to produce the fastest results in reducing conflict? Why?

10. Why should a manufacturer evaluate the performance of channel members? How could such an evaluation be used in making strategic decisions?

CASE APPLICATION

Franchising Ideas, Experts, and Caution

The growth of franchising has been phenomenal. In 1992, 35 percent of retail sales were made by franchises. Further, the International Franchising Association estimates that by the year 2000 more than 50 percent of retail sales will be made by franchises. The creativity that goes into franchising is endless. Every day, approximately 50 new franchises enter the market. For example, if you're an arm wrestling enthusiast with a bad grip or a short arm, guess what? You're in luck. Jack Barringer has developed and franchised a World Class Arm Wrestling Machine. He has already sold more than 35 franchises in the United States. Using the machine, which allows singles or doubles competition, competitors grab onto rubber hands, eliminating unfair grip advantages. Elbow pads can be adjusted so that each competitor, no matter how short his or her arms are, has a fair chance. Franchisees pay a $25,000 fee that allows them the right to market the machine in a restricted geographic area.

If you're looking to invest in a franchise opportunity that serves a $4 billion market and gets a lot of advertising for free, Sports Fantasy may be the one. Sports Fantasy offers officially licensed professional and college sports apparel, as well as sports-related gifts and novelties. Each outlet sells jerseys, jackets, hats, and other gear bearing the team logos and numbers of favorite sports personalities. Sports Fantasy has grown to 7 franchises and 13 company-owned stores. A $15,000 franchise fee and a 5 percent royalty on gross sales are needed to get started in business.

How would you like to wake up to an eight-foot birthday card in your front yard?

Michael Hoefinger is the president of Yard Cards, Incorporated. For $35, anyone can have a personalized anniversary, get well, birthday, or congratulations card placed in someone's yard, home, or office for 24 hours. Franchisers are required to buy one of each of the ten copyrighted cards for $225 each.

Leslie and Douglas Alvey decided to sell cinnamon rolls in a shopping mall. Mom's Cinnamon Rolls Shop, Incorporated, became a very popular place. Now Mom's has 35 franchised stores, and people are waiting in lines to get a franchise.

The accompanying table provides data on the ten fastest growing franchises.

Franchises do have their risks. A franchisor often makes promises. Buying a franchise, someone else's idea, or his or her expertise and support don't always lead to profits. One of the first steps a person must take is to carefully analyze the franchise. Here are 12 situations to approach with caution before you become involved in a franchise of any kind:

1. *Franchisors who say you don't need to read the disclosure document.* According to a study by the Federal Trade Commission (FTC), approximately 40 percent of new franchisees sign an agreement without reading it.

2. *Franchisors who say you don't need to have a lawyer or an accountant look at the agreement.*

3. *A franchisor who doesn't give you a copy of the disclosure document at your first face-to-face meeting to discuss the franchise.* Federal fines of up to $10,000 are levied for each violation of this procedure. Report violations immediately to the Bureau of Consumer Protection at the FTC.

	THE 10 FASTEST GROWING FRANCHISES Rank • Franchise • Location									
TOP TEN	**1** 7-Eleven Convenience Stores Dallas, TX	**2** Subway Milford, CT	**3** Snap-On Tools Kenosha, WI	**4** Matco Tools Stow, OH	**5** McDonald's Oak Brook, IL	**6** Chem-Dry Carpet Drapery & Upholstery Cleaning Logan, UT	**7** Little Caesars Pizza Detroit, MI	**8** Burger King Corp. Miami, FL	**9** Coverall North America Inc. San Diego, CA	**10** Mail Boxes Etc. San Diego, CA
Product or Service	Convenience stores	Submarine sandwiches & salads	Professional tools & equipment	Automotive tools	Hamburgers, chicken, salads	Carpet, drapery & upholstery cleaning/ fabric care	Carry-out pizza restaurant	Fast-food hamburger restaurants	Commercial office cleaning	Postal/ business/ communications services
Founded	1927	1965	1920	1979	1955	1977	1959	1954	1985	1980
First Franchised Unit Opened	1964	1974	1991	1993	1955	1978	1961	1961	1985	1980
Franchised Units (1993)	10,604	8,013	2,021	768	9,770	3,523	3,339	5,903	2,735	2,106
Company-Owned Units (1993)	3,156	2	430	0	3,665	0	1,193	912	0	1
Units Added (1993)	1,359	1,156	1,032	768	630	509	502	475	407	378
Franchise Fee ($)	Varies	10K	3K	0	22.5K	11.4K	20K	40K	3.25K– 33.6K	24.95K
Start-up Costs ($)	$12.5K up	38.9K– 80.7K	12.6K– 166K	42.5K	Varies	3.55K	170K	73K–511K	350–3.5K	28.18K– 67.18K
Royalty Fee	Varies	8%	$50/mo.	0	3.5%	$175/mo.	5%	3.5%	10%	5%

Source: "Entrepreneur Magazine's 15th Annual Franchise 500," *Entrepreneur*, January, 1994, pp. 115–211

4. *Pressure to sign before the legally required ten-day waiting period.*

5. *Any franchisor you don't feel good about.* "An important rule in franchising is know your franchisor. It's like a marriage, and you wouldn't marry someone you met one afternoon," says Patrick J. Boroian, president of Francorp, Incorporated, Olympia Fields, Illinois.

6. *Thin management.* Make sure you're going to get the support you're paying for. Boroian suggests that you look at the number of supervisors the franchisor has. For example, McDonald's has one supervisor for every 20 franchisees.

7. *A marginally successful prototype or no prototype at all.* "Most of those that fail are those that start franchising without a prototype," says Boroian.

8. *Franchisors who don't give you a list of all franchisees.* "Calling just one or two franchisees is a mistake," says John E. Kinch, author of *Franchising: The Inside Story.* Be sure to ask several franchisees about such things as start-up costs, income, and the quality of the franchisor's support.

9. *Franchisors who make projections about how much you can earn.* Projections have to be based on what the franchisor is earning in a company-owned store. If projections are based on what other franchisees have made, those specific figures must be disclosed in most states. "If they don't put it in writing and tell you orally, it's a violation of federal law," says Boroian.

10. *A franchisor who has no operations manual or a skimpy one.*

11. *A high franchise turnover rate.* Terminations of franchises should be reported in the disclosure document.

12. *Litigation against the franchisor.* The fact that the franchisor has been sued doesn't necessarily mean you should decide against buying a franchise. However, you should look at the nature and the number of suits. Be aware that only litigation that has to do with deceit, fraud, or cases where money or property were allegedly stolen have to be reported in the disclosure document.

Questions

1. Why is it fairly easy to present a franchise as an attractive business deal to a prospective franchisee?
2. Some claim that franchising is a complex distribution business. What do they mean?
3. Why would royalty fees and franchise fees differ across franchises?

Finding the Right Channels

Chapter 11 covers channels of distribution as they relate to the marketing of goods and services. You might wonder how these concepts apply to your career search. You face channels of distribution as you search for employment. By understanding the functions and variations in these channels, you will be better prepared for your job search.

The longest employment channel or pipeline is on-campus recruiting, which typically includes these segments:

Promotion. The organization gives a corporate presentation on campus and/or advertises that it will be interviewing candidates for certain entry positions.

Selection. The organization reviews résumés and decides whom to invite for first interviews.

Initial screening. The organization conducts short interviews on campus, typically lasting 30 minutes each, to identify the top candidates at the school.

Follow-up screening. The organization conducts more in-depth interviews to identify the top candidates from the finalists.

Bidding. The organization's management makes formal offers to those candidates it wishes to hire.

On-campus recruiting programs can vary considerably from one organization to the next. You need to review the organization's annual report and other company data and check with others (that is, counselors, students, alumni) to identify important specifics about the organization. You also need to know:

- Who decides who will be interviewed? What information is used? What are the major factors in selection decisions?
- Who will notify the school's finalists?
- Who will conduct the follow-up screening? What roles do they play in the process? Where will the interviews be held? How much time will be required?
- Who will make the final decisions? When will they make final offers? Who will make the offers?

To do your best in obtaining and conducting a job interview, you need to know the interviewer's role as well as his or her needs at each point in the pipeline. Also, in order to plan all your career search activities, you need to know the decision schedules of your target organizations.

The remaining major pipelines for your career search are job postings and the hidden job market. You can relate these to certain segments of on-campus recruiting. With job postings, the interviewing takes place at the organization's location. The interview process is usually the same as for an on-campus recruiting program. In the hidden job market, you have to generate the interview lead, and the interview will most likely occur at the organization's location.

Questions

1. What are the best ways for you to access each of the three employment pipelines (on-campus recruitment, job postings, and the hidden job market)?
2. Why is it to your advantage to pursue all three pipelines to employment at the same time?
3. In the typical on-campus recruiting program, what are the likely differences in roles and needs of the on-campus interviewer, the follow-up interviewer, and the final interviewer (the person making the job offer)?
4. In your research of the on-campus recruiting program for one of your target organizations, what did you identify as the most important feature(s) of the process pipeline?

CHapTeR 12

Wholesaling
and
Physical
Distribution

LEARNING OBJECTIVES

Upon completing this chapter, you will be able to do the following:

■ **Explain** the role that wholesalers serve and the functions they provide in the marketing of goods.

■ **Describe** the dimensions that can be used to classify wholesalers and classify the major types of wholesalers.

■ **Discuss** the trends that can be expected in wholesaling in the coming years.

■ **Understand** the objectives of physical distribution and how they influence decision making in this area.

■ **Identify** the five major functions of physical distribution.

■ **Illustrate** how the total quality management concept can be applied to physical distribution.

Marketing Profile

Wholesale Clubs Continue to Grow

If you were to open a small restaurant and needed ketchup, books of order pads, and a small computer, where would you get them? Traditionally, you would get the ketchup from a restaurant supplier, the order pads from an office-supply wholesaler, and the computer from a business machines specialist. These intermediaries would deliver the products to your restaurant and allow you to pay later by extending you a line of credit. This arrangement, while convenient, would be costly.

Today, you would most likely shop for the needed items yourself at a local wholesale club. Wholesale clubs are cash-and-carry intermediaries who sell to small retailers (and ultimate consumers). Clubs do not provide services like delivery and they do not typically extend credit. Their prices, however, represent significant savings for the small retailer.

The wholesale club concept began in 1976 in San Diego, California. Sol Price formed the Price Club, a warehouse that catered to small businesses. The warehouse was a no-frills operation targeted to area businesses that didn't have the volume to attract other wholesalers. The small businesses found the club attractive because costs were lower than those in conventional channels. In addition, new businesses did not have to work to develop relationships with suppliers, nor were they penalized for small orders. Thus, a new business could immediately enjoy all of the benefits of using a wholesaler. Distributors were not upset with the advent of wholesale clubs because the smaller businesses tended to be more of a burden than a source of revenue for them.

The wholesale club industry has grown dramatically. There are many competitors today but the major players are Costco (based in Kirkland, Washington), Sam's Club (owned and operated by Wal-Mart, Inc.), Price Club, and Pace (a subsidiary of Kmart Corporation). Sam's Club is the largest of the competitors in terms of number of warehouses, with 385 units and $12 billion in revenues in 1992. In June 1993 Costco and Price Club (the number two and three clubs in terms of size) announced a merger that created the sixth largest retailer in the United States. When stockholders of both companies approved the merger in October 1993, the newly formed Price/Costco operated 220 warehouses and had annual revenues of $15.3 billion. Sales for the industry in 1993 were reported to be $41.6 billion.

The success of the wholesale club can be attributed to many factors. Jack Shoemaker, former vice chairman of Wal-Mart Stores, Incorporated, has suggested that success stems from three factors. First, because fast turnover items sell before vendors are paid, clubs have an incentive to stock high volume, fast turnover items. Second, packaging saves costs for the club, and therefore the consumer. Manufacturers, for example, might shrink-wrap five items and put a tag on them, thus minimizing labor costs once the items are in the store. The third factor, suggests Shoemaker, is the lower costs for labor incurred by wholesale clubs. These lower labor costs result from the need for fewer personnel to provide service functions and the use of more efficient check-out and check verification systems.

The success of the wholesale club in the United States has enabled the industry to pursue plans for global expansion. Price/Costco has outlets in Canada, Mexico, and Great Britain. Further penetration of the European market is expected in the next few years, and following the merger in October 1993, plans were announced to expand into the Asian market. The first Price/Costco warehouse in Asia is planned for South Korea and should be open by fall of 1994.

Some buyers for wholesale clubs still report prejudice against the clubs from suppliers. In certain instances, buyers must continue to convince suppliers that the wholesale club is a viable outlet for their products. The tremendous volume that the wholesale club can promise suppliers, however, usually serves to sell producers on this type of intermediary.

Words taken from the original business plan for Costco, written before its entrance into the marketplace in 1983, appear to sum up the success of the industry:

> Through a combination of low prices and unique marketing, the company will gain a significant share of retail and wholesale sales.

Bill Matthews set out early one Saturday morning in Dallas to pick up a few food items, get a new radio speaker for his car, buy sunblock lotion, and purchase some vacuum cleaner bags. Since many stores and pharmacies carry these items, Bill's most difficult task was determining where to go. He easily bought these items and had an inexpensive, quick lunch, in about two hours. In many countries, it would be impossible to accomplish these tasks in such a short period of time.

Because of a system of intermediaries that bring goods and services to American consumers whenever and wherever they are desired, it is easy for Bill Matthews and most of the U.S. population to obtain goods. The system is all but invisible except when it does not work properly. We see retailers, though we do not often think about the functions they perform. Wholesalers, while less obvious to final consumers, are no less critical. For example, the sunblock that Bill Matthews purchased was handled by and delivered to his local retailer by McKesson Corporation, a wholesaler with more than $7.8 billion in annual sales.

Wholesalers such as McKesson differ from retailers in a number of ways. Most of the time, wholesalers sell to businesses. In most cases, retailers sell directly to final customers. Wholesalers spend less time and money on promotion than retailers because of their customer base. The geographical area that a wholesaler serves is usually larger than the geographical area served by a retailer. Some of the traditional distinctions between wholesalers and retailers have become less clear. McKesson may not be a familiar name, but one or more of the wholesale clubs mentioned in the Marketing Profile probably are familiar to ultimate consumers. Wholesalers such as Sam's Club, Pace, and Price/Costco are competing head-on with retailers.

The example of Bill Matthews and his purchase of sunblock suggests that wholesalers are also frequently involved in the physical process of getting goods to consumers. Physical distribution systems, in which wholesalers participate along with producers and retailers, are largely responsible for providing consumers like Bill Matthews with time and place utility.

In this chapter we look at how wholesaling works and the functions that wholesalers perform. In addition, we explore the organizational structure of wholesale institutions. We also examine the objectives, management, and organization of physical distribution systems and discuss how they operate as part of the marketing strategy of an enterprise.

WHOLESALING

As defined in Chapter 11, a wholesaler is a business unit that buys and resells merchandise to retailers and other merchants and to business, institutional, and commercial users. Wholesalers do not sell in significant amounts to ultimate consumers. Their main customers are other businesses. Sales by one manufacturer to another, or one retailer to another, are wholesaling sales. Approximately six million people are employed in wholesaling.[1] It is estimated that 60 percent of manufacturers' products shipped in a year went through wholesalers.[2] Wholesaling is important worldwide; international wholesaling by U.S. firms totaled $68.5 billion in 1993.[3] The size of the wholesaling trade in the United States reached $1.997 trillion in 1992, up from $1,258 billion in 1977, and from $181 billion in 1948.

In the 1990s major wholesalers are moving more and more to global operations. McKesson, for example, is a San Francisco-based company that derives 94 percent of its revenue from drugs and health and beauty aids. In addition to the United States, it currently operates in Canada, Japan, Austria, Germany, Sweden, the United Kingdom, and France. About 14 percent of the company's revenues now come from foreign markets. McKesson expects that more than 20 percent of its revenues will be from international markets by 1995. The firm's long-term strategic plan includes additional European and Asian markets as well as possible opportunities in Latin America.[4]

The cost of the services that wholesalers perform influences the prices charged to customers. A firm like McKesson has significant operating and other expenses in handling, distributing, and facilitating the sale of products like the sunblock lotion. These expenses include inventory charges, advertising, heating and lighting, rent, sales-force fees, and administrative charges. Although 23.6 percent of the price of Bill Matthews's sunblock lotion went to McKesson for sorting, transporting, and providing other services to the drug store, McKesson's before-tax profit on the $5.00 container of lotion Bill purchased was about $.14.

WHOLESALING FUNCTIONS

Wholesalers perform a range of marketing functions or services. Some wholesalers specialize while others engage in all functions. A full-service wholesaler might offer the following services to its manufacturers or suppliers:

1. Provide a sales force to sell the goods to retailers and other buyers
2. Communicate the manufacturer's advertising deals and plans
3. Maintain inventory to reduce the level of the inventory suppliers must carry
4. Arrange or undertake transportation of goods
5. Provide capital by paying cash or quick payments for goods
6. Provide suppliers with market information they cannot afford or are unable to obtain themselves
7. Undertake credit risk by granting credit to customers and absorbing bad debts
8. Assume the risk for the product by taking title

The wholesaler may perform the following services for its customers:

1. Buy goods that the end market will desire and make them available to customers
2. Maintain inventory to reduce customers' costs
3. Transport goods to customers quickly
4. Provide market information and business consulting services
5. Provide financing by granting credit (especially critical to small retailers)
6. Order goods in the types and quantities that customers desire

It is important to note that the functions and services listed are activities that wholesalers *typically* perform. Not every channel of distribution, however, includes a wholesaler. A channel without a wholesaler does not omit the functions and services listed here. If no wholesaler is present in the channel, someone else (at some other level) must perform the activities usually performed by wholesalers. That someone else might be the manufacturer, the retailer, or even the final consumer.

CLASSIFYING DIMENSIONS OF WHOLESALERS

There are many types of wholesalers. Four dimensions can be used to describe the differences among the various types of wholesalers.

▪ *Assumption of risk.* Some wholesalers take title or legal possession of goods; others do not. When a wholesaler takes title or legal possession it assumes risk for the products.

▪ *Type of ownership.* Wholesalers can be owned independently or owned by a manufacturer or retailer.

▪ *Breadth of functions or services offered.* Some wholesalers perform all the functions and services that were identified above, while others perform only a limited number of functions and services. (This difference in services performed is the main reason for the variation in operating expenses as a percentage of sales. In general, the more services performed, the higher the operating expenses.)

▪ *Degree of specialization in product lines carried.* Some wholesalers carry goods across many product lines, while others carry a smaller number of lines. Some wholesalers specialize in a very narrow product line.

CLASSIFYING WHOLESALERS

Using the dimensions described, we will now take a closer look at different wholesalers. Figure 12.1 illustrates the many types of wholesalers and their relationships to each other.

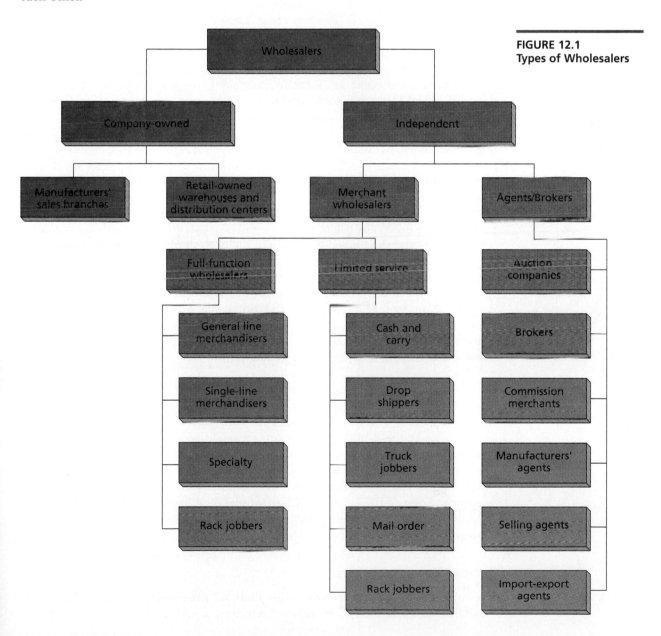

FIGURE 12.1
Types of Wholesalers

Company-Owned Wholesalers

Some manufacturers and some retailers prefer to own and operate their wholesaling operations. When the manufacturer or retailer owns the wholesaling function, wholesaling does not show up as a separate level in the channel of distribution. The activities typically performed by an independent wholesaler still take place however. Functions performed within a channel of distribution can be shifted among channel members but they cannot be eliminated. The two types of company-owned wholesalers are manufacturers' sales branches and retail-owned warehouses and distribution centers.

Manufacturers' sales branches. The U.S. Census Bureau treats **manufacturers' sales branches** as a separate wholesaling category. These branches are wholesale operations owned by manufacturers. The percentage of wholesaling work performed by manufacturers' sales branches is declining. In 1987 this type of wholesaler performed 31 percent of wholesaling work in the United States but by the year 2000, it is predicted that only 21 percent of wholesaling activity in the United States will be performed by manufacturers' sales branches.[5] These operations represent the actions of manufacturers to take over the functions of wholesalers by setting up separate businesses. IBM, for example, owns its own operation that provides wholesaling services for IBM's products. The wholesaling operation is a separate division from manufacturing and operates as a semi-independent business. Other manufacturers such as General Electric, Crane, and Hiram Walker perform wholesaling operations in a similar manner. Manufacturers' sales branches are common in product categories such as automobiles, chemicals, metals, commercial machines and equipment, farm machinery, paints, electrical equipment, tires, construction materials, and paper.[6]

Manufacturers' sales branches are usually justified when large retail or organizational customers are concentrated in large urban areas. By serving a smaller number of large customers in a fairly small geographical area, these branches are able to take the cream off the top of the market. The wholesale dollar volume accounted for by sales branches is much greater than the portion of total wholesale businesses they represent. Branches perform functions in the transactional, logistical, and facilitating areas. Transactional activities, you will recall from Chapter 1, include buying, selling, and risk-taking through taking title to the goods. Logistical activities involve transportation, storage, assembly, and sorting goods. Facilitating involves financing, providing information, grading, and providing postpurchase service of goods. Manufacturers' sales branches have lower costs as a percentage of sales than do merchant wholesalers and earn higher gross margins.

Retail-owned warehouses and distribution centers. Large chain retailers often perform wholesaling functions through company (retailer)-owned warehouses and distribution centers. A food retailer such as Vons, Safeway, or A & P, for example, may take on the responsibility for transactional, logistical, and facilitating functions at regional distribution centers. The retail chain buys directly from producers and growers, products are sorted and prepared at the distribution center for distribution to individual supermarkets in the region, and then are delivered to the stores in company-owned trucks. This form of wholesaling has enjoyed significant growth in recent years. (Distribution centers will be discussed in greater detail later in this chapter.)

Independent Wholesalers

In contrast to wholesalers that are owned and operated by manufacturers and retailers, independent wholesalers own and operate their own businesses.

Wholesaler Type	Takes Title to Goods	Stores and Delivers Goods	Provides Sales Force	Advertises and Promotes Goods	Provides Credit
Merchant Wholesaler					
Full function					
General line	yes	yes	yes	yes	yes
Single line	yes	yes	yes	yes	yes
Specialty merchandisers	yes	yes	yes	yes	yes
Rack jobbers	yes	yes	yes	yes	yes
Merchant Wholesaler					
Limited function					
Cash-and-carry	yes	stores (yes) delivers (no)	no	no	no
Drop shipper	yes	stores (yes) delivers (no)	yes	no	yes
Truck jobbers	yes	yes	yes	yes	no
Mail order	yes	yes	yes	no	sometimes
Agents and brokers					
Auction companies	no	yes	yes	yes	no
Brokers	no	sometimes	yes	yes	sometimes
Commission merchants	no	yes	yes	no	yes
Manufacturers' agents	no	sometimes	yes	yes	no
Selling agents	no	yes	yes	yes	sometimes
Import-export agents	no	sometimes	yes	yes	sometimes

TABLE 12.1
Functions and Characteristics of Independent Wholesalers

Traditionally about two-thirds of wholesaling operations have taken place through independent wholesalers. It is predicted that by the year 2000, however, this figure will have declined to 52 percent.[7] The main distinction among types of independent wholesalers is whether the wholesaler takes title to the goods. Table 12.1 summarizes the functions and characteristics of the different independent wholesalers.

Merchant Wholesalers

Merchant wholesalers are independent businesses that hold ownership to the goods they market. Total sales by merchant wholesalers in the United States in 1993 were $161 billion.[8] In 1987 they accounted for about 58 percent of wholesale trade, a figure that is expected to drop to 45 percent by 2000.[9] Wholesalers such as McKesson, Price/Costco, and Sam's Club are all merchants. They purchase goods from manufacturers or other wholesalers and hold ownership until the goods are resold to retailers or others. Merchant wholesalers who sell to producers rather than to retailers are *industrial distributors*. Industrial distributors may carry products such as electrical supplies, plastics, fasteners, machine tools, aluminum products, welding equipment, and bearings, which producers use in the manufacture of goods.

Some merchant wholesalers provide a substantial amount of aid to the retailers with whom they do business. Super Valu Stores, Incorporated, is a merchant wholesaler that considers itself more than a wholesaler because of the service it provides. In 1993 Super Valu had sales of $12.6 billion.[10] The company believes its continued success will result from helping retailers succeed. Super Valu offers retailers services such as financing, staff training, and store design. The wholesaler distinguishes itself from other wholesalers by calling itself "The Retail Support Company." The wholesaler carefully listens to retailers and closely measures retailers' buying behaviors. Super Valu then modifies its service and products to meet the needs of its retailer customers.[11] Super Valu retail support centers are engaged in wholesaling food, nonfood,

Super Valu considers itself more than a wholesaler because of the services it provides retailers. These include financing, staff training, and store design.

and pharmaceutical products primarily to grocery retailers. Super Valu serves more than 2,800 retail food stores, nearly all independently owned, in 33 states. It also operates 275 of its own company stores. The firm is also very committed to international expansion and is looking for acquisitions in Russia, Turkey, and Japan.[12] The Super Valu creed highlights its commitment to working with retailers:

> We shall so effectively serve our retailers both with merchandise and services that they may experience continuing success and satisfactory growth under all competitive conditions. The future successful growth of Super Valu must always result from our achievement of this meaningful goal. Since the future of both Super Valu and our retailers is relative to, limited by, and dependent upon the future success of each other, there must always exist between us a strong personal bond with mutual responsibilities to each other.

Full-function wholesalers.   Merchant wholesalers who are active in each major function of marketing are called **full-function wholesalers.** These wholesalers, sometimes referred to as *full-service* or just *service* wholesalers, perform transactional, logistical, and facilitating activities. Full-function wholesalers vary in terms of the assortment of merchandise they carry. Some carry a wide assortment of general merchandise and are referred to as **general-line merchandisers.** Some carry a single line of merchandise such as plumbing supplies, beverages, or snack foods. These wholesalers are **single-line merchandisers. Specialty merchandisers** carry only a limited assortment of a particular type of specialty good. Seventh Generation, an example of a specialty merchandiser, is a wholesaler that distributes a line consisting of only 22 products to 400 of the largest natural food retailers on the East Coast of the United States.[13]

Another type of full-function wholesaler is a rack jobber. **Rack jobbers** typically sell nonfood, staple items to grocery and drug stores. Staples include health and beauty aids, books, housewares, hardware products, and records. These items are usually displayed on racks, as the name rack jobber implies. The rack jobber maintains the inventory and prices the product. Note that rack jobbers who insist upon cash payments when the rack is stocked are limited-function wholesalers. For this reason, Figure 12.1 shows the rack jobber as both a full- and a limited-function wholesaler.

Rack jobbers came into existence to fill a need. As food stores began to offer more nonfood items, it became bothersome for retailers and traditional wholesalers to handle such merchandise. The sales of any of these items in a specific store were not large enough to justify the costs of recordkeeping and ordering incurred by the retailer or traditional wholesaler. Traditional wholesalers became concerned that their other customers would resent the time they spent serving the food stores. A drug wholesaler, for example, who sold to a supermarket would run the risk of losing the business of a nearby drug store. When serviced by a rack jobber, the retailer just provides floor space and collects money from customers at the check-out counter. Because rack jobbers perform both the traditional wholesaling functions and many retail services, their operating costs are high (about 16 to 20 percent of sales) but gross margins are also high, usually 12 to 16 percent.

12-1   Give examples of the risks that a merchant wholesaler assumes.

12-2   What kind of needs does a rack jobber satisfy for supermarkets? (You might ask the manager at a local grocery store.)

YOUR
MARKETING
KNOWLEDGE

Limited-function wholesalers.   Limited-function wholesalers are merchant whole salers who provide only a subset of the services of a full-function wholesaler. Often they specialize in the provision of certain functions. The major types of limited function wholesalers are (1) cash-and-carry wholesalers, (2) drop shippers, (3) truck jobbers, (4) mail-order wholesalers, and (5) certain types of rack jobbers. Because limited-function wholesalers provide less service than their full-function counter parts, they earn smaller gross margins.

Cash-and-carry wholesalers provide no credit, transportation, or selling effort. Customers come to them to buy and pick up purchased goods, for which they pay cash. Food and drug stores and garages that are too small to be serviced by full-function wholesalers have been able to stay in business because of cash-and-carry wholesalers. The wholesale clubs described in the Marketing Profile that begins this chapter are cash-and-carry wholesalers. Such wholesalers are becoming increasingly popular in Russia. Small retailers frequently buy from such wholesalers as Roditi Moscow Ltd., a cash-and-carry wholesaler.[14]

Drop shippers, sometimes called *desk jobbers*, take title to the goods they sell but do not hold possession. They do not store, transport, or assemble these goods. They obtain orders for goods from retailers, business buyers, and other wholesalers and then forward these orders to producers. This allows producers to avoid the time and effort involved in dealing directly with customers to obtain orders. Drop shippers operate almost exclusively with bulky products such as coal, lumber, fuel, chemicals, and building materials. These products are usually sold in carloads and have high transportation and handling costs relative to their value. Thus, avoiding an extra handling of the goods in the channel saves money.

Truck jobbers, sometimes called *wagon jobbers* or *truck wholesalers*, specialize in the quick delivery of perishable or semiperishable items such as candy, bakery items, fresh fruits, potato chips, and tobacco products. They use their own trucks and offer virtually all services except the provision of credit to their customers. They deal primarily with smaller retailers that large wholesalers choose not to sell to. The combination of small orders from their customers and the great deal of service they provide makes them a high-cost operation.

Mail-order wholesalers sell through catalogs that are distributed to small retailers and organizational buyers. They are most active in hardware, sporting goods, jewelry, and other general items. They sell mostly to smaller customers in outlying regions where the cost of undertaking a personal selling effort would not be supported by the sales that could be generated. A mail-order wholesaler specializing in jewelry, for example, might distribute catalogues featuring available items to retail jewelry stores in small towns throughout the West and Midwest.

We have already mentioned that rack jobbers can be full-function wholesalers. If they choose not to extend credit to their customers, however, they are better classified as limited-function wholesalers.

Agents

Agents are intermediaries that do not take title to goods. They also tend to perform far fewer services than merchant wholesalers, even limited-function merchants.[15] Their main function is transactional: they facilitate the buying and selling of goods and services. Agents and brokers provide knowledge of the market, usually have long-standing relationships with potential customers, and typically charge fees as low as 5 percent of their selling prices for their services. Their operating costs are low because of the limited services they provide. They account for about 10 percent of wholesale trade (approximately $220 billion), a figure predicted to decrease to 7 percent by 2000.[16]

The most important groups in this category are (1) auction companies, (2) brokers, (3) commission merchants, (4) manufacturers' agents, (5) selling agents, and (6) import-export agents.

Auction companies bring buyers and sellers together. There are only 1,700 such companies in the United States. Despite their relatively small number, auction companies are very important in such product classes as used cars, tobacco, livestock, fruit, and furs. For all these products, supply and demand change quickly, and inspection of the goods by prospective buyers is important. Auction companies charge a fee or commission for their services and the use of their facilities, which are usually spartan to help keep overhead low. Sometimes, especially in agricultural sales, the auction company will set up at the seller's location.

Brokers, like auctioneers, also bring buyers and sellers together for a sale, but they rarely need physical facilities to do so. Their main function is to provide buyers and sellers with information about each others' needs, market conditions, alternative products, and price levels. They do not take possession of, or handle, the goods. They earn a commission once a sale is completed and the party represented by the broker pays the commission. Brokers can work for the buyer or the seller, but they do not have a continuous relationship with either. The 4,800 brokers in the United States have low operating costs—about 3 percent of sales—because of the small number of functions they perform. They earn 3 to 6 percent gross margin.

Brokers are especially active in product categories where sellers are not continuously trying to sell their products. This includes real estate, financial securities, certain complex capital machinery, and seasonal food items such as fruits, vegetables, and seafood. For these categories, the seller has no solid relationship with prospective buyers and usually lacks market knowledge. The broker fills the gap. For

Auction companies bring buyers and sellers together. An auction for farm equipment is shown here.

example, a fruit cannery may operate only for a few months per year. The canner then hires a broker to sell the product to food wholesalers and chain stores. Once the year's production is sold, the broker's services are dropped until the next year. The "Marketing in Action: Snider, Hayes, Hurd Prospers in a Tough Market" describes the efforts of one broker operating in the food industry.

Commission merchants operate mostly in agricultural markets. Typically, commission merchants take possession of a commodity sent to them at a central market area by a small farmer. They handle the logistics of the goods, find a buyer, negotiate a price, and complete the sale. The monies earned (minus the commission earned) are returned to the farmer. For example, farmers in the Midwest might send livestock to a central market in Chicago. The livestock is met by commission merchants who negotiate with meat packers who are at the central market to buy. Commission merchants costs are relatively low—about 4.8 percent of sales—and they earn about 5 percent gross margin.

Manufacturers' agents or *manufacturers' representatives*, as they are often called, are agents designated by a manufacturer to sell all or some part of its product offering in a specified geographic area. In essence, they become the manufacturer's sales force in that territory. Manufacturers' agents earn 5 to 7 percent gross margin, with costs running 6.6 percent of sales. Commissions average 6 to 7 percent of sales, but may run as high as 20 percent for slow-moving items, or as low as 2 percent for large-volume products. Japanese camera companies first entered the American market by using these types of representatives.[17]

Manufacturers' representatives operate year-round. They usually carry many related product lines from several noncompeting manufacturers. Thus, they can spread the cost of a sales call among a number of different products. They do not set the sales price for items they sell and often do not carry inventories. They generally do not give technical advice or handle repairs or installations. Manufacturers' representatives are most active in business-to-business products, clothing, cameras, and food products.[18]

Manufacturers' agents who specialize in marketing processed foods are *food brokers*. The term *broker* is actually inappropriate because they now act on a permanent basis as manufacturers' representatives, calling on wholesalers and large retailers. These food brokers earn about 5 percent commission and are typically specialized geographically. A company like General Mills gains national distribution in the United States by using 70 to 100 food brokers.

In general, manufacturers' agents are used in situations such as the following:

- A manufacturer wants to develop a new sales territory and the cost of one's own sales force would be prohibitive, given early sales levels.
- A firm wishes to add a new and unrelated product line to its product offering and this product does not fit the experience or end customers of its current sales force. In this case the company's sales force and its agents will operate in the same geographic territory.
- A small firm has no sales force of its own.
- A large firm wants to operate in a territory that is too small to support a sales force.

Manufacturers' agents can sell across national boundaries. For example, M. J. Daniel Company, a manufacturers' agency in Dallas, Texas, ships Apple Computers to U.S. military PXs in West Germany for resale to military personnel there.[19] Paul E. Moss & Company concentrates on selling business goods and auto equipment in the Middle East. Quinto, Dawson & Associates of Orlando, Florida, specializes in the Caribbean market. There is a growing number of manufacturers' agents like these who are finding lucrative new opportunities for U.S. producers.[20]

Selling agents are independent intermediaries who perform the manufacturers' entire marketing. They set prices, determine promotional activities and distribution policies, and advise on product offerings. Selling agents are most active with financially weak producers who cannot afford their own marketing effort.[21] Selling agents are important intermediaries in coal and textiles and are found in the clothing, metal products, lumber, and food industries. There are about 1,700 selling agents in the United States doing about $6.5 billion in wholesale trade. Operating expenses are about 3.2 percent of sales, and gross margins are about 5 percent.

Import-export agents, numbering about 1,000 in the United States, are intermediaries who specialize in international trade. Some operate as brokers, while others are more like manufacturers' representatives or selling agents. Their understanding of foreign markets and their ability to provide financing make them crucial intermediaries in international trade.

TRENDS IN WHOLESALING

In the nineteenth century, wholesalers dominated the marketing scene. The small producers and retailers of the day found their services to be essential. However, as producers and retailers grew larger in the early years of the twentieth century, many manufacturers began to set up their own sales forces and to take over the wholesaling function. From 1929 to 1939 wholesale trade in the United States declined significantly.

During this period of decline, however, many manufacturers began to find it more expensive to bypass the wholesaler. This, combined with the growth in the economy from the 1940s through the 1980s, led to great growth in wholesaling during that 50-year period. Growth was especially significant among merchant wholesalers, the very group some had earlier predicted would disappear.

Type of Wholesaler	Percentage of Wholesaling Work Performed	
	1987	2000
Manufacturers' sales branches	31%	21%
Merchant wholesalers	58%	45%
Agents and brokers	11%	7%
Alternative channels	---	27%

Source: U.S. Department of Commerce, *U.S. Industrial Outlook*, 1993.

TABLE 12.2
The Decline of Wholesalers

The trend toward wholesale growth, however, appears to have somewhat reversed itself in the 1990s, a phenomenon predicted to continue at least through the remainder of the decade. As Table 12.2 illustrates, every major category of wholesaler is predicted to decline throughout the 1990s. As indicated by the table, this decline is attributable to growth in alternative channels.

One type of alternative channel is the retail-owned warehouse and distribution center described earlier in this chapter. In addition, technological advances have created alternative channels. Computerized systems, for example, make it easier than ever before for retailers to order and buy directly from manufacturers. Furthermore, computerized systems and mail-order operations enable final consumers to easily buy directly from manufacturers. Seventh Generation, the specialty merchandiser of natural foods, realizes $8 million in sales monthly through its wholesale operation. The firm also sells almost $5.5 million each month through a direct-to-the-consumer catalogue. Catalogue sales are predicted to increase to $8 million per month by 1997, an increase not anticipated for the wholesale operation.[22]

The growth in alternative channels and the subsequent decline in the use of traditional wholesalers, in itself, perpetuates additional decline. Arthur Andersen Consulting predicts 15 percent fewer wholesalers by the year 2000 due to mergers, acquisitions, and failures.[23] Wholesalers are motivated to merge in the current economic environment because of the management expertise and economies of scale that can be realized through merger or acquisition. In the electronics industry, for example, many semiconductor distributors have merged as a means of maintaining a "critical mass" as their sales have decreased.[24]

As threats to traditional wholesale operations increase, the emphasis on improving the quality of performance of wholesaling functions and services is a major concern. An example of the push for quality is the case of Sysco Corporation, the nation's largest food distributor supplying restaurants, hospitals, and other institutions. Between 1983 and 1993, Sysco grew at a compound annual rate of 16 percent. In 1993 the firm earned $10 billion.[25] Much of its success can be credited to the reputation it maintains for being quality-conscious. More than 80 food technologists in the United States and around the world continually evaluate and inspect products sold under the Sysco brand (Supreme, Imperial, Classic, and Reliance). Sysco has developed specifications for its brands so that customers are assured of high-quality brand products. Tuna sold under the Sysco label must be caught on fishing lines so that there are no struggle marks from the nets. Sysco has also turned down truckloads of ham that contained too much water. Samples from every product lot are tested at Sysco for quality.

For most wholesalers, future productivity gains and maintaining a reasonable profit margin seem to motivate the careful management of marketing information and the improved use of computers. Issues such as inventory turnaround are critical,

MARKETING *IN ACTION*

Snider, Hayes, Hurd Prospers in a Tough Market

Snider, Hayes, Hurd (SHH) is a brokerage business that focuses on the food industry. It works to bring together manufacturers and food processors and retailers, both chain grocery stores and independent grocers. In business in Denver since 1952, the small- to mid-size brokerage found itself struggling to survive in the late 1980s. In the food industry, the size of a broker is important. In this industry, larger firms enjoy economies of scale that enable them to beat out smaller rivals. Consequently, the number of food brokerage businesses has declined, while the relative size of each business has grown. In Denver, for example, the number of food brokers declined from 40 to 26 between the years 1987 and 1992. This decrease was the result of mergers, acquisitions, and in some cases, failures of smaller firms.

Part of the struggle that smaller brokers face results from expectations in the food industry that brokers provide services beyond bringing together buyers and sellers. For example, one of the services that food brokers regularly provide is computerized space management. This service uses the latest technology to guide chains or independent grocers on the number of cans, boxes, or bottles to display in a given space. Data on sales, size, and shape are factored into the recommendations. Larger brokers are better able to provide computerized space management services because their expertise increases as they work with a larger number of clients.

In 1987 Snider, Hayes, Hurd decided that it must grow if it was to survive. But how? It wasn't large enough to buy another broker. A merger might mean loss of control for management and loss of security for employees. Borrowing was not a possibility because lenders are reluctant to make loans in an industry where 30-day service contracts are the norm. Because brokers have only 30 days of guaranteed revenue, they are viewed as risky investments.

Snider, Hayes, Hurd looked for a niche that would set it apart from other brokers and would help it grow. In the spring of 1987 it created a marketing department. Marketing departments were rare at that time in the industry. The department did marketing research and placed and sometimes created advertising for clients' products. These services helped SHH salespeople persuade grocers to stock its clients' products and also proved helpful in persuading potential clients to sign up.

In 1989, Mars, Incorporated, was shopping for a food broker to handle its pet food, rice products, cookies, and candy in the Denver market. As the smallest broker to earn an interview, SHH knew that to win Mars's business, it needed more than the niche it had created through its marketing efforts. It used its size and desire to grow as selling points. Pointing out that revenues from Mars would represent 40 percent of its gross, the company emphasized that the account would get plenty of attention. It promised to reinvest all that it earned from Mars, allowing it to grow and add services. Mars approved of the approach and SHH got its business.

Between 1990 and 1992 sales of Mars products in the Denver area rose 62 percent with a consequent rise in SHH commissions. As for Snider, Hayes, Hurd, it has hired and promoted personnel with the reinvested Mars income. The increased size of the firm has helped it attract additional clients, thus enabling it to grow more.

and wholesalers are concerned about picking up not just weeks or days, but hours. Despite these needs, wholesalers have been slow to develop marketing information systems and adopt new technologies.[26] Wholesalers spend only an average of 1 percent of their revenues on developing and maintaining marketing information systems.[27] When they do institute such systems, however, the results are usually very positive. In 1992 Chrysler Corporation's wholesaling division implemented a PC-based decision management analysis system that allows the firm to analyze three years' worth of history regarding automotive parts, and then use the information when making inventory decisions. The result has been improved productivity.[28]

Many of the large wholesalers such as Sysco, Farm House Foods, Phibro-Solomon, Alco Standard, Amfac, and McKesson have installed complex computer networks for inventory control.[29] The store manager at your local supermarket doesn't have to talk directly to anyone when it's time to order more Wheaties. The manager waves an electric wand over the product label on the Wheaties box and then uses the telephone lines to relay that order to the wholesaler. This instant ordering helps the store manager satisfy customers' needs more efficiently. Many wholesalers today use electronic data interchange (EDI), described in Chapter 11.

Another form of technology that can improve the efficiency and productivity of wholesalers is the wearable bar-code scanning glove. McKesson Drug Company has installed such a system at its Spokane, Washington, distribution center. The innovative bar-code scanning glove fits on a worker's hand. It contains a laser scanner that allows the wearer to point and scan, a customized forearm-mounted keyboard display module, and a waist-mounted portable computer and battery power supply. The hand scanner and arm terminal together weigh less than 13 ounces. The worker can scan a purchase order and receive information on the display screen on the product's location. This is all done without paperwork and without manually entering information into the computer. Since its introduction the scanning glove has helped reduce errors in filling orders by at least 60 percent.[30]

PHYSICAL DISTRIBUTION

Up to this point we have studied various marketing channels of distribution and wholesaling. The physical transport of goods is increasingly important to marketing decision makers because physical distribution can account for as much as one-half of marketing costs. In 1991 U.S. industry spent an estimated $587 billion on physical distribution functions like transportation, warehousing, inventory-carrying costs, and general management.[31]

The creation of place and time utilities in an environment of change and increasing complexity is causing managers to pay more attention to physical distribution. By providing customers with place and time utilities, physical distribution implements the marketing concept. As Robert Woodruff, former president of Coca-Cola, put it, Coke's organization policy was to "put Coke within an arm's length of desire."

From a marketing viewpoint, physical distribution can be seen in two ways. One perspective views it as a support for a firm's marketing objectives. In this case, responsibility for physical distribution is usually dispersed throughout a firm as a backup function. Figure 12.2 shows the organization of a company where physical distribution activities are conducted in three departments. This dispersion often results in conflicting objectives: marketing wants more inventory to meet customer needs, while finance and accounting want to hold inventory down to reduce carrying costs.

Efficient physical distribution can give a firm a competitive edge in the marketplace. To achieve this competitive edge, some believe that physical distribution functions should be unified in a full-fledged organizational unit that provides service to other units. Figure 12.3 represents such a unit as a freestanding member of a firm's team.

There are stumbling blocks to the creation of freestanding physical distribution departments. In many firms, marketing or production is dominant. If the structure

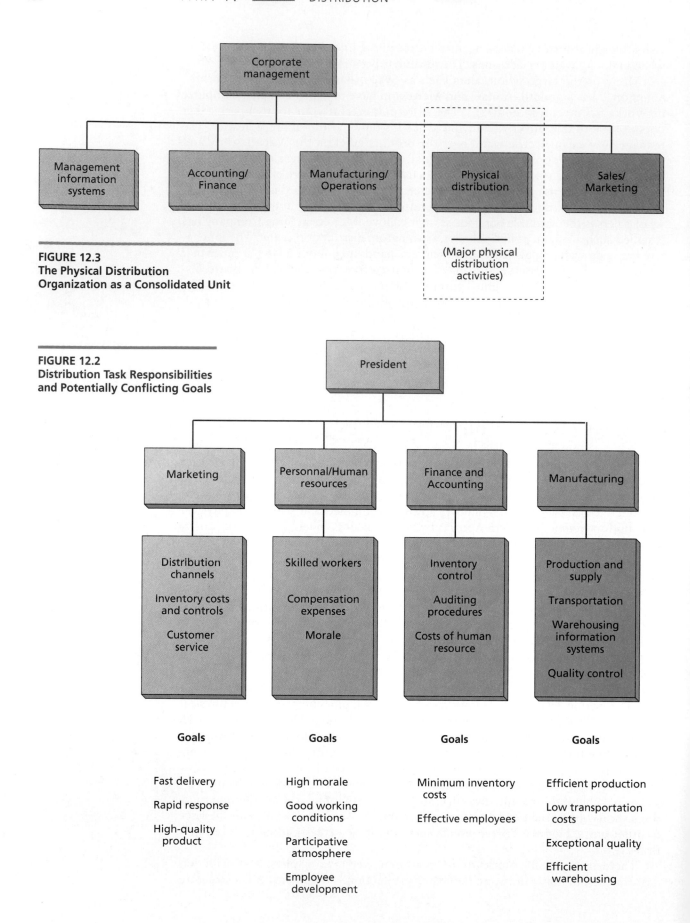

FIGURE 12.3
The Physical Distribution
Organization as a Consolidated Unit

FIGURE 12.2
Distribution Task Responsibilities
and Potentially Conflicting Goals

were changed from that of Figure 12.2 to the one presented in Figure 12.3, it might be perceived as a threat to the power of the dominant unit.

The debate about the fit between physical distribution and other areas like marketing, production, and finance will undoubtedly continue.[32] What's most important is that those involved in physical distribution must see it as a marketing function and, instead of competing with the marketing department, they must work together. Experts in physical distribution believe that, to compete effectively, firms should follow the structure shown in Figure 12.3. They believe the hard facts of rising physical distribution costs, growing customer service demands, increased competition, and shrinking profits will push physical distribution into a freestanding system that is equal to the other business units in the firm.

THE NATURE OF PHYSICAL DISTRIBUTION

The terms *physical distribution* and *logistics* are sometimes used interchangeably to refer to activities associated with the physical transfer of goods. The National Council of Physical Distribution Management (NCPDM) has defined **physical distribution** as

> the movement of an item from the place where it was made or grown to the place where it is consumed. . . . All the activities involved in moving goods to the right place at the right time (as opposed to manufacturing them) can be described under the broad term "distribution." The components of the physical distribution system include: customer service, demand forecasting, inventory control, materials handling, order processing, packaging, traffic and transportation, warehousing, and distribution communications.[33]

The term **logistics** is borrowed from the military and has a broader definition including "the procurement, distribution, maintenance, and replacement of material and personnel."[34] In marketing, physical distribution is the better term because it suggests concern with the physical movement and transfer of finished and semi-finished goods within and across marketing channels.

Physical distribution systems need to be flexible enough to meet the different needs of consumers. An important difference among markets, for example, is the volume in which they buy. Single consumers usually purchase small amounts of a product, while intermediaries and other companies often buy in large quantities. Physical distribution planners need to design systems that can accommodate both.

Physical distribution flow includes inventories sent directly to consumers, direct resale shipments from intermediaries, and shipments from field warehouses. If large quantities are needed, shipments are made from inventories, the production line, or vendors. Since transportation rates are lower when full vehicle loads are transferred, this method of movement is the least expensive.[35] If quantities requested will not fully load a vehicle, it may be more cost efficient to distribute through warehouses. By strategically locating warehouses as close to customers as possible, manufacturers can improve service and lower distribution costs.

The physical transferring of goods is not necessarily finished upon customer receipt. Sometimes goods are returned, necessitating a return-of-goods procedure as part of the physical distribution system. Reasons for returning products include damage, receipt of the wrong product, a customer's changing need, or failure of the customer to pay. Many goods are returned due to concerns for users' safety. Although such product recalls can create image problems for organizations, efficient handling, through a well-developed distribution chain, can actually work in a firm's favor. For example, in August of 1993 General Motors recalled 350,000 Saturn automobiles to replace a wire that could short-circuit and catch fire. Saturn

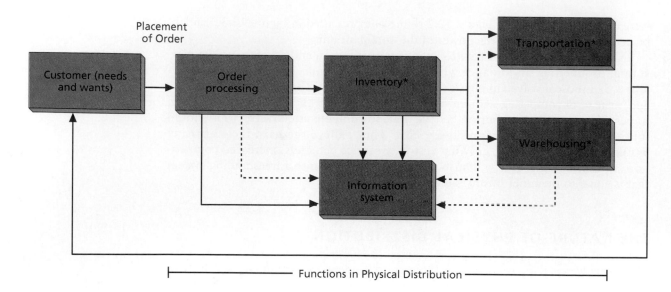

Placement of Order

Functions in Physical Distribution

*Materials handling function occurs in these three areas.

Note: Dotted lines indicate information flows. For example, orders flow into the system. Transportation data also flow into the system, but there is a reciprocal flow to the transportation point.

FIGURE 12.4
Functions in the Physical Distribution System

owners were instructed to return their cars to dealerships where the repair was performed in 25 minutes. Customers were served hot dogs, soft drinks, and doughnuts as they waited. Most owners of the recalled autos reported the experience to be a positive one.[36]

Figure 12.4 shows the typical functions of physical distribution systems. The figure, however, provides only a skeleton view of the flow of goods in the physical distribution system. Effective distribution of goods like home computers, automobiles, detergents, central air-conditioning units, and lamps involves a number of physical distribution elements not displayed. As with product, price, and promotion decisions, the starting point in physical distribution is the customer.

It is extremely important for a firm's physical distribution system to keep pace with the rest of its marketing mix. In other words, stimulating demand for a product through other components of the marketing mix, like promotion, can do more harm than good if the firm's distribution system is not operating efficiently to make the product available to consumers. Eastman Kodak, in the past, failed to efficiently serve its customers. The aggressive promotion of its instant camera resulted in rising customer interest. Customers liked the features of the Kodak product and wanted to buy it. The company, however, did not provide sufficient quantities of the camera to retailers. Polaroid, a competitor, stepped in and made the sales. The result was not only lost sales for Kodak, but also negative consumer attitudes toward the company because it advertised a product that was not readily available.

OBJECTIVES OF PHYSICAL DISTRIBUTION

The development of an efficient, market-driven physical distribution system is a major challenge. It is sometimes said that the goal of physical distribution is to maximize customer service while minimizing costs. Clearly both of these things cannot be accomplished simultaneously, hence constant trade-offs must be made among customer service, costs, and profits.

Balancing customer service, costs, and a firm's profits is a Herculean feat. The expenses in each phase of physical distribution are usually inversely related.[37]

▪ A firm decides to ship goods by motor carriers to reduce transportation expenses. Motor transport is only moderately fast but it's dependable, frequent, and available. However, because most customers want goods promptly and because motor carriers are slower than air carriers, customer satisfaction is often reduced.

▪ A firm plans to use air carriers to transport goods. However, the air carriers are far away from the source of the goods. Again, customer ill will results because goods must first be shipped from the plant by motor carrier to air carrier facilities resulting in more distribution time.

▪ A decision is made to place orders as soon as a customer needs a product. As a result, many small orders are placed which increases the administrative cost of ordering and overburdens the administrative staff. The overburdened staff makes errors, which results in an increase in returned goods because many customers receive the wrong orders. Dealing with the returned goods further increases administrative costs.

Each physical distribution activity must be studied in conjunction with other activities. Good customer service, minimal costs, and high profits are certainly worthy objectives, but it's hard to find the optimal mix of physical distribution activities that will produce all three.

The Customer Service Objective

The main objective of physical distribution is to provide customer service. Without customers, concerns about cost and profits are meaningless. Customers are interested in receiving goods when needed, receiving appropriate sizes of orders, receiving usable goods, being able to return goods when necessary, purchasing goods at fair and competitive prices, and placing orders easily.

Companies can emphasize their ability to fill these needs in terms of performance objectives. Victoreen, an electronics manufacturer in Chicago, has the following customer service objectives:

▪ The number of orders that are shipped within 24 hours of demand should represent 90 percent of orders placed.
▪ No customer will wait more than 96 hours to receive an order. Customers waiting longer than this will receive at least a 10 percent reduction in the total (full) cost of the order.
▪ At least 96 percent of goods delivered will be in perfect working condition.

Victoreen management has been setting specific, quantifiable, customer-service objectives every year for two decades. It believes this is one reason it has been successful in the highly competitive electronics parts industry.

To some firms, customer service is the ultimate objective that must be fulfilled; consequently, customer preferences must be determined.[38] Studies have shown that customer-service preferences can be determined by informal questioning and formal surveying.[39] The intent of such probing is to establish physical distribution objectives that are meaningful, timely, concise, and, if at all possible, quantifiable.

The Total Cost Objective

Total cost includes all costs incurred in accomplishing the customer-service objectives of the physical distribution system. Physical distribution experts believe it is less important to minimize the cost of any one component (for example, transportation

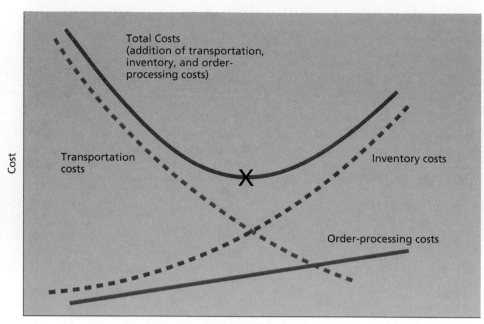

Customer Service
(Percentage of customers served within ten days of receiving order)

FIGURE 12.5
Total Cost Analysis for Providing Customer Service

or ordering) than to minimize the total cost.[40] Since the various physical distribution functions are interrelated, a change in one function affects other functions. Hence if management wants to increase the number of warehouses, it should study the effects on inventory, processing, and transportation.

Figure 12.5 presents a total cost analysis for customer service. A manager typically faces three types of costs: inventory costs, transportation costs, and order processing costs. In the figure, the minimum total cost is noted by an X. This point is different from the lowest points of the three components because it is the determination of the lowest total cost for the system, a combination of transportation, inventory, and order processing. A lower cost in one area may be offset by a higher cost in another.

Physical distribution managers must often weigh distribution cost trade-offs, which occur when cost increases in one area lead to cost decreases in other areas. As Figure 12.5 illustrates, costs often conflict with one another.

If a decision is made to increase the number of warehouses, transportation costs decline. At the same time, however, inventory and order-processing costs may increase. The cost of inventory increases with the number of warehouses because more stock is stored, and order-processing costs increase if orders are placed from each warehouse because more personnel are needed.

The more managers of physical distribution think in terms of total cost, the closer they will be to acceptance of the physical distribution concept. The **physical distribution concept** states that an organization should view all aspects of physical distribution as part of a single system. This systems view of the physical distribution function will enable the operation to run more smoothly and bring the organization closer to an appropriate balance between customer service, costs, and profits.

12-3   What is the difference between physical distribution and logistics?

12-4   Why is it important to balance customer service, costs, and profits?

12-5   When discussing physical distribution, some believe that a freestanding department can be effective, while others view it as a supportive activity. What are the strengths and weaknesses of these views of physical distribution?

FUNCTIONS OF THE PHYSICAL DISTRIBUTION SYSTEM

A physical distribution system consists of a set of interrelated functions with specific boundaries. Figure 12.4 shows how these functions interrelate. The physical distribution manager must address how orders should be placed (order processing), where goods should be located geographically (warehousing), what amount of goods should be on hand (inventory management and control), what mode of transportation should be used to move goods (transportation), how goods should be moved within company boundaries (materials handling), and what type of information system is needed to link producers, intermediaries, and customers.[41]

Order Processing

The old proverb that "time is money" points to the importance of order processing. The distribution of goods does not begin until customer orders have been received, processed, and filled. Carrying out these activities as quickly and efficiently as possible results in profits, customer satisfaction, and repeat business. **Order processing** refers to all activities involved in collecting, checking, and transmitting sales-order information. It is the handling of all paperwork associated with the sale of an organization's goods and services.

Order entry includes the completion of an order form by a salesperson or customer and the transmission of that form to the warehouse. Order processing includes preparing the bill of lading, checking credit, and carrying out the order. Order filling from warehouse inventory and delivering of the goods complete the order cycle.[42]

Order processing can be handled in many ways. In general, firms want to fill orders with speed and accuracy. However, these objectives need to be achieved within cost limits. Two types of systems, manual and automated, are used to achieve speed and accuracy.

The application of electronic technology to order processing has progressed rapidly. Sears, Roebuck & Company, for example, uses electronic data interchange to order furniture from its suppliers providing fast merchandising information and delivery to its customers at widely dispersed retail locations.[43]

The first step in Sears's electronic ordering system occurs when a customer at a Sears store finds a piece of furniture that he or she would like to purchase. The sales associate keys the item's number into a point-of-sale (POS) computer on the sales floor. The computer instantly displays information on the availability of the item and when it can be delivered to the customer's home.

The POS computer is just an end point in Sears's Source Availability System (SAS). SAS was created at Sears in 1989 to overcome problems with suppliers and inventory management. Prior to SAS, Sears's furniture sales associates wrote orders on paper order forms, which were delivered to one of 50 centers that stocked inventory in the United States. Personnel at these centers checked to see if the item was in stock and, if so, called the customer to arrange a delivery date. If the item was not in stock, staff would call the supplier to place an order and then call the customer to inform them of how long it would be until the item would be available.

When Sears instituted its Source Availability System, it required all of its suppliers to interface with the system through electronic data interchange. Hence, sales associates could have instantaneous information on product availability. Computerization also allowed Sears to instantly cross a calculation of the delivery space needed on a truck for any given piece of furniture with information regarding when a truck was scheduled to be in a given geographical location. This allowed sales associates on the retail floor to know not only whether the product was available but exactly when it could be delivered.

SAS has allowed Sears to operate from four consolidation centers nationwide, rather than from the 50 centers it previously operated. Inventory-carrying costs and personnel costs have been reduced by 75 to 80 percent, and 97 to 98 percent of merchandise is delivered on the date it was promised. The Sears system illustrates how order processing, inventory control, manufacturing, and transportation activities can be tied together. Because Sears's customers can just as easily purchase furniture at JCPenney or Montgomery Ward, it is important to keep this system running smoothly.

Warehousing

Warehouses maintained by intermediaries or by the manufacturers themselves must be strategically located in or near centers of demand. There are two types of warehousing facilities: private and public. Private warehouses are either owned or leased and are used when a large volume of goods must be stored regularly to meet customers' demands. Although owning warehouse space may be expensive, private warehouses are popular when a firm needs flexibility in the design of facilities, wishes to maintain control over its warehousing operations, has special handling and storage requirements, and has a high volume of goods flowing through its facilities.[44] In contrast, public warehouses, which are rented, are desirable for firms that do not want to be burdened with operating a warehouse. Public warehousing is also popular if a firm needs flexibility in placing its inventory because of uncertain or seasonal demand for goods. The customer using a public warehouse pays only for the amount of space used.

Distribution centers.   A major development in private warehousing has been the distribution center, which differs from a conventional private warehouse in several ways. A **distribution center** is a centralized operation that serves regional markets, processes and regroups products into customized orders, maintains a full line of products, consolidates large shipments from different distribution points, frequently uses computers, and is highly automated.[45] The consolidation centers referred to in the Sears example are distribution centers. Because the movement of goods at distribution centers is very rapid, with the focus on getting goods out rather than storing them, the term **throughput** is often used to describe the major activity of a distribution center.

Warehouses, such as that of a software distribution company shown here, must be strategically located in or near centers of demand.

Distribution centers are designed to accommodate rapid throughput. Hence, they look quite different from traditional warehouses. While a traditional warehouse may be several stories high and located in a "warehouse district" that is not easily accessible, distribution centers tend to be sprawling facilities located on the edges of urban areas so as to provide easy access by all major forms of transportation.

The costs of storage decrease when distribution centers are used because the center serves as only a temporary station for goods prior to their rapid movement to customers. Transportation costs may also be lowered. For example, instead of shipping to 90 key market locations, General Mills transports its products to only 15 locations. The loads are larger, and bulk loads usually are cheaper to transport than small loads.

Walgreen Company, an industry leader in revenues and profits, uses a network of six strategically located distribution centers to serve its 1,100 stores. The firm has been able to reduce its distribution costs by 35 percent by using this system.

Distribution centers, such as those of Sears, Wal-Mart, Montgomery Ward, Pillsbury, and Hallmark, typically use computerized information systems. Computers are involved in processing orders, guiding conveyor systems, and guiding stacker cranes to move goods from place to place. Distribution centers are costly to build but the improved customer service is generally well worth the investment. Greater order accuracy, better control, and improved efficiency, which come with a smoothly running, computerized distribution center, aid a firm's drive to expand business. Furthermore, while start-up costs may be high, operating costs for a distribution center may be less than for a traditional warehouse. Personnel costs, for example, are usually low because the automated system allows it to operate with a much smaller staff than would be required otherwise.

Inventory Management and Control

Businesses that deal in tangible goods must manage inventories. Managers must procure stocks of goods to meet demand. One challenge is minimizing total inventory costs within the constraints of demand, cost, and customer service. The major objective of inventory management and control is to inform managers how much of a good to reorder, when to reorder the good, how frequently to place orders, and what

One way to examine inventory management is to consider the demand for goods. Continuous demand products, like food products, require continual stock replenishment.

the appropriate safety stock is for minimizing stockouts. Thus, the overall goal of inventory is to have what is needed, when it is needed, and to minimize the number of times a firm is out of stock.

One way to examine inventory management is to consider the demand for goods. There are continuous, seasonal, and erratic demand patterns.[46] Products in **continuous demand** have a long history of sales with demand basically unchanged throughout the year. Products such as Wrigley's chewing gum, Tide detergent, and Crest toothpaste are continuously demanded and require continual stock replenishment. Inventory decisions involve forecasting the continuous demand level, judging when replenishment should occur, and determining the size of the replenishment order. When these decisions are made effectively, customer-service and profit objectives are met.

Products with **seasonal demand** experience high demand at regular points in time. Turkeys at Thanksgiving, stuffed bunnies at Easter, and wreaths at Christmas are examples. These products require accurate forecasting of the level of demand.

Erratic demand is a generally unpredictable pattern of demand. The unpredictable demand for compressors, cement mixers, automobiles, and trailers makes inventory management and control challenging. The time to fill orders, the size of the inventory, and the method of delivery are difficult to plan and implement.

Three important costs of inventory are carrying costs, procurement costs, and out-of-stock costs.[47] **Carrying costs** are all costs associated with holding a quantity of goods for some time. For example, there is the cost of capital that is tied up and could be used for other purposes. There are also the costs of taxes and insurance for carrying inventory. With the exception of a few states, a property tax is levied on all or some inventories in warehouses. Fire and theft insurance is needed to protect the inventory from losses. There are also costs for storage space. Finally, a risk cost must be considered because damage, obsolescence, and deterioration of inventory occur. Carrying costs can average as much as 25 percent of inventory value. Thus, there must be good reasons for carrying large inventories. Valid reasons include fulfilling customer-service objectives, increasing profit, or improving public image by having goods in stock.

Procurement costs occur when stock must be replenished. Costs for processing orders, transmittal expenses, handling materials, and the price of goods make up procurement costs.

If there is a demand for goods that are out of stock, a firm incurs an **out-of-stock cost** because of lost sales and back-order expenses. Customers prefer to receive goods as soon as possible. The customer who cancels an order because the firm is out of stock usually goes elsewhere. The lost sales cost is the profit lost at the time of the outage, as well as the ill will suffered by not having the goods available. Back-order costs result if clerical and ordering expenses must be incurred to fill the order as soon as possible.

Balancing carrying, procurement, and out-of-stock costs is an important objective of inventory management. The larger the inventory in a warehouse, the higher the inventory levels. Fewer, but larger, replenishment orders are needed to keep goods in inventory. Figure 12.6 illustrates the conflicting costs of inventory. The total cost curve is derived by vertically summing the other three curves. The optimal order quantity is represented as R_Q on the replenishment axis.

Channel integration.   Some companies, including Kmart, Kodak, and Lee Apparel have adopted *channel integration inventory control*. The process depends upon retailers sharing information on sales at the store level with their suppliers. This exchange of information enables suppliers to manufacture the amount of actual product needed. It allows suppliers and retailers to carry the barest minimum of inventory in their warehouses.[48]

Channel integration represents a significant departure from the old way of doing business. In the past, the manufacturer and the retailer would operate their channels separately, each trying to minimize its own transportation and distribution costs. Under channel integration the manufacturer and supplier work together to manage inventory throughout the pipeline from the factory to the store floor. For example, Kmart sends point-of-sale and inventory data to its largest suppliers on a daily basis. The suppliers then automatically ship replenished stock to the ten Kmart distribution centers that restock the individual stores. In this system, the suppliers make the replacement decisions.

FIGURE 12.6
Conflicting Costs Involved in Inventory Management and Control

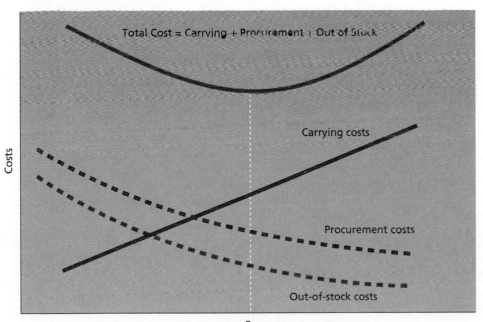

Size of Inventory Replenishment Quantity

Lee Apparel Company has a replenishment program with nine retailers. Using point-of-sale data, Lee supplies retailers according to their needs. Lee also uses the point-of-sale data to drive its production. Sales information triggers Lee's daily flexible manufacturing operation. If retailers and suppliers can overcome their reluctance to share data, channel integration may become widely used.

Just-in-Time (JIT).   **Just-in-Time** is an inventory control system in which the supplier's customer (a wholesaler, retailer, another firm, or a consumer) starts the process by calling for a product.[49] JIT was developed by Taiichi Ohno at Toyota Motor Company of Japan. Under Ohno's system, Toyota factories carried very little inventory. When parts were needed, they were delivered from other Toyota plants or from outside suppliers. An efficient JIT system can minimize administrative costs and result in low inventories of parts, raw materials, work in process, and finished goods. This contributes to savings in warehousing and work space.

Advocates of JIT point out that traditionally most manufacturing plants have been required to build up inventories to help weather barriers to the smooth flow of materials, such as capacity bottlenecks, machine breakdowns, and quality defects.[50] To hold down these barriers, the JIT approach includes maintaining cleaner plants, scheduling machine maintenance, simpler product designs, and much more. The application of these tools leads to a process of continuous improvement. Using JIT, Toyota reduced the times of critical die-change operations from several hours to a few minutes.[51] Other companies have also become converts to the virtues of JIT.

Just-in-Time is not without its critics. The "Marketing in Action: JIT—Panacea or Problem?" discusses the use of JIT by such giants as Proctor & Gamble, General Motors, and Mazda and explains why the system is controversial.

Managers inspired to implement JIT have had to overcome concerns about a radically different system. They fear the loss of an "inventory security blanket" that can meet high sales demands or missed production schedules. They also fear the long distances that suppliers must travel to make daily deliveries. The Japanese have those problems, too. For example, all of Toyota City production was shut down when a massive traffic jam tied up roads leading to the facility and suppliers' trucks couldn't get through.[52]

Transportation

The United States has the most sophisticated transportation network in the world. In 1992, 3.57 million people worked to transport goods in the United States.[53] Despite deregulation bills enacted between 1978 and 1986, the transportation network is still closely monitored by government agencies. The Interstate Commerce Commission (ICC) helps regulate railroads, pipelines, motor carriers, and inland water carriers. It also regulates the Federal Marine Board (FMB). The Civil Aeronautics Board (CAB), which was phased out in 1985, regulated air carriers. Some specific deregulation laws include the following:

- *Airline Deregulation Act of 1978.* Carriers can choose new routes or phase them out and can cut fares by half or raise them by 5 percent on routes where they control less than 70 percent of the traffic.

- *Motor Carrier Act of 1980.* Carriers can raise or lower rates by 10 percent without ICC approval. Any fit, willing, and able carrier who provides a public service can enter the regulated trucking industry.

- *Household Goods Transportation Act of 1980.* Moving companies can give customers guaranteed pick-up and delivery dates at an extra charge. They must pay the customer a specific amount if they miss these dates.

MARKETING *IN ACTION*

JIT: Panacea or Problem?

Just-in-Time (JIT) inventory management has been hailed as a builder of partnerships and a method to save billions for the manufacturers, wholesalers, and retailers who have instituted it.

Procter & Gamble, for example, has used the method to build strong relationships with retailers, relationships that did not exist prior to implementation of a JIT system. Procter & Gamble had developed a reputation as a tough bargainer when dealing with retailers who carry its products. The firm claims, however, that the institution of Just-in-Time delivery arrangements has improved its reputation among retailers and saved the company and its customers (the retailers) about $1 billion annually. The savings, claims Proctor & Gamble, comes from the use of data processing recordkeeping systems that have improved the efficiencies of shipments. The relationship between Procter & Gamble and Wal-Mart, the retail and wholesale giant, is an example of JIT's success. JIT has brought a smooth flow to shipment of goods from Procter & Gamble to Wal-Mart. This has improved customer satisfaction because desired products always seem to be available at Wal-Mart.

Just-in-Time has also been a success for General Motors. The automobile manufacturer spent almost $2 billion to make a plant in Ontario, Canada, one of the most efficient JIT facilities anywhere. Before installing JIT, GM attained 24 turns of inventory at the plant. The use of JIT resulted in 50 turns of inventory. Each inventory turn is worth $1 million. GM's goal is to have only one day's worth of material at its assembly plants. Maintaining such a lean inventory presents some

risks—being out of stock, delays, and potential shutdowns of assembly lines. GM has decided, however, that being lean in terms of inventory is worth the risks.

Not every firm that has instituted JIT has found trouble-free results. Problems have occurred not only as the result of the risks of maintaining a lean inventory, but also due to personnel issues that sometimes surround JIT. The experience of the Mazda factory near Detroit, Michigan, illustrates this situation. The United Auto Workers leadership at the factory had worked closely with Mazda's management to institute JIT. However, one year after implementing JIT, the UAW leaders were voted out. One of the issues raised by the slate of new union leaders was that JIT created less autonomy for workers and required a faster work pace. The new union leaders raised the issue of whether JIT is just a nice sounding, highly publicized way to squeeze more out of workers.

Such criticisms of JIT have been echoed at other companies as well. A number of U.S. and Japanese firms using JIT have found that sharp reductions in inventory buffers sometimes result in a regimented work flow and high levels of stress among employees. Proponents of JIT challenge such criticisms by countering that the method boosts workers' morale by increasing their involvement in decision making and scheduling.

Just-in-Time is likely to remain controversial. While it appears clear that it can and does result in cost savings for companies, its possible effects on worker morale make it a practice likely to remain at the center of lively debate.

- *Staggers Rail Act of 1980.* ICC jurisdiction over rates is limited to cases in which railroads exercise market dominance. Carriers were permitted to raise rates up to 6 percent per year through October 1984 and can now raise rates 4 percent annually.

- *Surface Freight Forwarder Act of 1986.* This act substantially deregulated the nonhousehold goods segment of the surface freight forwarder industry. This legislation retains federal regulation of all surface freight forwarders in the areas of cargo liability and claims settlement procedures. Freight forwarders are responsible for any loss or damage to the cargo they handle.

The deregulation trend in the United States affects all classes of carriers. **Common carriers** are transporters that maintain regular schedules and accept goods from any shipper. **Contract carriers** are for-hire transporters who carry goods for anyone for an agreed-upon sum. They are generally subject to less governmental regulation than common carriers. **Private carriers** are company-owned transporters that carry goods only for the company. Because the company owns them, private carriers are subject to little government regulation. **Exempt carriers** are shippers that are not required to operate according to state and federal regulation. They usually move unprocessed agricultural products by truck.

Rate regulation. Even with the general trend toward deregulating the transportation industry, there is still some rate control by the ICC. *Transportation rates* are the prices for-hire carriers charge for their services. *Class rates* are rates charged for goods that are shipped in small amounts. Only about 7 percent of the total revenue for railroads comes from class rates. *Commodity rates* are special low rates for the shipment of large quantities or regular use. About 90 percent of the total tonnage of railroads and a large percentage of the tonnage of inland water carriers is shipped under commodity rates.[54]

Most rates are based originally on supply factors or the costs of providing services—loading, special handling, product liability, and so on. The rates actually charged, however, are determined largely by competition among carriers and alternative modes of transportation. The physical distribution manager searches out, bargains for, and selects the best rate. By receiving the best rates, routes, and service, firms can best accomplish their objectives for physical distribution, customer service, cost, and profit.

Modes of transportation. Most goods are moved by rail, motor, water, pipe, or air.[55] Table 12.3 shows the relative importance of these five transportation modes. The latest available data indicate that railroads haul about 37 percent of total ton-miles. (A *ton-mile* is one ton of freight moved one mile.) Motor vehicles are second in ton-miles shipped at about 25 percent. Pipelines account for about 20 percent of ton-miles. Fourth are water carriers, accounting for approximately 16 percent of ton-miles. Air freight has shown the most dramatic growth, but, despite this growth, it still represents less than 1 percent of ton-miles shipped. As you can see, the order of rankings for the five modes of transportation have not changed in 25 years. The importance of a particular mode of transportation for moving goods depends largely on the type of freight being hauled.

Pipelines are efficient means for moving liquids, such as oil and gas products, over long distances (from Alaska to California, for example). More than 200,000 miles of pipelines (not including the Alaskan pipeline, which stretches about 900 miles from Prudhoe Bay, Alaska, to Valdez, Alaska) weave through the United States.[56]

In contrast, *air freight* is best suited for products that can trade off higher transport costs per ton-mile against improved service. Common goods shipped by air

TABLE 12.3
Domestic Freight Traffic by Major Transportation Modes

Mode of Transportation	Percentage of Ton-Miles Shipped		
	1970	1985	Today
Railroads	40.0%	38.0%	37.0%
Motor vehicles	21.0%	25.0%	27.0%
Pipelines	22.0%	23.0%	20.0%
Water carriers	16.0%	16.0%	16.0%
Airways	0.1%	0.2%	0.4%

Sources: Eno Foundation for Transportation, *Transportation in America*, 11th ed.,1993; *The 1994 Information Please Almanac*, New York: Houghton Mifflin, 1993.

are computing and accounting machines, special dies and tools, medical supplies, live lobsters, and electronic parts. These products generally have high value compared to their weight and must get to customers quickly. While the cost of transporting by air is significantly higher than by other modes of transportation, air freight rates fell a bit in the early 1990s. This is due to excess industry capacity and heavy competition.[57]

Air has grown, overall, as a means of transportation despite remaining last of the five modes in terms of ton-miles shipped. In some cases, the use of air as a mode of transportation has spawned entire industries. Overnight mail delivery is an example of this. Federal Express is the largest competitor in the overnight mail industry. In 1993 the company had revenues of $7.8 billion. It picks up, sorts, and delivers 1.8 million pieces of mail every day. Federal Express employs 96,000 people in 187 countries.[58] Some industry experts predict, however, that overnight delivery may lose its edge in moving mail as the use of facsimile (fax) continues to grow worldwide.[59]

Water carriers provide a major means of hauling products in bulk. Shipments by water carriers accounted for $10 billion in revenues in 1993.[60] Water carriers offer the least expensive mode of transport, especially when moving goods internationally, and are not expected to increase rates.[61] The trade-off, however, is that water carriers are a very slow means of moving goods. Coal, oil, grain, and sand in bulk amounts are shipped over waterways. These products are of low value relative to their weight and are not perishable. Time is typically not a crucial consideration in the transport of these goods.

Motor vehicles are a flexible mode of shipping a variety of products, including food, metal castings, rubber belts, and apparel. Motor vehicles can move goods short or long distances and offer customers relatively fast and consistent service. Motor vehicles are a more expensive form of transportation than modes such as water carriers that offer lower levels of service. Hence, while accounting for only 25 percent of ton-miles shipped in the United States, at $313 billion in revenues, motor vehicles' share of total shipping revenue was close to 78 percent.[62] Despite the popularity of motor vehicles for transportation, many trucking companies are finding it harder and harder to prosper. In 1992 expenses in the trucking industry rose faster than revenues, and more than 2,200 trucking firms failed.[63]

Railroads are the most widely used method of transportation, although this dominance has been weakened by the development of other modes of transportation. In 1993, for example, railroads carried about 37 percent of ton-miles shipped, a drop from 56 percent in 1950 and 44 percent in 1960. Railroad revenues in 1993 were approximately $32 billion.[64] Rail is a relatively low-cost form of transportation, especially for heavy cargoes. Rates for rail transportation declined from 3.23 cents per ton-mile in 1982 to 2.57 cents in 1992.[65]

Deciding how to transport goods. At some point a decision must be made about how to transport goods. Transportation modes can be used in combination as well as exclusively. To aid in making the best decision, six criteria are important: speed of delivery, dependability, frequency of shipments, availability in different locations, flexibility in handling products, and cost.

Table 12.4 rates the five modes of transportation on each of these six criteria. In selecting a mode of transportation, the physical distribution manager considers his or her objectives, the needs of consumers, and the consumers' willingness to pay for higher levels of service. For example, air is the most expensive mode of transportation, but it is also fast. Consumers who desire products very quickly and are willing to pay for a high level of service may be best served by air. On the other hand, water is the least expensive, but it is slow. Of course, any comparisons must consider the type of product shipped and the other criteria listed in Table 12.4.

Operating Characteristics	Ranking by Transportation Form[a]				
	Railroads	Motor Carriers	Waterways	Pipelines	Airways
Delivery speed	3	2	4	5	1
Number of locations served	2	1	4	5	3
On-time dependability[b]	3	2	4	1	5
Range of products carried	1	2	3	5	4
Frequency of shipments	4	2	5	1	3
Losses and damages	5	4	2	1	3
Cost per ton-mile	3	4	1	2	5

[a] 1 = highest ranking.
[b] Relative variation from anticipated delivery time.

Sources: Adapted by the authors from D. J. Bowersox, D. J. Closs, and O. K. Helferich, *Logistical Management*, 3d ed. (New York: Macmillan, 1986), p. 166; and R. H. Ballou, *Business Logistics Management: Planning and Control*, 2d ed. (Englewood Cliffs, NJ: Prentice-Hall, 1985), p. 194.

TABLE 12.4
Operating Characteristics of Five Transportation Modes

It is also important for a manager to remember that the total cost of physical distribution should be considered when making decisions about transportation. For example, although air is expensive, the speed it provides may mean the shipper can cut down on storage and warehousing costs prior to shipment. Hence, the combined cost of storage and transportation might be less with air.

Intermodal transportation.   In many instances the best choice of transportation is a combination of modes. This is *intermodal coordination of transport services*. Intermodal shipments have skyrocketed during the last two decades. In 1982 there were an estimated 3.5 million intermodal shipments in the United States. That figure jumped to 7.2 million in 1993.[66] To accomplish intermodal coordination, exchange of equipment between modes is necessary. For example, a truck might be carried aboard an airplane, or a rail car might be shipped fully loaded on a water carrier.

Piggyback is the most widely used form of coordinating modes. It is now available between 1,400 cities in the United States and Canada. Also known as *trailer-on-flatcars (TOFC)*, piggyback involves transporting truck trailers on railroad flatcars, usually over long distances. Piggybacking combines the flexibility of trucking with the economical long-distance rates of railroads. The overall cost per ton-mile is less than the cost for trucking alone, and the combination permits trucking to extend its range of service.

With another form of intermodal coordination, *birdyback*, motor carriers, picking up and delivering shipments of goods, are transported on air carriers. There is also *fishyback*, in which motor carriers are loaded on water carriers.

Yet another intermodal service is *containerized freight*. This involves the placing of goods in containers, which are then placed on a trailer's chassis. With a truck–rail combination it is possible to haul only the containers, thus eliminating the cost of the dead weight of the motor vehicle. This particular combination is called *container-on-flatcar (COFC)*.

On March 23, 1981, the ICC deregulated all truck and rail services provided by the railroads in connection with TOFC and COFC movements to give the railroads more marketing flexibility. This deregulation allowed the railroads to counteract the advantages in efficiency gained by motor carriers with their 1980 deregulation.

12-6   Could the Just-in-Time inventory management procedure be used between countries? Explain.

12-7   What mode of transportation would you recommend for appliances? Fresh flowers? Industrial lubricants?

Materials Handling

Materials handling is the physical handling of goods. It is an important activity in inventory, warehousing, and transportation. The characteristics of a product determine, to a large extent, how it will be handled. For example, radioactive wastes, bulk chemicals, and gases require special handling and storage.

A variety of equipment is used to handle a wide range of product sizes, shapes, volumes, and weights. The most popular materials handling equipment includes trucks, conveyors, and cranes, which minimize losses from breakage and spoilage. General Mills carefully monitors the handling by forklift operators in its warehouses. Rough and careless handling can break boxes that are being stacked. Damaged boxes are put in off-storage, the area reserved for boxes that must be destroyed. To minimize such losses, the company has its forklift operators attend classes for materials handling and periodically tests the operators.

Information Systems

The use of computerized information systems for physical distribution has become standard procedure in most industries. Computers, memory systems, display equipment, and other forms of information-processing technology link producers, intermediaries, and customers. Del Monte, Campbell's, R. J. Reynolds, and Standard Brands are among the many firms that rely heavily on computer information systems to manage their physical distribution.

Computer costs continue to decline while speed and reliability of equipment used in order processing, warehousing, inventory control, and scheduling transportation improve annually. Today minicomputers and even hand-held microcomputers provide the basis of most physical distribution systems. Advances in computer software and hardware are continuously making physical distribution systems faster and more efficient.

An example of a computer-based program that eases order processing for international shippers is Encompass.[67] Encompass is a joint venture of two transportation giants, CSX Corporation, owner of the CSX railroad and Sea-Land, and AMR, parent of American Airlines. The program allows shippers to communicate electronically with carriers, forwarders, and brokers worldwide through a single neutral interface. All participants use their own computers, regardless of which system they use or where the computers are located.

Using Encompass, a distribution manager can consolidate shipments, schedule, book carriers, and track shipments on a global basis from a single computer. The system helps international shippers clear customs through its interlink with customs services throughout the world.

As one example of how useful this system is, Digital Equipment Corporation (DEC) is using Encompass to manage airfreight shipments from its vendors through its distribution center in Massachusetts and on to manufacturing facilities in Scotland and Ireland.

The management of global physical distribution systems is made easier and more efficient through the use of programs like Encompass and other information systems that provide an electronic window to the world.

TOTAL QUALITY MANAGEMENT IN A MARKET-DRIVEN PHYSICAL DISTRIBUTION SYSTEM

Physical distribution is one area within organizations where the concepts of total quality management have seen great application. The precise, quantified objectives set for physical distribution performance lend themselves well to efforts to implement total quality programs. As programs of quality management continue to spread throughout the physical distribution industry, market-driven companies interested in satisfying consumers by improving their performance relative to that of competitors should continue to grow.

Firms begin by comparing their current performance to the current performance of competitors. This can be accomplished through benchmarking. **Benchmarking** is the process of analyzing each function of a system compared to those of competitors. This comparison has the potential to produce improvements if a firm is able to find the best industry practices and implement them. A survey of Fortune 1000 companies indicated that 65 percent of the respondents said their firms benchmarked to "gain competitive advantage." The International Benchmarking Clearinghouse in Houston, Texas, has been established to bring together benchmarking firms, reposition benchmarking data, and to promote the benchmarking process. Some believe that Xerox, by using competitive benchmarking, was able to regain the competitive edge it had lost to the Japanese. Two benchmarks for Xerox were L. L. Bean's shopping operations and Sears Roebuck's field distribution system.[68]

Benchmarking can be applied to the physical distribution system of an organization in the following way:

- *Determine which functions of physical distribution to benchmark.* For example, a firm may decide to consider its inventory management and control system and the impact of that system on customer service.

- *Identify key performance indicators that affect customers.* A key performance indicator might be the number of days it takes to fill a back order when an out-of-stock is reported.

- *Identify the best companies with respect to the identified performance indicators.* At this point the firm searches for firms whose performance on the key indicators is deemed to be superior. Perhaps a competitor fills orders resulting from out-of-stocks within 24 hours, 95 percent of the time.

- *Identify the practices of the best companies.* What are the policies of the superior companies? How is the competitor able to fill orders within 24 hours?

- *Take action to close the gap.* At this point the firm adopts the policies necessary to provide superior performance on the key indicators.

- *Reevaluate.* Benchmarking now provides an assessment of whether the firm has improved in satisfying customers' needs.

Areas	Companies
Inbound transportation	Digital Equipment Corporation Dow Chemical
Customer service	American Express L. L. Bean
Outbound transportation	Procter & Gamble 3M Corporation
Private fleet management	Frito-Lay Harley-Davidson
Warehousing	Hershey Foods Kodak
Materials management	Du Pont Motorola

Source: T. Foster, "Searching for the Best," *Distribution*, March 1992, pp. 31–34.

TABLE 12.5
The Best in Physical Distribution

- *Repeat the cycle.* Improvement doesn't mean a firm should stop the benchmarking process. Rather, it should continue to look for meaningful comparisons and work to improve.

Benchmarking physical distribution has become easier for firms according to a survey of 300 major firms.[69] The survey identified companies that were superior in each of six areas of physical distribution. Table 12.5 identifies two of the five firms identified as superior in each area. An analysis of these firms could serve as a good starting point for a firm interested in benchmarking to improve its physical distribution system.

PERSONAL COMPUTER EXERCISE

This PC Exercise asks you to choose an appropriate wholesaler for two companies and determine the price to the intermediary and the ultimate consumer. By analyzing how your decisions affect demand, expenses, and profits for both the company and the wholesaler, you will gain insight into the benefits and areas of potential conflict when using intermediaries.

KEY POINTS

■ Wholesalers perform many functions in the distribution channel but are not well known to ultimate consumers because they do not sell to them.

■ Wholesalers perform transitional, logistical, and facilitating roles. These roles involve buying, selling, taking title, transporting, storing, assembling, financing, and servicing. The wholesaler is the business unit that buys and sells merchandise primarily to retailers, other wholesalers, and business, institutional, and commercial users.

■ The functions typically performed by wholesalers can be shifted to other members of the distribution channel, but they cannot be eliminated.

■ There are many types of wholesalers. They can be classified on the basis of risk assumption, type of ownership, breadth of functions or services offered, and degree of specialization in product lines carried.

■ The major categories of wholesalers are company-owned and independent. The major distinction among independent wholesalers is between merchants, who take title to goods, and agents, who do not take title.

■ Physical distribution encompasses all activities involved in physically getting goods from producer to consumer. An organization's physical distribution system is critical to its ability to provide time, place, and possession utilities.

■ Maximizing customer service and minimizing cost are the two main goals of physical distribution. Because these goals are often in conflict, planning physical distribution requires many trade-offs.

■ To provide the highest level of service at the lowest price, managers of physical distribution should adopt the physical distribution concept and think in terms of total cost.

■ The five major functions of a physical distribution system are order processing, warehousing, inventory management and control, transportation, and information processing.

■ Computerization and other technological advances have allowed physical distribution planners to be more efficient in every area of their responsibility.

KEY TERMS

manufacturers' sales branches (396)
merchant wholesalers (397)
full-function wholesalers (398)
general-line merchandisers (398)
single-line merchandisers (398)
specialty merchandisers (398)
rack jobbers (398)
limited-function wholesalers (399)
cash-and-carry wholesalers (399)
drop shippers (399)
truck jobbers (400)
mail-order wholesalers (400)
agents (400)
auction companies (400)
brokers (400)
commission merchants (401)
manufacturers' agents (401)
selling agents (402)
import-export agents (402)
physical distribution (407)

logistics (407)
total cost (409)
physical distribution concept (410)
order processing (411)
distribution center (412)
throughput (412)
continuous demand (414)
seasonal demand (414)
erratic demand (414)
carrying costs (414)
procurement costs (414)
out-of-stock cost (415)
Just-in-Time (JIT) (416)
common carriers (417)
contract carriers (417)
private carriers (417)
exempt carriers (418)
materials handling (421)
benchmarking (422)

ISSUES FOR DISCUSSION

1. Why would a manufacturer decide to hire an agent or broker instead of a merchant wholesaler? Give an example of a situation where this decision might be made.

2. What types of services does a wholesaler provide to a retailer?

3. How would you transport the products listed below? Explain the reasons for your recommendations.
    (a) Fresh shrimp from the Gulf waters off the coast of Texas to restaurants in South Dakota
    (b) Eli's Cheesecake from Chicago to customers in Las Vegas
    (c) Medical equipment for heart surgery from San Francisco to St. Petersburg, Russia

4. What criteria should be used to evaluate how well a firm's physical distribution unit is performing?

5. Give an example of "total cost approach" thinking.

6. Discuss how computers have affected wholesalers.

7. What roles does physical distribution play in the provision of each of the four types of utility?

8. Why would a manufacturer want to hire a manufacturers' agent instead of having its own sales force?

9. Why would channel integration be a possible approach to reducing the cost of carrying inventory?

10. Explain the role of a distribution center in the sorting and delivery of goods with continuous, seasonal, and erratic demand.

CASE APPLICATION

Railroads Are Making a Comeback

America's railroads have been losing out to truckers and airfreight for over four decades. In 1993 rail transport accounted for approximately 37% of U.S. ton-miles shipped. This represented a decline, however, from 44% in 1960 and 56% in 1950. Railroad revenues in 1993 were $32 billion compared to $313 billion for trucking. Both air and trucking as modes of transportation have grown significantly during the last 40 years while rail transport has declined.

A couple of changes, however, have renewed the rail industry's optimism. First, during the summer of 1991, the U.S. government imposed a new labor contract that, for the first time, allowed the railroads to eliminate work rules that placed them at a competitive disadvantage. Second, the passage of the North American Free Trade Agreement (NAFTA) in 1993 is predicted to be good for railroads. It is believed that rail will be the transportation mode of choice between the United States and Mexico for many manufactured goods.

In fact, railroads started to see some improvement in their competitive position against trucks in 1981 when deregulation scrapped the old system of fixed rates, allowing railroads and trucks to negotiate tariffs with their big customers. In the mid-1980s, thousands of low-cost, non-union trucking firms flooded the market. The railroads survived by focusing on such stable businesses as coal, grain, and chemicals. They made little headway in the fastest growing market—shipments of manufactured goods on long hauls, typically 700 miles or more.

Throughout the 1980s, railroads lost against truckers by a wide margin. Truckers increased their intercity freight business, raising their revenues from $95 billion to $150 billion from 1980 to 1990. By contrast, rail revenues increased only 6% to $30 billion. Again, however, there is room for some cautious optimism in the 1990s. Freight costs, as a percentage of GDP, have remained relatively constant since 1984. Trucking expenses, on the other hand, have risen significantly. In 1993 the trucking industry experienced a $5.6 billion increase in revenues but also a $5.5 billion increase in expenses. Increasing costs have caused many of the trucking firms that entered the market in the mid-1980s to drop out. In 1992 an estimated 2,200 trucking firms failed in the United States.

During the 1980s railroads were focusing not only on competition, but also on higher productivity. Because of improvements in systems and management, railroads now transport the same volume of freight with fewer workers, switching yards, railcars, and miles of track. The seven largest railroads—CSX, Union Pacific, Burlington Northern, Norfolk Southern, Conrail, Santa Fe, and Southern Pacific—have cut their trackage by about 25% to 124,000 since 1981.

Labor costs are still cited by railroad executives as a problem. At $56,000 a year, including fringe benefits, heavily unionized railroad employees earn more on average than those of any other industry except stock brokerage, oil, and investment banking. For train crews (an engineer, a conductor, and one or two brakemen), a workday is defined as the time it took in the past to complete a 108-mile trip. This definition was developed when train speeds slower than 15 MPH were common. Today, trains carrying heavy loads of lumber, coal, or grain travel at speeds almost three times as fast.

Railroads believe their biggest boost will come from intermodal transportation. Intermodal transportation links truck and rail in a single package, combining the door-to-door convenience with long-haul efficiency. For example, trucks in Indianapolis take containers from a factory to a rail hub in Chicago. The railroad moves the freight to Denver, where a waiting truck moves the freight to its final destination in Colorado Springs. Since 1986, railroad's intermodal revenues have climbed 35% to $6.5 billion.

Growth is also expected from containers imported by ship and being moved from ports to U.S. warehouses and factories. Today an intermodal train nearly 1,700 yards long can carry 200 48-foot containers picked up at a seaport, compared to half as many in 1985. In 1985 it took 17 five-person crews who climbed on and off the train to run the Santa Fe's intermodal train from Chicago to Los Angeles. The same trains now can make the trip with just seven two-person crews, reducing the labor costs per trip from $19,000 to $8,400.

The railroad versus truck versus ship versus intermodal competition focuses on the issues of cost and service. Long-haul trucks offer frequent departures and deliver goods on time more frequently. Intermodal is less direct. Reducing costs and improving service is the key to winning more freight.

Questions

1. What types of service can a railroad provide to a shipper of coal, grain, or automobiles?
2. Why would an increase in exports from the United States, a possible result of NAFTA, result in an increase in railroad business in the United States?
3. What ethical issues are involved when railroads are cutting employees? Each of the railroads mentioned in this case has downsized its work force. Will new technology and joint ventures mean more cuts? What should the government do?

The Pipelines to Employment

Chapter 12 defines and describes the role of wholesalers in marketing goods. In promoting and supporting your career search, your school acts like a wholesaler. Some of the ways your school can assist you in effectively using the pipelines to employment are:

1. Schools cultivate relationships with organizations that can offer employment opportunities to their graduates. Through such relationships, schools are included in on-campus recruiting programs. If a particular school does not participate in such programs, it usually tries to encourage organizations to post job opportunities so students can apply for positions.

2. Schools cultivate relationships with alumni/alumnae so students can contact them for information or actual employment. Some schools have regional networks that students can access as well as computer programs that classify graduates according to such categories as occupation, industry, and location. Other schools have alumni volunteers who counsel students in specific career areas, while some institutions bring alumni to campus so that students can gather information and make contacts.

3. Many schools provide job counseling services for students. Professionals can help shape your career goals and effectively use the major employment pipelines.

In one sense, your school functions like a wholesaler in that it provides services to you as the *supplier* of your capabilities and to organizations as the *customers* for those capabilities. These services include promotion, information, logistics, systems, and counseling. The objective is to facilitate the best match between career desires and career opportunities.

Questions

1. Describe the program at your school for developing relationships with prospective employers.
2. What alumni networks has your school implemented? Identify the information and employment services of such networks.
3. Describe the programs for groups and counseling for individuals that your school offers to help you use the three major employment pipelines.

CHapTeR 13

Retailing

LEARNING OBJECTIVES

Upon completing this chapter, you will be able to do the following:

■ **Understand** the impact to the economy of retailing due to both its volume of activity and the number of people it employs.

■ **Explain** the primary responsibilities of retailers in the distribution channel.

■ **List** the six dimensions that can be used to classify retailers.

■ **Categorize** various retailers by different dimensions.

■ **Discuss** reasons for the growth in scrambled merchandising.

■ **Compare and contrast** the strategic management issues facing retailers and producers.

■ **Describe** the dynamic nature of retailing using the Wheel of Retailing hypothesis.

■ **Identify** some of the trends that are occurring in retailing in the 1990s.

Marketing Profile

Retailing in Japan

Both Japan and the United States have about two million retailers. Japan, however, has a population about half that of the United States and it is smaller than the state of California. The remarkable number of retailers in this small country can be explained by the structure of the Japanese retail industry. Eighty-one percent of Japanese retailers have four employees or fewer and 65 percent of the stores occupy less than 545 square feet of selling space.

Traditionally, retailing in Japan has been quite different from retailing in the United States and Europe. The industry in Japan has historically been dominated by a mixture of small family-owned shops and department stores. In the 1990s, however, Japan has begun to adopt a more westernized style of retailing. New players include mass merchandisers, discount stores, hypermarkets (large stores that sell a wide array of merchandise from automobile tires to candy bars), and specialty stores. This expansion to multiple types of retailing was a trend in the United States during the 1980s. In Japan, where tradition is extremely important, the trend is considered a revolution by many.

Several factors have combined to accelerate Japan's move to a less traditional, more expansive retail industry. First, Japanese consumers have evolved over the last decade. Their economic wealth has produced dramatic social changes and new patterns of consumerism. The Japanese middle class, which grew tremendously during the eighties, has fragmented, resulting in consumers with a wider variety of needs and interests. While its needs are more varied, the middle class as a whole has seen its purchasing power steadily increase. Social change has resulted in a new generation of Japanese consumers who tend to spend more and save less than their elders.

Despite what appears to be a newfound affluence, many young Japanese families are unable to buy homes in the expensive Japanese real estate market. As a result, they have more money to spend on televisions, VCRs, automobiles, home furnishings, and travel. In addition, these new consumers are more mobile than the previous generation. Travel has exposed them to international brands. This explains their growing attraction and demand for foreign products, like BMWs, Levis, and Gucci apparel. Like Americans in the 1970s and 1980s, more and more Japanese prefer foreign products to local brands and are searching for retailers who can provide them.

Japan is now being exposed to other social trends that the United States and Europe have already experienced. These include later marriage and postponed childbearing, longer lifespans, and new roles for women in society. These trends affect retailing in a variety of ways, including an increased demand for convenient alternatives to traditional retail institutions. The Japanese retail industry has also been challenged by several Japanese entrepreneurs who have been inspired by U.S. mass merchandisers.

The types of services that a Tokyo department store offers are very different from its American or European counterparts. Japanese department stores such as Mitsukoshi and Seibu operate not only as stores but also as public institutions, promoting cultural events through exhibitions and shows. The "depaato," as these major department stores are called, are also famous for their high levels of customer service, which they maintain through intensive staff training programs. The Japanese department stores have always occupied a leadership position. However, large discounters are competing on price rather than service, and this may result in lower market share for the department stores.

According to the *Japanese Economic Journal*, a large number of suppliers and retailers believe that the new discounters have the largest growth potential in the industry. In April 1990, Daiei, the leading mass merchandiser in Japan, opened Kou's, a giant store on the model of U.S. warehouse clubs such as Price/Costco. The store offers merchandise at discounts up to 80 percent of prices charged by traditional Japanese retailers. A dozen U.S.-made golf balls, for example, sell at Kou's for the equivalent of $26.80. Elsewhere in Japan, the same 12 golf balls sell for approximately $72.

Another form of mass merchandising, the "category killer," is gaining popularity in Japan. Category killers are retailers who offer such a complete selection of merchandise of a particular type that they effectively outdo any competition. An American example of a category killer is Toys "Я" Us. Its selection of toys and its competitive prices allows it to outperform almost any other toy merchandiser in the market. Toys "Я" Us has moved into the Japanese market and is doing very well. The company expects to open 26 stores in Japan by the end of 1995. Category killers can be found both in the United States and Japan in such retail industries as home electronics, cameras, and sporting goods.

The Japanese retail industry is changing more slowly than the U.S. retail industry, but it is moving toward a less traditional and more sophisticated approach. The Japanese are learning how to become innovative, aggressive, and up-to-date when competing with other retailers.

What was the last good or service you purchased? Perhaps it was a soda from a vending machine just before you settled down to read this chapter. Maybe it was a ticket to an upcoming football game or concert. Whatever it was, chances are good that you made that purchase, a retail transaction, sometime within the last 24 hours. In fact, you've probably purchased more than one thing during that time. The average consumer in the United States spends between $20 and $40 every day in retail establishments. It's easy to see how this is possible when you consider that the average drugstore carries more than 8,000 items, supermarkets carry about 12,000 items, and a department store like Macy's has more than 100,000 items.

Your experience with retailing may not be limited to your role as a consumer. In the United States, approximately one of every seven full-time workers is employed in retailing.[1] In Japan that number is one in four. Hundreds of thousands of entrepreneurs start their own retail businesses each year.

In this chapter we focus on the institution of retailing. Retailing is dynamic and exciting because it is constantly changing. New methods and ideas are continuously introduced and tested. Fads seem to come and go frequently. All business activities that involve the sale of goods and services to consumers for personal, family, or household consumption are part of retailing.[2] Note that by this definition stores such as Mervyn's, Wal-Mart, Nordstrom, and Safeway are retailers but the Avon representative, the orthodontist, and the CPA also are retailers.

When a manufacturer or wholesaler sells goods or services to the final consumer it is acting as a retailer. For example, L. L. Bean, a producer of casual clothes, sells its products to final consumers through a mail-order operation. By doing this, Bean is acting as a retailer as well as a manufacturer. A wholesale club like the Price Club sells to small businesses as well as to final consumers. Sales to the former are wholesale transactions, and sales to the latter are retail transactions.

THE IMPORTANCE OF RETAILING

Retailing plays a significant role in the global economy because of its size and pervasiveness. Annual retail sales in the United States alone were over $2.1 trillion in 1993. That represented an increase from $1.96 trillion in 1992 and $1.87 trillion in 1991. Total international retail sales for 1993 (outside the United States) were $468 billion.[3] Furthermore, there are about 2.0 million retail stores in the United States.[4] Table 13.1 presents sales data for some selected large food retailers.

Name	Sales ($ million)	Profits ($ million)	Net Income (% of sales)
Kroger	22,384	170.8	.76
American	18,743	239.1	1.27
Safeway	15,214	123.3	.81
Albertson's	10,909	318.4	2.92
A & P	10,397	−16.7	−.16
Winn-Dixie	10,040	239.7	2.39
Food Lion	7,610	3.9	.05
Supermarkets General Holding	4,259	−637.5	−14.97
Giant	3,521	91.7	2.60
Stop & Shop	3,508	59.6	1.70

Source: "Corporate Switchboard," *Business Week*, March 7, 1994, pp. 116–117.

TABLE 13.1
Sales and Income for Selected Food Retailers, 1993

In the past, the role and importance of retailing has varied by economy. Command economies like those found in the former U.S.S.R. tended to pay little attention to retailing. With the collapse of such economies and the establishment of Russia and Eastern Europe as free-market economies, however, retailing has grown in importance in these parts of the world. Faced with the challenge of planning effective strategy, retailers in Russia have found it necessary to learn from economies with more experience. The "Marketing in Action: Thriving in Hard Times" describes some U.S. retailers who have thrived despite difficult economic conditions and the lessons they may provide for novice retailers worldwide.

RETAIL FUNCTIONS

Retailers provide place, time, possession, and sometimes form utility to their suppliers and their customers by actively performing transactional, logistical, and facilitating functions. The retailer makes it easier, more pleasant, and quicker for the consumer to shop. This provides a value, or utility, to the consumer. Like wholesalers, not all retailers are active in each of these functional areas; some choose to specialize.

For suppliers, the retailer anticipates ultimate customer needs, provides inventory storage and transportation, finances inventories, breaks bulk, provides market information, assumes product risk, and provides personal selling and advertising effort. For ultimate consumers, the retailer anticipates product and service needs, provides product storage and delivery, breaks product bulk into acceptable size, provides credit, provides product and service information, and assumes risk by giving guarantees and after-sale service.

To be successful, retailers must develop an efficient marketing mix. Price, product, place, and promotion decisions must fit the firm's retail situation. The marketing mix of retailing firms is called the **retailing mix.** In this mix, price, product, place, promotion, and service decisions must be made. Like the manufacturer, the retailer must meet customers' needs while at the same time meeting the firm's goals. Table 13.2 describes the marketing mix decisions of the manufacturer and the retailer. As the table illustrates, there are some similarities and some differences in the kinds of decisions the two channel members must make in order to be successful. In the promotion area for example, both manufacturers and retailers are concerned with advertising, but personal selling issues are quite different. Later in this chapter we will consider the strategic planning issues facing a retailer. As you will see, the overall strategic planning process at this level in the distribution channel is quite similar to the type of planning that producers must do.

RETAIL COSTS AND MARGINS

There is, of course, a cost associated with the provision of retail functions. Average retail expenses, other than the cost of the retail goods themselves, run 25 to 30 percent of retail sales—two to three times the average cost of a wholesaling operation. This difference reflects the nature of doing business with ultimate consumers. Relative to a wholesaler, a retailer has higher costs for physical facilities (rent or purchase), has more personnel per dollar of sales, buys in smaller volume, and sells in smaller average volume per sale.

The gross margins and profit levels of retail operations are different for various types of retailers, as you can see from Table 13.3. Retailers in the same business can choose to operate in different ways. For example, one hardware store may take only 28 percent gross margin and have a 2.1 percent profit on sales. This "discount" dealer may earn more profit, however, than a competitor who takes 32 percent

	For Marketing-Oriented Manufacturer	For Marketing-Oriented Retailer
Product	Product-design characteristics Brand-name selection Packaging Creation of product line Labeling—level of information Other	Product design (for private label) Brand-name selection (private label) Selection of brands to carry Creation of assortments by departments Signing—level of information Other
Place	Which markets to distribute in Which intermediaries to distribute through Desirable shelf space or display location Other	Trade-area analysis Site location Number of branches Store layout Variations of assortment plan by store location Other
Promotion	Creation of national campaign—extended time period Promotional appeals for national market Should a sales force be used? Use of point-of-purchase (POP) materials and their nature Contests, coupons, stamps, and other sales promotions Shall co-op advertising be offered? Other	Typically, creation of local advertising—immediate time period Promotional appeals for local market Should sales clerks be available? Will manufacturer's POP materials be permitted in store? In-store promotions and mall-promotion participation Use of co-op advertising Other
Price	Price strategy over product life cycle Trade and functional discount structure Periodic promotional pricing Shall suggested retail price be established? Prepricing? Other	Full- or discount-price orientation Reduction plans for store employees and markdowns Periodic promotional pricing—off-retail strategies Shall suggested retail price be honored or promoted against? Other
Service	Nature of return policy Nature of warranty Delivery policies (to store) Credit policies Product-information availability Other	Nature of return policy Nature of warranties beyond manufacturer Delivery policies (to home) Credit policies Consumer-information availability Other

Source: R. W. Stampfl, "Marketing vs. Merchandising Mentalities in Retailing Management, *Proceedings of the American Marketing Association*, J. Gultenien and D. Achabal, Eds., (American Marketing Association, 1986).

TABLE 13.2
Marketing Management Decisions

margin and earns 4.5 percent on sales, because the discounter may do a much greater volume than its competitor. Appendix A provides a concise explanation of the tools commonly used by retailers to analyze cost, margins, and profits. It also explains markup, markdown, and stockturns that retailers use.

TYPES OF RETAILERS

The seemingly endless variety of retailers that we confront daily may be classified according to six dimensions, as Figure 13.1 shows. These dimensions are size of establishment, merchandise lines carried, level of service offered, method of operation, form of ownership, and location of facilities. In this section each dimension is briefly described.

Type of Retailer	Gross Margin (% Sales)	Net Profit After Tax (% Sales)
Motor vehicle dealer	13–15	1.1–1.5
Gasoline service station	23–25	2.4–3.0
Liquor stores	18–23	2.5–2.8
Food stores	18–21	1.0–1.8
Department stores	35–37	1.9–2.0
Variety stores	36–37	2.0–3.7
Jewelry stores	45–48	4.5–7.7
Drugstores	30–35	1.7–1.9
Hardware stores	28–32	2.1–4.5
Building materials dealers	24–27	2.4–3.5
Furniture stores	40	2.1–4.4
Appliance stores	28–35	1.5–3.6
Apparel and accessories stores	35–37	
Children's and infants' wear		2.0–4.8
Women's ready-to-wear		2.2–5.0
Men's and boys' clothing		2.8–4.0
Shoe stores		3.0–5.2
Restaurants	50	N.A.*

* N.A. = not available

Source: Dun and Bradstreet; Internal Revenue Statistics; Robert Morris Associates

TABLE 13.3
Margins and Profits for Selected Retailers

Size of Establishment

The total retail sales volume is, of course, not evenly spread across retailing firms. The ten largest retailers account for almost 10 percent of retail sales volume in the United States. Wal-Mart, the largest retailer in the United States with 1994 sales estimated at $68.8 billion, accounts for almost 3.5 percent of retail sales volume.[5] Table 13.4 ranks these ten retailers by their total sales. This concentration of sales among the large retailers means that the majority of retailers have relatively low sales volumes. Many small retailers do less than $100,000 in business per year.

One reason that so many small retailers exist is the ease with which the retailing business can be entered on a small scale. By renting a location and having product suppliers grant credit, the capital requirements can be held to a minimum. Virtually anyone can open a retail store.

The large retailer has advantages over the small retailer in the division of labor and management skills, buying power, efficient use of the media, financial resources, possible integration into wholesaling and manufacturing, and use of private brands. Small retailers have the advantages of greater flexibility in store layout, merchandise carried, and services offered. They have lower costs of operations with smaller overheads.

Merchandise Lines Carried

Retailers can also be classified according to the product lines they carry. Sales patterns can be thought of as flowing through three types of stores: (1) general-merchandise stores, (2) limited-line stores, and (3) single-line stores. Each type carries a different degree of depth and breadth in its product line. In retailing, **depth** refers to the selection of offerings available to a customer, and **breadth** refers to the variety of products carried. So, for example, a department store like Macy's has a wide number of offerings (breadth) compared to a specialty store that sells only men's ties (depth).

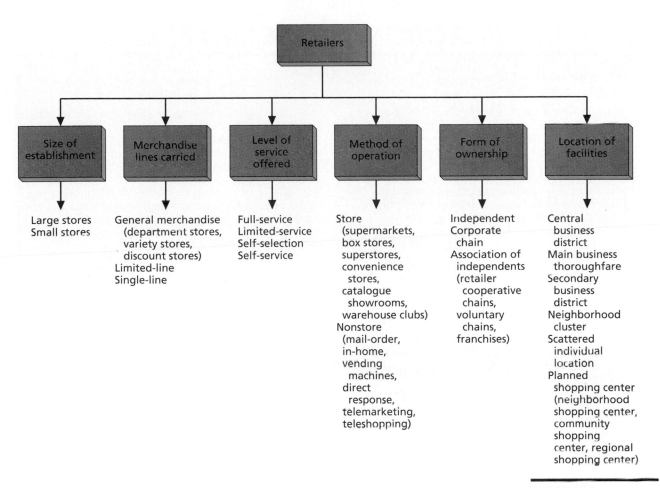

FIGURE 13.1
Types of Retailers

General-merchandise stores. General-merchandise stores carry many different products. The degree of depth depends on the specific type of store. Department stores, variety stores, and discount stores are all types of general-merchandise stores.

The **department store** is a large retail institution that carries a wide variety of merchandise grouped into well-defined departments, usually with substantial depth for each product line. Department stores usually offer many services such as credit,

Rank	Retailer	Total Sales ($ billions)
1	Wal-Mart Stores	$67.3
2	Sears, Roebuck & Co.	54.9
3	Kmart Corporation	34.1
4	Kroger	22.4
5	JCPenney Co.	19.6
6	Dayton Hudson Corp.	19.2
7	American Stores	18.8
8	Safeway	15.2
9	Albertson's	11.3
10	May Department Stores Co.	11.0

Source: "The 50 Largest Retailers," *Fortune*, May 30, 1994, p. 214.

TABLE 13.4
Top Ten Retailers of 1993

MARKETING *IN ACTION*

Thriving in Hard Times

Even under the worst economic conditions, when many retailers are suffering, some retailers continue to thrive. For example, in recent recessions, Sears Roebuck, Woolworth, and JCPenney suffered while The Gap, Nordstrom, and Home Depot did well. How can this happen? Success stories are usually attributable to careful planning, consumer orientation, and strategies designed to adapt to a rapidly changing environment.

The Gap, for example, is aptly named. Before it joined the retail ranks, there was a gap between boutiques and army-surplus stores in the market for young people's clothing. The Gap stepped in and provided moderately priced apparel at the precise time young adults were anxious for fashionable clothes at affordable prices.

Nordstrom is another success story. It is an upscale retailer that grew and prospered during the economic low times experienced in the United States in the 1980s and early 1990s. Nordstrom is a Seattle-based specialty retailer. In 1994 it had 77 stores spread across 14 states. Nordstrom's name has become practically synonymous with extremely high levels of customer service. The retailer takes the market-driven concept seriously. Stories abound of Nordstrom's employees going beyond the ordinary by helping customers find a ride home, start their cars in the winter, or dropping off packages at customers' homes. The store further responds to customer needs and desires through amenities such as a no-questions-asked return policy, oversized dressing rooms, and abundant inventories aimed to ensure that the right sizes and colors are in stock.

A strong consumer focus coupled with an offering well-suited to difficult economic times may explain the success of Home Depot during

the eighties and nineties. Home Depot is a do-it-yourself chain that specializes in the products consumers need to do their own home improvement projects. Facing a depressed housing market, many consumers in the 1980s and 1990s decided to fix up existing homes rather than seek new ones. Furthermore, doing the work themselves saved money. Home Depot caters to this market through employees who love to tinker, inform, and help customers. Employees are called "homers," and they like to think they are working to educate and help the customers.

The success of retailers such as The Gap, Home Depot, and Nordstrom is not limited to retailers in the United States. Other industrialized nations such as Japan, Germany, and Great Britain are homes to retailers who offer consumer goods for sales in pleasant atmospheres.

Such role models are valuable for retailers in fledgling economies. Eastern European and Russian retailers, for example, must learn more about service, fulfillment of customers' needs, and general retailing principles if they are to thrive. In Russia, immediately after the August 1991 coup that dissolved the U.S.S.R., many retailers sold by invitation only. Stores would issue to government officials special invitations that permitted access to the limited merchandise available. Even today, Russian retail establishments are often poorly maintained and offer inefficient service. There is some evidence that this is beginning to slowly change. GUM, the largest department store in Moscow, was famous for decades for its rude clerks and long lines. Today, driven by stockholders' demands for profits, friendly service and product assortment are much easier to find.

The department store carries a wide variety of merchandise grouped into well-defined departments, usually with substantial depth for each product line.

delivery, money-back guarantees, and personal selling assistance. There are well-known, national stores such as Sears, JCPenney, and Montgomery Ward as well as such regional ones as Filene's (Boston), Hudson's (Detroit), and Marshall Field's (Chicago).

The intense competition in retailing has led some to question whether the department store is doomed. Many department stores have failed to adapt to changes in the market. For example, while much of the competition has restructured prices to spur sales, many department stores have continued to use promotion alone to drive sales.[6] The "Marketing in Action: Sears Is Trying . . ." describes the efforts of Sears to survive and prosper in a very competitive environment.

Discount stores price merchandise at a relatively low markup and offer limited customer services. They handle many types of merchandise, but tend to concentrate on specialty and shopping goods and avoid convenience goods. Appliances, cameras, sporting goods, jewelry, silverware, and apparel are featured products in discount stores. Target, Toys "Я" Us, and Wal-Mart are examples of discount stores. As the Marketing in Action about Sears notes, the success of discounters such as Wal-Mart and Toys "Я" Us is one of the factors that has made it so difficult for traditional department stores to remain competitive.

Limited-line stores. Limited-line stores carry great depth in their merchandise but only in a few associated product lines. They tend to be named for the product lines they carry. Thus we have furniture stores, hardware stores, food stores, and jewelry stores. The advent of scrambled merchandising has complicated this classification scheme, however.

Scrambled merchandising occurs when retailers carry product lines that are unrelated to their primary business. For example, in addition to filling prescriptions and selling over-the-counter drugs, drugstores sell cameras and photo supplies. Scrambled merchandising is likely to continue to grow because it appears to benefit both retailers and consumers. Consumers benefit due to the added convenience of "one-stop" shopping. Instead of going to the service station to buy gas and the grocery store to buy bread and milk, scrambled merchandising allows the consumer to get all three of these items from a single retailer. Many retailers find scrambled

MARKETING *IN ACTION*

Sears Is Trying . . .

Sears Roebuck is a retailer that helped build modern America. A century ago, its mail-order catalogue brought together remote rural communities across the country. In more recent years, however, Sears has been floundering. For years the top U.S. retailer in terms of sales, the company was third in 1992 behind Wal-Mart and Kmart. Its total U.S. sales in 1992 were $25.4 billion (worldwide sales were $53 billion), less than half of Wal-Mart's. In 1991 Sears reported net profits of $1.3 billion, 22 percent less than it earned a mere four years before in 1987. The large department store has clearly been losing the battle against aggressive and innovative competitors.

Part of Sears's problem in recent years appears to be related to its unclear position in the market. Caught between upscale department stores that offer higher quality merchandise and better service and discounters featuring low prices, Sears has lost its reputation as the store "where America shops." The famous retailer found itself offering lower quality, less service, and less ambience than the upscale department stores but still charging higher prices than discounters such as Wal-Mart and Kmart.

Sears is not dead yet. It has attempted to fight back aggressively. The store's early efforts seemed directed at competing more effectively against the discounters who had usurped its position as a low-price leader. In the late 1980s Sears announced a new low-price policy. The basis of the policy was everyday low prices rather than a plethora of discounts and sales. In the 1990s, however, Sears appears to have reversed its strategy. Its fight-back efforts are targeted more at moving to a higher level of merchandising. By November 1992, 35 percent of the company's 860 stores had been renovated. Floors are now carpeted rather than covered with linoleum. Women's dresses are displayed in their own department instead of next to refrigerators, brand name appliances are common, and trendy blouses and dresses usually sold at upscale retailers such as Saks can be found. Sears has sold off its financial-services business and its real estate operations. It is realigning its core businesses in an effort to increase the percentage of its business from sales of apparel. In 1991, 41 percent of Sears's sales came from women's, children's, and men's apparel. A promotional campaign inviting consumers to "Come see the softer side of Sears," was designed to increase that number.

The move to a greater focus on soft goods (clothing, linens, etc.) is probably a good one since the areas where Sears was once king, home appliances and consumer electronics, represent shrinking retail industries. In addition, the firm was dealt a blow in one of its "harder" businesses in 1992 when California state officials threatened to revoke the company's license to perform auto repairs. The action followed an undercover investigation by California officials that turned up recommendations of unnecessary repairs 90 percent of the time. The compensation system under which Sears's auto-repair people worked encouraged them to meet repair quotas and has since been discontinued. Today Sears's auto-repair workers are compensated under a system based on customers' satisfaction.

Whether Sears succeeds in its efforts to regain its status as America's largest retailer remains to be seen. Early returns suggest some success. Sales grew 8.2 percent in 1993 over 1992. Retailing is an aggressive industry where both major and minor players must fight hard to compete and succeed.

merchandising appealing because it allows them to carry items that provide higher profit margins at the retail level. A grocery retailer, for example, makes little profit selling consumer staples such as bread and milk (thus it must rely on volume sales). Nonfood items that the grocer may choose to carry, however, typically provide much higher profit margins.

Single-line stores.   Single-line stores, sometimes called *specialty stores*, specialize in one product line. Florists, bakeries, automobile dealerships, and video rental stores are examples. Even single-line stores have experienced the effects of scrambled merchandising, leading to a broadening of their product assortment. Video rental stores like Blockbuster Video, for example, now carry soda, popcorn, candy, and pizza—natural accompaniments to an evening of movie viewing.

Level of Service

Another way to classify retail establishments is by the level of service performed for customers. Retailers can be categorized as full-service, limited-service, self-selection, or self-service. Table 13.5 describes the differences across the range of service levels and gives examples of retailers that fit into each category.

Because services cost money, the more services retailers offer, the higher their costs—and their prices. Hence, the major appeal of a self-service or self-selection retailer is likely to be its low prices. Retailers have a great deal of choice in the service level they offer, even within a category that, by tradition, provides a certain service level. Mail-order retailing, for example, is typically viewed as self-selection, offering a low level of service. Victoria's Secret, a merchandiser of women's apparel, however, has found success by providing a higher level of service on mail-order sales. The firm employs telephone sales representatives who work directly with customers, making suggestions and offering advice about size, fit, and color.

Method of Operation

Not all retailing takes place in stores. A fourth method of classifying retailers is method of operation—whether it is store or nonstore retailing.

Store retailers. Store or in-store retailers operate their businesses within a physical structure. They can be further categorized by type. There are many different types of in-store retailers. These include supermarkets, box stores, superstores, convenience stores, catalogue showrooms, and warehouse clubs.

**TABLE 13.5
Classification of Retailers
by Service Level**

| | Decreasing Services ← | | → Increasing Services | |
	Self-Service	**Self-Selection**	**Limited-Service**	**Full-Service**
Characteristics	Very few services	Restricted services	Very limited variety of services	Wide variety of services
	Price appeal	Price appeal	Much less price appeal	Fashion merchandise
	Staple goods	Staple goods	Shopping and convenience goods	Specialty merchandise
	Convenience goods			
Examples	Warehouse retailing	Discount retailing	Door-to-door	Specialty stores
	Supermarkets	Variety stores	Telephone sales	Department stores
	Mail-order	Mail-order retailing	Variety stores	
	Automatic vending			

Source: L. D. Redinbaugh, *Retail Management: A Planning Approach* (McGraw-Hill, 1976), p. 12.

Supermarkets such as Kroger's, Lucky Stores, and Albertson's are large self-service food stores that carry some nonfood items. Supermarkets developed during the Depression as low-cost, low-price alternatives to the small, personal-service food stores that were common until that time.

An excess of supermarkets, aggressive competitors, price wars, and more careful consumers have contributed to a cut in supermarket profit margins in the early 1990s.[7] American consumers have been spending less on food. The chains have had to come up with new methods of service, lower prices, more sales, and campaigns to attract customers. Many supermarket chains have gone high-tech in order to compete. Vons, for example, uses a labor-saving electronic price display that is linked to its check-out scanners. The device permits employees at a central location to change prices on products instantly. Additional technological advances, found in the food industry and other industries as well, will be considered later in this chapter.

One special type of discount supermarket is the **box store.** These stores are smaller, carrying fewer staple product lines and no perishables. The goods are displayed in their shipping boxes (hence the name), and few national brands are carried. Customers frequently bag their own groceries and sometimes even mark the prices on the items they select. The success of these stores has led some traditional supermarkets to have special "box" sections in their stores.

Superstores, sometimes called *hypermarkets*, combine general-merchandise discounts with a supermarket. Superstores are generally about twice the size of a supermarket and carry four times as many items. The merchandising technique was founded in France during the 1970s. The success of superstores has been considerable in Europe and Latin America, less so in the United States. Wal-Mart and Kmart each stopped their superstore programs in the United States after only a few stores were built. The lack of success in the United States has been attributed to size (customers complain that they get lost), and to the costs of operating these mammoth stores of 200,000+ square feet.[6]

It may be that the superstore merchandising technique just needs some adjustment to succeed in the United States. Despite the discontinuance of their hypermarket programs, both Wal-Mart and Kmart are pursuing what they call "supercenters." These are a traditional Wal-Mart or Kmart with a grocery added on. Kmart plans to build six supercenters, while Wal-Mart is planning approximately 40.

Convenience stores represent still another type of in-store retailing. **Convenience stores** carry a limited assortment of products, are usually quite small, and have higher prices than traditional supermarkets. Examples include 7-Eleven, Stop-N-Go, and Circle K. The emphasis in convenience stores is on proximity to the customer, long store hours, easy parking, and fast checkout.[9] The majority stake of Dallas-based Southland Corporation, operator of the 7-Eleven chain, is currently owned by a Japanese company, which rescued the firm from financial difficulties.[10]

Convenience stores have been quite successful in Japan after making necessary adaptations. In Japan, for example, 7-Elevens carry everything from magazines and milk to canned octopus and boiled tofu. Clerks take orders for expensive products such as Tiffany and Rolex watches. The average store in Japan is less than half the size of its American counterpart, yet it sells twice as much. Japanese 7-Elevens are able to carry about one-third of the inventory of U.S. convenience stores due to point-of-sale computers that allow just-in-time delivery.

Catalogue showrooms are discount retail stores that sell general merchandise using as their main promotional pieces large catalogues mailed to prospective customers. The customer identifies the item he or she wishes to purchase, from either the catalogue or an in-store display, and the order is filled from a warehouse attached to the showroom. Some of the larger catalogue showrooms are Spiegel, Service Merchandise, and Zales. These outlets grew dramatically in the 1970s and early

1980s. In recent years, however, sales have dropped. Total industry sales are approximately $8 billion annually.[11]

Warehouse clubs are retailers that offer customers a broad assortment of both food and nonfood items at low prices. The clubs keep prices low by buying and selling in volume and maintaining low overhead through limited customer service and decor. Sam's Club and Price/Costco are the major competitors. Warehouse clubs were described in Chapter 12 (Wholesaling and Physical Distribution) because a large part of their business is to small retailers and other small businesses. The clubs do, however, provide retail services, selling directly to final consumers. As documented previously, warehouse clubs have grown dramatically in the 1980s and 1990s.

Nonstore retailers.   Nonstore retailers sell to final consumers without the benefit of a physical structure. There are more than 33,000 nonstore retailers in the United States. Sales for many nonstore retailers have grown significantly in recent years. For example, QVC and Home Shopping Network, both retailers who sell to consumers via television, saw their sales increase by 53.4 percent and 15.8 percent, respectively, between 1988 and 1992. Likewise, Lillian Vernon Corporation, a retailer who reaches consumers through mail-order catalogues, experienced a 13.9 percent sales increase between 1988 and 1992.[12] The most important types of nonstore retailers are mail-order retailers, in-home retailers, automatic vending machines, direct-response merchandisers, and telemarketers.

Mail-order retailers sell through catalogues distributed to customers. More than 10,000 companies distribute catalogues each year. The average U.S. household receives two catalogues per week.[13] In 1993, U.S. catalogue sales were $60 billion, up from $51.5 billion in 1992. This figure is predicted to increase to at least $66 billion by 1996. The products most frequently purchased through the mail are clothing, home furnishings, toys, and games.[14]

The greatest success in mail-order retailing in recent years appears to have been realized by firms who use mail-order to reach very specific targeted markets. Firms such as Land's End (a casual apparel retailer), Williams Sonoma (upscale kitchenware), and Time Warner (books) have found their catalogue operations thriving. On the other hand, Sears dropped its generally positioned Big Book catalogue in 1993 after several years of declining profits.[15]

While customers receive promotion about products through the mail, they order merchandise by mail, phone, or at a store's catalogue-order desk, if the retailer maintains a store. The goods are shipped either directly to the customer or to the store for customer pick-up. Mail-order retailing has grown in the United States as the number of women in the work force has grown. Many shoppers find it a convenient means of obtaining goods when they have limited time for in-store shopping.

Mail-order retailing has also met with considerable success globally. Consumers in Canada, Europe, Japan, and Australia have been very receptive to buying through catalogues. Japanese consumers ordered $17 billion in merchandise through the mail in 1992.[16] Austad's, a South Dakota–based golf equipment company, mails more than 150,000 catalogues to Japanese consumers annually. In 1992, the first year the firm had its catalogue fully translated into Japanese, sales from that country rose 88 percent.[17] L. L. Bean, a producer of outdoor and casual wear, mails catalogues to 146 countries. Japan accounts for 70 percent of the firm's international sales.[18]

In-home retailers, sometimes called *direct retailers*, present goods to customers in a face-to-face meeting at the customer's home or by contacting the customers by telephone. This solicitation can be done without advance selection of consumers or by follow-ups based upon prior contact at stores, or by phone or mail. The well-known Tupperware party fits into this category. Here a person has a social gathering where everyone knows a sales presentation will be made. Besides Tupperware,

Land's End uses mail-order to reach very specific targeted markets.

some of the largest in-home retailers are Avon (cosmetics), Electrolux (vacuum cleaners), Amway (household products), and World Book (encyclopedias). Although the lack of a store and inventory can save costs, labor costs make this form of retailing expensive. Expenses are estimated to average 50 percent of sales, compared to about 26 percent for all retailing.[19]

As environmental factors have changed, some at-home retailers have found it necessary to expand their methods of operation. Avon, for example, found it increasingly difficult to sell its cosmetics door-to-door to women who worked outside the home. Today Avon sells in offices as well as in homes.

Automatic vending machine retailers in the United States had $26 billion in sales in 1992. There are more than 90,000 vending machine companies in this country with 4.5 million machines and a work force of 200,000.[20] Coffee and soft drinks account for about half of vending machine sales, which represented about 13 percent of all retail sales in 1992.[21]

Technology for vending machines has advanced in recent years. In Japan, for example, vending machines often play a tune or talk to buyers while dispensing up to 24 varieties of soda, fruit juice, sports drinks, and ready-to-drink canned coffee (hot in winter, cold in summer).[22] In the United States, vending machines now offer hot foods. Presto Pizzeria is a machine that cooks and serves a piping hot seven-inch pizza in 60 seconds for $2.50. Cafe Purck Enterprises, Incorporated, of Irving, Texas, has developed a machine that cooks french fries, pizza, and chicken.[23]

Direct-response retailers solicit customers through mass media promotion. Many of the goods offered are "not available in any store." The customer orders the goods either by a toll-free phone call or by mail. Broadcast media are sometimes paid a commission on sales or inquiries instead of being paid for the advertising time. QVC and Home Shopping Network are examples of television-based direct-response retailing. The success of these "shopping channels" in the United States has led to international expansion. In 1993 QVC entered a joint venture with Grupo Televisa, a Mexican media conglomerate. The joint venture will develop a home shopping program for the Mexican market.[24] QVC has also completed a joint venture with BSkyB satellite television network to develop a live broadcast home shopping channel that will target all European countries except Spain and Portugal.

Direct-response retailers also include those who sell products through infomercials. An infomercial is an extended television commercial for a product. Often 30 minutes long, the infomercial provides information about a product as well as encouraging consumers to order it. Infomercials accounted for $2 billion in sales in 1992.[25]

Telemarketing involves retailers selling goods and services to customers over the telephone. It is a growing form of retailing. In 1991 consumers spent an estimated $262 billion ordering goods and services over the phone.[26] Telemarketing has been the target of criticism for its intrusiveness. Calls that interrupt activities such as meals have caused many complaints by consumers. The federal government has investigated the establishment of industry guidelines for how and when telemarketing can be carried out.

In addition to the major forms of nonstore retailing described so far, technological advances have allowed the development of new types of nonstore retailers. Examples include videocassette catalogues, interactive cable television, and on-line computer services.

Videocassette catalogues display the printed pages of a catalogue on a home television screen through use of a VCR. An interactive cable television system allows viewers to buy products displayed on their television sets by pushing cable system

Home Shopping Network is an example of television-based direct response retailing. The success experienced by such "shopping channels" has led to international expansion.

buttons that record and charge the purchase to a credit card or bank account. Many similar systems are being established, or have been proposed, by such companies as AT&T, Cox Cable, Dow-Jones, and Time, Incorporated. This type of retailing is referred to as **teleshopping.** On-line computer services allow consumers access to catalogues and other forms of retailing through their home computers. Companies that provide this service, including Prodigy, Compuserve, and Comp-U-Card, have found many consumers so receptive that they are working to expand their offerings. Prodigy, a joint venture of IBM and Sears, has formed a partnership with the Home Shopping Network. Shoppers in the network's 60 million cable homes will be able to chat with the network's television hosts through Prodigy on their home computers beginning in 1995.[27] A recent study found 26 percent of consumers very interested in interactive shopping services and another 26 percent somewhat interested.[28] Recently Jewel Food Stores in Chicago and Safeway in San Francisco have experimented with allowing consumers to place grocery orders via computer. On-line services accounted for $1 billion in consumer shopping expenditures in 1992.

Form of Ownership

Another dimension that can be used to classify retailers is by form of ownership. The major distinctions are independents, corporate chains, and associations of independents.

An independent retailer owns a single store that is not affiliated in any way with other retailers. The local diner that serves your favorite hamburger is an example of independent retail ownership. Independent retailers are often, but not always, small businesses. When they are small, they typically survive despite their size because they have a special location, give better or more personal service, or carry unique products compared to larger competitors. This is the most common type of retailer in terms of numbers. About 90 percent of retail stores fall into this category.

A **corporate chain** is a group of two or more stores that is centrally owned and managed and that deals in the same line of merchandise. If your favorite hamburger is found at CoCo's, Marie Callendars, or another restaurant that is one of many owned by the same company, you are enjoying it at a chain retail establishment. The technical definition presented here is probably too broad for common use. Many merchants operate a few units and probably do not consider themselves chains. About 31 percent of retail store sales are made by chains. These sales account for about 90 percent of department store sales, and 45 percent of shoe store sales. The great majority of these sales are made by chains with more than ten stores. Since chains gain economies in purchasing goods and in promotion, they can often underprice independents.

To compete against the cost and promotion advantages enjoyed by chains, some independent retailers have combined to form **associations of independents.** The associations help independent retailers gain some of the advantages of a large-scale operation. There are various types of associations including retailer cooperative chains, voluntary chains, and franchise systems. These were discussed in Chapter 11.

Location of Facilities

The last dimension we will use to classify retailers is the location of their facilities. We can identify five types of location.

1. The *central business district* or *downtown shopping area* contains the larger chain and department stores in a city or town.
2. *Main business thoroughfares* or *string streets* are heavily traveled streets leading to the central business district or other important commercial areas.

3. *Secondary shopping districts* are usually located in outlying and suburban areas, closer to consumers' homes.
4. *Neighborhood clusters* are small groups of stores located in or near residential areas.
5. *Scattered individual locations* are held by some stores apart from other retailers, usually in residential areas (for example, a convenience store).

Up until about 1978 real estate developers were building shopping centers in the suburbs. Stores like Macy's, Dillard's, Marshall Field, and Foley's moved most of their glamorous and fully stocked stores to the suburbs. However, around 1978 a growing number of downtown malls started to appear. Places such as Water Tower in Chicago, Harborplace in Baltimore, Faneuil Hall in Boston, and Horton Plaza in San Diego have attracted thousands of customers.[29] Many of the downtown centers are combined with entertainment complexes, hotels, condominiums, and even boating facilities. Such shopping centers often target higher-income customers. Not all of these ventures have been successful. Union Station in Indianapolis, for example, has found that its clubs and restaurants draw traffic but many of the retail stores remain relatively empty. Thus, the resurgence of the downtown shopping area seems to reveal mixed results.

Another way to distinguish by location is to look at whether a store is located in a planned shopping center. A **planned shopping center** is an integrated unit, planned in advance, composed of different types of stores to satisfy customers' needs. Free, off-street parking is usually provided. Large centers are often enclosed and designed to be pleasant environments that will attract browsers. A single owner, frequently a developer or a large department store, owns and manages the center.

Centers vary greatly in size. The smallest is the *neighborhood shopping center*, consisting of 10 to 15 stores, selling mostly convenience goods such as food, drugs, and hardware items. A supermarket is often the anchor store. These centers serve from 2,500 to 20,000 people and average 54,000 square feet of selling space. Next largest is the *community shopping center*, which contains both specialty and convenience stores and has a small department or discount store as the anchor unit. These centers serve from 50,000 to 100,000 people and average 162,000 square feet of selling space.[30] The largest are the *regional shopping centers* or *malls* that are anchored by two or more department stores and have 100 or more stores. These centers serve as alternatives to downtown shopping and average 481,000 square feet of selling space. The largest ones can be one million square feet.[31] There is a trend toward larger centers. These centers feature shopping and specialty goods, but they have some convenience goods also and may serve from 100,000 to 200,000 people coming from distances as far as 50 miles.

The largest U.S. mall project opened in Bloomington, Minnesota, in 1992.[32] It is a $625 million retail extravaganza that includes a roller coaster, a bi-level miniature golf course, 2.5 million square feet of retail space in an area the size of 52 football fields. Anchor tenants include Bloomingdale's, Macy's, Nordstrom, and Sears. The mall developers hope to attract 40 million visitors per year. The only other mall comparable in size is West Edmonton Mall, located in Edmonton, Alberta, Canada. It claims about 23 million visitors annually.

The popularity of shopping malls has resulted in the growth of specialty malls. Factory outlet malls are an example. There are about 275 factory outlet malls in the United States. Factory outlet malls are comprised of stores owned by manufacturers who sell off-season, overrun, and irregular items at reduced prices. The outlet allows the manufacturer to capture price-conscious buyers without taking away from the higher-margin sales occurring in department stores. In recent years, factory outlets have had a harder time attracting bargain shoppers. This is because prices in the outlets have risen as manufacturers have upgraded their offerings and ambience to compete with warehouse clubs. At the same time, department stores

The West Edmonton Mall, located in Alberta, Canada, claims about 23 million visitors annually. In addition to the "Deep Sea Adventure," attractions include an ice rink, a swimming pool, miniature golf, and a fantasy theme park.

are offering more discounts. In many cases, the price differential between factory outlets and department stores is much smaller today than in the past.[33] Attracting bargain hunters is not the only reason that factory outlets exist. Manufacturers also use their outlet stores to monitor consumers' needs and preferences. Factory outlet malls are typically located away from major shopping areas where they would compete with higher-margin retailers. Though often small (the typical outlet mall has about 25 stores and 3,000 square feet), there are some very large factory outlet malls such as Sawgrass Mills in Ft. Lauderdale, Florida. Sawgrass Mills, the world's largest outlet mall, has more than 200 stores and provides more than a mile of shopping.[34]

Summary of Retail Classifications

The six dimensions we have discussed can be used to classify virtually any retailer. Table 13.6 compares a JCPenney store, a Timberland store, and Home Shopping Network according to the dimensions.

REVIEW

**YOUR
MARKETING
KNOWLEDGE**

13-1 Use the six dimensions of retail classification to describe a Pizza Hut.

13-2 Identify the last purchase you made from a nonstore retailer.

13-3 What would be some limitations of or reasons that some consumers might not like teleshopping?

Classification Dimension	JCPenney	Timberland (Footwear)	Home Shopping Network
Size of store	Large	Small	Nonstore
Merchandise lines	General merchandise	Limited line	General merchandise
Level of service	Self-selection	Limited to full service	Self-selection
Method of operation	Store and mail-order	Store	Phone and mail-order
Form of ownership	Corporate chain	Corporate chain	Independent
Location of store	Secondary shopping district—in a regional shopping center	Main business thoroughfare—in a neighborhood shopping center	Television-based

TABLE 13.6
Retail Classifications: Three Examples

RETAIL MANAGEMENT: STRATEGY AND DECISIONS

The retailer today doesn't simply find the best products, display them, and make it easy for customers to see and buy the goods. Like producers, retailers in the 1990s must devise strategic plans for areas such as target market selection, promotion, pricing, and selection of a location. The successful retailer addresses such questions as: What business are we in? How are we different from competitors? Who is our target customer? The "Marketing in Action: Old Navy—The Gap's Strategy for Reaching the Mass Middle Market" illustrates strategic planning at The Gap.

Developing a strategy means that a firm carefully plans how it will compete so that desired objectives are accomplished. Retailers should follow the strategic planning process as it is described in Chapter 3. The decision process should begin only after the mission of the firm is clearly stated. JCPenney's mission, adopted in 1913, is an example:

1. To serve the public, as nearly as we can, to its complete satisfaction;
2. To expect for the service we render a fair remuneration and not all the profit the traffic will bear;
3. To do all in our power to pack the customer's dollar full of value, quality, and satisfaction;
4. To continue to train ourselves and our associates so that the service we give will be more and more intelligently performed;
5. To improve constantly the human factor in our business;
6. To reward men and women in our organization through participation in what the business produces; and
7. To test our every policy, method, and act in this way: "Does it square with what is right and just?"[35]

The decision areas faced by a retailer once a clear mission has been stated are target markets, decision support systems, merchandise mix, pricing, store image and ambience, and technology. Table 13.7 identifies some of the issues that must be considered in each of these areas. Some of these decisions, target markets and pricing for example, parallel decisions that producers face. Other decision areas, such as store image and ambience, are relatively unique to retailing. In the following sections we will discuss the strategic considerations related to each of these areas.

Target Market Selection

Target markets are the segments of the population that management decides to serve. Retailers must specify target markets before they can decide on a positioning strategy. Market positioning in retailing refers to how the retail management team

TABLE 13.7
Retail Management Decisions: Some Issues to Consider

Target markets	What business should we be in? Who are our competitors (local, national, international)? How can we gain competitive advantage? How much of the target market are we satisfied with? How can we gain our target market share? How much will we spend to achieve our goals?
Decision support systems	What information do we have about our markets, competitors, and resources? What research information is available? How can information be formulated to achieve optimal value? When is information needed?
Merchandise mix	What products should be carried? What style, how many? What type of inventory system is needed? How should merchandise be displayed?
Pricing	What are competitors charging? What will our customers pay? What price is needed to attract more customers? If we use a pricing strategy, how will competitors respond?
Store image and ambience	What do our customers like in terms of ambience? What furniture, colors, and layout are most appropriate? Where will parking be? How many parking lots?
Technology	What technology is needed to compete effectively? What are the costs for technology? Can technology improve the services we provide?

plans to compete in its chosen target markets.[36] Retail target markets can be chosen according to any of the bases of segmentation described in Chapter 5. Usually in retailing demographics such as age, income, education, and occupation are important. McDonald's, for example, is in the fast-food business. It has used the demographics of age and income level to identify one of its target markets. Specifically, the company targets teenagers 15 to 19 years old who have average incomes. The positioning strategy for this target market is that McDonald's provides a high-quality meal at an average price in attractive and clean outlets. McDonald's has been very successful with this targeting and positioning strategy. Although the firm competes with other fast-food restaurants from the perspective of being in the same business, it does not directly compete with a restaurant such as Wendy's because the two have identified different target markets and positioning strategies.[37]

Geographical location is another common segmentation variable for retailers. A shopping center often defines its target market in terms of the distance that a consumer would be willing to drive to shop there. Generally, the larger the shopping center is, the farther consumers will travel to reach it. Retailers are increasingly identifying international target markets. In some instances international consumers are

MARKETING IN ACTION

Old Navy—The Gap's Strategy for Reaching the Mass Middle Market

In 1993, The Gap faced a major dilemma. Profits had dropped 8 percent in 1992, the first decline since 1984. The price of Gap, Incorporated, shares had also dropped, more than 50 percent between early 1992 and September 1993. Industry analysts attributed the company's decline to two related problems: fierce competition and the failure of The Gap to reach the "mass middle market" of U.S. shoppers. The mass middle market, defined as those with annual household incomes of $20,000 to $50,000, buy almost 50 percent of the $150 billion worth of apparel sold in the United States every year.

In recent years, The Gap's fiercest competition has targeted this middle market. Although many people view The Gap, with its focus on casual clothes, as a store for the "common shopper," it has, in fact, attracted a more upscale consumer. The Gap's own marketing research confirms this. Middle-market shoppers rarely buy in regional malls where most Gap stores are located. When they do shop in the malls, they purchase only sale items. Competitors such as Marshall's and Mervyn's were reaching out to these middle-market shoppers by locating stores in strip malls and selling apparel at discount prices. As Donald G. Fisher, founder, chairman, and CEO of The Gap, stated, "We just didn't see what was coming. We got kicked in the pants."

Enter Old Navy, specifically targeted at the mass middle market. It is, in essence, The Gap's response to its competition, which had produced lower-priced imitations of its merchandise. Old Navy matches the prices of its competitors in the middle market while trying to send a message of higher quality to the market.

The merchandise sold at Old Navy is made from high-quality fabrics. The attention paid to detail is uncommon from discounters. Still, 80 percent of the store's items sell for $22 or less. The 44 Old Navy locations that Gap, Incorporated, had opened by 1994 are located in working-class cities and suburbs, away from glitzy regional malls. The cement-floored stores, with features such as in-store playhouses, giant tic-tac-toe games, and a variety of child-sized distorted mirrors, are designed to attract the whole family. Promotion has also been designed to appeal to the mass middle market. Because marketing research told The Gap that this market does not read advertising circulars in newspapers (commonly used to promote Gap stores), sales promotions for Old Navy include such techniques as offering customers a free gift with a purchase.

Gap, Incorporated, sees Old Navy as the culmination of a three-tier consumer appeal. The company's Banana Republic chain is designed to appeal to the high end of the market, The Gap is in the middle, and Old Navy is at the low end. The Gap's strategy could, of course, backfire should Old Navy attract customers who currently shop at The Gap. Analysts predict that the chain will grow to at least the size of the Gap chain (which had 866 stores in August 1994). Early returns appear good. Parent company Gap, Incorporated, reported record second-quarter results in 1994. Net earnings for the second quarter of 1994 were up to 55 percent of earnings for the second quarter of 1993.

---

a target market for domestic retail operations. Upscale retailers in Dallas, Texas, for example, frequently advertise in tourist magazines that are available in the Mexico City International Airport. More often, retailers are choosing to go global with their retail operations. JCPenney operates in Mexico and several Latin American countries, sells licensed products through department stores in Spain and Japan, and is exploring a joint venture that would introduce Chinese consumers to the retailing giant.[38]

The Retail Decision Support System

Retailers need timely, accurate information about the environment, consumers' needs, tastes, perceptions, and competitors' merchandise. A retail decision support system consists of the people, equipment, and procedures needed to gather, analyze, and use information for efficient decision making. Hence, a retail decision support system is somewhat like a marketing information system. Arbor Drugs, a chain of drug stores based in Troy, Michigan, attributes much of its success to an effective decision support system. Computerized inventory analysis, for example, allows Arbor to identify and quickly respond to merchandising trends.[39]

Merchandise Mix Decisions

Managing the merchandise mix involves decisions about what products to carry, styles, models, colors, sizes, and price ranges, and how many units of each product to have in inventory. Many customers select one store over another because of the variety or assortment of goods available. The merchandise mix contributes to a store's character or atmosphere, its ambience.

The decisions about size and content of any store are determined largely by the space available. Adequate space to display an assortment of products is important for customers' comfort. Thus, an important decision involves the range of products that are essential to satisfy customers' needs. A small number of products will probably account for a large amount of sales volume. These products deserve special attention and need to be stocked. Being out of preferred and highly demanded goods creates a negative customer impression of the retailer.

In addition to a wide assortment of products on hand, retailers must also have stock depth—that is, sufficient quantity of each product on hand to support sales. For example, Oshman's sporting goods stores carry considerable depth in exercise equipment that ranges from rowing machines to universal gym sets to stretching ropes. A store that carries one line of merchandise, such as a ski shop, a scuba diving shop, or a sports clothing store, also has stock depth.

A major problem of merchandise management is that decisions about assortments, range, and depth often conflict with one another.[40] There is only so much money available to expand the product line and to maintain an inventory. On the other hand, building up an inventory takes money away from building adequate depth behind each product. Retailers must consider each of these factors as well as customers' satisfaction when making merchandise mix decisions.

Pricing Decisions

Pricing decisions are a major challenge for most retailers. Retail prices must match the expectations of the customers in the retailer's target market. Customers develop what they believe is an appropriate price range for various kinds of merchandise. If a retailer's prices do not fit into this range, few sales will be made. Furthermore, price is a major factor in dealing with competition from other retailers.

Many lines of merchandise have what is accepted as a market-level price. It is common to find prices for candy, groceries, hardware, automotive, and drug store items to be based on a standard markup percentage that is similar for all competitors. Supermarkets often adhere to almost identical prices so that competitors do not have a price advantage.

In some cases a store may offer something that permits it to set its prices higher than its competitors do. Some of the factors that permit pricing above the market are (1) more personal service, (2) exclusivity of the merchandise line (for example, petite ladies' clothing or big and tall men's clothing), (3) an especially attractive store atmosphere, (4) special promotions, such as triple coupon days or trading stamps, (5) a convenient location, and (6) special service, such as home delivery, free alterations, or 90-day free credit.

Pricing below market levels is used by retailers who have decided to focus on lower expenses, less service, and less ambience. The Wal-Mart strategy of being friendly to customers, in a rather bland store, is compatible with the strategy of offering customers lower prices. The no-frills discount retailer believes that lower prices will be sustained by volume selling and some cutbacks in service.

Pricing is further complicated for the retailer by the tendency of many consumers to engage in sale-shopping behavior. **Sale shopping** occurs when a consumer puts off a planned purchase until the desired item goes on sale. A recent study indicated that this behavior is extremely common in some product categories. In consumer electronics, for example, 82 percent of the respondents claimed to wait for a sale before purchasing. Likewise, 71 percent waited for a sale before purchasing women's clothes.[41] Sale-shopping behavior has been described as the consumer's response to rising retail prices.

The pricing decisions made by a retailer depend to a great extent on the value of products as perceived by the target market. Customers, whether paying market or above- or below-market prices, make decisions at the time of purchase about the value of the product. Price reflects the value of the product to the customer. Some customers are willing to pay more for services and atmosphere, while others are more price-sensitive and prefer lower prices, less ambience, and less service. Again, knowing the preferences of the target market and its thoughts about value is a factor that retailers always consider when making pricing decisions.

Store Image and Ambience Decisions

Customers invest more than money when they purchase something of value: they invest time and effort. In most cases, the merchandise and customer exchange occurs in a physical store. A store's ambience, reflecting its mood, character, tone, and atmosphere, is something the customer can feel.[42] The retailer can artfully create ambience. A jewelry store on Rodeo Drive in Beverly Hills, California, for example, has ambience because of its location.

Other factors that contribute to ambience are the merchandise, how merchandise is displayed, what is emphasized in a display, the interior design and decoration of a store, and the customer services. A comparison of Neiman Marcus and Kmart shows how these factors create a different feel or tone. Together they create a store's image in the minds of customers and potential customers—that is, a composite attitude customers have about the retail store (company).

Technological Improvements

Because competition is intense, retailers must stay attuned to the technological improvements that will help them survive. Decisions about which technological advances to adopt are an important part of a retailer's strategic planning. Computerized check-out systems are used routinely in most supermarkets and discount stores. A clerk uses a hand-held scanner or passes a bar-coded item over an optical scanner. The computerized register records the sale. The computer stores inventory information, and the customer receives an itemized receipt. The computerized system aids in inventory control, reduces clerk errors, and reduces the time spent by the customer in checking out. The system also provides up-to-date sales reports.

Caldor, a Norwalk, Connecticut, discount chain, uses the computer system and has incorporated a new design for the check-out area.[43] Caldor has incorporated a pull-bag system that allows the cashier to place a large plastic bag at waist height. Once the item is scanned, it is placed into the bag. The cashiers can now scan and bag in one motion. This has resulted in less time in line, which Caldor's shoppers prefer.

Retailers must stay attuned to the technological improvements that will help them survive. Caldor has incorporated a system whereby cashiers can scan and bag in one motion.

Smaller retailers have been the slowest to adopt or experiment with new technologies and automation.[44] However, more and more retailers are using scanners with bar codes, or touch-screen entry to assure that items are entered accurately and credit cards and checks are approved promptly.

Some small retailers have adopted the use of radio terminals to speed customer service. Videopad, for example, is a small hand-held terminal that allows waiters and waitresses to send orders directly from the customer's table to the kitchen. At Gregg's Restaurants the terminals are used to keep servers, the kitchen, and the cash register in constant communication.

Multimedia kiosks are also being used to improve service and customer satisfaction. A kiosk is a small, freestanding structure that can be used to sell a variety of products. Kiosks have been combined with the automated bank teller machine concept at R. Stevens Express, a photo developer in Charlotte, North Carolina. The customer enters his or her film, uses a touch screen to program the kiosk, pays for what is being requested, and developed photos appear. The kiosk is quick, personal, and easy to program. Kiosk sales and use are on the increase. In 1993, 135,540 kiosks were sold for use by retailers, an increase from 23,135 in 1990. Sales are predicted to be 518,780 annually by 1997.[45]

Winn-Dixie has developed videotape technology to introduce itself to customers.[46] Aimed at infrequent Winn-Dixie supermarket shoppers, a ten-minute videotape tours the store. Customers receive the videotape in the mail. The videotape is designed to get consumers to consider Winn-Dixie as more than a low-priced store. A personalized cover letter to the consumer accompanies the video and offers a special free gift to shoppers who watch the video. The age of electronic marketing is further highlighted in the "Spotlight on Technology: Electronic Retailing—Current Uses and Future Possibilities."

THE WHEEL OF RETAILING

Retailing seems to be characterized by cycles of growth and decline. New types of retail institutions are introduced, grow in popularity, and then vanish or at least become less important. An explanation for this pattern, called the wheel of retailing, has been offered by Malcolm McNair.[47] The **wheel of retailing** proposes that new retail institutions gain a foothold in the market by starting as low-cost/low-priced operators and then over time trade up in terms of services, costs, and prices. That is, retail innovators often first appear as low-priced operators with low profit-margin requirements and low costs. These operators keep costs low by locating in low-rent areas and offering few customer services. They typically have low status due to their simple operations, but are attractive to consumers due to their low

MARKETING *IN ACTION*

Electronic Retailing—Current Uses and Future Possibilities

A technological breakthrough for retailers has come with the use of in-store computers to gather data on consumers and to encourage sales. The use of computers in this way has been called electronic marketing. Electronic marketing has already proved successful in the grocery industry. Traditionally, supermarkets considered their target markets limited to those living within a three-mile radius of the store, with a rather predictable population. Today, however, shoppers are made up of a much wider variety of life styles, interests, and values. Evaluating these trends is more and more complex.

In-store computers, scanners, and customer ID cards now make it possible for retailers to gather and evaluate detailed client transaction data. This information is used to implement marketing merchandising strategies aimed at a particular consumer target. Such electronic marketing programs also allow retailers to track specific customer purchases and use this data, along with other demographic information, to analyze purchase behavior in specific areas.

Ukrops Supermarkets, Incorporated, of Richmond, Virginia, initiated what is called the Valued Customer Program, which essentially interfaces check-out scanners with its in-store computer, opening accounts of electronic coupons. Customers first complete an application that asks for certain household demographic information. Then they receive a Valued Customer Card to use when checking out. The computer automatically credits them with in-store and manufacturer specials. Shoppers also receive monthly lists of electronic coupons by mail. Ukrops has determined that using the card can save shoppers up to $500 annually.

This type of technological advance is not limited to the United States. In Sweden, Rolf Holmberg, owner of Flygfyren supermarket, has installed an interactive computer terminal used by customers enrolled in the store's frequent buyer

program. The machine, accessed with a card, provides customers a variety of benefits including special coupons, recipes, and free cake and coffee on their birthdays.

Studies have shown that issuing plastic cards to customers increases sales, image, and loyalty. In addition, shoppers with cards tend to spend up to four times more than those without them. At Flygfyren's, customers using their cards and the computer spend 95 percent more than other customers.

Retailers have also been able to take advantage of new technology to improve their ability to communicate. Imaging, or image-processing technology, is one way some retailers do this. Imaging is the process by which images are digitized from a video camera, stored in a computer, transformed, and then sent through networks and satellites without losing photographic quality. JCPenney has been using the Sony Still Image System, which transmits highly detailed colored pictures between its Dallas headquarters and other offices around the world in four minutes. If an office in Hong Kong wants to show a particular item to headquarters, it sends it through the Still Image System and is able to get feedback almost immediately. Similarly, if a buyer in the Dallas office sees a new style and would like to consider importing it, a picture can be transmitted instantly to the appropriate overseas office. Although JCPenney mainly uses imaging in the buying process, other uses such as improving the quality control process are in the works.

Another possible future use of imaging in retailing would give consumers opportunities to try products more easily. A customer might, for example, one day be able to "try on" clothes electronically. By manipulating high-resolution computer images of herself in a variety of styles, colors, and so on, the consumer could see how the clothes would look without actually putting on the garments.

prices. Gradually the new competitors start to add services, improve facilities, and create a more pleasant atmosphere. This is known as trading up. As time passes, they become higher-cost merchants and are then vulnerable to challenges from a new set of competitors who are using the low-end strategies that allowed the original competitors to enter the market. Thus the wheel continues to turn.

Retailers in several industries appear to have followed the pattern proposed by the wheel of retailing. Hotels, for example, were undercut by motels, which were in turn challenged by budget motels such as Motel 6, Days Inn, and Red Roof Inn. In recent years these budget motels have added amenities such as swimming pools and restaurants. In doing so they become targets for more basic, less expensive operations. Likewise, department stores have been challenged by discount stores, which have in turn been challenged by warehouse clubs. Many warehouse clubs however, which initially offered very basic, no-frills merchandising, now provide fresh produce and meat, in-store bakeries, and higher levels of customer service.

The wheel of retailing offers an explanation for the success realized by innovative retailers who discover ways to provide better, different, and lower-cost goods and services to consumers. The theory does suggest, however, that the great success of new types of retail institutions like warehouse clubs may continue only until some creative new type of lower-cost, lower-priced retailer comes along and becomes the new retailing rage.

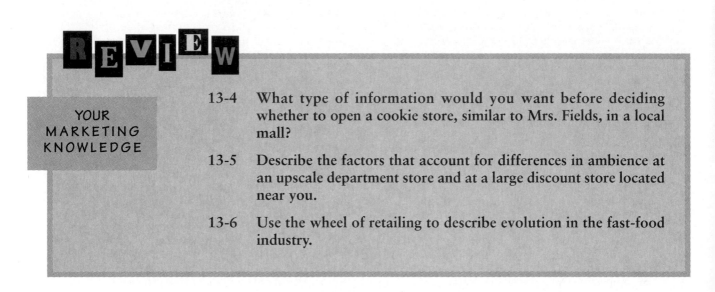

REVIEW

YOUR MARKETING KNOWLEDGE

13-4   What type of information would you want before deciding whether to open a cookie store, similar to Mrs. Fields, in a local mall?

13-5   Describe the factors that account for differences in ambience at an upscale department store and at a large discount store located near you.

13-6   Use the wheel of retailing to describe evolution in the fast-food industry.

TRENDS IN RETAILING

The United States retailing establishment has been called a "Baskin-Robbins" society; the market is so diversified that products and services are available in many different shapes, sizes, and forms.[48] This represents a change. The marketplace of the 1960s offered consumers few alternatives. There were three major television networks, a limited number of automobiles to choose from, and three or four major department stores in large cities. Today there are choices and more choices.

This range of choices has brought on a degree of marketplace fragmentation. In addition, some stores have had to close their doors and lay off employees. To survive the influx of new retailers, new forms of retailing, and changes in the life-styles of consumers, many stores have learned to manage more effectively. More than ever we see a strong consumer orientation in retailing. Simply minding the store and offering a limited assortment is no longer enough to run a profitable business. Retailers have to search continually for new ways to meet changing consumer needs. In this section we will consider some of the trends in retailing that have occurred during the 1990s as retailers have faced these challenges.

Productivity and Profit Margins

Retailers are seeking to increase their productivity and profit margins through improved merchandising practices, cost reductions, and strategic planning. Forecasters have agreed that only moderate growth in retail sales is expected throughout the 1990s.[49] This will place more emphasis on sustaining market-share performance at acceptable levels. The implications of moderate sales growth include:

- increased competition for consumers' patronage and spending
- more attention to improving productivity for increased profitability
- more awareness of consumer changes like the aging of the population, better informed and discriminating consumers, working couples, and nontraditional households

Retailers are responding to these "facts of life" through products and services designed to meet the needs of *today's* consumers. More working couples, for example, means that more people eat prepared foods. Grocery retailers in the 1990s are emphasizing prepared foods in their stores, especially foods that do not require in-store preparation.[50] There is some indication that retailers' efforts are paying off. Productivity, as measured in terms of sales in the thousands per employee, increased from 115.3 in 1989 to 125.7 in 1994.[51]

Increased Competition Versus Consolidation

Numerous niche retailers have created intensified competition. To compete better, many retailers are going the route of consolidation through merger. Merger can produce greater market access and larger size in terms of number of stores, higher sales, and a wider product assortment. While it is true that mergers such as the one undertaken by Price Club and Costco in 1993 initially reduce competition, they are typically undertaken in an effort to compete more aggressively against an influx of additional retailers. It has been predicted that by 2000 there will be only three big department store operators in the United States, competing against hundreds of smaller niche players.[52]

It has been noted that although there is increased competition, everyone seems to be going about competing in the same manner as in the past. There is what some describe as "very little creative, competitive marketing being executed in most retail lines of trade."[53] Innovation, creative styles, and decisions have been described as the keys to securing and holding on to a distinct market share throughout the 1990s. Nordstrom's success has been attributed to its ability to distinguish itself from other retailers through its reputation for customer service.

As competition continues to intensify, retail life cycles will likely be shortened. Store concepts reach maturity quickly and innovation is almost mandatory. Retailers must move rapidly to "change the scenery" in order to attract and keep customers. For example, JCPenney has attempted to shed its blue-collar image by altering its product mix, designing upscale in-store displays, and improving customer service.[54] Merchandise and promotional themes are also changing. Montgomery Ward stores have sublet space and Sears has invited shoppers to "come see the softer side of Sears," emphasizing the store's apparel and other soft goods over its traditional strongholds, appliances and tools. Changing the decor, the goods, and the overall scenery is likely to become more important as retailers face increased competition.

Increased Technology

Elsewhere in this chapter we discussed the important role technology is playing in retailing. Advances in technology have created new opportunities for nonstore retailing as well as challenges for the decision maker who must determine which new technologies to adopt. Technology will not slow down. If anything, retailers are going to face more opportunities and even greater decision-making challenges. There is likely to be more video technology and interactive monitors that customers can use to shop an entire store from one location. Walking around a store is not going to be necessary. A use code will deduct the cost of the merchandise from the customer's bank account. The customer will then pick up the bagged purchases at a central point. Pathmark Stores, a grocery chain, has already experimented with giving shoppers hand-held scanners to use while they shop. The consumer uses the scanner to read UPCs (Universal Price Codes) from products as they are put in the grocery cart. This eliminates the need for a checker to scan the products at the end of the shopping trip and expedites the check-out process.[55]

While advances in technology would appear to be an important trend in retailing, not all technological advances have been wholeheartedly embraced by retailers. One such example is the VideoCart. A VideoCart is a normal shopping cart with a small computer bolted onto its front rail and a battery pack underneath. Brand advertising occurs while the customer shops. The VideoCart screen flashes a Pepsi ad just when the customer is in front of the soda pop shelf. At other times, the screen displays a list of products with featured prices in whatever aisle the cart happens to be.[56] In 1988 the firm that produces VideoCart predicted that the carts would be placed in 10,000 U.S. supermarkets by 1991. At its peak in the early 1990s, however, VideoCarts could be found in only 222 supermarkets across the United States. By late 1993 the technology's penetration was down to 150 stores in six geographic markets.[57] Despite the decline, the company plans to continue the development of an upgraded model of VideoCart that provides touch-screen response for shoppers.

Some predict that the growth of interactive merchandising may put many traditional retailers out of business. Interactive merchandising allows consumers to shop from home through their televisions or home computers. Retailers such as AT&T, Time Warner, and Sam's Warehouse are expected to be major players in the promotion of interactive merchandising, which could make more than one-third of the United States' retailing space superfluous in the coming years.[58]

Environmental Concerns

Consumers' interest and concerns about the environment have resulted in retailers working harder to make environmentally sound strategic decisions. Many supermarkets, for example, are being built with recycling centers prominently featured in their design.[59] Fast-food restaurants have reduced their use of polystyrene in packaging and looked for ways to use recycled materials. The shingles used in building McDonald's restaurants, for example, are produced from recycled plastic waste.[60] Wal-Mart informs customers about products that are friendly to them and to the environment.

Some retailers have to be convinced that they should participate in the trend toward greater environmental concern. For example, Natural Chemistry of New Canaan, Connecticut, producer of environmentally safe household cleaning products, found it difficult to get adequate shelf space in supermarkets. The firm overcame the problem by teaming up with Statler Tissue Company, a firm well entrenched in supermarkets.[61] Despite difficulties it seems likely that greater retail support of green marketing will continue, especially if consumers demand it.

Carnival Food Stores represent a targeted market approach. This store offers foods and products that appeal to Hispanic customers.

Targeting Minorities

The minority population of the United States is growing much faster than the overall population. There are now more than 50 ethnic groups with sizable populations in the United States. There is also a growing number of retailers who have targeted minority groups. Minyard Food Stores, a 73-store chain in the Dallas–Ft. Worth area, has initiated a targeted market approach. The chain opened three stores under the banner, "Carnival Food Stores." Two of the stores target African American customers, and one store targets Hispanic customers. The store targeting Hispanics offers signs in English and Spanish. Foods and products preferred by the two groups are available in the stores.

Fiesta Mart, Incorporated, a Houston grocery chain, was started in 1972. The Fiesta stores have developed a sensitivity to the eating habits of ethnic groups. They have segmented the market on the basis of different countries and what kinds of foods are preferred. Fiesta attempts to provide foods and merchandise that customers are used to in their home countries. Korean, Cuban, Vietnamese, African, French, Greek, and Colombian products are among the different foodstuffs available.

Perhaps the most successful retailer targeting a minority market is Yaohan. Yaohan International Group, a Hong Kong–based company, has a chain of 130 Oriental food stores worldwide. Ten of them are located in the United States. Yaohan states its goal for the United States as, "exporting the Japanese life-style stateside by expanding its chain of all-Eastern food stores." The idea, says the manager of one of the U.S. locations, is "to provide one-stop shopping for the large pockets of Oriental consumers around the globe." The company's efforts to target the Asian market in the United States appears to be paying off. Sales in 1992 were $1.8 billion, a figure expected to increase to $6.5 billion by 1997.[62]

The use of price, productivity, and cost data can help you understand the low profit margins enjoyed by small retailers. Issues such as product offering and location can have a tremendous impact on sales and profits as this PC Exercise demonstrates.

KEY POINTS

■ The retail industry has an enormous impact on the economy. It employs one of every seven people employed in the United States and accounts for a significant portion of the country's GDP.

■ Any transaction involving an ultimate consumer is a retail transaction. The transaction does not have to occur in a store.

■ Retailers serve important transactional, logistical, and facilitating functions. A retailer typically provides form, place, time, and possession utility by making the desired goods and services available for purchase at a time and place convenient to consumers.

■ The many types of retailers can be classified using six dimensions: size, merchandise, level of service, method of operation, form of ownership, and location of facilities.

■ A single retailer can be classified in a variety of ways by using the six dimensions. A department store, for example, might be classified as large, general-merchandise, full-service, in-store, a chain, and located in a regional shopping center.

■ A retailer is engaged in scrambled merchandising when he or she carries product lines that are unrelated to his or her primary business. A drug store that carries photo supplies is an example of scrambled merchandising.

■ The strategic planning and management issues facing a retailer are similar to those facing a manufacturer. The retailer must define a mission, identify a target market, set objectives, and plan a marketing mix.

■ The wheel of retailing is a theory that attempts to explain the dynamic nature of retailing.

■ Technological advances such as the use of computers have given retailers new opportunities to better serve consumers.

■ Significant trends in retailing in the 1990s appear to include efforts to increase competition, technological advances, greater concern for the environment, and more frequent targeting of minorities.

KEY TERMS

retailing mix (432)
depth (434)
breadth (434)
general-merchandise store (435)

department store (435)
discount store (437)
limited-line store (437)
scrambled merchandising (437

single-line store (438)
supermarket (440)
box store (440)
superstore (440)
convenience store (440)
catalogue showroom (440)
warehouse club (441)
mail-order retailer (441)
in-home retailer (441)

direct-response retailer (443)
telemarketing (443)
teleshopping (444)
corporate chain (444)
association of independents (444)
planned shopping center (445)
sale shopping (451)
wheel of retailing (453)

ISSUES FOR DISCUSSION

1. What factors contribute to a department store's ambience? Describe a department store that you are familiar with in terms of these factors.

2. What customer needs might a regional shopping center fulfill that would not be fulfilled by a neighborhood shopping center?

3. Does a convenience store such as 7-Eleven use a scrambled merchandising approach? Explain.

4. How do a supermarket, a superstore, a box store, and a warehouse club differ? How are they the same?

5. What factors have contributed to the increase in mail-order retailing?

6. How have technological advances affected the retail industry?

7. What advantages might an independent retailer have over a corporate chain?

8. Which retail classification dimensions seem to offer the most valuable distinctions among retailers? Why?

9. How would the promotion decisions of a retailer be different from the promotion decisions of a manufacturer? How would they be similar?

10. What consumer behaviors do you believe have led to superstores (or hypermarkets) being less popular in the United States than in Europe?

CASE APPLICATION

The Wal-Mart Shadow Is Growing

In 1992 Wal-Mart was the number one U.S. retailer with sales of $55.5 billion, an increase of $11.6 billion from 1991. The 1991 sales figure of $43.9 billion had in itself represented a 26% increase over 1990. Estimated sales for 1994 are $68.8 billion. The firm's rise to the top has been quick and staggering. From its modest beginnings in Arkansas, Wal-Mart built its empire with stores located on the outskirts of small southern towns. In recent years, however, the firm has expanded throughout the country with much success.

Wal-Mart's success can be attributed to many factors. One particular strength for Wal-Mart is its excellent observation and response skills. The firm has closely observed consumers who are short on time and conscious of prices. Wal-Mart marketing managers devise a strategy aimed at these customers.

Wal-Mart is the acknowledged industry leader in information distribution. Its satellite communication network and computers allow it instant access to sales information. Wal-Mart broadcasts training and merchandising programs over the network. All ordering is done computer-to-computer. This has lowered the distribution costs of large Wal-Mart suppliers like Procter & Gamble and Colgate-Palmolive. The result is that Wal-Mart is able to buy goods more cheaply.

Wal-Mart is responsive to the interests of its customers as well as socially responsible in its own right. This orientation is demonstrated through its efforts on behalf of the environment. Wal-Mart uses signs and advertisements to inform its customers about suppliers who make packaging and products that are friendly to the environment.

Wal-Mart has not been without its problems during its rise to the top. In 1993 the firm was charged with predatory pricing practices. The federal government accused the firm of purposely keeping prices low, even when profits were being sacrificed, in order to run small competitors out of business.

Wal-Mart's success has come at the expense of some other retailers. Kmart Corporation, the number two retailer in 1992 with $37.7 billion in sales, struggled, sputtered, and stagnated throughout the 1980s while Wal-Mart was rising to fame. Kmart became known as the tired-looking store that merchandised lower quality apparel and housewares. The word *dowdy* was used to describe Kmart stores.

In the 1990s Kmart has fought to recover in the face of Wal-Mart's success. In 1991 Kmart began to spruce up and gave facelifts to many of its more than 2,300 stores. The facelifts began with 700 of Kmart's oldest stores. The remodeled stores featured brighter, more eye-catching displays, wider aisles, and taller and deeper shelves. This last change allows more customer access to the merchandise.

In addition to the remodeling, Kmart improved the quality of merchandise it carried. Women's apparel, for example, featured a line of clothing endorsed by entertainer Jaclyn Smith. Kmart also instituted a policy of drastically cutting prices in the 1990s. This was meant as a direct attack on Wal-Mart.

Another change was the addition of bar-code scanning at checkouts. This new technology (for Kmart) not only allows shoppers to reduce checkout time but also monitors Kmart's inventory. The improved technology helped Kmart lower its costs, thus permitting the price reductions instituted by the chain.

A second retail chain that has fought hard to combat the success of Wal-Mart is Target. Target is a chain of discount stores owned and operated by Dayton Hudson. Dayton Hudson was fifth in overall U.S. retail sales in 1992 with $17.9 billion.

Target's strategy in recent years has been to focus on quality and service as a means of communicating its commitment to being market-driven to consumers. Quality is important to Target. The firm performs scientific tests to assure it. Each year more than 2,500 garments are tested in Target's Minneapolis laboratory for shrinkage, color fastness, fiber content, and workmanship.

Target's management works to support an image for the store that positions it as a "life-style" merchandiser. This means that the firm wishes to have the reputation of presenting trends in merchandise before they peak. Management believes that Target anticipates trends because experts travel around the world looking for color changes, fresh silhouettes, and new items. The firm also studies demographic, social, and economic trends that produce life-style changes.

Kmart and Target have used different strategies to combat the threat presented by Wal-Mart's success. No doubt, the fierce battle of the giant discount chains continues and the results of the competitive retailing strategies remain to be seen.

Questions

1. What problems would a discount store such as Target face in attempting to become known as a "life-style" merchandiser?
2. What appears to be unique about Wal-Mart's strategy that could account for its success over Kmart and Target?
3. Which strategy, Kmart's aggressive price discounting, or Target's upscale approach, do you believe is likely to be most effective in combatting the threat posed by Wal-Mart?
4. How should Wal-Mart respond to the increased efforts of Kmart and Target?

Know Your Customer

Just as your school performs some wholesaling functions to aid your job search, you must take on some retailing functions in that pursuit. Your retailing functions include obtaining a screening interview with your target organization and selling yourself in a series of interviews with other screeners and the final decision makers.

To be successful, you have to take on the strategic planning and management task that retailers face: define a mission, identify a target market, set objectives, and design a marketing mix to show how you will be an asset to the organization that you have targeted.

Probably the most important task of your role as a retailer is to clearly define the needs of your customer. Who is the customer? You will probably identify the organization as your customer, but you must also view each interviewer as a separate customer. You must identify the needs and preferences of each individual. Then, you must present yourself so that each person can enthusiastically recommend you to the next interviewer. Each person must convey your "commercial" in a convincing manner.

How do you develop a commercial for yourself? Start by listing the four or five reasons, directly related to the organization's needs, that the organization should hire you. Think of each reason as a "sound bite." Next, determine how you can best introduce your commercial at each step in the screening process, beginning with your first letter to your targeted organization and ending with the final contact that brings you a job offer.

Questions

1. The person who screens letters of application must review many cover letter/résumé packages. How can you make it easy for that individual to select your package for further screening?
2. The person who conducts screening interviews works a long day filled with many brief interviews. With that in mind, how can you make it easy for that individual to identify you as a top candidate for the position?
3. What are some of the roles played by each person who conducts follow-up interviews, and how would you alter your presentation for each role?
4. Imagine that you have received a job offer and you are negotiating the terms of that offer. How can you sustain the positive impression that has led the organization to extend an offer while negotiating terms that are acceptable to you and meet the interviewer's needs?

Jobs in Retailing

Like other business functions, retail marketing is growing in importance, due to several factors. The retail industry has more than tripled in size over the past 30 years and some major failures have occurred. As more careful study goes into determining customers' wants and needs, retail institutions are demanding better educated and trained managers, and business-school graduates are being placed in more and more management roles.

Entering the field. Probably the best way to get into retailing is through one of the training programs offered by major department store chains such as Macy's, Lord & Taylor, Bloomingdale's, May Stores, and Filene's. These programs give you exposure to a broad view of retailing and substantial responsibility early in your career.

Types of positions. Retailing offers a variety of positions, including sales, buying, distribution, and staff functions such as advertising and marketing research. Entry-level jobs may involve some sales work, depending on the store and whether you have any background in retailing. The next-level positions may be those of assistant buyer and then buyer. In these, the job is like that of running your own ministore within a store—as the buyer often has control over types of merchandise displayed, nature of promotions, and even price levels. Another route up the retail ladder is to first manage a department, then gradually work your way up to store manager, and finally move to upper-level management.

Atmosphere and salaries. Work schedules vary with the season, but six-day work weeks are common during the fall and into Christmas. Entry level salaries are about average (below average for sales jobs). Management salaries can be high, and advancement and responsibility can come quickly.

The Story of Harley-Davidson: Distribution

"Get 'em to the Dealer!"

Even though it has a superior product and has excellent service capabilities, how does a company like Harley-Davidson transport its motorcycles and then distribute them to consumers worldwide?

Considering the number and global dispersion of its dealers and the size and weight of the product, distribution of its motorcycles is certainly a demanding task for the company. Harley-Davidson makes distribution decisions as frequently as necessary, in response to changes in the market and according to what suits the customer and the dealer network.

If Harley-Davidson chose to do so, it could make its motorcycles available to consumers through a vast network of wholesalers and retailers and could distribute the bikes only when sold. But that's not the way the company does it. Instead, Harley-Davidson relies on its extensive network of dealers (620 in the United States alone) who sell Harley-Davidsons in more than 30 countries.

Dealers as Independent Businesses

All dealers are independently owned businesses (not franchises) who carry Harley-Davidson parts and after-market accessories and service the company's motorcycle products. Training for both dealers and their employees originates at Harley-Davidson University,[1] while funding and credit helps dealers buy motorcycles and ensure availability.[2]

In the early 1980s, just after the AMF buyout, Harley-Davidson began for the first time to implement required, uniform standards for its dealers. By instituting this change, the company did not intend to take control of dealers, but rather to increase sales through a consistent message and image established across the entire dealer network. Both management and dealers agreed that for the product to achieve an enhanced and consistent identity, the dealers would have to coordinate their efforts with the company and sacrifice some of their traditional autonomy.

The Company–Dealer Relationship

Harley-Davidson has built close ties with its dealers–the company's customer-direct retailers. This valuable relationship allows Harley-Davidson to influence the quality and professionalism of the selling process while enabling dealers to customize selling efforts to their local markets. This relationship is a two-way street where the company and dealers respond to each other's needs. For its part, Harley-Davidson provides unique financial plans, product development, and service enhancements to its dealers. This type of relationship has fostered cooperation and mutual success.

Harley-Davidson management respects and facilitates the needs of each dealer by getting to know them individually. The company makes sure to do the following:

- deliver motorcycles that can sell in the dealer's area (and not bikes that it happens to have on hand)
- serve the special needs of the dealers' customers
- train dealers in merchandising and selling skills

Ultimately, the company builds a separate relationship with each dealer, much as the dealer builds relationships with customers.

Prior to 1985, Harley-Davidson supported its dealerships in selling and servicing motorcycles with only marginal results. However, in the mid-1980s, management recognized that the marketplace had changed and that competition was growing ever stronger. In response, they relied on their Dealer Advisory Council (DAC), 20 dealers who represent the needs and interests of all Harley-Davidson dealers. The council meets at least four or five times a year and discusses topics such as how stores and retail products are presented.

Harley-Davidson sees itself playing an active role in its dealers' success. If dealers do not do well, neither does Harley-Davidson. While the company often helps dealers with financing and business-management consulting, the dealers themselves invest considerable amounts of capital for dealership start-ups and upgrades. In

1988, stores that underwent renovations under the company's Designer Store Program saw an average 25 percent increase in sales, while stores that maintained their old design and decor gained less. Clearly, the additional investment in renovations heightened the visual appeal of dealerships and inspired more customers to come in and make a purchase.

Channels of Distribution

Harley-Davidson supplies its vast dealer network with motorcycles according to a complex allocation system that is based, at minimum, on each dealer's prior year's sales, Customer Satisfaction Index scores, and a variety of other performance-related criteria. The manufacturer ships motorcycles directly to the dealers, thus minimizing delivery time and keeping company costs down by eliminating "middlemen." Harley-Davidson motorcycles are transported by truck, train, ship, or any combination of distribution modes (depending on the distance and time allotted) from the final assembly plant in York, Pennsylvania. Motorcycles are rarely, if ever, shipped by airfreight.

In one sense, the actual distribution of motorcycles is the easy part of the business. The challenge lies in maintaining an adequate inventory of parts at dealerships around the world. The idea is to have enough, but not too much, of a product available at all times. A good supply system for parts and accessories is essential. Without it, Harley-Davidson's reputation among its customers for reliability and service would decline dramatically, along with sales. And without an effective computer system to track the product, inventory control would be nearly impossible, and overstocks would be all too frequent.[4]

The Management Information System (MIS)

To monitor inbound shipments of supplies and resources and outbound shipments of product (motorcycles, parts, and accessories), Harley-Davidson uses a computerized Management Information System (MIS). This state-of-the-art system, developed by IBM and Hewlett-Packard,[5] tracks sales, production, orders, shipments, and inventory.

The company rarely ships a product unless it is "spoken for" by a customer or a dealer. Because only a limited number of each model is produced each year, customers often wait anywhere from a couple of months to one or two years for delivery of their motorcycles. (By comparison, competitors such as Suzuki and Yamaha can usually deliver their bikes within a couple of weeks.) This is a delicate balance for Harley-Davidson to maintain. On the one hand, the company is careful not to overstock and thereby dilute the appeal of the motorcycle; on the other hand, it does not want to keep customers waiting too long for delivery. The MIS provides greater accuracy of records and predictability of delivery schedules, thus enabling Harley-Davidson to minimize inventories, shipments, and overstocking. As a service to dealers, Harley-Davidson coordinates the joint delivery of motorcycles with parts and accessories through the MIS to save on time and delivery costs.

Questions

1. What are the strengths of Harley-Davidson's channel management system?
2. Why does Harley-Davidson not use "middlemen?" Would you recommend they use them? Defend your answer.
3. What role does the dealer network play at Harley-Davidson? In what other industries could this arrangement be used?
4. If you were to make channel recommendations, what would they be?
5. With worldwide sales more than 25 percent of total sales, would you recommend that Harley-Davidson build a factory in a foreign country to reduce costs and shipping time? Defend your answer.
6. Make a visit to your local Harley-Davidson dealership and find out how long the delivery time is for your favorite motorcycle. Would you be willing to wait? Is the motorcycle's exclusivity an advantage or a disadvantage?

part V

Promotion

CHapTeR 14

Communication Strategies

LEARNING OBJECTIVES

Upon completing this chapter, you will be able to do the following:

■ **Explain** the concept of Integrated Marketing Communications.

■ **Define** the components of a promotional mix: advertising, sales promotion, publicity, and personal selling.

■ **Explain** how communication takes place and how it influences promotion.

■ **Describe** the components of properly stated promotional objectives.

■ **Discuss** the general concept of a response hierarchy to promotion.

■ **List** the factors that determine an organization's overall cost of sales promotion.

■ **Explain** the various budgeting procedures for determining promotional expense.

■ **Discuss** the factors that influence an organization's choice of a promotional mix.

■ **Comment** on promotional planning in a global setting.

Marketing Profile

Integrating Promotion to Bring Tourists Down Under

The Aussies are hard at work singing the praises of a down-under vacation through an alliance of groups known as Partnership Australia. The alliance is an information network designed to coordinate promotion of tourism efforts by the Australian Tourist Commission (ATC), the tourism authorities of the six states and two territories, and the advertising agency that represents the different entities. The purpose of the joint venture is to promote travel to Australia under one worldwide tourism marketing umbrella.

Partnership Australia has introduced a toll-free, centralized telephone information service called the Aussie helpline. The information service targets both travelers and travel agents in the key international areas of Chicago, Tokyo, Osaka, Hong Kong, Singapore, London, Paris, Frankfurt, Zurich, Rome, and Auckland. In addition to the helpline, Partnership Australia has coordinated more than 40 different promotional campaigns. The result is a clear, concise message to every consumer and prospect at a reduced cost.

Between January and June of 1994 the partnership invested a total of $8.4 million on 82 different joint campaigns in international markets. Partnership Australia has projected that it will spend a total of $20 million in 1994. The spending will, however, save the various tourism commissions money by eliminating much duplication of effort in getting the word out.

Early returns on the efforts of Partnership Australia are good. Six months after the alliance's inception, the ATC reported that it handled more than 130,000 requests for information during the first four months of operation. The commission also reported that the partnership's efforts had generated more than 15,000 bookings of Australian holidays.

More than 38 million overseas visitors are predicted to visit the country between 1994 and 2000, when Sydney will host the Olympic games. Those visitors represent the end users of Partnership Australia's communication efforts. These consumers need to receive an integrated, well-planned effort that meets their need for information. By starting with a consideration of end-user wants and needs and then backing into a strategy for addressing those needs, the groups that formed the alliance no doubt found it apparent that a partnership would provide a coordinated and connected communications effort.

his chapter examines the ways marketers communicate information to their target markets. **Promotion** is the communication arm of the marketing mix. The task of promotion is to inform, persuade, and remind consumers to respond to the product or service being offered. The desired response may take many forms, from awareness of the product or service to actual purchase.

Promotion is the most visible part of the marketing process; without promotion a target market may never hear about an organization's products. In a study of 100 marketing vice presidents and directors of marketing, 62 percent said they expect promotion to gain importance within their companies' marketing mix in the next three to five years.[1]

Making promotional decisions in marketing is both exciting and challenging. Imagine that you work for the American Heart Association where you must develop an advertising program that aims to get those teenage girls who smoke to stop. Or consider the challenge of being national sales manager for Pfizer, a large pharmaceutical firm, trying to develop programs of compensation, training, and evaluation for your sales force. This chapter and the two that follow focus on the dynamic and complex nature of promotional activity. In this chapter we introduce the concept of integrated marketing communications, a market-driven approach to promotion; we define the different types of activities that constitute promotion and examine the dynamics of the communication process. We introduce the concept of response hierarchies and discuss setting promotional objectives. Methods of determining promotional expenditures and selecting a promotional mix are explored. Chapter 15 focuses on the promotional tools of advertising, sales promotion, and publicity. Chapter 16 examines personal selling.

INTEGRATED MARKETING COMMUNICATIONS

In recent years, the need to be market-driven has caused firms to analyze every aspect of their businesses from the perspective of better serving consumers. While marketing-oriented firms strove to develop products and services that met consumers needs and wants, many of those firms still believed that the purpose of promotion was to convince consumers to buy the product.

In recent years organizations have begun to adopt the idea that promotion, or communication, like product development, should be rooted in the needs and desires of consumers. This led to the concept of **integrated marketing communications (IMC)**, defined as the process of developing and implementing over time various forms of persuasive communications programs with customers and prospects.[2] Don E. Schultz, of Northwestern University, explains IMC as follows:

> The goal of IMC is to influence or directly affect the behavior of the selected communications audience. IMC considers all sources of brand or company contacts which a customer or prospect has with the product or service as potential delivery channels for future messages. Further, IMC makes use of all forms of communication which are relevant to the customer and prospects, and to which they might be receptive. In sum, the IMC process starts with the customer or prospect and then works back to determine and define the forms and methods through which persuasive communications programs should be developed.[3]

By focusing on the consumer, IMC uses an "outside-in" approach to developing promotional strategies.[4] That is, promotional planning begins with the customer's view of communications rather than the company's view. The Marketing Profile that begins this chapter illustrates the use of integrated marketing communications by groups that promote Australian tourism.

Integrated marketing communication is critical to the overall strategic planning of an organization. In the study of 100 top marketing executives cited earlier, 60 percent of the respondents rated it (IMC) as the most important factor that will influence marketing strategy in the next few years. This rating placed integrated marketing strategies first in importance, ahead of such influential issues as consumer life-style changes, economic trends, and globalization.[5]

As its name implies, IMC uses a variety of techniques. In the following section we will discuss various tools that can be a part of the IMC efforts of a firm.

COMPONENTS OF PROMOTION

A marketing manager has four broad types of promotional devices available.[6] They are advertising, personal selling, sales promotion, and publicity/public relations.

1. *Advertising* includes any paid form of nonpersonal presentation and promotion of ideas, goods, or services by an identified sponsor in such media as magazines, newspapers, outdoor posters, billboards, direct mail, radio, and television.
2. *Personal selling* is an oral presentation in a conversation with one or more prospective purchasers for the purpose of making sales.
3. *Sales promotion* includes marketing activities other than personal selling, advertising, and publicity that stimulate consumers' purchasing and dealers' effectiveness. Examples are displays, shows and exhibitions, demonstrations, coupons, contests, and other non-routine selling efforts. These are usually short-term activities.
4. *Publicity/public relations* is nonpersonal stimulation of demand for a product, service, or organization by generating commercially significant news in published media or by obtaining a presentation on radio, television, or stage. Unlike advertising, the costs of this form of promotion are not paid for by the sponsor.

Marketing managers use a combination of these four promotional tools to communicate their messages to a target market. This combination is the **promotional mix.** Promotional mixes are tailored to the needs of the given target market, as well as determined by the resources of the organization. Not every promotional mix uses all available tools. A firm that engages in business-to-business marketing, for example, might develop a promotional mix that focuses exclusively on personal selling. A not-for-profit organization might opt for no advertising or personal selling due to cost constraints or the anticipated receptivity of its target market. The organization might choose, instead, to focus all its promotional efforts on publicity. Other organizations might use a very balanced promotional mix to reach certain target markets. Whatever the combination of promotional tools, the concept of integrated marketing communication reminds us that all promotional messages must be integrated and consistent. Many customers will be exposed to several or all of the promotional efforts and will naturally group them together when evaluating their needs for a particular product.

It has been suggested that the lines between promotional categories will become blurry in the future.[7] With the integration of promotional tools, this seems a reasonable prediction. We can see this change in the way that the various promotional tools have come to be evaluated. For example, advertising has always been expected to produce a quantifiable return, while publicity and public relations were viewed as "image-oriented" and not subject to being measured for effectiveness. But recently, image-oriented advertising has become common, while marketers have begun to gauge specific results from their public-relations efforts. For example,

American Airlines has used image-oriented ads to show how the professionalism it offers its business travelers can benefit leisure travelers as well. In introducing the Dodge Viper, Chrysler created a TV show around the car, and tried to reduce its image of stodginess.[8]

MARKETING COMMUNICATIONS

Because promotion is the communication arm of the marketing mix, it is important to understand some basic things about communication in order to plan effective promotional strategies. In this section we explore the communication process as well as a couple of basic distinctions regarding communication types.

The Communication Process

Figure 14.1 depicts the communication process.[9] All communications require a source and a receiver. The **source** (or sender) is the individual or organization with information to share. In a marketing communication, the source is likely to be an organization, one of its sales representatives, or someone (perhaps a celebrity) hired by the firm to communicate information. In the advertisement shown on the next page, Frank Perdue is the sender, speaking for Perdue Chickens. The **receiver** is the target of the communication. Marketing communications should be directed at a specific target market.

Communication can occur between a sender and receiver even if the sender did not intend for it to occur. Likewise, communication does not depend on the receiver's understanding the sender's intended message. For a communication to be judged successful, however, the receiver must understand the message that the sender intended

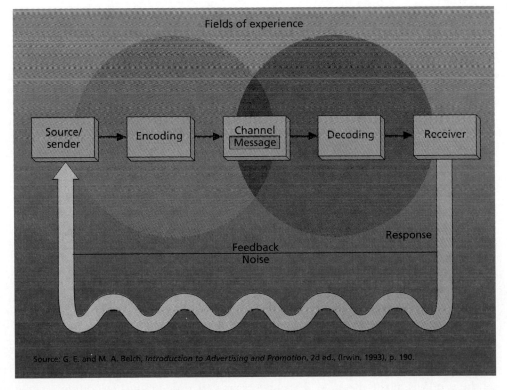

**FIGURE 14.1
A Model of the
Communication Process**

Source: G. E. and M. A. Belch, *Introduction to Advertising and Promotion*, 2d ed., (Irwin, 1993), p. 190.

All communications require a source (sender) and a receiver. In this ad, Frank Perdue is the sender and the reader is the targeted receiver.

to send. Using this rule, it is easy to see that many attempted communications fail because mutual understanding is not achieved. Consider the exchange depicted in the cartoon that is shown on the next page. A communication has occurred; would you judge it successful?

To make communication successful, a marketer faces three challenges: to communicate at the intended time, to communicate in the ways planned, and to communicate only the specific message intended.

To meet these challenges, the sender must arrange ideas into symbolic forms such as words, pictures, and gestures. This process is called **encoding.** Marketers must encode ideas in a form the intended receiver will understand. Symbols can be especially valuable for a firm that has global target markets. The golden arches of McDonald's, for example, are understood by people of many languages, worldwide. The "Marketing in Action: Communicating Clearly" also illustrates the power of a nonverbal message.

The encoded message, the exact set of symbols used by the sender, is then transmitted through a **channel.** Channels can be personal or nonpersonal. **Personal channels** are direct means of communication. They would include personal selling as well as word of mouth. **Nonpersonal channels** involve no interpersonal contact between sender and receiver. Advertising, publicity, and sales promotion fall into this category.

If the channel delivers the message to the receiver, the receiver assigns meaning to the symbols in the message. This process is called **decoding.** Decoding is most likely to be accurate (the receiver assigns the meaning intended by the sender) if the sender and receiver share common fields of experience. Belch and Belch point out that many advertising communications fail because the backgrounds of marketing people differ from those of people who constitute large markets. Can a college-educated New Yorker effectively communicate with a blue-collar, small-town, Midwesterner? The creative director of a large advertising agency commented on advertising people, "We pull them in and work them to death. Then they begin moving in sushi circles and lose touch with Velveeta and the people who eat it."[10] Without shared fields of experience, it becomes very difficult for marketers to communicate successfully with consumers.

Once the message has been received, the receiver will make some response to the message. The response could be a purchase, an attitude shift, or even just a physical gesture. The part of the overall response that is measured by the sender is called *feedback*. Feedback is very important to marketers because it tells them whether their communication efforts have been successful. In marketing communications, purchase is the ultimate type of desired feedback. It is important for marketers to remember, however, that not every individual communication is intended to produce a sale. Hence we cannot judge a communication as unsuccessful simply because it does not result in a sale. To measure the effectiveness of their communications, marketers must develop other means of obtaining feedback. These might include measuring inquiries, customer traffic, and telephone calls.

THE FAR SIDE   By GARY LARSON

An Example of Nonverbal Communication

Through mostly grunts and exaggerated gestures, two fishermen/gatherers attempt to communicate.

MARKETING *IN ACTION*

Communicating Clearly

Quick! What comes to mind when you see a crystal clear lake, a sparkling clear day, or a liquid product that's colorless? Pepsi, Coca-Cola, Procter & Gamble, Colgate-Palmolive, Amoco, and Coors all hope that the absence of color in their clear products communicates an unspoken message of purity and naturalness. All four companies hope that's the unspoken message communicated by the clear products they are marketing.

Sheldon E. Rysner, a partner in a Chicago-based package design firm, sees the trend to transparent products a result of what he calls a "New-Age Mentality." According to Rysner, transparency communicates the message that a product is "free of all that bad stuff." It also communicates a "less is more" look that has proved very popular with upscale markets.

The marketers of new clear products generally deny that uniqueness or fad, alone, led them to drain the color. Suzan Harrison, a spokesperson for Colgate-Palmolive, discussed the firm's launch of Palmolive Sensitive Skin, a clear dishwashing liquid. Harrison explained that the company set out to produce a product, as the name implies, for sensitive skin. She admits, however, that Colgate-Palmolive felt the best way to convey that the new product was free of dyes and other potential skin irritants was to make it clear.

Pepsi may well be the leader, at least in terms of accumulated notoriety, of the movement to transparent products. The firm introduced Crystal Pepsi, later renamed Crystal, during the 1993 SuperBowl. In an advertisement featuring the music of Van Halen, the line "You've never seen a taste like this before" challenged consumers to try the new product.

Pepsi's new clear drink was not a gimmicky attempt to spark flat soft-drink sales. Extensive consumer research was performed prior to introduction. Development, which took place over a 15-month period, involved almost 3,000 variations of the formula before arriving at the final taste. Pepsi conducted more than 5,000 consumer taste tests before test marketing ever began. Consumer research indicated likely success for the product, with one study predicting that 33 percent of the mass market would probably or definitely buy Crystal Pepsi. Clearly the firm did more than simply remove the color from Pepsi. But just as clearly, the absence of color was as important as the taste in communicating that Crystal Pepsi was different.

The Advantages of Clear Thinking.

An extra refining step. A crystal clear gasoline. A premium gasoline with reduced harmful impurities. A gasoline that gives unsurpassed performance. A driver that exhibits exhilaration. A sky with cleaner air.* A satisfaction within that comes only from driving your best. A premium gasoline unlike any other. Crystal clear Amoco Ultimate.* The result—and the advantage— of clear thinking.

AMOCO

You Expect More From A Leader.

Crystal Clear Amoco Ultimate

*The extra refining step results in a 13% reduction of hydrocarbon exhaust emissions.   © 1993, Amoco Oil Company

Not everyone predicts unqualified success for Pepsi's new entrant in the "transparency wars." David Lavinsky, a market research analyst with a New York–based firm, sees clear cola as a novelty that will pass in short order. Lavinsky argues that the message being communicated by a colorless liquid will not reach the health and fitness proponents to which he claims it is geared. The absence of color, predicts the analyst, will not cause this group to switch from mineral waters and fruit juices. Lavinsky believes that Crystal will entice existing soft-drink users, especially cola fans, but that such movement will only cannibalize cola sales and will not continue once the novelty wears off.

The jury is still out on clear products. Crystal Pepsi was predicted to garner nearly $1 million in sales in its introductory year. In fact, the product sold only $335,000. While foods and beverages are generally not well received, items that appeal to personal hygiene (like mouthwash and deodorant) seem to be faring better. In addition, ZIMA Clearmalt by Coors Brewing Company is an exception to the generally poor performance in the beverage category. Experts attribute this success to the newness of the product and its promotion as an alternative to beer and wine.

The long-run success of clear cola and other colorless products remains to be seen. One thing, however, is clear—the absence of dye plays an integral part in communicating a message.

Unplanned distortion, or interference, is known as **noise.** Construction on the street outside a classroom will most likely interfere with a professor's communication to the class. But, in the marketing communication process, noise need not be sound. Have you ever turned your attention away from the television when a television commercial came on? Getting up for a snack, for example, is noise in the communication between the advertiser and you. Or perhaps you're so engrossed in an article on the left-hand side of a magazine page that you overlook the advertisement on the right-hand side. The article is noise between you and the advertiser.

The process of communication is fragile. Successful communication of the source's intended message requires proper encoding and decoding plus a clear channel for transmitting the message. All these requirements are difficult to meet.

The communication process is relevant for each of the promotional tools marketers have at their disposal. Table 14.1 gives examples of the communication process for the four promotional tools.

Interpersonal Versus Mass Communication

In the previous section, we distinguished between personal and nonpersonal channels of communication. Personal or interpersonal channels of communication can occur in social settings when friends or acquaintances share information. Such word-of-mouth communication is a very powerful source of information for consumers.[11] Word-of-mouth communication is usually not under the control of the marketer.

**TABLE 14.1
The Communication
Process in Promotion**

	Source	Encoding	Media	Receiver	Decoding	Feedback
Personal selling	Hewlett-Packard sales manager	Words, gestures, appearances	Sales visit	Purchasing agent at Coopers & Lybrand	Mannerisms of sales-person distract buyer from fully understanding message	Buyer asks questions to clarify information
Advertising	General Foods' ad for Jello featuring Bill Cosby	Words, pictures, color, social setting	Television commercial	Viewer in Chicago	Consumer gets positive feeling about new Jello flavor	Consumer purchases Jello; sales increase
Sales promotion	Hallmark's coupon for Personalize it! greeting card	Size and shape of coupon, words, offer of free card	*People* magazine, *TV Guide*	Reader of *People*	Consumer clips coupon from paper	Consumer uses coupon towards purchase; sales increase
Publicity	Interview of GM Chairman John Smale	Words, gestures, appearance, office image	Television news show	Viewer in Portland	Viewer dislikes "big business" image of Smale	Consumer does not buy products. No research done so GM unaware of reaction

Factor	Interpersonal Communication	Mass Communication
Reaching a large audience		
Speed	Slow	Fast
Cost per individual reached	High	Low
Influence on the individual		
Attraction of attention	High	Low
Probability of interest and response	High	High
Accuracy of comprehension	High	Low
Feedback		
Direction of message flow	Two-way	One-way
Speed of feedback	High	Low
Accuracy of feedback	High	Low

Source: J. F. Engel, M. R. Warshaw, and T. C. Kinnear, *Promotional Strategy*, 7th ed. (Irwin, 1991), p. 78.

TABLE 14.2
Comparison of Interpersonal and Mass Communication

Commercial sources of interpersonal communication usually come in the form of personal selling efforts.

Nonpersonal channels of communication, as defined earlier, do not involve direct communication between sender and receiver. Instead, information is shared through mass communication. Advertising, sales promotion, and publicity use nonpersonal techniques. Both interpersonal and mass communication are important in marketing. Table 14.2 summarizes the advantages and disadvantages of the two communication modes.

A mass communication, such as an advertisement in a magazine, can more accurately deliver the same message to a larger audience than can an interpersonal communication such as a salesperson's presentation to a customer. The latter changes with each attempt to communicate. The cost of reaching an individual through the mass media is substantially lower as well. However, mass communication is one-way, it is less likely to gain the potential audience's selective attention, and it suffers from slow, and many times, inaccurate feedback.

Interpersonal communication has the benefits of being fast and allowing two-way feedback. A buyer can respond instantly to a salesperson's presentation, and the salesperson can ask for clarification of the response. This greater flexibility in feedback allows the communicator to counter objections from the buyer and thus attain a greater change in attitude and behavior than is possible with mass communication. Interpersonal communication is much more efficient than mass communication. Unfortunately, when used for a large audience, interpersonal communication is slow and very expensive. Hence marketers must compare the efficiency of using a particular type of communication with the cost involved. This comparison is referred to as the **communication-promotion paradox.** One set of authors noted:

> It is obvious that the mass media present some significant communication problems. Advertising and publicity through mass media will always represent inefficient communication, even with precise definition of market targets, motivation research, and feedback of results through various media. This is because of the very nature of the communication process. Nevertheless, a mass market generally can be reached economically only with mass media. This leads to the seeming paradox that advertising provides efficient promotion through inefficient communication.[12]

Because of this paradox, interpersonal and mass communication are often used in conjunction. A firm might use mass communication, for example, to introduce a new product to a large audience because it is cost effective. After consumers have become somewhat familiar with the product, the firm might switch to interpersonal communication (via personal selling) to actually close sales among a much smaller group of people.

The product itself and its distribution structure will also influence the choice of communication mode. The more direct the purchase transaction between buyer and seller, the fewer mass communication devices will be used. For example, a sale of a house is a very direct transaction and is thus dominated by interpersonal communication. At the other extreme is a packaged good such as shampoo, where the seller uses advertising and sales promotion to communicate with prospective buyers. Without devices, the seller would have no direct influence on the sale of the product. The choice between interpersonal and mass communication and the factors that influence the choice are discussed in more detail later in this chapter.

Controlled Versus Uncontrolled Communication

As the senders in marketing communications, marketers work to plan, execute, and control their communication. The marketer who is paying to air a television commercial will ensure that the commercial presents the product in a favorable light. Likewise, a sales representative, working for a firm, is unlikely to run down his or her company's products or services in a presentation to a potential customer. To control communication, the marketer must bear the costs.

When a marketer does not bear the cost of a communication, as with publicity, marketers must sacrifice some or all of the control. A news release about a new product or service might generate favorable television coverage and a number of positive newspaper and magazine articles. Or, it might go largely unnoticed. The coverage generated by the release depends on many factors the marketer cannot control. This might include the personal interest of journalists, or the other "news" occurring at the time. Certainly an astute marketer would never plan to release information about a new product on election day. However, the amount of "other news" cannot always be anticipated. A press conference to introduce a new product held on the day O. J. Simpson made his dash across the freeways of Los Angeles would probably have been very poorly attended.

Another uncontrollable aspect of publicity is the nature of what the promotion will contain. Favorable publicity is great—it's free and generally perceived as credible. But unfavorable publicity can be very damaging. A new restaurant can be killed by an unfavorable review, despite advertising that states what a great place it is. The "Marketing in Action: Fighting Back in the Face of Uncontrolled Communication" illustrates one company's response to negative publicity. We discuss publicity in greater detail in Chapter 15.

Another type of uncontrolled communication is word of mouth, a personal communication that involves consumers talking to other consumers about products and services. It is well documented and generally influential. For example, word of mouth is the most effective type of communication in the adoption of a new food product; it is twice as influential as television advertising and about four times as influential as store displays. Although this form of uncontrolled communication can be very helpful to a firm, it can also be very damaging. For example, if a friend told you about a new movie he saw and disliked, would you be inclined to go?

RESPONSE HIERARCHIES

The ultimate response for a promotional message (i.e., marketing communication) is a purchase. However, purchases occur because of the complex interaction of all marketing activity, not just promotion. Further, purchases are affected by uncontrollable environmental factors such as competition. Finally, as pointed out earlier, immediate purchase is not the intent of every promotional message a marketer

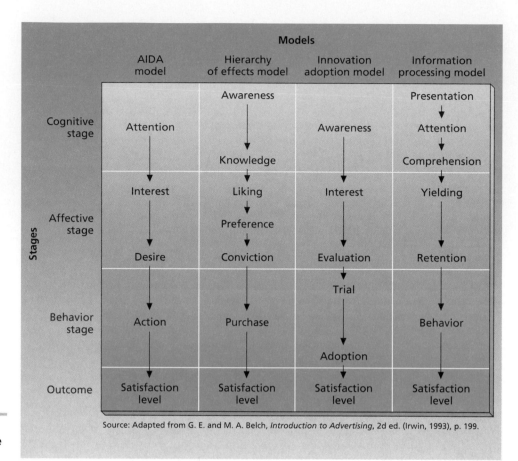

FIGURE 14.2
Four Models of the Response Process

Source: Adapted from G. E. and M. A. Belch, *Introduction to Advertising*, 2d ed. (Irwin, 1993), p. 199.

develops. Thus, in order to understand how a consumer might respond to a marketing communication, marketers look at a hierarchy of possible responses to their promotions. Figure 14.2 illustrates four common response hierarchies used by marketers.

Response hierarchies, in general, suggest that consumers must be led through a series of steps before reaching the point of action, or product purchase. The concept of integrated marketing communications has sometimes challenged this view of consumers' responses because the view suggests that all consumers move through the same steps, in the same sequence.[13] With its focus on consumers, IMC suggests that promotional efforts must be based on what consumers want to hear rather than where marketers wish to move those consumers. Despite this seeming discrepancy between IMC and more traditional promotion theory, an understanding of response hierarchies is very helpful to a marketer.

The AIDA Model

Before purchasing a product, a consumer is expected to go through four stages, the acronym for which is **AIDA:** Attention (sometimes called Awareness), Interest, Desire, and Action. Although this model was developed to describe the steps a salesperson must take a consumer through to close a sale, it is applicable to any promotional effort.[14] A promotion may have as its objective any part or parts of AIDA. A marketer may, for example, use a billboard to get people's attention, a television advertisement to create interest, and a cents-off coupon to motivate action. As the

This action-oriented ad asks the reader to see a physician, not to make a purchase.

advertisement for Cerenex shows, action does not specifically refer only to making a purchase. This action-oriented ad asks the reader to complete the hierarchy by seeing a physician.

The Hierarchy-of-Effects Model

The **hierarchy-of-effects model** was proposed by Lavidge and Steiner as a means to set and measure advertising objectives.[15] Like the AIDA model, it can be applied to any promotional effort. It is a more elaborate model than AIDA because it proposes more steps, or more potential responses. The steps in the hierarchy of effects, similar to AIDA, are proposed to occur in sequence. A consumer first becomes aware, then knowledgeable. Knowledge in turn leads to liking, liking to preference, preference to conviction, and ultimately, conviction leads to purchase. A single promotional effort could attempt to lead a consumer through all of the stages. A sales rep might, for example, plan a presentation with the goal of moving a prospective customer from one step to the next. A single advertisement is unlikely to move a consumer through all the steps in the hierarchy. More likely, an advertiser would need a series of advertisements, with each ad focused on accomplishing one step in the hierarchy.

The Innovation Adoption Model

The five stages proposed in the **innovation adoption model** were first suggested as stages through which a consumer passes on the way to adopting an innovation, such as a new product. The trial stage in this model is of interest because it differentiates this response hierarchy from the two previously introduced. Trial allows a consumer to experience a product or service through actual use. Sales promotions such as free samples can be extremely successful in accomplishing this stage.

MARKETING *IN ACTION* ▪▪▪▪▪▪▪▪

Fighting Back in the Face of Uncontrolled Communication

Foodmaker Corporation, Incorporated, the parent company of Jack-in-the-Box fast-food restaurants, faced a crisis during the fall of 1992 and winter of 1993. Several cases of *E. coli* poisoning were traced to hamburgers purchased from Jack-in-the-Box outlets in Seattle, Washington, and San Diego, California. The poisoning is a particularly insidious killer that springs from *E. coli* bacteria, which are in meat that has been tainted through contact with parasites often found in animal feces. The bacteria are killed when the meat is cooked to a sufficiently high internal temperature, but can remain when meat is rare. An infected individual does not show signs of being ill until several days after the bacteria enter his or her body. *E. coli* can be extremely dangerous; children are particularly vulnerable because of their small size.

In the case of the Foodmaker Corporation, two children died in the Seattle area and several in Seattle and San Diego recovered after critical illnesses. Local, national, and international media reported extensively on the children, their illnesses and deaths, and the link to the tainted Jack-in-the-Box hamburgers. Consumers' reactions were predictably fast. Jack-in-the-Box restaurants were empty. Equally predictable, Foodmaker Corporation's stock plunged.

Foodmaker had purchased the tainted meat from a long-time supplier of ground beef. Foodmaker did not have the luxury of time if it was to survive. The firm's response needed to be swift.

In the days after the first few poisonings were reported by the media and even before it had

been unequivocally proved that Jack-in-the-Box burgers were to blame, the firm took two actions. First, it changed meat suppliers and second, it raised the required internal cooking temperatures for hamburgers in all restaurants. Although very important, these actions were only the beginning of Foodmaker's response to the damaging uncontrolled communication.

During the weeks that followed, the firm expressed condolences to the families of the victims and offered to pay all medical expenses for anyone suffering from *E. coli* bacteria after eating at a Jack-in-the-Box. The most dramatic response by the firm, however, came in the form of its communication strategy. A large controlled communication effort was launched to combat the effects of the uncontrolled communication that had been occurring. Jack Goodall, president and CEO of Foodmaker, appeared on radio and television to apologize to all victims and their families, explaining the firm's intent to cover all medical expenses, and assuring consumers that appropriate steps had been taken to make eating at Jack-in-the-Box safe. Full-page advertisements that communicated this same information ran in local newspapers in the Seattle and San Diego areas.

Because of this aggressive response, many analysts expected Jack-in-the-Box and Foodmaker to recover fairly quickly. Unfortunately, this has not been the case. The firm lost $44.1 million or $1.15 per share in 1993. In the first quarter of 1994, the company lost an additional $.11 per share. One year after the outbreak, sales for stores that had been open at least a year were down 9.2 percent.

The Information-Processing Model

The last response hierarchy we will consider is the **information-processing model.** This model, like the hierarchy of effects model, contains six stages through which a consumer must pass. This information-processing model, proposed by McGuire,[16] however, proposes the retention stage, not found in any of the other response hierarchies discussed here. Retention refers to the consumer's ability to remember information in a promotional message. This stage may be quite important because consumers usually are not in a position to take immediate action when receiving information through a promotional effort.

Hierarchy Commonalities

The relationships among the four response hierarchies can be readily seen if you consider the general stages on the left-hand side of Figure 14.2. *Cognitive* refers to awareness, knowledge, and comprehension. *Affective* refers to interest, liking, preference, and other "pre-use" terms. *Behavior* refers to actual experience such as trial or purchase. *Outcome* refers to the degree to which the consumer is satisfied.

Achievement of the steps in the various response hierarchies generally increases in difficulty as one moves through the steps. Building awareness, for example, is perceived to be easier than obtaining interest or desire. Conviction and purchase are the most challenging stages to move a consumer through.

Diagnostic Power of Response Hierarchies

The response hierarchies can be extremely useful in helping a marketer determine where to direct promotional efforts. For example, using the hierarchy-of-effects model, consider the following response profiles in the market for two hypothetical products (total market = 100 percent). The percentages given are cumulative; that is, for Product 2, the 10 percent satisfied represents 10 percent of the target consumers, but 25 percent (10 percent of 40 percent) of those target consumers who were aware of the product.

Product 1		Product 2	
Awareness	90%	Awareness	40%
Knowledge	60%	Knowledge	30%
Liking	20%	Liking	25%
Preference	10%	Preference	20%
Conviction	8%	Conviction	15%
Purchase	4%	Purchase	12%
Satisfied	3%	Satisfied	10%

Product 1's profile suggests the consumers understand the communication about the product fairly well (60 percent knowledge) but do not particularly care for these attributes (only 20 percent liking). In this case, a major reworking of the message (or a new product with more liked attributes) may be needed. Product 2's profile suggests a product that needs to be better known (40 percent awareness) in the marketplace. Building awareness should be the prime objective for Product 2. As you can see, the power of the hierarchy in guiding promotional planning is considerable.

Alternatively Ordered Response Hierarchies

A **standard learning hierarchy** is any response model that posits that consumers progress through a series of steps beginning with something similar to awareness and ending with some type of action. The response hierarchies just discussed are all standard learning hierarchies. Every consumer does not automatically pass through the hierarchy of effects in order, however. In fact, researchers have found that this tends to occur only when the consumer is highly involved with the product and when there is a perception of significant differences among competing brands. Figure 14.3 illustrates this situation. The figure also presents two alternative hierarchies that can explain consumer behavior under certain circumstances.

The **low-involvement hierarchy,** on the right-hand side of Figure 14.3, assumes that the consumer has little involvement with the product or purchase process and perceives products as similar to each other. The ordering in this hierarchy is cognitive stage (awareness, knowledge), conative stage (purchase), and affective stage (liking, preference, conviction). Usually the product is in a late phase of maturity in the product life cycle and so broadcast media are important. For example, many consumers do not get involved with laundry detergent. Thus, switching from one brand to another is a feature of the low-involvement pattern. Suppose a Tide user becomes aware of a new brand through a television commercial or an in-store promotion. This person then purchases the product, perhaps because of a low introductory price. After making the purchase, the consumer reasons that because she has purchased the

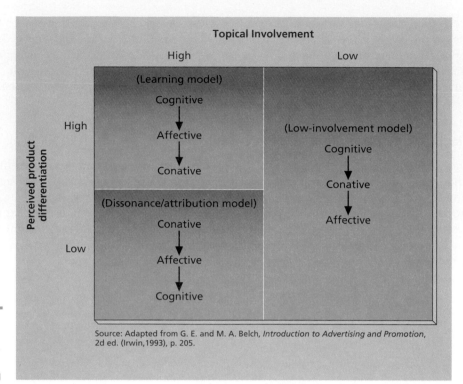

FIGURE 14.3
Alternative Response Hierarchies: The Three-Orders Model of Information Processing

product, the new brand is preferable. This accomplishes stages such as liking and preference.

In the lower left-hand side of Figure 14.3 is the **dissonance/attribution model,** or the *action-first* model, as it is sometimes called. This model assumes high consumer involvement but low perceived differentiation of competing brands. In this situation the steps are conative (purchase), affective (liking, preference), and then cognitive (knowledge, comprehension). It is called the dissonance hierarchy because the buyer is presumed to have some second thoughts about the purchase since so many similar products exist. These second thoughts are called dissonance. What follows in the hierarchy after the purchase is that consumers make their attitudes consistent with the purchase, thereby reducing the dissonance. This, of course, presumes that the purchase was not an obvious mistake.

Products to which this model apply are often in the early phases of maturity. A businessperson in charge of buying one of virtually hundreds of similar fax machines may make a quick decision because the task of assembling and processing information on all machines is just too overwhelming. In this situation, the decision is made first and then information is gathered to make the attitude consistent with the actual purchase. This may involve just noting ads or reading the brochure that accompanies the product.

Promotional Tools and Consumers' Responses

Various promotional tools generally affect the levels of a response hierarchy differently. This means that each stage may be served best by different promotional tools. Figure 14.4 shows the relationships of the four AIDA stages to the various promotional tools. Note that advertising has its greatest impact on creating attention or awareness and developing interest. This is true because mass media can reach large numbers of people at once with glitzy, attention-getting messages. Advertising is not as effective at inducing action. Personal selling shows just the opposite pattern: it

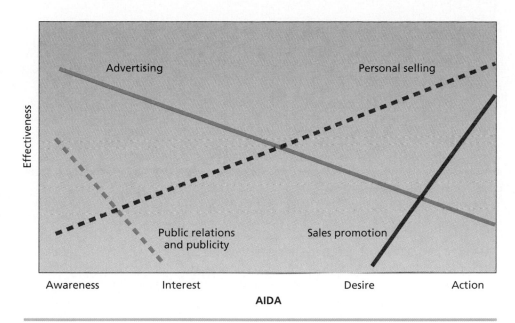

FIGURE 14.4
The Impact of Promotional Tools on Consumers' Responses

is less effective in the area of awareness and interest building, but much more effective in accomplishing higher-level steps such as motivating desire and action. One of the reasons personal selling does not lend itself to lower-level steps in the hierarchy is the cost. Although it might well be possible to build consumer awareness through personal selling, the cost would be prohibitive for all but the smallest, business-to-business target markets.

Sales promotion is most effective at stimulating action. Many blood banks, for example, give T-shirts to donors. This sales promotion helps move potential donors from the "I-intend-to-give-blood" stage (desire or conviction) to the actual act of donating. Finally, publicity is limited to creating awareness and generating a low level of interest.

SETTING PROMOTIONAL OBJECTIVES

Before strategies for promotion can be developed, the marketer must set objectives. Promotion objectives should be directly related to the response desired from a communication. Thus in developing objectives, marketers should look at the various steps in a response hierarchy. A given objective, for example, might be aimed at creating awareness, building interest or desire, or getting consumers to take action.

Elements of Good Promotional Objectives

Despite the fact that a promotional objective can be focused at a number of possible responses, some elements are consistently found in all good promotional objectives. The basic elements of good promotional objectives were first proposed in 1961 in a model called DAGMAR. **DAGMAR** is an acronym for Defining Advertising Goals for Measured Advertising Results.[17] The DAGMAR model suggests that a good objective should

1. be concrete and measurable
2. designate a target market
3. establish a benchmark and indicate degree of change sought
4. specify a time period

Consider the following hypothetical objectives:

- To increase awareness of the Ford Explorer from 50 percent to 75 percent among married women aged 25 to 45 years in San Diego County during the next six months.
- To increase sales, in units, of the Apple PowerBook notebook computer by 15 percent, from the present level of 750,000 to 862,500 among college students aged 20 to 25 years in the United States during the next year.

These objectives meet the DAGMAR criteria. Evaluation of the effectiveness of strategies to accomplish these objectives should be relatively straightforward. Now consider two more objectives:

- To increase interest in Stanford University among alumni
- To be the best new car dealership in Ann Arbor, Michigan

These are poor promotional objectives for a number of reasons. In the first case, while a target market is specified (Stanford alumni), the objective neither suggests a level of increase nor identifies a time period. The goal is vague. Is this increased interest intended to help raise funds? Is it intended to help recruit new students? The second example is a poor objective because it offers no benchmark or time frame. Thus, it is not measurable. "Best" can mean anything from highest in sales, open the most hours, or offering the lowest prices. Objectives must be realistic and attainable.

Promotional effectiveness should be determined based on the objectives originally established. Unfortunately, the criteria used to judge promotional success are often different from the original objectives. For example, the objective for a Welch's grape juice campaign was "to convince parents that the product was the best drink for children because of its nutritious value and good taste." Although increased knowledge and conviction were the objectives, success was measured in terms of sales; there were no measurements of knowledge and conviction. If sales were the true objective, then that objective should have been stated; otherwise, the sales criterion is an invalid measure of the worth of the campaign. This is a common mistake.

Objectives designed for each promotional element should be complementary. Marketers expect them to combine with other marketing-mix activities to reach overall marketing objectives. It is important that the role of each promotional tool be well thought-out and that each be assigned a well-stated objective. Once objectives are in place, marketers can turn their attention to determining how much money needs to be spent to achieve those objectives—the costs of promotion.

YOUR MARKETING KNOWLEDGE

14-1   Review the advertisement for Cerenex and describe the source, encoding, channel, receiver, decoding, and feedback.

14-2   What forms might noise take in the communication process between sender and receiver in the Cerenex advertisement?

14-3   Write a good objective for each stage in the AIDA hierarchy relative to promotional activity you might undertake as part of a job search.

Industry	Ad $ as % of Sales
Apparel	5.9
Building material/glass	1.7
Computer/office equipment	0.6
Food	1.9
Pharmaceuticals	2.3
Publishing/media	2.4
Toiletries/cosmetics	5.0
Toys and sporting goods	14.3

Source: Compiled from "Fortune 500," *Fortune*, April 18, 1994, pp. 257–276 and "Ad Age Fact Book," *Advertising Age*, January 3, 1994, \ 24.

TABLE 14.3
Advertising Dollars as Percentage of Sales for Selected Industries (1992)

UNDERSTANDING PROMOTION COSTS

The amount that organizations spend on promotion varies dramatically from firm to firm, within industries, and across industries. To give you an idea of how significant this variation can be, Table 14.3 shows advertising dollars spent as a percentage of sales for a few selected industries. Remember as you look at these numbers that variation also exists across firms within each of the industries listed.

Even in industries where the ratio of promotional spending to sales is relatively low, the dollars spent on promotion can still be enormous. Table 14.4 shows spending on advertising media for the top ten U.S. advertisers. These figures, when combined with the cost of advertising production, as well as personal selling and sales, help explain why a firm may spend so much on promotion. It is important to remember, however, that promotional expenditures are a necessary investment for an organization. Viewing promotional spending as an expense that cuts into profits reflects a basic misunderstanding of the role and purpose of promotion in marketing strategy. Unfortunately many companies fail to grasp this basic notion.

A number of factors influence the amount that a firm spends on promotion. The most important are:

- channel involvement in promotion
- overall strategy
- number and accessibility of customers
- complexity of decision-making units

TABLE 14.4
Top 10 National Advertisers ($ millions)

Rank 1992	Rank 1991	Advertiser, headquarters	Total U.S. Ad Spending 1992	Total U.S. Ad Spending 1991	% chg
1	1	**Procter & Gamble Co.,** Cincinnati	**$2,165.6**	$2,150.0	0.7
2	2	**Phillip Morris Cos.,** New York	**2,024.1**	2,071.3	−2.3
3	3	**General Motors Corp.,** Detroit	**1,333.6**	1,476.8	−9.7
4	4	**Sears, Roebuck & Co.,** Chicago	**1,204.6**	1,195.6	0.8
5	5	**Pepsico,** Purchase, NY	**928.6**	903.9	2.7
6	9	**Ford Motor Co.,** Dearborn, MI	**794.5**	689.7	15.2
7	11	**Warner-Lambert Co.,** Morris Plains, NJ	**757.5**	657.0	15.3
8	21	**Chrysler Corp.,** Highland Park, MI	**756.6**	547.1	38.3
9	8	**McDonald's Corp.,** Oak Brook, IL	**743.6**	695.7	6.9
10	14	**Nestle SA,** Vevey, Switzerland	**733.4**	643.4	14.0

Source: *Advertising Age*, March 3, 1994, p. 14.

Just about everyone who's ever used a computer has experienced the same thought: Wouldn't it be great if setting up or upgrading your machine was as easy as turning it on?

The idea is called "Plug and Play." People have been talking about it for years. But now, an ongoing partnership between Compaq and Microsoft, working with other industry leaders, is actually making it happen.

Plug and Play is the result of some very fresh thinking in both hardware and software – an accomplishment that tapped the combined engineering expertise of both companies. Together, Compaq® computers and the next version of the Microsoft® Windows™ operating system (code-named Chicago) will deliver the long-promised benefits of true Plug and Play: easy setup, easy expansion and easy connection to peripherals.

Which means no more configuration headaches. No more hidden switches, cryptic codes or mystery.

Even today, Compaq is shipping computers that will take full advantage of Plug and Play technology as soon as the forthcoming version of Windows is available. So the Compaq & Windows combination will quickly become the standard for Plug and Play computing. A welcome reassurance for people who buy computers.

COMPAQ Microsoft

COMPAQ AND MICROSOFT.
THE CONNECTION THAT'S MAKING
"PLUG AND PLAY" A REALITY.

Firms committed to continuous product innovation require greater promotional spending to maintain high consumer awareness of new products.

- standardization of products and customers' needs
- customers' recognition of product benefits
- product line turnover
- frequency and timing of purchases

Channel Involvement in Promotion

In some industries, all levels in the distribution channel carry part of the promotional load. The greater portion of that load the manufacturer can get other channel levels to accept, the lower the promotional expense of the manufacturer.

Overall Strategy

Other elements of a firm's marketing strategy affect the amount of dollars that must be spent on promotional activity. Some product and pricing decisions require more promotional support than others. For example, a firm committed to continuous product innovation requires greater promotional spending to maintain high consumer awareness of new products. Companies that frequently change prices, perhaps lowering prices or running discounts, find it necessary to spend more on promotion to inform consumers than those companies whose prices remain stable over longer periods of time.

Number and Accessibility of Customers

Promotional costs are lower in situations where there are fewer potential customers and where it is easier to reach those customers. This is one reason that business-to-business marketers typically spend less on promotion than do marketers who target ultimate consumers. Business-to-business markets, as we learned in Chapter 7, are generally smaller, better defined, and more geographically concentrated than are ultimate consumer markets. Review the industries listed in Table 14.3. You'll see that those whose advertising spending is a low percentage of sales revenue are all business-to-business marketers.

Complexity of Decision-Making Units

The more complicated the decision-making process of the consumer, the more costly promotion is. In business-to-business markets, for example, straight rebuy decisions made by a single purchasing agent in a firm require less promotional spending. A more complex decision that involves multiple buying influences such as a purchasing agent, office manager, engineer, and others requires greater promotional spending. The marketer may need to develop individual advertisements and sales presentations for each party involved in the decision because each has a different set of concerns and questions.

Standardization of Products and Customers' Needs

The more a product is standardized within an industry, and the more customers and their needs are similar, the less promotional activity there is. Commodities are highly standardized products whose industries reflect this characteristic through low levels of promotional spending. When a product or service is highly differentiated and has multiple uses, higher promotional spending is the rule of thumb. For example, McDonald's directs its products toward a wide range of consumers: children, teens, young adults, middle-aged adults, and seniors. The firm spends a great deal on promotion that delivers appropriate messages to each group.

Customers' Recognition of Product Benefits

When customers are familiar with a product or service, the need to promote it diminishes. For this reason, there is greater promotional spending in the introduction and growth stages of the product life cycle than in the maturity and decline stages. An industry like pharmaceuticals, known for rapid change and constant innovation, requires much greater promotional spending than a more stable industry, such as the airplane industry whose products are well known and understood by consumers.

Turnover of Product Line

When changes to a firm's product line are frequent, greater promotional spending is required to keep consumers informed. The automobile industry is an excellent example of this. With new models coming out every year, the industry must work almost constantly to keep potential customers up-to-date.

Frequency and Timing of Purchases

The more frequently a product is purchased, the greater the need for continuous promotion. Consumer packaged goods (like breakfast cereal or shampoo) that may be purchased weekly or monthly are examples of such products. Consider a consumer who purchases breakfast cereal every week. Every seven days the producer of the brand last purchased faces the challenge of convincing the consumer not to try something different the next time. Durable consumer goods or business-to-business goods that are purchased infrequently have less need for continual promotion.

It is clear that determining the correct amount to spend on promotion is a complex decision for a manager. Table 14.5 summarizes the information regarding the various factors that influence promotional spending. Understanding the impact of these factors can help a manager determine the total amount to spend on promotion.

ESTABLISHING THE PROMOTIONAL BUDGET

Just how much money should an organization spend on promotional activity in a given year? The methods that can be used to determine this figure fall into one of three broad approaches to budget determination:

1. the theoretical approach
2. top-down approaches
3. build-up approaches[18]

The Theoretical Approach

The theoretical approach uses marginal analysis to determine the promotional budget that will maximize profits for the organization. Figure 14.5 illustrates this approach. The horizontal axis is the number of units produced, and the vertical axis represents the dollars allocated to promotion. Since price seldom changes during a short-run planning period, price is presumed to remain constant over the possible range of production. Also, production costs are assumed to be constant at $.20 per

TABLE 14.5
Factors Affecting
Promotional Expenses

Factor	Increased Spending	Decreased Spending
Channel involvement in promotion	Low channel support	High channel support
Overall strategy change	Other marketing-mix activities change	Other marketing-mix activities change little
Number and accessibility of customers	Many, hard-to-reach customers	Few, easy-to-reach customers
Complexity of decision-making units	More complex	Less complex
Standardization of products and customer needs	Differentiated product and nonhomogeneous customer needs	Highly standardized product and very homogeneous customer needs
Customer recognition of product benefits	Not well known or recognized	Well known and recognized
Product line turnover	High level of turnover	Low level of turnover
Frequency and timing of purchase	Purchased often and in small quantities	Purchased infrequently and in large quantities

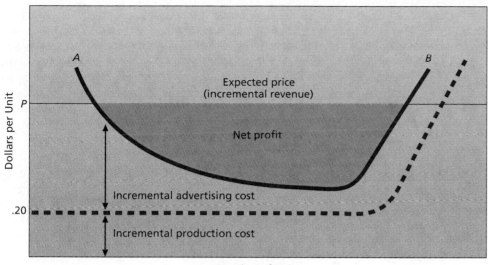

FIGURE 14.5
Short-Run Determination of Promotional Budget by Marginal Analysis

unit over the relevant range of production, but rise rapidly when certain capacity limits are reached. The line *AB* represents the promotional costs per unit. Promotional expenditures are usually substantial, no matter what sales volume is. Thus, at a very low sales volume we find the cost of promotion exceeding price (*AB* is above *P*). However, as sales prospects are won over, the promotion per unit drops rapidly. At some later point, the response to promotion diminishes as few additional prospective buyers are being motivated to buy, and the cost per incremental sale rises. At what point, then, should we stop spending on promotion? Notice that net profit is represented by the shaded area in Figure 14.5. Profits result when promotional costs per unit are below the production price per unit. Thus profit continues to be earned until the promotional-cost line *AB* exceeds the price per unit. In general, a firm should spend on promotion until the cost of acquiring new business (the marginal sale) equals the sales revenue per unit (the marginal revenue).

The theoretical approach helps us to understand that when we set a promotional budget, we are trying to get the most benefit for the dollars spent. This approach, however, is extremely difficult to implement. To do so would require determining the correct promotion response per unit sold.

Despite the difficulty of implementing the theoretical approach, the method does focus attention on profitability as the key criterion for setting budgets. Hence, it can serve as a standard against which to judge other procedures used to determine promotional budgets. As we discuss budgeting methods under the other two approaches, we will judge them against their capacities to approximate the theoretical approach.

Top-Down Approaches

Top-down approaches to setting promotion budgets determine a single budgetary amount that must be divided among the different promotional tools. The approaches are the *affordable method*, the *percentage of sales method*, *competitive parity*, the *ROI method*, and the *arbitrary method*.

The affordable method.   Some firms set promotional budgets on the basis of available funds. This is called the affordable or the all-you-can-afford method. With this method the company spends what is left after production and other expenses are accounted for. This method of budgeting may seem safe because firms will not spend more than they can afford on promotion. Unfortunately, this method is likely to result in a budget that does not meet the promotional objectives of the firm. With this method a firm could miss opportunities because of underspending. The firm could also spend too much. Either mistake would be easy to make because profitability is not the key criterion for setting the budget.

Percentage of sales.   Perhaps the most common top-down budgeting method is to use percentage of sales. The budget is determined by applying a fixed percentage to either past or forecasted sales. A common variation is to fix a dollar amount per unit for promotion and then multiply this by the sales forecast to obtain the budget (this variation is sometimes referred to as the *fixed sum per unit method*). The proportion of sales allocated to promotion may be based upon past results or on management's judgments about the future.

The percentage-of-sales method is popular primarily because it is simple to calculate, exact, and easy to explain to managers who are used to thinking of costs in percentages. Also, it is financially safe because it ties expenditures to sales revenue. It can provide a stable competitive environment. If it is used throughout an industry, promotional levels will be proportionate to market shares.

The major problem with the percentage-of-sales approach is its faulty logic regarding the relationship between promotional spending and sales. This method views promotion as a result of sales rather than as a cause of it. Using this method could result in a downward spiral for sales and profits, from which a firm might never recover. If sales are down in a given year, the percentage-of-sales method would mean that the organization would spend fewer dollars on promotion in the coming year. It may well be, however, that the very thing the firm needs to do to reverse the downward sales trend is to spend more on promotion! This basic problem holds even when future sales are used to determine the budget. How can one forecast sales without knowing the level of promotional spending?

Competitive parity.   With the competitive-parity method of budget determination, firms try to match the spending of their competition. This could be accomplished by spending according to the average ratio of promotion costs to sales for their industry (Table 14.3 gives examples of industry averages, which can be found in trade journals and other advertising industry periodicals), spending to match the percentage of sales of an important competitor, or spending the same absolute dollar amount as a competitor spends. In practice, the first of these three alternatives is the most common.

Competitive parity is a relatively safe approach and it does add the consideration of spending levels of competing firms to the budget-setting process. Its shortcomings, however, far outweigh these advantages.

The critical problem with this method is it assumes that a firm's competitors know how to expend promotional dollars properly. Another major flaw is that promotional spending is unrelated to objectives. It seems unlikely that all other firms in an industry, or even a single major competitor, would have the identical promotional objectives as your firm. Finally, short of corporate spying, the only available data will reflect past promotional spending, not future spending. A competitor could well be planning a big change in promotional activity. As with the other top-down approaches, competitive parity clearly does not base promotional spending on profitability.

Return on investment (ROI). Some people believe that promotion should be treated like any other decision about long-term investment by a business. Using this approach, firms view promotional expenditures in terms of their ability to generate profits over many years. Promotional budgets compete for scarce resources with other possible investments. This encourages gathering data to measure the impact of promotion and assures more objective decision making. Unfortunately, management can usually do little more than guess at the likely future returns for promotional dollars. Also, managers are conditioned to think of promotional spending as an expense for a given year. Overcoming this mind-set would be difficult; therefore, this method has received little managerial use.

The arbitrary method. Even in some of the weakest top-down methods described, some thought is given to a key factor such as the financial ability of the firm or its competitive position. With arbitrary allocation, however, no theoretical basis is considered. Top management is using a seat-of-the-pants approach to arrive at a figure. While there are no clear advantages to this method, it is included because it is used by organizations of all sizes across almost all industries.

Build-up approaches

Build-up approaches set a promotional budget by adding all the costs associated with various promotional tasks. The build-up approaches to be considered are the *objective and task method*, *payout planning*, and *quantitative modeling*.

Objective-and-task method. Unlike any of the top-down methods, the objective-and-task method specifically ties promotional spending to the promotional objectives of the firm. To implement this method the organization must follow three steps:

1. *Determine and set objectives.* The promotion manager must begin with clearly stated, quantifiable objectives. These objectives should be specific, arrived at after a complete situation analysis.
2. *Determine the specific program needed to reach the objectives.* This step is the key to the objective-and-task method. It requires an extensive program of marketing research and good judgment. Experience can also be extremely valuable. It is a challenging step.
3. *Determine the cost.* Using the results from step 2, costs are determined for the various tasks outlined in the specific program. If, for example, it is determined in step 2 that two sales representatives are required to complete the personal-selling component of the promotional program, the cost of hiring and training those representatives must be calculated. Once costs are determined for all components of the program, the total promotional budget is determined by totaling all costs.

This method avoids arbitrary thinking and emphasizes research and sound managerial judgment. It also requires managers to define explicitly what they believe to be the relationship between the desired objective and expenditures. The major weakness of this method is the difficulty managers have in defining the tasks that will achieve the stated objectives. Even with the best research, this remains a challenging process.

Payout planning. When introducing a new product, a firm might use payout planning to determine promotional expenditures. A payout plan determines the investment value of promotional spending. Beginning with an expected rate of return, the plan aids in determining how much to spend on promotion to achieve that return and when the return can be expected. Payout plans typically follow the theory that

	Year 1	Year 2	Year 3
Product sales	15.0	35.5	60.75
Profit contribution (@ $0.50/case)	7.5	17.75	30.38
Advertising/promotions	15.0	10.5	8.5
Profit (loss)	(7.5)	7.25	21.88
Cumulative profit (loss)	(7.5)	(0.25)	21.63

Source: From G. E. and M. A. Belch, *Introduction to Advertising and Promotion*, 2d ed. (Irwin, 1993), Exhibit 9–15, p. 309.

TABLE 14.6
Example of a Three-Year Payout Plan ($ millions)

greater than normal promotional spending is required when new products are introduced. Stimulating awareness and trial have been found to require more promotion than brand maintenance.[19] Table 14.6 shows a three-year payout plan that follows this pattern. Product sales and profits increase over the three years while advertising and other promotional expenditures decrease.

Similar to the objective-and-task method, payout planning does require the manager of promotions to determine the relationship expected between promotional expenditures and the desired result (i.e., a specific level of return). The approach is often used in conjunction with the objective-and-task method.

Quantitative modeling.   Some firms have attempted to use computer-simulated models to determine the relationship between promotional spending and sales or profits. To the extent that a model could accurately predict the amount of promotional spending necessary to produce a given level of sales, profits, or whatever objective had been stated, this method would represent a logical and scientific approach to budget determination. To date these attempts have met with limited success. They may, however, become more useful in the future.

Build-up approaches to promotional budgeting are superior to top-down approaches because they clearly relate spending to the objectives of the firm. Of the three build-up approaches discussed, clearly the objective-and-task method is the best developed and most thorough.

DETERMINING THE PROMOTIONAL MIX

The firm that has chosen to use the objective-and-task method of promotional budgeting never faces the challenge of deciding how to divide a lump sum amount across the various promotional tools. For those organizations that use top-down approaches to budgeting, however, determination of the total budget is just the starting point in promotional planning. These firms now face decisions regarding the relative emphasis to place on advertising, sales promotion, and personal selling. The exact combination of promotional tools is called the *promotional mix* or *promotional blend*. Even when a firm uses the objective-and-task method, determination of the promotional mix is important. For organizations using this approach, the decision about the blend of promotional tools comes as part of the budgeting process (step 2 in the objective-and-task method). Regardless of whether this issue is faced during the budgeting process or after, it is a critical aspect of a firm's promotional strategy.

There is no one correct promotional mix for a company. Whether a firm achieves success with greater use of personal selling, advertising, or a balanced blend of the two may not matter if indeed the firm does achieve the success it desires. In this section we consider the different types of blended strategies a firm might choose, as well as a number of factors that can guide the promotion manager toward the optimal mix.

Push Versus Pull Strategies

Whether an organization focuses the bulk of its promotional activity on personal selling or on advertising is often determined by whether it chooses to employ a push strategy or a pull strategy. A **push strategy** accomplishes the goal of product distribution and ultimately sales by focusing promotional efforts on channel members. A producer promotes the product to the next closest level (perhaps a wholesaler), and the wholesaler in turn focuses its promotional efforts on the retailer. It is then left to the retailer to promote the product or service to the ultimate consumer. Promotional efforts of this strategy concentrate heavily on personal selling. While the various channel members may choose to use sales promotions (contests for sales representatives, for example) or advertising in trade publications, the biggest part of the promotional effort involves persuading each subsequent channel level, through personal selling, to carry the product. The channel member who is the object of the selling effort must be convinced that it will be profitable to give shelf space to the product in question. This approach can work very well with products from established manufacturers whose reputation and image are well known among channel members as well as ultimate consumers. The manufacturers of ROC, a French line of hypoallergenic skin-care lotions, uses a push strategy. The firm, with 1992 sales of more than $125 million outside the United States, attempts to get doctors and pharmacists sold on the product, so it can push the lotions to other customers, clients, and patients.[20]

It is common for marketers to meet resistance from channel members when attempting to implement a push strategy. Particularly in industries where competition is intense, the last thing a wholesaler or retailer may wish to see is another new brand that will require space on already crowded shelves. In this case, a pull strategy may work more effectively. A **pull strategy** accomplishes the goal of product distribution and sales by bypassing intermediary channel members and focusing on ultimate consumers. Because ultimate consumers are typically so vast in number, this strategy makes primary use of advertising rather than personal selling. The manufacturer of a new brand of snack cracker might choose to launch an advertising campaign to stimulate awareness and induce trial. As consumers become aware of the product, through advertising, they begin to look for it on their local grocer's shelf. When the cracker is not found, consumers may begin to ask the retailer about it. The theory of a pull strategy is that the retailer, after receiving sufficient inquiries, will seek information (and the product) from his or her suppliers (either a wholesaler or the manufacturer). Through this process the product is pulled through the channel. Figure 14.6 illustrates these two strategies.

The decision about using a push strategy or a pull strategy depends on a number of factors including the manufacturer's reputation and relationships with other channel members, the resources the manufacturer has, and the characteristics of the target market and the product.

Of course, it is important to remember that push and pull strategies are opposite ends of a spectrum. Virtually all marketers use both approaches. A pharmaceutical producer may advertise to end users even though a personal-selling push is the key ingredient in the promotional plan. Merck, for example, advertises its drugs to end users so that consumers will accept them when they are prescribed by a physician.

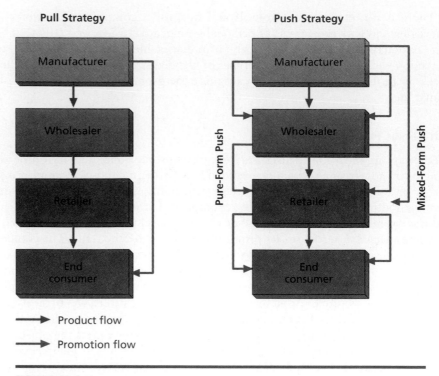

FIGURE 14.6
Push Versus Pull Strategies

The key to success for the firm, however, is its expert sales force, which trains for more than 12 months before approaching doctors, clinics, and hospitals. Even the most advertised packaged good also has push effort behind it. Procter & Gamble, the number one national advertiser (see Table 14.4), prides itself on a sales force that promotes its products to retailers, who in turn promote them to ultimate consumers. A combined strategy was used in marketing *The Flintstones* movie. Heavy radio ads and additional promotions to target audiences for the movie ensured that local theaters ran the film. Additional tie-ins with other companies (McDonald's, Mattel, Lee Apparel, Topps, and Thermos) ensured that channel members promoted the film through coupons, discounts, various activities, and events.[21]

Theoretical Optimum Mix

There is a theoretically optimal way to divide promotional dollars among the available elements. It involves a marginal analysis similar to that described in the section on budget determination. Simply put, an organization should spend any given dollar on the promotional element that has the highest marginal impact on the objective being sought. Every available dollar should thus be evaluated in terms of the marginal return available from each promotional element. The mix would be optimal when the total budget is used in such a way that the last dollar spent on each promotional element generates the same return.

Consider the two industries depicted in Figure 14.7. In the breakfast cereal industry, the returns to advertising/sales promotion, for the first dollar of the promotional budget spent, are much higher than those to personal selling. However, as more and more money is spent on advertising/sales promotion, the marginal results eventually diminish—new prospects become harder to motivate. At some point, they diminish so far that they fall below the marginal returns to personal selling, justifying spending money on personal selling. The returns associated with spending money

A combined push-pull strategy was used in marketing *The Flintstones* movie. Ultimate consumers were targeted through heavy radio ads and promotions, while channel members were targeted through tie-ins with other companies.

on personal selling diminish much faster in the breakfast cereal industry than those for advertising/sales promotion. Thus, the marginal impact of personal selling falls below that of advertising/sales promotion at a much lower dollar level. This process continues until the budgeted amount is spent. The marginal return patterns in the primary metals industry are, of course, just the opposite of the breakfast cereal industry. Here the marginal impact of personal selling diminishes much more slowly.

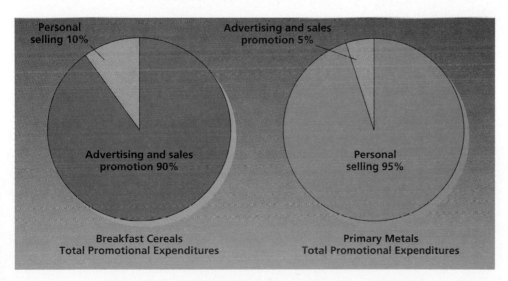

**FIGURE 14.7
Distribution of the Promotional Budget for the Breakfast Cereal and Primary Metals Industries**

Although this approach offers an optimum method for allocating promotional dollars, just as with budgeting, it is difficult to implement. In practice, determination of the response functions is difficult at best.

Factors in Mix Planning

In practice, a number of factors can provide guidance in choosing a promotional mix, including:

- the resources available
- characteristics of the product
- characteristics of the target market
- existing relationships with channel members
- stage of the product life cycle
- company policy
- degree of globalization

Resources available.   The amount of money available to an organization directly impacts decisions about promotional mix. Small companies with small budgets, or even small brands in large companies with small budgets, are unable to afford promotional choices such as television advertising. Thirty seconds on the Super Bowl goes for more than $900,000; all but the biggest spenders would find their annual promotion budget eaten up before January was over if they chose to focus advertising on this event. The dollar requirements of running an effective advertising campaign in almost any medium are not for those with small budgets, except for local spot ads or direct mail. The emphasis in such circumstances is usually on personal selling or other push activities, such as trade-level deals. A company could hire and support three salespeople for a whole year for the cost of one 30-second ad on prime-time television. The advertising may be a more efficient way to reach customers, but these marketers must turn to less efficient personal selling for lack of funds. Calyx and Corolla, a floral mail-order house in San Francisco, is an example of how a small company successfully used resources other than advertising. The company relies on a computerized information system, along with mailing lists and catalogues, to reach its customers.[22]

The next time you are in a large drugstore, count the number of brands that you have never seen advertised. The unadvertised brands are often "pushed" because these companies cannot afford to advertise. This also demonstrates the power of a pushing strategy, since all of these brands apparently sell well enough to hold their shelf space.

Product characteristics.   The nature of the product contributes greatly to the promotional mix decision. Personal selling tends to dominate when the product

- *has a high unit value.* In these circumstances, the consumer often needs intense persuasion to understand why the product justifies a high price. You would probably not buy a computer strictly on the basis of advertising. Also, a high revenue per product sold helps carry the cost of personal selling. With these consumer items, personal selling is critical. Because many business-to-business products also carry high unit values, personal selling dominates.

- *is technical in nature.* A highly technical product requires skilled sales personnel to explain it to customers. It is quite common for salespeople to have to explain the need for a new, technical business-to-business good to purchasing agents, engineers, and senior executives. A skilled sales force can sell technical products even over the telephone. Dell Computers has proved this with its success in the personal computer market, much of which can be attributed to the intense training it requires for its phone sales reps.

- *requires demonstration.* When a product's features "must be seen to be believed" and understood, the power of personal communication is needed. A sports car that has superior handling requires personal selling efforts.

- *must be tailored to the specific needs of customer groups.* In these cases the marketer must make personal contact with potential customers to understand their needs and explain how the product has been altered to satisfy those needs. Capital equipment systems such as computer controlled machines and investment analyst services are two areas where this factor is critical.

- *is purchased infrequently.* Here the product just cannot support a heavy advertising program relative to personal selling. Major home appliances are an example. Because consumers do not purchase stoves and refrigerators on a regular basis, personal selling is common.

- *involves the consideration of a trade-in for purchase.* The existence of a trade-in, in the purchase of a new automobile, for example, requires negotiation on the value of the old item.

As you read this list, it may occur to you that these characteristics match those of business-to-business products quite well. It shouldn't be surprising, then, that personal selling dominates the promotional mixes of most business-to-business firms. This is not to say that for business-to-business products, advertising is not important. Indeed, there is an important role for advertising in business-to-business marketing. Personal selling performance has been found to increase an average of 25 percent when supported by advertising. The advertising serves to open the door for the salesperson. The ad for McGraw-Hill reinforces this point.

Target market characteristics. The size and geographical dispersion of the target market has a direct effect on the promotional mix. If the target market is large and widely distributed, then advertising is, by far, the most economical means to reach the audience. The cost of personal selling would be prohibitive. Most consumer products have large, widely distributed markets. This is one reason advertising is so dominant for companies like Procter & Gamble, General Foods, General Mills, McDonald's, and Coca-Cola. Even some agencies of the government, like the U.S. Postal Service, use extensive advertising to reach their enormous, decentralized market.

At the other extreme, markets with small numbers of geographically concentrated customers can readily justify the cost of personal selling. Mass media here would lack the necessary target precision. Far too many people outside the target market would be reached by mass appeals. This is not to say that advertising cannot be useful in these circumstances. The advertising would be very specifically targeted, using special-interest media. For example, a company specializing in plant-cleaning equipment may place ads in *Plant Management* magazine.

Business-to-business markets tend to have small numbers of geographically concentrated customers. This fact, along with the characteristics of business-to-business products discussed previously, helps explain why personal selling is such a dominant promotional device for business-to-business products.

Promotional activity to wholesalers and retailers also tends to be dominated by personal selling for the same market-oriented reasons that business-to-business situations are. There are relatively few of these institutions and they are concentrated

"I don't know who you are.

I don't know your company.

I don't know your company's product.

I don't know what your company stands for.

I don't know your company's customers.

I don't know your company's record.

I don't know your company's reputation.

Now—what was it you wanted to sell me?"

MORAL: Sales start **before** your salesman calls—with business publication advertising.

McGRAW-HILL MAGAZINES
BUSINESS•PROFESSIONAL•TECHNICAL

As the ad suggests, when advertising supports personal selling, it can play an important role in business-to-business marketing.

enough to warrant personal attention. Also, the economic results of a successful sale help justify the cost, and often the specific sale may be quite complicated. For example, a sale to a retailer may involve coupons to the ultimate consumer, cents-off packages for the retailer to stock, and the use of a special end-aisle display. Personal selling is clearly needed. Managers at Procter & Gamble claim that the efforts of its sales force with retailers are as important to its success as advertising. Apple Computer has sold 12 million Macintosh machines through trade organizations and trade shows to wholesalers and retailers, along with additional promotions to ultimate consumers.[23]

Channel member relationships.   When a manufacturer has strong, personal relationships with other channel members, personal selling is likely to dominate the promotional mix. A manufacturer who is well liked can successfully implement a push strategy. Channel member cooperation, resulting in adequate shelf space and widespread distribution, can be achieved under these circumstances without the expense of a costly advertising campaign.

Strong relationships can, of course, be developed more easily if there are short channels and few channel members at any given level. Hence, not surprisingly, business-to-business marketers are often able to develop close relationships with channel members.

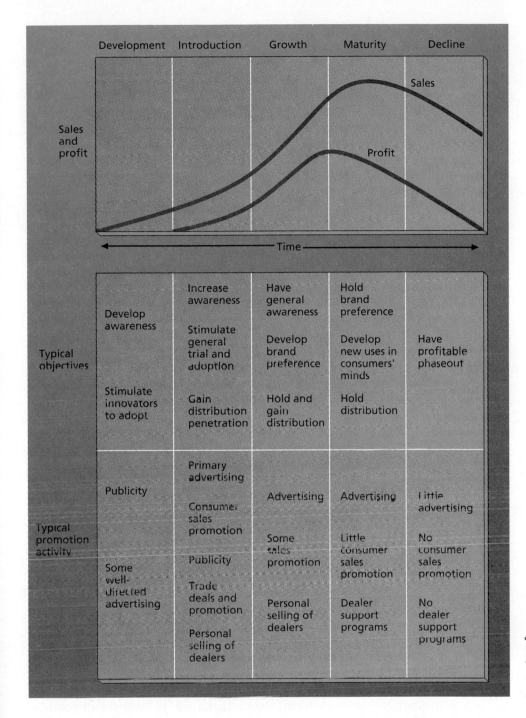

FIGURE 14.8
The Generalized Product Life Cycle and Promotional Activities

Product life cycle stages. In Chapter 9 we observed that products often follow a sales pattern called the product life cycle. Figure 14.8 illustrates how typical promotional activity varies by stage of the life cycle for a consumer good.

Note that both the promotional objectives and the specific promotional activities change over the life cycle. In the development stage, the objectives are to create awareness and develop interest in the product among targeted innovators—those who are expected to adopt first. The main methods are publicity and some well-directed advertising. Consider HDTV (high definition television), a major advance in television playback quality. Although it is available in only limited markets, virtually every major newspaper and news magazine in the country have carried articles about it. Advertisements have also been run in magazines that have high socioeconomic groups as readers.

At the introductory stage, the main objective is to increase awareness of the product in general and, to a lesser extent, to publicize the specific brands. The emphasis is on stimulating primary demand. Ads are often informative. Other objectives include generating product trials among consumers and gaining distribution penetration. Advertising and publicity are used to stimulate primary demand. Sales promotion is used to generate product trial (coupons, free samples, and rebates) and trade deals and personal selling to dealers are used to gain access to distribution channels. For example, when Southwest Airlines introduced service in San Jose, California, it used radio and print ads to focus on low fares and high frequency of flights.

As the product matures, the main objective of promotion changes to developing brand preference. Here ads become more persuasive and less informative. Selective demand becomes key. Holding and continuing to gain distribution are also important objectives. Advertising to a greater mass market than before becomes more important. Sales promotion and personal selling are still needed, but they are less important. In advertising its Smartsuite software, Microsoft offers bundled software, several "free" programs, and mentions the low price. These ads appear in trade and business publications.

At the maturity stage of the life cycle, holding brand preference and distribution, plus the possible communication of new uses for the product, become dominant objectives. Advertising and dealer support programs are key promotional activities. Advertising reinforces brand choice (Hallmark's "When you care enough to send the very best") and presents new uses. For example, Hallmark offers "Personalize It!" greeting cards and cards that use a small chip to present a voice message. Programs such as special discounts, rebates, and displays are designed to hold dealer support.

In the decline stage, the objective is to phase out the product profitably. Thus, all promotional costs are reduced dramatically. Some advertising is targeted to consumers still interested in the product; the goal is to remind them that the product is available. The pager is an example of a product in the decline stage. The pager is declining due to the widespread use of mobile phones. Existing ads focus on price and convenience.

Company policy.   Management choice can help to explain differences in promotional mixes. In these circumstances, long-standing preferences or traditions for one promotional approach can come into play. Some companies prefer to push while others prefer to pull. For example, Revlon emphasizes advertising and sales promotions while Avon emphasizes personal selling. Both companies are very successful. Northwestern Mutual Life Insurance Company is an organization that successfully follows a promotional mix different from those of its major competitors. Northwestern Mutual puts much more emphasis on its sales force relative to advertising. It advertises itself as "the quiet company," but its salespeople are anything but quiet. They consistently outperform the salespeople of competitors.

Degree of globalization.   Organizations face many unique challenges in promotional planning when they take their marketing efforts beyond domestic borders. Because of the external environment and cultural differences, a single global approach to communication is unlikely to work for any organization. (See Chapter 4.) Some firms have attempted to institute a single global marketing strategy, but companies have generally found that cultural differences call for promotional efforts unique to target markets.

The appropriate promotional mix or balance differs across international markets. In some parts of the world, for example, personal selling is by far the most important promotional tool for a marketer. To date, sales promotion has not been so important a component of the promotional mix in many foreign countries as it is in the United States. This may be due to the fact that legal restrictions on such activity are generally stricter in other countries than in the United States. Table 14.7 illustrates the legal status of various sales promotion activities in five European countries. Sales promotion does appear to be catching on in many international markets, however. Personal selling is very important in Mexico due to the poor postal service, and in Europe direct mail has dropped due to the rising cost of postage. In Japan, sales promotion is not an important strategy because it is considered inappropriate to ask another person to advertise your products. In preparing to market the new Korean car, KIA, in the United States, company officials realized they needed to "harden up" the advertisements. Its ads in Korea are less aggressive and include more comparison.[25]

Choosing the Mix: Advertising/Sales Promotion or Personal Selling?

In summary then, advertising and sales promotion is preferred for organizations or brands with large resources; for frequently purchased, low-cost items with low technical aspects, requiring little demonstration and no tailoring or trade-in; for large, widely dispersed target markets; and for the early stages of the product life cycle. On the other hand, personal selling is preferred for small organizations or brands; for infrequently purchased, high-cost items with high technical aspects, requiring demonstration and tailoring and having a trade-in; for small, geographically concentrated target markets; and for manufacturers who have strong relationships with other channel members.

TABLE 14.7
Sales Promotion in 5 European Countries

Promotion	U.K.	Spain	Germany	France	Italy
In-pack premiums	■	■	●	▲	■
Multiple-purchase offers	■	■	▲	■	■
Extra product	■	■	▲	■	■
Free product	■	■	■	■	■
Mail-in offers	■	■	●	■	■
Purchase-with-purchase	■	■	●	■	■
Cross-promotions	■	■	●	■	■
Contests	■	■	▲	■	■
Self-liquidating premiums	■	■	■	■	■
Sweepstakes	▲	▲	●	▲	▲
Money-off coupons	■	■	●	■	▲
Next-purchase coupons	■	■	●	■	▲
Cash rebates	■	■	▲	■	●
In-store demos	■	■	■	■	■

■ Permitted   ● Not permitted   ▲ May be permitted

Source: Adapted from G. E. and M. A. Belch, *Introduction to Advertising and Promotion*, 2d ed. (Irwin, 1993), Exhibit 22–24, p. 770.

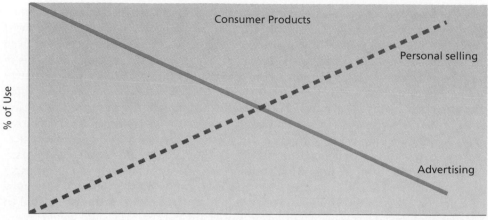

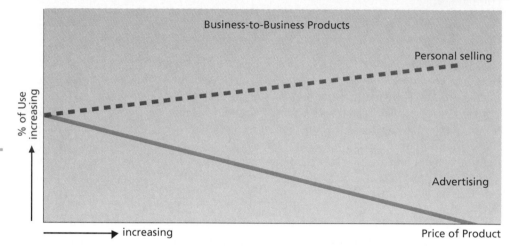

FIGURE 14.9
Typical Balance of
Advertising and Personal
Selling with Consumer
and Business-to-Business
Products

Because the set of characteristics associated with advertising/sales promotion dominance are more often found in consumer goods, consumer goods tend to rely more heavily on these promotional tools than do business-to-business products. Figure 14.9 illustrates, however, that even for consumer goods, personal selling begins to dominate as the cost of the product increases.

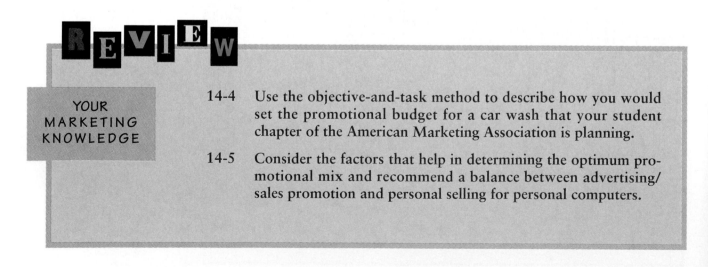

REVIEW

YOUR
MARKETING
KNOWLEDGE

14-4   Use the objective-and-task method to describe how you would set the promotional budget for a car wash that your student chapter of the American Marketing Association is planning.

14-5   Consider the factors that help in determining the optimum promotional mix and recommend a balance between advertising/sales promotion and personal selling for personal computers.

An effective promotional campaign requires the creative application of the concepts in this chapter and a detailed application of the procedures for mass and interpersonal communication discussed in the next two chapters. Thus, systematic planning is required. The steps involved are:

1. Analyze the situation facing the organization or brand.
2. Establish objectives.
3. Determine the budget.
4. Manage the specific programs for selling or advertising.
5. Measure effectiveness, evaluation, and follow-up.

The whole process is iterative and requires considerable skill from promotional managers and their staffs. The next two chapters discuss these issues in detail.

PERSONAL COMPUTER EXERCISE

Using integrated market communications to meet the company's well-defined promotional goals is the cornerstone of communications strategy. This PC Exercise asks you to develop a promotional mix for a product that sells in both consumer and business-to-business markets.

KEY POINTS

■ Effective marketing requires skillful communication between buyers and sellers. This communication is a key function of marketing activity. The marketing techniques used to communicate with potential customers are called promotion techniques.

■ Advertising, sales promotion, publicity/public relations, and personal selling all play important roles in promoting products and services.

■ Integrated marketing communication (IMC) requires that a marketer carefully plan so that all components of a promotional mix are integrated (present the same basic message) and represent a response to the target market's need for information.

■ Four major theoretical models explain consumer response to promotional activity: AIDA, the hierarchy of effects, the information-processing model, and the innovation adoption model.

■ Competing views of response suggest that consumers pass unidirectionally through a standard learning hierarchy only in the case of high-involvement products and services.

■ Good promotional objectives must include a designated target market; a statement of exactly what is to be accomplished; a goal stated in quantifiable terms; and a designated time period.

■ Promotional costs vary from industry to industry. The factors affecting costs are channel involvement in promotion; overall promotional strategy; number and accessibility of customers; complexity of decision-making units; standardization of products and customer needs; customer recognition of product benefits; product line turnover; and frequency and timing of purchases.

■ Of the many approaches to determining the promotional budget, the objective-and-task method (a build-up approach) is the most logical.

■ The promotional mix is the exact combination of advertising, sales promotion, personal selling, and publicity in a promotional strategy.

■ Factors that guide marketing managers in establishing the optimal promotional mix include available resources (the firm's budget), product characteristics, target market characteristics, relationships with other channel members, the product's stage in the life cycle, company policy, and the degree of globalization.

KEY TERMS

promotion (469)
integrated marketing
  communications (IMC) (469)
advertising (470)
personal selling (470)
sales promotion (470)
publicity/public relations (470)
promotional mix (470)
source (471)
receiver (471)
encoding (472)
channel (472)
personal channels (472)
nonpersonal channels (472)
decoding (472)
noise (475)
communication-promotion
  paradox (476)
AIDA (478)

hierarchy-of-effects model (479)
innovation adoption model (479)
information-processing model (480)
standard learning hierarchy (481)
low-involvement hierarchy (481)
dissonance/attribution model (482)
DAGMAR (483)
push strategy (493)
pull strategy (493)

ISSUES FOR DISCUSSION

1. What are the most fragile parts of the communication process? Why?

2. In what ways, besides purchase, does a customer give feedback to a retail salesperson while deciding to buy a new automobile?

3. What forms might noise take in the communication process between the purchasing agent for a business-to-business firm and his or her suppliers?

4. Consider your decision to attend the college or university in which you are enrolled. Identify all the communications you received that related to that purchase decision. What role in the AIDA model did each communication play? How could a marketer have communicated better with you?

5. Describe a recent purchase for which your behavior more closely paralleled one of the alternative response hierarchies rather than the standard learning hierarchy.

6. Why do marketers of bar soap spend more of each sales dollar on promotion than do appliance marketers such as Westinghouse?

7. Using recent newspapers or magazines, identify an example of publicity for a product that was probably initiated by the marketer and one that was probably beyond the marketer's control. Compare and contrast the value of each to the firm involved.

8. Why is it so difficult to set a budget for promotion?

9. "To get effective push, one must also pull." Do you agree with this statement? Give an example that supports your position.

10. What general mix of advertising/sales promotion and personal selling would you use for each of the following products? Assume you have a large budget. In each case, give reasons for your answer.
  (a) Birth control pills
  (b) Personal computers for business
  (c) Personal computers for home
  (d) Candy bars
  (e) Stereos

CASE APPLICATION

Promoting the Post Office

With a marketing communications department, a substantial advertising budget (that includes enough money for network television spots), and a new promotional campaign directly targeted at reaching business-to-business customers, you might think the organization involved was pretty sophisticated when it comes to the promotional component of the marketing mix. You'd be right. You might, however, be surprised to learn that the organization is the U.S. Postal Service, a government agency generally known in the past for its red tape, inefficiency, and bureaucracy.

Things have really changed around the Post Office! The changes could be attributed to a stated commitment of Postmaster General Marvin T. Runyon to decrease bureaucracy and improve customers' satisfaction. Realistically, however, the significant competition the post office has faced in recent years from such noteworthy opponents as Federal Express and UPS has clearly been instrumental in sparking the postal system's newfound interest in meeting consumers' needs and desires.

The post office's commitment to change goes beyond its efforts to communicate that it's trying to please. In recent years, new products and services have provided the foundation for the system's marketing efforts. In the area of consumer goods, for example, the Post Office engaged in some highly public marketing research to decide whether a young, thin Elvis or a more stately version would most please stamp buyers. Recognizing that Elvis is indeed a hot property, the organization has joined forces with the Presley estate to license more than 100 products bearing the new stamp's likeness.

It may, however, be in its efforts toward business-to-business consumers that the U.S. Post Office has really challenged the competition. With 50 Business Centers currently open and another 80 to 100 planned, the organization is working hard to meet the needs of the business-to-business consumers in the marketplace. The Business Centers offer services to help small- and medium-volume mailers get the best out of their business by "finding out how to improve their outgoing and incoming mail for price and efficiency."

With all these new products and services positioned to satisfy consumers' wants and needs, it is easy to see why marketing communications are so important for the Post Office. Communicating the organization's ability to satisfy those wants and needs is critical to the success of the Post Office's overall marketing strategy.

The postal system has used advertising, sales promotion, publicity, and personal selling to communicate with its target customers. Advertising, on both broadcast media (radio and television) and in print (newspapers and magazines), has compared the Post Office's speed and efficiency to the competition for overnight delivery, encouraged careful package wrapping, and promoted holiday mailing. The campaign designed to accomplish this last task was a knock-off of the Post Office's traditional advertising jingle, "We deliver for you." For the 1992 holiday season the slogan became, "We deliver for Yule."

Publicity surrounding the Presley stamp was significant, with the Post Office working diligently to control how the media reported items, to show the system in as favorable a light as possible. To increase the potential for publicity, the stamp was released for sale to post offices nationwide on January 8, 1993, the anniversary of Presley's 58th birthday.

Personal selling is also an integral part of the postal service's promotional efforts, especially for its business-to-business customers. The organization is working individually with clients such as the envelope industry to make sure that the products produced by that industry meet postal regulations and thus the needs of other firms and industries that buy envelopes. Similar efforts are being planned in collaboration with software firms and data base marketers who deal with preparation of address labels and mailing.

Questions

1. Using the hierarchy-of-effects model, suggest some reasonable objectives for the Post Office to promote its new Business Centers.
2. For the average ultimate consumer, do stamps appear to be a product for which a standard learning hierarchy or an alternative response hierarchy would apply? Why?
3. Cite factors that would help the Post Office determine the appropriate promotional balance between advertising/sales promotion and personal selling for its Business Center services. Which of the two types of promotion would you emphasize? Why?

Identify Your Communications Strategy

The principle that effective marketing requires skillful communication between buyers and sellers applies to your job search: To market yourself effectively you need to communicate skillfully with your target organizations.

It is easy to overlook communications between organizations and your school, and those between your target organizations and alumni working in those organizations. More easily recognized are communications between you and your target organizations via letters and informational meetings.

How can you maximize your communications network with your target organizations? You need to know what the members of your network have communicated to each of your target organizations. What message was sent, to whom was it delivered, and how was it received? For example, the strongest school-to-target-organization connection might be that the organization is completely sold on the quality of talent on the campus and has regularly conducted on-campus screening interviews. On the other hand, the weakest school-to-target-organization connection might be that the organization does not even post jobs on campus, much less come on site to conduct interviews. You also need to know the resources of your target organization. For example, the strongest school-to-alumni connection might be that several highly placed alumni are well aware of the quality of talent at your school and are receptive to "showcasing" individual students to their organizations. Of course, the weakest connection would be the absence of alumni in the target organization.

Where there are good sources of contacts with target organizations, you need to use them skillfully. The organizations most committed to your school will probably conduct group programs on campus (i.e., deliver presentations about employment) or participate in job fairs (i.e., provide a representative to answer questions). Attending these events gives you an opportunity to learn more about your target organization and to establish communication. If graduates of your school work at your target organizations, you usually can contact them for information: to find out about opportunities for someone with your background, to learn the best way to pursue those opportunities, and possibly to obtain introductions to suggested contacts.

Your ultimate goal is to generate employment opportunities with people in your target organizations with whom you interview. However, your objectives can vary with the situation. Sometimes your objective is merely to have someone remember you perhaps as "a person" at a group function, or to obtain information (from initial contacts with alums), or to obtain a first interview, perhaps with an employment contact.

To succeed, you must have an effective message. You need your professional "commercial" for each target organization. This commercial must be buyer-centered, letting the organization know why it should hire you. The commercial might be the same for similar target organizations. Your commercial should combine relevant highlights of your background, industry experience, and special skills. You need to send this message in all communications with your target organization, so that you can generate interest and work toward your objectives.

Questions

1. What are the sources of communications for each of the target organizations in your job search?
2. What audiences should you include in the job search and what should be your communication objectives with each?
3. What roles, if any, do advertising, sales promotion, publicity/public relations, and personal selling play in your job search?

CHapTeR

Advertising, Sales Promotion, and Publicity

Upon completing this chapter, you will be able to do the following:

■ **Understand** the role of advertising for the individual organization and for the economy.

■ **Identify** the major advertising decisions a marketing manager faces.

■ **Describe** how media decisions are made.

■ **Recognize** the role of the creative process in advertising.

■ **Discuss** how advertising effectiveness is measured.

■ **Illustrate** each of the different types of sales promotion techniques and define their roles in promotion.

■ **Explain** the nature, contribution, and role of publicity in the promotional mix.

■ **Comment** on the importance of integrating all promotional efforts into a single IMC plan.

LEARNING OBJECTIVES

Marketing Profile

Advertising Agencies: Integrating Marketing Communications

Advertising agencies have long been a strength behind the major promotions worldwide of products and services, especially consumer goods. Well-known agencies such as Leo Burnett and DDB Needham Worldwide have gained fame by planning and executing the advertising for equally well-known clients such as United Airlines and Volkswagen. But the advertising industry is changing. The media have traditionally compensated agencies for the ad space they purchase for their clients. Because of this ad agencies have traditionally focused their clients' advertising dollars on those media. But newspapers, magazines, radio, and especially network television also reached large audiences, so it made sense for these media to be the focus of agency efforts. This approach was safe in 1979 when 90 percent of the television audience was watching network TV. Today, however, that figure has dropped to only 60 percent. Television viewers have many alternatives to network TV including cable, public, and pay-per-view.

In the early 1990s, advertising budgets of even the largest consumer goods manufacturers plummeted. In 1991, ad spending declined for the first time in 30 years. The drop was followed by an even larger decline in 1992. Although ad spending increased 5.2 percent in 1993, companies are spending less of their promotional budgets on advertising, which means lower revenues for advertising agencies.

Advertising agencies are no longer the most important sources of market research information for their clients. Today, technological developments such as check-out scanners make it possible for companies to receive valuable information about consumer behavior from many sources. In addition, loyalty to the ad agency has decreased. Reasons include poor performance and the capacity of other organizations to provide superior results. In addition, there is a shift in the breakdown of promotional components that are used. In 1981, advertisements accounted for 43 percent of expenditures and trade and consumer promotions accounted for 57 percent. In 1993, the balance was 27 percent on advertising and 73 percent on trade and consumer promotions.

The future for advertising agencies is not necessarily bleak. Advertising agencies can play a central role in organizing and carrying out the integrated marketing communications (IMC) of their clients. The commitment to IMC has created opportunities for advertising agencies to expand beyond their historic focus on traditional media advertising. Agencies now play a pivotal role in coordinating all of a client's promotional efforts—TV ads, direct mail, special events, billboards, even publicity, public relations, and sales promotion. A single product or company image can be created and executed through all components of the promotional mix.

Johnson & Johnson hired the advertising agency, Lintas: USA, to plan and carry out an integrated strategy for Acuvue, the firm's disposable contact lenses. The IMC plan included simultaneous promotion to ophthalmologists and patients. Patients received messages on television, radio, and in magazines. The physicians were targeted with a direct-mail campaign and offered promotional allowances to set up office open houses where patients could gain personal information.

In 1993, Coca-Cola adopted a fully integrated campaign with the promotional theme "Always Coca-Cola." In addition to advertising, the firm launched a mail-in sweepstakes that would give away one million cases of Coca-Cola Classic. All the promotional tools implemented by the ad agency, McCann-Erickson, used the theme "Always Coca-Cola."

As evidence that an ad agency can do a better job, DDB Needham offers a program called "Total Creativity Guaranteed Results." The program guarantees the results of the agency's integrated marketing efforts by promising to rebate a substantial amount of its fee if sales do not improve. Conversely, if the program exceeds expectations, the client agrees to pay the agency a bonus.

Some clients prefer a traditional approach. Miller Lite uses Leo Burnett for its advertising; public relations, sales promotion, and direct marketing are handled by others. A spokesperson for Miller states, "We go to specialists. Burnett is the right agency for our advertising but not for sales promotion."

Despite the holdouts, IMC is the wave of the future. Advertising agencies that successfully integrate marketing communication efforts for their clients should thrive.

romotional tools directed at a mass audience include advertising, sales promotion, and publicity. Unlike personal selling, these promotion tools reach very large numbers of people at one time. These forms of promotion can be extremely effective in informing, persuading, and reminding consumers.

Most of this chapter discusses advertising, one of the two promotional tools firms use most. (Personal selling is the other.) We explore advertising decision making and the role of advertising in organizations and in the economy. We also consider some important advertisers and the role of advertising agencies.

We then discuss sales promotion and publicity. The use of these promotional tools, alone and in conjunction with a firm's advertising and personal selling efforts, remains an important component of promotion.

ADVERTISING

Advertising is any paid form of nonpersonal presentation and promotion of ideas, goods, or services by an identified sponsor. Advertising is the most visible marketing activity. Consequently, advertising and promotion, or even more broadly, advertising and marketing, are often viewed as synonymous. Despite the fact that marketing involves much more than advertising, the attention given to advertising is enormous. Advertising does play a significant role in many organizations and in the economy as a whole. Advertising decisions can be challenging, and advertising is usually an expensive budget item for a firm. It is often fodder for much controversy in our society.

Advertising is a highly visible part of marketing at least in part because companies regularly spend enormous amounts of money on it. In 1993, U.S. consumers were the targets of advertising messages whose total cost equalled an expenditure of more than $6 per week per person![1] The value of advertising expenditures in 1993 stood at $138 billion.[2] By the year 2000, U.S. advertising expenditures are predicted to stand at $350 billion.

Advertising expenditures in the United States represent almost 50 percent more per capita than any other nation in the world.[3] But advertising is a growth industry throughout the world. Global advertising expenditures (excluding that by the United States) rose from $55 billion in 1980 to $182 billion in 1993.[4] This figure is predicted to reach $450 billion by the year 2000.

The largest advertisers account for a disproportionate share of total advertising volume. Table 15.1 identifies the 25 leading U.S. advertisers in 1992, accounting for 15 percent of the advertising expenditures that year. As you might expect, the big names in consumer goods marketing lead the list of top advertisers: Procter & Gamble, Philip Morris, General Motors, Sears, Pepsi. Spending billions of dollars annually to reinforce their products and brand names has made these companies household names.

Advertising allows a company to control and direct its message. Advertising can also create images and symbolic appeals for products and services. It can be effective when other parts of the marketing effort are not successful. However, advertising is not right for every product or service. It is expensive, can lack credibility, and is easy to ignore.[5] Before planning an advertising campaign, marketing managers should consider several issues. Advertising is appropriate if

- the product or service possesses unique, salient attributes or "hidden qualities" important to prospects.
- consumers purchase the product or service on the basis of powerful, emotional motives.
- favorable primary demand exists for the product or service.
- there is a large potential market.

Rank 1992	Rank 1991	Advertiser, headquarters	Total U.S. ad spending 1992	Total U.S. ad spending 1991	% chg
1	1	Procter & Gamble Co., Cincinnati	$2,165.6	$2,150.0	0.7
2	2	Philip Morris Cos., New York	2,024.1	2,071.3	−2.3
3	3	General Motors Corp., Detroit	1,333.6	1,476.8	−9.7
4	4	Sears, Roebuck & Co., Chicago	1,204.6	1,195.6	0.8
5	5	Pepsico, Purchase, NY	928.6	903.9	2.7
6	9	Ford Motor Co., Dearborn, MI	794.5	689.7	15.2
7	11	Warner-Lambert Co., Morris Plains, NJ	757.5	657.0	15.3
8	21	Chrysler Corp., Highland Park, MI	756.6	547.1	38.3
9	8	McDonald's Corp., Oak Brook, IL	743.6	695.7	6.9
10	14	Nestle SA, Vevey, Switzerland	733.4	643.4	14.0
11	10	Eastman Kodak Co., Rochester, NY	686.0	666.0	3.0
12	6	Grand Metropolitan, London	680.2	746.5	−8.9
13	16	Unilever NV, London/Rotterdam	672.8	593.7	13.3
14	7	Johnson & Johnson, New Brunswick, NJ	659.6	733.2	−10.0
15	13	Toyota Motor Corp., Toyota City, Japan	648.9	649.0	−0.0
16	15	Time Warner, New York	637.9	617.1	3.4
17	17	Kellogg Co., Battle Creek, MI	630.3	578.0	9.1
18	12	AT&T Co., New York	623.7	649.3	−4.0
19	20	General Mills, Minneapolis	571.2	555.7	2.8
20	22	Anheuser-Busch Cos., St. Louis	555.8	510.8	8.8
21	18	Kmart Corp., Troy, MI	551.1	561.9	−1.9
22	30	JCPenney Co., Dallas	537.4	364.0	47.6
23	24	American Home Products Corp., New York	531.6	449.2	18.3
24	23	Walt Disney Co., Burbank, CA	524.6	495.0	6.0
25	25	Sony Corp., Tokyo	507.9	445.8	13.9

Source: *Advertising Age*, January 3, 1994, p. 14.

**TABLE 15.1
Twenty-five Leading
Advertisers in 1992
(in millions)**

- the company is not competing against products and services that already have very strong brand loyalty.
- economic conditions are favorable for this type of product or service.
- the organization is financially able and willing to spend the amount of money required.
- the organization possesses sufficient marketing expertise to market the product or service successfully.

If the marketing manager answers affirmatively to each of these criteria, advertising should become a part of the promotional mix for the product or service.

ADVERTISING DECISIONS

Once the marketing manager has determined that advertising should become a part of the promotional mix, a number of decisions regarding advertising must be made. These include setting advertising objectives, determining ad type, establishing the advertising budget, selecting the media, and choosing a creative approach. In the following sections, we will consider each of these decisions.

Setting Advertising Objectives

In Chapter 14 we discussed the importance of setting proper objectives for promotional activity. We can apply the same principles to setting objectives for advertising. Objective-setting requires very careful and accurate measurement both before and after the campaign. Advertisers who fail to do this will have only an intuitive feeling about the effectiveness of their campaigns. Research indicates that, unfortunately, many organizations do not set such objectives. One study examined the extent to which business-to-business marketers used advertising objectives that met the four DAGMAR criteria (discussed in Chapter 14). The study's authors concluded, "Advertising practitioners have only partially adopted the concepts and standards of objective setting and evaluation set forth over 25 years ago."[6]

The DAGMAR model provides criteria for setting objectives, and suggests that advertising objectives be built on the response hierarchy concept. Some marketers believe the sequence of stages in the response hierarchies can be reversed, with behavior (usually sales) preceding attitude change. Even those marketers who challenge the traditional response hierarchy for advertising and promotion objectives tend to agree that good objectives are specific and measurable.

Setting reasonable advertising objectives is part of the art of marketing. The first time a manager sets objectives, those objectives will probably represent an educated guess, despite the logical analysis that may have gone into the choice. As managers gain experience in setting objectives and observing the actual results of particular advertising programs, they will be equipped to set more realistic objectives as standards or norms of performance are developed.

Determining Ad Type

Advertising objectives lead directly to determining the types of ads that will be presented. In this section, we will consider the various orientations an advertisement can take.

Primary or selective demand. Ads directed toward primary demand are intended to affect the demand for a whole product category and not simply a specific brand. The American Dairy Association, for example, uses advertising to increase milk consumption. Selective-demand-oriented ads are intended to affect the demand for a specific brand. For example, Pepsi informs us, "Be Young. Have Fun. Drink Pepsi." The ad is attempting to build demand for Pepsi over other soft drinks, particularly Coca-Cola.

Direct or indirect action. Direct action ads are intended to cause the prospective consumer to purchase the product right away. Almost all direct-mail offers fit into this category. An advertisement for BMG Classical Music Service, focusing on incentives to join the club, is an example of a direct action ad. Indirect actions ads, on the other hand, are intended to attract attention, build awareness, or create favorable attitudes. Such ads are directed at levels below action in the response hierarchy. A Volvo advertisement that emphasizes the safety of its cars is an example of such an ad.

Consumer, business-to-business, or trade. Consumer ads are directed at end users in households. For example, Du Pont advertises its Rain Dance car wax to the readers of *Car and Driver* magazine. Business-to-business ads are directed at business consumers and at those who influence organizational purchases. For this purpose, Du Pont advertises Rain Dance to corporate car fleet managers in *Fleet Management* magazine. Trade ads are directed at wholesalers and retailers in the channel of distribution. Here, Du Pont advertises Rain Dance to retailers in *Discount Merchandiser* magazine, emphasizing advertising support, coupon availability, and a special trade price.

This ad is an example of a direct-action advertisement.

In this example of institutional advertising, Chevron promotes its sensitivity to the environment.

Sponsored by members of a group at the same level in a channel, this ad is a horizontal cooperative ad.

Product or institutional.   Product advertising is intended to promote a specific product or service and can be carried out by manufacturers or channel members. Chevron advertises its motor oil as reducing oil consumption. Institutional (or corporate) advertising is intended to build an overall favorable image about the organization and its product; it is not intended to sell specific products. Chevron advertises its sensitivity to the environment by explaining how it protects wildlife.

Vertical cooperative or horizontal cooperative.   Vertical cooperative advertising is undertaken by a wholesaler or retailer but is partially paid for by a manufacturer. The amount of support is usually based on sales levels. A camera store, for example, might get financial support from Nikon to run newspaper ads featuring Nikon cameras. Manufacturers consider this sort of advertising to be a type of sales promotion. Horizontal cooperative advertising is done by members of a group at the same level in a channel by pooling resources to sponsor ads. For example, the Florida Tomato Committee sponsors ads encouraging consumers to choose tomatoes grown in that state.

Commercial or public service.   With commercial ads, production and media are paid for by the sponsors. The advertiser may not be a business but the ad is paid for by its sponsors to facilitate an exchange between the organization and consumers. A nonprofit hospital might advertise its comfortable birthing rooms in an effort to attract expectant parents. In contrast, public service ads are paid for by the Advertising Council, television and radio stations, and other organizations. The advertisements are often intended to bring about behavioral changes. The Environmental Defense Fund, the March of Dimes, and the American Cancer Society are all recipients of public service ads (or announcements), often known as PSAs.

Choosing the ad type.   A single advertisement is likely to feature a variety of the orientations just described. Kellogg's might, for example, run an ad for Low-Fat Granola directed toward selective demand and direct action among final consumers. Advertisers choose the ad types they will feature by analyzing their objectives and then determining which types of ads are needed to accomplish those objectives. For example, Procter & Gamble has the following objectives: to increase awareness of Folger's coffee from 11 percent to 18 percent among young adults 18 to 25 years old in New York state during 1994. To meet these, it would appear to require a selective-demand, direct-action, consumer ad. It would probably also be a commercial, product ad.

Establishing the Advertising Budget

We have examined a number of approaches for determining the promotional budget for a product or service. These methods can also be used to plan an advertising budget. The objective-and-task approach is probably the best compromise between an ideal and a pragmatic procedure. Unfortunately, marketers often use the percentage-of-sales, competitive parity, and "all-one-can-afford" methods, because of the difficulty and expense of estimating the required response of sales or some communications measure of advertising.

When determining how much to spend on advertising, it is important for managers to recognize that advertising is an investment, not an expense. Managers who view advertising as an expense do not see the relationship between advertising and achieving the company's objectives (sales, for example). Viewing advertising as an expense can lead to cutbacks in hard times—at precisely the moment advertising is needed most. In 1993, the Saturn Corporation faced a decline in sales. At that time General Motors substantially increased the advertising budget for Saturn. The 1994

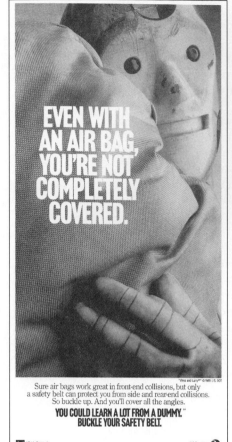

These are examples of public service ads paid for by the Advertising Council.

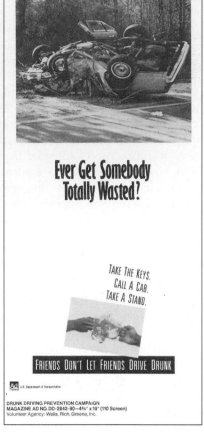

advertising budget was predicted to be $110–$120 million, as compared to $100 million in 1992. Similarly, in the wake of riots in 1992, fires in 1993, and the earthquake in 1994, the city of Los Angeles has stepped up its advertising. The goal is to regain the confidence of both domestic and international tourists.[7]

Selecting the Media

If the marketing manager is using the objective-and-task approach to budget determination, media selection will occur prior to or in conjunction with establishing the budget. In this case, the amount to spend can only be determined after a decision about what media to advertise in, how often to advertise in each medium, and what the costs will be.

Media decisions involve more than just choosing where to advertise. A firm's **media plan** for a product or service involves specifying the following:

- the **media types** to be used—Will the product be advertised on television, radio, in magazines, newspapers, by direct mail, or outdoors?
- the **media vehicles** to be used—What television station and program, what radio station and program, what specific magazines and issues will be involved?
- the **number of inserts**—How many specific ads will appear in each media vehicle?

Before considering the factors that influence good media planning, we must acknowledge some constraints that influence media decisions.

The size of the advertising budget influences both vehicle selection and the number of insertions. Even when the objective-and-task method of budgeting is used, a firm cannot spend more money than it has. A company might, for example, decide that network television is the best medium for reaching its target market. Because this form of media is very expensive, however, its use may not be feasible.

The concepts of reach and frequency are also important constraints affecting choice of media and vehicle. **Reach** refers to the total number of persons in the target market who are exposed to a particular ad. An advertisement for Michelin Tires run on the news magazine show *60 Minutes* might reach one million people. **Frequency** is the average number of times those who are reached in the target market are exposed. If Michelin places its tire ad on *60 Minutes* every week for a month, the regular audience for the show will be exposed four times. Given a fixed budget, both reach and frequency cannot be increased. Hence Michelin could choose to advertise one week on *60 Minutes*, another week on *PrimeTime Live*, a third week on *Nightline*, and a fourth week on *The Tonight Show*. This would increase reach because the ad would be seen by different audiences from each show. Alternatively, by advertising for four consecutive weeks on *60 Minutes*, frequency is increased but not reach.

A media planner on a fixed budget must decide whether reach or frequency is more important. Is it better to expose more people fewer times or fewer people more times? The answer affects media choice. For example, if reach is the primary goal, an advertiser will be most interested in people not previously exposed to the company's ad. The total number of people exposed just once to an ad is **unduplicated reach.** Such companies use more diverse media vehicles than those advertisers whose primary objective is frequency. If Michelin, in the earlier example, advertises on *Nightline* and *The Tonight Show*, it is likely to increase its unduplicated reach. These two shows attract diverse audiences and are shown at the same time in many markets. To increase frequency, an advertiser wishes to reach the same people more than once. When someone views an ad for a second time, this is known as **duplicated reach.** If Michelin advertises on two news programs such as *60 Minutes* and *PrimeTime Live*, some overlap is likely since the shows may attract many of the same viewers.

Figure 15.1 shows the concepts of reach and frequency by illustrating duplicated and unduplicated reach for two television shows. The more similar two TV programs are, the greater the overlap and duplicated reach. This situation will increase frequency. The less similar two TV programs are, the less overlap and the greater the unduplicated reach. Since duplicated reach increases frequency, a planner who wishes to emphasize frequency would opt for a situation where duplicated reach was great. Unduplicated reach would appeal to a planner more interested in reach than frequency.

The creative strategy a firm chooses can also constrain its choice of media. A scratch-and-sniff approach to introducing a new perfume limits the advertiser to print media. An advertisement that emphasizes the high-brow sophistication of BMW automobiles is not likely to be effective in *Modern Romance* magazine.

Having examined these constraints, we now turn to the factors at the heart of good media decisions. These are: characteristics of the product to be advertised, characteristics of the target market, characteristics of media types, and characteristics of media vehicles. Product characteristics and target market characteristics have been considered previously in this text so let us turn our attention to the last two factors.

Characteristics of media types.   The six major media types include television, radio, newspapers, magazines, outdoor (such as billboards), and direct mail. These media types can be characterized as **high involvement** or **low involvement,** depending on the amount of effort a receiver must exert to get the message. Print media, for example,

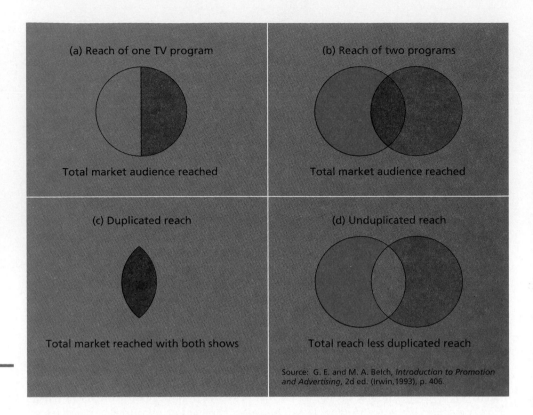

(a) Reach of one TV program

Total market audience reached

(b) Reach of two programs

Total market audience reached

(c) Duplicated reach

Total market reached with both shows

(d) Unduplicated reach

Total reach less duplicated reach

Source: G. E. and M. A. Belch, *Introduction to Promotion and Advertising*, 2d ed. (Irwin, 1993), p. 406.

FIGURE 15.1
Reach and Frequency

are high involvement because the target must actively work to get the message by turning the pages and reading. Direct mail can also be categorized as a high-involvement medium. Broadcast media (television and radio), on the other hand, are low-involvement media. Advertising messages that come to you through these vehicles require little, if any, effort. In fact, you must actively work not to get the message by turning off the radio or television. Outdoor advertising does not fall clearly into one of the two categories of involvement. While it does require some attention and effort from the receiver, the amount of active work required to get the message is typically minimal.

Whether a media type is high or low involvement influences when it might be the appropriate choice for an advertising campaign. Because low-involvement media expose consumers to an advertisement without their having to work to get the message, they are often ideal for increasing brand-name recognition. High levels of frequency through low-involvement media can be very effective in building brand name and product awareness. On the other hand, because high-involvement media require consumers to think and process information, they are a better choice when an advertiser is attempting to explain a product and its benefits to the target market. Table 15.2 lists the pros and cons of each media type.

Once the media planner understands the advantages and disadvantages of various media, it is possible to evaluate each medium on the basis of characteristics important to choice for a particular product or service. Important criteria to consider are:

- *intrusiveness*—the extent that the consumer cannot avoid being confronted with ads in that media.
- *product demonstration*—the extent that the use of the product being advertised can be shown.

Media	Advantages	Disadvantages
Television	Mass coverage High reach Impact of sight, sound, and motion High prestige Low cost per exposure Attention-getting Favorable image	Low selectivity Short message life High absolute cost High production costs Clutter
Radio	Local coverage Low cost High frequency Flexible Low production costs Well-segmented audiences	Audio only Clutter Low attention-getting Fleeting message
Magazines	Segmentation potential Quality reproduction High information content Longevity Multiple readers	Long lead time for ad placement Visual only Lack of flexibility
Newspapers	High coverage Low cost Short lead time for placing ads Ads can be placed in interest sections Timely (current ads) Reader controls exposure Can be used for coupons	Short life Clutter Low attention-getting capabilities Poor reproduction quality Selective reader exposure
Outdoor	Location specific High repetition Easily noticed	Short exposure time requires short ad Poor image Local restrictions
Direct mail	High selectivity Reader controls exposure High information content Opportunities for repeat exposures	High cost/contact Poor image (junk mail) Clutter

Source: Adapted from G. Belch and M. Belch, *Introduction to Advertising and Promotion*, 2d ed., (Irwin, 1993), p. 418.

TABLE 15.2
Media Advantages and Disadvantages

- *package identification*—the extent that the package, as it is available in the store, can be indicated to the audience.
- *short-term action*—the ability of ads in media types to generate a fairly immediate consumer response.
- *cost*—the expense of insertion relative to audience size.
- *economy of production costs*—the cost of preparing an advertisement for use in a media type.
- *coupon vehicle*—the ability to distribute coupons to consumers via the media.
- *major market penetration*—the ability of the media to reach the largest urban areas.
- *flexibility*—the ability to use media types for regional markets, test markets, seasonal brands, and major markets only.

Table 15.3 shows the results of considering each media type according to these nine criteria. This type of analysis helps the advertiser to select the best vehicle type. For example, assume you must develop a media plan for a product that (1) needs to

Characteristics	Broadcast		Print/Indoor/Outdoor		
	Television	Radio	Magazine	Newspaper	Outdoor
Intrusiveness	Very high	High	Low	Low	Very low
Product demonstration	Excellent	Poor	Fair	Fair	Poor
Package identification	Good	Poor	Excellent	Good	Good
Short-term action	Good	Excellent	Fair	Excellent	Fair
Cost per audience exposure	Good	Excellent	Fair	Good	Fair
Production cost, economy	Poor	Excellent	Fair	Fair	Poor
Coupon Vehicle	—	—	Good/exc.	Good	—
Major market penetration	Excellent	Excellent	Fair	Excellent	Good
Flexibility					
i. Regional buys	Good	Good	Fair	Excellent	Good
ii. Major markets	Excellent	Excellent	Poor	Excellent	Good
iii. Use of test cities	Excellent	Excellent	Poor	Excellent	Good

TABLE 15.3
Comparative Ratings for Media Selection

be demonstrated to be effectively sold, (2) needs a strong package identification because it will be purchased in a self-serve fashion, and (3) will be marketed only in major markets. Which medium seems appropriate for this product? The data in Table 15.3 suggest that television is the best choice.

Characteristics of media vehicles.   Once advertisers decide on the type or types of media, they must choose vehicles within the various types. A decision to use television is well and good but will it be network, cable, or local spot advertising? Which shows should be chosen? These decisions are influenced by the size of the vehicle audience, the size of the target audience, and the cost.

Vehicle audience and target audience are not the same. The former refers to the actual number of people exposed to a particular vehicle. What is the circulation of The *New York Times*, for example? Such information is usually available from the medium itself or from syndicated research services. These figures can be misleading. For example, more than one person is likely to read a single copy of a newspaper. Likewise, a measure of the number of television sets turned to a particular show does not tell the advertiser the number of people watching the show. Because not everyone in a vehicle audience is a member of the target market for a given product or service, the target audience will be smaller than the vehicle audience. Because the advertiser is really interested in the target market, the concept of target audience is more important than vehicle audience. It is, unfortunately, more difficult to obtain or calculate.

Knowing the vehicle's target market audience is not good enough. We must also consider the cost of reaching these audiences. Media planners generally compare potential vehicle choices using **cost per thousand (CPM)**, the cost of reaching a thousand people. Figures for CPM may be quoted for the total vehicle audience or for the target audience, but target audience CPM is a more meaningful figure. A media planner should choose vehicles that offer the lowest target audience CPM.

Vehicle and target audience figures, however difficult to determine, show only a portion of the picture for any medium. Consider that such figures offer measures only of exposure. But exposure does not ensure attention, interest, desire, or action—higher-order objectives in the response hierarchy.

The media planner is also faced with deciding how to schedule the ads in a particular vehicle once that vehicle has been selected. This decision depends on factors such as the seasonal nature of the product and competitive actions. Toy manufacturers, for example, are likely to concentrate their ads during the Christmas shopping season, whereas a product that has no seasonal fluctuations in sales would generally be advertised evenly throughout the year.

At this point you have seen that media selection is a complex process. This complexity has given rise to many computer models that attempt to help marketers make their media decisions. The models vary greatly, but, in general, follow the type of process outlined here. Advertisers constantly monitor the cost/benefit of alternative media types and media vehicles within media types.

Choosing a Creative Approach

Up to this point, advertising decision making has been described as a series of fairly scientific steps. First, objectives are determined; from the objectives come the type of ad to be used; budget determination and media selection proceed. Choosing the message and type of presentation an advertisement will have, however, requires creativity that cannot be found in a scientific formula. Nevertheless, decisions regarding an ad's creative approach are very important—the effectiveness of a whole campaign often depends on the specific message and presentation.

Selecting the appeal. The first step in choosing a creative approach is to decide on an advertising appeal. The **advertising appeal** refers to the basis or approach used in the advertisement to attract the attention or interest of consumers and/or to influence their feelings toward the product, service, or cause.[8]

The correct appeal results from a combination of analytical thinking based on a clear understanding of the brand situation and a liberal use of creativity and imagination. The appeal should be consistent with both the company and its advertising objectives. It must also be appropriate for the target audience, the product itself, and the media vehicle in which it will appear. Finally, the appeal must take account of competitive activity. Choosing an appropriate appeal can be especially challenging for the advertiser who is working to develop campaigns across the globe. The "Spotlight on Global Marketing: Pushing Products in Eastern Europe: But Will They Buy It in Poland?" describes the challenges advertisers face in Eastern Europe.

There are many types of advertising appeals:[9]

- *Informational/rational.* This appeal focuses on the consumer's practical, functional, or utilitarian need for the product or service. It emphasizes features of a product or service and/or the benefits or reasons for owning or using a particular brand. An ad for a Chevrolet Cavalier that emphasizes the car's practicality and good gas mileage offers an example of this type of appeal.

- *Emotional.* These appeals relate to the consumer's social and/or psychological need for purchasing a product or service. Such ads create a mood. The ad for Mass Mutual illustrates this type of appeal in life insurance.

- *Repeat assertion.* This is a hard-sell technique. Statements are made and repeated without specific evidence or explanations. A public service announcement emphasizing "Just Say No" is an example of a repeat assertion. Nonprescription drugs often use this style.

- *Command.* This approach presents the message in the form of an order. "Uncle Sam Wants You" and "Give to the United Way" are two well-known illustrations of this type of appeal.

Emotional appeals, like this one, appeal to the consumer's psychological needs for purchasing a product or service.

This ad combines the rational and emotional approaches. It appeals to the consumer's need for caring, yet presents factual information about the services the advertiser offers.

- *Symbolic association.* This links the product to a person, music, or a situation that target customers are likely to view positively. The product or service and the symbol become tightly connected in the consumer's mind. The Jolly Green Giant or the Rock of Prudential are examples.

- *Imitation.* In this approach, situations or people are offered for the prospective consumer to imitate. The use of famous people in ads is a common example of this appeal type.

These appeals are not mutually exclusive. Advertisers can and often do use a combination of appeals in a single advertisement. Even appeals as seemingly dichotomous as rational and emotional can be combined in a single ad.

Determining execution.   Once the advertising appeal has been determined, the best way to carry it out must be decided. **Execution** refers to the manner or way in which a particular appeal is turned into an advertising message that is presented to the consumer.[11]

An ad's execution may take the form of a direct comparison. In this case the company's product or service is evaluated against competitive offerings. This approach has become increasingly popular in recent years as the Federal Trade Commission has encouraged advertisers to consider it. A comparative ad typically follows a rational appeal, providing the consumer with factual information on which to base a decision.

The use of humor, fear, and sex are common in the creative execution of an appeal. Such approaches have been found more effective in ads whose objectives are lower in the response hierarchy. In other words, that funny ad that you enjoy may get your attention or build product awareness but it is less likely to build desire or spark action (sales). This fact has led to award-winning advertisements (based on creative execution or audience appeal) being discontinued by an advertiser who found that the ad did not produce the desired results (increased sales).

Other styles of execution include slice-of-life (showing the product used in a real-life context), testimonials, demonstrations, and fantasy. Advertisers are increasingly

MARKETING *IN ACTION*

SPOTLIGHT
ON
Global
Marketing

Pushing Products in Eastern Europe: But Will They Buy It in Poland?

Advertising in the emerging market economies of Eastern Europe is a unique challenge for Procter & Gamble and other marketers bold enough to try it. Persuading a population brought up to believe that just about everything one hears on TV is a lie is a task of gargantuan proportions. A recent public opinion poll in Poland found that 37 percent of respondents agreed with the statement, "Any product that is advertised is surely poor."

Nevertheless, many marketers from around the world appear eager to enter markets that have little competition and consumers eager for goods. However, a special sensitivity is needed to inform this vast market through advertising and other forms of promotion. Some Eastern European markets appear more difficult than others. In the Czech Republic, enterprising entrepreneurs have been met with a warm reception. Czechs react positively to TV commercials that cost as little as $1,000 for a 30-second spot. Belgian Jean-Claude Van Gansen, a former jeans retailer, went to Prague five days after the Communist regime fell in 1989. He has been enormously successful with a variety of ventures including the introduction of outdoor advertising. Van Gansen introduced the country's first billboard in 1990 and now owns 35 percent of the outdoor advertising industry, which appears to be burgeoning. Procter & Gamble has also met with success in the Czech Republic by using television advertising to sell its laundry detergent brands, Vizir and Ariel. Procter & Gamble encountered a rather surprising reaction to its sales promotion tactic of distributing free samples of the detergents through the mail. The postmaster of a small town sent the Procter & Gamble staff roses to express thanks for being part of the campaign. He included the explanation, "This is the most exciting thing that's ever happened in this post office—it's a terrific experience to be part of this new market economy that's coming."

Similar positive reactions to advertising and sales promotion efforts have been experienced by Procter & Gamble and others in Hungary, where Procter & Gamble is promoting Pampers disposable diapers. Reactions in the former East Germany have also been positive. Poland, however, appears to be a more formidable challenge. Initial reaction to the advertising and sales promotion efforts for Vidal Sasson Wash & Go shampoo

was good. Wash & Go was heavily advertised on television, radio, and in newspapers. After a strong introduction, however, the shampoo fell victim to a strange word-of-mouth campaign. Consumers began whispering that the product had been adulterated in some manner and caused the user's hair to fall out. Despite lack of evidence of any truth to this rumor, sales quickly died. Polish marketing experts suggested that the incident was a result of the strong belief that advertising is suspicious. The more a product is advertised, the more certainly there must be something wrong with it. A recent radio ad in Poland began with the disclaimer, "This is truth, not advertising." Poland also appears quite sensitive to advertising in certain product categories. While ads for women's feminine hygiene products, formerly taboo, are being tolerated, the Polish parliament recently voted to ban advertising of tobacco and alcohol in the country.

Advertisers in Eastern Europe have discovered that their ads require careful testing and must be customized for the cultural characteristics of the market. In Hungary, for example, a toothpaste ad that featured a dentist was reworked to downplay the authoritarianism of the doctor. Apparently the recently liberated Hungarians are quite sensitive when it comes to authoritarian figures telling them what to do. Procter & Gamble has developed comparative ads that contrast Pampers disposable diapers with cloth diapers, the predominant choice in the market.

Despite the fact that firms are working hard to design advertising unique to the Eastern European market, advertisers are moving toward greater acceptance of global messages. Though not a new idea, global advertising may be a concept whose time has finally come. Previous attempts at developing ad campaigns that spanned international borders have met with problems due to cultural differences as well as the practical problem of coordinating a worldwide campaign. Today international advertising agencies and globe-circling brand names are common.

The day may come when firms can develop truly global marketing communications campaigns, but for now, certain parts of the world (Eastern Europe, for example) will continue to require special attention.

using what are referred to as "reality ads" to sell certain products. Reality ads use subjects such as divorce and an execution style like slice-of-life. A bank or financial planning service might, for example, focus on a woman who needs to plan for the future because she is in the midst of a divorce.[11] The use of colors, particular actors, headlines, copy layout, and even graphics play a role in the execution of the message and appeal type. Clearly, the number of execution styles, as well as appeal approaches, are limited only by the creator's imagination.

MEASURING ADVERTISING EFFECTIVENESS

While it is difficult to approach the creative component of advertising scientifically, the amount of money involved in an ad's production and the cost of the media time still require that this process be subject to research evaluation. A 30-second television commercial costs about $75,000 to produce. Ads using special effects can cost far more than that. Some advertising agencies have begun using personal computers and commercial software to produce "rough" versions of ads. This approach can save a client thousands of dollars over the traditional approach of having a production house produce several interim versions of an advertisement.[12] Despite such innovations, however, ad production is still expensive. Media time is equally expensive. A 30-second spot on the Super Bowl in 1994 cost advertisers $900,000!

Despite these costs, some advertisers argue that it is inappropriate or unnecessary to attempt to measure the effectiveness of advertising. The cost of testing, the imprecise nature of available testing methods, and the time it requires have all been cited as reasons not to test. Even determining what to test can be a problem. Finally, some advertisers believe that testing stifles the creative process.[13]

While there may be some truth to these concerns, we take the position that good advertisers put considerable effort into testing an ad's effectiveness. Though measuring advertising effectiveness is important, what constitutes a good test of effectiveness is not always clear. First and foremost, any test of effectiveness should attempt to measure the extent to which the ad succeeded in accomplishing its objectives. This seems obvious, but many times ads have been judged ineffective when sales did not rise despite the fact that the ad was intended to build interest, liking, or desire.

In 1990 the Advertising Research Foundation (ARF) reported that "likability" was the most important measure in predicting a television commercial's success.[14] This finding has been disputed by researchers who believe that traditional measures such as persuasion and recall are better indicators of success.

Testing Methods

Ads may be tested at any one of a number of stages—as a concept, as a set of rough drawings, or as a finished ad, both before and after media exposure. An ad is pretested if the test occurs before media dollars are committed; tests after commitment of funds are designated as post-tests.

Pretesting.   Several testing procedures are available for this stage.

▪ *Focus-group interviews.* In this procedure, about six to ten target audience consumers are brought together with a group leader. They are then exposed to an ad or a part of an ad. The leader encourages group members to interact and asks probing questions about the ad. What do they understand from the ad? Does it interest them? Do they believe it? Would they try the product? This technique is most commonly used when an ad is being developed.

- *Folio tests.* This procedure takes place at the consumer's home. An interviewer shows the consumer a loose-leaf binder containing the test ad and others and asks the consumer to look through the ads, noting what he or she remembers or finds interesting. This technique is designed exclusively for testing print ads, usually when the ad is in a finished or nearly finished form. It measures an ad's attention-getting abilities. In addition, it provides insights into motivational and comprehensibility aspects and measures potential attitude changes.

- *In-home projector tests.* A rough or finished version of a television commercial is shown, in a consumer's home, as part of a short sequence from a television program or film. This procedure does not measure attention-getting aspects, but it does give a measure of comprehension, motivation, credibility, and possible consumer attitude change, if attitude measures are taken before and after the ads are shown.

- *Trailer tests.* Trailer tests are less expensive ways to evaluate television commercials. A trailer is parked in a shopping center parking lot, and people are asked to take part in a marketing research study. They are put in a waiting room with magazines and a television set. The set shows a closed circuit version of a prerecorded program in which the test ad is aired. The subject is then interviewed to determine the attention-getting impact of the ad, plus comprehension, credibility, and motivation. Alternatively, respondents may be shown an ad directly and asked for their reactions, but this procedure would not yield information about the attention-getting aspect of the ad.

- *Theater tests.* An audience is recruited to view a few test television programs. On arrival the participants fill out questionnaires about their opinions and preferences for the product categories and brands of interest. Then they see television shows into which the relevant commercials have been inserted. Following this, they complete another questionnaire. Comparing the before and after questionnaires gives measures of attention-getting power, credibility, motivation, and preference.

- *In-magazine recall tests.* Syndicated services regularly interview people who read magazines to determine which ads they remember seeing, how much of the ads they read, what associations they draw, and the interest level attained for the products advertised. They are asked questions about the ads they remember, then they're shown each ad and asked whether they remember it and to what extent they read it.

  Pretesting print ads is done in a similar fashion. The test ad is inserted into a dummy magazine containing editorial sections, other real ads, and some benchmark ads. The benchmark ads give reference points for meaningful comparisons with the test ad. This dummy magazine is placed in respondents' homes, and a few days later, an interview similar to the one for in-magazine recall takes place.

- *Live telecast tests.* An ad is shown, usually on a television program. The next day television interviews are conducted with respondents who viewed the show in question. They are asked what ads they remember seeing on the show (unaided recall). Those who remember the ad are asked to describe it, yielding measures of video impact, music, and other characteristics. This test is quite often the final pretest before full commitment of media dollars. Cable television has enabled research firms to expand this type of testing. Burke Marketing Services made this type of research well known under the name day-after-recall (DAR) test.

- *Test market.* A number of advertising approaches may be tested in the marketplace. Here, the intent is to measure the impact of the ads on sales. Communications measures are also usually taken in test areas at the same time. This approach requires a heavier commitment of funds to research than the other methods.

Post-testing.   In post-testing, people exposed to ads in such media as print, television, and radio are questioned to determine unaided recall, aided recall, recognition, comprehension, believability, brand awareness and preferences, product trial, satisfaction, and usage.

For example, the Starch Advertisement Readership Service gives post-measures of print ad effectiveness in at least three ways: (1) *noted*—a person who remembered having previously seen the advertisement in the issue being studied; (2) *seen-associated*—a person who not only noted the advertisement but also read some part of it that clearly indicates the brand or advertiser; and (3) *read most*—a person who read one-half or more of the written material in the ad. The service gives a number of measures, including the percentage of a magazine's readers in each of these three categories, and the number of "readers" an ad obtains per dollar spent. Many other syndicated organizations provide information on any of the measures we have discussed, or the impact of the campaign on sales. Of course, a company may do its own testing. Post-testing allows the advertiser to determine how well the objectives have been achieved.

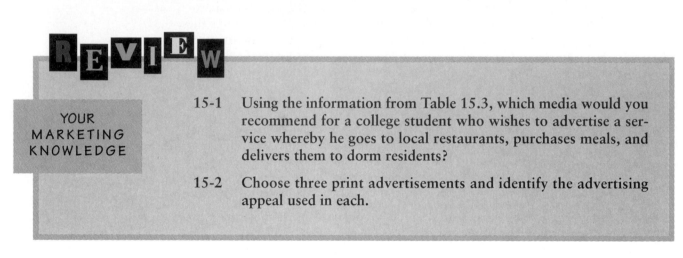

REVIEW

YOUR MARKETING KNOWLEDGE

15-1   Using the information from Table 15.3, which media would you recommend for a college student who wishes to advertise a service whereby he goes to local restaurants, purchases meals, and delivers them to dorm residents?

15-2   Choose three print advertisements and identify the advertising appeal used in each.

ADVERTISING AGENCIES

Many large firms perform all the functions necessary to carry out the advertising decisions described thus far in this chapter. When they do this, we say that they have an **in-house** [advertising] **agency.** However, most firms use some type of outside advertising agency to aid them in carrying out some or all of the advertising decisions. Companies that wish to perform some of their own advertising tasks may still use one of the following types of outside agencies:

▪ *Media-buying service.* This type of agency executes the media strategy developed by a firm by doing the actual purchasing of media vehicles.

▪ *Creative boutique.* This type of firm specializes in the development and production of the actual advertisements.

Alternatively, a company may hire a full-service agency. Full-service advertising agencies are capable of performing any or all activities related to a firm's advertising, including development of overall marketing strategy. These agencies are the most common form of advertising firm. Table 15.4 lists the ten largest advertising agencies. As we noted in the Marketing Profile that began this chapter, advertising agencies committed to working with clients to develop integrated marketing efforts are likely to be the most successful in the coming years.

Rank 1993	1992	Advertising organization, headquarters	Worldwide gross income 1993 ($ millions)
1	1	WPP Group, London	$2, 633.6
2	2	Interpublic Group of Cos., New York	2,078.5
3	3	Omnicom Group, New York	1,876.0
4	5	Dentsu Inc., Tokyo	1,403.2
5	4	Saatchi & Saatchi Co., London/New York	1,355.1
6	6	Young & Rubicam, New York	1,008.9
7	7	Euro RSCG Worldwide, Neuilly, France	864.8
8	8	Grey Advertising, New York	765.7
9	12	Hakuhodo Inc., Tokyo	667.8
10	9	Foote, Cone & Belding Communications, Chicago	633.7

Source: "World's Top 50 Advertising Organizations," *Advertising Age*, April 13, 1994, p. 12.

TABLE 15.4
World's Top 10 Advertising Organizations

Traditionally, advertising agencies have been paid a 15 percent commission on the value of the media they purchase for clients. If, for example, an agency buys television time worth $100,000, the network bills the agency for $85,000 ($100,000 less the commission). The network agrees to this arrangement because the agency has brought it business. The agency, in turn, bills its client for the full $100,000. The $15,000 represents the agency's compensation.

Many agencies still operate this way; however, many clients are turning away from sole reliance on traditional media for advertising. Because of this change and because of cost pressures and a great diversity in the functions of agencies, many different compensation systems have developed. In some instances, a negotiated system is used. With this approach, the agency and client negotiate the commission percentage which may be higher or lower than the standard 15 percent, or it may vary across the range of services the agency performs. Fee for service arrangements are also becoming increasingly common.

Historically, large firms such as General Motors, Levi Strauss, and Procter & Gamble rarely changed advertising agencies. However, for advertising to be effective, client and agency must work well together in an atmosphere of respect and trust. When this atmosphere does not exist, agencies may be fired or resign accounts. Today it is not uncommon for major clients to switch agencies on a fairly regular basis. Reasons that agencies lose clients include: poor performance or service by the agency; poor communication; unrealistic demands by the client; personality conflicts; personnel changes; changes in size of the client or agency; conflicts of interest; changes in the client's marketing strategy; declining sales; conflicting philosophies of compensation; and changes in policies.[15] Advertising agencies must monitor these danger signs if they hope to keep accounts.

ETHICAL ISSUES IN ADVERTISING

Many people see advertising as one of the most highly controversial activities of marketers. Despite the existence of numerous government regulations and industry guidelines, advertisers often face ethical decisions.

Because a firm's advertising decisions are so highly visible to its target market and others, morally questionable choices are likely to receive far greater attention than questionable decisions in other areas of the marketing mix. Issues related to the use of sex and violence in advertising, advertising to children, and the advertising of alcohol and tobacco products have all been raised and examined from this perspective. The "Spotlight on Ethics: The Battle Over Old Joe" describes the type of controversy that can arise when a company engages in what some contend are ethically questionable advertising practices.

Of course, no one can draw absolute conclusions with respect to what is right and wrong when it comes to ethical issues. Because every individual brings different values, standards, and frames of reference to a situation, whether something is unethical or not will lie, to a large extent, in the eye of the beholder. You may, for example, find it highly immoral and unethical for tobacco companies to advertise since cigarettes are known health hazards. Another person may feel that tobacco companies have every right to advertise their products, just as we, as citizens, have every right to choose or not choose to use their products.

Much of the criticism of advertising appears founded in the belief that advertising has the power to create needs and cause consumers to purchase products they do not really need or cannot afford. The American Association of Advertising Agencies has challenged this belief in advertisements of its own. Advertising is a powerful influence on consumers' wants and desires. Marketers who use this powerful tool must respect it and strive to make careful and considered choices. This is not only the right thing to do, it is also good business.

This advertisement is part of a campaign by the International Advertising Association aimed at convincing consumers that advertising is beneficial.

WITHOUT THE SPONSORS FOR ROCK CONCERTS, ALL YOU'D HEAR IS THE SOUND OF SILENCE.

When a company like Chevrolet or The Coca-Cola Company sponsors a concert, they actually bring you the concert. They help pay for the talent. The sets. The gaffers, grips, and roadies. Without these advertising sponsors, the only way to cover costs would be with enormously high ticket prices. Which wouldn't be music to anyone's ears.

Advertising. That's the way it works.

INTERNATIONAL ADVERTISING ASSOCATION

The global partnership of advertisers, agencies and media

LINTAS:WORLDWIDE

Monitoring the ethics of advertising is a global phenomenon. The International Advertising Association (IAA) launched a worldwide campaign in 1993 aimed at convincing consumers around the world that advertising is beneficial. The IAA's campaign message differed depending on the level of development of the economy in which their ads were being run. In less-developed countries such as China and Russia where the concept of advertising is still new, the IAA used the tag line, "Advertising—That's the Way It Works." In the United States and other more sophisticated economies, the featured tag line was, "Advertising—The Right to Choose."[16]

SALES PROMOTION

Sales promotion activities supplement both advertising and personal selling. **Sales promotion** is defined as a direct inducement to sell the product by offers of extra value or incentive to the sales force, distributors, or the ultimate consumer.[17] Sales promotion holds a middle ground between advertising and personal selling because it is usually not directed at as large an audience as advertising, but is directed at much larger groups than a personal selling effort. Hence, this form of promotion plays an important role in the company's scheme of integrated marketing communications. Sales promotion can help tie together the other planned promotional activities.

Although a firm's sales promotion activities are often designed to supplement its advertising and personal selling efforts, this does not mean that sales promotion expenditures take a back seat to spending on other areas in the promotional mix. It has been estimated that $140 billion was spent in 1991 on sales promotion activities.[18] Even more telling is the fact that sales promotion expenditures have skyrocketed in the last 15 years while advertising expenditures have declined or stayed constant. Today, of the total promotional dollars spent on advertising and sales promotion, sales promotion spending accounts for 73 percent, the remaining 27 percent goes to media advertising.[19] Table 15.5 illustrates the change in balance of expenditures for advertising and sales promotion that took place between 1981 and 1993.

Promotions focused at channel members are called **trade promotions**. Sales promotions focused at ultimate consumers, on the other hand, are referred to as **consumer promotions**. Figure 15.2 categorizes common sales promotion techniques as being either trade or consumer focused.

Consumer Promotions

Consumers like sales promotions. In fact, between 1988 and 1992 the percentage of ultimate consumers who reported feeling either much more favorable or somewhat more favorable toward brands of grocery products that offered sales promotions grew from 47 percent to 56 percent.[20] Consumer promotions take many forms.

| | Percentage of Expenditures on | |
	Advertisements	Trade/Consumer Promos
1981	43%	57%
1985	34	66
1990	28	72
1993	27	73

Source: A. Bryant, "Those Mind-Boggling Promotions," *New York Times*, November 14, 1993, p. F7.

TABLE 15.5
Twelve-year Comparison of Promotion Spending

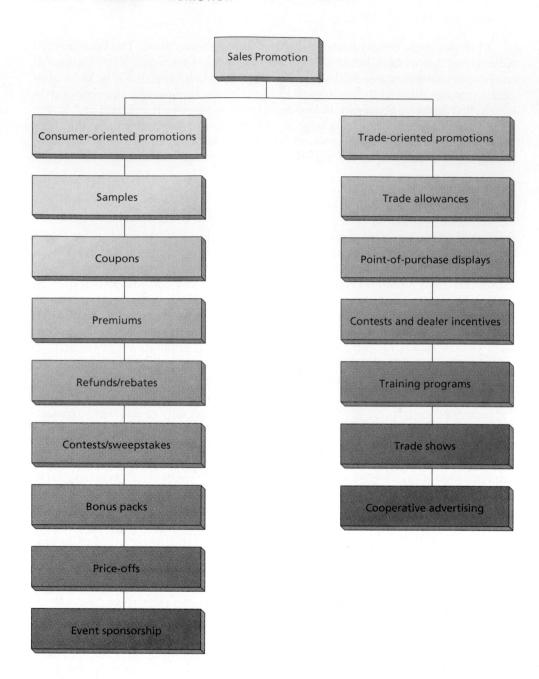

Source: Adapted from G. E. and M. A. Belch, *Introduction to Advertising and Promotion*, 2d ed. (Irwin, 1993), p. 576.

FIGURE 15.2
Types of Sales Promotion Activities

Samples.   **Sampling** a product means giving away free quantities of it. Few people throw away free items. In fact, one expert has estimated that 75 percent of house-holds that receive a sample will try the product.[21] Samples are usually, but not always, given in sizes that are smaller than regular packages. Keebler ran a sam-pling program in which consumers woke to find that the "Keebler elves" had deposited full-size boxes of Wheatables, a new snack cracker, at their front doors during the night. Sampling is expensive and presents a complex distribution problem. Mail, home delivery by private services, and distribution in stores are some examples of how it can be done. Some service firms distribute samples for companies. One such firm, Reuben H. Donnelley Corporation, can handle samples with mass mailings, handouts, or door drops.

Sampling typically makes the most sense for new products or for products with significant changes or modifications. For more mature, established products, a free sample is unlikely to induce a switch by a consumer already loyal to a competing brand. For consumers already loyal to the brand in question, sampling is simply giving away a product the customer would have purchased. Sampling also may not

MARKETING IN ACTION

SPOTLIGHT ON Ethics

The Battle over Old Joe

Is the controversy over Joe Camel just a puff of smoke? The popular cartoon character is spokescamel for Camel cigarettes, a product of the RJR Nabisco Company. Old Joe, as he is affectionately called, has been credited with reversing the fortunes of Camel, the U.S.'s oldest brand of cigarettes. Joe has been featured prominently on billboards and in magazine advertising that totaled more than $100 million in the single year, 1991.

Consumer advocates and antismoking activists, however, have been hopping mad at RJR Nabisco ever since Old Joe hit the media. They contend that the cartoon character appeals strongly to children and so encourages them to smoke cigarettes. In fact, argue Old Joe's opponents, the company has purposely targeted children by making a cartoon character the central figure in its promotional campaign. As early as 1991, the Federal Trade Commission started receiving petitions demanding that Old Joe be banned.

Research studies have sought to validate or disprove the contentions that children are unusually aware of or attracted to Old Joe. Results have been equivocal. Several studies, including one commissioned by *Advertising Age*, have indicated high levels of awareness of the character by children as young as elementary-school age. A study performed by Marketing Evaluations, an independent research firm, however, found Old Joe was familiar to 58 percent of children aged 6 to 11. By means of contrast, Tony the Tiger (Kellogg's Frosted Flakes spokestiger) was familiar to 91 percent of the children in the same age group and 83 percent knew the pink Energizer bunny. Furthermore, the study indicated that among children familiar with Old Joe, his "likability" index was quite low.

RJR Nabisco denies that it has targeted children with the Old Joe character. The company maintains that its own research shows only that Joe is appealing to adult smokers, its market of

interest. The firm not only emphasizes that the character wasn't aimed at children but, as expected, stands behind indications that Joe is not effective at reaching children or causing them to consider smoking.

The company may have decided to sidestep the controversy to some extent by decreasing its advertising spending altogether. Media purchases for late 1992, especially magazines, were dramatically cut. The move followed an industry trend (albeit spearheaded by RJR Nabisco) of shifting dollars away from magazines. Outdoor advertising, it has contended, is more regionally oriented. With the latest round of cuts in media spending, the company claims to have shifted focus to sales promotion tactics such as point-of-purchase displays. Speculation has been raised that the cutbacks in fact reflect a response to declining profits, perhaps resulting in part from the Old Joe controversy. RJR Nabisco denies this claim.

Meanwhile, the Federal Trade Commission, after investigating the issue for two years, decided not to have Joe Camel declared an unfair advertising practice. The commission voted down (3 to 2) a petition filed by the Coalition on Smoking and Health, an organization that opposes smoking. Despite the decision, Joe's life may not be a long one. The term of one of the commissioners who voted with the majority expires in September 1994, and a replacement who holds more of an antismoking view could make Joe an endangered species. In addition, it seems likely that by the end of 1994 the FDA will declare cigarettes a drug, due to their nicotine content.

Is the Old Joe campaign unethical? Even if it was not RJR Nabisco's intent to target children, should the firm have dropped the character when controversy arose? What responsibility should a company have in this type of situation?

be appropriate for perishable items, some personal-care products, or items with slow in-store turnover. Despite these problems, sampling is currently used by 64 percent of manufacturers.[22]

Coupons.   Coupon distribution grew dramatically in the 1980s and early 1990s. In 1980, 96.4 billion coupons were distributed in the United States. By 1993 that figure had grown to 323 billion.[23] In 1990, 95 percent of marketers reported using couponing.[24] There is some evidence, however, that coupon redemption rates may have peaked and that couponing in general is slowing. In 1992 7.7 billion, 2.4 percent of coupons distributed, were redeemed. In 1993 only 7.2 billion, or 2.2 percent of those distributed, were redeemed.[25] Coupons are distributed in newspapers and magazines, on packages and labels, and through the mail. They are usually returned to a retailer, although sometimes consumers must send them directly to the manufacturer for redemption. Price-sensitive consumers can be induced to purchase a product using a coupon without the manufacturers' having to reduce the overall price of the good. It is difficult, however, to avoid the use of coupons by established purchasers who would have bought the item even without a coupon.

Many marketers now use targeted couponing. With targeted couponing, a firm varies its cents-off offer or the copy in the coupon by region. Many firms are also issuing coupons on the backs of cash-register tapes based specifically on the purchase behavior of individual consumers. When you buy Coca-Cola, for example, the purchase may trigger the cash-register computer to issue you a Pepsi coupon on the back of your register tape.

Premiums.   A **premium** is the offer of an article of merchandise, either free or at a lower price than usual, as an inducement to purchase it instead of another product or to visit the location where the product is sold. The intent is to induce consumers to purchase the product to which the premium is tied. The goal may be to increase trial of a new product or encourage more consumption of an established product. Estimates of annual expenditures on premiums are $4 to $15 billion. In recent years the trend in premiums has been to offer items consistent with the image of the product and its position in the market. Premiums fall into three common categories.

- *Free premiums.* These are items that the consumer receives or may obtain as a result of buying the product. Small toys in cereal boxes are examples of in-pack free premiums. With each Sony AV Laser Player, Sony includes a "Take 5" Sampler Disc that has samples of the company's laser discs. Alternatively, the premium may be offered free in the mail. In this case the consumer mails a request to the manufacturer or a designated redemption center. In a promotion related to the one above, Sony offers consumers a mail-in coupon for two free laser discs when they buy a Sony AV Laser player.

- *Self-liquidating premiums.* Here the customer is offered the chance to buy merchandise at a special price, usually just enough to cover the cost of the premium. These offers can reinforce the brand's image and its advertising. Marlboro cigarettes, for example, has reinforced its rugged, western image by offering a variety of cowboy-related items (hats, shirts, belts, etc.) in this manner.

- *Reusable container premiums.* The product's package can be an effective premium. One product that employs this technique is Chubbs Stackables. A supply of baby wipes comes in brightly colored containers. When the baby wipes are used up, the child can stack the empty containers and use them as building blocks.

Refunds/rebates.   Refunds or rebates are offers to return some portion of the product's purchase price, usually after the customer supplies proof of purchase.[26] This type of price incentive allows the manufacturer to avoid using coupons. It is also easier to control than couponing. Such sales promotions may require considerable effort on the part of the consumer who usually is required to mail in a rebate form and proof of purchase. Some research has shown that many consumers do not like rebates because they feel it is not worth the bother required to obtain the refund.[27] On the other hand, a manufacturer who promotes the rebate at the point of sale may produce the perception of a lower price by the consumer, even though the consumer never bothers to send for the rebate. Producers need to be careful when using rebates; overuse can cheapen a brand's image.

Contests and sweepstakes. Promotional activities that involve consumers in games of skill are called **contests,** and those involving consumers in games of chance are called **sweepstakes.** Such sales promotions can produce high consumer involvement, added retailer support, and added excitement about or interest in products or advertising themes. Sometimes, however, the contest or sweepstakes can overshadow the product. These activities rarely involve more than 20 percent of the target audience. They are also prohibited by law in certain states.

Bonus packs. Bonus packs offer consumers an extra amount of the product either through a larger container or extra units. This type of sales promotion can be very effective in spurring purchase because it is immediately clear that value has been added. Neither the consumer or retailer has to deal with coupons or the delayed gratification of a rebate.

Bonus packs can have the added benefit of "stocking the consumer up" on the item. Hence, when a competitor later offers a special, the consumer may be temporarily out of the market for the item.

Price-offs. Price-offs are a promotional technique that offers consumers a reduced price for the item, right on the package. The package might indicate, for example, that the price marked is 25 cents below the regular retail price for the product. As with bonus packs, the consumer can see the immediate value of this type of promotion. Retailers, on the other hand, often dislike such promotions because they can cause pricing and inventory problems.

Many manufacturers are moving away from price-offs and other price incentives or deals. Instead the producers are using a pricing technique known as everyday low pricing. **Everyday low pricing (EDLP)** is a strategy in which the price charged for the item is lower than it would be if other sales promotions were being used. When a firm uses EDLP, it does not use coupons, rebates, price-offs, or other forms of price-related sales promotions. Growth in EDLP has been cited as a contributing factor in the slowdown of couponing discussed earlier.[28] Procter & Gamble has experimented heavily with this technique. In early 1993 the company discontinued all coupons for its disposable diapers, Luvs and Pampers, and reduced the price by 7 percent. (EDLP is discussed in greater depth in Chapter 17.)

Event sponsorship. In event sponsorship a company develops a business relationship with a particular event. Two-thirds of sponsorship is for sports events; however, companies have also sponsored music tours, festivals, and arts and cultural events. This type of sales promotion gets a firm's name in front of consumers and associates it with something popular in the target market. Event sponsorship has been particularly effective in reaching ethnic markets.[29]

Beer, cigarette, and automobile manufacturers have been the biggest users of this type of sales promotion. RJR Nabisco, for example, sponsors many automobile races across the country. Companies that sponsor events to promote sales benefit by reaching not only those consumers who attend the event, but also through publicity (news coverage) that reaches many additional consumers. The Grand Prix of Long Beach, sponsored in 1992 by Toyota, is reported to have generated $26 million worth of publicity.[30] Firms must plan carefully to ensure that the events they sponsor attract individuals with the characteristics of their target markets.

Trade Promotions

Trade promotions are designed to increase sales by motivating channel members to sell products more actively to their customers, to place larger orders, to feature these products in local advertising, and to allocate more shelf space or allow special displays for the product. They are a critical part of overall marketing success.

Trade allowances. Trade allowances are the most common form of trade promotion. They involve some type of monetary allowance or discount made to the channel member in exchange for displaying the manufacturer's product in a specific location, for promoting the product, or for stocking the product at all. These have grown increasingly common.

A special type of trade allowance, known as a slotting fee, has grown dramatically. **Slotting fees** are cash payments by the manufacturer to the retailer for access to shelf space in the store or warehouse, or for special shelf locations or displays. Retailers have been able to demand slotting fees as the power in the channel has shifted toward them. A slotting fee could be $1,000 to secure shelf space in a retail store for a new product. A manufacturer could pay a slotting fee as high as $50,000 for an entire retail chain. It's easy to see that the producer could face several million dollars in slotting fees for a national rollout of a packaged consumer good.

Slotting allowances are very unpopular with manufacturers and very controversial in the packaged goods business. Some consider these payments a form of extortion. The long-run viability and structure of slotting fees is very much an open question. Some retailers are even asking for failure or discontinuance fees when a product is dropped from retail distribution. This fight is likely to continue.

Point-of-purchase displays. Point-of-purchase promotions (POP) are special displays, racks, signs, banners, and exhibits placed in the retail store to support the sales of a brand. With the increasing popularity of self-service, POP has become more important. These promotions serve to remind customers that a product is available at a given location (a GE or Sony sign in the window or a Budweiser sign over the bar); as one final attempt to influence the customer to select a specific brand (the Gillette display right at the cash register); and to encourage impulse buying. Sometimes it is necessary to pay the retailer in order to obtain a prime POP location, such as right at the cash register. The payment may be in cash discounts or even free goods. With a proven, successful display, the retailer may pay to get the POP materials. Studies indicate that dollars spent on POP displays are worthwhile when effectively coordinated with advertising and other promotional activity. Retailers may choose not to use a firm's POP materials because

- too much material is supplied by too many firms.
- displays do not fit the retailer's needs in terms of size or durability.
- the quality of display material is inferior.
- the salesperson merchandises the display material badly to the retailer, it is not seasonally appropriate, or it is difficult to assemble.
- the profit available on the product is insufficient to warrant the space.[31]

If retailers put up every display offered to them, there would be very little room in the store for anything else. The next time you are in a food market or drugstore, notice the number of POP displays.

Contests and dealer incentives. Manufacturers often sponsor contests with prizes like free merchandise, trips, and plaques for dealers who reach specified sales levels. In addition, they may give free merchandise allowances or even monetary bonuses for reaching sales performance goals. Once in a while, there is a sweepstakes, where "lucky" dealers can win substantial prizes. For example, Fisher-Price Toys had great success with a sweepstakes that gave cooperating dealers a chance to win a trip to Puerto Rico. These types of programs may also be directed at in-store sales personnel for individual sales performances. A direct payment by a manufacturer to a channel member salesperson is called a *spiff*. This is very common at the consumer level for consumer durables and cosmetics, and at the wholesale level for beer. Another version of a spiff occurs when retailers pay their salespeople to push certain items. Clearly, this practice makes it possible for consumers to be deceived by a salesperson attempting to earn "push money." As a result, these types of payments are controversial.

Management assistance. Manufacturers may also provide channel members with management assistance in running their businesses. Among these services are personnel training, inventory control, store displays, and financial management.

The manufacturer's sales force, for example, might aid retail sales personnel by helping to educate them about various product lines. They could also provide selling tips or competitive information that will help the retail sales force do a more effective job.

Trade shows. Trade shows are exhibitions where producers display products and give information to current and potential customers in the distribution channel. Shows provide a significant opportunity for manufacturers to introduce new products and for channel members to gain knowledge. Inquiries at trade shows can provide sales leads to manufacturers. Shows can also be used to entertain customers and develop relationships.

Trade shows can provide a significant opportunity for manufacturers to introduce new products and for channel members to gain knowledge.

Cooperative advertising.   Cooperative advertising is an agreement so that a manufacturer pays a portion of a retailer's local advertising costs. These costs are shared on an equal basis up to a specified limit, usually related to the amount the retailer purchases from the manufacturer. An appliance manufacturer such as Whirlpool, for example, might enter into cooperative advertising with a retail appliance store. The store's advertisements feature Whirlpool appliances.

ADVANTAGES AND DISADVANTAGES OF SALES PROMOTION USE

Sales promotion has a few distinct advantages. First, it involves primarily the consumer or channel member. For example, consumers must return coupons to get the values, or they must use free samples or throw them away. Hence, sales promotion generally represents a more tangible form of promotion than advertising. These types of sales promotions are sometimes called forcing techniques, since they "force" the consumer to act. Additionally, sales promotions give true value to the user; actual savings of money usually occurs. Finally, they can be directed to narrowly defined market segments. For example, free samples can be mailed only to prospective users in high-income areas in Los Angeles.

Many marketing managers are concerned that use of too much sales promotion produces an overreliance on such techniques. The firm's promotional efforts end up being focused almost exclusively on short-term performance rather than on building of long-term brand equity. The latter is achieved better with advertising. As use of sales promotion grows, firms are fighting for the consumer's attention amid significant promotional clutter.

The extent to which a company chooses to use sales promotion is largely determined by the actions of its competitors. Figure 15.3 presents what has been called the sales promotion dilemma. Only if all firms in an industry simultaneously cut back on sales promotion is the industry likely to benefit. Consequently, we can expect to see the use of sales promotion continuing to grow.

FIGURE 15.3
The Sales Promotion Dilemma

All other firms	Our firm	
	Cut back promotions	Maintain promotions
Cut back promotions	Higher profits for all	Market share goes to our firm
Maintain promotions	Market share goes to all other firms	Market share stays constant; profits stay low

Source: G. E. and M. A. Belch, *Introduction to Advertising and Promotion*, 2d ed. (Irwin, 1993), p. 623.

15-3   Ask the manager at a local discount department store about his or her experience with rebates. Do consumers like them?

15-4   Talk to the manager at a large chain grocery store. Ask what type of trade deals would be required for a new product to get shelf space. Before asking, what do you think he or she will say?

PUBLICITY AND PUBLIC RELATIONS

Publicity refers to the generating of news about a person, product, or service that appears in broadcast or print media.[32] **Public relations** evaluates public attitudes, identifies the policies and procedures of an individual or an organization with the public interest, and executes a program of action to earn public understanding and acceptance.[33] Publicity and public relations are additional means that marketers use to promote their products, their services, and themselves to mass audiences. Publicity is a particularly attractive means of promotion for many organizations because the sponsor does not pay for it.

Many consumers find publicity more credible than advertising that has been generated and paid for by the firm. Consequently, positive publicity is a very valuable asset in promoting a company. Which are you more likely to believe, an advertisement for a new restaurant telling you how terrific it is, or a positive review by a restaurant critic?

The Relationship Between Publicity and Public Relations

Publicity and public relations are closely related. While the public-relations role in organizations involves many communications approaches including institutional advertising and personal selling by senior corporate executives, publicity is often the cornerstone of a company's public-relations efforts. A firm's successful public-relations efforts, for example, might be largely the result of publicity it has managed to attract. When Chevron Oil sponsors research aimed at improving the environment, news reports that carry the story (publicity) are instrumental in furthering the image of the company (public relations).

Publicity is generally a short-term strategy whereas a firm's public relations are ongoing. It is also important to note that a firm controls its public-relations efforts. The company designs its public-relations program to provide positive information about itself and its products. Because publicity is not generated internally, the organization cannot control it.

Both publicity and public relations are important components of an organization's integrated marketing communications. When carefully planned, with an understanding of the target audience's interests, publicity and public relations can effectively promote a company with little expense.

Topics Available for Publicity

Organizations use a variety of topics to generate publicity. Among these are new products, special events, changes in the marketing mix, charitable activities, athletic sponsorships, profit positions, and speeches by executives. For a topic to generate effective publicity, it must be truly newsworthy. But, unfortunately, stories that present the company in a negative light may sometimes be newsworthy. As we noted in Chapter 14, when two children died and several became ill from *E. coli* bacteria after eating at Jack-in-the-Box restaurants, a great deal of publicity was generated about Foodmaker Corporation (owner of Jack-in-the-Box). Because media attention is beyond the control of the firm, companies must be concerned not only about generating positive publicity but also about crisis management, responding to negative publicity.

Managing Publicity

Although publicity is not paid for or sponsored by the firm, it still needs to be managed carefully. A company should set objectives, target media, and evaluate the performance of its publicity efforts in the same way it would plan for any of its promotional tools. The firm's publicity efforts are generally undertaken by its public relations department. It is important to remember, however, that publicity and public relations are components of the overall promotional mix. Their objectives should be consistent with the overall IMC plan for the target audience. Publicity is a powerful promotional device if managed properly.

In this chapter we have focused on three of the four components of the promotional mix: advertising, sales promotion, and publicity. These components are similar in that each attempts persuasive communication with a mass audience. Personal selling, which we discuss in the next chapter, communicates one-on-one with target consumers. We have seen in this chapter how advertising, sales promotion, and publicity should be coordinated and integrated. It is equally important to coordinate the efforts of these mass audience techniques with the personal selling efforts of the company so that an integrated marketing communications effort presents a single image and message to the target audience.

PERSONAL COMPUTER EXERCISE

Preparing an advertising and sales promotion plan involves the careful analysis of the effectiveness, cost, and sales impact of various marketing vehicles. This PC Exercise gives you such data for a product and challenges you to prepare advertising and sales promotion plans. What are the advantages and disadvantages of alternative marketing approaches?

KEY POINTS

■ Coordinated advertising, sales promotion, and publicity are important to a firm's successful integrated marketing communications.

■ Advertising is a highly visible component of the promotional mix, in part due to the amount of money advertisers invest in the United States and around the world.

■ The first two steps in advertising decision making are setting objectives and determining the budget. These processes parallel the same tasks in planning the promotional mix.

■ Media planning involves determining which types of media to use (newspaper, television, etc.) as well as which specific vehicles to advertise in and the frequency and timing of the ads.

■ There are many types of advertising, including primary or selective demand; direct or indirect action; consumer, business-to-business, or trade; product or institutional; vertical or horizontal cooperative; and commercial or public service.

■ Measuring advertising effectiveness is an imperfect science but it is important for long-term success.

■ Many large and small companies use advertising agencies to plan and implement some or all of their advertising decisions.

■ Sales promotion techniques supplement the advertising and personal selling efforts of the firm. Companies typically invest a much larger percentage of their promotional dollars in sales promotion than in advertising.

■ Sales promotions can be directed at ultimate consumers (consumer promotions) or channel members (trade promotions).

■ Consumer promotions include sampling, coupons, premiums, refunds/rebates, contests/sweepstakes, bonus packs, price-offs, and event sponsorship.

■ Trade promotions include trade allowances, point-of-purchase displays, contests and dealer incentives, management assistance, trade shows, and cooperative advertising.

■ Publicity (positive) is very useful to marketers in the promotion of their products or organizations.

■ Publicity and public relations are related concepts but publicity has a more short-term focus while public relations has a more long-term focus.

■ Publicity is often perceived as more credible than advertising because it is externally generated and not paid for by the sponsor.

■ Marketers typically lack control over publicity, hence it may sometimes be negative.

KEY TERMS

advertising (511)
media plan (516)
media type (516)
number of inserts (516)
media vehicles (516)

reach (517)
frequency (517)
unduplicated reach (517)
duplicated reach (517)
high-involvement media (517)

ISSUES FOR DISCUSSION

1. A firm that markets a major packaged good was about to undertake a study of the relationship between its advertising dollars and its sales. One member of the management team argued that this could be misleading, because advertising factors beyond the amount of money spent also affected sales. These include the media used and the creative execution. Discuss.

2. Should advertising be viewed as an expense? Why or why not?

3. The cost per thousand of The *New Yorker* magazine is many times greater than that for *Time* magazine. Why, then, would one advertise in The *New Yorker*?

4. Pick a magazine ad for a consumer good and one for a business-to-business service.

   (a) What do you think each ad's objective(s) are?

   (b) Evaluate each ad's fit with the editorial environment of the magazine.

   (c) How would you measure the effectiveness of each ad?

5. The brand manager for a new entry into the shampoo market is planning her sales promotion strategy. Should she focus her efforts on trade or consumer promotions?

6. What type of sales promotion program would you recommend for a manufacturer of personal fax machines?

7. Would it be possible or advisable to develop a global sales promotion for a globally well-known product such as Coca-Cola?

8. Identify some publicity about a product or organization that is negative. How might the firm respond?

9. Would you advertise a dating service using high-involvement or low-involvement media? Why?

10. Analyze your favorite advertisement.

   (a) Who is the target audience?

   (b) What type of presentation is used?

   (c) How would you rate the execution?

   (d) Do you think the ad is effective in obtaining its objectives?

CASE APPLICATION

Where and How do you Advertise Automobiles?

Automobile advertising is big business. Where and how to allocate the millions of dollars spent by automobile companies is an issue that produces some disagreement among car marketers. J. D. Powers and Associates, a major marketing research firm, recently completed a survey of 877 automobile dealerships in the United States. Auto dealers are the front line in the battle to sell cars. The opinions of the dealers suggest some basic conflict between the advertising decisions of the manufacturers and the preferences of the dealers.

Eighty-two percent of the dealers who responded are happy with the brand image created by their manufacturer's national advertising campaign. Sixty-six percent agree the national advertising does a good job overall. When asked, however, whether they would prefer more advertising dollars be spent on national ads or on local dealer ads, the results reported in the first table were produced.

Dealers also had opinions regarding the forms of media to which national advertising dollars should be allocated. In the remaining tables, this survey's respondents expressed views on advertising spending across the media.

Questions

1. As an automobile manufacturer, how would you use the information about newspapers, radio, television, magazines, and direct mail?
2. Why do you think car dealers selling European models are so much more in favor of more TV spending and less in favor of magazine spending than dealers selling domestic cars?
3. How do the roles of national and local dealer advertising differ?
4. How should the appeals differ in national and dealer advertising for the same brand of car?

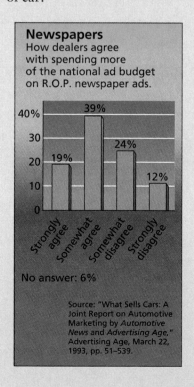

Dealer ads vs. national ads
Percent of respondents who agree they prefer dealer association ads.

Chrysler: 56%
Ford: 64%
GM: 56%
Japanese: 50%
European: 43%

Source: "What Sells Cars: A Joint Report on Automotive Marketing by *Automotive News* and *Advertising Age*," Advertising Age, March 22, 1993, pp. 51–539.

Newspapers
How dealers agree with spending more of the national ad budget on R.O.P. newspaper ads.

Strongly agree: 19%
Somewhat agree: 39%
Somewhat disagree: 24%
Strongly disagree: 12%

No answer: 6%

Source: "What Sells Cars: A Joint Report on Automotive Marketing by *Automotive News* and *Advertising Age*," Advertising Age, March 22, 1993, pp. 51–539.

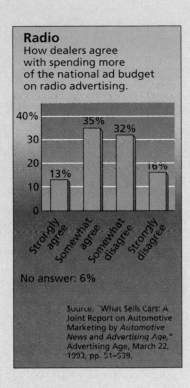

Radio
How dealers agree
with spending more
of the national ad budget
on radio advertising.

40%
35%
32%
30
20
16%
13%
10
0

Strongly agree
Somewhat agree
Somewhat disagree
Strongly disagree

No answer: 6%

Source: "What Sells Cars: A
Joint Report on Automotive
Marketing by *Automotive
News* and *Advertising Age*,"
Advertising Age, March 22,
1993, pp. 51–539.

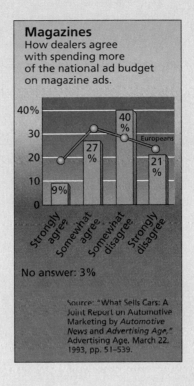

Magazines
How dealers agree
with spending more
of the national ad budget
on magazine ads.

40%
40%
30
27%
Europeans
20
21%
9%
10
0

Strongly agree
Somewhat agree
Somewhat disagree
Strongly disagree

No answer: 3%

Source: "What Sells Cars: A
Joint Report on Automotive
Marketing by *Automotive
News* and *Advertising Age*,"
Advertising Age, March 22,
1993, pp. 51–539.

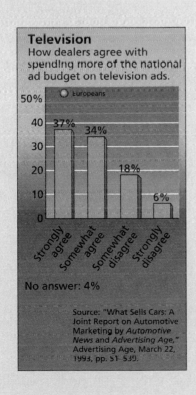

Television
How dealers agree with
spending more of the national
ad budget on television ads.

Europeans
50%
40
37%
34%
30
20
18%
10
6%
0

Strongly agree
Somewhat agree
Somewhat disagree
Strongly disagree

No answer: 4%

Source: "What Sells Cars: A
Joint Report on Automotive
Marketing by *Automotive
News* and *Advertising Age*,"
Advertising Age, March 22,
1993, pp. 51–539.

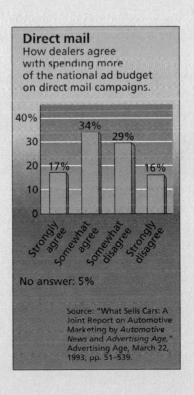

Direct mail
How dealers agree
with spending more
of the national ad budget
on direct mail campaigns.

40%
34%
29%
30
20
17%
16%
10
0

Strongly agree
Somewhat agree
Somewhat disagree
Strongly disagree

No answer: 5%

Source: "What Sells Cars: A
Joint Report on Automotive
Marketing by *Automotive
News* and *Advertising Age*,"
Advertising Age, March 22,
1993, pp. 51–539.

Advertisements for Yourself

Some of the principles of advertising in business marketing can be applied to the written communications required for your career search, specifically cover letters and résumés. The presence of "salient attributes and hidden qualities" is a factor in opting for advertising. How does this apply to your "advertising" activities? Your cover letters and résumés should feature your salient characteristics (your relevant education, experience, and personal profile) and your hidden qualities (evidence of intangible achievements in such areas as commitment, initiative, and leadership).

Business advertising also emphasizes the importance of objectives and approach. What is your objective when you send out cover letters and résumés? You will probably measure success by the number of interviews you receive. You can do a mass mailing of hundreds of letters and résumés or spend time developing high-quality contacts and then do a selective mailing. Experience suggests that the latter is a more productive use of time.

Once you have set your advertising objectives, think about the details of your "ads." The cover letter is the first document the reader sees. It should attract attention and generate interest. There must be a reason for the reader to read further. One way to interest the reader is to mention that an employee of the organization suggested you write. If you have no personal reference, then highlight your best skills and the work experience that would appeal to your reader's organization. Your cover letter and résumé provide an opportunity to demonstrate your creativity in what you say about yourself and how you say it.

In refining your advertising program, talk to people who could provide a "test market" for your plans. Consult school counselors, campus interviewers, fellow students, and recent graduates on the key features of your advertising program. Also, be creative. Think of the unique extras that make you stand out from others. For example, one student obtained a summer job with a large consumer products company because she sent along a copy of her class project, a review of the company's annual report. Some students have included news items on their achievements or special roles.

Questions

1. How would you rate the appeal of the openings of your cover letters? How can you strengthen those letters as attention-getters?
2. How would you rate the appeal of your skill and knowledge summary in your cover letters? How can you strengthen those letters to better feature your benefits and provide a more competitive focus?

Jobs in Advertising

Advertising has been called a glamorous profession. Those in it will tell you that it is also pressure filled and analytical, yet rewarding in its own way. In advertising, the product is communication, and advertising professionals must master its concepts and techniques.

Skills needed.   Many executives find that students come to agencies with distorted impressions of advertising. They stress the need to spend some time finding out the realities of the trade. A good way to do this is through the summer programs many agencies offer. Also, be sure to examine not only the management of an agency, but also its client roster and the quality of the work done for its clients.

Entering the field. Many ad agencies prefer to hire undergraduates instead of MBAs for several reasons. First of all, they can pay undergraduates less and then give them a chance to prove themselves before raising their salaries. Second, since most graduate business schools lack emphasis and course work in advertising, MBAs know little more about advertising than undergraduates, although they do have a broader background in business and, perhaps, more maturity.

Types of positions. One can begin as a media buyer, copywriter, or, less often, as a junior or assistant account executive. The media buyer chooses the media that will carry the client's ad and arranges for buying the time and space. Those who write the words for ads or the scripts for commercials are called copywriters. After a year or two in one of these positions—or sometimes in a position in the agency's marketing research department—you may become a junior or assistant executive. You will do some analytical work and have moderate contact with clients, usually with just one account. From this point on, the responsibility increases and the workload is heavy. Strategic thinking and planning, as well as implementation in a highly competitive, fast-paced environment, become very important. The next promotions are to full account executive, account supervisor, management supervisor, and then into various principal positions in the agency.

Atmosphere and salaries. Some agencies offer formal training programs, while others use on-the-job training. Although entry-level salaries are low, increases come quickly, and the fringe benefits and bonuses are often very good.

Jobs in Public Relations

Members of the public relations department must be kept fully advised of internal changes in marketing strategy, advertising, and new products. They must, at the same time, share this and information about products, labor policies, community activities, and social programs with the public. They must also deal directly with the news media and are often responsible for internal communication, including employee and management newsletters.

Skills needed. Although public relations is a part of the marketing function, a background in communications or journalism is necessary. Because the public relations department is the link between the organization and its various publics, effective communication skills are vital.

Entering the field. The entry-level position is usually as a public relations trainee, which could involve preparing press releases or working on company publications. People often specialize in certain areas within the public relations department and/or work their way up to vice president or director of public relations.

Atmosphere and salaries. Entry-level jobs in public relations are not highly paid, and the compensation for top jobs in public relations depends largely on the firm and its industry. In the past, industrial firms have tended to pay better than consumer marketers. Working toward the goal of projecting the desired company image to the public is an important and difficult task, but a creative and rewarding one.

CHapTeR 16

Personal Selling

LEARNING OBJECTIVES

Upon completing this chapter, you will be able to do the following:

■ **Understand** why personal selling is an important part of the promotion mix.

■ **Explain** how various types of sales jobs differ.

■ **Define** the three phases in the sale of a product.

■ **Describe** the steps in the personal selling process.

■ **Identify** the responsibilities of the sales manager and understand the importance of each area.

Marketing Profile

Forging Ahead Technologically at Forbes and Elsewhere

Imagine the following scenario: A sales representative for *Forbes* magazine is calling on a potential new customer. If the sales rep makes a persuasive presentation and answers all of the prospect's questions satisfactorily, the customer may decide to purchase advertising space in *Forbes*. The sales rep settles into a seat in the prospective client's office but instead of opening her mouth, she opens her briefcase. Inside is a Sony portable CD-I player, a form of compact-disc player that contains a complete presentation on *Forbes* magazine stored on CD-ROM. The material in the presentation is broken into chunks and the random access nature of the chunks allows the salesperson, or the prospect, to customize the presentation to meet the needs and interests of the prospective customer. Furthermore, the presentation is interactive. The CD asks the prospect questions and then proceeds based on the answers it receives.

The presentation used by *Forbes* was developed in 1993 by Murray Multimedia, Incorporated, of Blairstown, New Jersey. it cost *Forbes* $100,000. *Forbes* then equipped each of its sales reps with a $1,200 player so that the presentation could be taken into the field. So far *Forbes* is pleased with the results.

Interactive compact-disc presentations are the latest technological tool in the modern salesperson's bag of tricks. They follow on the heels of laptop computers, which began infiltrating the sales scene in the 1980s. Basic laptop computers do not offer the interactivity and amount of information made possible by the latest CD-ROM technology. Even so, laptop computers have offered significant improvements over traditional sales presentation tools such as flip charts and slide shows. Salespeople in the 1990s typically use laptops not only as presentation aids but also as means of instantly accessing information on inventory, shipping, and customer service.

In addition to the improvements brought about by advances in CD-ROM technology, downsizing has helped improve the value of the computer as a sales tool. In many instances laptops have been replaced by "smaller-than-laptop" subcompact computers. Palm-size, pen-based computers, for example, weigh only about one pound. The GRID Pad is one such machine. The hand-held computer uses a tethered pen stylus instead of a keyboard. The pen is used to select options by touching or directly writing on the screen. Best Foods Baking Group has its salespeople use the tablet to track deliveries of baked goods to supermarkets. Salespeople at Marrow Merrell Dow in Kansas City tote a GRID Pad instead of drug samples when calling on medical clients. The physicians use the pen to sign electronic forms to order samples.

The nature of future advances in computer technology is anybody's guess, though certainly they can be counted on to continue at a fast and furious pace. As pointed out by one *Forbes* sales representative, however, it should be remembered that computers are tools that are only as good as the salesperson who uses them.

Personal selling is promotion that relies on personal interactions between buyer and seller. Personal interaction is often the best way to persuade someone to purchase a good or service. Each of us has, at one time or another, used personal-selling skills. Telling a prospective employer about our abilities and skills, selling used furniture at a garage sale, and even persuading a friend to drive more carefully all require personal interaction and persuasion. In simple terms, personal selling uses human relations skills.

The old maxim "Nothing happens until a sale is made" is worth keeping in mind when considering personal selling. In this chapter we will see that personal selling is an extremely important and necessary part of the promotion mix. The job is done by salespeople, who attempt to establish two-way communication with potential buyers.[1]

We begin by discussing the importance of personal selling to an organization. The various types of sales jobs are reviewed, and each step in the personal selling process is considered. We then discuss the job of managing the personal selling force. This consideration includes decisions about the number of salespeople to hire, the kind of salespeople needed, how to motivate the sales team, and how to evaluate their performances.

THE IMPORTANCE OF PERSONAL SELLING

The salesperson must tailor the communication to fit the prospective customer's needs, expressions, and overall behavior. Because selling involves direct interactions between people, it is the most human, flexible, and dynamic part of the promotion mix.

The United States Census Bureau statistics suggest that about 8 percent of the labor force, or approximately 7 million people, work in sales. Many of those simply collect money at check-out counters, but others find customers, sell creatively, close sales, and provide service to customers afterward. Even those at the cash register help "sell" the store to the customers, though they are not always aware of their impact.

Historically many types of products have needed the creativity of personal selling to gain acceptance in the marketplace.[2] Most consumers are hesitant to change from old, familiar products or ways of doing things. Someone must communicate the advantages of and demonstrate new products before they are accepted. This type of communication and demonstration has occurred with many products most people take for granted such as television, microwave ovens, vacuum cleaners, videocassette recorders, exercise equipment, vacations to Hawaii, and long-wear, disposable contact lenses. Through the creative efforts of salespeople, these products have become integral parts of modern life.

Salespeople can be thought of as operating with one foot in a firm and one foot with a customer. They are **boundary spanners** who serve as a link between an organization and its customers. In this capacity, salespeople act as agents who continually receive, process, and transmit information back and forth between the public and the organization. The salesperson is the *image agent* of the company. He or she is the contact person, the representative of the company who affects and controls the customer's perceptions and evaluations of the company and its products and services. The salesperson is also the communication link from the customer to the company, hence he or she acts as a *liaison agent*. As liaison agent the salesperson should be trained to report customers' dissatisfactions with the company, its programs, products, and services. This feedback helps reduce unnecessarily lost sales and bad word-of-mouth reports. The salesperson is in a good position to act as *intelligence agent* and report to the company changes in the marketplace, such as changes in customers' choice criteria, competition, and the environment. As we saw in the Marketing

Profile that begins this chapter, new technology is making it easier for the salesperson to span the boundary between a firm and its customers.

The work of salespeople is related to the work of many other people in society. A chain reaction follows each sale, starting with the first reorder through the wholesaler to the larger replacement orders for factory production with basic items that come from farms and mines. Hence, salespeople affect the economic health of a society.

Personal selling and salespeople have frequently battled negative images despite the importance of the selling function to economic growth, a high standard of living, and full employment. Although these negative images have diminished, many people continue to possess perceptions of salespeople as being overly aggressive, high-pressure, fast-talkers. Interestingly, research has found that American salespeople are generally perceived as more pushy than their counterparts in other countries.[3] As our society advances its understanding of the role of personal selling and marketing in general in market-driven organizations, positive images should grow.

Another factor contributing to a change in perceptions about personal selling is the increase in professionalism. The professionalization of the sales job has come about gradually, with standards being established by various accreditation groups. For example, the American College of Life Underwriters offers a Chartered Life Underwriters certificate to salespeople who complete a rigorous course of training and study. Colleges and universities educate the public by offering courses in marketing and personal selling.[4] Today, the salesperson's responsibilities require more education and technical training than ever before.

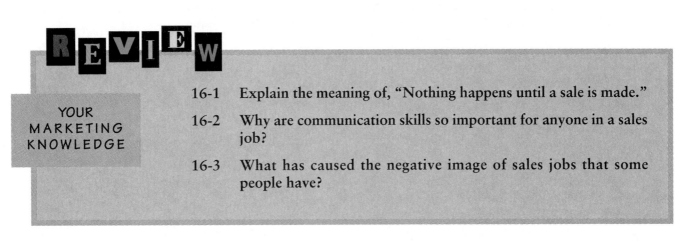

R E V I E W

YOUR MARKETING KNOWLEDGE

16-1   Explain the meaning of, "Nothing happens until a sale is made."

16-2   Why are communication skills so important for anyone in a sales job?

16-3   What has caused the negative image of sales jobs that some people have?

TYPES OF SALES JOBS

Personal-selling jobs differ on such dimensions as need for training, independence, compensation, location, creativity, and type of customers served. Generally, more complex products or products with high economic value rely more on the efforts of personal selling. Based on the functions they perform, salespeople can be classified into three groups: order getters, order takers, and support personnel.[5]

Order Getters

An **order getter** is a salesperson concerned with seeking out potential customers and persuading them to buy a product. The order-getting job requires finding new buyers and increasing sales to old customers by creative selling. In order to accomplish these tasks, the order getter must work closely with a potential customer. An order getter begins by consulting a potential customer, gaining insight into the potential customer's problems, and then working to demonstrate how his or her company's goods and services can solve those problems. Because of this process, order getters are often described as engaging in **consultative selling.**

Producers of all types of goods and services, but especially business products, need order getters to find new prospects, present the products, and facilitate the exchange of goods. Order getters often tell customers how a product can be used, reordered, and modified. The order getter's skillful ability to explain becomes especially important when many competitors exist. In these situations, order getters must clearly show how their products can solve a customer's problems better than products of the competition. For example, an order getter for GRID Systems Corporation, a producer of laptop computers, must be able to show why the company's pen-based GRID Pad meets the needs of the customer better than a Texas Instrument Travelmate 3000 or the Poget PC.

In wholesaling, order getters often serve as counselors to retailers, advising them how to sell goods. A food wholesaler, for example, might offer training seminars on how to display goods to independent retail grocers. Services such as checking inventory, performing product demonstrations, advertising, and conducting special promotions are also frequently offered.

At the retail level, order getters are needed to increase the sales of unsought goods. Convincing a customer that he or she needs a set of pots and pans or encyclopedias can be difficult. Order getters must persuade customers that the goods will satisfy important needs. For example, an encyclopedia is sold as a good that can provide information and enjoyment for many years. Reluctant customers must be persuaded that these needs are worth the cost.

Order getters are also needed at the retail level to sell shopping goods. Buyers of cameras, furniture, automobiles, and clothing are often looking for the best price

Order getters at the retail level must persuade customers that the goods will satisfy important needs.

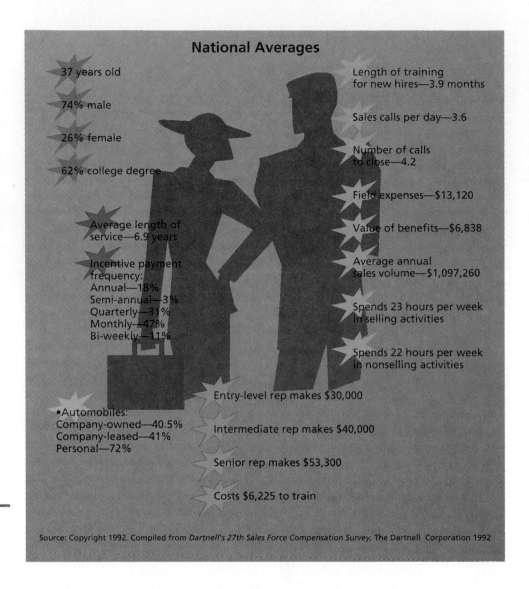

National Averages

37 years old

74% male

26% female

62% college degree

Average length of
service—6.9 years

Incentive payment
frequency:
Annual—18%
Semi-annual—3%
Quarterly—31%
Monthly—47%
Bi-weekly—11%

•Automobiles:
Company-owned—40.5%
Company-leased—41%
Personal—72%

Length of training
for new hires—3.9 months

Sales calls per day—3.6

Number of calls
to close—4.2

Field expenses—$13,120

Value of benefits—$6,838

Average annual
sales volume—$1,097,260

Spends 23 hours per week
in selling activities

Spends 22 hours per week
in nonselling activities

Entry-level rep makes $30,000

Intermediate rep makes $40,000

Senior rep makes $53,300

Costs $6,225 to train

Source: Copyright 1992. Compiled from *Dartnell's 27th Sales Force Compensation Survey*, The Dartnell Corporation 1992

FIGURE 16.1
Dartnell Profile:
The American Sales
Professional

and quality. Order getters who are helpful, informed, and interesting can be invaluable. Figure 16.1 presents some characteristics of order getters.

Many companies have found that their order getters' efforts can be made more effective through a process known as team selling. **Team selling** is the combination of sales and nonsales people under the direction of a leader who sets strategy and coordinates flows of information.[6] A sales team might consist of an order getter sales representative, an engineer, a technician, and a product manager. The team works together to identify and understand the problems and needs of a potential customer. Team selling has been described as the future of sales.[7] The "Marketing in Action: Teaming Up to Increase Sales" describes how team selling works.

Order Takers

Order takers are salespeople who complete sales made to regular or repeat customers. The customers do not need to be convinced that the product will meet their needs or solve their problems. Although order takers do fairly routine work, their responsibilities should not be underestimated. Without order takers, the regular or repeat customer might well purchase goods elsewhere.

Order takers at the manufacturing level often have a regular sales route. As part of the job and in the process of making calls, they often serve as sources of infor-

MARKETING *IN ACTION*

Teaming Up to Increase Sales

What does falling backward from a five-foot-high perch and hoping others will catch you have to do with selling? A lot, according to many proponents of team selling. Traditionally sales has been perceived as a fairly independent career. Success or failure, according to this view, is largely the responsibility of the salesperson alone. The "trust fall" exercise, however, is aimed at reeducating salespeople to see selling as a team effort.

Team selling has grown in the last decade, largely because of the complexity and global nature of corporate business.

For example, it took a team of 50 General Electric salespeople to win a large contract with General Motors' new Saturn subsidiary. The team represented eight divisions. A high-level executive coordinated the effort. This turned out to be more effective than having all salespeople calling on Saturn at once. Another example is Lotus Development Corporation, which composed teams of two members, a salesperson and a systems engineer, to introduce its Notes software package.

As these examples suggest, the team selling concept is more prevalent in organizations with high-tech product lines than in other industries. Digital Equipment Corporation and IBM have employed team selling for many years. Teams at Digital Equipment include sales representatives, engineers, technicians, and product managers. High-tech products often require considerable initial customer education. Hence, engineering and maintenance employees are needed for customer assistance.

The main advantage of team selling is that the company obtains the maximum benefit from selling to a large, diversified client. How? By synchronizing the work of all the salespeople representing the different product lines. A team is more likely "to spot a chance to fill a large corporation's emerging need for a tangential product than individual salespeople whose interest is to sell their own small array of products," says Stephen X. Doyle, a consultant in sales management. Companies involved in team selling also believe that it helps them forge solid relationships with their clients. Thus, "clients that make their buying decisions based only on price are not likely prospects for team selling," Doyle adds.

Team selling seems attractive, but it is not always easy. The first obstacle lies in the team formation. Forming a group with individuals who were originally hired on the basis of their abilities to work independently is a difficult task. "It's just awfully hard to get everybody singing out of the same hymn book," Doyle says. Resistance by salespeople is another major obstacle to team selling. The salespeople will likely resist team selling because it threatens their autonomy and their commissions.

The key to overcoming these obstacles appears to be training. Teams need to be trained in a range of skills and behaviors that stress partnership with each other and with customers. Training sessions should focus on topics such as team building and conflict resolution. Retreats focused on building or enhancing team spirit have included exercises such as the trust fall, having participants lead blindfolded colleagues around, and having participants fit with tethering harnesses leap from atop telephone poles. This latter is designed to prove to the jumper that much can be accomplished with the support of a team. In this case, the team support is provided by fellow participants standing around encouraging the jumper to believe that he or she can do it.

Team selling is seen by many as the future of sales. According to one proponent, "One person can't do it all anymore."

mation and trainers. They inform customers about prices, terms, and new developments and train them in the proper use and display of the products. A snack-food manufacturer, for example, might use order takers to serve retailers who regularly purchase from the company. In addition to taking and filling orders, the salesperson would alert retailers to new products coming out, sales promotions being planned, and suggest creative ways to display the company's offerings.

The wholesale order taker exists to serve the customer, regularly calling on business customers or retailers and then making sure the order is filled on time and accurately.[8] Similar to a manufacturer's order takers, wholesale order takers might act as sources of information and training for their customers.

Order taking at the retail level, for example at a Toys "Я" Us checkout counter or supermarket bakery counter, is routine. The goods are brought to the counter and sales are rung up. The order taker completes the sale by wrapping or bagging and making change. At the retail level the order-taking job is not so challenging or well-paying as other forms of order taking.

The distinction between order takers and order getters can get fuzzy. A good order taker often acts as an order getter. By paying attention to customers, he or she can enhance sales. A waiter or waitress at a restaurant, for example, can often sell more by suggesting appetizers, wine, or dessert with the meal.

On the other hand, efforts by order takers to become order getters can negatively affect sales. Some electronic stores are experimenting with a new approach to order taking that emphasizes making no sales pitch.[9] Best Buy, Tandy's Incredible Universe stores, and Highland Superstores are using noncommissioned sales staffs. The switch to straight salary is based on focus-group findings that people do not like high-pressure salespeople. Customers appear to want service, not self-service, but they want to deal with salespeople who are not aggressive in trying to make a sale. Such customers would appear to want the ultimate order taker.

Support Salespeople

Support salespeople are involved in the selling process but typically do not get orders themselves. They are used primarily to market business products. Support personnel usually locate prospects, educate customers, foster goodwill, and provide postsale service. Support personnel include missionary salespeople, trade salespeople, and technical specialists.

Missionary salespeople.   The missionary salesperson (also called the *detail person*) works for manufacturers and calls on their intermediaries and customers.[10] He or she visits professional people such as doctors and dentists, giving them literature and leaving samples of the company's products. Missionary salespeople describe the products, answer questions, and pave the way for later sales. They attempt to stimulate demand, build goodwill, and train their intermediaries' salespeople. Merck, Hospital Supply, Eli Lilly, and Smith Kline Beckman are manufacturers that use missionary salespeople to promote their products to retail druggists, physicians, and hospital pharmacists. These missionary salespeople hope their efforts will result in physicians' writing prescriptions for the drugs their companies sell.

Trade salespeople.   The trade salesperson is not only a support person, but often an order taker. The main part of the job, however, is to help customers promote products. Companies such as Nabisco, Kellogg's, and Sunshine Bakery use trade salespeople to arrange shelf space, set up displays, distribute samples, and provide in-store demonstrations.

Technical specialists.   Technical specialists act as consultants and often help design products or systems to meet a client's needs. A background in engineering or the physical sciences is often needed to be a technical specialist. For example, Brown & Root Engineering and Construction Company has technical specialists who work with customers to design highways, distribution facilities, and electrical utility plants.

The three types of sales jobs—order getters, order takers, and support sales-people—are used only as a general classification system. Many sales jobs do not fit neatly into one type. A salesperson, working in a retail store or showroom or calling

The missionary salesperson works for manufacturers and calls on his or her intermediaries and customers. Many pharmaceutical firms hire missionary salespeople to promote their products to retail druggists, physicians, and hospital pharmacists.

on a customer, may do all of these activities. The job may be routine in many respects but still require creativity.

The type of person needed to do the sales job and the compensation involved depend primarily on the mix of sales tasks, found in the job description. A **job description** is a general statement about the tasks and behaviors required to perform a specific job. A job description for a sales representative of FMC Corporation, which manufactures food-processing machinery, agricultural machinery, and chemicals, is presented in Figure 16.2. This describes the district sales representative as an order getter and order taker and a support to customers.

FIGURE 16.2
Job Description

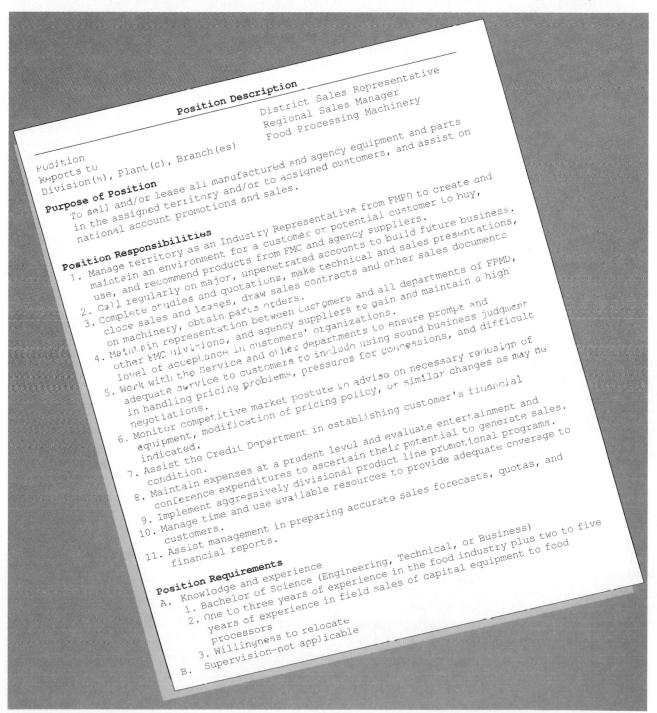

Position Description

Position: District Sales Representative
Reports to: Regional Sales Manager
Division(s), Plant(s), Branch(es): Food Processing Machinery

Purpose of Position

To sell and/or lease all manufactured and agency equipment and parts in the assigned territory and/or to assigned customers, and assist on national account promotions and sales.

Position Responsibilities

1. Manage territory as an Industry Representative from FMPD to create and maintain an environment for a customer or potential customer to buy, use, and recommend products from FMC and agency suppliers.
2. Call regularly on major, unpenetrated accounts to build future business.
3. Complete studies and quotations, make technical and sales presentations, close sales and leases, draw sales contracts and other sales documents on machinery, obtain parts orders.
4. Maintain representation between customers and all departments of FPMD, other FMC divisions, and agency suppliers to gain and maintain a high level of acceptance in customers' organizations.
5. Work with the Service and other departments to include using sound business judgment in handling pricing problems, pressures for concessions, and difficult negotiations.
6. Monitor competitive market posture to advise on necessary redesign of equipment, modification of pricing policy, or similar changes as may be indicated.
7. Assist the Credit Department in establishing customer's financial condition.
8. Maintain expenses at a prudent level and evaluate entertainment and conference expenditures to ascertain their potential to generate sales.
9. Implement aggressively divisional product line promotional programs.
10. Manage time and use available resources to provide adequate coverage to customers.
11. Assist management in preparing accurate sales forecasts, quotas, and financial reports.

Position Requirements

A. Knowledge and experience
1. Bachelor of Science (Engineering, Technical, or Business)
2. One to three years of experience in the food industry plus two to five years of experience in field sales of capital equipment to food processors
3. Willingness to relocate
B. Supervision—not applicable

THE PERSONAL SELLING PROCESS

It is an old adage that successful salespeople are born that way. For example, Colonel Sanders was a natural at selling fried chicken and Walt Disney was great at selling laughter. However, most successful salespeople are not born with the required attributes, style, intelligence, and personality. Rather they develop them through hard work, dedication, positive attitudes, and proper training. The personal-selling process includes a number of steps people can be trained to perform effectively.

The sale of a product or service has three major phases.[11] The activities in each phase differ for each type of sales job. The phases described here generally fit the order-getting type. First is the *preparation* phase, which includes everything that takes place before the customer is approached. Next is the *persuasion phase*, in which the potential customer is shown a need that the salesperson can help fill. Finally there is the *transaction* phase, in which the sale is finalized. Figure 16.3 presents the three phases and their respective activities.

Phase 1: Preparation

Before face-to-face, buyer-to-seller communication begins, the necessary groundwork must be done. This groundwork is done in two steps: The salesperson must find the prospective customers, then the salesperson must prepare for the interaction with the prospects.

Prospecting. **Prospecting** involves finding prospective customers. Prospects may come from many different sources: current customers, previous customers, friends and relatives, advertising leads, other sales personnel selling noncompeting lines, and newspapers. The prospects list identifies possibilities, but does not suggest which are most likely.

Another part of prospecting is deciding how much time to spend. Judgments must be made on the basis of potential sales, likelihood of repeat sales, and the financial situation of the prospect. The salesperson should develop some type of ranking from "live, good prospect" to "cold, unlikely prospect" since each prospect cannot be covered in the same way. Some prospects require continuous attention and cultivation; others can be checked with a telephone call.[12]

If a salesperson's product has widespread demand, he or she may resort to the **cold canvass** method of prospecting, in which calls are made to every person or company in a group. Since no advance information on the needs or financial status of each prospect is available, the salesperson relies on the law of averages to generate sales. H. J. Heinz Company was launched by cold canvassing.[13] Henry J. Heinz made his first big sale after a cold call on the largest supply house in London. Today, Heinz is a $7.1 billion business.[14] DEVCOR Software Development in San Diego has relied on cold calls to expand business. While DEVCOR initially developed software for

FIGURE 16.3
Three Phases of Making a Sale

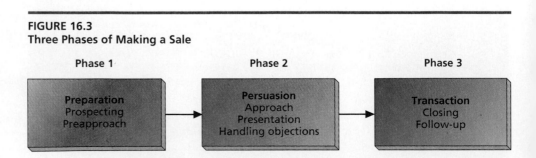

the automobile industry, cold calls to the general and commercial aviation industry enabled the firm to expand.[15]

The increasing cost of making personal visits has increased the popularity of telemarketing. **Telemarketing** is using the telephone to make personal sales calls. A single sales call can now cost as much as $300, and it may take five to seven personal visits to complete a sale.[16] Telemarketing is used in a variety of ways: communicating company and product information to prospects and customers, conducting marketing surveys, creating sales strategies, prospecting for new sales, screening sales leads, responding to toll-free (800) numbers for orders, and direct sales solicitations. A telemarketer can contact a daily average of 21 to 42 prospects; a sales rep will only be able to make three to six in-person calls.[17] In 1994 the telemarketing industry surpassed $600 billion. Heavy users include Apple Computer and Pitney-Bowes.[18] The "Spotlight on Ethics: Protecting Consumers from Telemarketing" describes some relevant legislation that has passed as telemarketing has grown.

Preapproach. Before making the contact, the salesperson should learn as much as possible about the prospect in order to anticipate questions and indicate to the prospect the salesperson's seriousness.[19] The process of gaining this information is the **preapproach.** The salesperson might want to know something about the products or brands the prospect is using, the personal likes and dislikes of the prospect, and the prospect's preferences for service. When calling on a company, a salesperson can consult annual reports, Dun and Bradstreet reports, the Census of Manufacturers, newspapers, and the salespeople of noncompetitive goods or services for information.

Phase 2: Persuasion

The persuasion phase of the selling process involves steps aimed at convincing a prospect to purchase the product. This phase includes the approach, the presentation, and handling objections.

The approach. The **approach** is the first direct contact between the salesperson and the prospect. Factors such as timing and tone are critical in laying the groundwork for the presentation. After all, if a prospect is not reached through the appropriate approach, the salesperson may never get the opportunity to make a presentation.

Some prospects are impossible to reach at certain times. Therefore, whether the approach is attempted in the morning, the afternoon, or the evening can be critical to its success. Some business customers identify a set time of the week or month when they will meet with salespeople. It is important that salespeople plan their approaches to coincide with the time a prospect will be willing to listen.

The tone of the approach is also a factor in its success. Some approaches seem to beg for rejection. A retail clerk, for example, who asks a browsing customer, "May I help you?" can probably predict what the response will be before it is uttered. The best approaches get a prospect's attention, peak interest, and pave the way for the salesperson to make a presentation.

The presentation. The **presentation** is the communication part of making the sale. In this step the salesperson communicates information to persuade the prospect. Presentations often include demonstrations. The presentation should be carefully planned by the salesperson. Several models of consumer behavior offer guidelines in planning a sales presentation. We will consider two such models, the *stimulus-response model* and the *need-satisfaction model*, in this section.[20]

The **stimulus-response model,** when used as a basis of a sales presentation, is also referred to as the **canned, packaged,** or **prepared presentation.** Such a presentation

MARKETING IN ACTION

Protecting Consumers from Telemarketers

Telemarketing is hot. With more than $600 billion in industry revenues in 1994 and more than 13 million employees, this form of selling has come into its own. These figures can be expected to continue to increase as the cost of traditional personal sales calls keeps climbing. Perceptions of the professionalism of most types of personal selling have improved in recent years; however, the telemarketing industry remains largely perceived as slightly sleazy. Consumers' views of telemarketing and telemarketers often range from mildly obnoxious to totally unethical.

In 1992, amid widespread reports of fraud in the telemarketing industry, a bill called the Telemarketing and Consumer Fraud and Abuse Prevention Act was introduced into the U.S. Congress. The act requires the Federal Trade Commission to establish rules on telemarketing activities, to prohibit fraudulent activities by the industry, and to empower state attorneys general to take action in cases where fraud is determined to have occurred. The FTC is particularly encouraged to:

1. consider a requirement that goods or services offered by telemarketing be shipped or provided within a specified period

2. authorize consumers to cancel telemarketing sales orders within a specified period

3. place restrictions on the hours of the day during which telemarketing calls can be made

4. prohibit telemarketing by computers that do not permit the consumer to terminate the call

Furthermore, telemarketers are restricted from representing themselves as marketing researchers.

The bill received the support of both houses of the U.S. Congress in 1992 but failed to become law before Congress adjourned that year. It was reintroduced in 1993 and passed the U.S. Senate. As this is written the bill is still pending in the U.S. House of Representatives but is expected to pass and be enacted before the end of 1994. The act would be put into action six months following its passage.

While some telemarketers feel the rules of this act are overly restrictive, many welcome the legislation. The rules, they reason, will help to "clean up the industry," thus improving the overall image of telemarketing and thereby benefitting honest and ethical telemarketers.

The Telemarketing and Consumer Fraud and Abuse Prevention Act is not the first piece of legislation aimed at protecting consumers from the telemarketing industry. In 1991 Congress passed the Telephone Consumer Protection Act, stating that a telemarketer must obey a consumer's request to "never call me again" even if the request is simply issued verbally. A recent lawsuit tested the act. Citibank Corporation settled out of court with Michael Jacobson after ignoring two requests from Mr. Jacobson not to call him again. The act also imposes restrictions on the use of autodialing devices. Autodialing devices call telephone numbers randomly. The autodialing clause of the Telephone Consumer Protection Act was overturned in May 1993 when a federal judge ruled that the limitation constituted a hardship for small businesses.

---

involves a salesperson delivering a standard commentary, designed to elicit a positive response, to all prospects. This notion is built on stimulus-response theory, first introduced in Chapter 6. It can be summarized as follows:

Drive ———————▶ Cue ———————▶ Response ———————▶ Reward

As you recall from Chapter 6, a *drive* is a stimulus strong enough to impel a prospect into activity, and a *cue* is a stimulus that guides the response of the prospect. Cues may be visual or auditory, or may rely on tasting, smelling, or feeling.

The logic behind the canned presentation is that a prospect will give the desired "yes" response to a persuasive presentation. In this theory, the prospect is passive and simply responds to the right stimulus. The encyclopedia salesperson (an order getter) describing learning as a lifetime experience that begins at birth and ends only at death, or the salesclerk who says, "That hat was made for you, it is simply beautiful," is using a canned approach. What goes on in the prospect's mind is not important; only finding the right stimulus to make the sale counts.

In contrast to the "me-oriented" stimulus-response model, need satisfaction is marketing-concept oriented. The **need-satisfaction model** emphasizes the internal motivation of the prospect, pinpointing specific wants, instead of throwing out cues in the hope that one or more will be on target.[21] A need-satisfaction presentation is often used to sell insurance, individual retirement accounts, stocks and bonds, and farm machinery.

Understanding what a prospect really needs or wants calls for skills such as excellent listening, problem-solving ability, careful observance of nonverbal communications, and an attempt to take the place of the other person. To fully develop the need-satisfaction approach, the salesperson must be a student of internal motivation and have a good understanding of human behavior.

Sometimes a salesperson using a need-satisfaction presentation may not recommend a product or service to a customer if it will not satisfy that customer's needs. This decision is made to avoid creating ill will after the sale. The astute salesperson, however, will report back to the company, providing information needed to create better products in the future.

Bruce Woolpert is an example of someone who uses the need-satisfaction approach to sales.[22] Mr. Woolpert is president and CEO of the Granite Rock Company. Granite Rock is a construction contractor and supplier of building materials. The firm begins the sales process by meeting with potential customers to understand their needs. Products and services are then designed to meet those needs. One customer, for example, was building a flood-control structure. Much of the concrete for the project would be under water. Granite Rock worked to solve the problem by delivering and pouring the concrete at 2:00 A.M., during low tide. Woolpert states, "Anytime a customer asks us to do something—unless it's illegal or immoral—we will do it."

Both of these models, used as the basis of a sales presentation, emphasize the importance of persuasion. Both models rely on communication skills. The two are quite different, however, in terms of how important it is for the salesperson to have good listening skills or an understanding of the prospect's thoughts and ideas. A comparison of the two models is presented in Table 16.1.

Whatever the type of presentation, it is usually supported with visual and audio-visual aids. Computer presentations, movies, brochures, manuals, slides, and product samples can all be effective in helping to persuade a customer. Anything within reason is used so the prospect can see, touch, or handle the product. A prospect who can handle a product will become better acquainted with it and remember its features and uses. Product demonstrations can be critical parts of a presentation.

Handling objections. Objections are excuses for not buying that slow down the momentum needed to make a sale. Usually they are polite ways of informing the salesperson, "I am not interested." Even if there is a match between the product or

TABLE 16.1
A Comparison of the Stimulus-Response and Need-Satisfaction Models

Model	Communication Skills	Listening Skills	Knowledge of Prospect's Thoughts	Stimulus Value	Example Application
Stimulus-response	Important	Not very important	Not important	Extremely important	Door-to-door sales and telephone canvassing
Need-satisfaction	Important	Extremely important	Extremely important	Important	Sales of business or home computers

Visual and audiovisual aids, when used as part of the presentation, can help to persuade the customer to make a purchase.

service offered and the needs of the prospect, psychological resistance to closing a sale may build up. Resistance to spending too much time with the salesperson, a preference for maintaining established routines or habits, a lack of desire for what the salesperson is offering, reluctance to spend money on the good or service, bad feeling about salespeople in general, resistance to being dominated by salespeople, a preconceived idea about the good or service, and dislike for having to make a final decision are just some of the causes. Other objections may be very logical, focusing on price, product characteristics, delivery schedule, or type of company selling the product.

Tactics for handling an objection, psychological or logical, require communication and negotiating skills. There are six techniques:

1. *Ignore* the prospect's remark.
2. Meet the prospect's statement *head on* and *deny* it.
3. First *agree* with the prospect, then go on to *refute* the objection.
4. *Convert* the objection into a logical reason for buying.
5. Ask the prospect *why* and attempt to stimulate further discussion.
6. Ask the prospect to *work through* the situation.[23]

These techniques stress calmness, minimal interruption of the prospect, no downgrading of competitors' products, and anticipation of objections before they are raised. In essence, the salesperson tries to reduce a customer's fears by being an astute communicator and a proficient negotiator.

Phase 3: Transaction

Transaction is the final phase of the selling process. It consists of two steps, the closing and the follow-up.

Closing.   Every step taken to this point moves toward one goal—making, or **closing** the sale. If the salesperson fails to close properly, everything is lost. After the prospect's objections are handled, the closing begins. The salesperson may attempt a **trial close,** which is designed to test the customer's willingness to buy by asking, "When would you like this delivery?" or, "Do you want the car with the stick or the automatic shift?" Answers to these questions indicate how close the prospect is to making a decision. The trial close can also bring out the most important objections, which can then be addressed.

Another closing approach is the **assumption technique.** The salesperson assumes that the prospect is going to buy and says, "Did you decide on the blue or the green model?" or, "What day of the week should we deliver your refrigerator?"

In today's economy, salespeople are using the **urgency close** more and more. This type of close encourages the consumer to purchase now by suggesting that the deal may not be as good later. A customer might be told, for example, "Prices are going up 15 percent next week," or, "Because of shortages, this is the last group we will have available for four months."

The best closers appear to be salespeople who are always in what can be called a state of closing. They know that closing begins the minute the salesperson and the prospect meet. The questions they ask are timed correctly and always lead to the close.[24]

Follow-up. A salesperson's tasks do not stop once the sale is made and the order placed. What happens after the sale is the **follow-up.** The salesperson must make sure promises of delivery, service, and performance are met. Most businesses depend on repeat sales, which depend on following up on promises.

The follow-up work is designed to reduce the buyer's **cognitive dissonance,**[25] or postdecision anxiety. According to cognitive-dissonance theory, once a decision is made, anxiety often occurs and the buyer seeks reassurance that the best purchase was made. The salesperson can reduce dissonance by emphasizing the positive features of the product or service, complying with all prepurchase promises, and relating comments from other satisfied customers. Companies use follow-up in different ways. Saab calls new car owners monthly for the first quarter after the sale, then once per quarter for the next three quarters, then annually in the following years. Chevrolet relies on after-purchase seminars that focus on warranties, service, and maintenance.[26]

Although the steps in the selling process seem logical, they are not always followed. Some salespeople take shortcuts or disregard some steps; others have never been adequately informed. Hints about making a sale and following a sequence of steps have been offered by theorists, researchers, and practitioners. The following guidelines are offered to those interested in learning more about the personal-selling process.

1. The more closely matched the physical, social, and personal characteristics of customer and salesperson are, the more likely there will be a sale.
2. The more believable and trustworthy the customer perceives a salesperson to be, the more likely there will be a sale. To be believable, a salesperson has to believe in the product or service.
3. The more persuadable a customer is, the more likely there will be a sale.
4. Be gentle and remove objections from a customer cautiously. Remove objections without the customers noticing.
5. The more a salesperson can make prospective buyers view themselves favorably, the more likely there will be a sale.

The "Marketing in Action: Sales Pros Know the Eight Keys to Success" emphasizes some important considerations for salespeople that relate to the steps in the selling process.

MARKETING *IN ACTION*

Sales Pros Know the Eight Keys to Success

Salesmanship may not be the world's oldest profession, but it may well be the least appreciated.

Let's face it: What image comes to mind when you hear the word "salesperson?" Some guy in a checkered sport coat and loud tie trying to peddle a used car that a little old lady drove only to church on Sundays and to bingo on Wednesday nights? A fast-talking insurance salesman you do your best to avoid? Probably nothing you would consider professional.

Anyone can be a salesperson. If you went out right now and began knocking on the doors of businesses, within 24 hours you'd have a job as a salesperson. You might be on straight commission with no salary, draw, or expense account, and you'd have to write in your name on the business cards, but you'd be able to say that you were employed as a salesperson.

It's a fact: Anyone can say he or she is in sales. However, there's a world of difference between "being in sales" and being a professional salesperson, a knowledgeable expert and consultant who brings business-building ideas to his or her clients. Those professionals know there are eight key points that differentiate the pros from average salespeople.

1. *Selling is a skill, not a talent.* You may have thought of someone as a natural salesperson or a born salesperson, but professional selling is a learned skill, not a natural talent. It starts with knowledge and expertise about your product or service, your customers and their needs, your competition, and your industry.

   Professional salespeople have developed effective communication skills, including the ability to ask questions and listen, to identify customers' needs, and to address product benefits that will satisfy those needs.

2. *You are the most important product of all.* I'm sure you've heard people say that you must sell yourself, and it's true. If a customer isn't sold on you, chances are he or she will buy from someone else.

   Professional salespeople accept personal responsibility for themselves and their lives, committing themselves to personal development and an effective, organized personal management style.

3. *Relationships, emotions, and feelings are the key factors in sales success.* People buy from salespeople they like and trust, and though we often justify our decisions with facts and logic,

the trigger to sales success is often vivid images and emotions. Professional salespeople not only have all the facts, they also create positive emotions about themselves and their products.

4. *You must effectively identify and develop prospects.* That means having an organized system for locating qualified decision makers, the discipline to contact those people to request appointments, and the skills to persuade them to see you in person.

   Don't forget to provide proper service and follow-up to your current customers to help build repeat business and referrals.

5. *A sales call is a performance.* Make sure you've handled all your meeting room arrangements and double-check to be sure all your equipment is working properly.

   When you open your presentation, begin with a bang to get your prospect's undivided attention and interest. Get the prospect to participate in your demonstration to discover the truth for him- or herself.

6. *Develop the skills of effective negotiation.* Anyone can make a sale by cutting the price, but the professional salesperson closes a profitable sale by developing and using negotiation skills that identify all points of agreement to weave them together into a mutually beneficial package.

7. *Objections are your friends.* By encouraging the prospect to express objections, you uncover concerns, benefits, and buying motives that can help make the sale.

   The professional salesperson loves objections and has the skill to move every content-based objection directly towards a closing scenario.

8. *Always be closing.* The professional salesperson begins closing at the outset of the presentation by building an agreement and helping the prospect decide how, not whether, to buy. Through the judicious use of closing questions, this professional helps the prospect complete all the points of a mutually beneficial transaction.

These eight points highlight the difference between being just a salesperson and being a sales professional. Make a commitment to developing those skills and joining the ranks of the pros. There's just no other way to go.

16-4   What type of customer response suggests to a salesperson that the buyer is ready to make a purchase?

16-5   Give some examples of order getters and order takers with whom you do business on a regular basis.

16-6   Do you believe that successful salespeople are born? Why or why not?

SALES MANAGEMENT

Sales management is the planning, organizing, controlling, and directing of the individual and collective efforts of a sales force. The selling process requires a great deal of managerial guidance and coordination, and is, therefore, costly. Because costs are high, efficient management of the sales force is a major concern for firms, as well as an important responsibility. Table 16.2 lists the costs of a sales call for consumer, business-to-business, and service salespeople as surveyed by *Sales & Marketing Management*. Compensation is presented as the total direct sales costs. A cost-per-call is calculated for A and B territories. An A territory is defined as a metropolitan area where customers and prospects are heavily concentrated. A B territory reflects an area where customers are widely dispersed.

One of the biggest personnel promotion mistakes that firms make is to assume that a successful salesperson can manage a sales force. In fact, the job of managing a sales force involves much more than learning and following the steps in the selling process. The sales manager must build his or her salespeople into a team that achieves objectives compatible with the firm's total promotion strategy and with the overall marketing strategy of the organization. Figure 16.4 lists the activities that sales force managers engage in and the relationship of those activities to the levels of marketing strategy within the organization.

TABLE 16.2
Sales Costs: Metro (A) and Nonmetro (B) Areas

Industry	Total Direct Sales Costs	Calls per Territory per Year		Cost per Call per Territory	
		A	B	A	B
Consumer					
Range	$25,000–$120,000	561–1,122	374–748	$22.28–$213.90	$33.42–$320.86
Median	$72,500	841.5	561	$118.09	$177.17
Business-to-Business					
Range	$20,000–$155,000	561–935	374–748	$21.39–$276.29	$26.73–$414.44
Median	$87,500	748	561	$148.84	$220.58
Service					
Range	$21,000–145,000	748–1,496	374–935	$14.04–193.85	$22.46–$387.70
Median	$83,000	1,122	654.5	$103.95	$205.08

Source: "A User's Guide to the Survey of Selling Costs," *Sales & Marketing Management*, February 20, 1989, p. 5.

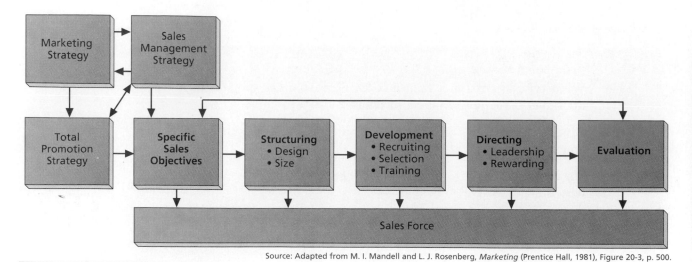

Source: Adapted from M. I. Mandell and L. J. Rosenberg, *Marketing* (Prentice Hall, 1981), Figure 20-3, p. 500.

FIGURE 16.4
Activities of Sales Force Managers

Setting Sales Objectives

The first activity a sales manager faces is the establishment of objectives. Objectives must be set both for the manager and for the sales team. Additionally, objectives that individual salespeople set for themselves are guided by the sales manager. All of these objectives should be specific, measurable, and have a deadline. Table 16.3 presents a few major target areas for which sales managers' objectives can be determined.

Sales managers expect salespeople to establish objectives for each step in the selling process. Guiding the sales force to set their objectives is a responsibility that requires the manager to understand each salesperson's ability, motivation, and goals. It also requires an ability to help develop meaningful, clearly stated, challenging, and timely objectives. For example, a set of *prospecting objectives* for a salesperson could be the following:

- To find at least six new prospects a week in the western territory for the period July 1 to December 31
- To close at least one sale from among these six prospects each week for the period July 1 to December 31
- To have at least one repeat sale every two months from the new group for the next year

TABLE 16.3
Target Areas for Establishing Sales Force Manager Objectives

Sample Target Areas*				
Total Sales	**Recruiting**	**Training**	**Motivation**	**Evaluation**
Increase volume	Improve job offer-acceptance ratio	Improve sales presentation	Reduce turnover	Develop equitable system
Increase repeat sales	Develop clear job descriptions	Develop subordinates	Improve sales performance	Provide personal development feedback to salespeople
Improve customer mix	Increase hiring of minorities	Train for new product	Develop sales contest	Improve counseling skills

* Target areas are short forms of more elaborate objectives that include a quantitative measure, time frame, and cost of accomplishment estimate. For example, the second recruiting objective could be written: Objective—To develop a complete set of job descriptions for sales representatives in eastern region by June 15, 1996, at a cost not to exceed $16,000.

Structuring the Sales Force

Establishing the structure of the sales force is another responsibility of sales managers. Two factors must be considered: the design of the sales force and the size of the sales force.

Design.   The design of the sales force has to do with how the salespeople are organized to sell the product. Organization can be by geographical territory, by product, or by customer.

The simplest design is one in which each salesperson sells the firm's full product line in a specific geographical territory and is responsible for successes and failures in that territory. Because of this direct responsibility, the salesperson is encouraged to work hard at selling and cultivating business ties. Worldwide Transportation Group, a consulting firm that focuses on the aviation industry, structures its clients into geographic territories. The firm uses these regions: West, Southwest, South, Upper Atlantic, and Upper Midwest.

The hierarchy of sales management by territory often includes a district sales manager, a regional sales manager responsible for several districts, and a national sales manager. This hierarchy serves as an incentive for those interested in being promoted from personal selling into administrative positions. It is typical for a technical representative to stay in the job for about six years and then to move to corporate headquarters as an instructor. After about two years as an instructor, a person could be moved to a staff position; after three years as a staff employee, the person might be promoted to a managerial position.

With sales management by product, the sales task is divided among different sales managers, each of whom directs operations for part of the product line. The decision to use the product line organizational structure depends on the benefits of product specialization outweighing the additional expenses. Because multiple sales forces are needed, this type of design could result in higher administrative and travel expenses.[27] A product design can also result in a prospect being called on by more than one salesperson from the same company. For the June 1994 introduction of Aleve, an analgesic designed to relieve headaches and compete with products like Tylenol, Procter & Gamble broke its sales force into product territories.

Companies sometimes design their sales forces along customer lines. This method is suitable when similar products are marketed to several types of customers. With the customer arrangement, special attention can be paid to the needs of each type of buyer. For example, the computer needs of colleges, manufacturing firms, retail stores, and banks are quite different. National Cash Register Corporation recognizes these differences and assigns its sales force on the basis of industry categories—retailing, financial, and educational. IBM uses two customer profiles to structure its sales force: those who are loyal to the company and product, and those who are considering other products or have recently bought other products.[28]

Few companies use a single design for structuring the sales force. Most use a combination, dividing the selling task into multiple arrangements. Nearly every sales department uses a geographical territory arrangement combined with the product or customer design. IBM also uses multiple bases. The company breaks its 40,000-member sales staff into 63 geographical regions, and then subdivides into areas that include distribution/finance, public/government sectors, manufacturing, and insurance.[29]

Size.   The second factor in structuring a sales force is size. A sales manager must decide how many salespeople to use. Sometimes the sales force is very large, which means larger market coverage, as well as more expense. For example, Nabisco has more than 3,000 salespeople.

A common approach to determining the size of the sale force is workload analysis. **Workload analysis** is a mathematical approach to determining sales force size. Using workload analysis, firms such as IBM, General Electric, or Polaroid might determine the necessary number of salespeople by estimating the extent of the selling task and dividing this by the amount a single salesperson could handle.

Suppose, for example, an appliance manufacturer sells toasters to two types of customers, discount stores and retailers. Suppose further that in a selected market there are approximately 600 retailers and 10 discount stores. The sales management team might, after careful analysis, decide to calculate how many salespeople are needed to make five calls on each retailer and five calls on each discount store in a year. A simple calculation would reveal that the sales force would have to make $5(600) + 5(10)$, or 3050 calls a year. If the average salesperson could make 750 calls a year, the manufacturer would need about four full-time salespeople (3050/750).

Another method of determining the size of the sales force is by the formula

$$SS = \frac{C \times F \times L}{A_T}$$

where SS = size of the sales force,
C = number of customers,
F = needed frequency of calls on customers,
L = length of average customer call, and
A_T = average amount of time each salesperson has available.

Suppose the number of customers is estimated to be about 5000 and about six calls per year should be made, with an average length of 30 minutes (.5 hour). The average salesperson works 2000 hours per year (40 hours a week × 50 weeks), but has only about 30 hours per week available for calls. The rest of the time is spent in meetings and traveling. Using the formula produces

$$SS = \frac{5000 \times 6 \times .5}{1500} = 10$$

This formula permits the sales manager to change variables and data as necessary. For example, the number of customers or the time for calls may change.

Developing a Sales Force

Three challenges must be met for an organization to compete effectively in securing sales talent. First, the organization must attract qualified candidates for sales positions. Second, it must identify potential selling talent, selecting the most qualified people from those who apply for sales jobs. Without qualified recruits and effective selection, the organization will never reach the third challenge, the training and motivation of the sales force.[30]

Recruitment.   **Recruitment** is the process of identifying and attracting candidates for sales positions. It is largely influenced by answers to two questions: What type of sales job is to be filled? What are the requirements of the sales position? The organization may attempt to locate candidates for the job from within the firm, but if this is not possible, an outside search must begin. Identifying and attracting candidates for screening are done through advertising, employee referrals, interviews with walk-ins, and referrals from public and private employment agencies and colleges and universities. Salespeople may also be located in other organizations in the same industry.

The selection process can include such steps as tests, interviews, background checks, and physical examinations.

Some organizations attempt to recruit and select candidates with what they consider ideal traits for the job. Identifying traits that will ensure success in sales is like identifying the stock purchases that will make you wealthy tomorrow. Some of the attributes frequently cited for sales success are high level of energy, ambition, tolerance, self-confidence, reflectiveness, intelligence, and friendliness. There still is no isolated and accurate model that can predict what makes a successful salesperson.[31]

Selection. **Selection** refers to the steps that the firm uses to identify and assess individuals and place them in sales positions. Such selection steps as tests, interviews, background checks, and physical examinations represent hurdles. If the candidate overcomes them, he or she is presumed able to do the job.

Psychological testing is a gauge many firms use to measure, in a consistent manner, characteristics related to effective sales performance and the degree to which a candidate possesses these characteristics. Such tests are only used as a supplement to other selection criteria, which include application forms, interviews, background or reference checks, and physical examinations. The decision to hire comes after every selection step has been passed. Applicants are rejected for many reasons (lack of ability, poor work record, criminal record).

Companies use a variety of selection processes. For example, Air South of Columbia, South Carolina, conducts extensive team interviews for prospective customer-contact employees. The airline seeks employees whose goals and abilities are compatible with the firm's emphasis on distinctive "southern service."[32] Executone, the nationwide telephone system company, seeks experience, technical knowledge, and the drive to sell by serving customers. Interviewing and role playing are critical parts of its selection process.[33]

Training. Once a person is hired, the sales manager must continue developing the sales force through training. Training usually takes one of three forms. First, new salespeople must often be taught what their job entails, how to do it, what their competition will be, and what is expected of them. This training involves some orientation, knowledge acquisition, and work on specific selling skills. Training goals are usually identified by analyzing the tasks of the sales job. An important principle to remember is that training should be done at the trainee's level.[34]

Sales training is essential to the ongoing development of the sales force.

Sales training increases product knowledge and improves selling skills; it also builds self-confidence among members of the sales force. When people know what is expected of them, they are better prepared for the challenges and disappointments of a sales career. Effective sales training can point out and reinforce positive behaviors that can contribute to a very successful sales career.

Finally, there is a need for long-term development, aimed at increasing the firm's long-run effectiveness. The organization's objectives, strategy, and environment are all considered when planning the program for sales force development. Development may involve providing salespeople with more responsible jobs, more autonomy, and more decision-making power. These are assumed to help salespeople prepare for future assignments. The ultimate long-term objective is to increase the sales of the firm. The direct relationship between sales and training is elusive, because so many factors influence sales (such as the economy, shortages, and size of sales territories). Some examples of how companies use sales training include:

▪ Kodak believes in "excellence through education." It has spent $20 million to send 50,000 employees through courses given by its Marketing Educational Centers. Sixty percent of the attendees are new hires and sales people. New-hire training alone takes six months and costs approximately $50,000 to $70,000 per employee.[35]

▪ Oldsmobile is putting its dealers and employees through team- and trust-building training used by General Motors' Saturn Division. The goal of the training is to convince dealers, traditionally independent, that they can better serve customers by considering their employees as "family."[37]

▪ Xerox Corporation attributes a $4.6 million increase in capital revenue to a four-hour computer-based training course. The course used the quality process to train sales representatives in selling a specific piece of software. The self-paced training program was adapted to each rep's background and integrated with other training.[37]

The Japanese view sales training differently from Americans and Canadians. Formal sales training as practiced in the United States is virtually nonexistent in Japan. Rather, Japanese salespeople learn through experience.[38] Going out with and observing successful salespeople is the Japanese model of training. The Japanese salesperson selling a product in New York or Tokyo has typically learned techniques on the job.

With the proliferation of multinational companies, it is essential that sales personnel be trained to understand cross-cultural differences. Such training stresses the avoidance of incorrect stereotypes. For example, Sprint provided cross-cultural training to 45 staffers in its international marketing group. Designed to provide the staff skills for doing business in particular countries and markets, the training focuses on acknowledging differences among cultures, avoiding stereotypes, overcoming language barriers, and becoming aware of the value systems of various cultural groups.[39]

Directing

The task of directing individual salespeople and integrating their needs and goals with the objectives of the firm is continuous. The exact style and procedures used to direct the sales force depend largely on the leadership and reward system.

Leadership. The ability to influence others to accomplish desired goals is called **leadership.** The responsibility of a sales manager to lead is derived from the formal position he or she has in the hierarchy and the respect and cooperation he or she inspires because of personal traits and expertise.

The extensive literature on leadership suggests there is no one best way to lead subordinates.[41] For years attempts were made to isolate and identify a "best" leadership style. It now appears that what is good leadership in one situation, or at one time, is often disastrous in another situation, or at a different time. Research suggests that situational and personal variables must be considered seriously before a style is adopted.[40]

An important aspect of applying a leadership style is determining how authority is used. Figure 16.5 indicates five styles of leadership and ways trade-offs between

**FIGURE 16.5
Leadership Styles and Situational Considerations**

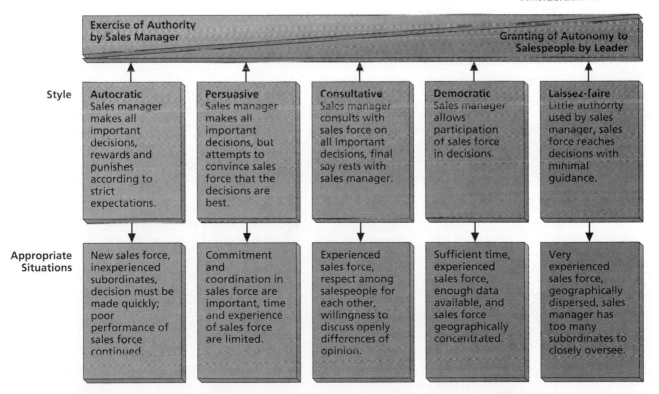

	Autocratic	Persuasive	Consultative	Democratic	Laissez-faire
Style	Sales manager makes all important decisions, rewards and punishes according to strict expectations.	Sales manager makes all important decisions, but attempts to convince sales force that the decisions are best.	Sales manager consults with sales force on all important decisions, final say rests with sales manager.	Sales manager allows participation of sales force in decisions.	Little authority used by sales manager, sales force reaches decisions with minimal guidance.
Appropriate Situations	New sales force, inexperienced subordinates, decision must be made quickly; poor performance of sales force continued.	Commitment and coordination in sales force are important, time and experience of sales force are limited.	Experienced sales force, respect among salespeople for each other, willingness to discuss openly differences of opinion.	Sufficient time, experienced sales force, enough data available, and sales force geographically concentrated.	Very experienced sales force, geographically dispersed, sales manager has too many subordinates to closely oversee.

Exercise of Authority by Sales Manager → Granting of Autonomy to Salespeople by Leader

Salespeople exchange their time, ability, skills, and effort for valued rewards that sales managers then distribute as they see fit.

authority and autonomy can be made. The *autocratic* style emphasizes top-down decision making, while the *consultative* places a premium on receiving input from subordinates before making a decision. Different situations lend themselves to different styles.

The style that works best depends on the sales manager, situation, and sales force. Whichever style is selected, the leader will eventually have to implement a reward system to motivate the sales force.

Rewards.   One directing activity a sales manager engages in is the administration of rewards. Rewarding salespeople is tied closely to evaluation. The objectives of a reward system are to attract people to join the firm, to keep them coming to work, and to motivate them to perform at high levels. Salespeople exchange their time, ability, skills, and effort for valued rewards that sales managers distribute as they see fit.

Extrinsic rewards are external to the job. Included in this category are financial rewards, such as pay, fringe benefits, and sales bonuses, as well as promotions and good working conditions. Intrinsic rewards are associated directly with the job itself. Being challenged and having freedom to make decisions are intrinsic rewards. Devising a reward approach that is effective is difficult. The "Marketing in Action: Personalizing Incentives" looks at what the sales manager can do to improve the probability that the reward will be motivational.

A reward must be important to the salesperson if it is to influence his or her behavior. In all occupations, an important reward is the compensation received for working. Sales compensation is an extrinsic reward distributed by a sales manager. The best mix and type of compensation programs depend on such factors as the compensation plans of competitors, costs of sales-force turnover and poor morale, compensation plans for nonsales personnel in the organization, and amount of non-salary selling expenses.

Many sales compensation programs reimburse salespeople for their selling expenses and provide some fringe benefits and compensation. Three popular methods of compensation are straight salary, straight commission, and a combination of salary and commission. In a **straight salary plan,** the amount received by salespeople is based on the time worked. A **straight commission plan** bases compensation on the sales generated during a specific period of time. The commission may

MARKETING *IN ACTION*

Personalizing Incentives

Most organizations offer incentives to motivate their salespeople. These incentives range from coffee mugs, watches, and trophies to electronic equipment and exotic trips. Companies can choose among thousands of premium, incentive, and gift products. Which ones should they offer? Will any incentive be considered a reward and act as a motivator?

Managers must realize that incentives do not always produce the results expected. Whether an incentive program works depends on many factors, one of which is the relationship between the giver and the receiver. According to Dr. Jerry Lanoil, a psychologist in private practice, "What is important about an incentive isn't what it is, but who gives it and how it's given." Lanoil believes that the relationship between the giver and the receiver should be based on mutual respect and trust. The incentive will be more effective if it comes from someone from whom the salesperson wants approval and praise.

A second factor is the salesperson type. The appropriate incentive should correspond to each salesperson type. Managers should consider the characteristics of the sales representatives who make up their sales forces. The reps may be self-motivated or outwardly motivated. Some may prefer extrinsic rewards, whereas others look for intrinsic rewards. Some believe in the product they sell, others do not. Some reps have many responsibilities and others have only themselves to consider. Each type of salesperson responds differently to the same incentive.

Jim Weitzul, a consultant specializing in managing sales forces, believes that two salesperson types cannot be motivated in the same manner. He provides two examples to support his theory. "The active-passive rep is kind, thoughtful, supportive, and energetic," says Weitzul. "This type of salesperson sees himself or herself as a professional who does not fall for gimmicks or the quick-and-dirty incentive." This salesperson can be contrasted with what Weitzul describes as "the young, smooth, polished, razor-cut hair, manicured-nails, monogrammed-shirt type." This type celebrates a closed sale as a victory and favorably responds to quick-and-dirty incentives. Whatever the reward, it should have some impact and be given every quarter, not every year.

The great majority of compensation specialists emphasize the need to set goals on an individual basis. Sales managers should try to identify the needs of their reps. How? By having a personal meeting with each rep during which the manager asks them what type of incentive would motivate them. The sales manager also should be a good listener. Listen to what the reps talk about, dream about, and envy in others. One salesperson may be motivated by a trip to Hawaii, another by a big screen TV, and yet another by a conversation with the president of the company.

This process seems quite simple, yet most sales managers do not bother to consult their reps about incentive programs. It is easier and often cheaper to choose an incentive for the whole group. Since most sales experts agree that the benefits of offering incentives on an individual basis are certain to outweigh the cost, it is worth taking the trouble.

be based on a straight percentage of sales or a sliding scale in which the percentage increases as sales increase. In a **combination plan,** salespeople are paid a fixed salary and a commission based on sales volume. Some combination plans require the salesperson to generate a certain level of sales (quota) before a commission is paid. Table 16.4 presents some advantages and disadvantages of the straight salary, straight commission, and combination plans.

Average compensation for salespeople varies greatly by the type of product and the level of the salesperson. Figure 16.6 illustrates these differences and reports average expenses for salespeople.

In addition to direct compensation, another extrinsic reward is the sales contest. Its purpose is to increase the volume of sales. Prizes in such a contest have included merchandise, vacation trips, honors such as being named "Salesperson of the Month," trophies, pins, and certificates. Of course, the success or failure of a sales contest is often influenced by the attractiveness of the award.

Compensation Method	Frequency of Use	Especially Useful	Advantages	Disadvantages
Straight salary	8.0%	When compensating new salespeople; when firm moves into new sales territories that require developmental work; when salespeople need to perform many nonselling activities	Provides salesperson with maximum amount of security; gives sales manager large amount of control over salespeople; easy to administer; yields more predictable selling expenses	Provides no incentive; necessitates closer supervision of salespeople's activities; during sales declines, selling expenses remain at same level
Straight commission	24.2%	When highly aggressive selling is required; when nonselling tasks are minimized; when company cannot closely control sales force's activities	Provides maximum amount of incentive; by increasing commission rate, sales managers can encourage salespeople to sell certain items; selling expenses relate directly to sales resources	Salespeople have little financial security; sales manager has minimum control over sales force; may cause salespeople to provide inadequate service to smaller accounts; selling costs less predictable
Combination	67.8%	When sales territories have relatively similar sales potentials; when firm wishes to provide incentive but still control sales force activities	Provides certain level of financial security; provides some incentive; selling expenses fluctuate with sales revenue; sales manager has some control over salesperson's nonselling activities	Selling expenses less predictable; may be difficult to administer

Source: The percentages are from *Dartnell's 27th Sales Force Compensation Survey*, (Chicago: The Dartnell Corporation, 1992), p. 27. Characteristics are based on J. P. Steinbrink, "How to Pay Your Sales Force," *Harvard Business Review*, July–August 1978, p. 119.

TABLE 16.4
Characteristics of Compensation Methods for Sales Personnel

In contrast to extrinsic rewards, **intrinsic rewards** are associated with doing the job. In essence, an intrinsic reward permits salespeople to reward themselves. Allowing the salesperson to make decisions without being closely monitored, encouraging the sales force to set challenging and realistic goals, and providing good feedback on performance are intrinsic rewards that can be built into the motivational package by creative sales managers. Sales managers need to foster the conditions necessary for salespeople to experience intrinsic rewards.

Behavioralists and practicing managers agree that both extrinsic and intrinsic rewards must be used to encourage sales performance.[42] It is clear that the following conditions must exist for rewards to motivate sales performance.

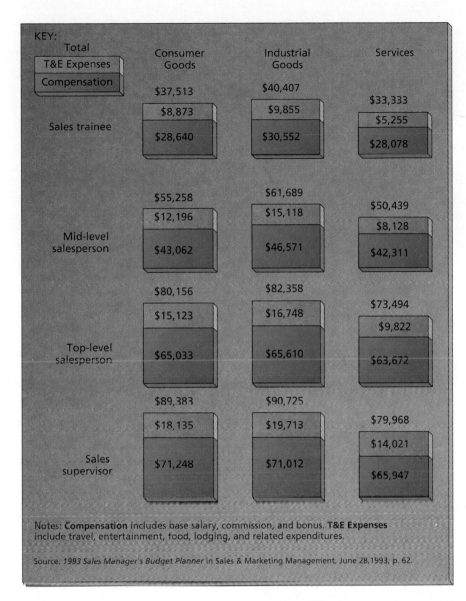

KEY:

	Total	Consumer Goods	Industrial Goods	Services
T&E Expenses				
Compensation				

Sales trainee
- Consumer Goods: $37,513 / $8,873 / $28,640
- Industrial Goods: $40,407 / $9,855 / $30,552
- Services: $33,333 / $5,255 / $28,078

Mid-level salesperson
- Consumer Goods: $55,258 / $12,196 / $43,062
- Industrial Goods: $61,689 / $15,118 / $46,571
- Services: $50,439 / $8,128 / $42,311

Top-level salesperson
- Consumer Goods: $80,156 / $15,123 / $65,033
- Industrial Goods: $82,358 / $16,748 / $65,610
- Services: $73,494 / $9,822 / $63,672

Sales supervisor
- Consumer Goods: $89,383 / $18,135 / $71,248
- Industrial Goods: $90,725 / $19,713 / $71,012
- Services: $79,968 / $14,021 / $65,947

Notes: **Compensation** includes base salary, commission, and bonus. **T&E Expenses** include travel, entertainment, food, lodging, and related expenditures.

Source: *1993 Sales Manager's Budget Planner* in Sales & Marketing Management, June 28, 1993, p. 62.

FIGURE 16.6
Compensation and Expenses for Sale Jobs by Industry (1992)

1. Rewards must be *important* to the sales force.
2. Both *extrinsic* (financial incentives) and *intrinsic* (allowing more autonomy in making decisions) rewards must be used by the sales manager.
3. Information must be made *public* (for example, through a company newsletter) about how rewards are distributed to the sales force.
4. Sales managers must be able to *explain* the firm's reward system to salespeople so that they can easily understand it.
5. Sales performance should be *measured* with the most objective system available, using specific numbers when possible. Keep in mind that perfectly objective systems are probably not feasible.
6. Rewards can be varied, depending on the conclusions reached with the *performance evaluation* system.

If these conditions do not exist, the sales manager is likely to have major problems directing the sales force. Management of an effective sales force and an efficient reward system requires evaluations of sales performance.

Evaluation

The evaluation of each person in the sales force is an important and difficult task for sales managers. The job is *judgmental*, because verdicts must be made about whether each person has met sales objectives. It is also *developmental*, because the professional growth of salespeople depends on performance evaluation and as well as on feedback.

The sales manager and each salesperson must know how well objectives are being met. To acquire this information, a formal evaluation program is usually developed and implemented. The search for the "perfect performance evaluation" has been going on and producing controversy for years.[43] The ideal evaluation continues to center on minimizing or eliminating traditional complaints from raters (sales managers) and ratees (salespeople). Specific complaints center on inequities in ratings, poorly trained evaluators, ambiguous performance standards, the subjective nature of evaluations, and excessive emphasis on weaknesses.

In spite of this controversy, there are a number of reasons that performance evaluations are necessary and should be done:

- They can provide feedback to salespeople on their job results, enabling them to match expectations to reality.
- They can provide information for training, compensation, and motivation programs.
- They serve as a basis of control. Projected efforts and results can be compared to actual efforts and results.
- They point out strengths to maintain, as well as weaknesses to correct.
- They provide information for the sales manager to use in working out a plan for career progress and development.

Formal evaluation programs used by firms like IBM, General Mills, Sears, JCPenney, First City National Bank, and Procter & Gamble usually follow five steps:

1. The sales job is analyzed and objectives are set.
2. A job description (a factual description of the duties, responsibilities, and requirements of the sales job) is prepared.
3. Sales performance measures (quantitative and qualitative standards) are developed.
4. The evaluator observes when possible, measures, and evaluates sales performance.
5. The evaluation is fed back to the salesperson, and some form of reward or sanction is distributed.

The role of the sales manager is crucial in an evaluation of the sales force's performance. Basically, the manager is asked to observe, evaluate, counsel, and coach the sales force as well as to administer rewards and sanctions. To accomplish these duties, the sales manager must use some standards.

Based on the situation, job analysis, and job description, quantitative and qualitative criteria can be developed to measure and evaluate sales job performance. Of course, the criteria used also depends on the objectives of the firm. *Quantitative* measures indicate specific levels of performance in objective terms—sales volume in dollars, number of new accounts, sales volume as a percentage of sales quota. The emphasis is on output or objective results. *Qualitative* measures involve more personal judgments about the contribution of the salesperson. Included in qualitative evaluations may be such factors as politeness, appearance, knowledge of products, knowledge of competitors, and creativity.

The sales manager making the evaluation needs to appraise sales performance on a range of measures. For example, the number of new accounts may tell the manager nothing about the average size of orders. Furthermore, the efforts of salespeople must be considered along with the results. A salesperson's effectiveness should be based on quantitative results, as measured by dollar sales volume and gross margin, and qualitative efforts, as indicated by enthusiasm, serving customer interests, and steps taken to expand the customer base. Thus, both outputs (quantitative) and inputs (qualitative) are considered in the evaluation of a salesperson.[44]

PERSONAL COMPUTER EXERCISE

The overall effectiveness of five salespeople will be examined, analyzed, and interpreted in this PC Exercise. You will be asked to develop an appropriate compensation system for this sales force. Which of the salespeople should be named salesperson of the year? If there is to be a reduction in the sales force of one person, which of the five should be let go? Suppose that the sales force wanted an explanation of the reasons behind your decisions—could you explain how your weights were determined?

KEY POINTS

■ Over the years, perceptions of selling have grown more favorable. There has been a shift from the view that sales work is unchallenging and "just a job" to the contemporary view that selling is a career, is challenging, and requires creative skills and abilities.

■ The order getter is a type of salesperson who generates sales by finding new customers or increasing sales to repeat customers. This kind of selling requires creativity and taking the initiative.

■ The order taker is a salesperson who works primarily in a routine manner with regular or repeat customers. There is less creative selling involved.

■ Support salespeople (e.g., a missionary salesperson) locate prospects, educate prospects, and create goodwill.

■ There are three phases in the selling process: preparation, persuasion, and transaction.

■ There are seven steps in the selling process: prospecting, the preapproach, the approach, the presentation, handling objections, the closing, and follow-up.

■ According to the stimulus-response model a sales prospect will decide to buy if the sales approach and presentation are persuasive. The sales prospect can be stimulated, encouraged, and persuaded to make a purchase.

■ The need-satisfaction model focuses on the needs of the customer. It is more marketing oriented than the stimulus-response model.

■ The major activities of a sales manager are setting objectives, structuring, developing, directing, and evaluating the sales force.

■ Common ways of organizing a sales force are by geographical territory, by product, or by customer.

■ Development of a sales force involves the recruitment, selection, and training of salespeople.

■ Rewards are major factors in directing a sales force. Compensation is an important part of the rewarding process.

■ Combination compensation plans combine a base salary with commissions, bonuses, or both. A commission is payment for achieving a given level of performance. A bonus is a payment made at the discretion of management for achieving or surpassing a set level of performance. The combination method of payment provides both a degree of financial security and an incentive. These two ingredients, security and incentive, make this type of plan popular.

■ Intrinsic rewards come from the job itself, such as the ability to sell without close supervision. Being professionally challenged, being able to create a personal selling technique, and receiving a personal thank-you from a major customer are job-specific or job-generated rewards. Extrinsic rewards, such as salary, are external to the job.

KEY TERMS

personal selling (549)
boundary spanners (549)
order getter (550)
consultative selling (551)
team selling (552)
order takers (552)
support salespeople (554)
job description (555)
prospecting (556)
cold canvass (556)
telemarketing (557)
preapproach (557)
approach (557)
presentation (557)
stimulus-response model (557)
canned presentation (557)
packaged presentation (557)
prepared presentation (557)
need-satisfaction model (559)
objections (559)

closing (560)
trial close (561)
assumption technique (561)
urgency close (561)
follow-up (561)
cognitive dissonance (561)
sales management (563)
workload analysis (566)
recruitment (566)
selection (567)
leadership (569)
extrinsic rewards (570)
straight salary plan (570)
straight commission plan (570)
combination plan (571)
intrinsic rewards (572)

ISSUES FOR DISCUSSION

1. How does the general public form perceptions of the work performed by a salesperson? Is there a generally accepted perception of the challenge offered by a sales career?

2. In preparing a compensation package for a young, recent college-graduate salesperson, what factors would you consider?

3. The sales presentation step in the selling process has attracted the attention of various theories. Which theory relies the most on what the sales prospect is thinking? Explain.

4. What approaches besides asking "May I help you?" might a retail salesperson use when first making contact with a prospect?

5. What amount of creativity is involved in selling a prospect a GRID Pad computer?

6. What can a sales manager do to make the job personally rewarding for a salesperson?

7. What communication skills are needed to overcome a vacillating prospect's objections to purchasing a product?

8. What type of closing techniques work on prospects who are purchasing a new suit (man) or new dress (woman)?

9. Why would a salesperson prefer to be paid a straight commission instead of a straight salary?

10. Should the criteria used in selecting a salesperson be different for Nike athletic shoes and Maytag washers and dryers? If so, how would they differ?

CASE APPLICATION

Personal Selling in France and Germany

Do cultural differences affect the personal selling process? Is the sales profession in other cultures the same as in the United States? Among all international business activities, selling is probably one of the most sensitive areas of cross-cultural communications. Although the use of a common language is an extremely important communication tool, it is not always enough to close a sale. The selling process also requires the ability to communicate through nonverbal cues such as posture, gestures, facial expressions, and visual behavior. An American salesperson selling in international markets also needs to know the customs involved in a typical sales negotiation with a foreign customer.

The European Community represents the largest export market for American companies. Thus, if a firm or business is to be successful, it is strategically important that U.S. firms understand selling techniques practiced by salespeople in countries such as France, Germany, and the United Kingdom. It is also important to study and learn about non-American sales professionals who sell American-made products in other countries. Jean Louis De Coix, a Frenchman, is the number one seller of American-made medical diagnostic equipment. His style emphasizes polish, customer service, and technical knowledge, a winning combination in any country. Two personal selling experts, Erich Norbert Detroy of Germany, head of a multinational training firm, and Jean Pierre Tricard of France, a top sales trainer and motivator, provide some examples of selling tactics of their respective countries and discuss the differences between French and German salespeople and American salespeople.

Characteristics

Tricard: "American salespeople are very direct. When you want something, you ask for it directly. In France, we follow different customs. We don't want to risk offending someone or show bad manners. As a result, we skirt the issues; we beat around the bush and it takes much longer to make a request. In our culture, the one thing we tend to be afraid of is to talk about money. When French salespeople get to the point of discussing price, they usually are uncomfortable because they have not been trained to talk about money. In my opinion, American salespeople are better equipped to talk about price. An American salesperson trying to sell to French prospects should spend more time listening to the clients, encouraging them to talk more, and trying to make them comfortable. French customers don't like to be pushed to a conclusion."

Detroy: "I see the typical American salesperson as a more money-oriented thinker. The German salesperson is more critical, more reflective, and often more skeptical. The most successful salespeople in Germany share such common characteristics as high ego drive and a great amount of inner motivation. The typical salesperson is usually someone without a college degree and who may have tried a number of different professions before going into sales. There are many former teachers and government workers, as well as East Germans, entering the profession.

Goals

Tricard: "In general, a salesperson is seen as someone who has failed at everything in life or someone who doesn't want to do manual labor because it's too hard. But a salesperson is also seen as someone who is congenial and able to relate well to other people. The French salesperson's dream is to become the sales manager. Because the image of a salesperson in France has been historically low, he wants to get out of sales and become the leader of the sales team. France is a country that values technical training more than anything else. For example, most CEOs in France have been trained as engineers and, as a result, their priorities are product first, service second, and sales third. Also, most salespeople love their companies. They tend to work hard for their companies, and they have a great desire to be well thought-of by their clients."

Detroy: "The dreams and goals of a German salesperson is to become the sales manager. That's often a tragic mistake because the company usually gains a poor manager and loses a great salesperson. Salespeople don't realize that and, as they move up in the hierarchy, the air gets thinner and people tend to get intoxicated as they get closer to power.

Levels and Methods of Sales Training

Tricard: "Every successful company in France is looking for good salespeople, and sales managers complain that they can't find enough. Most of the salespeople don't know how to sell. They are just getting by because they can talk a good game, but they don't know any techniques. When they lose a sale, it's never the salesperson's fault; they're always blaming it on the product, the price, the delivery, or the competition. They do, however, go out of their way to help a customer solve a problem. Their aim is to be of service, and salespeople in France see themselves more on the client's team. Also, we tell salespeople not to launch into a lengthy presentation about the product, but first find out what advantages the client is really looking for. Stop selling products and start selling images. A good salesperson is like a mirror that reflects the customer's ideas, and the job of the salesperson is to find the image that interests his client. For example, customers don't buy a Mercedes; they buy success."

Detroy: "We often take American methods for sales and management and apply them with great enthusiasm, only to find that these methods can backfire very quickly. For example, when Management by Objectives was introduced here, salespeople became driven to achieve higher quotas at any cost. When numbers become more important than people, hard-sell techniques drive out common sense. The media began to expose the hard-sell schemes of the German industry, and many customers got turned off. The image of German salespeople suffered greatly. Sales training and management had to focus again on establishing trust. We've developed what we call Reflective Selling. That means to take more time to listen to real customers' needs. We teach salespeople that their presentation should reflect 100 percent of the customer's logical and emotional needs. We see a great comeback to basic human values. German customers trust people who are friendly, well mannered, very knowledgeable, and very punctual."

Salesperson–Customer Relations

Tricard: "The client expects that the salesperson is thoroughly knowledgeable about the product or service he sells. For this reason, good salespeople have to be specialists in their fields. Customers have to be able to trust the salesperson. When an American customer gives a salesperson an appointment, he will see him more or less on time. In France, customers often leave salespeople waiting for 30 to 45 minutes. It's not uncommon for customers to forget about the appointment altogether."

Detroy: "In general, customers who have made an appointment with salespeople don't let them wait. The typical purchasing manager is trained to form a partnership with the salesperson. Any sales negotiation with a German customer is still tough, but today's customers show more respect for the salesperson as a human being."

Questions

1. In your opinion, what skills does a salesperson need the most to sell in France and in Germany. Why?
2. How are salespeople perceived in the United States? Compare and contrast these perceptions with what was described regarding French and German salespeople.
3. Should an American company expanding overseas send its own American salespeople or make up a sales force of local reps? Discuss the advantages and disadvantages of foreigners versus local people.

Selling Yourself

An employment interview is your opportunity to practice personal selling. When you apply for a position, you must understand the company's needs and how you can satisfy them. Preparation is the key to a successful employment interview. You need to answer two questions:

- Why do I want to work in this industry or company, and in this position?
- Why should this company hire me?

Answers to the first question tell an interviewer why you, the interviewee, chose his or her company and a particular job. The second question prompts you to think about the needs of the interviewer and determine how to sell yourself to him or her. If you can't answer these questions, you will not be able to illustrate a commitment and show your "professional commercial" to make a truly positive and powerful impact.

To sell yourself effectively, you must prepare a short commercial on why you should be hired. Be certain to present the message of the commercial during the interview. As in personal selling, you need to watch the interviewer's reactions, be good at listening and observing, and keep asking yourself, "Am I getting my message across? Is the interviewer comfortable with me?"

As you get control of your personal-selling skills in the interview process, your body language, voice level, and eye contact will enhance your ability to stand out. Recruiters give high marks to the ability to communicate a clear and memorable message.

Questions

1. Think back to some of your job interviews. How might you have improved your personal-selling performance?
2. Which aspects of interviewing trouble you? What steps can you take to address your concerns?

Jobs in Sales

What do you need to be successful in personal selling? Most firms look for an outgoing personality, a competitive spirit, sensitivity in dealing with people, a foundation in marketing, and the ability to understand one's clients.

Entering the field. There are more job opportunities, especially entry-level positions, in personal selling than in any other area. A college degree is becoming more and more necessary for a sales position. Company sales forces are benefiting more and more from the business and technical skills of their salespeople.

Types of positions. Selling positions are found in a variety of consumer and business-to-business organizations. These positions could involve calling on a number of customers each day, putting up and maintaining displays, checking inventory levels, or taking orders for stock. Problem solving for and with customers is increasingly a part of the sales job. There are two general career paths you can follow in sales. First, a salesperson may make sales a career and become a specialist in dealing with jobbers, chains, or vendors, or in selling to specialized target groups such as independent grocers and hospitals. The person may even specialize in selling particular types of products. The second path involves becoming the sales manager of a region or district, supervising sales representatives and managers who report to you. This path could ultimately lead to becoming national sales manager, vice president of sales, or perhaps even president of the company. Some companies—IBM and Eastman Kodak, for example—view a period in the field as a prerequisite to higher-level management positions, and offer sales training for a solid introduction to personal selling.

Atmosphere and salaries. Personal selling does have its hardships. It often involves a good deal of traveling, dealing with hostile or indifferent people, and work that occasionally seems tedious and unglamorous. It can be lonely, but, at the same time, you are so free of the constraints of an office job that it is almost like being your own boss. It can be very rewarding to know that you represent the company to your customers and have the chance to develop personal resourcefulness as well as product and customer knowledge.

The remuneration for a sales position can be very high, depending on your effort and the compensation plan. Many people, once in sales, spend their entire careers there, choosing the freedom and earning potential over the restrictions and often lower salaries of office management positions. Selling is hard work, but it also provides highly visible results, and the potential rewards, both personal and financial, are great. No job is more important to an organization's success.

Part Five

The Story of Harley-Davidson: Promotions

The Promotional Mix

Harley-Davidson is regarded as a consummate promoter with an excellent product in high demand. The company knows its product is good; it's up to the marketing and brand management teams to ensure that the public knows this, too. Like other successful companies, Harley-Davidson uses a carefully determined combination of advertising, sales promotion, personal selling, and public relations in its mix of promotional elements to communicate with its target audiences.

Advertising

In 1993, Harley-Davidson was recognized for its creative ads by *Adweek* magazine.[1] One example of the company's advertising is the following ad placed in a number of magazines to celebrate Harley-Davidson's 90th anniversary in 1993. The ad copy playfully expresses the attitude at the core of the Harley-Davidson mystique:

> We've survived four wars, a Depression, a few recessions, 16 U.S. Presidents, foreign and domestic competition, racetrack competition, and one Marlon Brando Movie.
>
> Sounds like a party to us.

Copy from a different ad provides yet another example of Harley-Davidson's print approach:

> When you put your hard-earned money into a Harley-Davidson, you're getting more than a motorcycle. You're buying into a motorcycling legend. And a feeling that's impossible to put a price tag on.[2]

As the choice of wording makes clear, Harley-Davidson makes an emotional appeal to customers in its ads. The language communicates the intangible benefits—status, image, attitude, charisma, tradition—of owning your own Harley-Davidson. Meanwhile, the company's competitors traditionally take a more rational, pragmatic approach. Instead of making an emotional appeal, competitors' ads often stress technology, speed, and price.[3]

In 1985, Harley-Davidson slashed its advertising budget from $1.2 million to $180,000, a drop of more than $1 million. Some of the funds saved by the cuts were allocated to other promotional activities, including public relations and sales promotion efforts. This shift in funds allowed it to stage more rallies and special events which brought the Harley-Davidson experience directly to the people.

Public Relations

Harley-Davidson believes that exposure of its brand name to the public enhances the success and profitability of the company. There is constant concern over controlling the corporate image in the marketplace, and the company is very particular about where and how its "product" is presented. Working closely with editors, Harley-Davidson places articles and pictures in motorcycle trade publications such as *CycleWorld* and *Motorcyclist,* as well as general-interest consumer magazines. In addition, Harley-Davidson successfully pursues local and network television coverage.

The patronage of famous personalities is usually a dependable boon to sales. Jay Leno of *The Tonight Show* rides a Harley-Davidson and has appeared at charitable benefits sponsored by the company. The late Malcolm Forbes, owner and publisher of *Forbes* magazine, was a great lover of Harley-Davidson motorcycles. His trip on a Harley-Davidson through China with other prominent dignitaries was well publicized.

Sales Promotion Efforts

Sales promotion efforts help Harley-Davidson "get close" to its customers. They help generate interest in motorcycling, expose the Harley-Davidson name and image to the public, and increase sales of motorcycles, accessories, and licensed goods. Local dealers hold promotions such as motorcycle shows and rallies and, together with Harley-Davidson, sponsor racing activities and special events. Harley-Davidson dealers often join local businesses and firms to hold joint promotions. Since each dealership is independently owned, these promotions are organized on a dealer-by-dealer basis and are not usually arranged by Harley-Davidson.

A good example of a promotion is a local Harley-Davidson dealer association's arrangement with In-N-Out Burgers, a successful non-franchise fast-food company in southern California. In-N-Out offers its fast-food fare in a setting reminiscent of 1950s "burger joints," with a contemporary emphasis on quality, service, and simplicity. Because Harley-Davidson identifies its product in much the same way, local Harley-Davidson dealers and In-N-Out representatives agreed they were a good match for a cooperative promotional effort. This promotion featured placemats with pictures of Harley-Davidson motorcycles, scratch-off cards with the chance to win a Harley-Davidson motorcycle, apparel, and accessories, and Harley-Davidson posters in the restaurants.

Harley-Davidson developed its SuperRide Demo program in 1985. A "demo ride" lets a potential customer try out a motorcycle and get a taste of the Harley-Davidson motorcycle experience before ever buying a bike. The company staged a three-weekend event across the country at more than 600 dealerships. The event provided more than 90,000 rides to 40,000 people, half of whom owned competitors' motorcycles at the time.

Planners encountered problems during the event: some stores were closed during normal hours, dealers were not properly trained how to "sell," and demonstrations were poorly organized. Although the company was unable to recoup immediately its initial $3 million investment in the project, more than 100,000 motorcyclists have taken advantage of the program, which eventually had a positive impact on sales.[4] The idea became such a hot concept that other motorcycle companies followed Harley-Davidson's lead and introduced their own versions of the SuperRide Demo.

Harley-Davidson's promotional efforts also include selecting a candidate for Ms. Harley-Davidson, part of its marketing program to women. One recent Ms. Harley-Davidson managed to log 39 corporate events, 65 dealer visits, 347 days on the road, and over 340,000 air miles.

Selling

Much of Harley-Davidson's recent boost in sales is due to improved quality and manufacturing systems and increased employee involvement.[5] However, while quality and sales are up and production has nearly tripled in the past six years, the company has not been able to supply enough motorcycles to satisfy total demand in the marketplace. Because Harley-Davidson knows that reliability and service play a critical role in its competitive advantage, it refuses to sacrifice quality for the sake of increased production and sales. Moreover, Harley-Davidson has learned from experience about the cyclical nature of market and customers' demand. By keeping growth under control, Harley-Davidson carefully avoids overexpansion. Meanwhile, the company develops parts, services, and accessories to maintain sales volume and profits for dealers.[6]

Harley-Davidson does research to keep track of its customers. Recent "guiding" research found that the average Harley-Davidson buyer is 41.6 years old and that 39 percent of all owners are college-educated. In order to increase brand-name awareness among 18- to 34-year-olds, the company has begun to address this age group. Although members of this demographic group rarely possess the discretionary income to purchase a Harley-Davidson motorcycle, the company feels that acquainting potential customers with the brand at an earlier age will sustain strong sales into the future.

Questions

1. Given Harley-Davidson's effective combination of promotional efforts, what else might you recommend to increase awareness of the brand and company image?
2. Would you recommend that Harley-Davidson advertise more heavily in magazines? Should the company downplay its activities with the customer? Explain your answer.
3. What level of success can you attribute to the "customer focus" of Harley-Davidson?
4. Investigate other companies that claim to be "customer focused." How are they similar to and different from Harley-Davidson?
5. Does Harley-Davidson need to introduce another motorcycle for 18- to 34-year-olds? If so, why? How would it go about introducing it? If not, why?

part VI

PRiCinG

CHAPTER 17

Basic Pricing Concepts

Marketing Profile

What's the Big Deal with Everyday Low Pricing?

Who controls the pricing of consumer packaged goods? What is a reasonable pricing policy? How much profit should a company make? And where should that profit come from? Throughout the world, supermarkets and their suppliers are locked in a continuing power struggle over these and related questions.

In the fall of 1991, Procter & Gamble announced its new "everyday-low-pricing" strategy (EDLP), a practice by which manufacturers sell their products to retailers at one, fixed low price. For example, P & G eliminated trade promotions for Dawn dishwashing liquid and then set the brand's price to a standard average of $1.32, rather than pricing it at $.99 one week and $1.49 the next. Let's see why P & G decided to make this dramatic change.

Discounts, allowances, and promotional deals are often used to control the flow of products through marketing channels. These "deals" generally translate into price cuts from manufacturers to retailers, who are expected to provide the manufacturer some benefit in return, such as more shelf space or special displays. However, such trade promotions have given rise to some practices that industry experts say are in the best interests of neither the manufacturers nor the retailers.

One example is *diverting*, where a manufacturer might sell its retailers a certain amount of merchandise for a 30-week promotion. A retailer may participate in the promotion, buying the product from the manufacturer at a discount, but offering it to customers for only 20 weeks. The retailer then sells the inventory for the last 10 weeks to another division of its company, where the promotion is not being held. This division sells the product at the regular price. The retailer benefits from the 30-week promotional discount, but the consumer only receives 20 weeks' worth of the product at the sale price. The difference—the extra profit for products sold during the last 10 weeks at regular price—goes to the retailer's bottom line and not to the consumer.

Another practice is *forward buying*. In this case, a manufacturer offers retailers the opportunity to get $2 "off-invoice" for ordering a certain number of cases of product. In return, retailers must purchase the manufacturer's product for a specified number of weeks—and give excellent shelf space, special promotional placement, and a cutback on the retail price to consumers. Sometimes retailers will order, say, four additional weeks of merchandise only to charge customers the regular price when the promotion is over—again, pocketing the profit. Understandably, manufacturers are disturbed by these practices that fail to give consumers the full value of the manufacturers' promotional efforts.

Forward buying and diverting are common, widespread practices. Industry studies show that about 40 percent of the wholesaler's bottom line comes from these types of activities. Studies also show that of the estimated $300 billion in annual grocery sales, between $75 billion and $100 billion in inventory is stuck in the pipeline between the manufacturer and the retailer as a result of such activities.

P & G was quickly followed by Philip Morris, which cut prices by $.40 per pack on Marlboro, Merit, Benson & Hedges, Virginia Slims, and other premium brands of cigarettes. How successful was the move for Philip Morris? Well, the numbers tell the story; Marlboro is a prime example.

Before the price change, Marlboro's U.S. market share dropped for eight months straight, from 24.9% to 22%. As soon as the price cuts took effect, Marlboro's fortunes began to improve. The brand gained 3.1% of market share at supermarkets and 4.1% at convenience stores. Within a few months, Marlboro's overall share improved to 22.6% on its way to 27.3% as of June 1994. It's estimated that had Marlboro continued on its high-priced path, its share would have dropped to less than 20% by the end of the year.

A study released in the spring of 1994 shows that EDLP does not drive volume sufficiently to compensate for lower profit margins. In the test case at Dominck's Finer Foods in the Chicago area, the researchers discovered that EDLP gave manufacturers a small win (3% increase in units sold) at the cost of a big loss for retailers (18% decrease in profit). In fact, the researchers calculate that volume must increase 39% for a supermarket to avoid losing money after a 7% price drop.

Research indicates that consumers are in a conservative mood with respect to prices; they do not want to see increases. Some manufacturers, such as Philip Morris, have experienced success with EDLP. Over the first one and one-half years of implementing the program, P & G lost both market share and unit volume for the brands involved. Most retailers believe that EDLP presents a bleak profit picture for them.

The Marketing Profile shows that price setting is not simply a matter of making a few calculations or even of simply pricing to cover costs and profits. It often involves relationships with other members of the marketing channel as well as with consumers. Channel leadership and power often influence pricing decisions, as do consumers' perceptions and purchase responses and competitors' actions. Even government regulatory action impacts most companies' pricing strategies. Balancing these factors to make successful pricing decisions is a difficult task.

In this chapter, we describe the basic concepts that underlie pricing decisions. This will provide a foundation for the pricing strategies that we examine in Chapter 18. The first step is to define *price* and discuss its importance in marketing. Then we examine the different factors that play a role in pricing strategy. These include the various objectives that a firm hopes to accomplish with its pricing, customer influences on pricing, cost and product characteristics that impact pricing, and competitive considerations. We close the chapter with a discussion of government regulation and legislation as related to pricing.

Before beginning Chapter 17, you may want to read the Appendix to Chapter 17. It contains a review of demand analysis, price elasticity, marginal analysis, cost analysis, and other principles of economics that are usually prerequisites for this course. This chapter assumes that you are familiar with the material in the appendix.

THE MEANING OF PRICE

Deceptively simple at first, pricing becomes more complicated the more we study it. Price can be defined in many ways and can take many forms. The actual price is what one party is willing to give up to acquire something of value from another party. We commonly think of price in monetary terms; however, it can be anything of value that is exchanged for something else (see Table 17.1). **Price** is the value one puts on the utility received for goods and services. The utility received can be of any type, as discussed in Chapter 1: form, time, place, and possession.

What Is a Price?

The price, or value, of a good does not have to be expressed in monetary terms. For example, **barter**—the exchange of goods or services in lieu of cash—was the basis for history's earliest pricing systems. Although monetary equivalents have supplanted barter as the basis of modern economies, bartering has made a resurgence as a small

Alternative Terms	What Is Given in Return
Price	Physical merchandise
Tuition	College courses; education
Rent	A place to live or the use of equipment for a specific time period
Interest	Use of money
Fee	Professional services: for lawyers, doctors, consultants
Fare	Transportation: air, taxi, bus
Toll	Use of road or bridge, or long-distance phone rate
Salary	Work of managers
Wage	Work of hourly workers
Bribe	Illegal actions
Commission	Sales effort

TABLE 17.1
The Meaning of Price

but increasingly important segment of the U.S. economy. Bartering is now used by companies, both large and small, to solve problems in operations, finance, and marketing. Examples of bartering in our society include:

- An independent consultant, who works with a manufacturer of fitness equipment, trades his time for a commercial-grade treadmill.
- A cardiovascular surgeon treats a pediatrician's mother, and the pediatrician treats the surgeon's children.
- A baseball team's pitcher is traded for a shortstop and an outfielder.
- A radio station trades commercial time to retailers in exchange for products to use in its station promotions.

Many transactions involve a price consisting of both money and goods. This practice frequently occurs in the purchase of durable goods, such as cars and appliances, where a trade-in is part of the price.

Price has a *subjective* and a *temporal* meaning. Consider the following examples:

- Bob and Carol each purchase a General Electric 27-inch color television set. Bob pays $650; Carol pays $525. Clearly, Carol made a better deal, right? Maybe not. Bob purchased his TV from a store that offers home delivery, in-home tuning, extended service at the store, and many different brands to choose from and is a convenient distance from Bob's home. Carol, on the other hand, bought her TV from a discount store 20 miles from her house that offers no service, no delivery, few brands to select from, and required Carol to take the set with her. Although they have both purchased the same TV, the bundles of utility each received are different, and the value each subjectively attached to his or her purchase also differs.

- In 1992, the Philadelphia 76ers of the NBA exchanged the team's only superstar, Charles Barkley, to the Phoenix Suns for three players: guard Jeff Hornacek,

TABLE 17.2
The Equation of Exchange

	Price Paid	Bundle of Utility Received
Consumer	**List Price Minus** store discounts coupons rebates trade-ins	**Product** features style quality packaging **Place** location delivery service **Promotion** image confidence of quality information about use
Retailer	**List Price Minus** quantity discounts seasonal discounts functional discounts advertising allowances display allowances return of goods allowances transportation allowances	**Product** brand recognition and preference warranties service support **Place** availability of inventory of models, sizes, etc. speed of delivery **Promotion** advertising support to end consumers sales promotion activity to end consumers sales training

Careful pricing is crucial for products that change rapidly, like home video games. Prices must be set to allow for the rapid movement thorough the product life cycle brought on by the pace of technological advance.

center Andrew Lang, and forward Tim Perry. In the 1992–1993 NBA season, the Suns won the Western Conference championship and lost in the NBA finals to the Bulls. The 76ers finished with one of the worst records in either league and had little meaningful contribution from the three acquired players. It now appears that the Suns got the better of the deal. However, *at the time of the exchange*, both parties received a price equal to the value they perceived.

Clearly, different sets of utilities are involved in different exchanges, and price may take a variety of forms. But in our society, price is typically a monetary amount in the equation of exchange. Table 17.2 shows an exchange from both the consumer's and the retailer's points of view. The table illustrates that price is the value assigned to a bundle of form, time, place, and possession utilities.

Why Is Price Important to Marketers?

Pricing decisions are very important because they have a direct impact on customers. Thus, prices play an important role in affecting the sales-and-profit dynamics of the firm. Here are examples of some instances where careful pricing is crucial:

▪ The pace of *technological advance* increases, pushing a product through its life cycle more quickly and making it more difficult to remedy pricing errors. Home video games and computer chips are two examples of products for which pricing is changing rapidly. This means that prices must be set to allow for early success, steep sales growth, quick market-segment penetration, and a fast recoupment of product-development costs.

▪ *Foreign competition* puts substantial pressure on prices. Many foreign-made goods such as shoes, clothes, toys, electronics, and automobiles compete to a great degree with American goods on a price basis.

- The firm is preparing to introduce a *new product*. Setting a proper price is difficult, and a mistake can irreparably damage the new product's chances for market acceptance.

- A *competitor attempts to gain market share* using price decreases. For example, Sanyo's low prices of microwave ovens forced competitors to reassess their pricing structures.

- A *substitute product* is introduced into the market. Dallas-based Southwest Airlines' no-frill fares have forced other carriers to lower their rates for routes on which these carriers compete directly with Southwest.

The role of price in a firm's profitability becomes clear in the equation:

$$\text{Profit} = \text{total revenue} - \text{total cost},$$

or

$$\text{Profit} = (\text{prices} \times \text{quantity sold}) - \text{total cost}.$$

As shown above, price is an essential determinant of total revenue in two ways. Obviously,

$$\text{price} \times \text{quantity sold} = \text{total revenue},$$

which means that, for a given quantity, the higher the price, the more sales dollars a company has coming in. More important, perhaps, is the notion that price is a factor that *causes* the sale. That is, marketers ask themselves the following questions:

- How much can I raise price without reducing volume (sales, profits)?
- How much do I have to lower price to get a beneficial increase in volume (sales, profits)?[1]

Thus the task is to set a price that generates enough total revenue to yield an acceptable profit.

We must recognize that the price set for goods and services has a direct impact on consumers for whom prices determine the cost of living. Consumers will get angry at some prices (e.g., gasoline, utility costs), show elation at others (e.g., appliances, home video equipment), and change their behavior (e.g., conversion to foreign cars, shopping at warehouse clubs) in response to others. Consumers' perceptions of how well they are doing financially from year to year are determined by measuring the prices they get for their labor (wages or salaries) against the prices they pay for goods and services.

Yet consumers' perceptions are likely to vary depending on the value each person attaches to certain bundles of utilities. For example, in 1994 fast-food chains in recession-pinched Japan struggled to build profits by slashing prices to attract consumers. KFC's research found that Japanese believed the food was good but the prices were expensive. So KFC cut prices by 16.8 percent. The result: the chain regained 10 percent of its lost customers.[2]

Zhen Xiaowen left her $100-a-month job as hostess at a Beijing restaurant to go to work for an American bank, where she earns $250 a month. Now she can afford to indulge her desire for American-made products. She buys Safeguard soap at 52¢ for 125 grams rather than Yu Tu soap at 15¢ for 125 grams because it "smells so much nicer than the Chinese kind." Soon she hopes to try Wella Balsam Shampoo at $4.60 rather than continuing to use Pan Ting Shampoo at $2.84. Zhen Xiaowen demonstrates that even at her small salary, some higher-priced products carry enough incremental utility to be worth the difference.[3] Figure 17.1 compares prices for a select group of products across national boundaries.

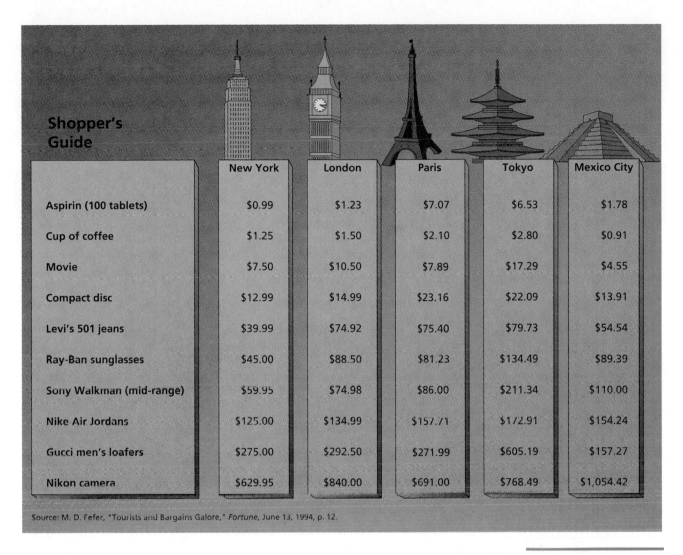

Shopper's Guide

	New York	London	Paris	Tokyo	Mexico City
Aspirin (100 tablets)	$0.99	$1.23	$7.07	$6.53	$1.78
Cup of coffee	$1.25	$1.50	$2.10	$2.80	$0.91
Movie	$7.50	$10.50	$7.89	$17.29	$4.55
Compact disc	$12.99	$14.99	$23.16	$22.09	$13.91
Levi's 501 jeans	$39.99	$74.92	$75.40	$79.73	$54.54
Ray-Ban sunglasses	$45.00	$88.50	$81.23	$134.49	$89.39
Sony Walkman (mid-range)	$59.95	$74.98	$86.00	$211.34	$110.00
Nike Air Jordans	$125.00	$134.99	$157.71	$172.91	$154.24
Gucci men's loafers	$275.00	$292.50	$271.99	$605.19	$157.27
Nikon camera	$629.95	$840.00	$691.00	$768.49	$1,054.42

Source: M. D. Fefer, "Tourists and Bargains Galore," *Fortune,* June 13, 1994, p. 12.

FIGURE 17.1
Comparison of Prices for Selected Items in Five World Capitals

KEY FACTORS IN PRICE DETERMINATION

Determining a specific price for a product or service involves a dynamic trade-off among certain key factors (see Figure 17.2). These include:

1. pricing objectives
2. customer influences
3. cost considerations
4. product characteristics
5. competitive forces
6. legal and regulatory constraints

In the remainder of the chapter, we discuss the basics of pricing in terms of each of these key factors. Because marketing situations vary widely, the impact of various factors may be more significant in one situation than in another. However, wise marketers have learned not to assume too much; it's better to consider factors that can then be discarded as having negligible impact than to ignore a factor that turns out to be the key to success.

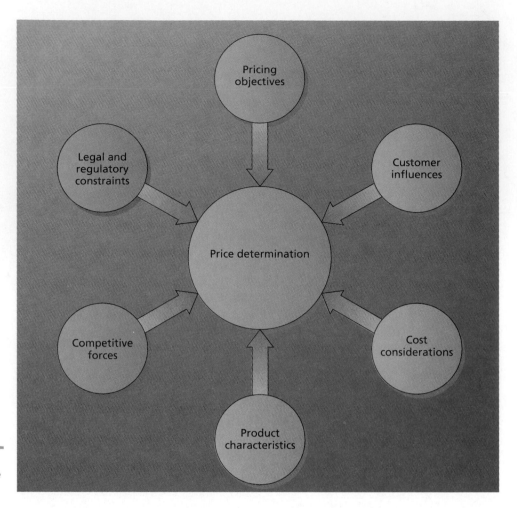

FIGURE 17.2
Key Factors in Price Determination

PRICING OBJECTIVES

Pricing objectives must be consistent with a company's overall corporate and marketing objectives. Pricing objectives must also be realistic in terms of the company's position in the marketplace and the product's target market and positioning strategy. For example, Lexus would not set a pricing objective that would make it the low-cost leader in the market. Lexus is a luxury car, positioned to command a higher price with a target market that expects to pay more for a car.

Regrettably, not many firms develop explicit, written pricing objectives. Instead, these objectives tend to be held as implicitly understood by the firm's management. Objectives, whether implicit or explicit, tend to fall into one of three broad classes: profit objectives, sales objectives, or competitive position objectives.

Profit Objectives

Profit maximization and target return on investment are two major types of profit objectives. **Profit maximization** means that the firm attempts to earn the largest profit possible. To do this, the firm sets the price at the point where the additional revenue generated by the sale of one more unit just equals the additional cost of producing and marketing this additional unit. Although this marginal analysis approach to profit satisfies many economists, businesspeople who have to make decisions under uncertainty rarely, if ever, can attain true profit maximization. To do so would require detailed information about customer demand and costs that is unlikely to ever be available.

Profit maximization would be an even more difficult objective to achieve in multiproduct companies (which is, of course, most companies). Trade-offs are often necessary in such cases. For example, the firm may accept little or no profit on one product to gain large profits on another, complementary product. Polaroid sells cameras at a low price and profit to gain high profitability on film; Gillette sells razors at a low price to sell many more replacement blades or cartridges.

Even if a firm did use a profit maximization objective, it would not necessarily mean a high price for the product in question. Profit maximization does not mean price gouging, excessive profits, and consumer rip-offs. Depending on demand and the costs associated with marketing the product, the firm might be most profitable selling a large volume at a small profit on each sale. Selling at a higher price could decrease demand and increase unit costs; profits might be far below what the lower price option would generate. Supermarkets and discount stores operate on this principle.

In view of the operational difficulties of the profit-maximization approach, many firms have turned to using a target return on investment (ROI) objective. ROI is the ratio of profits to capital investment, such as the manufacturing plant, production equipment, and accounts receivable.

One variation on this objective is to set a **target return on net sales,** where the targeted profit is a specific percentage of each sales dollar. Retailers and wholesalers often use this type of objective. The typical supermarket earns $.01 to $.02 profit on a $1.00 sale; the typical department store, about $.04; and wholesalers, about $.02.

Firms may also set other types of profit-related objectives. Some less aggressive companies may set price to *earn a satisfactory profit*. What is considered satisfactory varies by company and is affected by the attitudes of the managers, stockholders, and the financial community. Often the level of profit that managers believe the public will consider *fair* is part of the decision.

Sometimes pricing decisions reflect managers' desires to avoid an aggressive attack on competition. Other firms want to generate a positive cash flow, particularly when they have their liquidity tied up in inventory. For example, some condominium developers have sold off their already-built properties at distress prices just to get enough cash to stay in business. Automobile rebate programs are essentially price cuts that decrease profit, but they stimulate sales and move inventories.

Sales Objectives

Many organizations state their pricing objectives in sales-related terms. These goals can take a number of forms:

- Maintenance or growth in absolute sales
- Maintenance or growth in market share
- Minimum sales necessary to survive

Sometimes the firm's objective will be to address sales volume in terms of dollars or units sold. When industry sales are flat or the economy is in a recession, the best a company can hope for may be to keep sales volume flat instead of decreasing.

In other cases, larger volume can help a firm achieve economies of scale that lower the costs per unit sold. Excess plant capacity can be used and employee idle time is cut. Inventory turnover may increase, thus lowering average inventory carrying costs. Larger production runs may mean buying in larger quantities from sup-

MARKETING *IN ACTION*

EDLP at Procter & Gamble—The Saga Continues

Procter & Gamble is going through the $725 restructuring. Why $725? That's the premium a brand-loyal family paid in 1993 for a year's worth of P & G products versus private-label brands. These days, a premium like that spells big trouble with consumers. Similarly, with the growth of membership warehouse clubs, such as Price Club/Costco and Pace, and of discount stores like Wal-Mart, P & G was pulled in a different direction from the one that had worked with supermarkets and drugstores in the past.

P & G's new pricing strategy emphasizes value (no surprise there) at its new everyday low prices (EDLP). Introduced in 1991, EDLP was a shock to P & G's system. And for a while, things did not go too well. Market shares plummeted in liquid detergents, diapers, shampoo, fabric softener, shortening, and other categories. Some categories have recovered; others, such as diapers, are still having problems.

The key to EDLP is to maintain consistent pricing rather than high list prices punctuated by frequent, irregular, and costly promotional discounts. The wheeling and dealing had sent costs skyrocketing for P & G. The company was making 55 daily price changes on some 80 brands, necessitating rework on every third order. Ordering usually peaked at the end of a quarter (get those orders in during the discount period), sending factories into a frenzy of overtime followed by periods of underutilization. P & G plants ran at 55 to 60 percent of rated efficiency on average, with huge variations in output.

Furthermore, the paper trail became increasingly unwieldy. More and more retailers disputed more and more invoices as inaccuracies in billing multiplied. P & G treated these contested charges as accounts receivable, although 80 percent were

resolved in the customers' favor. The accountants were not happy!

Finally, problems escalated in the promotional arena. The quarterly sales promotional plan for health and beauty products alone ran to more than 500 pages and was sent to every salesperson. Moreover, P & G's sales force met U.S. retailers with five divisions in three sales layers, selling more than 2,300 stock-keeping units (SKUs) in 34 product categories with 17 basic pricing brackets and endless permutations. WHEW!

It quickly became apparent after the introduction of EDLP in 1991 that everyday low prices would require P&G to implement everyday low costs as well. Shock therapy for the organization! A team of P & G employees and consultants analyzed the costs of the sales organization. They analyzed the 41 work processes that comprise the company's customer management system (P & G had the highest overhead in the business), and they created a distribution chain linking supplier, wholesaler, retailer, and consumer in a partnering system. Now check-out stands are linked electronically with inventory control and re-ordering systems. Factories are more efficient; four plants can make as much detergent as 12 plants used to make. The company has downsized and eliminated more than 13,000 unnecessary jobs.

Procter & Gamble is looking forward to a new era of marketing—one in which customers receive more value for their money. With costs under control, P & G is as profitable as ever. Not all retailers are happy with the change; many miss the margins that the old promotions gave them. But eventually retailers too will be forced to become more efficient to compete successfully in an industry that is moving increasingly toward EDLP.

---

pliers with the accompanying discounts. These benefits translate into increased profitability for the company, provided that profits are not offset by increased costs.

Market share may be the objective for some companies. As we saw in the Marketing Profile at the beginning of this chapter, Philip Morris cut its price on Marlboro cigarettes and eventually increased market share from 22 percent to 27.3 percent in a matter of months.[4]

Robert Shaw, CEO of Shaw Industries, knows about pricing and about increasing his market share. Shaw Industries is located in Dalton, Georgia, where 80 percent of the nation's carpet is made. Shaw observes, "The carpet business has been overexpanded for a decade. Prices have been dropping for years." Carpet wholesales today for about $5.90 a yard, down from $6.40 in 1989. Shaw's profits, on the other hand, have ballooned from $22 million to $100 million in a decade.

Shaw's secret is domination. Shaw loves market share almost as much as he loves golf, and he built his own golf course.

Shaw also relies on economies of scale; that is, that larger operations achieve cost consolidations that translate into lower costs per unit sold. He believes that if a company grows big enough, costs will fall and profits will emerge. Since 1984, Shaw has expanded his market share from less than 5 percent to more than 30 percent and growing.[5]

For some companies, pricing is an essential element of survival. Commander Aircraft Company in Bethany, Oklahoma, builds single piston-engine, high-performance aircraft. Only a few hundred of these planes were manufactured in the United States last year; the business has been hit hard by product liability suits. And Commander is not having an easy time staying in business. Only 30 of its planes, priced at $285,000 plus extras, were sold in 1993—well below the break-even rate of about 40 a year. Its prices are reasonable, given the liability history of the industry: Commander's product liability insurance adds just $10,000 to the cost of the plane, well below industry averages. The goal of Commander's management is to stay aloft by marketing a superior product at a competitive price.[6]

Competitive Position Objectives

Some firms set pricing objectives in relationship to the actions of their competitors. Their goals may be the following:

- *To meet or prevent competition.* Many firms attempt to match the pricing of competitors. This pattern is very common in industries where one firm dominates and serves as the **price leader**—the firm that usually is first to change prices in the industry. U.S. Steel (USX) serves this role in the steel industry.

- *To stabilize prices.* Here the objective is to have similar prices throughout the industry, so that competition will not be based on price. This is often the objective of price leaders. Their power in the industry allows them to "police" the prices they set. Smaller firms fear a price reprisal from a large firm if they deviate from the normal price in the industry. Steel, paper, chemicals, and aluminum appear to follow such a pattern.

REVIEW

YOUR MARKETING KNOWLEDGE

17-1 What is being exchanged for your college tuition? How is this price determined? What are the long-term consequences of increases in tuition during the last ten years that have generally exceeded the inflation rate?

17-2 The same Macintosh personal computer can be purchased at a standard retail computer store, at a college computer sale, and from a mail-order supplier. In each case the price to the end consumer is different. Which price would you expect to be the highest, the second highest, and the lowest? What is being exchanged for the price in each instance? How can the lowest price retail institution stay in business with those prices?

CUSTOMER INFLUENCES

Of all the influences on price, the customer is unequivocally the dominant influence. If prices are so high that demand falls off dramatically, marketers are *forced* to change their pricing structures. After all, as the number of units purchased falls, revenue also drops. Consumers' willingness to buy is a major key to successful pricing. The "Marketing in Action: EDLP at Procter & Gamble—The Saga Continues" illustrates one company's attempts at price restructuring.

It's been called the "hardest task of the 1990s." Raising prices. As of spring, 1994, KFC had not had a price increase at the retail level since 1989. Other fast-food giants have had similar experiences. Retailers note that markets have become extraordinarily sensitive to price changes. Even the steel industry, which has enjoyed robust demand during the past few years, finds little reason to raise prices.[7]

So, after years of price hikes, marketers now find that consumers are extremely resistant to higher prices. How can marketers know what prices consumers are willing to pay for products? How does pricing affect consumer behavior? There are two broad areas that we will look at with respect to customer influences. These are: demand analysis and the impact on sales, and elasticity analysis and consumer price perceptions.

Demand Analysis and the Impact on Sales

According to economists, each price that a firm could set will result in a different level of demand. (See demand curves in the Chapter 17 Appendix.) These variations in demand impact the pricing strategy that a firm will choose to adopt. Usually, we assume that demand and price are inversely related. That is, the higher the price, the fewer units we can sell, and vice versa. In the case of some prestige products, of course, demand increases with a higher price. We believe that this occurs because customers interpret the higher price to mean a higher quality product, and they respond positively to this higher perceived value. Fur coats, exclusive restaurants, quality gemstones, and some automobiles fall into this category.

It is certain that price causes the volume sold to vary. The real question is: What price will cause the desired volume of sales? There are only two ways for a manager to discover the answer to that question. One is trial-and-error experimentation. Not surprisingly, there are many instances of pricing that appear to be guesswork. Saturn, Sears, and Northwest Airlines are recent examples that have turned out badly. Gillette introduced its Sensor razor wondering if customers would balk at the higher price, but the Sensor turned out to be one of the stars of the 1990s.

The second way to determine what price to charge is safer but more time consuming. Inevitably, the customer is the ultimate judge of whether your price, in combination with product quality and service, delivers real value. For this reason, it is essential that a firm obtain input from customers before setting a pricing strategy. The answers that a company gets are often unexpected and provide valuable direction for determining prices.

For example, two entrepreneurs were designing a mortgage-evaluation service. They called recent home buyers, described the idea to them, and asked two simple questions: What do you think this service would cost? Would you have bought the service when you were shopping for a mortgage? The answers were surprising. Customers expected and were willing to pay two to three times what the company was planning to charge.[8]

There are several practical reasons for forecasting demand at several price points. First, marketers will have an estimate of how much they can sell and should produce and an idea of what revenues will be and what will be their break-even point. They can also decide whether adding costly options to the product will be profitable and whether periodic discounting should be part of the pricing strategy.

Elasticity Analysis and Consumer Price Perceptions

Demand analysis gives an idea of how much can be sold at a given price. Elasticity analysis tells how seriously price changes will affect customers.

The theory behind elasticity analysis is discussed in the appendix to this chapter. Basically elasticity has to do with how sensitive consumers are to price changes. Will they continue to buy if the price is raised? If the price is lowered, will it achieve a large increase in sales? A small increase? Any increase?

To select the best pricing structure in a given situation, marketers must recognize the heterogeneity of buyers. These differences arise from at least three sources that are relevant to pricing and that affect how sensitive consumers are to price. First, consumers differ in the degree and nature of information they have about products and services—especially about prices. It takes effort and sometimes expense to obtain pricing information; thus we refer to this problem as consumers' **information costs.** Information costs may be high, and consumers would then buy without full information. Sometimes customers' lack of pricing information allows wide variations in the prices that producers can charge for products.

Research suggests many consumers have poor price recall, even at the point of purchase. However, some consumers are more vigilant than others. Price recall is influenced by correctly perceived promotion of the brand, use of the price in making the purchase decision, and income. Gender and age appear to have no impact on price recall.[9]

A second difference relates to the price that consumers are willing to pay; this is the **reservation price.** Reservation prices vary among consumers because of differences in perceived utilities derived from a given product. For example, Jim price-shops when he buys gasoline; he wants the lowest price he can find. Jim derives a great deal of utility from finding the lowest price and his reservation price is generally pegged to his perception of the lowest price currently available. Rob is willing to pay more. His income is higher, a few cents per gallon either way has little impact, and Rob derives more utility from convenience than does Jim. So Rob buys from a dealer that carries a well-known brand of gasoline. Rob's reservation price is quite flexible; only if a dramatic price increase occurred would he be likely to notice price.

Finally, consumers may have different transaction costs. These could include traveling costs, the costs of obtaining funds, the costs of switching brands, or the cost of uncertainty (risk) in investing in the product.[10]

To select the best pricing structure in a given situation, marketers must recognize the heterogeneity of buyers. For example, some consumers will price-shop for particular items, others will not.

Nagle has identified nine factors that affect buyers' sensitivity to price.[11] These are useful as guidelines for marketers:

1. *Unique value effect.* If the product is unique, buyers are less price sensitive.
2. *Substitute awareness effect.* If buyers are aware of acceptable substitute products, they are more sensitive to price.
3. *Difficult comparison effect.* If buyers have difficulty making price comparisons, they tend to be less price sensitive.
4. *Total expenditure effect.* The lower the expenditure as a percentage of total income, the less price sensitive buyers will be.
5. *End-benefit effect.* The less the expenditure in terms of the total cost of the end product, the less likely are customers to be price sensitive.
6. *Shared-cost effect.* When part of the cost is shared with another party, buyers are less price sensitive.
7. *Sunk investment effect.* When customers have assets that they have already purchased, they are less likely to be price sensitive to incremental purchases.
8. *Price–quality effect.* Buyers are less price sensitive about products that have more quality, prestige, or exclusive characteristics.
9. *Inventory effect.* When buyers cannot store the product, they are less price sensitive.

Note price sensitivity varies across market segments. Firms that "average price" their products across segments are losing sales by not exploiting to their advantage the fragmented nature of most markets. For example, a survey conducted among business travelers found that the most important considerations in choosing an airline were (1) large number of schedules from which to choose, (2) fast check-in, (3) physical comfort, (4) on-time flights, (5) safety, and (6) friendly service. On the list, price was number 14; yet much of airline pricing is across the board. Many discounts and deals do not differentiate between the tourist and the business traveler.[12]

For these reasons, price sensitivity should be measured for various targeted segments and under different marketing conditions. Pricing, as with any other variable in the marketing mix, must be adjusted to meet the expectations of each target market. The "Marketing in Action: Commercial Financial Institutions—Wake-Up!" discusses consumers' expectations in the purchase of financial services. Customer differences should never be assumed away!

COST CONSIDERATIONS

At the most basic level, a company has to cover its costs before it can make a profit. However, the process really is not that simple. First, the company must be able to identify its costs. Then it must allocate those costs among the products that it produces. As we have already pointed out, sometimes a cross-subsidizing or sharing of costs takes place. That is, one customer group or one product or product line may bear more of the costs than another, so that the firm may profitably serve a wider audience.[13]

Companies are changing their cost structures in order to set prices more competitively. This often means changing the entire approach to new-product development, so that costs are cut during the design and engineering stages of the product. Sometimes updated production equipment is necessary to lower production costs. The point to note here is that costs that marketers have assumed as fixed can actually be cut through creative design, engineering, and production.

At General Motors Corporation's Cadillac division, for example, marketers begin by setting a target price for a new model. Next a target profit is set and the new car development team *backs into* the cost. That is, sourcing, design, and production

MARKETING *IN ACTION*

Commercial Financial Institutions—Wake Up!

The results of a recent survey reveal a significant trend in the growth of member-owned credit unions. In a 1984 survey of midwestern bank customers, only 7 percent of the respondents said credit unions were their preferred financial institution. In contrast, the recent 1993 survey of these same customers found this preference had grown to 20 percent. What is accounting for this shift in customer preference?

It appears that fees charged by commercial banks for personal financial services have been rising nearly as fast as the cost of medical care. Since 1990, the cost of checking accounts and other bank services have climbed 18 percent, compared with a 21 percent increase in the price of medical care. Yet despite rising prices, commercial bank customers still retain a high degree of inertia. The 1993 study also found that more than 80 percent of respondents have maintained a banking relationship with their preferred financial institution for more than five years.

The research further finds that customers are increasingly using more than one financial institution to meet their banking needs. More than 70 percent of the midwestern bank customers responding to the survey reported using multiple financial institutions. These findings may portend a major shift in consumer banking.

Not only are commercial bank customers upset with rising service fees, their expectations of value are not being met. Commercial banks' attitudes toward customers may be characterized by a quote from Chris Lewis, banking policy director with the Washington, DC–based Consumer Federation of America. Mr. Lewis laments, "Bank customers are not real active shoppers and therefore are vulnerable to . . . price gouging by the industry."

But that situation may be changing. The results of the 1993 survey provide strong support that financial institutions are not meeting customers' expectations and perceptions regarding attributes such as friendliness and personal recognition. Overall customers' expectations of value are not being met. Further it was found that respondents overwhelmingly viewed convenience of location, service charges, and friendliness of employees as the most important considerations in bank selection.

On the other hand, credit unions offer lower service fees, no-fee or no-minimum-balance interest-bearing checking accounts, and lower interest on loans. Credit unions also pay higher rates on deposits.

It is suggested that commercial bankers continue to view their business as transaction-oriented rather than marketing-oriented based on strong customer relationships. But as American consumers become more and more accustomed to superior service at reasonable prices, commercial banks may find themselves with a severe case of declining market share.

---

are all geared toward building a car that incorporates an acceptable price and good value for the consumer.[14]

Cincinnati Milacron, Incorporated, is another manufacturer that is paying lots of attention to manufacturing during the design process. It now builds machine tools with 30 to 40 percent fewer parts. For the new Maxim 500, a machining center introduced in 1992, design streamlining reduced the number of fasteners from 2,542 to 709 and cut assembly time from 1,800 hours to 700 hours. Altogether, the new approach cut production costs by 36 percent! Milacron was then able to sell the Maxim 500 at the same price as the machine it replaced. Plus, the Maxim takes up 60 percent less floor space, can be installed and started up in two days instead of two weeks, and makes more rapid changeovers, which sharply increases user productivity. Impressive! But also an approach that has made the company extraordinarily competitive in its industry.[15]

Costs should be evaluated carefully to determine whether they are justified by added value to the customer. Sometimes unnecessary costs can be found in inefficient labor, in inefficient distribution, or in inefficient marketing practices. Even location can be the problem. Japanese companies caught in the double bind of a strong yen and a weak economy at home have been losing market share rapidly to U.S. rivals. That's why many Japanese exporters are adopting a strategy of moving factories—and jobs—out of Japan.[16]

PRODUCT CHARACTERISTICS

Three aspects of the product should be considered in determining a price: its positioning, its stage in the product life cycle, and whether it is a single product or part of a product line.

Positioning

In a survey commissioned by the *Wall Street Journal*, the Roper Organization surveyed 2,002 Americans. They were asked to name the "finest, most elegant" brand in each of five product categories. For men's clothing, 13% named Calvin Klein and 10% named Pierre Cardin. For women's clothing, 14% named Christian Dior and 11% named Calvin Klein. For leather goods, 37% named Gucci, 8% named Pierre Cardin. For watches, 45% said Rolex, 10% said Seiko. For perfumes, 18% cited Chanel, 9% mentioned Estée Lauder, and 9% named Georgio.[17] All of these are positioned as exclusive brands and command higher prices than many competitors in these product categories. Such products are targeted toward consumers who are willing to pay more for additional product benefits, which may simply mean a more exclusive image rather than real functional differences among brands.

Other brands are positioned and priced to take advantage of different opportunities. Bic makes reliable pens that are priced low enough to achieve high sales volume that generates high revenues for the brand. Profits per pen are low but high volume makes this brand highly profitable. Low-priced products are generally targeted toward price-sensitive buyers, who are unwilling to pay more for an item.

Low prices, however, do not always ensure high volume. The low-cost positioning that makes EDLP a success at Wal-Mart is not attainable for most retailers.[18] Thus other retailers will have to position themselves as adding value for customers to compensate for higher prices. Added value could be unique product offerings or additional services.

Stage in the Product Life Cycle

When a new product category is introduced, marketers often place a high price on the product for several reasons. First, they want to recover costs sunk in the development and initial marketing of the new product. Second, for a truly innovative product, consumers will often pay a premium price to acquire its unique attributes.

During the growth stage, new competitors enter the market. Often a firm has to lower its prices to keep pace with these new market entries. The degree to which this is likely to happen depends on how severe are the barriers to entry.

During the maturity stage of the product life cycle, profit margins are lower because of increased competition and the fact the consumers perceive many substitutes for the product. It is difficult to sustain high prices during the maturity stage.

Finally, during decline, marketers may try to exploit residual brand loyalty by maintaining prices. Alternatively, the strategy may be to lower prices and unload the remainder of product inventory as quickly as possible.

Single Product or Product Line

If a company produces a line of products that essentially serve the same customers' needs, an increase in price for one product in the line will serve to increase demand for other products in the line and vice versa. If the products, however, serve different market segments, the impact of a price change on one line item will have less impact on the demand for other line items. In this latter case, it is best if the company prices products more with a view toward competing in the different segments than toward competing with its own products.

If the company produces a single product in a given category, pricing will be oriented more toward maintaining a viable position against competitors than toward coordinating with the company's own product pricing. Lands' End, a catalogue retailer, offers several grades of men's dress shirts. Each item is priced according to specific benefits that may be desired by Lands' End customers. Of course, the company makes every attempt to convince its customers of the superior value attached to the higher-priced dress shirt by mentioning the quality of the cloth, the cut, and the workmanship.

COMPETITIVE FORCES

Probably the most important pricing role played by competitors is that they provide a reference price for consumers. That is, they do if consumers *know* at what level competitors are setting their prices. Research, however, indicates that most consumers have little memory concerning specific prices.[19] In some respects, this presents an opportunity for marketers who can tout low prices even if theirs are not necessarily the lowest.

Recently, Wal-Mart agreed to stop claiming that it always has the lowest prices. The nation's largest retailer said it would quit using its 5-year-old slogan, "Always the Low Price. Always." after the National Advertising Review Board, an advertising watchdog group, announced that the slogan might not be true. Wal-Mart denied that the slogan was misleading. But the company merely revised its slogan to read, "Always Low Prices. Always. Wal-Mart." Without consumer research, we can only speculate about whether the change in slogan will lead to any real change in consumers' perceptions about Wal-Mart's claims.[20]

LEGAL AND REGULATORY CONSTRAINTS

Virtually all aspects of pricing may be influenced by legislation and other government regulation. These occur in five major areas:

1. price fixing
2. price discrimination
3. price controls and guidelines
4. deceptive pricing
5. predatory pricing

Price Fixing

Section I of the Sherman Act states that every contract, combination, or conspiracy in restraint of trade or commerce is illegal. **Price fixing** may be thought of as a conspiracy, because it eliminates one major aspect of free competition among firms—competitive pricing. The conspirators are those competitors who work together to attempt to fix prices.

Here are two possible pricing strategies for selling men's jackets. Assume that these retailers are selling identical jackets. Further assume that this situation in each of the two stores takes place during the same time period.

	Everyday Low Prices	Frequent Sales
Initial price	$100	$120
Volume	× 60	× 20
Gross revenue	$6,000	$2,400
Sale price	$70	$80
Volume	× 40	× 80
Gross revenue	$2,800	$6,400
Total sales	$8,800	$8,800

17-3   Which of these two pricing strategies do you believe would be best for a retailer to adopt? Why? What are the advantages and the disadvantages of each?

17-4   Do you believe that consumers are likely to perceive these retailers as having different pricing strategies? What factors besides the price are likely to affect customers' choices in this situation?

17-5   What do you think will be the long-term effects on customers' perceptions of price as a result of these two strategies?

The standing legal precedent related to price fixing is the Sacony-Vacuum case.[21] In this case, the courts ruled that price fixing, or even the attempt to fix prices, was illegal per se (see Chapter 2). That is, the reasonableness or economic impact of the fixed prices is not a defense; the conspiracy itself is illegal. This per se illegality has been applied to many forms of cooperative price setting by competitors,[22] including efforts to lower prices; indirectly raising prices by taking excess supply of merchandise from an alternative channel; splitting markets by rotating who has the lowest bid for contracts; maintaining prices by distributing price lists to competitors; agreeing on markups or discounts; and for members of professions (for example, lawyers) publishing and circulating minimum fee schedules within the profession. All are illegal per se and have resulted in fines and sometimes prison terms for errant marketers. This is one area where the law is quite clear and the U.S. Justice Department's enforcement is vigorous.

We commonly think of price fixing among competitors at the same level in the channel. That is, manufacturers or retailers conspire to fix prices. This is *horizontal* price fixing, since the conspirators are at the same level in the channel.

It is also a conspiracy under Section I of the Sherman Act for organizations located at different levels of the channel to fix prices. However, for a period of almost 30 years, this *vertical* price fixing was expressly exempted from coverage by the Sherman Act. The Miller-Tydings Act of 1937 and the McGuire-Keogh Fair Trade

Enabling Act of 1952 allowed vertical price fixing to occur in states that passed laws allowing it. The practice was called either *resale price maintenance* or *fair trade*. It allowed a manufacturer, in effect, to set retail prices across an entire state. All retailers would be bound to this price, even if only one dealer in the state had agreed to the price with the manufacturer. Thus, no intrabrand competition could occur on prices in the state.

The major intent of the fair trade legislation was to protect small retailers from the price-cutting practices of large chains and discount stores. Also, it was intended to protect a manufacturer's brand name from being used as a discount item for attracting customers to stores. The image of the brand would thus be protected. But "fair trade" put constraints on free price competition and kept prices to consumers higher than they might have been. In 1975, the Consumer Goods Pricing Act was passed, repealing the Miller-Tydings and McGuire Acts and making vertical price fixing illegal per se.

Price Discrimination

Section II of the Clayton Act of 1914 and the amendments to Section II contained in the Robinson-Patman Act of 1936 prohibit price discrimination. **Price discrimination** is the practice of charging different prices to different buyers for goods of like grade and quality. This does not mean that all price differences granted to buyers in a market are illegal. On the contrary, most are legal. First, these statutes exclude sales to ultimate consumers. Second, in sales between businesses, certain bases for price differentials are explicitly allowed. Table 17.3 illustrates a number of bases for legal price discrimination among ultimate customers. Figure 17.3 shows an example of the many fares an airline can legally charge on the same flight.

TABLE 17.3
Types of Legal Price Discrimination

Class	Bases of Discrimination	Examples
Personal	Buyer's income or earning power	Doctors' fees, royalties paid for use of patented machines, professional association dues
Group	Age, military status, or student status of buyer	Children's haircuts, airline tickets, magazine subscription rates, theater admission charges, senior-citizen rates
	Location of buyers	Zone prices ("prices slightly higher west of the Rockies"), in-state vs. out-of-state tuition
	Status of buyers	New magazine subscriptions, quantity discounts to large-volume buyers
	Use of product	Railroad rates, public utility rates
Product	Qualities of products	Deluxe vs. regular models
	Labels of products	National, private, or unbranded
	Product size	Family, economy, giant size
	Peak–off peak services	Off-season resort rates, airline excursion rates, evening and holiday telephone rates

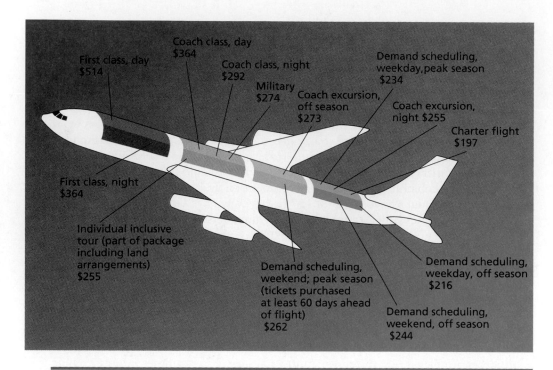

FIGURE 17.3
Typical Price Differentials in Airfares

Section II of the Clayton Act (1914) attempted to make price discrimination between firms illegal. Its purpose was to prevent sellers from cutting prices in areas with strong competition while maintaining higher prices in less competitive areas. It was found to have so many loopholes that the Robinson-Patman Act (1936) was passed to amend it.

Section II(a) of Robinson-Patman defines the conditions that constitute price discrimination. It must be shown that (1) the same seller, (2) charged different prices, (3) to two or more different purchasers, (4) for use, consumption, or resale within the United States or any territory, and that (5) there were two or more sales, (6) reasonably close in time, (7) involving commodities, (8) of like grade and quality, (9) and that at least one sale was in interstate commerce.

The Federal Trade Commission is empowered to act to stop the price discrimination if it believes these nine conditions hold. Even in these instances, though, the action is not illegal per se. The marketer may present a number of defenses. If any one of its defenses holds, then no illegal price discrimination exists. Also, Section II(f) makes it illegal for a buyer to knowingly induce or receive a discrimination in price. The intent here is to keep large buyers from coercing suppliers.

Defenses against the charge of price discrimination.   The seller may use eight defenses against a price discrimination charge. The first three attempt to refute some of the nine conditions in Section II(a) of the Robinson-Patman Act.

1. *The item in question is not a commodity* (physical product).

2. *The sale is not in interstate commerce.*

3. *The items being sold are not of like grade and quality.*

Products that are not physically identical may still be considered of like grade and quality. The relevant question is whether they are functionally or commercially equivalent.[23] Perceived product differences do not justify this defense. This was demonstrated in the Borden case, when the courts ruled that privately labeled milk manufactured by Borden was legally the same as Borden branded milk, even though consumers perceived the former to be inferior.

Other defenses against price discrimination charges arise out of the general wording and some specific provisions of the Robinson-Patman Act. At a general level, the effect of the price discrimination under Section II(a) must "be substantially to lessen competition or tend to create a monopoly, or to injure, destroy, or prevent competition" for the differences in price to be illegal. This leads directly to two more defenses.

4. *The buyers of the goods are not in competition with each other.* Competition cannot be injured if the buyers do not compete. This defense has three important dimensions:

   a. *Geographic location* of the markets. The buyers must compete in the same geographic area.

   b. *Timing of the sales.* The courts have held that both price quotes and the delivery of goods must be reasonably close in time.

   c. *Level of distribution.* The extent that retailers and wholesalers are not in competition constitutes the only justification of *functional* discounts in the channel. Robinson-Patman makes no explicit place for functional discounts; they must be justified on other bases. Thus, a functional discount given to one channel member who performs extra functions and not given to another at the same level who does not is illegal unless some other defense can be found; the argument that they perform different functions carries no weight.[24]

5. *No injury to competition has occurred.* The defendant may show that no significant injury to competition has occurred at any of three levels of distribution:

   a. The first, the *primary level injury*, occurs when a direct competitor at the same level in the channel as the price discriminator is hurt by discriminatory pricing.

   b. The advantage of one buyer over another buyer is called *secondary level injury*. The wholesalers who buy from the price discriminator may sell farther down the channel at different prices because of the price discriminator's different prices to them. Those getting a lower price may undercut those paying a higher price and thus gain a competitive advantage.

   c. Finally, *tertiary level injury* involves injury to the customer of a customer. This occurs when the seller has two separate channels of distribution. One channel uses wholesalers, the other involves direct sales to retailers. If the retailer receiving direct sales pays either a higher or lower price than the retailers buying from the wholesalers are paying, then one group has a potential advantage over the other. The classic case here involves Standard Oil, which sold its gasoline to jobbers at 1.5 cents below its price to retail service stations in the same area.[25] These jobbers then resold the gasoline to other retail outlets at a price below Standard Oil's price to directly competing stations, with resulting injury at the tertiary level.

In addition to the two general provisions about competitive effects, three specific defenses are allowed under Robinson-Patman.

6. *The differences in prices are based upon cost differences in serving the customers.* Section II(a) allows price differences "made only due to allowance for differences in the cost of manufacture, sale or delivery resulting from different methods or quantities." Thus, we see that *quantity discounts* have no legal standing in themselves. They must be justified by cost differences in serving buyers purchasing different amounts.

7. *The seller is meeting the equally low price of a competitor.* Section II(b) allows one to meet, but not beat, a competitive price.

8. *The price differential is caused by changing conditions.* Section II(a) states that prices may be changed to reflect "changing conditions affecting the market for or marketability of the goods." Included here would be such conditions as (1) actual or imminent deterioration of perishable goods, (2) obsolescence of seasonal goods, (3) distress sales under court process, and (4) sales in good faith in discontinuance of business in the goods concerned.

Deceptive Pricing

Marketers often use special low prices to promote their products. We are familiar with all types of retail "sales." Sale prices are potentially illegal under Section V of the Federal Trade Commission Act, which prohibits "unfair and deceptive practices." **Deceptive pricing** refers to specially promoted price deals that mislead consumers. The FTC is likely to act if it believes that the marketer has deceived the buyer about the true nature of his or her prices. These pricing practices, like price discrimination, are subject to the rule of reason. Five price promotions have the potential for legal action.

1. *Bait and switch.* This activity is "an alluring but insincere offer to sell a product or service which the advertiser does not intend or want to sell." The marketer offers a very low price on a product (the bait) in order to get the customer into the place of business. Once in the store, the prospective buyer is persuaded to purchase a higher-priced item (the switch). The switch is made by such devices as criticizing the quality of the promoted item, failing to have the item in stock, refusing to take orders for the item, or failing to deliver the item in a reasonable time. Sears recently signed an agreement with the FTC to take great care not to practice bait and switch in its sewing machine, washer and dryer, and major home appliance lines.

2. *Former price comparisons.* In one of the most-used forms of a bargain price, marketers offer a reduction from their own former price for an item. If the former price is the actual price at which the item was regularly offered to the public for a reasonably substantial period of time, it provides a legal basis for a price comparison. But if the former price is fictitious, then the discount being offered is deceptive.

3. *Comparable value comparisons.* Another common form of bargain price is to offer items at prices lower than those charged by others for the same merchandise in the same trading area. The person making the claim should be reasonably certain that the higher price, used as the reference price for the sale, does not appreciably exceed the price at which most of the item's sales are being made in the area. This also holds when comparisons are made to other brands of like grade and quality. For example, Retailer A promotes Brand X pen as having "comparable value of $15." Unless a reasonable number of the principal out-

lets in the area are offering Brand Y, an essentially similar pen, for $15, the price offer would be deceptive.

4. *Advertising manufacturer and retailer suggested retail prices.* The FTC holds that "many members of the purchasing public believe that a manufacturer's list price, or suggested retail price, is the price at which an article is generally sold." If these list prices do not correspond to prices at which a substantial number of sales of the item are made, the bargain price is deceptive.

5. *Bargain offers based upon the purchase of other merchandise.* Often marketers offer additional merchandise, to be given or sold at a special price to customers, on the condition that they purchase a particular item at a price usually offered by the marketer. Such offers as "Buy One–Get One Free," "2-for-1 Sale," "Half-Price Sale," "1 Cent Sale," and "50 Percent Off" all are relevant here. When the seller, in making these types of offers, increases the regular price of the item the customer must buy to qualify for the bargain, or decreases the quantity or quality of that item, or otherwise attaches conditions beyond the specified purchase, then the consumer may be deceived, according to the FTC. The Mary Carter Paint Company was found guilty of deceptive pricing of this type. Its claim was that for every can of paint purchased, the buyer would get a "free" can of equal size and quality. The FTC charged that Mary Carter had never sold single cans of paint and that the quoted one-can price was really a two-can price, thus deceiving consumers. The Supreme Court agreed.

In addition, retailers' use of such terms as *wholesale* and *factory* in referring to prices can also be considered deceptive. Unfortunately, all of us confront these pricing practices by some retailers. This fact reflects the difficulty of enforcing these provisions. The FTC's budget and priorities do not allow it to police deceptive pricing well. Enforcement is often left to state and municipal governments.

Predatory Pricing

Predatory pricing occurs when a firm charges a very low price for a product, with the intent to drive competitors out of business. Having driven out the competition, the firm raises prices. This practice is potentially illegal under Section II of the Sherman Act as an "attempt to monopolize," or under Section 5 of the Federal Trade Commission Act as an "unfair practice." It is likely to be judged illegal if the firm is selling at prices below its cost. Certain states have statutes that require minimum markups of about 2 percent at wholesale and 6 percent retail. Thus, the marketer must take care not to appear too aggressive in setting prices, or predatory intent may be inferred.

An important predatory pricing case is currently working its way through the appeal process in the courts. It is based on the impact that Wal-Mart pricing has had on the small retailers in the communities that Wal-Mart enters. An Arkansas court has found Wal-Mart guilty of predatory pricing and ordered that prices be increased. The specifics of this case and its potential ramifications for competition and consumer welfare are explored in the "Spotlight on Ethics: Wal-Mart—A Predatory Pricer?"

This chapter has laid the foundation for our discussion of pricing strategies in Chapter 18. Marketers make these decisions within the context of issues discussed here in Chapter 17: pricing objectives, customer influences, cost considerations, product characteristics, competitive forces, and legal and regulatory constraints. In the next chapter, we will examine the various pricing strategies that marketers use to set prices.

MARKETING *IN ACTION*

Wal-Mart: A Predatory Pricer?

In October 1993, a state court in Arkansas ruled that Wal-Mart had been engaging in predatory pricing. The suit, which originated in Conway, Arkansas, was brought by three independent Conway merchants: Dwayne Goode, owner of American Drugs, Jim Hendrickson, owner of Baker Drug Store, and Tim Benton of Mayflower Family Pharmacy. The trio charged that Wal-Mart crossed the line and violated Arkansas' 56-year-old Unfair Practices Law by cutting prices with the intent to drive them out of business.

The Wal-Mart case has been widely watched as a test of state predatory-pricing laws, which not only exist in Arkansas but in 22 other states. Pharmacies in many of the other states helped fund the suit against Wal-Mart.

In the past, federal courts have not been particularly receptive to alleged victims of predatory pricing. For example, in June 1993, the U.S. Supreme Court upheld lower-court rulings that tossed out a $150 million judgment against the Brown & Williamson Tobacco unit of B. A. T. Industries PLC for allegedly trying to drive Brooke Group Ltd. out of the generic-cigarette market with unfair price cuts. Similarly, in August 1993, a federal jury in Texas rejected claims that American Airlines was trying to drive weaker competitors out of business with its lower airfares.

For these reasons, there is widespread speculation that plaintiffs may turn more and more to state laws that are generally more accommodating. In some cases, state law defines selling below cost as *prima facie* evidence of predatory intent.

In the Wal-Mart case, Judge David Reynolds gave the following reasons for backing the plaintiffs:

- The frequency and large number of Wal-Mart's below-cost sales
- Wal-Mart's stated policy to "meet or beat the competition without regard to cost"
- Wal-Mart's below-cost sales intended to "attract a disproportionate number of customers to Wal-Mart"
- Wal-Mart's practice of displaying other stores' higher prices next to merchandise in its stores
- The very large price discrepancy between Wal-Mart's Conway prices and Wal-Mart prices in other towns

There are two very interesting sides to the argument concerning whether the predatory-pricing judgment should stand. One side reflects concerns for consumers, reflected in a statement by Robert Rhoads, Wal-Mart's attorney: "If this decision is allowed to stand, the result will be higher prices not just for Wal-Mart customers but customers of every retail store, large and small, in Arkansas." Rhoads went on to term Judge Reynolds decision as "anticonsumer." Chris Hoyt, retail consultant at Ryan Management Group, says, "I don't see how the judge can put the priorities of three bedraggled Arkansas druggists over the millions and millions of people who shop at Wal-Mart every day. The beauty of Wal-Mart is that it controls its costs, and it is able to sell at lower prices than other retailers."

Yet there is another side to the story. Local coalitions in Massachusetts, Vermont, and other parts of New England have been fighting to keep Wal-Mart out of their towns. Other predatory-pricing cases against Wal-Mart are pending (at time of this writing) in Pine Bluff, Arkansas, Pawhuska, Oklahoma, and Cortez, Colorado. Spokespeople for these groups claim that they are preserving the free-market economy. National Federation of Independent Business spokesman Terry Hill maintains, "A small business can return a lot more to a community than a mega-corp. Profits stay in the town instead of going off to company headquarters." Certainly, the demise of many small, local retailers after Wal-Mart moved into town can be documented. Many believe that Wal-Mart's low prices don't stay so low after its small-business competitors have gone out of business.

In March, 1994, Wal-Mart signed an agreement with Michigan to not make misleading price comparisons in its stores. A spokesman for the state's attorney general said Wal-Mart's in-store ads compared products that weren't the same sizes or models without noting the differences. He also said that advertisements sometimes inflated the prices that Wal-Mart claimed its competitors were charging. Wal-Mart agreed, among other things, not to claim its price on an item is lower without verifying the price a competitor is charging; not to leave in place signs comparing prices if it knows the comparison isn't accurate; to update comparisons weekly and post the date any comparison was made; not to compare products that aren't the same size or model; and not to lower an item's price just so it can claim a better price comparison.

In the predatory-pricing case in Conway, Arkansas, Judge Reynolds awarded the three pharmacists a total of $288,000 in damages, and Wal-Mart has been ordered to stop selling health and beauty products below cost. Wal-Mart will, of course, appeal the decision.

PERSONAL COMPUTER EXERCISE

When considering changing from traditional promotion-based pricing to everyday low pricing, manufacturers must consider the impact on consumers, intermediaries, and, of course, their own market share and profits. This PC Exercise will help you analyze the effectiveness of EDLP for a packaged goods manufacturer.

KEY POINTS

■ Pricing is an essential component of the marketing mix. In times of high inflation or of high unemployment, or both, the price decision takes on even greater importance.

■ The price set for goods and services serves as the basis of exchange in our society and is an index of value for goods. Price is the value assigned to a bundle of form, time, place, and possession utilities.

■ The price of goods and services goes by many names (other than price) including tuition, rent, interest, fee, fare, toll, and salary. In all cases, it is the index of value for the item.

■ Price plays an important role for the economy as a whole by bringing demand and supply into balance. When price is not allowed to move with supply and demand, imbalances occur. These may be shortages that result from prices that are too low, or surpluses that arise when prices are too high.

■ Price increases in importance to the organization with increasing technological advances, increased foreign competition, shortages of raw materials and energy, the advent of substitute products, and inflation.

■ Key factors in price determination are pricing objectives, customer influences, cost considerations, product characteristics, competitive forces, and legal and regulatory constraints.

■ Pricing objectives should be explicit but may be implicit. They are typically based on profits, sales, or competitive position.

■ Reservation price depends on the quoted price levels relative to the general market price and to the degree of price flexibility the consumer perceives as acceptable. Both aspects guide the specific price that is set.

■ Companies must set prices to cover costs in order to make a profit, but costs can be lowered by making production and marketing more efficient.

■ Product positioning, stage in the product life cycle, and relative placement of the product in the firm's total product mix impact the setting of a price that is acceptable to customers.

■ Competitive forces play an important role in price setting, but consumers often lack knowledge about actual prices.

■ Major areas of price regulation include price fixing, price discrimination, price controls and guidelines, deceptive pricing, and predatory pricing.

KEY TERMS

price (589)
barter (589)
profit maximization (594)
target return on net sales (595)
price leader (597)
information costs (599)
reservation price (599)

price fixing (603)
price discrimination (605)
deceptive pricing (608)

ISSUES FOR DISCUSSION

1. What is the price paid and what is exchanged for each of the following?

    (a) The principles of marketing course you are now taking

    (b) A free hot lunch program in a school

    (c) A standby flight from Boston to Atlanta

    (d) An exchange with a Russian firm of personal computers for oil

2. Evaluate EDLP from the point of view of the manufacturer, the retailer, and the consumer.

3. Evaluate the Arkansas court decision against Wal-Mart for predatory pricing from the perspective of consumer welfare, retail competition, and small community environment.

4. An old friend who now works for a firm that competes directly with yours invites you to lunch. At the luncheon, this friend begins to discuss prices of your competing products. What should you do? Why?

5. A manufacturer of machine tools is accused of illegal price discrimination. The charge is that different customers at the same level in the channel have been charged different prices per unit for their supplies of machine tools. On what basis can the manufacturer defend itself against this charge?

6. There has been a recent trend in automobile retailing for some dealers to post a final sale price on the car and allow no bargaining. This so-called value pricing has been quite controversial among dealers. Why would some dealers adopt this pricing structure? Is it in the best interest of competition or the consumer?

7. "Getting more bang for the buck is the ticket for business travelers as corporations keep a tight rein on costs . . . " announced *Advertising Age*, May 2, 1994, in an article entitled "Low Prices Alone Won't Fly in Biz Travel." The same article reported that Hyatt Hotels Corp. is promoting its "Business Plan product offering an in-room fax, and a copier and printer on every floor, plus free local phone calls and breakfast." What considerations is Hyatt likely to take into account when determining a price for its Business Plan, and who will be the targeted customer?

8. You are a consultant to a mid-sized manufacturer of camping equipment. The company president says that he wants to price to maximize the company's profit potential. What kinds of questions will you need to ask in order to offer him some intelligent advice?

9. When customers are extremely sensitive to price increases, what are some measures that producers can take to control prices?

10. Several years ago, an on-campus snack bar raised the price on its chicken sandwiches by 50 percent. In defiance of basic economics, demand went up. In fact, the first week of the new price, students were lined up outside the door to buy chicken sandwiches. How can this be explained?

CASE APPLICATION

Antitrust Dogfight: The Case of American Airlines

In April 1992, American Airlines implemented its new policy of value pricing. The new policy consisted of a four-tier fare structure, with only first-class, unrestricted-coach, and 14-day and 30-day advance-purchase tickets. All other special discounts were discontinued. First-class fares were to be 20 percent to 50 percent lower and coach seats 40 percent lower than current fares. According to Robert Crandall, AA's chairman, value pricing would stimulate traffic, eliminate special deals, establish a fairer fare structure, and increase American's revenue and profitability.

By August 1992, American had abandoned the pricing plan after competitors refused to match the program. But that wasn't the end of the story. Continental and Northwest Airlines filed suit against American, charging predatory pricing. The case was tried in Galveston, Texas, in Judge Samuel B. Kent's courtroom.

Northwest and Continental accused AA of adopting a value-pricing plan, then cutting summer excursion fares in half, in order to bleed them to death. Northwest attempted to show that AA knew it would lose money from value pricing and the half-price sale. Northwest and Continental charged that AA was trying to run them out of business. American says it was merely trying to lure reluctant people, especially businesspeople, into its seats. But Northwest and Continental contended that AA expected its net income to rise $1.7 billion over the following five years as other carriers collapsed and the industry consolidated.

The two airlines were asking for $3 billion in damages from American for the losses they say were imposed on them by the Value Pricing Plan. Judge Kent found in favor of American Airlines.

Questions

1. What do you think American Airlines' current pricing policy might be?
2. Do you believe that American Airlines was guilty of predatory pricing? What are the pros and cons to your position?
3. Assuming that airline prices are heavily influenced by supply and demand, what could each airline do to remain competitive? How might this case affect American Airlines' market share?

Determining Your Price

In employment, price includes all elements of monetary compensation, including salary, bonus, and benefits. Salary is a fixed amount paid on a regular basis, usually about every two weeks or once per month. Bonus pay is sometimes added to the fixed component. Many salespeople are paid a commission over and above a base salary, others are paid a bonus once per year. Benefits can include various categories of life and health insurance, tuition reimbursement, coverage of child care, use of a company automobile, product discounts, and the like.

Value in employment is determined by utility and market factors. Your value is influenced by how well you match the requirements of the job. Your education, experience, and interpersonal skills are the major areas that will be assessed when you are under consideration for a job. "Quality" is important is all three areas: in education, experience, and interpersonal skills.

To determine your employment value, you need to know something about the requirements of jobs that are high on your list. Some potential sources of information include, but are not restricted to, your school's placement office, your employment market's publications, human resource managers, and employment advertising.

Questions

1. What are the key requirements in education, experience, and interpersonal skills for each of your top-priority jobs?
2. What sources did you use for the above information?
3. What might you do to increase your employment value for your two or three top-priority jobs?

Appendix to Chapter 17

Fundamental Economic Analysis for Pricing Decisions

This appendix consists of material that combines basic principles of economic analysis with pricing considerations. The topics include analyzing demand and its impact on price elasticity, how revenues are affected by demand and price, marginal analysis and profit maximization, and competitive analysis. Discussion of these topics is placed in the appendix for two reasons: (1) the material is highly technical in nature, and (2) the material should be a review of prerequisite material that you have already covered in an economics course. However, for convenience, this appendix is organized to provide a succinct review and to place the discussion of pricing in Chapters 17 and 18 in the proper theoretical context.

DEMAND ANALYSIS

Price setting depends largely on how demand reacts to various prices. Estimates of demand allow one to forecast the revenue that will be generated for the firm at various prices. One basic tenet of economics and marketing is that as the price of an item increases, the demand for that item will decrease. This is a very intuitive concept and is one that real-world experience supports. We present this general result by means of a downward sloping **demand curve** showing the quantity of a product that is expected to be sold at various prices. Figure 17A.1 presents hypothetical demand curves for several products. Clearly, the responsiveness of these products to price varies greatly. What we need is a measure of the degree to which consumers respond to changes in prices. This measure is called the price elasticity of demand.

Price Elasticity of Demand

The **price elasticity of demand** is defined as the percentage change in quantity demanded relative to the percentage change made in price. This is expressed as:

$$\text{Elasticity} = \frac{(\text{original quantity} - \text{new quantity})/\text{original quantity}}{(\text{original price} - \text{new price})/\text{original price}}$$

or

$$E = \frac{(Q_1 - Q_2)/Q_1}{(P_1 - P_2)/P_1} = \frac{\Delta Q/Q_1}{\Delta P/P_1}$$

where P_1 = original price E = elasticity
P_2 = new price $\Delta P = P_1 - P_2$ the change in price
Q_1 = original quantity demanded $\Delta Q = Q_1 - Q_2$ the change in quantity
Q_2 = new quantity demanded

Let us illustrate this concept with two situations. First, assume that the price of a small computer in January 1994 was $800 and 20,000 units were sold during the year. In January 1995, the price dropped to $700 and 22,000 units were sold during the year.

$$E = \frac{(20,000 - 22,000)/20,000}{(\$800 - \$700)/\$800} = \frac{-2,000/20,000}{\$100/\$800}$$

$$= \left(-\frac{2,000}{\$100}\right)\left(\frac{\$800}{20,000}\right) = -.8$$

The minus sign reflects the fact that demand increases as price decreases, and vice versa. Since it is not customary to express the minus sign, we will not continue to use it here. Note that the total revenue generated at the 1994 price is greater than that generated at the 1995 price.

Old situation: $800 × 20,000 = $16 million (total revenue)

New situation: $700 × 22,000 = $15.4 million (total revenue)

In situations where the total revenue generated after a price decrease is smaller than the original total revenue, the product is said to be *price inelastic*. This is reflected in a calculated elasticity of demand of *less than one*, and is typically portrayed by a demand curve that is close to vertical. In Figure 17A.1, the demand for a required textbook and candy bars are price inelastic. The demand for the use of

617

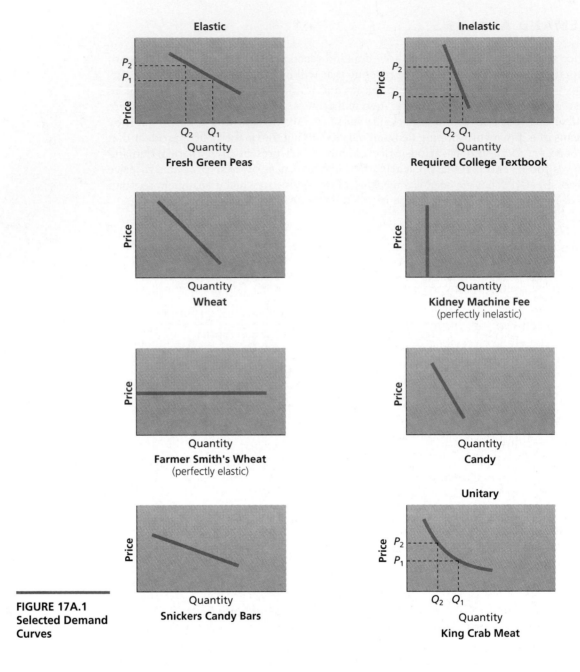

**FIGURE 17A.1
Selected Demand
Curves**

kidney machines is the extreme case of inelasticity: it is *perfectly inelastic*, which means that the same number of units will be sold regardless of price. A perfectly inelastic demand curve suggests that no matter how high price rises, consumers will not cut back on demand.

Now assume that in January 1996 the price of the computer is reduced further, to $550. The quantity sold in 1996 is 40,000 units.

$$E = \frac{(22{,}000 - 40{,}000)/22{,}000}{(\$700 - \$550)/\$700} = \frac{-18{,}000/22{,}000}{\$150/\$700}$$

$$= \left(-\frac{18{,}000}{\$150}\right)\left(\frac{\$700}{22{,}000}\right) = 3.8 \quad \text{(minus sign suppressed)}$$

Note that the total revenue after the price decrease is greater.

$$\text{Old situation: } \$700 \times 22{,}000 = \$15.4 \text{ million}$$

$$\text{New situation: } \$550 \times 40{,}000 = \$22 \text{ million}$$

In situations where the total revenue generated after a price decrease is larger than the original total revenue, the product is said to be *price elastic*. This is reflected in a calculated elasticity of demand of *greater than one*, and is typically portrayed by a nearly horizontal demand curve. In Figure 17A.1 note that the demand for fresh green peas, wheat, and Snickers candy bars is price elastic, and that the demand for Farmer Smith's wheat is the extreme case of elasticity. It is *perfectly elastic*, which means that Smith's wheat brings the same price regardless of how much he or she produces.

It is also possible for the total revenue generated before and after a price decrease to be identical. This is called *unitary price elasticity* and occurs when the elasticity of demand *equals one*. King crab meat illustrates this situation in Figure 17A.1. The small computer example points out a very important aspect of price elasticity of demand: in general, it is not the same value over all possible prices for a product.

The price elasticity of demand is determined by a number of factors. The first is the degree to which substitute products are available. If a product has close substitutes, it tends to be elastic; if a product does not have close substitutes, it tends to be inelastic. For example, apples have many possible substitutes in a meal and, therefore, are very elastic; gasoline has almost no substitutes and is very inelastic. Second, goods that are necessities, such as medical services and required textbooks, tend to be inelastic; luxuries like vacations and dining out tend to be elastic. Third, goods that constitute a large proportion of one's budget tend to be elastic while those that use little of the budget tend to be inelastic. Cars, housing, and television sets are elastic, while napkins, stationery, and matches are inelastic.

Primary versus Selective Demand

It is important to draw a distinction between the price elasticity for *primary* and *selective* demand. As we pointed out in Chapter 5, primary demand is the size of the market for a product class as a whole. (It is also called *generic demand*.) In Figure 17A.1 the demand curves for fresh green peas, a required textbook, wheat, candy, king crab meat, and kidney machine services all represent primary demand. The demand curves for Farmer Smith's wheat and Snickers candy bars represent the impact of price on *selective* or *brand demand*. This is demand for one specific brand offering within a product class.

The wheat and candy examples in Figure 17A.1 illustrate the distinction between primary and selective demand elasticity. They also point out that it is possible for primary demand to be inelastic while selective demand is elastic. That is, the total market may not be very responsive to price changes, but the choice of a specific brand may be affected very much by price differences among brands. This situation often occurs when primary demand is a *derived demand*, that is, when the demand for a product is affected by the demand for some other product. Business-to-business products fit this pattern very much. For example, the demand for steel is partially derived from the demand for new cars, and the demand for building products such as bricks and lumber is derived from the demand for new structures. The following generalization is important:

> For business-to-business products, the primary price elasticity of demand is often inelastic, while the selective price elasticity of demand is often elastic.

This same pattern can occur in consumer products when the market is mature and when brands are considered to be reasonable substitutes for each other. For example, candy and gasoline as categories are price inelastic while specific brands are price elastic. Also, although a required textbook is price inelastic, stores may sell the same book at different prices, creating a very elastic situation. In marketing it is important to know both the primary and selective price elasticity of demand.

Demand and Revenue

Demand level leads directly to the amount of revenue generated for the firm, and this, in turn, is related to the price elasticity of demand. We recognize three concepts of revenue:

1. *Total revenue (TR).*   This is simply the total amount of money received from all buyers of a product, or

$$TR = P \cdot Q \qquad \text{(Equation 17A.1)}$$

   where P = price of the product
   Q = quantity sold

   We noted earlier the effect price elasticity had on the total revenue generated.

2. *Average revenue (AR).*   This is simply the average amount of money received per unit sold, which we know is the price of the units sold. It is the total revenue divided by the quantity sold. As a simple manipulation of Equation 17A.1 we get:

$$P = TR/Q = AR$$

   Because average revenue equals price at any given quantity, the plot of the average revenue curve will be identical to the plot of the demand curve.

3. *Marginal revenue (MR).*   Marginal revenue refers to the amount of change in total revenue resulting from one additional unit of sales. In formula:

$$MR = \Delta TR/\Delta Q$$

   With the standard downward sloping demand curve, marginal revenue will be less than average revenue, because, in order to gain additional sales, the price has to be lowered on the entire quantity that would have been sold at the higher price. Table 17A.1 illustrates the impact of a downward sloping demand curve on total revenue, average revenue, and marginal revenue.

   Note that with the exception of the first unit, marginal revenue is always less than the price or average revenue at each sales level. This becomes clear if we look at the revenue effects of moving from a $9 price to an $8 price. On the incremental unit sold, the firm earns $8. However, to get this sale it gives up $1 on the two units that would sell at $9. Thus, the marginal revenue of the incremental unit sold is $8 − $2 = $6. Graphically, then, the marginal revenue curve will always lie below the demand curve (see Figure 17A.2).

   Note also, from Table 17A.1, that marginal revenue becomes negative when the amount of money given up on sales that could be made at higher prices exceeds the price of the incremental units. By moving from a price of $5 to a price of $4, we gain $4 for the incremental unit but give up $1 each on six units that would sell at $5. Thus marginal revenue equals $4 − $6 = −$2. When marginal revenue is negative, total revenue is decreased.

Price (P)	Quantity Sold (Q)	Total Revenue (TR = PQ)	Marginal Revenue (ΔTR/ΔQ)	Average Revenue (TR/Q) = P
$10	1	$10	$10	$10
9	2	18	8	9
8	3	24	6	8
7	4	28	4	7
6	5	30	2	6
5	6	30	0	5
4	7	28	−2	4
3	8	24	−4	3
2	9	18	−6	2
1	10	10	−8	1

Source: Adapted from R. E. Leftwich, *The Price System and Resource Allocation* (Holt, Rinehart and Winston, 1986), p. 191.

TABLE 17A.1
Impact of Downward Sloping Demand Curve on Revenue

Marginal Revenue and Elasticity

Marginal revenue and elasticity are related as follows:

$$MR - P - P/E$$

This leads to important generalizations about the impact on marginal revenue for price increases and decreases at various elasticities. These revenue effects of var-

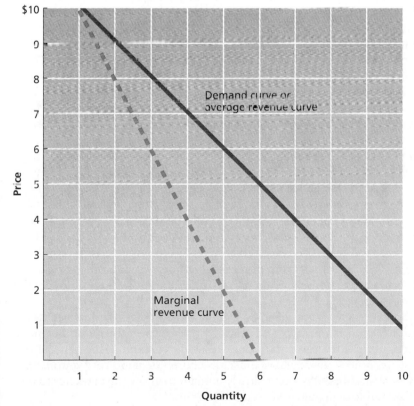

FIGURE 17A.2
The Relationship of Demand and Marginal Revenue Curves

Elasticity	Effect on Total Revenue		Effect on Marginal Revenue	
	Price Increase	Price Decrease	Price Increase	Price Decrease
Inelastic $E < 1$	Increase	Decrease	Positive	Negative
Unitary $E = 1$	Zero	Zero	Zero	Zero
Elastic $E > 1$	Decrease	Increase	Negative	Positive

TABLE 17A.2
How Elasticities Affect Revenue

ious elasticities are summarized in Table 17A.2. This summary makes clear that for total revenue to increase, marginal revenue must be positive and vice versa. Note that (1) if P and TR move in the *same* direction, demand is inelastic, and (2) if P and TR move in *opposite* directions, demand is elastic.

These concepts help explain why, in the 1980s and 1990s, the automobile companies undertook price rebate programs. With an elastic demand for cars (in the short run), the companies increased their total revenues by decreasing the price. But, why, then, do so many analysts believe the automobile companies actually lost money in their rebate programs? The answer probably lies in the cost dynamics of the industry.

Nonprice Competition and Demand

The other elements of the marketing mix, besides price, are intended to affect demand in two ways. First, the marketer hopes to sell more of a product at any given price than would be possible without the "nonprice" activity in channel availability, promotion, or product offering. This makes it possible, in effect, to shift the demand curve to the right, as illustrated in Figure 17A.3, Panel A. RCA has been able to increase the *demand* for $600 videotape systems from 100,000 to 120,000 units by effective promotion and distribution penetration and support. Effectively, they have shifted the demand curve D to D'. In contrast, by using price competition alone, RCA could only change the *quantity demanded* by moving up or down its demand curve (D).

A second major objective of nonprice competition is to make the firm's demand curve more inelastic (see Figure 17A.3, Panel B). Here RCA, due to effective promotion, has been able to change from demand curve D to curve D'. On curve D', it can increase price from $600 to $650 with demand only falling from 100,000 units to 95,000. Total revenue has increased from $60 million to $61.75 million. If RCA had remained on the original demand curve D, demand at $650 would have been 85,000 units. Total revenue would have fallen from $60 million to $55.25 million. The benefits of insulating oneself from price competition through other marketing activities thus becomes clear. Many firms aggressively attempt this, and it remains a very controversial area in marketing.

Any demand curve assumes a given and fixed environment with respect to all other elements of the marketing mix and consumer taste. We talk about a demand curve being accurate if "all other conditions are held constant." Since, in the real world, these other conditions change, we must also expect demand curves to change. Fortunately, these changes usually occur slowly enough to allow the marketer to deal with a reasonably stable demand curve in the short run.

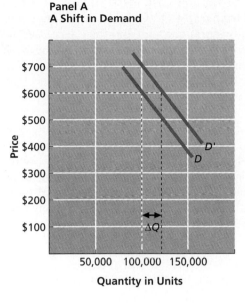

Panel A
A Shift in Demand

ΔQ = Change in Quantity

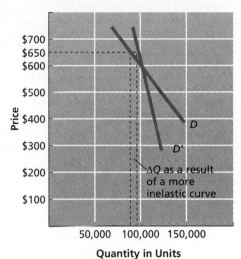

Panel B
A More Inelastic Demand Curve

ΔQ = Change in Quantity Demanded

**FIGURE 17A.3
Demand for RCA
Videotape Systems**

Estimating Demand

The importance of demand estimation should be very clear by now. How does one go about estimating the effects of price on demand? We addressed this issue to some degree when we discussed marketing research and demand forecasting in Chapter 8. Basically, the same techniques are available to help identify demand curves. These techniques include surveys of buyers' intentions, laboratory and field experiments measuring buyers' purchase behavior related to price, and the statistical analysis of past price and sales data.

COST ANALYSIS

The nature of the demand for a product determines the revenues that will be generated. However, whether these revenues will yield a profit depends on the costs associated with generating that revenue. In fact, some approaches to price setting only examine costs, as we will see in Chapter 18.

Types of Costs

We must develop an understanding of six different costs if we are to be good price setters.

▪ **Total fixed cost (TFC)** is the sum of the financial obligations of the firm that remains at the same level no matter how many units of a product are produced and marketed. Amortization charges for capital equipment and plant, plus such charges as rent, executive salaries, property taxes, and insurance are examples.

▪ **Average fixed cost (AFC),** or fixed cost per unit, is the amount of fixed cost allocated to each unit. It is simply the TFC divided by the number of units.

▪ **Variable cost (VC)** is directly tied to production. It includes direct labor and raw materials charges.

- **Average variable cost (AVC)**, or per-unit variable cost, is the variable cost per unit produced. It is simply the sum of all variable cost (TVC) at a given production volume divided by this volume. AVC usually starts out high and then decreases as production and purchasing efficiencies are obtained with increased volume. Beyond a certain point, the costs of trying to overwork labor or overcrowd a plant drive AVC up again.

- **Total cost (TC)** is the sum of TFC plus TVC at a given output.

- **Marginal cost (MC)** is the change in total cost of producing and marketing one additional unit. Usually MC will fall sharply at low volume levels but will level off and then rise sharply as volume increases. It could be defined equally well with identical results as the change in total variable cost associated with one additional unit of volume. This is true because this one unit increase raises total cost and total variable cost by the same amount. Note in Table 17A.3 that the increase from 1 to 2 units changes total variable cost from $40 (1 unit × $40) to $70 (2 units × $35). The difference is the MC of $30.

Table 17A.3 presents the costs associated with the production and marketing of a specific product. For these per-unit costs, graphed in Figure 17A.4, note the following generalizations:

- *Average fixed cost* (AFC) declines across the whole output level.

- *Average variable cost* (AVC) forms a U shape. Early economies in production and purchasing eventually give way to inefficiencies of overworked labor and overcrowded production facilities. A major calculator company lost control of variable cost in this way and eventually went bankrupt.

TABLE 17A.3
Types of Costs and Their Behavior

(1) Quantity Produced and Marketed	(2) Total Fixed Cost	(3) Average Fixed Cost (2) ÷ (1)	(4) Average Variable Cost	(5) Average Total Cost (3) + (4)	(6) Total Cost (5) · (1)	(7) Marginal Cost
1	$100	$100.00	$40.00	$140.00	$140.00	$30
2	100	50.00	35.00	85.00	170.00	15
3	100	33.33	28.33	61.66	185.00	11
4	100	25.00	24.00	49.00	196.00	8
5	100	20.00	20.80	40.80	204.00	6
6	100	16.67	18.33	35.00	210.00	5
7	100	14.29	16.43	30.72	215.00	5
8	100	12.50	15.00	27.50	220.00	6
9	100	11.11	14.00	25.11	226.00	8
10	100	10.00	13.40	23.40	234.00	11
11	100	9.09	13.18	22.27	245.00	15
12	100	8.33	13.33	21.66	260.00	20
13	100	7.69	13.85	21.54	280.00	26
14	100	7.14	14.72	22.86	306.00	33
15	100	6.67	15.93	22.60	339.00	41
16	100	6.25	17.50	23.75	380.00	50
17	100	5.88	19.41	25.29	430.00	60
18	100	5.55	21.67	27.22	490.00	71
19	100	5.26	24.27	29.53	561.00	83
20	100	5.00	27.20	32.20	644.00	

Source: Adapted from R. E. Leftwich, *The Price System and Resource Allocation* (Holt, Rinehart and Winston, 1986), p. 139.

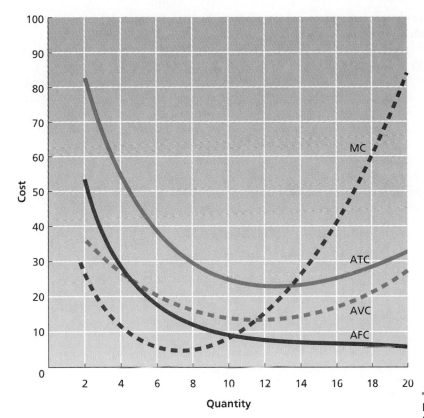

FIGURE 17A.4
Behavior of Average Cost Curves

Source: R. H. Leftwich, *The Price System and Resource Allocation* (Holt, Rinehart and Winston, 1986), p. 140.

- *Average total cost* (ATC) is the sum of AFC and AVC. As a result, it, too, is usually U shaped. Because AFC continues to fall after AVC starts to increase, the lowest point of ATC is at a higher level of output than AVC. For ATC, the lowest point is at 13 units at an ATC of $21.54. For AVC, the lowest point is at 11 units at a cost of $13.18.

- *Marginal cost* (MC) always equals ATC at the latter's *lowest level*. Note in Table 17A.3 that MC equals ATC at between 12 and 13 units of output. ATC decreases as long as MC is less than ATC and increases once MC is above ATC.

We can use these concepts of cost and the demand concepts we developed earlier to determine a profit-maximizing price. This approach is called *marginal analysis* because it uses the concepts of marginal revenue and marginal cost to reach the optimal pricing level.

MAXIMIZING PROFIT THROUGH MARGINAL ANALYSIS

Table 17A.4 combines relevant data on cost from Table 17A.3 and adds information on demand: price, quantity sold, total revenue, and marginal revenue. In addition, it shows maximum profits possible for various combinations of price and cost. It also demonstrates the overriding principle of profit maximization: *Profit is maximized when MC = MR.*

Up to this point, when $MC = MR$, the incremental total revenue generated from an extra unit of sales exceeds the total incremental cost of it. Thus, profitability increases. Beyond this point, however, the incremental cost exceeds the incremental revenue and profits decrease (see Figure 17A.5). In our example, $MC = MR$ at 10 units. The optimal price is then $40, and profit is $166.

Note that if we would have set a price based upon the *minimum average total cost*, we would have made less profit—at 13 units ($21.54 ATC, from Table 17A.3) and a price of $31, for example, profit is down to $123. Also, a price based upon *minimum average variable cost* is also not optimal. At 11 units ($13.18 AVC, from Table 17A.3) and a price of $37, profit is $162. The dangers of pricing based upon some markup over some average cost should be clear. Unfortunately, it is quite common for firms to set prices based upon average cost.

A more detailed look at cost analysis is presented in Appendix A, Financial Concepts for Marketing Analysis. It also discusses break-even analysis, operating statement analysis, analytical ratios, and computing markups and markdowns.

The marginal approach to price-setting does have some practical problems.

1. Demand curves are difficult to estimate accurately.

2. Costs often are not in the form needed for marginal analysis. Costs are much more accurate than demand estimates. However, there are many ways to account for costs, and costs assigned to products often include nonrelevant overhead.

3. Firms often have goals other than profit maximization, as noted in Chapter 17. For example, a firm, using the data in Table 17A.4, might set its price at $20 with the explicit understanding that it would take a loss in order to gain market share.

Most operating managers do not know exactly what their marginal revenue and marginal cost curves look like. They must approximate them using research and good judgment. However, some firms—including major airlines, catalogue retailers, and gas and electrical utilities—explicitly use marginal analysis to make

TABLE 17A.4
Using Marginal Analysis to Get Maximum Profit-Producing Price

	(1) Price	(2) Quantity Sold	(3) Total Revenue (1) · (2)	(4) Marginal Revenue	(5) Marginal Cost*	(6) Total Cost*	(7) Profit (3) − (6)	
	75.00	1	75	75	—	$140	−$65	
	70.00	2	140	65	$30	170	− 30	
	66.00	3	198	58	15	185	13	
	62.50	4	250	52	11	196	54	
	59.00	5	295	45	8	204	91	
	55.00	6	330	40	6	210	120	
	51.50	7	361	31	5	215	146	
	47.50	8	380	19	5	220	160	
	43.50	9	392	12	6	226	166	
(Optimal Price)	40.00	10	400	8	8	234	166	(Maximum Profit)
	37.00	11	407	7	11	245	162	
	34.50	12	414	7	15	260	154	
	31.00	13	403	−11	20	280	123	
	27.50	14	385	−18	26	306	79	
	24.00	15	360	−25	33	339	21	
	20.00	16	320	−40	41	380	− 60	
	16.00	17	272	−48	50	430	−158	
	12.00	18	216	−56	60	490	−274	
	8.00	19	152	−64	71	561	−409	
	4.00	20	80	−72	83	644	−564	

* See Table 17A.3.

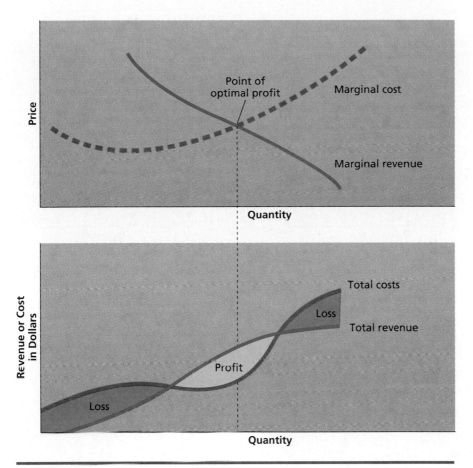

FIGURE 17A.5
Pricing for Maximum Profit

pricing decisions. In all these instances, they do have a good understanding of their demand and cost structures. Other organizations may attempt to make optimal pricing decisions in other ways. We will examine these procedures in Chapter 18.

Of course, all price setting, whether marginal analysis is used or not, takes place in a competitive environment. In the next section, we examine the role of competitive analysis in determining price.

COMPETITIVE ANALYSIS

The assessment of demand and cost must take place within the context of a specific competitive environment. That environment directly affects the demand curve faced by an individual firm. Two aspects of competitive analysis are important: the competitive structure of the firm and the pricing behavior of competitors.

Competitive Structure

Recall that there are four general classes of competitive structure: (1) pure competition, (2) monopoly, (3) oligopoly, and (4) monopolistic competition. (The characteristics of each were discussed in Chapter 2 as part of the marketing environment.) Figure 17A.6 shows the demand and associated marginal revenue curves for these structures.

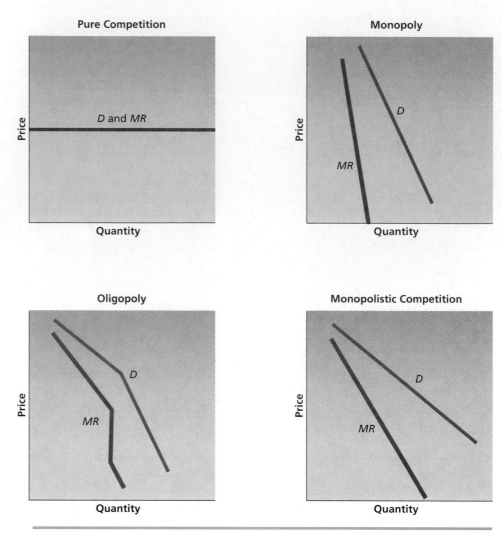

FIGURE 17A.6
Demand and Marginal Revenue Curves for Competitive Structures

The monopolist's demand curve in Figure 17A.6 is the least elastic, since this is where the fewest product substitutes are available. In the few cases for which the United States government permits monopoly, pricing policies are usually regulated. For example, the pricing of services provided by public utilities are strictly controlled. Also note the "kink" in the oligopolist's demand curve. With oligopolies, there is usually a uniform or market price at which most competitors sell a product. If one firm lowers its price below the market price, the competitors will match this price quickly so they won't lose sales. Thus, the sales gain from lowering price will be small or nonexistent, and total revenue will be less due to the price decrease. Below market price, then, the demand curve for the firm in an oligopoly is very inelastic. However, if one competitor raises prices above the market price, the competitors may not match this price. The result is that the competitor raising the price loses sales as customers switch to lower-priced competitive products. Thus, above the market price, the oligopolist's demand curve is very elastic.

The demand curve for an individual firm in pure competition is perfectly elastic, because the firm has no impact on price. Price is determined completely by the interaction of supply and demand in the total market (see Figure 17A.7), and the market

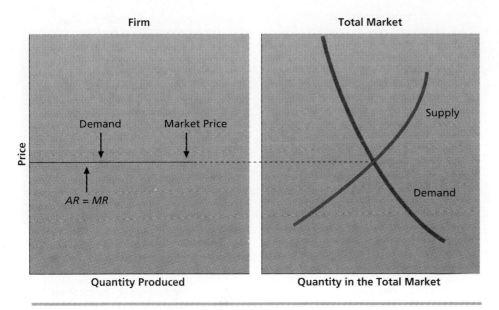

FIGURE 17A.7
Pure Competition

price, then, represents the demand curve for the firm. A marketer, as far as price is concerned, is completely at the mercy of the demand and supply conditions in the market. The agricultural sector of our economy, which comes closer to pure competition than any other, has even taken steps to mitigate the power of the overall market to set prices by forming cooperatives to try to differentiate products (for example, Sunkist oranges) or to agree on the amount of product that will be supplied to the market.

If we added the marginal cost curve of the individual firm to each of the competitive demand and marginal revenue curves shown in Figure 17A.6, we could find the profit-maximizing price. This is, of course, the point where marginal cost equals marginal revenue ($MC = MR$). It is illustrated in Figure 17A.8. The exact profit could then be calculated by taking the total revenue generated at this price and subtracting the total cost.

This approach to price setting suffers from the previously noted limitations of marginal analysis. However, it does serve as a conceptual standard because it considers demand, cost, and competitive environment.

Competitors' Pricing Behavior

Within the monopolistic competition and oligopolistic market structures that represent most of our economy, price choices are available to the firm and its competitors. In setting price, a firm must consider the pricing behavior of its competitors by asking questions like:

- How many competitors are there?
- What market share does each have?
- What are their total financial resources invested in and how much money has been committed to the competitive product?
- What is their cost position relative to ours?
- What pricing behavior have they exhibited in the past?
- How is demand affecting them?

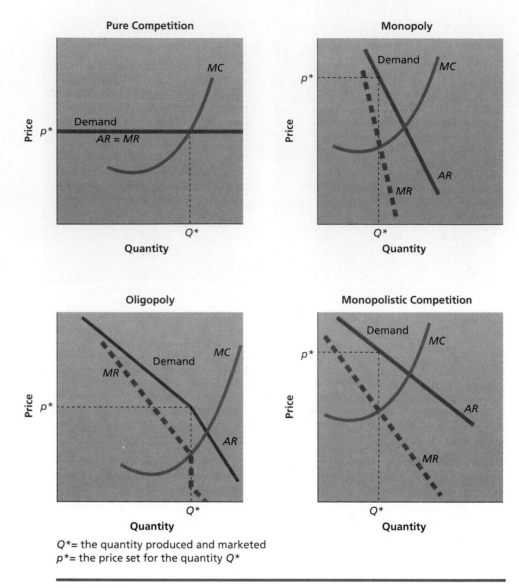

Q*= the quantity produced and marketed
p*= the price set for the quantity Q*

FIGURE 17A.8
Pricing for Maximum Profit in Different Competitive Structures

From the answers to these questions, the manager attempts to forecast competitors' prices. It is not an easy task.

OTHER ENVIRONMENTAL INFLUENCES ON PRICE

Other factors in the environment—such as government price supports, foreign conspiracies to fix raw material prices (OPEC), weather, and tariff policy—all have an indirect impact on price setting. They affect demand, cost/supply, or competition. Table 17A.5 presents examples of some potential influences on price and indicates how they affect demand, cost/supply, or competition.

With this background in the basic economics of demand, cost, market structure, and profit maximization understood, we are now in a position to continue the discussion of price setting as presented in Chapters 17 and 18.

	Factor	Impact
Demand	Government price supports for butter	Decrease in demand for butter
	Promotional program and tax incentives for home insulation	Increase in demand for home insulation
	Government drops support for air bags in cars	Decrease in demand for air bags; increase in demand for seat belts
Cost/supply	OPEC increases oil prices	Increase in cost of all products using oil in any form
	Freeze in Brazil's coffee fields	Increase in cost of coffee marketing
	Pollution standards lowered for the steel industry	Decrease in cost of doing business for the steel industry
Competition	Government subsidizes Texas Savings and Loans	A competitor kept in the market for financial services
	Government sells its own aluminum plants to Kaiser and Reynolds	New competitors for Alcoa enter market
	U.S. and Japan agree on limit on imports of Japanese cars	Aggressive competitors' actions on price are limited

TABLE 17A.5
The Effect on Price of Environmental Factors

KEY TERMS

demand curve (617)
price elasticity of demand (617)
total fixed cost (TFC) (623)
average fixed cost (AFC) (623)
variable cost (VC) (623)

average variable cost (AVC) (624)
total cost (TC) (624)
marginal cost (MC) (624)

CHapTeR 18

Pricing Procedures

Marketing Profile

Borland Strikes Out in a New Direction

Historically, computer software has sported hefty price tags. For example, the leading spreadsheet packages, such as Lotus 1-2-3 and Microsoft Excel, have been priced in the $300 range. But in August 1993, Borland International turned industry heads by offering the newest version of its spreadsheet program, Quattro Pro for Windows 5.0, at an unheard-of $49.95.

Borland's strategy—or gamble, as some industry experts see it—is to target the home market segment. This is the fastest growing market in the industry. For example, Glen Mells, vice president of marketing communications for WordPerfect Corporation says, "Right now it's about 1 percent of our total revenues, and we think it could go as high as 10 percent within five years. We know that this area is very price sensitive and believe that it makes sense to have software that retails for under $100."

Borland hopes to boost future revenues by offering subsequent upgrades at higher prices to customers who buy the current discounted package. But some have doubts about the success of this discounting strategy. Jeffrey Tarter, editor of the software industry newsletter *SoftLetter,* says, "Those prices make sense only if there is a significant follow-up. Otherwise, it won't mean a thing for Borland's revenues." Mr. Tarter continues, "Generally, there's always been a low interest in upgrades [among home users]. So it doesn't matter if [Borland] can come up with upgrades or lower prices."

Certainly the lower prices for the latest Quattro Pro version have hurt profitability, which has tumbled in the wake of price wars. For example, Borland's profits in the third quarter of 1993 fell 48 percent. So the big question remains: Will Borland's new pricing strategy help or hurt its bottom line in the long run?

Mark Calkins, vice president of product and strategic marketing at WordPerfect, has mixed feelings about Borland's pricing. "What Borland did with Quattro Pro was a good short-term strategy aimed at the home user. But it's not a good move if they're seeking to win over the larger users of business applications." Among business users, loyalty is strong for software programs. This loyalty develops as users have time invested in learning certain systems. Therefore, low prices are seldom a sufficient incentive to make business users switch brands.

For now, Borland is noncommittal about its next moves. But the company remains optimistic that its low-price strategy will pay off in the long run.

In the pricing of personal computer (PC) software, we see many of the factors that impact price determination and the success of pricing decisions: consumer demand in relation to the price and the product features, differential responses by market segments, competitive activity with respect to pricing, issues concerning profitability as a result of varying pricing strategies, and, in the background, the impact of advancing software technology on pricing strategy.

Balancing price with demand, competition, costs, and environmental conditions plays a major role in determining the profitability of the enterprise. Imagine that you have to analyze and balance all these factors to arrive at a successful pricing strategy for your company's products. A challenging assignment!

In this chapter we look at various options for setting prices. As we saw in Chapter 17, price setting occurs within a variety of constraints and considerations, such as pricing objectives, competition, and customer behavior. Legal and regulatory statutes must be taken into account, and the characteristics of the product itself will have a bearing on pricing strategy. Specifically, in this chapter we will examine how costs represent a starting point for pricing strategy. We then look at differential pricing, competitive pricing, product line pricing, and miscellaneous pricing methods.

PRICE SETTING IN PRACTICE

The complexity of setting prices in business practice is such that marketers commonly set prices with isolated information based only on demand, cost, or competition. Thus we end up with cost-based pricing, differential pricing, competition-based pricing, and product-line pricing. Some marketers do consider all of these factors, as well as important environmental dynamics in setting prices. We refer to this as **integrative pricing.** Table 18.1 summarizes the specific pricing methods within these classifications. We will look at each method in detail. Finally, we examine some of the reasons that marketers make adjustments to their pricing strategies.

As recently as 1988, advertising guru David Ogilvy commented, "Pricing is guesswork. It is usually assumed that marketers use scientific methods to determine the price of their products. Nothing could be further from the truth. In almost every case, the process of decision is one of guesswork."[1] In fact, sacrificed profits and strategic damage are the results.

TABLE 18.1
Classification of Pricing Methods

Cost-based Pricing	Differential Pricing for Consumers	Differential Pricing to Channel Members	Competitive Pricing	Product-Line Pricing	Miscellaneous Pricing Methods
Cost-plus pricing	Second-market discounting	Quantity and timing discounts	Penetration pricing	Price bundling	Value pricing
Intermediary pricing	Periodic discounting	Functional discounts	Experience curve pricing	Premium pricing	Customary pricing
Return-on investment	Random discounting	Credit and collection discounts	Price signaling	Complementary pricing	Odd-even pricing
		Multiple discounts	Geographic pricing		
		Allowances	Competitive bidding		
			Price leadership		

A good pricing strategy is a reasoned choice from a set of alternative prices. Usually the choice is made with profit maximization as the ultimate objective, while taking into account specific situations.[2] At the same time, marketers use certain assumptions about buyers that help determine what price to set.

First, marketers know that customers often engage in nonoptimal behavior when they buy. That is, customers may evaluate their choices incorrectly because of too little information. Consumers vary in their willingness to incur search costs (e.g., time) and transaction costs (e.g., traveling costs, cost of money, and switching costs). Incomplete information may lead to three types of behavior: consumers may purchase randomly, they may use a surrogate for an unknown attribute (e.g., price as a surrogate for quality), or they may evaluate choices incorrectly.[3]

Second, as we saw in Chapter 17, consumers vary in terms of their reservation prices. Some consumers are simply more price sensitive than others; some consumers are more price sensitive for a given product or in a given situation.

Finally, the best pricing strategy in certain circumstances is not apparent until any shared economies or cross-subsidies are taken into account. This means that one consumer segment bears more of the average cost than another, but the average price still reflects cost plus an acceptable profit to the marketer.[4] This may sound like price discrimination and in fact it is. As we saw in Chapter 17, differential pricing to marketing channel members under the conditions specified by the Robinson-Patman Act is illegal. However, as we shall see, differential pricing to consumers is common practice.

COST-BASED ORIENTATION AS A STARTING POINT

To determine a price without concern for cost is very dangerous. In fact, those who use other pricing methods must keep one eye on the cost of the products involved. Because costs are so important in determining profitability, and because they are much easier to estimate than demand, many marketers set prices using cost-based procedures. The most common are cost-plus pricing, intermediary pricing, and return-on-investment pricing.

Cost-plus Pricing

Cost-plus pricing is the most common form of price setting. One simply adds a specified amount to the cost of an item. The added amount is a percentage of the cost. Usually the cost is based on average total cost (ATC) for a planned number of sales. However, average variable cost (AVC) is sometimes used. Here is the formula:

Using average total cost $\text{Price} = \text{ATC} + m\,(\text{ATC})$

Using average variable cost $\text{Price} = \text{AVC} + m\,(\text{AVC})$

where m is the percentage added to cost. Thus, if the target markup on ATC was 25 percent and ATC was $100, then

$$\text{Price} = \$100 + .25\,(\$100) = \$125.$$

The simplicity of this approach to setting prices is its biggest strength. All one needs is a cost schedule and a set of decisions about the appropriate markup. It is also useful because marketers often do not know demand schedules or price sensitivity very well and so estimates of total revenue are often uncertain. In addition, it is easy to justify a price that covers total cost. This is especially important in competitive bidding situations, such as government contracts.

A cost-plus approach to pricing is most appropriate in product categories where demand and competitive activity are quite stable over time. This would include food (milk, bread) and other household staples. But the cost-plus approach has weaknesses, too. First, it assumes an accurate assessment of cost. In inflationary times and in high technology industries, assessing cost is not easy. For example, the inability to estimate cost accurately is a constant problem for military contractors.

Also, when using ATC, the product has some of the firm's general overhead allocated to it; but just how much of the president's salary or the employees' recreation area should be allocated to each product? There are many ways to allocate these costs, each way resulting in a different ATC. Price then becomes the slave of an arbitrary accounting system. Cost allocation systems are set up to absorb these overhead costs at some specified planning volume. If actual volume is below the planned volume, then not all overhead costs are covered.

Intermediary Pricing

In **intermediary pricing,** cost-plus pricing is the dominant mode among intermediaries in the marketing channel, wholesalers and retailers, where it is called *markup pricing*. These marketers deal with large assortments of products and do not have the resources to develop demand schedules for each item. (The way margins are quoted and calculated is presented in the Appendix to Chapter 17.) Channel members' prices are not totally unrelated to demand; they do assign different percentage markups to different items based upon sales experience and estimates of consumer price sensitivity. Wholesalers and retailers will quickly lower prices if an item is not selling. Also, the intermediary's price is based upon a markup on manufacturer's selling price, or discount from manufacturer's suggested retail price. (See the Appendix to Chapter 17 for details of these calculations.) The manufacturer may have researched demand and conducted a competitive analysis before setting the price and discount schedules.

Markups may be based, however, on profit margins that eventually are challenged by consumers. Take the beer cartel in Japan, for example. Until recently, the popular 633-milliliter bottle sold for 320 yen, or $3.11. In May 1994, the breweries raised that price by 10 yen. But some retailers rebelled. Kawachiya, a retailer that has cultivated its image as a renegade eager to smash the old price cartels, sells the 633-milliliter bottles for 220 yen, or $2.14. Even in Japan, consumers are making the pressure for lower margins felt.[5]

Return-on-Investment (ROI) Pricing

With **return-on-investment (ROI) pricing,** marketers attempt to set a price that will enable the firm to reach a specified return. Sometimes called *target ROI pricing*, this method requires the firm to forecast a planning volume to determine both cost and profitability levels. This planning volume is the quantity the firm expects to sell over the next year, or is some average of sales expectations over a number of years. Target ROI price is set using the following formula:

$$\text{Price} = AVC + \frac{TFC}{PV} + \frac{r(INV)}{PV}$$

where AVC = average variable cost
TFC = total fixed cost
PV = planning volume
INV = investment
r = target ROI

Let us illustrate how this formula can be used. Assume that for a 35mm film product, *AVC* is $1.50 per unit, the *TFC* is $2 million, total investment is $10 million, target ROI is 25 percent, and planning volume is 20 million units. Then the price should be:

$$\text{Price} = \$1.50 + \frac{\$2,000,000}{20,000,000} + \frac{.25\ (\$10,000,000)}{20,000,000} = \$1.73$$

Basically, this formula says that the set price must cover the average variable cost, the average fixed cost per unit, plus the average desired return on the investment per unit.

Note that if the targeted planning volume (*PV*) is not attained, then *AFC/PV* and *r(INV)/PV* will be larger than before. Thus, to reach the target ROI, the price must be raised. Therefore, one would raise prices when confronted with falling demand, a seemingly counterproductive action. Yet this is precisely what the automobile companies have often done to attempt to meet their target ROIs. Of course, this price increase could further depress demand, inventories could build up, and ROI could actually become negative. Like cost-plus pricing, this method is based on total costs being allocated to products; hence, distortions are not only possible but probable.

PRICING STRATEGIES

A Vermont grocery-store owner once shared his pricing philosophy with a sales rep: "What you charge tells me how low I can go. What my competitor sets prices at is how high I can go. I just pick a place in between, and that's my price."

That Vermont grocer picked an easy way to set prices, but it may not be the best way to optimize profits. Still, his statement reflects the confusion and lack of creativity associated with much that passes for pricing strategy. Many managers just do not think of pricing as a marketing tool to build their businesses. And yet for many companies (particularly start-ups or small, growing businesses) there is no other marketing decision that more immediately affects customers' acceptance or rejection of the company's products.[6]

Pricing difficulties are certainly not confined to small companies. Figure 18.1 shows that many companies across a wide range of industries are struggling with pricing issues and being forced to make changes that may or may not improve the firm's competitive position and profitability. The "Marketing in Action: Creative Marketing—Price Flexibility in the Mortgage Market" shows how one company has taken a positive, creative approach to pricing a mundane product—home mortgages.

As we have seen, determining successful pricing strategies depends on taking into account relevant factors: pricing objectives, how competition will react, levels of customer demand and price sensitivity, costs, and legal constraints. As we look at differential pricing, competitive pricing, and product-line pricing, we will discuss the advantages and disadvantages associated with these strategies. We will also examine the conditions under which each strategy should be considered.[7]

Differential Pricing for Consumers

Because of customer heterogeneity (the differences of search costs, transaction costs, and reservation prices), the same product can often be sold to consumers under more than one price. Transaction costs motivate second-market discounting, demand fluctuations motivate periodic discounting, and search costs motivate random discounting. These conditions result in price discrimination toward consumers. Although obvious price discrimination could lead to negative reactions from consumers, discounting in general enhances a company's sales. It should be noted, however, that a discounted price appears attractive to many consumers simply because it is discounted. If that price were the everyday price, many consumers would find the

Latest Reports from the Price Front (June 1994)

Products	Players	Pricing Situation	Prognosis
Airlines 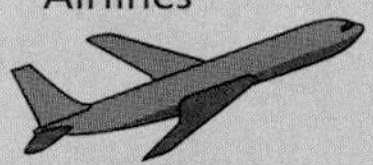	American, Delta, Northwest, USAir	Regular dogfights send prices crashing about every week. Summer fares fell 30% recently.	Lots of bruised bottom lines in industry.
Cigarettes 	Philip Morris, RJR Nabisco	A 40-cents-a-pack price cut on Marlboro last year burned up billions in market value for Philip Morris.	RJR raised prices by 5 cents a pack on Camel, pointing the way out of the pricing desert.
Computer Disk Drives 	Conner Peripherals, Quantum, Seagate	Wars forced prices to retreat some 30% in 1993.	Increasing PC sales to the rescue.
Diapers 	Kimberly-Clark, Procter & Gamble	Five percent to 15% decline on various brands since 1993.	P & G revamps and goes to war.
Frozen Dinners 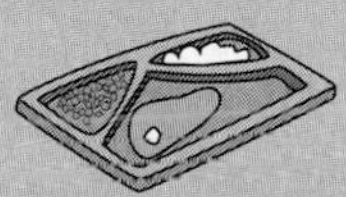	ConAgra, Heinz, Kraft General Foods, Stouffer	Prices dropped 5%; weapons included buy-one, get-one-free offers.	Slim returns for Lean Cuisine and Weight Watchers.
Laparoscopic Surgery Tools 	J&J's Ethicon, U.S. Surgical	Sharp cut in prices, 25% since 1993.	Intense competition from newer player lowers U.S. Surgical market share.
PCs 	Apple, Compaq, Dell, IBM	Prices have been falling about 8% every three months.	Affordability has pushed demand way up in the home market, but profits get chipped.
Soda 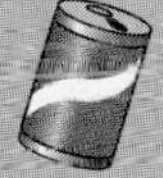	Coca-Cola, Pepsico	Prices dropped an average 2% in 1993.	Market share remains the same.
Software 	Borland, Lotus, Microsoft	In the "suite wars," companies have discounted prices more than 60% by bundling software.	Microsoft is leading, but Lotus is gaining with attractive value.
Vaginal Yeast Infection Treatments 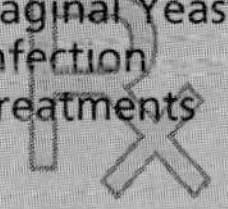	Miles, Ortho/J&J, Schering-Plough	Drug went over the counter. Prices shrank by 20%.	Good news for more than 13 million American women who suffer every year.

Source: A. Serwer, "How to Escape a Price War," *Fortune*, June 13, 1994, p. 85.

FIGURE 18.1
Latest Reports from the Price Front (June 1994)

price uninspiring and would refuse to buy. This will undoubtedly prove to be a major disadvantage for companies that adopt everyday low pricing.[8]

Second-market discounting. Oliver's Drug Store offers a 15 percent discount to senior citizens. The pharmacist believes that this price break makes senior citizens, who are heavy users of prescription drugs, more loyal to Oliver's. The local dry cleaner may offer student discounts. National advertisers pay more for an ad in your local newspaper than do local advertisers.

MARKETING *IN ACTION*

Creative Marketing—Price Flexibility in the Mortgage Market

In the mortgage market, what could matter to consumers besides price? And wouldn't a mortgage company have to offer the lowest rates just to stay in business? Certainly it's no wonder that the mortgage industry is in a state of perpetual price wars, particularly in recent months when rates are heading up and the demand is stalling.

That's why Arbor National Mortgage, a midsize company in Uniondale, New York, is such an interesting case. Arbor expects to have another banner year in 1994 because of its differentiated product. Differentiation in mortgages? How can this be? Nancy Boles, Arbor's senior vice president of marketing, declares, "We never sell products based on price. We focus on niche products, repackaging plain-vanilla mortgages, and relationships with the community."

We're about to find out how to charge average prices in a price-competitive industry, while suffering fewer defaults than competitors. In fact, Arbor maintains a delinquency ratio of 1.8 percent, which is one of the lowest in the industry. Arbor's revenues have jumped more than threefold since 1991, to $60 million. Net income has climbed even more, to $7.7 million in 1993, and Wall Street analysts look for $12 million in 1994. The key to all this is smart marketing.

Arbor will lend to consumers with poor credit ratings. Arbor does extensive appraisal work on potential customers' finances, and as a result suffers fewer losses. The company refuses to price its products like Money Store or Champion, which assume a high default rate. Instead, Arbor looks at the total picture and seems to have a knack for picking good customers.

Arbor takes a standard mortgage and repackages it into the Arbor Home Bridal Registry. Couples register with Arbor instead of a department store so friends and families can contribute to the newlyweds' first home. Boles confesses, "Running the registry is a lot of work, so we aren't as concerned with getting couples to register as we are in getting inquiries about purchasing a first home. Only three dozen couples have actually registered, but we've had over 5,000 couples call to ask about the service. Their names are now in our data base. We hope to have them as customers someday."

Arbor also holds mortgage seminars for real estate brokers, accountants, and consumers. And the company plants a tree for customers who want one, either in their yard or in a public forest. Successful marketing? Yes, but with a careful positioning strategy in mind.

With all the emphasis on low-price strategies coupled with cost-cutting, there are still companies that succeed with average-price strategies, even some that are successful with premium pricing. The key is to know your markets, customer demand and price sensitivity, and special needs that you can meet to provide added value for the price.

As illustrated by these examples, **second-market discounting** means (1) a differential price (2) offered to secondary market segments (3) to increase usage or build repeat purchase among those that might otherwise take their business elsewhere or simply not buy at all. Firms that use a second-market strategy have excess production capacity or inventory that means low costs associated with producing additional units of the product. This is the case with pharmaceutical companies that produce generic versions of branded drugs or producers of consumer packaged goods who make generic or private-label brands in addition to their national brands.

Excess capacity is also observed in international marketing where a firm's selling price or even current average costs may be higher in the home market than the selling price in the foreign market. At the extremes, "dumping" describes a firm's selling at a price in the foreign market that is below its average costs. Some allege that Japan used a dumping strategy in this country to drive U.S. television manufacturers out of business, then raised the price for television sets. The fact that only one U.S. company now manufactures televisions coupled with evidence that Japanese companies financed their losses in the United States by selling at inflated prices in Japan lends credence to this accusation.

Periodic discounting. Periodic discounting means that a firm initially prices high and then systematically reduces the price over some specified time period. One variation is **price skimming,** presumably named in honor of the phrase "skim the cream off the top"—in this case, the top of the market. By pricing high when a new product is introduced, a firm can expect to sell to all those who are less price sensitive than their neighbors and who want to be the first to try the item. (In behavioral terms, we often term these individuals *innovators* and *early adopters.*) Advantages to the marketer are faster recovery of development costs, improved cash flow, and higher profit margins during the introductory stage of the product life cycle when sales volume is low. However, price skimming is an open invitation to competitors to enter the market with a lower-priced substitute, thus appealing to the large number of price-sensitive consumers who are as yet uncommitted. As the product ages, more competitive products appear and prices tend to drop, as, for example, with personal computers.

Price skimming as a strategy works best when the new product represents a major breakthrough in terms of the functions it performs and/or it represents status to consumers. If there are significant barriers to entry into the market, competitors may be temporarily stalled. Barriers to entry include a large capital investment or technical knowledge that is not readily available, perhaps protected by a patent.

Peak-load pricing involves temporal markdowns, such as off-season merchandise, older models, and perishable items whose expiration dates are approaching. For example, Atkins's Homemade Buffet Restaurant runs a two-for-one pricing special every Monday evening. Mondays are Atkins's slow days, and the manager believes that this off-peak discounting improves revenues and profits for the Monday evening meal.

Homer's Six-Screen Theatre offers $3.00 tickets for showtimes before 6:00 P.M. every day. Homer's manager is using off-peak discounting to attract price-sensitive moviegoers who would refuse to pay the full $6.50 for evening showings.

A key to understanding periodic discounting is to note that these discounts are systematic and predictable. Consumers learn to know about them and take advantage of them. Consumers with a low reservation price are more likely to take advantage of the discounts; others are willing to pay full price. Firms should minimize the likelihood of discounting to segments that would pay full price.

Random discounts. Random discounts include coupons, cents-off offers, and other types of variable price merchandising.[9] These discounts may enable a company to solicit new business or increase cash flow in the short term. These price breaks should not be predictable, even to consumers who are "searchers." Marketers want to avoid encouraging regular, full-price customers to postpone their purchases until the item goes on sale.

At the retail level, supermarkets often offer discounts such as three cans of vegetables for $1.00 or a single can for $.37. Those buying appliances can easily bargain for a discount if more than one item is being purchased.

DIFFERENTIAL PRICING TO CHANNEL MEMBERS

In sales made between firms, it is common practice to quote a *list* or *base price* for a product and then quote discounts, or lower prices, that are available. These discounts occur in three circumstances:

1. sales made in different quantities, or at different times
2. sales made to different intermediaries performing different functions
3. sales made with different credit and collection terms

Coupons are an example of a random discount. These discounts may enable a company to solicit new business or increase cash flow in the short term.

Quantity and timing discounts.   As an incentive for their customers to purchase larger quantities of an item, marketers at all levels in the channel often offer quantity discounts. For example, one firm offered the following discount schedule to its customers on automatic temperature controls:

Annual Volume	Net Price
50–349	$17.35
350–999	16.45
1,000+	15.90

Quantity discounts may be either *cumulative* or *noncumulative*. **Cumulative quantity discounts** are based upon the total amount of a product purchased within a specified time, usually one year. The discount schedule for the temperature controls was cumulative. This type of discount is an incentive to the buyer to stick with one supplier, since the reduced price applies to the quantity purchased in the entire period. When a buyer's volume level qualifies him or her for a lower price, the seller makes an adjustment to account for items purchased earlier at a higher price.

Noncumulative quantity discounts relate to the size of an individual purchase. They encourage large purchase orders, but unlike cumulative quantity discounts, they do not tie the buyer as tightly to the seller over the long run. Quantity discounts sometimes give "free" amounts of the product being purchased instead of reducing the cash price. Thus, a retailer might get one free carton of Tang for every 24 cartons purchased.

Quantity discounts help producers gain economies of scale in production, marketing, and order handling. That is, since the fixed costs of getting and filling an order are the same whether the order is large or small, an order for a large number of units means lower order costs per unit. Also, fewer orders are obtained and processed during the period, giving additional cost savings. For noncumulative discounts, the buyer, of course, must compare the discount savings against the additional costs to carry more inventory associated with the larger orders.

Marketers may also give discounts based on the timing of a purchase order. Automobile rebates always have a specified cut-off date, as do most special retail sales (for example, Midnight Madness Sale, from midnight to 6:00 A.M.). **Seasonal discounts** are timed to get buyers to stock up on an item ahead of its selling season. Snow blowers, air conditioners, lawn mowers, coal, fuel oil, and toys are all sold in this fashion. This aids manufacturers in planning production and decreases their inventory carrying costs.

Functional discounts. **Functional discounts** or trade discounts are reductions off the list price given to resellers on the basis of the level they hold in the channel and the marketing activities or functions they are expected to perform. It is quite common to quote price in the following form:

List price: $300 less 30/10/5

The $300 is the manufacturer's suggested retail price. The 30 is the percentage of the suggested retail price available to the retailer to cover costs and provide a profit ($300 × .30 = $90). The first number given always refers to the retail end of the channel. The next number refers to the wholesalers closest to the retailer in the channel. These wholesalers get 10 percent of their selling price ($300 − $90 = $210). Thus, they get $21 per unit sold ($210 × .10). The next group of wholesalers (probably jobbers) in the channel who are closest to the manufacturer get 5 percent of their selling price of $189 ($210 − $21) or $9.45 ($189 × .05). Trade discounts are subtracted one at a time, starting with the manufacturer's suggested retail price and making sure that the relevant discount is applied to each level of the channel's selling price. We can then determine the manufacturer's selling price to the wholesaler closest in the channel. In our example, this price is $179.55 ($189 − $9.45). Table 18.2 presents the example more clearly.

This chain of discounts delivers what the manufacturer proposes the margin should be at the various levels in the channel. The channel members may vary from this schedule if they wish. Retailers or wholesalers may increase the discount from the producer's list price, while others may decrease it. Quite often trade discounts are determined by custom for a given product. Thus, these types of discounts tend to be very similar across brands.

Credit and collection discounts. **Credit and collection discounts** are additional deductions from list prices given if a buyer pays a bill for goods and services within a specified time frame. For example, a bill may be quoted as $800, 2/10, net 30. This means that the bill for the product is $800, but the buyer can take a 2 percent discount and pay $784 if payment is within ten days. Otherwise, the total $800 is due within 30 days. It is usually in the buyer's best interest to take this cash discount.

Terms	List price $300 less 30/10/15	
	Manufacturer's suggested retail price (MSRP)	$300.00
Less	Retail margin, 30 percent of MSRP	90.00
Yields	Retail cost price or wholesaler's selling price (WSP)	$210.00
Less	Wholesale margin, 10 percent of WSP	21.00
Yields	Wholesale cost price or jobber seller price (JSP)	$189.00
Less	Jobber margin, 5 percent of JSP	9.45
Yields	Jobber cost price or manufacturer's selling price	$179.55

TABLE 18.2
The Chain of Functional Discounts

If a buyer does not take advantage of it, he or she is paying a very high interest rate for the use of money. For example, 2/10, net 30, means the buyer would pay 2 percent interest to gain use of this money for 20 days. In a 360-day year, this translates to an effective annual interest rate of 36 percent ($2\% \times 360/20 = 36\%$). Because the effective rate is so high, a firm is usually wise to borrow money at bank rates to take advantage of cash discounts. **Cash discounts** involve both the financial management and marketing areas of a company, and these two divisions should make joint decisions about them.

Multiple discounts: An example.   To see how all these different types of discounts are related, let us consider the following situation: The Stepup Ladder Company sells five types of ladders priced at $30, $50, $90, $120, and $150. The channel for those ladders is through a jobber to a merchant wholesaler to department and hardware stores. Functional or trade discounts are 40/10/5. Additionally, Stepup gives a cash discount of 3/10, net 30 and gives a quantity discount of 5 percent for orders of $1,000 or more at list price. An order is placed by the Hardware Distributing Company. Table 18.3 shows how the discounts apply. Note that the quantity discount comes off first, as is customary, then the trade discounts, and finally the cash discount. If all the discounts are taken, an order that lists at $2,700 retail yields $1,276.36 to the manufacturer.

Allowances.   In addition to all the discounts already noted, the buyer may be able to obtain certain **allowances** from the seller. We are all familiar with trade-in allowances offered to consumers. These are quite common in purchases of cars, appliances, and even textbooks. A seller can change a true price substantially without altering list price by changing the value given on the trade-in item. It is also possible for a buyer to qualify for promotional allowances. These types of allowances are given as a discount in selling price, as "free" goods, or as a cash payment. In return, the wholesaler or retailer undertakes certain promotional activities for the seller.

TABLE 18.3
An Example of Multiple Discounts

The Hardware Distributing Company order	10 ladders @ $30	$ 300.00
	6 ladders @ $50	300.00
	10 ladders @ $90	900.00
	5 ladders @ $120	600.00
	4 ladders @ $150	600.00
	Total	$2700.00
Applying the quantity discounts	Total order amount	$2700.00
	Discounts, $2700 × 0.05	135.00
	Net order amount	$2565.00
Applying the trade discounts	Net order amount	$2565.00
	Less 40% discount	1026.00
		$1539.00
	Less 10% discount	153.90
		$1385.10
	Less 5% discount	69.26
	Amount due manufacturer	$1315.84
Applying the cash discount	Amount due manufacturer	$1315.84
	Less 3% discount	39.48
	Net remittance	$1276.36

Source: K. B. Monroe, *Pricing: Making Profitable Decisions* (McGraw-Hill, 1979), p. 171.

Competitive pricing focuses on a group of pricing strategies based on a company's competitive positioning in the market.

Competitive Pricing

The "Spotlight on Technology: Competitive Pricing in a High-Tech Industry" illustrates that competitors' pricing strategies can have a tremendous impact on the success of a company's products. In about two years, Compaq went from being an industry standard to a company that was losing money, and with the same pricing strategy. Now Compaq is recovering, largely due to its new competitive pricing strategy.

Competitive pricing focuses on a group of pricing strategies based on a company's competitive positioning in the market. In fact, it is virtually impossible to have market share objectives without an appropriate pricing strategy. [10] Penetration pricing and experience curve pricing allow marketers to take advantage of economies of scale or experience to price lower than competitors. Using economies of scale means that as larger volumes are produced during each period, the average total cost per unit declines. These savings result from superior technology, a more efficient organization, or quantity discounting when purchasing from suppliers. [11] (Of course, if the scale of the operation continues to grow, at some point average costs will again rise due to the investment in new plant capacity, warehouse space, and/or an expanded labor force.)

Experience curve or experience economies result from the decline in average total costs that occurs from cumulative production volume during the life of the product. Cost declines that accumulate through experience can be attributed to such factors as labor efficiency and newer process technology. [12]

A third strategy is price signaling, which communicates product quality to consumers who have little knowledge about the product. Fourth is geographic pricing and the differences in pricing for customers in different locations. Fifth is competitive bidding, and, finally, price leadership.

Penetration pricing. **Penetration pricing** involves introducing a product at a price below competition in order to establish market share. It is based on two logical principles. First, setting low prices may discourage competitors from entering the market. If prices are low and profit margins are small, the opportunities are not so interesting for competitors. Second, when consumers' reservation prices are low and product prices are well known, new products that carry low prices sell best. Thus, the company with a penetration price wins a large following of customers and enjoys high sales volume with the accompanying profits.

For these reasons, penetration pricing is often used with new products, and has also been used successfully by discount stores. It can be used by manufacturers whose products are in the mature stage of the product life cycle and who want to "shake out" weak competitors.

MARKETING IN ACTION

SPOTLIGHT ON Technology

Competitive Pricing in a High-Tech Industry

"We threw our old pricing policy overboard. We are now pricing to market," says Eckhard Pfeiffer, CEO at Compaq Computer Corporation, based in Houston, Texas. Once the victim of price wars, Compaq is now the aggressor. But the moves that Compaq has made since Pfeiffer became the CEO on October 24, 1991 have astonished the computer industry.

Earlier in 1991 Compaq was jolted back to reality when its first-ever quarterly loss was reported, the result of a 17 percent revenue slide and a belated cost-cutting campaign to match such upstarts as Dell Computer Corporation and AST Research, Incorporated. The success of other computer companies belied the notion circulating among some top executives at Compaq that the company's drop in sales was due to the recession. Clearly, customers were still buying computers, but from someone else.

Compaq was founded in 1982 by a group of engineers from Texas Instruments, and the company had sustained a meteoric rise as the most competent designer and builder of IBM clones in the industry. But this very success had made it difficult for Compaq to read the handwriting on the wall. The company couldn't acknowledge that its PCs had become overengineered, overpriced, and an easy mark for cheaper clones from Dell, AST, Gateway 2000, and others. Selling top-of-the-line PCs at premium prices to *Fortune* 500 companies—a magical formula in the 1980s—was out of gas. Compaq, therefore, was unprepared for price wars, the rise of mail-order and retail PC sales, and the growth of sales to small businesses and consumers.

But in 1991 Pfeiffer instituted a new law for Compaq employees, and it's paying off. Slash

bloated costs; forget gold-plated technology, except where it really makes a difference; and, most important, redirect Compaq's vaunted engineering to building high-quality computers at low prices. So they did.

With 41 new products announced in June 1992, Compaq's unit shipments leaped at a 40% annual clip, rebuilding market share, which had slipped from 5.3% to 4.5% in 1991. In the third quarter of 1992, revenues climbed 50% to a record $1.07 billion, and earnings hit $49.4 million. By 1994, Compaq was reporting second-quarter earnings of more than $185 million on sales of more than $2.4 billion, a huge 81% jump in profits and a 50% rise in sales from the same period in 1993.

Compaq's turnaround product was its ProLinea, unveiled in June of 1992. The ProLinea was the company's first low-price computer, with its entry-level machine a low $899 and priced below Dell's cheapest. Engineers took costs out by, for example, designing custom circuits to reduce the number of chips needed in each ProLinea. Fewer chips means less chance of faulty connections. And computer magazines gave the machines rave reviews. It wasn't long before Compaq was building 200,000 ProLineas a month and was still backlogged. During the fall of 1993, Compaq introduced its Presario home computer with similar success.

And the success formula is simple: quality products with standard industry features, fast product development, broad distribution, heavy brand-building advertising, and—most of all—low prices made feasible by intense cost cutting.

Penetration pricing works best for firms that have low average costs and whose markets contain large segments of price-sensitive consumers. Penetration pricing is often viewed as a defensive strategy against competitors but it can also work well as an offensive strategy for low-cost producers. Penetration pricing is the strategy Compaq used when it introduced its ProLinea line of computers.

Experience curve pricing. **Experience curve pricing** is similar to penetration pricing in that the basis for the low-price strategy is average total costs that are lower than competitors' costs. However, economies of scale contribute to lower costs in the penetration pricing scenario, while experience economies contribute to experience curve pricing. Although the outcomes are similar, the mechanisms for arriving at the final prices are different.

Average total cost (in constant dollars) of a product declines as the firm produces and markets more of it. This occurs because labor becomes more skilled, automated equipment can be used, and purchasing and marketing costs can be lowered on average because the firm is able to obtain discounts at higher volume. An *experience curve* is a representation of the relationship between average total cost and cumulative experience in producing and marketing a product.

With experience-curve pricing, the firm has more experience than its competitors and consumers are price sensitive. These conditions occur most often for non-essential durable goods in the introductory or growth stages of the product life cycle. As the industry matures, experience-curve pricing tends to cause weak competitors to drop out of the market. But some very astute marketers have also made experience pay in more mature industries.

The 104-year-old Emerson Electric Company, based in St. Louis, Missouri, makes refrigerator compressors, pressure gauges, and In-Sink-Erator garbage disposals. These are basic products, essential to industry, but few command premium prices based on proprietary technologies. Yet Emerson has engaged in a low-price strategy, operating without significant price increases since the mid-1980s. Emerson's chairman and chief executive, Charles (Chuck) Knight, has used his experience in the industry to keep costs low. A decade ago, for example, a Japanese plant in Malaysia could offer temperature sensors for washing machines for 20 percent below Emerson's prices. Today Emerson's costs are below the Japanese, and it has regained market share.

How was Knight able to make such strides? He located lower-priced suppliers for parts and materials. He shut down more than 30 high-cost plants, shifting product to low-cost regions in the United States or out of the country. Emerson divested itself of low-profit subsidiaries, such as defense and construction businesses and the Weed Eater gardening tools division. Now that Emerson has learned through experience to control its costs, the company is poised to concentrate on growth strategies.[13]

Price signaling. **Price signaling** represents a conscious effort by manufacturers to use price as an indicator of quality.[14] Research provides evidence that, at times, consumers do use price to infer quality.[15] Three conditions must be present for price signaling to be useful to marketers. First, consumers must find information about price more readily available than information about quality. Second, they must want high quality enough to risk buying at a higher price to get it, even though there is a risk that the high price does not necessarily ensure higher quality. Third, there must be enough consumers who do understand how to evaluate quality objectively, and these consumers establish behaviorally a positive correlation between price and quality. That is, they can tell if a product's quality warrants a higher price, and they find it worthwhile to pay that price.[16]

One version of price signaling is reference pricing. In this case, a marketer places a high-priced version of a product next to a much higher-priced version of the same product, so that the former may seem more attractive to risk-aversive, uninformed buyers.[17] The function of the latter version is to serve as a *reference price* to consumers, although some may actually purchase the product.

A reference price is one that the consumer uses to compare with the actual price of the product. A reference price may be the manufacturer's suggested retail price, the price at which the product is offered at another store, or the regular price of a sale item. Certainly the use of reference prices by consumers is documented.[18] It can also be shown that the influence of reference prices is mitigated by consumers' prior beliefs about price and the context in which the reference price appears. For example, consumers appear to be more influenced by reference prices in discount stores than in other stores.[19]

A higher price does not always reflect superior product quality.[20] For example, a study correlating quality ratings by *Consumer Reports* with brand prices found significant variation in the relationship between price and objective product quality.[21] Thus, some companies that sell low-quality products at high prices, relying on price signaling to mislead consumers, may do so with some success.

Although some companies use price signaling successfully, others attempt to use it but fail. Two manufacturers introduced skin moisturizers at prices well above industry averages: Estée Lauder's Future Perfect at $25.70 in the spring of 1988, and Ultima II's Megadose at $24.20 in the spring of 1989. (A sample of competitors' products ranged from $1.70 to $8.13.) Megadose experienced disappointing sales results; by contrast, Future Perfect performed well. Subsequent research provides compelling evidence that price signaling is successful only when multiple cues (other than merely price) consistently signal quality. In this case, these cues include: upscale packaging, advertising message appeal, exclusive distribution, and strong brand-name appeal. The conclusion is that price signaling where high price is the sole quality signal is a strategy of limited potential. An integrated promotion and distribution program is necessary to support price signaling.[22]

Geographic pricing.   Another major strategy that affects the way prices are quoted is the cost of transportation of goods from seller to buyer. Recall from Chapter 12 that this cost runs into billions of dollars annually. There are two general **geographic pricing** procedures for quoting prices related to transportation costs: F.O.B origin pricing and delivered pricing methods.

F.O.B. origin. F.O.B. means free on board, and **F.O.B. origin** means prices are quoted F.O.B. to some specific point. For example, F.O.B. Omaha means that the buyer becomes responsible for the transportation costs, plus picking the specific mode of transportation, designating a carrier, and handling all damage claims, once the seller delivers the goods to Omaha. Typically, the seller quotes a location at or near the seller's factory. The major advantage of such a system is that the seller obtains the same net amount from each sale of like quantity for a given channel level, since the buyer pays the freight from the F.O.B. location.

The big disadvantage is that this system effectively raises the price of goods more and more the farther away the buyer is from the seller. Sales can suffer, especially when demand is responsive to price differences and little product differentiation exists among competitors. If all sellers in a product class used an F.O.B. plant system, then sellers would have price advantages in their local areas. The net result could be regional monopolies.

Delivered pricing. In a **delivered pricing** structure, the price quoted by the seller includes transportation costs. The price is quoted as F.O.B buyer's location, and the seller maintains responsibility over all aspects of transportation of the goods. Under this general framework, four different delivered pricing methods are possible.

1. **Single-zone pricing**—Under a single-zone pricing method, each buyer pays the same delivered price for goods regardless of proximity to the seller. This system is also called *uniform delivered pricing* or *postage stamp pricing*, because this is in essence how American postage rates are established. A first-class letter from Detroit to Houston costs the same to mail as it would from Detroit to Chicago. Under such a system, those customers at greater-than-average distance from the shipper have their transportation costs subsidized by those who are closer than average to the seller. All buyers effectively pay the average transportation costs. The net return to the seller, then, varies depending on where the goods are being shipped. Pizza stores offering "free" delivery are really requiring all customers to pay an average delivery charge for their pizzas.

2. **Multiple-zone pricing**—Under a multiple-zone pricing method (sometimes called *zone-delivered pricing*), sellers divide their selling territory into two or more geographic areas called zones. Within any one zone, the delivered price to buyers is uniform, but prices across zones are different. For example, a long-distance call from San Francisco to Seattle costs less than one from San Francisco to Memphis. Similarly, metropolitan transportation systems often divide cities into zones, charging a specific amount for each zone traveled. Or, a manufacturer may quote different prices for New England, the Midwest, or other regions. The price quote for a zone reflects the average transportation costs within a zone and the competition and level of demand within the zone. A zone system makes it easier to sell in markets that are farther from the shipper.

3. **F.O.B. with freight allowed**—Under the system, called *freight absorption pricing*, prices are quoted as F.O.B. plant-freight allowed. The seller absorbs the transportation costs; the buyer is allowed to deduct freight expenses from the list price of the goods. This system is used by sellers trying to expand their geographical market coverage. A twist on this is to allow freight absorption equal to the freight costs of the competitive seller closest to the prospective buyer. This approach can severely cut into profit margins if freight costs are large relative to product selling price.

4. **Basing-point pricing**—The basing-point pricing system is also designed to expand a seller's geographical market area by giving distant buyers prices similar to nearby buyers. The seller may select either a single basing point or use multiple basing points.

With a *single basing point pricing system*, the price set by the seller is the list price for the product plus the freight charges from the selected basing point to the purchaser. The place where the goods are actually produced is not usually the basing point. Thus, the amount the seller charges the customer for freight is often quite different from the actual freight costs. Consider the example of a company with three mills (see Figure 18.2). The basing point used by the company is the location of Plant A. Thus, the price to the customer from all three mills is $500 base price plus the $50 of actual freight from Plant A to Customer X ($550). Under this scheme, Plant B must absorb $30 of freight charges because it actually costs $80 to ship to Customer X from Plant B. On the other hand, Plant C can collect $30 for freight beyond the actual $20 that it costs to ship to Customer X. This nonexistent freight is called *phantom freight*.

The most famous basing-point pricing system was the "Pittsburgh-plus" pricing system used in the steel industry for a long time. Although steel producers did have many mills around the country, prices were quoted containing freight charges from Pittsburgh. Thus, a steel buyer in St. Louis would pay freight charges from Pittsburgh even though the steel involved may have been produced and shipped from a mill in Gary, Indiana. After a time, buyers' objections to paying phantom freight led to the use of multiple basing-point systems.

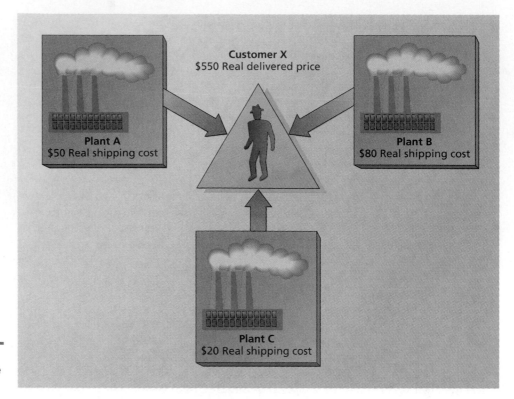

FIGURE 18.2
An Illustration of Single Base-Point Pricing

Under a *multiple basing-point system*, more than one geographic location is designated as a basing point. The price quoted to a customer is the base price plus the freight charges from the closest basing point to this customer. If the seller ships the goods from a plant farther away from the buyer than the closest basing point, then the seller absorbs the differential in actual freight charges. For example, assume that both Pittsburgh and Gary are basing points for steel. The buyer in St. Louis would pay the freight cost from Gary. If the seller shipped to St. Louis from Pittsburgh, the seller would pay the freight costs over and above the charges from Gary to St. Louis.

Competitive bidding.   In **competitive bidding** buyers or sellers can initiate the process. An auction is an example of a seller initiating competitive bidding. Auctions are often used in markets for livestock and commodity products. They are also used for antiques and one-of-a-kind items such as art and jewels. Sotheby's and Christie's are famous auction houses for art, antiques, and collectibles.

In December 1993, fashion arbiter Hubert de Givenchy put up several rooms of 17th- and 18th-century French furniture from his Paris mansion for auction. Christie's gave this offering the royal treatment, with exhibits in New York and Paris. The actual sale took place at a gala evening held at the Metropole Palace Hotel in Monte Carlo. A smashing success, the auction amassed $26 million in revenues. Some of Givenchy's pieces made records. A massive Louis XIV desk made in the early 1700s by André-Charles Boulle brought only $4,700 when last auctioned in 1953; in Monte Carlo, the desk sold for $3.2 million. A Louis XV tulipwood marquetry cabinet made in 1758 fetched a mere $604,000 in 1985, but the price ballooned to $1.8 million at the Christie's auction.[23]

Military purchases and government contracts are likely to be decided by a sealed bidding process. Buyers request bids, including the specifications of the products desired. Sellers are invited to submit competitive bids, with the result that typically the contract goes to the lowest bidder. There may be exceptions to this rule if a

CHAPTER 18 ███ PRICING PROCEDURES

An auction is an example of a seller initiating competitive bidding. Auctions are often used in markets for livestock, for commodity products, and for antiques and one-of-a-kind items such as art and jewelry.

particular seller offers special services or unique product benefits. When bidding for a job or an order, sellers must consider their costs and the competition's probable costs and bids. It is important, however, for companies to only submit bids that they can live with if they are awarded the contract. Winning low bids when costs are not covered or profit margins are unacceptable does not bode well for a company's long-term survival.

A year after founding the Delahaye Group, a $1 million public relations company located in Hampton, Falls, New Hampshire, Katharine Paine was in the black. But when she analyzed her company's profitability, she discovered one-half of her projects were misquoted, barely breaking even. Now Paine uses the following guidelines to price profitably:

- *Determine how much is being spent.* Factor in all employee time using detailed time sheets as well as costs for materials, equipment, utilities, etc.
- *Determine what future costs will be.* Quotes for the future must include employee raises, increased rent or utility bills, and new equipment and supplies.
- *Fix a realistic billing rate and stick to it.* Paine's pricing consultant advised her to look at industry statistics for sales, direct labor costs, and profit margins. She now uses a markup factor derived from these variables.[24]

Price leadership. In some oligopolistic industries the job of assessing competitors' prices has been made easier because of **price leadership** in the industry where a price leader takes the first step at raising and lowering prices in an industry. Others then generally follow. U.S. Steel plays this role in the steel industry, as does General Motors in the automobile industry. The price leader is usually the largest competitor in the industry, although it is not uncommon for the second or third largest firm to play some role in price leadership. Sometimes the leader is not the first firm to make a price change, but the leader's response to another price change will set the market price. For example, Chrysler often announces price increases first, but then adjusts its prices based upon what General Motors does in response.

It is quite common for competitors to signal (this is *not* the type of price signaling strategy discussed earlier) one another by announcing price changes effective at some specified time in the future. Deliberate collusion or price fixing is illegal, as we saw in Chapter 17. However, the fact that the competitors have the same price and change price together is not illegal per se. Under the Supreme Court doctrine of conscious parallelism, the FTC or Justice Department must also prove the existence of a conspiracy to make equal prices and/or price moves.

In setting prices, the price leader must consider the demand and cost situation of all competitors, not just its own. For example, a price level that would prevent some competitors from making a profit may cause these competitors to cut prices in an effort to gain needed volume. A price war might follow. The temptation to conspire to fix prices or divide the market increases in these circumstances. This would be illegal under Section I of the Sherman Act.

Product-Line Pricing

So far we have concentrated mostly on pricing individual products or services, but many firms market a complete product line or a number of interrelated product lines. For example, Kodak not only markets many different still cameras, but also film, projectors, movie cameras, screens, and other related items. These products are likely to have demand considerations, competitive characteristics, and cost interrelationships. In **product line pricing**, the marketer must (1) determine the lowest-priced product and its price, (2) determine the highest-priced product and its price, and (3) determine the price differentials for all other products in the line.

The role of each item in the product line must be understood. For example, the lowest-priced item may serve as a *price leader*, a low-priced version designed to get prospective purchasers to trade up to other items in the line. At the other end, the highest-priced item may serve to add prestige to the line. In both instances, the price of the item may bear little relationship to its cost. When pricing, the marketer seeks to cover the total cost of the full line, not necessarily of each specific item. Automobile companies have historically used prices that gave them much higher margins on larger cars, particularly on the most expensive models of the larger cars.

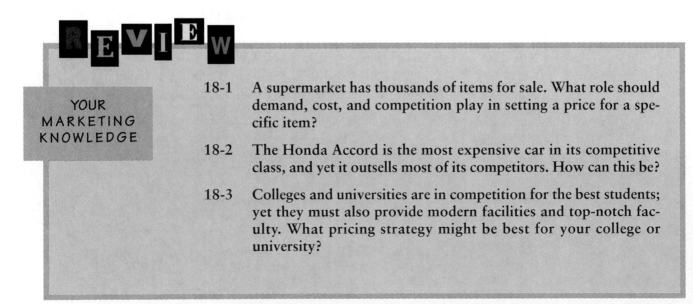

REVIEW

YOUR MARKETING KNOWLEDGE

18-1   A supermarket has thousands of items for sale. What role should demand, cost, and competition play in setting a price for a specific item?

18-2   The Honda Accord is the most expensive car in its competitive class, and yet it outsells most of its competitors. How can this be?

18-3   Colleges and universities are in competition for the best students; yet they must also provide modern facilities and top-notch faculty. What pricing strategy might be best for your college or university?

For the leader items in a product line, average variable cost is likely to be the floor below which prices will not be set. At prices above this level, the item makes a positive contribution to the fixed costs of the whole product line.

Both the lowest- and highest-priced item in a product line are critical for establishing the buyers' perceptions of the total line. With too low a price at the bottom, the whole line may be considered cheap; with too high a price at the top, buyers may perceive the line as above the mass market. Would you really take seriously a Porsche priced at $5,000? This price would cheapen the whole line's image. Additionally, price differentials between items in a line should be associated with perceptual differences in the value of the products offered. The price differences must make sense to customers. There is some behavioral evidence to suggest that the price differentials should get larger as one moves up the product line.

Price bundling.   **Price bundling** refers to marketing two or more products as a unit, with a single price for the entire package. For example, travel packages may include airfare, hotel, transfers, and some meals. Consumers often find that such deals lower their search and transactions costs, thus offering extra value as a total product. Sellers may be induced to use price bundling as a way of reducing their costs also— everyone benefits. And retailers can use bundling of interdependent products to maximize profitability.[25]

Price bundling refers to marketing two or more products as a unit, with a single price for the entire package. Consumers often find that such "deals" lower their search and transactions costs, thus offering extra value as a total product.

There are two types of price bundling: mixed bundling and pure bundling. In mixed bundling, only the package is available; with pure bundling, the price of one product is reduced only if the second product is purchased. Pure bundling may be illegal if it amounts to a tying contract because it requires the purchaser of one product to agree as a condition of purchase to buy another product. However, this does not apply to consumer purchases.[26]

Microsoft has recently bundled several of its popular business software programs, including Word, Excel, and Power Point, into a single package called "Microsoft Office." These software bundles are called "suites," and they offer a set of programs for a fraction of what they used to sell for separately. For example, Microsoft's Word word-processing program used to sell for as much as $495; now the "Office" can be purchased at some discount retailers for as little as $269, a significant savings for customers.

Bundling works best with nonsubstitute, perishable products and consumers who have varying demand structures for the products included in the bundle. The usefulness of such techniques with food items, concert seats, or hotel rooms is demonstrated by the fact that if these products are not sold on time, they essentially vanish.

Premium pricing.   **Premium pricing** is used in a variety of circumstances. The basic idea is that the consumers have heterogeneity of demand; thus, a firm can sell more than one version of a product at different price points. Relative to costs, the higher-priced version offers larger margins, while the lower-priced version may break even or sometimes may even lose money if volume is sufficient on the high-priced version to compensate for the loss. However, the additional features and attributes of the higher-priced model do not carry sufficient costs to objectively justify the higher price.

Premium pricing may be used with durable goods, perishable products, and even services. Retailers often use premium pricing to enable them to carry some otherwise unprofitable products that appeal to select market segments. Automobiles are a good example, because dealers may make very little or no profit on their low-priced models, while the higher-priced models are much more profitable.

Image pricing.   **Image pricing** is a composite of price signaling and premium pricing. In this case, a firm brings out a virtually identical version of its current product with a different name or model number and a higher price. The higher price is intended to signal quality; the cost aspects reflect premium pricing, except that differences between brands are not real, only illusory. Image pricing differs from price signaling in that a given firm has several products and varies its prices over the range of those products.

Early in 1994, Michelin, the world's largest tire company, launched a new tire called the Michelin Classic. The Classic was no different from its standard tire but was 15 percent cheaper. Retailers and distributors, accustomed to selling Michelins at premium prices, did not know what to make of the move. It is already cannibalizing sales of higher-priced Michelin lines. In this case, Michelin apparently felt that the higher-priced model, coupled with the Michelin quality mystique, would be enough to differentiate the tires in consumers' minds. This ineffective image pricing strategy appears to be on the road to becoming a disaster for the company.[27]

Complementary pricing.   The three related aspects of **complementary pricing** are captive pricing, two-part pricing, and loss-leader pricing. With **captive pricing,** the firm sells a basic product and the supplies that go with the product. Generally, the basic product is priced low, with the belief that consumers will continue to purchase the supplies throughout the life of the product and the price of the supplies would more than compensate for any losses incurred in the sale of the basic product. Obvious examples include razors and blades, cameras and film, automobile parts and servicing.

There are some drawbacks to captive pricing. First, a company must estimate its costs carefully, including the discounted value of future earnings and the possibility that some consumers will not continue to use the supplies. For some products, captive pricing is not practical, since shared economies in the production of the basic product and its supplies do not exist. If the profit margins are high on the basic product's complementary supplies, lower-cost competitors may enter the market and drive down prices.

Two-part pricing is basically captive pricing as it relates to the service industry. The service price includes a fixed fee plus variable costs according to subsequent usage. For example, a cellular telephone company may charge a fixed monthly fee of $21, plus $.25 per minute on all use that exceeds 30 minutes per month. A health club may charge monthly dues of $30 but place a $25 price on a massage.

In retailing, the corresponding strategy is called loss leadership. **Loss leaders** are items that are sold near or sometimes even below cost in order to generate increased store traffic. The rationale is that once customers are in the store, they will be induced to purchase additional products at the regular markup.

Price lining. In **price lining,** the marketer places items in a product line at specific pricing points to cover the whole range. One twist in this approach occurs when marketers identify a pricing point that consumers will respond to, but no items exist at that position. Research and production people are then asked to develop and produce an item that will sell at that retail price. Essentially, marketers subtract all relevant channel margins for the target retail price to determine the price they must charge. Then they subtract their expected profit per item to establish the cost at which the product must be produced. This type of pricing is sometimes called *market-minus pricing* or *demand-backwards pricing*. It is common for many retail products, especially when customary pricing or price lining is used. In addition, the gift market is one where customers seem to have upper limits on spending. So products are developed for the $10 gift or the $25 gift.

Integrative Pricing

Managers must take a sophisticated approach to pricing. They must exploit premium potentials, fine-tune price to the product's perceived value and competitive situation, and use price differentiation, price bundling, or discounting to make shrewd timing decisions. The following extract illustrates the complexity of selecting the best pricing strategy for even a single product:

> A leading agrochemical company planned to sell a new insecticide called Netex to different segments in different countries. The Netex pricing process had started, as usual, with the accountants' cost estimates. However, the various functional areas within the firm were divided on what the cost should be.
>
> The accounting and finance people, who traditionally had a strong influence on price decisions, thought and argued in cost-plus and unit-margin terms. Their remoteness from the customer made them uncomfortable with the "soft" information marketing provided. The product manager favored a penetration price. The sales manager concurred with some reservations; he saw price mainly as an obstacle to concluding deals. Top management tended toward slight premiums, though smaller ones than the accountants wanted.
>
> This case was especially complex because the product had several applications with different requirements, customer characteristics, and competitive structures. So each group could cite evidence in its favor.

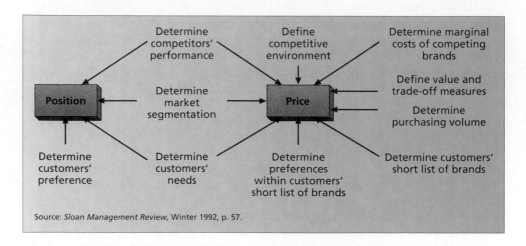

FIGURE 18.3
Framework for Consistent Pricing and Positioning

Discussion yielded a number of questions: How important are price and product attributes to farmers and dealers in the various segments? How does Netex's performance compare with that of competitors on these attributes? What are the values, in price terms, that Netex and competitive products deliver? How do farmers and dealers differ in purchasing volume, importance of attributes, perceptions, short lists of approved suppliers, preferences, price sensitivities, and so forth? What is the segment structure? Where are competitors positioned?

It is clear that a narrow price analysis could not answer these questions. Rather, the situation required a full-fledged market and competitive analysis. Figure 18.3 gives an overview of the main issues and their interconnections.

What did Netex management find? Well, the price structure turned out to be complex, reflecting the market's intricacies. On average, the price was slightly above the competition. In fact, there was no average price, but rather a set of highly differentiated price schemes. For example, in one major application, Netex's perceived value and thus the willingness to pay were markedly superior. This indicated a premium price. Because it was not possible to sell the standard Netex at different prices, the company developed a slightly modified version called Netex-Forte to sell at a higher markup. In certain developing countries Netex's perceived value and the farmers' willingness to pay were far below average, mostly because the farmers did not appreciate the product's superior safety and environmental characteristics. The company decided not to introduce Netex in those countries.

In another field Netex had to be used with a second, much cheaper product. By combining this agent with Netex to become Netex-Combi, the company saved farmers an additional spraying and raised the product's perceived value. The company found that light users were much less price sensitive than heavy users, so it offered pronounced quantity rebates and a bonus system, essentially a discount structure. Netex also introduced a seasonal pricing scheme.[28]

Such analyses are, of course, no guarantee for success, but they greatly improve the product's chances for survival and even maximum profitability. This example illustrates the need for an integrative approach to pricing, called **integrative pricing,** that incorporates careful research into the key factors in price determination examined in Chapter 17. It also shows that a mix of the pricing strategies may be the best approach for a company to use.

This integrative approach to pricing is designed to get marketers to think through all the aspects of setting a price. This approach emphasizes the importance of setting prices not in isolation but within the framework of other marketing decisions.

Since when do consumers believe that less is more? More often than you'd think. See if you can explain why consumers might accept the following pricing strategies.[29]

18-4   The phone company charges a monthly fee of, say, $3 for the privilege of having an unlisted phone number. The company won't print your name in the telephone book or give your number to anyone calling directory assistance, but will charge you extra for this lack of service—less service for more money. Can you explain that?

18-5   A credit card company thinks you should pay $70 a year for its card so that you have the honor of paying your bill every month without any interest. The other banks and companies charge you less or nothing for their cards and you also have the opportunity of paying your bill each month with no interest charges. Why do consumers choose to use this card?

18-6   Major banks charge you a service fee if you use an ATM instead of a human teller. Which is more expensive? Should they give you a discount if you use the ATM?

MISCELLANEOUS PRICING METHODS

Sometimes marketers have pricing considerations in addition to the strategies discussed above. These include value pricing, customary pricing, odd-even pricing, and unit pricing.

Value Pricing

Value pricing, or *value-in-use pricing*, works to assign a price to a product based upon its value to the consumer in the use of the product. For example, 3M Corporation's Post-It Notes is a high-priced product relative to its cost. However, a high price is consistent with the value that the customer places on the product. Companies like 3M and Hewlett-Packard have used this pricing method to gain a competitive edge in the marketplace.

However, because value involves the judgment by consumers of the worth of the product, it is not uncommon to find product and service benefits increasing as prices decline.[30] In late 1993, Mercedes-Benz introduced its new C-Class sedans. Based from $29,900 to $34,900, the four-cylinder C220 and the six-cylinder C280 represent the German company's boldest attempt at offering cars that are within reach of entry-level luxury-car buyers. These are buyers that the company has been losing for years to Lexus, Infiniti, and BMW.[31]

Odd-even pricing is common at the retail level and is based on the belief that consumers respond more positively to prices ending in certain numbers.

Customary Pricing

With **customary pricing,** all competitors use certain traditional pricing points. For example, retail prices for virtually all candy bars are $.50. Firms do not sell candy bars for $.51 or $.56. In times of changing costs, the product itself is changed, not the price. Thus, the size of an M & M's package changes with the cost of chocolate, but the retail price stays the same as long as possible. In periods of extreme cost changes, though, the customary pricing point can shift, as it has for candy bars in recent years from $.25 to $.40 to $.50. (Believe it or not, for many years candy bars stayed at $.05.)

Vending machines at the retail level give further impetus for customary pricing. One finds prices in these machines that are divisible by 5. For example, local phone calls are $.25, not $.17, and even on long-distance calls where one is actually putting coins in the phone, the charge is always a multiple of 5. Prices of beverages, food, and other vending machine products also conform to this pattern.

Although customary pricing occurs mostly at the retail level, it is still common at the wholesale and manufacturing levels. This is most true when all manufacturers of the same product type quote the same retail and wholesale margins. Tradition dictates what this margin should be, and one takes a big risk—competitively speaking—in deviating from it.

Odd-Even Pricing

Odd-even pricing is common at the retail level and is based upon the belief that consumers will respond more positively to prices ending in certain numbers. Thus, we see prices of $6.95 instead of $7.00, $2.99 instead of $3.00, and $499.99 instead of $500.00. For retail goods under $50, prices ending in 9 are the most common, followed by prices ending in 5 and 3. With products selling for more than $50, the most common prices are $1 or $2 below the even dollar amount. The presumption is that consumers will buy the same amount, or even less, of a product as prices are lowered below an odd-price point. Then, as the price approaches a new odd-price point, demand will increase dramatically. There is some evidence that consumers perceive these slightly reduced odd prices to be more below the even price above them than they really are.[32] However, the evidence is not compelling, and the practice may be based more on convention than anything else.

Unit Pricing

In retail outlets that offer many product classes—with many brands within a product class, and many package sizes within a brand—consumers may become confused about which item is the best price offer. Consider the following prices for two sizes of Frosted Flakes, along with a third option of a special deal: (a) 10-oz. box for $1.09; (b) 13-oz. box for $1.56; and (c) two 18-oz. boxes for $3.98. Which offer is the best deal? With **unit pricing** customers can tell, because both the price of the item and the ounce, pound, or other unit of measurement is marked on the shelf in the store. In our example, the unit prices are (a) 10.9 cents per ounce, (b) 12 cents per ounce, and (c) 11.1 cents per ounce. In this case, larger packages and special offers are really less of a bargain than the standard price on the smallest package. Unit pricing, which grew out of the consumer movement, is used by some large supermarkets. Although unit pricing does add to costs, retailers hope that the social benefit of consumers making better purchase decisions will offset this cost.

REVIEW

YOUR MARKETING KNOWLEDGE

18-7 For the PC ProLinea pricing example in the Marketing in Action on Compaq Computers, describe the demand analysis that might have led Compaq to introduce ProLinea at its $899 introductory price. What is the nature of the demand curve for PCs? (See Appendix to Chapter 17.)

18-8 Next time you are shopping in a drugstore, check the prices on the shelf for odd-even pricing and price lining. Report your findings to the class.

18-9 The value-in-use of a new industrial-machine tool product to the automobile industry is $15,000. The cost of manufacturing and marketing the product is $9,000. What should be the quoted price of the product to the automotive customers?

PERSONAL COMPUTER EXERCISE

Setting a specific price for a product or service involves the analysis of demand, cost, and competition. This PC Exercise allows you to analyze the impact of alternative prices for an item, given data on demand, cost, and competition.

■ Setting an appropriate price for a product has always been a difficult and complex task. In time of inflation and recession, this decision becomes even more complex and important.

■ A proper approach to setting prices involves a detailed analysis of demand, customer behavior, cost, and competition. The legal environment must also be clearly understood.

■ Cost analysis is an important starting point in price setting. Marketers need to understand fixed costs, variable costs, total cost, average fixed cost, average total cost, and marginal cost.

■ Profit is maximized by fitting the pricing strategy to the product and market characteristics. Pricing decisions must be evaluated on a targeted segment-by-segment basis in order to determine customized pricing strategies for each.

■ There are real-world strategies to setting prices. These include differential pricing methods, competitive pricing, product-line pricing, and integrative approaches. Differential methods include second-market discounting, periodic discounts, and random discounts. Various discounting methods can also be applied to channel members. Competitive pricing is comprised of penetration pricing, experience curve pricing, price signaling, geographic pricing, competitive bidding, and price leadership. Product-line pricing involves price bundling, premium pricing, image pricing, complementary pricing, and price lining.

■ Some miscellaneous tactics that marketers employ because of their psychological impact on consumers include value pricing, customary pricing, odd-even pricing, and unit pricing.

KEY TERMS

integrative pricing (635)
cost-plus pricing (636)
intermediary pricing (637)
return-on-investment
  (ROI) pricing (637)
second-market discounting (640)
periodic discounting (641)
price skimming (641)
peak-load pricing (641)
random discounts (641)
quantity discounts (642)
cumulative quantity discounts (642)
noncumulative quantity discounts (642)
seasonal discounts (643)
functional discounts (643)
credit and collection discounts (643)
cash discounts (644)
allowances (644)
competitive pricing (645)

penetration pricing (645)
experience curve pricing (647)
price signaling (647)
geographic pricing (648)
F.O.B. origin (648)
delivered pricing (648)
single-zone pricing (649)
multiple-zone pricing (649)
F.O.B. with freight allowed (649)
basing-point pricing (649)
competitive bidding (650)
price leadership (651)
product-line pricing (652)
price bundling (653)
premium pricing (654)
image pricing (654)
complementary pricing (654)
captive pricing (654)
two-part pricing (655)

loss leaders (655)
price lining (655)
integrative pricing (656)
value pricing (657)

customary pricing (658)
odd-even pricing (658)
unit pricing (659)

ISSUES FOR DISCUSSION

1. How do you think PC software marketers will be pricing their products in the future?

2. An industrial equipment marketer has developed a new product to clean industrial pipes. Its value-in-use to customers per unit is $150. The total cost of manufacturing and marketing this product is $75 dollars. What price would you recommend for this product?

3. From observing AT&T's promotional efforts, what do you think the company's pricing strategy might be with respect to other long-distance telephone carriers?

4. "Price competition is ethically superior to non-price competition." Comment.

5. Within your local retailing community, identify examples of premium pricing, odd-even pricing, price lining, and leader pricing.

6. The retail selling price of a small appliance item was quoted as $50, with trade margins of 25 and 15 percent. The variable cost of the product was $20, while the relevant fixed costs of production and marketing were $5 million:
   (a) What is the break-even unit volume and dollar volume?
   (b) How many units would have to be sold to earn a profit of $1 million?
   (c) What additional information would one need to determine the number of units required to reach maximum profit?

7. Explain why intermediaries in the marketing channel might lean toward cost-plus pricing as the dominant pricing mode.

8. If you were the president of a home mortgage company that is competing against Arbor National Mortgage, what type of pricing strategy would you adopt and why?

9. Identify two marketers in your area that practice peak-load pricing and two that practice second-market discounting.

10. Name three consumer brands that you believe are using price signaling as an indicator of product quality.

CASE APPLICATION

The Next Round in the Cola Wars

Cott Cola. No, that's not a misprint. That's the real name of a new combatant in the cola wars. The Toronto-based company makes remarkably good-tasting private-label colas and other soft drinks, packages them ingeniously, sells them for at least 25% less than Coke and Pepsi around the world, and is seizing supermarket shelf space from the big guys.

Cott recently rolled into seven countries, including Japan, Australia, and Spain. Although Spanish consumers are notoriously brand loyal, one would never suspect it observing shoppers in a Continente supermarket in Madrid, where shoppers loaded up on new Continente Gold cola from Cott. Why the big draw? Well, Continente Gold was selling for 115 pesetas ($.87 U.S.) for 2 liters, while Coke was going for 169 pesetas ($1.28 U.S.). So much for brand loyalty!

Cott has been doing particularly well in Great Britain, where it is featured prominently in Sainsbury's grocery stores. In one London store, huge red-and-white merchandise displays and dozens of red-and-white signs promote not "the Real Thing" but Sainsbury's Classic Cola, supplied by Cott. According to A. C. Nielsen, Classic has gained a 75% share of Sainsbuy's cola sales since early April 1994, while Coke's share sank from 44% to 9% and Pepsi's from 21% to 10%.

No surprise that Coca-Cola raised a monumental stink with Britain's largest grocery store chain: Those all-too-familiar reds and whites make the Sainsbury's Classic label look just like Coke's. And Coca-Cola was quick to retaliate by running an ad that warned, "If anyone tells you their cola's the same as Coke, don't buy it." Under pressure, Sainsbury's

agreed to alter the label—to un-italicize "Classic" and to remove a Coke-like red line that had underlined the word.

Cott has been busy in the U.S. markets also. It has increased its revenues to $665 million over the past three years, a tenfold increase due primarily to getting Cott's into retailers such as Wal-Mart, where it is labeled Sam's American Choice, and Safeway (Safeway Select).

Cott President Heather Reisman says, "There's an expanding group of consumers worldwide who will buy the best value, not pay extra just for a famous brand." Cott, who plans to expand into three more countries by the end of 1994, is looking to provide value choices for even more consumers.

Questions

1. What roles do demand, cost, and competition play in the pricing of Cott's colas?
2. Do Coca-Cola's and Pepsi's actions affect the marketing of Cott's soft drinks?
3. What types of pricing strategies do you think Cott will have to adopt to remain competitive?
4. What are the probable long-term consequences of Cott's competitive positioning in the market? Why?

Influences on Your Price

Every job has some sort of market range for direct compensation based on position requirements and market competition. You need to know the market range for each of your top-priority jobs. You can then estimate your employment value by positioning yourself in each range according to how well you match the job requirements. Some potential sources of this information include, but are not restricted to, your school's placement office, your employment market publications, human resource managers, and employment advertising. Keep in mind some nuances when you evaluate the direct compensation information. Some major considerations include:

Geographical variations. There can be differences in actual compensation but not real compensation between regions. For example, the Southeast might pay less, but the cost of living might be less, thus providing pay that is equally attractive when compared to other regions.

Organizational qualities. Some organizations might offer greater stability or better training than others. They may counter somewhat lower compensation levels with stronger opportunities for development and advancement.

Community features. Other companies might be convenient to residential areas that have excellent schools and recreational areas. These companies might factor these advantages into a lower pay scale.

Benefits. Decide which benefits are important to you and make a qualitative judgment as to the importance of differences in benefits against direct compensation. For instance, long-term retirement and savings plans might not be so important to one seeking an entry-level position whereas medical and life insurance might be critical for entry-level candidates. Organizations differ in whether they pay for moving expenses for entry-level employees. Also, some organizations pay extra compensation upon hire, usually as an incentive to join that organization.

Questions

1. What effect might demand versus supply or inflation versus depression have on your employment value and how can you assess these factors?
2. List the considerations that are of great value to you in determining your "price." Besides salary or wages, what do you want in exchange for doing the job you are seeking?

Part Six

The Story of Harley-Davidson: Pricing

Premium Product at a Premium Price

Pricing is taken very seriously at Harley-Davidson. Managers and employees recognize that not everyone can afford the price of a Harley-Davidson motorcycle, which ranges from $5,600 to $16,000 (without accessories). The company knows it must produce such an excellent product that enough customers say the price is worth it. Harley-Davidson has been able to prove the worth of its bikes, with more than 600,000 registered in the United States alone.

At Harley-Davidson, a lot of time, money, and effort go into settling on the right price for a motorcycle. Value, or the perception of value, greatly affects price. That's why the Harley-Davidson motorcycle costs a bit more than the competition. The price takes into account not only the cost of production, but also the value of the experience—the status, image, and life-style—that customers expect to enjoy upon ownership of a Harley-Davidson motorcycle.

Under such expectations, it can be to the company's advantage to charge a premium price for its product. A higher-than-average price can often "position" a product to look even more desirable, prestigious, and high-quality to the consumer than the competition looks. Of course, the company also has to take care not to alienate existing customers who are loyal to the brand, but whose pockets aren't quite so deep. Thus the company takes the customer's willingness and ability to pay into account in its pricing strategies and balances those considerations against the total worth of the bike on the market.

Not surprisingly, prices have increased over time. In 1977 a Street Super Glide cost $4,349; in mid-1994 a comparable motorcycle cost more than $12,000.[1] International prices of Harley-Davidson motorcycles can easily approach and exceed $25,000, as in Japan.[2]

Harley-Davidson plans to maintain a premium pricing strategy, but has a goal of keeping the rate of price increase slightly below the U.S. inflation rate.

Harley-Davidson recommends a manufacturer's Suggested Retail Price (MSRP) for each motorcycle model to its dealers. However, dealers may set their own final price by increasing or decreasing the amount of the MSRP. Prices can vary around the country due to local market conditions and regulations that may require special parts or production techniques. In southern California, for example, Environmental Protection Agency regulations are much more stringent than in other parts of the country and require special features on the bikes. As a result, the motorcycles cost more in California.

Supply and demand also affect pricing. For instance, between 1980 and 1983 inventory of unsold motorcycles climbed. In order to sell (or unload) the excess units, Harley-Davidson cut prices by 30 percent. Competition is yet another factor. Prices across the entire industry dropped in the early 1980s due to excessive dealer inventories of Japanese-manufactured motorcycles. Today, Harley-Davidson strictly controls its production capacity in order to ensure quality in the final product. Not surprisingly, this limit on supply creates an even higher demand for the bikes, which in turn, increases the value of the bikes.

While Harley-Davidson is very sensitive to costs in terms of production, it is certainly willing to pay for quality, improvement, and reliability in the final product. Thus Harley-Davidson motorcycles use better quality and higher-priced parts than other manufacturers to ensure that the reputation of the bikes and the company is not jeopardized by malfunctions. As a result, resale values of used Harley-Davidson motorcycles tend to be much higher than those of its competitors' products.

Breaking It Down

Since the buyout from American Machine and Foundry Company (AMF), Harley-Davidson has handled its costs and cash flow superbly. Fully allocating product costs is a monumental but necessary job. If done effectively, the task results in better cost control and bigger profits.

Let's consider that the purchase price of each motorcycle unit must contribute to the following costs:

- salaries and benefits
- accounting, finance
- travel
- training staff
- packaging
- service warranties
- debt payoff
- dividends
- production costs, including facilities
- equipment, supplies, and parts
- promotions
- dealer relations
- rent and mortgages
- parts and accessories sales
- storage
- environmental accommodations
- inventory control
- profit

Cost allocation determines how the purchase price of a product will defray operational costs. For example, on average, the price of each General Motors car sold in 1992 had to account for approximately $340 worth of advertising and promotions and $665 of employee medical and individual benefits. Likewise, Harley-Davidson must account for such costs and price its motorcycles accordingly.

One thing that must not be overlooked in these calculations is profit. Believe it or not, many companies often forget to plan for a profit, and, as a result, at the end of the fiscal year they break even, at best. In its calculations, Harley-Davidson must also include an allowance of dollars for discounting the product, in case discounting becomes necessary. Demand in recent years has been very high, and so discounts have not been offered, thus adding even more dollars to Harley-Davidson's profits.

Alternatives to Discounting

In the past, instead of offering discounts or rebates, Harley-Davidson has encouraged brand loyalty through occasional trade-in offers. For example, in 1987 Harley-Davidson celebrated the 30th anniversary of its Sportster model with a special trade-in offer. Anyone trading in a Sportster that was less than two years old could get $3,995 (the full price of the old Sportster) off the price of a new, larger Harley-Davidson model.[3]

While Harley-Davidson management recognizes that its motorcycles occupy the high end of the price spectrum, it is continuously evaluating the possible development of smaller, entry-level-priced motorcycles.[4] The hope is that these new bikes will attract more customers to the Harley-Davidson brand. Some of these new customers might eventually decide to buy a larger, more traditional Harley-Davidson model.

Questions

1. Knowing that the price of a Harley-Davidson motorcycle is so high, what course of action would you recommend to its competitors for them to capture part of the heavyweight market?
2. As the price of a motorcycle increases, what issues might the consumer consider?
3. Survey your classmates and identify the amount they would pay for a motorcycle.
4. What characteristics of a Harley-Davidson motorcycle make it worth the price?

part VII
MARKETING APLICATIONS: STATIONS, TRENDS, & ISSUES

CHapTeR 19

Marketing of Services

Marketing Profile

Flying the Virgin Skies: Virgin Atlantic Airways

Being a little guy in an industry dominated by a relatively small number of major competitors (a group that seems to be growing smaller every day) isn't easy. By focusing on meeting the needs and desires of its passengers rather than just meeting the prices of industry giants, however, Virgin Atlantic Airways appears to be beating the odds. Established in 1984, the airline grew significantly in its first ten years. Along the way it has earned a marketing achievement award from *Sales & Marketing Management* magazine (in 1992) for providing excellent consumer service. In 1994 the airline was given a number one rating for service by readers of the *Ashington-Pickett Airlines Report*.

According to Taylor Ingraham, the airline's vice president of marketing for North America, "What American is doing with fares, we're doing with service. They're reducing fares to meet the market. We're increasing service to meet the fares." Such a strategy, if it works, will give Virgin Atlantic increasing flexibility in an industry that has moved from government regulation to a deregulated free-for-all. Competition in promotional fares has led to price cutting and substantial losses for many carriers.

Virgin Atlantic is well aware that empty seats mean lost opportunity. Hence, Ingraham's task is to keep the seats full by attracting return customers and by reaching those who have never flown Virgin. Ingraham believes this latter challenge is the biggest hurdle the airline faces. She states, "We need to do things that rise above the noise out there. There's so much airline noise right now, and we have to make our little voice heard."

The airline works to achieve this goal through consumer research, promotion, and attention to service. Research identified a group of economy-class passengers who typically made reservations at the last minute. Often they paid full-fare in economy seating because they had found out about their travel needs only days before departure and so were ineligible for Virgin's Economy class price breaks that require pre-planning and stayover restrictions. These flyers, typically business travelers, were not candidates for the airline's Upper class seating since their companies would not pay the higher class fares; thus they seemed to fall between the cracks of Virgin's two-class system. To serve this group, Virgin created a Mid class that offers enhanced services such as more leg room, separate check-in, pre-takeoff drinks, and individual video players. Travelers who would normally fly full-fare in economy seating can now enjoy Virgin's enhanced service with no increase in price.

The airline's Upper class passengers also benefit from a host of value-added service features that make the offerings of competitors seem positively shabby by comparison. Virgin provides free chauffeured limousine service to and from the airport, four days of a free Avis rental car, sleeper seats, and an "infrequent flyer program" that provides every full-fare round-trip passenger in Upper class with a complementary one-way ticket in Economy class for any route Virgin flies except London to Tokyo.

Richard Branson, Virgin Atlantic's owner, explains his strategy with the following anecdote: "If I invite you to my home, I'd try to entertain you, not put a chicken in front of you and leave you staring at a blank wall."

In the area of promotion also, the airline appears to be on top of what's needed to make its service stand out in the competitive fray. It didn't happen overnight, however. Virgin Atlantic first promoted itself through advertisements that were slightly irreverent. One ad, for example, showed a picture of former President Richard Nixon, arms upraised, flashing a "V" for victory. The caption under the picture read, "At least he knew the best way to get to London." Such ads were memorable but didn't produce the ticket sales the firm had hoped for. Research indicated that consumers weren't being given reasons to choose Virgin. Today Virgin Atlantic's advertisements use humor but focus on the airline's virtues in no uncertain terms.

Virgin Atlantic Airways provides its customers with a service package that contains both tangible and intangible features. The transportation itself is intangible, as are offerings such as in-flight massages. Tangible items such as the pre-takeoff drinks and the individual stereo players, however, help Virgin's passengers to see, in a concrete way, what sets this service provider apart from the competition.

Since the end of World War II, the fastest growing part of the American economy has been the service sector. In 1992, more than 16.1 million employees worked in the services sector. Seventy-four percent of the GDP of the United States is service based and 79 percent of all jobs are service based. The Bureau of Labor Statistics predicts that all net job creation through 2005 will come from services.[1] According to Dun & Bradstreet, every one of the ten fastest growing categories of new businesses in the United States is a service-based business.[2] These include health clubs, beauty shops, medical care, investment management, real estate businesses, travel agencies, and hotels.[3] Furthermore, this growth has occurred not only in the United States but throughout the world, in all industrialized nations. In many such economies, service industries account for more than two-thirds of the gross domestic product.[4]

Despite these statistics, the marketing of services has received less attention than the marketing of goods. One reason has been the belief that product marketing techniques apply equally to services, hence it was viewed as unnecessary to study services marketing separately. Furthermore, many scholars and practitioners have believed that when a service does not add value to a physical product, it does not create value, and so is less important than the physical product itself.[5]

In the last 30 years these ideas and other misconceptions about services have begun to change.[6] While there are many similarities between goods and services, there are also significant differences.[7] The marketing challenges Virgin Atlantic Airways faces are considerably different from those encountered by producers of tangible goods. The use of marketing by health-care organizations, financial service companies, law firms and other professional service organizations, telecommunications companies, and other service firms has been the fastest growing area within the field of marketing. Although many service firms ignored marketing in the past, they are now embracing it, recognizing its ability to help them meet their goals.

In this chapter we look at the basic characteristics of services marketing. We identify methods of classifying services and examine some of the key issues and problems in developing a marketing strategy for services. We also discuss the marketing of professional services and how the issue of quality relates to services.

WHAT IS A SERVICE?

What does the term *service* mean? Despite the fact that the United States and many other industrialized nations have seen the service sector of their economies come to dominate, there is no widely accepted definition of the term in marketing. Indeed, there is no clear distinction between those firms that are part of a marketing channel for products and those firms that market services. For example, fast-food restaurants are often classified as food distributors because they compete with supermarkets, but these restaurants also provide services to customers.

In 1988, the American Marketing Association defined services as

> products such as a bank loan or home security, that are intangible, or at least substantially so. If totally intangible, they are exchanged directly from producer to user, cannot be transported or stored, and are almost instantly perishable. Service products are often difficult to identify, since they come into existence at the same time they are bought and consumed. They are composed of intangible elements that are inseparable, they usually involve customer participation in some important way, cannot be sold in the sense of ownership transfer, and have no title.[8]

In this text, we will briefly define **service** as an intangible activity that provides the user some degree of performance satisfaction but does not involve ownership and that, in most cases, cannot be stored or transported.

Services include activities such as accounting, banking, medical care, lodging, transportation, communication, advertising, consulting, and personal care. Activities in which the principal aim is the production of tangible products, such as cars, food, and appliances, are not services.

Intangibility is a very important aspect of services. The term refers to something that lacks form or substance. When something is intangible it cannot be felt or touched. Consumers may be more reluctant to purchase something they cannot feel or touch. Hence the fact that services are intangible provides many challenges to marketers. It affects how a service is delivered, promoted, and priced. A service provider, for example, might attempt to make a service more tangible so that it can provide customers a feeling of being able to touch something. The bank credit card creates a tangible representation of a service. Customers receive the service when a plastic encoded card is used to make purchases. VISA and others have thus overcome the drawbacks of intangibility; they allow customers to make credit purchases without having to visit the bank.[9]

In fact, despite the definition above, few products can be classified as strictly tangible or intangible. Instead, products can be thought of as existing on a goods-to-services continuum based on the concept of tangibility. At the ends of the continuum are products that would be viewed as wholly tangible or intangible. A chair, for example, is tangible, while teaching is intangible. In between these two extremes exist all consumer and business products, most of which contain some combination of tangible and intangible features. A fast-food restaurant, for example, offers tangible items such as the food itself, but also intangible benefits such as speed and convenience. Figure 19.1 uses the goods-to-services continuum as a system for comparing products on the basis of tangibility.

Services provide performance satisfaction. *Performance satisfaction* refers to the satisfaction experienced by the consumer of a service as a result of the performance of the intangible activities. When a hairdresser styles a customer's hair, the customer is typically pleased, thus performance satisfaction has occurred.

The performance of a service provides satisfaction, but it does not provide ownership of an actual product. Goods like Wheaties cereal, Crest toothpaste, or French's mustard are produced, sold, and consumed. Consumers take ownership of them after purchasing these products. Services are first sold and then performed

**FIGURE 19.1
A Goods-to-Services
Continuum**

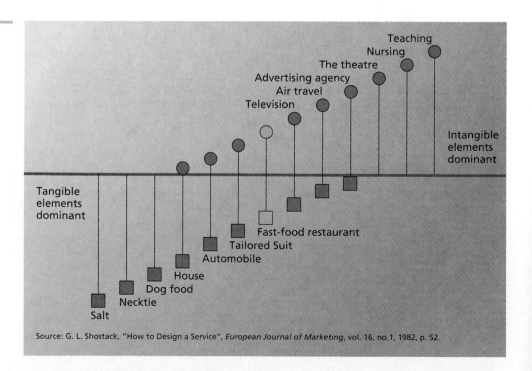

Source: G. L. Shostack, "How to Design a Service", *European Journal of Marketing*, vol. 16, no.1, 1982, p. 52.

and consumed simultaneously. So, for example, if you purchase a seat on an airplane to Hawaii, the airline transports you (performs the service) at the same time you consume the service. No actual ownership occurs.

Services cannot be stored or transported. Because Wheaties are produced first and then sold, the cereal can be stored until consumers are ready to purchase it. It can also be transported from where it is produced to a place more convenient for consumers to purchase it. The seat on the airplane to Hawaii, however, cannot be stored. If it is not used to transport someone, the potential to offer the service at that point in time is lost. Furthermore, the seat cannot be moved to a different airplane in a different location.

THE CHANGING SERVICES ENVIRONMENT

Ideas about services and about marketing services have changed markedly. Certain misconceptions, however, remain.[10] Services marketing scholar Christopher Lovelock offers six myths regarding the service sector of our economy:[11]

Myth No. 1:　A service economy produces services at the expense of other sectors.
Myth No. 2:　Service jobs are low paying and menial.
Myth No. 3:　Service production is primarily labor intensive and low in productivity.
Myth No. 4:　The growth of government is the main reason the service sector is dominant.
Myth No. 5:　Services are responses to marginal demands that people satisfy only after they meet their product needs.
Myth No. 6:　Service businesses are composed primarily of cottage industries and Mom & Pop operations.

As the service sector grows rapidly, it is in a state of transition. Lovelock suggests that the following factors are responsible: changing patterns of government regulation, relaxation of professional association standards, privatization, computerization and technological innovation, growth of franchises, expansion of leasing and rental businesses, manufacturers as service providers, and globalization.[12]

Changing Patterns of Government Regulation

In the past, many service industries were highly regulated by the government. Airlines, banking, and telecommunications are just three examples in the United States. In the eighties and nineties, however, this changed. As major service industries have been deregulated, the role of marketing has changed dramatically.

Relaxation of Professional Association Standards

Led by the United States, other nations joined the move to end restrictions on promotional activities for professional services. Physicians, attorneys, and other professionals now engage in advertising and other promotional activities. New-product development, competitive pricing strategies, and more customer-oriented delivery systems have become the rule of the day.

Privatization

The policy of returning nationalized industries to private ownership is **privatization.** The industries involved are mostly service industries. A country might, for example, transform a national airline to a private company, which must then com-

The relaxation of professional association standards has led to advertising by professionals, like this Big 6 accounting firm.

pete for business as would any private, for-profit firm. This action has become more common. In Great Britain, British Airways, once a government airline, was privatized in the late 1980s. In addition, Germany is currently selling off 25 percent of its postal service.[13] The move typically results in firms becoming more market-driven.

Computerization and Technological Innovation

The increase in computerization and the new technologies that often grow from it have changed the way many service industries do business. The banking industry, for example, is not the same business it was before the advent of automatic teller machines and other computerized services. Services can be provided to consumers more quickly, more efficiently, and with less personnel. The advent of many new types of services, new ways of dealing with customers, and the ability to standardize services to a greater degree are all the result of computerization and technological innovation. These innovations have changed the nature of marketing efforts. The "Marketing in Action: Hunting for That Dream House with Your Fingertips . . ."

describes a service offered to house hunters in the Boston area that has been made possible by the advances in computerization.

Growth of Franchising

Franchising as a means of financing growth of service businesses has grown dramatically, not only in the United States but worldwide. This growth has sparked many changes in marketing. Promotion that builds awareness globally, more challenging new-product development, and wider distribution systems are just examples of how service industries have had to adapt to this growth.

Expansion of Leasing and Rental Businesses

Growth in leasing and rental businesses provides evidence that customers are finding the benefits of service critical even in product categories traditionally viewed as manufacturing based. A business might choose to lease trucks rather than purchase them, for example. In addition, as the work force in the United States becomes more entrepreneurial, many small businesses lease office space and rent computer equipment.

MARKETING IN ACTION

Hunting for That Dream House with Your Fingertips . . .

House hunting has traditionally meant long hours of traipsing from house to house in search of the right combination of price, space, amenities, and neighborhood. The process is usually tedious for both the real estate agent and the potential home owner. Advancing technology is attempting to change how people buy houses, but it is meeting with resistance.

HomeView, a company based in Needham, Massachusetts, has fought to allow house hunters to do their searching by computer. Established in 1989, its service initially allowed Boston-area consumers to enter their requirements and preferences in the computer. An interactive system would provide a list of more than three hundred features from which buyers could choose. The list includes amenities such as skylights, spiral staircases, tennis courts, and "rooms with a view." The system would then search through a data base to find offerings that met the client's specifications. On a 20-inch digital color screen, the buyer could preview homes the system identified as appropriate, and see a variety of interior and exterior shots of the houses as well as photos of the neighborhoods. The computerized system also provides information about the tax rates, schools, and other pertinent details.

To establish its data base, HomeView approached real estate brokers in the Boston area. The firm offered to add all the listings of a real estate company to its computer data base for no charge. Membership in the service would continue, free, until a home from the company's listings was sold. When a house was sold, HomeView would get 40% of the broker's commission.

HomeView, however, met with resistance from real estate brokers who felt the firm was offering a service too similar to the brokers' services. Thus, many brokers perceived HomeView as a threat. As a result, HomeView found it difficult to expand its data base beyond the 10,000 homes it initially acquired from subscribing to multiple listings services.

HomeView is trying a different approach. The firm is attempting to set up licensing agreements with real estate brokers that would allow the brokers to use HomeView's technology. Licensees (brokers) would place computers containing HomeView's service in their offices, where home buyers could use the computer to do initial screening. Once potential buyers had identified homes they wished to visit, the broker would escort them to the houses. HomeView hopes this strategy will work to build alliances with the brokers.

Manufacturers as Service Providers

As the demand for service has increased, many traditional manufacturing firms have emerged as major service providers. A truck producer, for example, might manage its own leasing division. Xerox Corporation has a separate division that services accounts on-site. As the service component of the firm grows, many companies find it profitable enough to seek service customers even among those consumers who have purchased goods from competing manufacturers. This move has required many marketers of goods to become skilled at marketing services.

Globalization

Service firms are becoming global in their business efforts. Many service providers are expanding internationally with the aid of free-trade agreements. This move has required industries and the firms that comprise them to expand their marketing expertise to a global scope. For example, Kinko's Copy Services has grown both within the United States and in Canada, Europe, and Japan.

This is an exciting and challenging period in the evolution of services. Marketers can no longer afford to relegate efforts directed at services to second-class status. Services marketing is fast becoming the dominant arena for marketers and will continue to be so into the next century.

CHARACTERISTICS OF SERVICES

Consumer services and business services are themselves quite varied (ranging, for example, from a barber shop to corporate legal counsel). All services have certain characteristics in common. These include intangibility, simultaneous production and consumption, less standardization than goods, perishability, and the nature of the client relationship.

Intangibility

A microwave oven, a can of Coke, or a new car are products that can be seen, tasted, or test driven before they are purchased. A haircut, a visit to the doctor, or the cleaning of a soiled garment, on the other hand, cannot be evaluated by the consumer him- or herself in any meaningful way prior to purchase and consumption, which occur simultaneously. The latter items, of course, are services performed for the buyer by the seller. When a service is purchased, there is generally no object to show for it. The consumer does not walk away from the transaction with anything in his or her hands. As described earlier, services possess the quality of intangibility. Money is exchanged, but there is no new automobile in the driveway or microwave oven in the kitchen. This characteristic of intangibility is key to understanding the challenges that services marketers face.

Because there is nothing to touch, service providers often attempt to improve the buyer's feeling of receiving something of value. Insurance companies promote the benefits of having money available for a child's college education or having necessary dollars for retirement. Insurance policies are designed to look impressive so that customers feel they have bought something of value. Another way to enhance buyers' feelings about services is to use celebrities to promote the service. Sprint has used Candice Bergen to create confidence among consumers for its services by making the service tangible through the link to the celebrity.

Another way service companies make the service more tangible is through the dramatization of their "product," showing consumers the benefits of using it. For

She goes two blocks to pre-school. But college is just around the corner.

Your tomorrows depend on the consistent performance of your long-term investments. And that's why investors have made Kemper one of America's largest asset managers. For over forty years, the Kemper Family of Mutual Funds has been dedicated to the kind of steady, long-term performance that builds tomorrows today. Ask your financial representative or call Kemper Mutual Funds at 1-800-KFS-8600, ext. 77.

Kemper MUTUAL FUNDS

We're Building Tomorrows Today™

Before you invest in a fund, carefully read the brochure and prospectus for more complete information, including management fees and expenses. Fund performance cannot be guaranteed and will fluctuate. ©1994 Kemper Financial Services, Inc.   219632

NAT-72B 1/94

Service providers often attempt to improve the buyer's feeling of receiving something of value. This financial services firm promotes the benefits of having money available for a child's college education.

example, Carnival Cruise Lines uses television advertising showing happy consumers dining, dancing, and enjoying the pleasures of exotic places. Hence viewers are put "on the ship." Similarly, American Express, in advertising, has dramatized the unpleasant experience facing someone who does not use its service.[14]

Simultaneous Production and Consumption

Services are typically produced and consumed at the same time. The physician listens to the patient, analyzes the problem, and suggests a solution (production) while the patient explains symptoms and receives the doctor's evaluation (consumption). In the case of services, the provider is usually physically present when consumption occurs, unlike with tangible goods. This characteristic of services has implications for distribution.

Having the good at the right place at the right time to satisfy the customer is a vital concern of marketing management. With goods, these tasks are accomplished through distribution means such as transportation and storage. With services, special emphasis is also placed on distributing the service in the "right way." Because services are intangible, inventories cannot be created, hence transportation and storage to provide time and place utility are not important issues. Conduct in the presence of the customer, however, can influence future purchasing decisions and become key factors in the distribution of services. A CD player or a pair of sneakers is not rude, abrasive, or careless, but people who provide services during the decision to purchase can be. When this occurs, customers are likely to look for a more courteous service provider. The result is not only a lost sale, but a lost customer.[15]

Less Standardization

Consumers expect products to be standardized. For example, a tube of Crest toothpaste is the same every time it is bought. This consistency is reassuring to consumers and, in fact, represents a major benefit of the branding process for consumer goods. However, the consumer's expectation about medical service, hair styling, or car repairs is less certain. The skills of one doctor differ from the skills of another doctor; the quality of work your hair stylist exhibits may change from one visit to another based on increasing experience or even how tired the stylist is on a given day. Because each situation that requires the service is different, standardization is not wholly possible or even appropriate.

This general lack of standardization requires special techniques for monitoring quality. A firm can determine quality by monitoring customers' satisfaction. Banks often conduct attitude surveys, restaurants use opinion surveys, and airlines ask passengers to rate their services. Some service organizations pay close attention to the recruitment, selection, placement, and training of personnel, so that the best available people are hired and retained to provide services promptly, courteously, and continuously. These efforts to manage and develop human resources are attempts to provide as much standardization as possible, minimize uncertainty, and improve customers' confidence. Some service providers, such as the Haircut Store and Fantastic Sam's, have attempted to standardize their services by charging the same price to everyone for a standard haircut and emphasizing that you will get a good cut regardless of which particular stylist cuts your hair.

Of course, standardization is desirable and assuring for goods, but this is not always the case with services. As mentioned, it may not always be appropriate to standardize a service to the point where its uniqueness is gone. A few years ago Holiday Inn Corporation used a promotional theme that touted, "The Best Surprise Is No Surprises." The firm may have overlooked the fact that many travelers prefer unique accommodations when they stay at hotels across the country or around the world. Knowing that every room you stay in on a trip will look like every other room you've ever stayed in is not a benefit to all consumers. By contrast, Radisson Hotels International, as illustrated in the accompanying ad, touts its unique worldwide offerings with the advertising tag line, "When You've Seen One Radisson, You've Seen One."[16]

Perishability

A television set can be stored in a warehouse until it is sold, but an idle H & R Block tax accountant represents lost business. Physicians and dentists sometimes charge patients for missed appointments because the service value only existed at the time the patient was not present. An empty seat on yesterday's flight is lost; it cannot be used tomorrow when demand exceeds the plane's capacity. These examples represent the service characteristic of **perishability.**

The perishability of services is not a major problem if demand is continuous and steady. However, when demand fluctuates considerably, providers of services have difficult decisions to make about efficient use of resources. For example, how many city buses should be running during nonpeak times? How many tellers should be in the bank's drive-through section? When the variation in demand is less than

WHEN YOU'VE SEEN ONE RADISSON, YOU'VE SEEN ONE.

Radisson HOTELS INTERNATIONAL

You'll find more than 250 different Radissons around the world, each as individual as the people who stay in them. So why get just a room, when you can get yourself a Radisson in all these cities in the South:

- Asheville, NC
- Atlanta, GA
- Augusta, GA
- Birmingham, AL
- Boca Raton, FL
- Charlotte, NC
- Chattanooga, TN

- High Point, NC
- Huntsville, AL
- Jacksonville, FL
- Knoxville, TN
- Memphis, TN
- Miami, FL
- Mobile, AL

- Montgomery, AL
- Ocala, FL
- Orlando, FL
- Palm Beach Gdns, FL
- Port St. Lucie, FL
- Raleigh, NC

- Research Triangle Pk, NC
- Spartanburg, SC
- Tallahassee, FL
- Tampa, FL
- Warner Robins, GA
- West Palm Beach, FL

Radisson Plaza Hotel, Indianapolis

Why get a room when you can get a Radisson?

For reservations **800-333-3333** gets you every single Radisson worldwide, including leading hotels, conference centers and resorts on six continents. Or call your travel professional.

For services, standardization is not always appropriate. In this ad, Radisson touts the advantage of hotels that differ from one locale to another.

predictable, the challenge perishability represents becomes even greater. While a bank might expect its tellers to be busier on Fridays or on the last working day of the month, the computer center at your school may have no idea when the busiest times will be (unless it checks the syllabi of all instructors to see if and when computer assignments are scheduled).

Service marketers must analyze the nature of supply and demand in order to make necessary resource decisions in the face of service perishability.[17] Overdemand is not the only problem they face. As Figure 19.2 shows, a service provider may find itself in one of four cyclical variations of demand.

The following are means of managing demand for services:

- *Differential pricing.* Movie theaters attempt to shift some demand from peak to off-peak times by offering matinée rates; restaurants offer "early-bird" specials to entice dining before peak hours; telephone companies offer lower rates for long-distance calling at night and on weekends.

- *Developing nonpeak demand.* Ski resorts have attempted to develop demand when there is no snow by installing slides or promoting their lifts in summer as ways to view the scenery.

- *Complementary services.* Many banks now offer their customers investment services to complement basic services such as checking and savings accounts.

- *Reservation systems.* Preselling services is a way to determine demand in advance. This is used by airlines, railroads, buses, hotels, and restaurants.

- *Communication efforts.* Sometimes communication alone can aid in managing demand. The U.S. Postal Service, for example, encourages us, through advertising, to mail early for Christmas.

Services often use differential pricing to manage demand. For example, restaurants use early-bird specials to entice customers to dine before peak hours and all-you-can-eat dinners on nights when demand is typically slow.

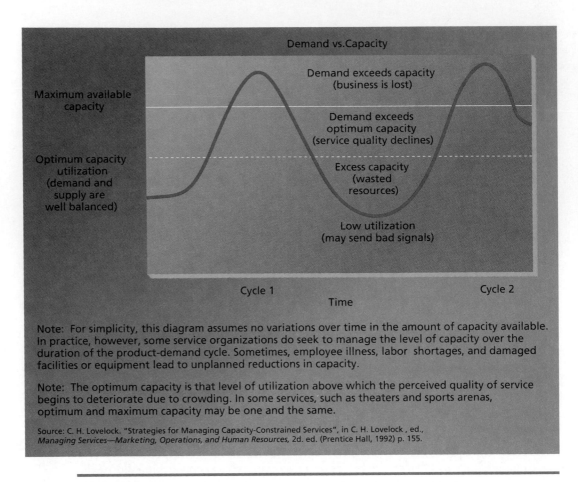

Note: For simplicity, this diagram assumes no variations over time in the amount of capacity available. In practice, however, some service organizations do seek to manage the level of capacity over the duration of the product-demand cycle. Sometimes, employee illness, labor shortages, and damaged facilities or equipment lead to unplanned reductions in capacity.

Note: The optimum capacity is that level of utilization above which the perceived quality of service begins to deteriorate due to crowding. In some services, such as theaters and sports arenas, optimum and maximum capacity may be one and the same.

Source: C. H. Lovelock. "Strategies for Managing Capacity-Constrained Services", in C. H. Lovelock , ed., *Managing Services—Marketing, Operations, and Human Resources*, 2d. ed. (Prentice Hall, 1992) p. 155.

FIGURE 19.2
Cyclical Variations in Demand Relative to Capacity

Marketers also face the challenge of perishability through the management of supply in the following ways:

- *Hiring part-time employees.* Seasonal help is hired by retailers during the Christmas season or by restaurants in resort towns during the summer.

- *Employing peak-time efficiency practices.* Employees may be encouraged to work faster at times of high demand or to practice only the necessary procedures at those times. A physician in an emergency room, for example, may have to choose a different course of action on a busy Saturday night than at a quieter time.

- *Increasing consumer participation.* Consumers may be asked to take a more active role in the service at times of high demand. Patients might fill out their own medical records, for example, or customers might bag their own groceries.

- *Sharing or renting facilities.* To avoid overinvestment in fixed assets, a firm may share facilities with another provider or lease the facilities. For example, several hospitals might use the same laboratory.

- *Cross-training of employees.* Training employees to perform more than one task enables them to assist during periods of overdemand. Stockpeople in a grocery store, for example, could run a cash register during a peak time if they have been trained to do so.

The "Marketing in Action: Creative Supply Solutions" describes a company that offers a solution to marketers who are attempting to synchronize demand and supply through supply management.

Nature of the Client Relationship

In many service transactions, the buyer is a client rather than a customer; when buying a service the client is "in the hands" of the seller. Consider a physician and patient or a hair stylist and customer. The buyers are not free to use the service

MARKETING *IN ACTION*

Creative Supply Solutions

Synchronizing supply and demand is a major challenge for service providers. Marketers attempt to deal with this by reducing or shifting demand so their supply is adequate, or by increasing supply. Because service providers must rely on personnel to increase supply, this latter solution to overdemand is often met through the use of part-time, seasonal, or temporary help.

The temporary services industry is booming and is projected to continue to increase during the next ten years. Temporary help has become common in the areas of clerical work, bookkeeping, light industrial applications, and janitorial and cleaning services. In Chicago, a firm called J & A Corporate Financial Services hired educated mothers of young children to do financial services work on a temporary basis. J & A offers flexibility to the women and reduces expenses for its client companies.

Creative Solutions, a Washington, DC–based firm, is bringing the solution of temporary supply to overdemand situations that require creative talent. Most of the company's temporary supply is talent in the company's traditional areas such as graphic artists, designers, and copywriters, but the agency can supply just about any type of creative talent, including a tattoo artist. A shopping center hired a man for the holidays whose talent was "talking like a bear." The primary target market for such temporary skills is midsized advertising agencies, which often do not have the capital to retain a full cadre of creative help on a permanent basis. When big jobs or rush orders come in, Creative Solutions can come to the rescue by supplying the help that allows the firm to meet the demand and retain business. In addition to ad agencies, Creative Solutions supplies retailers, law firms, corporations, and associations.

Steven Smith, president of Creative Solutions, feels the firm has benefitted from the recessionary economy of the early 1990s. Smith doesn't anticipate a "huge difference" as the economy turns around, however. He states, "The whole notion of à-la-carte services is becoming more important in business . . . There's really no one doing that [supplying temporary creatives], and it's a niche that seems to be needed to be filled as companies cut back on permanent marketing and communications staff."

Assignments for the creatively talented temporaries generally involve short-term projects such as newsletters, direct-mail pieces, annual reports, and logo designs. Really good temps are in high demand. That can be a disadvantage according to one of Creative Solutions' clients who states, "Once you find someone in their [Creative Solutions] stable that you like and want to use again, they're usually gone because everyone discovers the same one." Some clients have solved this problem by hiring the talented individual away from Creative Solutions, a practice the firm does allow, for a price. Most clients, however, are simply thrilled to have a source that can help when they're faced with a temporary need to synchronize supply and demand.

Creative Solutions is now expanding beyond the Washington, DC, area. Smith is selling licenses to operate Creative Solutions. For $6,000 to $12,000 (depending on the size of the market) and 5 percent of gross monthly sales, a licensee receives marketing materials that include brochures, direct-mail pieces, ad reprints for use in newspaper, magazine, and the yellow pages, and free-lancer recruitment ads. The licensee also receives exclusive territorial rights, access to national data bases of clients and talent, and tax, legal, and insurance advice. Smith estimates total start-up costs for a licensee would average $25,000.

when they wish, as would be true if a product were purchased. Nor can they return the service if they are not satisfied with it. So, service providers must work to establish and maintain the trust of their clients. If the service provider does not successfully instill this sense of trust in his or her clients, the provider's business will not be successful. This sense of trust generally takes time to develop, which is one of the reasons that service providers often work conscientiously to develop long-term relationships with customers. Consumers often refer to "my hairdresser," "my accountant," and "my doctor," and feel decidedly less comfortable if for some reason their provider is unavailable.

The importance of trust between provider and client is also the reason that word of mouth is such an effective means of promotion for services. Consumers feel more comfortable purchasing services, especially professional services such as medical care and legal care, from a provider who has been recommended.

Because of the client–provider relationship that exists with services, it is also true that buyers must abide by the conditions the seller establishes. Airplanes with passengers do not simply take off when passengers tell them to; they follow a departure and arrival schedule. They also have rules, procedures, and policies for passengers to follow. Passengers abide by these programs so that services, such as in-flight meals, can be performed on time and efficiently. The rules, procedures, and policies are usually in the best interests of the customer as well as the provider.

Each of the characteristics of services considered in this section affects the ways service providers market their "products." We now consider some of the ways to classify services.

CLASSIFICATION OF SERVICES

In Chapter 9, we saw that a classification scheme for products could help the marketer determine appropriate strategies. The same is true with services.

A classification system helps delineate services and can provide insight into how marketing principles apply to the service sector of society. There is no one generally accepted classification system for services and many classification schemes have been suggested.[18] In this section we consider three classification schemes, each of which provides insight into the nature of services and strategies for marketing them.

Equipment Versus People

The first classification scheme categorizes services as either people-based or as equipment-based. This distinction is determined by the extent to which special equipment is involved in the provision of the service. Figure 19.3 illustrates the classification scheme.

Equipment-based services.   **Equipment-based services** involve automated equipment (for example, an automatic car wash), equipment monitored by relatively unskilled operators (for example, dry-cleaning equipment), and equipment operated by skilled operators (for example, excavating vehicles). Successful marketing of an equipment-based service may depend on the uniqueness and superiority of the equipment itself.[19] Specifically,

- Equipment capabilities should be featured when uniquely superior equipment is present.
- Person-to-equipment interaction should be featured when the equipment is less unique but still not commonly available.

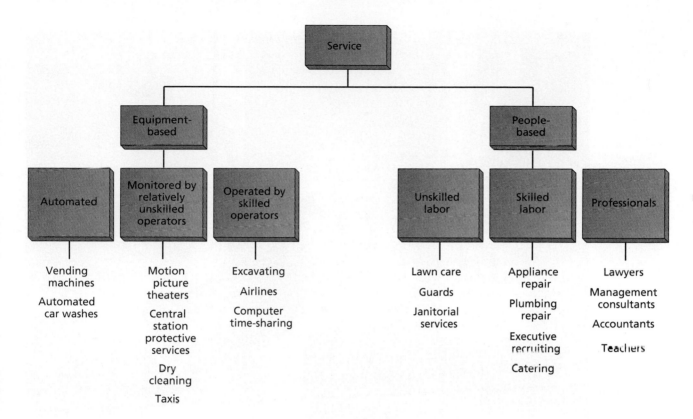

FIGURE 19.3
Types of Service Businesses

- Human capabilities should be featured when the equipment is common among competitive service suppliers.

People-based services. **People-based services** are provided by professionals (lawyers), skilled labor (plumbers), and unskilled labor (janitors and plant guards). In the case of people-based services, promotional efforts should focus on the producers, their capabilities, experience, and training, and anything that can convey cues to the successes of the providers.[20]

Classifying services as either people- or equipment-based places them in groups for further analysis. This can be useful in planning promotional strategies. Exact placement is difficult for two reasons, however. First, as service businesses evolve, they often move along the spectrum from people-based to equipment-based or vice versa. Automobile repair is an example of a service that has moved gradually from being people-based to being equipment-based. While good auto mechanics are still important, many of today's auto-repair services rely heavily on computers to diagnose a car's problems.[21] Second, the services that many companies provide may span a range of categories. For example, when transferring and storing funds, banks use equipment to perform services, but when financing a car loan, the bank's loan officers work directly with customers.[22]

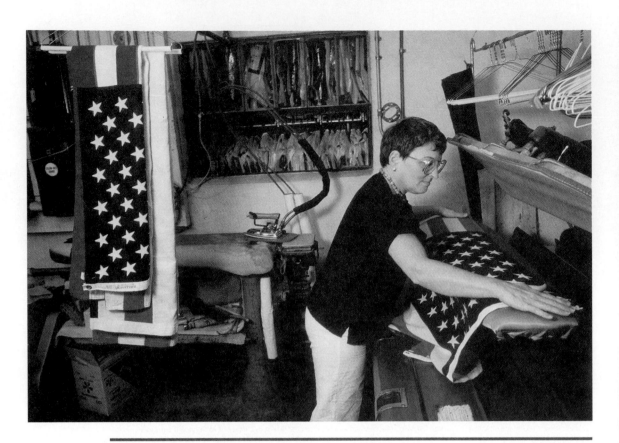

Dry cleaning is an example of an equipment-based service.

People Versus Things

Table 19.1 shows a classification scheme that looks at whether a service is directed at people or things. A surgeon who transplants a heart into a patient directs his or her service at a person. A janitor who cleans the floors of an office building directs his or her service at a thing. Both service providers are performing tangible actions. The second dimension of this classification scheme has to do with the action of the service: is it tangible or intangible? An intangible action, such as a bank transaction at a customer's account, might be directed at a thing rather than a person, or an intangible action, such as a television program, might be directed at a person (the viewer).

This classification scheme produces four types of service situations: tangible actions directed at people, tangible actions directed at things, intangible actions directed at people, and intangible actions directed at things.

What does this suggest for how a service should be promoted? By identifying, for example, what the service provider actually provides, the benefits of each service can be highlighted. The classification system also helps answer the question of whether the person must be present physically to receive the service. This in turn helps the person determine the distribution channel. For example, a provider of a tangible service directed at a person has little alternative but to use a direct channel of distribution. Intangible services, however, could use intermediaries, as when an educator teaches a correspondence or television course. When the recipient of the service is a thing rather than a person, there are more channel alternatives. The consumer need not be physically present to consume or receive dry cleaning or accounting services.

What Is the Nature of the Service Act?	Who or What Is the Direct Recipient of the Service?	
	People	**Possessions**
Tangible actions	*Services directed at people's bodies*	*Services directed at goods and other physical possessions*
	Health care	Freight transportation
	Passenger transportation	Industrial equipment repair and maintenance
	Beauty salons	
	Exercise clinics	Janitorial services
	Restaurants	Laundry and dry cleaning
	Haircutting	Landscaping, lawncare
		Veterinary care
Intangible actions	*Services directed at people's minds*	*Services directed at intangible assets*
	Education	Banking
	Broadcasting	Legal services
	Information services	Accounting
	Theaters	Securities
	Museums	Insurance

Source: C. H. Lovelock, *Services Marketing*, 2d ed., (Prentice Hall, 1991), p. 26.

TABLE 19.1
Recipients of Service

Service Delivery

A third method of service classification distinguishes the various methods of service delivery. This classification system, presented in Table 19.2, gives service marketers a better understanding of service distribution. The scheme recognizes three forms of customer-to-service organization interactions. Customers, in some cases, must travel to receive the service. A person may have a favorite beauty salon or restaurant, for example. In other cases, the service organization travels to the customer to provide the service, as is the case with a taxi cab or Federal Express. There is also the possibility that the person and service provider transact business without either engaging in travel. This is an *arm's-length interaction* and is usually accomplished through

	Availability of Service Outlets	
Nature of Interaction	**Single Site**	**Multiple Sites**
Customer goes to service organization.	Theater	Bus service
	Barbershop	Fast-food chain
Service organization comes to customer.	Lawncare service	Mail delivery
	Pest control service	AAA emergency repairs
		Taxi
Customer and service organization transact at arm's length (mail or electronic communications).	Credit card company	Broadcast network
	Local TV station	Telephone company

Source: C. H. Lovelock, *Services Marketing*, 2d ed., (Prentice Hall, 1991), p. 33.

TABLE 19.2
Methods of Service Delivery

some form of electronic media. For example, an airline can provide flight information, reservations, and tickets by telephone or computer instead of requiring customers to come to an office. Whether the service is offered from a single outlet or from multiple outlets is also a consideration of service delivery.

These variations in service delivery affect the level of quality a service provides as well as the consumer's perception of the convenience of the service. For example, providing a service from a single site probably provides the opportunity for the highest quality control. But it may also be extremely inconvenient for the customer. Hence, the provider must be able to convince the customer, through promotion, that the service is worth the effort. A retailer with only a single location in a city must work to convince customers that the store's ambiance, merchandise assortment, service, and prices are worth the extra effort of traveling to the single location. Conversely, a service that comes to the customer from one of many sites may be extremely convenient, but may also carry a higher price that the consumer must be willing to pay. If a retailer has multiple locations in the city, consumers will have to travel less, but the retailer's overhead is increased. The increase will probably be reflected in higher prices to the customer.

A firm may be able to split its services, centralizing some and not centralizing others. It might choose to centralize those services that require the greatest level of quality control and decentralize those that dispersed customers must deal with on a regular basis. A bank holding company centralized most of its marketing services. These included research, advertising, and international communications. Customer service and community relations, however, remained decentralized.[23]

DEVELOPING A PROGRAM FOR MARKETING SERVICES

Developing a sound marketing program for services is complex and requires decisions about the marketing mix that differ from those for marketing products. In describing the characteristics of services and considering some of the ways to classify services, we have already discussed many implications for marketing them. We now consider the four components of the marketing mix from the perspective of the service marketer.

Product

Product planning, development, and provision are just as important for a service marketer as they are for a marketer of tangible goods. Product-related issues such as branding and packaging are also considerations for the service marketer. The unique characteristics of services, however, can create special considerations when it comes to product decision making.

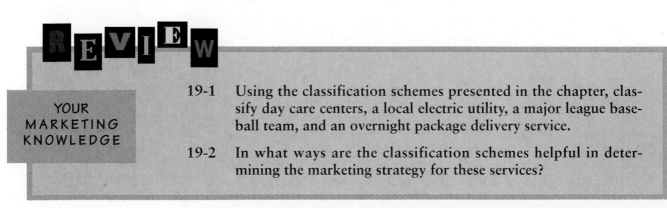

REVIEW

YOUR MARKETING KNOWLEDGE

19-1   Using the classification schemes presented in the chapter, classify day care centers, a local electric utility, a major league baseball team, and an overnight package delivery service.

19-2   In what ways are the classification schemes helpful in determining the marketing strategy for these services?

Intangibility not only makes it difficult for a customer to visualize the product prior to purchase but it also makes it difficult for a marketer to visualize the product as it is being developed. The service may be different each time it is produced, further hindering efforts at planning and development. Some service firms attempt to provide as standard a product as possible. Cleaning and laundry services, checking accounts at banks, automotive care, and overnight package delivery are virtually the same for all customers. Other service organizations vary the product for each customer. Attorneys, physicians, and consultants usually adapt the service to individual customers' needs. In these cases, product planning, development, and provision begins almost anew with each client. Some professionals like attorneys have standardized their services for routine procedures such as preparing a will or administering a simple divorce.

Because consumers may be uncomfortable purchasing an intangible item, service providers often attempt to **tangibilize** their offerings by including in the service package something that provides a tangible representation of the service. Such items may help the customer to visualize the product. A bank, for example, presents credit-line customers with a plastic charge card. The charge card represents the service of providing credit to the customer. It also makes it easy for retailers and others to see that the bank has extended credit to the cardholder.

Brand names are a means to product differentiation. This is especially important when there is no physical product to differentiate. Hence, brand names are very valuable to service providers. The names Holiday Inn, Hilton, H & R Block, United Airlines, Merrill Lynch, and Federal Express are important in establishing a competitive advantage for marketing services. The customer associates quality with the names of these well-known service providers.

The packaging of the service "product" is another marketing activity not usually considered; however, the impact of a package is important. Goods manufacturers constantly work on providing packages that will attract their customers' attention. Service marketers also must consider the effect their packaging efforts, or lack thereof, will have on customers. A preventive medicine center in Houston that caters to business executives had searched for months for a way to present results of medical examinations to patients. After a thorough, five- to six-hour physical exam, the center had used a personal letter and a visit with the physician to inform patients about their health. Patients complained about the impersonal tone and lack of clarity of this method. The center's director concluded that business executives were used to reviewing charts and figures; so, he created a bar-chart medical-report form. This director packaged the preventive medicine diagnostic report to provide patients with information in a convenient, clear, and familiar format.

Distribution

Some people assume that because services are intangible, heterogeneous, and perishable, distribution becomes much less important. It is true that most services are sold directly from the provider to the consumer or business user, although this is not necessarily always the case. (Recall the discussions associated with the classification schemes presented in Tables 19.1 and 19.2.) Although it is true that no intermediaries are used when an attorney or accountant evaluates a client's needs, prescribes some action, and follows up, it is also true that some service providers use agents, brokers, or other channel members as intermediaries. Figure 19.4 presents the channel alternatives for services. For example, companies that sell entertainment, insurance, or securities typically use independent brokers or agents to sell their services. In other instances, such as employment agencies, day care centers, or dance studios, individuals are trained to perform a service and are franchised to sell it.

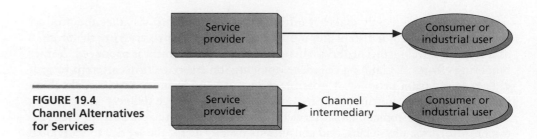

**FIGURE 19.4
Channel Alternatives
for Services**

Service marketers are less concerned than marketers of goods about physical distribution issues such as warehousing, transportation, inventory control, and materials handlings. On the other hand, service marketers are often more concerned with scheduling delivery than are goods marketers.[24] Service marketers cannot inventory their products to make them available when consumers wish to purchase and consume them. Hence, service provision must be scheduled to match consumer demand. Banks often schedule additional employees at the beginning of the month when demand for service is the greatest.

An important issue in the distribution of many services is location. Motels, hotels, physicians, dentists, and physical fitness facilities all seek convenient locations. Hotels and motels cluster near airports. Physical fitness centers attempt to locate facilities in areas that are easily accessible to customers, especially before and after work hours. For some services, the advent of electronic distribution channels has made location a less critical issue. Today many services such as banking, travel planning, education, and even consultation are distributed via television, telephone, and computer. On-line computer services such as Prodigy and America On-Line provide consumers access to a myriad of other services. In providing such access, the computer services themselves are intermediaries in the distribution channel.

Promotion

It is generally easier to promote something tangible. A product can be seen and demonstrated and lends itself to customers' evaluation. In fact, it has been argued that a key to successfully marketing a tangible item is developing an abstract image through promotion.[25] On the other hand, it is difficult to evaluate something that cannot be touched. To attempt to market a service (already an intangible) through the creation of an abstract, intangible image is asking for trouble.[26] Instead, marketers of services must make the service seem more tangible by focusing on concrete images and evidence in their promotion. Figure 19.5 illustrates this premise.

Some service firms use this idea by promoting the real benefits their services provide to users. For example, by using promotion, the insurance industry has made it easier for consumers to visualize what is being sold.[27] Think about these well-known efforts to promote insurance protection (an intangible) with a specific tangible object:

- Allstate—You're in good hands with Allstate
- Prudential—Buy a piece of the rock (the rock of Gibraltar)
- Travelers—Protected by the Travelers' umbrella
- Nationwide—The Nationwide blanket of protection.

Hands, rocks, umbrellas, and blankets give customers an object they can associate with an insurance firm.

Promotion can also build interest in benefits and help distinguish one service from another. Other forms of services like professional sports, travel agencies, and tax

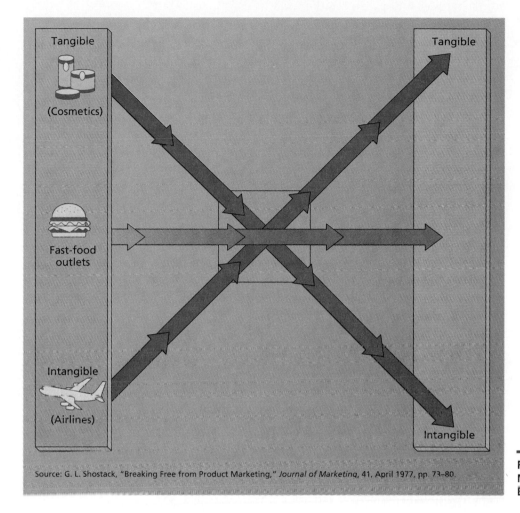

Tangible

(Cosmetics)

Fast-food outlets

Intangible

(Airlines)

Tangible

Intangible

Source: G. L. Shostack, "Breaking Free from Product Marketing," *Journal of Marketing*, 41, April 1977, pp. 73–80.

**FIGURE 19.5
Market Positioning
Emphasis**

preparation benefit from coverage on radio, television, billboards, and newspapers. These media build interest in watching a sports event like the World Series, or traveling to the Grand Canyon, or completing your tax returns properly.

An indirect form of promotion is the volunteer professional (pro bono) work and community activities by physicians, accountants, and attorneys to make themselves more publicly known. Eventual customers come in contact with the volunteers, who acquire reputations for helping the community.

Pricing

The word *price* is rarely used in marketing services. The payment component of the seller-to-buyer exchange is described in many different terms including *fee*, *charge*, *rent*, *interest*, *admission*, *rate*, *retainer*, and *tuition*. It may be that consumers are more comfortable with these synonyms for *price* when purchasing an intangible product.

Pricing strategies vary across service industries. Some, such as utilities (electricity and telephone), have their prices regulated by the government; other service firms charge users according to the season or time of day (resorts, motels, and movie theaters). Some service prices are based on age, with lower charges for children and senior citizens (restaurants and movies), while others (physicians, attorneys, accountants) may set rates on the basis of a customer's ability to pay.

In general, pricing services tends to be flexible but is similar to setting product prices. An important consideration is the cost of providing quality service. Most services, especially if they are people-based, are labor intensive (involving people's time, expertise, efforts), and prices must cover these labor costs, plus capital costs and an allowance for a satisfactory profit. Supply and demand also influence the price of services. The supply of outstanding diamond cutters is limited, and demand for their services is high. Thus, the supply–demand imbalance has resulted in high prices for this service.

Because services are intangible and consumers do not have a material good to evaluate value, price tends to be a very important indicator of quality.[28] Many consumers will assume that the higher the fee charged by the attorney, hairdresser, or private school, the better the quality of the service being rendered.

The method of paying for a product and a service often differs. Because a service cannot be repossessed like an automobile or a dining room set, some service firms require payment before the service is performed or at the time it is provided. A house painter usually requires at least a down payment before beginning the job. Sports teams and entertainers require payment before performing. Auto-repair businesses require payment at the time the service is provided. These advance or time-of-delivery payments are designed to prevent losses.

PROFESSIONAL SERVICES: A SPECIAL CASE?

A **professional service** is qualified; it is advisory, even though it may also encompass some routine work for clients.[29] Professional services are sometimes viewed as a special case of services marketing. This status is not due to the fact that these services differ in their characteristics from other services (they are in fact intangible, perishable, and so forth). Instead, the distinction may have to do with the fact that those who perform professional services see themselves as involved in occupations different from traditional commercial activities. The professional services—health care, law, accounting, engineering, and architecture—have been especially slow to accept and practice marketing. Some of this reluctance has been based on the following:

▪ *A disdain for commercialism.* Professionals view their areas of expertise as more scientific than business. Furthermore, many of them do not like to publicly discuss fees or rates for services, considering it crass or unprofessional.

▪ *Codes of ethics.* Many professional associations have established rules against advertising, direct solicitation, and referral commissions.

▪ *The notion that marketing is selling.* Many professionals have equated marketing with selling. As we have discussed throughout this book, marketing encompasses more than selling.[30]

These barriers have slowed the development of marketing professional services. However, the barriers have gradually come down and the use of marketing by service professionals is becoming more common. The U.S. Supreme Court, for example, ruled in 1977 that self-imposed ethical restrictions against advertising prices or services, intended to inhibit the free flow of commercial information and to keep the public ignorant, are illegal.

Increasing competition has also hastened the demise of barriers against marketing. In the health-care professions, for example, consumers now face many choices. Private physicians, health maintenance organizations, ready-care facilities, and other alternative methods of health-care delivery provide a person in need of health care with more choices than ever before. With this proliferation of choices, with free-flowing communication about prices and services, and with a national push for efficiency and accountability, it's not surprising that many health-care providers have become experienced marketers.

Changes in Professional Services Marketing

Since the 1977 Supreme Court ruling, professional services have dramatically increased their use of promotion. For example, a November 1993 poll that the Gallop Organization conducted for the *American Bar Association Journal* found that 61 percent of the ABA respondents said their firms engaged in some form of advertising. Eighty-seven percent said their firms expected to advertise as much or more in the future.[31] Other professions have also experienced similarly dramatic increases.

The professionals who are becoming more involved with marketing have accepted the following ideas:

- *Marketing is not only selling.* Marketing professional services involves decisions about pricing, promotion, and place.

- *Business marketing procedures are not only commercial.* Successful business leaders use scientific methods to analyze markets, provide people with what they want, and, after delivery of merchandise, handle complaints. They are as ethical, moral, and motivated as professionals.

- *Aggressive market analysis and planning is essential.* If marketing is to be effective, it requires marketing analysis and planning. As competition for professional services increases, marketing programs will have to be conducted in accordance with each profession's canon of ethics.

The real issue in professional services is not whether marketing is needed, but how it can be done effectively. Those professionals who accept the marketplace challenges will be better able to meet competition head on, cope with spiraling service costs, and improve the quality and delivery of their services. In general, the successful marketers of services are the people who can capitalize on what customers, clients, and patients want and need—which is what being market-driven is all about.

19-3 How does the marketing of professional services differ from the marketing of other services?

19-4 What suggestions would you make to the head of a local architectural firm concerning the marketing strategy the firm should use?

YOUR MARKETING KNOWLEDGE

SERVICE QUALITY

The importance of quality is just as great in the production of services as it is in the production of tangible goods. Everyone has been disappointed in the quality of a service, whether it was a poor meal at a restaurant, a noisy hotel, an auto-repair shop that did not repair a car properly, or a long wait at a doctor's office. A recent poll of Georgia residents conducted by Georgia State reported on residents' satisfaction with public and private sector service providers. Although there is a general impression that private sector service is superior to public sector service, responses to the poll indicated that residents were more satisfied with public sector service. Respondents gave the highest ratings to these providers: private mail carriers, fire departments, grocery stores, the United States Postal Service, and doctors' offices. The lowest ratings went to taxis, cable television providers, auto-repair shops, street maintenance, and public schools. The poll also found that if respondents had used the service within the last six months, they tended to rate that service more favorably.[32]

What determines a customer's perception of quality in service? There are five dimensions that differentiate good and bad service:

- *Tangibles*—the appearance of physical facilities, equipment, personnel, and communication materials.

- *Reliability*—the ability to perform promised services accurately and dependably.

- *Responsiveness*—the willingness to help customers and to provide services promptly.

- *Assurance*—the knowledge and courtesy of employees and their ability to convey trust and confidence.

- *Empathy*—the provision of caring, individualized attention to customers.[33]

Knowing the criteria that consumers use to judge quality in the services they shop for and buy does not mean that the service provider always provides that quality. Many service providers leave the provision of service quality to the discretion of their employees while providing little, if any, direction. One bank marketing officer commented, "There are no standards for quality [for branch office employees]. We tell them to provide a high level of service to the customer."[34] Other service providers, however, are very careful to spell out the standards that constitute quality service. Table 19.3 describes the standards set by the Rusty Pelican, a restaurant chain offering food and cocktails.

Five imperatives have been offered for firms interested in improving their quality of service:

1. *Define the service role.* Service standards must be determined and specified.

2. *Compete for talent, and use it.* Look for and hire the best service performers.

3. *Emphasize service teams.* An interactive community of coworkers can help the service provider perform better.

4. *Go for reliability.* Reliable, consistent service has been found to be the heart of excellent service.

5. *Resolve problems promptly and courteously.* Develop satisfactory means of correcting the situation when a problem occurs.[35]

Careful attention to quality is a mark of the market-driven service provider. Service marketers who recognize this and plan accordingly are on the road to success.

Food-service Standards
1. **First contact**—cocktail server speaks to customer within two minutes of customer seating.
2. **Cocktails delivered**—beverage service at table within four minutes of order. If no beverage order, request for food order within four minutes of first greeting.
3. **Request for order**—within four minutes after beverage service, customer should be asked whether he or she cares to order.
4. **Appetizers delivered**—salad, chowder, or wine delivered within five minutes.
5. **Entrée delivered**—entrée served within 16 minutes of order.
6. **Dessert delivered**—dessert and coffee or after-dinner drinks served within five minutes after plates are cleared.
7. **Check delivered**—check presented within four minutes after dessert course or after plates are cleared if no dessert.
8. **Money picked up**—cash or credit cards picked up within two minutes of being placed by customer on table.

Cocktail-service Standards
1. **First contact**—greeting given and cocktail order taken; seafood bar, happy-hour specials, and wine-by-glass menus presented within two minutes.
2. **Cocktails delivered**—cocktails delivered within five minutes after first contact.
3. **Seafood bar delivered**—seafood bar and happy-hour specials delivered within seven minutes of first contact; ten minutes for cooked items.
4. **Next contact**—check for reorder of cocktail, seafood bar, customer's satisfaction, and table maintenance within five minutes from delivery of first cocktail.

Source: D. D. Wyckoff, "New Tools for Achieving Service Quality," in C. H. Lovelock, *Managing Services—Marketing, Operations, and Human Resources*, 2d ed. (1992), p. 245.

TABLE 19.3
Rusty Pelican Standards of Service

PERSONAL COMPUTER EXERCISE

The level of service quality a firm provides can determine its success or failure. Often, companies that primarily provide services will conduct surveys to measure their level of service quality in comparison to that of their competitors. This PC Exercise allows you to analyze a firm's service quality on a number of factors relative to that of its competition.

KEY POINTS

■ The marketing of services is similar in many ways to the marketing of products. However, there are some distinct differences in promotion, pricing, and distribution.

■ The service sector is expected to continue to grow. It already accounts for $.50 of every dollar spent by consumers and 60 percent of private sector jobs.

■ Marketing concepts, tools, and programs have been slow to catch on in service firms. However, more service firms are beginning to incorporate their own forms of the marketing mix.

■ Several forces in today's environment account for increased interest in marketing by service firms: changing patterns of government regulation, relaxation of professional associations' standards, privatization, computerization and technological innovation, growth of franchising, expansion of leasing and rental businesses, manufacturers as service providers, and globalization.

■ The distinct characteristics of services include intangibility, simultaneous production and consumption, less standardization than for products, perishability, and client relationships.

■ Service businesses can be equipment-based (automated car washes) or people-based (legal counsel from a lawyer), by the recipient of a service or by the method of service delivery.

■ The marketing of professional services presents significant challenges. Many professionals are reluctant to engage in marketing activities; however, increased competition and customers' demands are placing pressure on professionals to market their services.

■ Service quality has become increasingly important. Tangibles, reliability, responsiveness, assurance, and empathy are the critical dimensions of service quality. It is important to deliver a level of quality consistent with consumers' expectations.

KEY TERMS

service (671)
intangibility (672)
privatization (673)
perishability (678)
equipment-based services (682)

people-based services (683)
tangibilize (687)
professional service (690)

ISSUES FOR DISCUSSION

1. List reasons that service-oriented firms generally are not as up-to-date and sophisticated in performing marketing activities as goods-marketing firms.

2. Which of the different ways of classifying services discussed in this chapter do you think is best? Why? Think of at least one other way of classifying services.

3. Discuss the characteristics of the following services:
   (a) KinderCare (franchised) day care centers
   (b) Sprint long-distance service
   (c) One of the "Big 6" accounting firms
   (d) H & R Block income-tax service
   (e) A small dry-cleaning establishment

4. How might each of the services in question 3 be tangibilized?

5. It is estimated that in 1995 there will be more than one million attorneys in the United States. What kind of changes in advertising and public relations do you foresee for the legal profession in the late 1990s?

6. What actions might a fast-food restaurant like Burger King take to increase its quality of service?

7. How would you respond to a physician who commented, "I don't believe in advertising, only bad doctors need to advertise."

8. When someone comments that maintaining an inventory of services is not feasible, what does he or she mean?

9. Think of the advertising for a local bank. Why do you suppose the bank advertises the way it does? How effective is it? Why?

10. Would being a marketing manager in a service firm involve different decisions and a different management style than being one in a product firm? How?

CASE APPLICATION

Is Hospital Marketing Dead?

Professional services such as those in health care were slow to view marketing as appropriate for them. In the 1980s, however, many health-care service providers seemed to overcome their reluctance with a vengeance. Hospitals, in particular, embraced marketing with increasing fervor throughout the decade of the 1980s. From 1980 to 1990 spending on hospital marketing in the United States quintupled. Expenditures reached a peak of $2.1 billion in 1991. With health-care reform on the horizon, however, the industry seems to be rethinking the situation. In 1992, marketing spending by hospitals declined 24 percent. Some hospitals have totally abandoned their marketing efforts, and many others have sharply cut back.

The change appears to be the result of more than one factor. First, many hospital administrators are questioning whether large marketing expenditures are the best way to use available dollars. Michael Jhin, president of Houston's St. Luke's Episcopal Hospital, states, "It's just not the best use of patient-care dollars." Health-care providers often agree. "It's diverting millions of dollars from the bedside," states Dr. Philip Lanzkowski, acting medical director of New York's Long Island Jewish Medical Center. For many, this debate regarding the use of available monies for marketing raises an ethical issue. The question of whether dollars should be spent on marketing rather than patient care is a hot ethical dilemma in many hospitals.

A second factor contributing to the decrease in hospital marketing appears to be a more pragmatic issue for many hospital administrators. There is increasing evidence that marketing spending aimed at ultimate consumers does not produce the hoped-for results. An estimated 70 percent of hospital admissions are based on physicians' rather than patients' choice. According to research, convenient location and affiliation with a patient's health plan are the major factors influencing the 30 percent of admissions that do result from patient choice.

Health-care reform, as proposed by the Clinton administration, is likely to further reduce the degree of patients' choice of hospital. Many hospitals are already regearing their marketing strategies to focus on attracting large health maintenance organizations (HMOs) and other managed-care organizations. Paul Keckley, a Nashville–based hospital marketing consultant, illustrates the futility of direct patient promotion in this evolving environment: "What happens when you spend all of your money promoting cardiovascular doctors and then managed-care companies say, 'you may have a big name, but we're not using you?'"

As the attitudes of hospital administrators toward marketing change, so does the nature of the hospital marketing that continues to exist. The freewheeling 1980s produced hospital marketing centered largely around gimmicky promotion. Celebrity endorsers in ads, candlelit dinners for new parents, and roadside billboards were common. While not all such promotions are gone, especially in heavily competitive markets, today's hospital marketing is more likely to focus on research and segmentation. Marketing research is used by hospitals to understand better not only consumers' needs but also the needs of health-care providers—the physicians and the HMOs that hospitals seek to attract. Segmentation has grown in sophistication also. Using psychographics and behavior patterns as well as demographics, many hospitals have identified markets for new services. Segmentation is especially effective for hospitals marketing discretionary services such as substance-abuse treatment and psychiatric services. Patients typically have greater direct choice in selecting a hospital for these types of services.

Hospital marketing is not dead. Its future, however, appears destined to be different from what its early years have been. The changing external environment and the increased sophistication of hospital marketers are bringing it to a new level. What the future holds remains to be seen.

Questions

1. Describe the five characteristics of services as they would apply to a hospital.
2. How would you classify the health-care services offered by a hospital using the three classification schemes discussed in this chapter? Would your answers change if you were classifying the services of an individual physician instead of an entire hospital? How?
3. In what ways might a hospital tangibilize its services through promotion?
4. What are the dimensions of the ethical debate regarding expenditures for hospital marketing? Do you think hospital marketing is unethical? Defend your position.

You're the Service

Because marketing yourself is closer to marketing a service than to marketing a product, the special considerations in the marketing of services deserve some discussion. Two of the properties of services have special meaning for marketing yourself to target organizations. First, what you are offering is an intangible. What you bring to an organization are capabilities to produce results. These capabilities cannot be touched or observed in a physical sense. Second, there is a lack of standardization in what you have to offer to organizations. Because each of your target organizations has unique needs, there are some differences in how you would package your capabilities for each of them.

The service buyer usually makes decisions based on past experience, word of mouth, reputation of the provider, and promotional campaigns. Think about how these factors apply to your job search. In making and nurturing contacts by letter and in person, you should

- emphasize the details in your background that your target company will see as success factors based on its experiences with new hires,
- use referrals and testimonials from other people to help you get introduced to and accepted by the employment decision makers in your target organizations,
- highlight the "brand-name" schools, organizations, and activities in your background,
- develop a real strategy for skillful communication between you and your target companies based on the principles covered in Chapter 14.

In short, look at yourself through the eyes of a service buyer. In addition, the presentation pattern for service can be useful in your self marketing:

- Think of the benefits you can bring to each of your target organizations as a result of your background. For example, if you have excelled in a relevant academic area, you have demonstrated the capability to learn quickly. Or, if you have some relevant industrial and functional experience, you have demonstrated capability for the work and can get "up to speed" fairly quickly
- Think about concrete evidence of your ability to make good on the benefits you have identified above. For example, in the academic area, be specific about such items as titles and numbers of courses; grades and honors in those courses; teaching or tutoring assignments that reflect superior proficiency; and any practicums or similar work projects in these areas. In the work areas, include the length and level of your responsibilities and what you learned from such experience.

In dealing with intangibles, you must feature benefits first because they can be more readily understood than features and then deal with the features in the most concrete terms that are possible.

Questions

1. In thinking about two or three of your target organizations, what do you understand to be the success factors for new hires in each?
2. What are the benefits for hiring you for each target organization?
3. What are some of the brand names (i.e., highly recognizable and respected items) in your education or experience?
4. What referrals and testimonials can you use for each target organization to reinforce your ability to produce the necessary and desired benefits?

CHapTeR 20

Marketing in the Social Sector

Upon completing this chapter, you will be able to do the following:

■ **Describe** the growth and development of marketing in the social sector.

■ **Identify** the reasons that social sector marketers are adopting marketing.

■ **Explain** why the exchange process is different in the social sector.

■ **Discuss** the characteristics of social sector organizations and how they differ from business firms.

■ **List** the marketing challenges faced by social sector marketers.

■ **Understand** the importance of marketing for social sector organizations.

■ **Illustrate** how marketing tools are applied in the social sector.

■ **Discuss** strategies for introducing marketing into social sector organizations.

Marketing Profile

The Girl Scout Promise: Meet the Needs of Today's Girls

The Girl Scouts of the U.S.A. is a thriving, market-driven organization. Membership numbers a healthy 3.44 million. That figure includes 2.6 million girls and 827,000 adult members. One in every nine girls in the United States (ages 5 to 17) is a Girl Scout. The former National Executive Director, Frances Hesselbein (she retired in 1990), has frequently been invited to give guest lectures to MBA students at Harvard Business School. Management guru Peter F. Drucker has suggested that Hesselbein would have been a good candidate to succeed Roger Smith as CEO of General Motors—given the strength of the Girl Scout organization.

In the late 1970s, the Girl Scouts of the U.S.A. were in serious trouble. Membership had been dropping for almost ten straight years. Not only was the organization unable to attract girls but finding adult leadership was equally challenging. Women were returning to the work force in droves, leaving no one to volunteer as troop leaders, the backbone of the organization's complex management structure (331 autonomous subsidiaries loosely associated under a common name). The organization was under attack by critics who saw it as irrelevant to modern tastes and concerns. Teenagers had lost interest and in an age of diversity, the organization was 95 percent comprised of white, middle-class members. Things were, in a word, a mess!

How did the Girl Scouts accomplish such an astonishing turn around? There was nothing mysterious about it. The Girl Scouts of the U.S.A. have applied some basic marketing and strategic planning techniques. Initially under Hesselbein's direction, the process began with a major re-examination of the Girl Scouts' mission. In response to the tough questions, "What is our business? Who is our customer?" the Girl Scouts of the U.S.A. concluded that helping girls reach their highest potential was the basis of what the organization was about. This clarification of mission led to clear goals and operating objectives. The Girl Scouts, for example, rejected pressures from women's rights groups who desired its support because it judged the support unrelated to the newly defined mission.

Following mission clarification, throughout the 1980s, marketing research was conducted to determine what would attract more members and how to retain the interests of teenage girls. Under the direction of the current National Executive Director, Mary Rose Main, the organization remains committed to marketing research as a means of improving its efforts. In 1993, for example, the Girl Scouts commissioned a study of perceptions about Girl Scouting in different communities nationwide. The study, *Toward a Broader Understanding of Racial and Ethnic Diversity in Girl Scouting*, has provided data to support efforts toward even greater diversity in membership.

Research findings have shaped the look of the new Girl Scouts. Girls were found to want a greater emphasis on science, business, and the environment. In response, proficiency badges in these areas have been developed. Furthermore, in 1993 the Girl Scouts of the U.S.A. began a three-year project, funded in part by the National Science Foundation, the goal of which is to promote interest in science among girls aged 8 to 13. Science museums in six states will sponsor special programs for the girls.

After reviewing findings that indicated that teenage girls did not find scouting relevant to their needs, programs were overhauled. Date rape, incest, AIDS, suicide, and eating disorders are only a few of the topics addressed in Girl Scouting today. Barbara Alderson, Executive Director of the San Diego-Imperial Girl Scouting Council states, "We want to address those things because if we can't, we're not doing our job." In addition to adding programs to increase retention of older scouts, the Girl Scouts of the U.S.A. have established a new level in Girl Scouting after learning that interest was strong in younger girls. Kindergarten-aged girls are now introduced to girl scouting through Daisy Girl Scouts, a level that precedes Brownie Girl Scouts, traditionally the first step in Girl Scouting. Uniforms at all levels have been redesigned after research indicated many girls were put off by the traditional Girl Scouting uniforms.

Delivery systems were also in radical need of an overhaul. Unable to establish troops in many neighborhoods where a tradition of Girl Scouting did not exist, Girl Scouts instituted Girl Scout Groups. Groups meet for short periods of time (perhaps 4 to 6 weeks) and then disband. This delivery system has made it easier to attract adult volunteers because the demand on their time is shorter. Some Girl Scout Councils hold troop or group meetings during school hours.

N ot long ago well-run, not-for-profit organizations like the Girl Scouts of the U.S.A. were rare exceptions. Not-for-profit organizations and governmental agencies were neither experienced nor comfortable with marketing. Today, the use of marketing in the social sector of our economy has grown significantly. Successful social sector marketer is no longer an oxymoron. Not-for-profit organizations are created for a purpose other than making a profit. They comprise an important part of what is called the **social sector,** or **public sector,** of our economy.[1] Additionally, the social sector includes government agencies. The social sector is also called the **concept sector** because most of the "products" that emanate from this sector of our economy are intangibles, particularly ideas.[2] The organizations and agencies that make up the social sector differ from companies in the commercial (for-profit) sector in several important ways. Such organizations, however, need to follow the same steps that a profit-oriented organization would follow in developing and implementing a marketing program. For example, Henry Ford Health Care Corporation, in the Detroit area, uses secondary research into demographics and patients' histories to forecast demand. The organization targets the inner-city and has developed programs (products) and delivery systems (distribution) to meet the needs of its target market.[3]

The same techniques used by private, for-profit companies can be used by government agencies, hospitals, charitable organizations, museums, and the arts to achieve their objectives. In this chapter, we study the characteristics of social sector organizations and how they differ from profit-making firms, focusing on how these differences affect marketing strategies. Because social sector marketing is a relatively new application in marketing, we briefly consider its history, growth, and development. We also consider the use of marketing techniques in the somewhat unique application of fund-raising. Finally, since many organizations have begun to recognize the contribution that marketing can make to an organization's effectiveness, we consider ways in which not-for-profit organizations and government agencies can introduce marketing into their operations.

THE NATURE, SCOPE, AND HISTORY OF SOCIAL SECTOR MARKETING

Social sector marketing includes marketing performed by not-for-profit organizations and government groups and agencies, and marketing techniques used to promote ideas and social causes. Examples of social sector marketing include marketing applied to intangible goods or services such as education, health care, entertainment, and religion, or to ideas or viewpoints such as prevention of forest fires, the use of seat belts, the prevention of cruelty to animals, and the importance of practicing safer sex. Social sector marketers also market tangible goods such as Girl Scout cookies, but this is not so common as marketing services or ideas. Marketers have used a variety of terms to refer to social sector marketing. **Nonprofit marketing, not-for-profit marketing,** and **nonbusiness marketing** are all common. In addition, when marketing techniques are used in association with ideas or social causes the term **social marketing** is frequently used. In this book we use the term *social sector marketing* because it encompasses more than the other terms.

Although no definitive sources exist that specifically measure the social sector as it is defined in this chapter, by all available measures the sector is enormous. Estimates suggest that there are more than 1.4 million not-for-profit organizations in the United States.[4] The public or governmental component of the social sector is even larger. Table 20.1 lists five industries that are heavily dominated by not-for-profit organizations and their sizes on three measures: number of establishments, number of employees, and payroll size.

Industry	Establishments	Employees	Payroll (in billions)
Museums and zoos	3,521	66,157	$ 1.2
Religious organizations	139,085	1,143,374	$ 11.1
Civic and social organizations	43,422	384,560	$ 4.1
Social services	124,833	1,861,985	$ 23.3
Hospitals	6,571	4,466,142	$108.6

Source: Economics and Statistics Administration, United States Department of Commerce, Washington, DC, 1991 figures which represent the most recent available data in mid-1994.

TABLE 20.1
Five Social Sector Industries

The social sector has lagged behind the commercial or business sector in marketing activities and expenditures. The social sector, however, will undoubtedly increase its spending on marketing as not-for-profit and governmental agencies continue to see how effective marketing is in helping them to achieve their goals and objectives. The realization that high ideals and dedicated volunteers may not be enough has begun to pervade not-for-profit organizations.[5] As we saw in the Marketing Profile, not-for-profit groups that have embraced marketing are enjoying considerable success.

Twenty-five years ago the suggestion that social sector organizations, such as police departments, countries, and museums, engage in marketing was met with resistance and denial.[6] Not-for-profit "purists" regarded the idea of business activities in their organizations as "near-obscenity." According to John R. Garrison, president of the National Easter Seal Society, "Some nonprofit people used to think that if you're doing good, somehow God will provide."[7] For many not-for-profit agencies, marketing had long been associated with corporate insensitivity, hence negative feelings about incorporating it into their organizations was understandable.[8] As the "Marketing in Action: Amnesty International Injects Pizzazz into Its Marketing Approach" illustrates, some organizations continue to move slowly and cautiously when it comes to marketing. The "taint of commercialism" is still a concern of many not-for-profit groups.

Although social sector practitioners may be reluctant to accept the notion of business in their organizations, the concept of exchange is generally more palatable. Hence social sector marketing applications have grown with the realization that the concept of exchange is the basis of marketing in the social sector, just as it is in marketing goods and services in the commercial sector. The nature of what is exchanged between a social sector marketer and his or her "customers," however, is quite different from the average exchange in the commercial sector. Kotler and Andreasen[9] define the products that could be offered by any organization (for-profit or not-for-profit) in terms of the benefits that a consumer receives from an exchange. There are three basic kinds of benefits:

1. *Economic.* In this case, the benefit could be a tangible good or a service. A consumer receives an economic benefit when he or she purchases a new car.
2. *Social.* This would be a benefit to the larger community as a result of an individual's contribution. Each contribution to the American Cancer Society brings us all closer to a cancer cure.
3. *Psychological.* Here the benefit to the individual is personal satisfaction. A blood donor feels good about himself or herself after donating blood.

In turn, the "price" an organization "charges" for these benefits also varies, for example:

1. Sacrifices of money or something of economic value.
2. Sacrifices of old ideas, values, or views of the world; giving up existing beliefs.
3. Sacrifices of old patterns of behavior; giving up existing ways of doing things.
4. Sacrifices of time and energy; allocating effort or time to obtain a benefit.

Table 20.2 identifies various types of exchanges that could occur within an assortment of products and payments. Commercial organizations typically operate in only the first two cells in the upper left-hand corner of the table. Social sector marketers, however, are regularly involved in all of the exchanges described in the table. The challenge to a social sector marketer's skills and creativity should be evident as you consider the diversity illustrated.

In addition to a growing acceptance of the concept of exchange and marketing's role in facilitating exchanges, several other factors account for the rise in social sector marketing activities.[10] These include competition, financial pressures, politics, changing technological and social patterns, and newly found self-confidence.

Competition.   Perhaps more than any factor, the increased competition most social sector marketers face now requires them to investigate somewhat more aggressive means of accomplishing their goals and objectives. Hospitals, for example, traditionally benefitted from an exclusive relationship with physicians that left patients without choices when it came to health care. In recent years, however, the patient/consumer is faced with a myriad of alternatives from hospitals offering different services and conveniences, health maintenance organizations, ready-care clinics, and a variety of other health-care delivery systems. The hospital that hopes to continue attracting patients in this new, competitive environment must look to becoming more marketing oriented.

Financial pressures.   Both government agencies and not-for-profit organizations have found themselves faced with increasing financial pressures over the last two decades. Taxes are often unable to keep up with the needs of government-sponsored groups, and politicians are understandably very reluctant to continue raising taxes. Not-for-profit organizations find it more and more difficult to generate sufficient

TABLE 20.2
Cost/Benefit Matrix for the Profit/Not-for Profit Sectors

Costs	Benefits			
	A Product	**A Service**	**Social**	**Psychological**
Give up economic assets	Buy a poster	Pay for surgery or an education	Donate to alma mater	Donate to charity
Give up old ideas, values, opinions	Receive free Goodwill clothing	Support neighborhood vigilantes	Support Republicans	Oppose abortion
Give up old behaviors, undertake or learn new behaviors	Practice birth control and receive a radio	Undertake drug detoxification treatment	Go to geriatric group once a week	Wear seat belts
Give up time or energy	Participate in a study and receive a coffeemaker	Attend a free concert	Volunteer for Junior League	Give blood

Source: P. Kotler and A. Andreasen, *Strategic Marketing for Nonprofit Organizations*, 4th ed., Prentice Hall, 1991, p. 27.

MARKETING *IN ACTION*

Amnesty International Injects Pizzazz into Its Marketing Approach

Amnesty International has spent 30 years working to stop torture and execution throughout the world and to ensure fair and prompt trials of political prisoners. John G. Healey, executive director of the New York–based not-for-profit organization, realizes, however, that the message of Amnesty International may be a bit dry for many audiences. Therefore, the organization has begun introducing more pizzazz into its marketing efforts. Healey states, "We will use any nonviolent means to free prisoners. I'm pretty much up for anything that works." The organization, however, is moving slowly on building relationships with corporate sponsors. It expresses concern about the potential of "besmirching its stellar reputation with crass commercialism." Joint efforts aimed at directly benefitting both Amnesty International and a corporate sponsor's bottom line (termed *cause-related marketing*) appear unlikely. Healey states, "They're [corporations] in business to sell, and I don't want to sell tennis shoes for Reebok." Any organization interested in donating money or affiliating itself in any way with Amnesty International must agree to a thorough background check on factors like investments and working conditions.

The organization has attempted to carry its message to new audiences by aligning with pop musicians at rock concerts. In 1988 the "Human Rights Now!" tour featured a number of rock stars including Bruce Springsteen, Peter Gabriel, and Sting. The tour visited 20 locations on five continents. Amnesty International did concede to a small level of corporate support to cover a

He raised his hands, above his head and said, "You have the wrong man." In 1975, Paul Hill, a twenty-one year old man from Northern Ireland, was sentenced to a lifetime in prison for pub bombings in Britain. It was the longest such sentence by a British court. As the years were taken from him, Hill could do nothing but hold onto his innocence. Fifteen years later, including four years in solitary confinement, Hill was set free when the British government finally admitted that officers lied at the original trial. It might not have happened without the help of family, friends, and Amnesty International. Let no one tell you your hands are bound. Pick up a pen and raise your voice for those who can't. Join Amnesty and become a Freedom Writer. Call 1-800-55-AMNESTY. It's your human right.

A M N E S T Y   I N T E R N A T I O N A L

portion of the $26 million in costs associated with the tour. In exchange for $3 million, a tag line on concert programs read, "Made possible by the Reebok Foundation." Rock bands continued to tout the Amnesty International message in a tour of college campuses throughout 1992 and 1993.

The organization has increased its use of public service announcements (PSAs) in recent years. Calling on celebrities who support the cause, Amnesty International has aired PSAs featuring Robin Williams, Carly Simon, and Meryl Streep.

In a continued effort to reach new markets with its message, Amnesty International is also working closely with *Spin* magazine. Editor and publisher Bob Guccione, Jr., a strong supporter of the organization, was instrumental in linking Amnesty International and clothing manufacturer, Z. Cavaricci. The fashionable designer is sponsoring full-page ads for Amnesty International in *Spin*. Created by Vertical Advertising of Los Angeles, the ads are profiles of prisoners of conscience. The first featured Aung San Suu Kyi, a prisoner in Burma, and winner of the 1991 Nobel Peace Prize. Amnesty International, of course, hopes that the effort will raise awareness of existing organizational supporters as well as those who know little about Amnesty International. Publisher Guccione does believe that the ads will bring a new audience to Amnesty's work.

Although Amnesty International may be cautious as it expands its marketing, the organization is clearly aware of the value of such efforts in advancing its organizational mission.

donations in an environment that is increasingly competitive, while less generous in terms of tax deductions for donations.

Politics. Government agencies who must answer to taxpayers and not-for-profit groups who must answer to donors feel increased pressure to maximize their effectiveness. Donors and taxpayers alike are demanding that social sector organizations operate at maximum effectiveness and efficiency.

Changing technological and social patterns. The need for rapid behavioral changes by people is forcing social sector organizations to turn to marketing. As global warming becomes a reality, for example, governments and environmental organizations must implement marketing techniques to accomplish social changes such as decreased use of aerosol spray cans. Legislation can do only so much to effect behavioral change.

Newly found self-confidence. Two prominent scholars in the field of social sector marketing, Kotler and Andreasen, argue that marketing has continued to spread rapidly across the sector in the 1990s due to a newfound self-confidence on the part of the discipline itself.[11] As social sector marketers have become aware of its widespread application, proud of their successes, confident in their power to be effective, and challenged by the circumstances they face, the growth of marketing in the social sector has skyrocketed.

The tools used by social sector marketers are the same as those used in marketing consumer or business products. Because of the differences between the sectors, however, the applications are often different.

HOW DOES THE SOCIAL SECTOR DIFFER?

Five key differences have been identified between social sector organizations and profit-oriented organizations.[12] These differences help explain many of the special challenges of marketing in the social sector. Social sector organizations are characterized by multiple publics, nonprofit objectives, services rather than goods, customers' satisfaction, and public scrutiny.

Multiple publics. A marketing manager for a consumer or business product is concerned with the exchange relationship between the company and its target market. A social sector marketer, on the other hand, must be concerned with exchange relationships between the company and a number of different groups or publics.

Figure 20.1 illustrates some of the publics with which a university would engage in exchanges. As you can see, the university must "keep many balls in the air" at once when it comes to exchange.[13] The university provides educational services to its current students and receives dollars in return. It provides the use of the university facilities and dollars to faculty in return for teaching and research services. The university gives alumni gratitude, recognition, and a feeling of "doing good," and receives contributions of money or time in return. Students, faculty, and alumni are thus all treated as consumers. This is also true for the many other publics of the university. Of course, the products offered in these exchanges are not all tangible goods. Instead, they are services, feelings, ideas, and other nontraditional items. In turn, the university is receiving a variety of nontraditional payments: services, publicity, time. Nevertheless, exchanges are taking place.

The various publics with which most not-for-profit organizations interact fall into two categories—funders (those involved with attracting resources) and users

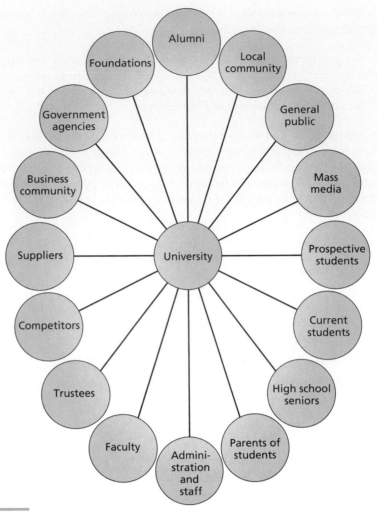

FIGURE 20.1
A University and Its Publics

Source: P. Kotler and A. Andreasen, *Strategic Marketing for Nonprofit Organizations,* 4th ed. (Prentice Hall, 1991), p. 90.

(those involved with allocating resources).[14] In Figure 20.1, graduates and the business community represent resource attraction while current and prospective students represent resource allocation (even though current students also give the university resources to pay for the services they receive). The American Cancer Society engages in fund-raising to attract resources and then provides many services in allocating its resources. It can be argued that businesses also have multiple publics, but their marketers are only involved in relationships of exchange with consumers. Although business firms must attract resources from the sale of stocks or bonds or the negotiation of loans from financial institutions, marketers are rarely involved in these exchanges.

Nonprofit objectives.   All marketing decisions should be evaluated in terms of ability to contribute to the organization's objectives. In a for-profit organization, strategies and tactics that contribute the most to the firm's profit are selected. Not-for-profit organizations have multiple objectives that do not involve profit. With multiple and often immeasurable objectives, it becomes difficult to evaluate alternative marketing programs and activities. For example, if a museum were deciding whether to enlarge its collection of Impressionist paintings or to add a room where children could create their own art works, the decision would depend on whether the museum were trying to increase total attendance (and revenues), maximize the satisfaction of visitors, or increase the educational value of a visit.

Services rather than physical goods.   Not-for-profit organizations are more involved in marketing services than they are in marketing physical goods. (Chapter 19 outlined the differences between the marketing of services and the marketing of physical products.) Marketers in not-for-profit organizations not only must adapt the marketing tools used by consumer-goods firms but also must make adjustments for the kind of products to be marketed. As one social sector commentator suggested, "It's not as easy to market counseling sessions as Nikes or Thunderbirds."[15]

Importance of customer satisfaction.   Often the objectives of not-for-profit organizations clash with consumers' preferences. A museum, for example, may define its mission as educating the public about various types of art. Patrons, on the other hand, prefer to view the work of familiar artists, which does not challenge their understanding. Offering programs that provide the greatest customer satisfaction may conflict with the organizational mission of the museum. Furthermore, because not-for-profit organizations typically possess separate publics for resource attraction and resource allocation, the short-term satisfaction of the resource-allocation public may not be critical to the healthy functioning of the organization. Both of these circumstances create an environment in which the importance of customer satisfaction may be viewed as less critical than it is in a for-profit organization.

Public scrutiny and nonmarket pressures.   Many social sector organizations and agencies are subject to close scrutiny because of their roles in providing public services. For example, the U.S. Postal Rate Commission's review of proposed price

The American Cancer Society engages in fund-raising to attract resources and then provides many services in allocating those resources.

increases for mail delivery illustrates how public hearings and testimonies from trade associations, special interest groups, and heavy users of mail services must all be involved in the price-setting process. In addition, not-for-profit organizations often are expected, or even required, to provide services or serve market segments that a profit-making organization would not find economical. The U.S. Postal Service is required to maintain rural post offices, and many mass transit companies are forced to maintain service on unprofitable routes.

Research indicates that the unique characteristics of the social sector do produce an environment with special marketing challenges, which include:[16]

1. Little, if any, data on consumer behavior is available. Secondary data regarding consumers' characteristics and behaviors relevant to social sector marketers is practically nonexistent.
2. Due to the nature of the issues in the social sector, reliable primary research data is difficult to obtain. Consumers are less likely to lie, for example, about their use of soft drinks than they are about their use of birth control.
3. Social sector marketers often find themselves asking for behavioral change in a situation where consumers are basically indifferent. For example, before social marketing could get you to conserve water, it must first convince you that you should care about this issue.
4. The behavioral changes asked for by social sector marketers are usually more dramatic than those desired by commercial-sector marketers. A commercial-sector marketer, for example, may ask a consumer to try a new brand of shampoo, a much simpler request than, say, asking consumers to practice safer sex. Marketers in the commercial sector can ignore consumers who are opposed to a product. Social sector marketers, however, are often trying to persuade people to accept and practice a behavior they resist. It's much easier to convince an individual to try a new brand of shampoo or soft drink than to practice safer sex or quit smoking.
5. Social sector marketers generally do not have the discretion to alter their product to accommodate the preferences of consumers. A soft drink manufacturer could make the drink sweeter if consumers so desired, but there is only one means of extracting blood from donors, no matter how much they dislike the needle.
6. The level of understanding, attitudes, and behaviors social sector marketers desire are often very complex in comparison to what is being asked of consumers by commercial-sector marketers. Trying a new soft drink because it tastes good and is refreshing is fairly straightforward. Sexual abstinence or practicing safer sex, on the other hand, requires an understanding of why the behavior is important, a positive attitude towards trying it, and a careful and detailed explanation of how to accomplish it.
7. The benefits to the consumer of social sector "products" are not always apparent. Having your thirst quenched is an obvious benefit of consuming a soft drink, but what is the obvious benefit of sexual abstinence or practicing safer sex? The consumer who engages in the behavior is presumably healthy to start with and will continue to be healthy—nothing has changed.
8. Social sector marketers often ask for sacrifices from consumers that benefit others far more than they benefit the individual. The 55-mile-per-hour speed limit, for example, produced energy savings that benefitted the government. It also caused consumers to take longer to get where they were going.[16]
9. Because many of the benefits offered by social sector marketers are social and psychological, it is difficult to communicate them through promotion. What could a symphony orchestra, for example, show in an advertisement that would illustrate the benefits of listening to a concert?[17]

MARKETING STRATEGIES FOR THE SOCIAL SECTOR

Marketing tools are just as applicable to social sector organizations as they are to organizations dedicated to making a profit. Strategic planning, an understanding of consumer behavior, market analysis, segmentation, product, distribution, pricing, and promotion strategies can be implemented effectively in such organizations.

Strategic Planning

When social sector organizations think of marketing, they sometimes consider only promotion. Not many managers (or volunteers) in not-for-profit organizations or governmental agencies think in terms of total marketing programs or in marketing language. For example, colleges tend to think in terms of educational programs, not products; tuition, not price; catalogues and brochures, not advertising or sales promotions; college recruiting, not personal selling; and branch campuses and correspondence courses, not distribution. In these cases, marketing is being applied at the tactical level rather than the strategic level. Churches, which have increasingly turned to promotion in the 1990s, also appear to be acting at the tactical rather than the strategic level. A church marketing consultant states, "Churches . . . have no idea who they're trying to reach or how to develop a strategy to reach them."[18]

Despite calls for not-for-profit agencies to increase their focus on strategic planning, many have made little progress in this regard.[19] This generally is the case because tactical approaches have a more immediate payoff for the organization and because many social sector organizations do not understand how to use or appreciate the necessity of implementing long-term strategic planning. The university with declining enrollment, for example, is likely to conclude that "doing marketing" (i.e., usually promotional activities) is the solution to its problem. With no strategic focus, however, any success is likely to be temporary.

The strategic planning process discussed in Chapter 3 is just as important to social sector organizations as it is to commercial-sector firms. The effectiveness of careful strategic planning was illustrated in the Marketing Profile. For the Girl Scouts, clarifying its mission and then using that mission as the guiding force of the planning process was crucial to the organization's success.

Commercial firms often use some type of portfolio analysis in their strategic planning. Many of the portfolio models discussed in Chapter 3 can be useful to social sector planners. Sometimes, however, models appropriate to for-profit firms that rely heavily on assessments of the firm's financial situation, market share, and so forth, are difficult to use with a not-for-profit organization whose bottom-line criteria are social rather than financial. Lovelock and Weinberg have suggested a portfolio model appropriate for not-for-profit organizations.[20] It is illustrated in Figure 20.2. This portfolio model challenges social sector marketers to consider their strategic business units in terms of the extent to which they advance the institutional mission, as well as whether they represent a cash drain or asset to the organization. This type of analysis can be extremely useful to the social sector marketer who is attempting to develop an overall strategic plan that includes advancement of organizational mission as well as financial solvency.

Understanding and accepting the importance of strategic planning is the critical first step for a social sector organization that wishes to embrace marketing and reap its benefits.

Consumer Behavior

Understanding consumer behavior is the basis of all marketing efforts. As we saw throughout Chapter 6, consumer behavior is unpredictable, inconsistent, and often not directly observable. Achieving an understanding of consumer behavior in the

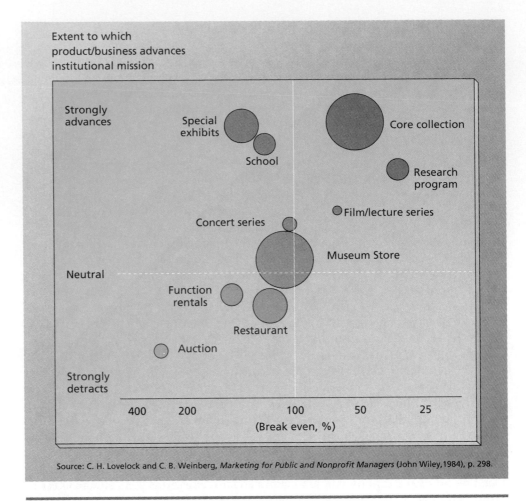

Source: C. H. Lovelock and C. B. Weinberg, *Marketing for Public and Nonprofit Managers* (John Wiley, 1984), p. 298.

FIGURE 20.2
Example of Portfolio Analysis for a Large Museum

social sector is doubly challenging because little secondary data is available and consumers are often reluctant to be straightforward with researchers on many of the sensitive issues addressed in the social sector. Despite these problems, social sector marketers must study the behavior of their consumers if they hope to develop successful marketing efforts. One social sector behavior that has been studied is blood donation.[21] Researchers have found that external factors such as reference group behavior and situational factors such as where the individual is when asked to donate can help explain an individual's likelihood to donate. Employees asked to donate at work, for example, are more likely to do so, especially if their co-workers are donating.

Market Analysis

Careful and conscientious marketing requires judicious use of marketing research. Market-driven organizations must acquire marketing information. Not-for-profit organizations, however, do much less research than they should.[22] Andreasen attributes this fact to five myths about research:

1. *The big decision myth* is the belief that it's only right to do research when it's something big. An organization might, for example, believe that research is justified if it is considering a site relocation or an across-the-board increase in client

fees. On the other hand, it may feel that relying on direct-mail promotion rather than advertising is a decision supported by historical precedence and not something worth planning a research study to investigate.

2. *The survey myopia myth* is the belief that a survey is the only legitimate type of marketing research. Surveys can be expensive and time-consuming so this attitude would seem to rule out research under many circumstances. In reality, many other forms of research may provide insight for an organization.

3. *The big bucks myth* is the belief that if you don't spend a lot of money, the research can't possibly be worth anything. This often stops an organization from doing research.

4. *The sophisticated researcher myth* is the belief that marketing research involves carrying out and understanding complex technical and statistical analyses and other processes that are beyond the knowledge base of the organization.

5. *The most research is not read myth* is the belief that it isn't worth bothering since "most research is not read anyway."[23]

Social sector marketers who get beyond these five myths still may run into problems. As noted, secondary data is generally not available and primary research is difficult to conduct. Consumers are reluctant to respond to many of the issues social sector marketers raise. Also, it is sure to be more difficult for consumers to explain why they gave money to a charity, what they expect from their churches, or what they expect from their hospitals.[24] Such questions require an individual to describe complex feelings and are much harder to discuss than desirable features in an automobile or camera.

Despite these challenges, many social sector marketers have successfully used marketing research techniques in their marketing planning. The Houston Grand Opera, for example, carried out a research study to determine whether a decrease in season subscription prices was warranted. After gathering and analyzing the data, the opera concluded that its decision to decrease prices was wrong. The research indicated that a price cut would not attract additional subscriptions. Instead, selective price increases were implemented.[25]

Segmentation

We know that meeting the needs of consumers is generally best accomplished by recognizing differences among them. Social sector marketers, however, frequently take an undifferentiated approach to segmentation. They may believe that their population is all similar, they may feel that it is inappropriate to focus efforts on only subsets of the overall population, or they may not have the resources to carry out segmentation. Whatever the reasons, in almost every instance the organization would be better able to accomplish its objectives and advance its mission if it did apply segmentation.

Not-for-profit organizations who have implemented segmentation strategies have typically found success. For example, many colleges treat all of their graduates equally in their fund-raising efforts. Stanford University, however, identifies different segments of alumni and develops separate marketing programs for each group.[26] The fund-raising effort first categorizes alumni by school (college, business school, medical school, etc.) and year of graduation. These groups are divided into subgroups according to their estimated potential for donations—$1000 or more, $100–$999, and less than $100. Personal contact is then used to solicit donations from the first two groups; mail solicitation is used to request funds from those likely to give less than $100. The last group is further divided into seven segments based on when the alumnus last donated money to Stanford, whether it was the first time he or she gave, and whether the amount was more or less than $25. Five letters are sent to those who gave more than $25 the year before for the first time, and only two letters are sent

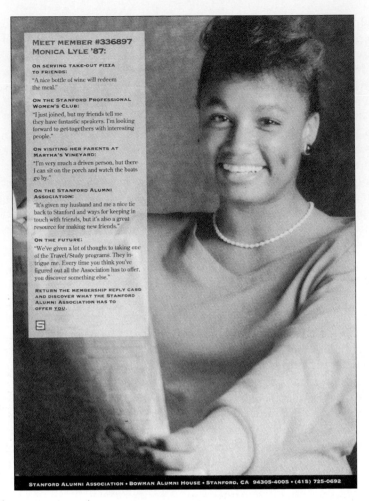

Stanford University identifies different segments of alumni and develops separate marketing programs for each group.

to those who have never given. The letters sent to each of the groups contain different messages and appeals.

Social sector organizations can use the whole range of segmentation bases and variables discussed in Chapter 5. As seen in the Stanford example, demographics such as year of graduation, and responsiveness factors such as potential to give can be very useful. Psychographic factors, such as extent of school spirit, could further define various segments.

REVIEW

YOUR MARKETING KNOWLEDGE

You have just been named director of marketing for a small, rural college that is struggling to attract sufficient students. Review the reasons students have for choosing a college.

20-1   How could these reasons help develop programs to attract students?

20-2   What marketing methods would be most appropriate for attracting students to your school?

Product

Social sector marketers are more likely to market services and ideas rather than physical goods. It is no less important, however, for government and not-for-profit marketers to define their products broadly, including such things as brand, packaging, and warranty. How the product is positioned plays a critical part in how it should be promoted, distributed, and priced. The concepts of product line, product mix, and product life cycle are as important for social sector organizations as they are for businesses.

A critical ingredient in product strategy is, of course, a definition of what the customer wants to buy. The U.S. Postal Service has conducted a substantial amount of research to determine what its customers want to buy and, based on that research, developed a series of new products. Recognizing that consumers really were buying the ability to transmit communications (rather than mail service), the postal service has developed and introduced Express Mail overnight delivery service (with money-back guarantee if not delivered the next day) and Zip + 4 Presort Mail for large mailers willing to sort their outgoing mail by nine-digit zip codes in return for a postage discount. These products have been branded and are heavily promoted to businesses. Other products developed by the U.S. Postal Service include stamp albums, first day covers, and commemorative stamps. The extent to which the Postal Service is willing to go in satisfying consumers' preferences was seen in 1992 when a national poll was conducted to determine whether a young Elvis Presley or an older Elvis Presley should appear on the Post Office's Elvis commemorative stamp.

Many not-for-profit organizations have increased their attention to their product mix. Universities have offered new product lines to meet the demand for degree programs in such new areas as information systems and health technology.

The U.S. Postal Service has conducted a substantial amount of research to determine what its customers want to buy. Based on that research, the Postal Service has developed a series of new products, including stamp albums, first day covers, and commemorative stamps.

Noncredit adult education courses of all types have been added and product lines such as MBA programs have been revised and expanded through the addition of evening programs and Executive MBA programs taught on weekends. Zoos have altered product mixes by adding categories of animals and more animals within each category as well as educational classes and programs. The San Diego Zoological Society offers classes to all age levels, including a KinderZoo program targeted at children aged 4 to 6 years. It also offers a program called "Snore and Roar" that allows families to spend the night camping in the zoo.

The product of many social sector organizations is an idea. Planned Parenthood, an organization that has been hailed for its successful strategic planning and marketing skills, understands the concept of idea as product very clearly. In fact the organization's past president, Faye Wattleton, had specifically stated, "I am selling our ideas, that is the product."[27] Not all social sector marketers understand the concept of idea as product quite so clearly.

When the product being marketed by a social sector organization is an idea or social cause, the effort is termed *social marketing*. Social marketing has been described as the most controversial of marketing applications.[28] Many critics contend that using marketing to promote social causes is unethical. Using marketing techniques to promote social causes that may be unpopular or in conflict with the views of some members of society is generally the basis of the controversy. For example, those who support the right to abortion and those who oppose it are likely to object to each others' use of marketing. It is important, when evaluating social marketing efforts, to try to separate the marketing techniques from the issue. Marketing techniques are themselves ethically neutral, and marketers cannot be accountable for how the techniques are applied.[29]

To keep the issue of social marketing in perspective, consider that marketing is in fact only one of a variety of means of accomplishing desired behavioral changes within society. Fox and Kotler identified four methods of achieving behavior change:[30]

1. *Legal.* With this method, change is legislated. For example, when the government wanted drivers to slow down, the legal speed limit was reduced from 70 to 55 miles per hour.
2. *Technological.* Here, new technologies that make it easier to change behavior are developed. For example, automobiles have breathalyzers built into the ignition system as a curb to driving under the influence of alcohol.
3. *Economic.* Monetary sanctions are used to encourage the behavioral change. For example, drivers who practice safe driving techniques may be eligible for reduced insurance premiums.
4. *Informational.* This approach employs marketing techniques to persuade consumers to change their behaviors. For example, organizations such as MADD (Mothers Against Drunk Driving) have attempted, through marketing, to convince consumers not to drink alcohol and drive motor vehicles.

Distribution

Because social sector marketers must distribute a variety of product types (tangible goods, services, and ideas), the diversity of their distribution challenges is considerable. Not-for-profits and governmental agencies who market tangible goods (such as Girl Scout cookies or postage stamps) face the same distribution decisions as do for-profit marketers of goods. Organizations must determine what, if any, intermediaries to employ in their channels of distribution, what intensity of market coverage to offer, and what means of physical distribution is best to help meet their objectives.

Most social sector marketers market services, hence, most channels of distribution in this sector of the economy are very short. The channel for services typically goes directly from producer to consumer without intermediaries. Thus, Planned Parenthood markets its information and services directly to consumers, colleges work directly with students and potential students, and museums and performing arts organizations deal directly with their patrons. Occasionally intermediaries are involved. For example, some performing arts organizations have independent firms market their tickets, and certain charities hire professional fund-raisers to implement programs for soliciting contributions.

Intensity of distribution is a very important issue for social sector marketers of services. The easier it is to donate money, for example, the more money will be donated. Thus, the Salvation Army is extremely successful in its fund-raising efforts during the Christmas season by accepting donations on many street corners around town. Universities have added branches in suburban areas, at corporate headquarters, and even on commuter trains. Symphony orchestras have tours that take concerts to people in rural areas and make recordings to distribute their music. Libraries have established branches in shopping malls and use large vans to create mobile branches throughout many cities. The U.S. Postal Service has opened self-service branches in the parking lots of many shopping centers. These facilities are open 24 hours a day and no employees are necessary. Stamps can also be purchased by mail. Figure 20.3 identifies the intensity of distribution alternatives that a social sector marketer might consider. The facilities from which the service is performed as well as the service itself are considered. The trend in delivery of social services has been away from exclusive distribution and more toward selective or intensive distribution. This movement suggests that social-service organizations are increasingly responsive to the needs of their consumers, that is, more market driven.[31]

FIGURE 20.3
Intensity of Distribution Alternatives

		Services		
		Intensive	Selective	Exclusive
Facilities	Intensive	Street lights Storm sewers Roads Neighborhood playgrounds	Supervised play at selected neighborhood playgrounds	Performing arts program in the major city park Interpretive nature programs
	Selective	Police Fire Welfare workers	Community health care Parks Schools Adult education classes Libraries Community centers	Blood donor drive Public agency day camps
	Exclusive	Garbage collection Housing inspectors Health inspectors College courses via mail or public TV	Bookmobiles	Hospitals Universities Judicial courts City Hall Zoo Animal shelter

Source: C. W. Lamb, Jr., and J. L. Crompton, "Distributing Public Services: A Strategic Approach," *Journal of the Academy of Marketing Science,* Summer 1985, p. 215.

It is desirable to distribute a product in locations attractive to consumers, but this is not always possible with social sector organizations. Many hospitals, performing arts organizations, and government agencies are saddled with physical structures in downtown locations that are unattractive to the suburban part of their market. Because the cost of creating new facilities in the suburbs would be prohibitive, the other parts of the marketing program must be designed to overcome the disadvantage created by the distribution of the product.

When the product being marketed by a social sector organization is an idea or cause, the distribution component of the marketing mix is often difficult to separate from the promotional strategy. Choice of media, specifically, could be argued to be either a promotion decision or a distribution decision. Although either view is acceptable, we will discuss this decision in the promotion section of the chapter.

Pricing

Pricing in social sector organizations is often determined differently from that in profit-oriented businesses. The differences between the two groups relate to their objectives. Often, for not-for-profit groups, the objective in setting a price is recovery of costs, and there are times when prices are set knowing that even this will not be accomplished. For example, tuition at public colleges and universities often covers less than one-third of the cost of educating a student. Performing arts organizations seldom cover their costs through ticket sales; they must rely upon grants and contributions from foundations, businesses, and individuals. If prices for buses and subways were set to cover operating costs, many individuals would not be able to afford to ride them.

It is also important to recognize that prices charged by social sector organizations involve more than money. Nonmonetary costs include time, effort, inconvenience, and pride. Alcoholics Anonymous, for example, charges a very high price—a public commitment to stop drinking and an admission of a drinking problem in front of one's peers.[32] Because the price of a good or service affects consumers' perceptions of it, social sector marketers must be careful not to undercharge in an effort to accomplish their mission. The San Diego Humane Society, for example, charges $37.50 to adopt a kitten or puppy. While the organization might be able to charge less and cover its costs through donations, it feels that the price will imbue new pet owners with a sense of commitment to their pets. Charging too low a price might cause a consumer to undervalue the pet and not care for it properly.

The nonmonetary components of the price equation are of particular concern to social marketers. In such cases, monetary cost is likely to be minimal or nonexistent. Perceived costs of "buying an idea," however, may be great, making the "product" "too expensive" for the targeted group. Table 20.3 provides an example of the perceived costs to a variety of target segments of adopting the idea of safer sex. Some economic price is involved, but the majority of the price in each exchange is nonmonetary.[33]

Promotion

Promotion is the one marketing mix factor that most social sector organizations use. Symphonies, theater groups, and the United Way as well as government agencies such as the Armed Forces have advertised for many years. In 1992 the federal government spent more than $331 million on its paid and public service advertising campaigns. In 1992 the federal government ranked number 34 on the list of the top 100 advertisers in the United States.[34] Other social sector organizations such as churches, hospitals, and social welfare groups have only more recently used this tool.

Social Exchange Approach	Type of Public			
	Input (condom manufacturers)	Internal (student volunteers)	Intermediary (university administrators)	Consuming (college students)
Use of condoms (technological)	1. Monetary if manufacturer gives away 2. Time to plan program	1. Time to disseminate information 2. Psychic—embarrassment alienation	1. Monetary to develop program 2. Psychic—angry parents 3. Time to plan/ implement	1. Monetary if not given away 2. Psychic—machismo embarrassment fear of rejection 3. Time interruption
Promotion of less promiscuity (informational)	1. Monetary if involved in program 2. Time to plan	1. Time to disseminate information 2. Psychic—embarrassment alienation	1. Monetary to develop program 2. Psychic—angry parents 3. Time to plan/ implement	1. Psychic—machismo femininity frustration fear of rejection 2. Energy restraint
Free STD screens (economic)	1. Monetary if involved in program 2. Time to plan	1. Time to disseminate information 2. Psychic—embarrassment alienation	1. Monetary to develop program 2. Psychic—angry parents 3. Time to plan/ implement	1. Psychic—fear of test positivity admission of life-style 2. Time to be tested

Source: M. L. Joyce and M. H. Morris, "Pricing Considerations in Social Marketing," in S. H. Fine, *Social Marketing*, Allyn and Bacon, 1990, p. 110.

TABLE 20.3
Perceived Costs of Social Exchange Programs Across Various Types of Public (A Safe-Sex Example)

Often these latecomers have come on strong, however. Several ads created by the Church Ad Project are shown on the following page. Although many not-for-profit groups and government agencies have used advertising, personal selling, public relations, and/or sales promotion, very few have developed strong communications programs that integrate all aspects of the promotion mix.

Advertising. Many not-for-profit organizations use **public service announcements (PSAs)**. PSAs are advertisements run by the media as a public service, at no cost to the advertiser. The not-for-profit agency, however, is responsible for production costs associated with development of the advertisement. Unfortunately, many PSA

Social sector organizations such as churches, hospitals, and social welfare groups have started to use promotion. These ads were created by the Church Ad Project.

campaigns are not effective, for a number of reasons.[35] Few public service advertisers pretest their ads. The ads are often created by committees, without clear objectives and no clear media strategy. The advertiser has no say about when or where the PSAs are run—they could be on TV in the daytime or in the middle of the night, and in magazines or newspapers, they go wherever there is space available. Because the number of not-for-profits requesting PSAs has increased, less time is given to each organization. This results in the ads not running with enough frequency to have much impact. Furthermore, often the not-for-profit does not have enough money to produce high-quality ads.

An exception to the problems of PSAs cited above are campaigns produced by the Advertising Council of America for not-for-profit organizations promoting social causes. The Advertising Council accepts several causes each year and solicits donated services from advertising agencies and media to prepare and broadcast the advertising. The Ad Council is financed by commercial-sector firms. The "Marketing in Action: Happy 50th Anniversary Advertising Council" describes the origins of the

Ad Council and some of its memorable campaigns. Over its 50-year lifetime, an estimated $64 billion in media time and space has been donated to Advertising Council campaigns.[36] Not-for-profit organizations and social causes lucky enough to be chosen by the Advertising Council are the beneficiaries of advertising campaigns that rival any produced by or for firms in the commercial sector.

Personal selling.   Many charitable organizations find that a small proportion of their donors contribute a large portion of the total funds raised. In such a case the organization will typically use personal selling to reach the large contributors. College alumni directors personally "sell" large contributors on their school, and the same holds true for fund-raisers in organizations such as the American Cancer Society, the United Negro College Fund, the Humane Society, and museums and performing arts organizations. The U.S. Army uses personal selling to recruit new soldiers. Certain religious groups use missionaries to sell their religions. College admissions personnel engage in personal selling when they visit high schools to recruit students. Kotler suggests that personal selling should be called *personal contact* in not-for-profit organizations.[37] It is crucial for social sector marketers to recognize that any staff person or volunteer that comes in contact with the publics of the organization is performing an important personal selling task.

Sales promotion.   Sales promotion can also be important for social sector marketers. The New Museum of Contemporary Art in New York held a fund-raiser that featured a limited edition of a T-shirt by artist Felix Gonzales. The shirt sold for $50. Rainforest Alliance held a celebrity auction where one of the items sold was Madonna's sequined brassiere.[38] A family planning agency operating in India offered a free set of pots and pans with each vasectomy it performed. Brochures, films, special events, contests, and catalogues can all be effective sales promotion tools.

Public relations.   Many not-for-profit marketers have become adept at getting publicity for their organizations by staging "events." Greenpeace, an environmental group, received press and media coverage for its cause by staging a protest at the Time-Life building in New York City. The organization was protesting *Time* magazine's use of "unhealthy paper." Not-for-profits have been encouraged to enhance their public relations by nurturing the press.[39] Public relations has the advantage for the social sector organization of not only being free, but also being perceived as more credible and more "appropriate" for not-for-profits because it doesn't carry the same "taint of commercialism" that advertising is sometimes seen as possessing.

20-3   Why do many not-for-profit organizations concentrate most of their marketing efforts in the promotion area?

20-4   How could a hospital use distribution and pricing concepts effectively? How might a public hospital go about adding products to its product mix?

YOUR
MARKETING
KNOWLEDGE

MARKETING *IN ACTION*

Happy 50th Anniversary Advertising Council

The Advertising Council of America celebrated its 50th anniversary in 1992. Founded in 1942 as the War Advertising Council, its value today is every bit as strong as it was at its inception. The council was originally proposed in 1941 as a means of responding to advertising industry critics. By developing advertising campaigns to promote not-for-profit organizations and social causes, "the critics of advertising will all be on the sending end, too, and they will all be on our side," according to James Webb Young, who originally proposed the Council. Mr. Young, clearly a visionary, foresaw that advertising would play an integral role in the promotion of governments, schools, and churches, and help wipe out disease and serve the arts. Shortly after Young's proposal was made, the United States entered World War II and the concept was quickly adopted with a focus on wartime issues. The council created several enormously successful campaigns during the war. These included A Slip of Your Lip Will Sink a Ship (urging U.S. citizens not to divulge information that might help the enemy) and The Kid in Upper Four (a campaign encouraging citizens to remember and communicate with soldiers overseas).

Because of the success enjoyed by the War Advertising Council, then President Franklin D. Roosevelt urged the Ad Council to continue its work after the war, concentrating on issues of national concern. Adopting the simple postwar name, Ad Council, the not-for-profit organization has continued to score success after success despite a sometimes rocky and controversial history. The controversies have stemmed from the fact that few social issues since World War II have garnered the degree of uniform support that the war effort enjoyed. For example, Ad Council campaigns surrounding the Vietnam War in 1970 drew sharply divided public reaction. A 1971 Ad Council campaign designed to promote support for Vietnam veterans and families of U.S. prisoners raised a storm of controversy and diverse opinions.

Throughout the years and the controversies, however, the Ad Council has continued to grow and produce outstanding advertising campaigns aimed at many sensitive issues. In the late 1970s the Ad Council attacked the national disgrace of child abuse. Advertisements begged Americans to Help Destroy a Family Tradition and informed us that Child Abuse Hurts Everybody. Between 1976 and 1982, the number of Americans who believed child abuse to be a major social problem increased from one in ten to nine out of ten, according to a Harris poll conducted in 1982. Having accomplished the important objective of awareness the Ad Council continued throughout the 1980s to focus on the issue by offering solutions. Advertisements advised parents to Stop. Take Time Out. Don't Take It Out on Your Kids and one memorable effort by the Council offered Twelve Alternatives to Lashing Out at Your Kid.

The Advertising Council has developed many other memorable and effective campaigns. A few of them are Only You can Prevent Forest

Fires with Smokey the Bear; A Mind Is a Terrible Thing to Waste for the United Negro College Fund; and Take a Bite Out of Crime featuring McGruff, the crime dog, for the National Crime Prevention Council.

With 50 years under its belt, the Ad Council has no intention of resting on its laurels. Ad Council President Ruth A. Wooden is committed to continuing to increase total donated media (estimated at $600 million in 1993) and to carrying out a series of innovative research studies on the effectiveness of public service advertising. In 1994 the Ad Council began using interactive television to measure viewers' opinions on important social issues. This allows the Ad Council not only to test the effectiveness of its ads but also to measure consumer sentiment regarding what social issues should receive attention. Wooden agrees with critics who describe the Ad Council as "the best public relations for business [the business of advertising]." She knows, however, and is anxious to point out, that it is also much more. She states, "It's a wonder to me that some of the most competitive businesspeople in the world leave the hatchets outside our conference room every day and work to move mountains, not because of what's in it for them but because the mountains are there."

FUND-RAISING

Early in this chapter, we described not-for-profit marketers as facing two types of publics—those involved with attraction of resources and those involved with allocation of resources. Resource-attraction publics consist of those who support the organization by providing funding that would not come from the sales of goods and services. Because few donors seek out an organization in order to donate money, not-for-profit organizations must engage in fund-raising activities. The marketing tools and techniques required to raise funds for an organization are no different from the tools and techniques to facilitate exchanges with the resource-allocation publics. An organization must do research, develop a segmentation strategy, and then plan appropriate marketing mixes for each segment. Many not-for-profit organizations, however, see their fund-raising activities as separate from their marketing activities directed at clients. Fund-raising, sometimes called development activities, is often under the direction of a separate department that may communicate only minimally with the marketing people in the organization.

But fund-raising is not a separate or different activity from marketing within social sector organizations. A brief example should serve to emphasize that the marketing efforts an organization undertakes to raise funds are the same types of efforts that must be expended to accomplish any facilitation of exchange.

Researchers used the concept of benefit segmentation to analyze and segment the market for fund-raising.[40] In the study, consumers were divided into segments based on the primary benefit they hoped to attain by giving to a charity. Five distinct segments were identified in the study:

1. *Managers*. These individuals are concerned primarily with supporting a charity that is well run, excels in administrative functions, provides services efficiently, and engages in research.
2. *Low involvement*. These individuals are fairly indifferent to any concerns about the organization itself and how it is run.
3. *Skeptics*. These individuals possess a negative attitude toward fund-raisers and resent any sign of pressure to give.
4. *Guardians*. These individuals are concerned with avoiding controversy that would have a negative impact on an organization's activities.
5. *Crusaders*. These individuals have high loyalty to the organization's mission. This segment gives the most money.

Once an organization has identified the various segments in its resource-attraction population, it can design marketing programs to maximize the contributions from each segment. Table 20.4 gives examples of fund-raising methods that might be used to obtain contributions from four segments of the market.

Cause-Related Marketing

Cause-related marketing is an activity undertaken by private, for-profit companies that is designed to increase the firm's sales and profits while also benefitting a not-for-profit organization. For example, in late 1993, Jenny Craig International, the weight management company, contributed $10 to the Susan G. Komen Breast Cancer Foundation for each new participant who enrolled in the company's weight management program.[41] Growth of this technique has produced a new source of resource attraction for not-for-profit marketers. As cutbacks in government subsidies, mergers and acquisitions, and economic recession have reduced the philanthropic activities of corporations, cause-related marketing has provided a means for not-for-profit organizations to continue benefitting from the generosity of corporate sponsors.[42]

Mass anonymous	Charity cans in stores	Raffles
Small gifts	Direct mail	Rummage sales
	Door-to-door solicitation	Sporting events
	Street and sidewalk solicitation	Tours
	TV and radio marathons	Walkathons, readathons,
	Thrift shops	bikeathons, danceathons,
	Plate passing	jogathons, swimathons
		Yearbooks
Members and their friends	Anniversary celebrations	Dances
	Art shows	Dinners, suppers, lunches, breakfasts
	Auctions	Fairs
	Benefits (theater, movies, sports events)	Fashion shows
		Parties in unusual places
	Bingo games	Telethons
	Book sales	
	Cake sales	
Affluent citizens	Convocations	Parlor meetings
	Dinners (invitational and/or testimonial)	Telephone calls from high-status individuals
	Letters from high-status individuals	
Wealthy donors	Bequests	Testimonial dinner for wealthy individuals
	Celebrity grooming	
	Committee visit to person's home, office	Wealthy person invited to another's home or club
	Memorials	

Source: P. Kotler and A. Andreasen, *Strategic Marketing for Nonprofit Organizations*, 4th ed., Prentice Hall, 1991. Reprinted by permission of Prentice Hall, Inc., Englewood Cliffs, NJ.

**TABLE 20.4
Fund-raising Methods for Different Market Segments**

Cause-related marketing has the potential to benefit both the commercial firm that sponsors it and the not-for-profit organization that it targets. Charities should be careful, however, not to become too dependent on this resource; any such program is likely to be terminated if it does not achieve the profit-related objectives the firm has set for it. Furthermore, the corporations might begin to eliminate their charitable giving, seeing cause-related marketing as a substitute for philanthropic activities.[43] Finally, no not-for-profit should rely too heavily on corporations as its major source of funding regardless of the means by which the resources are raised. One study indicated that 83 percent of charitable donations in the United States comes from individual givers, and only 5 percent comes from corporations (the remainder coming from bequests and foundations).[44]

INTRODUCING MARKETING INTO SOCIAL SECTOR ORGANIZATIONS

Since many social sector organizations do not have extensive experience with marketing, implementation can be a major issue. Implementation in such instances refers not only to the carrying out of marketing plans, but more globally, to the means by which marketing can be integrated into the entire organization. There are a number of ways to integrate marketing into social sector organizations, but it is first important to understand the role marketing is to play in the organization. Figure 20.4 presents an organizational chart for the marketing function within a transit authority.[45] Note the many aspects of marketing on the organizational chart and that a number of different people would be needed to execute all these functions. Although this organizational structure is recommended by the United States Department of Transportation, many mass transit organizations are not structured this way. Even though it makes sense to marketing people, pricing and service changes are probably not under the authority of the marketing manager in most transit systems.

Kotler recommends the following ways of introducing marketing into not-for-profit institutions.[46]

1. *Marketing committee.* A marketing committee examines the institution's problems and the potential for the marketing function. The committee objectives are

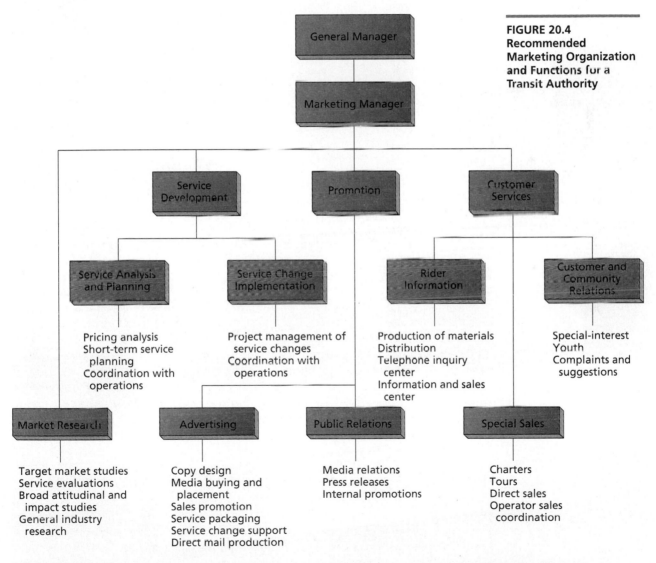

**FIGURE 20.4
Recommended
Marketing Organization
and Functions for a
Transit Authority**

General Manager

Marketing Manager

Service Development — Promotion — Customer Services

Service Analysis and Planning — Service Change Implementation — Rider Information — Customer and Community Relations

Pricing analysis
Short-term service planning
Coordination with operations

Project management of service changes
Coordination with operations

Production of materials
Distribution
Telephone inquiry center
Information and sales center

Special-interest
Youth
Complaints and suggestions

Market Research — Advertising — Public Relations — Special Sales

Target market studies
Service evaluations
Broad attitudinal and impact studies
General industry research

Copy design
Media buying and placement
Sales promotion
Service packaging
Service change support
Direct mail production

Media relations
Press releases
Internal promotions

Charters
Tours
Direct sales
Operator sales coordination

Source: Office of Transit Management, Urban Mass Transportation Administration, U.S. Department of Transportation, *Transit Marketing Management Handbook: Marketing Organization*, as excerpted in C. Lovelock and C. Weinberg, eds., *Readings in Public and Nonprofit Marketing* (The Scientific Press, 1978), p. 85.

to (1) identify the marketing problems and opportunities facing the institution, (2) identify the major needs for marketing services, and (3) explore the possible need for a full-time director of marketing.

2. *Task forces.* The chief administrator should appoint task forces to conduct an institutional audit to discover how the institution is seen by its key publics, what its constituencies want the institution to be, which programs are strong and which are weak, and so on.

FIGURE 20.5
Job Description: A University Director of Marketing

Position title: Director of Marketing

Reports to: Vice President, University Relations

Scope: University-wide

Position concept: The Director of Marketing is responsible for providing marketing guidance and services to university officers, school deans, department chairpersons, and other agents of the university.

Functions: The Director of Marketing will:
1. contribute a marketing perspective to the deliberations of the top administration in its planning of the university's future
2. prepare data that might be needed by an officer of the university on a particular market's size, segments, trends, and behavioral dynamics
3. conduct studies of the needs, perceptions, preferences, and satisfactions of particular markets
4. assist in the planning, promotion, and launching of new programs
5. assist in the development of communication and promotion campaigns and materials
6. analyze and advise on pricing questions
7. appraise the workability of new academic proposals from a marketing point of view
8. advise on recruitment of students
9. advise on current students' satisfaction
10. advise on university fund-raising

Responsibilities: The Director of Marketing will:
1. contact individual officers and small groups at the university to explain services and to solicit problems
2. prioritize the various requests for services according to their long-run impact, cost-saving potential, time requirements, ease of accomplishment, cost, and urgency
3. select projects of high priority and set accomplishment goals for the year
4. prepare a budget request to support the anticipated work
5. prepare an annual report on the main accomplishments of the office

Major liaisons: The Director of Marketing will:
1. relate most closely with the President's Office, Admissions Office, Development Office, Planning Office, and Public Relations
2. relate secondarily with the deans of various schools and chairpersons of various departments

Source: From *Strategic Marketing for Nonprofit Organizations*, 4th ed., by P. Kotler and A. R. Andreasen. Copyright © 1991 by Prentice Hall, Inc., p. 345. Reprinted by permission of Prentice Hall, Inc., Englewood Cliffs, N.J.

3. *Marketing specialist firms.* Specialist firms such as advertising agencies, direct mail consultants, and marketing research firms should be used on special projects to help the institution identify its mission, objectives, strategies, and opportunities.

4. *Marketing consultant.* An independent marketing consultant may be hired to conduct a comprehensive marketing audit of the organization and present findings and recommendations concerning the institution's marketing efforts.

5. *Marketing director.* Eventually the organization may accept the role of marketing to the extent that it becomes ready to hire a director of marketing. This requires the development of a job description containing the functions, responsibilities, and major liaisons of the position. Figure 20.5 presents a job description for a director of marketing for a university.

6. *Marketing vice president.* According to Kotler, an organization has reached the ultimate level of sophistication with the establishment of a vice president of marketing, an upper-level management position with more scope, authority, and influence for marketing.[47]

Social sector marketing is an exciting new area of application for marketing techniques. As this sector of our economy continues to embrace marketing as a means to accomplish goals and objectives, employment opportunities will abound for people with marketing skills. Many social sector organizations today realize that to succeed with their marketing efforts they need to hire individuals with marketing expertise and compensate those individuals similarly to the competition, in this case, the for-profit sector. As this realization continues to pervade the social sector, opportunities will multiply.

PERSONAL COMPUTER EXERCISE

This PC Exercise illustrates the tradeoffs that have to be made in social sector marketing. Deciding among program alternatives when faced with multiple objectives is difficult, especially in times of tight budgets. When you have completed this exercise, you will understand better the kinds of choices that managers of these organizations must make every day.

KEY POINTS

■ Social sector marketing has grown increasingly popular and accepted in the last 25 years.

■ The many reasons for the growth and development of social sector marketing include increased competition, financial and political pressures, and changing technological and social patterns.

■ The concept of exchange provides the basis of marketing by not-for-profit and public organizations. Marketing managers in businesses are concerned with the exchange between the company and its target market; social sector marketers are concerned with exchanges involving several different publics.

■ Social sector marketing differs from marketing in profit-oriented organizations in several other ways: it has a nonprofit objective, it focuses on services rather than physical goods, it must deal with public scrutiny and nonmarket pressures, and often customer satisfaction is less important.

■ The tools in marketing social sector organizations are the same as those used by businesses. How the tools are used differs, however, because of the differences in the products and organizations.

■ Strategic planning is a concept that often escapes social sector marketers who tend to make marketing decisions more at the tactical level.

■ It is important for social sector organizations to conduct market analyses and segment their markets, but marketing research is often difficult, and there is usually not much secondary information available.

■ Social sector organizations should develop strategies regarding product positioning, branding, packaging, and product mix.

■ When the product is an idea or social cause, marketing is only one means of achieving behavioral changes. Proponents may also attempt to change behavior via economic, technological, and legal means.

■ Channels of distribution for social sector organizations are very short, typically going directly from producer to consumer without intermediaries.

■ Social sector organizations often use promotional tools, including public service advertisements.

■ Pricing strategies for social sector organizations often differ from those of profit-oriented businesses because the objectives are not the same.

■ Fund-raising is an important marketing task for most not-for-profit organizations.

■ Marketing can be integrated into a social sector institution through a marketing committee, task forces, marketing specialist firms, marketing consultants, a marketing director, or a marketing vice president.

KEY TERMS

social sector (701)
public sector (701)
concept sector (701)
social sector marketing (701)
nonprofit marketing (701)
not-for-profit marketing (701)
nonbusiness marketing (701)
social marketing (701)

public service announcements
  (PSAs) (717)
cause-related marketing (721)

1. In what ways might the marketing manager's job in a public, not-for-profit hospital differ from his or her counterpart in a private, profit-oriented hospital?

2. Identify some relevant market segments for each of the following organizations:
   (a) The American Red Cross
   (b) A church
   (c) The United Way of America
   (d) Amtrak
   (e) The American Cancer Society

3. What tactics could be used by the Partnership for a Drug Free America for product, price, promotion, and distribution to get people to stop using drugs?

4. Think of some relevant publics for your college or university. For each, describe the exchange relationship that exists.

5. What do you think is the most compelling factor in explaining why social sector marketing has grown so rapidly?

6. Which method of inducing behavioral change do you think would work most effectively in the case of getting people to become organ donors? Why?

7. Why do people give money to organizations like the Society for the Prevention of Cruelty to Animals? What methods would you recommend to this organization to help it increase the amount of funds it raises?

8. Do you think cause-related marketing is a good way for not-for-profit organizations to raise funds? Why or why not?

9. Using the portfolio model depicted in Figure 20.2, diagram the situation that might be faced by the local YMCA. What strategic recommendations can you make?

10. In many not-for-profit organizations, marketing is a "dirty word," one associated with the rough world of commerce and with real or imaginary abuses. What would you say to a person who directs a not-for-profit organization who holds these attitudes?

CASE APPLICATION

Winning and Losing at the Lottery

State lotteries, a form of legalized gambling, have found widespread acceptance across the United States. The first officially sponsored state lottery took place in New Hampshire in 1963. Other early participants included New York (1965), New Jersey (1971), and Massachusetts (1972). Today 37 states and the District of Columbia have lottery programs. The typical state lottery offers a variety of games and designates a portion of its proceeds to state programs, often education. Some states have focused on the aid to education in their advertising but a far greater number have featured the thrill of playing or the opportunity to win as the key selling point.

California was a relatively late entrant into the state lottery game. After winning voter approval, California's lottery began in October 1985. The lottery in California is mandated to return a minimum of 50% of its revenues to players in the form of prizes and a minimum of 34% of its revenues to education in the state. The remaining 16% covers administrative and marketing costs. According to Joanne McNabb, the lottery's former Director of Public Affairs (she was replaced by Jeannie Winnick in January 1994), despite technically being a public, not-for-profit organization, "we don't market like a nonprofit." The California lottery's primary objective is to maximize revenues for education.

California lottery sales exploded between the introduction of the lottery in 1985 and June 1989. The fiscal year ending June 1989 represented a peak in sales, with the lottery realizing $2.6 billion in sales that year. Following that peak, however, the California State lottery took a nosedive. During fiscal year 1990–1991 sales dropped 18% from the previous year to $2.13 billion. Sales were predicted to fall another 6% during fiscal year 1991–1992. In fact, sales of $1.36 billion during that year represented a 36% decline over the previous year and a 48% decline over the peak sales year of 1988–1989. Since the lottery's advertising budget is tied to its level of sales, advertising expenditures also tumbled during this period. Between 1990 and 1991, for example, the lottery's advertising budget dropped 24% from $45 million to $35 million.

McNabb has attributed the decline in sales of the early 1990s to the recession, legal restrictions on types of games, and the fading novelty of the lottery. State Assemblyman Richard Floyd, a critic of the lottery, however, claims that the biggest factor in the lottery's decline occurred in 1990 when the odds on the Lotto game were doubled in order to boost jackpots. The move, planned to increase enthusiasm and excitement in the game, instead generated broad media attention about the poor odds of winning.

In October 1991, in the face of declining sales, Governor Pete Wilson hired a new director to replace Chon Gutierrez, who had been director since 1987. The replacement, Sharon Sharp, was previously the director of the lottery for the state of Illinois. In her first year, Sharp wrote an 18-month strategic plan for the lottery.

Between late 1992 and early 1994 the lottery increased the number of games it offered from four to nine. Product positioning focused on the lottery as a form of entertainment rather than a get-rich-quick scheme. Consistent with this positioning strategy, the lottery's competition was defined as "other low-cost entertainment options" (the average player spends $5 a week on tickets).

To carry out the strategic changes, the lottery's advertising efforts were changed. Prior to 1992 lottery advertising had often been the target of criticism. Advertising was frequently described as talking down to consumers with an attitude that positioned ticket buyers as "idiots" and "suckers." The agency of Dailey and Associates of Los Angeles had been handling the advertising, and it possessed a contract that ran through February 1994. The state reserved the right, however, to terminate the contract at any time with a 30-day notice. In June of 1992, the J. Walter Thompson agency in San Francisco was given the account.

The strategic planning efforts appeared to pay off. In 1992–1993 lottery revenues rose to $1.76 billion, a 29% increase over the previous fiscal year. Despite the increase, Sharp left her position as director in 1993. She was replaced by an interim director, Del Pierce. Despite personnel changes, sales continue to grow. The 1993–1994 fiscal year saw sales of $1.92 billion, a 9.1% increase from 1992–1993.

Questions

1. Describe the product of the California State Lottery. What are the core, tangible, and augmented components of the product?
2. What are the reasons that an individual might buy a lottery ticket? How could this information be used to plan a segmentation strategy for the lottery?
3. Suggest appropriate advertising strategies for each of the segments you considered in question 2.
4. What does McNabb mean, "We don't market like a nonprofit"? Do you agree with her? Why or why not?

Consider the Social Sector

Social sector marketing is a relatively new and exciting area. Many organizations in this sector are finding that effective marketing can help them to achieve their missions and goals. Organizations have also realized that marketing expertise and compensation in the social sector need to be more in line with that in the business (that is, the for-profit) sector. Increased competition, financial pressures, political demands, and changing technological and social patterns are cited as reasons for the greater attention to social sector marketing.

There are growing opportunities for satisfying, rewarding marketing careers in the social sector. Candidates for marketing careers owe it to themselves to identify the subsectors whose missions are of interest to them. There is a wide range of institutions delivering intangible goods and services, including education, health care, environmentalism, entertainment, and religion.

Why should you look at the social sector for career options beyond marketing positions? First, you might find goods, services, and ideas for viewpoints that are of special importance and meaning to you. Second, there is much diversity in the nature of exchanges. These exchanges might give you a greater professional challenge than those in the business sector. Finally, there is an especially close relationship between strategy and marketing in the social sector. This relationship might offer the chance to be more involved in the development of strategy than you might be in the business sector.

How could you identify the best opportunities for you in the social sector? First, you might conduct some library research to identify and evaluate the major subsectors that might interest you. Next, use your network of faculty, alumni, colleagues, and friends to learn more about the missions, needs, approaches, structures, and cultures of the subsectors that made it through your "first level" research. This step will help identify specific institutions that might provide you with the best opportunities. Once you have identified your target organizations, try to talk to someone in each of those institutions to give you a feel for such intangibles as the maturity and stability of the organization, the viability of the mission and resources, the opportunities for someone with your personal and professional profile, and the best way to access those opportunities.

In your career search, identification and consideration of opportunities in the social sector assures that you have a complete and current foundation for your career planning.

Questions

1. What areas of the social (not-for-profit) sector have missions of interest to you?
2. Identify positive and negative aspects of a career in the social sector versus those same factors in the business sector.
3. If you plan to pursue a career in the social sector, what major steps would you take to carry out an effective career search?

The Story of Harley-Davidson: Services

Servicing Suppliers, Dealers, and Distributors: The First Customers

Harley-Davidson's success is in large part due to its impressive service practices. One of the foremost goals for the company is to achieve the highest level of satisfaction among customers. However, the term "customer" doesn't simply refer to the individual who walks off the street and into the showroom. Harley-Davidson's corporate philosophy broadens the traditional definition of "customer" to include suppliers, dealers, and distributors, whom the company regards as equal stakeholders in Harley-Davidson's success.

This business-to-business approach emphasizes Harley-Davidson's commitment to producing motorcycles in the most cost-effective and efficient manner possible while maintaining a healthy "partnership" with each of its supplier companies. Harley-Davidson's dedication to getting closer to suppliers led the company to develop in 1992 a Supplier Advisory Council, a forum for better business-to-business communication and problem-solving.

Dealers and distributors are also a vital part of Harley-Davidson's drive for superior customer satisfaction. In 1992 the company established Harley-Davidson University, where dealers and their employees attend training programs covering all aspects of operating a competitive dealership, including improved service and business management practices. Through such initiatives as its Designer Store Program (discussed earlier in Part Four), Harley-Davidson makes every effort to provide dealers with the resources and support needed to run successful businesses.

Servicing Owners: The Ultimate Consumer

By training its dealers and their employees, Harley-Davidson makes a direct investment in satisfying its traditional customers—the product owners. The company recently expanded its Customer Service staff in order to meet the needs of customers and dealers in such areas as data analysis and reporting and improved warranty processing.

Buyers of motorcycles expect service in the initial purchase stage and, even more importantly, the post-purchase stage. Harley-Davidson's "close to the customer" marketing philosophy emphasizes its ability to provide maintenance and repair service for each client's bike, as well as its ability to service the client's personal needs. Post-sales services and products for customers include enthusiast organizations like the Harley Owners Group (H.O.G.) and Ladies of Harley, club-sponsored rallies, touring handbooks and free subscriptions to *Hog Tales* and *Enthusiast* magazines, and, for H.O.G. members, reimbursement for rider safety training courses. A variety of product lines comprise Harley-Davidson's ever-growing list of Parts and Accessories. The company offers Genuine Accessories for sale to owners who wish to customize their bikes according to particular tastes and styles, as well as other specialty lines, including Screamin' Eagle Performance Parts, intended for off-road, competitive racing.

The company provides fashion as well as functional riding products for its customers. With its MotorClothes accessory and apparel line, the company fulfills the more abstract, emotional needs of riders and non-riders alike by selling everything from keychains and watches to leather biking boots and jackets.

In the end, the Customer Satisfaction Index is the key indicator for Harley-Davidson of its success among consumers. The company clearly possesses a loyal, satisfied customer base, with over 90 percent of its customers claiming in a 1992 survey that they would purchase another Harley-Davidson. By maintaining a strong reputation for quality and reliability in its motorcycle products, Harley-Davidson will continue to grow and profit in the future.

Servicing the Community: Society as a Stakeholder

While other companies cater solely to profit-conscious shareholders, Harley-Davidson also promotes within its company the concept of society as a stakeholder. The notion of a stakeholder encompasses not only individuals who have a financial interest in the company, but also the customers who buy the products, the employees who produce those products, and the community in which the business functions and thrives. These people all possess an equal stake in the company's growth; without their hard work, patronage, and respect, the company would not be the success it is today.

Few companies are successful in the long-term without contributing to society at large. At Harley-Davidson, success and leadership in the business community are incomplete without demonstrating an equal degree of leadership within the local community as well. That's why the company has established long-term ties with many charitable organizations and heartily encourages its employees and dealers to contribute their time to different causes. Aside from the exposure they gain for the company, participants earn a great sense of personal satisfaction and accomplishment from their charitable work. The following are some of the activities in which Harley-Davidson has taken part:

1. Harley-Davidson has raised more than $20 million for the Muscular Dystrophy Association through corporate events, such as Harley-Davidson's 90th anniversary reunion, and dealer-sponsored and H.O.G. sponsored events including auctions and raffles.

2. In hundreds of cities across the United States, H.O.G. members coordinate and contribute to the annual Christmas Toys for Tots campaign. Thousands of motorcyclists ride to charitable organizations and hospitals with toys and teddy bears strapped to their motorcycles. The riders make a media event out of it, which encourages others in the community to participate.

3. In California, H.O.G. members and Harley-Davidson dealers participate in California's Benefit Miracle Ride. Donations and proceeds go to research on birth defects.

4. Led by Harley-Davidson CEO Richard F. Teerlink, the Next Door Foundation works to improve the quality of life in and around the Milwaukee neighborhood where Harley-Davidson's corporate headquarters are located.

5. The company is a sponsor of the "Reading Rainbow" children's series on public television.

6. The company supports the efforts of the Motorcycle Safety Foundation' to encourage riders to take its motorcycling safety course.

7. Harley-Davidson takes pride in preserving the history and heritage of the United States. As a result, it contributed heavily to the national campaign to restore the Statue of Liberty.

Employees and customers raised more than $250,000 for the cause.

8. As part of the company's Passport to America program, H.O.G. members in many chapters have made a commitment to the environment and adopted scenic highways, often in national forests, and work on cleanup projects.

These are just some examples of Harley-Davidson's commitment to community service. Surely, charitable causes boost the company's image and help maintain good public relations. But such efforts also reinforce the notion that business is not just about products, but about people, as well.

Investing in the Community

At Harley-Davidson, service is a concept that doesn't stop with the purchase. Like the Harley-Davidson motorcycling experience, service is a way of life — not just in the world of business but in the world at large, as well. Harley-Davidson lives by its corporate visions and values by sharing its good fortune with the community. In wrapping up this case, keep in mind that success in business depends on the right combination of various product, service, and community components. Whether a business is a corporation, manufacturer, service (such as a bank or hotel), or not for profit organization, community service is always good business.

Questions

1. The costs that go into working with charitable organizations are substantial, considering the capital and time expended. What are the benefits of such activities for a company like Harley-Davidson?

2. How could a company go about determining which charitable organizations it would like to support?

3. Some companies require that its employees devote a certain amount of time each month, out of their regular working hours, to charitable organizations. What is your opinion of this policy? Do you recommend it to Harley-Davidson?

Appendix A

Financial Concepts for Marketing Analysis

This appendix explains some of the financial concepts and methods that are of special importance in analyzing marketing problems. It covers three topics: cost analysis for evaluating specific projects or expenditures, including break-even analysis; operating statements; and analytical ratios based on financial statements.

COST ANALYSIS

Costs or expenses may be classified in many ways, as the Appendix to Chapter 17 shows. For analytical purposes, costs are customarily distinguished along the following lines: (1) total costs and unit costs and (2) variable, fixed, and discretionary costs.

Total Costs and Unit Costs

Total costs are all the costs associated with an activity. The total cost of manufacturing 1,000 widgets is, say, $480. It is divided into the following cost categories:

Direct material	$180
Direct labor	210
Factory overhead	90
Total	$480

The *unit cost* of producing these 1,000 widgets is $480 ÷ 1,000, or $.48 per unit. The direct-labor cost per unit is $.21, or $210 ÷ 1,000.

Unit cost is often a convenient and meaningful way of expressing costs. The total cost of a family reunion picnic may have been $150. But if it was attended by 100 people, it was only $1.50 per person (unit).

Variable, Fixed, and Discretionary Costs

Fixed costs (FC) are costs that remain unchanged during a given period of time or over a specified or relevant range of output. A store's annual rental payments of, say, $100 per month, are a fixed cost. If the store's sales in January are 100 units, and in February are 50, its rent is fixed at $100 in each of these months, although its rent per unit of sales rose from $1 in January to $2 in February.

For a manufacturing plant, fixed costs generally include the depreciation and amortization of investment in machinery, most of the cost of a maintenance crew, most of the management and supervisory payroll, real estate taxes, depreciation on the building, and similar expenses. These costs remain unchanged over a fairly wide range of plant output and over a given period of time. This range of output is generally called the *relevant range*. In Figure A.1, fixed costs are $10,000 between 1,000 and 2,999 units of output, $15,000 between 3,000 and 7,999, and $25,000 between 8,000 and 9,999. The relevant range is between 3,000 and 7,999 if that is the output range within which the firm will most commonly operate. Although *total* fixed manufacturing costs may be low under 3,000 units, *unit* fixed costs are relatively high in this range. Thus at 2,999 output, unit fixed costs are $10,000 ÷ 2,999 = $3.333. The lowest fixed costs per unit are at 7,999 output: $15,000 ÷ 7,999 = $1.885.

Variable costs (VC) are fixed *per unit* of output but vary in total amount directly with output. Suppose a toothpaste packager buys his empty tubes and bulk dentifrice at a total cost of $.10 per tube. If he fills 10,000 tubes per day, his total materials costs will be $1,000, or $.10 per tube filled. If he produces 100,000, it will be $10,000, also $.10 per unit. Thus a variable cost is generally uniform (or fixed) per unit, but fluctuates in total in direct proportion to change in total business. Figure A.2 shows this relationship.

Discretionary costs (DC) are costs that, unlike fixed or variable costs, arise mostly at the discretion of the management. Variable costs are caused by changes in output. Fixed costs are caused because a company has decided to go into business, but discretionary costs are different. Advertising expenditures are discretionary costs; research and development expenditures are discretionary costs. They are distinguished by the fact that management *wants* to incur them. Instead of being caused

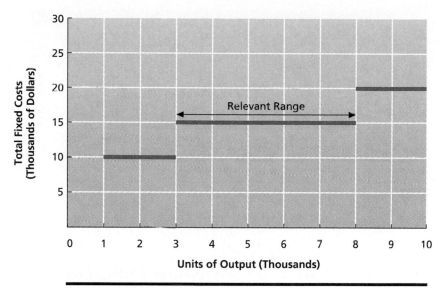

FIGURE A.1
Fixed Costs and Relevant Range

by changes in production and sales volume, their object is to *cause* changes in sales volume. A company advertises more in order to sell more. Hence, although successful advertising expenditures may seem to be like variable costs in that they vary with output and sales, they are different in that they are causes of volume changes, not caused by volume changes.

Break-Even Analysis

Break-even analysis attempts to determine the volume of sales necessary (at various prices) for the manufacturer or merchant to cover his or her costs or to break even between revenue and costs. Break-even analysis is useful in a variety of ways: to help set prices, to estimate profit or loss potentials, and to help determine the discretionary costs that should be incurred.

FIGURE A.2
Variable Cost Chart

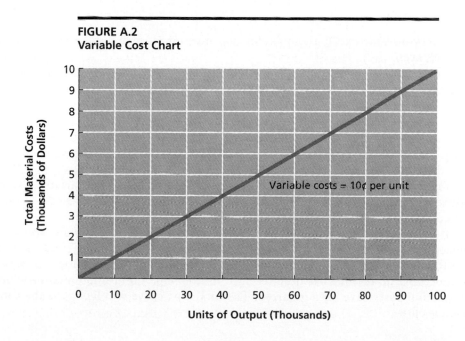

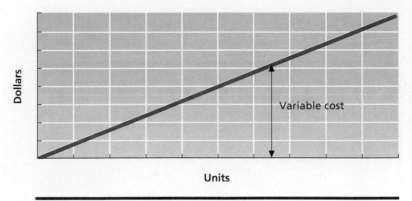

FIGURE A.3
Variable Cost

Our toothpaste packager had direct-material costs of $.10 per unit. Suppose that its other variable costs are $.05. Its total variable costs, therefore, would be $.15. Suppose that it had annual fixed costs of $50,000 and intended to sell the toothpaste to wholesalers for $.20. How many tubes must be sold to break even—that is, just exactly to cover all costs? The questions can be answered simply by using the following formula:

$$\text{Break-even units} = \frac{\text{fixed costs}}{\text{unit contribution}}.$$

Unit contribution is the difference between unit selling price and unit variable cost:

$$\text{Unit selling price} - \text{variable cost} = \text{unit contributions.}$$
$$(\$.20) \qquad\qquad (\$.15) \qquad\qquad (\$.05)$$

The word *contribution* refers to what this difference ($.05) contributes toward covering fixed costs and producing profits.

The break-even formula yields the following:

$$\text{Break-even units} = \frac{\$50,000}{\$.05} = 1,000,000 \text{ tubes.}$$

In other words, the toothpaste manufacturer must produce and sell 1 million tubes to break even.

This relationship between fixed costs, variable costs, revenues, and the break-even point can be shown graphically. Figure A.3 is a plot of total variable costs against units of output.

Figure A.4 plots total fixed costs against units of output. It is the relevant range cost segment of Figure A.1 stretched out to cover the full range of possible outputs. Thus, for the purposes of this illustration, we assume that fixed costs are constant over the whole range of possible outputs.

Figure A.5 is merely the fixed cost of Figure A.4 added to the variable cost of Figure A.3. This gives a combined graph of total cost at various levels of output. (Discretionary costs are ignored for the moment.)

It is important to recognize that the break-even volume is strictly an arithmetic concept. It assumes that this volume is both produced *and sold*. In Figure A.6, if 1,300,000 units are produced, but only 900,000 are sold, the firm does not break even because no revenue has been received for the 400,000 unsold units for which production costs have been incurred. The total cost curve will lie above the total revenue curve.

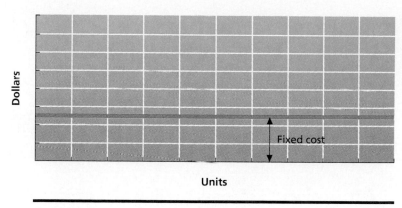

FIGURE A.4
Fixed Cost

The break-even logic can also be used to determine the volume of sales needed to yield a specific profit objective. Thus, the question might be, "At present prices ($.20 wholesale), what volume of sales is needed to earn a net profit of $30,000?" Using the break-even formula as a basis for answering this question, we get

$$\text{break-even units} = \frac{\text{fixed costs} + \$30,000}{\text{unit contribution}}$$

$$= \frac{\$80,000}{\$.05}$$

$$= 1,600,000 \text{ units.}$$

Proof:

1,600,000 × $.20	= $320,000
VC = 1,600,000 × $.15	= 240,000
Difference	= $ 80,000
FC	= 50,000
Net profit	= $ 30,000

FIGURE A.5
Total Cost

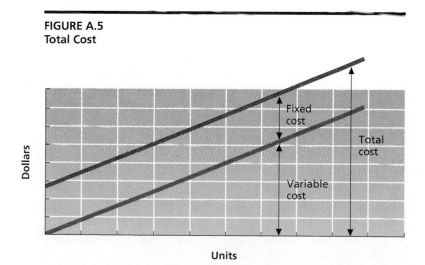

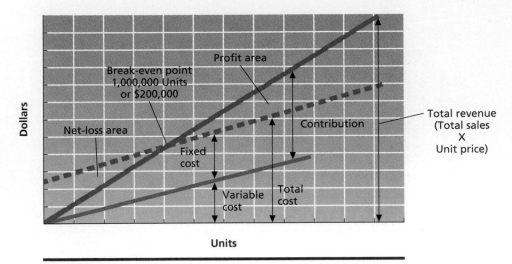

FIGURE A.6
A Break-Even Chart

Suppose that the question is, "What volume of sales do I need to yield a 10 percent profit; that is, a 10 percent profit on sales?" Using the break-even approach again we get

$$\text{break-even units} = \frac{\text{fixed costs} + 10\% \,(\$.20 \times \text{break-even units})}{\text{unit contribution}}$$

$$= \frac{\$50,000 + .10\,(\$.20\ \text{BE})}{\$.05}$$

$$= \frac{\$50,000 + \$.02\ \text{BE}}{\$.05}$$

$$\$.05\ \text{BE} = \$50,000 + \$.02\ \text{BE}$$
$$\$.03\ \text{BE} = \$50,000$$
$$\text{BE} = 1,666,666\ \text{units.}$$

Proof:

$1,666,666 \times \$.20$	$= \$333,333$
$VC = 1,666,666 \times \$.15$	$= \underline{249,999}$
Difference	$= \$\ 83,334$
FC	$= \underline{50,000}$
Net profit	$= \$\ 33,334$

$$\text{Profit} = \frac{\$33,334}{\$333,333} = 10\%.$$

The break-even formula is also useful in answering a variety of other questions, such as the following:

1. If fixed costs rise by x dollars and the price remains the same, how much sales increase is needed to break even?
2. If fixed costs rise by x dollars and unit sales remain the same, how much of a price increase is needed to break even?

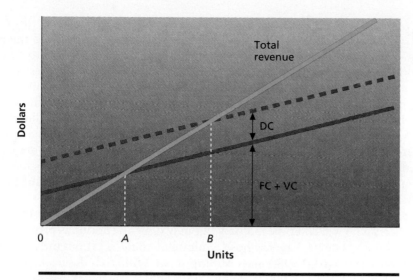

FIGURE A.7
A Break-Even Chart Showing the Addition of a Discretionary Expenditure

3. With an expected variable cost increase of *y* cents per unit, how much of a sales increase is needed at the present price to yield an operating profit of $40,000?

With products that the seller believes may respond favorably to advertising and other promotional efforts, he or she may try to achieve sales expansion via advertising expenditures. Thus in Figure A.7 he or she adds discretionary advertising expenditures (DC) to the present total cost (FC + VC). With total costs now higher, he or she must either sell more to break even (raising sales from 0*A* to 0*B*) or raise his or her prices at the present volume. The advertising expenditure was made in the expectation that sales would rise in response to that expenditure. Examination of Figure A.7 shows *how much* sales must increase to justify the increased expenditure, and permits the analyst to estimate the profit consequences of different changes in sales volume that might follow from the advertising effort. It does not, of course, say anything about what sales result it would be reasonable to expect.

Costs and Marketing Strategy

It was pointed out earlier that fixed costs are actually not fixed over the entire range of output, but variable costs are also seldom as stable and linear as shown in the break-even chart. For example, if a recession occurs, management is likely to tighten controls and cut variable costs. During good times it may be indulgent and careless and allow variable costs to rise. When competitive activity is severe and sales are endangered, advertising and selling expenditures might be raised to stem the downturn and recoup sales losses, although, in practice, the reverse is frequently done in order to "conserve cash." When the latter is done, management's assumption is obviously that sales will not adequately respond to advertising.

The bigger the unit contribution, the more likely marketing management is to spend more on sales-building promotions. This is not only because it is more likely to have the resources to spend this way, but also because high unit contributions will produce large total profits if sales are high.

The relative sizes of fixed and variable costs are also important in their other effects on marketing strategy. A high variable-cost ratio, and, therefore, a low fixed-cost ratio, makes getting into an industry (that is, *entry*) relatively easier than when the ratios are reversed. This produces extremely competitive conditions in the industry. Good examples are the garment manufacturing industry and the restaurant business. Because the variable-cost ratio is high, nobody is likely to "win" the competition (that is, destroy the competitors) because of the willingness to charge substantially lower prices. The reason is that a high variable-cost ratio generally means that there are few economies of scale; that is, there is little or no high-volume, low-cost productivity that is facilitated by mass technology or mass selling. Higher volume sales do not produce proportionately lower unit costs with which to outcompete the competition. Prices will tend to be low, and where they are substantially above variable costs, they reflect the seller's other advantages such as, in the garment industry, good styling or workmanship, and, in the restaurant business, quality food, service, and entertainment.

A relatively high initial fixed-cost ratio will not only tend to limit the number of producers who will enter the industry but may offer an enormous profit potential. Thus our toothpaste packager, whose equipment could fill thousands of tubes an hour, broke even at 1,000,000 units of output. At 1,600,000 the packager had net profits of $30,000, but at 2,000,000 units, with only a 25 percent increase in output, profits would rise to $50,000 or 67 percent. This is one reason that the packager is more willing to spend money for advertising. It is also the reason that machine-produced consumer goods are more heavily advertised than handcrafted consumer goods. A rising volume of output is spread over fixed costs, and this reduces the average total cost per unit. The higher the fixed-cost ratio, the greater the benefits of full utilization of productive capacity.

OPERATING (OR PROFIT AND LOSS) STATEMENT

An operating, or profit and loss, statement is a financial summary of business operations during a period of time. It shows how the various elements of the operation contributed to the final outcome. Like cost analysis, it is one measure of the effectiveness of the firm.

A retailer's operating statement is composed of the following major elements:

$$\text{Sales} - \text{cost of goods sold} = \text{gross margin}.$$

$$\text{Gross margin} - \text{expenses} = \text{profit}.$$

Each element of the operating statement can be expressed as a ratio of sales, and these ratios can be compared with those of other retail outlets of like size and product line to appraise the relative effectiveness of a retailer. Various trade associations and trade publications regularly publish detailed operating statistics and ratios of department and specialty stores, retail food chains, and other types of retail and wholesale firms.

A retail operating statement is much more detailed than the above example. Table A.1 is typical. Since accounting statements are governed by conventions that tend to reflect the peculiarities of the industries or business functions they portray, such a statement requires some explanation.

1. *Gross sales* represent the total value of sales made during the period.
2. *Returns* are the value of credit or cash given to customers for merchandise purchased but subsequently returned. (This may be resold and the revenue of that sale then appears a second time under gross sales.)
3. *Allowances* are the value of price adjustments given to customers who have brought back defective or other merchandise. The adjustments generally keep the items from becoming returns.
4. *Net sales* are gross sales less returns and allowances. This represents the merchant's real volume of business out of which all expenses must be met.

Gross sales		$7,580,340
Returns and allowances		745,325
Net sales		$6,835,015
Beginning inventory	$ 810,055	
Purchases	4,225,017	
Inward transportation costs	55,013	
Gross cost of goods handled	$5,090,085	
Ending inventory	907,153	
Gross cost of goods sold	$4,182,932	
Cash discounts earned	251,192	
Cost of goods sold		3,931,740
Gross margin		$2,903,275
Expenses:		
Payroll	$ 998,765	
Supplies	83,073	
Repairs and maintenance	55,073	
Advertising	184,111	
Delivery	33,582	
Interest	43,700	
Pensions and insurance	129,709	
Depreciation	37,853	
Losses and bad debts	6,211	
Real estate costs	191,403	
Utilities	11,382	
Taxes (other than income taxes)	53,052	
Services purchased	58,491	
Miscellaneous	4,011	1,890,416
Operating profit		$1,012,859
Other income		61,511
Net profit before income taxes		$1,074,370

TABLE A 1
Retail Operating Statement

5. *Cost of goods sold* is the cost to the merchant of the goods sold during the period. The merchant who has been in business before the year of the current statement will have started the year of the current statement with a carryover of last year's stock, that is, its *beginning inventory*.

When the cost of goods purchased during the year is added to the cost of transporting them into the establishment, the sum is gross cost of goods handled. Subtracting *ending* inventory at the close of the accounting period, the remainder is gross cost of goods sold.

The final net cost of goods sold is obtained by subtracting cash discounts earned from gross cost of goods sold. A cash discount is a reduction in the price of merchandise offered by a supplier for prompt payment. The reason for stating cash discounts earned separately as a subtraction from gross cost of goods rather than merely stating purchases at a lower figure is for control and analysis purposes. It shows how well the firm's financial management is capitalizing on a particular kind of profit or money-saving opportunity.

There is some difference among businesses about the treatment of these discounts—as merchandise discounts and, therefore, subtracted from gross cost of goods sold, or as *other income earned* and, therefore, added to operating profit. Most retail merchants use the former treatment.

Although the net profit outcome is identical, treating it as *other income* results in a higher *cost of goods sold* and, therefore, a lower operating profit. Thus, in Table A.1, what would happen to *cost of goods sold* and *operating profit* if *cash discounts earned* were treated differently?

Variety in Operating Statements

Although the purposes, format, and analytical approaches of operating statements are broadly the same regardless of the type of business, there are some differences among those of retailers, wholesalers, and manufacturers, and differences among types of each of these. The statement in Table A.1 is typical of a medium-sized department store.

ANALYTICAL RATIOS

A firm is interested not only in how much it sells and how much profit it makes but also in how efficiently various aspects of its operations are being managed compared with some previous time period or with other firms of a similar type and size. Such comparisons are facilitated by looking at various operating ratios or analytical ratios—that is, by stating certain elements of the operating statements as percentages of net sales. Common analytical ratios are gross margin percentage, expense ratio, profit ratio, and markup.

In nearly all cases such ratios use *net sales* as the base. Thus in the operating statement of Table A.1:

$$\text{Gross margin} = \frac{\$2,903,275}{\$6,835,015} = 42.5\%.$$

$$\text{Expense ratio} = \frac{\$1,890,416}{\$6,835,015} = 27.7\%.$$

$$\text{Returns and allowances} = \frac{\$745,325}{\$6,835,015} = 10.9\%.$$

Markup Computation

Markup is the amount by which the selling price of an item exceeds its cost to the seller. Thus an item the merchant buys for $.60 and sells for $1 has a markup (or markon) of $.40. For a manufacturer, markup is the difference between its fully allocated cost of producing the product and its selling price.

As pointed out earlier, operating or analytical ratios are generally expressed as percentages of net sales. In the preceding example, the markup percentage is $.40/$1.00 = 40%. It is *not* $.40/$.60 = 66⅔%.

In ordinary business parlance the term *markup percentage* is generally shortened simply to markup. Hence the answer to the question, "What is the markup on that $1 item?" is "40%." If there are no returns, allowances, or markdowns on the sale of that item, and no inward transportation costs, we would also say that its gross margin is 40%.

Many retailers use markup formulas in deciding how to price an item. Thus, in view of their expenses and profit objectives, retailers may have a standard practice of using a 50% markup for certain classes of furniture, 40% for men's suits, and 33⅓% for linens.

Suppose that the retailer buys a suit for $100 and uses a 40% markup formula. What will be the selling price? Not $140. Since the markup percentage is based on *selling* price, the retailer must price the suit such that the difference between that price and the cost is 40%. Therefore, to find the selling price of a $100 suit with a 40% markup, the merchant makes the following calculation.

Let

$$X = \text{selling price}$$
$$\$100 = \text{cost}$$
$$40\% = \text{markup.}$$

Therefore,

$$X = \$100 + .4X$$
$$X - .4X = \$100$$
$$.6X = \$100$$
$$X = 100 \div .6$$
$$= \$166.67 = \text{selling price}$$

since

$$\text{selling price} = \text{cost} + \text{markup}$$

and

$$\text{markup} = 40\% \text{ of selling price}$$
$$\text{cost} = 60\% \text{ of selling price.}$$

Hence given a desired markup, merchants find the selling price by dividing the dollar cost by the percentage cost—that is, the difference between 100% and the desired percentage markup. Therefore,

$$\text{selling price} = \frac{\text{cost}}{(100\% - \text{markup }\%)} = \frac{\text{cost in \$}}{\text{cost in }\%}$$

$$= \frac{\$100}{.6}$$

$$= \$166.67.$$

Proof that $166.67 is a 40% markup:

$$\$166.67 \quad = \text{price}$$
$$- \underline{100.00} \quad = \text{cost}$$
$$\$ \ 66.67 \quad = \text{margin}$$

$$\frac{\$66.67}{\$166.67} = 40\%.$$

If merchants know their selling price and markup and want to recall what their costs were, the reverse formula holds:

$$\text{Cost} = \text{selling price} \times \text{cost percent}$$
$$= \$166.67 \times .6$$
$$= \$100.00.$$

To convert a markup expressed as a percentage of selling price into one expressed as a percentage of cost, the following formula applies:

$$\text{Markup percent on cost} = \frac{\text{markup percent on price}}{\text{cost percent on price}}$$

$$= \frac{40\%}{60\%}$$

$$= 66\tfrac{2}{3}\%.$$

To convert a markup expressed as a percentage of cost into one expressed as a percentage of selling price, the following formula applies:

$$\text{Markup percent on price} = \frac{\text{markup percent on cost}}{100\% + \text{markup percent on cost}}$$

$$= \frac{66\frac{2}{3}\%}{166\frac{2}{3}\%}$$

$$= 40\%.$$

Hence a 40% markup on selling price is equivalent to a 66⅔% markup on cost. A 33⅓% markup on selling price is equivalent to a 50% markup on cost.

Markdown Computation

A markdown is the amount by which a merchant reduces the original selling price of merchandise in order to sell it more easily. Clearance sales, for example, generally involve heavy markdowns.

Just as markup is computed on net selling price, so is markdown. If a merchant buys an item for $.60 and prices it at $1, the markup is 40%. If the merchant subsequently reduces the price to $.90, there has been a markdown of $.10. The percentage markdown is based on the *net* sales price, or $.90. Hence the markdown percent is $.10/$.90 = 11.11%.

Markdowns do not appear on the operating statement, except for that portion which represents allowances made to customers who have already bought the item.

While regular markdowns do not appear on the operating statement, they are a significant measure of retail efficiency. All retailers *expect* to incur markdowns. The reason is that they must keep a relatively large inventory and assortment of all classes of goods, even toward the end of a regular buying season (say winter clothes during February), or run the risk of alienating and losing customers to stores that have a good selection at such times. At the end of February and early March, however, many people begin shopping for spring clothes. Hence, at some point the winter supply must be cleared out to make room for the spring supply. Markdown prices are one way to encourage people to buy this end-of-season stock.

Although markdowns are an expected part of retail life, maintaining the proper balance between adequate end-of-season stock and the markdown percentage is a sign of good management. Both high and low markdown percentages suggest some possible management shortcoming.

Most progressive merchants keep separate markdown records, broken down by departments. This is not only for control and evaluation but also for pricing. The fact that markdowns must be incurred requires that this be taken into consideration in the original pricing of the product. Therefore, the amount of typical markdown usually has some effect on the size of the original markup. Hence, the initial markup generally exceeds the expected rate of gross margin.

The markdown percentage of a store or a store department is computed on total net sales of the store or department, not just on the marked-down goods themselves. Thus, if a department buys 50 dresses for $10 each and prices them to yield a markup of 33⅓%, its selling price will be $15. If it sells 40 at $15 and marks the remaining 10 down to $12 each and sells these, its gross sales will be

$$40 \times \$15 = \$600.$$
$$10 \times \$12 = 120.$$
$$\text{Gross sales} = \$720.$$

If one of the $15 dresses is returned and then resold for $12, the final calculation will be

$$
\begin{aligned}
40 \times \$15 &= \$600 \\
11 \times \$12 &= \underline{\quad 132} \\
\text{Gross sales} &= \$732 \\
\text{Returns and allowances} &= \underline{\quad 15} \\
\text{Net sales} &= \$717
\end{aligned}
$$

$$
\text{Markdown} = 11 \times (\$15 - \$12) = 11 \times \$3 = \$33
$$

$$
\text{Markdown percent} = \frac{\text{markdown, \$}}{\text{net sales, \$}} = \frac{\$33}{\$717} = 4.6\%.
$$

Stockturn

Stockturn refers to the number of times a store's average inventory is sold during a given period, generally a year. A common synonym for stockturn is *turnover*.

The stockturn rate may be computed in several ways:

1. by dividing the cost of goods sold by the average inventory at cost
2. by dividing the net sales by the average inventory at selling price
3. by dividing the net sales in physical units by the average inventory in physical units

Average inventory is computed as follows, using consistently throughout the calculation either cost, selling price, or physical units:

$$
\text{Average inventory} = \frac{\text{beginning inventory} + \text{ending inventory}}{2}.
$$

What a "proper" stockturn rate is depends not only on the industry but also on the strategy of the company in question and on the particular department in the company. Thus, in a supermarket, the meat department's stockturn may be high at 30 times a year, but the canned food department's stockturn may be low at 1.5 times a year. A study by Dun and Bradstreet, Incorporated, of average annual stockturns is shown in Table A.2.

TABLE A.2
Average Annual Stockturns

Line of Retail Trade	Average Number of Stockturns
Bakeries	18.7
Small department stores (under $250,000 annual volume)	2.5
Drugstores	3.9
Dry goods and general merchandising	2.4
Furniture stores ($200,000–$300,000 annual volume)	2.5
Gasoline service stations	21.3
Grocery and meat stores	17.2
Meat markets	53.3
Restaurants	35.5
Women's ready-to-wear	4.1

Appendix B

Instructions for Using the Personal Computer Exercises Disk

The PC Exercises are computerized marketing exercises that are designed to reinforce one or more of the topics presented in each chapter. The software is available in either MS-DOS (IBM PC) or Macintosh format. Only the MS-DOS format is included with this textbook. (Your instructor can obtain the Macintosh version of the software from HarperCollins.) All the exercises are easy to use and comprehensive. On-line help is available in the software.

Each exercise consists of an introduction, a mini-case, a worksheet (which may include a graph and other options), and a follow-up quiz. The software includes two types of help. TOPIC HELP describes the objective of the exercise, the essential learning points, and the desired results (outcome) from completing the exercise. CONTEXT HELP provides assistance and descriptions for the specific problem that you are working on when you select HELP. You can print any of the parts of the exercise at any time by selecting the PRINT button or choosing PRINT from the FILE menu.

HARDWARE REQUIREMENTS AND OPERATING ENVIRONMENTS

The PC Exercises are available for use in MS-DOS 3.1+ and Macintosh Systems 6 and 7. Please make sure you are using the disk that is appropriate for your computer.

Hardware Requirements for the MS-DOS Version

To use the PC Exercises designed for the MS-DOS environment, you need to have at least the following computer configuration:
- An IBM-PC or compatible with 640K RAM and 3 1/2-inch disk drive
- A graphics card (CGA, EGA, VGA) and monitor
- A printer (if hard copy reports are desired)
- MS-DOS version 3.1 or higher

Hardware Requirements for the Macintosh Version

To use the PC Exercises designed for the Macintosh environment, you need to have at least the following computer configuration:

- A Macintosh Plus/SE with a hard drive is the minimum suggested configuration. Most versions of Systems 6 and 7 will work. (We were unable to test all versions.) Obviously, faster machines will improve performance and allow reasonable execution speeds on floppy disks.
- 2 megabytes of RAM.
- A high-density disk drive.

Printers Supported

MS-DOS printer drivers for HP Laserjet Series, Epson, and Okidata printers come with the software. These are necessary only to print graphs. Text reports can be printed on most printer models using the default printer driver. Because many of the latest printer models are able to emulate either HP or Epson printers, you may want to choose one of those drivers and test for your printer. Macintosh operating systems provide their own printer drivers and should work well with the PC Exercises. If you are using the MS-DOS version, please choose PRINTER SET-UP to select the appropriate printer for your computer hardware.

GETTING STARTED

You may use the PC Exercises either on a hard drive or from your floppy disk. If you decide to use a floppy disk drive, we recommend that you make a backup copy of the disk. Please refer to your operating system manuals for how to make a backup copy of a disk. In these instructions, the floppy disk drive is referred to as drive A (A>) and the hard disk as drive C (C>). However, your configuration may differ. If your floppy disk is drive B or your hard disk is drive D, just replace the A or C with the letter appropriate for your disk drive. In this section we present instructions for getting started in both the MS-DOS and Macintosh operating environments.

MS-DOS Environment

To run on a floppy disk:

1. Insert the PC Exercises disk, or a backup copy, into drive A.
2. Make the A drive the default drive by typing A: and pressing the ENTER key.
   C:\>A: ENTER

3. Start the PC Exercises program by typing PCX at the A> ("A prompt"), and pressing ENTER.
   A:\>PCX ENTER
4. The registration screen should appear. Now turn to the section of this appendix called The First Few Screens and follow the instructions.

To run on a hard disk:

1. Insert the PC Exercises disk into drive A.
2. Make the A drive the default drive by typing A: and pressing ENTER.
   C:\>A: ENTER
3. Install the program on the hard disk by typing INSTALL at the A> ("A prompt"), and pressing ENTER.
   A:\>INSTALL ENTER
4. A default directory indicating where the files will be installed will appear. To use that location, just press the ENTER key. You may also type in an alternative location.
5. The program will automatically start. To start the program the next time you use it, type in PCX from the directory where you've installed the files.
   C:\PCX\>PCX ENTER
6. The registration screen should appear. Now turn to the section of this appendix called The First Few Screens and follow the instructions.

Macintosh Environment

To run on a floppy disk:

1. Insert the PC Exercises (PCX) disk, or a backup copy, into the disk drive.
2. Once the PCX disk icon appears, double click on it to open the PC Exercises window.
3. Double click on the PCX icon to start the program.
4. The registration screen should appear. Now turn to the section of this appendix called The First Few Screens and follow the instructions.

To run on a hard disk:

1. Insert the PC Exercises (PCX) disk into the disk drive.
2. Once the PCX disk icon appears, copy it to the hard disk by clicking on it and dragging it to the hard disk (or the appropriate folder on the hard disk).
3. Open the PCX folder on the hard disk by double clicking on it.
4. Double click on the PCX icon to start the program.
5. The registration screen should appear. Now turn to the section of this appendix called The First Few Screens and follow the instructions.

THE FIRST FEW SCREENS

When the registration screen (Figure B.1) appears, please enter your name, class, and school. Because this information will be printed at the top of reports you print out, be sure to enter all information properly. You will not have a second chance to enter the information. Use either the mouse, the ENTER key, the TAB key, or ARROW keys to move among the fields. Select OK when you have finished. (On PCs without a mouse, this can be done either by pressing CTRL-O for OK or tabbing to the OK control button and pressing ENTER.)

After you register the software, the next screen will be the About PC Exercises Screen. This screen provides some basic information about the software, registration information, and available memory. You may select GETTING STARTED for a brief overview of the PC Exercises. If you do, a scrollable text box or window will appear. Information in this text box continues below the screen and can be viewed either by clicking on and holding the DOWN ARROW on the lower right side of the screen (at the bottom of the "scroll bar") or by pressing the DOWN ARROW key on your keyboard. Make sure you understand how to use this option because many of the exercises have scrollable windows.

Once you have mastered the scroll box and read the getting started text, select CANCEL or press the ESC key to continue. At this point, a list box will appear with Chapter 2 selected and the OK control button selected as the default. If you select OK you will start the exercise for Chapter 2. If you want to select another chapter, you could do so by clicking on the appropriate chapter (or scrolling down to see more) and then selecting OK. Since the examples that follow are from Chapter 6, select that chapter either by scrolling down the list box and clicking on Chapter 6 with the mouse or, in MS-DOS, by tabbing over to the list box, scrolling down with the arrow key until Chapter 6 is highlighted, and then selecting OK.

USING THE PC EXERCISES

Since each exercise uses the same basic approach, we will describe how to use the options common to all exercises. The sample data displayed in the exhibits is from the exercise for Chapter 6, Consumer Buying Behavior.

When you first select a chapter exercise, the introduction window for the exercise will be displayed. This description matches the PC Exercise description at the end of each chapter. A sample introduction screen appears in Figure B.2.

After you read the introduction, select CASE to read the specifics of the exercise. You may select the CASE control button either with your mouse, or by pressing CTRL-C (for case) or by pressing the TAB key in MS-DOS until the cursor is positioned on CASE and then pressing ENTER.

The information about the case is displayed in a scrollable text window. Most cases have more text than can fit on one screen. To see the part that is not in view, either select the DOWN ARROW on the lower right portion of the window with your mouse or press the DOWN ARROW key. You may print out the case by selecting PRINT. Figure B.3 shows a sample case screen.

After reading the case and possibly printing it out, select WORKSHEET to enter data related to the case. You'll always have the option of changing the data you enter, so don't worry about making data-entry errors or trying something a little out of the ordinary. Use the mouse or arrow keys to move around the screen. Usually after you enter data, you will advance to the next field automatically. If you need help on how to use the worksheet, select help with either F1 on MS-DOS or CMD-? (⌘-?) on the Macintosh. Selecting TOPIC will provide some guidance for the exercise. Figure B.4 displays a sample worksheet.

When you have completed the worksheet, print out the results and then select QUIZ. The quiz provides follow-up questions, some of which may require you to change data in the worksheet. The quiz is actually a simple word processor that allows you to enter your answers directly into the computer. Use the mouse or the arrow keys to move to the location you desire and then just type in your answer. The word processor is always in Insert mode. Therefore, you can always add new words wherever you want. Pressing ENTER will insert a new line. To delete, just use the DELETE key (to erase in front of the cursor) or backspace (to erase characters behind the cursor). Figure B.5 displays a sample quiz window.

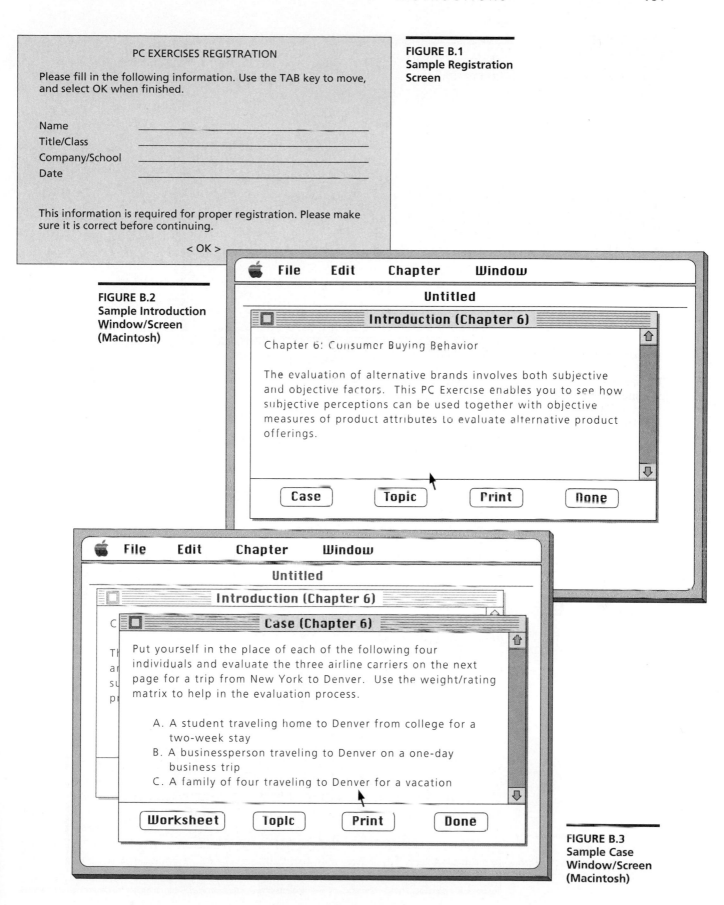

PC EXERCISES REGISTRATION

Please fill in the following information. Use the TAB key to move, and select OK when finished.

Name
Title/Class
Company/School
Date

This information is required for proper registration. Please make sure it is correct before continuing.

< OK >

FIGURE B.1
Sample Registration Screen

FIGURE B.2
Sample Introduction Window/Screen (Macintosh)

 File   Edit   Chapter   Window

Untitled

Introduction (Chapter 6)

Chapter 6: Consumer Buying Behavior

The evaluation of alternative brands involves both subjective and objective factors. This PC Exercise enables you to see how subjective perceptions can be used together with objective measures of product attributes to evaluate alternative product offerings.

Case   Topic   Print   None

 File   Edit   Chapter   Window

Untitled

Introduction (Chapter 6)

Case (Chapter 6)

Put yourself in the place of each of the following four individuals and evaluate the three airline carriers on the next page for a trip from New York to Denver. Use the weight/rating matrix to help in the evaluation process.

A. A student traveling home to Denver from college for a two-week stay
B. A businessperson traveling to Denver on a one-day business trip
C. A family of four traveling to Denver for a vacation

Worksheet   Topic   Print   Done

FIGURE B.3
Sample Case Window/Screen (Macintosh)

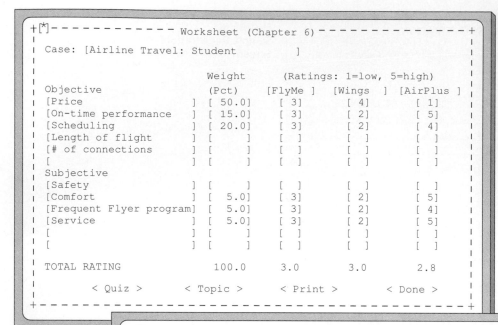

```
+[*]- - - - - - - - - - Worksheet (Chapter 6) - - - - - - - - - - - -+
| Case: [Airline Travel: Student                  ]                 |
|                                                                   |
|                    Weight    (Ratings: 1=low, 5=high)             |
| Objective          (Pct)    [FlyMe ]  [Wings ] [AirPlus ]         |
| [Price            ] [ 50.0]   [ 3]      [ 4]     [ 1]             |
| [On-time performance ] [ 15.0]  [ 3]     [ 2]     [ 5]            |
| [Scheduling       ] [ 20.0]   [ 3]      [ 2]     [ 4]             |
| [Length of flight ] [     ]   [  ]      [  ]     [  ]             |
| [# of connections ] [     ]   [  ]      [  ]     [  ]             |
| [                 ] [     ]   [  ]      [  ]     [  ]             |
| Subjective                                                        |
| [Safety           ] [     ]   [  ]      [  ]     [  ]             |
| [Comfort          ] [  5.0]   [ 3]      [ 2]     [ 5]             |
| [Frequent Flyer program] [  5.0]  [ 3]   [ 2]     [ 4]            |
| [Service          ] [  5.0]   [ 3]      [ 2]     [ 5]             |
| [                 ] [     ]   [  ]      [  ]     [  ]             |
| [                 ] [     ]   [  ]      [  ]     [  ]             |
|                                                                   |
| TOTAL RATING          100.0     3.0      3.0      2.8             |
|        < Quiz >      < Topic >     < Print >      < Done >        |
+- - - - - - - - - - - - - - - - - - - - - - - - - - - - - - - - - -+
```

FIGURE B.4
Sample Worksheet Window/Screen (MS-DOS with data entered)

FIGURE B.5
Sample Quiz Window/Screen (MS-DOS)

```
+[*]- - - - - - - - - - Quiz (Chapter 6) - - - - - - - - - - -^^
| 1) Do the ratings for each carrier vary by individual? Do the  | |
| weights?                                                       | |
|                                                               | |
|                                                               | |
| 2) Do all three decision makers come to the same purchase     | |
| decision? Why or why not?                                     | |
|                                                               | |
|                                                               | |
| 3) Do the results make sense to you? If not, try to explain why. | |
|                                                               | |
|                                                               | |
|                                                               | |
| 4) Use the brand evaluator to help you rate:                  | |
|                                                               | |
|     A. Soft drinks: Coke versus Pepsi                         | |
|     B. Fast-food restaurants: McDonald's, Wendy's, Burger King | |
+- - - - - - - - - - - - - - - - - - - - - - - - - - - - - - -vv
```

```
File        Chapter        Window
+-------------------------+
| Start New Exercise      |
|-------------------------|
| Printer Setup           |
| Print                   |
|-------------------------|
| Quit                    |
+-------------------------+
           +----------------------+
           | Introduction         |
           | Case                 |
           | Worksheet            |
           | Quiz                 |
           |----------------------|
           | Next Exercise        |
           +----------------------+
                    +----------------------+
                    | Switch to Window     |
                    | Close All Windows    |
                    | Font                 |
                    | Help                 |
                    | About                |
                    +----------------------+
```

FIGURE B.6
PC Exercises Software Menu Structure for Each Chapter

MENUS

Along with the windows and control buttons, which can direct the flow of the software, there is also a menu structure to select each aspect of the exercises. To select a menu option, either use the mouse, or, for the MS-DOS version, press F10, use the arrow keys to highlight a choice from the menu, then press ENTER. You may access the menu at any time, except when viewing a graph in MS-DOS, by using a mouse, or in MS-DOS, pressing F10. Figure B.6 displays the entire menu structure.

THE WINDOW MENU

Under the WINDOW menu, there are several choices you might use from time to time. If you have several windows open on the screen at the same time, SWITCH TO WINDOW will bring up a list of the open windows. Of course, you may be able to do this with your mouse as well. CLOSE ALL WINDOWS will close all open windows. HELP will access the help topics directly. Of course, you can also get context-sensitive help by pressing F1 on MS-DOS or the CMD-? (⌘-?) on the Macintosh. ABOUT will display current registration and free memory. ABOUT is also where you can access the Getting Started information.

The FONT menu choice may be useful if the font on your screen is not clear. Try using the small font on Macintosh machines. This supports the Monaco 9-point font, which should be available in all system folders. The Fit to Screen option will attempt to use the largest fixed-point font to fill the screen (and make it easier to read). Large will select one of the larger fixed-point fonts. Bold will show all displays in bold type, which may be helpful if you have a very high resolution screen. Experiment with these options. What works best for you will depend on your machine, screen resolution, and available fonts. On the MS-DOS version, the FONT menu choice allows you to select various color combinations for the menus, windows/controls, and reports.

SELECTING A PRINTER

Before printing any graphs in MS-DOS, you need to select a printer. Choose PRINTER SETUP under the FILE menu. Under Macintosh, the standard system dialog box will appear. Under MS-DOS, the default printer will be selected. Change this to either Epson (for most dot-matrix printers) or HP Laser (for most laser printers). You can print to a file with MS-DOS by selecting PRINT TO FILE and indicating a file name.

WHEN YOU ARE FINISHED

After you have completed the current exercise, you may either exit the software or start a new exercise. To exit the software, select QUIT under the FILE menu. To start a new exercise, select either NEXT EXERCISE under the CHAPTER menu or START NEW EXERCISE under the FILE menu. All of your changes to the current exercise will be saved to disk.

Notes

Chapter 1

1. Institute of Marketing. Definition of September 1966. In *Marketing in a Competitive Economy*, 3d ed., (London: Cassell/Associated Business Programmes, 1971), p. 47.
2. Peter D. Bennett, *Dictionary of Marketing Terms* (Chicago: American Marketing Association, 1988), p. 115.
3. William McInnes, "A Conceptual Approach to Marketing," in Reavis Cox, Wrote Alderson, and Stanley J. Shapiro, Eds., *Theory in Marketing* (Homewood, IL: Irwin, 1964), p. 56.
4. Adam Smith, *The Wealth of Nations*, Book IV (New York: Modern Library, 1937), p. 625.
5. General Electric Company, *Annual Report* (Fairfield, CT, 1952), p. 21. (Note: Certain language in the orginal, now considered sexist, has been changed.)
6. Robert F. Hartley, *Marketing Mistakes and Successes,* 5th ed., (New York: J. Wiley, 1992).
7. Theodore Levitt, "Marketing Myopia," *Harvard Business Review*, July/August 1960, p. 45.
8. The first formal argument for this appeared in Philip Kotler and Sidney J. Levy, "Broadening the Concept of Marketing," *Journal of Marketing*, vol. 33, January, 1969, pp. 10–15.
9. Committee on Definitions of the American Marketing Association. *Marketing Definitions*. Chicago: American Marketing Association, 1961.
10. E. Jerome McCarthy was the first to popularize this in E. Jerome McCarthy and William Perreault, *Basic Marketing: A Managerial Approach*, 11th ed., (Homewood, IL: Irwin, 1993). The first edition was published in 1960.
11. U.S. Department of Labor, Bureau of Labor Statistics, *Survey of Current Business* (Washington, DC: various dates).
12. This is a difficult number to estimate. Reavis Cox in *Distribution in a High-Level Economy* (Englewood Cliffs, NJ: Prentice-Hall, 1965), p. 149, put this value at 41.7%. I. Frederick Dewhurst in *Does Distribution Cost Too Much?* (Twentieth Century Fund, 1963), pp. 117–118, estimated this value at 58.9%.
13. Peter Drucker, *The Practice of Management* (New York: Harper & Row, 1954), p. 38.
14. Drucker, p. 38.

Chapter 2

1. S. C. Jain, *Marketing Planning and Strategy* (South Western, 1981), p. 69.
2. Glueck, *Business Policy and Strategic Management* (New York: McGraw-Hill, 1980), p. 88.
3. "The World According to Ernest," *The Economist,* April 6, 1991, p. 72.
4. Justin Martin, "Ulcer Update," *Fortune,* February 7, 1994, pp. 14–15.
5. *Wall Street Journal*, September 20, 1993, p. A9C.
6. The net migration to the United States of 500,000 persons per year excludes illegal immigration. The number of illegal immigrants has been increasing rapidly, and estimates range as high as 1 million per year.
7. Ani Hadjian, "Why It Will Be Hip to Be Old," *Fortune,* Autumn/Winter 1993, pp. 96–97.
8. Hadjian, *Fortune*.
9. Michael Mandel and Christopher Farrell, "How to Get America Growing Again," *Business Week*, Reinventing America 1992–Special Edition, pp. 22–44.
10. *American Demographics*, vol. 12, no. 2, February 1990, pp. 22–26.
11. Christina Duff, *Wall Street Journal*, December 17, 1993, p. B1.
12. "Households—A Special Report," *American Demographics*, 1992, pp. 15–16.
13. Pepper Miller and Ronald Miller, "Trends Are Opportunities for Targeting African Americans," *Marketing News*, January 20, 1992, p. 9.
14. "The Thirst of Champions," *The Economist*, June 6, 1992, p. 83.
15. Lawrence Mishel and Jared Bernstein, *The State of Working America* (New York: M. E. Sharpe, 1993), pp. 91–96.
16. William Lazer, "How Rising Affluence Will Reshape Markets," *American Demographics*, February 1984, pp. 17–21.
17. Robert D. Hershey, Jr., "How Accurately Does the Government Measure the Pinch of Inflation?" *The New York Times*, April 7, 1991, p. 4E.
18. Bureau of Labor Statistics, Office of Productivity and Technology.
19. Kenneth N. Wexley and Stanley B. Silverman, *Working Scared* (San Francisco: Jossey-Bass, 1993), pp. 73–74.
20. Al Ries and Jack Trout, *Bottom-Up Marketing* (New York: McGraw-Hill, 1989), p. 127.
21. "The Largest U.S. Corporations," *Fortune*, April 25, 1988, p. D17.
22. Faye Rice, "How Copycats Steal Billions," *Fortune*, April 22, 1991, pp. 157–164.
23. Tom Redburn, "Toys Are Us Stops Selling a Violent Video Game," *New York Times*, December 17, 1993, pp. B1, B6.
24. Study conducted by Market Facts and reported in "Who Should Police Videogame Violence?" *Advertising Age*, January 10, 1994, p. 28.
25. An additional 2.5% of the respondents indicated that they did not know who should rate videogames while 3.9% of the respondents refused to answer the question.
26. The assistance of Michael R. Pearce in the preparation of this section is gratefully acknowledged.
27. George Whie and Margaret B. W. Graham, "How to Spot a Technological Winner," *Harvard Business Review*, March–April 1978, pp. 146–52.
28. Ian M. Ross, "R & D: How to Stay Ahead in Technology," *Across The Board*, May 1987, pp. 8–15.
29. Information based on a telephone conversation between Tim A. Becker, Research Assistant to the authors, and a representative at the Polaroid Customer Service Line, January 1994.
30. Jon Roland, "Nantechnology: The Promise and Peril of Ultratiny Machines," *The Futurist*, March-April 1991, pp. 28–35.
31. Erich Block, "High-Tech Patriotism," *Omni*, April 1991, p. 10.

32. Candice Stevens, "Technoglobalism vs. Technonationalism: The Corporate Dilemma," *Columbia Journal of World Business*, Fall 1990, pp. 42–48.

33. Ford Motor Company, *Annual Report* (Dearborn, MI, 1992).

34. Frederick D. Sturdivant, *Business and Society* (Homewood, IL: Irwin, 1981), p. 119.

35. Barry Commoner, *The Closing Circle* (New York: Knopf, 1971), p. 33.

36. David Kirkpatrick, "Environmentalism: The New Decade," *Fortune*, February 12, 1990, pp. 44–53.

37. E. J. Muller, "Reuse It, Don't Lose It," *Distribution*, May 1992, pp. 20–21.

38. "The Greening of Detroit," *Business Week*, April 8, 1991, p. 59.

39. "Bib Oil Sees the Future—And It's Clean Gasoline," *Business Week*, April 8, 1991, p. 60.

40. William Tucker, "Shaking the Invisible Hand," *Forbes*, April 1, 1991, p. 64–66.

41. "What Price Posterity," *The Economist*, March 23, 1991, p. 73.

42. Paul Hofheinz, "The New Soviet Threat: Pollution," *Fortune*, July 27, 1992, pp. 110–114.

43. Alexander Hium and Charles D. Schewe, *The Portable MBA in Marketing* (New York: John Wiley, 1992), p. 49.

44. Murray Weidenbaum and Mark Jensen, *Threats and Opportunities in the International Economy* (St. Louis: Center for the Study of American Business, 1990), pp. 1–18.

45. Martin L. Bell, *Marketing Concepts and Strategy* (Boston: Houghton Mifflin, 1972), p. 18.

46. Carolyn Y. Woo, "Market Share Leadership—Not Always So Good," *Harvard Business Review*, January–February 1984, pp. 50–54.

47. Alex Taylor III, "U.S. Cars Come Back," *Fortune*, November 16, 1992, pp. 52–85.

48. Subrata N. Chakravarty, "We Had to Change the Playing Field," *Forbes*, February 4, 1991, pp. 82–86.

49. "The Best a Plan Can Get," *The Economist*, August 15, 1992, pp. 59–60.

50. Robert A. Glaclone and Stephen L. Payne, "Are Business Leaders Staging a Morality Play?" in Fred Mardment, Ed., *Management 91/92* (Guilford, CT: Dushkin Publishing Group, 1991), pp. 232–235.

51. Shelby D. Hunt and Scott Vitell, "A General Theory of Marketing Ethics," *Journal of Macromarketing*, Spring 1986, pp. 5–16.

52. Larue T. Hosner, "Does It Pay To Be Ethical?" Winter, 1991, pp. 3–4.

53. Peter Nulty, "How to Live by Your Wits," *Fortune*, April 20, 1992, pp. 119–120.

54. Gene R. Laczniak and Jacob Naor, "Global Ethics: Wrestling with the Corporate Conscience," *Business*, July–September 1985, pp. 3–10.

Chapter 3

1. Robert T. Davis, *Marketing Strategy (A): A Note* (Palo Alto, CA: Graduate School of Business, Stanford University, 1975), p. 3.

2. Davis, p. 3.

3. Theodore Levitt, "Marketing Myopia," *Harvard Business Review*, September–October, 1975.

4. Disney, *Annual Report* (Orlando, FL, 1992).

5. Apple Computer, Inc., *Annual Report* (San Jose, CA, 1992), p. 24.

6. Procter & Gamble, *Annual Report* (Cincinnati, OH, 1992).

7. Michael E. Porter, *Competitive Advantage* (New York: The Free Press, 1985).

8. "Gerstner's Near Vision for IBM," *Fortune*, November 15, 1993, pp. 119–126.

9. Laura Bird, "Marketers Sell Pen As Signature of Style," *Wall Street Journal*, November 9, 1993, p. B1.

10. Apple Computer, Inc., *Annual Report* (Orlando, FL, 1992), p.16.

11. "Dino-Mite Desires," *Advertising Age*, December 20, 1993, p. 12.

12. Gary Strauss, "Alternative Drinks Nudge Cola Giants," *USA Today*, November 9, 1992, p. 1.

13. *San Diego Union-Tribune*, September 16, 1993, p. C1.

14. A number of sources contain fuller descriptions of the Boston Consulting Group matrix including: George S. Day, *Analysis for Strategic Marketing Decisions* (St. Paul, MN: West, 1986) and David W. Cravens, *Strategic Marketing*, 3d ed., (Homewood, IL: Irwin, 1991).

15. Jennifer Lawrence, "Pepsico's Doritos Plots Worldwide Snack Attack," *Advertising Age*, November 15, 1993.

16. Stuart Elliott, "The Famous Brands on Death Row," *The New York Times*, November 7, 1993, Section 3, pp. 1, 6.

17. Elliott, *The New York Times*.

18. Bridget O'Brien, "Hot Suitcase Brings Success and Stress," *Wall Street Journal*, November 27, 1993, p. B1.

19. Elliott, *The New York Times*.

20. Cravens, p. 46.

21. A number of sources contain fuller descriptions of the GE Screening Grid including Day (see note 14) and Cravens (see note 14).

22. Although this analysis is discussed in many more recent texts, the original source is Igor H. Ansoff, "Strategies for Diversification," *Harvard Business Review*, vol. 35, September–October 1957, pp. 113–124.

23. *New York Times*, October 28, 1993.

24. Cyndee Miller, "Marketers Hoping Kids Will Join Club, Become Lifelong Customers," *Marketing News*, January 31, 1994, pp. 1–2.

25. Mrs. Field's Cookies, *Annual Report* (Park City, UT, 1992).

26. "The Age of Consolidation," *Business Week*, October 14, 1991.

27. *Japan Times Weekly International*, November 15–21, 1993, p. 16.

28. Cravens, *Strategic Marketing*.

29. Al Ries and Jack Trout, *Marketing Warfare* (New York: McGraw-Hill, 1986), p. 188.

30. This discussion on marketing control draws heavily from Philip Kotler and Alan R. Andreasen, *Strategic Marketing for Nonprofit Organizations*, 4th ed., (Englewood Cliffs, NJ: Prentice-Hall, 1991).

31. Kotler and Andreasen, p. 617.

32. Kotler and Andreasen, p. 80.

33. This example is based on information from the *1992 Annual Report* of the American Express Company.

34. American Express Annual Report, p. 3.

35. American Express Annual Report, p. 3.

36. Joshua Mills, "Parent Sets a Spinoff of Lehman," *The New York Times*, January 25, 1994, p. C1.

37. Gary Levin, "AmEx's new 'Plan' for charge cards relies on rewards programs," *Advertising Age*, October 11, 1993.

Chapter 4

1. Laura D'Andrea Tyson, "Competitiveness: An Analysis of the Problem and a Perspective on Future Policy," in Martin K. Starr, Ed., *Global Competitiveness* (New York: Norton, 1988), p. 97.

2. Roger Kokin, "For Coke, World Is Its Oyster," *The New York Times*, October 21, 1992, pp. D1, D6.

3. Harry Endsley, "After Eight Years the GATT Uruguay Round Concludes," *California Council for International Trade*, February 1994, pp. 1, 5.

4. Carla Rajioport, "Europe Looks Ahead to Hard Choices," *Fortune*, December 14, 1992, pp. 144–149.

5. Otto Johnson, Ed., *The 1994 Information Please Almanac*, 47th ed., (New York: Houghton Mifflin).

6. Al Reis and Steve Eisenbrown, "The Myths of the European Consumer," *Industry Week*, February 21, 1994, pp. 28–36.

7. Howard Schlossberg, "Canadians Urged to Be Patient, Award Long-term Trade Benefits," *Marketing News*, October 28, 1991, p. 24.

8. John Urquart and Gary Lamphier, "Canada," *The Wall Street Journal Reports*, September 21, 1990, pp. 32, 35–36.

9. U.S. Department of Commerce, Survey of Current Business, December 1993.

10. U.S. Department of Commerce, Survey of Current Business, December 1993.

11. Herbert M. Baum, "Borderless North America: One Company's Response," *Marketing Management,* Winter 1992, pp. 46–48.

12. Joseph Romn, "Japan's Flying Geese," *Forbes,* November 23, 1992, p. 108.

13. William J. Holstein, "The Stateless Corporation," *Business Week,* May 14, 1990, pp. 98–105.

14. Holstein, *Business Week,* op. cit., p. 103.

15. "P & G Makes a Run at Unilever Outside U.S.," *Advertising Age,* December 13, 1993, p. I–11.

16. James E. Ellis, "Why Overseas? 'Cause That's Where the Sales Are," *Business Week,* January 10, 1994, pp. 62–63.

17. Ani Hadjian and Lorraine Tritton, "Fortune 500 Performance," *Fortune,* July 26, 1993, p. 189.

18. Peter Marks, "Visionaries Offer Eyewear to Uzbeks," *The New York Times,* July 31, 1993.

19. Robert Farnighetti, Ed., *The World Almanac 1994,* Funk & Wagnalls, New Jersey.

20. Felix Rohatyn, "America's Economic Dependence, *America and the World 1988/1989* (New York: Council on Foreign Relations, 1989), pp. 53–65.

21. Rahul Jacob, "India is Opening for Business," *Fortune,* November 16, 1992, pp. 128–130.

22. U.S. Department of Commerce, Bureau of Economic Analysis, January 1994, Survey of Current Business.

23. Gillian Ann Findlay, "South Africa Dials Up Cellular Phones," *Advertising Age,* January 17, 1994, p. I–3, I–38.

24. "The Enigma of Japanese Advertising," *The Economist,* August 14, 1993, pp. 59–60.

25. Jane Perlez, "In East Europe, Kmart Faces an Attitude Problem," *The New York Times,* July 7, 1993, pp. D1–D2.

26. David J. Rachman and Elaine Romano, *Modern Marketing* (Chicago: Dryden Press, 1980), p. 552.

27. Arthur O. Fisher, "Advertising of New Products in Foreign Markets," in S. Watson Dunn, Ed., *International Handbook of Advertising* (New York: McGraw-Hill, 1964), p. 102.

28. Tom Redburn, "Luring Two Pigeons with One Bean," *The New York Times,* February 13, 1994; James C. Simmons, " A Matter of Interpretation," *American Way,* April 1983, pp. 106–111.

29. Allyson L. Stewart, "Toiletries, Cosmetics Marketing in Europe: Vive la Différence!," *Marketing News,* February 14, 1994, p. 6.

30. Ibid.

31. Yumiko Ono, "Pepsi Challenges Japanese Taboo as It Ribs Coke," *The Wall Street Journal,* March 6, 1991, pp. B1, B5; telephone conversation with PepsiCo's Director of International Marketing, April 1994.

32. "How to Analyze Political Risk," *Business Marketing,* January 1987, pp. 52–53.

33. Richard D. Lamm, "Crisis: The Uncompetitive Society," in Martin K. Starr, Ed., *Global Competitiveness* (New York: Norton, 1987), pp. 12–42.

34. Cyndee Miller, "U.S. Firms Rush to Claim Share of Newly Opened Vietnam Market," *Marketing News,* March 14, 1994, p. 11; Philip Shenon, "New Vietnam Combat: Coke vs. Pepsi," *The New York Times,* February 7, 1994, pp. D1–D2.

35. Harry Endsley, "After Eight Years the GATT Uruguay Round Concludes," *California Council for International Trade Newsletter,* pp. 1, 5.

36. Ideas for this section from: Philip Kotler and Gary Armstrong, *Marketing: An Introduction,* 3d ed., (Englewood Cliffs, NJ: Prentice-Hall, 1993), pp. 477–478.

37. James S. Howard, "West Meets East—The Competition, That Is," *D & B Reports,* May/June 1993, pp. 334–337.

38. U.S. Congress, Omnibus Trade and Competitiveness Act of 1988 (102 Statute 117), Public Law 100-418 [HR4848], August 23, 1988.

39. Earl H. Fry, "Is the United States a Declining Economic Power?," *Business in the Contemporary World,* Summer 1989, pp. 38–47.

40. U.S. Department of Commerce, Survey of Current Business, December 1993.

41. U.S. Department of Commerce, Survey of Current Business, December 1993.

42. Alex Taylor III, "The U.S. in Fighting Shape," *Fortune,* April 24, 1989, pp. 42–48.

43. Mark Pendergrast, "A Brief History of Coca-Colonization," *The New York Times,* August 15, 1993.

44. Yoshi Tsurumi, "A Japanese–American Grand Bargain," *Pacific Basin Quarterly,* Fall 1993, pp. 5–10.

45. "Will Big Mac Meet Its Match in the Land of the Rising Sun?" *Forbes,* May 15, 1978, p. 118; Martin Tolchin and Susan Tolchin, *Buying into America* (New York: Times Books, 1988).

46. Diane Lindquist, "Pillsbury in Joint Mexican Venture," *The San Diego Union-Tribune,* September 2, 1993, p. C1.

47. "Coke Joint Venture With Moscow," *Marketing News,* February 17, 1992, p. 10.

48. Bryan Batson, "Chinese Fortunes," *Sales & Marketing Management,* March 1994, pp. 93–98.

49. Robert Farnighetti, Ed., *World Almanac 1994,* Funk & Wagnalls, New Jersey.

50. Hirotaka Takeuchi and Michael E. Porter, "Three Roles of International Marketing in Global Strategy," in Michael E. Porter, Ed., *Competition in Global Industries* (Boston: Harvard University Press, 1987), pp. 111–146.

51. Paul W. Beamish, J. Peter Kelling, Donald J. Lecraw, and Harold Crookell, *International Management* (Homewood, IL: Irwin, 1991), p. 39.

52. Brad Durham, "CIS is Next Battlefield in Cola Wars," *We,* June 29–July 12, 1992, p. 6; Philip Shenon, "New Vietnam Combat: Coke vs. Pepsi," *The New York Times,* February 7, 1994, pp. D1–D7.

53. Allyson L. Stewart, "Toiletries, Cosmetics Marketing in Europe: Vive la Différence!," *Marketing News,* February 14, 1994, p. 6.

54. Cacilie Rohwedder, "Ethnic Food Whets Appetites in Europe, Enticing Producers to Add Foreign Fare," *The Wall Street Journal,* November 1, 1993.

55. Warren J. Keegan, *Multinational Marketing Management* (Englewood Cliffs, NJ: Prentice-Hall, 1984), p. 321.

56. Robert E. Hite and Cynthia L. Fraser, "International Advertising Strategies of Multinational Corporations," *Journal of Advertising Research,* August–September, 1988, pp. 9–17.

57. Ali Kanso, "International Advertising Strategies: Global Commitment to Local Vision," *Journal of Advertising Research,* January–February 1992, pp. 10–14.

58. George E. Belch and Michael A. Belch, *Introduction to Advertising & Promotion,* 2d ed., (Homewood, IL: Irwin, 1993), p. 736.

59. Allyson L. Stewart, "Toiletries, Cosmetics Marketing in Europe: Vive la Différence!," *Marketing News,* February 14, 1994, p. 6.

60. Belch and Belch, op. cit., p. 753.

61. Robert L. Simison, "Huge Market Potential in China Lures Auto Makers," *Wall Street Journal,* January 11, 1994, p. B4.

62. Reported on ABC News, March 31, 1994.

HARLEY-DAVIDSON CASE STUDY

1. Malia Boyd, "Harley-Davidson Motor Company," *Incentive,* September 1993, pp. 26–31.

2. Bob Woods, "Hog Wild," *Profiles: The Magazine of Continental Airlines,* July 1994, p. 31.

3. Thomas Gelb, "Overhauling Corporate Engines Drive Winning Strategies," *Journal of Business Strategy,* vol. 19, no. 6, November/December 1993, pp. 6–12.

4. Boyd, op. cit., pp. 26–31.
5. Adam Blankenship, "Harley-Davidson Riding High on the Hog," *The Japan Times Weekly International Edition*, November 29–December 5, 1993, p. 18.
6. Gary Slutsker, "Hog Wild," *Forbes*, May 24, 1992, pp. 45–46.
7. Pablo Del Nibletto, "Case Study: Historical Data Needed to See into Harley-Davidson's Future," *Info Canada*, July 1992, p. 42.
8. Brian Moskal, "Born to Be Real," *Industry Week*, August 2, 1993, pp. 14–18.
9. Ibid.
10. Harley-Davidson, Inc., *Annual Report* (Milwaukee, WI, 1992).

Chapter 5

1. "Transportation's Toll, *American Demographics*, Reference Series, no. 5: *American Spending*, July 1993, p. 12.
2. "Transportation's Toll," (see note 1), p. 13.
3. Michael Hartnett, reported in "Travel Tips", *Direct*, January 1994, p. 59.
4. Calvin Sims, "Giving Denny's a Menu for Change," *New York Times*, November 1, 1993, p. 17.
5. *Wall Street Journal*, Educational Edition 1993, p. 1.
6. Thomas W. Osborn, "Analytic Techniques for Opportunity Marketing," *Marketing Communications*, September 1987, p. 54.
7. This information was obtained from an interview by Tim A. Becker, authors' research assistant, on January 13, 1994, with Martin Kolsky, regional manager for UniBev, U.S. importers of XXXX Beer.
8. Fara Warner, "In the Fast Lane," *BrandWeek*, vol. 34, no. 27, July 5, 1993, pp. 20–24.
9. "New Ford Mustang Designed to Attract More Female Buyers," *Marketing News*, January 3, 1994, p. 27.
10. Terence P. Pare, "Mature Mainstreaming", part of the article, "The Tough New Consumer/Winning Companies," *Fortune*, Autumn/Winter 1993, p. 24.
11. Cyndee Miller, "Cosmetics Firms Finally Discover the Ethnic Market," *Marketing News*, August 30, 1993, p. 2.
12. Materials provided by VNU Business Information Services, Claritas/NPDC, Alexandria, VA.
13. Thomas Moore, "Different Folks, Different Strokes," *Fortune*, September 16, 1985, pp. 65–68.
14. Information from VNU Business Information Services, Claritas/NPDC, Alexandria, VA.
15. This information is from company materials provided by CACI Market Research, 3333 N. Torrey Pines Ct, San Diego, CA, January 1994.
16. Michael P. Solomon, *Consumer Behavior* (Needham, MA: Allyn and Bacon, 1992), p. 492.
17. *The VALS 2 Segmentation System* (Menlo Park, CA: SRI International), 1989.
18. This discussion is partially adapted from George E. Belch and Michael A. Belch, *Introduction to Advertising & Promotion*, 2d ed., (Homewood, IL: Irwin, 1993), p. 165.
19. Tom Bayer, "American Accent," *Advertising Age*, July 28, 1986, p. 30.
20. Aimee Stern, "Marketers Question Value of Psychographics," *Adweek*, August 3, 1987, p. 41.
21. Patricia Selig, "News Flash/Trends," *Fortune*, August 23, 1993, pp. 52–56.
22. Solomon, p. 489.
23. This section is based on Russell Haley, "Benefit Segmentation: A Decision-Oriented Tool," *Journal of Marketing*, July 1968, pp. 30–35.
24. Joseph D. Brown, "Benefit Segmentation of the Fitness Market," *Health Marketing Quarterly*, vol. 9, no. 3/4, 1992, pp. 19–28.
25. Mark Landler, "Move Over Boomers," *Business Week*, December 14, 1993, pp. 74–82.

26. Information on First Cabin Travel was obtained from a personal interview by Tim A. Becker, research assistant, of Robert Kenyon, company president, in January; 1994.
27. Allen E. Schultz, "Wall Street Courts Women With Pitch They Have Different Financial Needs," *Wall Street Journal*, June 11, 1992, pp. C1, C16.
28. James F. Engel, Martin R. Warshaw, and Thomas C. Kinnear, *Promotional Strategy*, 7th ed., (Homewood, IL: Irwin, 1991), p. 230.
29. Engel, Warshaw, and Kinnear, p. 231.
30. David A. Aaker and J. Gary Shansby, "Positioning Your Product," *Business Horizons* (May–June 1982), pp. 56–62.
31. Eric N. Berkowitz, Roger A. Kerin, Steven W. Hartley, and William Rudelius, *Marketing*, 4th ed., (Homewood, IL: Irwin, 1994), p. 252.
32. Stephanie Strom, "Image and Attitude Are Department Stores' Draw," *New York Times*, August 12, 1993.
33. George E. Belch and Michael A. Belch, *Introduction to Advertising & Promotion*, 2nd ed., (Homewood, IL: Irwin, 1993), p. 182.

Chapter 6

1. Michael R. Solomon, *Consumer Behavior Buying, Having, and Being* (Needham Hts, MA: Allyn and Bacon, 1992), p. 4.
2. E. Jerome, Michael R. McCarthy, and William D. Perreault, Jr., *Basic Marketing*, 10th ed., (Homewood, IL: Irwin, 1990), p. 170.
3. James Engel, Roger Blackwell, and Paul Miniard, *Consumer Behavior*, 5th ed., (Fort Worth, TX: The Dryden Press, 1986), p. 28.
4. For an excellent review of consumer external search, see Joseph W. Newman, "Consumer External Search: Amount and Determinants," in Arch Woodside, Jagdish Sheth, Peter Bennett, Eds., *Consumer and Industrial Buying Behavior* (New York: Elsevier North Holland, 1977), pp. 79–94.
5. For more detail on the concept of evoked set, see John Howard and Jagdish Sheth, *The Theory of Buyer Behavior* (New York: Wiley, 1969).
6. Del Hawkins, Roger Best, and Kenneth Coney, *Consumer Behavior Implications for Marketing Strategy*, 4th ed., (Homewood, IL: BPI/Irwin, 1989), p. 664. Postpurchase dissonance is a subset of the theory of cognitive dissonance. An overview can be found in W.H. Cummings and M. Venkatesan, "Cognitive Dissonance and Consumer Behavior: A Review of the Evidence," *Journal of Marketing Research*, November 1978, pp. 650–655.
7. Howard and Sheth, *Theory of Buying Behavior*, pp. 27–28.
8. Henry Assael, *Consumer Behavior and Marketing Action*, 4th ed., (Boston: PWS-Kent, 1992), pp. 16–17.
9. Assael, pp. 16–17.
10. See Abraham H. Maslow, "A Theory of Human Motivation," *Psychological Review*, vol. 50, 1943, pp. 370–96; and Abraham H. Maslow, *Motivation and Personality* (New York: Harper & Row, 1954).
11. Kenneth Runyon and David Stewart, *Consumer Behavior and the Practice of Marketing*, 3d ed., (New York: Merrill, 1987), p. 423.
12. Thomas Robertson, Joan Zielinski, and Scott Ward, *Consumer Behavior* (Glenview, IL: Scott, Foresman, 1984), pp. 166–71.
13. Edward Grubb and Gregg Hupp, "Perception of Self, Generalized Stereotypes, and Brand Selection," *Journal of Marketing Research*, February 1968, pp. 58–63.
14. Nancy Gibbs, *Time*, June 27, 1988, p. 54.
15. Kent Monroe and Susan Petroshius, "Buyers; Perceptions of Price: An Update of the Evidence," in Harold Kassarjian and Thomas Robertson, Eds., *Perspectives in Consumer Behavior*, 3d ed., (Glenview, IL: Scott, Foresman, 1981) pp. 43–55.
16. This section is based on Thomas Robertson, et. al., *Consumer Behavior*, pp. 192–199.

17. Reported in Marketing Briefs—"New Coke II on Sale in Midwest," *Marketing News*, vol. 26, no. 11, May 25, 1992, p. 1.

18. Harold H. Kassarjian and Mary Jane Sheffet, "Personality and Consumer Behavior: An Update," in Harold H. Kassarjian and Thomas S. Robertson, Eds., *Perspectives in Consumer Behavior*, 3d ed., (Scott, Foresman, 1981), p. 160.

19. Harold H. Kassarjian, "Personality and Consumer Behavior: A Review," *Journal of Marketing Research*, November 1971, pp. 409–19.

20. Martin Fishbein and Icek Ajzen, *Belief, Attitude, Intention, and Behavior: An Introduction to Theory and Research* (Reading, MA: Addison-Wesley, 1975), p. 6.

21. Milton J. Rosenberg, et. al., *Attitude Organization and Change* (New Haven, CT: Yale University Press, 1960).

22. George Katona, *The Powerful Consumer* (New York: McGraw-Hill, 1960), pp. 80–83.

23. This example is from "Don't Gouge the Customer," by Patricia Sellers, *Fortune*, Autumn/Winter 1993, p. 29.

24. David A. Ricks, "International Business Blunders: An Update," *Business and Economic Review*, January–March, 1988, pp. 11–14.

25. Additional blunders have been collected by David A. Ricks of Ohio State University and reported to United Press International by Rosemary Armao, October 28, 1980.

26. John A. Howard, *Consumer Behavior in Marketing Strategy* (Englewood Cliffs, NJ: Prentice-Hall, 1989), p. 231 as noted from T. S. Robertson, et. al., *Consumer Behavior* (Glenview, IL: Scott, Foresman, 1984).

27. Engel, Blackwell, and Miniard, *Consumer Behavior*, p. 328.

28. Robertson, et. al., 1984, *Consumer Behavior*, pp. 518–21.

29. This example came from "Downscale Consumers, Long Neglected, Start to Get Some Respect From Marketers," *Wall Street Journal*, May 31, 1990, p. 81 as reported in Henry Assael, *Consumer Behavior & Marketing Action*, 4th ed., (Boston: PWS Kent, 1992), p. 344.

30. Robertson, et. al., 1984, *Consumer Behavior*, p. 521.

31. Francis S. Bourne, "Group Influence in Marketing," in Louis E. Boone, Ed., *Classics in Consumer Behavior* (PPC Books, 1977), pp. 211–225.

32. Elihu Katz and Paul F. Lazarsfeld, *Personal Influence* (New York: The Free Press, 1955).

33. Assael, *Consumer Behavior and Marketing Action*, p. 442.

34. George P. Moschis and Roy L. Moore, "Decision Making Among the Young: A Socialization Perspective," *Journal of Consumer Research*, September 1979, pp. 101–112.

35. Scott Ward and Daniel B. Wackman, "Children's Purchase Influence Attempts and Parental Yielding," *Journal of Marketing Research*, August 1972, pp. 316–19.

36. This section is based on Assael, *Consumer Behavior and Marketing Action*, 4th ed., chapter 18 and Hawkins, Best, and Coney, *Consumer Behavior Implications for Marketing Strategy*, 4th ed., chapter 13.

37. R. W. Belk, "Situational Variables and Consumer Behavior," *Journal of Consumer Research*, December 1975, p. 158.

38. Assael, *Consumer Behavior and Marketing Action*, pp. 527–529.

39. R. W. Belk, "Situational Variables and Consumer Behavior," *Journal of Consumer Research*, December 1975, p. 161 as reproduced in D. I. Hawkins, R. J. Best, and K. A. Coney, *Consumer Behavior Implications for Marketing Strategy*, 4th ed., (Homewood, IL: BPI/Irwin, 1989), p. 506.

40. R. E. Milliman, "The Influence of Background Music on the Behavior of Restaurant Patrons," *Journal of Consumer Research*, September 1986, p. 289.

41. J. B. Palmer and R. H. Cropnick, "New Dimensions Added to Conjoint Analysis," *Marketing News*, January 3, 1986, p. 62.

42. E. Dupnick, "The Effect of Context on Cognitive Structure," (Ph.D. dissertation, University of Arizona, Tucson, 1979).

43. J. A. Cote, J. McCullough, and M. Reilly, "Effects of Unexpected Situations on Behavior-Intention Differences," *Journal of Consumer Research*, September 1985, p. 193.

44. R. E. Nisbett and D. E. Kanouse, "Obesity, Food Deprivation, and Supermarket Shopping Behavior," *Journal of Personality and Social Psychology*, August 1969, p. 290.

45. B. E. Mattson, and A. J. Dubinsky, "Shopping Patterns," *Psychology and Marketing*, Spring 1987, pp. 42–62.

46. Mattson and Dubinsky, also S. M. Smith and S. E. Beatty, "An Examination of Gift Purchasing Behavior," in 1985 *Marketing Educators Conference*, R. F. Lusch, et. al., Eds., (Chicago: American Marketing Association, 1985), pp. 69–74; and D. M. Andrus, E. Silver, and D. E. Johnson, "Status Brand Management and Gift Purchase," *Journal of Consumer Marketing*, Winter 1986, pp. 5–13.

47. E. M. Tauber, "Why Do People Shop?," *Journal of Marketing*, October 1972, p. 47.

Chapter 7

1. R. W. Haas, *Business Marketing Management*, 5th ed., (Boston: PWS-Kent, 1992), p. 2.

2. Haas, p. 214.

3. John R. Johnson, "Promoting Profits through Partnerships," *Industrial Distribution*, March 1994, pp. 22–24.

4. "McKesson Erects Computer Wall Against Competition," *Sales & Marketing Management*, March 11, 1985, pp. 123–24.

5. Johnson, p. 22.

6. Theordore Levitt, "After the Sale Is Over . . .," *Harvard Business Review*, September–October 1983, pp. 87–93.

7. Haas, pp. 17–23.

8. U.S. Department of Commerce, Survey of Current Business, January 1994.

9. U.S. Department of Commerce, Survey of Current Business, January 1994.

10. Warren Suss, "How to Sell to Uncle Sam," *Harvard Business Review*, November–December, 1984, pp. 136–144.

11. AMA Information Center, June 1994.

12. Haas, p. 16.

13. Amy Stone, "Hot Growth Companies," *Business Week*, May 23, 1994, pp. 92–98; *The Economist*, July 3, 1993, p. 59.

14. Haas, Chapter 4.

15. Haas, Chapter 4.

16. Figures for this comparison came from Boeing Company documents and the U.S. Department of Transportation, Washington, DC, 1994.

17. B. Charles Ames and James Hlavacek, *Managerial Marketing for Industrial Firms* (New York: Random House, 1984), p. 21.

18. See Patrick Robinson, Charles Faris, and Yoram Wind, *Industrial Buying and Creative Marketing* (Needham Heights, MA: Allyn & Bacon, 1967) and Frederick Webster and Yoram Wind, *Organizational Buying Behavior* (Englewood Cliffs, NJ: Prentice-Hall, 1972).

19. Thomas Bonoma and Benson Shapiro, *Industrial Market Segmentation: A Nested Approach*, Marketing Science Institute, February 1983.

20. Cornelis A. de Kluyver and David B. Whitlark, "Benefit Segmentation for Industrial Products," *Industrial Marketing Management*, 15(1986): 273.

21. Sally Dibb and Lyndon Simkin, "Implementation Problems in Industrial Market Segmentation," *Industrial Marketing Management*, February 1994, pp. 55–63.

22. Dibb and Simkin.

23. Haas, p. 297.

24. J. D. Hlavacek and N. M. Reddy, "Identifying and Qualifying Industrial Market Segments," *European Journal of Marketing*, vol. 20, 1986, pp. 8–21.

25. Rodney L. Griffith and Louis G. Pol, "Segmenting Industrial Markets," *Industrial Marketing Management*, February 1994, pp. 39–46.

26. Rowland Moriarty and David Reibstein, "Benefit Segmentation in Industrial Markets," *Journal of Business Research*, December 1986, pp. 463–486.

27. Haas, p. 287.
28. Jean-Marie Choffray and Gary L. Lilien, "Industrial Marketing Segmentation by the Structure of the Purchasing Process," *Industrial Marketing Management*, 9, (1980): pp. 331–342.
29. This section is adapted from Robert W. Haas, *Industrial Marketing Management* (Petrocelli/Charter, 1976), pp. 56–60.
30. W. J. Baley, Moss Maden, and Graham Scholefield, *Regional Studies*, vol. 27, no. 3, June 1993, p. 179.
31. Robinson, Faris, and Wind, *Industrial Buying and Creative Marketing*, pp. 28–32.
32. S. Joe Puri and C. M. Sashi, "Anatomy of a Complex Computer Purchase," *Industrial Marketing Management*, February 1994, pp. 17–27.

Chapter 8

1. In addition to the specific references made in this section to the Malhotra text (see cite 2), the author also referred to *Contemporary Marketing Research*, 2d ed. by Carl McDaniel, Jr. and Roger Gates, (Minneapolis–St. Paul: West, 1993), in preparing this section.
2. Naresh K. Malhotra, *Marketing Research: An Applied Orientation* (Englewood Cliffs, NJ: Prentice-Hall, 1993), p. 13.
3. Ibid.
4. "Marketers Increasing Their Use of Decision Support Systems," *Marketing News*, May 22, 1989, p .29; "More Marketers Are Going On Line for Decision Support," *Marketing News*, November 12, 1990, p.14; Terrence O'Brien, "Decision Support Systems," *Marketing Research*, December 1990, pp. 51–55.
5. Robert F. Hartley, *Marketing Mistakes*, 5th ed., (New York: Wiley, 1992), pp. 140–159.
6. "New Marketing Research Definition Approved," *Marketing News*, January 2, 1987.
7. Jack Honomichl, "Combined Revenues for '93 Hit $3.7 Billion," *Marketing News*, June 6, 1994, p. H2, and "Three Factors Drive Growth of Top 50 Research Firms, *Marketing News*, June 7, 1993, p. H2.
8. E. H. Demby, "ESOMAR Urges Changes in Reporting Demographics, Issues Worldwide Report," *Marketing News*, January 8, 1990, pp. 24–25.
9. Malhotra, p. 772.
10. "Hotel Chains Capitalize on International Travel Market," *Hotels and Restaurant International*, June 1989, pp. 81S–86S, and "Target Marketing Points to Worldwide Success," *Hotels and Restaurants International*, June 1989, p. S87.
11. Raymond Serafin, "VW Considers a New Bug-inning in U.S. Car Market," *Advertising Age*, January 10, 1994, p. 6.
12. "Co-operation North," *Marketing Practice: The Republic of Ireland and Northern Ireland*, Third Study Series, Report No. 3, 1991.
13. H. Aftab Ahmad in "Readers Speak Out on CMOR," in *Marketing News*, August 16, 1993, p. A4.
14. Robert F. Hartley, *Marketing Mistakes*, 5th ed., (New York: Wiley, 1992), pp. 294–310.
15. McDaniel, p. 17 (see note 1).
16. Jack Honomichl, "Three Factors Drive Growth of Top 50 Research Firms," *Marketing News*, June 7, 1993, p. H2.
17. Malhotra, glossary, G1–G10.
18. For a more thorough catalogue of secondary data sources, see Kinnear and Taylor, *Marketing Research: An Applied Approach*, 4th ed., (New York: McGraw-Hill, 1991), pp. 163–176, 194–207.
19. George E. Belch and Michael A. Belch, *Introduction to Advertising & Promotion*, 2d ed., (Homewood, IL: Irwin, 1993), p. 761.
20. Malhotra, p. 780.
21. McDaniel, glossary, G1–G10.
22. Adapted from Malhotra, glossary, 811–825.
23. McDaniel, glossary, G1–G10.

24. Terence P. Pare, "How to Find Out What They Want," *Fortune*, Autumn/Winter 1993, pp. 39–41.
25. Laura Bird, "Marketing," *Wall Street Journal*, February 4, 1994, p. B1.
26. This research was reported in the Pare article in *Fortune* (see note 24).
27. Malhotra, glossary, 811–825.
28. Ibid.
29. Adapted from Malhotra, glossary, 811–825.
30. Susan Carroll, "Questionnaire Design Affects Response Rate," *Marketing News*, January 3, 1994, p. 14.
31. Malhotra, p. 190.
32. Peter J. DePaulo and Rick Weitzer, "Interactive Phone Technology Delivers Survey Data Quickly," *Marketing News*, January 3, 1994, p. 15.
33. For a more thorough discussion, see special section on CMOR in the *Marketing News*, August 16, 1993.
34. Harry W. O'Neill, "Dinosaurs Thought They Had It Made, Too," *Marketing News*, August 16, 1993, p. A5.
35. Nicolaos E. Synodinos and Jerry M. Brennan, "Computer Interactive Interviewing in Survey Research," *Psychology and Marketing*, vol. 5, Summer 1988, pp. 117–138.
36. Malhotra, p. 429.
37. Adapted from McDaniel, glossary, G1–G10.
38. Charles D. Parker and Kevin F. McCrohan, "Increasing Mail Survey Response Rates: A Discussion of Methods and Induced Bias," in *Marketing: Theories and Concepts for an Era of Change*, Eds. John Summey, R. Viswanathan, Ronald Taylor, and Karen Glynn; (Atlanta: Southern Marketing Association, 1983), pp. 254–256.
39. McDaniel, glossary, G1–G10.
40. E. R. Morrissey, "Sources of Error in the Coding of Questionnaire Data," *Sociological Methods and Research*, vol. 1, 1982; James McDonald, "Assessing Intercoder Reliability and Resolving Reliability and Resolving Discrepancies," in B. J. Walker, *An Assessment of Marketing Thought and Practice* (Chicago: American Marketing Association, 1982), pp. 435–438.
41. J. A. Sonquist and W.C. Dunkelberg, *Survey and Opinion Research: Procedures for Processing and Analysis* (Englewood Cliffs, NJ: Prentice-Hall, 1977), pp. 100–105.
42. Gilliann Ann Findlay, "South Africa Dials Up Cellular Phones," *Advertising Age*, January 17, 1994, p. I–3, p. I–38.
43. Matthias J. Kotowski, "Accident Trend Analysis by Cumulative Rates Calculation," *Professional Safety*, December 1987, pp. 15–18.
44. For a complete discussion of the Survey of Buying, the Buying Power Index, and how to use it, see *Sales & Marketing Management*, August 30, 1993.
45. Alexa Ball, "Will KFC's Latest Test Spawn a Change?" *Restaurant Business*, June 10, 1993, pp. 23–24.
46. Paul Meller, "Pepsi Tests Global Launch in the UK," *Marketing News*, March 4, 1993, p. 3.
47. This incident was reported during an interview with a marketing researcher at a major cookie and snack food company. The individual prefers to remain anonymous.

HARLEY-DAVIDSON CASE STUDY

1. Thomas Bolfert, Buzz Buzzelli, M. Bruce Chubbuck, Martin Jack Rosenblum, Eds., *Harley-Davidson Historical Overview* (Milwaukee, WI, 1994).
2. Bob Woods, "Hog Wild," *Profiles: The Magazine of Continental Airlines*, July 1994, p. 31.
3. Vaughn L. Beals, "Operation Recovery: How Customers Helped Us Turn Around Harley-Davidson," *Success*, January/February 1989, p. 16.
4. Richard L. Stern, "The Graying Wild Ones," *Forbes*, January 6, 1992, p. 40.
5. Kevin Kelly and Karen Lowry Miller, "The Rumble Heard Round the World: Harleys," *Business Week*, May 24, 1993, pp. 58–60.
6. Company documents, 1994.

Chapter 9

1. Rodman Sims, "Good Marketing Aided by a Good Product," *Marketing News*, November 22, 1993, p. 4.
2. Philip Kotler and Gary Armstrong, *Marketing: An Introduction*, 3d ed., (Englewood Cliffs, NJ: Prentice-Hall, 1993).
3. G. Lynne Shostack, "Breaking Free From Product Marketing," *Journal of Marketing*, 42 (July 1977), pp. 73–80.
4. Peter Bennet, Ed., *Dictionary of Marketing Terms* (Chicago: American Marketing Association, 1988), p. 95.
5. Melvin Copeland, "Relation of Consumers' Buying Habits to Marketing Methods," *Harvard Business Review*, April 1923, pp. 282–289. For additional information on this classification structure, see Louis Bucklin, "Retail Strategy and the Classification of Consumer Goods," *Journal of Marketing*, January 1963, pp. 50–55; Richard Holten, "The Distinctions between [sic] Convenience Goods, Shopping Goods, and Specialty Goods," *Journal of Marketing*, July 1958, pp. 53–56; and Patrick Murphy and Ben Enis, "Classifying Products Strategically," *Journal of Marketing*, July 1986, pp. 24–42.
6. "1992 Annual Market Survey of Waterbed Manufacturers," prepared by BDO Seidman for the Waterbed Manufacturers Association, Washington, DC, July 1993.
7. David Biemesderfer, "Fast Track," *World Traveler*, November 1993, pp. 21–26.
8. Pat Dailey, "Bread Machines Becoming Not Just Wants But Kneads," *San Diego Union-Tribune*, May 19, 1994, p. F-2.
9. Laurie M. Grossman, "Soda Pop Sales Sparkle at Fountain Outlets," *Wall Street Journal*, November 18, 1993, pp. B1, B5.
10. "'Red Hot Summer'", *Marketing News*, May 9, 1994, p. 1.
11. Peter Bennet, Ed., *Dictionary of Marketing Terms* (Chicago: American Marketing Association, 1988), p. 18.
12. Patricia Sellers, "Yes, Brands Can Still Work Magic," *Fortune*, February 7, 1994, pp. 133–134.
13. Manager of Public Information at the United States Patent and Trademark Office, telephone conversation with Tim A. Becker, research assistant, June 17, 1994.
14. Maxine Lans, "Protecting Your Product's Shape," *Marketing News*, March 14, 1994, p. 12.
15. Larry McShane, "Who Owns 'Nothing But Net'?," *The San Diego Union-Tribune*, April 29, 1994, p. C1.
16. American Marketing Association Information Center, Chicago, Illinois, telephone report obtained by Tim A. Becker, research assistant, June 1994.
17. James McNeal and Linda Zeren, "Brand Name Selection for Consumer Products," *MSU Business Topics*, Spring 1981, pp. 35–39.
18. Kim Cleland, "Multimarketer Mélange an Increasingly Tasty Option on the Store Shelf," *Advertising Age*, May 2, 1994, p. S-10.
19. "Out of Control," *Marketing News*, November 22, 1993, p. 1.
20. Adrienne Fawcett, "The Consumer Mindset in the '90s: DDB Needham's Lifestyle Study," *Advertising Age*, April 18, 1994, pp. 12–13.
21. Kevin J. Clancy, "Marketing With Blinders On," *Across the Board*, October 1993, pp. 33–38.
22. Riccardo A. Davis, "Private Label Treated Like National Brand," *Advertising Age*, December 13, 1993, p. 25.
23. Emily DeNitto, "Brand Names Learn from Hard Times to Rise Again," *Advertising Age*, April 18, 1994, pp. 3, 46.
24. This range of estimates is offered in two articles: Julie Liesse, "Private Label Losing its 'Enemy' Status, *Advertising Age*, October 11, 1993, p. 15; and Julie Liesse, "Private Labels Appear Less Omnipresent in GMA Study," *Advertising Age*, April 25, 1994, p. 8.
25. Marcella Rosen, "Net TV's Answer to Private Label Growth," *Advertising Age*, March 21, 1994, p. 24.
26. Richard Cardozo, *Product Policy: Cases and Concepts* (Reading, MA: Addison-Wesley, 1979), pp. 44–45.
27. Julie Liesse, "Private Label Losing its 'Enemy' Status," *Advertising Age*, October 11, 1993, p. 15.
28. Liesse, ibid.
29. J. McNeal and L. Zeren, op. cit. (see note 17), p. 37.
30. Dennis J. Moran, "How A Name Can Label Your Product," *Advertising Age*, November 10, 1980, pp. 53, 56. Also see Daniel L. Doeden, "How to Select a Brand Name," *Marketing Communications*, November 1981, pp. 58, 61.
31. For information on the history and development of generic brands, see Brian F. Harris and Roger A. Strang, "Marketing Strategies in the Age of Generics," *Journal of Marketing*, Fall 1985, pp. 70–81.
32. B. Harris and R. Strang, ibid., pp. 70–71.
33. Julie Franz, "Ten Years May Be Generic Lifetime," *Advertising Age*, March 23, 1987, p. 76.
34. Marc Levinson, "Stand By Your Brands," *Newsweek*, April 19, 1993, pp. 38–39.
35. "Copying the Copycats: Merck," *The Economist*, September 12, 1992, p. 78.
36. Frank Tobolski, "Packaging Design Requires Research," *Marketing News*, June 6, 1994, p. 4.
37. "L'Eggs to Scrap Plastic 'Egg' Package," *Marketing News*, August 19, 1991, p. 20.
38. Robert Opie, *Packaging Sourcebook* (London, England: MacDonald Orbis), 1989.
39. Hollis Brooks, "Used Clothing, (Skiwear Made from Polyester Pile Taken from Recycled Plastic Soda Bottles)," *Skiing*, December 1993, p. 30.
40. Anastasia Toufexis, "Know What You Eat," *Time*, May 9, 1994, p. 68.
41. Suzette Sherman, "'EcoAlert' an Udderly Great Idea," *I.D.*, March 4, 1993, p. 23.

Chapter 10

1. Alan Farnham, "America's Most Admired Company," *Fortune*, February 7, 1994, pp. 50–54; "Rubbermaid, Breaking All the Molds," *Sales & Marketing Management*, August 1992, p. 42.
2. Jennifer Lawrence, "P & G Losing Ground in Product Innovation," *Advertising Age*, November 15, 1993, p. 44.
3. Kenneth Labich, "The Innovators," *Fortune*, June 6, 1988, pp. 50–64.
4. Rahul Jacob, "Ways To Kill New Product Ideas," *Fortune*, December 14, 1992, pp. 93–94.
5. Joseph P. Guiltinan and Gordon W. Paul, *Marketing Management: Strategies and Programs*, 5th ed., (New York: McGraw-Hill, 1994), pp. 198–200; Edward Tauber, "Brand Franchise Extension: New Product Benefits From Existing Brand Names," *Business Horizons*, March/April, 1981, pp. 36–41.
6. C. Merle Crawford, *New Products Management*, 4th ed., (Homewood, IL: Irwin, 1994), pp. 48–63.
7. Stephanie Losee, "Closing the Innovation Gap," *Fortune*, December 2, 1991, pp. 56–62.
8. Losee, "Closing the Innovation Gap," p. 61.
9. Losee, "Closing the Innovation Gap," pp. 61–62.
10. Thomas Kuczmarski and Arthur G. Middlebrooks, "Innovation Risk and Reward," *Sales & Marketing Management*, February 1993, pp. 44–51; Bob Donath, "The Customer as Consultant," *Sales & Marketing Management*, September 1992, pp. 84–90; David Tanner, "Applying Creative Thinking to Everyday Problems," *Journal of Consumer Marketing*, vol. 9, Fall 1992, pp. 23–28; Losee, "Closing the Innovation Gap," p. 61.
11. "How 3M Manages for Innovation," *Marketing Communications*, November/December, 1988, p. 22.
12. Crawford, *New Products Management*, 4th ed., pp. 150–160.
13. Edward Tauber, "Forecasting Sales Prior to Test Market," *Journal of Marketing*, January 1977, pp. 80–84.
14. See for example, Terry Dworkin and Mary Jane Sheffet, "Product Liability in the '80s," *Journal of Public Policy and Marketing*, vol. 4, 1985, pp. 69–79; Michael Brody, "When

Products Turn into Liabilities," *Fortune*, March 3, 1986, pp. 20–24; and Carolyn Lochhead, "All Are Liable in Product Liability," *Insight*, February 15, 1988, pp. 46–47.

15. "3M Will Pay $325 Million to Settle Implant Suits," *The New York Times*, Tuesday, April 12, 1994, vol. 143, p. B8.

16. Jay Klompmaker, G. David Hughes, and Russell Haley, "Test Marketing in New Product Development," *Harvard Business Review*, May/June, 1976, pp. 128–38.

17. Christopher Power, "Will It Sell in Podunk? Hard To Say," *Business Week*, August 10, 1992, pp. 46–47.

18. "1993 Edison Best New Products Awards Winners," *Marketing News*, April 25, 1994, p. E3.

19. Power, "Will It Sell in Podunk? Hard to Say."

20. Power, p. 47.

21. Pam Weisz, "P & G Puts Crest on Ice," *BrandWeek*, January 10, 1994, p. 12; Judith Spunge, "Jergen's Tests New Skin Line," *BrandWeek*, October 11, 1993, p. 10; Roy Furchgott, "McDonald's Tests Fried Chicken, Supported by Advertising," *AdWeek*, July 12, 1993, p. 2; Jennifer Lawrence and Pat Sloan, "P & G Plans New Ivory Pad," *Advertising Age*, November 23, 1992, p. 12.

22. Booz, Allen, & Hamilton, *New Products Management for the 1980s* (Chicago: Booz, Allen, & Hamilton, 1982).

23. Booz, Allen, & Hamilton, *New Products Management for the 1980s*, 1982.

24. Cyndee Miller, "Little Relief Seen for New Product Failure Rate," *Marketing News*, June 21, 1993, pp. 1, 10–11.

25. Patricia Winters, "$116 Million Intro for Bayer Select Isn't Just Ads," *Advertising Age*, November 23, 1992, p. 37.

26. David Hopkins, *New Product Winners and Losers* (New York: The Conference Board, 1980). For a review of the many ways of defining product failures, see C. Merle Crawford, "New Product Failure Rates: Facts and Fallacies," *Research Management*, September 1979, pp. 9–13.

27. Christopher Power, "Flops," *Business Week*, August 16, 1993, pp. 76–82.

28. Bill Abrams, "Despite Mixed Record, Firms Still Pushing for New Products," *The Wall Street Journal*, November 12, 1981, p. 31.

29. Christopher Power, "Flops."

30. R. G. Cooper and E. J. Kleinschmidt, "New Products: What Separates Winners from Losers?" *Journal of Product Innovation Managment*, no. 4, 1987, pp. 169–84; F. Axel Johne and Patricia Snelson, "Success Factors in Product Innovation: A Selective Review of the Literature," *Journal of Product Innovation Management*, no. 5, 1988, pp. 114–28; Calvin Hodock, "Rx for New Product Survival," *Marketing Communications*, February 1986, pp. 27–32; C. Merle Crawford, "Marketing Research and the New Product Failure Rate," *Journal of Marketing*, April 1977, pp. 51–61; J. Hugh Davidson, "Why Most New Consumer Brands Fail," *Harvard Business Review*, March/April 1976, pp. 117–22; and David Hopkins, *New Product Winners and Losers* (New York: The Conference Board, 1980).

31. Bob Donath, "Customer as Consultant," *Sales & Marketing Management*, September 1992, pp. 84–90.

32. Chet Kane, "Accessing Latest Trends? It's Attitude, Not Behavior," *BrandWeek*, February 21, 1994, p. 15; Alexa Smith, "Doomed to an Early Death by Wrongheaded Research," *BrandWeek*, September 13, 1993, p. 18; Amy L. Halliday, "Product Change: The Perils of Moving Too Fast," *Harvard Business Review*, July/August 1993, p. 10; Hopkins, *New Product Winners and Losers*.

33. Steven C. Wheelwright and Kim B. Clark, "Creating Project Plans to Focus Product Development," *Harvard Business Review*, March/April 1992, pp. 70–82; Don Frey, "Learning the Ropes: My Life As a Product Champion," *Harvard Business Review*, September/October 1991, pp. 46–56; Crawford, "Marketing Research and the New Product Failure Rate," (see note 30 above).

34. Christopher Power, "Flops."

35. Hopkins, *New Product Winners and Losers*, p. 17.

36. Jon Berry and Edward F. Ogiba, "It's Your Boss. (Why New Products Fail)," *BrandWeek*, October 19, 1992, pp. 16–25.

37. Jon Berry and Edward F. Ogiba, "It's Your Boss. (Why New Products Fail)."

38. Laura Jereski, "Block That Innovation!" *Forbes*, January 18, 1993, p. 48.

39. Cooper and Kleinschmidt, "New Products: What Separates Winners from Losers?"

40. Kenneth Derow, "Prolonging the Product Life Cycle," *Marketing Communications*, October 1981, p. 108.

41. Bernice Kanner, "Moonlighting," *New York*, November 30, 1992, pp. 26–27.

42. Bernice Kanner, "Moonlighting."

43. Nariman Dhalla and Sonia Yuspeh, "Forget the Product Life Cycle Concept!" *Harvard Business Review*, January/February 1976, pp. 102–12.

44. Richard Cardozo, *Product Policy: Cases and Concepts* (Reading, MA: Addison-Wesley, 1979), pp. 31–60.

45. Bernice Kanner, "Moonlighting."

46. Richard Cardozo, *Product Policy*, p. 31.

47. Heather Ogilvie, "Brand Marketing: The Big Chill," *Journal of European Business*, March/April 1994, pp. 25–30.

48. Richard Cardozo, *Product Policy*, p. 47.

49. "The Best of 1993," *Business Week*, January 10, 1994, pp. 111–130.

50. For more information on discontinuing products in the product lines, see Douglas Lambert and Jay Sterling, "Identifying and Eliminating Weak Products," *Business*, July/September 1988, pp. 3–10; Richard Hise, A. Parasuraman, and R. Wiswanathan, "Product Elimination: The Neglected Management Responsibility," *Journal of Business Strategy*, Spring 1984, pp. 56–63; and George Avlonitis, "Industrial Product Elimination: Major Factors to Consider," *Industrial Marketing Management*, February 1984, pp. 77–85.

51. ANSI/ASQC. 1987. *Quality Systems Terminology, American Normal Standard*. A3, 1987.

52. Philip Crosby, *Quality Is Free* (New York: McGraw-Hill, 1979).

53. Valarie A. Zeithaml, A. Parasuraman, and Leonard L. Berry, "A Conceptual Model of Service Quality and Its Implications for Future Research," *Journal of Marketing*, Fall 1985, pp. 41–50.

HARLEY-DAVIDSON CASE STUDY

1. Michael L. McCracken and Brian H. Kleiner, "Enhancing Quality Control," *Industrial Management and Data Systems*, vol. 91, no. 6, 1991, pp. 20–25.

2. "Mounting the Drive for Quality," *Manufacturing Engineering*, January 1992, pp. 92, 94.

3. Harley-Davidson, Inc., *Annual Report* (Milwaukee, WI, 1993).

4. Robin Bergstrom, "Machining Centers with Guts," *Products*, May 1991, pp. 58–61.

5. Thomas Bolfert, Buzz Buzzelli, M. Bruce Chubbuck, Martin Jack Rosenblum, Eds., *Harley-Davidson Historical Overview* (Milwaukee, WI, 1994).

6. Ibid.

7. Video of meeting held March 1994 between Harley-Davidson and HarperCollins Publishers, New York.

Chapter 11

1. Committee on Definitions, *Marketing Definitions: A Glossary of Marketing Terms* (Chicago: American Marketing Association, 1960), p. 10.

2. Louis W. Stern and Adel I. El-Ansary, *Marketing Channels* (Englewood Cliffs, NJ: Prentice-Hall, 1989), p. 10.

3. Donald J. Bowersox, M. Bixby Cooper, Douglas M. Lambert, and Donald A. Taylor, *Management in Marketing Channels* (New York: McGraw-Hill, 1980), p. 11.

4. Carrie Goerne, "Coffee Consumption Down, But Sales of Exotic Blends Perk Up," *Marketing News*, July 20, 1992, pp. 1, 22.

5. Wroe Alderson, "The Analytical Framework for Marketing," in Delbert Duncan, Ed., *Proceedings: Conference of Marketing Teachers from Far Western States* (Berkeley: University of California, 1968), p. 15.

6. Carolyn T. Geer, "Eliminating Middlemen," *Forbes*, March 2, 1992, pp. 92–93.

7. Carrie Goerne, "More Computer Marketers Taking the Direct Approach," *Marketing News*, October 26, 1992, p. 6.

8. Peter Burrows, "Beyond Rock Bottom," *Business Week*, March 14, 1994, pp. 80–82.

9. Philip Kotler and Gary Armstrong, *Principles of Marketing*, 6th ed., (Englewood Cliffs, NJ: Prentice-Hall, 1994), p. 396.

10. Patricia Sellers, "Winning Over the New Consumer," *Fortune*, July 29, 1991, pp. 113–124.

11. Gul Butaney and Lawrence H. Wortzel, "Distribution Power Versus Manufacturer Power: The Customer Role," *Journal of Marketing*, January 1988, pp. 52–63.

12. Robert L. Heilbroner and Lester C. Thurow, *Economics Explained* (New York: Touchstone, 1987), pp. 59–60.

13. James D. Hlavacek and Tommy J. McCuistion, "Industrial Distributors: When, How, and Where?" *Harvard Business Review*, March/April, 1983, p. 97.

14. Laurie M. Grossman, "Soda Pop Sales Sparkle at Fountain Outlets," *Wall Street Journal*, November 18, 1993, p. B1.

15. Allan J. McGrath, "Differentiating Yourself via Distribution," *Sales & Marketing Management*, March 1991, pp. 50–57.

16. William G. Zikmund and William J. Stanton, "Recycling Solid Wastes: A Channels of Distribution Problem," *Journal of Marketing*, July 1971, p. 34.

17. Jessica Hamburger, "Reverse Vending Machines Pay for Cans," *Dallas Morning News*, October 14, 1990.

18. "Ways into Fortress Japan," *The Economist*, October 22, 1988, pp. 18–19.

19. Andrew Tanzer, "Just Get Out and Sell," *Forbes*, September 28, 1992, pp. 68–72.

20. James A. Narus and James C. Anderson, "Strengthen Distributor Performance Through Channel Positioning," *Sloan Management Review*, Winter 1988, pp. 31–40.

21. Carrie Goerne, "Cheap Eats and Quick Service," *Marketing News*, August 3, 1992, pp. 1, 20.

22. Christopher Power, "How to Get Closer to Your Customers," *Business Week*, Enterprise 1993, pp. 42–45.

23. Louis P. Bucklin, "Retail Strategy and the Classification of Consumer Goods," *Journal of Marketing*, January 1963, pp. 50–55.

24. Robert C. Weigand, "Fit Products and Channels to Your Channels," *Harvard Business Review*, January/February 1977, pp. 101–102.

25. Leo Aspinwall, *Four Marketing Theories* (Boulder: University of Colorado, 1961).

26. Kenneth G. Hardy and Allan J. McGrath, *Marketing Channel Management* (Glenview, IL: Scott, Foresman, 1988), p. 437.

27. Ravi S. Achol and Louis W. Stern, "Environmental Determinants of Decision-Making Uncertainty in Marketing Channels," *Journal of Marketing Research*, February 1988, pp. 36–50.

28. Mary Charlies, "Existing Distributors Are Being Squeezed by Brewers, Retailers," *Wall Street Journal*, November 22, 1993, p. A1.

29. Allan J. McGrath and Kenneth G. Hardy, "When Mergers Rock Your Distribution Channels," *Business Marketing*, June 1987, pp. 68–75.

30. Martin L. Bell, *Marketing: Concepts and Strategy* (Boston: Houghton-Mifflin, 1979), p. 282.

31. McGrath, *Sales & Marketing Management*, (see note 15).

32. Allan J. McGrath and Kenneth G. Hardy, "Six Steps to Distribution Network Design," *Business Horizons*, January/February 1991, pp. 48–52.

33. Scott Smith, president of Old Snowmass Food Company, Aspen, Colorado, interview with Tim A. Becker, research assistant, December 1993.

34. U.S. v. Arnold Schwinn & Company 388 U.S. 365 (1967).

35. Carol M. Larson, Robert E. Wegend, and John S. Wright, *Basic Retailing* (Englewood Cliffs, NJ: Prentice-Hall, 1976), p. 525.

36. "41st Annual Report on American Industry," *Forbes*, January 9, 1989, p. 148.

37. See Stern and El Ansary, *Marketing Channels*, Chapter 7 and John Gaski, "The Theory and Poser of Conflict in Channels of Distribution," *Journal of Marketing*, Summer 1984, pp. 9–29.

38. Maynard Garfield, "A Warning to Manufacturers: Don't Pass the Buck to Dealers," *Marketing News*, March 4, 1991, p. 18.

39. This section draws information from Hardy and McGrath, *Marketing Channel Management*, pp. 101–111, (see note 26).

40. Phyllis Berman, "The Steel Behind Steelcase," *Forbes*, October 17, 1985, pp. 90–99.

41. Cynthia R. Milsap, "Conquering the Distributor Incentive Blues," *Business Marketing*, November 1985, pp. 122–125.

42. Stern and El-Ansary, *Marketing Channels*, p. 408.

43. Molly Wade McGrath, *Top Sellers U.S.A.* (New York: William Morrow, 1983), pp. 66–67.

44. This figure was provided by the controller of Kraft Foods in a telephone conversation with Tim Becker, research assistant, December 13, 1993.

45. "What's Behind the Global Franchise Boom?" *World Trade*, April 1993, p. 148.

46. "Rising-Star Franchise," *Working Women*, November 1993, p. 85.

47. Barbara Presley Roble, "The Women Behind McDonald's," *The New York Times*, March 27, 1994, p. F23.

48. Jeffrey M. Hertzfeld, "Joint Ventures: Saving the Soviets from Perestroika," *Harvard Business Review*, January/February 1991, pp. 80–91.

49. Damon Darlin, "South Koreans Crave American Fast Food," *Wall Street Journal*, February 22, 1991, pp. B1, B3.

50. Jeffrey M. Hertzfeld, "McDonald's in Latvia," *The New York Times*, April 20, 1994, p. D19.

51. Stanley A. Brown, "Standchising is New Wave in Franchise Expansion," *Marketing News*, April 1, 1991, p. 10.

Chapter 12

1. Richard A. Melcher, "Cut Out the Middleman? Never!" *Business Week*, January 10, 1994, p. 96.

2. *Census of Wholesale Trade*, May 1985, p. 207.

3. U.S. Department of Commerce, International Trade Administration, *U.S. Industry Outlook 1994*.

4. McKesson Corporation, "Communications with the Public," (San Francisco, April 19, 1991).

5. U.S. Department of Commerce, *U.S. Industrial Outlook*, 1993.

6. Kenneth G. Hardy and Allan J. McGrath, *Marketing Channel Management* (Glenview, IL.: Scott, Foresman, 1988), p. 325.

7. U.S. Department of Commerce, *U.S. Industrial Outlook*, 1993.

8. "Monthly Wholesale Trade," *Current Business Reports*, U.S. Department of Commerce, December 1993.

9. U.S. Department of Commerce, *U.S. Industrial Outlook*, 1993.

10. Melcher, *Business Week*, January 10, 1994, p. 96.

11. Steve Weinstein, "Coping with Change," *Progressive Grocer*, March 1994, pp. 81–86.

12. Steve Weinstein, "Spanning the Globe," *Progressive Grocer*, October 1992, pp. 65–70.

13. "More Sales Through Wholesale," *Catalog Age*, July 1993, p. 54.

14. "Foreign Market Briefs: Russia," *Business America*, November 15, 1993, p. 25.

15. Jim Gibbons, "Selling Abroad with Manufacturer's Agents," *Sales & Marketing Management*, September 9, 1985, pp. 67–69.
16. U.S. Department of Commerce, *U.S. Industrial Outlook*, 1993.
17. Donald A. Ball and Wendell H. McCullock, Jr., *International Business* (Plano, TX: Business Publications, 1988), p. 55.
18. Harold J. Novick, "Yes, There Is a Perfect Rep," *Business Marketing*, February 1989, pp. 73–76.
19. Richard W. Noel, "From Peddlers to Professionals," *Electrical Wholesaling*, April 1986, pp. 42–46.
20. "The Ratios," *Dun's Review*, October 1989, pp. 144, 146.
21. "The Business Week Top 1000," *Business Week*, April 1988, p. 252.
22. "More Sales Through Wholesale," *Catalog Age*, July 1993, p. 54.
23. Christine Forbes, "Acquisitions Drive Industry Changes," *Industrial Distribution*, March 1993, pp. 22–24.
24. Barnard Lavine, "$1992," *Electronic News*, December 6, 1993, p. 58.
25. Toni Mack, "VP's of Planning Need Not Apply," *Forbes*, October 25, 1993, p. 84.
26. "The MANA Communications Survey," *Agency Sales Magazine*, January 1994, pp. 8–14.
27. "Lagging Behind on MIS," *Global Trade and Transportation*, March 1993, p. 30.
28. Megan Santosus, "Learning Their Parts," *CIO*, October 15, 1993, p. 88.
29. Michael Granturco, "The Supernets Are Coming!" *Forbes*, February 27, 1989, pp. 112–114.
30. "Workable Technologies for the 1990s," *Traffic Management*, August 1992, pp. 31–32.
31. Thomas A. Foster, "In a Difficult Year, Logistics Shine," *Distribution*, July 1992, p. 6.
32. "The Not-So-Nifty '90s," *Distribution*, January 1989, pp. 30–35.
33. *Careers in Distribution* (Oak Brook, IL: National Council of Physical Distribution Management, Careers in Distribution, 1983), p. 3.
34. William Morris, Ed., *The American Heritage*, 1982.
35. Ronald H. Ballou, *Basic Business Logistics* (Englewood Cliffs, NJ: Prentice-Hall, 1987), p. 27.
36. Ray Serafin, "Saturn Recall a Plus—for Saturn!" *Advertising Age*, August 16, 1993, p. 4.
37. Philip Kotler, *Principles of Marketing* (Englewood Cliffs, NJ: Prentice-Hall, 1989), p. 369.
38. Graham Sharman, "The Rediscovery of Logistics," *Harvard Business Review*, September/October 1984, pp. 71–79.
39. Tom Eisenhart, "Advanced Research Funds a New Market," *Business Marketing*, March 1989, pp. 51–61.
40. Robert J. Bowman, "Going the Extra Mile," *World Trade*, Winter 1988/1989, pp. 34–43.
41. Donald F. Wood and James C. Johnson, *Contemporary Transportation* (New York: McMillan, 1989), p. 81.
42. Tom Eisenhart, "Automating the Last Frontier," *Business Marketing*, May 1989, pp. 41–46.
43. "Sears Takes Direct Approach," *Chain Store Age Executive*, March 1994, pp. 168, 173.
44. Walter Weart and Robert Steiler, "Warehousing: A Review for Management," *Distribution*, June 1988, p. 72.
45. "Wake Up to Computers," *Distribution*, May 1989, pp. 25–28.
46. "Casebook: Hewlett-Packard," *Distribution*, March 1989, p. 66.
47. Hal F. Mather, "The Case for Skimpy Inventories," *Harvard Business Review*, January/February 1984, pp. 40–42, 46.
48. James A. Cooke, "Supply-Chain Management '90s Style," *Traffic Management*, May 1992, pp. 57–60.
49. William J. Stevenson, *Production and Operations Management* (Homewood, IL: Irwin, 1990), p. 624.
50. Paul H. Zipkin, "Does Manufacturing Need a JIT Revolution?" *Harvard Business Review*, January/February 1991, pp. 40–50.

51. Taiichi Ohno, *Toyota Production System: Beyond Large-Scale Production* (Cambridge: University Press, 1988), p. 81.
52. Jackson C. Grayson, Jr. and Carla O'Dell, *American Business: A Two-Minute Warning* (New York: Free Press, 1988), p. 149.
53. U.S. Department of Commerce, *U.S. Industry Outlook*, 1993.
54. Samuel P. Delise, "Interstate Commerce Commission Regulation, 1887–1987: The Carrier Viewpoint," *Transportation Practitioners Journal*, Spring 1987, pp. 262–291.
55. Robert J. Bowman, "A Survey of International Carriers," *World Trade*, Spring 1989, pp. 56–62.
56. Charles A. Taff, *Management of Physical Distribution and Transportation* (Homewood, IL: Irwin, 1986).
57. Peter Bradley, "Transportation Links All the Parts," *Purchasing*, July 15, 1993, pp. 62–73.
58. Federal Express Corporation, *Annual Report* (Memphis, TN, 1993).
59. Mark B. Solomon, "Is Overnight Delivery Slipping As Air Freight's Mode of Choice?" *Traffic World*, January 7, 1991, pp. 40–41.
60. U.S. Department of Commerce, *U.S. Industry Outlook*, 1993.
61. Bradley, op. cit.
62. Thomas Donuhue, "Let States Decide if They Want Big Trucks," *USA Today*, January 8, 1991, p. 11A.
63. Bradley, op. cit.
64. U.S. Department of Commerce, *U.S. Industry Outlook*, 1993.
65. Bradley, op. cit.
66. Bradley, op. cit.
67. "A World of Changing Data at Your Fingertips," *Traffic Management*, August 1992, pp. 36–37.
68. Daniel V. Hunt, *Quality in America* (Homewood, IL: Business One Irwin, 1992), p. 216.
69. Thomas Foster, "Searching for the Best," *Distribution*, March 1992, pp. 31–34.

Chapter 13

1. Otto Johnson, Ed., *The 1994 Information Please Almanac*, 47th ed., (New York: Houghton Mifflin).
2. Willian R. Davidson, Daniel J. Sweeney, and Ronald W. Stampfl, *Retail Management* (New York: Wiley, 1988), p. 5.
3. U.S. Department of Commerce, Bureau of the Census and the International Trade Administration, "Monthly Retail Trade, Sales, and Inventories," December 1993; Organization for Economic Cooperation and Development, "Main Economic Indicators 9/93."
4. U.S. Department of Commerce, Bureau of the Census, Statistical Abstract of the United States 1993, Washington D.C., pp. 751–757.
5. Bill Saporito, "And the Winner Is Still . . . Wal-Mart," *Fortune*, May 2, 1994, pp. 62–70.
6. Walter K. Levy, "Are Department Stores Doomed?" *Direct Marketing*, May 1991, pp. 56–60.
7. Laura Jereski, "Food Fight," *Forbes*, May 27, 1991, pp. 178–180.
8. Lauri M. Grossman, "Hypermarkets: A Sure-Fire Hit Bombs," *The Wall Street Journal*, June 25, 1992, p. B1.
9. Martin I. Horn, "Old Ways Expected to Die as the New Century Dawns," *Marketing News*, March 28, 1988, p. 11.
10. James Steingold, "New Japanese Lesson: Running a 7-Eleven," *The New York Times*, May 9, 1991, pp. 1–2E.
11. "Catalog Showrooms Enter '90s with New Vigor," *Discount Store News*, July 2, 1990, p. 71.
12. Douglas J. Eldridge, "Non-Store Retailing: Planning for a Big Future," *Chain Store Age Executive*, August 1993, pp. 34A–35A.
13. Vivian Marino, "Shop Around the Clock," *San Diego Union Tribune*, November 8, 1993, pp. C1, C2.
14. Patrick M. Reilly, "TV Shopping Hooks High-Toned Viewers," *Wall Street Journal*, November 16, 1993, pp. B1, B4.
15. Cyndee Miller, "Catalogs Alive, Thriving," *Marketing News*, February 28, 1994, pp. 1, 6; Karen J. Marchetti, "Customer

Information Should Drive Retail Direct Mail," *Marketing News*, February 28, 1994, p. 7.

16. David Evans, "Yes, You Can Sell Directly to Japan," *Direct*, April 1994, p. 67.
17. Easy Klein, *Dunn & Bradstreet Reports*, May/June 1993, pp. 20–23.
18. Gregory A. Patterson, "U.S. Catalogers Test International Waters," *Wall Street Journal*, April 19, 1994, p. B1.
19. "Direct Markets Adapt to New Lifestyles," *Marketing News*, June 19, 1989, p. 7.
20. National Automatic Merchandising Association, Chicago, 1993.
21. Robert Emproto, "Alternative Ad-vend-tures," *Beverage World*, February 1994, pp. 32–37.
22. Andrew Tanzer, "War of the Sales Robots," *Forbes*, January 7, 1991, pp. 294–296.
23. Kevin Helliker, "High-Tech Vending Machines Cook Up a New Menu of Hot Fast-Food Entrees," *The Wall Street Journal*, May 13, 1991, p. B1.
24. Maribeth Haynam, William Battino, and Scott Killips, "Going Electronic," *Chain Store Age Executive*, Special Issue, 1993, pp. 52–54.
25. Ibid.
26. Howard Schlossberg, "Researchers See Lucrative Possibilities in Telemarketing," *Marketing News*, September 2, 1991, p. 9.
27. Jared Sandberg, "Home Shopping Network to Offer Wares on Prodigy," *Wall Street Journal*, April 25, 1994, p. B6.
28. Haynam, Battino, and Killips, op. cit.
29. Gaynell Terrell, "Puttin' on the Glitz in the Downtown Area is a Risky Business," *The Houston Post*, September 2, 1991, pp. A21, A24.
30. John Branston, "Malls: Urban Fad of 1970s Raises Questions for '80s," *The Commercial Appeal*, Memphis, TN, September 4, 1986, pp. A1, A8.
31. Faneuil Hall Marketplace, Inc., "Fact Sheet," Boston, MA, 1988.
32. "Guys and Malls. The Simons' Crapshoot," *Business Week*, August 17, 1992, pp. 52–53.
33. Christina Duff, "Brighter Lights, Fewer Bargains: Outlets Go Upscale," *Wall Street Journal*, April 10, 1994, p. B1.
34. Gretchen Morgenson, "Cheapie Gucci," *Forbes*, May 27, 1991, pp. 43–44; Sawgrass Mills Directory.
35. *J. C. Penney Annual Report*, 1992.
36. Al Ries and Jack Trout, *Bottom-Up Marketing* (New York: McGraw-Hill, 1989).
37. Jason Zweig, "Bunnyburgers," *Forbes*, March 20, 1989, pp. 42–43.
38. Michael Gade, Jacquelyn Bibins, Ronald Shapiro, and Vanessa Cohen, *Chain Store Age Executive*, Special Issue, 1993.
39. Faye Brookman, "Arbor Drugs," *Stores*, April 1994, pp. 16–19.
40. Heikki Rinne and William R. Swingard, "Retailing Strategy: Developing a Desired Fidelity," *Exchange*, Fall 1988, pp. 8–11.
41. Sandra J. Skrovan, "Consumers in the 1990's: No Time or Money to Burn," *Chain Store Age Executive*, August 1993, pp. 15A–16A.
42. Patricia Sellers, "Getting Customers to Love You," *Fortune*, March 13, 1989, pp. 38–49.
43. "Checkstand Pushes Caldor's Productivity," *Chain Store Age Executive*, February 1991, p. 78.
44. Ripley Hotch, "New Directions in Retailing," *Nation's Business*, October 1992, pp. 48–50.
45. Debra Aho, "Kiosks: The Good, Bad & Ugly," *Advertising Age*, January 17, 1994, pp. 13, 16.
46. Jeffrey D. Zbar and Jennifer Lawrence, "Winn-Dixie Mails Video to Shoppers," *Advertising Age*, October 9, 1992, p. 18.
47. Malcolm P. McNair, "Significant Trends and Development in The Post-War Period," in A. B. Smith, Ed., *Competitive Distribution in a Free, High-Level Economy and Its Implication for a University* (Pittsburgh: University of Pittsburg Press, 1958), pp. 1–25; Malcolm P. McNair

and Eleanor May, "The Next Revolution of the Retailing Wheel," *Harvard Business Review*, September/October, 1978, pp. 81–91.
48. Sallie Hook, "Retailers Turn to Narrowcasting to Survive," *Marketing News*, February 15, 1988, p. 9.
49. Russell Vernon, "Fighting Boredom in Retailing," *Retailing Issues Letter*, July 1991, pp. 1–4; Francine Schwadel, "Shop Talk: What's in Store for Retailers," *The Wall Street Journal*, April 9, 1991, pp. B1, B6.
50. Gerald Lewis, "Strategic Management Concepts in U.S. Food Retailing and Wholesaling," *International Journal of Retail and Distribution Management*, vol.19, iss. 6, pp. 21–26.
51. Wendy Zellner, "Learning to Survive the 90's," *Business Week*, January 10, 1994, p. 95.
52. Stephanie Strom, "Retailers' Drive to Consolidate," *New York Times*, January 11, 1994, p. C1.
53. Margaret A. Gilliam, "The Future of the Discount Industry," *Direct Marketing*, May 1991, pp. 46–48, 50, 82.
54. Allan J. Magrath, "Born-Again Marketing," *Across the Board*, June 1991, pp. 33–36.
55. "Do It Yourself Grocery Checkout," *Wall Street Journal*, January 31, 1994, p. B1.
56. Joshua Levine, "The Ultimate Sell," *Forbes*, May 13, 1991, pp. 108–110.
57. Ira Teinowitz, "Videocart Shrinks Again as Kroger, Vons Leave," *Advertising Age*, September 13, 1993, p. 62.
58. Sherman Stratford, "Will the Information Superhighway be the Death of Retailing?" *Fortune*, April 18, 1994, pp. 98–110.
59. "Store Design Forecast," *Chain Store Age Executive*, January 1991, pp. 26–28.
60. Deborah Bihler, "Not Business As Usual," *Business Ethics*, May/June 1992, p. 14.
61. Ellie Winninghoff, "Greening the Supermarket Shelves," *Business Ethics*, July/August 1992, p. 14.
62. Frank Green, "Japan Lifestyle Joins Local Mall," *San Diego Union-Tribune*, August 3, 1993, pp. C1, C4.

HARLEY-DAVIDSON CASE STUDY

1. Video of meeting held March 1994 between representatives of Harley-Davidson and HarperCollins Publishers, New York.
2. Harley-Davidson financial reports, 1993 10K.
3. Peter C. Reid, *Well Made in America* (New York: McGraw-Hill, 1990).
4. Michael Jenkins, "Gaining a Financial Toothhold Through Public Warehousing," *Journal of Business Strategy*, May/June 1992.
5. Karen Auguston, "America on the Move: Part 3: Building Bridges to Greater Competitiveness," *Modern Materials Handling*, November 1992, pp. 68–72.
6. E. J. Muller, "Harley's Got the Handle on INbound," *Distribution*, March 1989, pp. 70, 74.
7. Pablo Del Nibletto, "Case Study: Historical Data Needed to See Into Harley-Davidson's Future," *Info Canada*, July 1992, p. 42.

Chapter 14

1. Scott Hume, "Integrated Marketing: Who's in Charge Here?" *Advertising Age*, March 22, 1993, p. 3.
2. Don E. Schultz, "Integrated Marketing Communications: Maybe Definition Is in the Point of View," *Marketing News*, January 18, 1993, p. 17.
3. Schultz, *Marketing News*, January 18, 1993.
4. Don E. Schultz, "Integration Helps You Plan Communications from Outside-in," *Marketing News*, March 15, 1993, p. 12.
5. Hume, *Advertising Age*, March 22, 1993.
6. Adapted from *Dictionary of Marketing Terms* (Chicago: American Marketing Association, 1988).
7. Karen Herther, "Survey Reveals Implications of Promotion Trends for the '90s," *Marketing News*, March 1, 1993, p. 7.
8. Adam Bryant, "Advertising," *The New York Times*, p. C8; James Bennet, "The Car's the Star, on Fridays at 8," *The New York Times*, December 21, 1993, p. C1.

9. This section is adapted from Chapter 6 of George E. Belch and M. A. Belch, *Introduction to Advertising and Promotion*, 2d ed., (Homewood, IL: Irwin, 1993).

10. Quote from Gorden S. Bower in *Fortune*, October 14, 1985, p. 11, reported in G. E. Belch and M. A. Belch, *Introduction to Advertising and Promotion*, 2d ed., (Homewood, IL: Irwin, 1993).

11. Barry L. Bayrus, "Word of Mouth: The Indirect Effect of Marketing Efforts," *Journal of Advertising Research*, June/July 1985, pp. 31–9.

12. James F. Engel, Martin R. Warshaw, and Thomas C. Kinnear, *Promotional Strategy: Managing the Marketing Communications Process*, 6th ed., (Homewood, IL: Irwin, 1987), p. 52.

13. Schultz, *Marketing News*, March 15, 1993, (see note 4).

14. E. K. Strong, *The Psychology of Selling* (New York: McGraw-Hill, 1925), p. 9.

15. Robert J. Lavidge and Gary A. Steiner, "A Model for Predictive Measurements of Advertising Effectiveness," *Journal of Marketing*, vol. 3, February 1966, pp. 13–24.

16. William J. McGuire, "An Information Processing Model of Advertising Effectiveness," in *Behavioral and Management Science in Marketing*, Harry J. Davis and Alvin J. Silk, Eds., (Ronald Press, 1978), pp. 156–80.

17. R. H. Colley, *Defining Advertising Goals for Measured Advertising Results* (New York: Association of National Advertisers, 1961).

18. This section is adapted from Chapter 9 of Belch & Belch, (see note 10).

19. James O. Peckham, "Can We Relate Advertising Dollars to Market Share Objectives?" in *How Much to Spend for Advertising*, M. A. McNiven, Ed., (New York: Association of National Advertisers, 1969), p. 30.

20. Andrea Adelson, "Advertising," *The New York Times*, February 14, 1994, p. C7.

21. Kevin Goldman, "Mammoth Marketers and Merchandisers Are Leaving No Flintstones Unturned," *Wall Street Journal*, February 14, 1994, pp. B1, B6.

22. Stephanie Strom, "Advertising," *The New York Times*, February 14, 1992, pp. C1, D12.

23. Eric Nelson, "Battered Apple Grapples to Regain Magic Touch," *The New York Times*, November 15, 1993, p. 56.

24. Interviews with various foreign business executives, San Diego, Spring 1994.

25. Daniel S. Levine and Moser O'Neill Goldberg, "Seoul Men," *Adweek*, v. 43, iss. 31, August 2, 1993, pp. 1, 5.

Chapter 15

1. Thomas R. King, "Spending on Ads Expected to rise Only 4.6% in '91," *The Wall Street Journal*, December 11, 1990, p. B1.

2. George Belch and Michael Belch, *An Introduction to Advertising and Promotion*, 2d ed., (Homewood, IL: Irwin, 1993), p. 4; Robert J. Cohen, "Ad Gain of 5.2% in '93 Marks Downturns's End," *Advertising Age*, May 2, 1994, p. 4.

3. Thomas R. King, *The Wall Street Journal*.

4. "Survey of World Advertising Expenditures: Twenty-fourth Edition," (New York: Starch INRA Hooper & The Roper Organization, 1991); Craig R. Endicott, "US Income Growth Outduels Foreign Side," *Advertising Age*, April 13, 1994, p. 1.

5. Belch and Belch, pp. 11–15.

6. Steven W. Hartley and Charles H. Patti, "Evaluating Business-to-Business Advertising: A Comparison of Objectives and Results," *Journal of Advertising Research*, 28, April/May 1988, p. 25.

7. Raymond Serafin, "Saturn Turnabout Doubles Ad Budget," *Advertising Age*, January 17, 1994, p. 1; Cleveland Horton, "City of Angels Is Less Than Heaven," *Advertising Age*, February 14, 1994, p. 12; Seth Mydans, "Japanese Tourists Shunning Southern California; Violence Blamed," *The New York Times*, May 14, 1994, p. 9.

8. Belch and Belch, p. 352.

9. Julian L. Simon, *The Management of Advertising* (Englewood Cliffs, NJ: Prentice-Hall, 1971), pp. 174–206; Belch and Belch, p. 353.

10. Belch and Belch, p. 352.

11. "Divorce Appears as Part of Pitch in 'Reality' Ads," *The Wall Street Journal*, December 3, 1992, pp. B1, B8.

12. Robert E. Calem, "Desktop Computers Reshaping the Way Ads Are Made," *The New York Times*, June 19, 1994, p. 9.

13. Belch and Belch, p. 681.

14. Cyndee Miller, "New Study Downplays 'Likability' as Major Factor in Ad Success," *Marketing News*, April 13, 1992, p. 2.

15. Belch and Belch, p. 100.

16. Cyndee Miller, "The Marketing of Advertising: Two Trade Groups Tout Its Benefits for Consumers, Marketers," *Marketing News*, December 7, 1992, p. 1.

17. Belch and Belch, p. 574.

18. Belch and Belch, p. 577.

19. Adam Bryant, "Those Mind-Boggling Promotions," *The New York Times*, November 14, 1993, p. 7.

20. Howard Schlossberg, "Coupons Likely to Remain Popular," *Marketing News*, March 29, 1993, pp. 1, 7.

21. Reference cited in John P. Rossiter and Larry Percy, *Advertising and Promotion Management* (New York: McGraw-Hill, 1987), p. 360.

22. Karen Herther, "Survey Reveals Implications of Promotion Trends for the '90s," March 1, 1993, p. 7.

23. Schlossberg, *Marketing News*, March 29, 1993; Len Egol, "Is Coupon Growth Flagging?" *Direct Marketing*, March 1, 1994, p. 13.

24. Michael Burgi, "Trade Spending Tops," *Advertising Age*, April 15, 1991, p. 36.

25. Len Egol, *Direct Marketing*, p. 13.

26. Belch and Belch, p. 604.

27. Survey by Oxtoby-Smith, Inc., cited in "Many Consumers View Rebates as a Bother," *The Wall Street Journal*, April 13, 1989, p. B1.

28. Len Egol, *Direct Marketing*, p. 13.

29. Howard Schlossberg, "Event Sponsorships Prove Reliable in Targeting Ethnics," *Marketing News*, January 18, 1993, p. 8.

30. Howard Schlossberg, "Firms Using Research to Assess Sponsorship Value," *Marketing News*, October 26, 1992, p. 13.

31. For detailed evaluation see "Display Effectiveness: An Evaluation," *The Nielsen Researcher*, Number 2, 1983, pp. 2–8; and "Display Effectiveness: An Evaluation Part II," *The Nielsen Researcher*, November 3, 1983, pp. 2–10.

32. Belch and Belch, p. 643.

33. Bertrand R. Cansfield and Frazier Moore, *Public Relations: Principles, Cases, and Problems*, 6th ed., (Homewood, IL: Irwin, 1973), p. 4.

Chapter 16

1. Frank V. Cespedes, Stephen X. Doyle, and Robert J. Freedman, "Teamwork for Today's Selling," *Harvard Business Review*, March/April 1989, pp. 44–54, 58.

2. C. Robert Petty, *Managing Salespeople* (Reston Publishing, 1979), p. 3.

3. Stephan Schiffman and Michele Reisner, "Selling: An International Perspective," *American Salesman*, November 1993, pp. 14–15.

4. Douglas J. Dalrymple, *Sales Management: Concepts and Cases* (New York: Wiley, 1982).

5. E. Jerome McCarthy and William D. Perreault, *Basic Marketing: A Managerial Approach*, 11th ed., (Homewood, IL: Irwin, 1993), p. 447.

6. Mark A. Moon and Garry M. Armstrong, "Selling Teams: A Conceptual Framework and Research Agenda," *Journal of Personal Selling and Sales Management*, Winter 1994, pp. 17–30.

7. "The Selling Game," *The Wall Street Journal*, March 29, 1994, p. A1.

8. Joseph J. Verno, "Sales People or Order Takers: Which Is Best?" *Beverage Industry*, November 1992, p. 35.

9. Carrie Goerne, "Customer-Friendly Sales Reps Get Tryout," *Marketing News*, October 26, 1992, pp. 1, 3.

10. Michael Waldholz, "How a Detail Man Promotes New Drugs to Tennessee Doctors," *The Wall Street Journal*, November 8, 1982, pp. 1, 18.

11. Ronald D. Balsley and E. Patricia Birsner, *Selling: Marketing Personified* (Chicago: Dryden Press, 1987), p. 47.

12. Thomas V. Bonoma, "Major Sales: Who Really Does the Buying?" *Harvard Business Review*, May/June 1982, pp. 111–19.

13. "The Fortune 500," *Fortune*, April 30, 1984, p. 182.

14. "The Fortune 500," *Fortune*, April 18, 1994, p. 222.

15. Personal interview with Brian Gahran, general manager for DEVCOR. Completed by Tim A. Becker, research assistant, May 1994.

16. Malcolm Fleschner, "Powerlines," *Personal Selling Power*, May/June 1994, pp. 14–24.

17. "Telemarketing Is 'Smarter' When Used with Other Tools," *Marketing News*, August 15, 1988, p. 8.

18. Fleschner, p. 17.

19. Ralph E. Anderson and Joseph F. Hair, Jr., *Sales Management* (New York: Random House, 1983), pp. 582–86.

20. For an expanded discussion of sales presentations as they relate to several consumer behavior models, see Philip G. Zimbardo, *Psychology and Life* (Glenview, IL: Scott, Foresman, 1985), pp. 190–194.

21. A. H. Maslow, *Motivation and Personality* (New York: Harper & Row, 1954).

22. Tim Triplett, "Satisfaction Is Nothing They Take for Granite," *Marketing News*, May 9, 1994, p. 6.

23. Daniel K. Weadock, "Your Troops Can Keep Control—and Close the Sale—By Anticipating Objections," *Sales & Marketing Management*, March 17, 1980, pp. 102–106.

24. Helen Berman, "To Close Sales Ask Questions," *Personal Selling Power*, March 1991, pp. 48–49.

25. Original thoughts about cognitive dissonance can be found in Leon Festinger, *A Theory of Cognitive Dissonance* (Stanford, CA: Stanford University Press, 1957).

26. The SAAB example is based on the personal experience of one of the authors; Krystal Miller, "Chevy's Latest Revival Effort Is Customer-Driven," *Wall Street Journal*, November 9, 1993, p. B1.

27. Scott Matulis, "Building a Sales Force," *Entrepreneur*, September 1988, pp. 43–48.

28. Johanna Ambrosio, "IBM Pushes Sales Team Specialists," *Computer World*, July 12, 1993, pp. 1–2.

29. Ambrosio, p. 2.

30. John M. Ivancevich, *Foundations of Personnel/Human Resource Management* (Homewood, IL: Irwin, 1992).

31. Patricia Sellers, "How IBM Teaches Technies to Sell," *Fortune*, June 6, 1988, pp. 141–146.

32. Personal interview with Thomas Volz, vice president of marketing, Air South, Columbia, South Carolina. Interview conducted by Tim A. Becker, research assistant, July 1994.

33. Personal interview with Richard Brayband, general manager of Executone. Interview conducted by Tim A. Becker, research assistant, March 1994.

34. Maynard M. Garfield, "Make a Salesperson and You Make a Sale," *Marketing News*, February 27, 1989, p. 16.

35. Carol R. Riggs, "New Team Approach to Sales Training," *Dun & Bradstreet Reports*, September/October 1993, p. 62.

36. James Bennet, "Team Spirit Is New Message at Olds," *New York Times*, June 23, 1994, pp. D1, D15.

37. Carlene Kleinhart, "Developing CBT—The Quality Way," *Training and Development Journal*, November 1989, pp. 85–89.

38. Mauricio Lorence, "Assignment USA: The Japanese Solution," *Sales & Marketing Management*, October 1992, pp. 61–64.

39. Cyndee Miller, "Going Overseas Requires Marketers to Learn More Than a New Language," *Marketing News*, March 28, 1994, p. 8; Margie Markarian, "Cultural Revolution," *Sales & Marketing Management*, May 1994, pp. 127–129.

40. Victor H. Vroom and Arthur G. Jago, *The New Leadership* (Englewood Cliffs, NJ: Prentice-Hall, 1988).

41. In the leadership literature, this is called a "contingency approach."

42. Edward E. Lawler, III, "Reward Systems," in J. Richard Hackman and L. Lloyd Suttle, Eds., *Improving Life at Work* (Glenview, IL: Scott, Foresman, 1977), pp. 163–226.

43. Martin Levy, "Almost-Perfect Performance Appraisals," *Personnel Journal*, April 1989, pp. 76–83.

44. Beth Pekaine and John Von Arnold, "Output vs. Input," *Sales & Marketing Management*, February 1991, pp. 10–11.

HARLEY-DAVIDSON CASE STUDY

1. Beth Heitzman, Dave Kiley, Jim Kim, "Adweek's Midwest Creative Team All-Stars," *Adweek*, June 4, 1993, pp. 41–46.

2. Peter C. Reid, *Well Made in America* (New York: McGraw-Hill, 1990).

3. Ibid.

4. Ibid.

5. Judann Dagnoli, "Philip Morris Thinks Movie Title's a Drag," *Advertising Age*, August 26, 1991, p. 10.

6. Malia Boyd, "Harley-Davidson Motor Company," *Incentive*, September 1993, pp. 26–31.

7. Warren Striegatch, "Identity Crisis," *World Trade*, July 1992, pp. 74–78.

8. Bristol Voss, "Marketers of the Month—William G. Davidson: Born to Ride," *Sales & Marketing Management*, April 1991, pp. 26–27.

9. Christine Brown, "Then and the Art of Motorcycle Maintenance," *Forbes*, March 4, 1991, p. 134.

Chapter 17

1. George Leaming, "In the Real World, Price Is a Cause, Not an Effect," *Marketing News*, May 13, 1991, p. 11.

2. Jack Russell, "U.S. Fast-Food Giants in Japan Slice Prices," *Advertising Age*, June 13, 1994, p. 64.

3. Sheila Tefft, "China's Savvy Shoppers Load Carts with Expensive Imported Goods," *Advertising Age*, June 20, 1994, p. I 21.

4. Andrew E. Serwer, "How To Escape a Price War," *Fortune*, June 13, 1994, pp. 82–90.

5. Andrew E. Serwer, *Fortune*, p. 88.

6. William M. Stern, "A Wing and a Prayer," *Forbes*, April 25, 1994, pp. 42–43.

7. Robert D. Hershey, Jr., "Hardest Task of the 1990s: Raising Prices," *The New York Times*, March 1, 1994, pp. C1, C14.

8. Michael D. Mondello, "Naming Your Price," *Inc.*, July, 1992, pp. 80–83.

9. Peter R. Dickson and Alan G. Sawyer, "The Price Knowledge and Search of Supermarket Shoppers," *Journal of Marketing*, July 1990, pp. 42–53; Jeffrey J. Inman, Leigh McAlister, and Wayne D. Hoyer, "Promotion Signal: Proxy for a Price Cut?" *Journal of Consumer Research*, June 1990, pp. 74–81; Aradhna Krishna, Imran S. Currim, and Robert W. Shoemaker, "Consumer Perceptions of Promotional Activity," *Journal of Marketing*, April 1991, pp. 4–16; Tridib Mazumdar and Kent B. Monroe, "The Effects of Buyers' Intentions to Learn Price Information on Price Encoding," *Journal of Retailing*, Spring 1990, pp. 15–32; Ken Partch and David Litwak, "Prices: How Much Do Shoppers Really Know or Care?" *Supermarket Business*, June 1990, pp. 15–21; Joel E. Urbany and Peter R. Dickson, "Consumer Normal Price Estimation: Market Versus Personal Standards," *Journal of Consumer Research*, June 1991, pp. 45–51; Kirk L. Wakefield and J. Jeffrey Inman, "Who Are the Price Vigilantes? An Investigation of Differentiating Characteristics Influencing Price

Information Processing," *Journal of Retailing*, Summer 1993, pp. 216–233.

10. Gerard J. Tellis, "Beyond the Many Faces of Price: An Integration of Pricing Strategies," *Journal of Marketing*, October, 1986, pp. 146–160.

11. Thomas T. Nagle, *The Strategy and Tactics of Pricing* (Englewood Cliffs, NJ: Prentice-Hall, 1987), Chapter 3.

12. Allan J. McGrath, "Ten Timeless Truths About Pricing," *Journal of Consumer Marketing*, Winter 1991, pp. 5–13.

13. Gerard J. Tellis, "Beyond the Many Faces of Price: An Integration of Pricing Strategies."

14. Christopher Farrell, Zachary Schiller, Richard A. Melcher, Geoffrey Smith, Peter Burrows, and Kathleen Kerwin, "Stuck! How Companies Cope When They Can't Raise Prices," *Business Week*, November 15, 1993, pp. 146–155.

15. Farrell, et al., *Business Week*, pp. 146–155.

16. Michael J. Mandel, "For Japanese Companies, A Double Whammy," *Business Week*, November 15, 1993, p. 154.

17. D. Kneale, "Glitzy Brands Make Small Impressions," *The Wall Street Journal*, December 15, 1989, p. 81.

18. "Everyday Low Profits: Why Manufacturers Should Leave Pricing to the Retailers," *Harvard Business Review*, March/April, 1994, p. 13.

19. Peter R. Dickson and Alan G. Sawyer, "The Price Knowledge and Search of Supermarket Shoppers," *Journal of Marketing*, July 1990, pp. 42–53; Valerie Zeithaml, "Consumer Perceptions of Price, Quality, and Value: A Means–End Model and Synthesis of Evidence," *Journal of Marketing*, July 1988, pp. 2–22.

20. "Always a Slogan," *Marketing News*, June 20, 1994, p. 1.

21. U.S. v. Sacony-Vaccuum Oil Co., 310 U.S. 150. (1940).

22. Joe L. Welch, *Marketing Law* (PCC Books, 1980), p. 55.

23. Welch, *Marketing Law*, p. 73.

24. Welch, *Marketing Law*, p. 74.

25. Standard Oil Co. v. FTC, 350 U.S. 231. (1951).

Chapter 18

1. David Ogilvy, *Ogilvy On Advertising* (New York: Vintage Books, 1988), p. 170.

2. Gerard J. Tellis, "Beyond the Many Faces of Price: An Integration of Pricing Strategies," *Journal of Marketing*, October 1986, pp. 146–160.

3. Tellis, *Journal of Marketing*, p. 147.

4. Tellis, *Journal of Marketing*, p. 147.

5. James Sterngold, "New Concept for Japan's Beer Drinkers: Discounts," *The New York Times*, April 21, 1994, p. C5.

6. Michael D. Mondello, "Naming Your Price," *Inc.*, July 1992, pp. 80–83.

7. Much of this section's structure and content is owed to "Beyond the Many Faces of Price: An Integration of Pricing Strategies," by Gerard J. Tellis, *Journal of Marketing*, vol. 50 (October 1986), pp. 146–160.

8. Tibbett Speer, "Do Low Prices Bore Shoppers?" *American Demographics*, January 1994, pp. 11–13; Richard Thaler, "Mental Accounting and Consumer Choice," *Marketing Science*, Summer 1985, pp. 199–214.

9. Paul E. Nelson and Lee E. Preston, *Price Merchandising in Food Retailing* (Berkeley, CA: The Special Publications, 1966); Lee E. Preston, *Markets and Marketing* (Glenview, IL: Scott, Foresman, 1970).

10. Allen J. McGrath, "Ten Timeless Truths About Pricing," *The Journal of Consumer Marketing*, vol. 8, Winter 1991, pp. 5–13.

11. Edwin Mansfield, *Principles of Microeconomics*, 4th ed., (New York: Norton, 1983); Kristian S. Palda, *Economic Analysis for Marketing Decisions* (Englewood Cliffs, NJ: Prentice-Hall, 1969).

12. Derek F. Abell and John S. Hammond, *Strategic Market Planning: Problems and Analytical Approaches* (Englewood Cliffs, NJ: Prentice-Hall, 1979); M. E. Porter, *Competitive Strategy, Techniques for Analyzing Industries and Competitors* (New York: The Free Press, 1980).

13. Seth Lubove, "It Ain't Broke But Fix It Anyway," *Forbes*, August 1, 1994, pp. 56–60.

14. Frank Alpert, Beth Wilson, and Michael T. Elliott, "Price Signaling: Does It Ever Work?" *Journal of Consumer Marketing*, vol. 10, no. 4, 1993, pp. 4–14.

15. Kent B. Monroe and S. M. Petroshius, "Buyers Perceptions of Price: An Update of the Evidence," in *Perspectives in Consumer Behavior*, H. H. Kassarjian and T. S. Robertson, Eds., (Glenview, IL: Scott, Foresman, 1981), pp. 43–45; J. C. Olson, "Price as an Informational Cue: Effects on Product Evaluations," in *Consumer and Industrial Buying Behavior*, A. G. Woodside, et al., Eds., (New York: North-Holland, 1977), pp. 267–286.

16. R. Cooper and T. W. Ross, "Prices, Product Qualities and Asymmetric Information: The Competitive Case," *Review of Economic Studies*, vol. 51, 1984, pp. 197–207; K. B. Monroe and W. B Dodds, "A Research Program for Establishing the Validity of the Price-Quality Relationship," *Journal of the Academy of Marketing Science*, vol. 16, Spring 1988, pp. 151–168; G. J. Tellis and B. Wemerfelt, "Competitive Price and Quality Under Asymmetric Information," *Marketing Science*, vol. 6, Summer 1981, pp. 240–253.

17. Tellis, *Journal of Marketing*, p. 153.

18. Monroe and Petroshius, *Perspectives in Consumer Behavior*.

19. Abhijit Biswas and Edward A. Blair, "Contextual Effects of Reference Prices in Retail Advertisements," *Journal of Marketing*, vol. 55, July 1991.

20. Alpert, Wilson, and Elliott, *Journal of Consumer Marketing*, p. 4.

21. E. Gerstner, "Do Prices Signal Higher Quality?" *Journal of Marketing Research*, vol. 22, May 1985, pp. 209–215.

22. Alpert, Wilson, and Elliott, *Journal of Consumer Marketing*, pp. 6, 11.

23. Christie Brown, "Marie Antoinette Sat Here," *Forbes*, March 28, 1994, pp. 126–128.

24. Susan Greco, "Pricing Your Service for Profits," *Inc.*, June 1992, p. 107.

25. Francis J. Mulhern and Robert P. Leone, "Implicit Price Bundling of Retail Products: A Multiproduct Approach to Maximizing Store Profitability," *Journal of Marketing*, vol. 55, October 1991, pp. 63–76.

26. F. M. Schere, *Industrial Market Structure and Economic Performance* (Chicago: Rand McNally College Publishing, 1980); Ray O. Werner, "Marketing and the United States Supreme Court," *Journal of Marketing*, vol. 46, Spring 1982, pp. 73–81.

27. Roula Khalaf, "Le Tire, Ç'est Moi," *Forbes*, August 1, 1994, pp. 48–49.

28. This case is excerpted from Hermann Simon, "Pricing Opportunities—And How to Exploit Them," *Sloan Management Review*, Winter 1992, pp. 55–65.

29. Questions are based on Jeffrey Teich and Albert A. Blum, "Perverse Pricing: Paying More for Less," *Marketing News*, May 23, 1994, p. 4.

30. Joseph B. White, "Value Pricing Is Hot as Shrewd Consumers Seek Low-Cost Quality," *The Wall Street Journal*, March 12, 1991, pp. A1, A5.

31. Oscar Suris, "Mercedes-Benz Tries to Compete on Value," *The Wall Street Journal*, October 20, 1993, p. C1.

32. "Strategic Mix of Odd-Even Pricing Can Lead to Increased Retail Profit," *Marketing News*, March 7, 1980, p. 24.

HARLEY-DAVIDSON CASE STUDY

1. Hap Jones, *Motorcycle Blue Book*, July/December 1993, (San Jose, CA: Hap Jones).

2. Kevin Kelly, Karen Lowry Miller, "The Rumble Heard Round the World: Harleys," *Business Week*, May 24, 1993, pp. 58–60.

3. *Harley-Davidson Historical Overview* (Milwaukee, WI, 1993), p. 122.

4. Video of meeting held March 1994 between representatives of Harley-Davidson and HarperCollins Publishers, New York.

5. Peter C. Reid, *Well Made in America* (New York: McGraw-Hill, 1990).
6. Company documents, 1994.

Chapter 19

1. Ron Henkoff, "Service Is Everybody's Business," *Fortune*, June 27, 1994, pp. 48–60. For statistics on service industries see "Annual Service Survey," U.S. Department of Commerce Bureau of the Census.
2. "Entrepreneurs Find Success in the Service Sector," *Business Week*, September 28, 1987, p. 68.
3. *Business Week*, September 28, 1987, p. 68.
4. Christopher Lovelock, "Are Services Really Different?" in Christopher Lovelock, *Managing Services—Marketing, Operations, and Human Resources*, 2d ed., (Englewood Cliffs, NJ: Prentice-Hall, 1992), pp. 1–8.
5. Lovelock, p. 4.
6. Some of the earliest thoughts and research on services marketing can be found in Robert C. Judd, "The Case for Redefining Services," *Journal of Marketing*, January 1964, pp. 58–59; John M. Rathmell, "What Is Meant by Services?" *Journal of Marketing*, October 1966, pp. 32–36; William J. Regan, "The Service Revolution," *Journal of Marketing*, July 1963, pp. 57–62.
7. See Leonard Berry, "Services Marketing Is Different," *Business*, May/June 1980, pp. 24–28; Christopher Lovelock, "Distinctive Aspects of Services Marketing," *Services Marketing* (Englewood Cliffs, NJ: Prentice Hall, 1984), pp. 1–9; G. Lynn Shostack, "Breaking Free from Product Marketing," *Journal of Marketing*, April 1977, pp. 73–80.
8. Peter Bennett, Ed., *Dictionary of Marketing Terms* (Chicago: American Marketing Association, 1988), p. 184.
9. James H. Donnelly, Jr., "Service Delivery Strategies in the 1980s—Academic Perspective," in Leonard L. Berry and James H. Donnelly, Jr., Eds., *Financial Institution Marketing: Strategies in the 1980s*, Consumers Bankers Association, 1980, pp. 143–150.
10. Lovelock, 1992, and Ronald K. Shelp, "The Service Economy Gets No Respect," *Across The Board*, February 1984, p. 5.
11. Lovelock, 1992, p. 4.
12. Lovelock, 1992, pp. 2–3.
13. National Public Radio, June 1994.
14. Leonard Berry and Terry Clark, "Four Ways to Make Services More Tangible," *Business*, October/December 1986, pp. 53–54.
15. Berry, "Services Marketing Is Different," p. 25.
16. Cyndee Miller, "Hotels Booked Solid with Brand Equity Campaigns," *Marketing News*, July 8, 1991, p. 6.
17. See Leonard Berry, A. Parasuraman, and Valerie Zeithaml, "Synchronizing Demand and Supply in Service Businesses," *Business*, October/December 1984, pp. 35–37; W. Earl Sasser, "Match Supply and Demand in Service Industries," *Harvard Business Review*, November/December 1976, pp. 133–140; Christopher Lovelock, "Strategies for Managing Capacity-Constrained Services," in Christopher Lovelock, *Managing Services—Marketing, Operations, and Human Resources*, 2d ed., (Englewood Cliffs, NJ: Prentice-Hall, 1992), pp. 154–168.
18. An excellent discussion of service classifications is provided by Christopher H. Lovelock, "Classifying Services to Gain Strategic Marketing Insights," in *Managing Services—Marketing, Operations, and Human Resources*, 2d ed., (Englewood Cliffs, NJ: Prentice-Hall, 1992), pp. 50–63.
19. Kenneth P. Uhl and Gregory D. Upah, "The Marketing of Services: A Set of Propositions," unpublished workshop discussion at Association of Decision Sciences Conference, New Orleans, 1979.
20. Uhl and Upah, op. cit.
21. Julie Edelson Halpert, "Who Will Fix Tomorrow's Cars?" *The New York Times*, November 7, 1993, p. F4.
22. Dan R. E. Thomas, "Strategy Is Different in Service Businesses," *Harvard Business Review*, July/August 1978, pp. 158–165.
23. Sybil F. Stershic, "New Imperative for Services Management," *Marketing News*, May 9, 1994, pp. 22–23.
24. Christopher H. Lovelock, "Why Marketing Management Needs to be Different for Services," in Christopher H. Lovelock, *Services Marketing* (Englewood Cliffs, NJ: Prentice-Hall, 1984), pp. 479–488.
25. G. Lynn Shostack, "Breaking Free from Product Marketing," *Journal of Marketing*, April 1977, pp. 73–80.
26. Shostack, op. cit.
27. Berry, "Services Marketing Is Different," p. 27 (see note 7).
28. Ibid.
29. Evert Gummersson, "The Marketing of Professional Services—25 Propositions," in Christopher Lovelock, *Services Marketing* (Englewood Cliffs, NJ: Prentice-Hall, 1984), pp. 125–132.
30. Philip Kotler and Richard A. Connor, Jr., "Marketing Professional Services," *Journal of Marketing*, January 1977, pp. 71–76.
31. Tim Triplett, "Lawyers Face Pressure to Become Marketers," *Marketing News*, March 14, 1994, p. 9.
32. Lenore Skenazy, "Jury Is Still Out," *Advertising Age*, April 11, 1988, p. 76.
33. W. Randolph Baker, "Counsel to Counsel," *Public Relations Journal*, February 1988, pp. 24–27, 43.
34. "Americans Voice Opinions on the Services Industry," *Marketing News*, November 20, 1987, p. 18.
35. Leonard L. Berry, Valarie A. Zeithaml, and A. Parasuraman, "Five Imperatives for Improving Service Quality," in Christopher Lovelock, *Managing Services—Marketing, Operations, and Human Resources*, 2d ed., (Englewood Cliffs, NJ: Prentice-Hall, 1992), pp. 224–235.
36. Berry, Zeithaml, and Parasuraman, p. 225.
37. Ibid.

Chapter 20

1. Seymour H. Fine, *Social Marketing—Promoting the Causes of Public and Nonprofit Agencies* (Needham Heights, MA: Allyn & Bacon, 1990), p. 10.
2. Fine, *Social Marketing*.
3. John A. Byrne, "Profiting from the Nonprofits," *Business Week*, March 26, 1990, pp. 66–74.
4. This statement is made based on an estimate of 1.37 million found in: Philip Kotler and Alan Andreasen, *Strategic Marketing for Nonprofit Organizations*, 4th ed., (Englewood Cliffs, NJ: Prentice-Hall, 1991), p. 11.
5. Karen Schwartz, "Nonprofits' Bottom-line: They mix lofty goals and gutsy survival strategies," *Marketing News*, February 13, 1989, p. 1.
6. One of the earliest articles promoting marketing in the social sector was Philip Kotler and Sidney J. Levy, "Broadening the Concept of Marketing," *Journal of Marketing*, January 1969, pp. 10–15. Early criticism came from David J. Luck in his article, "Broadening the Concept of Marketing—Too Far," *Journal of Marketing*, July 1969, pp. 14–17.
7. John A. Byrne, "Profiting from the Nonprofits," *Business Week*, March 26, 1990, pp. 66–74.
8. Kathleen Vyn, "Nonprofits Learn How-To's of Marketing," *Marketing News*, August 14, 1989, p. 1.
9. Kotler and Andreasen, p. 27.
10. Kotler and Andreasen, pp. 28–29.
11. Kotler and Andreasen, p. 30.
12. Christopher Lovelock and Charles Weinberg, "Public and Nonprofit Marketing Comes of Age," in G. Zaltman and T. Bonoma, Eds., *Review of Marketing 1978* (Chicago: American Marketing Association, 1978), pp. 413–52.
13. This example is drawn from Kotler and Andreasen, p. 90.
14. Katherine Gallagher and Charles B. Weinberg, "Coping with Success: New Challenges for Nonprofit Marketing," *Sloan Management Review*, Fall 1991, pp. 27–41.

15. Cyndee Miller, "Nonprofit Agencies Shun Marketing to the Poor," *Marketing News*, August 1, 1994, p. 2, 5.
16. Kotler and Andreasen, p. 28.
17. This example is taken from Kotler and Andreasen, p. 29, point #8.
18. Cyndee Miller, "Churches Turn to Research for Help in Saving New Souls, *Marketing News*, April 11, 1994, pp. 1–2, 5.
19. Lourdes Lee Valeriano, "Non-Profit Management," *Wall Street Journal*, November 11, 1993, p. A1.
20. Christopher H. Lovelock and Charles B. Weinberg, *Marketing for Public and Nonprofit Managers* (New York: Wiley, 1984), p. 298.
21. Kathleen A. Krentler, Mary L. Joyce, and J. W. Allen, "Causal Modeling Techniques in Health Care Marketing: A Case Study in Blood Donation," *Journal of Ambulatory Care Management*, May 1990, pp. 58–67.
22. Kotler and Andreasen, p. 222.
23. Alan R. Andreasen, "Cost-Conscious Marketing Research," *Harvard Business Review*, July/August 1983, pp. 74–77.
24. Paul Bloom and William Novelli, "Problems and Challenges in Social Marketing," *Journal of Marketing*, Spring 1981, pp. 79–88.
25. John B. Elmer, "Nonprofit Groups Can Profit from Commercial Techniques," *Marketing News*, September 3, 1990, p. 16.
26. The original description of Stanford's efforts came from: "Stanford University: The Annual Fund," in C. Lovelock and C. Weinberg, Eds., *Cases in Public and Nonprofit Marketing* (Palo Alto, CA: Scientific Press, 1977), pp. 73–88; this information was confirmed as still accurate in a telephone conversation between Tim A. Becker, research assistant, and Christine Valdez-Smith of Stanford University, August 4, 1994.
27. John A. Byrne, "Profting from the Nonprofits," *Business Week*, March 26, 1990, pp. 66–74.
28. Karen F. A. Fox and Philip Kotler, "The Marketing of Social Causes: The First 10 Years," *Journal of Marketing*, Fall 1980, pp. 24–33; Gene R. Laczniak, Robert F. Lusch, and Patrick E. Murphy, "Social Marketing: Its Ethical Dimensions," *Journal of Marketing*, Spring 1979, pp. 29–36.
29. Laczniak, Lusch, and Murphy, p. 30.
30. Fox and Kotler, p. 30.
31. Charles W. Lamb, Jr., and John L. Crompton, "Distributing Public Services: A Strategic Approach," *Journal of the Academy of Marketing Science*, Summer 1985, pp. 107–123.
32. Benson Shapiro, "Marketing for Nonprofit Organizations," *Harvard Business Review*, September/October 1973, pp. 123–32.
33. Mary L. Joyce and Michael H. Morris, "Pricing Considerations in Social Marketing," in Fine, *Social Marketing*, pp. 101–113.
34. "100 Leading National Advertisers," *Advertising Age*, January 3, 1994, p. 14.
35. American Marketing Association Information Center, Chicago, IL, telephone report to Tim A. Becker, research assistant, June 1994; Joe Adams, "Why Public Service Advertising Doesn't Work," *Ad Week*, November 17, 1980, p. 72.
36. Warren Berger, "Ad Council: A Grand Idea That Worked," *Advertising Age*, November 11, 1991, pp. A2–A8.
37. Kotler and Andreasen, p. 595.
38. Alexandra Peers, "Charities Draw Younger Donors with Hip Events and Door Prizes," *The Wall Street Journal*, April 25, 1994, p. B1.
39. Doug McPherson, "Twelve Tips to Stretch Your Nonprofit Media Relations Dollar," *Public Relations Quarterly*, Fall 1993, pp. 41–42.
40. James W. Harvey, "Benefit Segmentation for Fund Raisers," *Journal of the Academy of Marketing Science*, Winter 1990, pp. 77–86.
41. Cyndee Miller, "Tapping into Women's Issues Is Potent Way to Reach Market," *Marketing News*, December 6, 1993, pp. 1, 13.
42. Howard Schlossberg, "Surviving in a Cause-Related World: Social Agencies Grown into Sophisticated Marketers," *Marketing News*, December 18, 1989, p. 1.
43. Kathleen A. Krentler, "Cause-Related Marketing: Advantages and Pitfalls for Nonprofits," in Virginia A. Hodgkinson and Richard W. Lyman, Eds., *The Future of the Nonprofit Sector* (San Francisco, CA: Jossey-Bass, 1989), pp. 363–374.
44. Harvey, p. 77.
45. Office of Transit Management, Urban Mass Transportation Administration, U.S. Department of Transportation, "Organizing the Marketing Function for Transit Authorities," in C. Lovelock and C. Weinberg, Eds., *Readings in Public and Nonprofit Marketing* (Palo Alto, CA: The Scientific Press, 1978), pp. 81–86.
46. Philip Kotler, "Strategies for Introducing Marketing into Nonprofit Organizations," *Journal of Marketing*, January 1979, pp. 37–44.
47. Kotler, "Strategies for Introducing Marketing into Nonprofit Organizations," p. 43.

HARLEY-DAVIDSON CASE STUDY

1. Company documents, 1994.
2. Clay Dog, "The Miracle Road," *Easy Rider*, April 1994, pp. 170–173.
3. Marie McCaren, "Living the Family Legacy," *Diabetes Forecast*, April 1994, pp. 16–19.
4. Mark Sauer, "Big Wheels," *San Diego Union-Tribune*, May 23, 1994, p. C1.

Glossary

Number in brackets indicates chapter where term appears.

Absolute monopoly: a type of competitive environment with only one seller. [2]

Accessory equipment: goods required for individuals in the firm to "get the job done," but not permanently affixed to the customer's physical plant. [7]

Administered vertical marketing system: a system where coordination of marketing is achieved through the size and power of the channel leader(s). [11]

Advertising: any paid form of nonpersonal presentation and promotion of ideas, goods, or services by an identified sponsor. [14, 15]

Advertising appeal: the basis or approach used in the advertisement to attract the attention or interest of consumers and/or to influence their feelings toward the product, service, or cause. [15]

Agents: independent wholesalers who work to bring buyers and sellers together but who do not take title to goods [12]

Agents: wholesaler who does not take title but who facilitates the flow of a product from producer to user. [11]

AIDA: an acronym for a consumer response model to promotion: Attention, Interest, Desire, Action. [14]

AIO inventory: survey of consumers that provides researchers insight into consumers' activities, interests, and opinions. [5]

Allowances: reductions in the actual price paid resulting from a trade-in or an agreement to participate in promotional activity. [18]

Approach: the first direct contact between the salesperson and the prospect. [16]

Aspiration groups: a type of reference group that an individual aspires to join. [6]

Association of independents: a group of independent retailers that band together to gain some of the advantages enjoyed by large-scale operations. [13]

Assumption technique: a closing technique in which the salesperson assumes that the prospect is going to buy. [16]

Attitudes: learned tendencies to perceive and act in a certain consistent way toward a given object or idea, such as a product, service, brand, company, store, or spokesperson. [6]

Auction companies: agent wholesalers who bring buyers and sellers together usually at the auction company's facilities. [12]

Augmented product: a product with additional features and psychological benefits that enhance it in the eyes of the consumer. [9]

Average fixed cost (AFC): also called fixed cost per unit, the amount of fixed cost allocated to each unit. It is simply the TFC divided by the number of units. [17A]

Average variable cost (AVC): also called per-unit variable cost, the variable cost per unit produced. It is simply the sum of all variable cost (TVC) at a given production volume divided by this volume. [17A]

Backward integration: a method of forming a corporate vertical marketing system in which a wholesaler or retailer purchases and owns a component upstream in the channel. [11]

Balance of trade: the difference between the value of a country's exports and imports. [4]

Barter: a price set in terms of something other than money. [17]

Basing-point pricing: prices quoted as list price plus freight from a specific location. [18]

BCG matrix: a matrix developed by the Boston Consulting Group that plots an organization's SBUs on a two-dimensional grid using the factors of market share and growth rate. [3]

Behavioral segmentation: segmentation of markets on the basis of actual behavior instead of attitudes or demographics [5]

Benchmarking: comparison of a company's performance with that of other firms, units, or departments. [12]

Benefit segmentation: the identification of market segments by causal factors rather than descriptive factors. Using this approach, marketers determine what benefits consumers are seeking from products or services. [5]

Black Box Model: depiction of an individual's decision-making process as stimulus–response behavior. [6]

Bonus packs: extra amounts of a product offered to a customer either in a larger container or extra units packaged together. [15]

Boundary spanners: an individual who serves as a link between an organization and its customers. Salespeople are boundary spanners. [16]

Box store: a small food store that displays its low-priced goods in shipping boxes. It carries no perishables and fewer staple product lines than a supermarket. [13]

Brand: a name, term, symbol, design, or combination that identifies a seller's goods and services and distinguishes them from a competitor's products. [9]

Brand image: a consumer's subjective evaluation of a brand based on the perceived benefits it provides. [6]

Brand loyalty: a favorable attitude toward an exclusive purchase of a single brand over time. [5, 6]

Brand mark: the part of a brand—in the form of a symbol, design, or distinctive letters—that is seen but not spoken. [9]

Brand name: the part of a brand that can be vocalized, including letters, words, and numbers. [9]

Breadth: the variety of products carried by a retailer. A retailer that offers a large variety of products is said to have great breadth of assortment. [13]

Breadth of product mix: number of product lines marketed by an organization. [9]

Bribery: the act of giving, offering, or taking rewards for the performance of an activity that is known to be illegal or unjust. [4]

Brokers: agents who bring buyers and sellers into agreement for a sale, usually without buyers and sellers meeting at the broker's physical facilities. [12]

Buildup forecasting: a procedure for developing an overall sales forecast by adding up estimates made at the lowest level of interest—usually product lines, customer groups, or geographic areas. [8]

Business analysis: the evaluation of ideas for new products to determine estimated sales, market share, profit, and return on investment. [10]

Business definition: the answer to the question, "What business are we in?" The definition provides an organization with its thrust and direction. [3]

Business marketing: marketing efforts directed at any consuming group other than ultimate consumers. [7]

Business market(s): businesses, individuals, or organizations that purchase products or services to use in the production of other products and services, in their day-to-day operations, or for resale. [5, 7]

Business or organizational consumers: consumers who purchase products or services for use in the production of other products or services, for use in their day-to-day operations, or for resale. [5]

Business product: products sold to other businesses for use in producing other goods or in rendering services. [9]

Buyclass: a type of buying decision based on the newness of the problem to the organization, the amount of information required, and the consideration of new alternatives. [7]

Buyers: members of the organization that have formal authority for actually selecting the supplier and arranging the terms of the purchase. [7]

Buying center: the individuals involved in the organizational buying behavior process, including users, influencers, buyers, deciders, and gatekeepers. [7]

Canned presentation: a type of sales presentation that involves delivering a standard commentary, designed to elicit a positive response, to all prospects. [16]

Cannibalization: sales of a new product that take away sales of another product in the product line. [10]

Captive pricing: a type of complementary pricing whereby a basic product is sold at a low price with the belief that sales of accompanying supplies will compensate for any losses incurred in the sale of the basic product. [18]

Carrying costs: all costs associated with holding a quantity of goods for some period of time. [12]

Cash-and-carry wholesalers: a wholesale store where small retailers make cash purchases and carry the merchandise away themselves. [12]

Cash cows: strategic business unit with a big share of a low-growth market. [3]

Cash discounts: reduction from the list price given to the buyer for paying for the goods or services within a specified time period. [18]

Catalogue showroom: a discount retail store that sells general merchandise displayed in a catalogue and, to a lesser extent, displayed at the showroom. [13]

Cause-related marketing: marketing carried out by a for-profit firm designed to benefit both the firm's bottom line and a targeted not-for-profit organization or organizations. [20]

Channel: the media used to transmit a communication. [14]

Channel captain: the member of the distribution channel with the most power and authority, who directs, leads, and supports other channel members. [11]

Channel of distribution: organizations or individuals who participate in the flow and transfer of title of goods and services as they move from a producer to an ultimate consumer or a business-to-business user. [11]

Closing: the step in the selling process at which the buyer is asked for and makes a commitment to purchase. [16]

Co-branding: the pairing of two brand names from two producers on a single product. [9]

Coding: the process of grouping and assigning numeric codes to the various responses to a particular question. [8]

Cognitive dissonance: the anxiety a buyer experiences after making a decision. [16]

Cold canvass: a method of prospecting in which calls are made to every person or company in a group with no advance information on the needs or financial status of each prospect. [16]

Combined approach: consolidation of two or more market segments that have been determined to be responsive to a single marketing effort despite some degree of heterogeneity. [5]

Commercialization: the introduction of a new product into the marketplace. [10]

Commission merchants: a wholesaler who takes possession of and sells agricultural commodities in central markets. [12]

Commodity marketing: an approach to the study of marketing that concentrates on the functions performed in moving specific goods from producers to the ultimate consumers. [1]

Common carriers: transporters who maintain a regular schedule and accept goods from any shipper. [12]

Common market: *see* E.C. [4]

Communication network: a connected system of computers that can send and receive information. [8]

Communication-promotion paradox: the paradox that suggests that mass media promotion is efficient in reaching large audiences but a single message is not effective communication to large audiences. [14]

Competitive advantage: a factor or combination of factors in a company's product or marketing strategy that gives the firm an edge over competitors. [3]

Competitive bidding: price is determined through a process whereby potential buyers or sellers compete with each other. [18]

Competitive pricing: a group of pricing strategies that base price on an organization's competitive positioning in the market. [18]

Complementary pricing: a group of pricing strategies that involve setting a price for a product or service that is designed to influence demand for another product. [18]

Complementary products: products that have demand that is related to other products in the line. [10]

Component parts: goods incorporated with little or no change into other manufactured products. [7]

Concentrated marketing: selection of a single target market from all segments that have been identified in the population. [5]

Concept sector: *see* Social sector. [20]

Concept tests: reactions from selected groups of consumers to new product ideas and concepts, which are sought before new products are released. [10]

Conclusive research: research designed to help the decision maker evaluate alternative courses of action. [8]

Consistency of product mix: extent to which the various products in the product mix are similar to each other in use, distribution, target market, and so forth. [9]

Consultative selling: selling that involves consulting with a potential customer, gaining insight into the potential customer's problems, and then working to demonstrate how a company's goods and services can solve those problems. [16]

Consumer behavior: actions of individuals or groups who select, purchase, use, or dispose of products, services, ideas, or experiences to satisfy their needs and/or desires. [6]

Consumer education: attempts to make consumers good marketplace decision makers by exposing them to materials that explain good consumerism. [2]

Consumer market: buyers who intend to use or benefit from the product or service themselves. [5]

Consumer product: products purchased for use by ultimate consumers. [9]

Consumer promotion: sales promotions focused at ultimate consumers. [15]

Consumer protection: legal action designed to give consumers reasonable rights in their dealings with businesses. [2]

Consumer socialization: process by which (young) people acquire skills, knowledge, and attitudes that help them function as consumers. [6]

Consumerism: the consumers' movement for more fairness in relations with businesses. [2]

Contests: games requiring some skill on the part of the participant. [15]

Continuous demand: demand for products that have a long, relatively stable history of sales. [12]

Contract carriers: for-hire transporters who move goods for any shipper for an agreed-upon amount. [12]

Contractual vertical marketing system: a system where coordination of the marketing is the result of a contract among channel members. [11]

Controllable variables: the four general categories (product, distribution, promotion, and price) in which marketers make decisions, so called because they represent areas over which the marketer has control. [1]

Convenience goods: products that the consumer buys frequently with a minimum of time and effort. [9]

Convenience store: a small food and staples store with a limited assortment of products, locations near the consumer, long store hours, and fast checkout. [13]

Core product: the underlying benefits sought by a consumer in an exchange. [9]

Corollary product index: uses the known sales for one product to forecast the sales potential of another product. [8]

Corporate chain: a group of two or more stores that is centrally owned and managed and that deals in the same line of merchandise. [13]

Corporate vertical marketing system: a vertical marketing system where coordination of the marketing channel results from single ownership of channel levels. [11]

Cost per thousand (CPM): a measure used to summarize the cost-effectiveness of media vehicles; it gives the cost per thousand persons in the vehicle's audience. [15]

Cost-plus pricing: a price-setting method that adds a markup to average total cost or variable cost. [18]

Cost structure: the balance between fixed costs and variable costs. [3]

Coupons: a type of sales promotion that provides a certain amount off the price of an item. [15]

Credit and collection discounts: an additional deduction from a list price for a bill paid in full within a specified time frame. [18]

Cue: a stimulus in the environment that determines the type of response to a drive. [6]

Culture: the sum total of a society's beliefs, morals, laws, customs, language, and art forms that are transmitted from one generation to another within a society. [4, 6]

Cumulative quantity discounts: discounts based on buying a specified amount of product within a given time frame. [18]

Customary pricing: a practice in which all competitors use certain traditional pricing points. [18]

Customer satisfaction measurement (CSM): performance-monitoring research that provides ongoing assessment of how satisfied customers are. [8]

Custom-made index: a buying-power index constructed of factors chosen by the forecaster. [8]

DAGMAR: an acronym for Defining Advertising Goals, Measuring Advertising Results. DAGMAR is a model that suggests the characteristics of good promotion objectives. [14]

Data base: a storage depot for the information flowing into a decision support system. [8]

Data entry: the process of converting information from a form that cannot be read by a computer to a form than can be read by a computer. [8]

Deceptive pricing: specially promoted price deals that mislead consumers. [17]

Deciders: people who determine the final selection of products, services, and suppliers. [7]

Decision support system (DSS): a system that collects and interprets information for decision making. It enables decision makers to interact directly with both data bases and analysis models. The important components of a DSS include hardware and a communication network, data base, model base, software base, and the DSS user (decision maker). [8]

Decoding: assigning meaning to a communication by the receiver. [14]

Delivered pricing: a type of geographic pricing where the price quoted by the seller includes transportation costs. [18]

Delphi Technique: a technique whereby a group of experts are asked individually to make forecasts, which are then circulated to others in the group, who are then allowed to modify their initial forecasts. [8]

Demand curve: a graph of the quantity of products expected to be sold at various prices, given that other factors are held constant. [17A]

Demarketing: making an exchange with the objective of decreasing consumption of a product. [1]

Demographic segmentation: segmentation of markets on the basis of demographic characteristics such as age, income, occupation, and gender. [5]

Demography: the study of people in the aggregate. A demographer is concerned about size, birthrate, age, geographic migration patterns and education levels of the population. [2]

Department store: a large retail institution that carries a wide variety of merchandise grouped into well-defined departments, usually with substantial depth for each product line. [13]

Dependent variable: the variable that is acted upon in an experiment. [8]

Depth: refers to the selection of offerings available from a retailer. A retailer that offers a large selection of offerings is said to offer great depth. [13]

Depth of product mix: number of sizes, models, and colors offered within each product line. [9]

Derived demand: demand for one product that arises from the demand for another product. The demand for many business products is derived from the demand for consumer goods, such as the auto companies' demand for tires, which is a function of consumers' demand for cars. [7]

Developed nations: nations that enjoy a level of economic development characterized by private enterprise and a distinct consumer orientation. Countries in Western Europe, the United States, Canada, and Japan are developed nations. [4]

Developing nations: nations that are moving from economies based on agriculture or production of raw materials to economies based on industry. [4]

Differentiated marketing: an approach that attempts to reach the entire population by developing unique marketing mixes for each segment of the larger population. [5]

Direct channel: a distribution channel that has no intermediaries; products flow directly from producer to consumer. [11]

Direct ownership: a method of global operation that involves a company owning and operating a facility in a foreign country with no local partner involved. [4]

Direct-response retailer: a retailer who solicits customers through mass media promotion. [13]

Disaggregation: a segmentation approach that views each consumer or business as an individual segment. [5]

Disassociative groups: a type of reference group that an individual wishes to avoid. [6]

Discount store: a retail institution that offers only a few services and features low prices. [13]

Disposable personal income (DPI): a consumer's total income minus taxes paid to all levels of government. [2]

Dissonance/attribution model: a response hierarchy in which purchase occurs only after awareness, and attitude change occurs after purchase. [14]

Distribution: the component of the marketing mix that is concerned with delivering the product or service to the consumer. Sometimes referred to as place. [1]

Distribution center: a large, centralized warehouse that serves regional markets and processes and regroups products into customized orders that can be shipped in large quantities to various distribution points. [12]

Distribution channel: a set of firms and individuals who participate in the flow of goods and services as they move from producer to user. [1]

Distributor's brand: a brand owned and controlled by a retailer, wholesaler, or other type of reseller. [9]

Diversification: a growth strategy that requires an organization to introduce new products into markets that are also new to the organization. [3]

Dogs: strategic business unit with a small share of a low-growth market. [3]

Domestic firms: companies who restrict their efforts to within the borders of the country where they are based. [4]

Drive: a state of tension caused by an unfulfilled need. The drive will stimulate action to reduce the tension. [6]

Drop shippers: wholesalers who arrange the sale of goods, passing orders to their customers without ever taking possession of the goods. Also called Desk jobbers. [12]

Dual distribution: a manufacturer selling to intermediaries while at the same time competing with them and selling directly to consumers. [11]

Dumping: selling a product at a lower price in foreign markets than at home. [4]

Duplicated reach: the number of people exposed to one ad more than once. [15]

E.C. (European Economic Community): a group of twelve European nations—Belgium, France, Italy, Luxembourg, the Netherlands, Germany, Great Britain, Ireland, Denmark, Spain, Portugal, and Greece—that have a common antitrust law, no restrictions on movement of capital and labor, and uniform tariffs on imports from nonmembers. [4]

Ecology: the study of the relationship between living things and their environments. [2]

Economic community: a group of countries that agree to operate as a single entity for economic purposes. [4]

Editing: the process of assuring maximum accuracy and clarity in the wording and format of a questionnaire. [8]

80/20 rule: the common occurrence of 20 percent of a product's users accounting for close to 80 percent of sales. [5]

Emergency goods: convenience goods purchased as the result of an unexpected situation that requires immediate possession of a product. [9]

Encoding: the symbolic representation of the ideas in a communication. [14]

Environmental analysis: the process of monitoring external environmental forces. [2]

Environmental diagnosis: making marketing decisions by assessing data of the environmental analysis. [2]

Environmental scanning: collecting information on the elements of a firm's environment. [2]

Equipment-based services: a service that depends primarily on specific equipment for performance. An automated car wash is an equipment-based service. [19]

Erratic demand: an unpredictable pattern of demand for a good, such as the demand for large automobiles. [12]

Ethics: an individual's personal beliefs of what is right and wrong. [2]

Everyday low pricing (EDLP): strategy whereby the price charged for the item is lower than it would be if other sales promotion's were being used. [15]

Evoked set: the group of brands a consumer will consider when deciding to make a purchase. [6]

Exchange: all the activities associated with receiving something from someone by giving something in return. [1]

Exchange rate: the value of a country's currency relative to other currencies in the world. [4]

Exclusive dealing contract: an agreement whereby the manufacturer prohibits an intermediary from carrying competing products. This is illegal in some situations. [11]

Exclusive distribution: a distribution approach in which one or very few outlets are selected to resell a product or service. [11]

Exclusive sales territories: restriction, by a manufacturer, of the geographic territory of its intermediaries. This is illegal if it restricts competition. [11]

Execution: the manner or way in which a particular appeal is turned into an advertising message. [15]

Exempt carriers: shippers who are not required to operate by state and federal regulations. They usually move unprocessed agricultural goods. [12]

Experience-curve pricing: a price-setting method using a markup on the average total cost as forecast by the cost trends as sales volume increases. [18]

Experiment: a means of data collection in which the researcher manipulates one or more independent variables and measures their effects on one or more dependent variables, while controlling for the effect of extraneous variables. [8]

Exploratory research: research whose primary objective is to provide insights into the problem. [8]

Exporting: sending products that have been produced in one country to a different country and selling them there. [4]

External environment: all forces and events outside an organization. [2]

Extrinsic rewards: rewards, such as salary, that are external to the job. [16]

Facilitating functions: functions of marketing that serve to bridge perceptual, ownership, and values separations. The functions include financing products, risk-taking by holding ownership, providing market information, developing standards, and grading products against these standards. [1]

Family brand: a brand applied to one or more lines of products of one seller. [9]

Flanker brand: the introduction of a new brand to a product category in which the organization already has products. [10]

F.O.B. with Freight Allowed: "free on board," meaning that the seller pays freight charges to a designated location and the buyer pays the remaining freight expenses. [18]

F.O.B. origin: a type of geographic pricing where prices are quoted F.O.B. (Free On Board) to some specific point. [18]

Focus group: a group of eight to twelve participants who are led by a moderator in an in-depth discussion of one topic or concept. [8]

Follow-up: what happens after the sale. [16]

Form utility: the satisfaction derived from having a product that possesses the physical characteristics desired by a consumer. [1]

Forward integration: a method of forming a corporate vertical marketing system by a manufacturer's operation of its own channel intermediaries. [11]

Four Ps: product, place (distribution), promotion, and price. [1]

Franchise extension: the introduction of a product into a new category, using an existing brand name. [10]

Franchising: a form of contractual vertical marketing system in which a parent company (franchisor) grants an individual or small company (franchisee) the right to do business in exchange for revenues from fees or royalties. [11]

Frequency: the average number of times a person is exposed to an ad. [15]

Full-function wholesalers: merchant wholesalers who are active in each major marketing function (facilitating, logistical, transactional). [12]

Functional discounts: reductions from list price given to a firm because of the position it holds in the channel or because of the activities it is expected to perform. Also called *trade discounts*. [18]

Functional marketing: an approach to marketing that emphasizes the basic functions of marketing and how they are performed by various intermediaries. [1]

Gatekeepers: individuals who control the flow of information into the buying center. [7]

GATT: the General Agreement on Tariffs and Trade (GATT) is an agreement to encourage unrestricted multilateral trade by binding participating nations to negotiating trade rules and by mandating penalties for any deviation. [4]

GE screening grid: a grid that plots an organization's SBUs on the two dimensions of industry attractiveness and company strengths. [3]

General buying power indexes: a forecasting technique that attempts to identify factors that have affected sales in the past, and use those factors to predict future sales. [8]

General-line merchandisers: full-function wholesalers who carry a wide assortment of merchandise across many product lines. [12]

General-merchandise store: a store that carries many different product lines with varying degrees of depth. [13]

Generic brand: products sold with no identification other than the contents of the package. [9]

Geodemographic segmentation: division of the market on the assumption that people with similar economic and cultural backgrounds and perspectives tend to cluster in neighborhoods. [5]

Geographic pricing: a pricing strategy that affects the way prices are quoted depending on the cost of transportation of goods from seller to buyer. [18]

Geographic segmentation: division of the total market into segments on the basis of location. [5]

Global marketing: the practice of marketing with a view to the entire world as a market. [1, 4]

Green marketing: the carrying out of marketing activities with consideration for the environmental consequences of those activities. [1]

Hardware: the computer (the actual machine) that is part of a decision support system. [8]

Heavy equipment: products used directly in the production of other goods and often attached to the physical plant of the businesses using them. [7]

Heterogeneous shopping goods: shopping goods perceived by the consumer to vary significantly among a number of attributes. [9]

Hierarchy-of-effects model: a consumer response model to promotion: awareness, knowledge, preference, conviction, purchase. [14]

High-involvement media: media that require active participation by the consumer in order for the message to be communicated (e.g., newspapers, magazines). [15]

High-involvement purchases: purchases that are important to the consumer and are closely tied to the consumer's ego and self-image. [6]

Homogeneous shopping goods: shopping goods perceived by the consumer to possess similar attributes across all alternatives. [9]

Horizontal conflict: conflict among intermediaries who operate at the same level in a channel (for example, two or more retailers.) [11]

Idea generation: a stage of the product development process during which ideas for new products are sought. [10]

Ideal point: the place on the perceptual map that represents the combination of attributes most desired by the consumer. [5]

Image pricing: attaching a higher price to a product, similar to premium pricing, except differences in brands or models is illusory. [18]

Import-export agents: agent wholesalers who specialize in international trade. [12]

Impulse goods: convenience goods purchased on sight, without forethought. [9]

In-home retailer: a retailer who presents goods to customers in a face-to-face meeting at the customer's home or by contacting the customers by telephone. [13]

In-house agency: a department in an organization that does the work otherwise performed by an advertising agency. [15]

Independent variable: a variable that is manipulated by a researcher in an experiment. [8]

Indirect channel: a distribution channel that uses one or more intermediaries. [11]

Industrialized nations: *see* Developed nations. [4]

Inflation: a general rise in the prices that people must pay for goods and services. [2]

Information costs: the price of searching for more price information. These costs may include both time and money. [17]

Information-processing model: a consumer response model that proposes the following sequential steps: presentation, attention, comprehension, yielding, retention, behavior. [14]

Innovation adoption model: a consumer response model that proposes the following sequential steps: awareness, interest, evaluation, trial, and adoption. [14]

Innovation: a new product that represents a new and different means of satisfying consumers' wants and needs. [2, 10]

Input/output analysis: analysis based on the concept that the output (sales) from one industry is the input (purchases) of other industries. [7]

Institutional marketing: an approach to marketing that concentrates on the organizations that perform various marketing functions. [1]

Institutional markets: organizations that buy goods and/or services in order to serve the needs of large groups of people in institutional settings. [7]

Intangibility: a feature of most services. It means that the service of a physician or other performer cannot be touched or handled. Financial advice is an intangible, as is an education. [19]

Integrated marketing communications (IMC): the process of developing and implementing over time various forms of persuasive communications with customers and prospects. [14]

Integrative pricing: a price setting practice that includes consideration of demand, cost, and competition as well as important environmental factors. [18]

Intensive distribution: a distribution strategy in which as many outlets as possible are used to resell the product or service. [11]

Intermediaries: channel members operating between the producer and consumer that facilitate the flow of goods and services. Wholesalers and retailers are intermediaries. [11]

Intermediary pricing: the price charged by a channel member which represents a markup on the manufacturer's selling price. [18]

International firms: firms that engage in trade and marketing outside the borders of their home countries. [4]

International marketing: *see* Global marketing. [4]

Interviewing error: error that results from conscious or unconscious bias in the interviewer's interaction with the respondent. [8]

Intrinsic rewards: rewards associated with doing the job, like having autonomy to make important decisions. [16]

Job description: a statement about the tasks and behaviors required to perform a job. [16]

Joint venture: a partnership between two firms from different countries. The partners share ownership and control in proportion to the investment they have made. [4]

Just-in-Time (JIT): an inventory control system in which the supplier's customer (a wholesaler, retailer, another firm, or a consumer) starts the process by calling for a product. [12]

Laddering: a technique that attempts to identify benefits sought by beginning with specific product attributes and then encouraging consumers to "climb the ladder" between these attributes and benefits or desired end states. [5]

Leadership: the ability to influence others to accomplish desired goals. [16]

Learning: changes in an individual's behavior resulting from experiences. [6]

Less-developed nations: countries that exhibit a level of development characterized by populations with very low literacy rates, limited technology, and low per-capita GDP. Many nations in Africa and Asia fit this description. [4]

Licensing: a practice whereby a company authorizes a foreign firm or individual to produce its product locally. [4]

Life-style: a set of values or tastes exhibited by a group of consumers, especially as they are reflected in consumption patterns. [5]

Light equipment: *see* Accessory equipment. [7]

Limited-function wholesalers: merchant wholesalers who provide only a subset of the services of full function wholesalers. [12]

Limited-line store: a retail store that carries great depth of merchandise but only a few associated product lines. [13]

Line extension: the introduction of new flavors, sizes, or models into an existing product category, using an existing brand name. [10]

Localized approach: an approach to global marketing that views marketing as a local issue, emphasizing differences among countries in customers, distribution systems, and marketing techniques, and advocates tailoring a marketing program for each country. [4]

Logistical functions: functions of marketing that serve to bridge spatial and temporal separations. Storage and transportation are logistical functions. [1]

Logistics: a concept borrowed from the military to refer to the procurement, distribution, maintenance, and replacement of material and personnel. [12]

Loss leaders: the practice of setting very low prices on one product with the intent of stimulating sales of it and complementary products by attracting customers to the purchase location of both products. [18]

Low-involvement hierarchy: a response hierarchy in which purchase occurs before liking, preference, and conviction. [14]

Low-involvement media: media through which a consumer can receive an advertisement without actively participating (e.g., television, radio). [15]

Low-involvement purchases: purchases that are not very important to the consumer, who perceives available alternatives as being similar. [6]

Macromarketing: an approach that concentrates on the broader aspects of marketing and its effects on groups within society, on the economy, or on society as a whole. [1]

Mail-order retailer: a retailer who sells through a catalogue distributed to customers. [13]

Mail-order wholesalers: an intermediary who sells to retailers through catalogues. [12]

Majority fallacy: false assumption that the bigger a segment is, the more potential it offers to a marketer. [5]

Managerial approach: an approach that focuses on the way managers make decisions about the marketing mix. [1]

Manufacturer's brand: a brand owned by the manufacturer. [9]

Manufacturers' agents: representatives designated by a manufacturer to sell all or some part of their product line in a specified geographic area. [12]

Manufacturers' sales branches: a wholesale operation owned by a manufacturer. [12]

Marginal cost (MC): the change in total cost of producing and marketing one additional unit. [17A]

Market: people or businesses with the potential interest, purchasing power, and willingness to spend money for a product or service to satisfy a need or desire. [1, 5]

Market development: a growth strategy that requires an organization to introduce its existing products into markets that are new to the organization. [3]

Market-driven or **customer-driven organization:** a company that focuses all activities of the organization directly on satisfying and anticipating the needs and wants of customers. [1]

Market growth: a measure of the rate at which a market's size is increasing. Can be expressed in terms of units or dollars. [11]

Market penetration: a growth strategy that involves an organization's selling more of its existing products in its existing markets. [3]

Market potential: the maximum sales possible for all sellers of a product to an identified customer group within a specified time frame in a given environment. [8]

Market segmentation: the process of dividing large heterogeneous markets into smaller subsets of people or businesses with similar needs and/or responsiveness to marketing mix offerings. [5]

Market share: the percentage of total market size enjoyed by a single competitor. Can be expressed as "us/us + them." [11]

Market share analysis: a control analysis that considers how the firm is doing compared to the competition. Is the firm gaining or losing ground? [3]

Market size: the total number of people, companies, or organizations that possess the willingness, ability, and authority to purchase a product. Can be expressed in terms of number of units or as a dollar figure determined to be the amount of revenue generated by the units. [11]

Market stability: a description of the degree of volatility of a market's needs. [11]

Market structure: a description of the units comprising a market. Can be expressed in terms of geographical dispersion, size of the units, or any other relevant attribute. [11]

Marketing: the process of planning and executing the conception, pricing, promotion, and distribution of ideas, goods, and services to create exchanges that satisfy individual and organizational objectives. [1]

Marketing audit: an overall assessment of the organization's marketing environment, organizational capabilities, objectives, and strategy. [3]

Marketing concept: the philosophy that if all of an organization's activities are focused on satisfying consumers' needs, long-run profits will be achieved. [1]

Marketing control: feedback on how an organization's plans are progressing. The purpose of marketing control is to maximize the probability that the organization will achieve its short-run and long-run objectives in the marketplace. [3]

Marketing environment: all factors that affect an organization directly or indirectly. [2]

Marketing ethics: the application of ethical standards to all marketing activities and decisions. [2]

Marketing expense-to-sales analysis: a tactical control method that compares the ratio of various marketing expenses (such as advertising, marketing research) to the sales being generated. [3]

Marketing functions: activities that bridge the separations between products (of goods, services, and ideas) and consumers. [1]

Marketing information system (MIS):   a formalized set of procedures for generating, analyzing, storing, and distributing information on an ongoing basis to marketing decision makers. [8]

Marketing management: the planning, direction, and control of the entire marketing function, specifically the formulation and execution of marketing objectives, policies, programs, and strategy. Responsibilities include product development, organization and staffing, supervision of marketing operations, and control of marketing performance. [1]

Marketing mix: activities in the areas of the four Ps as decided by a marketing decision maker for a given target market. [1]

Marketing myopia: the failure of an organization to take a broad view of its business. Marketing myopia can result in missed opportunities. [1]

Marketing opportunity: a "challenge to specific marketing action that is characterized by a generally favorable set of environmental circumstances and an acceptable probability of success." [2]

Marketing research: the systematic and objective development and provision of information to be used in the marketing management's decision-making process. [8]

Marketing strategy: the long-term plan for developing a marketing mix that will achieve the organization's objectives by meeting the target market's needs. [3]

Marketing tactics: specific decisions that follow from an organization's marketing strategy and provide a blueprint for implementation. [3]

Mass marketing: a marketing approach that assumes all consumers are sufficiently similar that they will respond to a single marketing mix effort. [5]

Materials handling: activities involved in the physical handling of goods. [12]

Media plan: the media types, vehicles, and inserts used to advertise a product or service. [15]

Media type: distinctions among broad classes of media—newspapers, magazines, television, radio, and so forth. [15]

Media vehicles: the specific unit for purchase within media types (the *CBS Evening News* or the December issue of *Life*). [15]

Membership groups: a type of reference group of which an individual is currently a member. [6]

Merchants: an independently owned wholesaler who takes title to the products as they pass through the channel of distribution. [11]

Merchant wholesalers: independent businesses that hold ownership to the goods they market to retailers, other merchants, or business customers. [12]

Me-toos: a product new to the firm but not new to the marketplace, and usually very similar to a competitive product. [10]

Micromarketing: *see* Managerial approach. [1]

Microniche marketing: identification of a very small segment as a target market. [5]

Mission statement: *see* Business definition. [3]

Model base: the component of a decision support system that contains operations research models that represent the real marketing world. [8]

Modifications: a significant change in an existing product that, in effect, makes it a new product. [10]

Modified rebuys: a buying situation in which a new evaluation is made of suppliers' offerings, prompted by the conviction that it is worthwhile to seek additional information and alternatives before a decision is made. [7]

Monopolistic competition: state of the market in which many sellers account for smaller percentages of total sales. [2]

Most-favored nation principle: this principle ensures that all GATT nations will receive the most favorable terms in trading with another GATT member. [4]

Motivation: reason for activity directed toward a goal. [6]

MRO products: *m*aintenance, *r*epair, and *o*perating products. *See* Supplies. [7]

Multilevel marketing: a distribution system that consists of distributors that recruit additional distributors and receive a commission based on the sales of their recruits as well as their own sales. [4]

Multinational corporations: companies engaged in a variety of business activities including sales, manufacturing, and research outside the borders of their home countries. [4]

Multiple-zone pricing: a system in which prices vary depending on the buyer's geographical area. [18]

NAFTA: the North American Free Trade Agreement is an agreement between Canada, the United States, and Mexico to allow free trade among the three nations. [4]

National brand: *see* Manufacturer's brand. [9]

Need-satisfaction approach: an approach that can be used to develop a sales presentation that relies on the notion that customers have needs that must be satisfied. The good or service must be able to satisfy these needs if this approach is used. [16]

New product: a product that has a new brand name and is in a product category new to the organization. [10]

New task buys: a buying situation in which the buyer has no experience, needs considerable information, and considers alternatives. [7]

Noise: unplanned distortion or interference in the communication process. [14]

Nonbusiness marketing: marketing conducted by not-for-profit organizations. [20]

Noncumulative quantity discounts: discounts offered for purchasing in large quantities in a single order. [18]

Nonpersonal channels: communication involving no interpersonal contact between sender and receiver. [14]

Nonprofit marketing: *See* Social-sector marketing. [20]

Nonresponse error: the difference on measures of interest in a study between those who respond and those who do not. [8]

Not-for-profit marketing: *see* Social-sector marketing. [20]

Not-for-profit organization: an organization whose bottom-line objective is to attain some measure of success other than profits. [1]

Number of inserts: the number of specific advertisements that appear in a given media vehicle. [15]

Objections: excuses for not buying that slow down the momentum needed to make a sale. [16]

Observation: the collection of data with no communication between the respondent and the recorder of the behavior. [8]

Odd-even pricing: the practice of setting prices to end in certain odd numbers. [18]

Oligopoly: a market in which a few large sellers account for a large percentage of the market. [2]

Opinion leaders: individuals who, because of their knowledge or expertise in certain product or service areas, are able to exert personal influence on other consumers of these products or services. [6]

Order processing: all activities involved in collecting, checking, and transmitting information about sales transactions. [12]

Order getter: a salesperson who seeks out potential customers and persuades them to buy a product. [16]

Order takers: a salesperson who completes sales made to regular or repeat customers. [16]

Original equipment manufacturers (OEMs): manufacturers who produce heavy and light equipment. OEMs are typical purchasers of component parts. [7]

Out-of-stock cost: costs of lost sales and back orders resulting from not having goods available. [12]

Packaged presentation: *see* Canned presentation. [16]

Packaging: an important part of the product that serves two functions: utility to distribution channel members and final consumers and promotional communication. [9]

Peak-load pricing: offering seasonal, temporary markdowns during slow periods or for outdated merchandise. [18]

Penetration pricing: setting a low initial price for a new product. [18]

People-based services: a service that relies on people and requires no special equipment. A by-hand car wash is a people-based service. [19]

Perceived risk: the amount of risk a consumer perceives in a purchase, which is related to the uncertainty associated with the purchase and potential negative consequences. [6]

Perception: the process of receiving and deriving meaning from stimuli in internal and external environments. [6]

Perceptual map: a graph of consumers' perceptions of product attributes across two or more dimensions. [5]

Performance-monitoring research: research that provides feedback on the operation of a marketing program. [8]

Periodic discounting: offering a lower price at certain times of the day, days of the week, or seasons of the year with the fact that a markdown will occur being predictable by consumers. [18]

Perishability: the quality of a service that results in an inability to warehouse or store it. [19]

Personal channels: direct, person-to-person communication. [14]

Personal selling: selling that relies on personal interactions between buyer and seller. [14, 16]

Personality: the set of consistent and enduring behavioral responses exhibited by an individual to the stimuli he or she encounters. [6]

Physical distribution: the physical movement and transfer of finished and semifinished goods within and through marketing channels. [12]

Physical distribution concept: a concept of physical distribution as a systems approach, hence all activities should be viewed as parts of a single effort. [12]

Place utility: the satisfaction derived from using a product at the place the consumer wishes to use it. [1]

Planned shopping center: a group of stores that is planned in advance as an integrated unit. [13]

Point-of-purchase promotions (POP): special displays, racks, signs, banners, and exhibits placed in the retail store to support the sales of a brand. [15]

Political stability: the extent to which a country's government can be expected to remain strong and unchallenged. [4]

Portfolio analysis: a method of assessing a firm's strategic business units by comparing them on some determined criteria and then using that assessment to guide overall strategy planning. [3]

Positioning: the perception that targeted consumers have of a firm's offering relative to that of competitors. [5]

Possession utility: the satisfaction derived from having the ability to purchase or use a product. [1]

Postpurchase dissonance: doubt or anxiety experienced after making a difficult, relatively permanent decision. [6]

Post-testing: advertisement testing methods that involve people who have been exposed to a given ad. [15]

Preapproach: the process of gaining information about a prospect, prior to contact, in order to anticipate questions and indicate to the prospect the salesperson's seriousness. [16]

Premium pricing: attaching a higher price to one brand or model of a product that has some additional attributes but whose costs do not demand a premium price. [18]

Premiums: offer of an article of merchandise either free or at a lower price than usual to encourage consumers to buy it instead of another product or service. [15]

Prepared presentation: *see* Canned presentation. [16]

Presentation: the communication part of making the sale. This is the step where information is communicated to the prospect with the intent to persuade him or her. [16]

Pretesting: any method used to test an advertisement prior to the commitment of media dollars. [15]

Price: the value that one puts on the utility one receives for goods and services. [1, 17]

Price bundling: marketing two or more products as a unit with a single price for the entire package. [18]

Price decisions: decisions involving price determination as well as setting price policies and developing specific pricing stragtegies, including choices about discounts. [1]

Price discrimination: the practice of charging different prices to different buyers for goods of like grade and quality. [17]

Price elasticity of demand: the percentage change in quantity demanded relative to the percentage change made in price. [17A]

Price fixing: a conspiracy among competitors to set prices for a product either at the same level in the channel (horizontally) or at different levels in the channel (vertically). [17]

Price leader: the firm that usually is first to change prices in the industry. [17]

Price leadership: the tendency in some industries for one firm to take the first step at raising and lowering prices. [18]

Price lining: the practice of placing items in a product line at specific pricing points. [18]

Price-offs: a consumer promotion technique that offers a reduced price for the item, right on the package. [15]

Price signaling: using a price as a surrogate indicator of product quality. [18]

Price skimming: a pricing strategy that involved introducing a new product at a high price and then systematically reducing the price over time. [18]

Primary data: data collected expressly for the study at hand. [8]

Private carriers: company-owned transporters who carry goods for only that company. [12]

Private label: *see* Distributor's brand. [9]

Privatization: the policy of returning nationalized industries to private ownership. [19]

Problem children: strategic business unit with a small share in a high-growth market. [3]

Processed materials: manufactured products used in the production of goods by OEMs and other manufacturers. [7]

Procurement costs: costs that occur in replenishing stock. [12]

Product: every want- or need-satisfying attribute a consumer receives in making an exchange, including psychological as well as physical benefits. [1, 9]

Product adaptation: a strategy for global marketing that involves modifying a product to meet local preferences or conditions. [4]

Product development: a growth strategy that requires an organization to introduce new products to their existing markets. [3]

Product extension: a strategy for global marketing that involves offering the same product in all markets, domestic and foreign. [4]

Product innovation charter (PIC): strategy statement regarding new products that includes parameters for goals and programs to achieve the goals. [10]

Product invention: a strategy for global marketing that involves developing a new product to meet a market's needs and preferences. [4]

Product life cycle (PLC): according to a hypothesis based on the premise that products change over the period of time they are in the marketplace, the product life cycle is the series of stages that a product class goes through from its introduction until it is taken off the market. [9]

Product line: a group of closely related products offered by an organization. [9]

Product-line pricing: price determination for a line of products. Product-line pricing involved determining prices for the highest-priced and lowest-priced products in the line and determining price differentials for all other products in the line. [18]

Product mix: all of the individual products available from one organization. [9]

Production concept: the idea that organizations produce and distribute those products they are able to provide most efficiently, while presuming that a market exists for them. [1]

Productivity: an estimate of output per labor hour worked. [2]

Professional service: an activity performed by a practitioner such as a physician, accountant, engineer, lawyer, or architect. [19]

Profit Impact of Market Strategies (PIMS): computerized data bank of strategic information that is collected and analyzed by the Strategic Planning Institute. [3]

Profit maximization: the firm's attempts to earn the largest profit possible. [17]

Promotion: the communication mechanism of marketing designed to inform and to persuade consumers to respond to the offered product or service. [1, 14]

Promotional mix: the combination of promotional techniques used in a campaign. [14]

Prospecting: the step before any buyer–seller communication, during which likely customers are found for the good or service. [16]

Protectionism: political and legal maneuvers designed to shield a home country's businesses from foreign competition. [4]

Psychographics: a segmentation variable based on consumers' activities, interests, and opinions. [5]

Public relations: activities that evaluate public attitudes, identify the policies and procedures of an individual or an organization, and execute a program of action to earn public understanding and acceptance. [15]

Public sector: all agencies and departments that are part of a government. This includes all levels of government: federal, state, and local. [20]

Public service announcements (PSAs): advertising run by the media as a public service, that is, at no cost to the advertiser except for production. [20]

Publicity: the generation of news about a person, product, or service that appears in broadcast or print media, which is not paid for by the organization involved. Publicity can be positive or negative. [15]

Publicity/public relations: nonpersonal stimulation of demand for a product, service, or business unit by generating commercially significant news about it in a print medium or obtaining favorable presentation of it in radio, television, or on stage. This form of promotion is not paid for by the sponsor. [14]

Pull strategy: promotional strategy, such as advertising, that is primarily directed at the end consumer. [14]

Purchase decision process: the steps a consumer goes through when deciding whether to purchase a product or service. [6]

Pure competition: a market in which many sellers account for small percentages of total sales. Sellers are producing homogeneous products. [2]

Push strategy: promotional strategy, such as personal selling and trade deals, that is primarily directed at channel members. [14]

Qualitative data: data not subject to quantification or quantitative analysis. [8]

Quality: the totality of features and characteristics of a product or service that bear on its ability to satisfy stated or implied requirements. [10]

Quantitative data: data in the form of numbers. [8]

Quantity discounts: reduction from list price based upon the amount of purchases a buyer makes. They may be based upon a specific purchase (noncumulative) or on total purchases over a period (cumulative). [18]

Question marks: *see* Problem children. [3]

Quota: a limit set by a country that restricts the amount of a product that can be brought into or sent out of a country. [4]

Rack jobbers: a full-service wholesaler who sells nonfood items to grocery and drug retailers. [12]

Random discounts: using coupons, cents-off offers, and other unpredictable price-cutting devices to entice price-sensitive consumers to buy a product. [18]

Raw materials: products mined or produced by extractive industries for use, with little or no alteration, in the production of other goods. [7]

Reach: total number of persons exposed to a particular ad. [15]

Rebates: a firm's offer to return some portion of the purchase price to the consumer, usually after the consumer supplies proof of purchase. [15]

Receiver: the person or persons who attend to a communication. [14]

Recruitment: the process of identifying and attracting candidates for sales positions. [16]

Reference group: a group that the individual uses as a reference point in the formation of his or her beliefs, attitudes, values, and/or behavior. [6]

Reinforcement: reduction in a drive that results from a satisfactory response to a stimulus. [6]

Relationship marketing: efforts by organizations to have such a strong link between the marketer and customer that purchases are seen as part of a continuing relationship and not a series of independent transactions. [1]

Replacement rate: the rate at which a good or service is purchased and consumed. Milk is a high replacement rate product, a set of china is a low replacement rate product. [11]

Reservation price: the subjective price that consumers are willing to pay for a product. [17]

Response: an individual's reaction to cues or drives in the environment. [6]

Retailers: an intermediary who sells to ultimate consumers. [11]

Retailer-sponsored cooperative: a type of contractual vertical marketing system in which retailers organize and operate their own wholesale companies which then perform services for the member retailers. [11]

Retailing mix: the marketing mix of retailing firms. [13]

Return-on-investment (ROI) pricing: a price-setting strategy aimed at reaching a target ROI. [18]

Revenue analysis: a method of tactical control that involves measurement and evaluation of the actual revenue in relation to the revenue objectives. [3]

Reverse channel: a channel in which goods flow from consumers or business-to-business users to producers or other marketing intermediaries. [11]

Sale shopping: delaying a planned purchase until the desired item goes on sale. [13]

Sales concept: the idea that organizations should aggressively sell those products they want to produce. [1]

Sales-force composites: a buildup method of forecasting by obtaining from each sales representative an estimate of sales in his or her territory for a specified future period. [8]

Sales level: the expected level of sales of a company's product within a specified time frame given a designated marketing plan and a specific environment. [8]

Sales management: the planning, organizing, controlling, and directing of the individual and combined efforts of salespeople. [16]

Sales potential: the maximum sales to an identified customer group for one company during a set time period given a specified environment. [8]

Sales promotion: marketing activities—other than personal selling, advertising, and publicity—that stimulate consumers' purchasing and dealers' effectiveness such as displays, trade shows and exhibitions, demonstrations, coupons, contests, and other nonroutine selling efforts. [14, 15]

Sampling: giving away quantities of a product to encourage consumers to try it. [15]

Scrambled merchandising: the carrying of product lines that are unrelated to a retailer's primary business. [13]

Seasonal demand: product demand that is high only at certain regular points in time. [12]

Seasonal discounts: reduction from list price based upon the time of year a purchase is made. [18]

Secondary data: published data collected for reasons unrelated to the present study. [8]

Second-market discounting: offering a product to another market segment at a lower price than it is being offered to the primary target market. [18]

Selection: the steps that the firm uses to identify and assess individuals and place them in sales positions. [16]

Selective distribution: a distribution strategy in which only a limited number of outlets are allowed to resell a product or service. [11]

Selective perception: the process of perceiving only a small number of the stimuli to which an individual is exposed. The perceptions depend upon external stimuli and personal factors. [6]

Selling agents: an independent intermediary who performs the manufacturer's entire marketing task. [12]

Service: an intangible activity that provides the user some degree of performance satisfaction but does not involve ownership and which, in most cases, cannot be stored or transported. [19]

Service mark: a symbol, design, or a group of distinctive letters that designate a service rather than a tangible good, is being offered. [9]

Shopping goods: products usually purchased only after the consumer has compared the price, quality, and style of alternatives in several stores. [9]

Single-line merchandisers: a full-function wholesaler who carries items in only one product line. [12]

Single-line store: a retail outlet that carries only one line of goods. [13]

Single-zone pricing: a scheme in which all buyers pay the same price no matter what their location. [18]

Situational factors: factors particular to a time and place of observation which do not follow from a knowledge of personal (individual) and stimulus (alternative) attributes and which have a demonstrable and systematic effect on current behavior. [6]

Situation analysis: an analysis of the environment in which an organization is operating. The environment consists of factors operating internally (within the organization itself) and factors operating externally (outside the organization). [3]

Slotting fees: cash payments by a manufacturer to a retailer for access to shelf space in the store or warehouse, or for special shelf locations or displays. [15]

Social class: relatively permanent and homogeneous divisions in a society comprised of individuals or families who share similar values, life-styles, interests, and behavior. [6]

Social marketing: the marketing of ideas or social causes. [20]

Social responsibility: the obligation a business assumes to optimize the positive effects and minimize the negative effects of their actions on society. [1]

Social sector: organizations, agencies, and departments whose bottom-line goal is something other than profit. This would include both not-for-profit organizations and public-sector (government sponsored) organizations and agencies. [20]

Social-sector marketing: marketing performed by not-for-profit organizations and government groups and agencies, and marketing techniques used to promote ideas and social causes. [20]

Societal marketing concept: a view that focuses the organization's attention on the broader societal consequences of its marketing actions. [1]

Source: the originator of a communication. [14]

Specialty goods: products for which no reasonable substitutes exist because of unique characteristics and/or brand identification. Consumers are thus willing to expend considerable effort to buy these goods. [9]

Specialty merchandisers: a full-function wholesaler who carries a limited assortment of goods focusing on a particular type of product. [12]

Standard Industrial Classification code (SIC): a detailed numbering system for classifying American industry according to its economic activity. [7]

Standardized approach: an approach to global marketing that views marketing as know-how that can be transferred across borders, hence a tailored marketing program for each country is not necessary. [4]

Standard learning hierarchy: the standard hierarchy-of-effects response model. [14]

Standchising: a small retail outlet, often a cart or kiosk, positioned in a high-traffic area in a shopping mall. [11]

Stars: strategic business unit with a large share of a high-growth market. [3]

Store brand: *see* Distributor's brand. [9]

Straight commission plan: a system in which a salesperson's pay is based solely on the amount of sales he or she generated for a period of time. [16]

Straight rebuys: a buying situation involving a continuing or recurring purchase requiring little, if any, new information. No new alternatives are considered. [7]

Straight salary plan: a system in which a salesperson is paid on the basis of time worked. [16]

Strategic alliance: an enduring relationship between a business marketer and a customer that represents a planned, mutual effort to solve problems and meet the needs of the customer. [7]

Strategic business units (SBUs): a self-contained part of a larger organization, it has its own set of customers and competitors, separate costs, and a distinct marketing strategy. [3]

Strategic control: assessment of the effectiveness of the organization's long-term marketing strategy. [3]

Strict liability: a doctrine stating that if a defect in a product is legally established, the manufacturer is liable, regardless of precautions it has taken. [10]

Subculture: a category of people who share a sense of identification distinguishable from that of the total culture. [6]

Supermarket: a large, self-service food store that often carries some nonfood items also. [13]

Superstore: an extra-large supermarket and a general-merchandise store under one roof. [13]

Supplies: goods consumed by a business in its day-to-day operations. [7]

Support salespeople: a salesperson who is not directly responsible for closing sales. [16]

Survey: a structured questionnaire given to a group of people and designed to elicit specific information from them. [8]

Survey of buyers' intentions: a forecasting technique which involves asking target consumers whether they intend to purchase the product during a specified time period. [8]

Surveys of executive opinion: a forecasting technique by which company executives predict sales levels. [8]

Surveys of expert opinion: a forecasting technique by which independent experts predict sales levels. [8]

Sweepstakes: games of chance. [15]

SWOT analysis: an analysis that identifies the *s*trengths, *w*eaknesses, *o*pportunities, and *t*hreats facing an organization. It is often done as the conclusion to a situation analysis. [3]

Tactical control: concerned with the short-term marketing plan of the organization, it assesses the effectiveness of the tactics developed to carry out strategy. [3]

Tangibilize: the process of making services seem more tangible to the consumer by including in the service package some type of tangible representation. [19]

Tangible product: the actual features of a product that facilitate exchange of the core product. [9]

Target market: a specific group of people for whom a marketer develops a marketing mix. [1]

Target return on net sales: the targeted profit is a specific percentage of each sales dollar. [17]

Tariff: a tax imposed on products entering a country. [4]

Team selling: the combination of sales and nonsales people under the direction of a leader who sets strategy and coordinates flow of information. [16]

Technoglobalism: the internationalization of industrial activities due to technological needs. [2]

Technological extension: a type of new product created by introducing an existing technology into a new product category. [10]

Technological innovation: all activities involved in translating technical knowledge into a physical reality that can be used on a societal scale. [2]

Technology: a nation's accumulated competence to provide goods and services for people. [2]

Technonationalism: efforts to maintain domestic technological competitiveness. [2]

Telemarketing: selling goods and services to customers over the telephone. [13, 16]

Teleshopping: sales of goods and services via television presentation, and consumers can place orders via telephone. [13]

Test market: the introduction of a new product and marketing program into a limited market as a way of determining probable sales and profits under actual market conditions. [10]

Test marketing: a forecasting technique of actually marketing a product in a few select cities and then using the sales levels in these cities to predict national sales. [8]

Throughput: the movement of goods through a distribution center. [12]

Time utility: the satisfaction derived from using a product at the time the consumer wishes or needs to use it. [1]

Top-down forecasting: an overall approach to forecasting whereby predictions are allocated by product lines, customer groups, or geographic areas based upon some index of the potential in these subunits. [8]

Total cost (TC): the sum of TFC plus TVC at a given output. [17A]

Total cost: a concept that physical distribution costs should be viewed together rather than individually. [12]

Total fixed cost (TFC): the sum of the financial obligations of the firm that remains at the same level no matter how many units of a product are produced and marketed. [17A]

Total quality management (TQM): an operating philosophy that strives to imbue every aspect of organizational activity with quality. [1, 10]

Trade allowances: some type of monetary allowance or discount made to the channel member in exchange for displaying the manufacturer's product in a specific location, for promoting the product, or for stocking the product at all. [15]

Trade deficit: the result of an imbalance of international trade so that imports exceed exports. [4]

Trade promotion: sales promotion activity directed at wholesalers and retailers. [15]

Trade surplus: the result of an imbalance of international trade so that exports exceed imports. [4]

Trademark: a brand or part of a brand that has been given legal protection for the seller's exclusive use. [9]

Trading bloc: a group of countries that band together to trade as a single unit with other countries. [4]

Transactional functions: the buying and selling of products, services, ideas. [1]

Trend analysis: a forecasting technique based on the assumption that whatever unspecified factors caused sales in the past will continue to affect sales in the same way. [8]

Trial close: a sales technique designed to test the customer's willingness to buy. [16]

Truck jobbers: a wholesaler who operates from a truck and specializes in the quick delivery of perishable items. [12]

Two-part pricing: captive pricing applied to services. [18]

Two-step flow of communication: process of using the mass media to reach opinion leaders, who then communicate the information to the followers. [6]

Tying contract: a contract by which a manufacturer or franchisor sells a product to an intermediary only if the intermediary also buys other (possibly unwanted) products from the manufacturer or franchisor or from another specified manufacturer. [11]

Ultimate consumers: a buyer or potential buyer who intends to use or personally benefit from the product or service rather than buying for the purpose of reselling the product. [5, 6, 7]

Uncontrollable variables: environmental forces that are external to the firm and hence beyond the control of decision makers. [2]

Undifferentiated marketing: *see* Mass marketing. [5]

Unduplicated reach: the total number of people exposed just once to an ad. [15]

Unit pricing: retail prices that are posted to show customers the actual price of the smallest measurement of the product, e.g., ounces or pounds. [18]

Urgency close: a sales technique that encourages the consumer to purchase now by suggesting that the deal may not be as good later. [16]

Usage rate: the frequency with which consumers buy or use a product or service. [5]

Utility: a measure of the extent to which a particular good, service, or idea satisfies the needs or wants of a particular individual or organization. [1]

Value pricing: the method of setting price based upon the relative value the product gives a specific consumer or group of consumers. [18]

Values: likes, dislikes, beliefs and prejudices that determine a person's view of the world. [2]

Variable cost (VC): includes charges for items such as direct labor and raw materials. [17A]

Vendor: a marketer who sells to business customers. [7]

Vertical conflict: conflict among channel members at different levels (for example, between a producer and a wholesaler). [11]

Vertical marketing systems: a professionally managed and centrally programmed channel of distribution designed to achieve operating economies and maximum market impact. [11]

Warehouse club: retailers offering members a broad assortment of both food and nonfood items at low prices. [13]

Wheel of retailing: the theory that new retail institutions start as low-cost/low-price operators and "trade-up" services (costs) and prices over time. [13]

Wholesalers: an intermediary who does not sell to ultimate consumers. Wholesalers sell to retailers, other wholesalers, and business-to-business users. [11]

Wholesaler-sponsored voluntary group: a type of contractual vertical marketing system in which a wholesaler organizes a number of independently owned retailers into a group and then provides goods and services far more economically than if the wholesaler dealt with each retailer separately. [11]

Workload analysis: a mathematical approach to determining number of salespeople needed for a sales force. [16]

World corporation: a firm that has so fully integrated its operations into markets worldwide that its "home country" is of little consequence. [4]

Acknowledgments

Literary Credits

Page positions are as follows: (T)top, (C)center, (B)bottom, (L)left, (R)right.

4 Personal interview with representative of Carnival Cruise Lines, December 1993; Brook Hill Snow, "21 Cruise Trends for the 21st Century," *Cruise Travel*, January/February 1993, pp. 48–52; Constance A. Gustke, "How Carnival Stacks the Decks," *Fortune*, January 16, 1989, pp. 108–116; James F. Engle, Martin R. Warshaw, and Thomas C. Kinnear, *Promotional Strategy*, 7th ed., (Homewood, IL: Irwin, 1991), pp. 36–43.

7 Howard Schlossberg, "AIDS—Prevention Ads Spark Battle Over What's Proper," *Marketing News*, April 29, 1991, p. 2. Reprinted by permission of the American Marketing Association.

28 Gifford Claiborne, "How Marketing Rescued an L.A. Rescue Mission," *Marketing News*, December 18, 1989, p. 13.

32 Allyson L. Stewart, "U.S. Food, Drink Marketers Can Gain an Advantage in Europe," *Marketing News*, July 5, 1993, p. 8; Cyndee Miller, "U.S., European Shoppers Seem Pleased with Their Supermarkets," *Marketing News*, June 21, 1993, p. 3; Cyndee Miller, "The 'Real Food' Movement," *Marketing News*, June 7, 1993, pp. 1–2.

38 *Fortune*, Special Issue: The Tough New Consumer; Autumn/Winter 1993, page 87. Copyright 1994 Time, Inc.

39 From: Diane Crispell, "Student Supplies," *American Demographics*, August, 1993, p. 63. Reprinted with permission. Copyright August 1993, *American Demographics* magazine, Ithaca, New York.

56 Faye Rice, "The New Rules of Superlative Service," *Fortune*, Autumn/Winter 1993, p. 50; Robert Bixby, "The Incessant Office," *Omni*, April 1991, p. 104; "Journeying Deeper into the Minds of Shoppers," *Business Week*, February 4, 1991, p. 85; Jerry Kanter, Stephen Schiffman, and J. Fayl Horn, "Let the Customer Do It," *Computer World*, August 27, 1990, pp. 75–78.

61 Laurie Freeman, "P & G Zeros in on Green," *American Demographics*, July 1991, p. 11; Ed Hardy, "Eco-Entrepreneurs," *American Demographics*, Special Report on Green Marketing, 1992, p. 6; Joan Oleck, "The Great Clamshell Debate," *Restaurant Business*, November 1, 1992, pp. 68–72, David Stipp, "Life-Cycle Analysis Measures Greenness, But Results May Not Be Black and White," *The Wall Street Journal*, February 28, 1991, pp. 70–72; David Stipp, "Lunch-Box Staple Runs Afoul of Activists," *The Wall Street Journal*, March 14, 1991, pp. B1 and B4.

67 Adapted by the authors from Shelby D. Hunt and Scott Vitell, "A General Theory of Marketing Ethics," *Journal of Macromarketing*, Vol. 6 (Spring 1986), p. 8. The *Journal of Macromarketing* is published by The Business Research Division, University of Colorado at Boulder.

74 Roger Cohen, "EuroDisney in Danger of Shutdown," *The New York Times*, December 23, 1993; "Eisner to Shareholders: EuroDisney Dreadful," *The San Diego Union-Tribune*, December 23, 1993; "The Not-So-Magic Kingdom," *The Economist*, November 25, 1991, pp. 73–74; Steven Greenhouse, "Playing Disney in the Parisian Fields," *The New York Times*, February 17, 1991, Section 3, pp. 1, 6, 7; Lisa Gubernick, "Did Mickey Shaft Kermit?" *Forbes*, April 29, 1991, p. 44; Nicholas Powell, "Much Ado About Rules at EuroDisney," *Houston Chronicle*, March 10, 1991, p. 9H; Kathleen Kerwin and Antonio N. Fins, "Disney is Looking Just a Little Fragilistic," *Business Week*, June 25, 1990, pp. 52–54; Stewart Toy, "An American in Paris," *Business Week*, March 12, 1990, pp. 60–64.

78 First appeared in *Working Woman*, September 1993. Written by Suzanna Andrews. Reprinted with permission of *Working Woman* Magazine. Copyright 1993 by WWT Partnership.

84 "Lookout, World, Philips is on a War Footing," *Business Week*, January 15, 1990, pp. 44–45; Andrew Kupfer, "Japan Blinks on HDTV," *Fortune*, March 31, 1994, p. 14; Wilton Woods, "IQ Lighting," *Fortune*, February 21, 1994, p 107; "EU: Commission Proposed Approval for Joint Venture Between Philips and Osram," *Reuter Textline, Agence Europe*, February 1, 1994; Tony Jackson, "Can Europe Compete?: Gains via R&D, Market Share and Cost-Cuts—Three Leading European Manufacturers Employ Very Different Strategies Against Their International Competitors," *The Financial Times Limited*, February 25, 1994, p. 19.

89 Based on excerpts of a talk by Donald M. Wilchek, "Bic's Strategy for Growth."

98 John Labate, "Companies to Watch: Gymboree," *Fortune*, February 7, 1994, p. 137. Copyright 1994 Time, Inc.

100 Philip Kotler, and Alan Andreasen, *Strategic Marketing for Nonprofit Organizations*, 4/e, Copyright 1991, p. 617. Reprinted by permission of Prentice Hall, Englewood Cliffs, New Jersey.

106 Joseph Pereira and Randal Smith, "Heard on the Street," *The Wall Street Journal*, September 2, 1993, p. C1; Joseph Pereira and Pauline Yoshihashi, *The Wall Street Journal*, August 20, 1993, p. A3; Richard Teitlebaum, "Children A Mixed Blessing to These Stocks," *Fortune*, November 29, 1993; Research report compiled by the Kresge Business Administration Library, December 1990; Bill Saporito, "How Quaker Oats Got Rolled," *Fortune*, October 8, 1990, pp. 129–138; Keith Hammonds and Lois Therrien, "Fisher-Price: Fighting to Recapture the Playpen," *Business Week*, December 24, 1990, pp. 70–71; Kate Fitzgerald, "Fisher-Price Suffers from Turmoil in Toyland," *Advertising Age*, November 20, 1989, p. 12.

110 Bryan Batson, "Chinese Fortunes," *Sales & Marketing Management*, March 1994, pp. 93–98. Reprinted with permission of Sales & Marketing Management, 355 Park Avenue South, New York, NY 10010-1789. Andrew Tanzer, "Ding-dong, Capitalism Calling," *Forbes*, October 14, 1991, pp. 184–186. Reprinted by permission of *Forbes* magazine. Copyright Forbes Inc., 1991.

114 Reprinted from: The New Global Consumer," *Fortune*, Autumn/ Winter, 1993, p. 67. Copyright 1993 Time Inc. All rights reserved.

115 Reprinted with permission from the February 21, 1994 issue of *Advertising Age*. Copyright, Crain Communications Inc., 1994.

117 From: Eric S. Hardy and Steve Kichen, "The Forbes Foreign Rankings," *Forbes*, July 19, 1993, p. 182. Reprinted by permission of *Forbes* magazine, Copyright Forbes, Inc. 1993.

123 Thomas Donaldson, "Global Business Must Mind Its Morals," *The New York Times*, February 13, 1994. Copyright 1994 by The New York Times Company. Reprinted by permission.

127 Reprinted with permission from The World Almanac and Book of Facts 1994, Copyright 1993 Funk & Wagnalls Corporation. All rights reserved.

129 Reprinted from: The New Global Consumer," *Fortune*, Autumn/ Winter, 1993, p. 71. Copyright 1993 Time Inc. All rights reserved.

134 Cindy Kano and Thomas J. Martin, "Revolution in Japanese Retailing," *Fortune*, February 7, 1994, pp. 143–146; Frank Green, "Japanese Have Yen For Amway," *The San Diego Union-Tribune*, March 9, 1994, pp. C1–C2. Reprinted with permission from the The San Diego Union-Tribune.

138 Richard W. Stevenson, "Tapping a Rich Smoking Frontier," *The New York Times*, November 12, 1993, pp. D1–D2; Nina Munk, "Smuggled Smokes," Forbes, December 7, 1992, pp. 47–48; Mike Levin, "U.S. Tobacco Firms Push Eagerly into Asian Market," *Marketing News*, January 21, 1991, p. 3; "Red in Tooth and Claw," *The Economist*, May 18, 1991, pp. 79–80; "Asia: A New Front in the War on Smoking," *Business Week*, February 25, 1991, p. 3; Laura Sessions Stepp, "In Search of Ethics," *The Washington Post*, March 31, 1991, pp. H1, H4.

146 Susan Caminiti, "A Star is Born," *Fortune*, Autumn/Winter 1993, pp. 44–47. Copyright 1993 Time, Inc. All rights reserved.

154 Christy Fisher, *Advertising Age*, December 6, 1993, p. 30; Thomas G. Exter, *American*

Demographics: Special Report—Households, 1992, p. 15; Christy Fisher, "Coke Taps Latin Beat," *Advertising Age*, April 1991, p. 57; Jacqueline Sanchez, "Some Approaches Better Than Others When Targeting Hispanics," *Marketing News*, 5-25-92, pp. 8, 11; Chester. A. Swenson, "How to Speak to Hispanics," *American Demographics*, February 1990, pp. 40–41; "The Hispanic Market," *Stores*, May 1988, pp. 53–56; U. S. Bureau of the Census, "Projections of the Hispanic Population: 1983–2080," *Current Population Reports*, Series P-25, No. 995, p. 2; Pepper Miller, "Myths Discourage Marketing to African Americans," *Marketing News*, 1-20-92, p. 4; Pepper Miller and Ronald Miller, "Trends Are Opportunities for Targeting African Americans," *Marketing News*, 1-20-92, p. 9.

160 Russell Haley, "Benefit Segmentation: A Decision-Oriented Tool," pp. 30–35. *Journal of Marketing* (July 1968). Reprinted by permission of the American Marketing Association.

168 Stephanie Strom, "Image and Attitude Are Department Stores' Draw," *The New York Times*, August 12, 1993. Copyright 1993 by The New York Times Company. Reprinted by permission.

174 Arthur Buckler, "Tyson Foods Isn't Chicken Hearted About Expansion," *The Wall Street Journal*, January 18, 1994, p. B4.; Christy Fisher, "Tyson Stirs Food Pot," *Advertising Age*, November 11, 1991, p. 4; Julie Liesse, "ConAgra vs. Big Mac," *Advertising Age*, August 12, 1991, p. 3; Judann Dagnoli, "Healthy Soups Cut in at Campbell," *Advertising Age*, April 6, 1992, p. 12.

178 Cyndee Miller, "Perfume Maker Bucks Trend With Centsless Ad Campaign," *Marketing News*, January 6, 1992, p. 7.

188 Mary L. Carnevale, "A Baby Bell Gets Some Gray Hairs as Older People Buyers' Guide Flops," *The Wall Street Journal*, May 16, 1989, p. 26; Vicky Goodhead, "Marketing to Mature Adults Requires a State of Being," *Marketing News*, December 9, 1991, p. 10; Cyndee Miller "Misconception, Fear Stall Advance Into Mature Market," December 9, 1991, p. 11; Rod Riggs, "Agency Refines Targeting of the Over-50s," *The San Diego Union-Tribune*, October 5, 1993, P. D4; D. B. Wolfe, *Serving the Ageless Market: Strategies for Selling to the Fifty-Plus Market.*

195 Cyndee Miller, "P.F. Flyers Relaunch Targets Nostalgic Baby Boomers," *Marketing News*, February 17, 1992, p. 2

206 Howard Schlossberg, "Illinois Bell Predicts More Americans Will Start Doing Their Homework," *Marketing News*, September 16, 1991, p. 10; "L.A. Shaken, But Not Bowed," *Advertising Age*, January 24, 1994, pp. 1, 42; Calvin Sims, "Quake Provides Glimpse of Future of Commuting," *The New York Times*, January 25, 1994, p. A12.

210 From: John R. Johnson, "Strategic Alliances Revive Duskes, Inc., *Industrial Distribution*, January 1991, pp. 24-26

213 Bart Ziegler, "A Device Worth Checking Out," *Business Week*, February 1, 1993, p. 68D; Gene G. Marcial, "This Stock Doesn't Scan," *Business Week*, January 11, 1993, p. 50; "Symbol Technologies: Decoding Its Customers' Needs," *Sales & Marketing Management*, August 1992, p. 46.

214 From: John R. Johnson, "Promoting Profits Through Partnerships," *Industrial Distribution*, March 1994, pp. 22–24.

220 From: Jan Jaben, "Marketing's New Fast Lane Emerges," *Business Marketing*, October

1993, pp. 20–25. Reprinted by permission.

221 "American Express, the Sleeping Giant Wakes and Spooks the Travel Industry," *The Wall Street Journal*, February 24, 1994, p. B1; Emory Thomas, Jr., "Ryder Moves Back Home to Truck Leasing and Renting," *The Wall Street Journal*, December 14, 1993; "Ryder Trucks: Best Over the Long Haul," *Sales & Marketing Management*, August 1992, p. 47.

228 From: R.W. Haas, *Business Marketing Management*, 5/e PWS-Kent Publishing Co., 1992.

230 Adapted from: R. Haas, *Business Marketing Management*, 5/e, 1992 pp. 173–173, PWS-Kent.

232 From: Bob Donath, "Probing Buyers in this Post-Yuppie Age," *Marketing News*, October 14, 1991, p. 4; and "Satisfaction Obsession: How Biz-to Biz Marketers Must Compete in the 90's," *Marketing News*, November 25, 1991, p. 19. Reprinted by permission of the American Marketing Association.

236 From: Edward O. Welles, "Quick Study," *Inc.*, April 1992, pp. 67–76. Reprinted with permission, *Inc.* magazine, April, 1992. Copyright 1992 by Goldhirsh Group, Inc., 38 Commercial Wharf, Boston, MA 02110.

240 Terence P. Pare, "How to Find Out What They Want," *Fortune*, Autumn/Winter 1993, pp. 39–41. Copyright 1993 Time, Inc. All rights reserved.

242 Naresh K. Malhotra, *Marketing Research An Applied Orientation*, Prentice-Hall, 1993, Figure 1-3, p. 14.

247 Naresh K. Malholtra, *Marketing Research An Applied Orientation*, Prentice-Hall, 1993, p. 773.

248 CMOR—Council for Marketing & Opinion Research, special pull–out section published in *Marketing News*, August 16, 1993.

250 Carl McDaniel, Jr., and Roger Gates, *Contemporary Marketing Research*, 2/e, West, 1993, Table 1-2, p. 17.

251 Based on Thomas C. Kinnear and James R. Taylor, *Marketing Research: An Applied Approach*, 4/e, McGraw-Hill, 1991, p. 133. Reprinted by permission of McGraw-Hill, Inc.

252 Based on Thomas C. Kinnear and James R. Taylor, *Marketing Research: An Applied Approach*, 4/e, McGraw-Hill, 1991, p. 16. Reprinted by permission of McGraw-Hill, Inc.

256 Terence P. Pare, "...And Way Out on the Leading Edge," *Fortune*, Autumn/Winter 1993, pp. 39–41. Copyright 1993 Time, Inc. All rights reserved.

259 Cyndee Miller, "Sometimes a Researcher Has No Choice But to Hang Out in a Bar," *Marketing News*, January 3, 1994, p. 16; Cyndee Miller, "X Marks the Lucrative Spot, But Some Advertisers Can't Hit Target," *Marketing News*, August 2, 1993, pp. 1, 14; Cyndee Miller, "Xers Know They're a Target Market, And They Hate That," *Marketing News*, December 6, 1993, pp. 2, 15; Junu Bryan Kim, "Generation X Gets Comfortable with Furnishings, Housewares," *Advertising Age*, January 10, 1994, p. S–2.

270 Cyndee Miller, "Churches Turn to Research for Help in Saving New Souls," *Marketing News*, April 11, 1994, pp. 1–2, 5; Cyndee Miller," Church Keeps Message But Changes Medium," *Marketing News*, April 11, 1994, pp. 5, 7. Reprinted by permission of the American Marketing Association.

278 David Biemesderfer, "Fast Track," *World Traveler*, November, 1993, pp. 20-26; "How I Did It," First appeared in *Working Woman* in December 1991. Written by Anetta Miller.

Reprinted with the permission of *Working Woman* Magazine. Copyright 1991 by *Working Woman*, Inc.

280 Philip Kotler, and Gary Armstrong, *Marketing: An Introduction*, 3/e, Prentice-Hall, Inc., 1993, p. 221. Adapted by permission of Prentice Hall, Englewood Cliffs, New Jersey.

281 Deborah L. Jacobs, "The Titans of Tint Make Their Picks," *The New York Times*, May 29, 1994, p. 8; Randall Lane, "Does Orange Mean Cheap?" *Forbes*, December 23, 1991. Reprinted by permission of *Forbes* magazine. Copyright Forbes, Inc. 1991.

297 Clyde H. Farnsworth, "Quality: High. Price: Low. Big Ad Budget? Never.," *The New York Times*, February 6, 1994, p. 10; Ricardo A. Davis, "Private Label Treated Like National Brand," *Advertising Age*, December 13, 1993, p. 25; Jennifer Lawrence, "Grocers Pitch Private-Label Brands," *Advertising Age*, January 24, 1994, p. 15.

301 From: "Standard Farm Fare Sells in New Package," *Marketing News*, January 31, 1994, p. 6. Reprinted by permission of the American Marketing Association.

302 From: Anastasia Toufexis, "Know What You Eat," *Time*, May 9, 1994, p. 68. Copyright 1994 Time Inc. Reprinted by permission.

306 From: Amy Feldman, "Hello Oprah, Good-bye Iman," *Forbes*, March 16, 1992, pp. 116–117. Reprinted by permission of *Forbes* magazine. Copyright Forbes, Inc. 1992; Valli Herman, "Retailers Begin to Think Big," *The San Diego Union-Tribune*, August 28, 1992, p. E3. Reprinted with permission of The Dallas Morning News.

310 Kim Cleland, "Multimarketer Mélange an Increasingly Tasty Option on the Store Shelf," *Advertising Age*, May 2, 1994, pp. S–10; "ConAgra's Healthy Choice, Getting to the Heart of the Matter," *Sales & Marketing Management*, August 1992, p. 43; Julie Liesse, "ConAgra's New Ethic Brings Return to Ads," *Advertising Age*, January 10, 1994, p. 4.

313 Reprinted with permission. Copyright 1992, *American Demographics* magazine, Ithaca, New York.

314 From: Joseph P. Guiltinan and Gordon W. Paul, *Marketing Management: Strategies and Programs*, 5/e, 1994, p. 198. Reproduced with permission of McGraw-Hill, Inc.

315 From: "New Products Management for the 1980's," (1982) Booz, Allen, and Hamilton, Chicago, IL. Reprinted by permission.

317 From: Peter R. Dickson, *Marketing Management*, The Dryden Press, 1994, p. 299.

318 From: Rodger L. DeRose, "New Products—Sifting Through the Haystack," *The Journal of Consumer Marketing*, Summer 1986, pp. 81–84.

321 From: Jennifer Lawrence, "Whatever Happened to Olestra?" *Advertising Age*, May 2, 1994, pp. 16–18; and Jennifer Lawrence, The Clock Ticks on P&G's Olestra Patents." Reprinted with permission from the May 2, 1994 issue of *Advertising Age*. Copyright, Crain Communications, Inc.

323 Berkowitz, et. al: *Marketing*, 4/E, Richard D. Irwin, Inc., 1994, p. 308.

324 From: Judith Winthrop, "All-American Markets. Reprinted with permission. Copyright 1992, *American Demographics* magazine, Ithaca, New York.

327 From: Christopher Power, "Flops," *Business Week*, August 16, 1993, pp. 76–82.

328 From: Bob Donath," The Customer as Consultant," *Sales & Marketing Management*,

September 1992, pp. 84–90. Reprinted with permission of Sales & Marketing Management, 355 Park Avenue South, New York, NY 10010-1789.

331 Sandra Salmans, "Museum Houses Shattered Dreams," *Chicago Tribune*, March 10, 1985; Cyndee Miller, "Toy Companies Release 'Ethnically Correct' Dolls," *Marketing News*, September 30, 1991, p. 1; "Kellogg to Roll Out New Cereals," *Marketing News*, January 6, 1992, p. 1; "Offbeat Marketing," *Sales & Marketing Management*, July 1992, p. 111; Patricia Winters, "Fast Break for Crystal Pepsi," *Advertising Age*, April 12, 1993, p. 10; Tim Triplett, "Consumers Show Little Taste for Clear Beverages," *Marketing News*, May 23, 1994, p. 1.

332 From: Jennifer Lawrence, "P & G Makes New Push With Tide." Reprinted with permission from the February 7, 1994 issue of *Advertising Age*. Copyright Crain Communications, Inc. 1994.

333 Reprinted by permission of *Harvard Business Review*. An exhibit from " Forget the Product Life-Cycle Concept," by K. Nariman Dhalla, and Sonia Yuspeh, (January/February, 1976). Copyright 1976 by the President and Fellows of Harvard College; all rights reserved.

339 Reprinted by permission of *Harvard Business Review*. An excerpt from "Competing on the Eight Dimensions of Quality," by David A. Garvin, (November/December 1987). Copyright 1987 by the President and Fellows of Harvard College; all rights reserved.

340 A. Taylor III, "Iacocca's Minivan," *Fortune*, May 30, 1994, pp. 56–66.

344 From: "Campbell Shapes Up All Around, *The New York Times*, January 29, 1992.

352 "Joy of EDI," *Progressive Grocer*, April 1993, p. 110; Robert Salerno, Gayle Jones, Bret Raltray, and Stirling Rosario, Eds., Special Issue of *Chain Store Age Executive*, 1993, "Quick Response: What It Is; What It's Not," *Chain Store Age*, March 1991, pp. 4B–5B; Lisa H. Harrington, "The ABCs of EDI," *Traffic Management*, August 1990, pp. 49–51.

368 Claire Poole, "Pepsi's Newest Generation," *Forbes*, February 18, 1991, pp. 88–92. Reprinted by permission of *Forbes* magazine. Copyright Forbes Inc., 1991; and 1992 Annual Report, PepsiCo.

373 Paul M. Barrett, "Anti-Discount Policies of Manufacturers are Penalizing Certain Cut-Price Stores," *The Wall Street Journal*, February 27, 1991, pp. B1, B4. Reprinted by permission of *The Wall Street Journal*, Copyright 1991 Dow Jones and Company, Inc. All Rights Reserved Worldwide.

375 *Marketing Channel Management*, p. 104 by Kenneth G. Hardy and Allan J. McGrath. Copyright 1988 Scott Foresman. Reprinted by permission of Harper Collins College Publishers.

379 Reprinted by permission of Mr. Andy Trincia, Public Relations Manager, International Franchise Association, Washington, D.C.

386 Man Wrestles Machine," *Entrepreneur*, February 1988, p. 119; "Attention Sports," *Entrepreneur*, March 1988, p. 108; Echo M. Garrett, "Franchises on a Role," *Venture*, March 1988, pp. 39–47; Jeannie Ralston, "Promises, Promises," *Venture*, March 1988, pp. 55–57; Jennifer S. Stack and Joseph E. McKendrick, "Franchise Market Expands as Rest of Economy Slumps," *Marketing News*, July 6, 1992, p. 11. Lisa J. Moore, "The Flight to Franchising," *U.S. News & World Report*, June 10, 1991, pp. 68–71.

387 From: "Entrepreneur Magazine's 15th

Annual Franchise 500," Reprinted with permission from *Entrepreneur*, January, 1994.

392 Michael Kinsman, "South Korea May Get a Price Club, Too," *The San Diego Union–Tribune*, October 28, 1993, pp. C1–C2; Michael Kinsman, "Price and Costco Votes OK Merger," *The San Diego Union–Tribune*, October 22, 1993, pp. C1–C2; David W. Fuller, "Dedication to a Clear Mission Links Costco's Past, Present, and Future," *Costco Connection*, October 1993, pp. 1, 7; Stephanie Sullun, "Wholesale Clubs," *Institutional Distribution*, November 1, 1992, pp. 52–53; James M. Degen, "Warehouse Clubs Move From Revolution to Evaluations," *Marketing News*, August 3, 1992, p. 8; Charles J. Fombrun, *Turning Points*, New York: McGraw-Hill, 1992, pp. 57–58, 220; Matthew Wald, "Steinway Changing Amid Tradition," *The New York Times*, March 28, 1991, pp. D1, D8; Danny Miller, *The Icarus Paradox: How Exceptional Companies Bring About Their Own Downfall*, New York: Harper Business, 1990.

404 From: "Snider, Hayes, Hurd: A Food Broker's Big Break," *Nation's Business*, 1992, pp. 183–184.

417 Barnaby J. Feder, "Moving the Pampers Faster Cuts Everyone's Costs," *The New York Times*, July 14, 1991, p. 5F; "Partnering That Touched a Nerve," *The New York Times*, July 14, 1991, p. 5F; Andrew Tausz, "How GM–Canada Makes JIT Go," *Distribution*, March 1988, pp. 38–40; Joseph J. Fucini and Suzy Fucini, *Working for the Japanese*, (New York: Free Press, 1990), p. 106.

418 Table from *1994 Information Please Almanac*. Copyright 1993 by Houghton Mifflin Co. Reprinted by permission of Houghton Mifflin Co. All rights reserved.

420 From: Donald J. Bowersox, David J. Closs, and Omar K. Helferich, *Logistical Management*, 3/e, Macmillan, 1986, p. 166; and Ronald H. Ballou, *Business Logistics Management Planning and Control*, 2/e, Prentice-Hall, 1985, p. 194.

423 From: Thomas Foster, "Searching for the Best," *Distribution*, March, 1992, pp. 31–34. Reprinted with permission from *Distribution* Magazine.

426 Peter Bradley, "Transportation Links All the Parts," *Purchasing*, July 15, 1993, pp. 62–73; *U.S. Industry Outlook*, U.S. Department of Commerce, 1993; Shawn Tully, "Comeback Ahead for Railroads," *Fortune*, July 17, 1991, pp. 107–113; James R. Norman, "We've Got a Clock On It," *Forbes*, June 25, 1991, pp. 116–120.

430 "Revolution in Japanese Retailing," *Fortune*, February 7, 1994, pp. 143–146; Yumiko Ono, "As Discounting Rises in Japan, People Learn to Hunt for Bargains," *The Wall Street Journal*, December 31, 1993, p. 1; "Japan," *Chain Store Age Executive*, January 1991; Peter E. Monask and Masayoshi Ikemoto, "Japanese Discounting," *Direct Marketing*, May 1990.

431 The Top 1000 US Companies Ranked by Industry," *Business Week*, March 7, 1994, pp. 116–117.

435 From: "The 50 Largest Retailers," *Fortune*, May 30, 1994. Copyright 1994 Time, Inc. All rights reserved.

436 Ann Imse, "Across from Lenin's Tomb, A Monument to Capitalism," *The New York Times*, September 19, 1993, p. 5; *Chain Store Age Executive*, Special 1993 issue; Interview with Lucy McPherson, Nordstrom advertising manager, February 28, 1994; "Home Truths," *The*

Economist, August 17, 1991, p. 63; Peter Gumbel, "Soviet Retail Systems Get Strikingly Worse in Era of Perestroika," *The Wall Street Journal*, July 23, 1990, pp. A1, A6; Stuart Elliott, "Figuring Out the Russian Consumer," *The New York Times*, April 1, 1992, pp. D1, D19.

438 Laura Zinn, "The Limited: All Grown Up With Nowhere to Go?," *Business Week*, December 20, 1993, p. 44; 1992 Sears Annual Report; "Minding the Store," *The Economist*, October 3, 1991, p. 75; Stephanie Storm, "Signs of Life at Sears Roebuck," *The New York Times*, October 25, 1992, pp. 1, 6; Gregory A. Patterson, "Sears's Brennan Accepts Blame for Auto Flap," *The Wall Street Journal*, June 23, 1992, p. 12.

439 From: Larry D. Redinbaugh, *Retail Management: A Planning Approach*, McGraw-Hill, 1976, p. 12. Reprinted by permission of McGraw-Hill, Inc.

449 Alice Z. Cuneo, "Gap Floats Lower-Price Old Navy Stores," *Advertising Age*, July 25, 1994, p. 36; "Gap Reports Record Second Quarter 1994 Results," *Business Wire*, San Francisco, August 11, 1994; Pamela Street, "Three Tiers for The Gap," *Women's Wear Daily*, March 23, 1994, p. 5; Stephanie Strom, "Gap's New Chain, Old Navy, Aims at Masses," *The San Diego Union-Tribune*, April 24, 1994, pp. I-1, I-2; Stephanie Strom, "How Gap Inc. Spells Revenge," *The New York Times*, April 24, 1994, Section 3, pp. 1, 5, 6.

453 Murray Raphel, "Sweden's Green Grocer," *Direct Marketing*, May 1992, pp. 38–39; William C. Johnson, "Electronic Marketing Enters Supermarket Aisles," *Marketing News*, April 1991, p. 14; Renee Rouland, "Image Technology," *Discount Merchandiser*, March 1990, p. 55.

460 Bill Saporito, "And the Winner Is Still . . . Wal-Mart," *Fortune*, May 2, 1994, pp. 62–70; Bill Saporito, "Is Wal-Mart Unstoppable?", *Fortune*, May 6, 1991, pp. 50–60; "Kmart Gets a Facelift, New Concepts," *The Houston Post*, September 1, 1991, pp. D1, D6, Jay L. Johnson, "Target's New Dynamics," *Direct Marketing*, August 1991, pp. 30–40, 45–46; Subrata N. Chakravarty, "A Tale of Two Companies," *Forbes*, May 27, 1991, pp. 86–96; Renee Covino Rouland, "Target's Distribution Expert," *Direct Marketing*, August 1991, pp. 48, 94; Howard Schlossberg, "Kmart's New Approach Aims Straight for the Heart," *Marketing News*, April 1, 1991, pp. 8, 21.

468 Geoffrey Lee Martin, "Aussie Tourism Industry Links Up," *Advertising Age*, January 17, 1994, p. 1–36; Don E. Schultz, "How Communications Dis-integrate," *Marketing News*, June 20, 1994, p. 12; Don E. Schultz, "'Real' Integration's Benefit: Reducing Transaction Costs," *Marketing News*, March 28, 1994, p. 12; Additional information provided by the Australian Tourist Commission.

471 From: George E. Blech, and Michael A. Belch, *Introduction to Advertising and Promotion*, 2/e, Richard D. Irwin, 1993, p. 190. Reprinted by permission of Richard D. Irwin, Inc.

473 FAR SIDE copyright FARWORKS, INC./Dist. by UNIVERSAL PRESS SYNDICATE. Reprinted with permission. All rights reserved.

474 David Lavinsky, "When Novelty Wears Off, Soft Drinks Clearly Will Fail," *Marketing News*, March 15, 1993, p. 4; Marketing Briefs—"Clear Cola to Go National," *Marketing News*, January 4, 1993, p. 1; Cyndee Miller, "Trendy Marketers Want Consumers to See Right Through Their Products," *Marketing News*, February 1, 1993, pp. 1–2; Howard Schlossberg, "Researchers Forced to Seek Answers to Things They Once Took for Granted," *Marketing News*, March 29, 1993, pp. 3, 14; Tim Triplett, "Consumers Show Little Taste for Clear Beverages, " *Marketing News*, 28, no. 11, May 23, 1994, p. 1, 11; Anon., "Clear Fad is Fading Fast," *The Food Institute Report*, 67, no. 12, March 21, 1994, p. 3.

480 Updated information from Donald C. Bauder, "Foodmaker Puts a Struggling Company on Its Plate," *The San Diego Union-Tribune*, March 20, 1994, pp. I1–I2.

485 Compiled from "Fortune 500," *Fortune*, April 18, 1994, pp. 257–276 Copyright 1994 Time, Inc. All rights reserved; and "Ad Age Fact Book," *Advertising Age*, January 3, 1994, p. 24. Reprinted with permission from the January 3, 1994 issue of *Advertising Age*. Copyright, Crain Communications, Inc. 1994.

485 Reprinted with permission from the January 3, 1994 issue of *Advertising Age*. Copyright, Crain Communications, Inc., 1994.

492 From: George E. Blech, and Michael A. Belch, *Introduction to Advertising and Promotion*, 2/e, Richard D. Irwin, 1993, p. 309, Exhibit 9-15. Reprinted by permission of Richard D. Irwin, Inc.

506 From: Cyndee Miller, "U.S. Postal Service Discovers the Merits of Marketing," *Marketing News*, February 1, 1993, pp. 9, 18. Reprinted by permission of the American Marketing Association.

510 Faye Rice, "A Cure for What Ails Advertising?," *Fortune*, December 16, 1991, pp. 119–122; Patricia Winters, "Coca-Cola Classic Spring Giveaway Gets Local Accent," *Advertising Age*, March 22, 1993, p. 8; "Ad Spending Estimate Reduced for 1992; 6.9% Jump Seen for 1993," *Marketing News*, January 4, 1993, p. 5; Laura Bird, "The Clients That Exasperate Madison Avenue," *The Wall Street Journal*, November 22, 1993, p. B1; Adam Bryant, "Those Mind-Boggling Promotions," *The New York Times*, November 14, 1993, p. F7; Robert J. Coen, "Ad Gain of 5.2% in '93 Marks Downturn's End," *Advertising Age*, May 2, 1994, p. 4.

512 Reprinted with permission from the January 3, 1994 issue of *Advertising Age*. Copyright, Crain Communications, Inc., 1994.

518 From: George and Michael Belch, *Introduction to Promotion and Advertising*, 2/e Irwin, 1993, p. 406. Reprinted by permission of the publisher.

519 From: George and Michael Belch, *Introduction to Promotion and Advertising*, 2/e Irwin, 1993, p. 418. Reprinted by permission of the publisher.

523 Michael Lev, "Advertisers Seek Global Messages," *The New York Times*, November 18, 1991; "Poland to Ban Tobacco and Alcohol Ads," *Advertising Age*, February 22, 1993, p. 41; Stephen Engelberg, "Advertising Pervades Poland, Turning Propaganda to Glitz," *The New York Times*, May 26, 1992; Roger Cohen, "Still Another Spring," *The New York Times*, May 31, 1992; Jennifer Lawrence, "Proctor & Gamble Marches into Eastern Europe," *Advertising Age*, September 30, 1991, p. 10; Kevin Cote, "East Germans Return to Familiar Brands," *Advertising Age*, September 30, 1991, p. 10; "Free Samples Get Emotional Response," *Advertising Age*, September 30, 1991, p. 10.

527 From: "World's Top 50 Advertising Organizations." Reprinted from the April 13, 1994 issue of *Advertising Age*. Copyright, Crain Communications, Inc., 1994.

529 From: Adam Bryant, "Those Mind Boggling Promotions," *The New York Times*, November 14, 1993, p. F7.

530 From: George and Michael Belch, *Introduction to Promotion and Advertising*, 2/e Irwin, 1993, p. 576. Reprinted by permission of the publisher.

531 Scott Donaton and Riccardo A. Davis, "RJR Ad Spending for Fourth Quarter Goes Up in Smoke," *Advertising Age*, August 3, 1992, p. 3, 27; Gary Levin, "Joe Camel Can't Light Up Children in 'Q' Ratings," *Advertising Age*, March 1, 1993, p. 8; "FTC to Decide Whether to Sue RJR Tobacco for Old Joe Ad," *Marketing News*, May 10, 1993, p. 6; Maria Mallory, "That's One Angry Camel," *Business Week*, March 7, 1994, pp. 94, 96; Stuart Elliott, "The F.T.C. Explains Its Joe Camel Decision," *The New York Times*, June 8, 1994, p. D8.

536 From: George and Michael Belch, *Introduction to Promotion and Advertising*, 2/e Irwin, 1993, p. 406. Reprinted by permission of the publisher.

542 From: "What Sells Cars: A Joint Report on Automotive Marketing by *Automotive News* and *Advertising Age*." Reprinted with permission from the March 22, 1993 issue of *Advertising Age*. Copyright, Crain Communications., Inc., 1993.

550 Robert E. Calem, "New! Improved! Laptops Change the Art of the Pitch," *The New York Times*, March 13, 1994, p. 9; Tom Eisenhart, "An Interplay of Information", *Business Marketing*, September 1992, pp. 90–92; Thayer C. Taylor, "The PC Revolution: Desktop . . . Laptop . . . Palmtop . . . ? Top," *Sales & Marketing Management*, February 1991, pp. 50–56; Jack Falvey, Thayer C. Taylor, "How the Best Sales Forces Use PC's and Laptops," *Sales & Marketing Management*, April 1988, pp. 64–74.

555 James Bennett, "Team Spirit Is New Message at Olds," *The New York Times*, June 23, 1994, pp. D1, D15; "The Selling Game," *The Wall Street Journal*, March 29, 1994, p. A1; Beverly Geber, "The Whys and Wherefores of Team Selling," *Training*, January 1991, pp. 72–78; Tom Murray, "Team Selling: What's the Incentive?" *Sales & Marketing Management*, June 1991, pp. 89–92.

560 Telephone conversation with Marcia Goldberger, Direct Marketing Association, Government Affairs Division, Washington DC, July 1994; Associated Press, "Consumer Advocate Gets Even With Telemarketer," *Marketing News*, January 17, 1994, p. 12; Diane K. Bowers, "Amendment to Telemarketing Bill Outlaws Sugging," *Marketing News*, August 16, 1993, p. A9; Phaedra Hise, "What Telemarketers Must Know," *Inc.*, October 1993, p. 29.

564 From: "A User's Guide to the Survey of Selling Costs," *Sales & Marketing Management*, February 20, 1989, p. 5.

565 From: Maurica I. Mandell and Larry J. Rosenberg, *Marketing*, Prentice-Hall, 1981, Figure 20-3, p. 500.

566 Reprinted from: Bob Kimball, "Sales Pros Know the Eight Keys to Success," *Marketing News*, March 28, 1994, pp. 4–5. Reprinted by permission of the American Marketing Association.

571 Reprinted by permission of *Harvard Business Review*. An excerpt from "How to Choose a Leadership Pattern," by Robert Tannenbaum and Warren H. Schmidt. Copyright 1973 by the President and Fellows of Harvard College; all rights reserved.

573 Malcolm K. Fleshner, Il., "To Reach Your Sales Goals Consider Compensation in Your Incentive Mix", *Sales & Marketing Management*, October 1992, pp. 16–17; Rachel Thayer, "What's in It for Me?" *Sales & Marketing Management*, April 1991, pp. 79–83, and Steve Blount, "Incentives: Compensations's 'Plus Factor,'" *Sales & Marketing Management*, April 1991, pp. 66–76

574 *Dartnell's 28th Sales Force Compensation Survey*, (Chicago: The Dartnell Corporation, 1992), p. 27; reprinted by permission of *Harvard Business Review*. An exhibit from "How to Pay Your Sales Force," by John P. Steinbrink. Copyright 1978 by the President and Fellows of Harvard College; all rights reserved.

575 From: 1993 Sales Manager's Budget Planner in *Sales & Marketing Management* June 28, 1992, p. 62. Reprinted by permission of Sales & Marketing Management, 355 Park Avenue South, New York, NY 10010-1789.

580 Cyndee Miller, "Going Overseas Requires Marketers To Learn More Than a New Language," *Marketing News*, March 28, 1994; Gerhard Gschwandtner, "Portrait of a World Class Sales Professional," *Personal Selling Power*, July/August 1992, pp. 55–63; Gerhard Gschwandtner, "How to Sell in France," *Personal Selling Power*, July/August 1991, pp. 54–60; Gerhard Gschwandtner, "How to Sell in Germany," *Personal Selling Power*, September 1991, pp. 54–60.

588 Melissa Campanelli, "What's in Store for EDLP?" *Sales & Marketing Management*, August, 1993, pp. 56–59; James Cox "Companies Cut Costs to Survive Cutting Prices," *USA Today*, November 24, 1993, p. 28; "Everyday Low Profits: Why Manufacturers Should Leave Pricing to the Retailers," *Harvard Business Review*, March/April, 1994, p. 13; Julie Liesse, "EDLP Leaves Trade Efforts in Big Flux," *Advertising Age*, May 10, 1993, pp. 4, S–2, S8; Jeffrey K. McElnea, "When Price Cutting is Brand Strategy," *Advertising Age*, August 23, 1993, p. 14; Andrew E. Serwer, "How to Escape a Price War," *Fortune*, June 13, 1994, pp. 82–90.

593 From: Mark D. Fefer, "Tourists and Bargains Galore," *Fortune*, June 14, 1994, p. 12. Copyright 1994 Time, Inc. All rights reserved.

596 From: Bill Saporito, "Behind the Tumult at P & G," *Fortune*, March 7, 1994, pp. 74–82. Copyright 1994 Time, Inc. All rights reserved.

601 From: Craig Shoemaker, "Higher Bank Fees Don't Equal Value," *Marketing News*, June 20, 1994, p. 4. Reprinted by permission of the American Marketing Association.

604 Problem from: Stephanie Strom, "Retailers' Latest Tactic: If It Says $15, It Means $15," *The New York Times*, September 9, 1993, p. 1.

610 Ellen Neuborne, "Retail Giant's Loss May Hurt Consumers," *USA Today*, October 13, 1993, pp. B1–B2; Bob Ortega, "Wal-Mart Loses a Case On Pricing," *The Wall Street Journal*, October 13, 1993, p. A3; Bob Ortega, "Wal-Mart to Settle Dispute in Michigan Involving In-Store Price Comparisons," *The Wall Street Journal*, March 21, 1994, p. B3.

614 Kathryn Jones, "Crandell's Testimony Ends," *The New York Times*, July 30, 1993, p. C3; James T. McKenna, "Crandall Fends Off Lawyers at Tial," *Aviation Week & Space Technology*, August 2, 1993, p. 40; Bridget O'Brian, "Predatory Pricing Issue Is Due To Be Taken Up In American Air's Trial," *The Wall Street Journal*, July 12, 1993, pp. A1, A6.

621 From: Richard E. Leftwich, *The Price System and Resources Allocation*, Holt, Rinehart and Winston, 1986, p. 91.

624 From: Richard E. Leftwich *The Price System*

and Resources Allocation, Holt, Rinehart and Winston, 1986, p. 139.

626 From: Richard E. Leftwich, *The Price System and Resources Allocation*, Holt, Rinehart and Winston, 1986, p. 140.

634 From: Dave Gorak, "Software Price Wars Take Toll," *Advertising Age*, Nov. 15, 1993, p. S-10. Copyright, Crain Communications Inc., 1993.

639 From: Andrew E. Serwer, "How to Escape a Price War," *Fortune*, June 13, 1994, pp. 82–90. Copyright 1994 Time, Inc. All rights reserved.

640 From: Andrew E. Serwer, "How to Escape a Price War," *Fortune*, June 13, 1994, pp. 82–90. Copyright 1994 Time, Inc. All rights reserved.

644 From: Kent B. Monroe, *Pricing: Making Profitable Decisions*, McGraw-Hill, 1979, p. 171.

646 Catherine Arnst and Stephanie Anderson Forest, "Compaq: How It Made Its Impressive Move Out of the Doldrums," *Business Week*, November 2, 1992, pp. 146–151; Bradley Johnson, "Compaq Climbs into No. 1's Hot Seat," *Advertising Age*, July 18, 1994, p. 4; Christopher Farrell and Zachary Schiller, "Stuck! How Companies Cope When They Can't Raise Prices," *Business Week*, November 15, 1993, pp. 146–155; Andrew E. Serwer, "How to Escape A Price War," *Fortune*, June 13, 1994, pp. 82–90.

656 From: *Sloan Management Review*, Winter 1992, p. 57

662 From: Patricia Sellers, "Upstart Cott Challenges the Cola Kings," *Fortune*, August 8, 1994, p. 75. Copyright 1994 Time, Inc. All rights reserved.

670 "From: "Virgin Atlantic Airways—The Iconoclastic Carrier," *Sales & Marketing Management*, August 1992, p. 45. Reprinted with permission of Sales & Marketing Management, 355 Park Avenue South, New York, NY 10010-1789; *Washington Pickett Airlines Report*, Orlando, Florida, Spring/Summer 1994, p. 3.

675 From: Carrie Goerne, "Service Eases House-Hunting Hassles," *Marketing News*, February 3, 1992, p. 10. Reprinted by permission of the American Marketing Association.

680 From: Christopher H. Lovelock, "Strategies for Managing Capacity-Constrained Services," in *Managing Services Marketing, Operations, and Human Resources*, 2/e by Christopher H. Lovelock, Prentice-Hall, 1992, p. 155.

681 From: Cyndee Miller, "Temp Service for Creatives Finds a Niche in Poor Economy," *Marketing News*, January 20, 1992, pp. 8–10. Reprinted by permission of the American Marketing Association; Barbara Marsh, "A Consulting Business Thrives by Hiring Mothers Part-Time," *The Wall Street Journal*, February 23, 1994, pp. B1–B2. Reprinted by permission of The Wall Street Journal, Copyright 1994 Dow Jones & Company, Inc. All Rights Reserved Worldwide.

683 Reprinted by permission of *Harvard Business Review*. An exhibit from Strategy is Different in Service Businesses," by Dan R. E.. Thomas. Copyright 1978 by the President and Fellows of Harvard College; all rights reserved.

685 Christopher H. Lovelock, *Services Marketing*, Prentice-Hall, 1991, p. 26.

685 Christopher H. Lovelock, *Services Marketing*, Prentice-Hall, 1991, p. 33.

689 From: Lynn G. Shostack, "Breaking From Product Marketing," *Journal of Marketing*, 41, April 1977, pp. 73–80. Reprinted by permission of the American Marketing Association.

693 From: Daryl D. Wyckoff, "New Tools for Achieving Service Quality," in *Managing Services Marketing, Operations, and Human Resources*, 2/e by Christopher H. Lovelock, 1992 Prentice-Hall, p 245.

696 Melinda Henneberger, "Hospitals Learning the Not-Subtle Art of Self-Promotion," *The New York Times*, July 4, 1994, pp. 1, 22; Scott Hample and Rich Lapin, "Marketing Health Care: Operation Segmentation," *Marketing Tools*, April/May 1994, pp. 18–20; Christopher Palmeri and Terzah Ewing, "When It Doesn't Pay To Advertise," *Forbes*, December 20, 1993, pp. 234–236.

700 "GSUSA's Annual Report," *Girl Scout Leader*, Summer 1994, p. 30; "Responding to Change—Girl Scout Groups," *Program News*, San Diego–Imperial Girl Scout Council, August 1994, p. 1; E. Jahn, "Girl Scouts Break the Mold, Deal with Sordid Side of Life," *The San Diego Union–Tribune*, July 27, 1993, p. B–3; John A. Byrne, "Profiting from the Nonprofits," *Business Week*, March 26, 1990, pp. 66–74.

702 From: Philip Kotler and Alan Andersen, *Strategic Marketing for Nonprofit Organizations*, 4/e, Prentice-Hall, 1991, p. 27.

704 From: Cyndee Miller, "Amnesty International Injects Pizzazz into its Marketing Approach," *Marketing New*, February 17, 1992, p. 9. Reprinted by permission of the American Marketing Association.

706 From: Philip Kotler and Alan Andersen, *Strategic Marketing for Nonprofit Organizations*, 4/e, Prentice-Hall, 1991, p. 90.

710 From: Christopher H. Lovelock and Charles B. Weinberg, *Marketing for Public and Nonprofit Managers*, John Wiley & Sons, 1984, p. 298.

715 From: Charles W. Lamb, Jr., and John L. Crompton, "Distributing Public Services: A Strategic Approach," in *Journal of the Academy of Marketing Science*, Summer 1985. Copyright 1985. Reprinted by permission.

717 Seymour H. Fine, *Social Marketing*, "Promoting the Causes of Public and Non Profit Agencies," Copyright 1990, p. 110. Reprinted by permission of Prentice Hall, Englewood Cliffs, New Jersey.

720 Tim Triplett, "Marketing Briefs," *Marketing News*, May 23, 1994, p. 15; Interview with K. Haugero, Ad Council, New York City, June 3, 1994; Warren Berger, "Ad Council. a grand idea that worked,"; Warren Berger, "Campaign Sheds Light on a 'Hidden' Crisis; Ruth A. Wooden, "For the future—a commitment to ideals and effective advertising," last three articles in "Ad Council at 50," *Advertising Age*, November 11, 1991, pp. A–1–A–16.

722 From: Philip Kotler and Alan Andersen, *Strategic Marketing for Nonprofit Organizations*, 4/e, Prentice-Hall, 1991.

724 From: Philip Kotler and Alan Andersen, *Strategic Marketing for Nonprofit Organizations*, 4/e, Prentice-Hall, 1991, p. 345.

728 Some information for this case was provided during a telephone conversation with "Arthur" in the California State Lottery Office of Public Affairs, Sacramento, CA, August 5, 1994; John J. Rohs, "Gaming Industry: Why the Continuing Explosion," Institutional Investor, February 1994, pp. 6–7; Personal communication with Joanne McNabb, Director of Public Affairs, California State Lottery, October 1992; Bradley Johnson, "Lagging Lotto in California," *Advertising Age*, August 12, 1991, p. 4.; Dharmendra T. Verma and Frederick Wiseman, "Massachusetts State Lottery", in Philip Kotler, O. C. Ferrell, and Charles Lamb, Eds., *Cases & Readings for Marketing for Nonprofit Organizations*, (Englewood Cliffs, NJ: Prentice–Hall, 1983), pp. 141–154.

Appendix B (Figures B.1–B.5) Reprinted by permission of Interpretive Software, Inc., Charlottesville, Virginia.

Photo Credits

Page positions are as follows: (T)top, (C)center, (B)bottom, (L)left, (R)right.

Cover Copyright Clint Clemmens, Inc. 1992; all rights reserved.

Inside Front Cover
Left Photo Courtesy of Harley-Davidson.
Middle Photo Ad: Courtesy of Harley-Davidson. Photo: Copyright Dennis Manarchy, Ltd.
Right Photo Courtesy of Harley-Davidson.

ix Courtesy Carnival Cruise Lines
x Pierre Toutain-Dorbec/SYGMA
xi Copyright Allan Tannenbaum/SYGMA
xii Photos courtesy of Avon Products, Inc.
xiiiT Courtesy Black & Decker, Inc.
xiiiB Copyright 1991 Tom Young/The Stock Market
xiv Copyright M. Douglas/The Image Works
xv Copyright Jeff Greenberg/The Picture Cube
xvi Copyright W. Hill/The Image Works
xvii Copyright Tony Freeman/PhotoEdit
xviii Amy C. Etra/PhotoEdit
xvix Courtesy of Price Club de Mexico
xx Courtesy of Toys "R" Us
xxi Copyright Paul McKelvey/Tony Stone Worldwide
xxii Copyright Elena Rooraid/PhotoEdit
xxiii Copyright Myrleen Ferguson/PhotoEdit
xxiv Copyright Mary Kate Denny/PhotoEdit
xxv Copyright Tony Freeman/PhotoEdit
xxvi Copyright Michael Newman/PhotoEdit
xxvii Courtesy of the Girls Scouts of the U.S.A.
1TL Photos courtesy of Avon Products, Inc.
1CL Courtesy Carnival Cruise Lines
1BR Copyright Allan Tannenbaum/SYGMA
1R Pierre Toutain-Dorbec/SYGMA
2 Courtesy Carnival Cruise Lines
7 Courtesy U.S. Department of Health & Human Services
8 Copyright Bryn Campbell/Magnum Photos
13 Courtesy Kellogg U.S.A. ® 1992.
15 Courtesy San Diego Aerospace Museum
20 Courtesy of XEROX Corporation
30 Pierre Toutain-Dorbec/SYGMA
33 Courtesy DEVCOR Software Design and Development
41BR Courtesy of Maytag, Newton, Iowa
41TL Courtesy of Remington
41BR Courtesy of Weider Sporting Goods, Inc.
41TR Courtesy Thomasville Furniture Industries, Inc.
42 Courtesy of the Quaker Oats Company
47 Copyright Richard Megna, 1991, Fundamental Photographs
50 AP/Wide World Photos
56 Courtesy Marriott International
57 Courtesy Airbus Industrie of North America, Inc.
60 Courtesy of The Body Shop
64 Courtesy of Saturn
66 Courtesy of Hoechst Celanese Corporation
70 Courtesy of the Ronald McDonald House of New York
76 Copyright Allan Tannenbaum/SYGMA
82 Courtesy of United Parcel Service
87 Courtesy Kentucky Fried Chicken (KFC) Corporation, Louisville, KY.
91 Reprinted with the permission of Lexus, A Division of Toyota Motor Sales, U.S.A., Inc.
96 Courtesy University of Phoenix
102 Courtesy of American Express Travel

Related Services Company
108   Photos courtesy of Avon Products, Inc.
115   Reuters/Bettmann
116   Riclafe/SIPA Press
118   Courtesy Cohen's Fashion Optical
120   Joseph Treaster/NYT Pictures
142TL   Copyright 1991 Tom Young/The Stock Market
142CL   Copyright Jeff Greenberg/The Picture Cube
142BL   Copyright M. Douglas/The Image Works
142R   Courtesy Black & Decker, Inc.
144   Courtesy Black & Decker, Inc.
149L   Courtesy Hyatt Hotels Corporation
149R   Courtesy Hyatt Hotels Corporation
151   Advertisement courtesy of KIWI International Air Lines
154   Naum Kazhdan/New York Times Pictures
162   Courtesy of the Brooklyn Brewery
166   Reprinted Courtesy of American International Group, Inc.
176   Copyright 1991 Tom Young/The Stock Market
181   Copyright Granitsas/The Image Works
183   Courtesy Motorola
185   Copyright Rhoda Sidney/PhotoEdit
189   Reuters/Bettmann
193   Copyright Zbigniew Bzdak/The Image Works
196   Copyright Rob Crandall/Stock, Boston
198   Copyright Bob Daemmrich/The Image Works
200   Copyright Tony Freeman/PhotoEdit
202   Courtesy Hunt Wesson, Inc.
208   Copyright M. Douglas/The Image Works
213   Courtesy of Symbol Technologies
215   Courtesy of Kelly Services, Inc. All rights reserved.
221   Courtesy of Ryder Truck Rental, Inc.
223   Courtesy of Toshiba America Information Systems, Inc.
226   Courtesy of Minolta Corporation
238   Copyright Jeff Greenberg/The Picture Cube
247   Courtesy Volkswagen United States, Inc.
255   Copyright Spencer Grant/Stock, Boston
256   Courtesy of The Pre-Testing Company, Inc.
259   Courtesy of Converse
271L   Copyright W. Hill/The Image Works
271R   Copyright Tony Freeman/PhotoEdit
276   Copyright W. Hill/The Image Works
283   Copyright R. Lord/The Image Works
285L   Copyright Michael Newman/PhotoEdit
285R   Copyright Willie L. Hill, Jr./Stock, Boston
292   Courtesy of the Coca-Cola Company
293   Used by permission of General Mills, Inc.
295   Courtesy of Radio Shack, a division of Tandy Corporation
297   Courtesy of PRESIDENT'S CHOICE INTERNATIONAL, a Division of Loblaw Brands Limited
299   PhotoEdit/Courtesy of Ralphs Grocery
308   Copyright Tony Freeman/PhotoEdit
312   Courtesy of Ben & Jerry's Homemade, Inc.
322   Courtesy of the Lever Brothers Company
331   Copyright 1994 by OCSAR & ASSOCIATES, INC.
340   Courtesy of the Chrysler Corporation
347TL   Amy C. Etra/PhotoEdit
347BL   Courtesy of Price Club de Mexico
347R   Courtesy of Toys "R" Us
350   Amy C. Etra/PhotoEdit
354   Copyright 1992 Starbucks Coffee Company

357   Courtesy Mary Kay Cosmetics, Inc.
360   Copyright John Eastcott/YVA Momatiuk/The Image Works
367   Courtesy Champ Products, Inc.
368   Courtesy Pepsi-Cola Company
374   Copyright Bob Daemmrich/The Image Works
380   Reuters/Bettmann
381   Copyright Dave Young-Wolff/PhotoEdit
390   Courtesy of Price Club de Mexico
398   Photo courtesy of Cub Foods
401   Copyright Bob Daemmrich/Stock, Boston
413   Copyright MCMXCI Richard Pasley/Stock, Boston
414   Copyright Robert Brenner/PhotoEdit
428   Courtesy of Toys "R" Us
436   Copyright Michael Newman/PhotoEdit
437   Copyright Tim Barnwell/Stock, Boston
442   Courtesy of Land's End, Inc.
443   Courtesy of Home Shopping Network, Inc.
446   Courtesy West Edmonton Mall
452   Photo courtesy of The Caldor Corporation
457   Courtesy of Miniyard Food Stores, Inc.
465L   Copyright Paul McKelvey/Tony Stone Worldwide
465C   Copyright Elena Rooraid/PhotoEdit
465R   Copyright Myrleen Fergunson/PhotoEdit
466   Copyright Paul McKelvey/Tony Stone Worldwide
472   Courtesy of Perdue Farms, Inc.
473   FAR SIDE copyright FARWORKS, INC./Dist. by UNIVERSAL PRESS SYNDICATE. Reprinted with permission. All rights reserved.
474   Courtesy of Amoco Oil Company
479   Courtesy of Cerenex ™ Pharmaceuticals, a division of Glaxco, Inc.
486   Courtesy of the Compaq Computer Corporation
495   Globe Photos, Inc.
498   Reprinted by permission of McGraw-Hill, Inc.
508   Copyright Elena Rooraid/PhotoEdit
514TR   Courtesy of BMG Direct
514L   Courtesy of Chevron
514BR   Courtesy of the Florida Tomatoe Committee
516   Courtesy of The Ad Council
522L   Printed by permission of CIGNA
522R   Copyright 1990 Massachusetts Mutual Life Insurance Company. Reprinted by permission.
528   Courtesy of the International Advertising Association
535   Courtesy of The Interface Group
546   Copyright Myrleen Fergunson/PhotoEdit
553   Copyright Michael Fergunson/PhotoEdit
555   Copyright David Young Wolff/PhotoEdit
556   Copyright David J. Sams/Texas Imprint/Stock, Boston
562   Copyright C. Gupton/Stock, Boston
569   Copyright Michael Newman/Photo Edit
570   Copyright David Young Wolff/PhotoEdit
572   Copyright John Coletti/Stock, Boston
585L   Copyright Mary Kate Denny/PhotoEdit
585R   Copyright Tony Freeman/PhotoEdit
586   Copyright Mary Kate Denny/PhotoEdit
591   Copyright David Young Wolff/PhotoEdit
599   Copyright Bob Daemmrich/The Image Works
632   Copyright Tony Freeman/PhotoEdit
642   Copyright J. Greenberg/The Image Works
645   Courtesy of DeVito/Verdi
651   Copyright Steve Benbow/Stock, Boston

653   Copyright 1994 AT&T
658   Copyright Ogust/Image Works
667L   Copyright Michael Newman/PhotoEdit
667R   Courtesy of the Girl Scouts of the U.S.A.
668   Copyright Michael Newman/PhotoEdit
674   Reprinted with the permission of Deloite & Touche
677   Copyright Kemper Financial Services, Inc., 1994
679T   Courtesy of Radisson Hotels International
679B   Copyright Tony Freeman/PhotoEdit
684   Copyright M. Greenlar/The Image Works
698   Courtesy of the Girl Scouts of the U.S.A.
704   Courtesy of Amnesty International
707   Courtesy of the American Cancer Society, Inc.
712   Copyright Stanford Alumni Association. Reprinted with permission.
713   Copyright 1994 US Postal Service. Photo by Renee Comet
718   Photos courtesy of The Church Ad Project, 3410 Federal Drive, Suite #104, Eagan, MN 55122. (800) 331-9391
720   Courtesy of The Advertising Council, Inc.

Subject/Name Index

Company / Product / Service Index

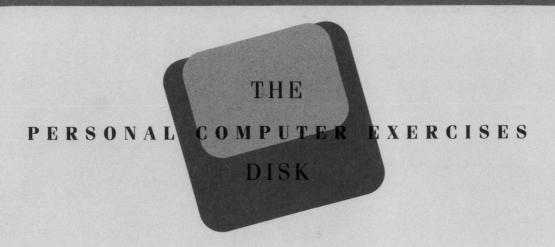

THE
PERSONAL COMPUTER EXERCISES
DISK

The Personal Computer Exercises Disk contains computerized marketing exercises designed to reinforce one or more topics in each chapter. The program is available in either MS-DOS (IBM PC) or Macintosh format. The MS-DOS version is enclosed in the facing sleeve. All of the PC Exercises are easy to use and comprehensive. All options are easily selected either by a mouse or through a keyboard. Many of the exercises include graphics and on-line help is available in the software.

Each chapter exercise consists of an introduction, a mini-case, a worksheet (which may include a graph and other options) and a follow-up quiz. The software includes two types of help: topic help and context help. *Topic help* provides the objective of the exercise, key points to grasp, and the essential elements that you should have mastered once you have completed the exercise. *Context help* provides directions about the specific task that you are working on at the time. The follow-up quiz has a built-in word processor that allows you to enter your answers directly into the quiz layout. You can print any of the parts of the exercise at any time by selecting the print button or choosing PRINT from the FILE menu. This feature enables you to submit your completed exercise in a standard format.

Appendix B of the text includes complete instructions for using the Personal Computer Exercises Disk.